Geographica's Pocket

WORLD REFERENCE

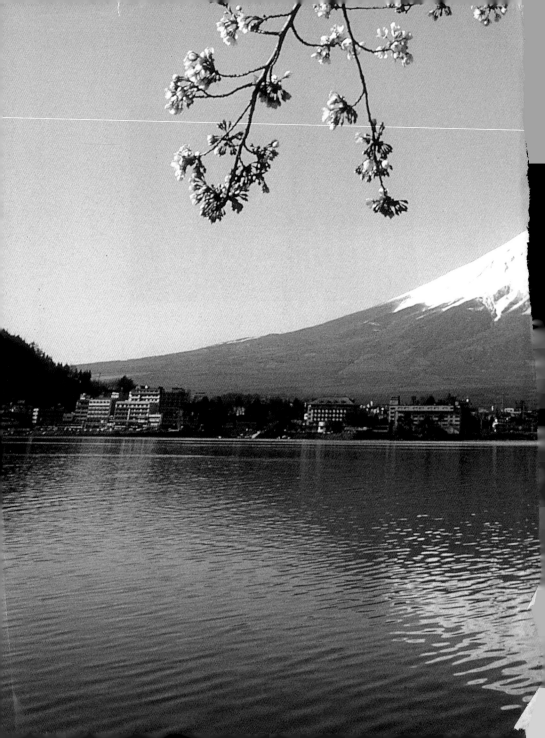

Geographica's Pocket

WORLD REFERENCE

Over 1,000 pages of global information

RAINCOAST BOOKS
Vancouver

Published in Australia by Random House Pty Ltd
20 Alfred Street, Milsons Point, NSW Australia 2061

First published in Canada in 2001 by
Raincoast Books
9050 Shaughnessy Street
Vancouver, B.C.
V6P 6E5
(604) 323-7100
www.raincoast.com

Canadian Cataloguing-in-Publication Data

Thom, B. G. (Bruce G.)
Geographica's pocket world reference

Includes index.
ISBN 1-55192-413-7

1. Geography. I. Title.

G123.T46 2001 910 C00-9115536

Publisher: Penny Martin
Editors: Karen Enkelaar, Susan Page, Penny Martin, Caroline Hunter
Production Manager: Linda Watchorn
Design: Ramsay MacFarlane, James Mills-Hicks, Kim Webber
Page makeup: Kim Webber, James Mills-Hicks
Photolibrarian: Susan Page
Photo research: Susan Page
Researcher: Tamsin Martin
Cartographic manager: James Mills-Hicks
Gazetteer: Susan Page
Production assistant: Wendy Canning
Flags: Flag Society of Australia

Printed by Dah Hua Printing Co Ltd, Hong Kong
Film separation: Pica Colour Separation, Singapore

Raincoast Books gratefully acknowledges the support of the Government of Canada, through the Department of Canadian Heritage and the Book Publishing Industry Development Program.

Contributors

GENERAL EDITORS

Dr Patrick Hesp BA, MA (Hons), PhD (University of Sydney); Geography Programme, School of Global Studies, Massey University
Professor Tom McKnight BA, MA, PhD (University of Wisconsin); Professor Emeritus of Geography, University of California, Los Angeles
Professor Bruce Thom BA, PhD (Louisiana State University), FIAG; Emeritus Professor of Geography University of Sydney, Visiting Professor of Geography, University of New South Wales
Professor William Wonders BA (Hons), MA, PhD (University of Toronto), Fil.Dr.h.c. (Uppsala); University Professor and Professor Emeritus of Geography, University of Alberta

CONSULTANTS

Professor Joan Clemons PhD (University of Minnesota); Visiting Professor, Graduate School of Education and Information Studies, University of California, Los Angeles
Professor Ray Hudson BA, PhD, DSc (University of Bristol), DSc (Honoris Causa, University of Roskilde); Department of Geography, University of Durham
Professor Tom McKnight BA, MA, PhD (University of Wisconsin); Professor Emeritus of Geography, University of California, Los Angeles
Professor John Overton MA, PhD (Cambridge); Professor, Institute of Development Studies, School of Global Studies, Massey University
Professor Toru Taniuchi BA, MSc, DSc, (University of Tokyo); Professor of Human Geography, University of Tokyo, Japan
Professor Bruce Thom BA, PhD (Louisiana State University), FIAG; Emeritus Professor of Geography University of Sydney, Visiting Professor of Geography, University of New South Wales
Professor William Wonders BA (Hons), MA, PhD (University of Toronto), Fil.Dr.h.c. (Uppsala); University Professor and Professor Emeritus of Geography, University of Alberta

CONTRIBUTORS

PART 1 PLANET EARTH
Professor Bruce Thom BA, PhD (Louisiana State University), F.I.A.G.
Dr John O'Byrne BSc, PhD (University of Sydney)
Dr Noel de Souza BSc (Hons), MSc., Doctorat de Specialité (University of Paris)
Dr Ron Horvath BA, MA, PhD (University of California, Los Angeles)
Dr Scott Mooney BSc (Hons), PhD (University of New South Wales

PART 2 PEOPLE AND SOCIETY
Dr Ron Brunton BA, MA, PhD (La Trobe University)
Associate Professor Sybil Jack MA, BLitt (Oxon), DipEd (University of New England)
Dr Ron Horvath BA, MA, PhD (University of California, Los Angeles)
Tess Rod BA (Hons), MA, BComm
Roger Sandall BA, MA (Columbia University)

PART 3 REGIONS OF THE WORLD
Robert Coupe MA, DipEd
Dr Noel de Souza BSc (Hons), MSc, Doctorat de Specialité (University of Paris)
Professor John Flenley MA (Cambridge) PhD (Australian National University);Professor of Geography, School of Global Studies, Massey University
Dr Robert Garnham, MSc (London), PhD (Massey University); Lecturer in Tourism, School of Business & Public Management, Victoria University
Dr Terry Hearn, MA (Hons) (Otago), PhD (Otago); Historian, Historical Branch, Department of Internal Affairs, Wellington
Manuka Henare BA (Hons); Maori Business Development, Department of Management and Employment Relations, University of Auckland
Dr John Holland BA Hons, MA, PhD (University of Natal); Institute of Natural Resources, Massey University
Dr Patrick Hesp BA, MA (Hons), PhD (University of Sydney); Geography Programme, School of Global Studies, Massey University
Grant Hunter BSc (Hons); Landcare Research New Zealand Limited, Lincoln University Campus
Dr Terry C. Kelly BSc, MSc, PhD (University of Florida); Institute of Natural Resources, Massey University
Professor Richard LeHeron MA (Hons), PhD (University of Washington, Professor of Geography, University of New Zealand
Dr Megan K. McKenna BA (Hons), MA (Carleton), PhD (University of Ottowa); Post-Doctoral Fellow, Geography Programme, School of Global Studies, Massey University
Professor Simon Milne BA, MA (Auckland), PhD (Cambridge); Professor of Tourism, School of Business & Public Management, Victoria University and Adjunct Professor of Geography, McGill University, Montreal, Canada
Professor John Overton MA, PhD (Cambridge); Professor, Institute of Development Studies, School of Global Studies, Massey University
Mike Page BSc (Hons), Landcare Research New Zealand Limited, Massey University Campus
Dr Katie Pickles BA, MA, PhD (McGill University); Department of History, University of Canterbury
Associate Professor Michael Roche MA (Hons), PhD (Cantuar); Associate Professor of Geography, School of Global Studies, Massey University
Roger Sandall BA, MA (Columbia University)
Professor Bruce Thom BA, PhD (Louisiana State University), F.I.A.G. Emeritus Professor of Geography University of Sydney, Visiting Professor of Geography, University of New South Wales
Noel Trustrum BSc, Dip Soil science; Landcare Research New Zealand Limited, Massey University Campus
Dr Clel Wallace PhD, Lecturer in Earth Science, Institute of Natural Resources, Massey University
CARTOGRAPHIC CONSULTANTS
Henk Brolsma, Associateship in Land Surveying;

Contributors

Australian Antarctic Division, Tasmania, Australia
Antarctica
Dr John Connell BA, PhD (University of London)
Papua New Guinea, Pacific Islands, Island Nations and Dependencies
Tony Davidson
Europe, Russian Federation, former Soviet Republics
Dr Noel de Souza BSc (Hons), MSc, Doctorat de Specialité (University of Paris)
India, Sri Lanka, Nepal, Bangladesh, Bhutan, Pakistan
Dr Joan Hardjono BA, LittB, PhD (University of New England); Padjadjaran State University, Bandung, Indonesia
Indonesia, Malaysia, Singapore
Dr Philip Hirsch BA, PhD
Thailand, Laos, Myanmar, Cambodia, Vietnam, Philippines
Professor Naftali Kadmon BA, MSc, PhD (University of Wales); Professor Emeritus, The Hebrew University of Jerusalem, Israel
Israel, Turkey, Iran, Cyprus, Afghanistan
Gerry Leitner
South America, Central America
Dr Zhilin Li BEng, PhD (University of Glasgow); Assistant Professor, The Hong Kong Polytechnic University, Hong Kong
China
Professor Tanga Munkhtsetseg; International Relations Institute, Ulan Bator, Mongolia
Mongolia
Chonghyon Paku MA BSc; Baito-Bunka University, Tokyo, Japan
Korea
Karen Puklowski NZCD/Survey; Massey University, New Zealand
New Zealand
Professor Chris Rogerson BSc (Hons), MSc, PhD (Queens), FSAGS; University of Witwatersrand, Johannesburg, South Africa
SubSaharan Africa
Dr Nasser Salma PhD (University of Washington, Seattle); Associate Professor, King Saud University, Riyadh, Saudi Arabia
Arabic speaking countries of the Middle East and Saharan Africa
Brian Stokes BBus (Tourism), AssDipCart
Australia
Professor Toru Taniuchi BA, MSc, DSc (University of Tokyo); Professor of Human Geography, University of Tokyo, Japan
Japan
Glenn Toldi BSc, DipCart&GIS
United States of America, Canada
Lillian Wonders BA, MA
Canada

CAPTIONS TO OPENING PAGE PHOTOGRAPHS

PART 1 (EARTH)

Pages 2–3 Mount Fiji, Five Lakes District, Japan.
Pages 12–13 View of the lake district in Chile.
Pages 14–15 Earth rising over the Moon's horizon, taken from *Apollo 11*.
Pages 54–5 Rice cultivation in the valley of the Yangtze River, China.
Pages 106–7 Lake shore in Banff National Park, Calgary, Canada.

PART 2 (PEOPLE)

Pages 134–5 View of Singapore from the harbor.

PART 3 (A–Z)

Pages 206–7 Antiquarian Map of America, Africa and Europe.
A Pages 208–9 Still night in summer at Cape Bird, Antarctica
B Pages 242–3 Iguaçu Falls, Brazil.
C Pages 276–7 Bow Lake in Banff National Park in the Canadian Rockies.
D Pages 326–7 Forested hills and bay around Soufrière, Dominica.
E Pages 336–7 Mountain terrain and steps carved into rock looking to San Vincente volcano through Puerta del Diablo (Devil's Door), El Salvador.
F Pages 354–5 Belcastel overlooking Ouysse and Dordogne River, France.
G Pages 368–9 Acropolis Ruins, Athens, Greece.
H Pages 396–7 Houses and colonial church (center), Santa Lucia village, Honduras.
I Pages 404–5 Lake Palace and Shiv Niwas Palace, Udaipur, Rajastan, India.
J Pages 434–5 One of the many rock-cut facades in the ancient city of Petra in Jordan.
K Pages 446–7 Zebra grazing at dawn in the Masai Mara National Reserve, Kenya.
L Pages 456–7 Fertile foothills of the Maluti Mountains, Lesotho.
M Pages 470–1 Crowded houses from Medina de Fèz (old part of Morocco), Morocco.
N Pages 504–5 Melting stream in the Sharkiphu River valley, Nepal.
O,P Pages 534–5 70 Islands Group, Rock Islands, Palau.
Q,R Pages 554–5 Pushkin Palace, Moscow, Russian Federation.
S Pages 572–3 Pyramids at Meroe, Sudan.
T Pages 626–7 Women in traditional dress, Thailand.
U,V Pages 646–7 St Peter's Square, The Vatican, Vatican City.
W Pages 688–9 Area of confrontation in Hebron, West Bank.
Y,Z Pages 694–5 Great Zimbabwe Ruins, Zimbabwe.

PART 4 (MAPS)

Pages 704–5 Antiquarian Map of the World.

PART 5 (GAZETTEER)

Pages 870–1 The snow-covered Great Sand Dune, Colorado, USA.

Contents

Contents

Contents

Contents

Contents

Part 1

Planet Earth

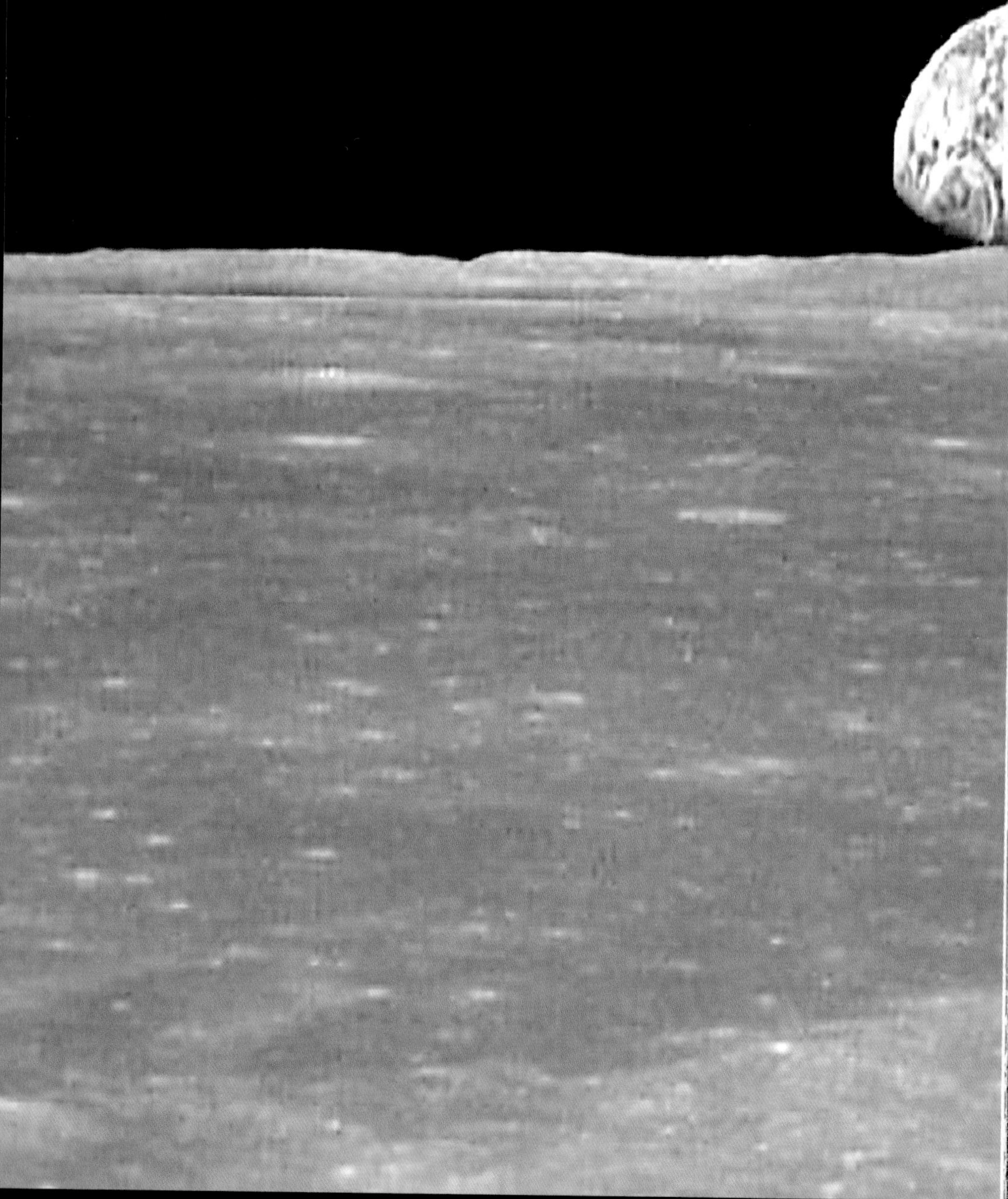

Earth in Space

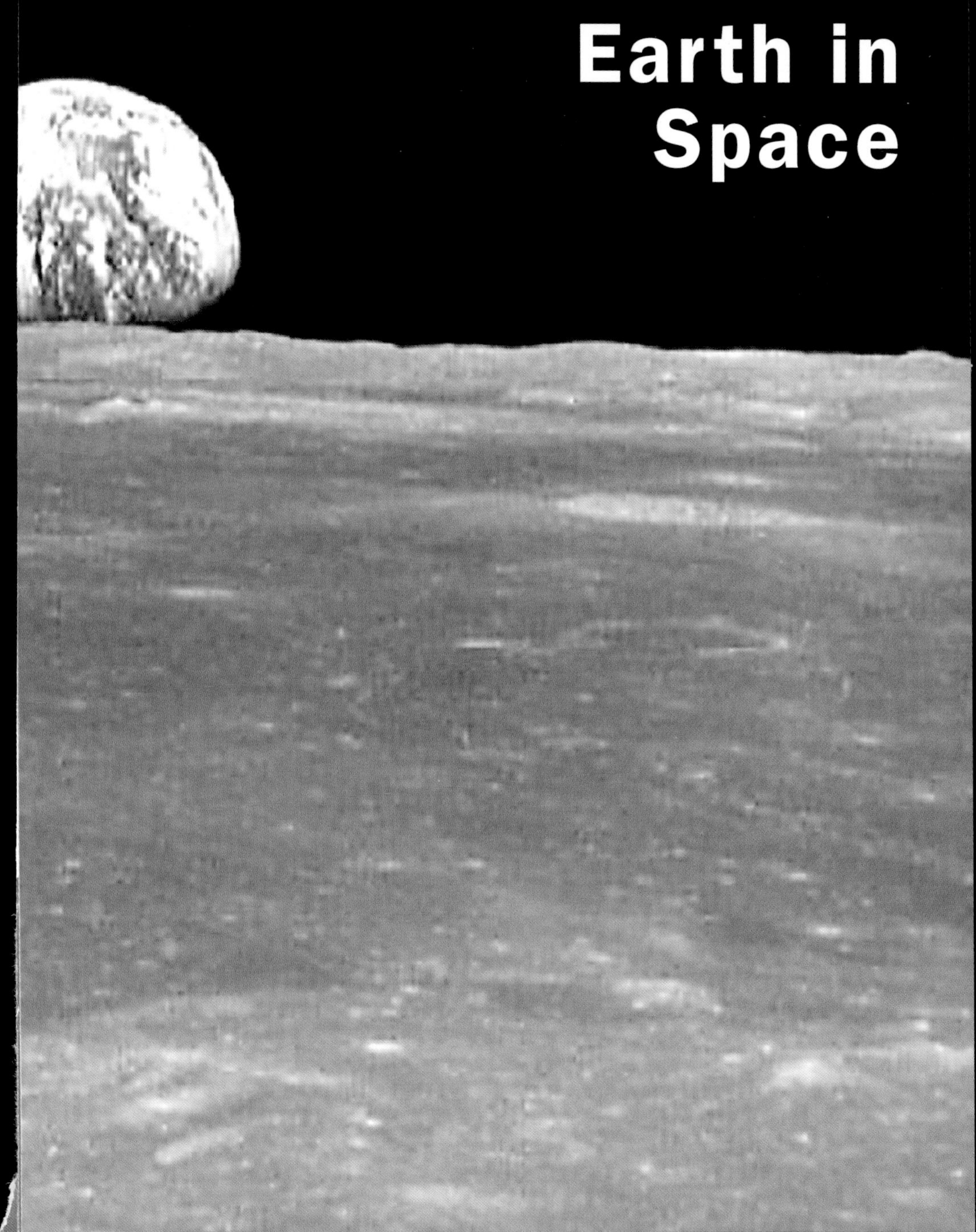

EARTH IN SPACE

Ideas on the origin of Earth, other planets, the Sun and stars can be traced to the time of classical Greece. They range from an Earth-centered universe to one where the position of this tiny, life-generating planet is placed in a context of an expanding universe populated by billions of stars, with an unknown number of planets similar in composition and structure to ours.

It was late in the eighteenth century that the great early geologist James Hutton (1726–97), a Scot, captured in a few poignant words the vastness and the immensity of time over which Earth, the Sun, the solar system, the galaxies, and the universe have evolved. He noted that there is "no vestige of a beginning, no prospect of an end". This phrase challenged the established thinking of a very limited time for the creation of the natural world and opened up a new era of geological and cosmological thought.

We live on a planet that is circling a single star of apparently limitless energy. Yet we now know that the engine of nuclear heat driving the Sun has a birth and a stable phase, and, as it runs short of hydrogen fuel, will go through enormous cataclysms. This process will absorb the Sun's dependent planets, and eventually lead to its own slow "death".

Our views of Earth as part of the universe have varied over time. New concepts and theories, such as Einstein's general theory of relativity, have offered scientists different perspectives on the origin of the universe and all matter. New technologies ranging from telescopes to satellites have opened up vast vistas within and beyond our solar system. Scientists now have tools to measure the composition and structure of matter racing through space. We understand much better the characteristics of various forces at work, such as those driving the expansion of the universe, the clustering of stars, the condensation of gases, the orbits of planets, and the movement of meteorites.

The Big Bang model for the universe is based on a number of observations. It is not speculation. Yet, as a model of how the universe evolved, it has been modified by cosmologists and scientists over time. New observations should lead to further changes as we continue to explore whether there is enough matter and energy in the universe to slow and stop the expansion started 10 billion or 15 billion years ago.

As gases condensed to form stars, there was a distinct tendency for these stars to cluster. The Milky Way Galaxy is an example of a large spiral galaxy or cluster of stars composed of a thin, circular disk surrounding a central bulge. Interestingly, new technologies show that many galaxies, including the Milky Way, have more mass than can readily be seen. There also appears to exist at the core of some galaxies a central powerhouse generating narrow jets of high-energy particles streaming outwards. Only more observations and theorizing will help us understand the significance of these phenomena.

Yet it is the stars themselves which offer so many clues to the origin of the universe and, ultimately, ourselves. They vary widely in size, color, and temperature. Stars are powered by nuclear reactions whereby hydrogen is fused to helium. We now possess knowledge of sequences through which stars may change from one state to another. Our Sun is no exception and can be seen as representative of an average star in the Milky Way Galaxy. It generates light and heat, which are transmitted through space to help transform life on the surface of one of its planets, Earth.

Radiometric dating of ancient rocks on Earth and its moon give some clue as to the age of the solar system—about 5 billion years. Cooling and consolidation under gravity of interstellar gases and dust created the Sun and progressively hardened objects accreted and condensed to form the nine planets and their moons. Early in the period of planet formation, the sweeping up of solar system debris led to bombardment of planet and moon surfaces, a phenomenon dramatically depicted today by photographs of the cratered surface of Earth's moon.

The Sun is the ultimate source of energy for life processes on planet Earth. As the Sun formed, it captured most matter in the Solar system, leaving only 0.1 percent to form the planets, their moons, asteroids, comets and dust. The Sun possessed sufficient mass needed to generate electromagnetic or radiant energy at various wavelengths. The hot Sun mostly radiates shorter wavelength energy especially at visible wavelengths. There are also large sunspots caused by magnetic storms on the Sun's surface. They can be observed as visible dark patches and as areas of X-ray activity ejecting electrically charged particles, the solar wind. Sunspot activity is not constant—it is actually cyclic in behavior. When these particles meet the Earth's atmosphere dramatic visual displays occur, especially in polar latitudes. Whether sunspots influence the weather is uncertain.

The spinning Earth orbits the Sun, traveling a distance of approximately 150 million km (93 million miles). Energy is received at a more or less constant rate, but is distributed unevenly because of the tilt of Earth's axis, yielding seasonal changes in temperature away from the equator. Yet Earth processes its own heat engine: radioactive processes within its core help generate gases into the atmosphere and drive movements of its crustal plates. The presence of different gases, including water vapor, has provided that vital mixture of substances from which life has evolved, as well as the thin protective envelope high in oxygen and nitrogen which forms the atmosphere.

Thus spaceship Earth, spinning systematically around the Sun, receiving heat, generating gases and driving its crust into mountains, offers various life forms an environment for evolution. Over time these environments change. Ultimately the future of the planet itself is tied to that of its solar system and its Sun.

Humans have always been fascinated by Earth's place in the universe. Earth is just one of many planets, moons, and stars that form our solar system. We still have much to learn about how the solar system formed, and about how it will end.

ORIGINS OF THE UNIVERSE

When we look out across the universe, we look back in time. Light traveling from distant galaxies, speeding across 300,000 km (186,000 miles) every second, has taken billions of years to reach Earth. We see the most distant galaxies across billions of light years, as those galaxies were when the universe was younger.

What is the universe really like? The modern view of the origins and future of the universe is based on the idea of a Big Bang that marked the beginning of the ongoing expansion of the universe. The popular view of the Big Bang, however, imagines galaxies flying away from one another out into empty space after a massive explosion. This naturally leads to questions about what happened before the Big Bang, and where it occurred. However, these questions arise from a misunderstanding of the Big Bang concept. Galaxies do not fly away from each other through space; rather, space itself expands, carrying the galaxies with it. The Big Bang was not an explosion *in* space, but an explosion *of* space and time. All of space and time arose in the Big Bang. There was no time before the Big Bang, and all of space was involved.

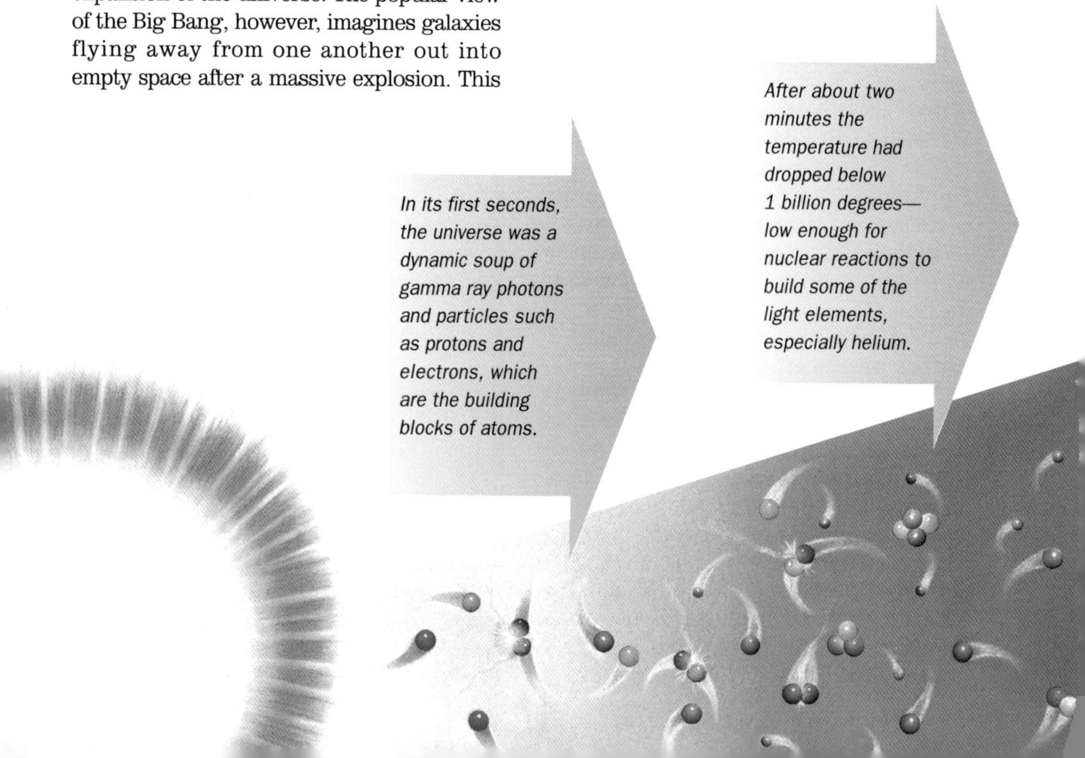

In its first seconds, the universe was a dynamic soup of gamma ray photons and particles such as protons and electrons, which are the building blocks of atoms.

After about two minutes the temperature had dropped below 1 billion degrees—low enough for nuclear reactions to build some of the light elements, especially helium.

A brief history of the universe

Ten to fifteen billion years ago, the universe of space and time began, as a hugely hot cauldron of energy governed by physical laws that we do not yet understand. Within a tiny fraction of a second the expansion had moderated the conditions to a point from which (we believe) our current understanding of physical laws can begin to describe what happened. The universe was expanding and cooling, but there may also have been a brief spurt of dramatic inflation in size—this is critical to understanding today's universe. If this sudden growth spurt *did* occur, then the part of the universe that telescopes can survey today was merely a tiny fraction of the total.

After no more than 10 millionths of a second, the universe had become a sea of high energy radiation—gamma ray photons characteristic of a temperature well over 1 trillion degrees. At such energy, photons can produce a pair of particles, a matter

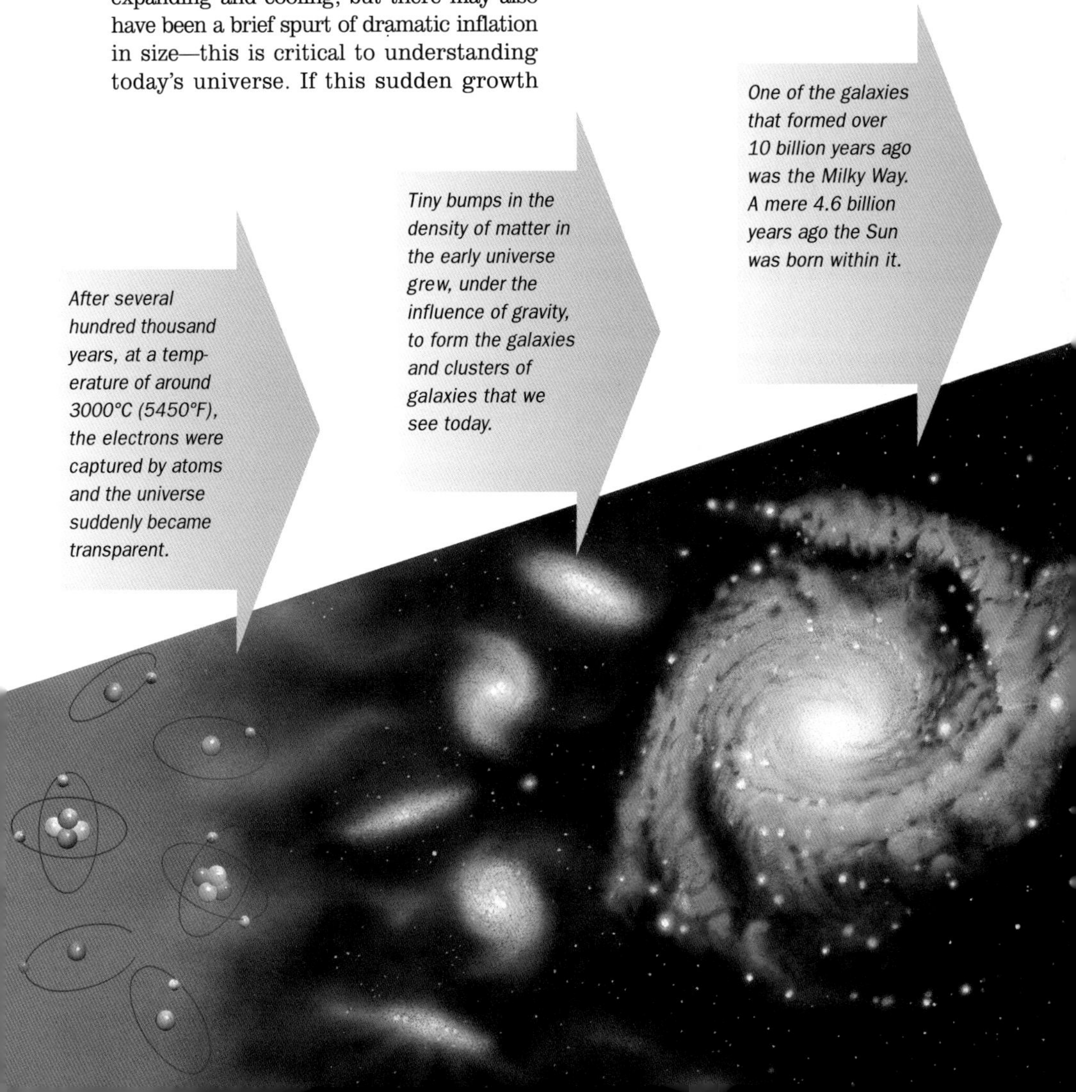

After several hundred thousand years, at a temperature of around 3000°C (5450°F), the electrons were captured by atoms and the universe suddenly became transparent.

Tiny bumps in the density of matter in the early universe grew, under the influence of gravity, to form the galaxies and clusters of galaxies that we see today.

One of the galaxies that formed over 10 billion years ago was the Milky Way. A mere 4.6 billion years ago the Sun was born within it.

Each speck of light in this Hubble Deep Field picture is a distant galaxy.

particle and its anti-matter partner, which exist fleetingly before annihilating each other in a flash of gamma ray radiation.

As the universe continued to expand, the photons dropped in energy as the temperature fell. Particle production ended, first for the heavy particles and then for the light ones. Most of the particle and anti-particle pairs were annihilated, leaving only a small residue—the protons, neutrons, and electrons that we see today.

As the temperature dropped further, some of these particles combined to build simple atomic nuclei. Within half an hour this phase was over, and, for the next few hundred thousand years, the universe was an expanding gas of light nuclei and electrons in a sea of photons. It was an opaque fog until continued cooling allowed the atomic nuclei to capture electrons and form atoms of simple elements, mostly hydrogen and helium. Without the free electrons to scatter them, the photons streamed freely through space and the fog cleared.

Matter was then free to respond to the influence of gravity alone. The first generations of individual stars formed from small knots in larger gas clouds that became whole galaxies of stars. The galaxies formed into clusters and superclusters that are still scattered through the universe today.

Are we sure of this picture?

This view of the universe is rather different from earlier versions. Ancient Egyptian cosmology featured the sky goddess Nut arched over Earth, with the Sun god Ra traveling across the sky every day. Greek thinkers removed gods from their cosmology, and constructed their world view largely on philosophical grounds. A more scientific approach to cosmology began to emerge after Copernicus, in the sixteenth century, discovered that it was the Earth that traveled around the Sun. The current view is the latest step in scientific cosmology, but can we be sure that the modern picture will not also be superseded?

Three important observations form the basis of the Big Bang model. The first emerged early in the twentieth century, when observations revealed the expansion of the universe. This fits into Einstein's theory of General Relativity, which describes the nature of space and time. The second key observation is recent measurements of the abundance of light elements, especially helium, in the universe. These observations agree with the amount that the Big Bang model predicts to have been formed in its first few minutes.

Perhaps the most compelling plank supporting the Big Bang concept was the discovery in 1965 of cosmic background radiation—an all-pervasive glow coming from all parts of the sky. It is our view of radiation from when the universe became transparent. It is the glow of the Big Bang itself, cooled by the universe's expansion.

Recent years have been exciting in cosmology, because new observations have begun to allow us to choose between variations of the basic Big Bang cosmology and some alternative concepts to the Big Bang itself. In particular, the Cosmic Background Explorer (COBE) satellite revealed the incredible smoothness of the cosmic background radiation, in all directions, challenging us to explain how the clumpy distribution of galaxies we see today could have had time to develop. Exactly how much time has passed in building this pattern remains uncertain, since astronomers are only now beginning to agree on just how fast the universe is expanding. This is a time of dramatic developments for cosmology.

Will the expansion continue?

Will the universe go on expanding until all the stars have died? The force of gravity governs the fate of the universe, so the question becomes: is there enough matter and energy in the universe to slow and stop the expansion?

Gravitational lenses

In recent years astronomers have discovered a new way in which to probe further into the universe and at the same time seek out dark matter nearer home. Einstein's theory of General Relativity predicted that the straight line path of light across the universe is affected by gravity. This was first observed in 1919, when light from stars was observed to be minutely deflected as it passed the Sun.

Recent observations have revealed the gravitational effect of whole galaxies and even clusters of galaxies, which can act as a lens to bend and focus light coming from more distant galaxies. Although the images produced by these gravitational lenses are distorted, they do enable us to study light from galaxies that would otherwise be far beyond the reach of our telescopes.

This gravitational lensing has also been seen—on a smaller scale—when the light of distant stars brightens briefly; this is because of gravitational lensing caused by an intervening object. Knowing this allows us to study the lensing objects that are part of the halo of dark matter believed to encircle our galaxy. What is this dark matter? It seems that gravitational lensing may be able to tell us.

This Hubble Space Telescope image shows a large galaxy. Its gravitational force is so strong it can bend light, changing what we see from Earth. The blue images are one galaxy, not scattered objects.

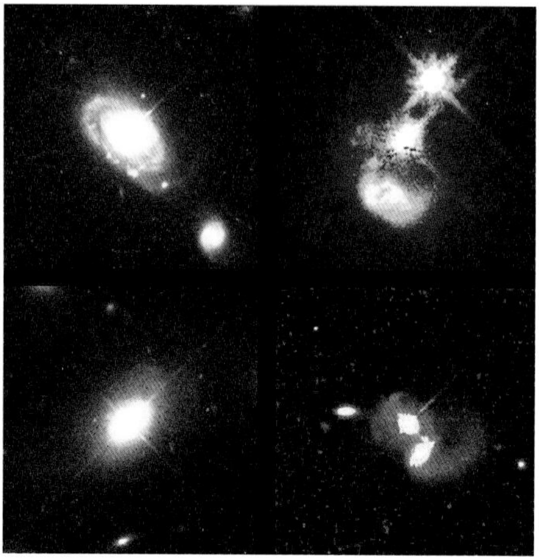

Although rather different in appearance, each of these galaxies harbors an intensely bright quasar. These quasar images show events that happened more than a billion years ago.

In mapping the distribution of matter, it is now clear that there is more matter out there than is apparent. This "dark matter" must surround many galaxies, including the Milky Way, to explain the motions of stars within them. There is more in clusters of galaxies, helping to hold them together. Studies are seeking further evidence of this matter, trying to determine what it is: small dark planets, star-sized bodies, or something less familiar.

Adding all this together, normal forms of matter appear to account for less than 10 percent of the matter needed to halt universal expansion. However, many cosmologists think that less than 10 percent is quite close to 100 percent in this instance. Moreover, there are theoretical reasons for thinking the universe may in fact be on that balance point between eternal expansion and ultimate halt and collapse. It may be that most of the matter in the universe is in forms as yet unseen.

The history of the Sun and Earth play only a small part in this picture. Born long after the Big Bang, both will die long before the universe changes much from the way it looks today.

GALAXIES

Many people today are city dwellers whose view of the night sky is hindered by the bright lights of the modern world. When we are fortunate enough to look at the night sky from a dark place, we see thousands of stars and the faint starry band of the Milky Way meandering across the sky. We now know that this is an insider's view of the vast collection of more than 100 billion stars we call the Milky Way Galaxy.

A dark sky will also reveal the huge Andromeda Galaxy, an even larger star system lying beyond the boundaries of the Milky Way. Both are members of the small cluster of galaxies called the Local Group, which lies on the edge of a supercluster of galaxies. Beyond lies the vast expanse of the universe—countless more distant galaxies.

The Milky Way

In 1785, William Herschel, the astronomer who discovered Uranus, counted stars in various directions across the sky and decided that the Sun lay near the center of a flattened disk of stars. In 1917, Harlow Shapley studied the distribution of globular clusters—clusters of hundreds of thousands of stars—and concluded that they clustered around the center of the galaxy in the direction of the constellation of Sagittarius. Herschel had been deceived by the clouds of

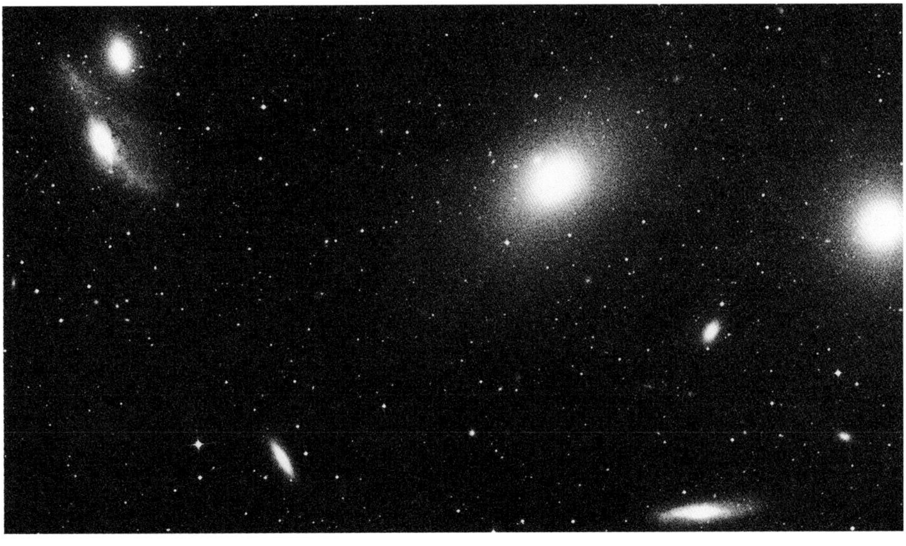

Some of the bright galaxies of the Virgo cluster.

dust which are scattered throughout the Milky Way and which obscure our view of more distant stars.

The modern view reveals the Milky Way to be a large spiral galaxy composed of a thin circular disk surrounding a central bulge, with a halo of stars and globular clusters. Light would take about 100,000 years to speed across the disk: a distance of 100,000 light years. Traveling as fast as the fastest spacecraft, a trip across the galaxy would take well over a billion years! The Sun lies in the disk, some 28,000 light years from the center, completing an orbit around the central bulge every 240 million years.

Around 95 percent of the visible mass of the galaxy is composed of stars, in particular the vast mass of faint Sun-like stars that contribute the yellowish background glow of the disk and bulge. Despite their vast numbers, the distances between the stars are immense, compared with their sizes. The nearest stars to the Sun are 4.3 light years away (40 trillion km; 25 trillion miles). Traveling on the fastest spacecraft, this trip would take some 60,000 years.

The heart of the galaxy is a mystery being slowly unveiled by observations using radio and infrared telescopes which can pierce the veil of dust which hides it from

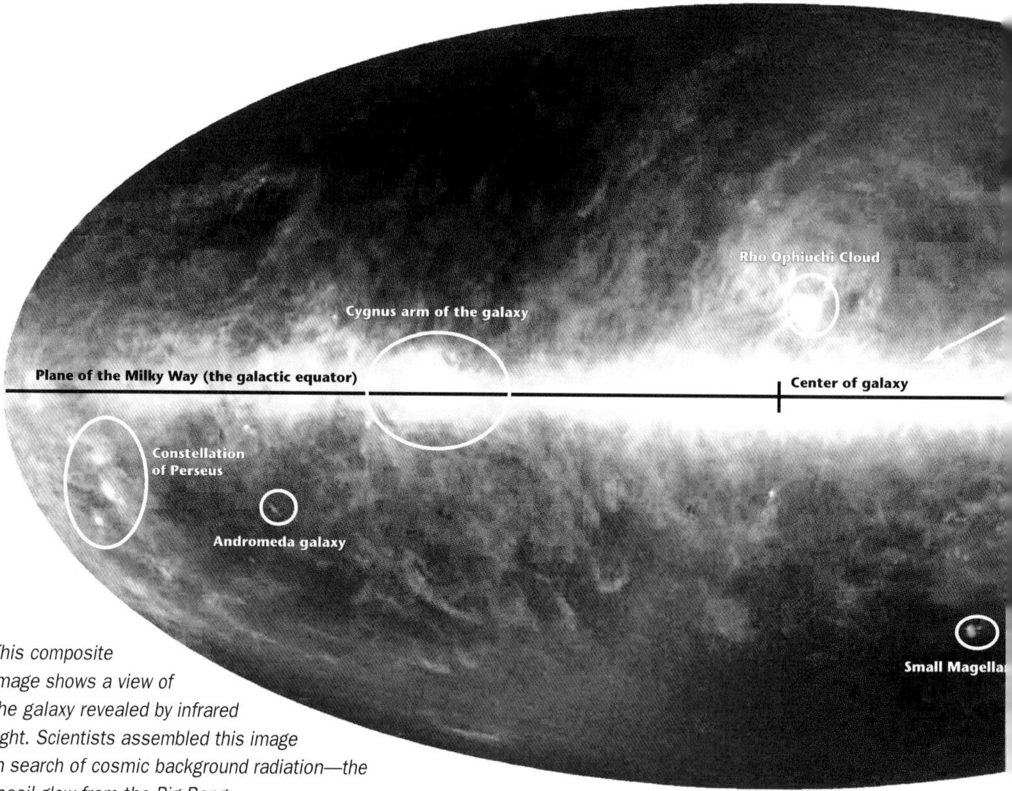

This composite image shows a view of the galaxy revealed by infrared light. Scientists assembled this image in search of cosmic background radiation—the fossil glow from the Big Bang.

our eyes. Astronomers suspect that it harbors a black hole with the mass of more than a million suns.

The remaining mass we see in the galaxy is the thin interstellar medium of gas and dust lying between the stars. Most of this is compacted into dense, cold clouds of gas laced with traces of dust.

The Milky Way system originated in a vast condensation of gas, which began to form stars within a billion years of the Big Bang. Early generations of stars in this cloud included those that form the halo of stars and globular clusters surrounding the galaxy. Successive generations of stars had orbits much closer to the thin disk we see today. When the Sun was formed 4.6 billion years ago, the galaxy was already middle aged, and would have looked much as it does today.

This spiral galaxy has two prominent arms, showing red patches of ionized hydrogen where stars have formed.

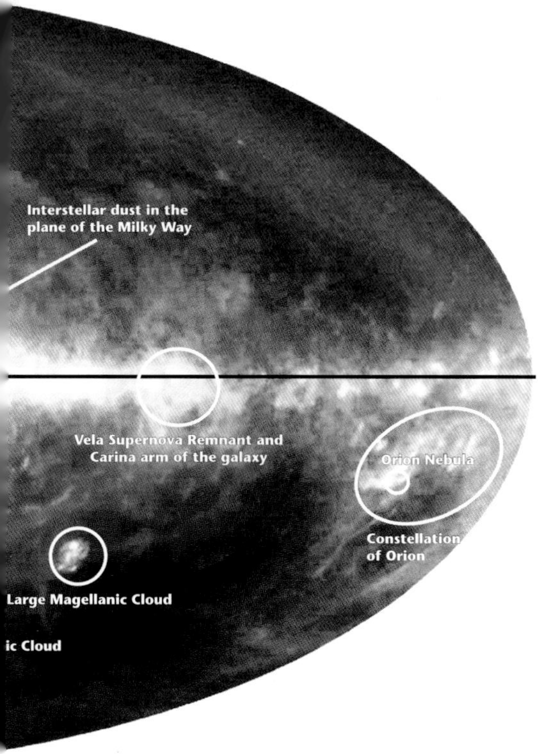

New stars are still being born from clouds of gas. While they live, these beacons and their gaseous birthplaces trace out the spiral arms within the background glow of the disk.

Individual stars will live and die, but the Milky Way will probably continue to look much as it does today for billions of years, until stars such as the Sun are long dead.

Other galaxies

The existence of galaxies other than the Milky Way was long suspected, but only became accepted in the 1920s, when Edwin Hubble measured the distance to some nearby galaxies. We classify galaxies according to their overall appearance, since only in the nearest ones can even the brightest stars be discerned individually.

Most familiar are the spiral galaxies like the Milky Way. Photos of these galaxies reveal that they are in beautiful spiral patterns, traced out by bright stars and gas, hiding the fainter background glow of the disk in which they lie. The spiral patterns range from loosely wound S-shapes to arms so tightly wound that the spiral cannot be discerned. The Milky Way falls midway in this range. Some spirals have a distinct bar across the nucleus from which the spiral arms trail.

Other galaxies show no apparent structure beyond a smooth spherical or elliptical shape. Unlike the spirals, these elliptical galaxies usually lack any significant signs of recent star formation or the gas to promote it. Giants of this class are rare, but are the most massive galaxies known. On the other end of the scale, faint dwarf ellipticals, little larger than a globular star cluster, are probably the most common type of galaxy.

Perhaps a quarter of all galaxies are classified as irregular because they do not fit neatly into either of these categories. They are typically faint, but with a mix of old and young stars, gas, and dust.

Many galaxies, including the Milky Way, show signs of more mass than can readily be seen. Some galaxies hide another enigma—a central powerhouse at their core that generates narrow jets of high-energy particles streaming outward. These active galaxies are believed to be powered by matter swirling around a massive black hole. It may be that many large galaxies have a central black hole with a mass equal to millions of suns, but in most of them, as in the Milky Way, this lies dormant unless brought to life by an inflow of gas.

Clusters of galaxies

Galaxies, like some stars within galaxies, tend to exist in clusters. The Milky Way's Local Group is a small cluster, with 30 or so members, most of them small elliptical or irregular galaxies. The nearest large cluster of galaxies is the Virgo cluster, with some 2,500 members, lying about 60 million light years away. The Virgo cluster is a major component of the Local Supercluster.

Compared with the amount of space between the stars, galaxies in these clusters are relatively close together. As a result of this proximity, they sometimes run into one another, causing cosmic fireworks. The stars within the galaxies almost never collide, but the tenuous interstellar clouds crash together and form new stars, changing the appearance of the galaxy and possibly triggering the nuclear powerhouse into activity.

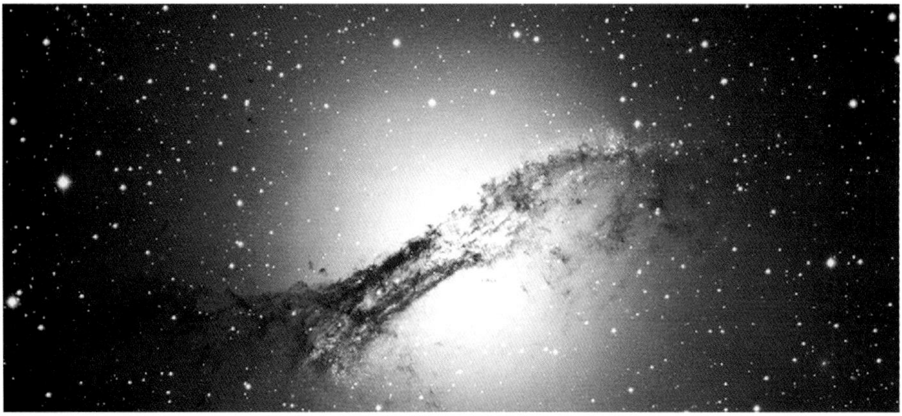

This galaxy, Centaurus A, features an unusual obscuring dust cloud and is a powerful source of radio, X- and gamma rays.

Exploring Space

Before the telescope, astronomy consisted largely of measuring and predicting the positions of stars and planets observed by eye. In 1609 a revolution began, when Galileo Galilei used a telescope to reveal mountains on the Moon, Jupiter's moons, and countless stars in the Milky Way. Despite these amazing discoveries, however, for the next 250 years astronomy was predominantly devoted to measuring positions and cataloging data.

Almost 150 years ago, the first identification of a chemical element in the Sun was made using a spectrograph, which separates sunlight into its component colors. This marked the start of our ability to deduce the composition of the stars. The science of astrophysics was born.

Today, spectrographs are used on optical telescopes hundreds of times the size of Galileo's first instruments. One of these, the Hubble Space Telescope, views the sky from above the distorting effect of Earth's atmosphere. Optical telescopes joined by radio telescopes on the ground and in space can be used to form large radio arrays. Other observatories in space search for sources of infrared and ultraviolet light, X-rays, and gamma rays.

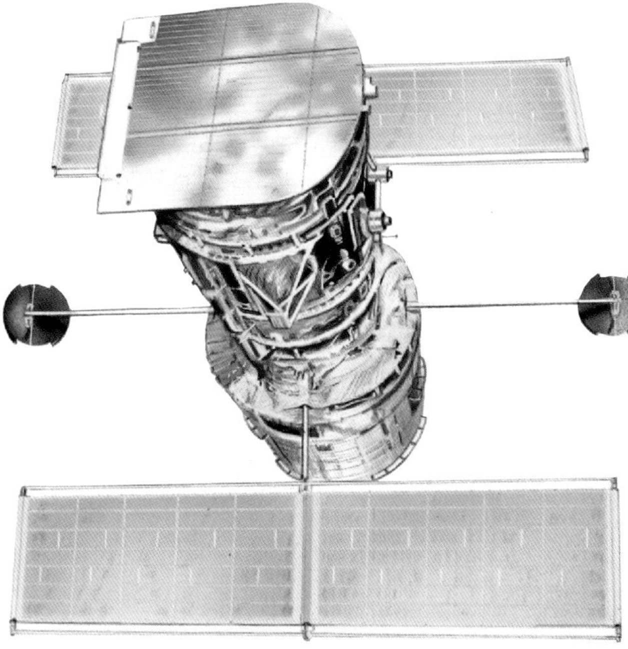

Launched in 1990, the Hubble Space Telescope was repaired in December 1999, and will continue to observe developments in space from above the distorting effects of Earth's atmosphere.

STARS

When we look at the stars in the night sky, it is easy to understand how people in ancient times imagined them to be flickering lights attached to the dark vault of the sky. It was not until 1838 that the first stellar distance was measured and the enormous distances of the stars from Earth and from each other were confirmed.

The first half of the twentieth century saw the development of the physics necessary to understand the composition and structure of the stars and the sources of nuclear energy that power them. As a result, astronomers today have an extensive understanding of the stars and the way they have evolved.

Types of star

While stars vary widely in size, color, and temperature, they are all essentially vast balls of hot gas powered by nuclear reactions deep in their cores. For most of the life of a star, these reactions fuse hydrogen into helium. Late in its life, a star leaves behind this main sequence phase and develops into a giant, converting helium into carbon and heavier elements. In both

Star birth begins deep in a tenuous cloud of interstellar gas and dust. Perhaps triggered by the birth or death of stars nearby, the cloud begins to collapse.

As the gas falls in under the force of gravity, it heats up, becoming a protostar, glowing warmly with infrared light through an obscuring cocoon of gas and dust.

A star like the Sun takes millions of years to form. It then embarks on the main part of its existence, living for 10 billion years as a stable main sequence star.

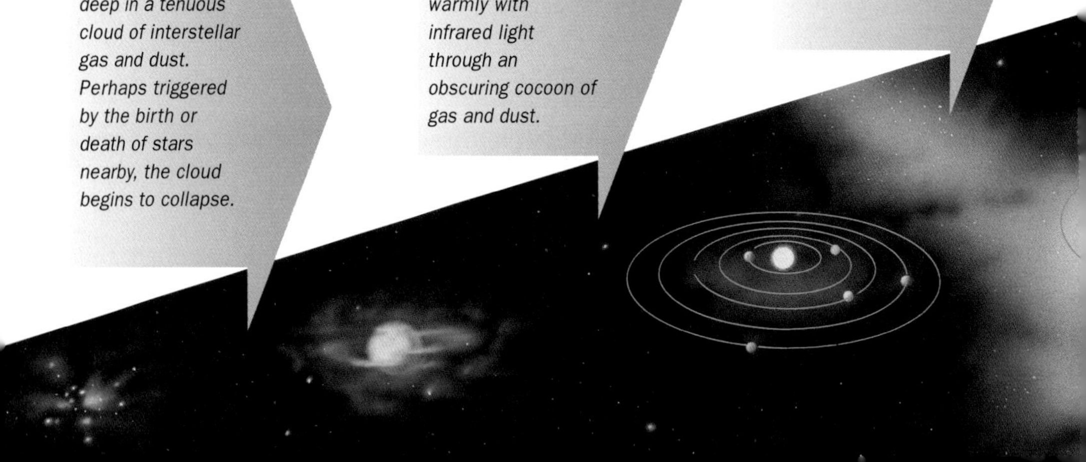

processes, a small fraction of the matter is converted into energy. The temperatures that are required in a star's core in order to achieve this are measured in tens of millions of degrees.

The main factor determining the characteristics of a main sequence star is its mass—how much matter it contains. Stars range in mass from less than one-tenth of the Sun's mass to perhaps more than 50 times its mass. At the top end of the range are the rare massive stars, which are a few times the size of the Sun but radiate hundreds of thousands of times more energy from their blue–white surfaces. The Sun itself has a slightly yellow color to its 6,000°C (10,800°F) surface. A less massive main sequence star will be somewhat smaller than the Sun, perhaps less than 1 percent as bright, with a cooler, red hue. Red dwarfs of this sort can only be seen from relatively nearby, but are the most common stars in the galaxy.

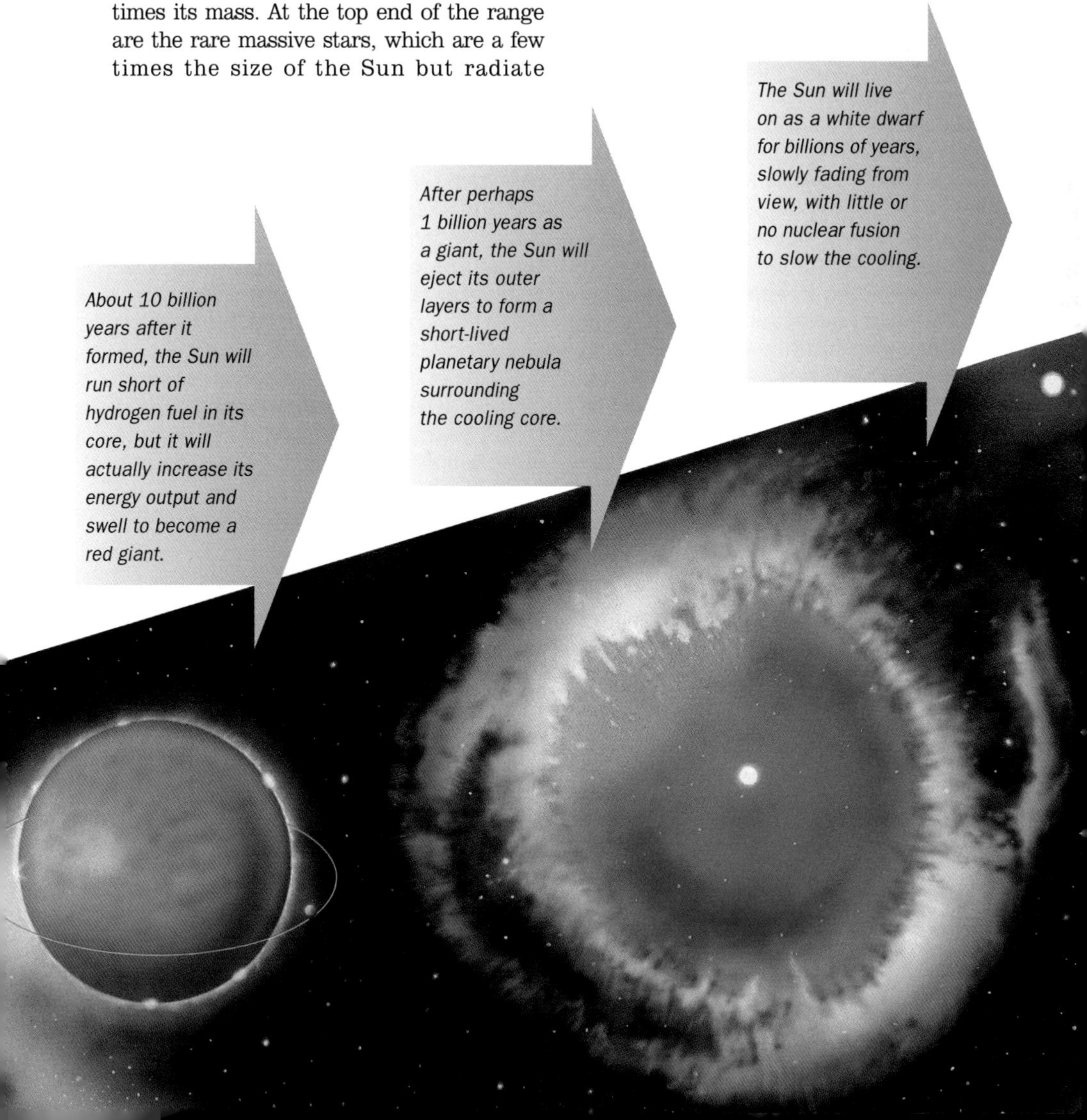
About 10 billion years after it formed, the Sun will run short of hydrogen fuel in its core, but it will actually increase its energy output and swell to become a red giant.
After perhaps 1 billion years as a giant, the Sun will eject its outer layers to form a short-lived planetary nebula surrounding the cooling core.
The Sun will live on as a white dwarf for billions of years, slowly fading from view, with little or no nuclear fusion to slow the cooling.

At the end of their main sequence lifetimes, stars swell to become giants and supergiants. The largest of these are cool red stars, which are more than a thousand times larger and a million times brighter than the Sun. Many of the giants will end their days as white dwarfs only as big as Earth—the faint glowing embers of old stars.

The nearest star

The Sun, which is the only star that we can readily see as anything other than a point of light, is representative of an average star in the Milky Way. Its surface displays a cycle of activity that is roughly 11 years long. The most obvious manifestations of the cycle are sunspots, the numbers of which rise and fall during the course of the cycle. Sunspots are often larger than Earth, and are relatively dark in appearance because magnetic effects make them slightly cooler than their surroundings. They are also centers of other activity—powerful solar flares, for instance, which last for a few minutes, glowing brightly and pouring hot gas into space. This gas is channeled by the solar magnetic field and sometimes strikes Earth, causing intense auroral displays near the poles and disrupting radio communication and, sometimes, electrical power systems.

The sudden outburst of a flare punctuates a more general outflow from the Sun's hot outer atmosphere, known as the corona. This solar wind is relatively mild when compared with the massive outflows from certain other stars. While the Sun will lose little mass through the solar wind during the course of its life, larger stars can blow away a sizeable proportion of their mass in this way.

Observations reveal that some other stars have cycles of activity that resemble those of the Sun. Although we are unable to see sunspots on their surfaces, we can detect the slight changes in brightness that accompany changes in activity.

The Sun's magnetism arises from the flow of electrical currents within its outer layers, but most of its material is packed closer to the core, where the energy is generated. In recent years, astronomers have begun to probe beneath the surface of the Sun using

This globular cluster—47 Tucanae—is an enormous group of stars formed early in the life of the Milky Way; it contains some of the oldest known stars.

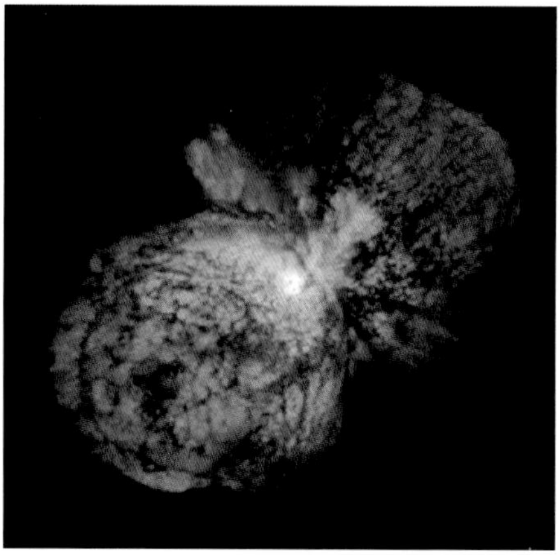

One hundred and eighty years ago, the massive star Eta Carinae experienced an outburst which created the lobes of gas now surrounding it.

After a supernova

Massive stars die spectacularly in a supernova explosion. If the remnant after the explosion is less than about three times the mass of the Sun, a neutron star will result. Despite the intense force of gravity, the neutrons making up much of the star refuse to collapse any further than a dense ball 20 km (12 miles) across. Neutron stars are sometimes seen as pulsing sources of radiation—they are then called pulsars.

If the remnant of the star contains more than three solar masses of material, the strength of the gravitational force cannot be resisted, and the collapse produces a black hole. Not even light can escape from within a black hole. Any matter that falls within the boundary of a black hole is lost from view.

The importance of black holes and neutron stars to astronomy lies more in what happens in the intense gravitational field around them than in what is inside them. Gas falls onto black holes or neutron stars with tremendous energy, producing intense radiation. The largest black holes are believed to be millions of times the mass of the Sun, and reside in the nuclei of active galaxies. They are the powerhouses of these beacons that shine across the universe.

a technique called helioseismology. This is helping to clarify our picture of the Sun's structure.

The life of a star

A constant battle takes place between gravity, which is attempting to pull a star inward, and the pressure of hot gas pushing outward. The battle starts when gravity begins to collapse a small part of an interstellar gas cloud. As the cloud falls in, the temperature at its core increases, and eventually hydrogen begins to fuse together to form helium. The collapse slows as the growing pressure of the hot gas resists the gravitational force. Finally the collapse comes to a halt; the protostar has become a stable main sequence star.

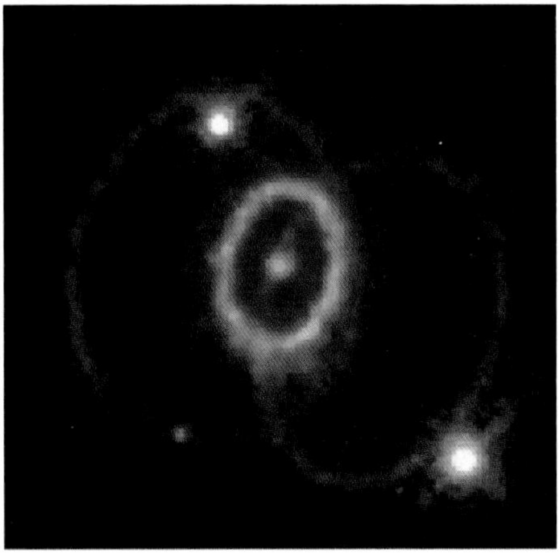

These rings of glowing gas surround an exploded star which was first observed in 1987—a supernova. It is 169,000 light years away.

A star such as the Sun will remain balanced in this state for around 10 billion years, constantly converting hydrogen to helium at its core and by degrees growing a little bigger and a little brighter. The Sun is currently about halfway through its main sequence phase.

In approximately 5 billion years, after it has circled the center of the galaxy some 20 more times, the Sun will begin to grow quite rapidly. By the time it has doubled in size, the oceans on Earth will have completely boiled away. Eventually, the Sun will become a red giant, perhaps 100 times larger and 1,000 times brighter than it is at the moment. It will envelop Mercury, Venus, and Earth, evaporating Earth's atmosphere and eventually causing the planet to spiral inward to oblivion.

Cooler, lower-mass stars will follow much the same path, but over spans of time so long that not even the oldest of them has yet had time to complete its sedate main sequence life. In contrast, massive stars consume their nuclear fuel at a prodigious rate and become red giants in a matter of only a few million years.

Once it has become a red giant, the Sun will begin to fuse helium to carbon in its core. However, this new energy source will only delay the inevitable victory of gravity. Within about a billion years the Sun will peel off its outer layers to reveal a white dwarf remnant that will cool slowly, over billions more years.

Stars that begin life larger than about eight times the mass of the Sun will blow away much of their mass during the course of their lives, but will still end up too large to survive as white dwarfs. Instead, they blow up in brilliant supernova explosions, leaving neutron stars or black holes to mark their passing.

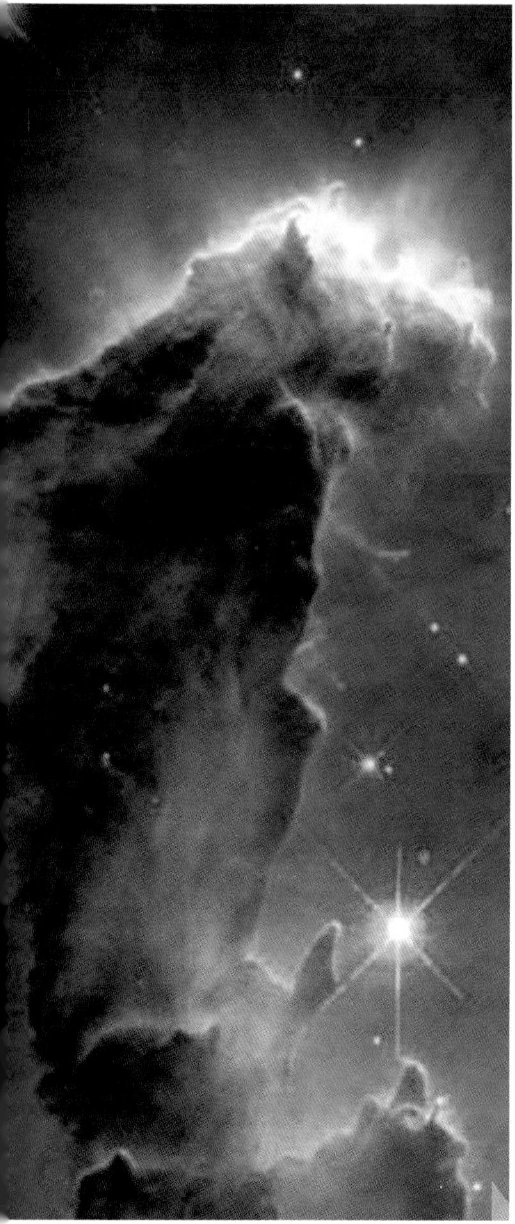

This gas pillar contains cool hydrogen gas and dust and can incubate new stars. It is a part of the Eagle Nebula, a star-forming region 7,000 light years away.

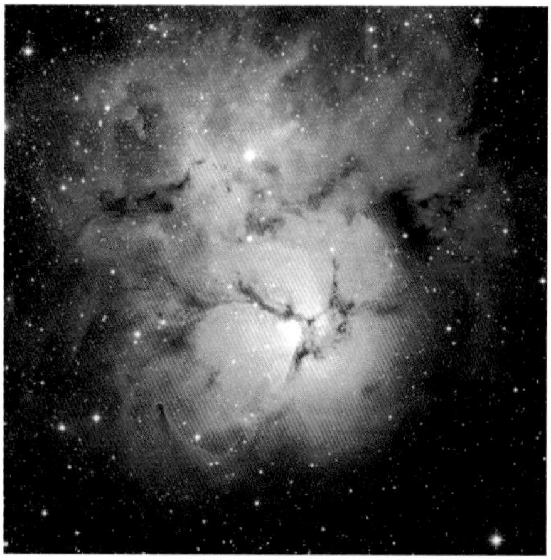

The Trifid Nebula contains hot young stars which cause the gas to emit red light, and cooler gas and dust reflecting blue light.

THE SOLAR SYSTEM

Among more than 100 billion stars in the Milky Way Galaxy, one is unique. It is the Sun—the only star that we know has a planetary system, including at least one planet which can support life as we know it. That planet is Earth, of course, although Mars may also be a candidate.

Until recently, the Sun's family was the only planetary system we knew of, but evidence that large planets circle several Sun-like stars is now accumulating. In time, observations may reveal that they also have Earth-sized planets.

The solar system's formation

A little less than 5 billion years ago, the Sun was formed in a cloud of interstellar gas. The infant Sun was surrounded by a cooling disk of gas and dust—the solar nebula—where knots of material were forming, colliding, breaking, and merging. The larger objects, called planetesimals, grew by accreting smaller particles, until a few protoplanets dominated. The protoplanets from the warm inner parts of the disk became the small rocky planets. Further out, in a cooler region where ices of water, ammonia, and methane could condense, the giant planets formed. These planets grew in mass more rapidly, forming deep atmospheres around rocky cores. The giant planets copied the Sun's accretion disk in miniature to create their moons.

As the Sun settled into its present stable state, the pressure of radiation and the gas of the solar wind streaming outward blew away the remains of the solar nebula. The newborn planets swept up the larger debris. In the process they were subjected to an intense bombardment, evidence of which we see in the craters on the rocky surfaces of the inner solar system and the icy surfaces of the moons of the outer solar system.

The solar system today has been largely swept clean of the debris of its formation. It is dominated by the Sun, at its center, which constitutes almost 99.9 percent of the solar system's mass. Most of the remainder is contained in the two giant planets Jupiter and Saturn, while Earth represents less than 0.0003 percent of the Sun's mass.

The region of space inhabited by the planets is a flat plane centered on the Sun and about 15 billion km (just under 10 billion miles) across. This is almost 50 times the span of Earth's orbit. Vast as this sounds, it is only 0.02 percent of the distance to the nearest star! The great void of interplanetary space is sparsely populated by debris orbiting the distant Sun, ranging in size from particles of dust to rocky asteroids and icy comets—these may be tens or even hundreds of kilometers across.

The family of planets

The inner rocky planets and asteroids and Earth's Moon share a common heritage, yet visits by spacecraft have revealed their histories to be quite different. The smaller ones, Mercury and the Moon, are geologically dead worlds retaining little or no atmosphere. Mars has had more geological activity and features Olympus

Mons, the solar system's largest volcano. The larger inner planets, Venus and Earth, are similar in size but differ geologically. Both show evidence of volcanic activity, but Earth's activity includes moving plates of rock causing active mountain building; this has not occurred on Venus.

The common thread in the surface histories of the rocky planets is the heavy bombardment they underwent early in their existence. Occasional impacts still occur, as was dramatically illustrated in 1994 when Comet Shoemaker-Levy 9 broke into fragments and crashed into Jupiter.

Of the inner planets, Venus, Earth, and Mars have significant atmospheres, although these are only thin veneers over their rocky surfaces. The atmospheres of Venus and Mars today are mostly carbon dioxide. Earth's atmosphere is unique in having nitrogen and oxygen. A combination of oceans of liquid water, an active geological history and abundant plant life has stripped

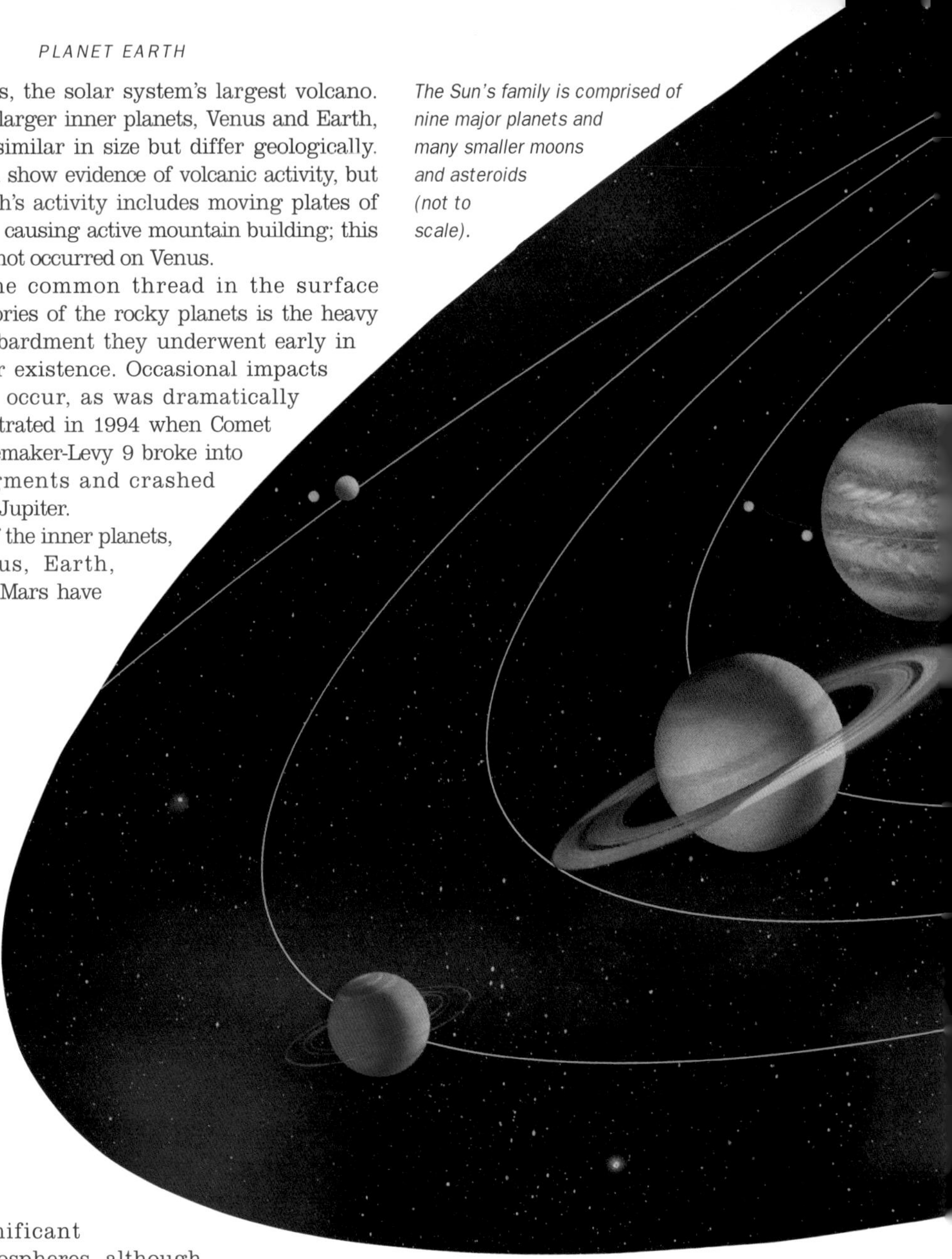

The Sun's family is comprised of nine major planets and many smaller moons and asteroids (not to scale).

the atmosphere of much of its carbon dioxide, and released oxygen.

In stark contrast, the faces presented by the giant outer planets, Jupiter and Saturn, are clouds of ammonia compounds and water in layers riding high in deep atmospheres. These gaseous envelopes are believed to surround a mantle of liquid metallic hydrogen overlying a rocky core. The clouds are split into bands by high-speed winds circulating in regular patterns within the atmosphere. They are punctuated now and then by cyclonic storms, the best known being Jupiter's Great Red Spot, which has survived for at least 300 years.

The smaller, colder giants, Uranus and Neptune, have few atmospheric features, and their blue–green coloring results from methane in the atmosphere.

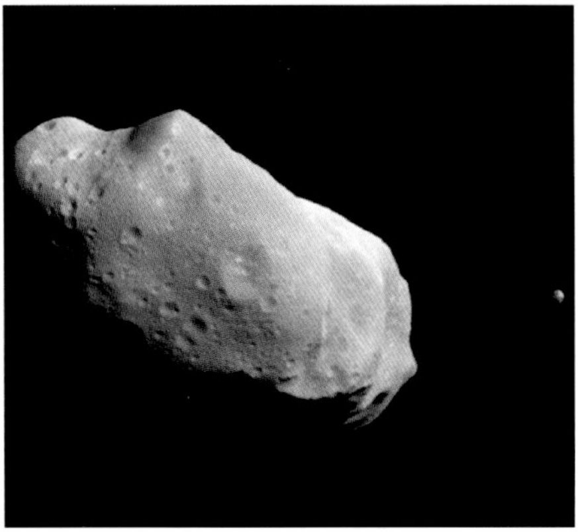

The asteroid Ida seen by the Galileo spacecraft; a tiny moon can be seen to the right.

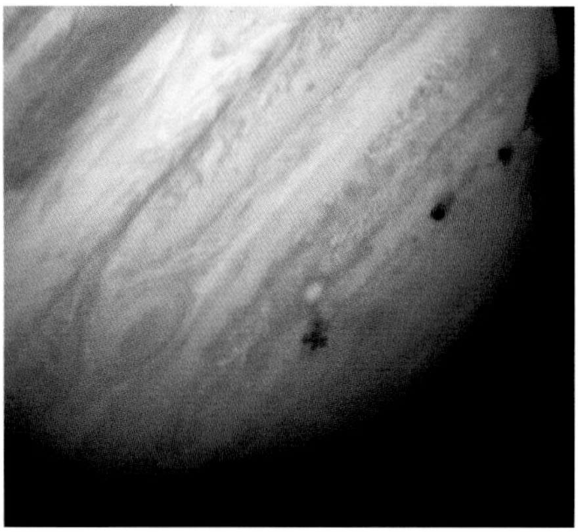

Jupiter, showing the short-lived scars of the impact of Comet Shoemaker-Levy 9.

Their atmospheres overlie an icy core of water, methane, ammonia, and rock.

The giant planets all have large moons in orbit around them which were formed in their surrounding nebulae, plus smaller objects that are probably captured asteroids. The largest moons, Jupiter's Ganymede and Saturn's Titan, are larger than the planet Mercury. Most of the moons have thick, icy crusts pitted with craters that date from the heavy bombardment which scarred the inner planets. Distant Pluto and its moon Chiron are much like them, but Pluto's elongated orbit grants it status as a planet. The one exception is Jupiter's large inner moon Io, which has a surface covered in sulfur-rich rock. Io is locked in a gravitational embrace with Jupiter and its neighboring moons, Europa and Ganymede, which causes heating and results in it being the most volcanically active place in the solar system.

All four giant planets have systems of thin rings orbiting over their equators. Saturn's famous rings are by far the most substantial, but none of the rings is solid. They are composed of icy particles that range in size from tiny specks to blocks as large as houses, and their orbits are shepherded by the gravitational influences of nearby moons.

What the future holds

As in the past, the future of the solar system will be dominated by the evolution of the Sun. About 5 billion years from now, the Sun will suddenly increase in size and brightness, ultimately encompassing most of the inner planets, causing their orbits to decay and the planets to spiral into the Sun. The outer planets and their moons will be subjected to 1,000 times the current energy output from the Sun; this will melt icy surfaces and alter their atmospheres. Within a few hundred million years the Sun will decrease in size to become a white dwarf, only feebly illuminating the remains of its family.

Planetary facts

Mercury

Diameter: 4,878 km (3,031 miles)
Average distance from Sun: 0.4 AU*
Known moons: None

Venus

Diameter: 12,104 km (7,521 miles)
Average distance from Sun: 0.7 AU*
Known moons: None

Earth

Diameter: 12,756 km (7,925 miles)
Average distance from Sun: 1.0 AU*
Known moons: 1

Mars

Diameter: 6,787 km (4,217 miles)
Average distance from Sun: 1.5 AU*
Known moons: 2

Jupiter

Diameter: 143,800 km (89,400 miles)
Average distance from Sun: 5.2 AU*
Known moons: 16

Saturn

Diameter: 120,660 km (75,000 miles)
Average distance from Sun: 9.5 AU*
Known moons: 18

Uranus

Diameter: 51,120 km (31,765 miles)
Average distance from Sun: 19.2 AU*
Known moons: 17

Neptune

Diameter: 49,500 km (30,760 miles)
Average distance from Sun: 30.1 AU*
Known moons: 8

Pluto

Diameter: 2,360 km (1,466 miles)
Average distance from Sun: 39.4 AU*
Known moons: 1

**AU stands for astronomical unit: an AU is the average distance between Earth and the Sun—about 150 million km (93 million miles). Below, the planets' relative distances from the Sun.*

PLANET EARTH

With the exception of Pluto, all the planets in the solar system lie in almost the same plane. This reflects their common origin in the disk surrounding the infant Sun. Pluto wanders far from this disk, indicating a history we can only suspect, but clearly one that differs considerably from those of the other planets. Earth is a better-behaved member of the Sun's family but, like the rest of the planets, it has its own particular characteristics and history.

Earth's motion

The orbits of all the planets around the Sun are elliptical, but, like those of most of the planets, Earth's orbit is quite close to circular. The distance between Earth and the Sun varies between 147 and 152 million km (92 and 95 million miles), known as 1.0 AU (astronomical unit). The point of closest approach occurs on 2 January each year, during the southern hemisphere's summer. It is a common misconception that the small change in distance produces the Earth's seasons.

Apart from its revolution around the Sun, Earth also spins around a rotation axis which passes through the north and south geographic poles. Seen from above the north pole, the Earth spins on its axis in a counterclockwise direction, and it circles the Sun in the same counterclockwise direction. Most of the other planets and major moons behave in the same way, which again points to their having common origins.

Earth travels around its orbit at 30 km per second (18 miles per second). At this speed, it takes 365.25 days to complete one

A total solar eclipse occurs when the Moon passes in front of the Sun and obscures it.

circuit—that period defines our calendar year. The period of a day is defined by the rotation of Earth on its axis relative to the stars—once every 23 hours and 56 minutes. In that time, however, Earth has also advanced 2.6 million km (1.6 million miles) along its curving orbit, so it has to turn a little further to rotate once relative to the Sun. This takes about 4 extra minutes, and makes the time from midday one day to midday the next exactly 24 hours.

Changing seasons

Earth's axis is tilted relative to the plane of its orbit by 23.5°. This axis remains pointed in the same orientation relative to the stars as Earth circles the Sun. As a result, Earth's northern hemisphere is tilted more directly toward the Sun in the middle of the calendar year.

From the ground, the Sun then appears higher in the sky and the direct sunlight leads to warmer weather—the northern summer. At the same time, the southern hemisphere has a more oblique view of the Sun, resulting in cooler winter weather. The situation is reversed six months later when Earth is on the opposite side of its orbit.

The direction of Earth's axis is not strictly fixed, but swings around in a circuit lasting 26,000 years. As a result of this precession, our seasons today would seem out of step to the ancient Egyptians, who lived some 5,000 years ago. Their seasons would have differed by around two months from ours, Earth's rotation axis having changed its direction somewhat since that time.

Other effects also operate over periods of tens of thousands of years to slightly change Earth's tilt and how close Earth gets to the Sun. Acting together, these effects produce changes in the amount of heat Earth receives from the Sun, and these changes may significantly affect Earth's climate. There is some evidence that these changes result in periodic ice ages, but the concept remains controversial. Links between the Sun's 11-year sunspot numbers cycle and the Earth's climate also remain speculative.

The largest rocky planet

Earth is a ball of rock 12,756 km (7,925 miles) in diameter at the equator, but its rotation causes it to be slightly flattened at the poles. It is the largest of the rocky planets in the solar system and, as a result of its bulk, it retains a hot interior; the temperature may reach 6,000°C (10,830°F) at the core—as hot as the surface of the Sun.

As the Sun is finally eclipsed, rays of sunlight filtering through the hills and valleys on the Moon's edge create an effect known as Baily's beads.

A lunar eclipse occurs when the Earth moves between the Sun and the Moon and its shadow darkens the Moon.

Earth's orbit: Earth orbits the Sun in 365.25 days, or one calendar year. It also rotates in slightly less than 24 hours on an axis which is tilted relative to the orbit. This tilt leads to the progression of the seasons each year.

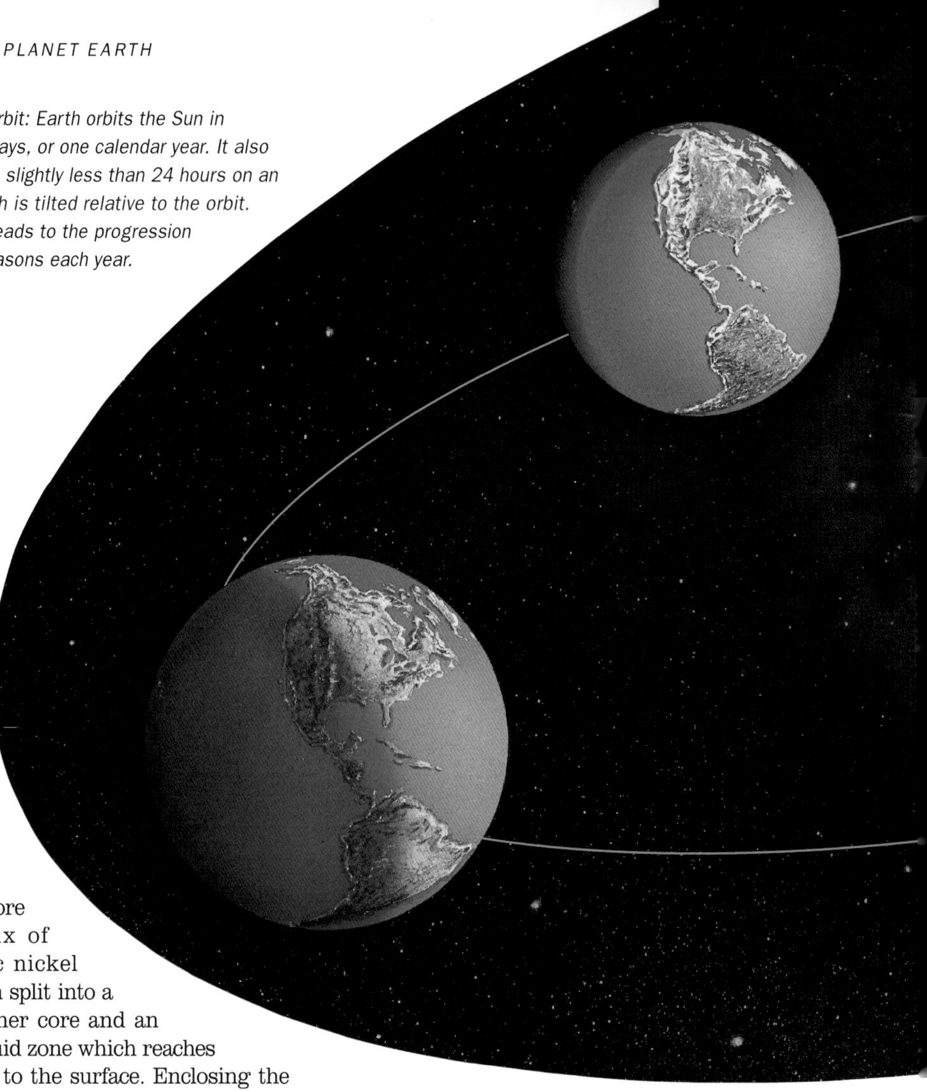

The core is a mix of metallic nickel and iron split into a solid inner core and an outer fluid zone which reaches halfway to the surface. Enclosing the outer core is Earth's mantle. The dense rocks in this zone flow, over geologic time, under the intense heat and pressure. Overlying the mantle, Earth's crust is a skin of lightweight rocks: a mere 60 km (36 miles) deep at its thickest.

Its inner heat makes Earth one of the most seismically active objects within the solar system. On the surface, it causes volcanic activity, and at depth, it drives the separate plates of the crust into motion. This motion—folding the rocks of the crust—creates mountain ranges. At the perimeters of the plates, new crust is created or old crust destroyed. Atmospheric forces such as wind and water flow also act to reshape Earth's surface, by eroding rock and depositing weathered material to form new sedimentary rock strata.

All these processes together act to renew the planet's surface over hundreds of

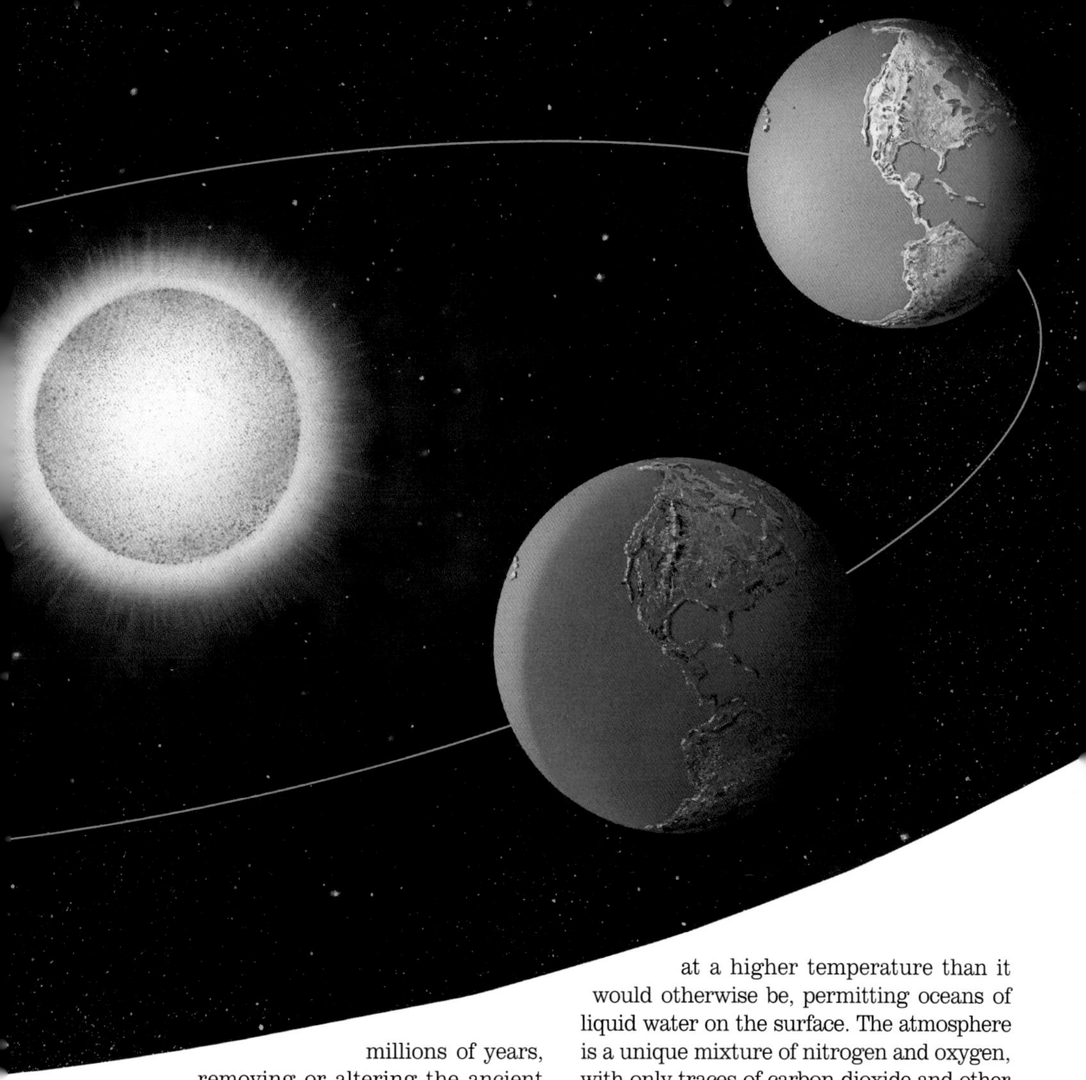

millions of years, removing or altering the ancient impact scarring that can be seen on the surfaces of so many other objects in the solar system. Only a few recent impact craters are visible, providing hints of Earth's turbulent early history.

Earth's atmosphere

Earth is surrounded by a thin atmospheric envelope which tapers off into space and is all but gone 100 km (62 miles) above the surface. This envelope maintains the surface at a higher temperature than it would otherwise be, permitting oceans of liquid water on the surface. The atmosphere is a unique mixture of nitrogen and oxygen, with only traces of carbon dioxide and other gases, and is certainly not Earth's primeval atmosphere. Oxygen only began to build up when primitive forms of life developed photosynthesis. Oxygen reacts to form ozone, which protects the surface of the planet from intense ultraviolet radiation. Life has crafted the environment of the blue planet to suit itself.

Above the atmosphere lies the protective cocoon of the magnetosphere—the domain of Earth's magnetic field. While most of the particles flowing from the Sun are deflected by the magnetosphere, some become ensnared and are channeled onto the north and south poles, forming the glowing aurorae.

The magnetic field originates in electrical currents within Earth's outer fluid core, and its axis is at a slightly different angle from the planet's rotation axis. As a result, Earth's magnetic and rotation poles are not quite the same, creating a difference between magnetic north, as measured by a compass, and "true" north.

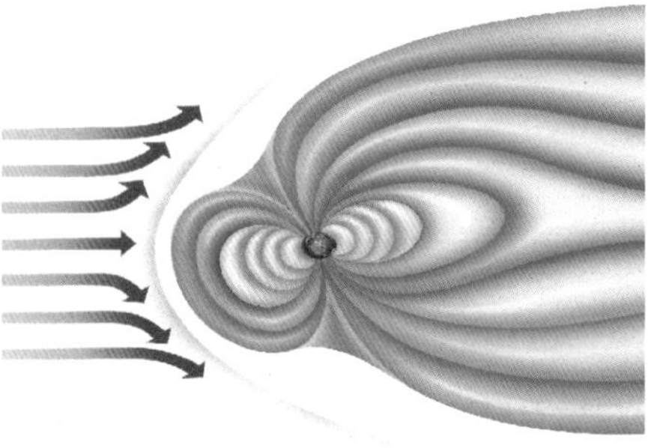

Earth is surrounded by a protective magnetic envelope called the magnetosphere (in blue and brown, top). Some charged particles from the Sun (red arrows) tend to be channeled down onto Earth's poles where they cause the air to glow as an aurora, as seen from a space shuttle (above).

Magnetic reversals

When molten lava from a volcano cools and solidifies, it captures the orientation and strength of the Earth's magnetic field at that time and place. This built-in compass needle has proved a powerful tool for studying the gradual drift of Earth's continents. It has also revealed periods, usually spaced by a few hundred thousand years, when Earth's magnetic field has briefly disappeared. Within a geological instant of only about 5,000 years, the field shrinks to zero and then reappears with magnetic north and south swapped. The magnetic imprint of this swapping is found in alternating bands of rocks along mid-oceanic ridges. Each band is made of rocks formed around the same time, and with the same magnetic signature. This provides dramatic confirmation of the picture of continents drifting apart with new crust forming between them. The origin of this change in magnetic directions lies in the electrical dynamo working in Earth's outer core to create the field. How it happens so quickly and why the interval is so irregular remain unknown.

How this change would affect those migratory animals that seem to use the direction of the magnetic field to navigate on their journeys, we do not know. And what if we lost the protective cloak of the Earth's magnetosphere? Cosmic ray particles from the Sun and interstellar space that are normally deflected or trapped by the magnetosphere would reach the surface of Earth. This would cause dramatically higher rates of genetic damage to animals and plants and lead to mutations and perhaps extinctions.

THE MOON

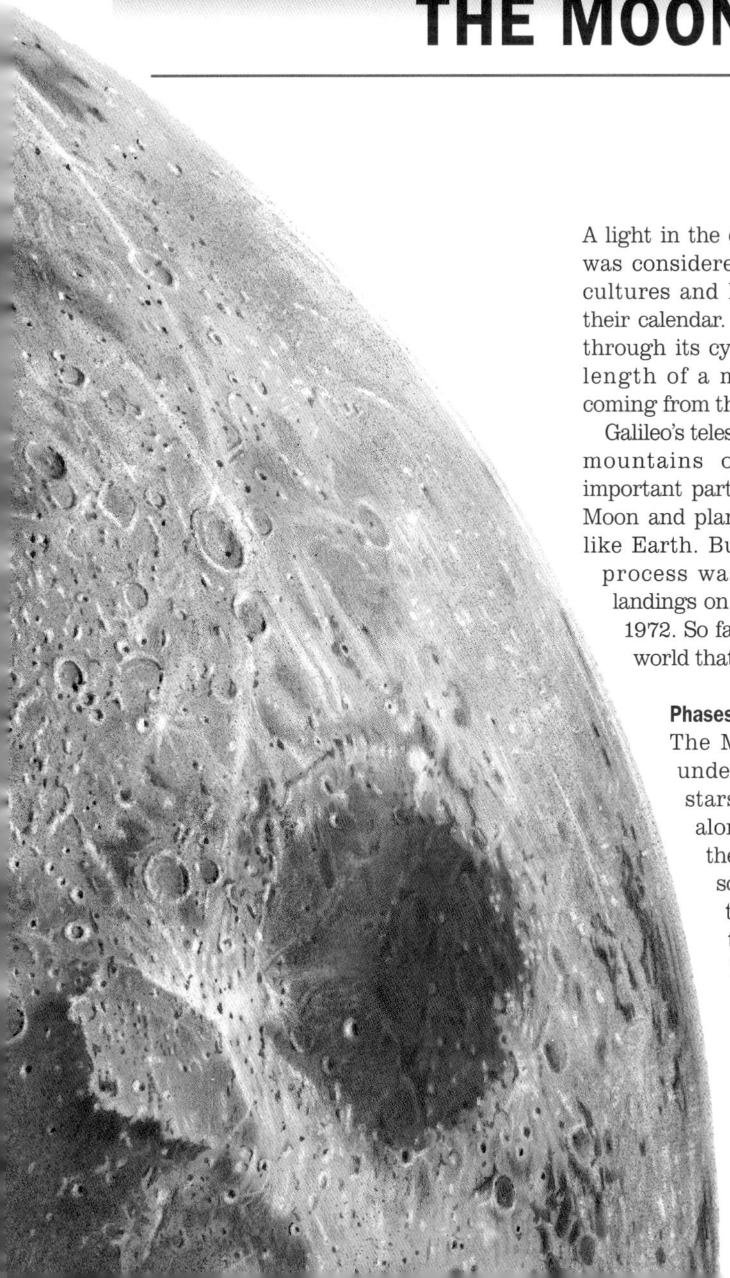

A light in the darkness of night, the Moon was considered a deity in many ancient cultures and has provided humans with their calendar. The 29.5 days it takes to go through its cycle of phases is close to the length of a month, the word "month" coming from the word "moon."

Galileo's telescopic observations in 1609 of mountains on the Moon played an important part in showing people that the Moon and planets were worlds something like Earth. But the greatest step in this process was the series of six Apollo landings on the Moon between 1969 and 1972. So far, the Moon is the only other world that humans have visited.

Phases of the Moon

The Moon orbits Earth in just under 27.5 days relative to the stars. Earth moves appreciably along its curving path around the Sun in that time, however, so the Moon needs to travel for two more days to get back to the same position relative to the Sun and Earth and complete its cycle of phases. At the same time, the Moon is rotating on its own axis, but the strong gravitational pull of Earth has locked these two motions together. As a result, the Moon always

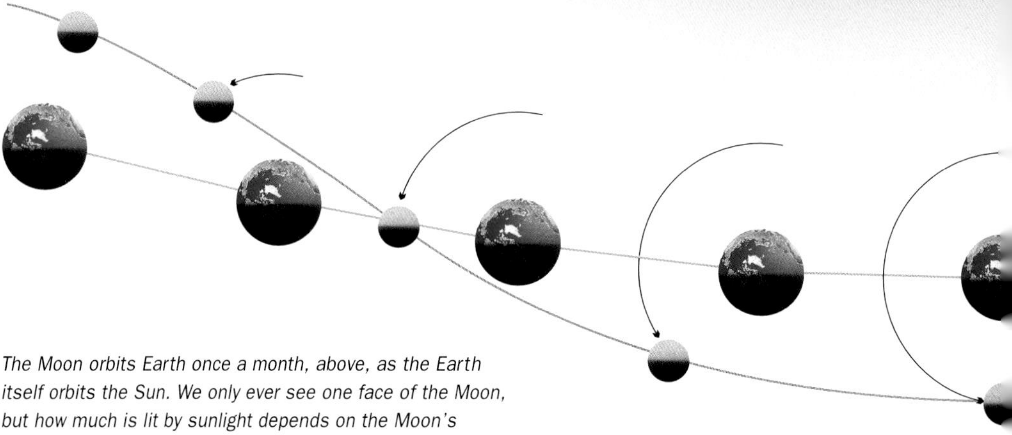

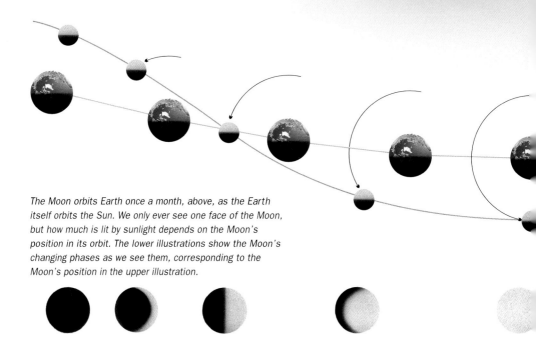

The Moon orbits Earth once a month, above, as the Earth itself orbits the Sun. We only ever see one face of the Moon, but how much is lit by sunlight depends on the Moon's position in its orbit. The lower illustrations show the Moon's changing phases as we see them, corresponding to the Moon's position in the upper illustration.

presents the same familiar face to us on Earth: apart from a little around the edges, we never see the "far side" of the Moon. It also means that a "day" on the Moon is two weeks long!

Half of the Moon is always lit by the Sun, and the amount of that sunny half we can see from Earth depends on where the Moon is in its orbit. If it lies directly sunward of the Earth, the Moon's night side (not the far side) is presented to our view. It appears dark and invisible when it is near the Sun in the sky. This is New Moon. Over the following days the sunlight begins to illuminate one edge of the visible face and the Moon appears as a crescent shape in the twilight sky. The crescent expands through First Quarter and on to Full Moon, when the fully illuminated disk is opposite the Sun in the sky. Over the following two weeks the sunlit portion of the disk shrinks back through Third Quarter towards New Moon.

Solar and lunar eclipses

The Moon's orbit is tilted by just over 5° to the plane of Earth's orbit. As a result, the New Moon usually passes close to the Sun in the sky, but does not cross it.

About twice a year, however, the orbital angles converge—the Sun and Moon line up and the Moon's shadow is cast towards Earth. Sometimes the shadow only just reaches Earth, as a dark spot no more than 270 km (170 miles) across. As Earth turns underneath it, the spot draws a thin line of darkness across the globe.

The Earth-bound observer sited somewhere along the total eclipse track sees the Moon as just big enough to cover the disk of the much larger but more distant Sun. Day turns to night for a few minutes as the solar disk is covered, revealing the faint glow of the surrounding corona.

Observers usually find the few minutes of a total solar eclipse a remarkable

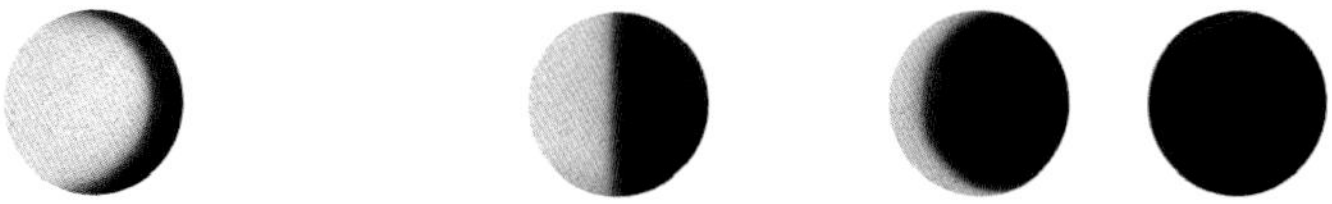

experience, and some have felt compelled to travel around the world, chasing further opportunities to see one.

A wider swath of Earth's surface lies off the track of totality, and sees the Sun only partly eclipsed. Also, about half the time, the shadow falls short of Earth, causing the Moon to appear too small to cover the Sun in the sky; this is called an annular eclipse, and it lacks the darkness of a total eclipse.

When the situation of Earth and the Moon are reversed, the Full Moon can be eclipsed by Earth's shadow. Sky watchers on the whole night side of Earth will see the Moon darken for several hours as it traverses Earth's wide shadow. The effect is somewhat less dramatic than a solar eclipse, but more commonly seen.

The motions of the tides

The most obvious effect of the Moon on Earth is the tides. These alterations in sea level twice a day are caused by the gravitational pull of the Moon on water and on Earth itself.

The water on the side of Earth nearest the Moon feels a stronger force from the Moon than does the center of Earth, which is itself more strongly attracted than water on the side away from the Moon. This results in water accumulating in two high tides: one on the side of Earth facing the Moon, and one on the far side. In between these regions of high tide are regions of low tide, where the water level is at its lowest. Tide heights vary greatly because of local effects, but they can range as high as 10 m (33 ft) in some locations. Tides of a few centimeters are also raised in the rocky crust of Earth itself.

But tidal forces have even more profound consequences. The Earth's rotation slows by 0.0023 seconds per century. This makes a day now four hours longer than a day was when the first complex life forms arose in

Earth's oceans. The same effect on the smaller Moon has already slowed its rotation to make its "day" equal its orbital period. Tidal forces are also causing the Moon to recede from Earth by about 4 cm (1.5 in) a year. As a result, solar eclipses will eventually all be annular, because the Moon will be too far away to ever fully cover the Sun's disk.

Lunar history

The origin of the Moon has long been a subject of debate, but current theory imagines a collision over 4 billion years ago between the infant Earth and another planetesimal as large as Mars. Some of the lighter debris then collected in orbit around Earth to become the Moon.

Both Earth and the Moon were subjected to intense bombardment early in their histories, as the solar system was swept clear of most of the debris of its formation. On the Moon, the last stages of this cosmic storm are still recorded in the bright highland areas of the surface, which are covered with impact craters. Other areas suffered large impacts late in the bombardment; these gouged enormous basins in the surface. Many of the basins on the side nearest Earth were soon flooded by dark lava flows from within the Moon. Rocks brought back to Earth by Apollo astronauts reveal that the youngest of these maria (singular mare, Latin for "sea") is over 3 billion years old, despite being marked by relatively few craters.

Since that time, the Moon has cooled to inactivity, with only occasional impacts changing the scene. The last large impact occurred perhaps 100 million years ago, creating the crater Tycho and splashing debris across the surface.

A new generation of spacecraft has recently begun to build on the legacy of the Apollo missions, by studying the Moon again. The most exciting finding from these recent studies has been the apparent discovery of water ice on the Moon's cold crater floors. These crater floors are shielded from the glare of radiation from the Sun, which bombards the rest of the surface unhindered by any atmosphere.

Earthrise—taken from Apollo 11. This picture shows Earth coming up over the Moon's horizon.

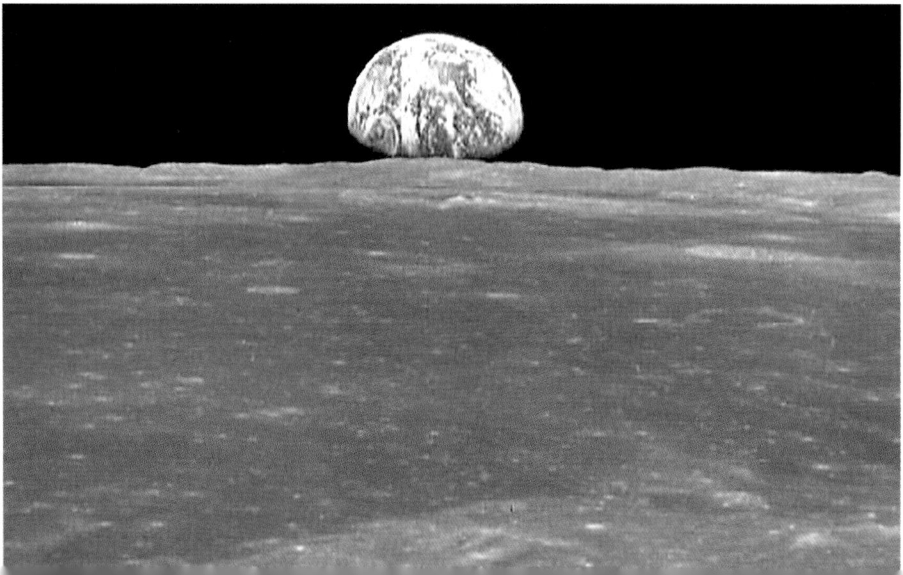

Man on the Moon

Man's first step on the Moon was taken on July 20, 1969, during the US Apollo 11 mission, and was watched by millions around the world as it was broadcast live on television.

The excitement this event generated may seem extraordinary now, but man seems to have always dreamt of walking on the Moon.

Since that first landing, when Buzz Aldrin and Neil Armstrong both stepped onto the Moon, there have been six other Apollo Moon missions, all between 1969 and 1972. One was aborted, but on each of the others, two more astronauts walked on the surface of the Moon.

Buzz Aldrin taking a historic step on the Moon, watched by millions of television viewers on July 20, 1969.

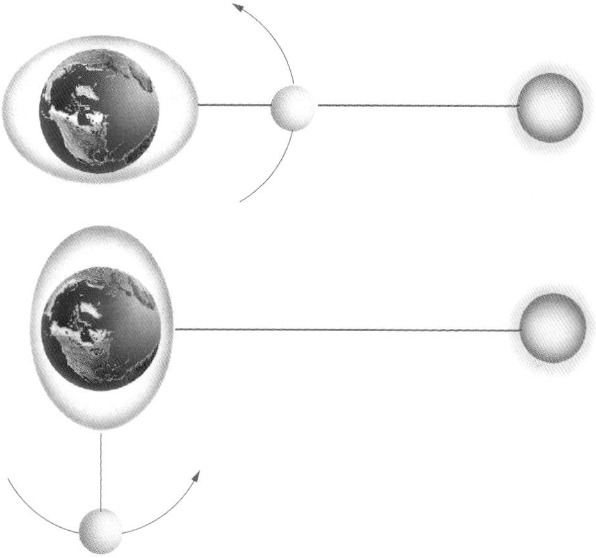

Tides in the oceans, and even in the rocky crust of Earth's surface, are caused by the changing gravitational pull of the Sun and Moon as the Earth circles the Sun and the Moon circles Earth. High tides as Earth faces the Moon, top, and low tides in the same places when the Moon has moved.

SPACE EXPLORATION

Our view of the solar system and the wider universe has improved dramatically in recent years. The exploration of the solar system by robot probes has revolutionized our perspective on the planets and their moons. Closer to home, telescopes in Earth orbit have studied the universe using ultraviolet, X-ray and gamma-ray radiation which is invisible from the ground. Arrays of radio telescopes, including one in space, probe the radio universe at finer resolution than any single optical telescope can achieve. On the ground, optical astronomers are

continually building new generations of larger telescopes which will probe the visible universe more deeply than ever before, and scan the infrared radiation coming from the sky to study regions hidden from visible light.

The nucleus of Halley's comet, taken by Giotto spacecraft in 1986.

Exploring the solar system

The space age began with the beeping voice of Sputnik 1 circling Earth in 1957. In retrospect, it seems a small step, but Sputnik led to a series of Soviet Luna and American Pioneer and Ranger spacecraft over the next few years; they sped past the Moon or deliberately crashed into it.

The exploration of the planets began with attempts to reach Venus and Mars in the early 1960s. In 1973, the US Mariner 10 spacecraft successfully flew past Venus and then continued to Mercury, where it captured what are still the only close-up images we have of the surface of that planet. The surface of Venus is hidden by perpetual clouds, but in 1975 the Soviet Venera 9 and 10 landers returned images of a rocky, desolate surface. More recently, radar maps of the surface have been produced by the Pioneer Venus and Magellan spacecraft.

While the Soviets explored Venus, the Americans were visiting Mars. In 1976, the Viking 1 and 2 orbiters arrived to map the surface from space for several years, while their accompanying landers studied two sites on the surface and tested, unsuccessfully, for evidence of life. This exploration of the surface was not resumed for another 21 years until, in 1997, the Mars Pathfinder landed, with its rover Sojourner. The exploration of Mars continues today with renewed vigor.

The exploration of the giant outer planets began in 1973 with the launch of Pioneer 10, followed soon after by Pioneer 11. They returned the first stunning images of Jupiter's colorful clouds and the surfaces of its major moons. Pioneer 11 continued on to a repeat performance at Saturn in 1979. By that time a new generation of explorers, Voyager 1 and 2, had already reached Jupiter. Both journeyed on to Saturn, and Voyager 2 then made a foray to the realms of Uranus and Neptune. All four of these interplanetary explorers are still journeying outward, reaching in different

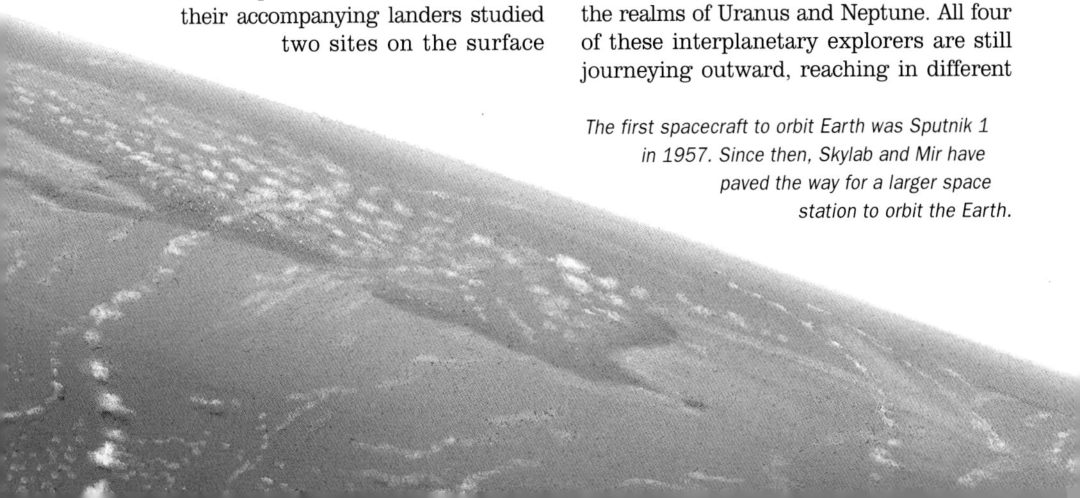

The first spacecraft to orbit Earth was Sputnik 1 in 1957. Since then, Skylab and Mir have paved the way for a larger space station to orbit the Earth.

Search for life

One of the reasons for exploring the solar system is to search for life beyond Earth. The desolate surfaces of Mercury, Venus, and the Moon are not promising sites. Mars, historically the most popular source of alien neighbors, remains a far more likely candidate after the discoveries of the space age. Although the surface is cold and dry today, evidence indicates it was once warmer and water flowed on it. The Viking landers searched for life in 1976 without success. There is no evidence yet that life ever arose on Mars.

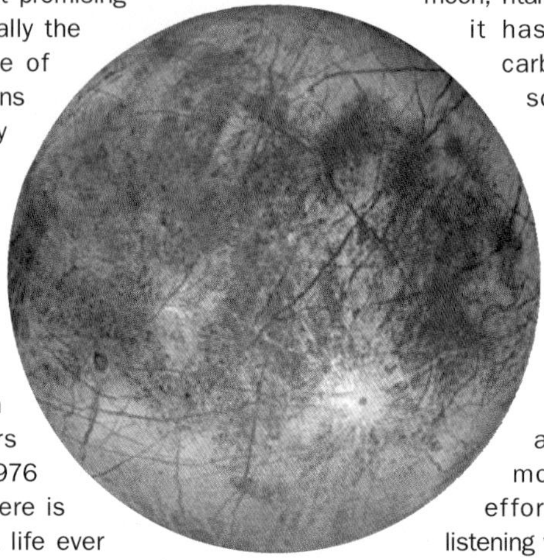

The Galileo mission to Jupiter has enlivened speculation that Europa (above) may have a warm ocean of water under its icy crust. Perhaps life could arise there. The Cassini spacecraft will soon examine Saturn's moon, Titan, and may show whether it has lakes or oceans of carbon compounds where some sort of life might have appeared.

Life elsewhere in the solar system is likely to be primitive, but its discovery may be within reach of interplanetary spacecraft from Earth. The search for life among the stars is far more difficult. Current efforts are directed at listening with radio telescopes for signals from distant civilizations. This project is known as SETI—the Search for Extra-Terrestrial Intelligence.

directions towards the edge of the Sun's domain. Meanwhile, the exploration of the giant planets continues, with the Galileo spacecraft surveying Jupiter and Cassini on its way to a rendezvous with Saturn.

While the outer reaches of the solar system were being explored, objects closer to home were also under investigation. Comets, asteroids and the Moon have all recently been explored.

Humans in space

The exploration of the solar system by robot spacecraft has been paralleled by a program of human spaceflight closer to Earth. It began in 1961, four years after Sputnik 1, with the flight of Yuri Gagarin in a Vostok spacecraft. The Soviets continued with the Voskhod and Soyuz programs. After being beaten into orbit, the US rapidly developed the techniques of working in space in the Mercury and Gemini programs, with the ultimate goal of satisfying President Kennedy's challenge of landing a man on the moon before the end of the 1960s.

A lunar landing was the objective of the Apollo program. It began disastrously with a fire in early 1967 which killed three astronauts. The first piloted mission was Apollo 7 in 1968, followed in rapid succession by Apollo 8, 9, and 10, which tested the equipment needed for the landing. On July 20, 1969, the program reached its culmination, with the landing of the Apollo 11 lunar module Eagle on the dusty floor of the Moon's Sea of Tranquillity. Soon afterward, Neil Armstrong became the first human to set foot on the Moon.

The Apollo program continued through five more successful landings, returning 382 kg (844 lb) of lunar rock and soil, plus photographs and other data which have shaped our current understanding of the history of the Moon.

The 1970s were the in-between years of US manned space activities: between the Apollo program and the advent of the reusable space shuttle. In 1981 the much-delayed space shuttle Columbia was launched for the first time, and regular launches have continued since then, but with a break of more than two years after the loss of all seven crew members in the Challenger accident in 1986.

The Soviet human spaceflight program concentrated on learning how to cope with long periods in space aboard the Salyut and Mir space stations. The US program featured Skylab in the early 1970s and then lapsed until US astronauts began to visit Mir during the 1990s. The future of long-term human presence in space lies with the international space station.

Exploring the universe

One function of an orbiting space station is to serve as an astronomical observing platform. However, most astronomical observations from within Earth's orbit are performed by unmanned telescope observatories controlled from the ground. The best known is the Hubble Space Telescope (HST), a 2.4 m (95 in) aperture telescope which offers views of unprecedented sharpness in infrared, visible, and ultraviolet light. It orbits at a height of about 600 km (375 miles) above the Earth's

As part of the Pathfinder mission, the unmanned Sojourner rover took X-ray measurements of Martian rocks.

surface—well above the blurring effects of Earth's atmosphere.

Equally important is the range of astronomical satellites studying other radiation from space. Satellites such as the International Ultraviolet Explorer (IUE) and the InfraRed Astronomical Satellite (IRAS) have made major contributions in the past. More recently, the Cosmic Background Explorer (COBE) has probed the glow of the Big Bang, while satellites such as BeppoSAX have hunted down elusive sources of energetic gamma-ray bursts. The Japanese Halca satellite is a radio telescope which observes the sky in conjunction with Earth-bound telescopes to create a radio telescope thousands of kilometers across. The Solar Heliospheric Observer (SOHO) observes the Sun from a point 1.5 million km (1 million miles) closer to the Sun than Earth.

Astronauts carrying out repairs on the Hubble Space Telescope, 1993.

Planetary science spacecraft

PAST MISSIONS

Mariner 9 *1971, NASA*
The first spacecraft to orbit Mars. Carried out detailed photography of the surface and of Phobos and Deimos, Mars' two moons.

Apollo 11, 12, 14, 15, 16, 17
1969–72, NASA
Manned landings on the Moon and sample returns.

Pioneer 10 *1973, NASA*
First spacecraft to flyby Jupiter. Now about 10.6 billion km (6.6 billion miles) from the Sun.

Pioneer 11 *1974–79, NASA*
Followed Pioneer 10 in 1974; first probe to study Saturn (1979). Now about 7.6 billion km (4.7 billion miles) from the Sun.

Mariner 10 *1974–75*
Used Venus as a gravity assist to Mercury; returned the first close-up images of the atmosphere of Venus in ultraviolet; made three flybys of Mercury.

Venera 9 *1975, USSR*
Landed on Venus, returned pictures of the surface.

Pioneer Venus *1978, NASA*
An orbiter and four atmospheric probes; made the first high-quality map of the surface of Venus.

Viking 1 *1976, NASA*
Probe in Martian orbit and lander set down on the western slopes of Chryse Planitia; returned images and searched for Martian microorganisms.

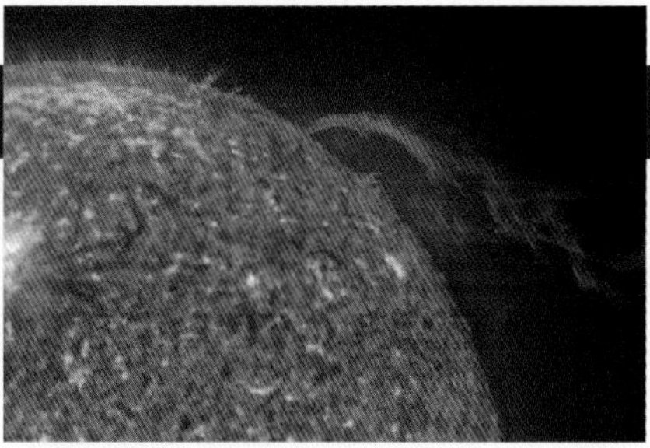

Viking 2 *1976, NASA*
Arrived in Martian orbit a month after Viking 1: lander touched down in Utopia Planitia; same tasks as Viking 1, plus seismometer.

Magellan *1989, NASA*
Mapped 98 percent of the surface of Venus at better than 300 m (1,000 ft), and obtained comprehensive gravity-field map for 95 percent of the planet.

ONGOING MISSIONS

Voyager 1 *1977– , NASA*
Flew past Jupiter (1979) and Saturn (1980). At mid-1998, the craft was 10.7 billion km (6.6 billion miles) from Earth.

Voyager 2 *1977– , NASA*
Launched just before Voyager 1, Voyager 2 flew by Jupiter (1979), Saturn (1981), Uranus (1986), and Neptune (1989). At mid-1998, the craft was 8.3 billion km (5 billion miles) from Earth.

Galileo *1989– , NASA*
While in transit to Jupiter, returned the first resolved images of two asteroids (951 Gaspra and 243 Ida), plus pictures of the impact of Comet SL9 on Jupiter (1994). Now in Jupiter orbit. Atmospheric probe has studied Jupiter's upper atmosphere. Mission hampered by antenna problems.

Ulysses *1990– , ESA/NASA*
Launched to investigate the Sun's polar regions. Gravity boost from Jupiter in 1992 took it out of the plane in which the planets orbit and over the Sun's south, then north, poles.

SOHO *1996– , ESA/NASA*
Solar Heliospheric Observatory (for studying the Sun and its structure), in solar orbit 1.5 million km (1 million miles) from Earth.

Pathfinder *1996–7, NASA*
A low-cost planetary discovery mission, consisting of a stationary lander and a surface rover. Operated on Mars for 3 months in 1997 measuring wind and weather, photographing the surface and chemically analyzing rocks.

Mars Surveyor Program *1996– , NASA*
Mars Global Surveyor is the first mission of a 10-year program of robotic exploration of Mars. It entered polar orbit in September 1997 and is mapping surface topography and distribution of minerals, and monitoring global weather.

Cassini *1997– , ESA/NASA*
Consists of an orbiter to study Saturn's clouds and a probe to land on Titan, Saturn's largest moon. Will use gravity to assist flybys of Venus, Earth, and Jupiter before arriving at Saturn in 2004.

Stardust *1999– , NASA*
Launched on February 7 1999, Stardust is scheduled to flyby Comet Wild 2 in 2004, collect particles from the comet's tail and return to Earth in 2006.

Earth as a Biophysical System

EARTH AS A BIOPHYSICAL SYSTEM

There are many factors that make Earth a unique planet. Its atmosphere, oceans, moving plates, escaping gases, diverse life forms, soils, and the presence of humans all contribute to a distinctive biophysical system. Above all else, it is the dynamic, ever-changing ways in which the air, land, and oceans interact that create particular landscapes available for human use and abuse. From the equator to the poles, from mountains to the depths of ocean basins, plants and animals go through their life cycles nurtured by the climates and the nutrients in soils and waters.

Yet what we observe today has not always been present. The world humans inhabit has been transformed not once, but many times since the hard, rocky crusts of continents and the watery masses of oceans first formed, around 4 billion years ago.

Charles Darwin was one of many scientists who conceptualized patterns of evolution. Organisms did not immediately find their place in the world, he proposed; rather, there were countless histories of evolving life for the different plants and animals that have occupied space on land or in the sea over geological time. These patterns of evolution were not uniform. Past life histories show punctuated successions of periods dominated by particular organisms, followed by extensive extinctions of various species. The cause and meaning of such changes are often a mystery and remain to be explained.

It is very difficult to unravel Earth's history. Geologists and paleontologists are like detectives. They are required to piece together fragmentary evidence using their imagination, and their sense of adventure and curiosity, exploring the world and discovering for themselves what has happened in the past. Some geologists, such as Charles Lyell, have had the ability to synthesize masses of information and develop generalized histories from field observations and interpretations. Increasingly, new technologies, including the capacity to calculate accurately the age of rocks using radiometric dating methods, have opened new vistas of thought, allowing the testing of theories such as that of continental drift.

Discoveries of magnetic reversals in rocks on the floor of oceans, the volcanic character of mid-oceanic ridges, and the age of oceanic basalts covered by a veneer of geologically young sediment, have contributed to our understanding of the processes of sea-floor spreading and hence to the development of plate tectonic theory. This was one of the most remarkable scientific advances of the twentieth century. It formalized the grand dreams of those who could see evidence for the validity of continental drift theory in the rock record and in the distribution of plants and animals. Yet, for decades, these geologists and biologists were not able to convince the skeptics, because they had no mechanism to explain the movement of the relatively light continental crust over vast distances. New technologies in ocean research changed all that; with plate tectonics, it is possible to explain much more satisfactorily the formation of mountains, as well as the distribution of earthquakes, volcanoes and many life forms.

Plants and animals, or biota, occur in particular groups, reflecting their adaptation to each other and to the environment. Interaction of biota with climatic, soil, landform, and other conditions has been the subject of much ecological discovery. Competition and predation are just two of the ways in which species function—on a range of scales from microorganisms in the soil to whales at sea. On land and in the ocean, there are clear regional groupings of biota which contribute to the differences between places. But even these differences are not static—they too are subject to change.

Changes in climate, for instance, whether it be over millions of years or tens of years, require organisms to adjust. On a global scale, it is possible to document periods of Earth cooling and the consequent expansion of ice sheets and falls in sea level. Vast areas of Europe and North America were under 1 km (5/8 mile) of ice as little as 15,000 years ago. Yet Earth warmed, and the glaciers retreated. Today, these areas are home to millions of people.

Rising sea levels flooded continental shelves and river valleys, creating new habitats for plants and animals; in the fertile deltaic plains of many countries, for instance. Such changes have taken place many times over the past 2 million years, the so-called Quaternary period of Earth's history. Understanding why these and other, smaller-scale climatic fluctuations such as the El Niño phenomenon occur is still the subject of much scientific debate.

Against the background of natural variability in climate, another factor comes into play—the impact of humans disturbing the chemistry of the atmosphere and inducing global warming, or the greenhouse effect.

The animals we know today—such as this Chinstrap Penguin in Antarctica—have evolved over thousands of years to adapt to their surroundings.

Plants, animals, and human productivity are highly dependent on the state of soils. Continental rocks are of varied chemical composition; on exposure to the atmosphere, they disintegrate or weather into different mixtures of mineral matter combined with decayed matter from plants and animals. The close inter-relationship between soils and climate, vegetation, landforms, and rock type is well known, and this knowledge has helped us develop crops which can be grown successfully in different soils. Again, however, we are confronted with lands that become transformed as soils are overused and exploited, losing their productive capacity and causing populations to decline and migrate.

Landscapes derived from the changing yet distinctive combinations of these biophysical factors constitute part of the human inheritance. Increasingly, we are recognizing our responsibility towards the management or stewardship of this heritage.

EVOLUTION OF EARTH

Earth is believed to have developed, along with the rest of the solar system, some 4,500 to 5,000 million years ago, when whirling dust aggregated to form the Sun and the planets. In the process, Earth may have attracted a primordial gaseous atmosphere around itself. The planet was then dominated by volcanic eruptions pouring out gases, including water vapor, onto its surface.

These gases gave rise to Earth's present atmosphere. As Earth's surface cooled, the water vapor condensed to form oceans. The oxygen content of the atmosphere was built up through photosynthesis by primitive life forms. Earth's plant life, through photosynthesis, gives off oxygen, which is then available to help sustain animals, including humans.

Earth's average density is approximately 5.5 g/cu cm (3.2 oz/cu in), although this is not uniformly distributed. Earth is formed of concentric layers, the innermost layers having the greatest densities. The density of Earth's crust is only

The core of Earth is made of solid iron, and has a temperature of 4,000°C (7,230°F). This is surrounded by liquid iron, and it is this layer that generates Earth's magnetic field. Above this is the mantle, made of rocks. This is topped by Earth's crust, which is made of lighter rocks.

about 2.7 g/cu cm (1.6 oz/ cu in), about half its average density; the highest densities (around 12.5 g/cu cm—7.2 oz/cu in) lie at the planet's core, which is believed to consist of iron and nickel, both of which are dense materials.

The surface of Earth

When compared to its diameter, Earth's crust is very thin—only 5 to 40 km (3 to 25 miles) thick. Much of Earth's surface is covered by water bodies, such as oceans, inland seas, lakes, and rivers, and these constitute the hydrosphere. The atmosphere and the hydrosphere together sustain plants and animals, which form the biosphere.

Earth's crust is cool on the surface, with temperatures in most cases not exceeding 30°C (86°F), but its deepest parts have temperatures as high as 1,100°C (2,010°F). The material of which the crust is composed can be divided into light continental material and heavier oceanic material. Light continental material has a density of 2.7 gm/cu cm (1.6 oz/cu in), and is often granitic. Heavier oceanic material has a density of 3.0 gm/cu cm (1.7 oz/cu in), and is mostly basaltic.

The thickness of Earth's crust is very variable; it is much thicker under the continents (an average of 40 km [25 miles]) and much thinner under the oceans (an average of 5 km [3 miles]). The crust is thickest below young, folded mountains such as the Alps and the Himalayas. In places such as these, it can be as thick as 64 km (40 miles).

Below Earth's crust

Below Earth's surface lie the mantle and the core. The mantle is a thick, mostly solid layer. It is about 2,895 km (1,800 miles) thick, with temperatures ranging from 1,100°–3,600°C (2,010°–6,510°F). The upper mantle is about 670 km (420 miles) thick and contains pockets of molten material. In some places, this molten material finds its way to Earth's surface through fractures, causing volcanic eruptions such as those along the mid-oceanic ridges or in isolated hot spots. A feature of the upper mantle is the low-velocity zone, as defined by the decrease in seismic waves penetrating through the Earth. The rock here is near or at its melting point, and forms material known as "hot slush", which is capable of motion or flow. It is a mobile layer, over which crustal plates can move. In contrast to this, the much thicker lower mantle (2,230 km; 1,385 miles) is entirely solid.

Earth's core is divided into an outer liquid core (2,250 km; 1,400 miles thick) and an inner solid core (1,255 km; 780 miles thick). The outer core has temperatures ranging between 3,600°C (6,510°F) and 4,200°C (7,590°F). Its liquid nature has been deduced from earthquake information.

Earthquakes transmit seismic P- and S-waves. S-waves cannot pass through liquid layers and are therefore deflected from Earth's core. In contrast, P-waves, which can be transmitted through liquids, pass through the liquid outer layer and eventually emerge on the other side of Earth.

Above Earth's surface

Earth's present atmosphere and water make it unique amongst the other planets of the solar system. The atmosphere, however, has undergone many changes in its long history. If Earth still had an atmosphere of primordial gases, that atmosphere would resemble the gaseous mix which occurs elsewhere in the solar system. This mixture contains an abundance of hydrogen and helium, as well as of carbon.

These gases, however, occur in small amounts in Earth's present atmosphere. It is very likely that primordial gases were lost from Earth's atmosphere and that a secondary atmosphere developed from gases emitted by volcanoes and produced by chemical and biological processes.

It is significant that the elements which form Earth's atmosphere are also found in its crust and thus an exchange between the two can take place. For example, carbon occurs in carbon dioxide in the atmosphere and in the oceans, in calcium carbonate in limestones, and in organic compounds in plant and animal life. Both carbon dioxide and oxygen form part of the cyclic process that involves photosynthesis by plants and respiration by animals. Oxygen was actually absent or present only in very small amounts in Earth's early atmosphere, but became abundant much later. The abundance of plant life that had developed by about 400 million years ago must have boosted oxygen supplies to their current level in Earth's atmosphere. It now seems that oxygen levels which could sustain animal life may possibly have existed as early as some 700 million years ago.

The atmosphere, which rises above Earth's surface to 100 km (60 miles), is mainly made up of nitrogen (78 percent) and oxygen (21 percent), with the remaining 1 percent made up of small quantities of carbon dioxide (0.04 percent), hydrogen, water vapor, and various other gases such as argon. The atmosphere has a layered structure: the densest layers lie close to Earth's surface and the atmosphere becomes more and more rarefied as one moves upwards.

The layer of most concern to us is the troposphere. It is about 12 km (7.5 miles) thick, and contains 75 percent of all the atmospheric gases, including those essential for life. It is within this layer that all our weather occurs. The temperature falls as one rises in this layer.

The stratosphere lies above the troposphere and is about 40 km (25 miles) thick. It contains a narrow layer of ozone molecules. This ozone layer protects life on Earth by shielding it from harmful ultraviolet radiation from the Sun. This ozone layer is under threat from the emission of chemicals produced by human activities—especially chlorofluorocarbons (CFCs), which have been used in aerosol cans and refrigerators. When chlorine is released from CFCs, it rises to the ozone layer and destroys ozone molecules.

In 1985, a large hole (7.7 million square km; 3 million square miles) was discovered in the ozone layer over Antarctica. The depletion of ozone in the area where the hole is has been linked to the increase in skin cancers, especially in Australia. Damage to the ozone layer implies that human impact reaches out 15 to 55 km (9 to 35 miles) into the atmosphere. Worldwide concern about ozone depletion has led to government action; there are now international agreements relating to phasing out the use of CFCs.

Human contribution to Earth's evolution

The changes in the composition of Earth's atmosphere, and the damage to the ozone layer, vividly demonstrate that since the advent of industrialization, humans have had considerable impact on Earth's environment and, as a consequence, on its biosphere. Many of these adverse effects were not foreseen.

It is becoming increasingly clear that human behavior can have far-reaching consequences; not only on our own local environment, but on the entire evolution of Earth. Therefore, all proposed industrial, agricultural, and other developments need to be carefully evaluated in terms of their impact on the environment before they are approved and implemented.

The gaseous mix of the troposphere has also been inadvertedly altered by humans, particularly since the acceleration of industrialization in the nineteenth century. The principal change is the increase of carbon dioxide due to emissions from the burning of fossil fuels (coal, natural gas, and petroleum) by factories, power plants, railway engines, and automobiles.

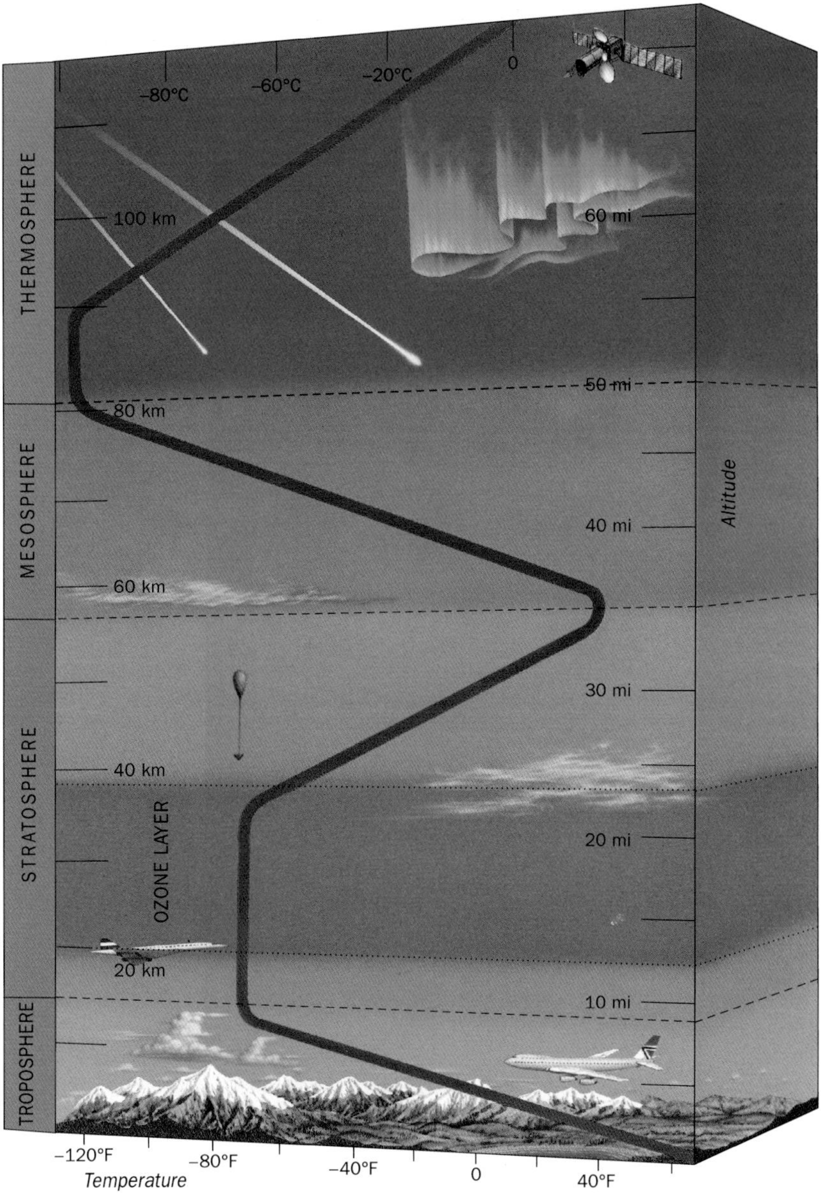

The troposphere is the layer of the atmosphere where life exists. The stratosphere is the next layer. The ozone layer, which absorbs most of the Sun's harmful ultraviolet rays, is in the stratosphere. The next layer is the mesosphere. The thermosphere is the outer layer of our atmosphere. Gases are very thin here, and this is where auroras and meteors are seen. The red line shows the decreases and increases in temperature through each layer of the atmosphere.

Although carbon dioxide forms only about 0.04 percent of Earth's atmosphere, it is a critical component because, along with the other greenhouse gases, it acts as a blanket, trapping some of the heat of the Earth that would otherwise escape into space.

The emission of carbon dioxide and other gases (methane, nitrous oxide, and ozone) is believed to have caused global warming—the greenhouse effect. Global temperatures have risen by 0.3° to 0.6°C (32.5° to 33.1°F) since the mid-nineteenth century and, at the current rate of increase of greenhouse gases, this figure could double by the middle of the twenty-first century. Some predictions place the increase at between 1.5°C (34.7°F) and 5.5°C (41.9°F).

The weather patterns in the world have shown great disturbance in recent decades, according to some observers. This also is being attributed to the greenhouse effect. If global warming continues, it could result in the melting of polar ice sheets and the consequent rising of sea levels, which in turn would seriously threaten low-lying areas, including quite a number of major coastal cities.

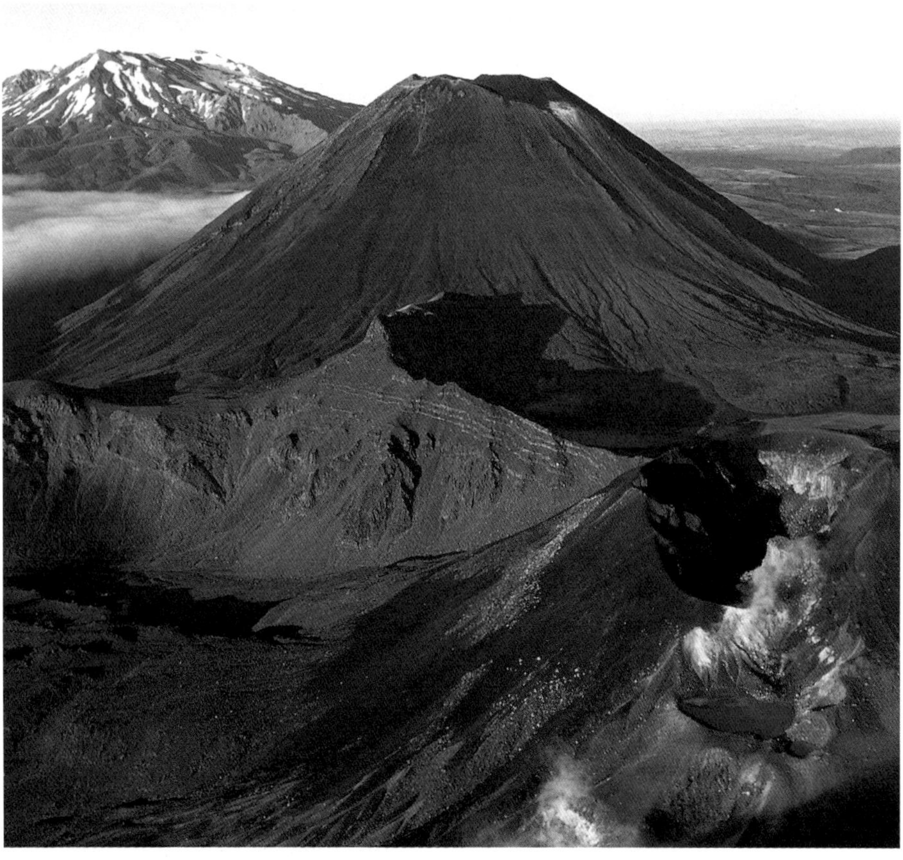

Volcanoes, such as this one in the North Island of New Zealand, can provide geologists with clues to the puzzle of Earth's history.

MOVEMENT OF PLATES

Earth is a dynamic planet, and forces within it are continuously active. Continents and oceans have changed in position and shape over time. Earthquakes and other evidence prove that Earth's crust, which is a solid and rigid layer, is broken up into parts called lithospheric or tectonic plates. Plate boundaries coincide with major earthquake zones, many of which also have volcanic chains along them. Seven major plates (Pacific, North American, South American, Eurasian, African, Indo-Australian, and Antarctic), and perhaps twice as many minor plates, have been identified.

Over many millions of years, crustal plates have moved considerably. They have separated (divergent plates), giving rise to oceans, collided (convergent plates), forming the world's highest mountains and the deep oceanic trenches, and slid past each other along fault lines. Thus Earth's crust has spread at divergent plate boundaries and contracted at convergent plate boundaries.

Divergent plate boundaries

In the middle of the Atlantic and Indian oceans, and in the eastern part of the Pacific Ocean, long rifts exist where molten material has risen to form undersea chains of volcanoes. This molten material originates from magma pockets

Earth's crust is made up of rigid tectonic plates. Their movement, over millions of years, has determined the structure of our continents and oceans, the formation of mountains and volcanoes, and the distribution of earthquakes.

within Earth's upper mantle, and crystallizes as basalt on cooling. These oceanic volcanic chains, called mid-oceanic ridges, form an interlinked system about 60,000 km (37,300 miles) long. In some places, the volcanoes have erupted above the water level, forming islands such as Iceland and the Azores.

Mid-oceanic ridges are not continuous features, but are fractured at several places, with parts being offset by transform faults. Shallow-focus earthquakes, recorded by sensitive instruments, occur frequently along mid-oceanic ridges.

Each time a new series of volcanic eruptions takes place, the existing ridge is split in two and the parts are pushed apart, spreading the sea floor. The corresponding parts of the early ridges are now far apart, on opposite sides of the current mid-oceanic ridge. The separated bands can be identified on the basis of their recorded magnetic directions and age. When the basaltic bands crystallized, Earth's magnetic direction at the time of formation was imprinted in them. Such data proves that Earth's magnetic direction has reversed many times during geological history.

Sea-floor spreading is believed to have produced the Atlantic and Indian oceans, and to have enlarged the Pacific Ocean. Plates move very slowly—on average, only about 2–5 cm (3/4–2 inches) per year—with the spreading of the Atlantic Ocean having taken about 65 million years. Some plates are separating much more quickly—the Nazca and Pacific plates move at about 18 cm (7 inches) per year.

Compared with the continental crust, which is more than 1,000 million years old, most of the oceanic crust (at less than 65 million years old) is geologically very young, the youngest parts being those that lie along the mid-oceanic ridges.

The Red Sea is an example of new sea-floor spreading, whilst the elongated Great Rift Valley in Africa, which extends for more than 2,890 km (1,800 miles), possibly

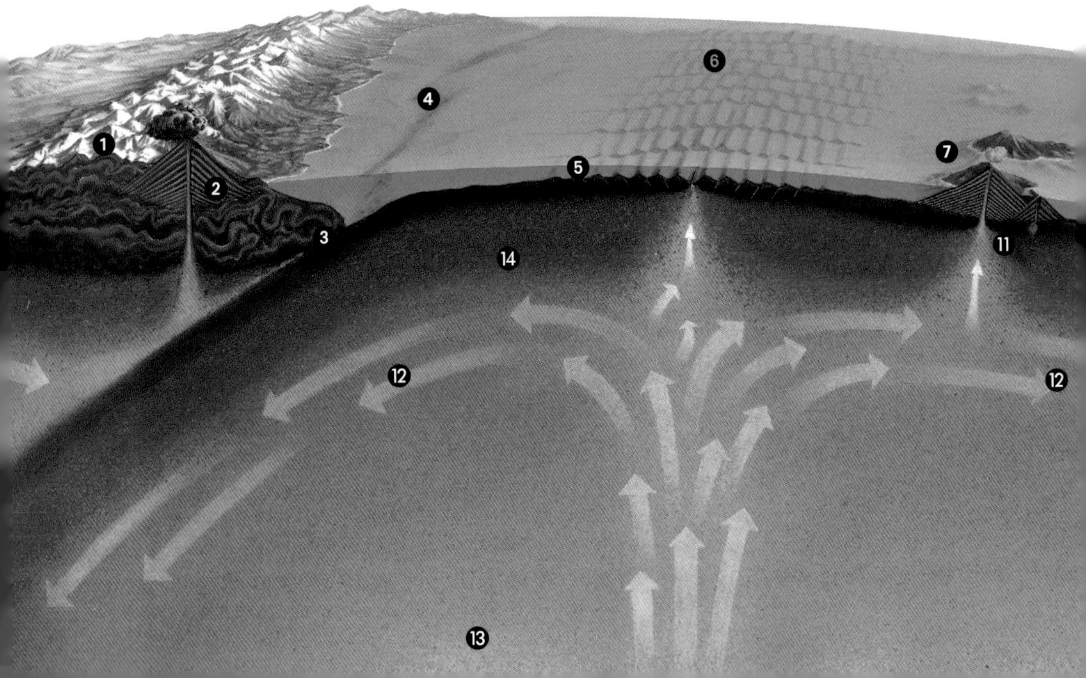

represents new continental rifting and splitting. There are several centers of volcanic eruptions along the Rift Valley; to the north and south of Lake Kivu, for example.

Convergent plate boundaries

Crustal plates may split and diverge on one side, and collide with other plates on the opposite side, giving rise to volcanic chains and oceanic ridges.

When plates collide, one plate slides under the other one in a process called subduction, the subducted plate being pushed deep into Earth's mantle. As a result of subduction, collision zones are marked by deep focus earthquakes, such as have occurred in recent times in Japan, Iran and Afghanistan. Subducted plates are dragged deep into the Earth, where they melt. This molten material later rises to form volcanoes.

The deep oceanic trenches lying parallel to the volcanic island arcs, which formed as a result of oceanic-to-oceanic plate collisions, are the deepest features on Earth's surface, ranging from 7,000 to 11,000 m (23,000 to 36,000 ft) deep. The Marianas Trench in the West Pacific is nearly 11,000 m (more than 36,000 ft) deep. There are several trenches in the western Pacific, along the coasts of Japan and the Philippines.

Where continental and oceanic plates collide, the continental plate is crumpled and the oceanic plate buckles downward deep into Earth, where it melts and mixes with the molten material inside the Earth. Lavas from this mixed molten material are lighter in density and color than oceanic basalt. The rock formed is andesite and it is found along a long chain around the Pacific Ocean. Several plates have collided with the Pacific Plate, giving rise to folded mountain chains, including the Cascade Range in the western USA, and the Andes in South America. This circum-Pacific zone is often referred to as the "Ring of Fire" because of the presence of active volcanoes.

Continent-to-continent plate collisions result in the formation of mountain ranges

The processes and results of plate movement: 1. Fold mountains 2. Active volcano 3. Subduction zone 4. Subduction trench 5. Spreading sea-floor 6. Mid-oceanic ridge 7. Hot spot island chain (volcanic) 8. Oceanic crust 9. Colliding plates form mountain chain 10. Rift valley 11. Hot spot 12. Magma (convection currents) 13. Asthenosphere 14. Lithosphere

such as the European Alps and the Himalayas, in Asia. The process gives rise to crustal thickening.

The stupendous Himalayan range arose when the Indo-Australian Plate collided with the Eurasian Plate. The Eurasian Plate rode over the Indian side, pushing up huge sedimentary strata from the then-existing sea into great mountain folds, some of which were thrust towards the south and almost overturned.

Three parallel ranges were formed in successive geological epochs. The southernmost chain is the lowest, ranging from 900 to 1,200 m (2,950 to 3,935 ft) in height, whilst the middle chain rises 2,000 to 4,500 m (6,560 to 14,765 ft).

The chain of highest elevation, lying in the north, has the world's highest peaks (topped by Mount Everest, at 8,848 m [29,028 ft]), which are about 8,500 m (27,885 ft) in height. Its average altitude is 6,000 m (19,685 ft). It adjoins the high Tibetan Plateau, which has an average altitude of 4,000 m (13,125 ft).

Transform fault boundaries

The third type of plate boundary involves two plates sliding past each other along a fault line. There is no collision or separation involved, but earthquakes result from the movement of these plates. The best-known example of this is the San Andreas Fault in California, which has been associated with major earthquakes in San Francisco and Los Angeles. Along that fault line, the Pacific Plate is sliding northwards in relation to the adjacent North American Plate.

Continental drift

It was in 1915 that Alfred Wegener fully developed his theory that the continents had drifted to their present positions. His hypothesis centered on the close jigsaw fit of Africa and South America. The English philosopher and essayist Francis Bacon had drawn attention to this much earlier and, in 1858, so did Snider-Pellegrini, who pointed to the similarities in the characteristics of plant fossils in coal deposits found in both continents.

A panoramic view of the Himalayas, the world's highest mountain range. The Himalayas are actually made up of three parallel ranges, formed at different times.

Wegener marshalled evidence to show that the fit involved the juxtaposition of river valleys, mountain chains, and similar rock formations and mineral deposits. Those rock formations contained similar fossils. Wegener hypothesized that all the continents once formed a single landmass, which he named Pangaea, and which, he claimed, began breaking up in the Carboniferous Period (divided into the Pennsylvanian and Mississippian epochs in the United States) about 300 million years ago. That split first resulted in two continents: a northern one called Laurasia and a southern one called Gondwanaland. The various supposed parts of the southern continent (South America, Africa, India, Australia, and Antarctica) showed a much better geological fit than did the supposed parts of the northern one.

Wegener's theory was based on the premise that the light continents floated on a denser underlying crust, and that these continents thus drifted to their present positions. The absence of an acceptable mechanism for drifting was used as an argument against Wegener's ideas—it was thought physically impossible that the solid continents could have moved through an underlying rigid, denser layer.

Nevertheless, many scientists accepted that the continents had moved to their present positions because there was mounting geological evidence, such as that marshalled by Alex du Toit of South Africa, which proved similarities in areas which had been said to have once been joined together.

During the past 50 years, modern technology has provided much new information about the sea floors. In particular, evidence has emerged leading to the acceptance of sea-floor spreading. This, in turn, has led to the development of plate tectonics, which may be considered an update of Wegener's ideas about continental movement. As a result, his main ideas about the original juxtaposition of the continents have now been largely vindicated.

The koala, which is unique to Australia, may be an animal that became isolated after the break-up of the supercontinent Gondwanaland.

Active volcanoes, such as Volcan de Pacaya in Guatemala, generally occur along fault lines between plates or along mid-oceanic ridges. Molten lava bursts through the Earth's crust and flows downwards, sometimes causing great loss of life and the destruction of entire towns.

ROCKS

Earth's crust consists of rocks. These rocks combine a variety of minerals that may or may not be crystalline, and which can form in several ways. Igneous rocks are made of crystalline minerals which originate during the cooling of molten material called magma. In contrast, sedimentary rocks result from the compaction or consolidation of loosened minerals, rock fragments, and plant and animal matter. Metamorphic rocks are formed when existing rocks are altered through pressure and temperature—they result either from compaction under pressure or from partial remelting, when new minerals can be formed from crystallization.

Minerals

Minerals are inorganic substances with defined chemical and atomic structures. When magmas cool, minerals crystallize. Each mineral exhibits its own unique crystalline shape. Minerals can also originate in the breakdown of pre-existing minerals, as in the case of clays, or from the reconstitution of existing materials, as in the case of metamorphic rocks.

A common mineral is quartz (an oxide of silica), which occurs as large crystals in some rocks and as sand on sea shores. It is a light-colored mineral. Other light-colored minerals include felspars, which are silicates combining silica, aluminum, potassium, sodium, and calcium. These light-colored minerals are commonly found in rocks of light density, such as granite. Dark-colored silicates, which are combinations of silica, magnesium, and iron

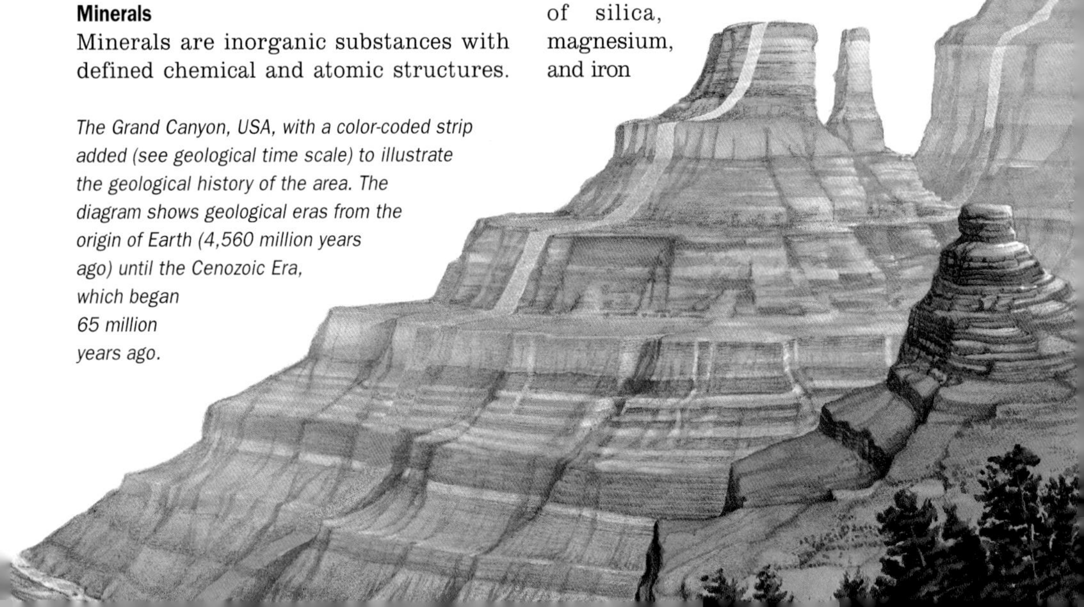

The Grand Canyon, USA, with a color-coded strip added (see geological time scale) to illustrate the geological history of the area. The diagram shows geological eras from the origin of Earth (4,560 million years ago) until the Cenozoic Era, which began 65 million years ago.

(pyroxenes, amphiboles, olivine, and dark micas), predominate in dark-colored rocks such as basalt.

Igneous rocks

When molten material lying deep within the Earth's crust cools, minerals form large crystals, because of slow cooling, producing plutonic igneous rocks. The most common plutonic rock is granite, which is also the rock that is most widespread in the continental crust. Granite is light colored and low in density because it contains silica and felspars.

When magma is extruded onto the Earth's surface as lava, faster cooling takes place, resulting in smaller crystals, even glass. The most common volcanic rock is basalt, which is dark colored and dense because of dark-colored minerals such as biotite, pyroxenes, amphiboles, and olivine. The ocean floors are largely made up of basalt.

Era	Major geological events	Period	Millions of years ago
CENOZOIC	• Ice age • First humans	Quaternary	1.6
	• Rockies, Alps and Himalayas begin to form • First hominids	Tertiary	65
MESOZOIC	• First flowering plants • Extinction of giant reptiles	Cretaceous	145
	• Pangaea splits into Gondwanaland and Laurasia • First birds and mammals	Jurassic	208
	• First dinosaurs • Supercontinent of Pangaea in existence	Triassic	245
PALEOZOIC	• First amphibians	Permian	288
	• Extensive forests which later formed coal deposits	Carboniferous	360
		Devonian	408
	• First land plants	Silurian	438
		Ordovician	508
	• Age of the trilobites, the first complex animals, which had hard shells and were marine	Cambrian	570
PRE-CAMBRIAN	• Oldest rocks on Earth's crust identified • First life forms: single cell forms like bacteria and algae • Continents and oceans formed • Extensive sedimentary rocks like iron ore deposits were laid down		4,560

Large pockets of magma inside the crust give rise to large rock bodies called batholiths, which are mostly made of granite and are often found in great mountain ranges. Smaller igneous intrusions may form in cracks and joints in other rocks. When these intrusions cut through sedimentary strata, they are called dikes; intrusions between the bedding planes of strata are known as sills.

The vapors emanating from igneous intrusions often crystallize in neighboring rocks as valuable minerals—gold, silver, copper, lead, and zinc. Such deposits are found in recent geological formations such as those around the Pacific "Ring of Fire", as well as in more ancient rocks such as those near the Kalgoorlie goldfields of Western Australia. A rare igneous rock called kimberlite, which occurs in pipe-like shapes, contains diamond deposits such as those found in South Africa.

Sedimentary rocks

Sedimentary rocks can be made up of either organic or inorganic particles. Organic sediments are the remains of plants and animals—one example of a sedimentary rock made up of plant remains is coal. Large deposits of limestone are mostly the result of the precipitation of calcium carbonate, but can also be the result of the agglomeration, or clustering, of sea shell fragments and the building of coral reefs. Inorganic sedimentary rocks include those made up of sand (sandstone), clays (shale), or pebbles cemented together (conglomerate).

Sedimentary strata deposited in large basins like the sea sometimes become exposed through vertical uplift, in which case the strata may remain horizontal. When strata are folded in the process of mountain formation, however, they form complex structures such as anticlines

An area of the East Sussex, United Kingdom, coast known as the Seven Sisters consists primarily of limestone, a sedimentary rock.

(dome-shaped folds) and synclines (basin-shaped folds). Anticlines have often become reservoirs for petroleum, while basin-type structures can often contain artesian water.

Several valuable minerals are found in sedimentary rocks: iron ores; oxides of aluminum (bauxite); and manganese. Coal deposits are sedimentary accumulations of transformed ancient forests. Building materials such as sandstones and materials for producing cement and fertilizers also come from sedimentary rocks.

Metamorphic rocks

When sedimentary rocks are subjected to high pressure they alter to become metamorphic rocks. Thus shale is converted to the more solid slate, sandstone to the very hard rock called quartzite and limestone to the crystallized rock known as marble. The presence of chemical impurities in limestone can result in marbles of a variety of colors and patterns.

When sedimentary and igneous rocks are subjected to high pressure as well as high temperature, partial melting can take place. This partially remelted material gives rise to crystalline metamorphic rocks called schist and gneiss. Gneiss resembles granite in appearance, but it generally has a layered structure. Schists are made of platy minerals, including micas.

Large igneous intrusions often change the rocks into which they intrude to metamorphic rocks through the effects of the heat and the gases that they carry. Batholiths, the largest igneous intrusions, have created metamorphic aureoles in contact zones such as are found in the Alps.

Two important building materials, slate and marble, are metamorphic rocks. Other commercially valuable metamorphic

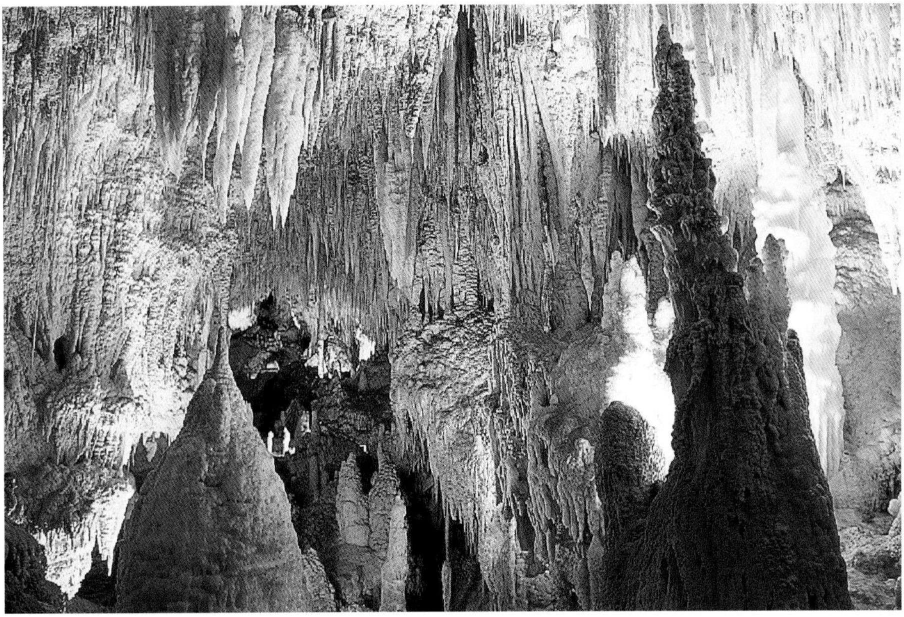

Limestone caves at Waitomo, North Island, New Zealand. The appearance of limestone varies according to the depositional environment in which it was formed.

mineral deposits include talc (used for cosmetics) and graphite (used for making pencils).

The rock cycle

In recent years, the concept of the rock cycle has proven useful. It represents the continuous recycling of rock materials and their conversion into different rock types, and helps link the various kinds of rocks found on Earth's surface.

When igneous rocks are exposed on the surface of Earth, they become weathered. Solar radiation, running water, ice, wind, and waves all weather rocks mechanically. Water acidified through the absorption of carbon dioxide and organic acids weathers rocks chemically. Over a long period, mechanical and chemical weathering produces pebbles, sands, and clays, which often consolidate into sedimentary rocks.

When these rocks are then dragged deep into Earth's crust by the process of plate subduction, they enter zones of very high pressure and temperature, resulting in partial melting and producing crystalline metamorphic rocks. If the rocks are carried still deeper into the Earth, however, where the temperatures are high enough to melt the rocks completely, a new magma is formed. This new magma may either crystallize deep inside Earth and form new plutonic igneous rocks, or be extruded as volcanic lavas.

Where volcanoes have erupted along zones of plate subduction, a rock named andesite has formed from lavas; this rock is a mixture of dark- and light-colored minerals, as it reflects the mixing of light continental and dark oceanic materials.

Banded limestone boulders in the Canadian Rockies.

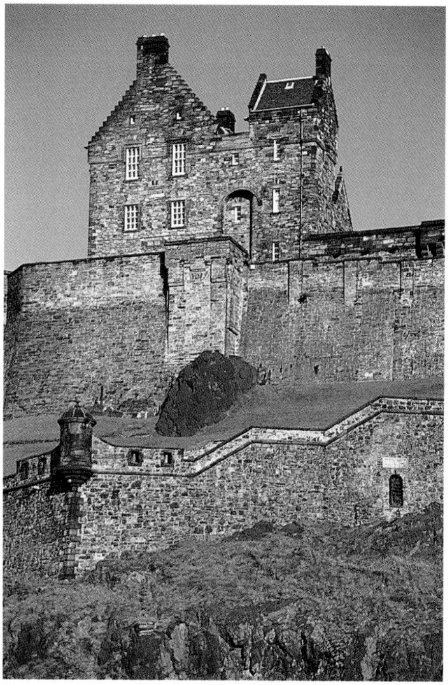

Edinburgh Castle is built on a plug of basalt, which seals the vent of an extinct volcano.

LANDFORMS

Earth's surface is constantly being transformed by falling rain, glaciers, rivers, underground water, wind, and waves. These constantly erode the land, transporting debris and depositing it elsewhere. The land is moulded into new forms through erosion, and new landforms are also created by the deposition of eroded debris.

Rainfall and water flow in creeks and rivers are the main agents of landform creation in humid areas; glaciers are the most important agents at high latitudes and in mountainous areas of heavy snowfall; and wind is important in arid areas.

Landforms of erosion

Glaciers, rivers, winds, and waves are powerful erosive agents. Glaciers pluck pieces of rock from valley sides, rivers carry rock fragments along in their current, and winds lift and transport particles of dust. Air and water velocities determine the erosive force of winds and rivers, and the rock fragments they carry with them make these agents additionally abrasive.

Rock fragments embedded in glaciers scour rock surfaces on the glacier's floor and sides; sand and gravel in fast-flowing rivers erode their floors and banks; and wind-borne sand blasts rock surfaces, creating intricate structures. Platforms, caves, and cliffs are formed by the action of waves carrying sand, pebbles and boulders and beating them against rocky coasts.

Rivers in mountainous areas flow rapidly because of steep slope gradients. Such streams may be highly erosive, and may cut their channels vertically, producing V-shaped valley profiles.

Glaciers are made of solid ice, and result from the compaction of snow. Some of the longest glaciers remaining, at 39 to 73 km (24 to 46 miles) in length, are found in the Karakoram ranges in the Himalayas. Although they generally move very slowly (2 to 3 cm [3/4 to 1 1/4 in] per day), glaciers are powerful eroders, and can move 4 to 5 m (13 to 16 1/2 ft) a day.

Glaciers typically create U-shaped valleys called troughs. Glaciers at the head of sloping valleys give rise to basin-shaped features known as cirques. When cirques from two opposing sides meet through erosion, a pass, or col, is formed. Between glacial valleys, sharp ridges, known as arêtes, develop. At the top of glacial mountains, arêtes meet at sharp peaks called horns, such as those on the Matterhorn and Mt Everest.

Where glaciers have disappeared, troughs are exposed, along with tributary glacial valleys, and these form hanging valleys perched above scarps. They often have streams cascading over them as waterfalls, and frequently are used as sites for the generation of hydroelectric power.

Depending on their velocity, winds can lift loose rock particles or soils. Generally speaking, the wind transports particles which are dry and not protected by plant cover—so wind action is mostly restricted to arid and semiarid regions, and some coastal areas. Strong winds can scoop out hollows in loose, dry soil. This process is known as deflation, and the hollows formed are called blowouts. These can range in diameter from about a meter to a kilometer or more.

When waves approach a coastline made up of headlands and bays, they gather around the headlands and spread out in the bays. Wave energy becomes concentrated on the headlands, where the steady pounding carves platforms and cliffs. In bays, by contrast, wave energy is dissipated, and the waves deposit sand and other detritus. These may also be transported along the shore, depending on the angle of the coast in relation to the direction of the waves.

Rock debris—such as loose, unsupported material and waterlogged soil—tends to move down hill slopes through the action of gravity. Slow movements known as soil creep are often imperceptible, and are indicated only by the changed position of fixed objects—trees, fences, and houses. The shaking of sloping ground by earthquakes can trigger a more rapid movement of loose materials. Fast movements such as landslides (or snow avalanches) tend to occur after heavy rains (or snowfalls) on steep slopes. In contrast to landslides, slumps are formed when slopes slip in a backward rotation, a phenomenon sometimes found in waterlogged soils.

Transportation and deposition of rock debris
The debris resulting from erosion is transported by glaciers, rivers, winds, and waves. A glacier carries assorted rock debris (boulders, pebbles, or finer materials) on or beneath its solid surface.

As a glacier moves, it plucks rocks from the valley walls, and the rock debris falls along the sides of the glacier to form what are known as lateral moraines. When two glaciers meet and coalesce, two lateral moraines join in the center of the new, larger glacier, forming a medial moraine.

The following features are those typically found in glacial areas, showing the close interconnection between current landforms and past glaciers: 1. Cirque basin 2. Hanging valley in a glacial trough 3. Outwash plain from glacial meltwater 4. Terminal moraine of a valley glacier 5. Lateral moraine 6. Medial moraine 7. Ground moraine 8. Arête or sharp-crested ridge 9. Horn or sharp peak

As mountain glaciers reach lower, warmer levels, they melt and drop their debris, which forms terminal moraines. The resulting meltwater carries a fine glacial flour, which may be spread as a vast depositional plain. Rich soils have developed in such plains in both northern Europe and the northern United States.

The amount of rock particle rivers and winds carry is determined by velocity; in general, larger particle sizes need greater velocities. At lower speeds, rivers deposit their sediment load, which then forms fertile alluvial flats and broad alluvial plains. These areas may be periodically inundated by floods. Much of the sediment carried by rivers in flood is deposited at the coast as deltas. Several major rivers carry high sediment loads—the Huang River in China carries more than one-and-a-half million tonnes annually.

Wind

Other landforms result from wind. Strong winds can lift and carry sands, while lighter winds lift and carry silts and clays. High winds rework sand masses into dunes of various types, depending on sand availability and wind direction. Sand dunes in deserts include crescent-shaped barchans, which have gentle windward slopes and abrupt leeward slopes—the crescent's horns point downwind. Silt-sized particles are transported by the wind to form thick, fertile deposits known as loess. Extensive deposits of loess are found on the edges of some deserts and in areas once glaciated (northern China and the Mississippi Valley, for instance).

Waves

Waves tend to approach a beach perpendicularly. The movement of the wave as it runs onto the beach is known as swash; the water, or backwash, then returns to the sea. Swash and backwash move sand along beaches, which contributes to littoral or longshore drift (when waves approach the beach at an angle). Along coastal plains, waves tend to build sand barriers by the shore. Lagoons develop behind these barriers, which are connected to the sea by tidal inlets. These lagoons can later fill with sediment, a stage in the gradual seaward extension of the coastal plain. The sea-level rise, on the other hand, along with storm wave erosion, can drive the sand barriers landward.

During the next several decades, because of global warming, the sea level may rise at rates up to 100 mm (4 in) per year. This would cause the loss of sand barriers and adjacent lagoons and wetlands, and the loss of some islands on coral reefs.

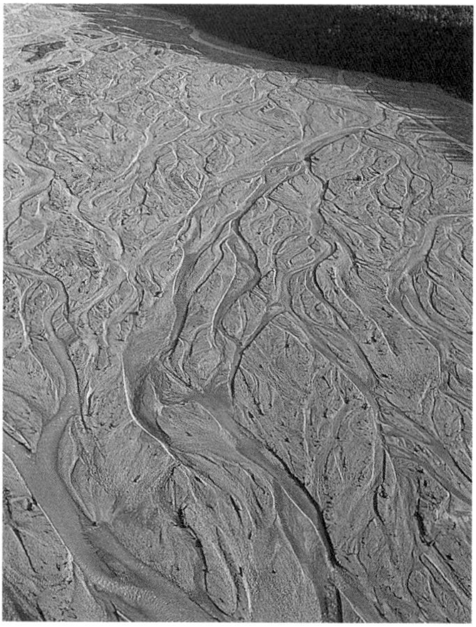

An aerial view of a braided river channel showing the build up of sediment on the river bed (above), and a coastline dramatically eroded by wave action (below).

CLIMATE

Just as weather is the day-to-day condition of the atmosphere, climate consists of the long-term average of weather conditions, including seasonal and year-to-year variability, and extremes. Many distinctive climatic types can be identified. These vary with regard to incoming solar radiation, temperature, wind, precipitation (rainfall and snowfall), evaporation, storms (type, frequency and magnitude), and seasonal patterns.

Solar radiation

Solar radiation (insolation) is received unequally in different parts of Earth. The equatorial belt receives strong solar radiation uniformly throughout the year, whilst places close to the poles, in contrast, have great differences between summer and winter solar radiation; perpetual ice climates exist at the poles. Along the equator, the lands are warm throughout the year, but, in the latitudes further away from the equator, seasonal variations become more discernible, with marked differences in the temperate zone.

General atmospheric circulation

The large amount of heat received at the equator means that air becomes heated and expands, and this air rises and flows towards the poles. Some of this air flows

Monsoon flooding in Vietnam. Monsoons are usually annual events, and deliver 85 percent of East Asia's annual rainfall, but can also cause devastation to low-lying areas.

back to the equator in the form of trade winds as part of the Hadley Cell circulation. Flowing from the east, these winds are called easterlies. The subtropical belt (up to about 30° latitude), is the zone of large high-pressure cells from which winds move through more temperate latitudes towards the poles. Cold, dense air from the poles flows, as polar fronts, back through these latitudes towards the equator. These fronts clash with tropical air masses in the temperate zones, giving give rise to cyclones (low-pressure cells), which bring inclement weather and rainy days. Such weather conditions are more common in the northern hemisphere, where there are extensive landmasses. In the southern hemisphere, in contrast, there are more extensive oceans. In that belt, between 40° latitude and Antarctica, a westerly wind blows eastward along an almost unbroken stretch of seas throughout the year.

Climatic types

Of the several proposed climatic classifications, the best known is that devised by Köppen, who divided climates broadly into five classes: A, B, C, D, and E. The humid climates are A, C, and D, with A being the warmest and lying in the tropics, C being found in the warm temperate regions, and D covering cold climates with

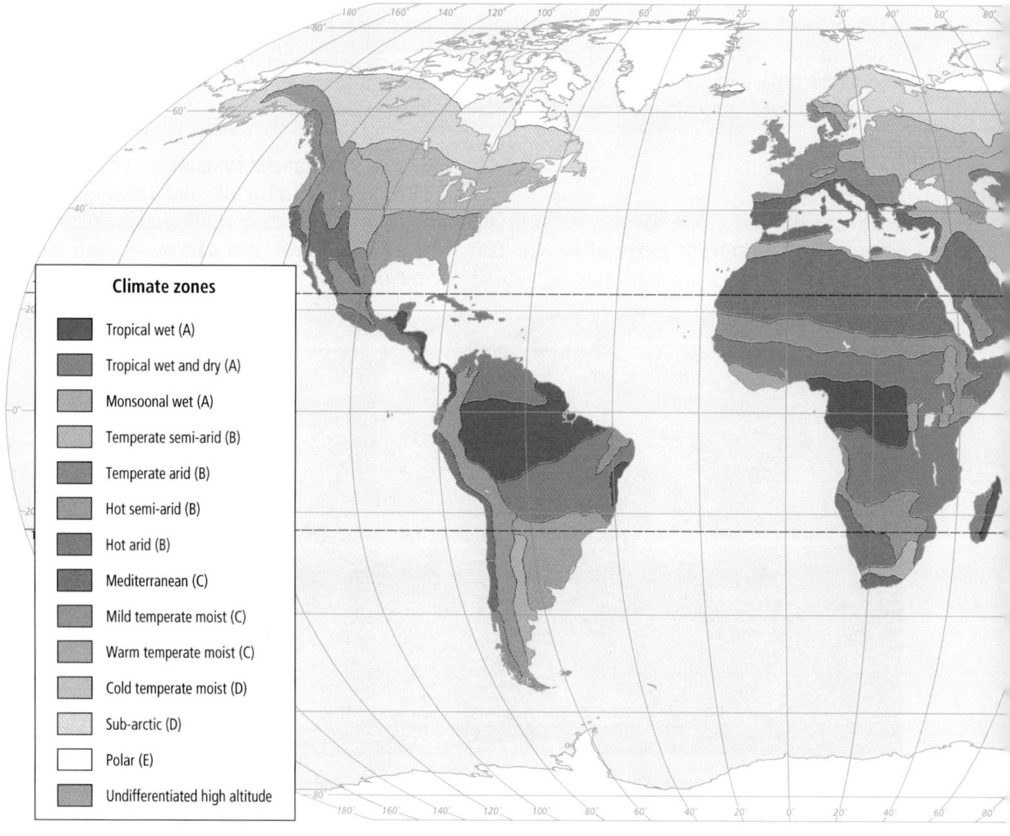

regular winter snowfall. Arid climates, both tropical and temperate, are classed as B climates. Ice sheets are represented by E climates.

Humid tropical climates (A)

Type A climates are found between 25°N and 25°S latitudes. These humid tropical climates receive abundant rainfall and have year-round high temperatures, with the areas further away from the equator having hot summers and mild winters.

These areas favor the abundant growth of vegetation, particularly rainforest. This climatic belt has extensive agriculture and often large populations. Heavy rainfall and high temperatures, however, leach soils of their valuable nutrients, which is detrimental for agriculture.

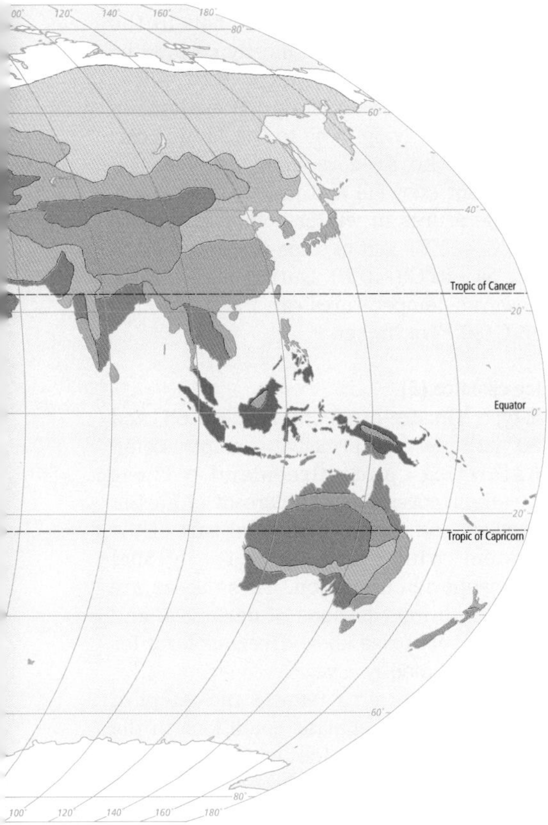

A typical A climate is the tropical monsoon climate that is found in Southeast Asia. It is characterized by a distinct season of heavy rainfall, preceded and followed by dry months; for example, large parts of India and Southeast Asia receive most of their rain between June and September, while March to May are typically dry months. Along the west coast of India, annual rainfall can be as high as 25,400 to 28,800 mm (9,900 to 1,123 in).

Desert climates (B)

Deserts are found in subtropical and temperate zones, and are classified by Köppen as B-type climates. Being areas of low rainfall, deserts have either few plants, or only small plants that are particularly well suited to dry environments.

Hot deserts lie in the subtropics—in the belt extending from North Africa (the Sahara Desert) and the Middle East to northwestern India (the Thar Desert)—and in the Central Australian Desert. These deserts have high daily temperature ranges; it can be very hot during the day and quite cool at night. The Gobi Desert, which lies in central Asia, is the best-known cold desert.

Humid temperate climates (C)

Type C climates lie between latitudes of 25° and 45°. They have marked seasonal variations, with temperature differences between summer and winter being quite large. The Mediterranean climate is a good example of a C-type climate; summer temperatures can on occasions soar to 40°C (110°F) in southern Greece and Italy, while winter temperatures can fall to 10°C (50°F). The Mediterranean climate is characterized by cold, wet winters and hot, dry summers.

The temperate zone close to the tropics (25° to 35° latitudes) is warm. It is now common to find that belt referred to as the

An ice floe, with walrus, in Arctic Siberia.

Lush mountainous terrain in Bolivia.

subtropics. The subtropical areas lying along the eastern sides of the continents are particularly warm, as they receive the warm easterly tropical winds, and warm ocean currents flow along their coasts. This east coast climate is found in southeast China, eastern Australia and South America.

In contrast, the westerlies in the higher latitudes (35° to 60° latitudes) give rise to a cooler west coast climate. Year-round rainfall and adequate temperatures promote the growth of forests in both east and west coast climates.

Grasslands generally occur in the continental interiors of C climate areas, where annual rainfall is moderate (300 to 400 mm; 12 to 16 in), and water in the soil is not abundant. These areas lie in the rainshadows of major mountain ranges. Seasonal temperature ranges are usually sizeable.

Cold temperate climates (D)

Moving into the temperate zone close to the poles, temperatures fall because there is reduced solar radiation. This is exacerbated by cold polar winds. Polar winds are easterlies, although their directions can be variable in temperate latitudes. Such type D climates lie between 45° and 65° latitudes, and are only significant in the northern hemisphere—the equivalent belt in the southern hemisphere is mostly covered by the oceans.

The taiga climate is a good example of this climate; lying close to the Arctic polar region, the area is characterized by abundant snowfall and unique woodlands. Temperatures in winter commonly fall to –30°C (–22°F), and in some places can go as low as –40°C (–40°F). During midsummer, however, temperatures can rise to around 15°C (60°F) or higher.

Ice climates (E)

E-type climates are found between 65° and 90° latitudes, the principal examples being Antarctica and Greenland. These ice sheets cover about 10 percent of Earth's surface, and form an essential part of the system which regulates the global atmospheric circulation. These areas are subject to long periods of darkness, and temperatures rise above freezing level for only 2 to 4 months a year.

If global warming reduces the extent of these ice sheets, climatic conditions in the world will alter: ice melting would contribute to rises in sea level, with adverse effects on low-lying areas.

The Valley of the Moon, in the high-altitude Atacama Desert, Chile, said to be the driest desert on Earth.

The El Niño phenomenon

Deviations from normal temperature patterns of the waters in the southern Pacific Ocean, between Australia and South America, result in the phenomenon called El Niño. Under normal conditions, eastern trade winds blow across the Pacific. These drive the sun-warmed surface water from the central Pacific to the coast off northern Australia. When clouds form above this area of warm water and move over Indonesia, Papua New Guinea, and Australia, they bring rain with them.

Every two to seven years, however, this pattern is interrupted by the El Niño event. During El Niño, the Pacific Ocean off Australia does not warm as much as it normally does. Instead, it becomes warmer right up to the coast of Peru in South America. At the same time, the easterly trade winds that blow across the Pacific reverse their direction. This causes high-pressure systems to build up to the north of and across the Australian continent, preventing moist tropical air reaching the continent. These conditions in turn result in storms, and in rain falling in the eastern Pacific Ocean and in South America instead of in Australia, Papua New Guinea, and Indonesia, which then suffer drought conditions.

While the effects of El Niño are sometimes weak, at other times they are very strong. During a severe El Niño period, extreme drought conditions prevail, as in 1982–83 and 1997–98. In contrast, heavy rainfall and flooding occurred in parts of North and South America. In 1997, there were severe storms and floods in Mexico and further north along the west coast of the United States.

The converse of the El Niño effect is the La Niña effect, which is an exaggeration of normal conditions. This takes place when trade winds blow strongly and consistently across the Pacific towards Australia. This pushes the warm waters from the central Pacific, off the northern Australian coast, to build up into a mass that is bigger than normal. Thus, much more cloud develops than usual, and this brings considerably more rain to Australia and neighboring countries.

THE WATER CYCLE

Earth, in contrast to all the other planets in the solar system, has an abundant supply of water. Much of this, of course, lies in the oceans and seas (more than 97 percent), and is saline. The polar ice caps lock up slightly more than 2 percent of the remaining water, leaving less than 1 percent of fresh water to sustain life on Earth. Human needs are met by the water from rainfall, rivers, and underground supplies (plus a small amount from desalination plants).

Water falls as rain and snow, and flows as rivers and glaciers before ultimately reaching the sea. It also sinks into the ground to form underground water reservoirs, to emerge as springs or to seep into river water. Fresh supplies of water are continuously needed and nature provides this supply through the water cycle.

How the water cycle works

Solar energy evaporates exposed water from seas, lakes, rivers, and wet soils; the majority of this evaporation takes place over the seas. Water is also released into the atmosphere by plants through

photosynthesis. During this process, known as evapotranspiration, water vapor rises into the atmosphere.

Clouds form when air becomes saturated with water vapor. The two major types of cloud formations are a stratified or layered gray cloud called stratus, and a billowing white or dark gray cloud called cumulus. Nimbostratus clouds and cumulonimbus clouds are the cloud types that are associated with rainy weather; nimbostratus clouds will bring steady rain, and cumulonimbus clouds will bring stormy weather.

Precipitation as rain, snow, or hail ensures that water returns to Earth's surface in a fresh form. Some of this rain, however, falls into the seas and is not accessible to humans. When rain falls, it either washes down hill slopes or seeps underground; when snow and hail melt, this water may also sink into the ground.

Rainfall also replenishes river water supplies, as does underground water. Snowfall may consolidate into glaciers and ice sheets which, when they melt, release their water into the ground, into streams, or into the seas.

Water in river courses

Rivers pass through several phases on their journey from hilly and mountainous areas to the seas and oceans. In their early phases—that is, close to their sources in the hills and mountains—they have steep slope gradients and, therefore, move with high velocities. They carry rock fragments and have high erosive force.

In these areas, the energy from these streams provides the potential for hydroelectric development. This potential has been harnessed in many places, such as in the foothills of the Himalayas in Nepal.

The water cycle: the sun heats water, which evaporates and rises into the atmosphere as water vapor, only to fall again later as rain and snow. The rain and snow then concentrate in rivers, or flow as ground water to the sea.

Artesian wells

When rain falls, some of it sinks into the ground and is held in the soil—this water is known as ground water. A layer under the ground becomes saturated with this seeped water; the surface of this layer is called the water table. Wells are mostly dug to tap water in the water table. There is another way, however, that water can seep under the ground to form water reservoirs. Some types of rock are porous, and this allows them to hold water; water can move through such permeable rock.

Sandstone is a permeable rock. If a sandstone bed is dipping at an angle, rainwater can penetrate the exposed part of the rock and travel along the stratum into the ground. The water will be retained by the sandstone layer if the rocks above and below it are impermeable. If this water reservoir lies well below the ground, it is held under pressure; if a well is bored to the reservoir, the water will gush out under this pressure. These reservoirs are called artesian wells. The permeable strata that carry the water are called aquifers; the impermeable layers which lie above and below the aquifers are known as aquicludes.

Artesian waters are important where rainfall is low and water supplies uncertain. Overuse of artesian water can result in the ground sinking, and if the reservoir is close to the sea, excessive removal of water can allow saline water to penetrate the reservoir, reducing water quality.

A hot water artesian bore.

On flat plains, rivers tend to wind their way in meandering courses. Here, the water flow has now lost most of its erosive capacity. Massive clay deposits may also give rise to fertile alluvial plains. During times of heavy rainfall, flooding can take place, and this is a serious issue along some of the major rivers of the world, such as the Mississippi in the United States, the Yangtze in China and the Ganges in India.

Human interference in the water cycle

There has been considerable human interference in the water cycle throughout recorded history, but far more so since the beginning of the twentieth century. For centuries, humans have built dams across rivers to store water, which is then used for irrigation, or for domestic or industrial water supply. Dams have also been built to control river flooding, such as across the Huang River in China, and to produce electricity.

The Aswan Dam across the Nile provides arid Egypt with essential water. The two highest dams in the world, more than 300 m (985 ft) in height, have been built across the Vakhsh River in Tajikistan. The dam with by far the largest reservoir capacity—2,700 million cubic meters (3,530 million cubic yards)—is the Owen Falls Dam, across the Nile, in Uganda.

Hydroelectric power is generated in several parts of the world, such as at Itaipu, across the Parana River, in Brazil—this dam can generate 12,600 megawatts of power. The building of dams in areas prone to earthquakes, such as Japan, however, causes great concern because of the potential for serious damage.

Water is necessary for agriculture, industry, and domestic use. Agriculture depends on rainfall, as well as on irrigation from stored water. The provision of water for domestic use—particularly the need for clean drinking water—has become very important with the spread of urbanization. Reservoirs are often built to ensure urban water supplies and water is purified before being channeled to consumers.

The discharge of industrial, agricultural, and domestic effluents into streams and lakes (especially in the twentieth century) has reduced water quality and damaged aquatic life. These effluents include metallic substances. One of the most dramatic examples has been the discharge of mercury into rivers in Japan. This mercury has now entered the food chain through fish, creating serious health problems. The discharge of pesticides has also been detrimental to aquatic life, and excessive use of fertilizers, along with salts released into rivers and lakes by poor land use practices, have also altered the ecological balance.

Changes in air quality brought about by humans have also affected the water cycle. The use of fossil fuels to generate electricity and power transport has resulted in substantial sulfur dioxide and nitrogen oxide emissions. When these gases and water react, sulfuric and nitric acids are produced. These pollutants are present in clouds and fog, and fall with rain and snow as acid rain. A pH value of 5 in water is acidic enough to damage aquatic life.

This acid rain phenomenon is most likely to occur in dense industrial centers such as those in the United States, Canada, and Europe. The problem, however, is not confined to these areas, as winds blow polluting gases over long distances. Acids can become concentrated in still waters and threaten aquatic life. The entire ecology of affected lakes, including the natural food chains, can be very seriously harmed.

Snowmelt from the Arrigetch peaks and glacier, in Alaska, finds its way to the sea as ground water.

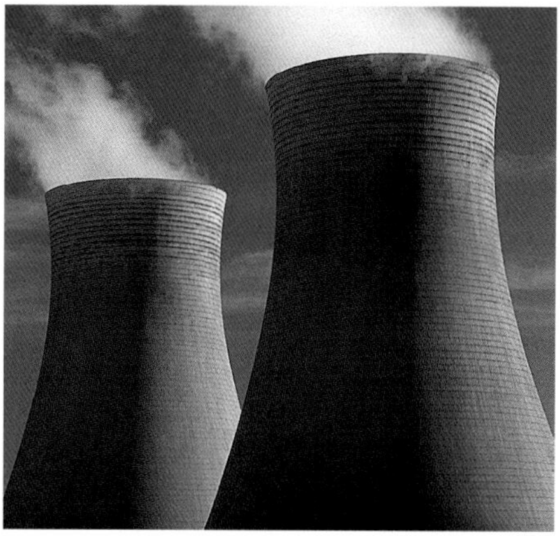

Water is released as steam into the atmosphere from electric power plants.

OCEANOGRAPHY

Earth is the only planet of the solar system with seas and oceans, and these cover more than 70 percent of its surface. The oceans lie in large and deep basins in Earth's crust. The seas, however, spread to the margins of the continents, drowning their shelves. The melting of the ice sheets following the end of the last ice age (about 15,000 years ago) resulted in a rise in sea levels and thus an increased area covered by seas.

Ocean currents

The waters of the oceans are in constant motion. This motion takes the form of ocean currents. These currents move at an average of 8 km (5 miles) per hour, and redistribute heat energy, thus influencing climate. Winds are the most important originators of ocean currents in the upper layers of the seas: they produce a frictional drag on the water which pushes it along.

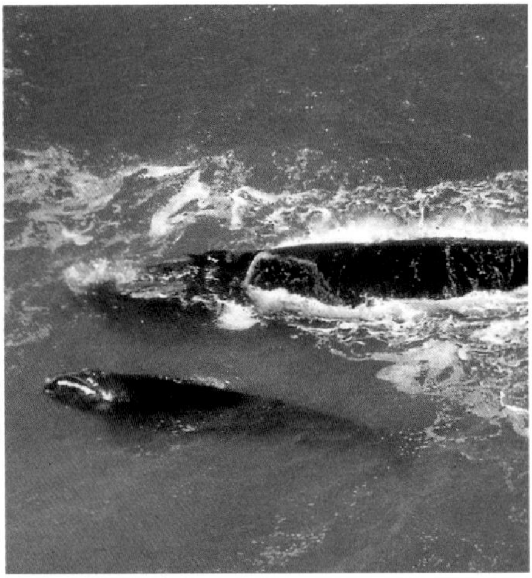

The southern right whale feeds off aquatic life that thrives in the nutrient-rich Antarctic waters, which are now threatened by ozone depletion.

As water is a fluid, it is subject to the Coriolis effect (caused by Earth's rotation)—that is, currents tend to move towards the right in the northern hemisphere and towards the left in the southern hemisphere. The resulting deflection is 45° to that of the direction of the wind. In the deeper parts of the oceans, it is water density that produces ocean currents. Water density depends upon two factors: temperature and salinity. The colder the water is, the denser it is; and the higher the salinity, the higher the density. The circulation which results from temperature and salinity difference is referred to as thermo-haline circulation.

There are broadly two types of ocean current: warm currents, which originate in tropical areas; and cold currents, which originate in polar areas. Warm currents are mostly located in the upper 100 m (330 ft) of the seas. Cold currents, on the other hand, are often encountered at greater depths. They move more slowly because of the overlying pressure exerted by surface water. The exchange of heat energy occurs as equatorial currents move towards the poles and polar currents move towards the equator. This exchange moderates Earth's heat patterns, preventing the equatorial belt becoming unbearably hot and the waters in the temperate zone becoming much colder than they are today.

Ocean water temperatures are a major influence on climatic conditions; warm currents bring warmth to the coastlines along which they flow and, likewise, cold currents reduce temperatures in the lands along which they flow.

Warm tropical ocean currents

Winds blowing westward along the equatorial belt generate west-flowing ocean currents called equatorial currents. When water from the equatorial currents piles up against land, the current reverses its direction and flows eastward, resulting in equatorial counter currents.

Equatorial currents turn towards the right in the northern hemisphere and towards the left in the southern hemisphere as a result of the Coriolis effect, and because of that motion, they develop into huge, circular, whorl-like rotating systems. These systems are known as gyres. Gyres rotate in a clockwise direction in the northern hemisphere and an anticlockwise direction in the southern hemisphere.

The distribution of the continental landmasses influences the size and shape of these gyres. There are major gyres in the northern and southern Atlantic and Pacific oceans, and in the southern Indian Ocean. There is also a gyre in the northern Indian Ocean, but it is restricted by the landmasses surrounding it, and so is much smaller.

Gyres carry warm equatorial water into the temperate zone. These currents carry about 25 percent of all the heat that moves polewards from the equator. In the North Atlantic, the Gulf Stream or North Atlantic Drift, which flows from the Gulf of Mexico towards Western Europe, warms the seas around those countries, making their climates warmer. Thus London (51°32'N) is warmer than New York, even though New York lies at a much lower latitude (40°43'N), because of this warming effect.

The Japan Current, flowing from Southeast Asia, warms the eastern coasts of China and Japan. The west coast of Japan, on the other hand, is cooled by cold currents originating in northern areas. The magnitude of large ocean currents is demonstrated by the enormous amount

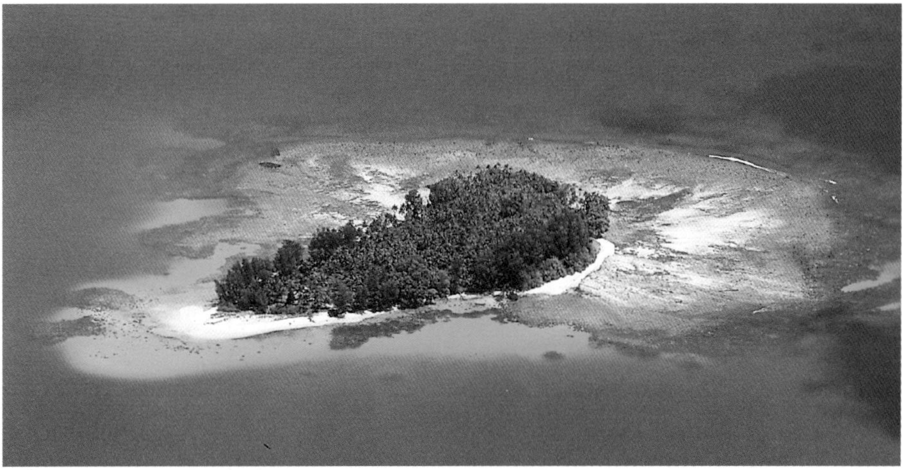

Coral islands are at risk if sea levels rise because of the greenhouse effect.

of water they can carry—for example, the Gulf Stream carries more than 50 million cubic meters (65.5 million cubic yards) per second.

The build-up of warm waters can have significant effects on climate. For example, tropical cyclones or hurricanes or typhoons develop in the areas of warm water in Southeast Asia. These can have devastating effects on those areas.

Also, temperature changes in the waters of the South Pacific Ocean provide indications of the El Niño and La Niña weather disturbances. The onset of El Niño is heralded by unusually high water temperatures in the central Pacific, with the warm water spreading across to South America.

Cold polar currents

Cold ocean currents originate in polar regions. They flow deep in the oceans and only surface through upwelling—when winds blowing from the land drive warm surface water back out into the ocean. Cold water then rises to the surface.

Two well-known upwelling sites, both on the western sides of continents, are the Humboldt or Peru Current along the coast of South America and the Benguela Current in southern Africa. Their nutrient-laden waters are rich breeding grounds for fish.

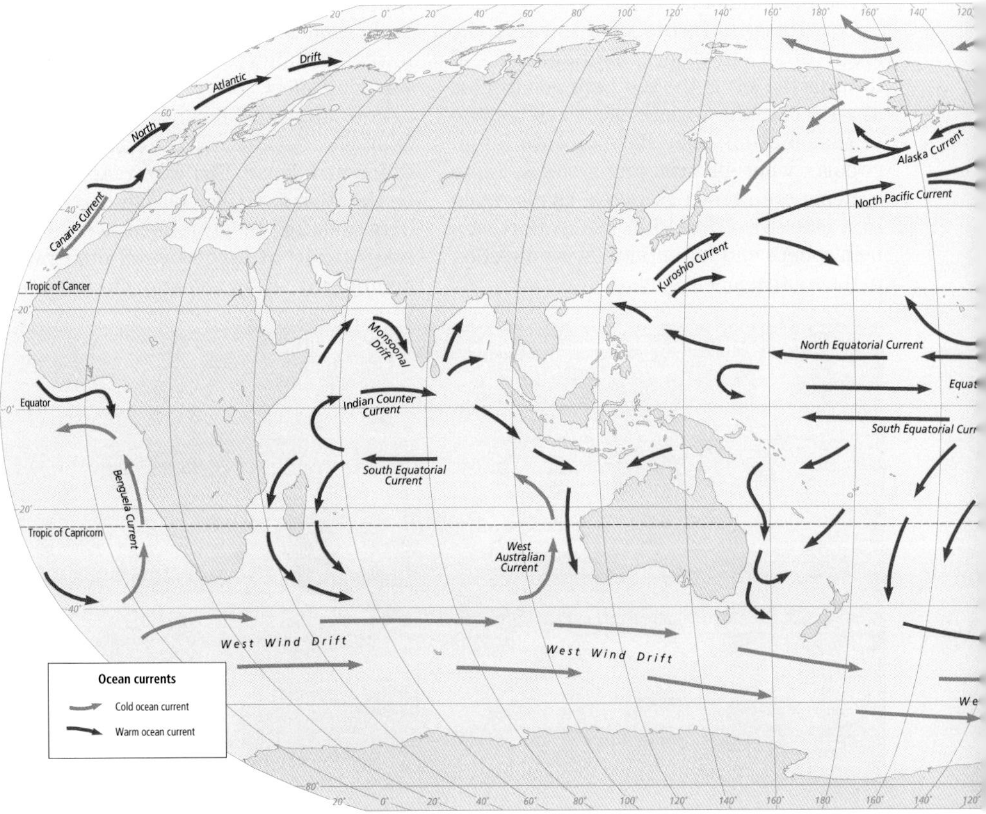

Two important cold currents flowing on the eastern sides of continents are the Kamchatka Current, which flows alongside Siberia and Japan, and the Labrador Current, which flows along the east coasts of Canada and the United States.

Icebergs and ice floes

Seas in the polar zones can freeze, forming pack ice that covers the sea surface. If subjected to strong currents or winds, this pack ice can break into pieces, called floes. Ice broken from ice sheets can also be seen floating in the seas as icebergs. Ice floes are mostly less than 5 m (161/2 ft) thick—much thinner than icebergs.

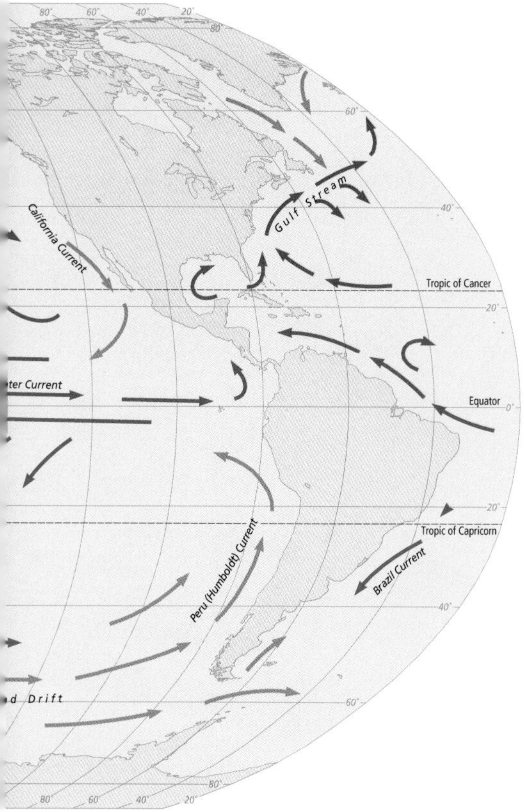

Icebergs can be very thick indeed—up to hundreds of meters in thickness—but only about one-sixth of an iceberg floats above water. The rest of it remains submerged or hidden below the water. This makes icebergs a major navigational hazard. There are always likely to be icebergs in the North Atlantic; they originate from the Greenland ice sheet and its glaciers.

The Antarctic zone

The waters around Antarctica flow in an unbroken band around the globe because there are no land areas to obstruct them. The West Wind Drift, as the winds blowing incessantly from the west to the east are called, results in some of the world's most turbulent seas. The seas in latitudes between 40°S and 60°S have been referred to as the "Roaring Forties", the "Furious Fifties", and the "Screaming Sixties".

In the Southern Ocean around Antarctica, between the latitudes 50°S and 60°S, cold currents interact with the warm currents coming from the tropics. The cold, nutrient-rich waters are driven upwards by this convergence, becoming the breeding ground for abundant oceanic life. These waters are thus a vital component of the food chain which depends upon that aquatic life.

Polar bears in Arctic Siberia survive on the ice floes, which are broken off icebergs by strong currents and winds.

PLANTS AND ANIMALS

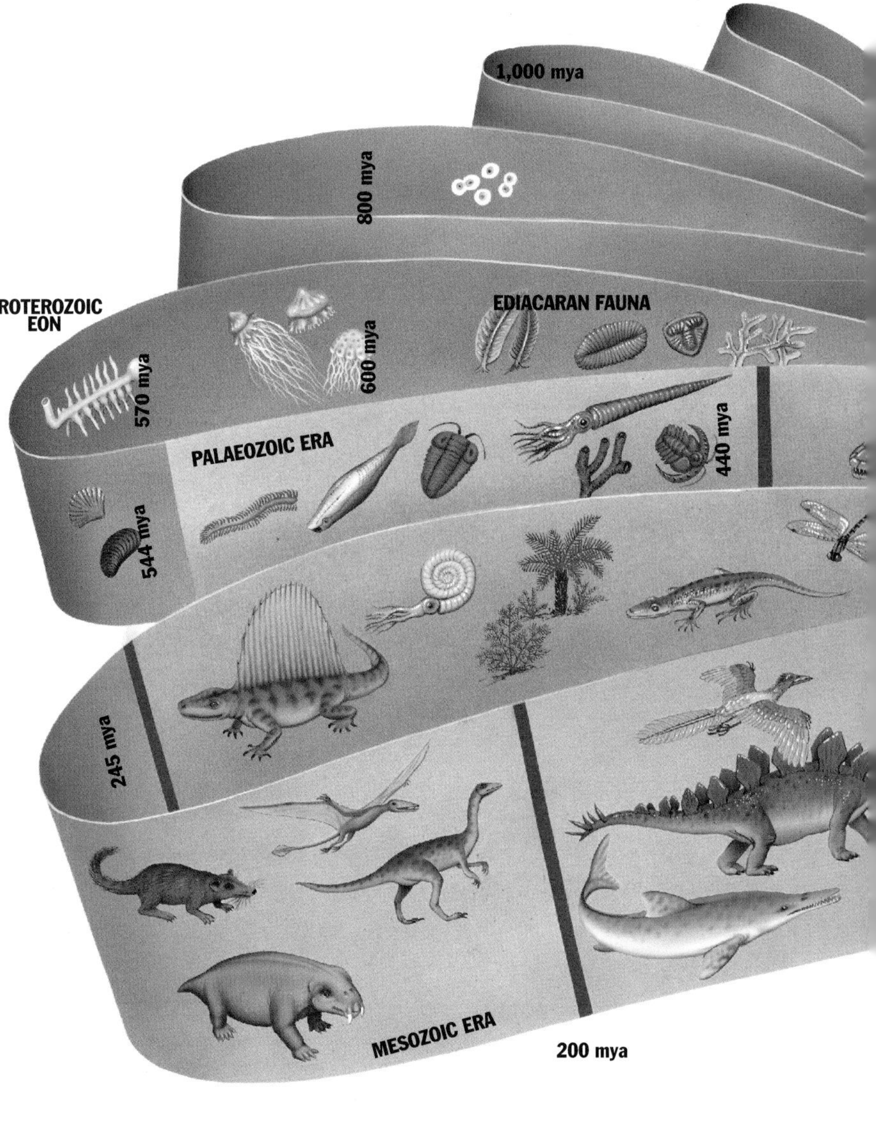

1,000 mya
800 mya
PROTEROZOIC EON
EDIACARAN FAUNA
600 mya
570 mya
440 mya
PALAEOZOIC ERA
544 mya
245 mya
MESOZOIC ERA
200 mya

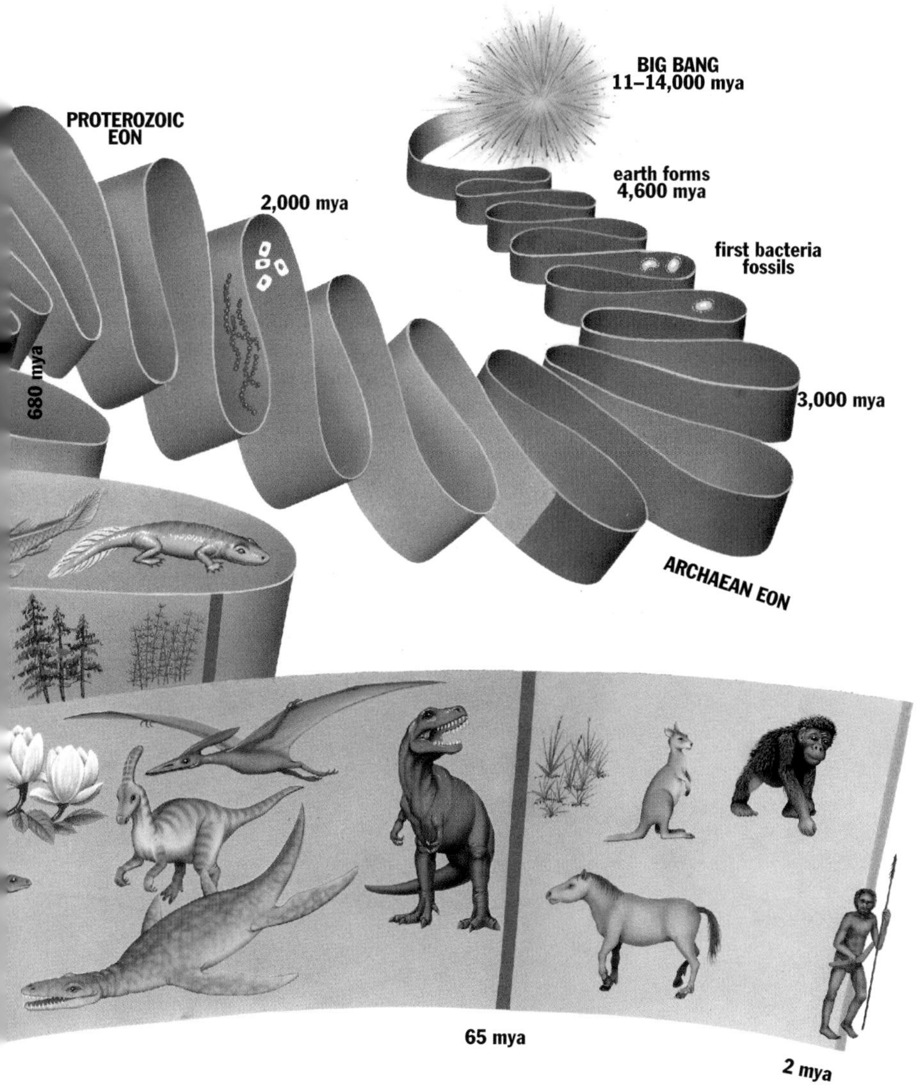

This diagram illustrates all the major stages in the evolution of plants and animals, from the first bacteria-like organisms, around 3,500 million years ago (mya), till humans, who first appeared in the late Quaternary Period.

Earth is about 4,500 million years old. After about 1,000 million years, most of the basic metabolic processes on which modern life depends were in place. The first eukaryote cells (cells that were capable of resisting oxidation) appeared about 1,500 million years ago. After about 4,000 million years, multicellular animals and plants appear in the fossil record. In the past 600 million years, life has exploded into a vast array of forms, but many of the animals and plants we are familiar with are relatively recent arrivals.

To deduce the history of Earth's life forms (collectively known as biota), and the prevailing environmental conditions, scientists primarily rely on physical evidence: the character of rocks or the fossils contained within them. Increasingly, however, biochemical evidence is also used.

The first life forms

Life is defined as a self-contained system of molecules that can duplicate itself from generation to generation. In Earth's early history, the elements that make up the vast majority of living tissues (hydrogen, carbon, oxygen, and nitrogen) were available in some form, and energy was abundant. Also, the concentration of atmospheric oxygen was low, which probably allowed a period of chemical evolution before the development of life. The earliest life forms may have resembled the bacteria-like organisms that exist today in hot springs associated with volcanic activity.

The first bacteria-like microfossils are dated to be 3,500 million years old. Stromatolites, or fossilized mats of cyanobacteria (a bacteria secreted by blue–green algae), first appear in the fossil record at about this time. These are the dominant fossils found in rocks older than about 550 million years. Between about 3,500 and 1,500 million years ago, cyanobacteria and blue–green algae were probably the main forms of life. Importantly, they slowly contributed oxygen to the atmosphere.

The build-up of free oxygen, hazardous to most life forms, may have stimulated the

Stromatolites in Hamelin Pool, Shark Bay, Western Australia.

development of organisms with more complex cellular organisation (the eukaryotes) about 1,500 million years ago. The eukaryotes could reproduce sexually, thus allowing evolutionary change. They generated more oxygen and eventually (by about 1,300 million years ago) an ozone shield—this is probably what enabled further biotic evolution.

The earliest fossil record of protozoans, which are animals and so derive their energy from ingesting other organisms, is from about 800 million years ago. By about 680 million years ago, the protozoa were a highly diverse and complex range of multicellular animals—mostly coral- or worm-like life forms.

Invertebrates and vertebrates

During the late Proterozoic or early Paleozoic Era, the principal groups (or phyla) of invertebrates appeared. Trilobites were probably the dominant form of marine life during the Cambrian Period. The seas teemed with a huge diversity of animals, including a group with an elongated support structure, a central nerve cord, and a blood circulatory system—members of the phylum to which humans belong, the Chordata.

A major extinction event ended the Cambrian Period. The Ordovician Period (500 to 435 million years ago) is characterized by another increase in species diversity. The fossil record is dominated by marine invertebrates, but vertebrates also appear. The primitive jawless fish of 485 million years ago are the first ancestors of all advanced life forms: fish, amphibians, reptiles, birds, and mammals. Another major extinction event ended this period.

From ocean to land

The first land plants—probably similar to modern liverworts, hornworts, and mosses—seem to have arisen about 450 million years ago. The move onto land was a significant evolutionary step; life on land was very different, demanding innovation and evolutionary change.

During the Silurian Period (435 to 395 million years ago), algae diversified and all the major fish groups appeared. Fossils of vascular plants (with specialized systems for moving nutrients, liquids, and so on) are found at about 430 million years ago. *Cooksonia*, a small moss-like plant common at this time, may have resulted in two distinct lines of evolution, one leading to all other higher plants. Floras of the late Silurian to early Devonian time are very similar worldwide, and may constitute evidence that the supercontinent Pangaea existed then.

During the mid-Devonian Period (395 to 345 million years ago), plants underwent a remarkable diversification, resulting in the development of Devonian "forests", which included giant clubmosses (lepidodendrons) and horsetails (calamites). The fossil record of the amphibians also begins here—animals were moving onto land—and the first fern-like foliage and gymnosperms appeared. The late Devonian was also marked by a mass extinction event.

Fossils from the Carboniferous Period (345 to 280 million years ago) suggest that the clubmoss forests teemed with spiders, scorpions, and centipedes. Amphibians gave rise to the first reptiles about 300 million years ago—vertebrates were no longer dependent on returning to water to reproduce. A trend towards an ice age occurred in the late Carboniferous Period, leading to low-diversity flora dominated by primitive seed ferns.

The Permian Period (280 to 245 million years ago) is dominated by the fossil remains of primitive members of the conifer line. By this period, reptiles with skeletal features characteristic of mammals were present.

The Age of Reptiles

The largest mass extinction event on record marks the end of the Permian Period. During the Mesozoic Era (245 to 65 million years ago), the "Age of Reptiles," flowering plants, dominated by cycads and gymnosperms early on, developed. Birds and mammals also appeared.

During the Triassic Period (245 to 200 million years ago), mammals, lizards, and dinosaurs appear in the fossil record. Some long-established reptiles were replaced by new groups, including the turtles, crocodilians, dinosaurs, and pterosaurs.

Dinosaurs date from early in the Triassic Period. From about 220 million years ago they dominated land habitats—for almost 160 million years. Mammals (initially small, perhaps nocturnal, shrew-like creatures) appear to have arisen from mammal-like reptiles. There was another mass extinction event (about 200 million years ago) in the late Triassic Period. Frogs and toads may have appeared around this time.

Pangaea began to break up during the Jurassic Period (200 to 145 million years ago). Ocean currents and the global climate were altered. The position of the continents and the break-up sequence determined the migration routes available and, therefore, the interrelation or common features of the plants and animals that we now see in the modern world.

The Stegosaurus lived during the late Jurassic period and ate plants that grew near the ground.

Jurassic rocks include Earth's earliest fossils of flies, mosquitoes, wasps, bees, and ants; modern types of marine crustaceans were abundant. It was also a critical point in the evolution of birds, which evolved either from the dinosaurs or from an earlier group of reptiles. The Archaeopteryx, which existed about 150 million years ago, is perhaps the most famous early bird-like animal.

The early Cretaceous Period (145 to 65 million years ago) had a cosmopolitan flora. The first record of bats appears at this time. From about 80 million years ago, gymnosperms and angiosperms expanded at the expense of cycads and ferns. Mammals were also becoming dominant.

The Cretaceous Period also saw the apparent rise of the monotreme and marsupials and placentals, and the first predatory mammals. The diversification and spread of angiosperms provided the impetus for the co-evolution of animals.

The Age of Mammals

A great extinction event occurred at the end of the Cretaceous Period, causing the demise of the dinosaurs and the loss of about 25 percent of all known animal families. This change marks the beginning of the Cenozoic Era (65 million years ago to the present). This era saw the formation of the famous mountain systems of the world, the movement of the continents to their present positions and a cooling trend that culminated in the ice ages of the Quaternary Period.

After dinosaurs died out, mammals quickly expanded into newly vacated habitats and roles, adapting and diversifying. Eventually, the warm-blooded animals came to dominate, so the Cenozoic Era is often called the "Age of Mammals". Late in the era, humans finally appear.

The Tertiary Period (65 to 1.8 million years ago) saw major new groups developing within pre-established plant families. Grasses appeared (about 50 million years ago), expanding particularly in the Miocene Period.

The development of grasslands resulted eventually in a proliferation of grazing mammals. Hoofed, placental herbivores are first recorded as fossils 85 million years ago. The first horses appeared about 55 million years ago. A similar explosion in small rodents also occurred from about 40 million years ago.

Although birds have been essentially modern since the start of the Cenozoic Era, the first songbirds seem to appear at about 55 million years ago; all the major bird groups of the modern world had evolved by 50 million years ago. At about the same time (mid-Eocene Period), the carnivorous mammals split into two major lines: the dogs and the cats, basically. The first toothed whales are from the Oligocene epoch and the first plankton-feeding whales are from the Miocene.

The first primates seem to date from the end of the Cretaceous Period, though it seems that both monkeys and apes did not separate from earlier groups until the Oligocene epoch. The oldest biped yet found—usually taken as the start of the hominids—is from about 4.4 million years ago.

Nearly 2.5 million years ago, stone tool users—the hallmark of our own genus, *Homo*—seem to have arisen. *Homo erectus*, dating from about 1.8 million years ago, migrated from Africa as far as China and Southeast Asia. Our species, *Homo sapiens*, seems to have evolved in Africa within the past 200,000 years and to have migrated out of that continent only during the past 100,000 years.

Around 750 BC Teotihuacán in Mesoamerica was one of the largest cities in the world

EARTH'S BIOSPHERE

The biosphere is the zone where all living organisms on Earth are found. It includes parts of the lithosphere (Earth's crust and mantle), the hydrosphere (all the waters on Earth), and the atmosphere. The term "biosphere" can also refer collectively to all Earth's living organisms.

Imagine a sort of biological spectrum, arranged from the simple to the complex; it would start with subatomic particles, then

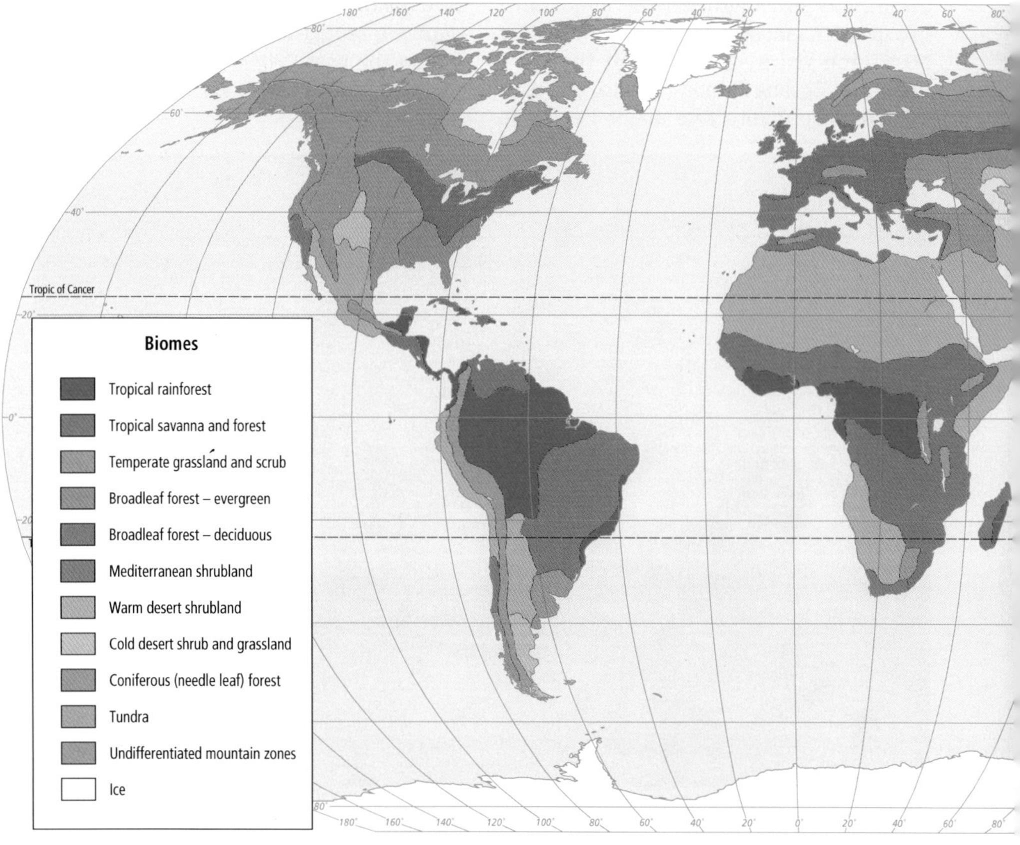

move through atoms, molecules, compounds, protoplasm, cells, tissues, organs, organ systems, organisms, populations, communities, and ecosystems, to, eventually, the biosphere. Each stage represents another level of organization, and each level implies new attributes and different properties.

"Population" refers to a group of organisms of a particular kind that form a breeding unit. Not all individuals of a kind (or species) can mix—for example, due to geographic isolation—so a population is the functional group that is capable of breeding. A "community" is all the populations of plants, animals, bacteria, and fungi that live in an environment and interact with one another. Populations within a community are linked by their interaction and effects on each other, and by their responses to the environment they share.

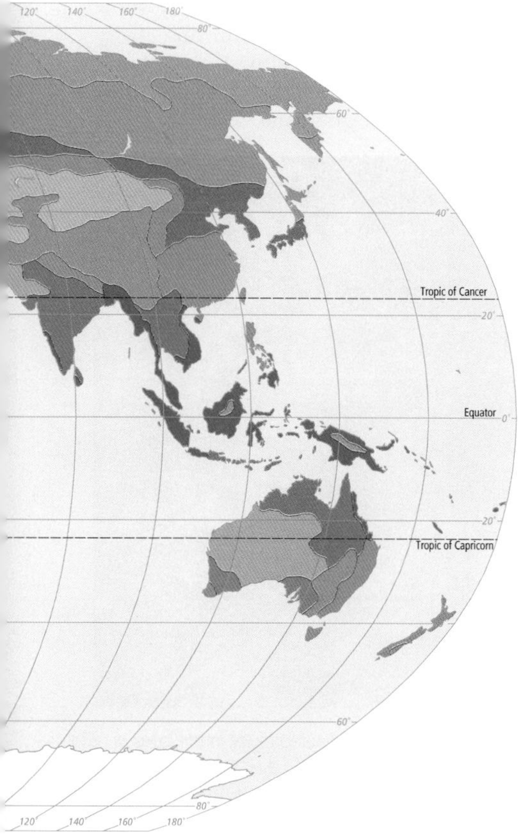

"Ecosystem" is a shortening of "ecological system", the concept that the living (biotic) community and the non-living (abiotic) environment are a functioning, integrated system. An ecosystem involves transfer and circulation of materials and energy between living and non-living systems. There is almost infinite variety in the magnitude of ecosystems, from a global ecosystem that encompasses the entire biosphere to the ecosystem of a fallen log or of the underside of a rock, or even of a drop of water.

Environmental conditions influence the distribution of individual organisms. Limiting factors may be physical (such as temperature and moisture availability) or biotic (such as competition, predation, and the presence of suitable food or other resources). A limiting factor is anything that tends to make it more difficult for an organism to grow, live, or reproduce—that makes some aspect of physiology or behavior less efficient and therefore less competitive.

The distribution of organisms is strongly influenced by the fact that each kind can tolerate only a certain set of conditions. For many organisms, distribution is critically associated with, or determined by, relationships with other organisms. A community of organisms is thus likely to include a loose collection of populations with similar environmental requirements, and possibly another, tighter, collection of organisms that are dependent in some way upon each other.

Due to genetic variation, individuals within a population have a range of tolerances around their ecological optimum, but beyond a particular tolerance limit, the species is unable to live. Importantly, this spread means a group may be able to cope with environmental change. A species must be able to complete all phases of its life cycle in a given region if it is to persist for a prolonged period, and different species vary in their tolerance of environmental factors.

The major biomes

Communities are strongly linked to their physical environment or habitat; this habitat is also modified by its communities. Since climate, soils, and biotic factors vary around the world, communities are bound to change. Vegetation is often the most visible aspect of communities, so they are often classified on the basis of vegetation. Communities recognized by their vegetation structure are termed "associations" or "formations"; when the definition also implies the consideration of animal communities, the term "biome" is used.

A biome is a grouping of communities or ecosystems that have similar appearances or structures (physiognomy). As physiognomy generally reflects the environment, the environmental characteristics of a specific biome on one continent will be similar to that same biome on any other. Furthermore, widely separated biomes are likely to include unrelated animals with a similar role and possibly similar morphology (form and structure), due to convergent evolution (animals evolving separately, but having similar characteristics).

A frill-necked lizard from Australia is well adapted to live in its dry environment.

At the global level, a number of distinctive features are generally recognized. There are several forest biomes, ranging in diversity and ecological complexity from tropical rainforest to the coniferous high-latitude forests of the northern hemisphere. In regions with seasonal contrasts in rainfall, trees become more widely spaced, species less diverse, and savanna grasses more characteristic of grassland areas develop. Other grassland biomes occur in temperate climates. Shrublands are dominated by shortish, scraggly trees or tall bushes, and may have an understorey of grasses. In drier climates, scrub vegetation may be quite scattered and small in size.

The boundaries of Earth's biomes are rather blurred and maps can only show approximate distributions. Human activity has greatly disturbed natural ecosystems, often leaving mere remnants of once-vast areas of forest or grassland.

These monkeys have adapted to life in the trees in Lombok, Indonesia. They find their food there, sleep there, and can move quickly through the branches at considerable heights above the ground.

The ecological niche

An ecological niche is the role that an organism plays in the ecosystem. Whereas habitat is the physical position of the organism, the ecological niche represents its functional position. For example, within grasslands, the kangaroo in Australia occupies the same niche as the bison in North America. They have the same role—large herbivores. Natural selection has often resulted in organisms adapting to their role, which means that the morphology of an animal can often be a good indicator of its niche.

Species vary in the breadth of their niche—some are specialists, others are generalists. Specialists are usually more efficient in the use of resources, due to adaptation, but they are also more vulnerable to change.

Importantly, two species with similar ecological requirements cannot occupy the same niche within an environment. This principle, called competitive exclusion, means that cohabiting organisms either use different resources, behave in such a way that resources are shared, or exist in a variable environment that favors each species alternately. Species that do have similar niches must compete for resources.

Specialization reduces this competition and, given time, adaptation to this new role may result in an altered morphology. Competitive exclusion is thus an extremely important evolutionary force.

This diagram illustrates the food chain in the tundra. At the top of the chain is the wolf, who has no predators. At the bottom is the vegetation. In between are insects, small mammals (such as lemmings, ground squirrels, and Arctic hares) and birds, followed by other larger mammals such as caribou and Arctic foxes.

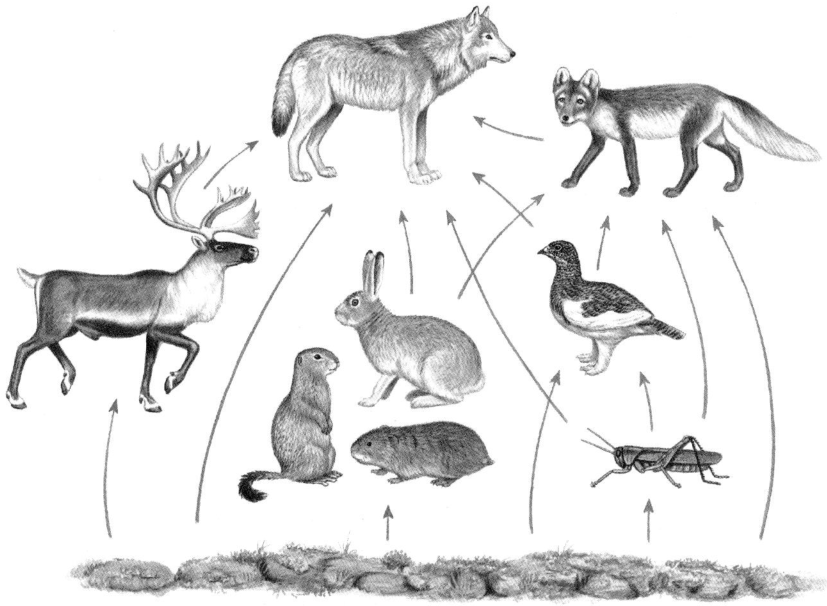

Energy in the biosphere

Most life on Earth is supported by the continuous flow of energy from the Sun into the biosphere. A tiny proportion of this radiant energy is used by plants, which are then able to maintain the biomass and the vital processes of the entire biosphere. Energy is eventually converted to heat and lost from the system.

Plants are capable of capturing and storing energy from sunlight. In the process called photosynthesis, plants absorb the radiant energy of the Sun and transform it into the energy of chemical bonds. The energy left after that used for the vital processes of the plant may accumulate as organic matter, and is available for harvest by animals and decomposition by bacteria and fungi.

As only plants can trap solar energy, their productivity determines the energy limits of the entire biosphere, and the total size of all consumer populations, including humans. The amount of this leftover energy is highest in regions with optimum conditions for plant growth.

On land, productivity is controlled primarily by water availability; in aquatic environments, nutrient availability is crucial. The most productive regions are found at the interface between the land and the sea. Generally, terrestrial communities are much more productive than aquatic systems.

The energy stored by plants as organic matter sustains other organisms. This transfer of energy, as food, from plants to herbivores, and from herbivores to carnivores, is a food chain. At each level of a food chain, a large amount of energy is degraded into heat and other forms of non-recoverable energy, so there is a steep decrease in productivity for each step up the sequence of the food chain. Correlated with this is usually a decrease in the number of organisms, and thus a decrease in total biomass.

The Weddell seal in Antarctica has few predators, and finds plenty of food in the nutrient-rich waters of the Ross Sea.

SOILS

Soil formation is a very complex process. It involves the interaction of climate, type of rock, topography and biota (the total plant and animal life of a region). These factors operate over time, and the amount of time required for soil formation varies substantially from place to place—some soils and their associated weathered products have been forming for millions of years. Soils are formed from weathered materials, usually with the addition of organic matter. The disintegration or weathering of rocks is the result of both physical and chemical processes. Physical weathering breaks rocks down into fragments, while chemical weathering leads to the transformation of rock minerals into products of different composition.

Climate and soils

Weathering products are most often determined by climatic conditions. Mechanical weathering is particularly powerful in drier environments; in hot deserts, the heating of rocks induces expansion and subsequent breakdown of exposed surfaces; freezing has a similar effect. Salt crystallization in crevices mechanically disintegrates rocks. Root growth also leads to mechanical dislodgment.

In wet climates, moisture helps remove particles from exposed rocks, and provides a means by which minerals in those rocks can

This plant from the desert of Angola and Namibia has adapted to life in desert soil.

Layers of soil are exposed in this weathered escarpment, Australia.

be attacked chemically to form clay minerals. Pure water is not a significant chemical agent; but the presence of dissolved carbon dioxide and complex organic substances in soil waters generates a chemical environment able to decompose, remove and redeposit rock (clay-rich) materials and salts.

Hot wet climates, plus the opportunity for plants to grow on stable surfaces for long periods of time, leads to extensive decomposition of rocks. In humid tropical climates, mineral decomposition results in the formation of oxides of aluminum and iron-producing red soils, sometimes cemented into a brick-like substance known as laterite. Such soils are much less fertile than those formed under somewhat drier grassland climates, where organic (or humic) matter and calcium-rich salts accumulate into a nutrient-rich soil capable of growing crops such as wheat and barley.

Rock type and soils

Within one climate area, soil type can vary as a result of the weathering of rocks of different mineral composition. Granites, basalts, quartz-rich sandstones and limestones are common rock types containing distinctive minerals. Chemical decomposition of these rocks over time will yield soils with different types and

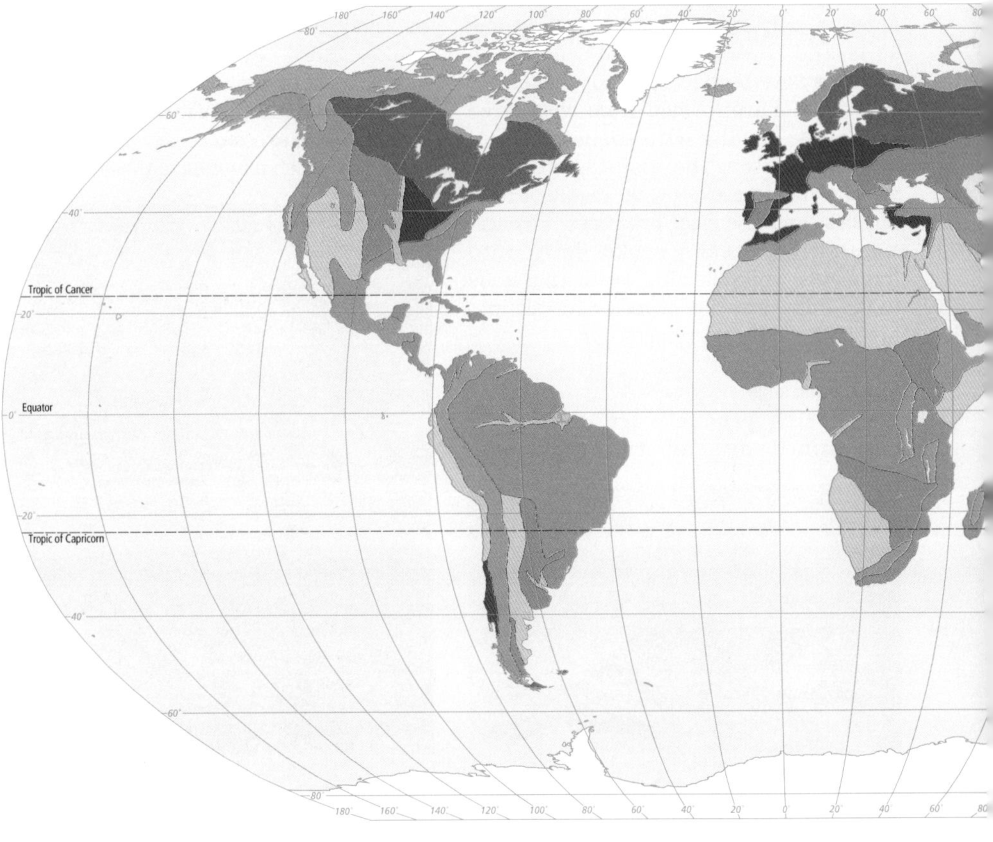

quantities of clays, varying amounts of precipitated salts, and different degrees of water retention and mobility (due to the existence of pore spaces and the capacity of minerals to absorb moisture).

Similar rock types in contrasting climate zones may also produce different soils. For instance, different rates and intensities of weathering can yield dark, organic-rich soils in grassland areas, underlain by basalt, whereas basalt soils in tropical areas are likely to be red and iron-rich.

Soil processes

The essence of soil formation is the breakdown and mobilization of mineral and organic matter in the presence of water. Living and dead organisms, both microscopic and larger (such as earthworms), assist in this process. The result is the formation of layers, or horizons. Each horizon has distinctive color, grain size (texture), chemical composition, organic matter content and pore space size (porosity). In some soils, binding agents such as organic colloids or iron oxides harden the layers. Over time, these layers may thicken, depending on slope position and the rate of landscape removal or deposition. Ground water movements can lead to precipitation of salts in soil layers, or even on the surface, leading to reduced soil productivity, as happens in lands bordering the Aral Sea.

Well-structured soils generally display "A", "B" and "C" horizons; A and B horizons are the real soil layers, known as the solum, while the C horizon consists of the weathered parent rock. The A horizon—the exposed soil—is often dark at the top because of the accumulation of organic

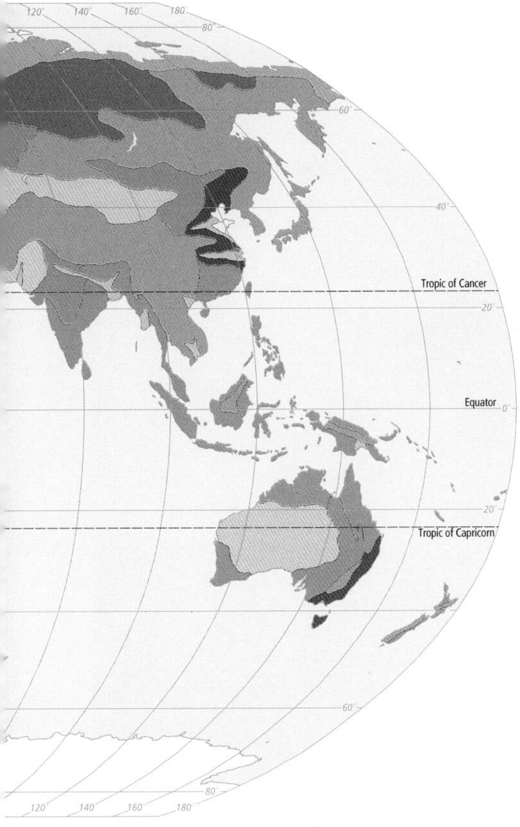

Soil zones

- Warm to cool temperate forest soils, moderately to highly leached, moderate to low in mineral bases and organic material, well developed horizons [Alfisols, Gray-brown podzolics].
- Cool temperate forest soils with highly leached upper profile, acidic accumulation of humus, iron and aluminum in illuvial horizon [Spodosols, Podzols].
- Grassland soils of subhumid and semiarid areas, often mixed with shrubs, organic rich in upper profile in more moist regions, also rich in mineral bases, fertile [Mollisols, Chernozems, Vertisols].
- Latosolic soils of tropical and subtropical climates with forest and/or savanna cover; highly to moderately leached profile, low in mineral bases but high in oxides [Ultisols, Oxisols, Red Podzolics, Laterites—some relic of past climates].
- Desert soils of arid areas with little soil profile development and very low organic material but may contain abundant salts [Aridisols].
- Alluvial soils in all climates especially in deltas, subject to frequent flooding and new deposition of river silt, fertile (only major areas shown), [Entisols].
- Tundra soils in subpolar areas with permanently frozen subsoils; subject to mass movement on slopes (solifluction) [Inceptisols].
- Mountainous areas: soils are typically shallow and stony and highly variable in profile and thickness depending on climate and slope position; includes localiz ed areas of fertile soils especially in mountain basins and near volcanoes.
- Ice sheets

material. A horizons are subject to leaching (eluviation). Leached material is transported to the B horizon, where it is deposited (illuviation); some B horizons are poor in organic material. Eluviation is assisted by the organic acids produced by decaying vegetation.

Soil nutrients

Soil texture and composition influence plant growth and therefore the suitability of a soil for agricultural use. Chemical and organic materials form colloids. Colloids are negatively charged, and attract plant nutrients such as calcium, magnesium, and potassium, which are positive ions (or cations). These nutrients are essential to the existence of all life on Earth.

Gray sandy soils of temperate regions are generally acidic; these soils are not rich in plant nutrients such as calcium and potassium, but this can be corrected by adding lime and fertilizers. On the other hand, some dry desert soils, which often contain mineral accumulations such as calcium carbonate and salts, are alkaline. Whilst many such soils have excessive salt levels, some are quite fertile and, irrigated, can be used for agriculture.

Soil types

Many attempts have been made to classify soils. Properties such as color, texture, composition, horizon thickness and porosity are used to define soil types. But even locally there can be considerable variation in soil type, given changes in elevation, slope angle, rock type and vegetation. In mountainous or hilly areas, for example, many different soil types may exist within short distances over a range of altitudes and slope positions.

At the global scale, soil types largely reflect climatic conditions. However, the history of a land surface may also be significant. The "fresh" deposits of recently deglaciated places in North America and Europe contain relatively poorly leached

Parched, eroded ground leaves trees unable to tap into food and water in the soil, Papua New Guinea.

minerals, contrasting markedly with ancient unglaciated tropical plateaus, from which nutrient-rich minerals have long been removed.

Any world map of soil types must be a broad generalization. Iron-rich weathered soils can occur in areas where past climates have had a significant effect (for instance, southwest Western Australia). Alluvial soils, on the other hand, are constantly forming and reforming as new sediments are deposited in flood plains. Yet soils in both areas may be extremely rich in nutrients and thus of great agricultural significance. By way of contrast, the sparsity of moisture and biota in desert regions, or the presence of ice on the ground, will greatly inhibit soil development.

A soil section, showing horizons enriched by organic matter (A1), and leached of humus and minerals (A2). A horizon of accumulation (B) contains mineral matter leached from above. The bedrock (D) is decomposed into a weathered horizon (C).

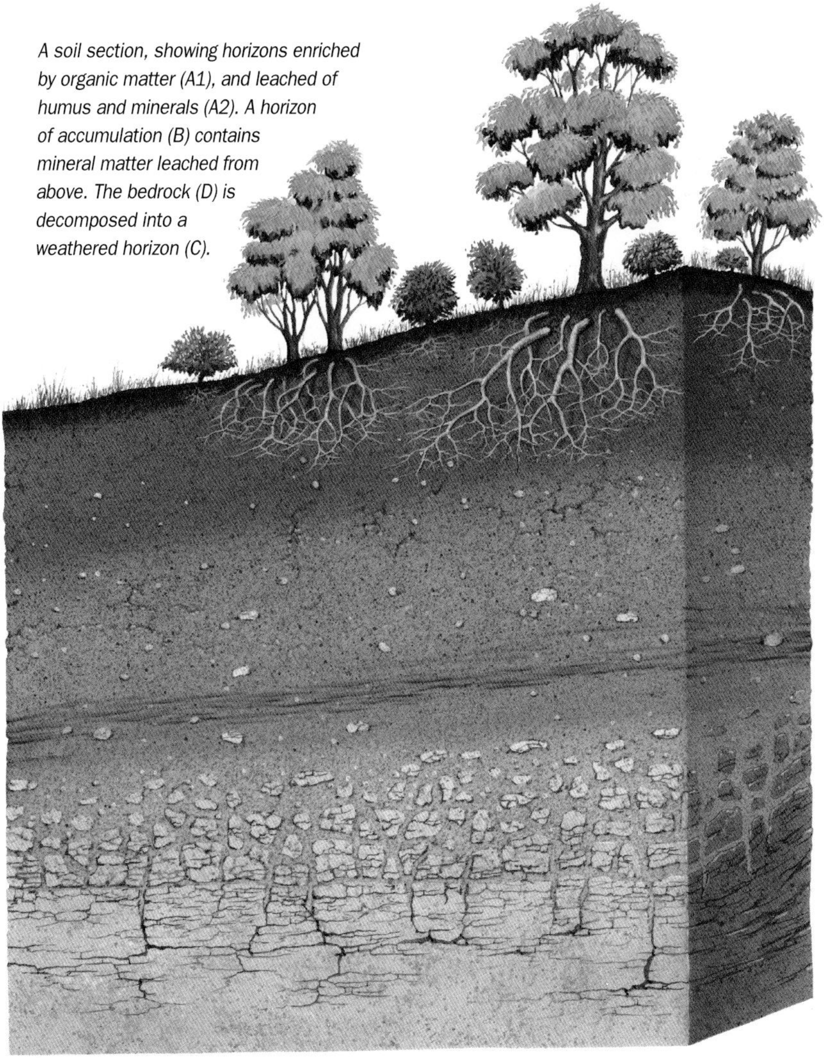

Earth as a Home for Humans

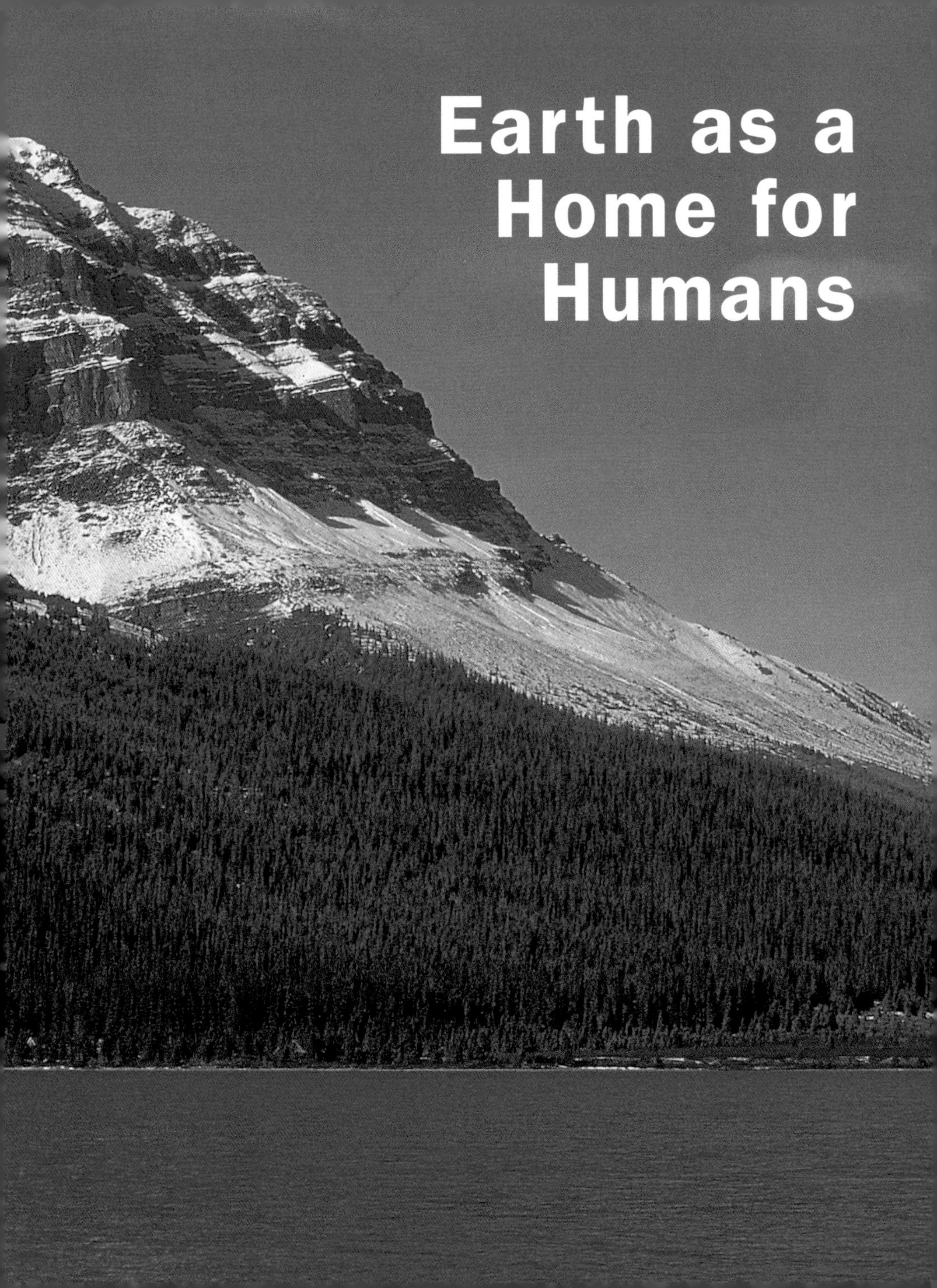

EARTH AS A HOME FOR HUMANS

As humans, we dominate our planet. There are very few places where our impact is not felt. Even the atmosphere has now been altered by gases produced by humans, and some of these—such as chloroflurocarbons (CFCs)—are the result of chemical processes alien to natural systems. Many who travel or work at sea are aware of human debris in our waters. Lakes are drying up and are often heavily polluted, as are rivers. Much of the forests and grasslands of Earth have been disturbed. Over the past 200 to 300 years, in particular, we have transformed this planet in ways which at times enhance our welfare, but at others threaten the existence of societies.

As the human race evolved, so did its capacity to utilize natural resources. The mineral uranium was of little use to societies for much of human history, but, from the end of the Second World War, its value as a destructive force and as a source of power has grown immensely. In contrast, the fertile soils of river floodplains and deltas have long been utilized in some areas, and civilizations such as those of Egypt have depended upon their richness. But as a resource, soils need nourishment. Without appropriate care, their ability to maintain the levels of productivity necessary for agriculture will decline. History is full of accounts of battles waged to maintain social structures and population levels in the face of soil degradation. On the other hand, other societies, such as in China, Japan, and Western Europe, have carefully nurtured their soil resources.

For the early humans, the vast forests of Earth were largely avoided. There is some evidence that forests displaced human activities during the period of global warming immediately following the Ice Age in Europe. Progressively, however, forests in tropical, temperate and high latitude areas have been removed or exploited to create new land uses. Today, fires sweep across vast areas of Amazonian and Indonesian rainforests as more timber is removed and land is cleared for cattle grazing and crops.

Marine life has long provided food for humans. Fishing in shallow waters using primitive lines and spears has developed into sophisticated technologies enabling large ships to roam the oceans capturing fish over a vast range of depths. Fears of exploitation and the reduction of stocks to levels at which particular species will not survive have resulted in international agreements on resource use, although the effectiveness of these agreements is in question, with countries such as Japan and Norway still actively hunting whales, for example. Other forms of more sustainable fishing have been developed to feed societies which are heavily dependent upon food from the sea. This includes various forms of aquaculture at sea, in sheltered bays, and on reclaimed land.

Pressures placed on natural resources are closely linked to population growth. One of the most amazing and environmentally significant aspects of the twentieth century has been the rate of increase in population.

With 6 billion people alive at the moment and perhaps close to 10 billion by the year 2050, it is no wonder that environmental managers, planners, and scientists are deeply worried about the consequences. Also, population increases are not distributed evenly across the world; it is often in developing countries already suffering from depleted resources that the impacts of many new mouths to feed will be most harshly felt. The effective and equitable distribution of food to those in need will become increasingly important. Unfortunately, major health problems also arise in countries where food supplies are threatened. The impacts of poverty and disease, and the capacity of international aid and economic organizations to support developing countries, create further uncertainties in a world beset with environmental and other problems.

Higher standards of living using available natural resources have been made possible through human inventions, including those designed to increase food production and to resist the ravages of pests and diseases in plants and animals. Many areas of high population have benefited from the so-called Green Revolution, but the ability of pathogens and parasites to undergo genetic change and therefore develop resistance to controls reminds us of the need for constant vigilance and research. Undertaking this research and acting on knowledge gained from other countries remain issues of global concern.

What has changed dramatically in recent years is the ability of individuals and groups to communicate quickly across vast distances. In one sense, space has "shrunk". Geographical isolation—such as that imposed by mountain ranges—no longer impedes the information flow; in the past, such barriers meant that separate languages developed in regions which, although physically close, were separated by their inaccessibility. Today, satellite television communications, electronic mail facilitated by fiber optic networks, and 24-hours-a-day business transactions are part of a global economic system which enables information to flow within and between nations.

Exploiting Earth's natural resources: small-scale fishing in Malawi.

The ability of societies to respond to natural hazards is another issue of great concern to international aid agencies and governments. Natural hazards may be insidious (droughts) or virtually instantaneous (earthquakes). Great loss of life and property can ensue; the impacts do not respect national economic strength (for example, the number of deaths as a result of tornadoes in the United States). Yet some areas, such as Bangladesh, are subject to frequent disasters of a scale which disturbs the economy. Greenhouse-effect-induced rises in sea level are another more insidious hazard which potentially threatens the futures of coral island nations such as the Maldives.

LAND RESOURCES

Humans meet their principal needs—for water, minerals, and plants—from the land. Inorganic resources include minerals, water, and various elements in soils, whilst organic or biotic resources include plant and animal life. Fossil fuels (coal, petroleum, and natural gas) are of biotic origin. Both mineral and biotic resources are unequally distributed throughout the world—while some

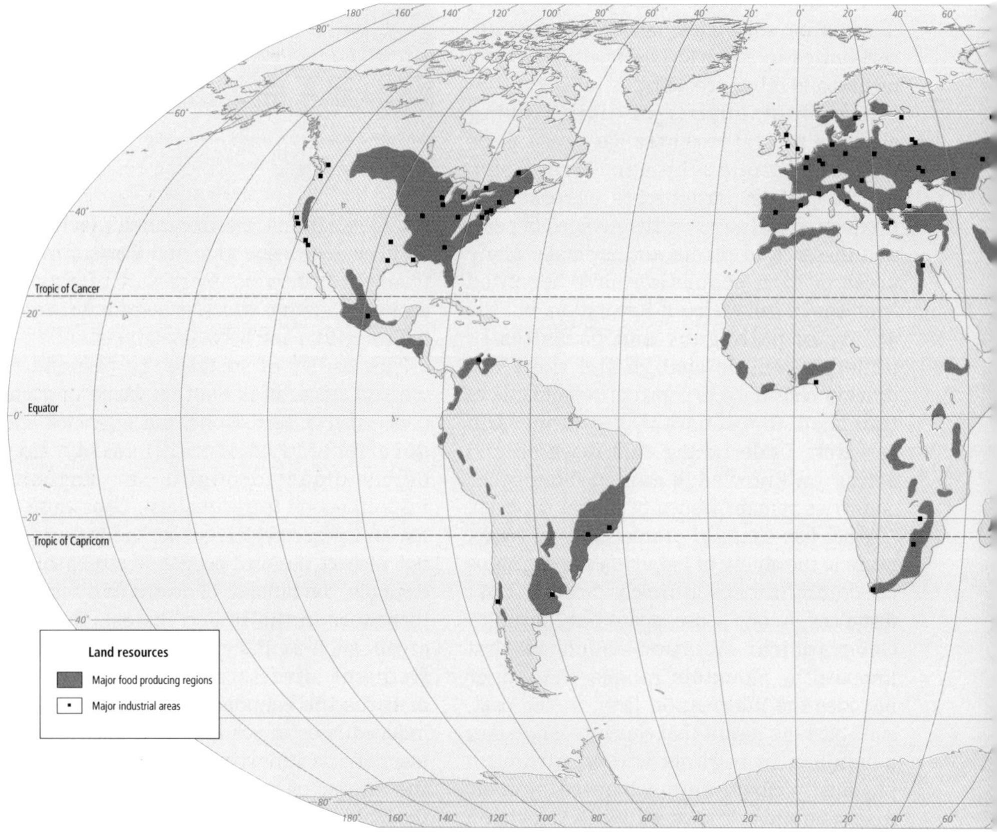

countries have abundant plant and water resources, others do not.

The presence or absence of water is often reflected in population densities, with high rainfall areas generally attracting, and being able to support, greater concentrations of people. China, for example, lacks water in its western half, but has a water surplus in its eastern half, and this is reflected in its population distribution.

Mineral resources are also very unevenly distributed. Some countries possess abundant reserves of certain minerals (such as petroleum in the Middle East), and others have gold reserves (Russia and South Africa).

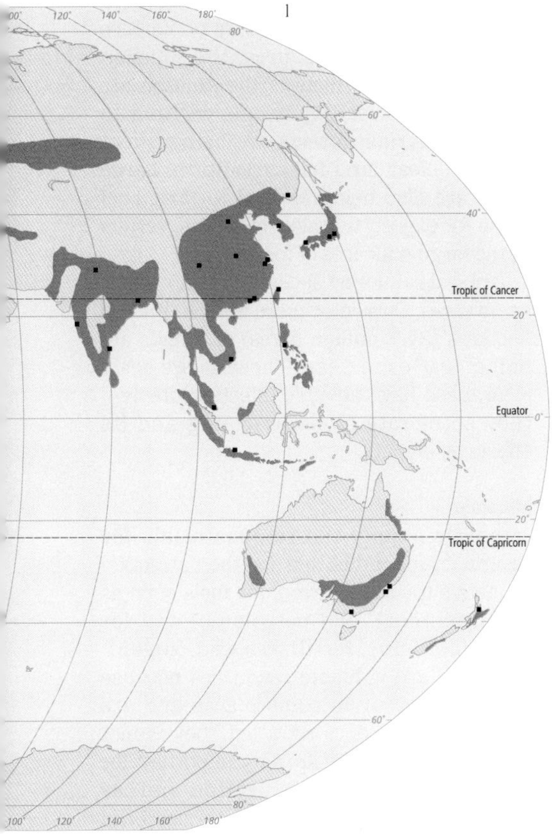

The fact that resources are unequally distributed means that countries must trade what they have for what they need. The highly industrialized countries of Western Europe and Japan, for instance, import raw materials to run their industries. Also, many countries depend upon fossil fuel imports for their energy supplies.

Climate

Climate can be considered a resource because agriculture is so highly dependent on climate. The world's industries and urban centers are mostly located where there is a favorable climate—in areas which have comfortable temperature ranges and adequate rainfall.

Agricultural products can, generally, only be grown economically in suitable climatic conditions. Since the middle of the nineteenth century, plantations in the tropics have produced sugar, tea, coffee, and rubber for international consumption—these areas have been exploited for the production of crops that do not grow elsewhere and are much in demand. Likewise, wheat and other cereals are produced in temperate climates and exported internationally.

Landforms

Human settlement concentrates along river plains and deltas because of fertile soils and available water. In Japan, flat land is prized because of its scarcity. In some places, such as in Japan and on the island of Java in Indonesia, hillsides have been terraced for agriculture. In Europe and North America, deposits of sediment, encrusted with ice age glaciations, form fertile plains.

Agriculture

A long-established agricultural practice is "slash-and-burn". This involves clearing a forest patch, then burning to fertilize the soils; cultivation only lasts a few seasons as the soils become depleted of nutrients. The exhausted patches are then abandoned and a new patch of forest is cleared. Secondary forests grow in these abandoned sites and, after some years, the reafforested areas can be used again. This rotating system can only support small numbers of people. It is not suitable for the type of food production that is needed for large, or growing, populations.

The development of grain farming, some 10,000 years ago, ensured food production for large populations. It led to sedentary settlements and, ultimately, to some of the great ancient civilizations such as Egypt, northern China, and the Indus Valley. Since the nineteenth century, agriculture has seen the development of mechanization, the use of fertilizers and pesticides, and improved varieties of both plant and animal species. These new developments paralleled the great milestones in industrialization, such as the invention of steam engines, the internal combustion engine, electric power and, more recently, the silicon chip.

A beef cattle feedlot in California, USA. This is a method of intensive agriculture; less land is needed, but cattle lead a more restricted existence.

The population explosion in several developing countries within the past 50 years greatly increased their demand for food, and it became necessary to increase crop yields per unit of land. This ushered in the so-called Green Revolution, which involved using high-yielding seeds, fertilizers, and pesticides. Although these products increased grain output, the increase has been at some environmental and social cost.

Brazil is a good example of changing uses of the land. Before becoming a colony, its agriculture was of the slash-and-burn type practiced by forest Indians. Colonialism brought in plantation agriculture. The development of coffee plantations boosted Brazil's economy. Great increases in population have placed pressure on its once largely untapped resource, the Amazon rainforest. Large tracts of the Amazon are being transformed by people wishing to establish farms; forests are being burnt down to clear land for agriculture. Large areas are also being cleared to raise beef cattle for export; this also, of course, results in the large-scale loss of forests.

Tropical rainforest clearance cannot easily be reversed. Currently, more than 10 million hectares (24.7 million acres) of forests are being lost each year. These large-scale clearances have adverse effects globally—they accelerate global warming and its effects on climate.

Minerals

Minerals supply the raw materials for several major industries: for the extraction of metals (primarily iron); for fuels such as uranium, coal, and petroleum; and for manufacturing fertilizers and cement. Minerals are valuable resources because they only occur in some places and are finite in nature: once extracted, they cannot be renewed. Minerals are very important for sustaining modern civilization and, as standards of living continue to rise on a global scale, so too does the demand for minerals. In fact, more minerals have been mined in the twentieth century than in all previous centuries. As demand for minerals increases and they become more scarce, their strategic importance to industry—including, especially, the defense industry—also increases, placing even greater strain on already vulnerable finite resources.

The principal metal in demand is iron for making steel; steel forms the basis of much of the world's manufacturing, and every major industrial country produces steel. Other important metals include aluminum, copper, lead, and zinc.

Coal, petroleum, and natural gas provide energy supplies, and, in recent decades, uranium has provided the basis for nuclear energy. Coal is used for electricity generation and in the manufacture of steel. The ever-growing use of automobiles ensures continuing demand for petroleum, while natural gas is being used extensively for heating. Nuclear energy is currently the subject of much controversy because of dangers associated with nuclear power generation, the problems of nuclear waste disposal, and the potential for using nuclear materials from such plants for nuclear weapons.

Near Beijing, China, people use donkeys to plow—a pre-industrial farming method still used in less developed countries.

The greatly increased use of minerals by the developed countries, and the increasing use by newly industrializing countries, has led to concerns about there being adequate mineral supplies for the future. Substitution of new materials for metals and the search for new or renewable energy sources—such as solar power or wind generation—are amongst the developments aimed at conserving our mineral resources.

Vast wheatfields like these in Saskatchewan, Canada, show human interference with the environment, and depend on high levels of mechanization.

OCEAN RESOURCES

The oceans, covering more than 70 percent of Earth's surface, are the source of enormous amounts of valuable resources. These broadly fall into two main categories: marine life and minerals. Marine life can be divided into pelagic forms and benthic forms. Pelagic forms move about in the waters—these resources include fish and marine mammals. Benthic forms, which live on the sea floor, include corals, molluscs,

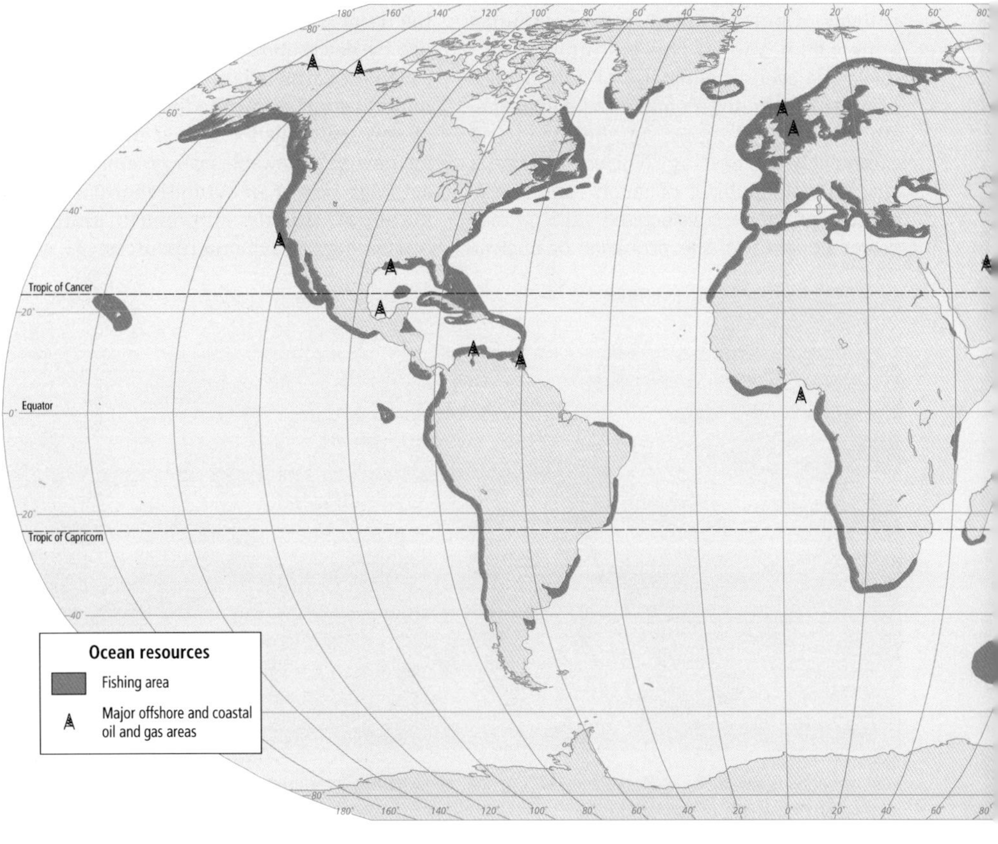

and crustaceans. There are also marine plants such as kelp that are harvested and used by humans.

The oceans also contain mineral deposits, including petroleum and gas, and mineral nodules. These resources are more difficult and expensive to obtain, generally, than marine life, but they are of great economic importance.

Within the past 50 years, modern technology has meant that detailed mapping of the oceans has become possible. Recent studies of the oceans, using this technology, have revealed some well-defined physiographic patterns: close to the land lie continental shelves which often end in steep continental slopes; these are followed, further from the shore, by gently sloping features called continental rises, which end in deep ocean basins; and the latter are intersected by mid-oceanic ridges. There are different marine resources commonly found in the different zones where these physiographic features are found.

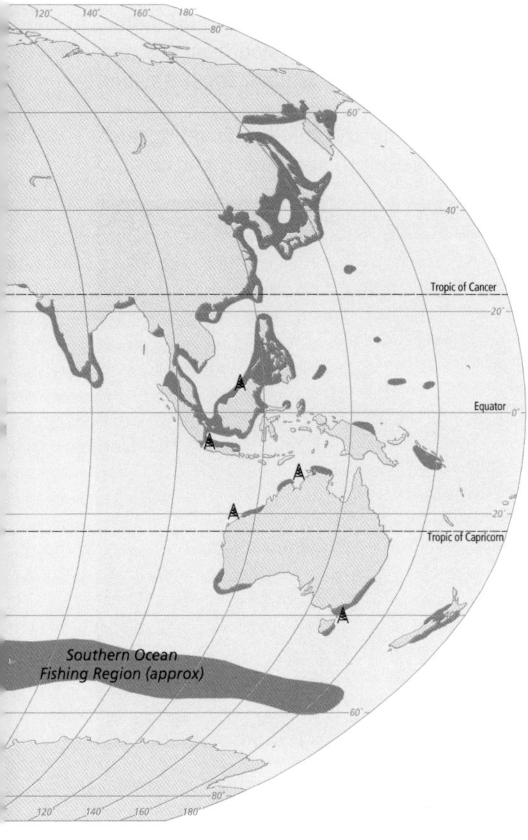

Many nations, realizing the potential riches of the oceans, have declared resource boundaries under the United Nations' Law of the Sea Convention. Territorial seas are normally set at 12 nautical miles (22 km), whilst exclusive economic zones extend to 200 nautical miles (370 km). These mostly include the resource-rich continental shelves.

Continental shelves, however, can vary in width from 110 to 170 nautical miles (200 to 320 km); the shelves in the Atlantic Ocean and the Gulf of Mexico are exceptional in being up to 260 nautical miles (480 km) wide. A nation can legitimately claim all its adjacent continental shelf, even if that shelf extends beyond 200 nautical miles (370 km), as is the case with the United States and Australia. As a result of this law, some small island nations, such as in those in the South Pacific, have maritime claims that far exceed their land areas.

Fishing

Fishing is the most important resource-gathering activity from the seas. In recent decades, however, overfishing of the seas has reached, in some places, crisis proportions. For example, the North Pacific haddock catch dwindled in 1974 to less than 10 percent of what it had been a decade earlier, and the once highly productive cod fishing industry in Canada, employing an estimated 40,000 people, collapsed in 1992.

Several nations grant licenses to foreign fishing fleets to fish in their waters, and this can exacerbate the situation, as has been the case with the southern bluefin tuna from the waters of Australia, New Zealand,

and the Southern Ocean. Overfishing is threatening the very existence of this tuna species; the numbers of this species have fallen, it is estimated, to just 2 to 5 percent of its original population.

Until recently, whales were one of the most threatened species of marine life, but a huge international outcry against whale hunting has resulted in most whaling nations giving up whaling altogether and international agreements for whale protection being enacted. The outcry was generated not only as a result of concern for preservation of whale species, but also because of the horrific nature of the hunting itself.

By the time that whale protection measures were agreed upon, however, several species—including the bowhead, gray and right whale species—had been hunted almost to extinction.

An extensive whale sanctuary in the Southern Ocean now covers the territory of more than 90 percent of the world's whale population. Japan and Norway, however, continue to hunt whales. Japan justifies its whaling operations on the grounds of scientific research, but this explanation is not generally accepted by conservation groups, many of which continue to campaign against all forms of whale hunting.

Coastal fishing

Seas close to shore are usually rich in a wide variety of marine organisms, and have traditionally been fishing grounds for coast-dwelling communities. These are also the areas, not surprisingly, where shellfish farming, aquaculture (fish farming), and salt extraction have, more recently, been widely undertaken.

Kelp, which is rich in potash and iodine, is another product harvested from the seas in coastal areas. It is used for both food and fertilizer.

Fish breeding and shellfish farming, such as oyster breeding, are carried out close to

Human predation has seriously affected creatures like the humpback whale, though international agreements aiming to reduce commercial hunting of whales may help to restore numbers.

Fish farming of Atlantic salmon in Australia is a relatively new commercial use of ocean resources.

the land. Aquaculture can provide reliable and convenient fish supplies, in contrast to fishing—it is no longer possible to depend upon the ever-dwindling supplies from the seas. Fish farming has been practiced for a long time—the breeding of fish in freshwater lakes in China, for instance, has been carried out for a great many years.

Modern aquaculture is a high-technology industry, as it requires meticulous monitoring of water conditions (such as salinity, oxygen levels, and water temperature) and nutrition. Only a limited number of species—salmon in the Outer Hebrides of Great Britain, for example—are being farmed at present.

In the Inland Sea of Japan, an arm of the sea has been completely cut off by metal nets, thus creating a confined space in which fish can be bred. In Japan particularly, seaweed is another important product of aquaculture.

Coastal countries that do not have sufficient supplies of fresh water can extract fresh water from sea water. However, the capital equipment required to establish these desalination plants is costly. There are several such plants for producing fresh water from salt water in the oil-rich countries bordering the Persian–Arabic Gulf—Kuwait, for instance, has desalination plants.

Continental shelves

These shallow, gently sloping features range in depth between 120 and 180 m (400 and 600 ft). When surface sea water is blown away from the land by offshore winds, colder nutrient-rich water rises to the surface. Where such waters are sunlit—these are known as epipelagic or euphotic zones—they make excellent breeding grounds for the minute marine organisms known as plankton. Plankton are tiny plant (phytoplankton) and animal (zooplankton) organisms that provide nutrition for other larger marine organisms.

Although sunlight can penetrate as far as 1,000 m (3,300 ft) below the ocean surface, photosynthesis can only take place in depths of up to 200 m (660 ft). As a result, phytoplankton can only survive within this shallow layer of ocean water. Small zooplankton feed on the phytoplankton in this layer and they, in turn, are preyed upon by larger organisms such as anchovies and squid. Larger fish such as tuna feed on the smaller marine life, only to be, in turn, consumed by still larger fish. This marine food chain extends even beyond the seas, to the seabirds which are the predators of fish.

The cold and extremely nutrient-rich waters surrounding the continental shelves of Antarctica are the breeding ground for small crustaceans known as krill. Species including seals and whales, as well as penguins, feed on krill.

In recent decades, rich petroleum and natural gas deposits have been discovered in the continental shelves. The petroleum deposits originated from the debris of marine organisms in oxygen-free shelf bottoms millions of years ago. Amongst the well-known deposits that are currently being exploited are those in the North Sea, the Gulf of Mexico, and off the city of Bombay on India's west coast.

Improvements in drilling technology have enabled exploration in ever-deeper seas; drilling for natural gas deposits is currently being carried out at depths of more than 1,700 m (5,600 ft) in the Marlim field, off Brazil.

Ocean basins

The ocean basins are made up of large, flat areas called abyssal plains. These abyssal plains lie at depths of about 4,000 m (15,000 ft). In these dark and cold areas, temperatures are low, perhaps only 4°C (40°F), compared with around 20°C (68°F) at the ocean surface.

These deep ocean basins lack plankton and are, therefore, not rich in marine life. Large parts of these plains, however, are covered with minerals, the most important of which are manganese nodules in the Pacific, Atlantic and southern Indian oceans. These nodules could be exploited at depths of up to 5,000 m (16,500 ft) using technology that has already been developed, but this is currently not economically viable.

The ocean basins are intersected by mid-oceanic ridges, which are formed by volcanic eruptions. The sea water and sediments around them often contain concentrations of zinc, lead, copper, silver, and gold. While these minerals are of considerable economic value and, therefore, importance, no method has yet been devised to extract them economically.

Ocean pollution

The seas have, unfortunately, long been considered convenient dumping grounds for waste—anything from urban sewage to nuclear materials. Chemicals from factories, fertilizers and pesticides from agricultural areas, and oil slicks from ships are also being released, often illegally, into the seas. Ballast water taken on by large ships on one side of the world is released on the other, with all its attendant marine organisms thus finding their way into other environments. The effects of such pollution are quite severe already in some areas, particularly in the semi-enclosed waters of the Mediterranean Sea.

Pollution threatens the existence of marine life, and as marine ecological systems are entwined with land-based ecological systems, it will eventually affect life on land, including human life. There are more immediate effects, too, in some cases: dangerous oil spills such as that from the *Exxon Valdez* in Alaska threaten the livelihood of the nearby fishing communities who depend on the sea for their economic existence. Fishing communities in the Gulf of Mexico have also experienced this threat following oil spills from offshore petroleum wells.

COMMERCE

The movement of goods and services from place to place has long been a characteristic of human endeavor. The exchange of products, information and ideas within an economic system extends beyond subsistence societies, and into the "global village" of today. The scale of transactions has changed, though—it now ranges from village or tribal bartering to the almost instantaneous transfer of vast sums of money on the international foreign exchange market. The size and bulk of trade also varies with the commodity, and there are great contrasts—camel trains range across deserts and huge bulk carriers roam the oceans.

Trade is the transport and/or communication of commodities from place to place, and is generally measured in terms of the monetary value of the items moved. Until the advent of steam-driven trains and ships and the extensive use of iron and steel for the manufacture of such carriers, the time taken and capacity to move large volumes of materials was limited. These technological limitations helped determine what could be traded, and what could be traded economically.

The volume and scope of trade, the movement of people, and the flow of information increased enormously in the nineteenth century, and continue to do so.

Container ships like the Katie *transport all manner of goods worldwide today.*

The effects of the increasing numbers of roads, cars, and trucks since the Second World War, for example, are so all-encompassing that it is difficult for many people to imagine life without these relatively recent transportation innovations. Add to these changes the enormous advances in electronic communication technology, and it is easy to see why today's modern suburbanites have become almost completely dependent upon their cars and their electronic communication devices.

The communication of information (ideas, images, audio signals, and written texts), especially as it converges with computer technology to produce information technology (IT), is undergoing another vast technological revolution. Information technology, combined with cable, satellite, optical fiber, and other technologies, can now transmit digitized information (including money) over cyberspace from one part of the globe to another instantaneously, and with potentially staggering effects. Entire national economic systems can suffer very quickly as a result of currency crises facilitated by the use of such technologies—this happened in parts of Asia during 1997 and 1998.

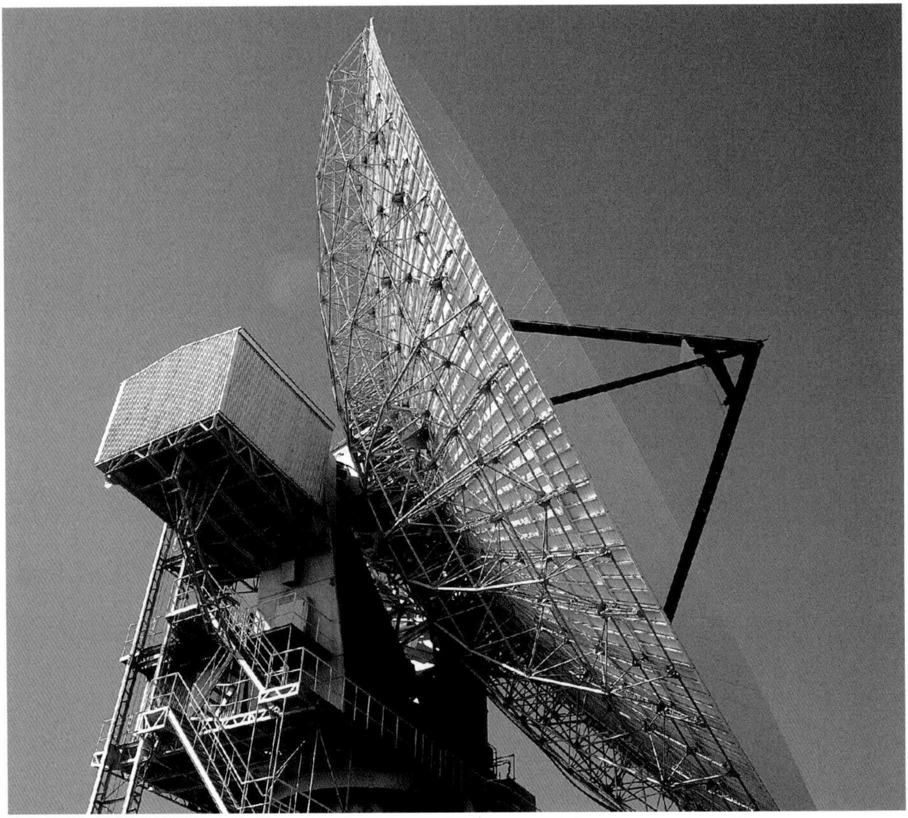

Satellite receiving dishes like this one are more common now, as international trade becomes increasingly dependent on satellite communications.

International trade imbalances

To appreciate the effects of recent changes in transportation and communication technology on trade, it is useful to compare trade between highly industrialized nations (such as the United Kingdom) and other parts of the world in the 1950s with that today.

An international division of labor existed then. Some countries produced manufactured goods in factories, using a highly skilled and well-paid labor force. These goods were traded for primary commodities (coffee and gold, for instance), which were produced by poorly paid and relatively unskilled labor. This unbalanced market system generated an unequal exchange: wealth accumulated in the industrialized areas, leading to unprecedented levels of development, while the other regions remained underdeveloped, largely because of these trade imbalances. That is, the Western world became richer and the Third World remained underdeveloped and poor.

Recent developments

In the 1960s, manufacturing jobs began to move to selected sites in the so-called developing countries, resulting in deindustrialization in the center, and selective industrialization in the periphery, of the global economy. The textile industry was an early industrial sector to move to the periphery, so some "banana" republics became "pajama" republics. The term "newly industrialized nation" applied to former peripheral nations such as Singapore, South Korea, Taiwan, Mexico, and a dozen or so other countries that were undergoing sustained, rapid growth in manufacturing.

The term "economic tiger" also arose, to describe the performance of some countries in the Pacific Rim. Their economies grew faster than those of the USA or Europe during the 1980s and early 1990s, but as those economies were export-oriented, they

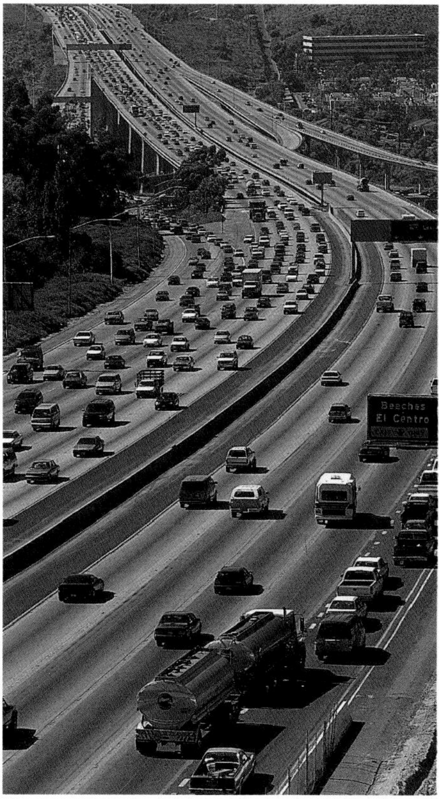

Increased freeway traffic (in San Diego, California, US) and the pollution it causes are a result of increased technology use in many countries.

Simpler forms of transport, such as those that are used in Agra, India, are still used in developing countries.

"E" stands for "electronic"

Email and e-commerce (electronic mail and electronic commerce) are still quite new to many, but they represent changes in the way business and communication are conducted, worldwide, that will soon affect everyone.

Email allows people to write messages on their computer screens and then, via a telephone connection, and for the cost of only a local telephone call, send those messages instantaneously to any person (or group of people) anywhere in the world who has the equipment to receive them. It is therefore cheaper (and of, course, faster!) than mailing a letter, cheaper than faxing written material overseas, and cheaper than telephoning overseas. And it is user-friendly—a genuine revolution in communication.

E-commerce means the buying and selling of goods and services via the Internet. It is even newer than email, and has not yet won the acceptance that email has. There are issues—credit card security (the majority of purchases made on the Internet are made by credit card), censorship and copyright, to mention just three—that are as yet unresolved. These issues are particularly difficult as the Internet does not reside in any country; it exists only in "cyberspace", and it is not clear who has jurisdiction to regulate behaviour on it, or how, in practical terms, such regulation could occur effectively. Despite these uncertainties, e-commerce is growing at a very rapid pace.

The attractions of e-commerce are many: the buyer can, from home, view and compare a range of alternative products; there are web sites that specialize in comparison shopping, so the purchaser can find very low prices for some products; and consumers can buy products that are not available locally at all. The sorts of things that are succeeding in this brave new market range from groceries to clothes, books and compact discs, computers, airplane tickets and shares.

While it is claimed that at present only 1 percent of commercial activities take place on the Internet, online consumer sales will soon reach $US20 billion, and online commerce between companies will reach $US175 billion. A 1998 US survey found that 46 percent of commerce-related web sites were currently profitable, and an additional 30 percent were expected to be within two years. Consumers will determine, as time passes, what sorts of products can be successfully sold this way.

suffered greatly as a result of the withdrawal of foreign funds after 1987.

International commerce is led by the wealthy economies; it increasingly involves service industries based on innovation and technology—finance, insurance, transport, marketing and information flow. Trade in raw materials, including those from countries heavily dependent on agriculture or mining, today accounts for little more than 20 percent of total world trade.

Manufactured goods are now produced and supplied by a range of developed and developing countries with former closed economies—China, for instance, is becoming more market-oriented and is contributing significantly to world trade.

Multinationals and trade blocs

Another major trend is the spread of multinationals. This is occurring in a number of fields that are engaged in world trade. This process is epitomized by the internationalization of stock markets—they operate around the clock and now even penetrate countries such as Russia.

A further feature of world commerce has been the emergence of powerful trade groups or blocs. These represent collections of countries which, as groups, have accepted rules and regulations that permit a freer exchange of goods and services between the countries in the group. Three main trade blocs are the European Union (EU), the signatories to the North American Free Trade Agreement (NAFTA), and the Association of South-East Asian Nations (ASEAN). The release of a single currency, the Euro, in parts of the EU in 1999 signalled another major development in the concept of trade between and within blocs.

Adverse effects of the global economy

Despite the benefits which have arisen from the growth and development of international trade, there are many areas where market liberalization and the availability of funds for investment and growth have created problems.

The replacement of subsistence agriculture by a limited range of "cash" crops is one. This change has placed many societies at the mercy of declines in commodity prices, or the failure of the crop itself, due to climatic or other factors.

The need for capital has raised debt levels in countries such as Thailand, Mexico, and Indonesia to amounts which, at times of crisis, may induce political and social instability. International funding agencies such as the International Monetary Fund (IMF) and the World Bank, as well as aid agencies operating through the United Nations (UN), have become critical in sustaining these economies in the face of changes in technology and the global marketplace, which they may not have survived or been able to exploit.

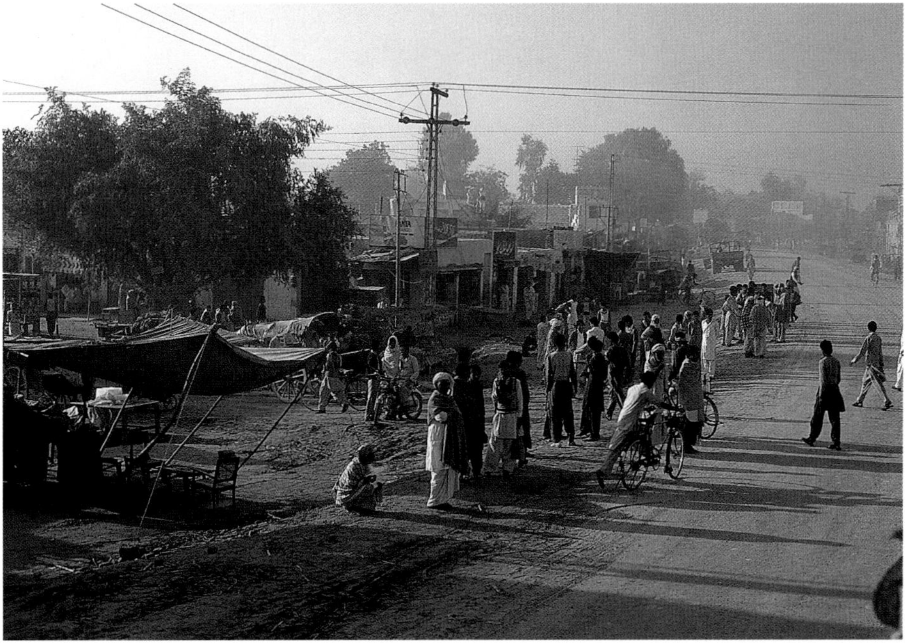

Low GNP and low rates of literacy coupled with a high debt burden and high defense spending make it difficult for countries such as Pakistan to join the electronic revolution.

POPULATION AND HEALTH

The growth of the human population in just the last 50 years has been staggering. In 1950, the global population was 2.5 billion, and it is currently 5.5 billion. It is projected that 8.5 billion people will live on the planet in 2025 and perhaps 10 billion people by 2050. If you are 30 years of age or less by the year 2000 and living in a developed country, according to current life expectancy figures, you will probably live through the

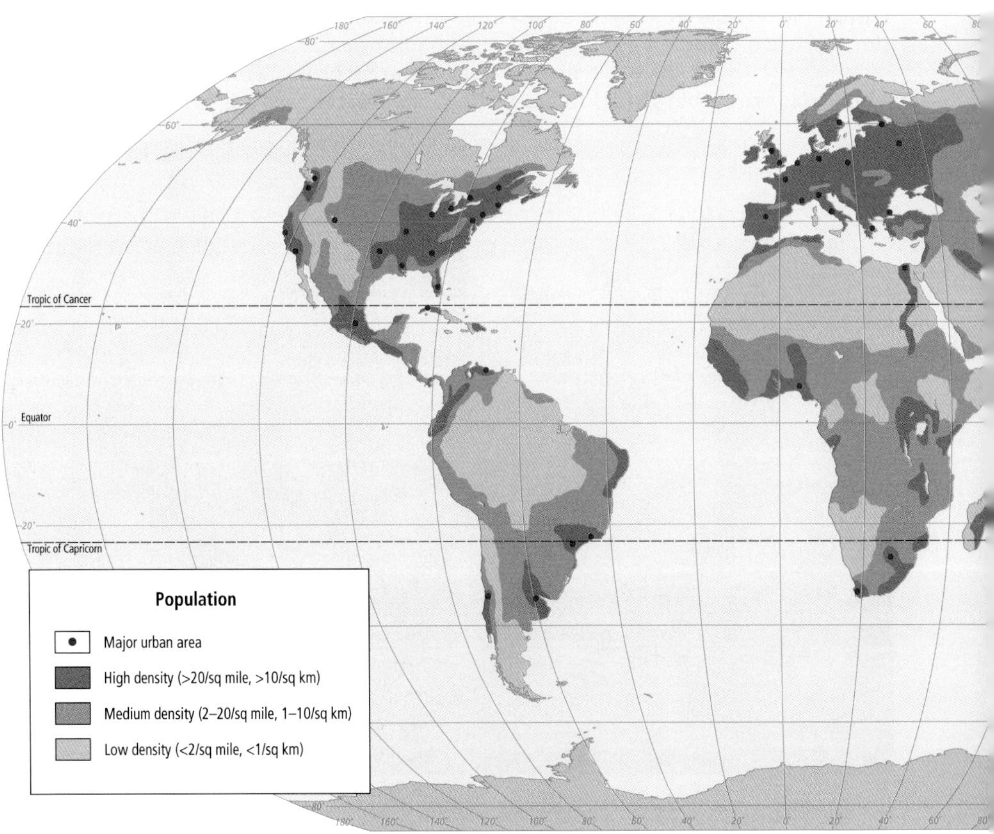

final exponential surge in the human population—it is estimated that the total number of people may start to decline in the second half of the twenty-first century.

Exponential growth refers to the doubling of a population over a given time period. The growth of the human population is of deep concern, as 5.5 billion people at current levels of resource consumption and waste generation are already causing major environmental problems.

Factors causing population growth

How is the growth in population explained? Demographers and population geographers generally explain world population growth by discussing its two immediate causes: increased fertility rates and changes in mortality rates. Fertility refers to the number of children born to women of childbearing age. Mortality refers to various aspects of death, including how long people tend to live (life expectancy) and the causes of death (viruses, cancers, accidents, etc.).

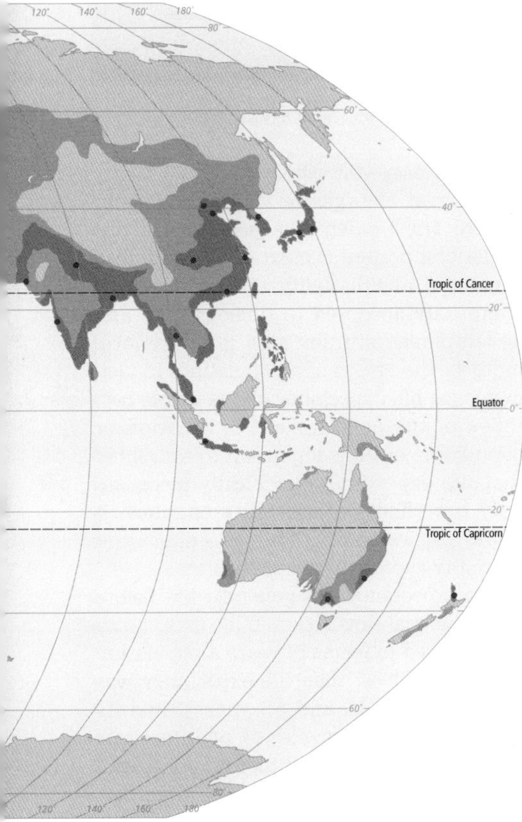

Other factors that play a part in any explanation of population growth include the level of economic development of a given place, the availability of birth control, and the way people in different societies think about children.

Before the Industrial Revolution, the world's population grew slowly, or not at all. Although fertility was high in pre-modern societies—women commonly gave birth to between 8 and 12 children—mortality was also high. One out of four children died before reaching its first birthday (infant mortality) and perhaps another one out of five died before reaching 5 years of age (child mortality). Infectious diseases and poor diet were the major causes of high mortality rates, including infant and child mortality.

Why was the fertility rate so high then? If a family wanted or needed six children, mortality rates alone would require them to have ten or more. Families required the children for agricultural and domestic labor, and as a source of support when a parent grew old—children were the only pension fund available.

The early exponential growth of population resulted from a substantial improvement in the health of populations, especially with respect to the control of infectious diseases and the improvement of nutrition, both of which reduced the mortality rate without a corresponding decline in the fertility rate. Infant and child mortality plummeted, and population growth surged.

As economic and social development moved into a more advanced stage, the

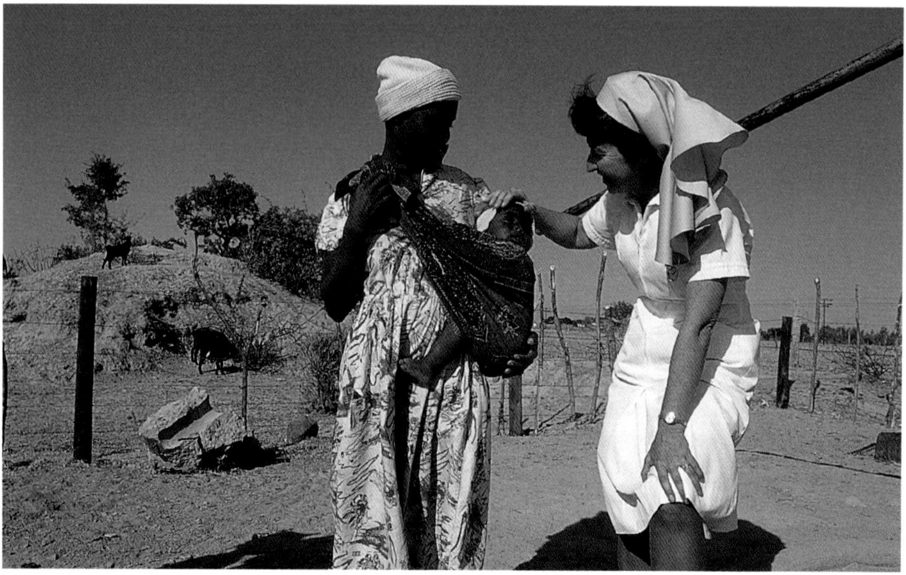

Communities in Zimbabwe work to improve their overall health by reducing the infant mortality rate.

economic meaning of children also changed. As children began attending school, they were no longer available for labor, and children became an expense rather than an asset. Raising a child today in a developed country may now cost between $US250,000 and $US750,000. Thus, fertility rates have declined with advanced development because of the increased survival rates of children (increased health) and because parents become economically poorer by having many children (though not necessarily socially poorer) today, as against the past, when children labored for their parents for a substantial portion of their lives.

The advent of modern birth control has also played an important role in the decline of the fertility rate. Most developed countries have fertility rates below that required for maintaining current levels of population; immigration is the major factor responsible for continued population growth within developed countries.

Life expectancy—the individual

Looking at changes in health in greater depth, the health of a population has three components: mortality, morbidity (sickness), and disability. Life expectancy is commonly accepted in demography and development studies as a good general index of the health of a population. In fact, many see life expectancy as the single best index of the development of a nation or population, but it is important to remember that life expectancy specifically measures only the effects of mortality changes; it does not relate to the sickness and disability aspects of human health.

Life expectancy was generally low before the Industrial Revolution. If life expectancy is expressed in terms of years a population as a whole lives, then life expectancy was low (between 45 and 55 years), mainly because of the prevalence of infectious diseases (measles, pneumonia, polio, and malaria, for instance), poor nutrition, lack of family planning, and the like.

Substantial advances in the reduction of a range of infectious diseases, coupled with improvements in nutrition, represent what the United Nations Children's Fund describes in their annual publication *The Progress of Nations* as simply that—the progress of nations. Life expectancy increased by 10 to 15 years because of these improvements to health.

Further increases in life expectancy—when compared with, say, life expectancy in the late 1960s and into the 1970s—are the result of advances in the reduction of death due to degenerative diseases (strokes, cancers, and heart attacks, for example) and the greater emphasis on improving lifestyle—a healthy diet, regular exercise and a reduction in smoking.

For a few nations, life expectancy is slightly more than 81 years at present. At the global scale, life expectancy at birth was 46 years in 1950, 65 years in the late 1990s, and is projected to be 77 years in the year 2050.

Life expectancy—the global view

Considerable regional diversity in the causes of population growth and life expectancy is evident in the late 1990s. Generally speaking, North America, Australia and Europe have high life expectancy and have internal growth rates below population replacement; South America and East and Southeast Asia are not far behind; and Africa south of the Sahara has low life expectancy, but population growth remains explosively high.

Many of the countries in the former communist world are experiencing deterioration in health, and life expectancy is actually declining in some of those nations, including Russia. It is interesting to compare the two most populous nations, China and India. Changes to population growth and life expectancy in China resemble those in other East and Southeast Asian nations, whereas India continues to have a very high growth rate and a moderately low life expectancy.

Exponential population growth occurs when rising prosperity coincides with high fertility rates, as in Bangladesh.

The future for life expectancy

Is there a limit to life expectancy? This is a most controversial topic about which there is no agreement. Under natural conditions, all life forms have a limit, called senescence: the point where an organism simply wears out. For the human population, senescence was believed to be roughly 85 years; however, a few population groups live into the low 90s. Genetic and other medical research, however, may well change the upper limit of life expectancy during the first half of the twenty-first century.

Of course, all of this optimistically assumes that improvements in health will continue. It remains to be seen whether or not the impact of diseases such as AIDS will retard or even reverse the historical improvement in human health, the resistance of some forms of bacteria to antibiotics, in particular, will give rise to deaths from diseases or infections previously thought to be under control, and whether the advances that come through medical research will be affordable to a sizeable proportion of the world's population.

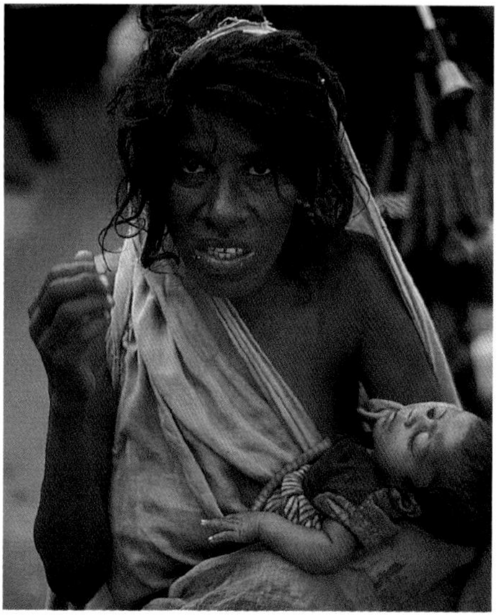

Some countries, such as India, continue to suffer low life expectancy.

Famine

Famine can be defined as a high degree of lack of food within a population, and it often goes along with widespread mortality. Malnutrition, on the other hand, refers to levels of nourishment that are below those needed to maintain health, and can apply to a whole population or part of a population.

Both are thought to be the results of population pressure—the pressure that builds, in developing countries particularly, between the size of the population and the economic resources (especially food) of the country. Falling living standards can be an early sign, in countries with rapidly growing populations, of this pressure. Many societies have suffered famines; in modern times, famine has most often affected societies in Africa.

The links between famine and malnutrition and mortality and fertility now seem not nearly as clear as may previously have been thought. Investigations into mortality in developing countries have found that it is the combination of malnourishment and infectious disease that is responsible for high mortality among infants and children, not simply lack of food.

It seems that populations are able to maintain their rates of fertility despite quite large reductions in nutritional levels—metabolic rates actually appear to readjust when there are food shortages.

NATURAL HAZARDS

Natural events which cause damage and loss of life are classified as natural hazards. These hazards are generally unpredictable—they strike suddenly and can therefore leave the affected populations traumatized. Natural hazards can result from movements taking place inside the Earth or on its surface, or in its atmosphere.

Movements within the Earth result in volcanic eruptions and earthquakes. Changing weather conditions generate wind storms, cyclones, tornadoes, heavy rainfall, and snowfall, as well as lightning strikes, which can trigger forest fires. River floods and tsunamis can cause loss of life and serious damage to property.

Earthquakes

Plate collision along the Japanese archipelago makes that area vulnerable to earthquakes and to tsunamis generated by earthquakes on the ocean floor. Plates sliding past each other can also cause earthquakes, such as along the San Andreas Fault in California, where earthquakes have occurred in San Francisco and in Los Angeles.

Earthquakes strike suddenly, and if they are of high intensity, buildings can be toppled and life and property lost. The famous San Francisco earthquake of 1906 was devastating to that city and its people—hundreds of buildings were destroyed and

Wildfires (bushfires) consume large tracts of forest in many countries every year. Often lives are also lost, and millions of dollars worth of property is destroyed.

the resulting fires swept through the city center, leaving about 3,000 people dead and many thousands more homeless.

An intense earthquake in 1995 toppled and wrecked the tall buildings and infrastructure of Kobe, in Japan, killing more than 6,000 of its inhabitants and injuring more than 35,000 others. The worst scenarios involve earthquakes located close to inhabited areas, notably cities.

On the Richter scale, earthquakes are serious when they exceed a magnitude of 4, cause damage when they exceed 5 and are intensely destructive when they are between 7 and 8.6. Although more than a million earthquakes occur every year, most of these are of low magnitude, and cause no loss of life or damage. High-intensity earthquakes, on the other hand, are capable of causing great damage and therefore receive the most publicity, particularly when they are centered on densely populated areas.

Tsunamis

Earthquakes taking place on the sea bed can trigger tsunamis (tidal waves) which, on reaching land, can assume enormous proportions and result in great damage. Such waves may be less than 1 m (3 ft) in height where they begin, in the deep oceans, but they can reach the enormous heights of more than 30 m (100 ft) as they approach

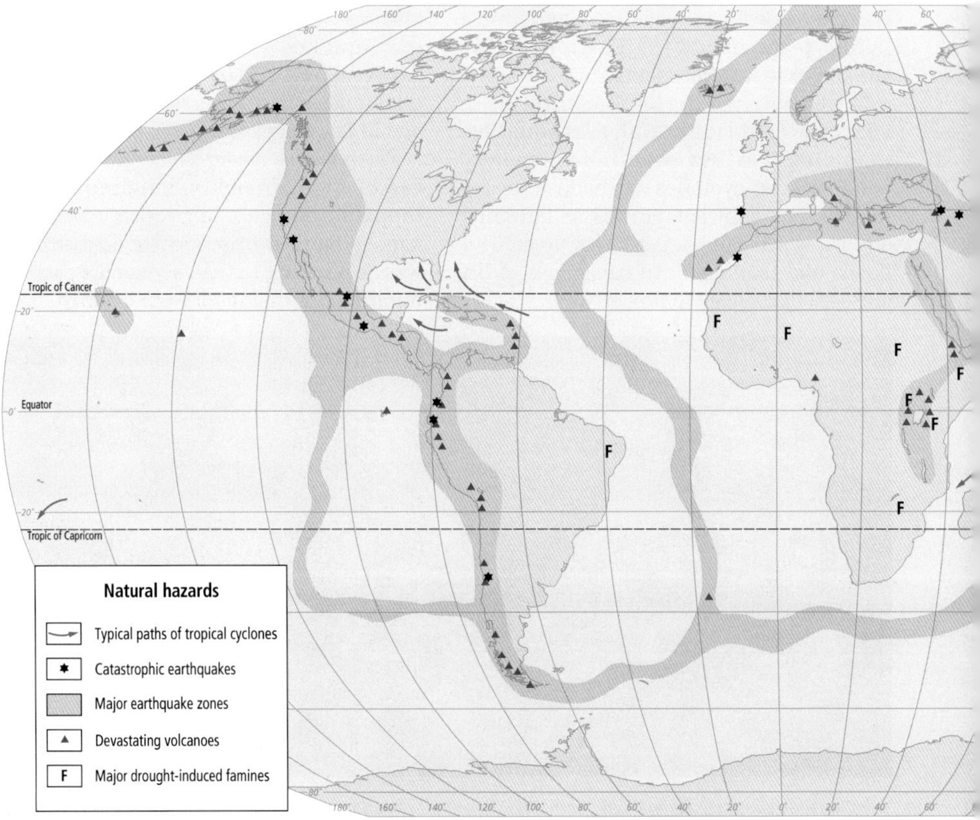

land, and they cause devastation to low-lying areas. Worse still, within seconds, more than one such giant tidal wave can strike.

In 1983, a tsunami resulted in the deaths of 30,000 people in Japan. On 17 July 1998, a tsunami struck the northern coast of Papua New Guinea, sweeping over the village of Arop and others nearby, which lay on a low-lying sandy spit; entire villages and their populations were swept away, and it is estimated that the death toll was approximately 4,000 people.

Volcanoes

Volcanic eruptions are common along certain paths, which are also seismic zones.

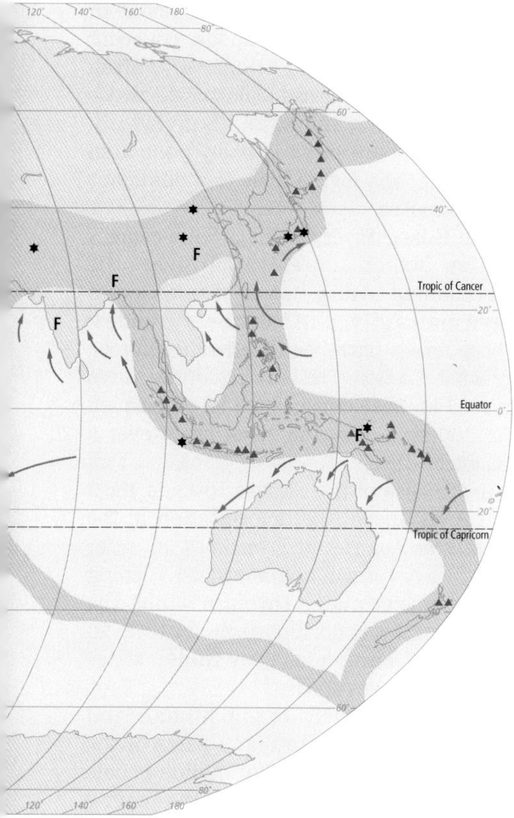

Here, crustal plates separate and collide. Volcanoes erupt where molten material (magma) accumulates just below Earth's surface and then rises to the surface. A volcanic explosion ejects ash and superheated steam into the atmosphere and cascades very hot lava along the sides of the volcanic cones. Volcanic eruptions are another natural disaster that can be devastating to life and property.

In AD 79, lava and ash destroyed the ancient city of Pompeii in southern Italy when Mt Vesuvius erupted. Mt Pelée, in Martinique, erupted in 1902, destroying the city of St Pierre and killing most of its inhabitants. Mt Pinatubo, in the Philippines, erupted in 1991, ejecting steam, ash, and lava, and threatened hundreds of thousands of people just 27 km (17 miles) away in Angeles; its ash even blanketed parts of Manila. Volcanic eruptions are also common in Bali and Java (Indonesia).

Volcanic eruptions are rated on the Volcanic Explosivity Index. The Krakatoa eruption of 1883 in Indonesia, one of the most spectacular on record, is rated at 6. No recorded eruption has reached 8, which is the highest possible rating. The Krakatoa eruption was heard more than 4,500 km (2,800 miles) away; it generated tsunamis, and more than 30,000 people are believed to have perished as a result.

Tropical cyclones and tornadoes

Tropical cyclones, known as typhoons in East Asia and hurricanes in the Caribbean, are also very destructive atmospheric hazards. Tropical cyclones are whirling, low-pressure vortices that can be up to 500 km (310 miles) in diameter and have wind speeds reaching more than 200 km (125 miles) per hour. They can pick up trees, rooftops, light boats, and planes and destroy them. This flying debris is enormously dangerous to people and property, too.

In coastal areas, large waves, or surges, which sweep the land may be generated,

Mt Pinatubo in the Philippines erupted in 1991 causing widespread damage with devastating mud slides.

resulting in considerable damage. These cyclones have a calm center, called the "eye" of the cyclone; when the eye passes over an area there is a period of calm, after which the storm returns in all its fury, but with the winds now reversed in direction.

The coastal areas of Southeast and East Asia, the Bay of Bengal, the Pacific Ocean west of Mexico, the Caribbean and Florida, plus island groups of the Pacific Ocean such as Fiji, and northern Australia, are amongst the areas most prone to tropical cyclones.

Cyclones have struck with great fury along the coast of Bangladesh, a small country which mostly consists of the combined deltas of the Ganges and Brahmaputra rivers. That low-lying deltaic area is particularly vulnerable to the surges which cyclones can generate. This has resulted, on several occasions, in considerable loss of life and damage to property.

In contrast to tropical cyclones, tornadoes are small low-pressure cells, not more than 0.5 km ($^3/_{10}$ mile) across. They are, however, very intense, and their wind speeds can exceed 400 km (250 miles) per hour. They thus have the potential to inflict sudden and serious damage. Their vortices become vividly visible as they whip up soil and other debris. The most damaging tornadoes occur in the central parts of the United States, although mini-versions are also found in parts of eastern Australia.

River floods

River floods are a common hazard in floodplains. Spectacular floods, covering thousands of square kilometers, often occur over the immense plains of the major rivers of China, India, and Bangladesh. These areas are often densely populated because of the fertile soils and abundant water supplies.

The Huang River in China flows along a course which is elevated over the surrounding plains; this is because levees have naturally built up on its sides. These levees have been further reinforced by human action. The bursting of the levees in 1887 inundated more than 130,000 sq km (50,000 sq miles) and resulted in over a million deaths.

In the case of the Ganges River in India and Bangladesh, the deforestation in the Himalayas has resulted, at times, in water from heavy rainfall and snowmelt rushing onto the vast plains through which the Ganges runs and flooding them. In 1988, 90 percent of Bangladesh lay under water when the Ganges flooded.

Floods regularly bring human and economic disasters to many parts of the world—in 1998 alone, 250 million people were affected by the flooding of the Yangtze River in China—and dams and irrigation networks have been built across many flood-prone rivers in an attempt to mitigate and control flood damage.

Wildfires

Wildfires or bushfires strike when forests are dry. These fires can cause serious damage and result in significant air pollution. The 1997 wildfires in the tropical forests of Sumatra, Indonesia, for instance, released a dense pall of smoke over a large area, including parts of Malaysia and Singapore. These fires were lit by humans clearing land for agriculture or wood-chipping. Normally, rains ensure that wildfires are temporary, and restricted to a small area. In Sumatra, however, the prolonged drought, blamed on the El Niño effect, resulted in the uncontrollable spread of the wildfires.

The naturally occurring eucalypt forests of Australia and the eucalypt forest plantations of California are also particularly prone to wildfires, as the volatile oil the eucalypts contain makes them highly flammable. Every year, wildfires wipe out large areas of these forests and damage human settlements or property in the process.

Drought is a more predictable natural hazard.

Remote sensing, using satellites and highly sophisticated monitoring techniques, is now being used to track possible natural disasters. It provides data to ground centers about the development of tropical cyclones, the spreading of flood waters from rivers, and the build-up of lava in volcanoes. Such advance warning systems have already helped save lives and limit damage.

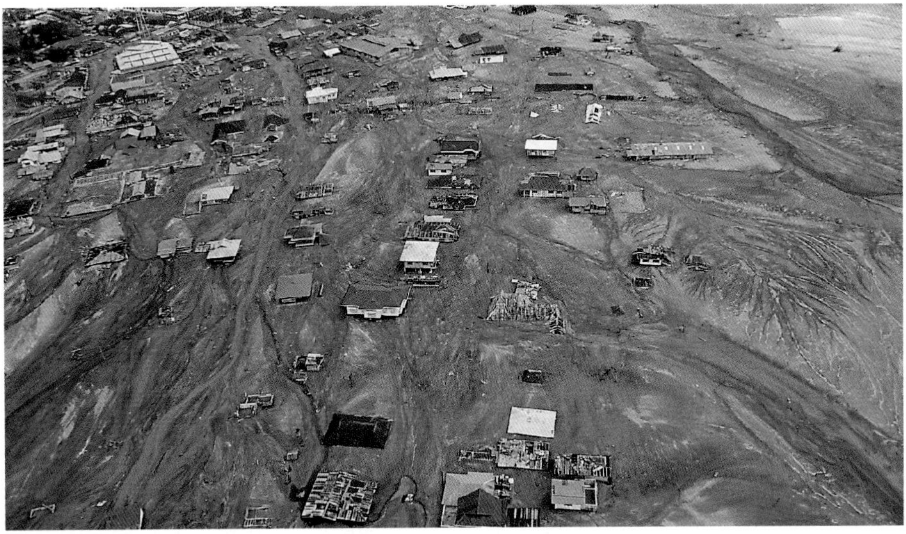

The town of Lahar in the Philippines, which was swamped by mud slides from Mt Pinatubo's 1991 eruption.

HongkongBank

Part 2

People and Society

THE CHANGING SCENE

Today's global pattern of peoples and nations rests on a long process of social evolution, going back about 2 million years. It was then that humanity began to clearly distinguish itself as something special on the planet—and unlike the great apes—by physical and mental changes such as a fully upright way of walking, and much bigger brains than the apes possessed. Then, some time in the past 40,000 years, the great evolutionary breakthrough occurred—a fully developed capacity for language, an ability to create new tools for new purposes, and a talent for forward planning. Previously nomadic, hunting wild animals and foraging for seeds, humans now chose to live a more settled existence. They lived in regular campsites and made shelters. In some places they dug pits for food storage, and had well-built, regularly used fireplaces as far back as 20,000 years ago. Art and religion also appeared, with remarkable cave paintings and evidence of ritual associated with the burial of the dead.

It is thought that *Homo sapiens sapiens* (the technical name for modern humans) originated in Africa. From there waves of migration carried people to every corner of Earth: to distant Australia perhaps 50,000 years ago, to North America across a land bridge (where the Bering Strait is now) perhaps 20,000 years ago. As they moved, they took their languages with them, and when they settled, their languages continued to evolve, many soon becoming mutually unintelligible. Then, around 10,000 years ago came a major development—the rise of agriculture and of permanent settlements. In Turkey and Iraq, in China, and in Mexico, farmers began to grow wheat and barley, or rice. At around the same time, the first farm animals were domesticated: pigs and cattle, goats and sheep, and llamas in South America.

Permanent farming settlements transformed human life economically, and on this foundation civilizations arose in different parts of the world. In Egypt and Iraq, in China and India, in Mexico and Peru, some towns became cities, with centralized political systems, strong rulers, and monumental buildings. The buildings were often religious temples associated with a class of priests, and in Egypt they were tombs for divine kings. These social and political developments were accompanied by equally significant developments in science and technology.

The Stone Age came to an end. First bronze was invented, then people found out how to make iron—by 500 BC, iron tools and weapons were spread throughout Europe and Asia. Metals and metallurgical science gave those who had them a huge military advantage over those who did not, as did the wheel, when it appeared around 3,500 BC. Horses harnessed to chariots changed the nature of warfare in ancient times.

War and conquest were normal conditions of life. Victory often went to those whose weapons were most advanced. Some dominant cities developed into empires, subjecting other cultures to their rule. The Roman Empire, at its height, included large areas of Europe, North Africa, and the Middle East. By 206 BC, China was united under the Qin Dynasty, while by 1,520 AD the Incas controlled some 2,000 miles (3,330 km) of territory west of the Andes in South America. The military advantages of steel weapons and guns were demonstrated by the easy victories of Cortez over the Aztecs (1521) and Pizarro over the Incas (1533) against vastly greater numbers of the ill-equipped Amerindian forces. The consequences of empire were that the knowledge, ideas, religion, technology and language of the dominant civilization were spread far and wide.

The spread of the main world religions has also been of major importance in the past two thousand years. These religions have been responsible for the most enduring examples of the art, literature, and architecture of civilization. A distinction can be made between proselytizing religions, which actively seek to convert people to their beliefs (such as Chistianity, and Islam) and those which do not, such as Hinduism and Judaism.

In the past 200 years, industrialization has been the biggest force for social change. Beginning in England with textile manufacturing in the 1780s, then progressing to manufacturing based on iron and steel in the nineteenth century, industrialization now combines science with technology in an unending cycle of invention and discovery. What began in Europe has now spread to every country in the world. Industry, which takes raw materials and then turns them into products to be traded, has provided millions of jobs for peasants who would otherwise be tied to the land. But in order to take those jobs they have moved into the cities. Urbanization has created huge concentrations of people in Asia and in South America, and while raising incomes, it has brought social problems too.

Human societies have changed more during the twentieth century than during any previous one, but mechanized facilities are not yet available to all—no running water for these Indian women in Varanasi.

Political changes have come thick and fast. The nation-state arose as a political movement in Europe in the nineteenth century, where it superseded an earlier pattern of city-states such as Venice, Antwerp and Amsterdam. After the Second World War it spread through Asia and Africa during the process of decolonization, and since 1989 it has disrupted the domains of the former Soviet Union. Conflicts born of nationalism continue to plague troublespots in Africa, Indo-China, the Balkans, and the Middle East. However, there has been at the same time a balancing move towards large, over-arching international organizations. The European Union steadily moves towards greater political and economic unity. Meanwhile, the United Nations, its resources and abilities increasingly overstretched, its goals more honored in the breach than in the observance, endeavors to keep international peace.

HUMAN EVOLUTION

The oldest primate fossils found in Africa and Asia date from between 45 and 50 million years ago. Around 15 million years ago, Asian and African hominoids (the earliest known ancestors of both humans and apes) diverged. The African hominoids adapted to woodland and savanna habitats and developed the ability to walk on two legs, while the Asian hominoids continued their tree-climbing existence. Although the fossil record is incomplete, a later divergence probably occurred among African hominoids between gorillas and the common ancestors of humans and chimpanzees.

Early hominids

The first hominids (the earliest ancestors of modern human beings not also related to modern great apes) developed about 5 to 6 million years ago. During the earliest phases of their evolution, hominids underwent anatomical changes that resulted in an erect posture, allowing them to walk habitually on two legs. Other changes included the reduction of canine teeth and the development of a comparatively vertical face. Features that are widely accepted as hominid hallmarks, such as a larger brain and the capacity for cultural life (indicated by stone or bone tools), appeared later.

The earliest hominid fossils have been found in southern and eastern Africa. The Olduvai Gorge in the Great Rift Valley of Tanzania has proved to be a rich source. In the 1930s, the anthropologist Louis Leakey began excavations there, and, in the ensuing years, he and others found a large number of hominid fossils and stone tools. The most famous find occurred in 1959 when his wife Mary uncovered a hominid fossil she called *Zinjanthropus*, believed to be 1,750,000 years old. Most scholars now believe that *Zinjanthropus* is an example of *Australopithecus* (specifically *Australopithecus boisei*), the earliest group of hominids yet found.

Handy man

Other hominid fossils found at Olduvai Gorge were more clearly identifiable as members of our own genus, *Homo*. These hominids were tool users and have been classified as *Homo habilis* ("handy man"). Tools similar to those found at Olduvai have been found at sites elsewhere in Africa and dated at between 1,800,000 and 2,340,000 years old.

Fossils of species that are more recognizably like ourselves have also been found in Africa and dated at about 1.9 million years ago. The best example is a nearly complete 1.6-million-year-old skeleton found in northern Kenya and known as Turkana Boy. The boy died in adolescence, but, had he lived to maturity, he would have been tall (about 1.8 m [6 ft]), with long, slender limbs, and well adapted to living on the open savanna.

Turkana Boy and other similar fossils found in Africa were originally thought to resemble specimens discovered in Java and China. All were classified as *Homo erectus* and it was believed that *Homo erectus* had evolved in Africa and then migrated to Asia about 1 million years ago. Discoveries in China in the past decade, however, together with the application of more sophisticated dating methods to previously excavated Asian sites, have pushed back the date of the first appearance of early hominids in Asia to about 2 million years ago. Hominid fossils found in Longgupo Cave in Sichuan province in China, dated at around 1.9 million years old, more closely resemble the earlier hominid species *Homo habilis*. This suggests a much earlier migration out of Africa. As a result, some scholars now believe that *Homo erectus* evolved independently in Asia and was not an African species. African hominid fossils of a more modern appearance, such as Turkana Boy, are now classified as a separate species, *Homo ergaster*.

Although there are a number of early hominid sites in Europe, they have yielded few fossils. Sites containing tools have been dated at around 1 million years old, with the earliest being about 1.5 million years old. Until recently, some of these were classified as *Homo erectus* sites.

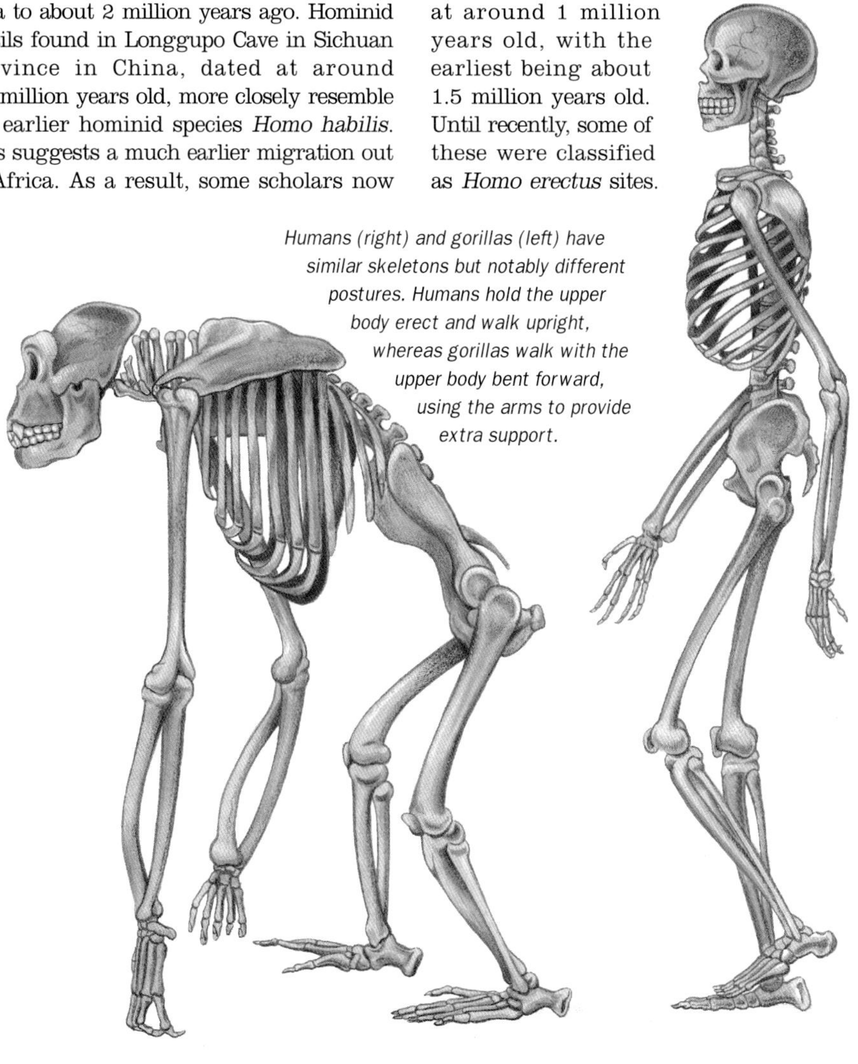

Humans (right) and gorillas (left) have similar skeletons but notably different postures. Humans hold the upper body erect and walk upright, whereas gorillas walk with the upper body bent forward, using the arms to provide extra support.

Since this species is now considered to be an Asian evolutionary sideline, however, the fossil record is being reassessed. In 1994, excavations in northern Spain produced numerous simple stone tools and some hominid fossils subsequently classified as a separate species, *Homo heidelbergensis*. This find has been dated at more than 780,000 years old and may provide evidence for the European ancestors of the Neanderthals.

Archaic *Homo sapiens*

The earliest archaeological discoveries made in Europe were fossils of archaic *Homo sapiens*. The fossils were named Neanderthals, after the Neander Valley near Düsseldorf in Germany, where they were first discovered in 1865. This find caused widespread excitement as it was the first discovery of an extinct ancestor of modern humans. Since then, numerous Neanderthal sites have been found throughout Europe and the Middle East. The Neanderthals are generally considered to be a subspecies of *Homo sapiens*, known as *Homo sapiens neanderthalensis*. However, some scholars believe that the Neanderthals' less evolved physical characteristics and less sophisticated technology indicate that they were a separate species, *Homo neanderthalensis*.

The Neanderthals lived in Europe and Western Asia approximately 35,000 to 130,000 years ago, overlapping with the modern human species (*Homo sapiens sapiens*). They had larger brain cases and smaller back teeth than earlier populations, but differed from modern humans in their receding forehead and large, protruding face with front teeth and forward-projecting jaw. The Neanderthals had a relatively short, bulky stature and considerable strength, and showed evidence of complex cultural traits and social organization. For example, they used planning and cooperation to hunt large mammals. They

The classification of primate f

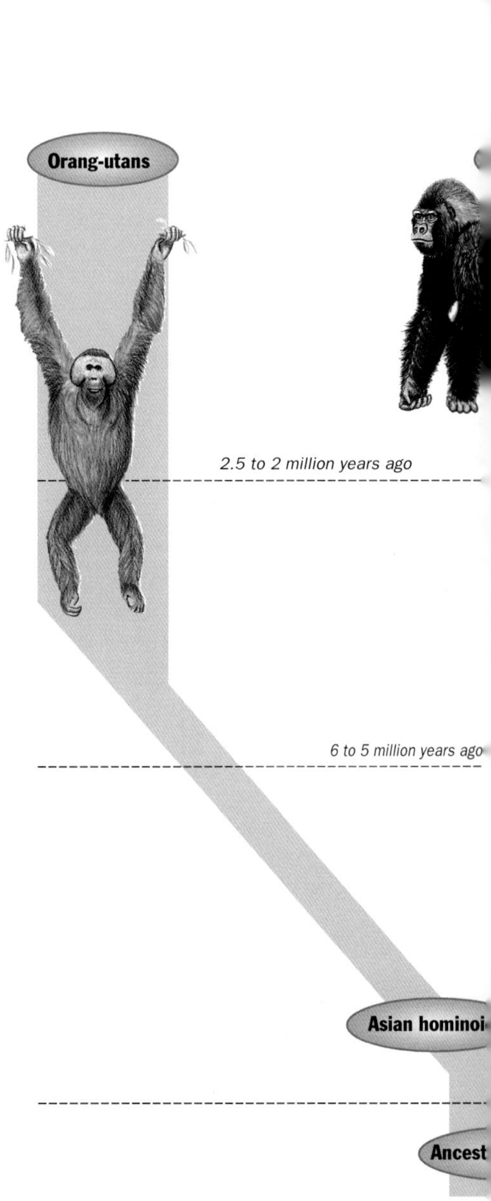

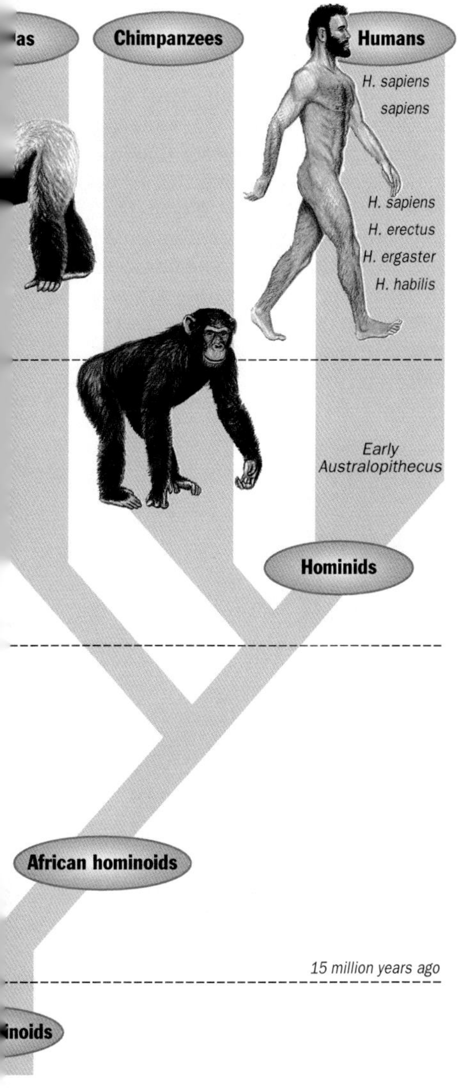

In 1735, the Swedish naturalist Carl Linnaeus caused a public outcry when he classified human beings as part of the animal kingdom. Today, however, his taxonomy—which has been extensively revised and expanded—is the accepted way of classifying all forms of plant and animal life.

The human species, *Homo sapiens sapiens*, belongs to the genus *Homo* (which includes our hominid ancestors) in the family *Hominidae* (which includes the apes). This family is in turn part of the Primate order. The relationship between humans, apes, and early hominid fossils is problematic. Recent studies by molecular biologists have shown that there is a much closer genetic link between humans and the African great apes (especially chimpanzees) than might have been predicted from comparing their anatomies. This has led some taxonomists to place humans, gorillas, and chimpanzees in one family, *Hominidae*, and Asian apes such as the orang-utan in another, *Pongidae*.

The currently accepted classification of hominid fossils establishes a chronology for modern humans from the development of the first australopithecine species (appearing around 5 million years ago), to early *Homo* species such as *Homo habilis* and *Homo erectus* (from around 2 million years ago), through to later *Homo* species (around 1 million years ago) and archaic *Homo sapiens* such as the Neanderthals (about 130,000 years ago). Both the classification and the chronology are likely to be revised as new fossil discoveries are made.

also buried their dead and seem to have had some knowledge of art, demonstrating a capacity for symbolic behavior. Their vocal apparatus and neurological structure provide indirect evidence that they may also have developed speech.

Neanderthals disappear from the archaeological record around 40,000 years ago in the Middle East and 35,000 years ago in Europe. They may have evolved slowly into modern humans, contributing to the gene pool of present-day inhabitants of Europe and the Middle East. However, many scholars now think they were gradually overwhelmed and replaced by incoming populations of a more advanced species classified as *Homo sapiens sapiens*.

Out of Africa

The early history of modern humans is still uncertain, as the fossil record is far from complete. Some scholars argue that *Homo sapiens sapiens* developed independently, in a number of different geographical locations. Other scholars consider that what is popularly called the "out of Africa" theory better reflects what is now known about the process of evolution. This proposes that modern human populations are all descended from a single ancestral population that emerged at one location between 150,000 and 100,000 years ago. Increasing archaeological evidence suggests that the place of origin of modern humans was somewhere in Africa. From this homeland, *Homo sapiens sapiens* migrated northward into Europe some 40,000 to 100,000 years ago, and then spread throughout the world, gradually replacing more archaic populations wherever they encountered them.

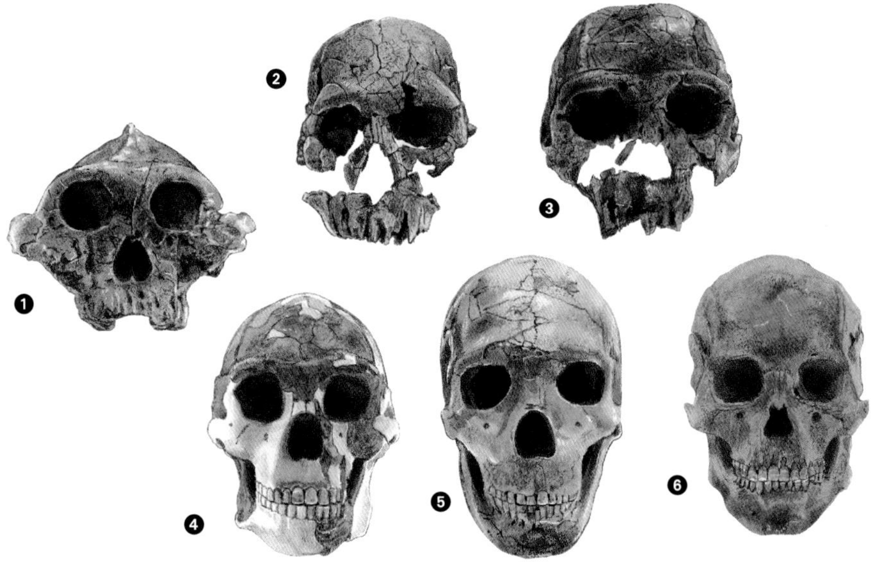

Human fossil skulls: 1. Australopithecus boisei. *2.* Homo habilis. *3.* Homo ergaster. *4.* Homo erectus. *5.* Homo sapiens neanderthalensis. *6.* Homo sapiens sapiens. *Note the gradual disappearance of the thick brow ridges, and the growth of the cranium—indicative of increasing brain capacity and intelligence.*

THE FIRST MODERN HUMANS

The success of modern humans, *Homo sapiens sapiens*, in colonizing Earth's landmasses owes much to the evolutionary changes that occurred in the physical form and mental capacity of hominids. Although the basic hominid anatomy changed little, the features that distinguished hominids from other hominoids, such as their erect posture, ability to walk habitually on two legs, vertical face, smaller teeth and enlarged brain, were refined in each successive species and subspecies. By far the most significant change, and the one that signaled the emergence of *Homo sapiens sapiens*, was the progressive enlargement of the brain, which was out of all proportion to changes in body size. In absolute terms, the average brain capacity of modern humans is three times that of the great apes.

Increased brain capacity allowed *Homo sapiens sapiens* to develop greater intelligence and problem-solving capabilities. This led to the appearance of tools as well as speech and language (although full language capacity emerged less than 40,000 years ago). It also enabled modern humans to develop strategies for coping with harsh environments, such as camp fires, clothing, natural food storage facilities, and primitive cooking methods. Further intellectual development resulted in a flourishing cultural life and increased capacity for social organization, which in turn stimulated the growth of civilizations and led to the evolution of modern society.

Making and using tools

Many people believe that it is the presence of tools that distinguishes early humans (*Homo* spp.) from other hominids, but a number of other animals also make and use tools. Chimpanzees, for instance, have demonstrated an ability to make and use tools for digging for food. More specifically,

Fertility figures, such as the 20,000-year-old Willendorf Venus from Austria, are among the earliest indications of a human concern with rituals and symbols.

some scholars have argued that it is the power and complexity of human tool assemblages that distinguishes humans. However, the simplicity of the tool assemblages of archaic humans and certain hunter–gatherers of the recent past makes this explanation inadequate. What is unique about human tool making and tool use is that the tools were made for particular purposes. Moreover, they were constantly improved and adapted for new purposes, to the extent that tools eventually pervaded all aspects of human life. This is not the case among chimpanzees.

The first hominid fossils associated with hand-made tools were those of *Homo habilis*, found at Olduvai Gorge in Tanzania, and dated at about 2 million years old. Tools have been found in older East African sites, but without any fossil remains. Although earlier hominid species knew how to make and use tools, it was probably only with the emergence of the genus *Homo* that tools became part of daily life.

The early *Homo habilis* tools were crude, stone hand-axes. Unsurprisingly, stone and some bone tools dominate the archaeological record. Tools made of perishable materials such as wood are found occasionally at water-logged, frozen, or arid sites, but such finds are rare. From about one million years ago, tool assemblages became more

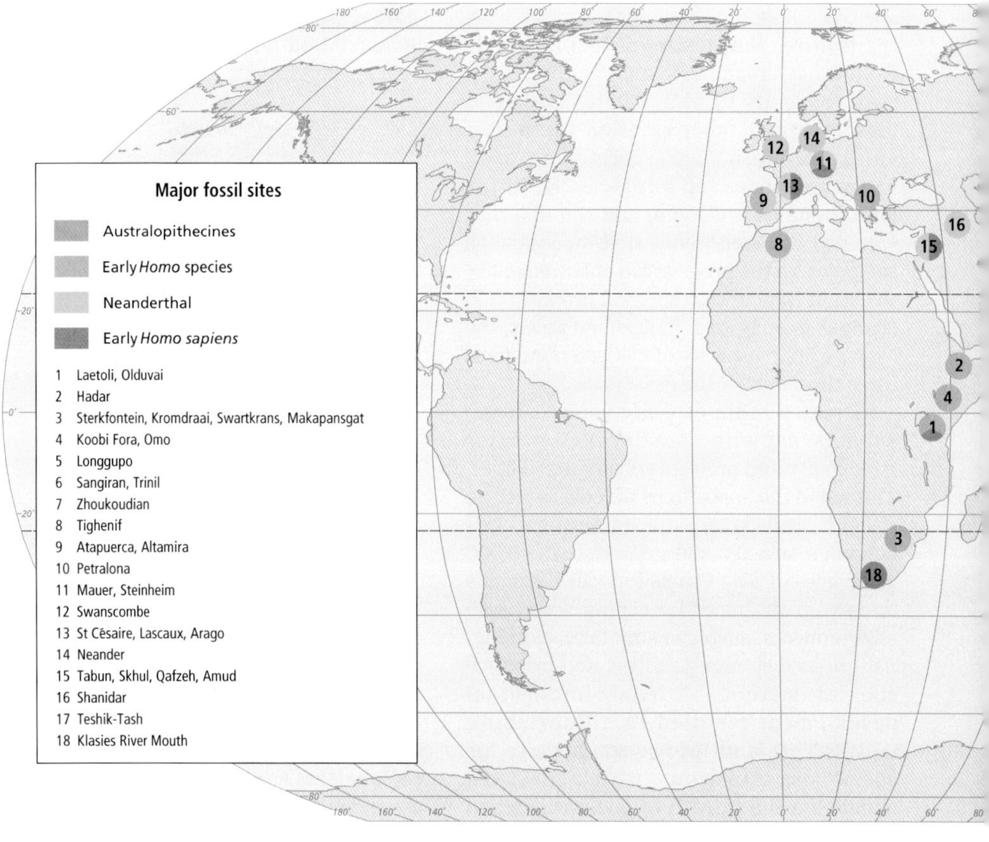

specialized, but it is only in the past 40,000 years that there has been a proliferation of designs.

The simplicity of early tools clearly indicates that hominids obtained their food by foraging and scavenging. The traditional view that the hunting of animals accompanied and influenced the evolutionary development of modern humans has been reassessed in the light of this evidence. Regular hunting, particularly the killing of large mammals, probably began later. Far more important at this stage in the evolution of modern humans was the development of an ability to plan ahead. Although this would become essential for organizing hunts, it was also required at an earlier stage to enable humans to forage for food and store supplies for lean times.

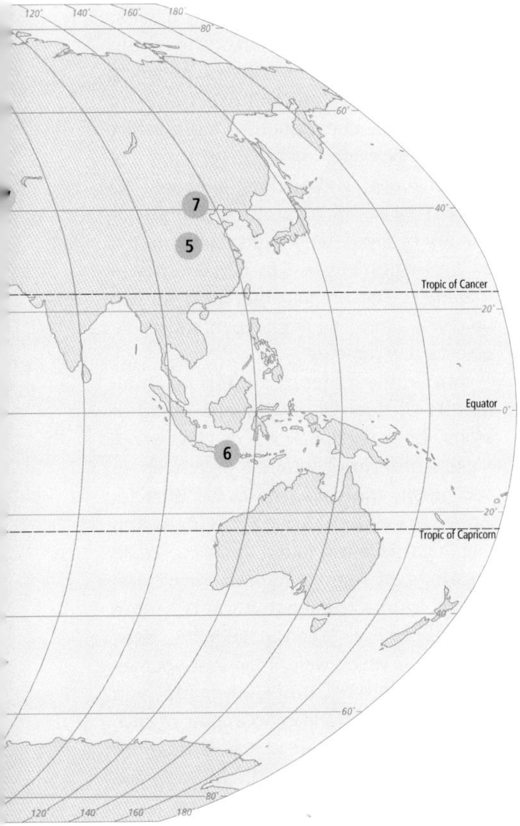

Art and cooking skills

There seems to have been a watershed in the development of modern humans around 40,000 years ago. This is reflected in a dramatic worldwide change in the archaeological evidence. Not only did tool assemblages become more sophisticated, but art, in the form of jewelry, figurines, paintings, and engravings (often depicting hunting scenes), also become prevalent. The widespread use of raw materials that could only have been obtained from distant sources suggests that trade networks had expanded. Campsites show evidence of more settled living, including artificial shelters, food storage pits, and well-built, regularly used fireplaces. Burial sites become more elaborate, containing ornaments and other cultural objects. The disposal of the dead clearly involved some form of ritual, reflecting metaphysical concerns and symbolic behavior.

There also appears to have been a "culinary revolution", with stone knives being used to cut up food. This allowed for more thorough cooking, which may in turn have resulted in changes in the cranial structure of humans, as large teeth would no longer have been necessary for tearing raw or partially roasted meat.

These cultural and physical changes occurred during the last ice age, which culminated about 15,000 to 20,000 years ago, when glaciers covered large areas of the world. Successful strategies developed by modern humans to cope with the deteriorating climate gave them a clear advantage over more archaic forms of *Homo sapiens*. Despite the spread of hostile environments during the ice age, *Homo sapiens sapiens* succeeded in colonizing the world far more rapidly and extensively than earlier hominid migrants.

Colonization on the scale undertaken by *Homo sapiens sapiens* required all of the species' new-found technical and social skills. Its success depended not just on tools and an ability to plan ahead, but also on the existence of extensive social structures which could provide the support and cooperation necessary for the completion of long, hazardous journeys into unknown lands.

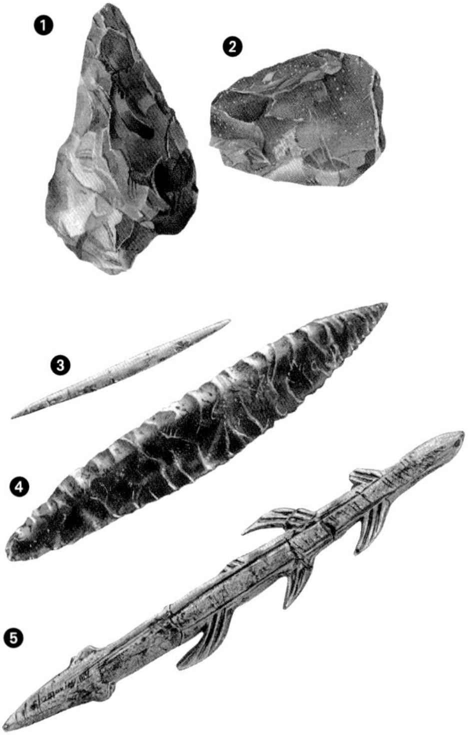

Many people believe that the invention and use of tools marked out the early humans from other hominids. The development of human technology is reflected in these tools: 1. Scraper from Swanscombe, England; 300,000–200,000 BP. 2. Sidescraper from Le Moustier, France; 70,000–35,000 BP. 3. Bone point from Aurignac, France, 35,000–23,000 BP. 4. Bifacial stone knife from Solutré, France; 20,000–17,000 BP. 5. Bone harpoon from Le Morin, France, 16,000–8,000 BP

Early art

Art is widely believed to have originated during the last ice age and appears to have flourished mainly in Europe and the southern hemisphere (southern Africa and Australia). Little has been found at ice-age sites in North Africa, China, or elsewhere in Asia. This does not mean, however, that art did not exist in these areas—it may simply be that the forms of artistic expression were more temporary or that the materials used did not survive.

Ice-age art is linked with major innovations in tool technology, including well-crafted and highly efficient blades, and hafted spears. With the rapid evolution of hunting techniques, obtaining food would no longer have been as difficult and, consequently, more effort could be expended on the development of art, language, and spiritual interests. No record remains of stories, songs, or dances of these pre-literate cultures, nor of artworks made out of perishable materials. The art that has survived can be divided into two main types: moveable objects and rock art.

Moveable objects comprise small figures or decorated weapons made of stone, bone, antler, ivory, or clay, which were sometimes placed in graves to accompany the deceased in the afterlife. Rock art, such as engravings and paintings, is often found in caves. While drawings of human figures have been found, most rock art depicts game animals such as bison, mammoths, deer, and bears, which were important sources of food, clothing, tools, weapons, and ornaments. Outstanding examples of cave art were discovered in the nineteenth century at Altamira in northern Spain and at Lascaux in southwestern France.

HUMAN MIGRATIONS

Recent research undertaken on fossil and genetic evidence suggests that hominids migrated "out of Africa" on many occasions, probably beginning with *Homo erectus*, *Homo habilis*, or the taller and more slender *Homo ergaster* more than 2 million years ago. Changes in the climate may have been a major factor in these early migrations. One theory suggests that between 2 million and 3 million years ago, a widespread drop in temperature led to the replacement of the tropical woodlands in eastern Africa by savanna grassland. This change in vegetation favored the *Homo* species over the australopithecines. With their larger brains, more generalized diets, and greater tool-using ability, the *Homo* species adapted more readily to the open terrain and soon began to roam widely. Initially, they probably followed the land mammals on which they scavenged, as the animals moved north and east following the expansion of the grasslands.

To date, early *Homo* sites have been discovered at several Asian sites in the Republic of Georgia, in China, and on the island of Java in Indonesia. Early humans did not make an appearance in Europe until some time later (around 1 to 1.5 million years ago), and this region remained sparsely populated until 500,000 years ago.

During their migrations, early *Homo* species would have crossed various land bridges that appeared during the recurring ice ages of the past 2 million years. However, to explain the presence of 800,000-year-old stone tools on the Indonesian island of Flores, which would have remained at least 20 km (12 miles) offshore even at the height of the ice ages, scientists have tentatively suggested that *Homo erectus* made use of simple vessels such as bamboo rafts to cross short stretches of sea.

Migrations by modern humans

Compared with the migrations made by archaic populations, the spread of modern humans during the last 100,000 years occurred remarkably rapidly. Furthermore, *Homo sapiens sapiens* ventured much farther than earlier hominids, eventually reaching the Americas and Australia. These more extensive migrations were made

The first people to settle in North America would have had a lifestyle similar to that of present-day Inuit.

possible by this species' greater adaptability and by the exposure of numerous land bridges during the last ice age.

Scientists are still debating when and how the Americas were colonized, although it is generally accepted that hunting groups crossed into Alaska via a land bridge in the Bering Strait. This could have occurred either between 63,000 and 45,000 years ago or between 35,000 and 10,000 years ago. Although some argue that the earlier crossing is more likely because the Alaskan ice sheet would not have been as extensive as during the later period, the earliest reliable dates for archaeological sites in North America are no more than 20,000 years old. Consequently, the more widely held view is that the crossing occurred between 12,000 and 20,000 years ago, with people gradually drifting south down the continent. Recent evidence suggests that Monte Verde in southern Chile may have been settled as early as 12,500 years ago.

The question of whether there was one or more crossings is also unresolved. Some researchers believe that genetic variations among the indigenous peoples of the Americas are so great that they suggest three or four waves of migration. A more recent assessment cautiously suggests that there were no more than two waves—one arriving about 20,000 to 25,000 years ago

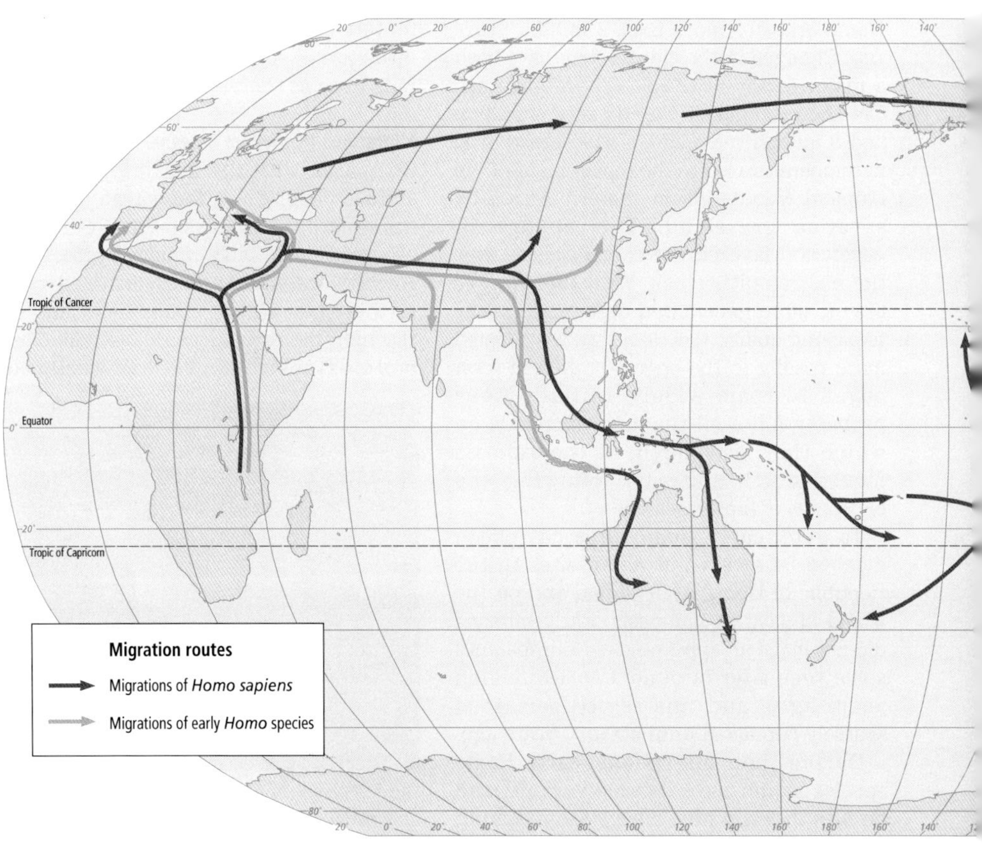

and the other around 11,300 years ago. These early settlers were probably of more diverse origins than previously thought, and some may even have arrived by sea rather than across the land bridge.

Debates of a similar nature surround the colonization of Australia. The earliest direct evidence of humans is about 40,000 years old (claims that various artefacts and sites in the Northern Territory date from around 60,000 years ago have not been confirmed). Since some of these sites are in the south of the continent, dates of up to 50–60,000 years ago for the initial arrival of humans from Southeast Asia have been proposed to allow for the settlement of large areas of the continent by 40,000 years ago. The absence of Asian fauna in Australia indicates that there must have been a substantial stretch of sea between the two continents for millions of years.

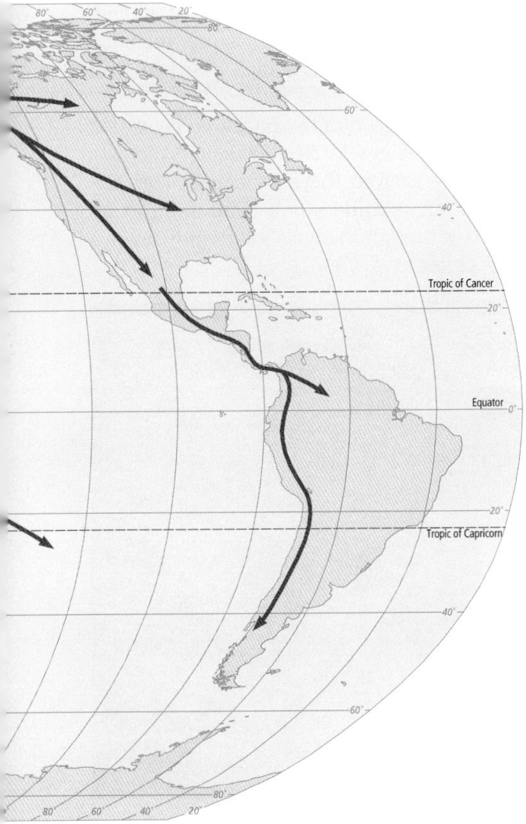

Colonizing the Pacific

The islands along the western rim of the Pacific were probably colonized around the same time as Australia and New Guinea, when sea levels were sufficiently low for them to be linked to the Asian mainland. Of course, *Homo erectus* may also have occupied these islands while they were linked to the mainland during earlier periods of glaciation, but the earliest signs of human occupation in Japan have been dated at around 30,000 years ago. Based on the evidence currently available, it appears that other islands on the western Pacific rim, such as most of the Philippines, were probably occupied 10,000 to 15,000 years later.

By the time European explorers reached the Pacific region in the early sixteenth century, virtually every inhabitable island was populated. Exactly when and how all the islands of the Pacific were first settled, however, is not entirely clear. The archaeological evidence is still meager, and there is considerable speculation about early migrations.

Not long after the Second World War, in an attempt to prove that the population of the Polynesian islands originated in South America, the Norwegian ethnologist and adventurer Thor Heyerdahl and his small crew sailed from the Pacific coast of South America to Polynesia on a balsa raft named *Kon-Tiki*. Although Heyerdahl showed that such a voyage was possible, most scholars still believe that the great bulk of linguistic and botanical evidence suggests that the populations originally came from Southeast Asia rather than South America.

The Pacific Islands are customarily divided into three ethnogeographic areas:

Melanesia, Micronesia, and Polynesia. Melanesia includes the predominantly dark-skinned peoples of New Guinea, the Bismarck Archipelago, the Solomons, Vanuatu, New Caledonia, and Fiji. Micronesia comprises the very small islands and atolls in the northern Pacific, including the Marianas, Carolines, and Marshalls. Polynesia forms a large triangle in the eastern Pacific, from Hawaii in the north, to New Zealand in the south, and Easter Island in the east. Despite these classifications, however, archaeological evidence, linguistic studies, and blood group analyses all suggest similar origins for the people of the three areas. The physical and cultural differences between modern-day peoples may result from the fact that the islands were occupied by successive waves of migrants.

The Lapita people

The earliest dates for settlement of the Pacific Islands in Micronesia and Polynesia go back no further than the second millennium BC. As they moved eastward, these early settlers took with them a well-developed agricultural tradition based on taro, yams, and pigs. This agricultural tradition was associated with a coarse, finely decorated pottery known as Lapita ware. By studying the distribution of this pottery, archaeologists have been able to trace the movement of this people across the Pacific.

One theory suggests that the Lapita people began to make their way eastward from eastern Indonesia or the Philippines about 4,000 years ago and then spread farther eastward through New Guinea to the southwestern Pacific. It is thought that they may have been forced to keep moving as a result of pressure from incoming groups of rice-growers. As they moved, they gradually developed distinctive Polynesian characteristics, which included complex hierarchical social, political, and religious systems.

The last region of the Pacific to be settled by Polynesians was New Zealand. Colonists probably arrived there by canoe from the Hawaiian islands some time around ad 1,000, although many scholars now favor a date closer to AD 750.

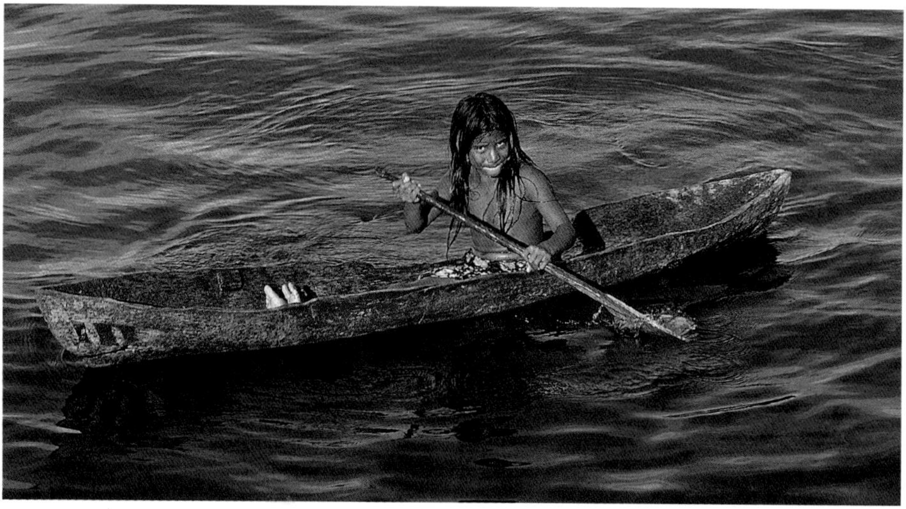

Early Polynesian watercraft may have resembled this canoe from the Solomon Islands.

LANGUAGES AND WRITING

As with many other questions about human evolution, there is still no consensus about the origin of speech and language. A number of scholars have suggested that art and language must be closely intertwined because they both require the ability to understand abstract ideas and symbolic concepts and to share these understandings with others as part of a cultural system. According to this theory, fully fledged languages would not have existed before the appearance of art—which first emerged about 40,000 years ago. If this argument is correct, archaic *Homo sapiens* such as the Neanderthals, who coexisted for some time with *Homo sapiens sapiens* and also created primitive art, would have possessed some form of language. Certainly, no one doubts that the Neanderthals were able to communicate with each other,

As a result of geographical isolation, the Papuan tribes that gather at traditional sing-sing ceremonies may speak many different languages.

although changes to the brain and facial structure would have meant the linguistic ability of *Homo sapiens sapiens* was markedly superior.

The complexity of human language and speech is dependent on a number of neural and anatomical mechanisms found only in *Homo sapiens sapiens*. These include a vocal tract that permits a wide range of speech sounds, areas of the brain that control and interpret these sounds, and an efficient memory that can use past experiences as a guide to the future. Although scientists believe that earlier hominid species were able to communicate both vocally and by gestures (just as animals do), their use of words, concepts, and sentence construction (syntax) would have been limited. Even chimpanzees can be taught to use words when placed in a human-like environment, yet they never progress beyond the vocabulary or grammatical ability of an average 3-year-old child. Humans alone are able to talk to each other, rather than just transmit words.

Although fully fledged linguistic ability would have been found only among *Homo sapiens sapiens*, it is still possible that language of some sort existed among the first anatomically modern humans in East Africa as early as 130,000 years ago. Some scientists even argue that *Homo habilis* may

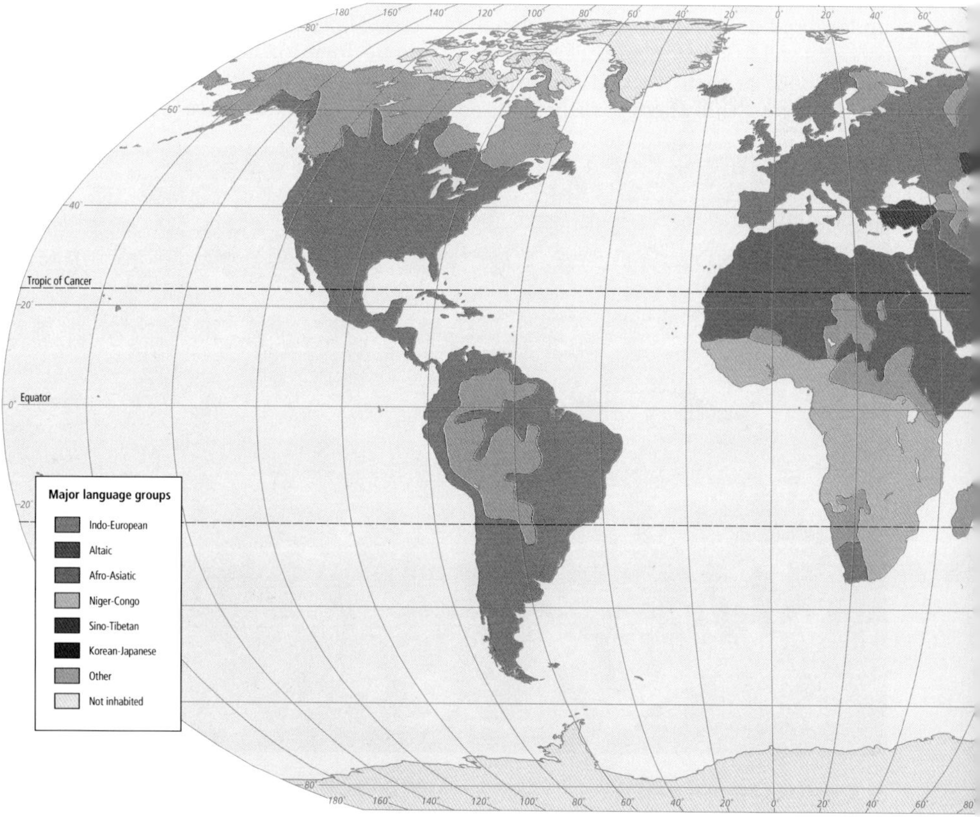

have been able to communicate vocally, albeit in a much simpler fashion. In other words, early humans may have had speech, but not a complete language.

Further evidence that early hominids were able to communicate verbally has recently emerged from what may at first seem an unlikely source: scientific research into the evolution of dogs. Studies in molecular biology suggest that wolves evolved into domestic animals more than 130,000 years ago, and wolf bones have even been found with 400,000-year-old hominid bones. These facts suggest that the association between humans and canines goes back a very long time. Some scientists now think that the domestication of canines had a profound effect on human evolution. The close association with dogs would have made it less crucial for early hominids to have a keen sense of smell that would alert them to other hominids or animal predators. In turn, this would have allowed the development of the facial and cranial modifications necessary for speech.

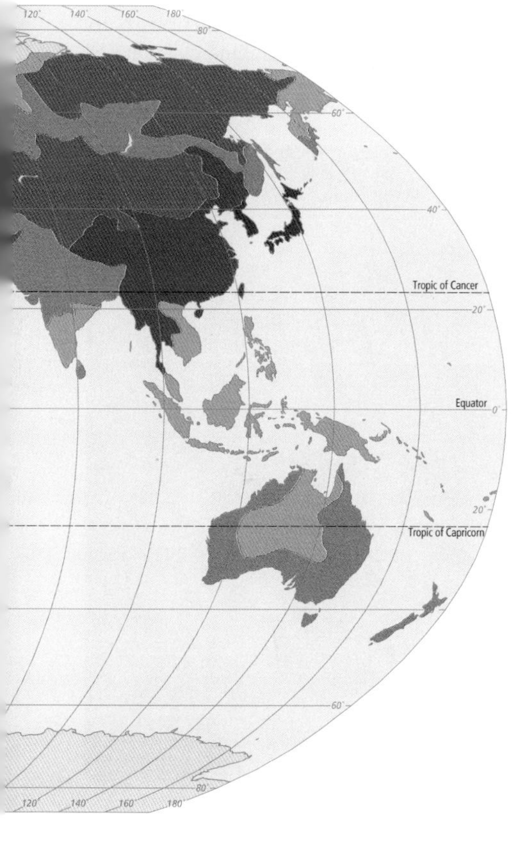

Languages of the world

Thousands of languages are spoken in the world today. Populations that share similar cultures and live only a short distance apart may still speak languages that are quite distinct and not readily understood by neighboring populations. For example, the inhabitants of New Guinea and adjacent islands speak approximately 1,000 different languages, or about one-fifth of the world's total.

At the same time, similarities exist between languages used in different parts of the world, which suggests that they developed from a common source. Scholars group such languages in families on the basis of similarities in vocabulary, sound systems, and grammar. English, for example, is part of the Indo-European family, which includes languages of antiquity, such as Sanskrit and classical Greek, as well as contemporary languages in both Asia and Europe, such as Hindi and Russian. Other geographically dispersed language families are Malayo-Polynesian (also known as Austronesian), which includes Hawaiian, Javanese, as well as the languages of Madagascar, and Uralic, which includes Finnish, Hungarian, and the Samoyed language of Northern Siberia.

The first languages were disseminated in a number of ways. The most obvious was migration. As they spread out across the globe, early peoples carried their languages into uninhabited territory. Languages would also have spread as a result of contact between different peoples. For example, the invention and adoption of food production would have encouraged agricultural peoples to migrate into territory occupied by hunter–gatherers, who may then have adopted both the cultivation techniques and language of the immigrants.

A third form of language dissemination involves the replacement of an existing language by one spoken by a dominant group. The development of more complex societies allowed incoming minorities with some form of centralized organization to dominate larger populations, who, in many cases, subsequently adopted the language of the elite. For example, the adoption of the Chinese language family in southern China in historical times occurred as a result of the military expansion of the Chinese empire.

The origins of writing

Writing is thought to have arisen around 5,000 to 6,000 years ago in Sumeria (southern Mesopotamia), and to have appeared shortly afterward in widely separate parts of the world, including Egypt (3000 BC), the Indus Valley (2500 BC), and China (2000 BC). Writing may have spread from Sumeria to the Indus and probably also to Egypt, but it was almost certainly independently invented in both China and, later, Mesoamerica, where it first appeared in the third century AD. Writing was unknown elsewhere in the Americas, even in the highly developed Inca civilization of the central Andes which flourished in the fifteenth century.

Scholars usually distinguish three broad kinds of writing systems, although in practice some systems combine elements of more than one kind. They are known as logographic, syllabic, and alphabetic writing.

Egyptian hieroglyphs are a form of pictorial writing.

In logographic writing, separate symbols are used to represent single words. This can complicate the representation of even simple statements. Because most of the symbols in logographic writing have a pictorial basis, it is believed that this is the earliest form of writing. Examples of logographic writing include early Sumerian cuneiform, Egyptian hieroglyphs, and modern Chinese characters.

In syllabic writing, symbols represent syllables. Examples of this type include later Sumerian cuneiform and the remarkable Cherokee syllabary developed by a Native American called Sequoyah in Arkansas in the early nineteenth century.

The third, and now most common, form of writing is alphabetic, in which symbols represent units of sound, or phonemes. Widespread alphabetic systems include Arabic, Roman (which is used for English and most other European languages), and Cyrillic (used for Russian and some other Slavic languages).

It has been suggested that these three types of writing reflect an evolutionary progression, from logographic to alphabetic; however, most scholars now regard this view as too simplistic. For instance, in a number of writing systems, logographic elements have been adopted, discarded, and then reintroduced.

The development of writing is closely associated with the rise of hierarchical societies. Literacy contributed to the formation of more complex state structures and bureaucratic institutions. In its early stages, it was often closely linked to religious activities and to authorities. In Sumeria, for instance, the recording of economic transactions was controlled by religious officialdom. Writing also arose as a religious practice in Mesoamerica, remaining the preserve of the elite until the Spanish conquest in the sixteenth century.

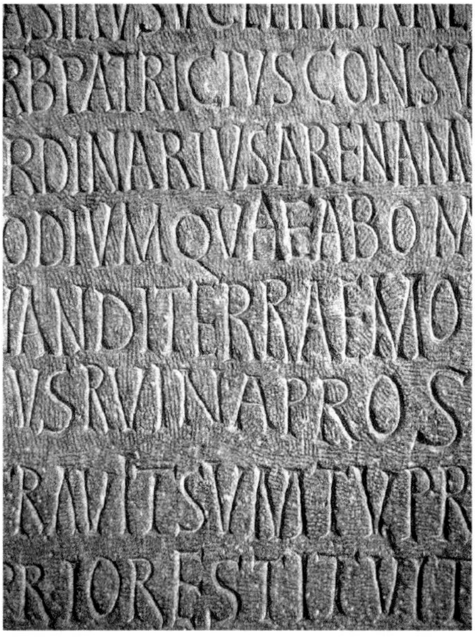

Latin script on this tablet from the Coliseum illustrates alphabetic writing.

The world's major languages

Language	**Speakers *(millions)***
Mandarin (Chinese)	885
English	322
Spanish	266
Bengali	189
Hindi	182
Portuguese	170
Russian	170
Japanese	125
German	98
Wu (Chinese)	77
Javanese	75.5
Korean	75

THE RISE OF AGRICULTURE

Humanity's transition from a mobile life of hunting and gathering to a sedentary farming lifestyle in settled communities was not a sudden "revolution". It took place by degrees, with the dependence on cultivation increasing slowly as selective breeding modified wild plant species. Nevertheless, in terms of the prehistory of modern humans (100,000 years or so), the emergence of full-scale agriculture, which includes the

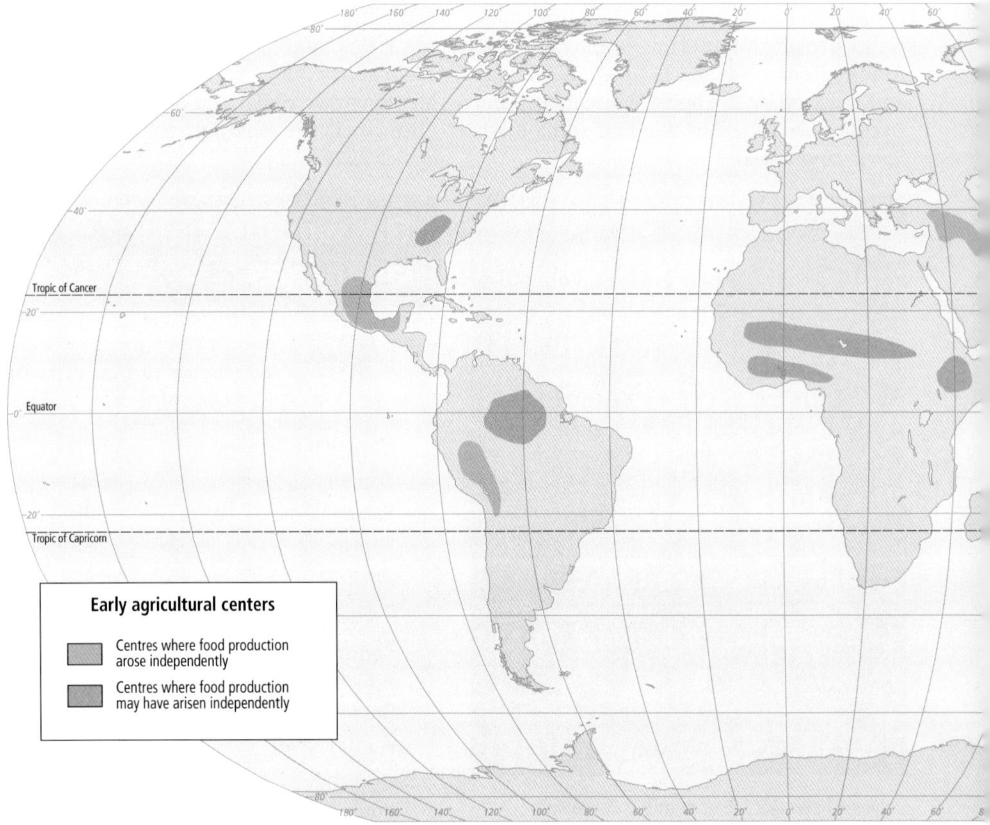

development of both plant cultivation and animal husbandry, was relatively rapid.

It is probable that the cultivation of plants developed independently in a number of different regions, including the Fertile Crescent (a region stretching from present-day central Turkey southeastward through Iraq to the Persian Gulf), China, Mesoamerica (roughly present-day Mexico and Guatemala), and the Central Andes. Some scholars suggest that food production also originated in other centers such as New Guinea and West Africa.

Plant cultivation first occurred in the Fertile Crescent, where evidence for the domestication of grains such as wheat and barley, and other foods such as pulses and olives, begins to make an appearance in the archaeological record around 11,000 years ago. Flax was also cultivated as a source of fiber for making cloth. Although much of this area was then, as it is now, rocky and rather arid, the fertility of the river floodplains probably encouraged an increasing reliance on cultivation. In the region between the Tigris and Euphrates rivers in present-day Iraq, the development of canal-based irrigation allowed farming centers to flourish. From there, agricultural methods spread throughout the Mediterranean, across the Balkans, and along the Danube River into central Europe. By 7,000 years ago, farming was also firmly established in Egypt's Nile Valley.

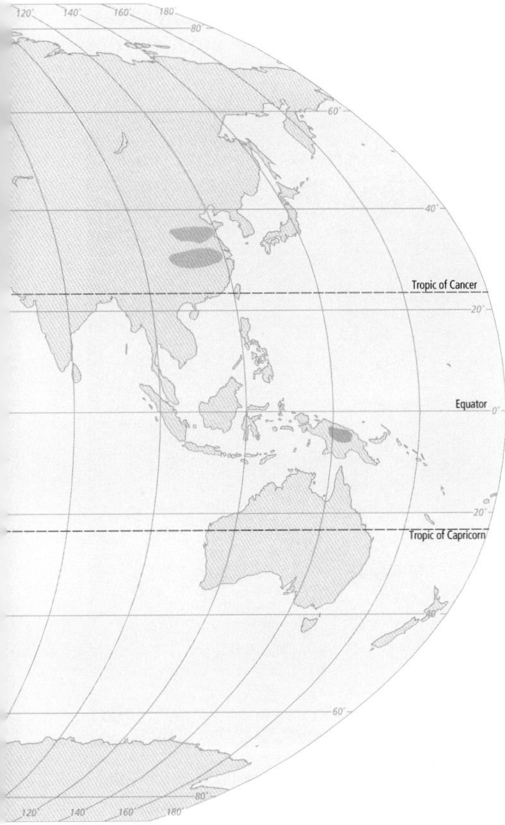

Recent archaeological finds have indicated that plant cultivation may have begun in Asia not long after it began in the Fertile Crescent. For example, it is possible that rice was cultivated along the middle Yangtze of central China as early as 9,500 years ago. In northern China, there is evidence that millet and rapeseed were grown around the same time. Farming practices spread along the fertile floodplains of Chinese rivers, where many early sites have been found. At about the same time, local people also began to domesticate animals, including pigs, cattle, sheep, dogs, and chickens.

Food production may have arisen independently in at least two parts of the Americas. One of these is the Peruvian Andes, where beans were cultivated perhaps as early as 7,000 years ago. At around the same time, people in Mesoamerica also started to grow beans, together with squash and pumpkins. Maize, which became the most important staple, may not have been cultivated until more than a thousand years later. The early archaeological record is sparse in South America, but it appears that plants such as manioc, amaranths, peanuts, potatoes, cotton, and chilli peppers were slowly domesticated in different parts of the continent.

Agriculture may have begun earlier in New Guinea. In the island's central highlands, archaeologists have discovered evidence of irrigation ditches in areas of swamp which date from around 9,000 years ago. They remain uncertain about the types of crops grown there, although taro and other native noncereal plants are likely candidates.

The domestication of animals

Although the dog was domesticated somewhat earlier, the process of rearing animals for food—and later for clothing and as draft and pack animals—began at around the same time as plant cultivation. Many animals hunted by humans were unsuitable for breeding as a result of such factors as their diet, growth rate, ability to breed in captivity, or behavioral disposition. Domestication therefore had to proceed by trial and error, and gradually it modified many species.

Some animals, such as the wild pig and the auroch (a large, long-horned wild ox), were distributed over a wide area of Europe and Asia, and were probably domesticated independently in a number of places. Others, such as goats and sheep, were confined largely to the Middle East and western Asia, and were later introduced into Europe. The people of the Andes domesticated llamas for use as pack animals and guinea pigs for food. The earliest evidence for the domestication of cats has been found in Greece. Cats were subsequently domesticated in many areas, usually to protect grain stores from rodents.

Food production began independently in China when rice was cultivated about 9,000 years ago in the valley of the Yangtze River. From there, rice cultivation spread throughout Southeast Asia, reaching Indonesia about 4,000 years ago.

The shift from hunting–gathering to agriculture resulted in the development of new technologies, including animal-driven pulley systems like the one on this well in Egypt.

Why choose agriculture?

Not all communities switched to agriculture as soon as they came into contact with it. Many early peoples remained dependent on food collecting and hunting, and hunter–gatherer societies continue to exist to this day. These communities may modify their environment—for example, by burning vegetation to encourage growth that attracts game—and some also undertake minimal husbanding of plant resources, such as replanting rootstock cuttings and protecting fruit-bearing trees. But despite this and the fact that they may have often come into contact with people practicing agriculture, they have chosen not to switch to a sedentary lifestyle based on farming.

The reason for this is that subsisting as a hunter–gatherer usually requires less work than subsisting as a farmer. As long as population densities remain low, a food-collecting lifestyle can be more attractive and efficient, and provide a more balanced and diverse diet. In fact, scientists find it hard to explain why certain populations ever became totally dependent on farming. However, once the switch had been made, the demographic and social consequences of an agricultural lifestyle would have made it difficult to reverse the trend.

The consequences of agriculture

Agriculture transformed both human societies and landscapes. The need to make cultivation more efficient encouraged rapid technological innovations. The use of clay, which was already known in pre-agricultural times, became widespread and people began to make large receptacles for food and water. In turn, these receptacles transformed diets, as grains and pulses could be soaked and boiled, making them easier to eat and digest. Other innovations that emerged in agricultural societies were metalworking, the wheel (which improved the making of pots and stimulated progress in transport), and the use of sails on boats. Small copper objects have been found at early agricultural sites in the Middle East, but extensive metalworking activities and

Despite the attractions of new technologies, many communities, including the San of the Kalahari desert in southwestern Africa, rejected agriculture and continue to follow a hunting–gathering lifestyle to this day.

purification techniques were not developed until a few thousand years later.

Early agricultural societies were based on small village communities. As the range of domesticated plants and animals grew, the village economies became increasingly diverse and food production techniques improved. These developments enabled communities to create surpluses which could be used to support full-time craftspeople. Specialization led to internal barter and to trade with other communities. Items and commodities that were found or produced in only certain localities were traded over considerable distances. Social divisions also increased and, in many areas, complex hierarchies, headed by hereditary leaders, came into existence. In some societies, elite classes emerged who were able to devote their time to religious, cultural, and military pursuits while living off the surplus produced by subordinate groups.

Agriculture and demographics

Some scholars believe that population growth encouraged the adoption of agriculture, while others think that it was agriculture that triggered an increase in population. Although there is no firm demographic evidence to decide the question, archaeological research suggests that the number and size of settlements usually increased following the appearance of food production in a region.

The rapid expansion of agriculture affected the environment, in some cases quite catastrophically. For example, archaeologists have found that the barren landscape of modern Greece is the result of more than 5,000 years of farming, during which deforestation and land clearance led to the loss of topsoil and severe soil erosion.

Foods and their origins

Most agricultural products were native to one part of the world and then spread gradually to other regions. The following list shows the origins of selected foods.

wheat	Fertile Crescent
potatoes	Central Andes
rice	China
corn	Mesoamerica
sugar	New Guinea
coffee	Ethiopia
tea	China
apples	Western Europe
oranges	Southeast Asia
sheep	Fertile Crescent
turkey	Mexico

EMERGING CIVILIZATIONS

The first civilizations arose on the fertile alluvial basins of major rivers such as the Tigris-Euphrates in Iraq, the Nile in Egypt, the Indus in Pakistan, and the Yellow (Huang Ho) in China. These regions shared many common features, including arid environments that made agricultural communities dependent on irrigation, and readily available supplies of raw materials such as stone, metal, and wood. The Tigris-Euphrates, Nile, and Indus regions were probably linked by trade well before the appearance of the early cities, but Chinese civilization developed in relative isolation.

The first urban societies

Cities emerged in all four regions during the third millennium BC as villages and towns slowly grew into cities with large public buildings and developed specialized and well-organized production and trade, forms of writing, hierarchical social structures, and centralized political systems. This process of evolution varied, although the cultural attributes of emerging cities were similar.

In most cases, cities arose following the emergence of a social elite. As a class or family became dominant, it usually sought to create a power base in one region. This power base attracted immigrants and businesses, resulting in the rapid growth of the urban community. Scholars have suggested various reasons for the emergence of social elites. Some propose that the construction and maintenance of the large-scale irrigation works needed to support a growing population would have required considerable organization and so it encouraged the development of a

Early Mesopotamian artworks such as this ivory carving often include portraits of members of the ruling elite.

managerial class. Others emphasize the role of specialized production and trade in creating a dominant commercial class. Another explanation is the growing influence of warfare: as settlements were overrun by invading peoples, their inhabitants were often forced to become the subjects of their conquerors. It was probably a combination of all these factors that led to the development of the first "upper classes" and the first sophisticated urban societies.

Cradles of civilization

In the region between the Tigris and Euphrates rivers known as Mesopotamia, farming gradually became more productive, canals were built, large temple platforms (called ziggurats) were erected, and the cuneiform script was simplified and standardized. Crafts, such as pottery and metalwork, became more specialized and production more organized, leading to greater social divisions in society. The city-states had their own monarchs, and were often heavily fortified. Their ascendancy came to an end, however, around 2350 BC, when Sargon, a military ruler from Agade in central Mesopotamia, forcibly amalgamated them into the Akkadian empire.

In Egypt, by contrast, it was the unification of the cities and towns of Upper and Lower Egypt at the beginning of the third millennium that caused civilization to flourish, giving rise to a well-developed political and administrative system, writing, and a complex religion. During this period, the massive stone pyramids of Giza were constructed to preserve the bodies, knowledge, and wealth of the Egyptian

kings in the afterlife. The pyramids also symbolized the structure of Egyptian society, with the god-king at the apex, officials in the middle levels, and the mass of the population at the bottom.

The emergence of the Indus civilization was marked by the appearance of distinctive artistic styles in pottery, copper, and bronze (a copper–tin alloy). These objects were traded with nomadic pastoral peoples who, in turn, transported the merchandise into central Asia and along the coast of the Arabian Sea. Around 2400 BC, the different cultural traditions of the Indus merged into one, called Harappa by archaeologists after the first city to be excavated in this region. Harappa culture had writing, a form of centralized control for administration and commerce, and large buildings made out of baked brick. In contrast to other early civilizations, however, Harappan society does not seem to have included a priest-king class, nor did its spread depend on military conquest.

In China, it is likely that villages merged to form states in several areas, but legend and archaeological evidence locate the first civilization, that of the Xia, in the middle and lower valleys of the Yellow River, from about the end of the third millennium BC. Texts written much later suggest that the Xia united a number of groups in a loose confederation. One of these was the Shang, who gained ascendancy in the second millennium BC. They developed an early form of Chinese script and expanded their territory through military campaigns. They were defeated by the Zhou, another Xia confederate, at the end of the second millennium BC.

Culture and trade

The expansion of civilizations was assisted by trade and migration as well as conquest. Trade routes in particular allowed knowledge and practices to be dispersed across sometimes vast distances. They were particularly significant in the expansion of Chinese culture into Southeast Asia, and in the spread of Egyptian and Middle Eastern traditions as far as North Africa, southern Asia, and Europe.

The first major European civilization emerged in Crete at the end of the third millennium BC. The Minoans, whose powerful navy controlled the Aegean Sea for much of the second millennium BC, constructed large cities centered on elaborate palaces including those at Knossos, Malia, and Phaistos. Later, urban societies also sprang up on the Greek mainland, the most notable being the Mycenean civilization, which came to prominence during the late second millennium BC. Classical Greek civilization emerged during the first millennium BC in a number of self-governing cities such as Athens and Sparta. These urban societies were distinguished by the formal constitutions that directed their political life and by the increasing power held by the male citizenry at the expense of a centralized leadership.

The pyramids at Giza in Egypt were built during the Fourth Dynasty to house the remains of the rulers Khufu, Khafra, and Menkau-re.

Civilizations also developed independently, but much later, among the agricultural communities of Mesoamerica and the central Andes. Mesoamerican civilizations emerged during the first millennium BC. The most important was that of the Maya, who developed a form of writing around AD 300. The Maya maintained commercial ties to city-states developing elsewhere in the region. One of these, Teotihuacán, in central Mexico, was an important trade center with a population that peaked at more than 100,000 around AD 600. During the same period, several interrelated civilizations existed in the central Andes, with territories that are now in present-day Peru and Bolivia. These societies created monumental buildings and elaborate crafts, but left no evidence of any written languages.

The meaning of "civilization"

In eighteenth-century Europe, "civilization" meant cultural refinement—the opposite of barbarism. Nineteenth-century social philosophers found this meaning too restrictive, so they used the term in the plural sense to refer to large-scale societies. This usage is followed by present-day sociologists and anthropologists.

Human societies can be classified in terms of their size and complexity. Small-scale or tribal societies comprise small bands loosely coordinated by kinship relations. These groups often live together at permanent settlements, although some may be nomadic. Medium-sized communities are usually made up of clusters of villages or small towns united under some form of confederation or chiefdom. In large-scale societies, at least some of the inhabitants live in large urban societies which are linked by a network of social, economic, and cultural ties, and normally unified under a centralized political organization.

Greek city-states such as Athens emerged around 750 BC

THE IMPACT OF CIVILIZATION

The main impetus for rapid progress over the past few thousand years was the development of large-scale urban societies. Their benefits in enriching human experience through technological innovation, scientific knowledge, and diversity in social life appear obvious. Certain consequences of civilization were less benign, however. These include the increasing destructiveness of warfare, the spread of disease, and the life-long bondage imposed on certain classes of people.

Innovation and adaptation

Many thousands of years elapsed between the development of specialized stone and bone tool assemblages and the beginnings of food production. After the adoption of agriculture and a sedentary lifestyle, however, the widespread diffusion of the latest innovations occurred remarkably rapidly. This was partly due to the obvious usefulness of the technology. Many inventions were developed in one location and then rapidly dispersed because of their

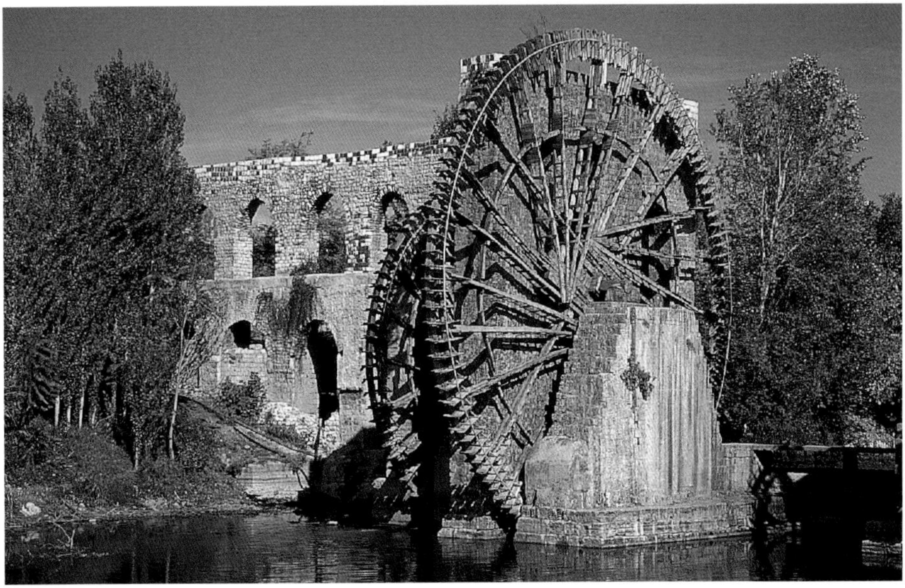

Invented in western Asia, the wheel was rapidly adapted to create devices such as the water wheel.

immediate utility. The wheel, for example, appears to have been invented near the Black Sea around 3400 BC, and within a few hundred years, was used throughout Europe and Asia.

Another reason for the exponential growth of technology was that new inventions were rapidly adapted to diverse local needs. For example, shortly after the emergence of the wheel, innovations based on this technology—such as pulleys, water wheels, and windmills—appeared and

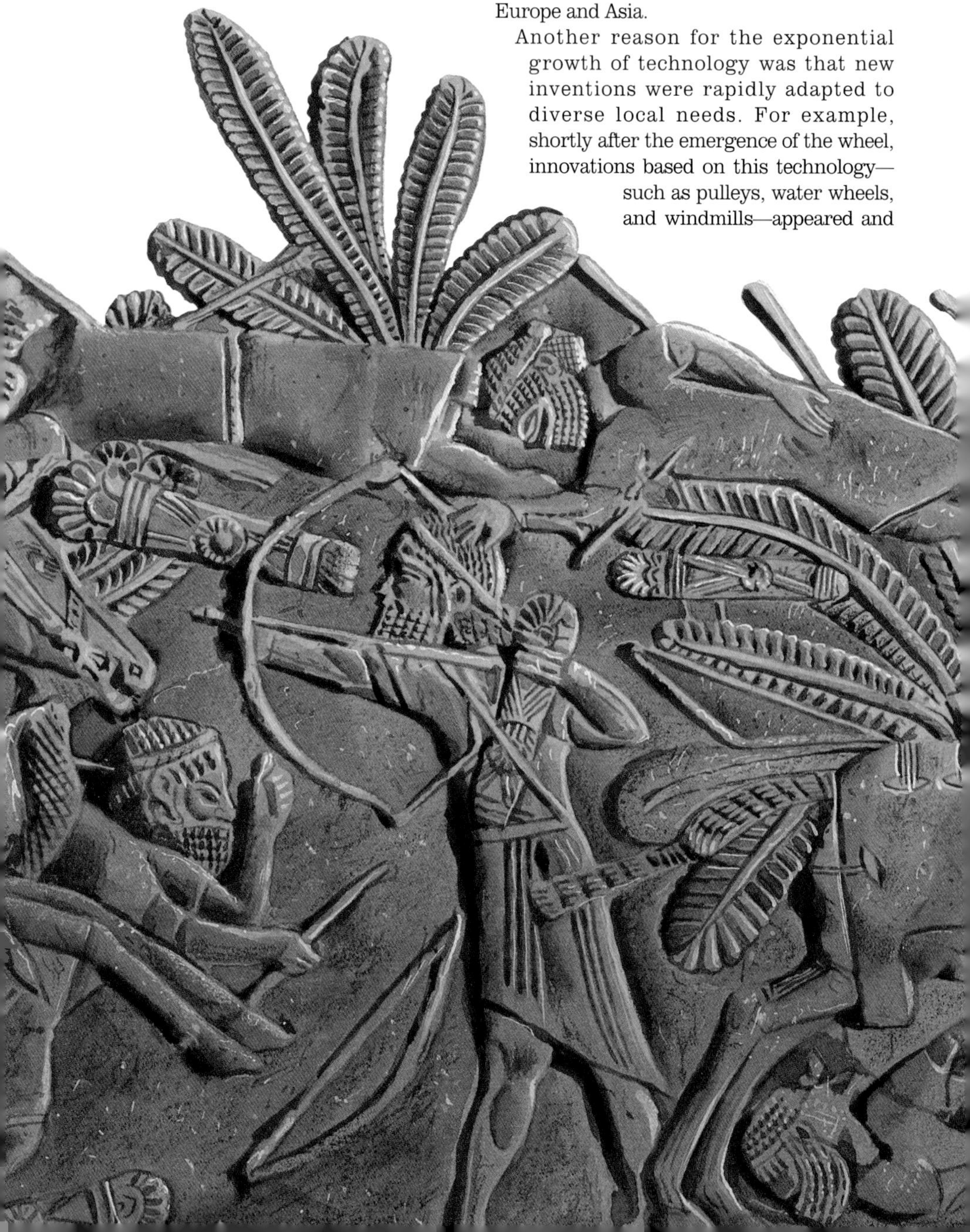

then spread quickly along ever-expanding trade routes.

Some innovations, however, did not travel as extensively as may be expected. For example, the wheel was probably also invented independently in Mesoamerica, where it was used in children's toys, but it was never adopted for transportation in this region due to the lack of draft animals. Nor did the wheel spread from Mesoamerica to South America, even though the people of the Andes had the Americas' only beast of burden—the llama—and despite the fact that technologies such as metallurgy had already spread northward from the Andes to Mesoamerica.

Technology and warfare

New technologies led to the expansion of production and, consequently, an increase in the size of urban populations. As cities grew in size, conflict over land with neighboring agricultural and pastoral peoples often led to warfare. In turn, this stimulated the manufacture of weaponry.

Early weapons were made of bronze, but by the beginning of the first millennium BC, iron weapons were being widely produced in the Fertile Crescent, and smelting techniques, which produced an early form of steel, were already well understood there. By 500 BC, iron tools and weapons were widespread throughout Europe and Asia.

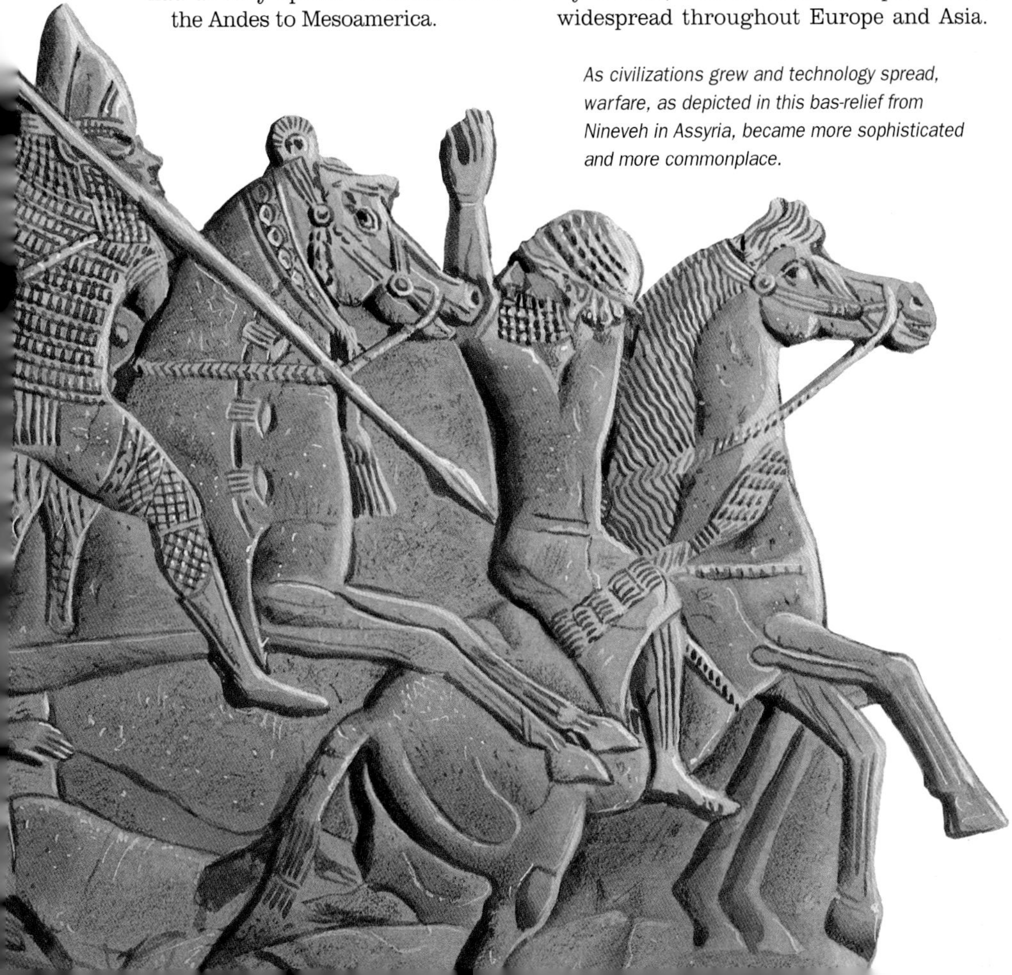

As civilizations grew and technology spread, warfare, as depicted in this bas-relief from Nineveh in Assyria, became more sophisticated and more commonplace.

However, ironworking did not appear in the Americas until after the Spanish conquests of the sixteenth century. The devastating effectiveness of steel weaponry was demonstrated by the Spanish conquest of the Incas. In 1532, the conquistador Pizzaro, with an army of only 168 soldiers, was able to defeat the Inca army of more than 80,000 soldiers and capture their emperor Atahualpa. The Spanish soldiers had chain mail, helmets, steel swords, lances, daggers, and horses, whereas the Inca army was protected by quilted padding, armed with blunt clubs, and traveled on foot.

Science and disease

Although many advances in the domestication of plants and animals and in technology were the result of accidental discoveries or trial and error, written records indicate that early civilizations were making careful observations of natural phenomena. For example, the Maya developed a calendar based on the solar year and lunar month, and could predict eclipses—a feat that required advanced mathematical skills. The Egyptians acquired considerable medical knowledge and surgical skills. Among the sophisticated techniques they developed was the practice of trepanation. This involved the cutting of bone in the skull to relieve pressure on the brain resulting from a skull fracture, or to treat headaches or epilepsy.

A sedentary lifestyle enabled ailing individuals to receive better care than they would receive if they remained nomadic. However, large concentrations of people living in close proximity to domestic animals and (initially, at least) dependent on a relatively limited range of foods created the perfect environment for the spread of disease. When human populations are small and move frequently, the opportunities for parasitic infections to spread are limited. Urban lifestyles, in contrast, with their permanent housing and large refuse dumps, attract disease-carrying vermin and

As a result of their preference for cooler climates, llamas never spread northward to Mesoamerica.

insects, and allow parasites to spread more quickly. Land clearance, irrigation, and the use of natural fertilizers would also have encouraged certain diseases in sedentary communities, particularly where diets were deficient and the population less resilient. Even more significant was the domestication of animals. Today, people associate animals with diseases such as rabies and anthrax, but domestic animals were also the original source of infections that are now commonly transmitted by humans, such as smallpox and measles.

The spread of disease was encouraged by trade, migration, and conquest. For example, bubonic plague is thought to have been restricted to Asia until it was spread to other parts of the world by traders. When it reached Europe in the mid-fourteenth century, it wiped out one quarter of the population. Diseases carried by conquering armies were often more destructive than their military campaigns. For example, in 1520, the Spaniards under Cortés inadvertently brought smallpox to the Aztecs, causing a massive epidemic that killed more than half the population and led to the demise of the empire.

Social hierarchies

The increasing division of labor and the steady enhancement of specialized skills in urban communities led to the development of ever-more sophisticated social hierarchies. People directly involved in food production—the commoners—were often obliged to provide tribute payments to a centralized authority. This did not necessarily mean that commoners were physically separated from the elite—in many early cities, they lived in close proximity to each other and even shared in decision-making. But as urban populations increased and relationships became more complex, so the social distinctions became more marked.

In China, for instance, the Shang, and later the Zhou, administered a feudal system of vassal states. Members of the royal clan, and others who assisted the king, were granted fiefdoms over parts of the kingdom. Below these nobles and loyal administrators were the farmers from whose ranks the soldiers were recruited. At the lowest end of the social scale were the slaves, who were usually nomadic pastoralists captured by the ruling elite. This pattern of enslaving captives was common in these evolving nation-states, probably because mass production and large-scale public works provided many uses for slaves in menial occupations.

Domestic horses

Today's domestic horses are descended from wild species native to southern Russia. Horses were first domesticated there around 4000 BC—much later than most other domestic animals—and before long had become the principal means of transportation throughout much of Asia and Europe. Horses transformed warfare, providing formidable military advantages when yoked to battle chariots or ridden. At the same time, however, they transmitted several diseases to humans, including tetanus and the common cold.

Mongolian horses are the only surviving relatives of the species from which all domestic horses are descended.

FROM CITY-STATES TO EMPIRES

There is no doubt that warfare was a part of human experience long before historical records were kept—even the small-scale societies of Melanesia that existed at the time of the first European contact were involved in frequent and violent tribal conflicts. However, the scale, range, and destructiveness of war increased significantly with the development of the first states. High population density, advances in transport and weapons technology, centralized decision-making, and a new fervor among troops willing to die for a powerful leader allowed extensive resources to be mobilized for warfare. This in turn meant that military engagements could take place much farther from home. Whereas war had previously involved only the annexation of adjacent territories from enemies who had either been chased away, killed, or enslaved, now they could lead to the amalgamation of entire societies into larger political units. Furthermore, the subjugated peoples could be forced to pay tribute, thereby increasing the ruler's resources for further campaigns. In this way, empires were born.

The rise of empires greatly enhanced the diffusion of knowledge, ideas, technology, languages, and cultural traditions. It also expanded trade links and imposed administrative and political unity on previously dispersed communities, laying the foundations for future nation-states.

There are three broad reasons why rulers of small city-states and medium-sized kingdoms ventured into empire-building. One was to create alliances that would

Construction of the Great Wall of China began during the Qin Empire (221–206 BC). Extensive sections of the wall were rebuilt during the fifteenth and sixteenth centuries.

provide protection against an external threat—the formation of the Chinese Empire is a good example of this. Another reason was to subdue a persistent enemy—this is why Alexander the Great began his conquests. The third was to acquire control over desired commodities, trade routes, and other resources—Roman expansion can be explained in this way. All three reasons

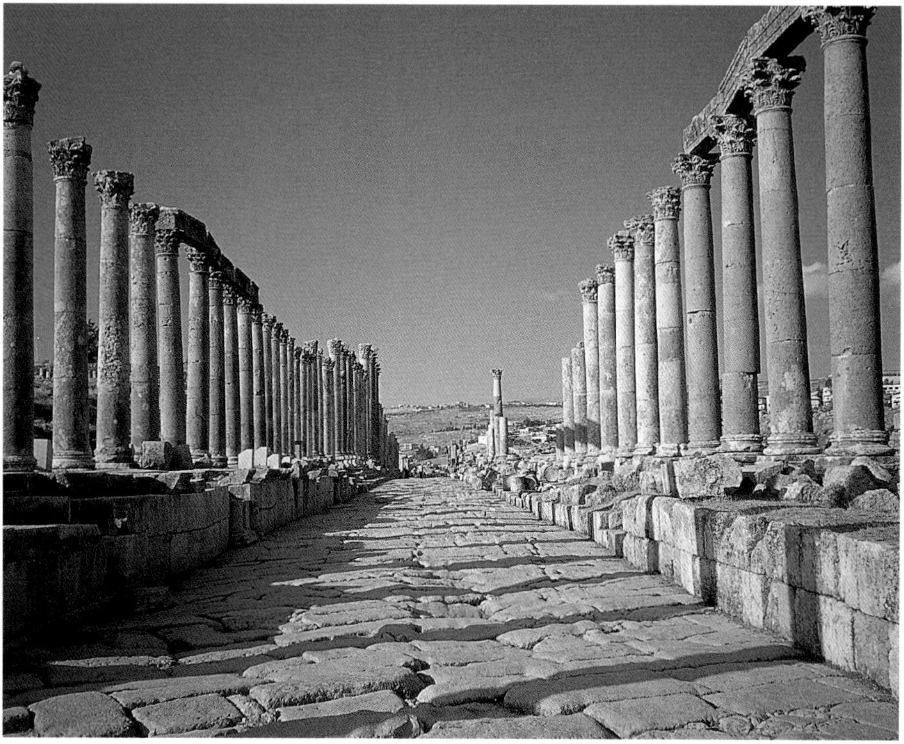

During the first century BC, the Roman Empire expanded rapidly. Under Pompey, Roman armies seized parts of the Middle East, including Syria, in 64 BC; in the west, Julius Caesar led the conquest of Gaul in 58–50 BC. Both generals subsequently laid claim to the title of emperor. Victory in a short civil war allowed Caesar to begin his reign in 48 BC.

influenced most expansionist ambitions, but one tended to be more dominant than the others in the building of individual empires.

The threat from the north

By the third century BC, the Zhou kingdom of northeastern China was breaking up, having been weakened by years of attacks perpetrated by warring tribal peoples to the north and northwest. Following the collapse of the kingdom, wars broke out between rival states and various alliances were formed and severed. Eventually, one of the Zhou vassal states, the Qin (221–206), gained ascendancy and brought the other states under their control. They then set about uniting the states into a single Chinese empire. The principle objective of this policy was to secure Qin territory against the foreign invaders that had plagued the Zhou. To ensure the protection of the empire, the Qin began to construct an enormous physical barrier to invasion by linking defensive structures originally built during the Zhou period. The Great Wall, as this barrier became known, would eventually stretch 3,000 km (1,860 miles) across northern China. The Qin also built an extensive network of highways and

Caesar's reign was short: he was murdered in 44BC.

canals to improve communications throughout their empire.

Following the death of the First Emperor, the Qin Empire was taken over by the Han in 206 BC. The Han expanded their empire further south beyond the floodplains of the Yellow (Huang Ho) and Yangtze rivers, and also defeated tribes to the west. This helped silk merchants to create a new trade route through central Asia which eventually extended all the way to Europe.

Alexander the Great

The rise of the Persian Empire in the sixth century BC posed a significant threat to Greek city-states such as Athens and Sparta. They responded by forming strategic alliances, which they managed to maintain long enough to defeat the Persians during the following century. However, subsequent disputes between the cities allowed Philip II of Macedon to take advantage of their disunity and unite Greece with Macedonia in 338 BC. In the following year, Philip declared war on Persia to revenge the Persian devastation of Greece, but before the war could begin he was assassinated.

Philip was succeeded by his son, Alexander, who realized his father's plans to crush Greece's formidable enemy. He successfully engaged the Persian army in Turkey and the eastern Mediterranean, moved westward to Egypt where he founded the city of Alexandria, and finally crushed the Persians in a decisive battle at Gaugamela in Mesopotamia in 331 BC. His conquests continued to the Indus River before he turned back, only to die suddenly at the age of 33 in Mesopotamia in 323 BC. Alexander's vast empire was divided up between his generals, and, without a strong leader, it soon disintegrated, although the kingdoms of Egypt, Persia, and Macedonia persisted.

Despite his short reign, Alexander left a long-lasting legacy. His decision to take scholars and scientists on his campaigns ensured that Greek learning, language, and cultural traditions were disseminated widely. He founded a number of Hellenic cities with Greeks and Macedonians, the most notable being Alexandria, which became a renowned center of learning.

Although the Greek city-states had previously established trade centers throughout the northern Mediterranean, they had largely left the southern shore to the Phoenicians. Alexander's conquests extended Hellenistic influence into North Africa and the Middle East. In this way, Alexander imposed a cultural unity on the Mediterranean region which stimulated trade and learning and which later played a significant part in the advancement of the Roman Empire.

The Roman Empire

In the seventh century BC, Rome was one of several small towns in the Tiber Valley that were situated on a strategically important road leading to saltworks at the mouth of the River Tiber. During the following two centuries, Rome gained control of neighboring territories, including the valuable saltworks, and became a potent force in local politics and commerce. Like other Mediterranean cities in that era, Rome was strongly influenced by Greek culture, but it never came under Greek control.

In the fifth century BC, Rome became a republic ruled by a Senate formed by an aristocratic clique. From that time, Rome gradually expanded its territory to encompass the whole of the Italic peninsula—while Alexander was conquering Persia, Rome was winning decisive battles for the control of southern Italy.

Success in southern Italy encouraged the Romans to seize Sicily, which was then under the influence of the North African city of Carthage. Over the next 100 years, the Romans fought three major wars—known as the Punic Wars—against Carthage to gain control of the western Mediterranean. By the end of the Third Punic War (146 BC), Carthage had been completely destroyed and Rome had emerged as by far the strongest force in the region. The empire subsequently extended eastward to Greece and the Middle East, where it benefited greatly from Greek advances in art, learning, and technology. Later still, the empire expanded to include large areas of present-day France, Germany, and England, spreading Hellenic culture and Roman political and social institutions across most of Europe.

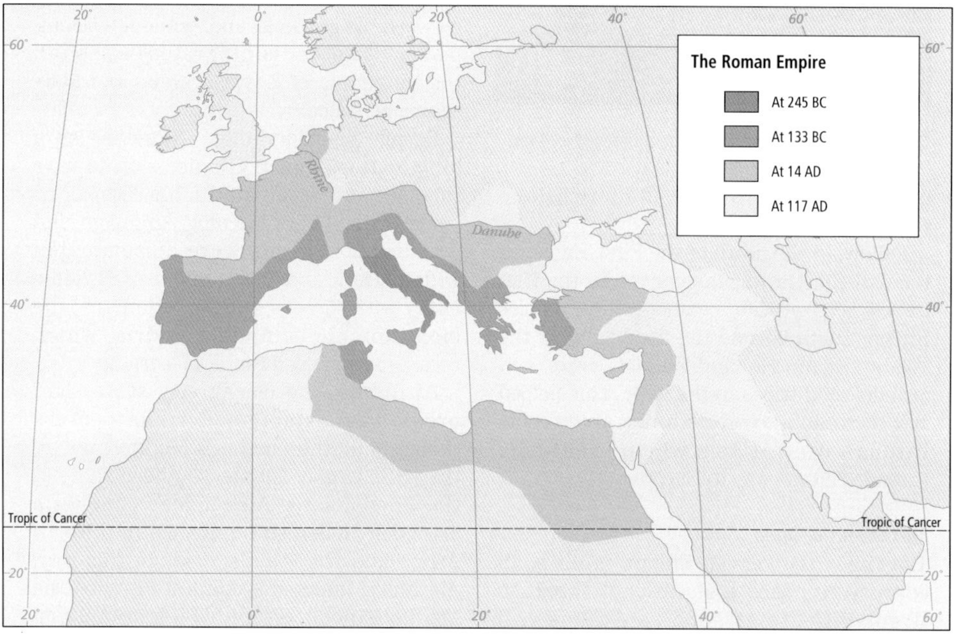

This map shows the gradual expansion of the Roman Empire, which reached its greatest extent during the reign of Trajan (AD 98–117).

RELIGIONS OF THE WORLD

Religions are a feature of almost all of the world's cultures. They have been the inspiration for much of the world's great art, music, architecture, and literature, but also the source of longstanding disputes and local, regional, and international conflicts.

The tenets and forms of religious belief vary widely. While most religions involve the worship of a deity or deities, supreme beings play only a minor role in some faiths such as Theravada Buddhism. Nor do all religions have practices, core doctrines, and moral codes that are common to every follower. For example, while Hinduism retains a self-identity developed historically through confrontation with other religious traditions such as Buddhism, Islam, and Christianity, it remains extremely diverse internally.

The great majority of the world's religions evolved among particular peoples who had no interest in attracting converts. Few tribal peoples, for instance, would attempt to persuade their neighbors to

Christianity spread rapidly through Europe after the fall of the Roman Empire; churches can be found all over Britain.

adopt their religious beliefs and practices. Similarly, some prominent religions such as Hinduism and Judaism make no effort to seek converts. However, religion is frequently the cause of great social conflict, particularly where two or more proselytizing religions are in competition. Even within religions that have a core doctrine, comparatively minor differences of faith or practice can cause bitter divisions—past tensions between Christian denominations are a good example of this. Frequently, religious conflicts are aggravated by historical factors and by the extent to which religious divisions are overlaid by other divisions, such as language, ethnicity, and class.

World religions

One-third of the world's population identify themselves as Christians, with about half belonging to the Roman Catholic Church. The next largest religious group is Islam, which includes nearly one-fifth of the world's population. These two major faiths are monotheistic—that is, they are based on the belief that there is only one God—and both developed out of Judaism. Hinduism, a non-proselytizing religion that is followed by almost 13 percent of the world's population, is the third largest faith. Buddhism, which is the third largest proselytizing religion, has approximately 325 million adherents.

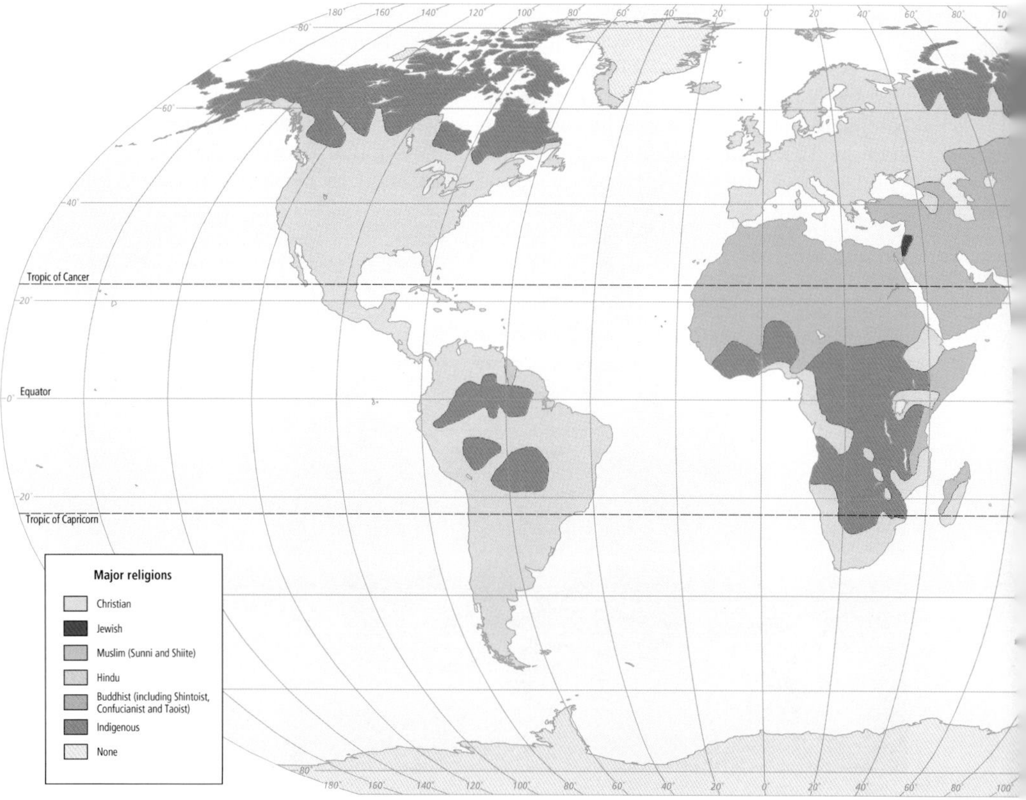

Judaism was originally the tribal religion of a people who traced themselves back to Abraham. Abraham is said to have migrated with his clan from the city of Ur in Mesopotamia to Canaan in the eastern Mediterranean. His descendants moved to Egypt, where they were later enslaved, and were then led back to Canaan by Moses around 1200 BC. Although Judaism has a comparatively small number of contemporary adherents (around 14 million), it is significant both for its role in the development of Christianity and Islam and for its continuing influence on cultural and historical events.

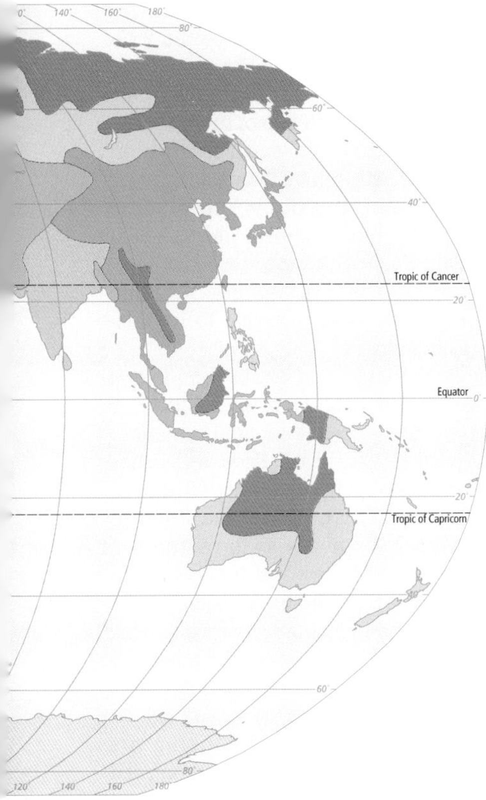

Christianity originated as a movement within Judaism. Fundamental to its doctrine is the belief that Jesus Christ was the Messiah prophesied in the Old Testament. After Christ's crucifixion, Christian doctrines were disseminated throughout the Mediterranean by the apostles and by missionaries, the most prominent of whom was Saint Paul (also known as Saul of Tarsus). Christianity then spread throughout the Roman Empire, first among Jewish communities and then into the general population.

Early persecution of Christians by the Romans gave way to tolerance early in the fourth century AD when the Emperor Constantine converted and Christianity became the official state religion. Christianity continued to spread after the fall of the empire in the fifth century, reaching most of Europe by the end of the first millennium. Later, particularly during the era of European expansion in the fifteenth and sixteenth centuries, missionary activity disseminated Christianity to other parts of the world. Over the centuries, theological disputes have resulted in major schisms, out of which have grown the Orthodox, Catholic, Protestant, and other traditions.

Islam was founded early in the seventh century AD by Muhammad, a merchant from the prosperous Arabian city of Mecca.

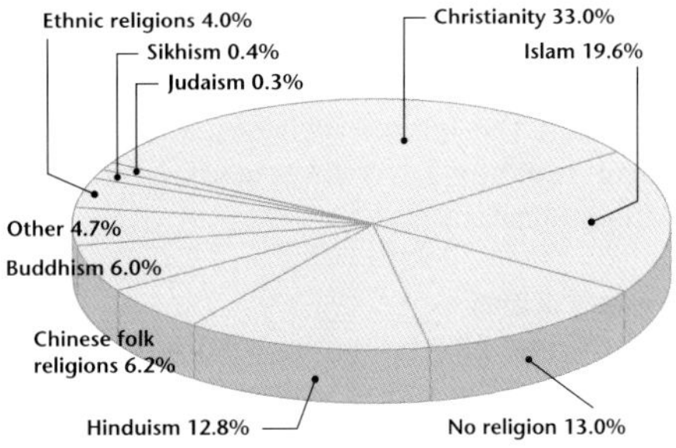

This pie chart shows the percentages of the world's population belonging to the major religions.

Islam spread to Southeast Asia along trade routes, reaching Malaysia in the fourteenth century.

Muhammad had contact with both Jewish and Christian communities, and he came to regard the Judaeo-Christian prophets, including Christ, as forerunners of Islam. After receiving revelations about the worship of one God (Allah), Muhammad began to preach against the polytheistic practices of his home city. Persecution then forced him and his followers to flee to Medina. This migration (Hegira), which took place in AD 622, marks the beginning of the Muslim calendar. By the time of his death in AD 632, Muhammad had become the political and spiritual leader of much of Arabia. After his death, Muslims expanded their territory beyond the Arabian peninsula. At its peak, the Arabic empire stretched from Spain and Morocco in the west to Afghanistan and central Asia in the east, but the Islamic religion was carried even farther into Asia and Africa by Muslim traders.

Eastern deities

Hinduism has its roots in Vedism, the religion of the Indo-European peoples who inhabited northern India during the second millennium BC. The religion's sacred texts are the Vedas which explore humankind's place in the cosmos and describe the roles played by various gods in the functioning of the universe. During the first millennium AD, cults associated with two of these deities, Vishnu and Shiva, spread throughout the continent. Hinduism has a large and faithful following among the diverse peoples of the Indian subcontinent, but it has relatively few adherents elsewhere, except among the descendants of Indian emigrants. This is in part due to its non-proselytizing nature.

Like Christianity and Islam, Buddhism, the third major proselytizing religion, is also based on the religious enlightenment experienced by one man. However, it has much earlier origins. According to tradition, Siddhartha Gautama lived in northeastern India in the sixth century BC, and was reared in the royal household. In his adulthood, Siddhartha is said to have sought enlightenment, which he achieved through a night of meditation, thereby becoming the Buddha or Awakened One. For 45 years he traveled India as an itinerant teacher while formalizing his religious precepts. His teachings spread into southern Asia, where the first Buddhist tradition, the Theravada (meaning "doctrine of the elders"), still prevails in Sri Lanka, Myanmar, Cambodia, Laos, and Thailand. However, it retains few followers in India. Buddhism also spread to the east (Tibet, China, and Japan), where the second tradition, Mahayana (meaning "great vehicle") Buddhism, emerged in the second century BC. A more liberal tradition, Mahayana is said to express greater compassion and social concern than the more aloof Theravada Buddhism.

What is religion?

Scholars have found it extremely difficult to come up with a definition that will allow a clear-cut distinction between religious and nonreligious phenomena. In broad terms, religion covers the beliefs and associated practices that focus on the relationship between humans and the supernatural, represented by a god or gods. These beliefs and practices address the ultimate questions of human existence, providing a sense of meaning and purpose to life. Frequently, they also create a feeling of fellowship and community with others who share the same beliefs and practices.

Approached in these terms, religions or religious activity can be found in all, or nearly all, eras and places, although the emphasis placed on religion by particular communities may vary greatly. Scholars have sometimes been surprised to discover that certain tribal or peasant peoples, who might have been assumed to be preoccupied with religion, are in fact relatively indifferent to it.

Religious practices may also have their origins in the need to regulate or control communities. Religion may enforce "taboo" or unacceptable behavior in order to preserve a peaceful and sustainable society.

Tibetan Buddhism is based on a tradition called Tantric Buddhism which emerged in India in the seventh century AD.

Despite their small number, the Jews have had a major influence on history, culture, and other religions.

TRADERS AND TRAVELERS

Humans moved from place to place either individually or in groups long before written records existed. The earliest records show they were impelled by a desire to occupy more fertile areas, by a desire for booty, by an urge to trade, by religious piety which took them on pilgrimages, by a thirst for knowledge, and sometimes by the fear of invasion.

Before the Christian era, Buddhism led monks from the East to travel to India to visit sites where Gautama had been. Nearly 2,000 years later, Ibn Battúta, an Islamic qadi (religious judge), after setting out in AD 1325 to go to Mecca, as all good Muhammedans sought to do, found that he could not rest until he had visited every Muslim state in Asia, Africa, and Europe. Although on his return to Fez, the sultan's court was incredulous at Battúta's stories, they were written down, and in such ways knowledge of the world was spread.

The spread and decline of empires

The growth of empires fostered trade and treaties, both with neighbors and with more distant powers. The Han Empire in China, for example, traded with Phoenicians,

Venice, a major trading power in the thirteenth century, is, today, an Italian tourist mecca.

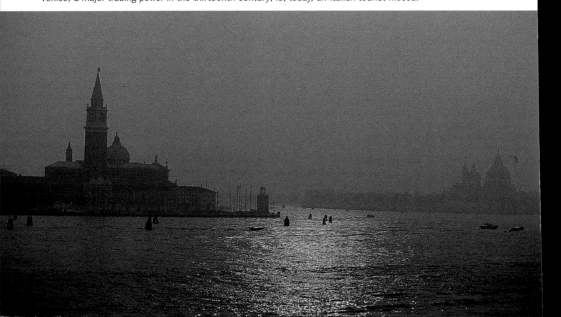

Carthaginians, Syrians, and the Roman ∏in silks, iron, furs, glass, and other exotic goods. Merchants also brought back knowledge—in the first century AD, a Greek navigator wrote of the Indian Ocean, where Hindu traders competed with merchants from the Red Sea and Arabs dealing in wax and ivory, rhinoceros horns, tortoiseshell, and palm oil.

However, nomads were always pressing at the frontiers of such empires, seeking to loot and ransack. Loose confederations of "barbarians"—as the civilized empires considered them—hungry for plunder, breached the defences. The Roman Empire bought their "barbarians" off for a time by settling some on the borders, as confederates, to keep out other tribes, but eventually pressures caused the Empire's defences to tumble. In AD 410, Rome itself was overrun.

The influx of mixed Germanic tribes was precipitated by the driving force of the Huns, who, according to the Goths, were the offspring of witches and evil spirits. No one knows where they originated. From the Carpathian mountains, however, they moved into the Mediterranean region and, by AD 450, under Attila, were poised to crush and drive out the Goths. Then their alliances crumbled, and they disappeared from Europe as quickly as they had come.

Instead, waves of Ostrogoths, Visigoths, Franks, and Saxons arrived and settled in England, France, Spain, Italy, and parts of North Africa, mixing with the local inhabitants, quarreling amongst themselves and moving on to settle in new areas.

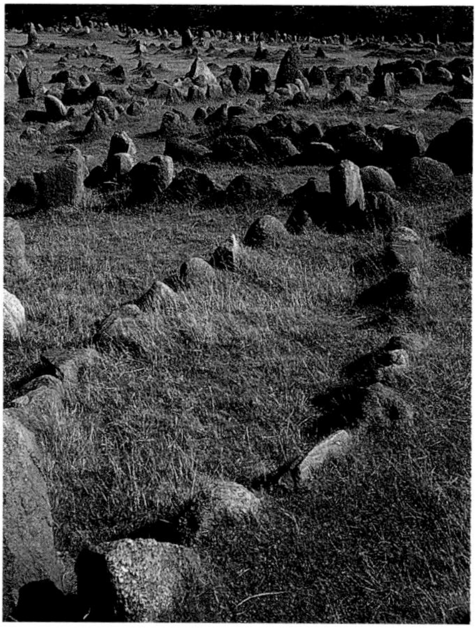

Viking graves in Denmark are a reminder of the early European territorial wars.

The Arab Empire

While Western Europe was fragmented and trade was declining, in the East, the Byzantine Empire remained the bulwark of Christianity against the rising Arab Empire. Mohammed's followers were spurred on by the idea of jihad, or Holy war, which combined religion with military exploits. After taking Syria and Egypt, they swept along the North African coast, took the Maghrib, and crossed into Spain. They attacked Byzantium by sea and blockaded Constantinople between AD 673 and 678. In the eighth century, the Caliphs of Damascus and Baghdad ruled an empire that stretched from Persia to Morocco.

The Arabs were also starting to dominate Africa by the eighth century. The peoples of the plateau between the Niger and the Benin had mined and used gold and copper, and later iron, long before Christ. Exotic archaeological finds and the presence of Asian food plants clearly show that trade began early in these areas. Tribal organization became more sophisticated, in order to control and tax trade and the trade routes. By the eighth century, empires such as Ghana had emerged. The Arabs had been pushing their way down the east coast of Africa well before Muhammad. They visited trading posts such as Sofala and dealt with the inland kingdoms, exchanging exotic goods for gold. After AD 700, they began colonizing the coast, establishing settlements such as Mogadishu and Mombasa. They also moved south across the Sahara, and established Arabic kingdoms.

The Arabs next pushed east across the Indian Ocean, carrying Islam to India and overwhelming the Hindu trading colonies of Sumatra, Java, and Borneo, and eventually acquiring a firm footing in Canton and other major Chinese cities.

The Chinese Empire

In the period after the Han, successive empires had been established in China, some ruled by nomad invaders. The Tang had subdued their neighbors and ruled from Korea to the frontiers of Persia. They had also established extensive links with the West. When Canton was sacked in 879, the slaughtered included large numbers of Nestorian Christians, Arabs, Jews, and Zoroastrians.

Western Europe

In the eighth century, driven by population pressure, Viking settlers from Scandinavia set out along the inland rivers to Constantinople to fight for the Emperor, and by sea in longboats to prey upon the coasts of Northern Europe. Sturdy fighters and skilled sailors, the Vikings explored the western routes via Iceland and Greenland towards the American continent, perhaps even landing there. In time, they settled—in Scotland, Ireland, northern England, and Normandy—and turned to trading.

After the spread of the Arab Empire had been halted in the West by the battle of Poitiers in 732, a new and fragile balance of power saw trade reviving in Western Europe. In 1095, the West felt strong enough to challenge Islam for possession of Jerusalem, and two centuries of Crusades (religious wars) began. The Crusades, however, did not hinder the growing trade in the Mediterranean.

Zanzibar, an island south of Mombasa, was for many years the center of the slave trade in Africa.

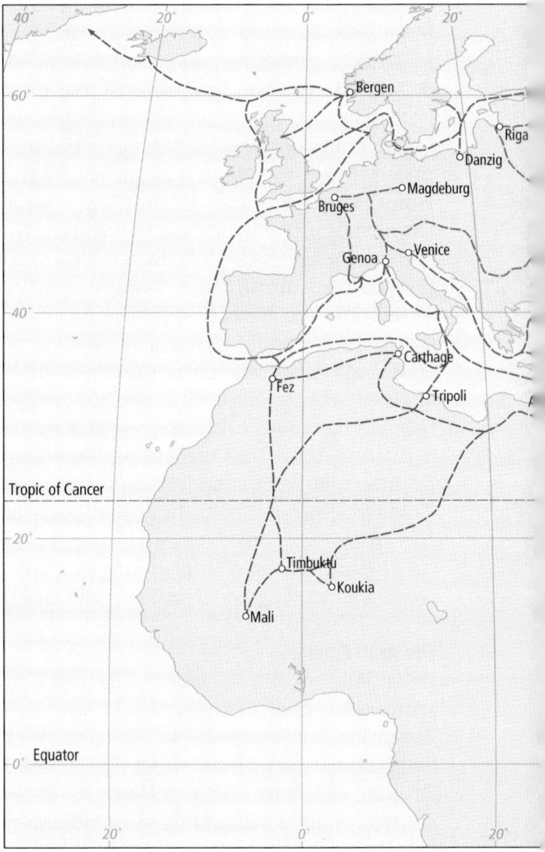

Merchants sought protection behind city walls and, by the twelfth century, fought for the right to govern themselves as independent communities. In Italy, luxury goods brought overland from the mythic Eastern lands of India and Cathay could now be imported from the Near Eastern ports. Genoa, Florence, and Venice became the starting point for travelers and pilgrims going to Jerusalem. In the north, cities along the great rivers and the Baltic coasts joined in a federation called the Hanse to strengthen their power and regulate trade in the fish and forest products they exported.

Even so, it was the Arabs who could move freely and upon whose knowledge the West relied—few Western merchants traveled to Asia.

The Mongols

Paradoxically, it was the Mongols who reopened the great land trade routes to the West and enabled Western merchants and missionaries to visit the East. The nomads who inhabited the great steppes were united by Genghis Khan in the first part of the thirteenth century into a powerful empire, with its capital at Korokaras. The Mongol hordes provided an extremely effective

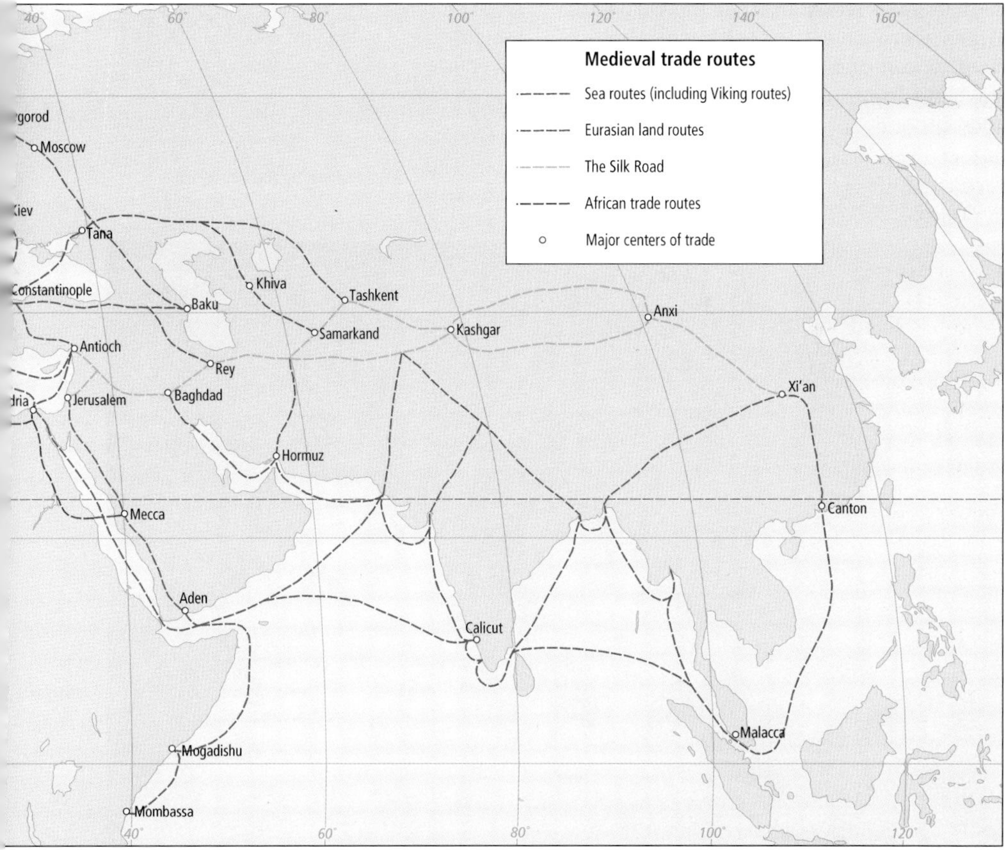

army, whose tactics left all who faced it outmatched—so much so that that it was seen as an instrument of divine will and punishment. They annexed Russia, ravaged Hungary, overwhelmed China, and set up the Mongol Empire. This empire was ruled in Marco Polo's time by Kublai Khan, whose ambitions stretched to conquering Java and Japan. In 1258, the Mongols defeated the Turks and took Iraq and Persia. They controlled communications between these centers and enticed or forced skilled workers and traders to live with them.

It was only when the Mongols were eventually converted to Islam and became more sedentary that the Ottoman Turks were able to retake the Arabic Empire and once again cut off Western travelers from land routes to both India and China.

Marco Polo

Marco Polo, a thirteenth-century Venetian, is possibly the most famous of early Western travelers. His journey to the Mongol Empire followed a long trading journey that his father and his uncle had made. He learnt Mongolian, and for many years served as an official for the emperor Kublai Khan. He returned to Venice in 1295, traveling via Sumatra, India and Persia. His account of his travels, which he dictated while in prison after having been captured by the Genoese, was the major source of Western knowledge of the Far East until the nineteenth century. The book became the basis for some of the first accurate maps of Asia made in Europe and inspired a number of great explorers.

Khiva was a trading post on the trade route between East and West. Khiva was taken by the Arabs in AD 680 and later by the Mongol leader Genghis Khan.

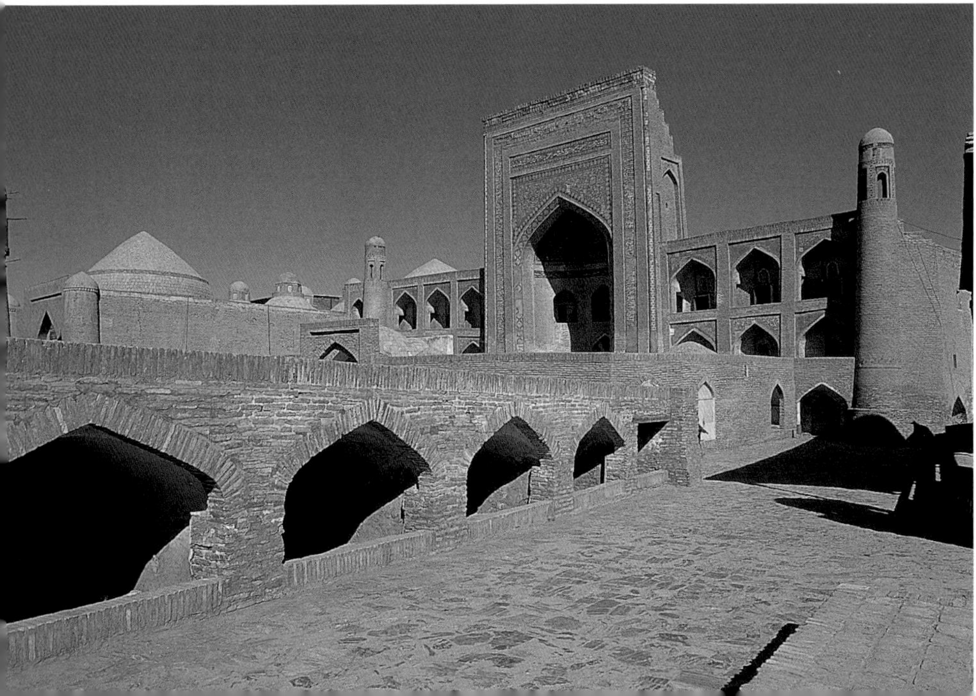

EXPLORERS AND SETTLERS

Carrying goods by water may have been cheap in the days of the great empires, but it was fraught with difficulties. Sailing out of sight of land required astronomical and mathematical skills, and sophisticated instruments. The combination of wind, tide, and current with a difficult and rocky shore could be a lethal one.

At the height of the era of world exploration, no one ruled the seas, and pirates were a constant threat. Many of the most honored explorers, such as Vasco da Gama, Alfonso de Albuquerque, and Francis Drake, were also pirates. Seaborne empires such as that of Sri Vijaya had existed before, but during this time, the European empires were unparalleled in their domination of the oceans.

Early explorers

The disruption of overland trade that occurred as a result of the Turks taking Constantinople in 1453 stimulated the search for sea routes to the east. Portugal had long been pushing down the western coast of Africa, albeit slowly, and had established a military hold on that coast which excluded traders from other countries. In 1488, Bartholomew Dias reached the Cape of Good Hope.

Many had sailed west from Europe by this time, and all had been lost. But in 1492, Christopher Columbus found a route and, upon his return, brought the unexpected news of "unknown lands" which were not part of Asia. However, the eastward passage was still of more immediate promise, and in 1497, Vasco da Gama, with the help of an Arab pilot, penetrated the Arab-dominated Indian Ocean.

In an epic voyage that took from 1519 to 1522, Ferdinand Magellan, sailing westward, showed that the world was indeed round. French, Dutch, and English explorers and seafarers were soon blocking the Spanish and Portuguese attempts to monopolize these trading routes.

Southeast Asia

In Asia, trade was the primary objective of exploration. The existing highly developed, wealthy, sophisticated empires were largely invulnerable. However, many Portuguese

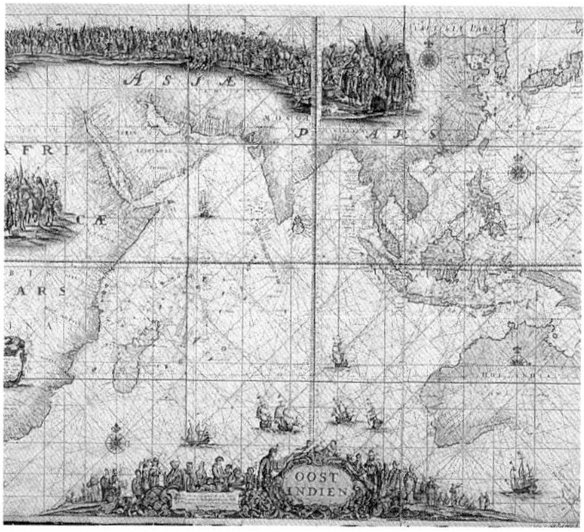

This Dutch map of the East Indies is from the early colonial days.

merchants, in well-armed ships, and protected by forts and royal fleets, did succeed in competing with the established Arab merchants.

In 1500, the Portuguese obtained trading rights on the west coast of India. In 1510, they settled in Malacca, the great emporium from which ships went to Borneo, Ternate, Tidore, and Amboina, and eventually to China and Japan. About 1565, the Spanish established an alternative route, with ships regularly crossing the Pacific to the Philippines. As the market for spices became saturated, trade in gold, ivory, silks, Indian cotton textiles, Chinese porcelain, tea, and coffee developed. By 1600, the Dutch and English East India companies had entered the competition, and eventually the Dutch controlled most of the spice trade from Batavia.

For more than two centuries, the costs of governing a distant state restricted colonization. In India, for instance, the British East India Company hesitated to assume direct rule until pushed by French competition. Only in the nineteenth century did direct rule become common.

South and Central America

The discovery of gold, silver, pearls, and industrial raw materials made the Americas attractive to the Europeans. The conquest of the Aztec and Inca empires enabled Spain to establish its rule from the Caribbean to Mexico, Peru, and Chile, while the Portuguese colonized Brazil. A steady trickle of fortune hunters from Spanish dominions in Europe took over the land and its inhabitants, causing an economic and cultural transformation. Despite the humanitarian protests of missionaries, exploitation of local labor, plus epidemics and diseases brought by the Europeans, resulted in up to 95 percent of the indigenous population dying.

African slaves were imported to work the mines whose silver had such profound effects on sixteenth-century Europe. Sugar, cotton, and tobacco production also required intensive labor, and so the slave trade grew. Hides, indigo, cochineal, forest products, dyes, and drugs also went east in return for manufactured metals, guns, and textiles. By the seventeenth century, the Dutch, English and French were also involved.

North America

The temperate areas of North America, already inhabited by Native American Indians, were initially less interesting to the European states. Cod fishing off Newfoundland did not require shore

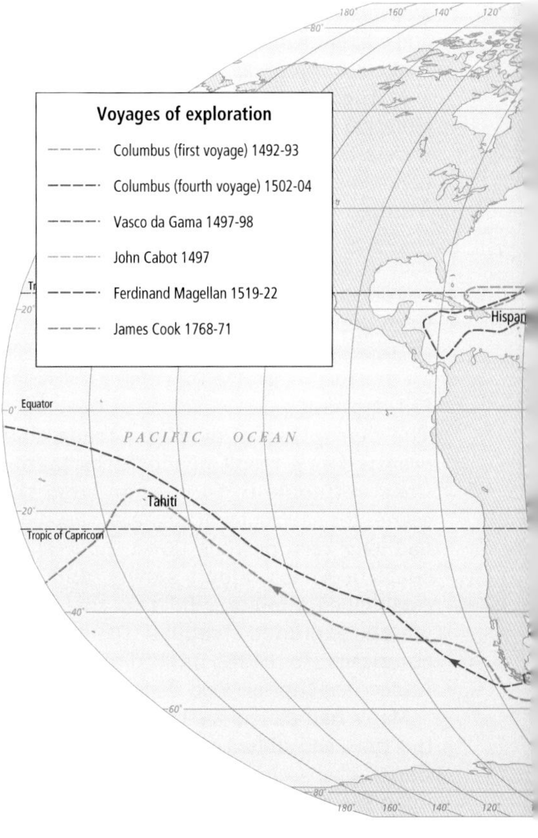

settlements. The French, Dutch, and English, however, all eventually established east coast settlements, from the early seventeenth century. There was royal supervision, but no state financing of these colonies. Each of the colonies had its own government, constitution, and purpose. Many were established as a refuge from religious persecution, and sought self-sufficiency. Staple exports were hard to find, migrants hard to entice, and transportation of convicts was an unsatisfactory solution. So total populations remained low.

A replica of Captain Cook's Endeavour *reminds us of the vessels sailed during the age of exploration.*

Southern colonies such as Virginia grew tobacco and, later, cotton, and increasingly

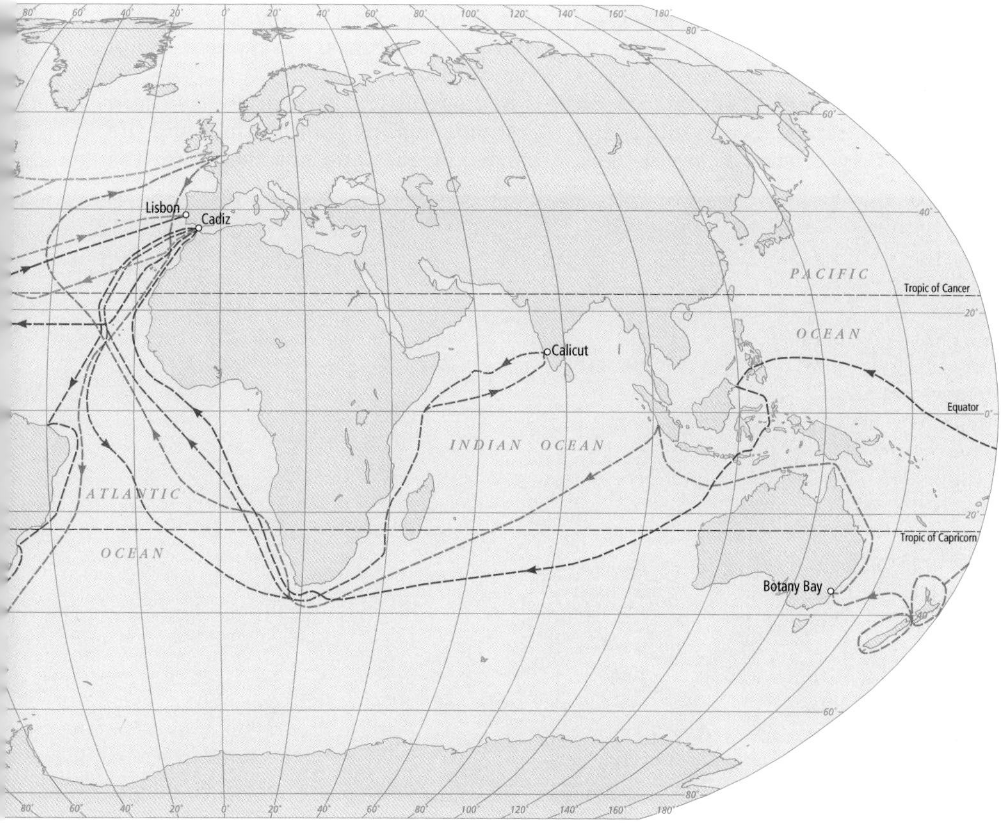

used slave labor. The other colonies supplied basic foodstuffs to the Caribbean. In the eighteenth century, sugar, cotton, and tobacco still dominated as exports. Migration was becoming more attractive, though, as the economic revolution in Europe displaced laborers. The wars of independence opened the United States to migrants from all over Europe, and as the numbers of migrants grew, settlers moved west. In the nineteenth century, this trickle became a flood.

Growth of a world system

European exploration established a worldwide network—regular long-distance trading voyages took up to two years or more, so exploiting the new discoveries required some form of settlement. Europeans established trading posts wherever they went. They also soon required more capital, bigger ships, and new forms of organization. Shipyards alone required the kind of complex organization that was soon used in the factories of the Industrial Revolution. European merchants became global carriers, meeting local requirements and introducing new commodities—horses and cotton to America; maize and turkeys to Europe.

Australasia was the last area to be drawn into this global network. In 1787, the British government chose Australia as a destination for convicts; the plan included the colonies being self-supporting. Initially, there was little but timber to offer world trade, and Europeans struggled to adapt the livestock and crops they brought with them to local conditions. Eventually, minerals were discovered as the interior of Australia was explored, wool became a staple, and convict transportation was replaced by free migration.

Ecologically, the world has been transformed by exploration and its consequences—and not always for the

Workers in Cochin, India, still deal in spices—here, turmeric.

better. In many places, the indigenous population has been largely swept aside through disease, displacement, and massacre, and survives today only as a small minority.

As worldwide trading routes developed, so too did the movement of people attracted by the prospect of personal betterment. During the nineteenth and twentieth centuries, population pressure and sometimes persecution in the homeland pushed millions, mainly young males, to move to new countries. The Scots and Irish went to the United States and Australia; Jews left Eastern Europe for Israel, Britain, and America; Indian workers settled in South Africa, the South Pacific islands, and East Africa; and Chinese laborers went to the goldfields in America, Australia, and elsewhere. Cultures have become mixed and modified as people intermarried and adapted to new conditions.

Machu Picchu, in Peru, is a moving record of a long-dead civilization.

The world is round

On September 20, 1519, the *Trinidad*, *San Antonio*, *Victoria*, *Concepción*, and *Santiago*, under the command of Ferdinand Magellan, set out to travel west from Spain and return from the east. News of the terrors and dangers of the journey—the empty Pacific, the difficulties of finding water and victuals, the strange cultures of the natives—only served to increase Western fascination with new horizons.

Magellan himself died en route in 1521, and it was del Cano who brought the single surviving ship back to Spain in September 1522. The expedition members had suffered mutiny and desertion, disease and famine, attacks by natives, involvement in local wars, and the treachery of supposed allies. They had proven that the Spice Islands could be reached by sailing west, but concluded that the length of the voyage made it uneconomic.

THE INDUSTRIAL WORLD

Modern industrial societies were born in the eighteenth century, when an expanding workforce and rapid developments in technology resulted in the transformation of the social and economic structure of British society. Over the past 200 years, industrialization has spread to other parts of the globe, distributing the commercial benefits of technology and improving the lifestyles of many, but also creating social and political problems, particularly in urban areas.

Preindustrial Britain

The Industrial Revolution began in Great Britain in the second half of the eighteenth century. Several factors made Britain ripe for industrial development. Improvements in agricultural methods during the first half of the century had reduced the number of workers required to produce sufficient food for the population, making agricultural laborers available for industrial production. At the same time, the wealth for investment had accumulated to a

The Firth of Forth bridge in Scotland was built in 1890 and is a marvel of Victorian engineering.

considerable degree, and much of it was concentrated in the hands of commercially minded individuals. A growing class of artisans and practical scientists possessed a high level of expertise in technologies, such as machinery, that could be readily applied to production processes. Continuing improvements in inland transportation, particularly river, canal, and road transport, allowed the rapid distribution of goods. Finally, Britain's growing empire provided it with access to vast overseas markets.

The Industrial Revolution

The first phase of the Industrial Revolution took place between the 1780s and 1830s, and was based on the early mechanization of production processes. The new industrial system focused on textiles (especially cotton) and textile machinery, and employed waterpower as its principal source of energy. It centered on the city of Manchester, in northern England. Here, in 1780, Richard Arkwright, inventor of the water-powered spinning frame, opened the largest factory yet built, employing 600 workers. Britain's position as head of the world's largest empire gave it a massive advantage in the textile trade; it could ensure a plentiful and cheap supply of cotton from the slave-labor-based plantations in the American South, and its powerful navy could protect its trade.

This first phase of industrial development was limited in two senses: it was narrowly focused (upon the textile industry), and it applied existing knowledge and skills rather than transforming the country's technological base. It was, however, revolutionary in that new economic relationships were forged between people, a new system of production was created, and a new society and historical epoch emerged.

Textile mills are a potent symbol of early industrial growth.

The evolution and spread of industry

The second phase of the Industrial Revolution occurred between the 1840s and 1880s, and was revolutionary in technological terms. Iron and steel manufacture in factories powered by steam engines represented a major innovation. When this technology was used to develop railroads and steamships, the country entered a new phase of production and transport. Britain became "the workshop of the world", supplying the materials for a remarkable burst of railroad-building activity in Europe and in former colonies of European nations. Factories now employed thousands of workers, rather than hundreds. The effects of this iron-and-steel-based Industrial Revolution on Britain were much more pronounced than were those of its predecessor. The employment generated was considerably greater, wages and living standards increased significantly, and British exports, which included foreign investments in railroads, rose phenomenally.

The revolution soon spread, with Germany and the USA among the first nations to industrialize on a large scale. Railroads helped achieve the integration of nation-states in Europe and opened up the Americas, as well as new colonies elsewhere. In the USA, the expansion and settlement of the frontier beyond the Mississippi River is closely associated with the penetration of the new railroads, the "Iron Horse".

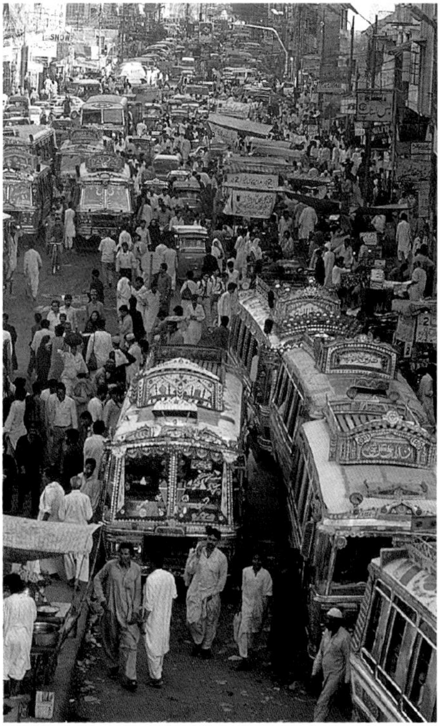

In countries such as India, modern technologies are replacing those of earlier times.

Modern industrialization

The third phase of the Industrial Revolution began in the last decades of the nineteenth century up to the First World War. Advances in electrical and heavy engineering and industry, and the exploitation of steel alloys and heavy chemicals, allowed warfare on an unprecedented scale. New factory systems combined electricity with power tools, overhead cranes, and more durable materials. Giant firms, cartels, and monopolies became the leading commercial organizations, and the ownership of capital rapidly became concentrated. The map on the right shows major European industrial centers at the time of the war. Germany and the USA had already began to rival the United Kingdom for industrial supremacy. At the same time, other nations, including Switzerland and The Netherlands, industrialized. Soon, Europeans introduced industrial practices to other parts of the world.

The Industrial Revolution continues to this day with the industrialization in the last few decades of nations like Taiwan, Korea, Singapore, Mexico, Brazil, and Thailand. This process has created a somewhat artificial but widely adopted distinction between "developed" countries—

those which are industrialized—and "developing" countries, which still depend largely on agriculture.

The consequences of industrialization

The application of industrial technology to an economy generally results in a population shift from rural to urban areas, as agricultural employment dwindles and people move to cities to work in industries and services. This process is known as urbanization. In the nineteenth century, the population of London, for example, rose from about 1 million in 1800 to almost 7 million in 1900.

While new industries raised living standards for many, the urban poor suffered overcrowding, poor sanitation, and pollution. There are many parallels between the social conditions in nineteenth-century United Kingdom cities and those in newly industrialized cities today. For example, the rapid expansion of an urban area such as Mexico City, which has grown from 3 million inhabitants in 1950 to about 10 million today, has resulted in acute social problems—water shortages, severe air pollution, and a chronic lack of adequate housing.

Recently, the industrialization of certain developing countries has had an interesting effect on the economies of the world's first industrial nations. Newly industrialized nations, particularly in Southeast Asia, have attracted manufacturing investment from the older developed countries; to such an extent that there has actually been a decline in the number of manufacturing jobs—a deindustrialization process—in the countries where the first and second phases of the Industrial Revolution initially occurred. The United Kingdom, Germany, and the USA have all deindustrialized to some extent.

But today's era of industrialization differs significantly from its earlier phases. Owing to new forms of technology, particularly in transport and communications, the contemporary industrial system extends to all corners of the globe, and encompasses most commodities. The Industrial Revolution has now entered its worldwide phase, integrating selected localities as workshops of emerging global factories.

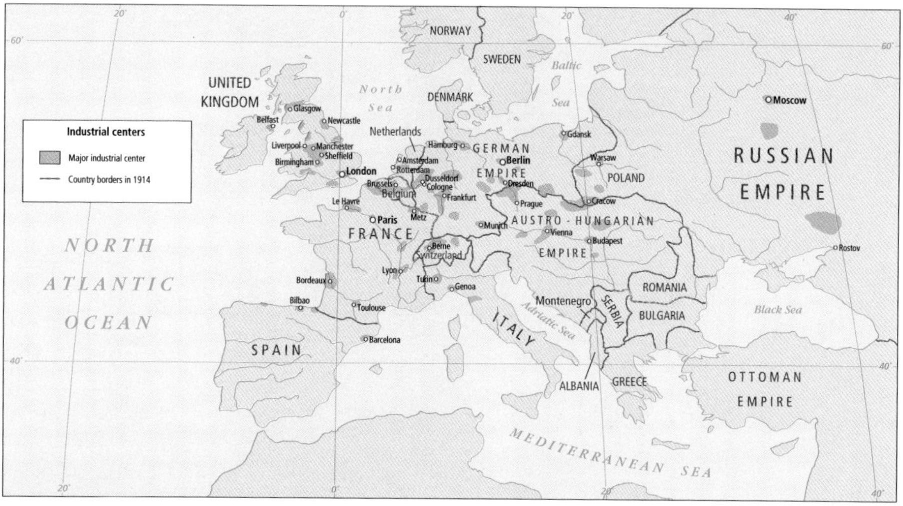

The major European industrial centers in 1914.

THE NATION-STATE

The world's nation-states, as represented today by the lines on a political map of the world, evolved over the past 500 years. Sixteenth-century Europe, for example, consisted of approximately 1,500 politically independent units. Yet by the start of the twentieth century, the continent was made up of only 20 nation-states. Since then, nation-states have flourished—today there are 191 nations and 58 territories on the

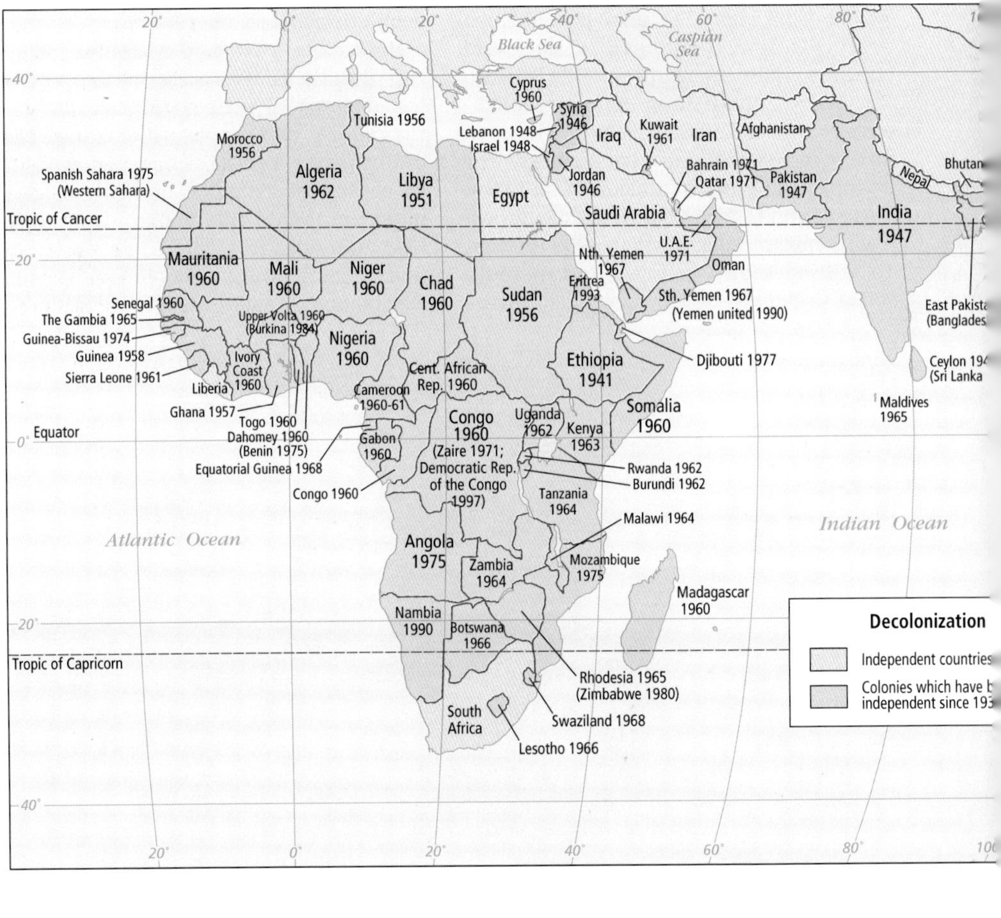

political map of the world. New supranational groups emerging at the end of the twentieth century have led many commentators to question the ability of nation-states to solve problems within their own borders and deal with the powerful forces operating at a regional or worldwide level.

From city-state to nation-state

Before the appearance of the nation-state in Europe, city-states such as Venice, Antwerp, and Amsterdam occupied centre stage in politics and economics. For much of the seventeenth and eighteenth centuries, Amsterdam was the control center for local, regional, and even worldwide affairs. The creation of the first nation-states, or more accurately, the territorial nation-states, occurred during the 1770s and 1780s.

The catalyst was competitive rivalry between Amsterdam, England, and France. The incorporation of national territory was a new feature of the political landscape, and it gave nation-states major economic and military advantages over city-states. In economic terms, for example, the nation-state could profit from its national market for goods. In military terms, it could more readily raise an army from its citizenry.

What do we mean by the term nation-state? It is useful to think of a nation-state as a combination of three elements: nation (ethnicity), state (the institutionalized regime of power), and territory (the spatially bounded area of state control).

A nation is a group of people who believe that they are an ethnic community with deep historical roots and the right to their own sovereign state. Nationalism is the cause through which such groups claim their right to be a sovereign power within a particular territory. Nationalism has its origins in the convergence of capitalism with print technology in the sixteenth century. The creation of separate vernacular

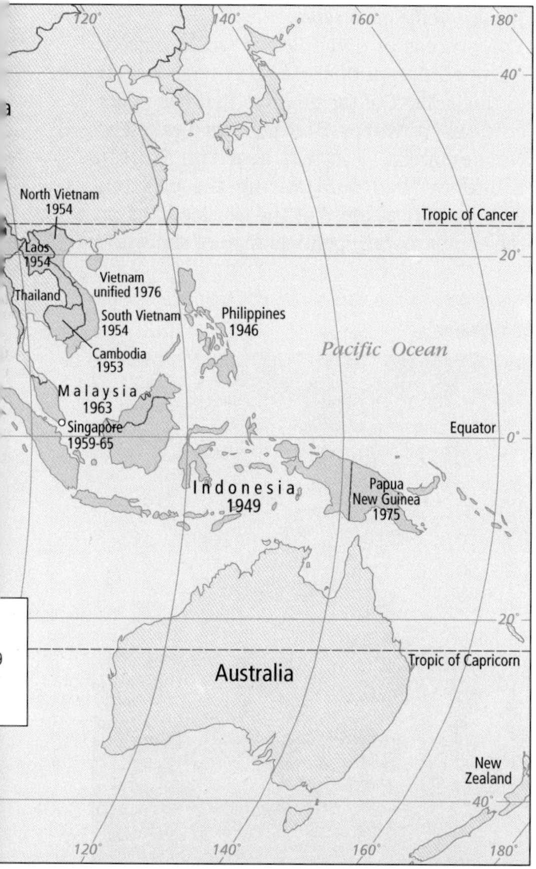

print communities led to the decline of Latin as a lingua franca, and played a critical role in forming national identities.

Although ethnic identity was a significant factor in the formation of many nation-states, nations seldom consist of a single ethnic group. Indeed, such entities are extremely rare, Iceland being one of very few contemporary examples. A survey of 164 nations in 1984 counted 589 ethnic groups, an average of more than three ethnic groups per nation. A major role of mass education has been to integrate diverse ethnic groups and regional minorities into a single community, often called the "melting-pot approach" to nation-building.

The second element of a nation-state, the state, refers to the institutions of political power within a country. These include its legislature, judiciary, political parties, and security forces. State power is organized into a wide variety of regimes, including constitutional monarchies, republics, theocracies, and totalitarian dictatorships. In the 1990s, three out of five states in the world were democracies—this is a historic high.

The third element that is used to define a nation is its territory, the physical area over which it has control. This area is normally marked out by geographical boundaries. Nation-state territories have typically been viewed as economic, political, social, and cultural containers that are largely sovereign and entitled to be free from outside interference. However, disputes over boundaries and national sovereignty have led to a number of major conflicts, particularly during the years of the twentieth century.

The rise of the nation-state

The process of dividing the world outside Europe into nation-states occurred largely in the context of the empires that the major colonial powers—Spain, Portugal, The Netherlands, France, and the United Kingdom—had built during the previous four centuries. Most of the border lines on the contemporary political map of the world

Internal conflicts between groups who consider themselves to be of a separate nation can lead to a state fragmenting into smaller ones, as happened in the former Yugoslavia.

have their origins in two major phases of decolonization.

The first phase unfolded over the half-century following the American War of Independence in 1776. About 100 colonies combined to form the current nation-states in the Americas. Little further decolonization occurred for more than a century, until around the time of the Second World War. Notable exceptions were the British settler colonies of Canada, Australia, and South Africa. The second major phase of decolonization began after the Second World War, when "the winds of change" blew through Africa, South and Southeast Asia, and islands in the Caribbean and the Pacific and Indian Oceans. This resulted in the formation of another approximately 110 nation-states.

Nation-states continued to be created in the 1990s—15 nations were created as a result of the break-up of the Soviet Union in 1991, for example. Eritrea, Slovenia, Croatia, and Macedonia became independent in 1991, as did the Czech Republic, Slovakia, and Namibia in 1994. The final outcome of the break-up of Yugoslavia is still uncertain. Internal ethnic tension in some areas has grown enormously, and ethnic-based nationalist movements continue to emerge. This kind of conflict is currently the most common—of the 89 armed conflicts that occurred between 1989 and 1992, only 3 were between nations.

At the same time, in Europe, where the nation-state first began, the European Union, a supranational regional state, continues to transform the European political landscape. Most of Western Europe has now been combined within the European Union, while a number of other European states have applied for admission and await entry. Some commentators see the European Union as the beginning of the end of the territorial nation-state as we have known it; it has undoubtedly changed long-held ideas on what makes a nation.

These Dutch-style buildings in Suriname hint at the nation's past history when it was part of the Dutch colonial empire.

Indian Sikhs on parade: the world's largest democracy is home to a wide range of ethnic groups.

The city-state of Venice was an important trading center from the tenth century onward. Today it forms part of a modern nation-state, the republic of Italy.

INTERNATIONAL ORGANIZATIONS

During the second half of the twentieth century, international organizations, including intergovernmental and nongovernmental bodies, have grown significantly in both number and stature. Today, there are about 500 intergovernmental organizations, such as the United Nations and the International Monetary Fund, and approximately 5,000 nongovernmental organizations, including the Red Cross and Amnesty International. That represents roughly five times the number that were active at the end of the Second World War.

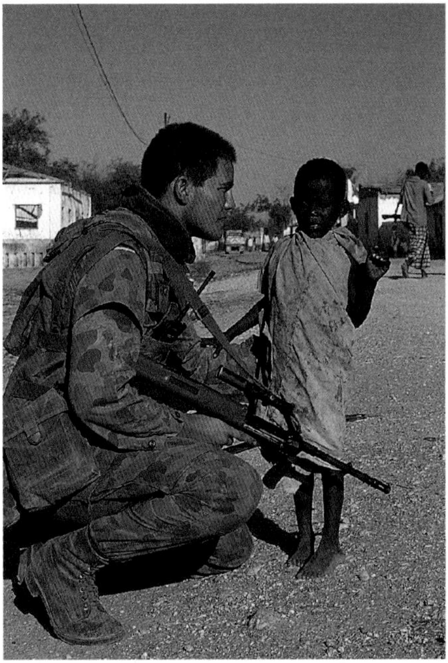

UN peacekeeping forces in Somalia.

International organizations form an important part of the social glue that binds the nations and peoples of the world together. They create a set of rules, norms, and procedures—encapsulated in international law, particularly in the form of treaties and conventions signed by nation-states—that define the expected conduct of participants in the international community.

The United Nations

The largest and most influential intergovernmental organization is the United Nations. Its predecessor was the League of Nations, which was founded at the end of the First World War, in an attempt to prevent further international conflict. Based in Geneva, the League gradually expanded its membership and became a focus for growing numbers of nongovernmental bodies. However, the refusal of the United States to ratify the League's covenant, and the League's inability to prevent expansion by Germany, Italy, and Japan in the 1930s led to its ceasing operations during the Second World War.

The United Nations (UN) was established in San Francisco in 1946, and now has its headquarters in New York. As with the League of Nations, the main motivation for the creation of the UN was collective security. Half a century later, the membership of the UN has grown to 185, and only a small number of nations (such as Switzerland and Taiwan) and territories (including French Polynesia and the Channel Islands) are not formal member states.

On the world stage, the UN is critically important, but relatively weak and often controversial. At times it has appeared to be an impotent and ineffective institution that more resembles a debating society for the superpowers, their client states, and major power blocs than anything remotely like a "world government".

It is, of course, important to remember that the UN is *not* a world government, in that its member states remain independent and sovereign entities. Furthermore, most of the member states clearly have an ambivalent attitude towards the organization. For example, the Norwegians are strong supporters of the UN, but refuse to accept UN directives on whaling. The USA frequently seeks UN support for military intervention abroad, but constantly defers payment of its UN dues. Resulting financial difficulties hamper UN operations. Even after the Cold War, when it seemed to have grown enormously in importance and stature, the UN operated on about the same budget as the Tokyo fire department.

During the half-century following the establishment of the UN, other collective issues, including environmental, economic, and legal issues, have been placed under the umbrella of the intergovernmental system. For example, the World Bank and the International Monetary Fund (IMF) have become responsible for managing a wide variety of international economic issues: the IMF coordinates international currency exchange and the balance of international payments, and the World Bank borrows the savings of rich nations and lends them to poor nations under conditions not available on the private capital markets.

Refugees in the Sudan are likely to receive assistance from international organizations—via UN peacekeeping forces.

Nongovernmental organizations

Nongovernmental organizations (NGOs) are private organizations that are today regarded as legitimate players on the world stage alongside nation-states and intergovernmental organizations. Generally, however, NGOs have significantly less power and far fewer financial resources.

Most NGOs are primarily concerned with the empowerment of marginal and impoverished sectors of the world's population through increasing those peoples' participation in resolving their own problems. NGOs tend to focus upon specific issues. For example, Greenpeace raises awareness of environmental issues, Planned Parenthood campaigns for reproductive rights and family planning, groups such as the International Federation of the Red Cross and the Red Crescent Societies provide disaster relief, and Médecins Sans Frontières provides medical care.

International organizations and human rights

Human rights is one highly significant area where international organizations have created the emerging rules, norms, and legal instruments that link nations and their citizens together in an embryonic worldwide system. Human rights are the laws, customs, and practices that have evolved to protect people, minorities, groups, and races from oppressive rulers and governments.

Before the Second World War, international human rights issues were restricted to matters such as slavery or armed conflict, and discussions about human rights (and recognition of them) took place mainly within the borders of particular nation-states. A turning point in the history of human rights occurred on December 10, 1948, when the Universal Declaration of Human Rights was adopted by the General Assembly of the UN without a dissenting vote.

Over the next half-century, major advances were made. Most significantly, a series of international covenants was drafted and adopted by the UN and subsequently ratified by individual nation-states. Once ratified by a nation-state, the human rights legislation was usually incorporated within the state's own legal system.

A land rights protest in Australia. International human rights organizations are increasingly exerting pressure on governments to recognize indigenous peoples' rights.

Although the UN has been prominent in creating human rights legislation, private individuals and nongovernmental organizations such as Amnesty International have frequently provided the political pressure that has persuaded intergovernmental and national agencies to act. Often, though, such action has been taken only reluctantly and retrospectively. The fact that countless millions of people have suffered (and many still do) terrible violations of their rights as human beings, even since the Declaration of Human Rights, is something of an indictment of the Declaration and of the UN's ability and will to enforce it. Most observers still regard the Declaration of Human Rights as inadequate and in need of enforcement. Its emergence, and the opportunity it created to bring such issues to world attention, are one positive result of the growth in importance of international organizations. While this has certainly produced a world that is better than it was, it is still by no means all that it could be.

Again, the ambivalent attitudes of nation-states to international organizations is a significant factor, affecting their ability to function effectively. For example, when concerns about human rights in Afghanistan were raised by the UN and NGO representatives in 1998, the ruling Taliban militia asked the organizations to leave the country. Yet, when it appeared that Iran might be ready to invade Afghanistan to protect some of its own citizens, the Taliban sought support from the UN to keep Iran out. At the end of the twentieth century, the idea of setting up global governance was still on the world's agenda, but only just.

The United Nations System

International Court of Justice

Secretariat

General Assembly
Committees

Trusteeship Council

Security Council
Peacekeeping Operations
International Tribunals
Military Staff Committees
Standing Committees

Economic and Social Council (ECOSOC)

UN Programs:

INSTRAW	UN International Research and Training Institute for the Advancement of Women
ITC	International Trade Center
UNCHS	UN Center for Human Habitats
UNCTAD	UN Conference on Trade and Development
UNDCP	UN Drug Control Program
UNDP	UN Development Program
UNEP	UN Environment Program
UNFPA	UN Fund for Population Activities
UNHCF	UN High Commission for Refugees
UNICEF	UN Children's Emergency Fund
UNIFEM	UN Development Fund for Women
UNITAR	UN Institute for Training and Research*
UNU	UN University
WFP	World Food Program
WFC	World Food Council

Functional Commissions
Regional Commissions
Standing Committees
Expert Bodies

Specialized Agencies:

FAO	Food and Agriculture Organization, Rome
ICAO	International Civil Aviation Organization, Montreal
IFAD	International Fund for Agricultural Development, Rome
ILO	International Labor Organization, Geneva
IMF	International Monetary Fund, Washington
IMO	International Maritime Organization, London
ITU	International Telecommunications Union, Geneva
UNESCO	UN Educational, Scientific, and Cultural Organization, Paris
UNIDO	UN Industrial Development Organization, Vienna
UPU	Universal Postal Union, Berne
WHO	World Health Organization, Geneva
WIPO	World Intellectual Property Organization, Geneva
WMO	World Meteorological Association, Geneva
WTO	World Trade Organization,Geneva*

World Bank Group, Washington

IBRD	International Bank for Reconstruction and Development
IDA	International Development Association
IFC	International Finance Corporation
MIGA	Multilateral Investment Guarantee Agency

**Does not report to ECOSOC*

GLOBALIZATION

Globalization refers to a change of scale in human processes and activities which has occurred during the last quarter of the twentieth century—one in which the nation-state is giving way, in many fields, to global organizations. Until recently, it was generally felt that such human and environmental affairs could and should be conducted at a national level. Nation-states were, in principle at least, sovereign or independent units. Of course, nation-states had relations with one another, and these were referred to as international, as in the terms "international trade"

and "international relations". In the 1990s, however, the terms "international" and "internationalization" have been increasingly replaced by the terms "global" and "globalization", as national boundaries have begun to seem less significant in economic, political, cultural, and environmental ways.

The global economy

Transnational corporations—companies that operate in a large number of countries—are the movers and shakers of the modern global economy. Among the firms with operations that are nearly worldwide are Exxon and Royal Dutch Shell in petroleum; McDonald's, Seagrams, Sara Lee, Nabisco and Nestlé in food and beverages; BMW, Ford, Volkswagen, and General Motors in automobiles; and Mitsubishi and Mitsui in banking, manufacturing, and trade.

Although few (if any) companies can be described as truly global at this time—most still focus on certain markets and report to shareholders in their home country—the term "global" is commonly used in business circles to identify a level of operations that many companies hope to attain in the not-too-distant future. This would involve a truly international workforce, shareholders in a number of nation-states, and products that are sold in all markets.

The flow of money from country to country is also encouraging the surge in economic globalization. National boundaries are no barrier to the movement of funds; thanks to modern telecommunications and computer technology, funds can now be rapidly transferred to any part of the globe. Such transactions have, it now appears, created a much more volatile and less secure world. In a matter of weeks in the middle of 1997, the Asian economic miracle became the Asian economic meltdown as a result of the massive and rapid withdrawal of global funds.

The phenomenal growth of the Internet has created opportunities for even small companies to operate at a global level. By selling goods via the World Wide Web, a firm can now compete in markets where it could not previously have established a presence, whether for geographical, political, or financial reasons. Governments are struggling to cope with the implications of this for the regulation of trade within their countries. How, for example, do they impose sales taxes on goods or services that are purchased in the virtual market of cyberspace?

Many commentators assert that globalization will transform the world economy in the twenty-first century, leaving

Financial centers such as Chicago are experiencing the globalization of trade.

no national products, no national corporations, no national industries, and no national economies. To succeed in the global marketplace, countries will have to depend entirely on the skills of their inhabitants, and will have to deal with powerful external forces that could create an ever-widening gulf between skilled, globally aware citizens and a growing unskilled, out-of-touch underclass.

World politics

The globalization of politics has resulted in the decline of the nation-state and the growth of international organizations. Although they remain the principal players on the world political stage, nation-states now appear less independent and less sovereign than they used to. One response to this has been to look to international organizations such as the United Nations to assume some of the roles previously played by nation-states.

Advertising signs in this village in Peru are an example of the penetration of multinational corporations into a developing country.

Perhaps the most significant political event in the 1990s was the end of the Cold War. During the Cold War (1946–91), most nation-states belonged to one of three geopolitical worlds: the First World, consisting of developed capitalist nations, and dominated by the USA; the Second World, consisting of developed communist nations, and dominated by the Soviet Union; and the Third World, consisting of developing nations that were in theory not aligned with either of the superpowers. The demise of the Cold War brought an end to these divisions, and created a geopolitical situation no longer driven by the rivalry of two opposing superpowers.

Some commentators believe that this has created a vacuum, where no effectively organized power system exists. In the past, when major geopolitical shifts occurred, one dominant power was typically replaced by another: Great Britain (as the United Kingdom then was) replaced Amsterdam, and the USA later replaced the United Kingdom. Globalization has produced a world so complex and integrated that it no longer seems possible for a single nation-state to play the dominant role that these nations once played. The growing emphasis on and allocation of power to international organizations can be seen as an attempt to fill this power vacuum.

The global village

Discussions of the globalization of culture often begin with the expression "global village", a term coined in the 1960s by Marshall McLuhan, an American commentator. He believed that television would replace the printed word as the primary medium of wider social integration, eventually uniting the people of the world through their collective participation in media events. In the 1990s, events such as the Gulf War, the annual Academy Awards, the death of an English princess, and certain sporting competitions were watched on television by people in almost all the world's countries—an audience of between 1 and 2 billion people.

The fact that a rapidly growing number of people are involved in maintaining the global village raises a number of questions. For instance, will globalization mean an inevitable cultural homogenization? Opinion is sharply divided on this question. A great deal of evidence supports the view that a global culture is developing. On the other hand, powerful movements which actively resist this cultural homogenization have also emerged—militant Islamic, Hindu, and Zionist organizations, for example.

One issue that has played a major role in raising awareness of the ways in which we truly are a global community is the environment. The first Earth Day in 1970 marked the beginning of mass awareness of the global significance of environmental issues. Over the next three decades, evidence of the extent of degradation of Earth's natural environment caused by human activity has mounted. This has forced governments and individuals to examine their impact on the natural world, and has encouraged political cooperation at a global level to effect change.

A series of international environmental forums have been held, including Stockholm (1972), the Earth Summit at Rio de Janeiro (1992), and the Population Conference at Cairo (1994). All stressed the worldwide and interconnected nature of the growing environmental crisis. The Earth Summit was attended by an unprecedented 130 heads of state, 1,500 nongovernmental organizations, and 7,000 accredited journalists. However, despite the willingness of many nations to discuss these issues globally, the desire or ability to act locally may be absent.

The slogan "Think globally, act locally" has been widely employed to express the scale shift involved in this transformation of economics, politics, culture, and nature—from what used to be thought local or national concepts to what are now recognized as (or have become) international, global concerns.

Globalization may prove to be the key change in the twenty-first century.

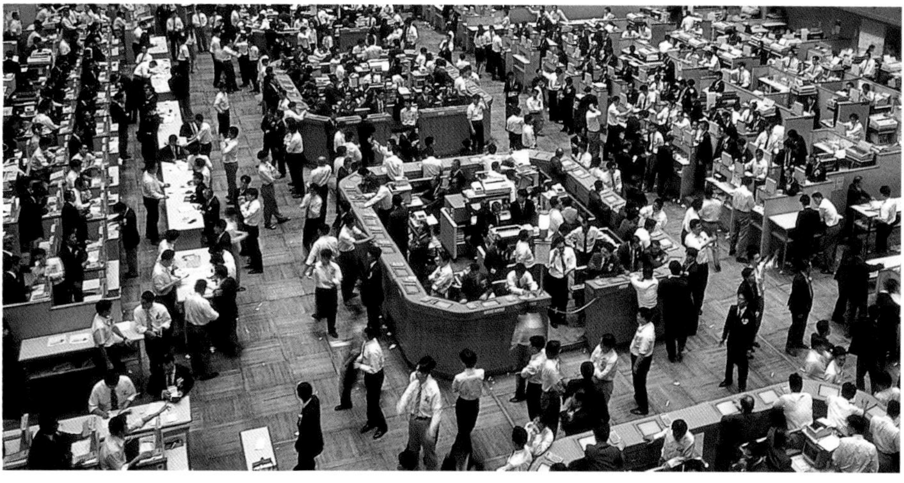

Dealings on the Tokyo Stock Exchange can affect the economy of many other countries.

ASIÆ
PERSIA
MOG
Ormus
Guadel
Gouzeratte
CAMBAIA
EGYPTEN
YEMEN
ARABIA FELIX
Fartaque
AFRI CÆ
MAGADOXA
Linea Æquinoctialis
MELINDE
MOMBAZA
QUILOA
MOZAMBIQUE
CUAMA
SOFFALA
MADA GAS CAR
BIS ARS INA
Abrolho
San Brandao
Diego Rodrigues
Dos Romeiros
D DE BONA
STERDAM, BIJ
ER GOOS
Water inde
gulde Zee
Spiegel

Part 3

A–Z Country Listings

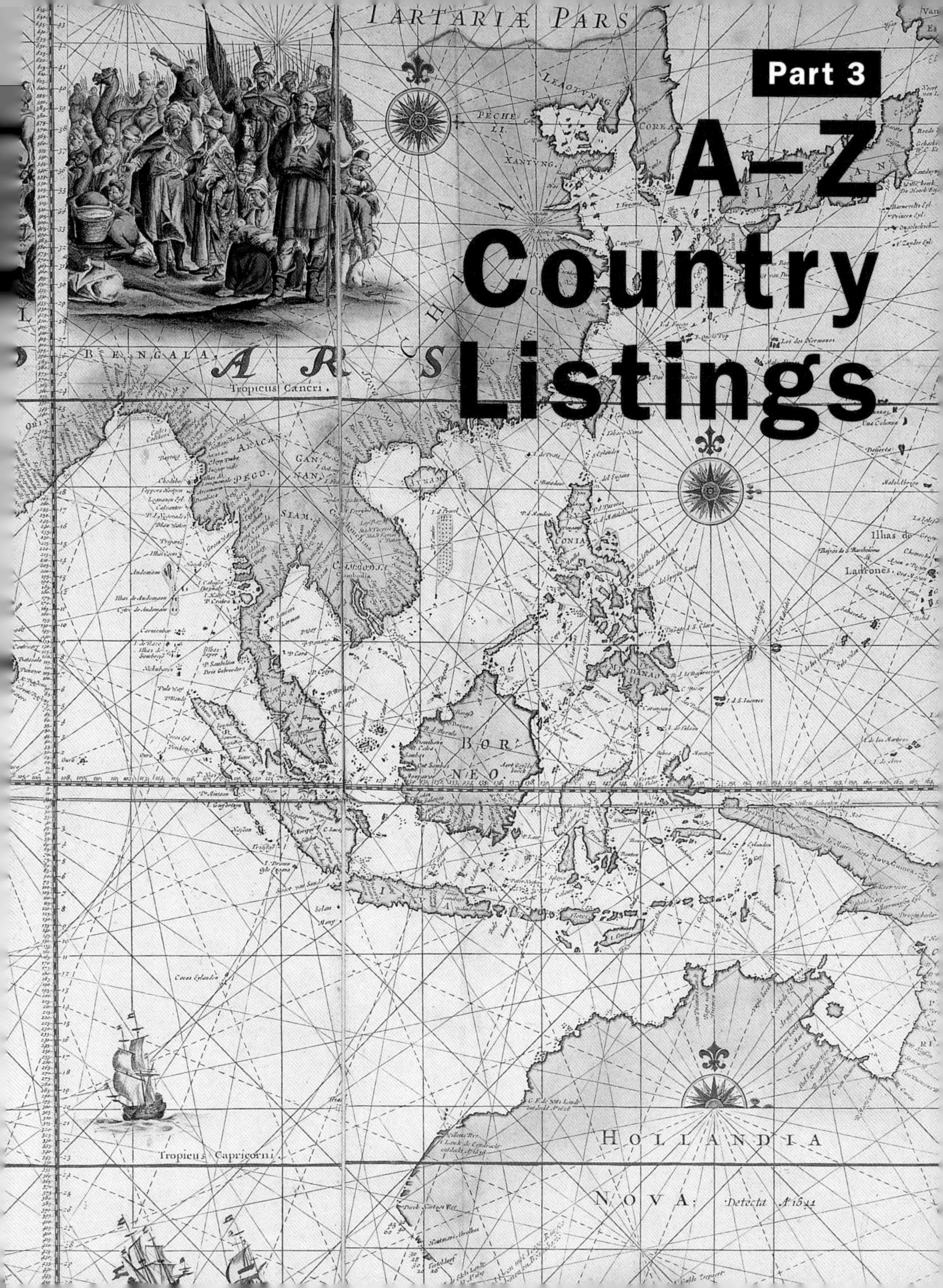

TARTARIÆ PARS
LEAOTUNG
COREA
PECHELI
XANTUNG
BENGALA
A R S
Tropicus Cancri
PEGO
SIAM
BOR NEO
MINDANAO
Ilhas de Ladrones
Tropicus Capricorni
HOLLANDIA
NOVA
Detecta Aº 1644

A

AFGHANISTAN

OFFICIAL NAME Islamic State of Afghanistan
FORM OF GOVERNMENT Transitional government
CAPITAL Kabōl (Kabul)
AREA 647,500 sq km (250,000 sq miles)
TIME ZONE GMT + 4.5 hours
POPULATION 25,824,882
PROJECTED POPULATION 2005 30,189,273
POPULATION DENSITY 39.8 per sq km (103 per sq mile)
LIFE EXPECTANCY 47.3
INFANT MORTALITY (PER 1,000) 140.6
OFFICIAL LANGUAGES Dari (Afghan Persian), Pashto
OTHER LANGUAGES Uzbek, Turkmen, Indi and Pamiri languages, Dravidian
LITERACY RATE 31.5%
RELIGIONS Sunni Muslim 84%, Shi'a Muslim 15%, other 1%
ETHNIC GROUPS Pashtun 38%, Tajik 25%, Hazara 19%, Uzbek 6%, other 12%
CURRENCY Afghani
ECONOMY Agriculture 61%, services 25%, industry 14%
GNP PER CAPITA Est. < US$765
CLIMATE Mainly semiarid, but arid in southwest and cold in mountains; hot summers and cold winters
HIGHEST POINT Nowshak 7,485 m (24,557 ft)
MAP REFERENCE Page 757

Afghanistan

Afghanistan is a landlocked country in the central part of South Asia with nearly three-quarters of its territory mountainous. It shares a western frontier with Iran, while Pakistan is across the southeastern border. Once a part of the ancient Persian Empire, Afghanistan was conquered by Alexander the Great in 328 BC. In the seventh century AD it adopted Islam, today the country's dominant religious and cultural force. From 1953 it was closely allied with the former Soviet Union. In 1979 the Soviet government intervened to install a communist faction more to its liking, and though constantly besieged by mujahideen guerrilla fighters, maintained its military occupation until 1989. After the overthrow of the communist government in 1992 the mujahideen began fighting among themselves along ethnic lines. Twenty years of internal war appeared to have ended in 1998 with the Sunni Muslim Taliban militia, associated with the majority Pashtun, in control of the country. The Taliban has imposed strict Islamic rule.

Geographically, the country's largest area is the thinly populated central highlands. This comprises most of the Hindu Kush, the second highest range in the world, with several peaks over 6,400 m (21,000 ft). The northeast is seismically active. Much of the rest is desert or semidesert, except for a few fertile and heavily populated valleys, among them Herāt in the northwest. Most agriculture takes place on the northern plains, near the frontiers of Turkmenistan, Uzbekistan, and Tajikistan. The country's main river basins are those of the Amu Darya, Helmand, and Kābol.

Afghanistan is very poor: a list of 192 countries ranked for calorie intake in 1995 placed Afghanistan 191. It depends largely on wheat farming and the raising of sheep and goats. During the Soviet occupation and the subsequent internecine conflict, one-third of the population left the country, with 6 million refugees fleeing to Pakistan and Iran. Many have now gone home to an economically devastated land. Millions of people lack food, clothing, housing, and medical care. Though data are shaky, it is likely that the country's most profitable crop is opium, Afghanistan reputedly being the world's second largest producer after Myanmar (Burma), and a major source of hashish.

The city of Kābol in Afghanistan, devastated by years of warfare.

Albania

Albania shares borders with Greece to the south-east and Macedonia to the east. Yugoslavia wraps around the northern part of the country. At its western edge it has a coastline 362 km (225 miles) long along the Adriatic Sea. For 500 years until 1912, when it became independent, Albania was part of the Ottoman Empire, and a large majority of the population is Muslim. In 1939 Albania was invaded by Italy. After the Second World War the country came into the Soviet sphere of influence. From 1946 until 1992 Albania was part of the Soviet bloc, although it often adopted policies independent of, and sometimes at odds with, the Moscow line. When the European communist system unraveled in the early 1990s Albania, in 1992, was the last country in Europe to abandon a communist regime.

Except for a narrow strip of plains along its coastline, Albania is hilly and mountainous. Most Albanian people eke out an existence through farming on the plains, which contain the only cultivable land. Even here, much of the country is marshy and difficult to access. Corn, wheat, barley, and fruits are among the main crops. Little is exported because transport methods are primitive. In most

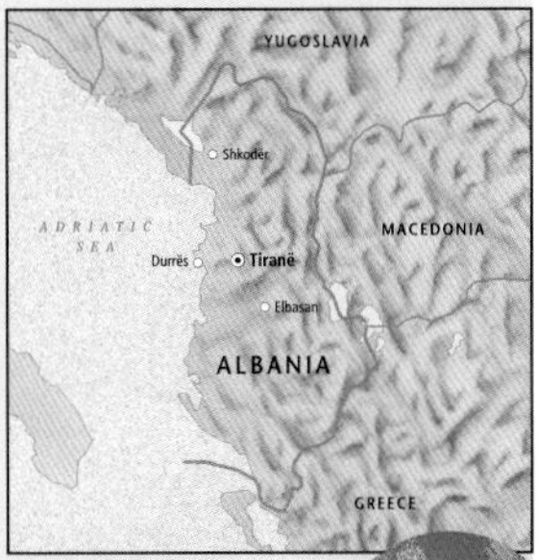

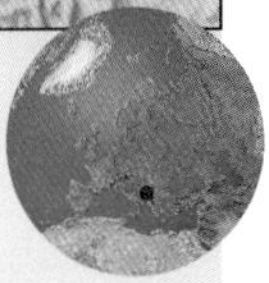

ALBANIA

OFFICIAL NAME Republic of Albania
FORM OF GOVERNMENT Republic with single legislative body (National Assembly)
CAPITAL Tiranë
AREA 28,750 sq km (11,100 sq miles)
TIME ZONE GMT + 1 hour
POPULATION 3,364,571

(continues)

A

ALBANIA *(continued)*

PROJECTED POPULATION 2005 3,591,121
POPULATION DENSITY 117 per sq km (303 per sq mile)
LIFE EXPECTANCY 69
INFANT MORTALITY (per 1,000) 42.9
OFFICIAL LANGUAGE Albanian
OTHER LANGUAGE Greek
LITERACY RATE 85%
RELIGIONS Muslim 70%, Albanian Orthodox 20%, Roman Catholic 10%
Ethnic groups Albanian 95%, Greek 3%, other 2%
CURRENCY Lek
Economy Agriculture 55%, industry 27%, services 18%
GNP PER CAPITA US$670
CLIMATE Mild temperate with cold, wet winters and warm, dry summers; colder in mountains
HIGHEST POINT Maja e Korabit 2,753 m (9,032 ft)
MAP REFERENCE Pages 780–81

areas people use horse- or mule-drawn vehicles. Mountains cover seven-tenths of the country. In the north are the Albanian Alps, and there are highlands in the center and south. Numerous rivers, notably the Drin in the north, and the Vijose in the south, flow to the coast from the highlands. Albania has significant reserves of natural resources such as petroleum, iron, and other mineral ores, plus natural gas, but most remain undeveloped.

The mountainous landscape makes land access difficult, and marshes restrict access to much of the coast. Rail links are few and there are no railway lines to neighboring countries. This has contributed to Albania's relative cultural and linguistic distinctness. Despite its conversion to free market ideals, Albania has failed to emerge from the cycle of poverty, continuing food shortages, and violence, fed to a large extent by the flood of refugees from the troubles in former Yugoslavia.

ALGERIA

OFFICIAL NAME Democratic and Popular Republic of Algeria
FORM OF GOVERNMENT Republic with single legislative body (National People's Assembly), but currently governed by military-backed council
CAPITAL Alger (Algiers)
AREA 2,381,740 sq km (919,590 sq miles)
TIME ZONE GMT
POPULATION 31,133,486

Algeria

The largest state in the north of Africa, Algeria was once a province of the Roman Empire known as Numidia, and since early times it has been the home of nomadic Berber peoples. Arabs came to the region during the seventh century, bringing Islam, and in the sixteenth century Algeria was incorporated into the Ottoman Empire. From the sixteenth to the nineteenth centuries Algeria posed a significant threat to all who used the nearby regions of the Mediterranean Sea. The pirates of what was at that time called the Barbary Coast made a lucrative living by trading in slaves and by attacking passing ships.

A French colony from 1848, Algeria won its independence in 1962 after eight years of bitter war. Then followed 30 years of peace, but since 1992 the country has been torn by violence once more. In a ruthless civil conflict between the government and an outlawed fundamentalist party, the Islamic Salvation Front (FIS), tens of thousands of people have died.

More than 90 percent of Algeria's people live on the narrow, fertile, discontinuous coastal strip on the Mediterranean. One-third of the population lives by farming, and it is here that most of the country's arable land is found—only 3 percent of the whole country. Inland,

and to the south, are the Maritime Atlas Mountains. Their northern slopes have a relatively reliable rainfall and support a shrinking forest of pines, cedars, and evergreen and cork oaks. A high plateau about 250 km (150 miles) wide lies between the coastal range and the Atlas Saharien Mountains. Beyond these, all the way to the boundaries of Mali and Niger, stretches the sandy, rocky waste of the Sahara Desert, dotted here and there with small oasis settlements.

As much as 85 percent of Algeria's land area is desert. In many parts of the country rain almost never falls and the summer heat is intense. Along the Mediterranean coast, however, while the summers are hot and dry the winters are wet. Wildlife on the inland plateaus includes wild boar and gazelle; in the desert there are small mammals such as the jerboa and the Saharan hare.

Oil and natural gas are the foundation of Algeria's economy and over the years revenue from these sources has encouraged a wide range of industrial development. From the late 1960s, the country's economy was run as a centrally controlled state system along Soviet lines. This began to change following 1989 with the introduction of market mechanisms. The farming region along the northern coast produces wheat, barley, oats, grapes, and olives, and supplies a wide variety of early fruit and vegetables to markets in Europe.

Projected population 2005 35,118,111
Population density 13.1 per sq km (33.9 per sq mile)
Life expectancy 69.2
Infant mortality (per 1,000) 43.8
Official language Arabic
Other languages French, Berber languages
Literacy rate 59.2%
Religions Sunni Muslim 99%, Christian and Jewish 1%
Ethnic groups Arab–Berber 99%, European 1%
Currency Algerian dinar
Economy Services 75%, agriculture 14%, industry 11%
GNP per capita US$1,600
Climate Mild temperate in north, with cool, wet winters and hot, dry summers; arid in south
Highest point Mt Tahat 2,918 m (9,573 ft)
Map reference Pages 800–801

The Algerian town of Ghardaïa lies at the eastern end of the Grand Erg Occidental, on the fringe of the Sahara Desert.

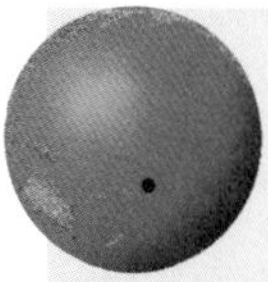

American Samoa

Official name Territory of American Samoa
Form of government Unincorporated and unorganized territory of the USA
Capital Pago Pago
Area 199 sq km (77 sq miles)
Time zone GMT – 11 hours
Population 66,475
Life expectancy 72.9
Infant mortality (per 1,000) 18.8
Literacy rate 97.3%
Currency US dollar
Economy Fishing 34%, government 33%, other 33%
Climate Tropical; wet season November to April
Map reference Pages 722, 727

American Samoa

A group of five volcanic islands and two atolls in the South Pacific, midway between Hawaii and New Zealand, American Samoa has been settled by Polynesian peoples since about 800 BC. The first European contact was made by the Dutch in 1722. British missionaries were active in the region from 1830. In 1872 the USA won exclusive rights from the High Chief to use Pago Pago as a strategic base for the American fleet. Pago Pago has one of the best natural deepwater harbors in the region, sheltered by surrounding mountains from rough seas and high winds. About 90 percent of American Samoa's trade is with the USA, which heavily subsidizes the economy. Tuna fishing, processing, and export are the foundation of private sector economic activity.

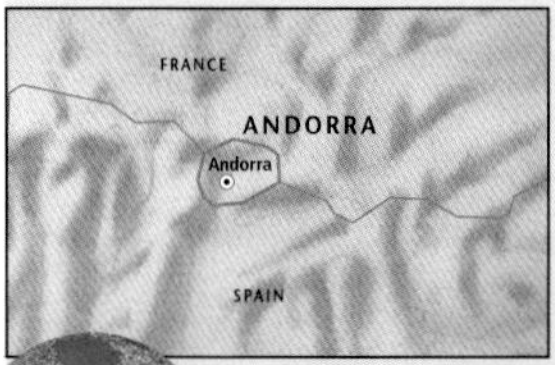

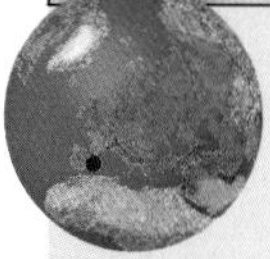

Andorra

Official name Principality of Andorra
Form of government Co-principality with single legislative body (General Council of the Valleys)
Capital Andorra la Vella
Area 450 sq km (174 sq miles)
Time zone GMT + 1 hour
Population 65,939
Projected population 2005 79,608

Andorra

The tiny landlocked principality of Andorra sits high in the Pyrenees, between France and Spain. From 1278 Andorra's government was shared between France and Spain. For 300 years it was jointly administered by the Bishop of Urgel in Spain and the Count of Foix in France. In the sixteenth century sovereignty passed to the French king and, after the French Revolution of 1789, to the French head of state. Today the Bishop of Urgel and the French president are official chiefs of state. Since 1993, however, when the first democratic elections were held, authority has been vested in a 28-member General Council of the Valleys. France and Spain are responsible for defence, and both have a representative on the General Council.

Andorra is mountainous with spectacular peaks. The country is snow-covered for six months in winter, but its summers are warm and dry. Two south-flowing branches of the River Valira—the Valira del Nord and the Valira d'Orient—flow through a series of valleys and gorges between ranges. They join in the center of the country and flow as one stream into Spain. The Valira is a major source of hydroelectric power.

About one in five in the population are citizens of Andorra: the rest are foreign residents, mainly French and Spanish. Almost two-thirds of the population live in the capital and the cities of Les Escaldes and Encamp. Tourism is the mainstay of the economy, and every year there are more than 12 million visitors, mainly skiers. Goods are duty-free in Andorra. This acts as a magnet to tourists and is vital to the economy, as is the sale of hydroelectricity to neighboring Catalonia. Banking services are significant, but there is little secondary industry, apart from cigarette and cigar making. As well as tobacco, some fruit, vegetables, and other crops are grown on the tiny amount of land that can be cultivated. Many of the village-dwellers are small farmers. Their sheep, cattle, and goats graze in the upland meadows during summer.

Population density 146.5 per sq km (375.6 per sq mile)
Life expectancy 83.5
Infant mortality (per 1,000) 4.1
Official language Catalan
Other languages French, Spanish
Literacy rate 99%
Religions Roman Catholic
Ethnic groups Spanish 61%, Andorran 30%, French 6%, other 3%
Currency French franc, Spanish peseta
Economy Tourism, financial services, tobacco production
GNP per capita Est. > US$9,386
Climate Temperate; snowy winter, warm summers
Highest point Coma Pedrosa 2,946 m (9,665 ft)
Map reference Page 777

Angola

A large country on Africa's southwest coast, Angola is bordered by the states of the Democratic Republic of the Congo to the north, Zambia to the east, and Namibia to the south. The small but resource-rich province of Cabinda lies separated from the rest of Angola to the north of the Congo River. A Portuguese colony since the sixteenth century, Angola was the source of an estimated 3 million slaves who were sent to Brazil and other places across the Atlantic, largely to work on sugar plantations. The country received its independence in 1975 and for the next 20 years was wracked by civil war. The government, having established a Marxist one-party state, was then challenged by the forces of Jonas Savimbi, who was backed by the USA. The truce between the two parties, which came into force in 1994, did not last for long. In the late 1990s violence escalated, verging on civil war.

Angola can be divided into two main regions. There are the relatively narrow coastal plains from which rise an extensive tableland that dominates the rest of the country. Divided roughly east to west across the center, this tableland drains into the Congo Basin to the north, and into the rivers of the Zambeze Basin to the south and east. While the tableland is fairly level in the south, the highlands become mountainous in central and southwestern Angola. In the province of Cabinda there are dense tropical rainforests, and heavy rains can be expected for seven

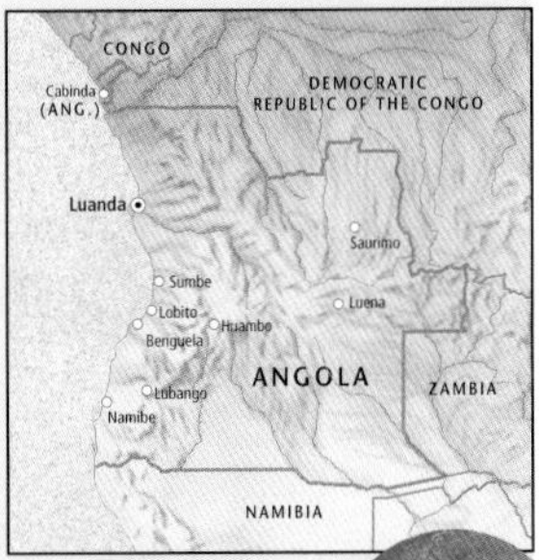

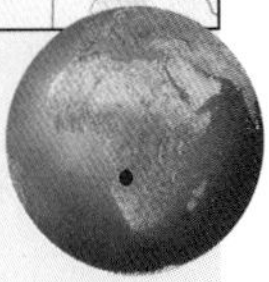

Angola

Official name Republic of Angola
Form of government Republic with single legislative body (National Assembly)
Capital Luanda
Area 1,246,700 sq km (481,351 sq miles)
Time zone GMT + 1 hour
Population 11,177,537
Projected population 2005 13,104,239
Population density 9 per sq km (23.3 per sq mile)
Life expectancy 48.4
Infant mortality (per 1,000) 129.2

(continues)

A

ANGOLA *(continued)*

OFFICIAL LANGUAGE Portuguese
OTHER LANGUAGES Bantu, other African languages
LITERACY RATE 42.5%
RELIGIONS Indigenous beliefs 47%, Roman Catholic 38%, Protestant 15%
ETHNIC GROUPS Mainly indigenous, including Ovimbundu 37%, Kimbundu 25%, Bakongo 13%; mixed European–African 2%, European 1%, other 22%
CURRENCY Kwanza
ECONOMY Agriculture 69%, services 21%, industry 10%
GNP PER CAPITA US$410
CLIMATE Mainly tropical with wet season November to April; semiarid in south and along coast
HIGHEST POINT Mt Môco 2,620 m (8,596 ft)
MAP REFERENCE Pages 808, 810

months of the year. Savanna woodland is found on much of the tableland, becoming mainly grassy plains to the south, dotted with acacia and baobab trees. The cold Benguela current that flows north from the southern Atlantic Ocean has a moderating effect on the heat of the coastal region. Toward Namibia on the southern border the coastal strip becomes desert.

Angola is rich in petroleum, gold, and diamonds, and has reserves of iron ore, phosphates, feldspar, bauxite, and uranium. It has large areas of forest, productive fisheries off the Atlantic coast, and extensive areas of arable land. While the country is capable of producing coffee, sisal, and cotton, the years of civil war have resulted in economic disarray and the country's output per capita is one of the lowest in the world. Subsistence agriculture supports up to 90 percent of the people and much of the nation's food has to be imported.

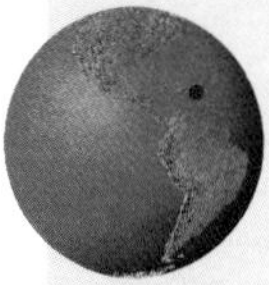

ANGUILLA

OFFICIAL NAME Anguilla
FORM OF GOVERNMENT Dependent territory of the United Kingdom
CAPITAL The Valley
AREA 91 sq km (35 sq miles)
TIME ZONE GMT – 4 hours
POPULATION 11,510
LIFE EXPECTANCY 77.7
INFANT MORTALITY (PER 1,000) 18.7
LITERACY RATE 80%
CURRENCY East Caribbean dollar
ECONOMY Services 65%, construction 18%, transportation and utilities 10%, manufacturing 3%, agriculture 4%
CLIMATE Tropical, moderated by trade winds
MAP REFERENCE Page 837

Anguilla

Anguilla's name comes from the Spanish *anguil* meaning "eel." The country is a long, thin, scrub-covered coral atoll in the Caribbean, north of St Kitts and Nevis. First colonized by Britain in 1690, its status as a dependent territory of the United Kingdom was formalized in 1980. While the governor is a crown appointee, a local assembly manages internal matters.

Anguilla has few natural resources and depends heavily on tourism, offshore banking, lobster fishing, and overseas remittances. The pleasant subtropical climate, which is tempered by trade winds, has attracted tourists and consequently tourism has multiplied in recent years, reflecting the generally healthy economic conditions in both the United States of America and the United Kingdom. As a result, annual growth has averaged about 7 percent. The offshore finance sector was strengthened by comprehensive legislation enacted in 1994.

Antarctica

The fifth largest continent, Antarctica is the coldest and most inhospitable, and differs in important respects from the polar regions of the northern hemisphere. Whereas the Arctic consists of a frozen sea surrounded by land masses, the Antarctic consists of a foundation of continental rock surmounted by a massive ice cap thousands of meters thick, separated from all other major land masses by the wild and stormy waters of the Southern Ocean. Again in contrast to the northern polar region, which was inhabited by hunting peoples within the Arctic Circle, Antarctica had never seen a human being before around 1800. Even today only about 1,000 people, all of them temporary visitors, live there during the long, severe Antarctic winter. Although a number of countries active in the exploration of the continent made territorial claims to parts of it, all such claims were indefinitely deferred after the signing of the Antarctic Treaty in December 1959.

Several factors make the climate uniquely harsh. Although Antarctica receives plenty of sunlight in

ANTARCTICA

AREA 14,000,000 sq km (5,405,400 sq miles)
POPULATION No permanent population
ECONOMY Research stations
CLIMATE Extremely cold and windy
MAP REFERENCE Page 862

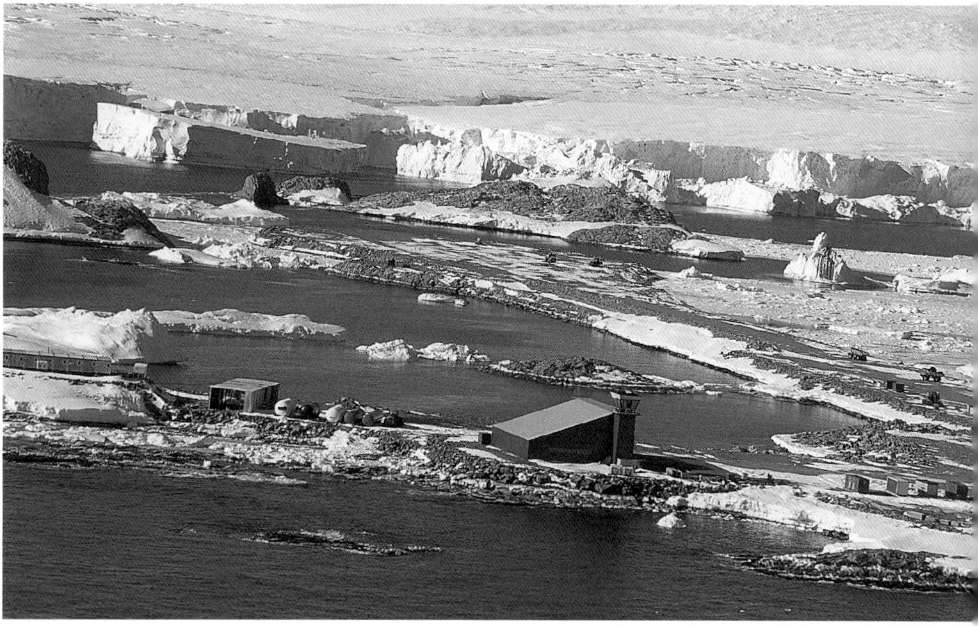

The French Antarctic research station at Dumont d'Urville, built in 1956.

A

midsummer, 80 percent of this radiation is reflected back by the permanent cover of snow. Altitude also plays a part: Antarctica has by far the greatest average elevation of any of the continents—2,300 m (7,500 ft)—which helps to produce the high winds prevailing over much of the region. Called katabatic (or downflowing) winds, these are gravity-driven, and consist of air pouring down at high speed from the elevated interior toward the coast. At one location the annual mean windspeed recorded was over 70 km/h (44 mph). Although some 90 percent of the world's fresh water is locked up in the ice cap (at places 4,800 m [15,700 ft] thick), Antarctica is also the world's driest continent, the very low temperatures limiting the moisture the air can hold. In fact only 120–150 mm (5–6 in) of water accumulates over the entire continent in the average year. Unique dry valleys, where the rock is exposed and rain has not fallen for about 2 million years, are the driest places in the world. Mummified animal carcases in these valleys have changed little in thousands of years.

The Transantarctic Mountains, which form a boundary between East and West Antarctica, are one of the world's great mountain chains, many peaks exceeding 4,000 m (13,000 ft). Geologically, East Antarctica consists mainly of an ancient continental shield with a history going back

New Zealand's Scott Base, in Antarctica.

3,000 million years. This was once part of the supercontinent known as Gondwana, from which Africa, South America, India, Australia, and New Zealand broke away. Many Antarctic rocks and fossils match up with those found in other southern continents, showing that the continents were once joined together. Ancient crystalline rocks of the shield are closely similar to those along the east coast of the Indian peninsula and Sri Lanka. Forming the base of the Transantarctic Mountains, and facing West Antarctica, is a belt of folded sediments 500 to 600 million years old.

It is a sedimentary formation dating from about 280 million years ago, however, that is most revealing. Up to 300 m (1,000 ft) thick, it is found in Australia, India, South Africa, and South America, as well as Antarctica. About 80 million years ago a series of earth movements accompanied extensive volcanic activity and it is thought that eruptions between 20 and 15 million years ago may be linked to the formation of the Transantarctic Mountains.

Plant life on the continent today consists almost entirely of mosses, lichens, and algae. Though soil mites and midges are able to survive, not a single land vertebrate can endure the winter. In contrast, life in the ocean is very rich, with a variety of seals and whales. Antarctica has five species of true or "earless" seals, including the predatory leopard seal, and both orcas and blue whales, the latter an ocean giant growing to a length of 30 m (100 ft). There are 43 species of bird, the best-known being the penguins. The Emperor Penguin, which breeds during the months of Antarctic darkness, is the only warm-blooded animal to remain on the continent during the bitter winter months. The most numerous birds are the Antarctic petrels, among which are the albatrosses.

The Antarctic Treaty of 1959 provides the legal framework for the management of Antarctica. This treaty superseded and indefinitely deferred the political partition of the continent among a number of separate nations. At present there are 42 treaty member nations, with 26 consultative nations and 16 acceding. Important Articles of the Treaty include No 1 (that the region is to be used for peaceful purposes only), No 2 (that freedom of scientific investigation and cooperation shall continue), and No 4 (that it does not recognize, dispute, or establish territorial claims, and that no new claims shall be asserted while the Treaty is in force). Agreed-to measures adopted at consultative meetings include several conventions on the conservation of Antarctic flora and fauna.

The Gerlache Strait on the western shore of the Antarctic Peninsula; this sheltered spot has allowed some ice to melt.

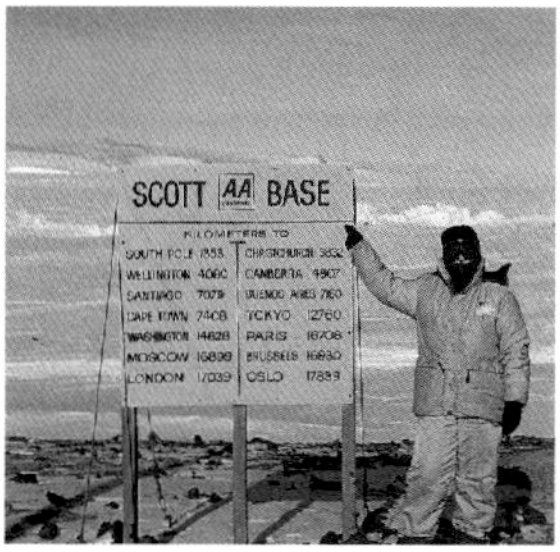

Scott Base, Antarctica.

A

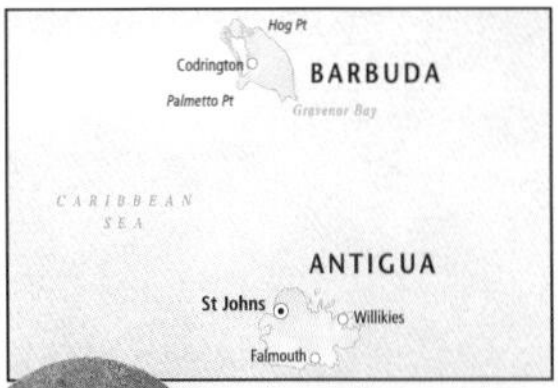

Antigua and Barbuda

Official name Antigua and Barbuda
Form of government Democracy with two legislative bodies (Senate and House of Representatives)
Capital St Johns
Area 440 sq km (170 sq miles)
Time zone GMT – 4 hours
Population 64,246
Projected population 2005 65,285
Population density 146 per sq km (378.1 per sq mile)
Life expectancy 71.5
Infant mortality (per 1,000) 20.7
Official language English
Other languages Indigenous languages
Literacy rate 96%
Religions Protestant 90%, Roman Catholic 10%
Ethnic groups African 94.5%, other 5.5%
Currency East Caribbean dollar
Economy Services 67%, industry 21%, agriculture 12%
GNP per capita US$7,290
Climate Tropical, moderated by sea breezes
Highest point Boggy Peak 405 m (1,328 ft)
Map reference Page 837

Antigua and Barbuda

Antigua and Barbuda consists of three islands in the eastern Caribbean. In 1493 the largest of the group was visited by Columbus, who named it Antigua. It became a British colony in 1667 and in the eighteenth century flourished under a plantation system using African slaves to produce sugar. Once populated by Arawak and Carib Indians, today the islands are peopled by Afro-Caribbean descendants of the plantation days. They are run by the Antiguan Labour Party and the Bird family, a combination that has held power almost constantly since 1956. Full independence was obtained in 1981.

Antigua rises to 405 m (1,328 ft) at Boggy Peak, a volcanic prominence in the southwest. Unlike the other Leeward Islands, to which it belongs, Antigua was denuded of forest long ago, and lacks both trees and rivers. In contrast, the flat coral-island game reserve of Barbuda, 40 km (25 miles) to the north, is fairly well wooded. Barbuda's one town is Codrington. The third island, Redonda, is an uninhabited islet southwest of Antigua. The tropical climate and palm-fringed beaches make Antigua and Barbuda an attractive tourist location. There is, however, little fresh water, and the region is hurricane-prone, with one in 1995 causing much damage.

Since the sugar industry closed in 1971 the islands have relied almost entirely on tourism, with some income from two US military bases on Antigua. The Bird family's hold on power, allegations of corruption and a high level of external debt, are causes for concern.

Nelson's Harbour in Antigua.

Argentina

With its northern extremity just north of the Tropic of Capricorn, but lying mainly within the temperate zone, Argentina becomes narrower and colder as it tapers south to Tierra del Fuego. The largest Spanish-speaking country of Latin America, it is named for the silver deposits that were sought by early explorers (Argentina means "land of silver"). In the nineteenth century Argentina attracted many Spanish and Italian immigrants in search of a better life, and today it contrasts with some of its neighbors in having a population that is mainly middle-class, with cosmopolitan interests, and strongly European in background and culture. Most Argentinians are of Spanish and Italian descent, but there are also people of German, Russian, French, and English background, as well as a Jewish community in Buenos Aires and a Welsh community in Patagonia.

Argentina's politics have been much influenced by the legacy of Colonel Juan Domingo Perón. A major force in Argentine politics from 1946 to 1976, "Perónism" was a mild form of fascism which combined military rule and statist economic policy with progressive labor legislation. After Perón's death in 1974, he was succeeded by his widow. The government was ousted by a military coup in 1976. A 3-man junta was then installed. Under this government thousands of people "disappeared" in a violent campaign against left-wing elements. Their fate is a vexatious issue for President Menem's more moderate government.

Physical features and land use

There are four main regions. In the north lie the subtropical woodlands and swamps of the Gran Chaco, a zone that spills over the northeastern border into Paraguay. Swampy in parts, dry in others, and covered with thorny scrub, the Chaco is known as "Green Hell." To the west are the wooded slopes and valleys of the Andes; in the far south is the cold, semiarid Patagonian Plateau. It was the temperate region to the west and south of Buenos Aires that made Argentina famous. Here are the plains of the pampas—moist and fertile near the capital, drier but still productive elsewhere. These grasslands, where the gauchos (part Indian, part Spanish cattleherders) once lived and worked, are the basis of Argentina's cattle industry.

The pampas was largely created by gravel and sand brought down by streams from the Andes. A large native

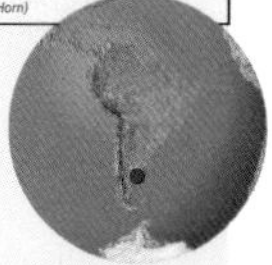

ARGENTINA

Official name Argentine Republic
Form of government Federal republic with two legislative bodies (Senate and Chamber of Deputies)
Capital Buenos Aires
Area 2,766,890 sq km (1,068,296 sq miles)
Time zone GMT – 3 hours
Population 36,737,664
Projected population 2005 39,625,870
Population density 13.3 per sq km (34.4 per sq mile)
Life expectancy 74.8
Infant mortality (per 1,000) 18.4
Official language Spanish
Other languages English, Italian, German, French
Literacy rate 96%
Religions Roman Catholic 90%, Protestant 2%, Jewish 2%, other 6%
Ethnic groups European 85%, indigenous, mixed indigenous–European, other 15%
Currency Argentine peso
Economy Services 53%, industry 34%, agriculture 13%
GNP per capita US$8,030
Climate Mainly temperate; subtropical in northern Chaco, cold and arid in Patagonia; snow on Andes
Highest point Aconcagua 6,960 m (22,834 ft)
Map reference Pages 856–57, 858

clump-grass called pampas grass, with coarse gray blades and silvery plumes, provided stock feed when the Spanish settlers arrived. They brought horses and cattle, and began to fence off the more productive land for ranching and cultivation. While beef raising is still important, much of the fertile parts of the pampas are now used for growing wheat, maize, alfalfa, and flax.

Argentina has many lakes on the slopes of the Andes, and the alpine terrain attracts tourists and skiers from elsewhere in South America. The Andes are widely affected by volcanic activity and there are several active volcanoes along the border with Chile, as well as Aconcagua, the highest mountain outside the Himalayas. The huge Paraguay–Paraná–Uruguay River system, the second-largest on the continent, drains south from the Chaco and west from the highlands of Uruguay before emptying into the estuary of the River Plate (Río de la Plata). The three cities located here, two of them national capitals (the ports of Buenos Aires and Montevideo), mark the historic importance of this estuary.

Autumn colors in Tierra del Fuego.

A

People and culture

Hunters and fishermen occupied the Argentine region from 12,000 years ago, and in recent times the Yahgan and Ona people made their home in Tierra del Fuego, despite its bitter climate. In the sixteenth century Spanish settlers began moving into Argentina from Peru, Chile, and Paraguay, and in the nineteenth century a ferocious war cleared the pampas of its remaining Indians.

Today, more than one-third of the population is descended from Italian immigrants. Argentinians are overwhelmingly urban: 88 percent live in towns and cities, with 40 percent in Buenos Aires itself (an urban agglomeration of over 11 million). The European orientation of cultural life is reflected in their art, music, and literature.

Buenos Aires, a national capital city of Argentina.

Economy and resources

Although the rural sector remains important, today industry makes a major contribution to the economy. Roughly one-fifth of the workforce is in manufacturing, mainly in industries producing frozen meat, canned meat,

The Moreno Glacier in Argentina.

A

tallow, and leather for export. Wheat and fruit are also major exports. Energy available for industry includes nuclear power, hydroelectric power, and petroleum. There are oilfields in Patagonia and in the Mendoza area near the Andes, directly west of Buenos Aires.

Argentina has varied mineral resources—lead, zinc, tin, copper, silver, and uranium. It has a well-educated workforce and a diversified industrial base. Buenos Aires has a thriving computer industry. Episodes of hyperinflation have shaken investor confidence but increased political stability and reduced inflation in recent years are again attracting overseas investment. Reforms introduced by President Menem have seen a general restructuring, and there are signs that the economy has begun a period of stable and sustained growth.

Timeline Argentina

12,000 BP Small human communities live by hunting and fishing in territory now known as Argentina

AD 600 Northwest settled by communities with complex social organizations—some have 10,000 to 20,000 members

900 Native populations living in Andes in small-scale communities; culture has total population of 250,000–500,000

1516 Spanish explorer Juan Díaz de Solís, first European to land on what is now Argentine soil; killed by Querandi people

1553 Permanent settlements established in northwest by Spanish arriving from Peru in search of gold and silver

1573 Towns of Córdoba and Mendoza develop on trade routes between Chile and Argentina

1580 Spanish colonists establish settlement of Buenos Aires on La Plata Estuary

1816 Argentina declares independence from Spain

1830 Argentina lays claim to Islas Malvinas (the Falkland Islands), which were then occupied by Great Britain in 1833

1866 San Roque Dam built on the Primero River providing irrigation and hydroelectric power

1876 Exports of meat and grain to Europe grow rapidly following introduction of refrigerated shipping

1910 Large numbers of European migrants arrive to farm and work on estates in the southern Pampas region

1914 First World War followed by export-led boom in agricultural produce; Argentine population reaches 8 million

1944 Earthquake kills 5,000 people in San Juan province in the Andes

1946 Colonel Juan Perón is elected President and later assumes the powers of a dictator

1955 Perón dismissed in military coup; he flees the country with his first wife, Eva

1973–74 Perón returns, is re-elected, dies; his third wife, "Isabelita", governs until arrested in a coup in 1976 in which thousands die

1982 Argentina invades Falklands after talks with Britain over sovereignty break down—Britain retakes the islands

1990 Full diplomatic relations with Britain are restored

1994 Paraguay and Argentina jointly build Corpus Posados Dam on the Pananá River to create hydroelectric power

Armenia

Armenia is a small, mountainous, Christian country, landlocked between hostile Muslim neighbors. To the east is Azerbaijan, and to the west is Turkey, which inflicted genocidal massacres on the Armenian people between 1894 and 1915. The legendary resting place of Noah's Ark after the Flood (its capital supposedly founded by Noah himself), Armenia had already existed as a distinct country for 1,000 years when, in the fourth century AD, it became the first in the world to make Christianity its state religion. The country has been fought over at various times by Romans, Persians, and Mongols. It became a Soviet Socialist Republic in 1922 and gained its independence from the Soviet Union in 1991.

In 1988 there was a devastating earthquake which killed 25,000 people and destroyed power stations and other infrastructure and in the same year conflict began over Nagorno-Karabakh, an internal Azerbaijani area largely populated by Christian Armenians, which is claimed by Armenia. The conflict continued into the 1990s. In 1998 the OSCE Minsk Group developed draft proposals for the resolution of the conflict; however, political unrest and international pressures continue, and the issue is not yet peacefully resolved.

The mountains of the Lesser Caucasus (Malyy Kavkaz) cover most of the country. The landscape is rugged, and includes extinct volcanoes and high lava plateaus cut with ravines. An active seismic area, the frequency of earthquakes in Armenia indicates that mountain-building is still taking place. Although the city of Ararat is in Armenia, Mt Ararat itself is across the border in Turkey. The centrally located Lake Sevan (Sevana Lich) lies nearly 2,000 m (6,000 ft) above sea level, but its use for hydropower has drained it to a point where drinking water supplies are threatened. Steppe vegetation is the main cover and drought-resistant grasses and sagebrush grow on the lower mountain slopes, where jackals, wildcats, and the occasional leopard are found.

As a Soviet Republic, Armenia developed an industrial sector, supplying machine building tools, textiles, and other manufactured goods to other republics in return for raw materials and energy. It has few natural resources, although formerly lead, copper, and zinc were mined, and there are deposits of gold and bauxite. Agriculture is an important source of income. In irrigated areas around

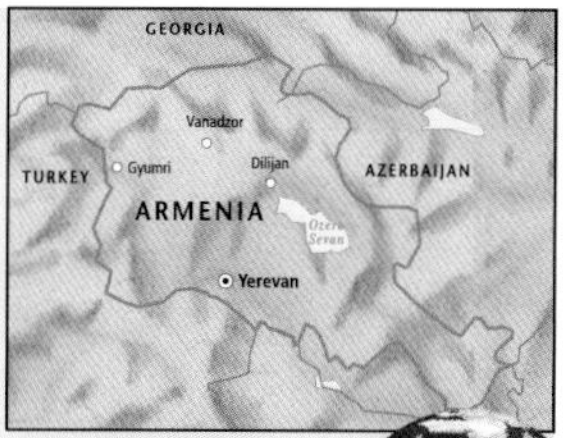

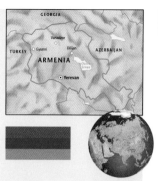

Armenia

Official name Republic of Armenia
Form of government Republic with single legislative body (National Assembly)
Capital Yerevan
Area 29,800 sq km (11,506 sq miles)
Time zone GMT + 4 hours
Population 3,409,234
Projected population 2005 3,351,982
Population density 114.4 per sq km (296.2 per sq mile)
Life expectancy 66.6
Infant mortality (per 1,000) 41.1
Official language Armenian
Other language Russian
Literacy rate 98.8%
Religions Armenian Orthodox 94%, other (Russian Orthodox, Muslim, Protestant) 6%
Ethnic groups Armenian 93%, Azeri 3%, Russian 2%, other (mainly Kurdish) 2%
Currency Dram
Economy Industry 28%, agriculture 27%, services 26%, other 19%
GNP per capita US$730
Climate Mainly dry, with cold winters and warm summers; cooler in mountains
Highest point Aragats Lerr 4,090 m (13,419 ft)
Map reference Page 758

View over the city of Yerevan in Armenia, with Mt Ararat in the background.

Yerevan, crops include grapes, almonds, figs, and olives, while apples, pears, and cereals are grown on higher ground. Armenia is also known for its quality brandies and wines. Economic decline in the period 1991 to 1994 was a direct result of the ongoing conflict over Nagorno-Karabakh. In retaliation for Armenia's military activities in the region, Turkey and Azerbaijan blockaded pipeline and railroad traffic into the country, causing chronic energy shortages. There have been improvements, but full economic recovery is unlikely before Armenia's conflict with its neighbors is settled. In 1999, foreign debt exceeded $740 million with imports 3.5 times higher than exports. The elections held in mid 1999 held the prospect of change, after General Motors (USA) announced a decision to manufacture in Armenia. However, calls to dissolve the parliament over political killings, libel and other charges have increased the tensions within the country. Human rights abuses are being examined, with military prison officials accused of beating prisoners, allowing poor conditions and detaining inmates without sentence. Several peacetime deaths caused international concerns over the abuses. Political party infighting is ongoing. This, and assassination attempts on key parliamentary members, has contributed to the instability of the economic situation, which is likely to remain unstable whilst the unemployment rate is 50% despite a rising Gross Domestic Product.

Aruba

Aruba is most unusual among the islands of the Caribbean in that it has a 1 percent unemployment rate, numerous employment vacancies, and a high gross domestic product. A flat, limestone island lying off the Venezuelan coast at the mouth of the Gulf of Venezuela, Aruba is barren on its eastern side and more lush on the west. It was once a part of the Netherlands Antilles, but is now a separate but autonomous part of the Dutch realm. The population is mainly of African, European, and Asian descent.

Closed in 1985, the oil refinery on the island was reopened in 1993. This is a major source of employment and foreign exchange earnings and has greatly spurred economic growth. Tourism is extensive on the western side of the island, known as the Turquoise Coast, and its rapid development has seen an expansion of other activities.

Chapel of the Alto Vista, on the eastern side of Aruba.

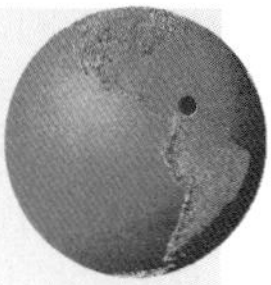

Aruba

Official name Aruba
Form of government Self-governing part of the Kingdom of the Netherlands
Capital Oranjestad
Area 193 sq km (74 sq miles)
Time zone GMT – 4 hours
Population 68,675
Life expectancy 77
Infant mortality (per 1,000) 7.8
Literacy rate Not available
Currency Aruban florin
Economy Tourism, financial services
Climate Tropical
Map reference Page 837

Ashmore and Cartier Islands

These uninhabited islands in the Indian Ocean northwest of Australia, Ashmore and Cartier Islands are at no point higher than 3 m (10 ft) above sea level. The terrain consists of sand and coral.

Despite the mild tropical climate, there is no development of tourism. The islands are surrounded by reefs and shoals that can pose a maritime hazard. The Australian government monitors the state of the Ashmore Reef National Nature Reserve. The Royal Australian Navy and Air Force make visits from time to time.

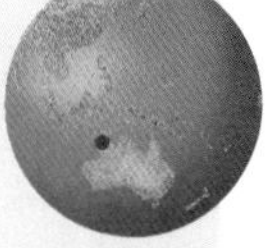

Ashmore and Cartier Islands

Official name Territory of Ashmore and Cartier Islands
Form of government External territory of Australia
Capital None; administered from Canberra
Area 5 sq km (2 sq miles)
Time zone GMT + 8 hours
Population No permanent population
Climate Tropical
Map reference Page 720

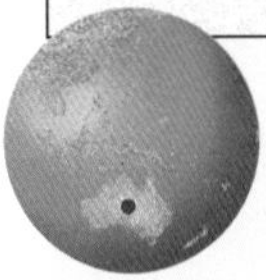

AUSTRALIA

OFFICIAL NAME Commonwealth of Australia
FORM OF GOVERNMENT Federal constitutional monarchy with two legislative bodies (Senate and House of Representatives)
CAPITAL Canberra
Area 7,686,850 sq km (2,967,893 sq miles)
TIME ZONE GMT + 10 hours
POPULATION 18,783,551
PROJECTED POPULATION 2005 19,728,533
POPULATION DENSITY 2.44 per sq km (6.3 per sq mile)
LIFE EXPECTANCY 80.1
INFANT MORTALITY (PER 1,000) 5.1
OFFICIAL LANGUAGE English
OTHER LANGUAGES Indigenous languages, Italian, Greek
LITERACY RATE 99%
RELIGIONS Roman Catholic 27%, Anglican 22%, other Christian 22%, other 12.4%, none 16.6%
ETHNIC GROUPS European 95%, Asian 4%, other (including Aboriginals) 1%
CURRENCY Australian dollar
ECONOMY Services 78%, industry 16%, agriculture 6%
GNP PER CAPITA US$18,720
CLIMATE Hot and arid in center; tropical in north with one wet season (November to March); temperate in southeast and along southern coasts
HIGHEST POINT Mt Kosciuszko 2,229 m (7,313 ft)
MAP REFERENCE Pages 720–21

Australia

Ancient yet young, isolated yet connected, Australia is a nation continent gaining in confidence. It is one of the most stable, yet culturally diverse, nations in the world with a good record of economic growth, political stability and social harmony, sometimes termed a 'lucky country'. Australia has, over the past two centuries, demonstrated remarkable resilience to those forces of change that could all too easily have disrupted its development, such as poor resource management by early migrants, land and water limitations and degradation, the threat of a population explosion, and rapidly changing conditions for Australia's market economy. However, in the twenty-first century innovative solutions are still needed to overcome remaining problems in areas such as exploitation of natural resources, the economic dichotemy between urban and rural areas, sustainable management of land and water resources, and reconciliation with its indigenous inhabitants, the Aboriginal peoples.

Geographically, Australia is both the world's smallest continental landmass and the sixth-largest country. Most of it consists of low plateaus, and almost one-third is desert. The Western Plateau region constitutes the western half of the Australian continent. Made of ancient rocks, the plateau rises near the west coast—the iron-rich Hamersley Range representing its highest elevation in the northwest—and then falls eastward toward the center of the continent. The arid landscape alternates between worn-down ridges and plains, and depressions containing sandy deserts and salt lakes. There is little surface water. The

Evidence of Aboriginal occupation at Lake Mungo in New South Wales dates back almost 40,000 years.

flatness of the plateau is interrupted by the MacDonnell and Musgrave ranges in the center of the continent and the Kimberley and Arnhem Land plateaus in the north. Sheep and cattle are raised on large holdings in parts of this western region.

The Central Lowlands forming the Great Artesian Basin, and river systems including the Carpentaria, Eyre, and Murray basins, constitute a nearly continuous expanse of lowland that runs north to south. The river systems feed into Lake Eyre, the Bulloo system, or the Darling River. While the Murray Basin is the smallest of the three, its rivers—the Murray and its tributary the Darling—are Australia's longest and most important. Artesian bores make cattle and sheep raising possible through much of the semiarid Central Lowlands region.

The Eastern Highlands (known as the Great Dividing Range) and the relatively narrow eastern coastal plain constitute Australia's third main geographic region. This has the greatest relief, the heaviest rainfall, the most

STATES

New South Wales • Sydney
Queensland • Brisbane
South Australia • Adelaide
Tasmania • Hobart
Victoria • Melbourne
Western Australia • Perth

TERRITORIES

Australian Capital Territory • Canberra
Northern Territory • Darwin

OVERSEAS TERRITORIES

Ashmore and Cartier Islands
Christmas Island
Cocos (Keeling) Island
Coral Sea Islands
Heard and McDonald Islands
Norfolk Island

Finke Gorge National Park in the Northern Territory.

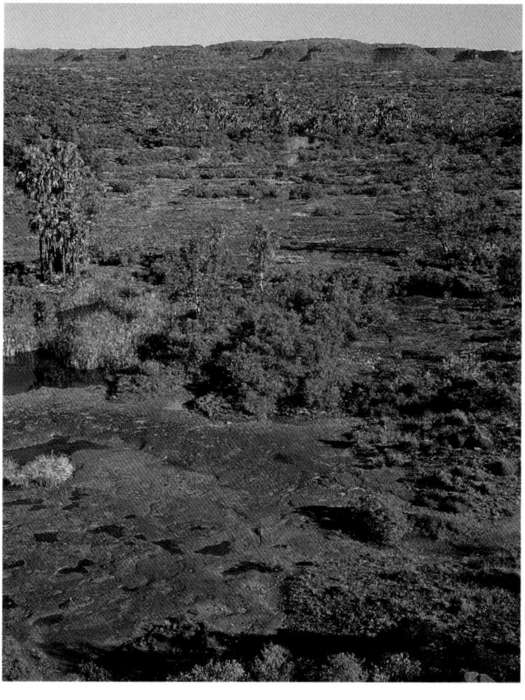

The Sydney Harbour Bridge.

The original inhabitants of Australia, Aboriginal peoples, have fostered deep links with the land that has supported them for thousands of years. Australia's fauna and flora, including eucalypt trees and ferns contribute to the country's unique natural environment.

Australia's vastness is highlighted by the distances shown on this street sign in the Northern Territory.

abundant and varied vegetation, and the densest human settlement. A notable feature of the eastern marine environment is the Great Barrier Reef. The world's biggest coral reef complex, it lies off the northeast coast, stretching some 2,500 km (1,550 miles) from the Tropic of Capricorn to Papua New Guinea. A major tourist attraction, with over 400 types of coral and 1,500 species of fish, it is now protected as the Great Barrier Reef Marine Park.

The island of Tasmania, to the southeast of mainland Australia, has spectacular mountain wilderness areas and more than 30 percent of the state is protected World Heritage areas, national parks, and reserves.

Prehistorians agree that the first human beings to inhabit Australia were migrants to the continent, as independent human evolution is ruled out by the absence of any primates from which a human species could have

Coastline from the area of The Twelve Apostles, Port Campbell National Park, Victoria.

An important financial center, Melbourne provides an Australian base for numerous transnational corporations.

Eucalypt trees are the food and homes of the native koala.

The bizarre-looking, spine-encrusted lizard known as the thorny devil can absorb moisture through its skin and has channels in its scales that direct water to its mouth.

developed. It was first occupied about 40,000 to 50,000 years ago by peoples from Southeast Asia (the ancestors of today's Aboriginals). The early migrants would have required watercraft to cross sea passages as a complete land connection between Asia and Australia has not existed for several million years. They were hunters, gatherers and fishers. They tended to move from place to place, thereby taking advantage of seasonal increases in resources.

With roots reaching back so far, Aboriginal communities have indisputable claim to the status of being the first Australians. It has been estimated that at the time of European settlement the Aboriginal population was in the vicinity of three-quarters of a million. This included some 700 different communities, speaking more than 200 distinct languages and many more dialects. In recent years, appreciation has grown for both the ancient origins of Aboriginal society and the diversity, complexity and dynamism of Aboriginal culture.

The traditional Aboriginal economy, which is still adhered to by some communities, is based on hunting, gathering, and where possible fishing. Early Aboriginal peoples developed knowledge, techniques and technologies to exploit effectively the broad range of environmental niches found across Australia. Aboriginal society was

A

organised to manage and utilize seasonal variations in water and food resources. Ceremonial gatherings often centred on seasons of plenty. The traditional economic system provided an efficient means of securing daily subsistence, leaving time for leisure, and spiritual and cultural activities.

The discovery of Australia by Europeans marked a turning point in the flow of Aboriginal life. Failing to appreciate the sophistication of Aboriginal political and social organization, the newcomers perceived the indigenous people as primitive. The absence of permanent dwellings, agricultural practices, and other land development was used by whites to argue that Australia was *terra nullius*—the land of no one. The ensuing European settlement of the country was to have a devastating impact on Aboriginal people by introducing diseases, frontier violence and dispossession of land.

In these days of cheap and efficient international air services, overseas travel on ocean liners such as the QE2 is now the preserve of those with an abundance of funds and time.

Australia was visited by Dutch explorers in the seventeenth century, including Abel Tasman in 1642 and 1644, and by the Englishman William Dampier in 1688

and 1699. After being claimed for Britain by Captain James Cook in 1770, a penal colony was established by the British in what is now Sydney in 1788. The First Fleet, consisting of 11 vessels carrying a total of 1,475 passengers including 722 convicts, made landfall in what was to become known as Sydney Cove in January 1788. The first years of the colony were a tough battle for survival. Conventional European farming methods were found to be inappropriate in the new environment, and the growing colony struggled to support itself. Some 160,000 convicts arrived before "transportation" from Britain was phased out in the nineteenth century. By then many free settlers had also arrived, and the gold rushes of the 1850s attracted still more people. Within two decades of the discovery of gold in New South Wales in 1851, the population increased from 437,000 to 1.7 million, and associated demand for food and manufactured goods greatly stimulated economic development. With both wool and wheat exports providing economic security, the settler population sought greater independence from Britain, and a measure of self-government was granted in 1850.

In 1901 the six states formed themselves into the Commonwealth of Australia. Slowly, a sense of nationhood was engendered, most notably by external wars. More than 16,000 Australians fought under British command in the Boer War (1899–1902), and over 500 volunteers helped counter the Boxer Rebellion in China (1900–1901). During the First World War, Australians served in New

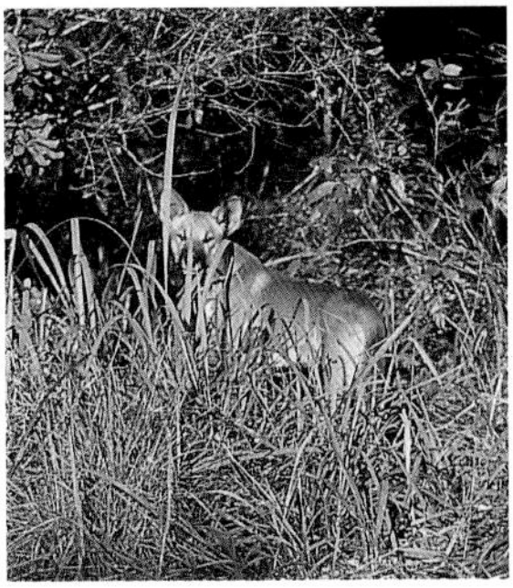

The dingo was introduced from Asia by seafarers about 4,000 years ago. Its arrival led to the demise of mainland populations of the Tasmanian tiger and the Tasmanian devil. These species were able to live on in Tasmania only because it was cut off from the mainland by rising seas about 10,000 years ago.

More than half of Australia's land is used for grazing cattle and sheep.

In just over 200 years, Sydney has developed from an isolated penal colony into a vibrant city with more than 3 million inhabitants.

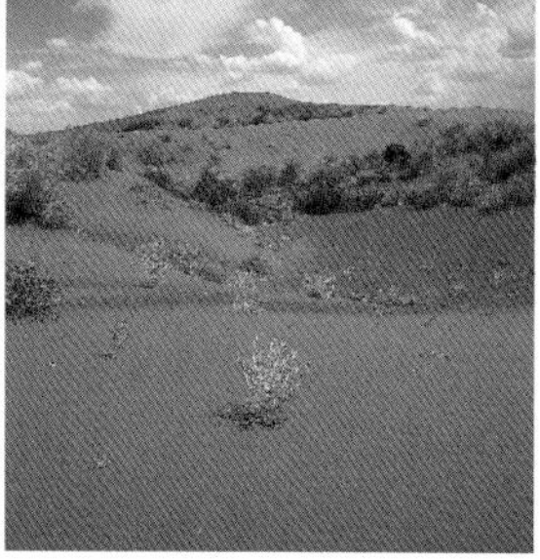

Hummock grasses, more commonly known as spinifex, thrive in arid and semiarid regions of Australia.

Guinea, the Pacific and Indians Oceans, Turkey and the Middle East, and France. The disastrous but heroic landings at Gallipoli in 1915 consolidated the Australians' reputation for courage, in turn boosting national pride at home. Almost 1 million Australians enlisted in the armed forces during the Second World War (1939–1945). They served in Europe, the Middle East, North Africa, the Pacific and at home, where they and their fellow citizens faced the threat of a Japanese invasion. A total of 37,500 Australians lost their lives during this war, and about 60,000 were wounded. In May, 1965, the Federal Government's decision to send 800 Australian troops to the Vietnam conflict provoked hostile reaction from the Opposition, and sparked a heated debate nationwide.

Despite the turmoil created by the country's involvement in external wars, in the 100 years since federation the country has become a successful, prosperous modern democracy. Current concerns include the consequences of economic dependence on Asian markets at a time of recession, demands for the frank acknowledgment of the history of Aboriginal displacement and dispossession, and whether or not there should be a republican government.

Australian plant and animal life is distinctive. The most common trees are the gums (*Eucalyptus*) and wattles (*Acacia*). Highly adaptable, *Eucalyptus* varieties range from the tall flooded gum, found on rainforest fringes, to the mallee which grows on dry plains. Most native mammals are marsupials, and include kangaroos, koalas, wombats, and possums. Australia's monotremes—the platypus and the echidna—which lay eggs and suckle their young, are unique. There are also about 400 species of reptile and some 700 species of bird. Australia's vulnerability to introduced plant and animal species was dramatically shown by the spread of prickly pear, which took over vast areas of rural New South Wales and Queensland in the 1920s, and the plagues of rabbits that devastated pastures for a century until the 1960s. Both scourges have been tamed by biological controls.

Once heavily dependent on the pastoral industry—nearly one-third of Australia is still used for grazing sheep—the nation's economy is now diversified, with an important manufacturing sector. Australia is rich in mineral resources, the leading export earners being iron ore from Western Australia and coking coal from Queensland and New South Wales, while bauxite is mined

Australia's fauna and flora, including eucalypt trees and ferns, contribute to the country's unique natural environment.

The 1988 bicentenary was marked by the unveiling of a new Parliament House.

A

Australia's wine producers generate over $900 million export revenue each year.

in the Northern Territory and Queensland. In recent years Australia has produced more than one-third of the world's diamonds, 14 percent of its lead, and 11 percent of its uranium and zinc.

Because commodities account for more than 80 percent of exports, falling commodity prices have severe economic effects: an apparently irreversible decline in world demand for wool has cast a shadow over the pastoral industry. The government has been encouraging increased exports of manufactured goods—cars are being exported to the Gulf States—but international competition is intense. The 1998 Asian economic downturn affected the tourist industry, which was the largest single foreign exchange earner, with 12.8 percent of the total.

Timeline Australia

c.40,000 BP First Australians arrive in log canoes or sail boats from southeast Asia

c.25,000 BP Earliest evidence of cremation, Lake Mungo, New South Wales

c.15,000 BP Rock art paintings created in shelters and caves of northwest Australia

c.13,000 BP People of robust appearance with thick skulls and large jaws living at Kow Swamp, Murray Valley, Victoria

c.6–5000 BC Dingoes brought to Australia, probably domesticated dogs belonging to people migrating from southeast Asia

1606 Dutch navigator Willem Jansz, first European to set foot in Australia, lands on Cape York Peninsula

1642 Dutch navigator Abel Tasman lands in Van Diemen's Land (now Tasmania), taking possession for Holland

1770 James Cook explores the east coast of Australia and the New Zealand islands, claiming both for Great Britain

1788 First Fleet under Captain Arthur Phillip arrives; penal colony set up in Port Jackson. Aboriginal population c.750,000

1813 First European crossing of the Blue Mountains, west of Sydney, opens up inland plains to pastoralists

1829 Charles Sturt explores the Darling River system and later travels inland to disprove the myth of an inland sea

1851 Gold discoveries first in New South Wales and then Victoria; gold rushes generate wealth and population increase

1855–56 Augustus Charles Gregory makes first west-to-east land crossing of the continent

1868 Transportation of convicts abolished; last ship lands in Fremantle, WA

1914–18 Australia sends 416,809 troops to fight in First World War; 53,993 killed in battle and 155,133 wounded

1919 More than 6,000 people die in the worst influenza epidemic in New South Wales history

1933 Aboriginal population reduced to 66,000 as a result of suppression and disease

1939 Australia's involvement in Second World War dominated by entry of Japanese after Pearl Harbor

1949 Construction of Snowy Mountains hydroelectric scheme, Australia's largest (completed 1972)

1967 Referendum accords citizenship to Aboriginal people for the first time by a vote of 90.8 percent of the population

1974 Cyclone Tracy destroys most of Darwin, Northern Territory

1991–92 Severe drought associated with El Niño climate pattern affects eastern Australia

1992 High Court ruling (*Mabo*) that Australia was not "empty" when Europeans arrived allows native title claims to proceed

2000 Council for Aboriginal Reconciliation delivers a document of reconciliation to the Howard Government.

Austria

The present borders of this landlocked central European country date back to the Treaty of Versailles of 1919, which presided over the dismantling of the Austro-Hungarian Empire. Germany lies directly to the north of Austria's narrow western boundary, Switzerland and Liechtenstein to its west, and Italy to its south. At its wider eastern end Slovenia lies to the south, Hungary and Slovakia to the east, and the Czech Republic to the north.

Austria's history for most of the last millennium is bound up with the fortunes of the Hapsburg family who ruled it, and at times much of Europe, from 1278 until the First World War. Roman conquest of most of present-day Austria was followed in the fourth and fifth centuries AD by invasions by Germanic and Celtic tribes and by the Franks under Charlemagne during the eighth century. The land fell to the King of Bohemia in 1252, only to be wrested from him by Rudolf of Hapsburg 26 years later. Rudolf named himself Archduke and declared the title hereditary.

From then until the sixteenth century the Hapsburg Empire expanded until it dominated much of Europe, including Spain (as well as its American colonies), part of Italy, the Netherlands, and Burgundy. During the sixteenth century Hungary and Bohemia came under Hapsburg rule and a Turkish siege of Vienna was repulsed. Catholic Austria's forced capitulation to German Protestantism at the end of the Thirty Years War saw Austria take second place to France as the leading European power. However, it remained a significant force with dominion over much of Europe, despite its loss of control over Spain in the early eighteenth century, a debilitating War of Succession between 1740 and 1748, and defeat by Prussian forces in 1763.

Napoleon's victory at the Battle of Austerlitz was a low point for Austria, but on Napoleon's defeat in 1814 Austria emerged as leader of a new German Confederation. Following the Austro-Prussian War of 1866, Austria and Hungary were combined under Hapsburg rule to form the Austro-Hungarian Empire. The Austrian annexation of Bosnia and Herzegovina in 1908 created the circumstances which culminated in the assassination of the heir to the Austro-Hungarian throne in Sarajevo in 1914 and the outbreak of the First World War. When the empire ended after the war, the Hapsburgs were expelled and Austria became a republic bounded by its present borders.

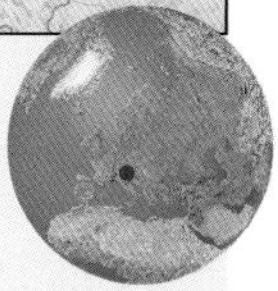

AUSTRIA

Official name Republic of Austria
Form of government Federal republic with two legislative bodies (Federal Council and National Council)
Capital Vienna
Area 83,850 sq km (32,374 sq miles)
Time zone GMT + 1 hour
Population 8,139,299
Projected population 2005 8,194,253
Population density 97.1 per sq km (251.4 per sq mile)
Life expectancy 77.5
Infant mortality (per 1,000) 5.1
Official language German
Literacy rate 99%
Religions Roman Catholic 85%, Protestant 6%, other 9%
Ethnic groups German 99.4%, Croatian 0.3%, Slovene 0.2%, other 0.1%
Currency Schilling
Economy Services 64%, industry 28%, agriculture 8%
GNP per capita US$26,890
Climate Temperate with cold winters and mild to warm summers; colder in mountains
Highest point Grossglockner 3,797 m (12,457 ft)
Map reference Page 778

A

Village in the Austrian Tyrol.

Annexed by Nazi Germany in 1938, Austria was part of the Third Reich until occupied by Allied forces in 1945. The Allies did not withdraw until 1955, when Austria was recognized internationally as an independent, democratic, and permanently neutral state. Today Austria is governed by a bicameral parliament elected for four-year terms. The president, whose role is essentially ceremonial, is directly elected for a six-year term.

Physical features and land use

Almost two-thirds of Austria consists of the Alps, which sweep west to east across the country in a succession of ranges almost as far as Vienna. Much of the alpine area is characterized by snowfields, glaciers, and snowy peaks. About one-third of the country's population lives in the valleys between the ranges. To the north of the Alps, the lower, heavily forested mountains of the Bohemian Massif, which cover about one-tenth of the land area, extend across the borders of the Czech Republic and Slovakia. Lowland areas lie along the eastern end of the Alps, extending into Hungary, and in the Danube Valley in the north. Most of Austria's main transport routes traverse this northern "corridor," which links Germany with Vienna and countries farther east. Almost all the arable land is in the northeast, and is divided between pasture and croplands. Root crops, such as potatoes and cereals, are the principal crops. There are also extensive vineyards which supply a significant wine industry. The main livestock are cattle and pigs.

Aerial view of the old city of Salzburg, on the south bank of the Salzach River

A

Industry, commerce, and culture

Austria is not rich in mineral resources, although it has some reserves of oil, iron ore, brown coal, and magnesite—a major resource in chemical industries. It imports most of the raw materials it needs for the manufacturing industries that form the backbone of its economy. More than 70 percent of electricity is generated hydroelectrically. Iron and steel making are the principal heavy industries and are large export earners. Aluminum, chemicals, and food processing are also significant. Tourism, based largely on the many alpine ski resorts, but also on the cultural attractions of such cities as Vienna and Salzburg, contributes greatly to the country's economic well-being. There are about 18 million visitors each year.

Austrians are generally conservative in their social attitudes and financial habits. They are savers rather than spenders or investors and the country has a high proportion of its wealth in savings deposits. Much of the country's industry, including iron and steel, and energy production is nationalized and there is a well-developed system of state social services. Most Austrians enjoy a comfortable lifestyle, exceptions being the many refugees

Snow on the mountains overlooking the town of Zel am Zeere in Austria.

from the former Yugoslav republics who have been entering the country during the 1990s.

The conservatism of the people came to the forefront when, in a politically settled and economically stable era, the right wing again came to hold government. The leader of the right wing party, Jorg Haider, publicly declared his ties with Nazi principles and preached isolationism, particularly against the European Union. Haider's statements attracted the attention of the international media. (Haider, who was born to parents who were both active in the Nazi Youth movement, graduated with a Law degree from Vienna University. Never practicing law, he immediately moved into politics, becoming one of the youngest members of Parliament. Elected Governor of Carinthia, his home state, in 1989, Haider served only a short term in office before being forced to step down because of his pro-Nazi statements. Ten years later Haider was re-elected as Governor of Carinthia, and drew international attention when his right-wing party captured a large percentage of seats in the last national elections.) In early 2000 Haider stepped down amid international calls for his resignation. It is possible that he may still run for Chancellor.

AZERBAIJAN

Official name Azerbaijani Republic
Form of government Federal republic with single legislative body (National Assembly)
Capital Baki (Baku)
Area 86,600 sq km (33,436 sq miles)

Azerbaijan

Oil was being collected from the Caspian Sea near Baku at least 1,000 years ago, when the area was known as "the land of eternal fire" because of burning natural gas flaming out of the ground. Today oil from Baku continues to be the mainstay of the Azerbaijani economy. The home of an independent Azeri state as early as the fourth century BC, the region later fell under the influence of Persia, then in the eleventh century Turkic-speaking people moved in and assumed control. A period of affiliation with the Soviets following the Russian Revolution led to Azerbaijan becoming a member of the Soviet Union in 1936. In 1991 it was one of the first Soviet Republics to declare independence.

Since 1988 there have been troubles with Armenia over the region of Nagorno-Karabakh in southwestern Azerbaijan. This territorial dispute (Armenia now holds 20 percent of the region, most of the people in Nagorno-

Karabakh being Christian Armenians) remains a major political problem for the newly independent state.

A range of the Great Caucasus (Bol'shoy Kavkas) running at an angle toward the Caspian Sea separates Russia from Azerbaijan, and reaches almost as far as Baku. South of this range, draining out of the foothills of the Caucasus in Georgia, the Kura (Kür) River reaches a broad floodplain, some of it lying below sea level. The mountains of the Lesser Caucasus (Malyy Kavkaz) form much of Nagorno-Karabakh in the southwest and also stand between Azerbaijan and its isolated enclave-territory Naxçivan. Although a Naxçivan independence movement exists, this territory, which is surrounded by Iran and Armenia, is regarded by the government as part of the Azerbaijan state.

Dry and subtropical, the lowlands experience mild winters and long, hot summers, and are frequently affected by drought. Plant cover consists of steppe grassland in the drier lowland regions, woods in the mountains, and swamps in the southeast.

Early this century Baku supplied as much as half the world's oil, but production declined steadily during the final years under Soviet control as plant became antiquated and maintenance was neglected. The 1994 ratification of a $7.5 billion deal with a consortium of Western oil companies marked a turning point, and should see a revival in this sector. Baku was the fifth biggest city in Soviet Russia and had a well diversified industrial sector. It is hoped the oil deal will stimulate new production of chemicals, textiles, and electrical goods.

Though Azerbaijan has only a small amount of arable land, it is a major producer of cotton, tobacco, grapes, and other fruit. Sturgeon from the Caspian was an important source of caviar but this industry is threatened by serious water pollution. One hundred years of intensive oil production, plus overuse of toxic defoliants in cotton growing, have taken a severe environmental toll. Azerbaijani scientists consider the Abseron Peninsula, where Baku stands, to be one of the most ecologically devastated areas in the world.

Time zone GMT + 4 hours
Population 7,908,224
Projected population 2005 8,171,979
Population density 91.3 per sq km (236.5 per sq mile)
Life expectancy 63.1
Infant mortality (per 1,000) 82.5
Official language Azerbaijani
Other languages Russian, Armenian
Literacy rate 96.3%
Religions Muslim 93.5%, Russian Orthodox 2.5%, Armenian Orthodox 2%, other 2%
Ethnic groups Azeri 90%, Dagestani peoples 3%, Russian 2.5%, Armenian 2.5%, other 2%
Currency Manat
Economy Services 42%, agriculture 32%, industry 26%
GNP per capita US$480
Climate Mainly semiarid
Highest point Bazardüzü Dağ 4,466 m (14,652 ft)
Map reference Page 758

B

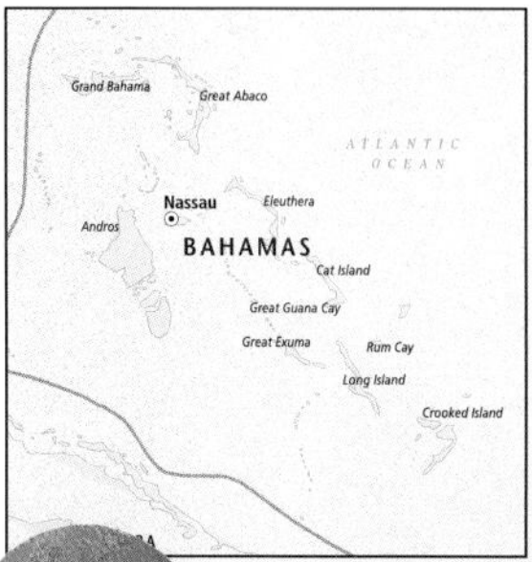

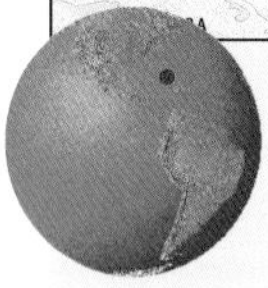

BAHAMAS

OFFICIAL NAME Commonwealth of the Bahamas
FORM OF GOVERNMENT Constitutional monarchy with two legislative bodies (Senate and House of Assembly)
CAPITAL Nassau
AREA 13,940 sq km (5,382 sq miles)
TIME ZONE GMT – 5 hours
POPULATION 283,705
PROJECTED POPULATION 2005 306,153
POPULATION DENSITY 20.4 per sq km (52.8 per sq mile)
LIFE EXPECTANCY 74.3
INFANT MORTALITY (PER 1,000) 18.4
OFFICIAL LANGUAGE English
OTHER LANGUAGE Creole
LITERACY RATE 98.1%
RELIGIONS Baptist 32%, Anglican 20%, Roman Catholic 19%, Methodist 6%, Church of God 6%, other Protestant 12%, other 5%
ETHNIC GROUPS African 85%, European 15%
CURRENCY Bahamian dollar
ECONOMY Tourism 40%, government 30%, business services 10%, agriculture 5%, industry 4%, other 11%
GNP PER CAPITA US$11,940
Climate Subtropical, with warm summers and mild winters
HIGHEST POINT Mt Alverina 63 m (207 ft)
MAP REFERENCE Page 835

Bahamas

Off the southern tip of Florida in the western Atlantic, the Bahamas consists of 700 islands and about 2,400 cays. Once the home of Arawak Indians, the islands were claimed by Britain in 1690, but have had a checkered history. A pirates' haven in the seventeenth century, they were held for short periods by the USA and Spain before Britain resumed control in 1783. They have been independent since 1983. The 25-year administration of Lynden Pindling ended in 1992 amid allegations of involvement in narcotics trafficking and money laundering. One of the most prosperous of the Caribbean's island states, the Bahamas has attracted many illegal immigrants from nearby Haiti. This influx has placed severe strain on government services.

All the islands are fragments of a large coralline limestone shelf. Most are only a few meters above sea level. Their coastlines are fringed with lagoons and coral reefs. Water is scarce. There are no rivers and rainfall disappears into the limestone. Much of the big islands are covered with pine forest. On the smaller islands people work mainly in fishing and agriculture.

In 1995 there were more than 3,600,000 foreign arrivals. Tourism in turn has given rise to the manufacture of garments, furniture, jewelry, and perfume. All energy resources must be imported into the country. Offshore banking, insurance, and financial services generate income and provide one of the region's highest standards of living. In addition, the Bahamas has a large open-registry fleet.

Southern right whales breed in the warm waters surrounding the Bahamas.

Bahrain

A cluster of 35 small, low-lying islands in the Persian Gulf, Bahrain is 28 km (17 miles) from the west coast of the Qatar Peninsula. The islands were once the heart of the ancient Dilmun civilization and have been a trading center for over 4,000 years. Bahrain was the first of the Gulf states to export oil, soon after oil was discovered in 1932. A 25 km (16 mile) causeway links the main island to Saudi Arabia.

After the 1970s' collapse of Beirut in Lebanon, previously the region's main commercial center, Bahrain began to provide banking and financial services, at the same time increasing its transport and communication facilities. When the elected assembly was dissolved in 1975 and the country reverted to traditional authoritarian rule, there was growing unrest among the fundamentalist Shi'ite Muslim majority. Encouraged in their resistance by Iran, the Shi'ites resent their low status under Bahrain's Sunni Muslim ruling family. In the opinion of Shi'ite fundamentalists this family is unacceptable for a number of reasons—it belongs to a branch of Islam they regard as oppressive, it is liberal and modernizing in its economic policies, and it is a supporter of US policy. US air bases on Bahrain were vital military assets during the 1990–91 Gulf War.

Consisting of barren rock, sandy plains, and salt marshes, the landscape of Bahrain is low-lying desert for the most part, rising to a low central escarpment. Winters are dry and mild, summers hot and humid. There are no natural freshwater resources. All the country's water needs must be met by groundwater from springs and from desalinated sea water. Imported soil has been used to create several small fertile areas, and domestic agricultural production is capable of meeting local demand for fruit and vegetables. However, the degradation of existing arable land is an environmental concern, along with damage to coastlines, coral reefs, and sea life resulting from spills of oil and oil-tanker discharges.

Waning oil production since the 1970s has forced Bahrain to diversify. Since the opening of the causeway linking the country to Saudi Arabia in 1986 there has been a boom in weekend tourism, visitors pouring in from the Gulf states. Bahrain is now the Arab world's major banking center, and numerous multinational firms with business in the Gulf have offices in the country. Ship

Bahrain

Official name State of Bahrain
Form of government Traditional monarchy
Capital Al Manamah (Manama)
Area 620 sq km (239 sq miles)
Time zone GMT + 3 hours
Population 629,090
Projected population 2005 701,662
Population density 1,014.6 per sq km (2,627.8 per sq mile)
Life expectancy 75.3
Infant mortality (per 1,000) 14.8
Official language Arabic
Other languages English, Farsi (Persian), Urdu
Literacy rate 84%
Religions Shi'a Muslim 75%, Sunni Muslim 25%
Ethnic groups Bahraini 63%, Asian 13%, other Arab 10%, Iranian 8%, other 6%
Currency Bahraini dinar
Economy Industry and commerce 85%, agriculture 5%, services 7%, government 3%
GNP per capita US$7,840
Climate Mainly arid, with mild winters and hot, humid summers
Highest point Jabal ad Dukhan 122 m (400 ft)
Map reference Page 756

A spice seller in a Bahrain market.

repairs are also undertaken in Bahrain. Petroleum production and processing account for 80 percent of export receipts. Natural gas has assumed greater importance, and is used to supply local industries, including an aluminum smelting plant. However, unemployment among the young, especially among the Shi'ite majority, is a cause of social unrest and continuing economic concern.

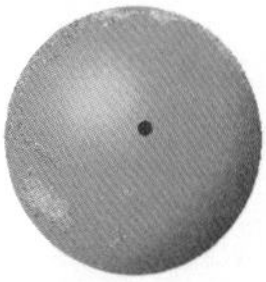

Baker and Howland Islands

Official name Baker and Howland Islands
Form of government Unincorporated territory of the USA
Capital None; administered from Washington DC
Area 3 sq km (1.2 sq miles)
Time zone GMT – 10 hours
Population No permanent population
Climate Hot, dry, and windy
Map reference Page 725

Baker and Howland Islands

Baker Island is an uninhabited atoll in the North Pacific, midway between Hawaii and Australia. The terrain consists of a low coral island surrounded by a narrow reef. Climate is equatorial with little rain, constant wind, and burning sun. Used by the US military during the Second World War, it is now mainly a nesting habitat for seabirds and marine wildlife. Howland Island is an uninhabited atoll nearby. Another low coral island surrounded by a narrow reef, it has no fresh water. Entry to Baker and Howland Islands is by special-use permit only.

Bangladesh

Known for tropical cyclones and endemic poverty, the small and densely populated country of Bangladesh lies north of the Bay of Bengal. Most of its frontier is with India and it has a short border with Myanmar (Burma) in the southeast. The name Bangladesh means "the land of the Bengalis," a people who have contributed a great deal to Indian history. Once a part of the Mauryan Empire of the fourth century bc, Bengal has been mainly Muslim since the thirteenth century, and during its more recent history its Muslim people have often been ruled by Hindu overlords. At the time of the partition of India in 1947, this situation led to the founding of East Pakistan, the oriental wing of the Muslim state that was set up following independence. In 1971 resentment of the power and privileges of West Pakistan resulted in East Pakistan breaking away and forming the independent state of Bangladesh. Since then its history has been one of political coups, dissolved parliaments, and civil unrest, compounded by natural disasters. In 1991 the worst cyclone in memory killed over 140,000 people.

Bangladesh is low and flat, its physiography determined by three navigable rivers—the Ganges (Padma), Brahmaputra (Jamuna) and the smaller Meghna. At their confluence they form the biggest delta in the world. The western part of this delta, which is over the border in India, is somewhat higher, and is less subject to flooding. What is called the "active delta" lies in Bangladesh and this region is frequently flooded. During monsoons the water rises up to 6 m (18 ft) above sea level, submerging two-thirds of the country, and the delta's changing channels are hazardous to life, health, and property. However, the floods are also beneficial in that they renew soil fertility with silt, some of it washed down from as far away as Tibet. Whole new islands are formed by alluvial

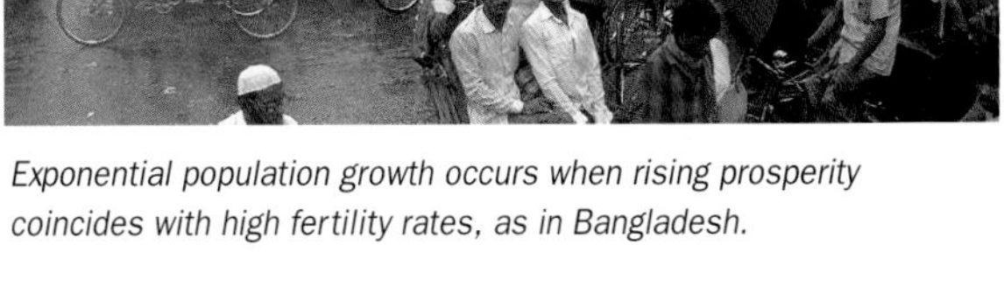

Exponential population growth occurs when rising prosperity coincides with high fertility rates, as in Bangladesh.

BANGLADESH

OFFICIAL NAME People's Republic of Bangladesh
FORM OF GOVERNMENT Republic with single legislative body (National Parliament)
CAPITAL Dhaka (Dacca)
AREA 144,000 sq km (55,598 sq miles)
TIME ZONE GMT + 6 hours
POPULATION 129,859,779
PROJECTED POPULATION 2005 142,921,111
POPULATION DENSITY 901.8 per sq km (2,335.7 per sq mile)
LIFE EXPECTANCY 57.1
INFANT MORTALITY (PER 1,000) 95.3
OFFICIAL LANGUAGE Bangla
OTHER LANGUAGE English
LITERACY RATE 37.3%
RELIGIONS Muslim 83%, Hindu 16%, other (mainly Buddhist, Christian) 1%
ETHNIC GROUPS Bengali 98%, Biharis and tribal peoples 2%
CURRENCY Taka
ECONOMY Agriculture 57%, services 33%, industry 10%
GNP PER CAPITA US$240
CLIMATE Tropical, with three seasons: cool, dry winter (October to March); hot, humid summer (March to June); and cool, wet monsoon (June to October)
HIGHEST POINT Mt Keokradong 1,230 m (4,035 ft)
MAP REFERENCE Page 755

deposition, and the highly fertile silt can yield as many as three rice crops a year. The far south-eastern region of Chittagong has the only high country in Bangladesh, with forested ridges and rubber plantations.

Bangladesh is a major recipient of international aid. Disbursements of aid are currently running at more than 1,000 times the annual value of foreign investment. Despite the efforts of the international community, however, it remains one of the world's poorest and least developed nations. Rice is the main crop in the country's basically agrarian economy, followed by jute, tea, and sugarcane. Bangladesh is the world's largest supplier of high quality jute. About half the crop is exported in its raw form and the rest is processed for export as hessian, sacking, and carpet-backing. A modern paper industry uses bamboo from the hills. Other industries include textiles, fertilizer, glass, iron and steel, sugar, cement, and aluminum. Fishing is also economically important. However, there are a number of serious impediments to progress. They include frequent cyclones and floods, inefficient state-owned enterprises, a labor force growing (as a consequence of a steady population growth) faster than it can be absorbed by agriculture alone, and delays in developing energy resources such as natural gas.

Bus station in Dhaka, Bangladesh.

Bangladeshi women doing agricultural work.

Issues in Bangaldesh

After 15 years of military rule multi-party politics returned to Bangladesh in 1990, and the country's first woman prime minister, Begum Khaleda Zia, leader of the Bangladesh Nationalist Party (BNP), was elected in 1991. However, factionalism divides the nation and Bangladesh remains politically unstable.

Despite the country's prominent female politicians (the opposition Awami League is also led by a woman), women in Bangladesh face discrimination in health care, education, and employment. In addition, dowry-related violence against women does occur.

Religious divides exist, as elsewhere in the region. Tension between Bangladesh's Hindus and the Muslim majority is a problem, and Buddhist tribes in the southeast are agitating for autonomous rule. Relations with neighboring India are also strained, although in 1996 the countries signed a treaty agreeing to share resources after an Indian dam on the Ganges River reduced the amount of irrigation water available to Bangladesh.

An exodus of refugees from Myanmar (Burma)—as many as 200,000 by early 1992—stretched the scarce resources of Bangladesh even further.

International aid finances 90 percent of state capital spending and an economic liberalization program has been introduced.

B

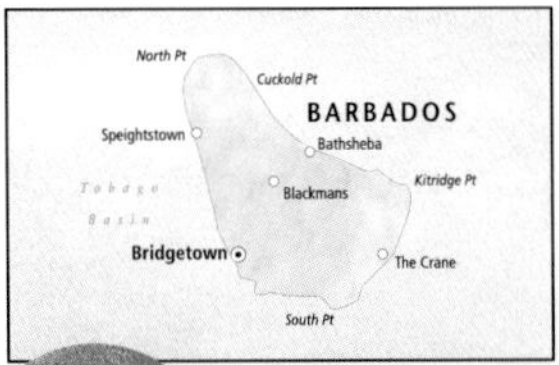

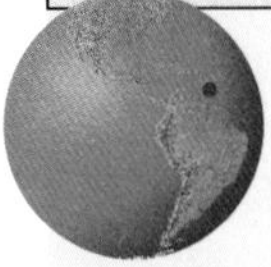

Barbados

Official name Barbados
Form of government Parliamentary democracy with two legislative bodies (Senate and House of Assembly)
Capital Bridgetown
Area 430 sq km (166 sq miles)
Time zone GMT – 4 hours
Population 259,191
Projected population 2005 260,535
Population density 602.8 per sq km (1,561.2 per sq mile)
Life expectancy 75
Infant mortality (per 1,000) 16.7
Official language English
Other language English Creole
Literacy rate 97.3%
Religions Protestant 67% (Anglican 40%, Pentecostal 8%, Methodist 7%, other 12%), Roman Catholic 4%, none 17%, other 12%
Ethnic groups African 80%, European 4%, other (mixed African–European, East Indian) 16%
Currency Barbadian dollar
Economy Services 76%, industry 18%, agriculture 6%
GNP per capita US$6,560
Climate Tropical, with wet season June to November
Highest point Mt Hillaby 336 m (1,102 ft)
Map reference Page 837

Barbados

Northeast of Trinidad and 435 km (270 miles) off the coast of Venezuela, Barbados is the most easterly of the Caribbean Windward Islands. It is also one of the most orderly and prosperous. After becoming independent from the UK in 1966, power has alternated between two centrist parties, the Democratic Labor Party and the Barbados Labor Party. Both elections and freedom of expression are accepted features of Barbados life. Originally inhabited by Arawak Indians and later settled under the British in the seventeenth century, its population is mainly descended from African slaves brought to work on the sugar plantations. The governor-general of Barbados represents the British sovereign and the country has a strong colonial influence. Its neighbors sometimes refer to it as "little England."

The foundation of the island consists of coral deposits formed around a rocky core, and a fringe of coral reef has produced dazzling white beaches. Inland, the rolling terrain rises to hills in the north and center. About 50 percent of the land area is arable, sugar plantations accounting for 85 percent of the cultivated terrain. Barbados is sunnier and drier than many of its neighbors. There is a shortage of water. Surface water is negligible, though when it rains heavily gullies form natural reservoirs.

A small oil industry provides about one-third of the country's needs. Sugar refining is an important source of

A view of the coast of Barbados.

employment and revenue but has recently been overtaken by the rapid growth in tourism. Facilities are being upgraded to cope with the surge in visitors. Most arrive from Europe and North America and cruise-ship traffic is increasing. Recently, light industrial manufacture has been developed, much of it component assembly for export. The government has promised to build "a modern, technologically dynamic economy."

With literacy rates reaching 97% in the late 1990s, with health and lifestyle being similar to that of a developed nation, and with a welfare structure in place, the government's promise appears to be coming into fruition. Partnerships with USA companies for oil have helped the economy. Some concerns exist within the nation as discussions for a Caribbean Single Market proceed. The Caribbean Single Market has been proposed by members of CARICOM, the Caribbean Community. CARICOM aims to unite Caribbean economies as a trading block in the international market. Small businesses are concerned that competition in such a market could be detrimental, as competition with large multinational companies would be difficult.

Belarus

Until 1991, when it declared its independence of the disintegrating Soviet Union, Belarus was known as the Byelorussian (which means "White Russian") Soviet Socialist Republic. Throughout its extensive and troubled history, Belarus has been dominated, invaded, and sometimes devastated by a succession of foreign powers. Initally settled by Slavic tribes in the sixth century AD, the country came under the control of Kiev in the ninth century. Three centuries later it was conquered by invading armies from neighboring Lithuania and in the sixteenth century, with the merging of Lithuania and Poland, Polish influences were also dominant. During the course of the eighteenth century the region came under Russian control and even today Belarus is economically dependent on its huge and powerful eastern neighbor.

Belarus was ravaged in the First and Second World Wars. The German invasion of 1941 saw the deaths of 1.3 million people and the virtual annihilation of the country's Jewish population. Many of Belarus's buildings were reduced to rubble and its capital, Minsk, was razed. Further devastation, in the form of nuclear contamination,

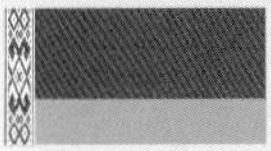

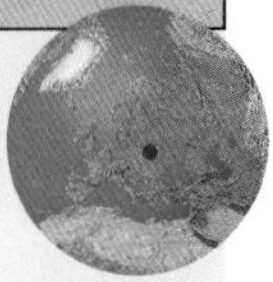

BELARUS

OFFICIAL NAME Republic of Belarus
FORM OF GOVERNMENT Republic with single legislative body (Supreme Soviet)
CAPITAL Minsk
AREA 207,600 sq km (80,154 sq miles)
TIME ZONE GMT + 3 hours
POPULATION 10,401,784

(continues)

B

BELARUS *(continued)*

PROJECTED POPULATION 2005 10,380,321
POPULATION DENSITY 50.1 per sq km (129.8 per sq mile)
LIFE EXPECTANCY 68.1
INFANT MORTALITY (PER 1,000) 14.4
OFFICIAL LANGUAGE Belarusian
OTHER LANGUAGE Russian
LITERACY RATE 97.9%
RELIGIONS Eastern Orthodox 60%, other (including Roman Catholic and small Muslim and Jewish communities) 40%
ETHNIC GROUPS Belarusian 78%, Russian 13%, Polish 4%, Ukrainian 3%, other 2%
CURRENCY Belarusian rouble
ECONOMY Industry 40%, services 39%, agriculture 21%
GNP PER CAPITA US$2,070
CLIMATE Temperate, with cold winters and mild, wet summers
HIGHEST POINT Mt Dzyarzhynskaya 346 m (1,135 ft)
MAP REFERENCE Pages 771, 783, 784

Old well, Smarhon, Belarus.

occurred in 1986 after the Chernobyl disaster in Ukraine, its neighbor to the south. Much of the farming land in the southern part of Belarus remains contaminated by fallout from the accident and is unsafe for cultivation.

The country is generally low-lying, the landscape varying from sandy hills in the north to swampy areas in the south, many of which have been drained and their rich soils cultivated. There are about 11,000 lakes and the country is traversed by numerous rivers, which complement the extensive road and railway networks as a major means of transportation. Forests and woodland cover about 30 percent of the country and almost half the land area is devoted to agriculture, the main crops being barley, rye, potatoes, sugar beet, and flax. There are large numbers of livestock, and dairy and pig farming are important industries.

Belarus is relatively poor in natural resources although it has significant reserves of peat and rock salt and small reserves of coal. It is deeply in debt to the Russian Federation and relies on Russia for the electricity needed to power its industries, which include vast petrochemical plants and truck manufacturing.

Strikes and industrial and political unrest have been a significant feature of Belarusian life during its short period as an independent nation, sometimes aggravated by the inability of the government to pay many of its workers. A controversial treaty that was signed with Russia in 1996 resulted in a substantial merging of aspects of the economy with that of its large neighbor. This was seen by many as a sign of a progressive whittling away of the country's independence.

A winter view of the Svislach River in Minsk, Belarus.

Belgium

This small, densely populated country has a 60 km (40 mile) coastline on the North Sea and is bounded by France to the west and south, Luxembourg at its southeastern corner, Germany to the east, and the Netherlands to the north. Its name derives from the Belgae, the Gallic race that occupied the area when invading Roman armies arrived in the first century BC. For over more than 2,000 years the region has been dominated by a succession of foreign powers, which explains Belgium's linguistic diversity. From the eighteenth century, Belgium was ruled by Austria, France, then the Netherlands. In 1830 the Belgians declared their independence and installed Leopold I, a relative of the future English Queen Victoria, as their king. Today the country is a parliamentary democracy with a monarch as head of state.

Belgium's population is divided into two main groups. The larger group, the Flemings, lives mostly in the north

Buildings in Antwerp.

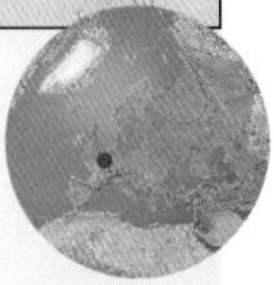

Belgium

Official name Kingdom of Belgium
Form of government Federal constitutional monarchy with two legislative bodies (Senate and Chamber of Deputies)
Capital Brussels
Area 30,510 sq km (11,780 sq miles)
Time zone GMT + 1 hour
Population 10,182,034
Projected population 2005 10,164,106
Population density 333.7 per sq km (864.3 per sq mile)
Life expectancy 77.5
Infant mortality (per 1,000) 6.2
Official languages French, Dutch, German
Literacy rate 99%
Religions Roman Catholic 75%, Protestant or other 25%
Ethnic groups Fleming 55%, Walloon 33%, mixed or other 12%
Currency Belgian franc
Economy Services 77%, industry 20%, agriculture 3%
GNP per capita US$24,710
Climate Temperate, with mild, wet winters and cool summers
Highest point Mt Botrange 694 m (2,277 ft)
Map reference Pages 772, 775

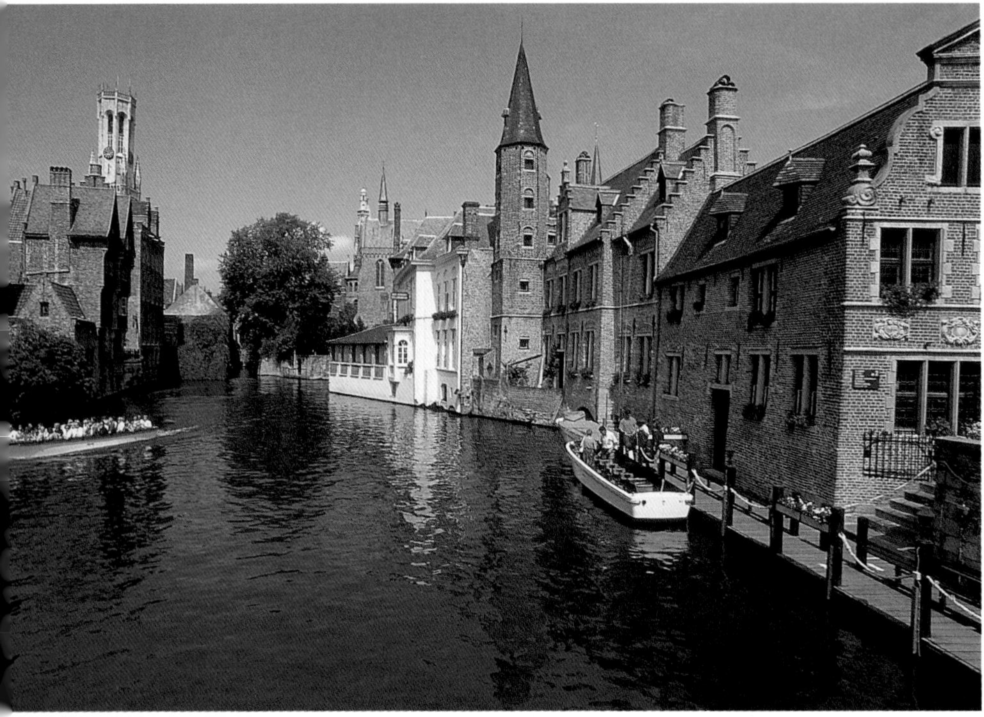

The historic city of Bruges.

Cathedral in Bruges, Belgium.

of the country and speaks Flemish, which is closely related to Dutch. The south is inhabited by the French-speaking Walloons. There is also a German-speaking community to the east of the city of Liège. Brussels, the capital, is officially bilingual and it is the headquarters of the European Union (EU) and the North Atlantic Treaty Organization (NATO).

Inland of the beaches and sand dunes along the North Sea lies a narrow strip of drained, reclaimed marshland, intespersed with dikes and traversed by canals. This region gives way to a central, fertile low-lying plain that rises to a low plateau north of the Meuse–Sambre river system. South of these rivers lie Belgium's uplands. In this rugged, sparsely populated area there are a number of mountain ranges, the most extensive of which is the Ardennes. This heavily wooded high plateau of sandstone and shale is punctuated by flat-topped peaks and cut by deep chasms and valleys. Forestry is the main industry in this southern region, where oak and beech trees predominate. Coal-mining, once important around the city of Charleroi, is now declining.

Belgium's agriculture is centered on its rich northern plain, where crops are secondary to livestock rearing. Although about half the land area has been cleared for agriculture, its contribution to the economy is not significant. Sugar beet, potatoes, wheat, and barley are the main crops and livestock consists largely of pigs and cattle.

Belgium is a heavily industrialized country and its population is highly urbanized. Except for coal, it is poor in natural resources and relies heavily on imported raw materials to fuel its industries. Almost all the industrial centers are in the Flemish area, in the north of the country. Antwerp, Europe's third-largest port and the most populous city in Belgium, is the center of numerous heavy industries, including petroleum refining, plastics, petrochemical, and heavy machinery manufacture. The manufacture of textiles is particularly associated with the cities of Ghent and Bruges. Iron and steel making, food processing, and glass manufacture are other important industries. Many of the major industrial centers are connected by a network of canals, along which barges transport cargo. One of the most celebrated of these is the Albert Canal, which links Liège with Antwerp.

While heavy industry has contributed significantly to Belgium's export earnings, it has had a decidedly negative impact on the environment. The Meuse River, which is a major source of drinking water, has been severely polluted by industrial wastes and fertilizers. The acid rain that falls on Belgium and its neighboring countries has been attributed largely to the air pollution that is caused by Belgian industry.

Bicycles in Bruges, Belgium.

Cows grazing in the Belgian countryside.

Belize

Belize lies on the eastern side of the Yucatan Peninsula. It was the last country in the Americas to achieve independence (1981). Formerly known as British Honduras, its original inhabitants were Maya Indians, with a few Carib Indians along the coast. Though adjacent territory was conquered by the Spanish in the sixteenth century, the first recorded European settlers in the area were British woodcutters in the seventeenth century. At a later date sugar plantations worked by African slaves were established. When Guatemala became independent in 1821 it laid claim to British Honduras and the sovereignty issue strained relations between the two countries until Guatemala officially recognized Belize as an independent country in 1993.

The northern part of the country is a swampy plain. In the south the Maya Mountains divide the coastal plain from the interior. Victoria Peak, on a spur of this range, is flanked by tropical forest, grasslands, and farming regions. Rainforests containing jaguar still cover nearly half the country and in the rivers there are crocodile and manatee. The world's second longest coral reef lies offshore. Belize is much affected by hurricanes. After the 1961 hurricane that destroyed Belize City the capital was moved inland to Belmopan.

Agriculture employs more than a quarter of the labor force, and is the mainstay of the economy. The domestic staples are maize, rice, kidney beans, and sweet potatoes. Belize enjoyed a boom in the years following independence, citrus-fruit processing and tourism helping to reduce the country's earlier dependence on timber, bananas, and sugar. Sugar still accounts for about 30 percent of export earnings. Forests produce valuable rosewood, mahogany, and the gum used for chewing gum, chicle.

Caye Caulker, off the coast of Belize that is popular with scuba divers.

BELIZE

OFFICIAL NAME Belize
FORM OF GOVERNMENT Constitutional monarchy with two legislative houses (Senate and National Assembly)
CAPITAL Belmopan
AREA 22,960 sq km (8,865 sq miles)
TIME ZONE GMT – 6 hours
POPULATION 235,789
PROJECTED POPULATION 2005 270,561
POPULATION DENSITY 10.3 per sq km (26.7 per sq mile)
LIFE EXPECTANCY 69.2
INFANT MORTALITY (PER 1,000) 31.6
Official language English
OTHER LANGUAGES Spanish, Mayan and Garifunan languages, German
Literacy rate 70%
RELIGIONS Roman Catholic 62%, Protestant 30%, none 2%, other 6%
ETHNIC GROUPS Mixed indigenous–European 44%, African 30%, Maya 11%, Garifuna 7%, other 8%
CURRENCY Belizean dollar
ECONOMY Services 60%, agriculture 30%, industry 10%
GNP PER CAPITA US$2,630
CLIMATE Tropical, with wet seasons June to July and September to January
HIGHEST POINT Victoria Peak 1,160 m (3,806 ft)
MAP REFERENCE Page 838

Benin

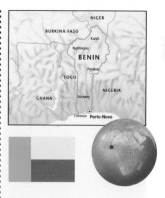

Benin is a small west African country facing the Gulf of Guinea. It was once part of the Kingdom of Benin, famous for the brass portrait heads made for the Oba and his court in the fifteenth century. By 1625 it was known as Abomey (later Dahomey). Slavery and slave-raiding were endemic, and grew when firearms and external slave markets became available. The town of Ouidah became the shipping point for several million slaves, mostly prisoners captured in raids by the Dahomeyans against their enemies. The captives were sent mainly to Brazil, and most Afro-Brazilian religious cults derive from this area. Under French control from 1850, the country became independent in 1960, eventually falling under the control of General Mathieu Kerekou, who changed its name to Benin. In the 1990s there were moves toward multi-party rule.

The Atakora Range (Chaine de l'Akatora) lies in northwestern Benin. To the northeast are the plains of the Niger, part of the boundary with the state of Niger being formed by the Niger River itself. Further south there are plateaus, and then a fertile plain where the Fon and Yoruba people live as subsistence farmers. Still further south, toward the Bight of Benin, lies a sandy strip with many lagoons. In the country's far north small numbers of Fulani people continue to live as nomads. Also in the north are two wildlife parks—the Parc National de la Pendjan and the Parcs Nationaux du W. du Niger—shared with Burkina Faso and Niger.

Children in a canoe paddle through a village of stilt houses, situated on a river in Benin.

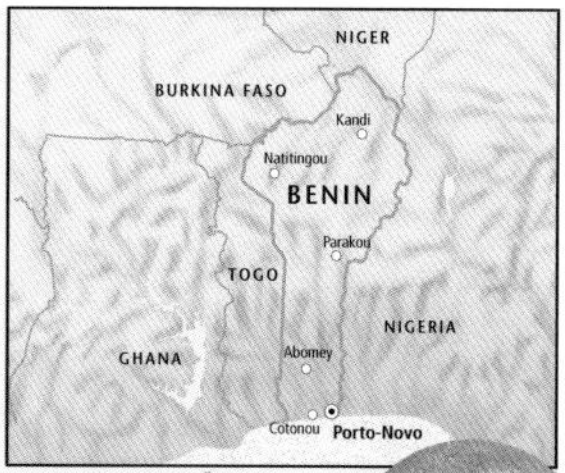

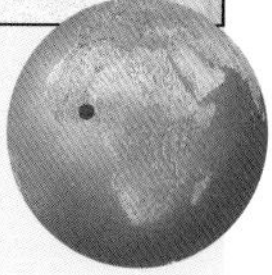

Benin

Official name Republic of Benin
Form of government Republic with single legislative body (National Assembly)
Capital Porto-Novo
Area 112,620 sq km (43,483 sq miles)
Time zone GMT + 1 hour
Population 6,305,567
Projected population 2005 7,662,158
Population density 56 per sq km (145 per sq mile)
Life expectancy 54.1
Infant mortality (per 1,000) 97.8
Official language French
Other languages Indigenous languages
Literacy rate 35.5%
Religions Indigenous beliefs 70%, Muslim 15%, Christian 15%
Ethnic groups Indigenous 99%, European and other 1%
Currency CFA (Communauté Financière Africaine) franc
Economy Agriculture 70%, services 23%, industry 7%
GNP per capita US$370
Climate Tropical; hot and humid in south, drier in north
Highest point Mt Tanekas 641 m (2,103 ft)
Map reference Page 805

Subsistence agriculture, cotton production, and regional trade remain fundamental to Benin's economy. Offshore oilfields promised much when they began producing in 1982, but were soon affected by a fall in petroleum prices. As well as crude oil Benin sells cotton, palm-oil products, cocoa, and peanuts. Goods in transit through the port of Cotonou to Niger are charged a fee, and this is an additional source of revenue. Although a World Bank reform program was adopted in 1991, inefficient state enterprises and an overstaffed civil service are inhibiting economic progress.

BERMUDA

OFFICIAL NAME Bermuda
FORM OF GOVERNMENT Dependent territory of the United Kingdom
CAPITAL Hamilton
AREA 50 sq km (19 sq miles)
TIME ZONE GMT – 4 hours
POPULATION 63,503
LIFE EXPECTANCY 75
INFANT MORTALITY (PER 1,000) 13.2
LITERACY RATE Not available
CURRENCY Bermudian dollar
ECONOMY Clerical 25%, services 29%, laborers 21%, professional and technical 13%, administrative 10%, agriculture 2%
CLIMATE Subtropical; windy in winter
MAP REFERENCE Page 866 (P5)

Bermuda

Bermuda is an island in the Atlantic Ocean 900 km (560 miles) off the coast of South Carolina, USA. It has one of the highest per capita incomes in the world, its balmy location and lush vegetation drawing tourists and its financial services offering tax-haven advantages. Bermuda also has one of the world's biggest flag-of-convenience fleets. The largest of some 360 low-lying coral islands which have grown atop ancient submarine volcanoes, it was discovered by the Spaniard Juan Bermudez in 1503, was later taken over by the British, and has a tradition of self-government going back to its first parliament in 1620. Its people are mainly descendants of former African slaves or British or Portuguese settlers. A move for full independence was rejected by 73 percent of voters in 1995, partly for fear of scaring away foreign business. With 90 percent of tourists coming from the US, links with that country are strong.

Islands of the Great Sound in Bermuda.

Bhutan

A tiny landlocked kingdom nestling in the Himalayas between India and Tibet, Bhutan remains largely closed to the outside world. It is the world's most "rural" country, with less than 6 percent of its population living in towns and over 90 percent dependent on agriculture for a living. Despite its isolation and apparent tranquillity, the country is torn by fierce ethnic tensions which its absolute monarch does little to mitigate. Bhutan's longest-resident ethnic group consists of the Tibetans who probably migrated there 1,000 years ago. Early in the twentieth century, in order to end continual fighting between rival warlords in the area, the British administration in neighboring India established a hereditary monarch in Bhutan, the "Dragon King," in 1907.

The monarch is both head of state and government. Though a modernizer, intent on changing Bhutan's feudal ways, his emphasis on a sense of national identity founded on the language, laws, and dress of his own Drukpa group has stirred up bitter opposition among the resident Hindu Nepalese in southern Bhutan. Many have been deported, and others have fled to refugee camps in southeast Nepal. Dzongkha, which has been proclaimed the official language, is the natural language of only 16 percent of Bhutanese. In 1998 the king announced that in future Bhutan's rulers would have to step down if they received a no-confidence vote from the National Assembly.

There are three main regions distinguished largely by altitude—the Great Himalayas, crowned by huge peaks along the border with Tibet; the slopes and fertile valleys of the Lesser Himalayas, which are divided by the Wong,

Young monks at Paro Festival, Bhutan.

Bhutan

Official name Kingdom of Bhutan
Form of government Monarchy with single legislative body (National Assembly)
Capital Thimphu
Area 47,000 sq km (18,147 sq miles)
Time zone GMT + 5.5 hours
Population 1,951,965
Projected population 2005 2,226,481
Population density 41.5 per sq km (107.5 per sq mile)
Life expectancy 52.8
Infant mortality (per 1,000) 109.3
Official language Dzongkha
Other languages Tibetan, Nepalese
Literacy rate 41.1%
Religions Lamaistic Buddhism 75%, Hinduism 25%
Ethnic groups Bhote (Tibetan) 50%, ethnic Nepalese 35%, indigenous or migrant tribes 15%
Currency Ngultrum
Economy Agriculture 93%, services 5%, industry and commerce 2%
GNP per capita US$420
Climate Tropical on southern plains; cool winters and hot summers in central valleys; cold winters and cool summers in mountains
Highest point Kula Kangri 7,554 m (24,783 ft)
Map reference Page 755

B

Sankosh, Tongsa and Manas rivers; and the Duars Plain which opens out toward India from the foothills of the mountains. The central uplands and foothills are cultivated, food staples including maize, wheat, barley, and potatoes. This area supports the bulk of the population. Below this the Duars Plain falls away into broad tracts of semitropical forest, savanna, and bamboo jungle. Forests still cover nearly 75 percent of Bhutan's land area, and timber is exported to India.

Almost all trade is with India. As an export, timber is outweighed in importance by cement. Other revenue-earning activities include a closely supervised and limited tourist industry (visitors are restricted to 4,000 per year), and the sale of stamps. Bhutan has huge hydropower potential but most of its manufacturing is of the cottage-industry type. Development projects such as road construction rely on Indian migrant labor. Though stable at a low level (the economy is one of the world's smallest and poorest) the country's balance of payments is strong, with comfortable reserves.

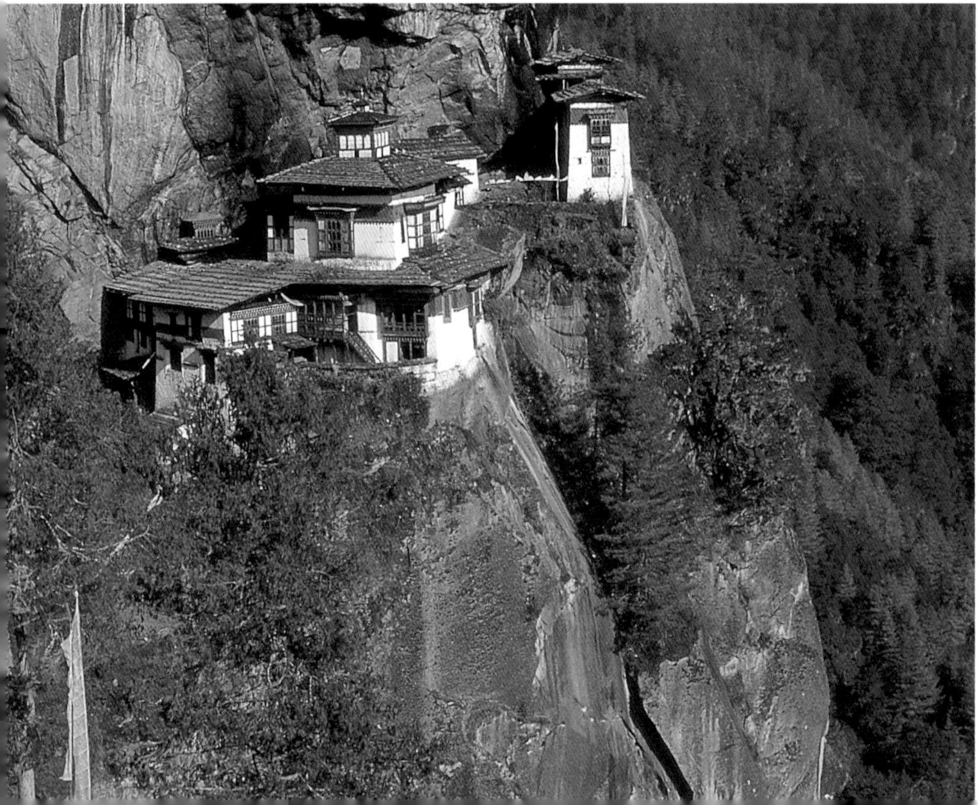

The Taksang monastery high in the mountains of Bhutan.

Bolivia

Sitting high on the Altiplano, a plateau nearly 3,600 m (12,000 ft) above sea level, La Paz is the world's loftiest capital city. In the sixteenth century, when the Spanish conquistadores arrived in Bolivia, they found silver and the mine they established at Potosi soon became famous. But the silver boom passed, the prices for the minerals and metals that replaced it (mainly tin) have been volatile, and Bolivia is now South America's poorest nation. Bolivia is landlocked, and its rugged terrain makes it doubly inaccessible. Notorious for its political instability (192 coups between 1824 and 1981), and for the hyperinflation that rose to 11,700 percent in 1985, it now appears to have a democratic government that is trying to establish economic order.

Quechua and Aymara Indians together form 55 percent of the population. Subsistence farmers, they grow maize, potatoes, and coca on the Altiplano. This cold, treeless region runs 400 km (250 miles) north to south between two major Andean ranges, the Cordillera Oriental and the Cordillera Occidental. At its north, Indians still fish in Lake Titicaca from boats made of reeds. In the south are salt flats.

The vegetation of the Altiplano is grassland which changes to scrubland at higher elevations. To the east lies the Oriente, reaching down across the Andean foothills and the plains. It includes the semi-arid Chaco of the southeast, the savanna country of the center, and the plains of the northern forests whose rivers feed into the Amazon Basin.

The hyperinflation of the 1980s damaged the country's tin industry, causing Boilivia to fall from first producer in the world to fifth. Government efforts reduced inflation to 20 percent by 1988, and to 9.3 percent by 1993. In the mid-1990s the state airline, railroad, and telephone companies were privatized, as were state mining and oil companies.

Metals, natural gas, soybeans, and jewelry are officially the main exports but coca grown for cocaine may well be the biggest export earner—Bolivia is the world's second-largest cultivator of coca leaf. This has affected aid arrangements because the main aid donor, the United States of America, demands proof of Bolivian efforts to eradicate coca farms as one of the conditions for further assistance.

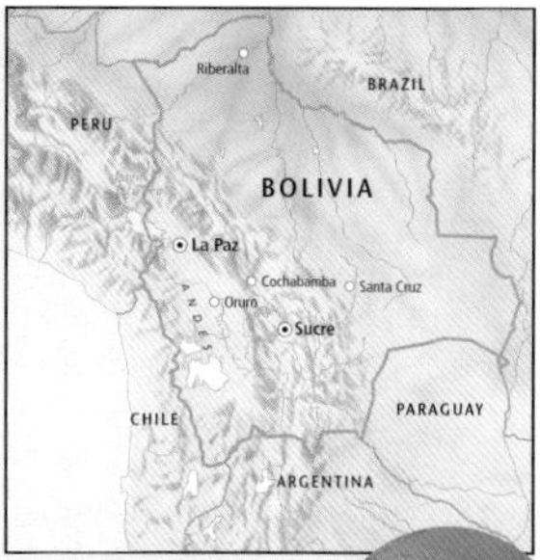

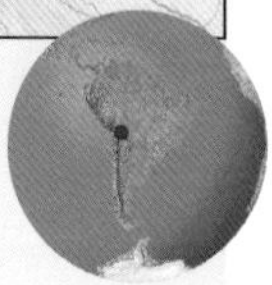

Bolivia

Official name Republic of Bolivia
Form of government Republic with two legislative bodies (Senate and Chamber of Deputies)
Capital Sucre (official); La Paz (administrative)
Area 1,098,580 sq km (424,161 sq miles)
Time zone GMT – 4 hours
Population 7,982,850
Projected population 2005 8,920,665
Population density 7.3 per sq km (18.8 per sq mile)
Life expectancy 61.4
Infant mortality (per 1,000) 62.0
Official languages Spanish, Quechua, Aymara
Literacy rate 82.5%
Religions Roman Catholic 95%, other 5%
Ethnic groups Quechua 30%, Aymara 25%, mixed indigenous–European 30%, European 15%
Currency Boliviano
Economy Agriculture 50%, services 36%, industry 14%
GNP per capita US$800
Climate Tropical north and east; cold, arid west of Andes
Highest point Nevado Sajama 6,520 m (21,391 ft)
Map reference Page 853

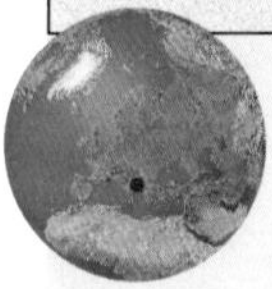

Bosnia and Herzegovina

Official name Republic of Bosnia and Herzegovina
Form of government Federal republic with two legislative bodies (Chamber of Municipalities and Chamber of Citizens)
Capital Sarajevo
Area 51,233 sq km (19,781 sq miles)
Time zone GMT + 1 hour
Population 3,482,495
Projected population 2005 3,758,243
Population density 68 per sq km (176.1 per sq mile)
Life expectancy 67
Infant mortality (per 1,000) 24.5
Official languages Serbian, Croatian
Literacy rate 82%
Religions Muslim 40%, Orthodox 31%, Catholic 15%, Protestant 4%, other 10%
Ethnic groups Serb 40%, Bosnian Muslim 38%, Croat 22%
Currency Dinar
Economy Not available; war has disrupted employment
GNP per capita Est. < US$765
Climate Cold winters and warm summers; cooler in the north and southern mountains
Highest point Mt Maglic 2,386 m (7,828 ft)
Map reference Pages 778, 780

Bosnia and Herzegovina

The federation of Bosnia and Herzegovina has a mere 20 km (12 miles) of coast at its southern tip on the Adriatic. It borders Croatia to the north and west and to the east it shares a border with what remains of the former Yugoslavia. Serbs first settled in Bosnia in the seventh century AD. In the twelfth century the country came under Hungarian control, and Ottoman Turks conquered it two centuries later. It was ceded to the Austro-Hungarian Empire in 1908, and in 1918 became part of the Kingdom of Serbs, Croats, and Slovenes, which was later renamed Yugoslavia.

The republic was formed in 1994 when, after several years of fighting, sparked by the breaking up of Yugoslavia in 1991, Bosnian Croats and Muslims agreed to joint control of the region. Fighting went on for a further 18 months as Bosnian Serbs, backed by Serbia, sought to have a portion of the country incorporated into Serbia. The war came to an end uneasily in 1995 when Serbia abandoned its claims on Bosnian territory. However, conflict continued. The Implementation Force (IFOR) troops entered the territories to assist with humanitarian aid. Elections were held in 1996 under the Dayton Peace Accord, controlled by the Organisation for Security and Cooperation in Europe (OSCE). With the North Atlantic Treaty Organisation (NATO) acting as peacekeepers, a moderate government was elected. With the focus now on rebuilding the shattered infrastructure, refugees from Yugoslavia placed a strain on resources. The Balkan Summit was held to increase commitment to peace and stability, with both Bosnia and Croatia signing the accord, and Croation elections in early 2000 led to hopes of rejoining the European Union, as the government declared peace and dealing with the high crime rate a priority. Now named Bosnia and Herzegovina, the country is divided for purposes of administration almost equally between the Muslim-Croat Federation and the Bosnian Serbs.

Much of the land is mountainous and the south consists largely of a harsh limestone plateau. About a quarter of the land, especially in the mountains, is covered in forests of pine and beech. Before the economy collapsed, forestry products were a major source of earnings. Most agriculture is centered in the fertile valley of the Sava River, which forms the border with Croatia. Crops include grapes, other fruit, and cereals. Sheep-raising is also significant. Most farms are small and, with the disruption caused by warfare, tend to be inefficient.

Bosnia-Herzegovina imports food and relies heavily on United Nations aid. Years of warfare have brought industry virtually to a standstill. Health and education services have also been severely disrupted.

Botswana

A large, dry, landlocked tableland, Botswana is bordered on the south by South Africa, a country with which it has strong historical and economic links. To the west is Namibia (the border touches on Zambia in the north near Victoria Falls) and to the northeast lies a 600 km (370 mile) frontier with Zimbabwe. Originally peopled by the nomadic San, also known as Bushmen, Botswana's more fertile eastern parts later became settled by Bantu Tswana. In the nineteenth century, after gold had been discovered near the Tati River, the area became the focus of a colonial dispute between the British and the Boers of neighboring Transvaal (now Gauteng) in South Africa. Britain established the British Bechuanaland Protectorate in 1885. This name and status within the British Empire was retained until independence in 1966, when Bechuanaland became Botswana.

Geographically a part of the southern African plateau, more than half of Botswana consists of the Kalahari Desert. Substantial parts of the remainder of the country consist of saltpans and swamps. There is little surface water except in the north and east, in the basins of the Okavango, Chobe, and Limpopo Rivers. Variations in

Aerial of village between Maun and Moremi, Botswana.

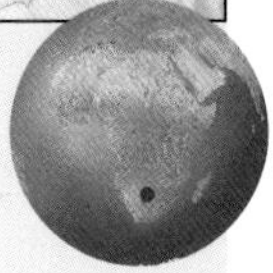

BOTSWANA

OFFICIAL NAME Republic of Botswana
FORM OF GOVERNMENT Republic with two legislative bodies (House of Chiefs and National Assembly)
CAPITAL Gaborone
AREA 600,370 sq km (231,803 sq miles)
TIME ZONE GMT + 2 hours
POPULATION 1,464,167
PROJECTED POPULATION 2005 1,537,747
POPULATION DENSITY 2.4 per sq km (6.2 per sq mile)
LIFE EXPECTANCY 60
INFANT MORTALITY (PER 1,000) 59.1
OFFICIAL LANGUAGE English
OTHER LANGUAGES Setswana and other indigenous languages
LITERACY RATE 68.7%
RELIGIONS Indigenous beliefs 50%, Christian 50%
ETHNIC GROUPS Tswana 94%, Khoikhoin 2.5%, Ndebele 1.3%, other 2.2%
CURRENCY Pula
ECONOMY Services 51%, mining and agriculture 49%
GNP PER CAPITA US$3,020
CLIMATE Semiarid to arid, with warm winters and hot summers
HIGHEST POINT Tsodilo Hill 1,489 m (4,885 ft)
MAP REFERENCE Pages 810–11

B

climate and a limited rainfall enable a certain amount of scrub and thornbush to grow in the Kalahari. The dominant vegetation in Botswana is savanna grassland, which provides sufficient grazing for about 100,000 widely scattered Bantu cattle herders to make a living.

At the time of independence, cattle were almost the country's only export, and Botswana was one of the poorest countries in the world. Since that time the economy has been transformed by the development of mining. Both copper and nickel are exported but the main earner has been diamonds, providing as much as 80 percent of export revenue. Tourism is also important, the 17 percent of Botswana's land area that is given over to national parks and game reserves attracting numerous visitors. A large proportion of the population still live as subsistence farmers raising cattle and growing crops such as maize, sorghum, vegetables, and fruit. Difficulties include an unemployment rate of 20 percent, overgrazing, and desertification.

A traditional dugout boat on the shore of the Okavango Delta in Botswana.

Lions and vultures around a kill, Ghobe National Park, Northern Botswana.

Bouvet Island

Bouvet Island is named for its discoverer, Jean-Baptiste Charles Bouvet de Lozier, who came across it on 1 January 1739. Imagining that he had found a cape of the fabled Great Southern Land, he had in fact stumbled on the loneliest island on earth—the nearest land, in South Africa, being over 1,600 km (1,000 miles) away. Uninhabited except for occasional visiting meteorologists, it rises 935 m (3,068 ft) out of the Southern Ocean, and is largely covered with snow and ice.

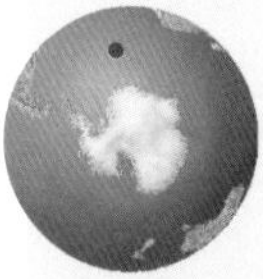

Bouvet Island

Official name Bouvet Island
Form of government Dependent territory of Norway
Capital None; administered from Oslo
Area 58 sq km (22 sq miles)
Time zone GMT
Population No permanent population
Economy Meteorological station
Climate Cold and windy
Map reference Page 862

Brazil

Brazil is the fifth largest country in the world and comprises nearly half of South America. Originally the home of numerous Amerindian tribes, Brazil was ruled by the Portuguese after their arrival in 1500. Political independence of a sort came in 1822, but a form of monarchy, sponsored by Portuguese royalty and featuring a self-styled Emperor of Brazil, existed until the first republic was declared in 1889.

Today, the well being of the Amazon Basin is a cause of international concern, yet for most of Brazil's history this huge region was virtually ignored. In the eyes of the first settlers the most valuable land was the fertile coastal strip from Recife to Rio de Janeiro. In the north of this area they established huge sugarcane plantations, brought 4 million African slaves to do the work, and became so dependent on slavery that it was only abolished in 1888. In the south, around São Paulo (now the world's third largest city), a huge coffee-growing industry became established. Ethnically mixed and rich in resources, Brazil has the potential to play a major role internationally.

Physical features and land use

Brazil has two major and several minor regions. In the north is the vast tropical area—once an inland sea—

Rio de Janeiro, capital city until 1960, when Brasilia was built in the highlands of the interior.

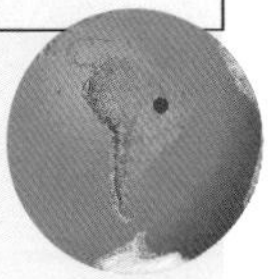

BRAZIL

OFFICIAL NAME Federative Republic of Brazil
FORM OF GOVERNMENT Federal republic with two legislative bodies (Senate and Chamber of Deputies)
CAPITAL Brasília
AREA 8,511,965 sq km (3,286,470 sq miles)
TIME ZONE GMT – 3/5 hours
POPULATION 171,853,126
PROJECTED POPULATION 2005 182,836,908
POPULATION DENSITY 20.2 per sq km (52.3 per sq mile)
LIFE EXPECTANCY 64.1
INFANT MORTALITY (PER 1,000) 35.4
OFFICIAL LANGUAGE Portuguese
OTHER LANGUAGES Spanish, English, French
LITERACY RATE 82.7%
RELIGIONS Roman Catholic 89%, Protestant 7%, other 4%
ETHNIC GROUPS European 55%, mixed European–African 38%, African 6%, other 1%
CURRENCY Real
ECONOMY Services 55%, agriculture 29%, industry 16%
GNP PER CAPITA US$3,640
CLIMATE Mainly tropical, but temperate in south
HIGHEST POINT Pico da Neblina 3,014 m (9,888 ft)
MAP REFERENCE Pages 848–49, 850–51, 852–53, 854–55

drained by the Amazon and its more than 1,000 tributaries. Occupying the entire northern half of the country, this river system passes through vast regions of rainforest. A greater variety of plant species grows here than in any other habitat in the world and the forest is home to a phenomenal range of animals and birds. More than 1,000 bird species are found here and as many as 3,000 species of fish swim in the rivers, along with other animals such as caiman (alligator), freshwater dolphin, and the endangered manatee, which is a large herbivorous mammal.

At present it is estimated that the rainforest is being reduced at a rate of between 1.5 and 4 percent per year as a result of logging, mining, ranching, and the resettlement of Brazil's many landless peasants. In early 1998 forest fires raged through the the northern state of Roraima. Ignited partly by traditional Amerindian slash-and-burn horticulture, partly by settlers clearing land, and aggravated by unusually dry conditions, much devastation was caused.

The second main region, the Brazilian Highlands, lies in the center and south of the country. This is an extensive plateau of hard, ancient rock in which weathering has formed deep river valleys. Much of the interior is covered by savanna woodland, thinning to semi-deciduous scrub in

The Iguaçu Falls, from the Brazilian side of the border.

the northeast. There are spectacular waterfalls on the Uruguay River on the southern side of the plateau and on the Paraná River west of the coastal highlands.

The interior of the Nordeste (northeast) region is the most undeveloped and drought-stricken corner of Brazil, and it is from here that large numbers of subsistence farmers who can no longer make a living have emigrated to the industrial center of São Paulo, looking for work.

The swampy Pantanal, in the southwest, flooded for seven months of the year, is the largest area of wetland in the world and has a striking diversity of wildlife.

People and culture

As in the Caribbean, the sugar industry's demand for slaves strongly influenced the ethnic composition of Brazil. But to a greater extent than in the slave-owning South of the USA, the result has been both economic and social integration. While Brazilian society shows extremes of wealth and poverty, the divisions are drawn along socio-economic rather than ethnic lines. Culturally, Brazil is a mixture of elements. This is particularly reflected in its religious life. Most people are Christian, mainly Roman Catholic. But a variety of African popular cults exist, such as candomblé, which are often mixed with Christianity.

Brazil also has the largest population of Japanese outside Japan. Arriving as poor farmers in the 1920s, 2 million of them now live in São Paulo and are prominent in commercial life. In the upper reaches of the Xingu, Araguaia, and Tocantins Rivers, small groups of Indians such as the Tapirapé survive in forest refuges. Gold prospectors have driven off or killed those Yanomami Indians in Roraima State who have stood in their way.

Economy and resources

Traditional rural activities continue to be important, the rural sector employing 29 percent of the labor force. Brazil is the world's largest producer of coffee and Brazilian livestock numbers are among the world's largest—mainly cattle and pigs—but trends show a steadily falling agricultural contribution to gross domestic product. Industry is increasing in importance, particularly manufacturing, with 90 percent of power coming from hydroelectric schemes. Despite some development of domestic sources, gasoline is still imported. Brazil attempted to substitute ethanol made from sugar for gasoline during the 1980s but falling oil prices made this uneconomical.

B

With South America's largest gross domestic product, Brazil has the potential to play a leading international role. Yet it must still be considered a developing country as it does not have a fully modern economy. Some difficulties have arisen from heavy state borrowing for unproductive projects; others stem from runaway inflation in the 1980s. Fiscal reforms are difficult to carry through politically—many need constitutional amendments. However, these problems are being addressed (consumer prices rose by 23 percent in 1995 compared with more than 1,000 per cent in 1994) and investor confidence is returning.

Timeline Brazil

12,000 BP Humans inhabit forests, living in small groups, hunting and fishing in rivers, and eating wild fruit and vegetables

3500 BC Amerindian people live in Amazon Basin, growing crops of potatoes and maize, and domesticating guinea pigs and llamas

AD 1500 Portuguese land in Brazil naming it after the brasa ("brazil-wood" in Portuguese); the native population is about 2 million

1530 Portuguese settle on Atlantic coast; establish sugarcane plantations, and grow tobacco and cotton for markets in Europe

1690 Prospectors find gold, diamonds in Minas Gerais and Mato Grosso; thousands of Portuguese settle in these regions

1790 Native peoples used as slaves on plantations; slaves also brought from Africa and elsewhere (slavery abolished 1888)

1808 John, ruler of Portugal, flees to Brazil, names Rio de Janeiro capital of Portuguese Empire; returns to Portugal 1821

1822 John's son Pedro declares independence and is Emperor until 1831; his son Pedro II rules 1841–89

1870 Rubber production soars in Amazon area, attracting migrants from the east and from Europe

1889 Don Pedro II overthrown and Brazil is proclaimed a republic

1917 Brazil sides with the Allies in the First World War and declares war on Germany

1934 Republic ends; Vargas is President as Depression hits; he becomes dictator (1937) and embarks on major public works

1942 Brazil joins Allies in Second World War and sends 25,000 troops to fight in Italy

1946 New constitution creates democratic system

1950 Industrialization in southeast results in rural depopulation; by 1960 about 80% of Brazilians are living near Atlantic coast

1960 Capital moves from Rio de Janeiro to Brasília, a new city built in the highlands of the interior

1973 Trans-Amazon Highway links remote western areas to the rest of the country

1975 Population reaches 108 million (rising from 53 million in 1950)

1982 Itaipú Dam on Paraná River, one of the world's largest, completed, provides hydroelectric power for growing industries

1992 Brazil hosts UN summit on global environmental issues, particularly global warming and green-house gas emissions

1998 Clearing of rainforest in Roraima attracts international attention—attempts are made to halt the process

British Indian Ocean Territory

Otherwise known as the Chagos Islands, and the location of the major US–UK military base of Diego Garcia, the British Indian Ocean Territory is a group of 2,300 islets located about 1,600 km (1,000 miles) from southern India and 600 km (400 miles) south of the Maldives. The islets are coral atolls and once supported a few people who produced copra for export. The islets were bought for $3 million by Britain from Mauritius but have been uninhabited since the copra plantations were closed and the population relocated to Mauritius in 1973.

British Indian Ocean Territory

Official name British Indian Ocean Territory
Form of government Dependent territory of the United Kingdom
Capital None
Area 60 sq km (23 sq miles)
Time zone GMT + 5 hours
Population No permanent population
Economy Air Force base
Climate Tropical, moderated by trade winds
Map reference Page 708

British Virgin Islands

East of Puerto Rico in the Caribbean, the British Virgin Islands are the most northerly of the Lesser Antilles. There are four low-lying islands—Tortola, Anegada, Virgin Gorda, and Jost Van Dyke—and 36 coral islets and cays. Most are the peaks of a submerged mountain chain, and they share a subtropical climate moderated by trade winds. With the exception of Anegada, which is flat, the landscape is hilly, with sandy beaches and coral reefs around the coasts.

Visited by Columbus in 1493, the British Virgin Islands were for 200 years pirate bases used by the English and the Dutch, until Tortola was annexed by the British in 1672. Today, they are a British dependency enjoying a large measure of self-government, and highly dependent on the tourism which produces some 45 percent of national income.

International business makes use of offshore services, incorporation fees generating substantial revenues. Livestock raising is agriculturally important. Soil fertility is low and much food must be imported.

British Virgin Islands

Official name British Virgin Islands
Form of government Dependent territory of the United Kingdom
Capital Road Town
Area 150 sq km (58 sq miles)
Time zone GMT – 4 hours
Population 13,732
Life expectancy 72.9
Infant mortality (per 1,000) 18.7
Literacy rate 98.2%
Currency US dollar
Economy Tourism, agriculture
Climate Subtropical, moderated by trade winds
Map reference Page 837

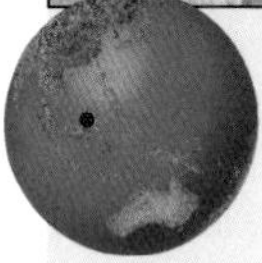

BRUNEI

OFFICIAL NAME State of Brunei
FORM OF GOVERNMENT Sultanate with advisory council of Cabinet Ministers
CAPITAL Bandar Seri Begawan
AREA 5,770 sq km (2,228 sq miles)
TIME ZONE GMT + 8 hours
POPULATION 322,982
PROJECTED POPULATION 2005 369,691
POPULATION DENSITY 56 per sq km (145 per sq mile)
LIFE EXPECTANCY 71.8
INFANT MORTALITY (PER 1,000) 22.8
OFFICIAL LANGUAGES English, Malay
OTHER LANGUAGE Chinese
LITERACY RATE 87.9%
RELIGIONS Muslim 63%, Buddhism 14%, Christian 8%, indigenous beliefs and other 15%
ETHNIC GROUPS Malay 64%, Chinese 20%, other 16%
CURRENCY Bruneian dollar
ECONOMY Services 87%, industry 9%, agriculture 4%
GNP PER CAPITA Est. > US$9,386
CLIMATE Tropical
HIGHEST POINT Gunong Pagon 1,850 m (6,070 ft)
MAP REFERENCE Page 737

Brunei

Oil was discovered in the sultanate of Brunei in 1929. By the time it became independent on 1 January 1984 this small country on the north coast of Borneo was already prosperous. Today its oil revenues have made Brunei's sultan perhaps the richest man in the world, and given its people one of the highest per capita incomes in Asia. There is no income tax, the government subsidizes food and housing, and provides free medical care. The downside is that all government employees (two-thirds of the work-force) are banned from political activity, and the Sultan of Brunei rules by decree. Some non-governmental political groupings have been allowed but the sultan remains firmly in control.

Brunei consists of two semi-enclaves on the northwest coast of Borneo which are bordered by the Malaysian state of Sarawak. They are separated by a few kilometers of coastline where the Limbang River enters Brunei Bay. The topography in both consists of hills bordering a narrow, swampy coastal plain. More than two-thirds of the country is tropical forest.

Brunei is almost entirely supported by exports of oil and natural gas. Petroleum revenues account for more than 40 percent of gross domestic product. Production is carried out by Brunei Shell Petroleum in which the government holds a 50 percent stake. Most crude oil is exported to Japan, South Korea, Taiwan, and the USA. Liquefied natural gas is produced in one of the world's biggest plants, at Lumut in Malaysia, and is sold to power and gas companies in Tokyo and Osaka. About 80 percent of Brunei's food is imported, but there has been a push to achieve agricultural self-sufficiency. Small farms grow rice, fruit, and vegetables. The government Forestry Department, which controls all forest reserves, is expanding into value-added activities such as furniture production.

After the economic downturn of the late 1990s, a major change in economic policy was proposed. The government planned to create a hub of services for regional and international markets, including communications and transport; an independent oil company was slated, and there were developments in the fields of aviation and engineering. A more transparent government, with a stronger corporate focus, was part of the restructuring. The economy appears to be responding favorably to the changes.

Bulgaria

Bulgaria is situated on the east of the Balkan Peninsula with a coastline along the Black Sea. To the west it shares borders with Yugoslavia as well as Macedonia. Turkey lies to its southeast, and Greece to its southwest. In the north the River Danube forms most of the border between Bulgaria and Romania.

Modern Bulgarians are descendants of the Bulgars, who arrived from north of the Danube in the late seventh century AD and established dominance over the Slavic races that had settled the area over the previous two centuries. The Christian religion, which is still dominant in the country, was established in the ninth century. A century of Byzantine domination in the eleventh and twelfth centuries was followed by a period of independence. In 1396 Turkish armies invaded and Bulgaria was then dominated for five centuries by the Turks until Russian intervention ended Ottoman rule in 1878. Full independence, however, did not come until 1908, when Prince Ferdinand of Saxe-Coburg, the elected ruler of Bulgaria, assumed the title of Tsar.

Bulgaria sided with the losing sides in both the First and Second World Wars, and as a result its boundaries changed several times as territories were ceded to it or confiscated. Its present boundaries were established by a 1947 treaty. From then until the fall of the Soviet Union in the early

Thoroughfare in Sophia.

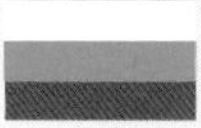

Bulgaria

Official name Republic of Bulgaria
Form of government Republic with single legislative body (National Assembly)
Capital Sofia
Area 110,910 sq km (42,822 sq miles)
Time zone GMT + 1 hour
Population 8,194,772
Projected population 2005 8,034,301
Population density 73.9 per sq km (191.4 per sq mile)
Life expectancy 72.3
Infant mortality (per 1,000) 12.4
Official language Bulgarian
Other languages Turkish, Romany
Literacy rate 93%
Religions Bulgarian Orthodox 85%, Muslim 13%, Jewish 0.8%, Roman Catholic 0.5%, Uniate Catholic 0.2%; Protestant, Gregorian–Armenian and other 0.5%
Ethnic groups Bulgarian 85.3%, Turkish 8.5%, Gypsy 2.6%, Macedonian 2.5%, Armenian 0.3%, Russian 0.2%, other 0.6%
Currency Lev
Economy Services 45%, industry 38%, agriculture 17%
GNP per capita US$1,330
Climate Temperate, with cold, wet winters and hot, dry summers
Highest point Mt Musala 2,925 m (9,596 ft)
Map reference Pages 780–81

B

1990s, Bulgaria remained one of the most loyal of Soviet satellites. A new constitution came into force in 1991 and the following year the first free elections were held.

The country's landscape is defined by three ranges of mountains and two extensive expanses of lowland. The Danube Valley is the country's richest agricultural area, producing significant yields of wheat, maize, and other cereal crops. The Balkan Mountains, running east–west across much of central Bulgaria, reach heights of up to 2,000 m (6,500 ft). They divide the Danube Valley from the southern lowlands, where, in the fertile valleys around the Maritsa River, tobacco and grapes are among the principal crops. The vineyards in this region produce some of southern Europe's finest wines. In the southwest the Rhodopi Massif, which contains the country's loftiest peak, forms the mountainous border with Greece.

More than 10 million tourists, attracted to its Black Sea coastline, visit each year and contribute significantly to the economy. Most of the country's export earnings stem from its machinery and other manufacturing industries. While there have been tentative moves towards the establishment of a free market economy, high inflation, foreign debt, and worker unrest have contributed to a short-term economic outlook that is far from robust.

One of the many churches in Sofia, Bulgaria.

Burkina Faso

Burkina Faso is a landlocked African country on the southern edge of the Sahara Desert. It is the size of Italy but has difficulty supporting its people. The desertification of the Sahel—the fringe of the Sahara running from Senegal to Chad—has severely affected large areas, though the parched savanna of the north and east still supports a nomadic population of cattle-herding Fulani. French colonial control was established between 1895 and 1897, and independence came in 1960. There have been many military coups in the last 40 years, accompanied by waves of executions, mostly the result of tribal power struggles.

Near the capital city of Ouagadougou live the Mossi, the traditional rulers and the dominant tribal group, who have been in the region since the twelfth century. They grow sorghum and millet for food, and cultivate cash crops such as peanuts, cotton, and sesame seeds.

In the west and south is a sandstone plateau, while in the southwest are the spectacular Banfora Cliffs. The plateau is cut by the watercourses of the Red, White, and Black Volta Rivers (Volta Rouge, Blanche, and Noir), draining toward Ghana. Although these valleys have more farming potential than the arid north, they cannot yet be developed because of the tsetse and simulium flies that flourish near their rivers. At present the diseases carried by these insects prevent settlement.

Grass huts are used to store grain in a rural village in Burkina Faso.

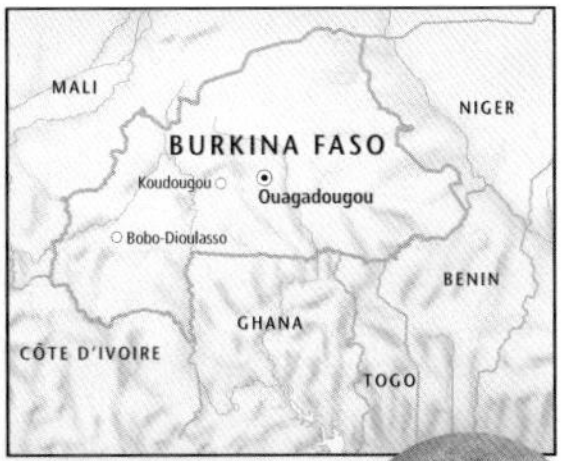

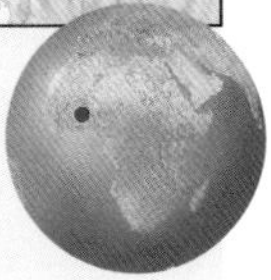

Burkina Faso

Official name Burkina Faso
Form of government Republic with single legislative body (Assembly of People's Deputies)
Capital Ouagadougou
Area 274,200 sq km (105,869 sq miles)
Time zone GMT
Population 11,575,898
Projected population 2005 13,565,940
Population density 40.7 per sq km (105.4 per sq mile)
Life expectancy 45.9
Infant mortality (per 1,000) 107.2
Official language French
Other languages Indigenous languages
Literacy rate 18.7%
Religions Muslim 50%, indigenous beliefs 40%, Roman Catholic 8%, Protestant 2%
Ethnic groups More than 50 indigenous tribes: the largest Mossi 48%, Fulani 10%, Mande 9%; other including Gurunsi, Senufo, Lobi, Bobo 33%
Currency CFA (Communauté Financière Africaine) franc
Economy Agriculture 87%, services 9%, industry 4%
GNP per capita US$230
Climate Tropical, with warm, dry winters and hot, wet summers
Highest point Tena Kourou 749 m (2,457 ft)
Map reference Page 804

Cascades outside of Banfora.

Irrigation system fed by the Cascades outside of Banfora.

Rice paddies watered by irrigation system fed by the Cascades outside of Banfora.

Burkina Faso has few natural resources. There is manganese in the far northeast, but to develop it a 350 km (220 mile) extension of the Côte d'Ivoire railway from Abidjan is needed. Industries consist of unprofitable state corporations, a legacy of the country's years as a one-party socialist state. About 10 percent of the land area is arable and more than 80 percent of the people work on the land. Drought has caused acute agricultural difficulties and the country depends heavily on foreign aid. Many people have emigrated, their wages, sent back from places such as the Côte d'Ivoire, providing much-needed income for their families. Tourists visit the Parcs Nationaux du W. du Niger, in the east—a reserve shared with Niger and Benin.

Hairdresser in Ougadougou, Burkina Faso.

B

Burundi

Burundi is a small, landlocked country in central Africa. Some time in the past a tall cattle-herding people known as the Tutsi (or Watussi) moved into Burundi from the north. Originating on the Upper Nile, the Tutsi established themselves as a ruling class over the much more numerous and physically shorter Bantu farmers called Hutu. This deeply divided social order has been the source of periodic outbreaks of violence, with hundreds of thousands of people having been massacred by both sides. The region's original inhabitants were the forest-dwelling Twa (or Pygmy), but few remain.

Burundi's topography resembles other lands along the Rift Valley. A narrow strip along the northeastern shore of Lake Tanganyika forms one boundary, which then extends up the valley of the River Ruzizi in the direction of Lake Kivu. From this lowland area an escarpment rises steeply up to the highlands which make up the rest of the country. The mountainous ridge east of Lake Tanganyika forms a watershed between the river systems of the Congo and the Nile. On its eastern slopes the land then falls away into the valley of the Ruvuvu River as it makes its way toward Tanzania and Lake Victoria. Malaria in the lowlands is endemic, a situation the continuing civil disorder makes difficult to change.

About 90 percent of Burundi's people depend on subsistence agriculture, growing corn, sorghum, sweet potatoes, bananas, and manioc. The Tutsi herders produce meat and milk. Export earnings come mainly from coffee, which contributes 81 percent, along with tea, cotton grown in the Ruzizi Valley, and hides. Three factors affect foreign exchange earnings and government revenue: the vagaries of the climate, international coffee prices, and civil unrest. Even when the first two are favorable, the struggle between Tutsi and Hutu which has been a continuing feature of Burundi life since 1993 has virtually brought cash cropping to a halt. Under the direction of the International Monetary Fund the government has tried to diversify exports but continuing discord makes it difficult to implement reforms.

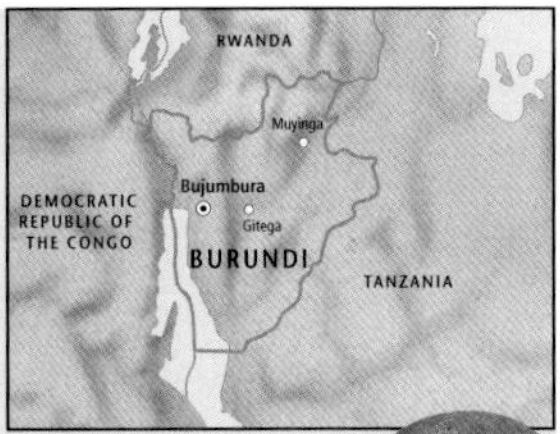

Burundi

Official name Republic of Burundi
Form of government Republic with single legislative body (National Assembly)
Capital Bujumbura
Area 27,830 sq km (10,745 sq miles)
Time zone GMT + 2 hours
Population 5,735,937
Projected population 2005 6,703,652
Population density 206.1 per sq km (533.8 per sq mile)
Life expectancy 45.4
Infant mortality (per 1,000) 99.4
Official languages Kirundi, French
Other languages Swahili
Literacy rate 34.6%
Religions Roman Catholic 62%, indigenous beliefs 32%, Protestant 5%, Muslim 1%
Ethnic groups Hutu 85%, Tutsi 14%, Twa (Pygmy) 1%
Currency Burundi franc
Economy Agriculture 92%, services 6%, industry 2%
GNP per capita US$160
Climate Tropical, with wet seasons March to May and September to December
Highest point Mt Heha 2,760 m (9,055 ft)
Map reference Page 809

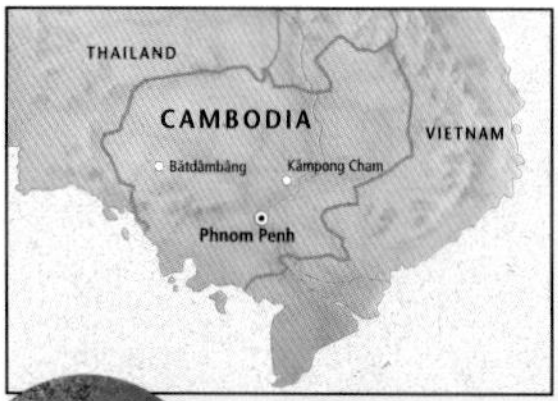

C

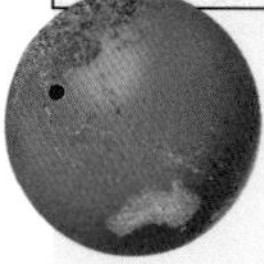

Cambodia

The Southeast Asian country of Cambodia is famous both culturally and politically. At Angkor Wat and Angkor Thom it has the world's largest group of religious buildings, a priceless relic of the Hindu Khmer Empire (AD 802 to 1432). It also, in the 1970s, saw an outbreak of communist fanaticism in which over 2 million people died. Under French rule from 1863, Cambodia won independence in 1954. In the late 1950s and during the 1960s there was a short period of relative stability in which the country developed its agricultural resources and rubber plantations and managed to achieve self-sufficiency in food.

Years of internal political struggles, plus its involvement in the Vietnam War, led to a takeover by the Khmer Rouge under Pol Pot in 1975. With the aim of creating a classless agrarian society, money and private property were abolished, the professional classes were murdered (anyone with glasses was at risk), and townspeople were brutally moved into the countryside and left to fend for themselves. Half a million refugees fled to Thailand, and between a quarter and one-eighth of the entire population died. The regime fell in 1978 and Pol Pot went into hiding but civil war continued for some years; Pol Pot died in 1998. A devastated and desperately poor nation, stripped of what little economic infrastructure and trained personnel it once had, Cambodia is now trying to put itself together again.

Cambodia

Official name Kingdom of Cambodia
Form of government Constitutional monarchy with single legislative body (National Assembly)
Capital Phnom Penh
Area 181,040 sq km (69,900 sq miles)
Time zone GMT + 7 hours
Population 11,780,285
Projected population 2005 13,786,677
Population density 65.1 per sq km (168.6 per sq mile)
Life expectancy 51.1
Infant mortality (per 1,000) 102.4
Official language Khmer
Other language French
Literacy rate 35%
Religions Theravada Buddhism 95%, other 5%
Ethnic groups Khmer 90%, Vietnamese 5%,
Chinese 1%, other 4%
Currency Riel
Economy Agriculture 80%, services and industry 20%
GNP per capita US$270
Climate Tropical, with wet season May to November
Highest point Phnum Aôral 1,771 m (5,810 ft)
Map reference Page 739

Angkor Wat is the largest of the many temples built by the Khmer people in Cambodia about 1,000 years ago.

The country's heartland consists of a wide basin drained by the Mekong River. In the center of this lies the Tonlé Sap (Great Lake), surrounded by a broad plain. When the rain is meager and the Mekong is low—from November to June—the lake drains south toward the sea. But during the rainy season when the Mekong is high—from July to October—the flow reverses, and the lake doubles its area to become the largest freshwater lake in Southeast Asia. The wealth of the fabled "gentle kingdom" of Cambodia consists of fish from the lake and rice from the flooded lowlands, a year-round water supply being provided by an extensive system of irrigation channels and reservoirs. Directly south of the lake the Cardamom (Chuŏr Phnum Kravan) and Elephant (Chuŏr Phnum Dămrek) Mountains look out over a narrow coastal plain.

Reconstructing the Cambodian economy is bringing almost as many costs as benefits. Tropical rainforest timber, especially teak and rosewood, is Cambodia's most important resource. For 20 years it was sold in huge quantities by all factions to finance their war efforts. Now indiscriminate tree-felling is a major environmental problem, a 1992 moratorium on logging largely being ignored. Gems are another resource but strip mining is causing habitat loss, and the destruction of mangrove swamps threatening fisheries. Starting from a very low base, growth was strong in the early 1990s, but a lack of skills at all levels of administration and management is slowing progress.

Cameroon

The African state of Cameroon is on the Gulf of Guinea, with Nigeria to the west and Equatorial Guinea and Congo to the south. The Portuguese arrived in 1472, and Cameroon is named after the prawns, *camarãos*, they found here. A German colony from 1884, and later ruled by both British and French, Cameroon became an independent republic in 1960. Although it was a one-party state for 30 years, opposition parties have been allowed since 1991.

One of the more prosperous African countries, Cameroon is home to more than 200 distinct tribes and peoples. There is also a broad distinction between the English- and French-speaking parts of the population. In response to the demands of the former, and the protests and demonstrations they made in 1996, Cameroon applied for entry and was admitted to the British Commonwealth.

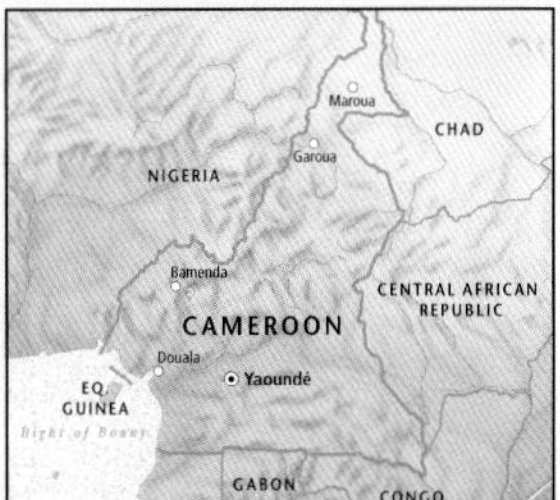

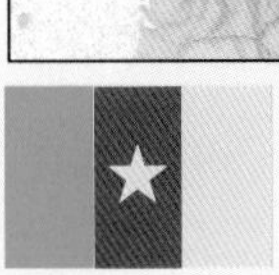

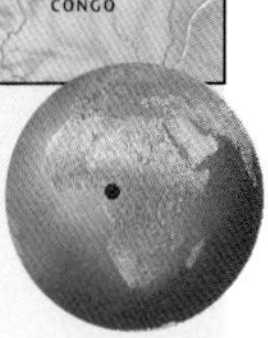

CAMEROON

OFFICIAL NAME Republic of Cameroon
FORM OF GOVERNMENT Republic with single legislative body (National Assembly)

C

CAMEROON *(continued)*

OFFICIAL NAME Republic of Cameroon
FORM OF GOVERNMENT Republic with single legislative body (National Assembly)
CAPITAL Yaoundé
AREA 475,440 sq km (183,567 sq miles)
TIME ZONE GMT + 1 hour
POPULATION 15,456,092
PROJECTED POPULATION 2005 18,175,654
POPULATION DENSITY 32.5 per sq km (84.2 per sq mile)
LIFE EXPECTANCY 51.3
INFANT MORTALITY (PER 1,000) 75.7
OFFICIAL LANGUAGES French, English
OTHER LANGUAGES 24 African languages
LITERACY RATE 62.1%
RELIGIONS Indigenous beliefs 51%, Christian 33%, Muslim 16%
ETHNIC GROUPS Cameroon Highlanders 31%, Equatorial Bantu 19%, Kirdi 11%, Fulani 10%, Northwestern Bantu 8%, Eastern Nigritic 7%; other African 13%; non-African 1%
CURRENCY CFA (Communauté Financière Africaine) franc
ECONOMY Agriculture 75%, industry and transport 12%, services 13%
GNP PER CAPITA US$950
CLIMATE Tropical in south and along coast, semiarid in north
HIGHEST POINT Mt Cameroon 4,095 m (13,435 ft)
MAP REFERENCE Page 805

The country can be divided into four regions. First, an area of tropical forest, plateau, and coastal plain extends from the southern frontier to the Sanaga River. Most of the population is concentrated in this southern part. Second, north of this river and Lake Mbakaou (M'Bakaou Reservoir), the land rises to the highlands of the Adamaoua Massif. Third is the mountainous western extension of the Adamaoua Massif which includes Mt Cameroon. Occasionally active, this 4,070 m (13,353 ft) volcanic cone is the highest mountain in west Africa. Fourth is the arid savanna north of the Benue (Bénoué River and toward Lake Chad (Lac Tchad). This region of savanna supports elephant, lion, and leopard, and a national park—the Parc National de la Bénoué—has been established there.

Cameroon's prosperity was helped by the oil boom between 1970 and 1985. Since then conditions have been more difficult, with prices falling for coffee, cocoa, and petroleum, the country's major exports. Three-quarters of the population are farmers who, in addition to coffee and cocoa, grow bananas, oilseed, grains, and manioc. Cameroon is self-sufficient in food, but a range of other economic difficulties exists. Serious inflation occurred in 1994. The dismantling of unproductive state industries has been slow to show results, and the swollen ranks of the civil service remain a fiscal burden.

A small village on Cameroon's arid savanna.

Canada

Canada is a country of geographic superlatives. It is the second-largest country in the world, its 9,976,200 sq km (3,851,800 sq miles) extending through six time zones, and its coastline is one of the longest—if not the longest—in the world. It has the greatest amount of fresh water surface (7.6 percent of its area) of any nation in the world, its two million lakes ranging from the five Great Lakes (the largest body of fresh water in the world, most of it shared with the united States) to the thousands of smaller bodies of water which blanket the Canadian Shield. Its forested area (4.4 million sq km; 1.7 million sq miles) is three times as large as that of all Europe, with over 2 million sq km (849,000 sq miles) being productive. In this vast country, there are only some 31 million people, roughly one-tenth of the population of its large southern neighbour, the United States. Looking at this statistic, Canada might be seen as a near empty country, with an overall population density of only 3 people per sq km (11.6 per sq mile). However, most of Canada will never be able to support a large population. A number of environmental, economic and social constraints mean that there are very limited habitable areas for a large, permanent resident population.

Some 90 percent of the Canadian population live within 500 km (310 miles) of its southern border with the United States. Its citizens enjoy a standard of living second only to that of the US itself, but the huge scale of Canada's land area, the small, spread out population, and the division between the British and the French have made national unity more difficult to achieve. Strong regional compartmentalization of Canada means that some areas seem at

Ottawa, on the banks of the Ottawa River.

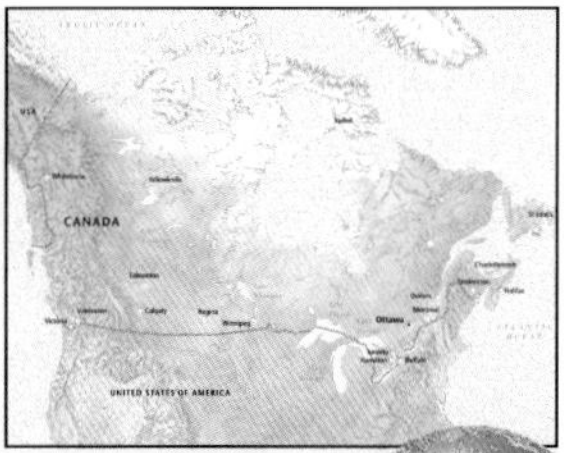

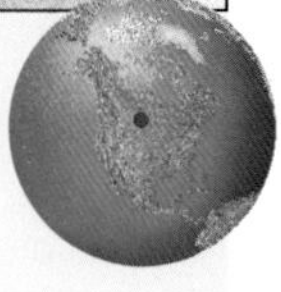

C

CANADA

OFFICIAL NAME Canada
FORM OF GOVERNMENT Constitutional monarchy with two legislative bodies (Senate and House of Commons)
CAPITAL Ottawa
AREA 9,976,140 sq km (3,851,788 sq miles)
TIME ZONE GMT – 3.5/9 hours
POPULATION 31,006,347
PROJECTED POPULATION 2005 32,855,230
POPULATION DENSITY 3.1 per sq km (8 per sq mile)
LIFE EXPECTANCY 79.4
INFANT MORTALITY (PER 1,000) 5.5
OFFICIAL LANGUAGES English, French
OTHER LANGUAGES Chinese, Italian, German, Polish, Spanish, Portuguese, Punjabi, Ukrainian, Vietnamese, Arabic, indigenous languages
LITERACY RATE 99%
RELIGIONS Roman Catholic 45%, United Church 12%, Anglican 8%, other 35%
ETHNIC GROUPS British 40%, French 27%, other European 20%, indigenous 1.5%, other 11.5%
CURRENCY Canadian dollar
ECONOMY Services 78%, industry 19%, agriculture 3%
GNP PER CAPITA US$19,380
CLIMATE Ranges from cool temperate in south to polar in north; long, cold winters; wetter and more temperate on coasts
HIGHEST POINT Mt Logan 5,950 m (19,521 ft)
MAP REFERENCE Pages 820–21, 822–23, 824–25, 826–27

C

times to have stronger ties with adjacent areas of the United States than with the remainder of their nation.

When Europeans first arrived in what is today's Canada, they found a country already inhabited by indigenous peoples—"First Nations", as they are now known. Perhaps 20,000 Inuit (Eskimo) occupied the Arctic Region, with Amerindians (as distinct from immigrant East Indians) in the Canadian areas further south. These Amerindians spoke some 50 languages (there were many dialects as well), which are collectively grouped into 12 linguistic families, including Inuktitut in the Arctic. At the time of first European contact, most indigenous Canadians relied on hunting and fishing, and the population was dispersed and migratory. However, through intimate knowledge of the varying resources available, distinct cultural differences existed.

The Pacific Coast provided abundant food resources in its fish (especially salmon), shellfish and sea mammals. Cedar provided an excellent building material for housing, sea-going dugout canoes and totem poles. These resources, plus a mild climate, made for relatively easy living, compared with the rest of Canada, and supported the largest population (perhaps 200,000) of First Nation people in the country, a culture with a sophisticated social

Canadian spring thaw.

Niagara Falls seen from the Canadian side.

structure and art. Large, multi-family plank houses formed permanent villages of 200 to 700 people. Some village sites in the coastal landscape show evidence of occupation over 4,000 years, and large shell middens are still to be found on many shores.

The other region where favourable environmental conditions encouraged larger than usual population numbers and a non-migratory way of life was what is now known as southern Ontario. There, the climatic and soil conditions made a farming way of life possible for several branches of the Iriquois peoples. Corn, beans and squash, supplemented by deer and fish, supported a population of 60,000 or more. These people lived in multi-family longhouses made of elm bark, grouped into palisaded villages of up to 1,500 inhabitants. When supplies of productive land or firewood became exhausted, a new site would be developed. Though the passage of time later erased village structures, incoming European settlers often found that former crop mounds were still discernible on the land.

Other indigenous peoples were nomadic or semi-nomadic hunters and gatherers, living typically in small groups and moving seasonally to take advantage of the availability of mammals, fish and birds. Deer, moose, and caribou were important resources. In the grassland region of the Western interior, herds of bison supported a highly specialised cultural area, involving eight principal tribes of Amerindians. As they were completely dependent on the

This native North American totem pole is a reminder of Canada's first inhabitants.

Bighorn sheep, Jasper National Park, Alberta.

migratory bison, they required portable dwellings in the form of tipi, or large, hide-covered conical tents, supported on slender poles. Following their acquisition of horses from the south in about 1730, these tribes' mobility was greatly increased. As they were migratory, these people left limited physical evidence of their presence on the landscape —only evidence such as circular tent rings of stone, relic bison pounds and accumulations of bison bones at jump sites, and large stone "medicine wheels" in the grass.

European settlement began in 1541 after Jacques Cartier's 1534 discovery of the St Lawrence River. In the eastern sector of the St Lawrence Lowlands, the establishment of initial fur trade posts of Québec, Trois-Riviéres and Montreal were followed by an agricultural settlement in farms along the river. Soon, French explorers pushed inland, in search of furs and trade. The French were still in a majority when British victory in a war with France, in 1763, gave Britain control of French settlements in Québec. Following the independence of the United States in 1783, however, many British settlers came north, and this marked the start of the long-resented domination of a French minority by a larger English-speaking population. There have been various Francophone initiatives for the secession of Québec in recent years. A 1995 vote in the province failed by 50.6 to 49.4 percent to settle the matter.

By contrast to the imprint left on the landscape by the First Nations, the effects of European settlement is clearly visible in today's Canadian landscape, for example in the removal of most of the local tree cover on the Atlantic coastline to meet the needs of the coastal communities for wood—for boat construction, building and firewood; and the transformation of the St Lawrence Lowlands from a natural landscape into a man-made one, as forest land was cleared for farms and settlements.

Physical features and land use

There is much variety among Canada's geographic regions. In the east lie the Atlantic Provinces of New Brunswick, Nova Scotia, Prince Edward Island, and Newfoundland, as well as Québec. The geological foundation of the Atlantic Provinces is ancient worn-down mountains, along with sectors of the still older Canadian Shield. Although farming settlements are common, agriculture in this region has always been marginal (with the exception of such places as the Annapolis Valley in Nova Scotia and Prince Edward Island), and is in decline. Pulp and paper is produced from Québec's coniferous forests and the state is also a major producer of hydropower.

West and south lie the most temperate inland parts of Canada, the St Lawrence–Great Lakes lowlands, including the Ontario peninsula. This fertile agricultural region reaches west from southern Québec along Lake Ontario and north from Lake Erie. Rural settlement is more dense here than elsewhere and, given the large urban

A grizzly bear in part of the untamed landscape of Alberta.

Forestry has changed the aspect of parts of the Subartic region—logs floating downriver to the mill.

Polar bears inhabit Canada's far north.

concentrations of Toronto and Montréal, these lowlands are the most heavily populated part of Canada.

The Canadian, or Laurentian, Shield is an extensive, ancient region floored with some of the world's oldest known rocks. Centered on Hudson Bay, it covers nearly 50 percent of Canadian territory. Except for some low mountains in eastern Québec and Labrador, this is a rolling landscape typified by outcrops of rock and a great amount of surface water in summer. There are hundreds of thousands of water bodies, ranging in size from gigantic to tiny, connected by thousands of rivers and streams. The shield's southern half is covered by boreal forest, whereas the northern half (including the islands of the Canadian Arctic Archipelago) is beyond the tree line and has a cover of rock, ice, and ground-hugging tundra. The Arctic Archipelago Islands range from high mountains in the east to low plains in the west.

West of the Canadian Shield lie the central plains. The southern portion of the "Prairie Provinces"—including Saskatchewan, Manitoba, and Alberta—has a natural vegetation of prairie grasses. The northern part is forested. In the prairies the mechanization of wheat farming long ago reduced the need for rural labor, and population densities are low.

The Canadian Cordillera, reaching from the northern Yukon to southern British Columbia and southwest Alberta, dominates western Canada, and contains a number of national parks including Yoho, Banff, Jasper, and Kootenay. On the Pacific side the Coast Mountains run south through British Columbia, the coastline deeply embayed by fjords. Off the coast lies Vancouver Island, the peak of another mountain range, now cut off by the sea.

Although most of Canada is not suitable for agriculture, it is one of the world's largest wheat exporters. These Albertan grain silos can be seen for miles across the prairies.

Smaller fields on the outskirts of Vancouver.

C

People and culture

With its major British and French components, its other Europeans who are largely from eastern and southern Europe, its Asians, and its indigenous First Nations, Métis, and Inuit, Canada is home to many peoples. Most now live in urban settings but this is quite a new development. At Confederation in 1867, when Britain granted home rule, 80 percent of the population was rural, and only Montreal had more than 100,000 people. It was not until after the Second World War that rural and urban populations became about equal in size. The war years stimulated the economy, industrialization was rapid, people moved into the cities to work in factories, and Canada emerged from the conflict with a powerful industrial base. It was at this time that British influence began to decline and the USA became of increasing economic and cultural importance in Canadian life.

In the past 25 years Canada's ethnic mix has changed significantly, resulting from a move toward a less restrictive immigration policy that welcomes people with money and skills. Under this policy many Asians have come to settle. The government defines Canada as a "community of communities" within which each ethnic group is encouraged to maintain its own culture. While generally welcomed, these liberalization measures have also produced problems. Since the Supreme Court recognized "aboriginal title" First Nations land claims have been or are being negotiated with the governments concerned where prior treaties did not exist, and in some cases demands are being made for revision of existing

A lakeshore in Banff National Park, Calgary.

Street scene, Dawson City, Yukon Territory.

treaties. Canada's most intractable political problem, however, remains the unsatisfied demand of many Québécois for autonomy.

Economy and resources

Canada has been richly endowed with natural resources. It is the world's third largest mineral exporter and has enormous energy resources – coal, petroleum, natural gas, and water power. Its resource base includes nickel (Sudbury, Ontario, usually provides some 20 percent of the western world's supply), while Canada is also a world leader in the output of zinc, potash, uranium, sulphur, asbestos, aluminum and copper. Alberta produces more than 75 percent of the nation's oil, and is an important source of natural gas and coal. Hydroelectric power has led to the expansion of pulp and paper industries. Canada is one of the world's leading exporters of wood products.

Agriculture is an important activity, though it only employs around 3 percent of the labor force. Grain, dairying, fruit, and ranching all flourish. In addition to pigs and sheep, Canadian ranches support about 13 million head of cattle. Fruit-growing is found in British Columbia's irrigated southern plateau and the Fraser Delta lands. In addition to wheat, other export crops include feed grains, oilseeds, apples, potatoes, and maple syrup.

The country's high taxes, regulatory structures, and low productivity have, however, led to ongoing problems. Starting the 1990s in recession, Canada's real rates of growth have averaged only 1 percent through much of the decade. A traditional commitment to high public service and welfare spending is proving hard to maintain. The

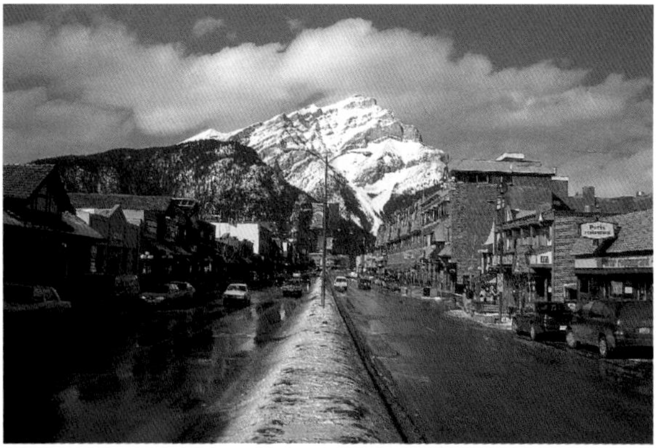

The spring thaw has come for a Canadian town.

Timeline Canada

35,000–12,000 BP Humans migrate to North American continent from Asia via land bridge across Bering Strait

5000 BP Communities in east survive by trapping caribou and bears, and fishing; use fur clothing and build wood and skin kayaks

1200 BC Ancestors of today's Inuit spread east and north as far as Arctic Circle

AD 1100 Inuit meet Vikings in Greenland; as a result, more than one-third of Inuit die of such diseases as smallpox and measles

1497 John Cabot lands near the mouth of the St Lawrence River and claims land for England

1534 Jacques Cartier sails up St Lawrence River to site of present-day Montréal

1663 New France made a French colony by Louis XIV; French, English settler rivalry over fur trade; native population c.200,000

1670 Hudson's Bay Company established

1791 British divide Canada into Upper and Lower Canada; French mainly in Lower Canada, along lower St Lawrence

1829 Welland Canal links Lakes Erie and Ontario, allowing ships to avoid Niagara Falls

1867 Britain creates Dominion of Canada, bringing together New Brunswick, Nova Scotia, Ontario, and Québec

1870 Dominion of Canada acquires the North West Territory

1871 British Columbia becomes sixth province; Prince Edward Island later made the seventh (1873)

1898 Yukon Territory added to Canada's official land area

1905 Saskatchewan and Alberta become provinces; Canada's population grows with European immigrants settling western prairies

1914 Canada fights alongside Britain and Allies against Germany in First World War

1930s Depression hits; new national bodies set up including Bank of Canada (1934) and Canadian Wheat Board (1935)

1939–45 More than 1 million Canadian troops aid Allies on European and Pacific fronts in Second World War

1945–55 Postwar migration from Europe boosts Canada's population by more than 1 million

1949 Newfoundland becomes tenth province; Canada joins North Atlantic Treaty Organization (NATO)

1959 Completion of St Lawrence Seaway creates waterway from Lake Superior to Atlantic of 3,767 km (2,340 miles)

1960 Demands for French–Canadian rights grow both peacefully and in form of terrorist attacks on public buildings

1982 Constitution Act, signed by Queen Elizabeth II, grants Canada sole power to amend its constitution

1988 Canada and USA sign free trade agreement ending wrangling over foreign investment, banking, and agriculture

1993 Parliament grants Inuit people (numbering around 30,000) self-governing homeland, Nunavut, effective 1 April 1999

current account deficit and national debt have led to the slashing of federal transfers to the provinces in the areas of health, education, and welfare. The continuing debate over Québec's future, and the possibility of a split in the confederation, also damages investor confidence.

Environmental issues, too, continue to be the subject of political debate in Canada, and a force for change. Most Canadians today are urban dwellers in the southernmost parts of the nation. They rarely, if ever, see the natural environments, which are still present in this vast country. Growing numbers of them, however, are concerned with the rapidity of transformation of even their immediate area, and with the ever-growing number of species that are now listed as endangered or extinct. Politically, this concern is reflected in widespread support for the creation of additional national parks to protect representative areas of the environment, and support for legislation protecting endangered species. Yet the potential conflict between environmentalists and conservationists, on the one hand, and resource developers seeking to provide employment opportunities and monetary gain on the other, will always be present in a resource-rich country such as Canada.

Canary Islands

Canary Islands

Official name The Canary Islands
Area 7447 sq km (2904 sq mi)
Population 1.605 million
Capital Las Palmas de Gran Canaria (pop 356,000)
Language Spanish
Religion Roman Catholic
Ethnic groups Spanish, North African, small Latin American and north European communities
Government Spanish autonomous region
Highest point Teide volcano 3718 m (12,195 ft)
Climate Mean winter termperature 18°C (64°F), mean summer temperature 24°C (75°F)
Time zone GMT/UTC
Currency Peseta (pta)
GNP US$219 million
GNP per capita US$14,000
Annual growth 3.5%
Inflation 4..3%
Major industries Tourism
Major trading partners France, Germany, Italy
Map reference Pages 800, 813

The Canary Islands, grouped off southern Morocco, are an autonomous community of Spain. There are seven large islands and numerous smaller islands, the nearest of which are within 100 km (60 miles) of the African coast. The "inshore" islands of Lanzarote and Fuerteventura are low lying. The more mountainous outer islands of Gran Canaria and Tenerife include the volcanic cone of Pico de Teide (3,718 m; 12,198 ft).

With a subtropical climate and fertile soils, the islands support farming and fruit growing, and such industries as food and fish processing, boat building, and crafts. The islands' mild climate makes them a major tourist destination year round.

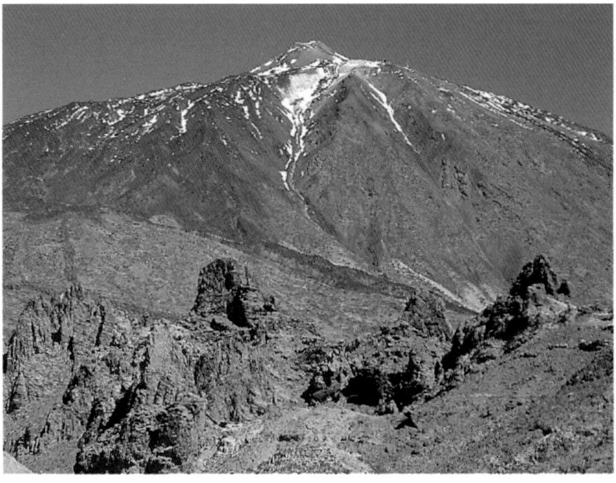

Pico de Teide on the island of Tenerife in the Canary Islands.

Cape Verde

Cape Verde consists of two small groups of islands 560 km (350 miles) off Dakar, on the westernmost part of west Africa. These islands were discovered, uninhabited, by Portuguese navigators in 1456. For several centuries, until 1876, the islands were used by slave-traders as a depot for assembling slaves and provisioning ships. As with other places involved in the slave trade, this activity influenced the composition of the population, with 71 percent being today of Afro-Portuguese background. Portuguese colonial administration came to an end with independence in 1975, but because of limited opportunities on the islands more Cape Verdeans now live abroad than at home. Remittances are an important source of domestic income.

The northern group of islands is called the Barlavento or windward group; the southern is called the Sotavento or leeward group. Volcanic, with slopes weathered into unusual shapes by the wind, the land leads steeply up from the sea to mountainous heights. The active volcano of Mt Cano on the island of Fogo in the southern group is the highest point.

The most densely populated areas are the coastal plain of São Tiago in the southern group, and Santa Antão and São Vicente in the northern group. A chronic lack of water makes agriculture difficult, most of the productive farming being done in a small number of irrigated inland valleys. Droughts regularly devastate the crops of maize, beans, and sweet potatoes on which the majority of Cape Verdeans live. The effects of the drought that lasted from 1968 to 1982 were so severe that some 40,000 people emigrated to Portugal.

On the economic front Cape Verde faces a number of severe problems. The natural resource base is limited. The only minerals of any significance are salt and pozzolana, a volcanic rock that is used for making cement. Only two food products are exported—fish and bananas, each representing one-third of total exports. Although almost 70 percent of the population lives in the countryside, the gross national product share of agriculture is only 13 percent, the tuna catch accounting for 4 percent of that figure. About 90 percent of food is imported and Cape Verde is heavily dependent on foreign aid.

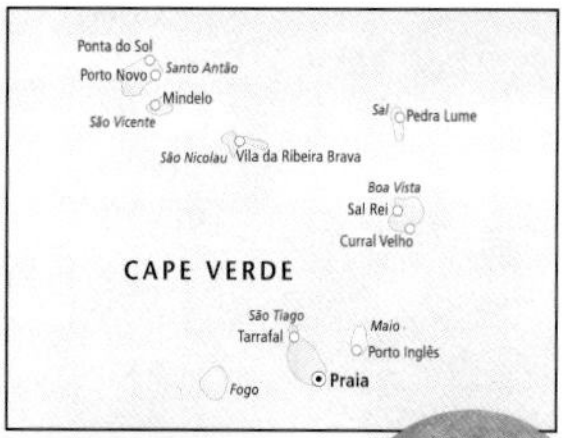

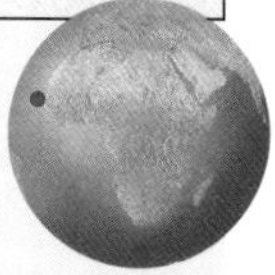

Cape Verde

Official name Republic of Cape Verde
Form of government Republic with single legislative body (People's National Assembly)
Capital Praia
Area 4,030 sq km (1,556 sq miles)
Time zone GMT – 1 hour
Population 405,748
Projected population 2005 438,465
Population density 100.7 per sq km (260.8 per sq mile)
Life expectancy 71
Infant mortality (per 1,000) 45.5
Official language Portuguese
Other languages Crioulo (blend of Portuguese and West African languages)
Literacy rate 69.9%
Religions Roman Catholic and indigenous beliefs, often in combination 98%; Protestant 2%
Ethnic groups Mixed African–European 71%, African 28%, European 1%
Currency Cape Verdean escudo
Economy Agriculture 66%, services 20%, industry 14%
GNP per capita US$9,602
Climate Arid, with warm, dry summers
Highest point Pico (Mt Cano) 2,829 m (9,281 ft)
Map reference Page 800

CAYMAN ISLANDS

OFFICIAL NAME Cayman Islands
FORM OF GOVERNMENT Dependent territory of the United Kingdom
CAPITAL George Town
AREA 260 sq km (100 sq miles)
TIME ZONE GMT – 5 hours
POPULATION 39,335
LIFE EXPECTANCY 77.1
INFANT MORTALITY (PER 1,000) 8.4
LITERACY RATE Not available
CURRENCY Caymanian dollar
ECONOMY Services 20%, clerical 20%, construction 13%, finance and investment 10%, directors and business managers 10%, other 27%
CLIMATE Tropical, with cool, dry winters and warm, wet summers
MAP REFERENCE Page 839

Cayman Islands

The largest of Britain's dependencies in the Caribbean, the Cayman Islands consist of three low-lying coral islands south of Cuba and 300 km (186 miles) west of Jamaica. Until the 1960s the main occupations were farming and fishing. Today the islands are one of the world's biggest offshore financial centers, offering a confidential tax haven to some 35,000 companies and several hundred banks. Tourism is also a mainstay, accounting for 70 percent of gross domestic product and 75 percent of foreign currency earnings. Tourism is aimed at the luxury end of the market and caters mainly to visitors from North America. The Cayman Islands were uninhabited when first discovered by Europeans. Most residents today are of mixed Afro-European descent, while an immigrant Jamaican labor force makes up about one-fifth of the population.

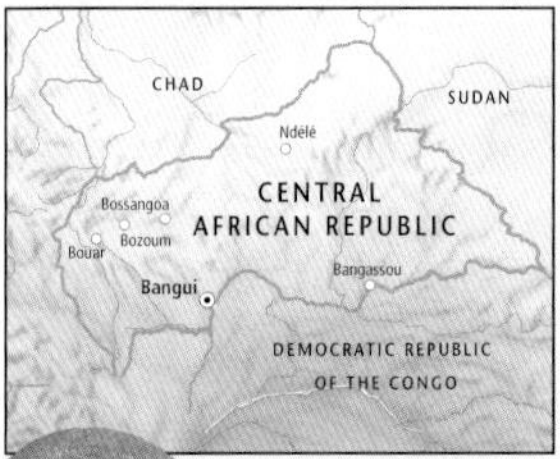

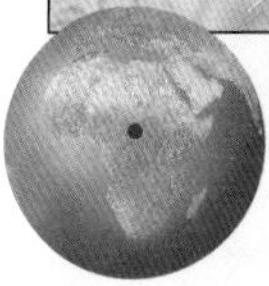

CENTRAL AFRICAN REPUBLIC

OFFICIAL NAME Central African Republic
FORM OF GOVERNMENT Republic with single legislative body (National Assembly)
CAPITAL Bangui
AREA 622,980 sq km (240,533 sq miles)
TIME ZONE GMT + 1 hour

Central African Republic

The Central African Republic (CAR) is a land-locked plateau just north of the equator. It is bordered on the west and north by Cameroon and Chad, and on the east and south by Sudan, the Democratic Republic of Congo, and Congo. By the time of European exploration the population of forest-dwelling Pygmies was much reduced, having been largely replaced by Bantu and Azande people. The region was for centuries used as a slave source by African slave-traders from the Sudan. When France took control in 1911 it ended slave-trading. The CAR was run as part of French Equatorial Africa until independence in 1958.

The average elevation of the CAR plateau is between 2,000 and 2,500 m (6,500 and 8,000 ft). These uplands form a watershed dividing the Congo and Nile river basins. North of the high ground of the Massif des Bongos the land drains toward the interior along water courses into swamps in southern Chad. South of this massif, numerous rivers feed into the Ubangi. To the west the Massif du Yadé forms a boundary with Cameroon.

In the south and southeast are forests containing hardwoods such as mahogany and ebony. Dense rainforest in this area provides one of the last homes of the lowland gorilla. Much of the rest of the land is savanna. Plantation forestry undertaken by foreign timber interests has in some places added significantly to natural soil erosion.

The CAR economy is based on subsistence agriculture combined with forestry. Food crops include manioc, yams, millet, maize, and bananas. Cotton, coffee, and tobacco are grown for cash. Industries include sawmills, textiles, footwear, and bicycle assembly. About 80 percent of export revenue comes from diamond mining.

The country's economic prospects are constrained by its position, its limited resources, its unskilled workforce, and its poor infrastructure. In addition, tuberculosis, leprosy, and sleeping sickness are widespread. These factors are likely to keep the CAR dependent on foreign aid for some time.

Population 3,444,951
Projected population 2005 3,904,795
Population density 5.5 per sq km (14.2 per sq mile)
Life expectancy 47.2
Infant mortality (per 1,000) 103.4
Official language French
Other languages Sangho, Arabic, Hunsa, Swahili
Literacy rate 57.2%
Religions Protestant 25%, Roman Catholic 25%, indigenous beliefs 24%, Muslim 15%, other 11%
Ethnic groups Baya 34%, Banda 27%, Mandjia 21%, Sara 10%, Mboum 4%, M'Baka 4%
Currency CFA (Communauté Financière Africaine) franc
Economy Agriculture 85%, services 12%, industry 3%
GNP per capita US$340
Climate Tropical, with hot, dry winters and hot, wet summers
Highest point Mt Kayagangir 1,420 m (4,659 ft)
Map reference Pages 805, 806

C

Falls on the Kotto River in the Central African Republic.

C

CEUTA

AREA 20 sq km (8 sq miles)
POPULATION approximately 75,000
GOVERNMENT Spanish autonomous region
MAP REFERENCE Page 801

Ceuta

In 1912 the Sultan of Morocco signed a treaty with France making Morocco a French protectorate. At the same time the French, recognizing Spanish interests in the region, gave Spain several enclaves along the Moroccan coast. Two of these enclaves remain under Spanish administration—Ceuta and Melilla.

The high promontory of Jebel Musa at Ceuta, on the African side of the Strait of Gibraltar, stands opposite Gibraltar on the northern side. Legend has it that Jebel Musa and the Rock of Gibraltar were the two "Pillars of Hercules", set there by Hercules to commemorate his travels and achievements. Today, Ceuta is a military station and seaport with a population of about 75,000.

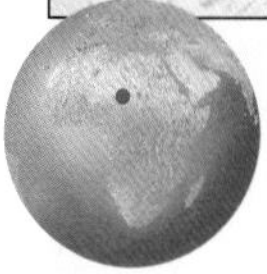

CHAD

OFFICIAL NAME Republic of Chad
FORM OF GOVERNMENT Republic with single legislative body (Higher Transitional Council)
CAPITAL Ndjamena
AREA 1,284,000 sq km (495,752 sq miles)
TIME ZONE GMT + 1 hour
POPULATION 7,557,436
PROJECTED POPULATION 2005 8,846,000
POPULATION DENSITY 5.9 per sq km (15.3 per sq mile)

Chad

Chad is a landlocked north African country twice the size of France. Much of it is semidesert and thinly populated, and it is one of the poorest and least developed countries in the world. Chad was conquered by the Sudanese warlord Rabah Zobeir late in the nineteenth century, but with 200 distinct ethnic groups in the population a sense of national unity has been slow to emerge. After France established control of the region in 1911 it became for 50 years part of French Equatorial Africa, achieving independence in 1960. Since then there has been almost constant civil war, aggravated by the main ethnic divide—that between the desert-dwelling Muslim Arabs in the north and the non-Muslim African farmers in the south.

The country can be loosely divided into four regions. In the center are broad, arid savanna plains. To the north are deserts with large areas of mobile sand dunes along the southern Sahara. In the northwest are the volcanic mountains of the Tibesti, rising to the 3,415 m (11,204 ft) peak of Emi Koussi. Though surrounded by desert these mountains attract rain, and some farming takes place in the valleys. In the south the valleys of the Chari and Logone Rivers support most of Chad's agriculture, including cotton-growing. Both these rivers drain into

Lake Chad (Lac Tchad). However, a series of droughts has reduced them to little more than streams, while the shallow and marshy Lake Chad itself is steadily shrinking as the desert advances.

Chad's economic difficulties have both political and climatic causes. Civil war in the 1980s disrupted agriculture and spread lasting division, while continuing government corruption and its inability to pay its employees have led to resentment in the civil service. Desertification has had an impoverishing effect, especially among pastoral peoples like the Fulbe in the Sahel. While oil production from a field discovered at Doba and additional mining of gold, iron ore, marble and uranium might provide significant long-term sources of revenue, 80 percent of the population is likely to depend on subsistence farming for some time and the country will continue to rely on foreign aid.

LIFE EXPECTANCY 48.6
INFANT MORTALITY (PER 1,000) 115.3
OFFICIAL LANGUAGES French, Arabic
OTHER LANGUAGES More than 100 indigenous languages
LITERACY RATE 47%
RELIGIONS Muslim 50%, Christian 25%, indigenous beliefs 25%
ETHNIC GROUPS More than 200 indigenous groups: north mainly Arabic, south mainly African
CURRENCY CFA (Communauté Financière Africaine) franc
ECONOMY Agriculture 85%, services and industry 15%
GNP PER CAPITA US$180
CLIMATE Tropical in south, arid in north
HIGHEST POINT Emi Koussi 3,415 m (11,204 ft)
MAP REFERENCE Pages 802, 805, 806

A nomadic family in Chad outside their home.

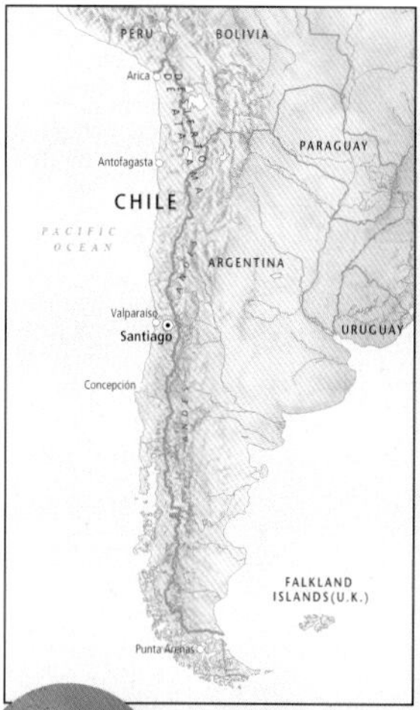

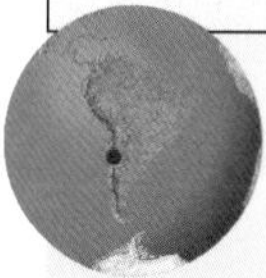

Chile

Chile lies between the Andes and the sea. It stretches 4,350 km (2,700 miles) along South America's Pacific coast, yet is never more than 180 km (110 miles) wide. In the fifteenth century, the Incas from Peru tried but failed to subjugate its Araucanian Indian population. This was gradually achieved by the Spanish, against strong resistance, after their arrival in the sixteenth century. The Spanish established mining in the north and huge estates in the Central Valley; by the nineteenth century produce was being exported to California, Australia and elsewhere. Today, fruit and vegetables remain important exports, along with wine.

The Atacama Desert (Desierto de Atacama), in the north, has one of the lowest rainfalls in the world. In the nineteenth century it was the world's main source of nitrate for fertilizer, an export which underwrote Chile's early economic development. Santiago and the port of Valparaíso form an urban cluster midway along the length of the country. Santiago lies in a sheltered, temperate valley between a coastal range of mountains to the west and the high Andes in the interior. This fertile 800 km (500 mile) valley is where Chile's main vineyards are located, and where 60 percent of the population live. It is also where most manufacturing industry is located. Volcanoes, active and inactive, mark the length of the

A view of the Lake District in Chile, with Volcán Villarrica in the background.

CHILE

OFFICIAL NAME Republic of Chile
FORM OF GOVERNMENT Republic with two legislative bodies (High Assembly and Chamber of Deputies)
CAPITAL Santiago
AREA 756,950 sq km (292,258 sq miles)
TIME ZONE GMT – 4 hours
POPULATION 14,839,304
PROJECTED POPULATION 2005 15,716,337
POPULATION DENSITY 19.6 per sq km (50.8 per sq mile)
LIFE EXPECTANCY 75.2
INFANT MORTALITY (PER 1,000) 12.4
OFFICIAL LANGUAGE Spanish
LITERACY RATE 95%
RELIGIONS Roman Catholic 89%, Protestant 11%
ETHNIC GROUPS European and mixed indigenous–European 93%, indigenous 5%, other 2%
CURRENCY Chilean peso
ECONOMY Services 63%, agriculture 19%, industry 18%
GNP PER CAPITA US$4,160
CLIMATE Arid in north, cold and wet in far south, temperate elsewhere
HIGHEST POINT Ojos del Salado 6,880 m (22,572 ft)
MAP REFERENCE Pages 856, 858

Chilean Andes to the east. In the southern third of the country the coastal range disintegrates into a maze of islands, archipelagoes, and fiords.

In 1970 President Allende nationalized the copper industry and other large enterprises, raised wages, and fixed prices. By 1973 inflation had reached 850 percent. Fearing a Cubanization of Chile, the political right under General Pinochet staged a coup and ruled for the next 17 years. During that time, over 2,000 political opponents "disappeared." Economically, the coup's effects were more positive. The regime restored economic liberalism and dismantled state controls. Democracy was restored at a general election in 1989.

After two decades of political turmoil, Chile is now one of the more economically progressive of South America's democracies. It is the world's leading supplier of copper, and high copper prices remain vital to the nation's economic health. Growth in gross domestic product averaged more than 6 percent annually from 1991 to 1995, and in recent years an estimated 1 million Chileans have ceased to be classed as poor.

Mountains in the Torres del Paine National Park, Chile.

China

The third largest country in the world, and the most populous, China is today something of an enigma: it has an increasingly capitalistic economy but with an old-style Communist Party leadership remaining in political control. Much depends on how successfully this "socialist market economy" works. With a civilization going back 5,000 years, China's history has combined long periods of dynastic stability with shorter periods of sudden change. In the last 100 years it has gone through a series of convulsive social, political, and economic transformations. Once isolated, agrarian, and indifferent to other societies and cultures, China's future is now that of a modern industrial nation trading with much of the world, particularly through the recently regained economic centers of Hong Kong and Macao. Politically it remains a one-party state. The political reforms needed for greater democracy are widely discussed in western media, as are civil liberties and human rights issues, but they are not yet on the agenda of China itself.

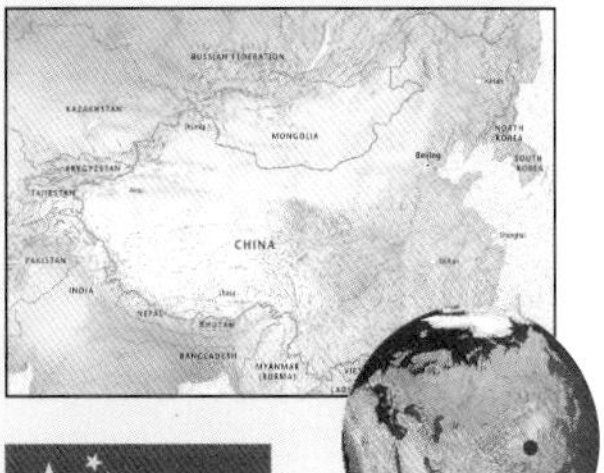

CHINA

OFFICIAL NAME People's Republic of China
FORM OF GOVERNMENT Communist republic with single legislative body (National People's Congress)
CAPITAL Beijing
AREA 9,596,960 sq km (3,705,386 sq miles)

continued overleaf

Time zone GMT + 8 hours
Population 1,246,871,951
Projected population 2005 1,296,199,683
Population density 129.9 per sq km (336.4 per sq mile)
Life expectancy 69.9
Infant mortality (per 1,000) 43.3
Official language Mandarin Chinese
Other languages Yue (Cantonese), Wu (Shanghaiese), Minbei (Fuzhou), Minnan (Hokkien-Taiwanese), other minority languages
Literacy rate 80.9%
Religions Officially atheist; traditionally Confucian, Taoist, Buddhist; small Muslim and Christian minorities
Ethnic groups Han Chinese 92%, other (including Zhuang, Uygur, Hui, Yi, Tibetan, Miao, Manchu, Mongol, Buyi, Korean) 8%
Currency Yuan
Economy Agriculture 74%, industry 14%, services 12%
GNP per capita US$620
Climate Varies widely: subtropical in southeast; temperate in east; cold and arid on southwestern Tibetan plateau; arid in northern deserts; cold temperate in northeast
Highest point Mt Everest 8,848 m (29,028 ft)
Map reference Pages 741, 742, 746–47, 748–49, 750–51

Physical features and land use

China can be divided into three major regions: the mountains to the west, including the vast Plateau of Tibet; the series of deserts and desert basins starting in the northwest with the Tarim Basin and the Taklimakan Desert, reaching across the Nei Mongol Plateau (Nei Mongol Gaoyuan) to Manchuria (Taklimakan Shamo) in the northeast; and the largely low-lying eastern region consisting of the valleys and floodplains of the Chang Jiang (Yangtze) and Huang (Yellow) rivers, extending to the coastal plains including the Pearl River in the south.

The melting snows of the Plateau of Tibet feed several major rivers—the Brahmaputra, flowing south to India, the Salween (Nu) of Myanmar (Burma), and the Mekong which skirts Laos and Thailand before passing through Cambodia and reaching the sea in Vietnam. In addition it is the source of both the Huang (Yellow), and the mighty Chang Jiang (Yangtze), China's two main rivers which drain into the East China Sea. In some parts permanently covered in snow, the Plateau of Tibet is the highest region in the world, averaging about 4,900 m (16,000 ft), with ranges rising from 6,100 to 7,300 m (20,000 to 24,000 ft). It is bounded to the north by the Kunlun Shan Range, and to the south along the borders of India, Nepal, and Bhutan by the mountain system of the Himalayas. A

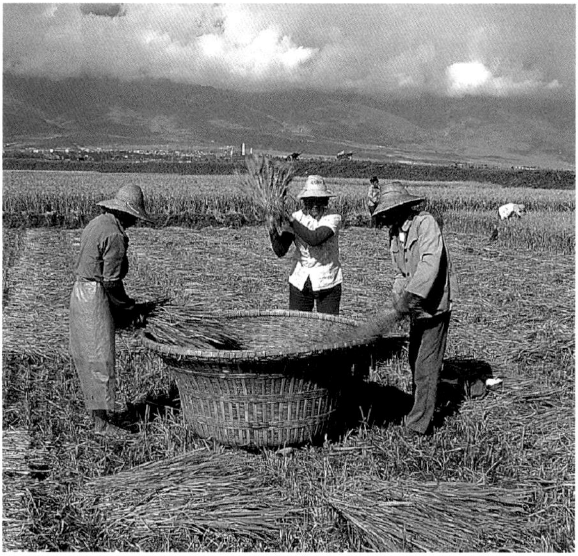

Threshing rice after harvesting.

harsh environment, hostile to human settlement, most of the plateau's 2 million people live in the south. The Himalayan ranges also have a political significance. Forming a massive rampart along China's southwestern frontier, for centuries they have provided a natural defensive barrier against the west. This is one reason why China is unwilling to allow the pressure for Tibetan independence to take it beyond the status of an "autonomous region."

The second region, stretching from the Tarim Basin and Dzungarian Basin (Junggar Pendi) in the northwest, past the southern fringes of the Gobi Desert to Northern Manchuria, is mostly too arid and cold for agriculture. Here, pastoralists such as the Uighurs of Xinjiang keep sheep, goats, and herds of horses. Some oasis crops, however, are grown around the rim of the Taklimakan Desert, and there are small farming settlements in the Gansu corridor to the north of the Qilian Mountains. The Turfan Depression (Turpan Pendi) (both the lowest and the hottest place in China at –154 m [–505 ft]) lies northeast of the Tarim Basin. East of the Gobi Desert lies the agricultural area of the Manchurian Plain, where coarse grains and soya beans are cultivated. In Northern Manchuria the growing season is short: only 90 days a year are frost free.

Buddhist prayer flags overlooking the Potala Palace, in Lhasa, Tibet.

The eastern region of central China is where two-thirds of the country's people live. This was the cradle of Chinese civilization. On the region's fertile alluvial plains the most distinctive features of China's economic and social life developed—intensive irrigated agriculture and the Chinese peasant family. Known as "China's Sorrow," the Huang (Yellow) River makes its way across the North China Plain. For hundreds of years it caused frequent flooding, with serious loss of life, but today there are modern flood-control schemes that have reduced this danger.

Further south, near the Chang Jiang (Yangtze) delta, the plain changes into a land of large lakes and intricate networks of canals, many of them centuries old. The Chang Jiang is China's largest and most important river, much of it navigable. When the river level is high, vessels of 10,000 tonnes may reach Wuhan; and 1,000-tonne barges can reach Chongqing in Sichuan. What is called the "Red Basin" of Sichuan is a fertile and highly productive area far up the Chang Jiang, separated from the lower valley by steep-sided gorges. It is intensively cultivated, the landscape dominated by rice fields arranged in terraces up the hillsides. Summer weather in the central valley of the Chang Jiang is hot and humid, temperatures at Nanjing reaching 44°C (111°F).

A distinctive landscape in southern China (famous for centuries as an inspiration for Chinese landscape painters) is found in northeastern Guizhou Province, where limestone spires and pinnacles rise above small, intensively cultivated plains. This heavily eroded area is marked by sinkholes, caverns, and underground streams.

A shopkeeper outside her fruit and vegetable store.

Provinces and Capitals

Anhui • Hefei
Fujian • Fuzhou
Gansu • Lanzhou
Guangdong • Guangzhou
Guizhou • Guiyang
Hainan • Haikou
Hebei • Shijiazhuang
Heilongjiang • Harbin
Henan • Zhengzhou
Hubei • Wuhan
Hunan • Changsha
Jiangsu • Nanjing
Jiangxi • Nanchang
Jilin • Changchun
Liaoning • Shenyang
Qinghai • Xining
Shaanxi • Xi'an
Shandong • Jinan
Shanxi • Taiyuan
Sichuan • Chengdu
Yunnan • Kunming
Zhejiang • Hangzhou

Autonomous Regions

Guangxi Zhuangzu • Nanning
Nei Monggol • Hohhot
Ningxia Huizu • Yinchuan
Tibet (Xizang) • Lhasa
Xinjiang Uygur • Ürümqi

Special Administrative Region

Xianggang (Hong Kong) • Xianggang (Hong Kong)
Macao • Macao

Municipalities

Beijing, Shanghai and Tianjin

In the coastal lowlands of Guangdong Province, in the far south, the climate is tropical and farmers enjoy a year-round growing season. On Hainan Island, flanking the Gulf of Tongking, three crops of rice per year are possible, while other crops in the south include sugar, bananas, and tropical fruits. During the summer, cyclones and typhoons often strike the southeast coast.

Young Buddhist monks collect food donations, Yunnan province.

Early history

Civilization arose along the margins of the North China Plain. Here, about 1700 BC, the Shang Dynasty originated in the Huang Valley. Noted for craftsmanship in bronze, along with the use of the wheel, the calendar, and a form of writing, the Shang lasted until 1122 BC. During the next dynasty, the Zhou, the teachings of the philosopher-teacher Confucius (551–479 BC) provided a pattern for Chinese society for centuries to come. Iron casting, metal coinage, and silk were also introduced at this time. During the short-lived Qin Dynasty (221–206 BC) a ruler arose named Qin Shihuang. He unified the nation, fortified China's northern boundary with the Great Wall, established the civil service, and was buried at Lintong with an army of 6,000 terracotta warriors which are today a major tourist attraction.

The Forbidden City, Beijing.

C

Temple, Wushi, Kiangsu province.

In 206 BC the Han Dynasty began. During the four centuries of the Han, paper and the seismograph were invented, steel was first made, Buddhism was introduced from India, and the boundaries of China were extended nearly to their present limits. Under the Sui (AD 581–618) a large part of the Grand Canal linking the north with the Chang Valley was built. During the 300 years of the Tang Dynasty which followed, China became the world's biggest empire. Paper money was adopted, block printing invented, and priceless ceramic vases produced. In these centuries, and those of the Song Dynasty (AD 960–1269) China's population, threatened by incursions of nomads from the north, began to concentrate in the warmer, more productive south. By the thirteenth century most people lived in the south, including the Chang Valley. The Song Dynasty is sometimes regarded as China's Golden Age. Trade expanded, and Chinese shipping took porcelain and silk to the East Indies, India, and Africa.

Northern invaders ended the Song Dynasty. By 1223 Ghengis Khan's Mongols held much of the north and in 1260 Kublai Khan proclaimed himself emperor, with Beijing as his capital. Unified by the conquests of the Mongol tribes, the empire by 1300 reached from Kiev to the Persian Gulf, and from Burma to Korea. Muslims, Christians, and Armenians all came to China at this time—among them was the Italian diplomat Marco Polo, who served under Kublai Khan. After the Mongols were

Rice pickers, Jinghong.

Basket loads of goods to sell at the Yangshou market.

Part of the Great Wall of China.

overthrown, Chinese rule was re-established under the Ming Dynasty in 1368, and the Great Wall was restored and extended to its present length of 6,400 km (4,000 miles). In the three centuries of Ming rule many palaces were built, including the Imperial Palace at Beijing, and ships explored as far afield as the Red Sea. It was during this period that the first Christian missions began to appear in China, the Jesuits establishing themselves with the Portuguese at Macao in the sixteenth century.

Chinese civilization's main features, however, had been laid down in the time of the Han, Tang, and Song. During their rule Confucianism became the pervasive social ethic, the individual becoming subordinated to both family and state; porcelain manufacture and silk production reached a rare perfection; and various inventions were made which found their way to the West, notably that of gunpowder. Despite the development of large cities, and the growth of an educated bureaucratic elite, Chinese society was largely agricultural, and its economic base depended on the productivity of the rural peasantry.

The Qing Dynasty (1683–1912) represented a return to power of northern people, the Manchus, descendants of the Mongols. Aggressive at first, seizing Taiwan and garrisoning Tibet, by the nineteenth century the Qing

Timeline China

1.9 MYA Appearance of early hominids who closely resemble *Homo habilis* (Longgupo Cave, Sichuan Province)

460,000 BP Earliest claimed evidence of controlled use of fire (Zhoukoudian Cave) by so-called *Homo erectus* Peking Man

800,000 BP Hominid *Homo erectus*, now considered to have evolved in Asia; present in China possibly 1.8 MYA

68,000 BP Homo sapiens sapiens present in China

1200 BC Writing system based on pictograms in use—many characters similar to those still used today

7500 BC Farmers of central and southern China domesticate foxtail millet and rice

5500 BC First thick clay pottery used in fishing villages along southern coastline

800 BC Populat under the Chou Dynasty more tl 13 million

214 BC First part of Great Wall of China completed under Qin Dynasty to protect against Turkish and Mongol invasions

206 BC Shi Huangdi (First Emperor) is buried with 6,000 life-size terracotta warriors at Chang-an near Xi'an

c.100 AD Paper made from hemp and rags in use with solid inks in northwest China

618 Tang Dynasty sees great economic development; Grand Canal links Huang and Chang rivers (completed 1283)

1213 Genghis Khan leads Mongolian invasion—up to 30 million Chinese are slaughtered

1279 The Mongols under Kublai Khan (grandson of Genghis) take control of all China; Beijing now the capital

1275 Marco Polo, a Venetian, visits China (until 1292) to establish trade links with the country he calls "Cathay"

1644 The Manchus establish Qing Dynasty, bringing peace and prosperity; the population rises to 400 million by 1700

1800 British smuggle in opium; war breaks out when Chinese object. Treaty in 1842 ends war; China cedes Hong Kong to Britain

1887–88 Huang River floods killing as many as 2.5 million people. It has flooded 1,500 times in the last 3,500 years

1900 Chinese "Boxer" rebellion in Peking (Beijing) against foreign interests put down by British and Russian forces

1911 Rebels proclaim republic—Emperor Pu Yi leaves throne 1912. In 1913 Sun Yat-sen founds Kuomintang (Nationalist Party)

1927–28 Civil War between Communist party and Kuomintang under Chiang Kai-Shek; Nationalists take Beijing

1934 Mao Zedong leads Long March of the Communists across China

1949 Mao Zedong proclaims People's Republic of China after a four-year civil war costing 12 million lives

1950 China invades Tibet; the Dalai Lama, Tibet's spiritual leader, flees to India

1958 "Great Leap Forward" to foster development damages economy and leads to severe food shortages; 20 million die by 1962

1979 "One-child families" policy introduced to curb population growth

1989 Pro-democracy demonstrations crushed by the use of tanks in Tiananmen Square, Beijing, with hundreds killed

1990 Census shows population of China exceeds 1.1 billion people

1997 China regains control of Hong Kong, imposes "One China, two systems" policy

1998 Chang Jiang River floods kill 3,000 with 250,000 homeless government had become weak and corrupt. Famine and unrest had made the country vulnerable to outside pressure and by the century's end China had been divided into spheres of influence among the major Western powers, a disintegration hastened by peasant uprisings (the Taiping Rebellion of 1850–64), and military defeats (the Sino-Japanese War of 1894–95). In 1912 the last of China's emperors abdicated and a republic was proclaimed.

Downtown Hong Kong, seen from the air.

Modern history

Political and military disorder prevailed during the next 40 years. At first the country was fought over by rival warlords. Two competing political movements offered solutions to this chaos—the Kuomintang (or Chinese National Party), and the Communist Party (founded in 1921)—but neither gained overall control. Then in 1931 Japan seized Manchuria, and in 1937 war broke out between China and Japan. During this time the communists sharpened their military and political skills, Mao Zedong winning the support of the peasantry and showing it was possible to succeed at guerrilla warfare. Hostilities between the Kuomintang and the communists were suspended in order to defeat Japan. But once this was achieved, in 1945, civil war broke out, costing 12 million lives. Victory went to the communists, and the People's Republic of China was proclaimed in October 1949.

Mass starvation, malnutrition, and disease were all brought under control in the initial years of communist rule and land reform began. As part of a planned economy the rural population was organized into 50,000 communes—smaller units that farmed the land collectively. Communes also ran rural industries, schools, and clinics. During these years morale and dedication were high. Many of the old middle classes suffered grave privations in "re-education camps" but living standards improved for most people, and corruption and bureaucratic sloth were not a major problem. But Mao Zedong was determined to push ahead with radical programs of industrialization and political change. In 1958 the "Great Leap Forward" movement tried to industrialize the country using the organization of the communes, and increase steel production by using backyard furnaces. It was a disaster. Between 1959 and 1961 failed economic policies led to famine, disease, and attempted rebellion. As many as 20 million people died.

Inner Mongolia.

Mao increasingly suspected his associates of disloyalty, believing some wanted to take "the capitalist road." In

C

Riding down ice slide, Harbin.

1966 he launched the Great Proletarian Cultural Revolution to extirpate "old thought, old culture, old customs and old habits." China's local authorities were, in effect, put on trial, many community members were abused and tormented, and the Red Guards rampaged through the many cities destroying property and wrecking ancient works of art. In 1967 the army was called in to restore order. Mao's death in 1976 brought change. There was even, in 1978, a brief flirtation with free speech. Deng Xiaoping, a new leader with a different vision of Chinese communism but no less determined to assert his power, began the process of economic liberalization which has led to today's state-managed capitalism and rigid political regime.

Taiwan and Tibet complicate China's relations with the West. China insists that Taiwan must rejoin the mainland as a province. Tibet has suffered under the regime, and thousands of its people have been killed, China's historic use of the region as a defensive bulwark in the west means that independence is unlikely. Civil rights do not exist in China. Law is arbitrary, the courts usually being conducted by army personnel without legal training. Students demonstrating in Beijing in 1989 for greater democracy were met with tanks and hundreds were killed and injured. In 1998 an attempt to organize an independent political party was crushed and its leaders were jailed.

The economy

Coal deposits exist in most provinces, and there are 70 production centers, of which Hebei, Shanxi, Shandong, Jilin, and Anhui are the most important. China also has deposits of iron ore, and is a major producer of tungsten. Industries produce iron, steel, coal, machinery, armaments, textiles, and petroleum, while the main exports are textiles, oil and oil products, chemicals, light industrial goods, and armaments. Questions about the economy are not centered on resources, skills or capacity. They concern the ideological clash between a market-oriented economy and the rigid controls of the Communist Party.

Cow grazing near an old Buddhist monument in China.

In 1978 the leadership began moving away from Soviet-style central planning. In agriculture, household responsibility replaced collectivization and brought an immediate rise in productivity. In industry, the power of plant managers and local officials was increased, small-scale private enterprise was allowed, and foreign investment and trade encouraged. As a result, agricultural output doubled in the 1980s and industry made major gains. Gross domestic product has tripled since 1978.

The present system, however, combines some of the worst features of communism (bureaucracy, inertia, and corruption) and of capitalism (windfall gains and high inflation). Additional difficulties arise from extortion and other economic malpractices; and from inefficient state enterprises. Up to 100 million rural workers are adrift between country and city. The amount of arable land continues to decline. Serious environmental problems exist, such as air pollution from the use of coal, and water pollution from industrial effluents; falling water tables and nation-wide water shortages; and the fact that less than 10 percent of sewage is treated.

Christmas Island

A small island in the Indian Ocean, Christmas Island is about 300 km (200 miles) south of Java. Coastal cliffs rise steeply to a central plateau. Formerly uninhabited, Chinese and Malayan labor was brought in to mine the island's rich phosphate deposits in the 1890s. The mine now operates under strict environmental controls to preserve remaining rainforest. After heavy Australian government investment, a hotel and casino complex was opened in 1993, drawing visitors mainly from Southeast Asia.

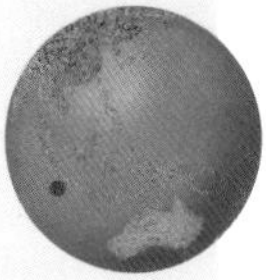

Christmas Island

Official name Territory of Christmas Island
Form of government External territory of Australia
Capital The Settlement
Area 135 sq km (52 sq miles)
Time zone GMT + 7 hours
Population 1,906 (1996)
Currency Australian dollar
Economy Mining, tourism
Climate Tropical, moderated by trade winds
Map reference Page 720

Cocos (Keeling) Islands

The Cocos (Keeling) Islands are a group of 27 coral atolls in the Indian Ocean midway between Australia and Sri Lanka. When discovered in 1609 by the East India Company's Captain William Keeling they were uninhabited. In 1827 the Scot John Clunies-Ross brought some Malays with him and established a settlement. The inhabited islands today are Home Island, where the Cocos Malays live, and West Island, with a small European community. The group has been administered directly by the Australian government since 1984. Coconuts are the sole cash crop, copra and fresh coconuts the major export earners. Though local gardens and fishing make a contribution, additional food and other necessities come from Australia.

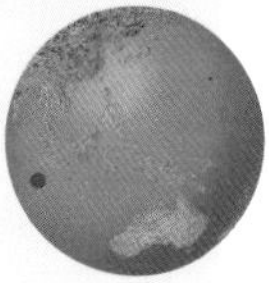

Cocos (Keeling) Islands

Official name Territory of Cocos (Keeling) Islands
Form of government External territory of Australia
Capital West Island
Area 14 sq km (5.4 sq miles)
Time zone GMT + 7 hours
Population 655 (1996)
Currency Australian dollar
Economy Coconut and copra production
Climate Tropical, moderated by trade winds
Map reference Page 720

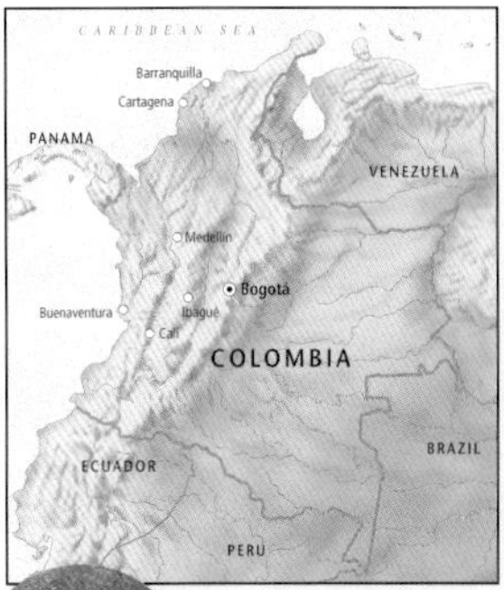

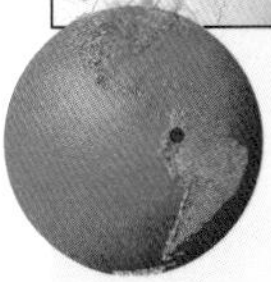

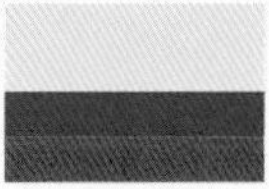

Colombia

Official name Republic of Colombia
Form of government Republic with two legislative bodies (Senate and House of Representatives)
Capital Bogotá
Area 1,138,910 sq km (439,733 sq miles)
Time zone GMT – 5 hours
Population 39,309,422
Projected population 2005 43,662,177
Population density 34.5 per sq km (89.4 per sq mile)
Life expectancy 70.5
Infant mortality (per 1,000) 24.3
Official language Spanish
Literacy rate 91.1%
Religions Roman Catholic 95%; Protestant, Jewish, other 5%
Ethnic groups Mixed indigenous–European 58%, European 20%, mixed European–African 14%, African 4%, mixed indigenous–African 3%, indigenous 1%
Currency Colombian peso
Economy Services 46%, agriculture 30%, industry 24%
GNP per capita US$1,910
Climate Tropical along coast and on plains, cool to sometimes cold in highlands
Highest point Nevado del Huila 5,750 m (18,865 ft)
Map reference Pages 848–49

Colombia

Visited by Christopher Columbus in 1499 and named after him, Colombia straddles the South American continent south of the isthmus of Panama. Once the home of the Chibcha Indians, the country came under Spanish control in 1544, after which it became their chief source of gold. Colombia achieved independence in 1819. From that time on the political and economic fortunes of the country have been contested by the anticlerical free-trading Liberals and the Conservatives, upholders of protectionism and the Church. While Colombia is notorious for its drug cartels and exports of cocaine, it has a diversified and stable economy that has, for 25 years, shown Latin America's most consistent record of growth.

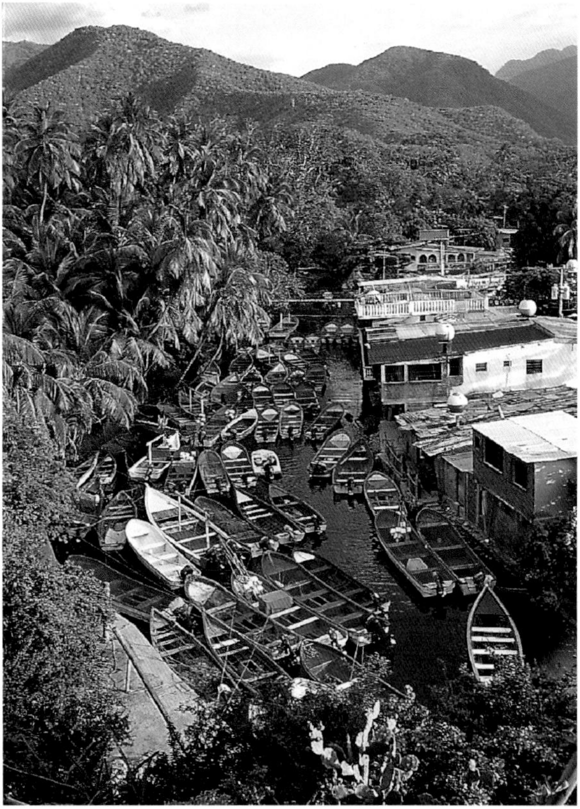

Riverboats in Puerto, Colombia.

The country can be divided into three regions. The hot, wet Pacific lowlands run south from the Panamanian border; to the north they merge into drier lowlands along the Caribbean. The cities that face the Caribbean—Barranquilla, Santa Marta, and Cartagena—are tourist resorts. Inland, the parallel Andean ranges running north from the Ecuadorian border define the second region, the high valleys of the Cauca and Magdalena Rivers. This is where most people live. The third region comprises the foothills east of the Andes, where the land falls away into the forested basins of the Amazon (Amazonas) and Orinoco Rivers. This region amounts to almost two-thirds of Colombia's area but only a few cattle ranchers and Indians live here.

With Latin America's largest proven reserves of coal, Colombia is the region's biggest coal exporter. Some 80 percent of the world's emeralds also come from here. Coffee, however, remains the biggest legitimate revenue-earning export. Since 1990 growth in gross domestic product has averaged 4 percent annually, led by expanding construction and financial service industries, and inflows of foreign capital. Nevertheless, earnings from processed cocaine probably exceed all others. Problems include a poverty index of 40 percent, and a continuing political crisis related to allegations of drug connections at high levels.

Comoros

The Comoros are a group of islands in the Mozambique Channel, lying between northern Madagascar and the African coast. Some of the smaller ones are coral islets. The larger islands are volcanic, and three of the four largest constitute the Republic of the Comoros. (Another large island, Mayotte, decided to remain a French dependency.)

For centuries, Indian and Arab traders have sailed across the Indian Ocean and worked their way along the coast of east Africa, visiting the Comoros as they went. The Comoran population reflects this history. There are large groups with African, Arab, Indonesian, and Madagascan backgrounds, and even a minority with Polynesian ancestors. France controlled the islands after

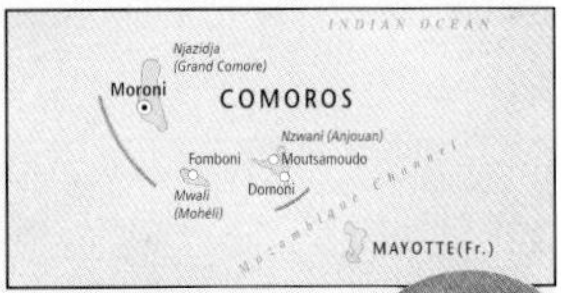

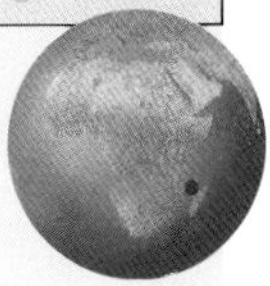

Comoros

Official name Federal Islamic Republic of the Comoros

Form of government Federal republic with single legislative body (National Assembly)

(continues)

C

COMOROS *(continued)*

AREA 2,170 sq km (838 sq miles)
TIME ZONE GMT + 3 hours
POPULATION 562,723
PROJECTED POPULATION 2005 676,257
POPULATION DENSITY 259.3 per sq km (671.5 per sq mile)
LIFE EXPECTANCY 60.9
INFANT MORTALITY (PER 1,000) 81.6
OFFICIAL LANGUAGES Arabic, French
OTHER LANGUAGE Comoran (blend of Swahili and Arabic)
LITERACY RATE 56.7%
RELIGIONS Sunni Muslim 86%, Roman Catholic 14%
ETHNIC GROUPS Mixture of Malagasy, African, Malay and Arab groups
CURRENCY Comoran franc
ECONOMY Agriculture 80%, government 3%, other 17%
GNP PER CAPITA US$470
CLIMATE Tropical, with wet season November to May
HIGHEST POINT Kartala 2,361 m (7,746 ft)
MAP REFERENCE Page 812

declaring them a colony in 1912. They obtained their independence in 1975.

The island of Njazidja (formerly Grande Comore) consists mainly of a rocky lava plateau, rising at its southern end to the active volcano of Kartala. On the coast is the national capital, Moroni. Because of the porous volcanic soils, rain quickly drains away, and despite heavy seasonal falls rainforests are found only on the mountain's upper slopes. On the island of Nzwani (formerly Anjouan) soils are more fertile but clearing of land without proper terracing has led to serious erosion. The island of Mwali (formerly Mohéli) is the smallest of the group. It has dense forests and fertile valleys.

Comoros has few natural resources. Subsistence agriculture is the traditional way of life, the main food crops being cassava, mountain rice, and sweet potato. Nevertheless, the islands are not self-sufficient in food, and rice accounts for 90 percent of all imports. Cattle and goats are kept—the latter are another cause of erosion. There are a few small hydroelectric plants; otherwise, fuel must be imported. Revenue-earning exports are vanilla, cloves, perfume oil, and copra.

The government is trying to diversify exports, privatize industrial enterprises, and reduce the high population growth rate, but its authority has been weakened by chronic political instability and several attempted coups. Foreign aid is likely to be needed for some time.

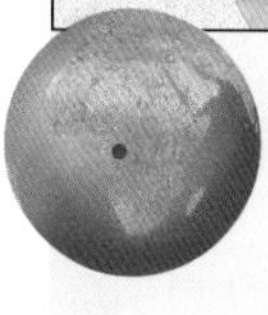

Congo

From the Atlantic coast, Congo extends 1,000 km (600 miles) inland to the border of the Central African Republic. Its history is obscure, although the first inhabitants may have been Pygmies. Later it was home to the Kongo peoples who supplied slaves for Portuguese traders. In the nineteenth century it was explored by the French-Italian Pierre Savorgnan de Brazza, who gave his name to the capital city, and whose activities led to the region becoming part of French Equatorial Africa in 1891. Congo has been independent since 1960.

Ten years after independence, Congo declared itself a People's Republic and Africa's first communist state. Since 1991, however, there have been attempts to introduce the principles of legal opposition and multi-party democracy. Road transport within Congo is hampered by tropical rains that make the unpaved roads unuseable, but water transport to the interior and the northeast is comparatively easy. Two mighty rivers, the Congo and the Ubangi, provide a commercially navigable highway along virtually the entire eastern frontier.

From a coastal strip on the Atlantic seaboard, the Rivers Kouilou and Niari lead up to the heights of the Massif du Mayombé. This range is crossed by a spectacular French-built railway joining Brazzaville with the port of Pointe-Noire. The Congo below Brazzaville has many cataracts, and the railway was built to carry freight around them. Beyond the massif the land falls away northward to the central plateau, where numerous rivers drain east into the Ubangi and the Congo itself.

Though more than half the Congolese live in towns, subsistence agriculture engages one-third of the workforce, and most of the food produced and consumed is cassava. Rice, maize, and vegetables are also grown, and coffee and cocoa are exported. Some 60 percent of the country is still covered in tropical forest. Timber was once a leading export, but today 90 percent of exports consists of oil. Despite its comparative wealth, the government has mortgaged a large part of its oil earnings for expensive development projects.

Congo

Official name People's Republic of the Congo
Form of government Republic with two legislative bodies (Senate and National Assembly)
Capital Brazzaville
Area 342,000 sq km (132,046 sq miles)
Time zone GMT + 1 hour
Population 2,716,814
Projected population 2005 3,072,457
Population density 7.9 per sq km (20.5 per sq mile)
Life expectancy 47.1
Infant mortality (per 1,000) 100.6
Official language French
Other languages African languages (particularly Lingala, Kikongo and Monokutuba)
Literacy rate 73.9%
Religions Christian 50%, indigenous 48%, Muslim 2%
Ethnic groups About 75 different tribes: Kongo 48%, Sangha 20%, Teke 17%; other 15%
Currency CFA (Communauté Financière Africaine) franc
Economy Agriculture 75%, industry and services 25%
GNP per capita US$680
Climate Tropical, with wet season March to June
Highest point Mt Berongou 903 m (2,963 ft)
Map reference Page 808

C

A village in the Congo highlands.

C

Cook Islands

Official name Cook Islands
Form of government Self-governing territory of New Zealand
Capital Avarua
Area 240 sq km (93 sq miles)
Time zone GMT – 10 hours
Population 20,200
Life expectancy 71.1
Infant mortality (per 1,000) 24.7
Literacy rate Not available
Currency New Zealand dollar
Economy Agriculture, services, industry
Climate Tropical, moderated by trade winds
Map reference Pages 722–23, 725

Cook Islands

About 3,500 km (2,175 miles) northeast of New Zealand, the Cook Islands consist of 24 widely separated coral atolls in the north, and hilly, volcanic islands in the south. The Polynesian inhabitants are believed to have settled the islands around AD 500 to 800. They were visited by the Spanish in 1595; explored by Captain James Cook in 1773 and 1777; Christianized by British missionaries after 1821; and annexed to New Zealand in 1901. Since independence in 1965 the islands have been self-governing in free association with New Zealand. They have a fully responsible government, with elections every five years to a 25-member parliament, based on full adult suffrage. The climate is tropical with plentiful rainfall. Agriculture provides the economic base, and the main export earners are fruit, copra, and clothing. Marine culture has recently led to the production of black pearls and trochus shell. Financial services are available. New Zealand is both the main trading partner (taking 96 percent of exports) and the source of substantial aid. Tourism is expanding.

Pristine waters off the Cook Islands.

Coral Sea Islands

These uninhabited sandy islands and coral reefs are located in the Coral Sea northeast of Australia's Great Barrier Reef. The numerous small islands and reefs are scattered over a sea area of about 1 million sq km (386,000 sq miles), with Willis Islets the most important. Nowhere more than 6 m (20 ft) above sea level, the area is an important nesting area for seabirds and turtles. There are no permanent freshwater resources and the islands are occasionally subject to cyclones. Although there are no indigenous inhabitants, three meteorologists are stationed there. Defense is the responsibility of Australia, the islets being regularly visited by the Royal Australian Navy. Australia controls the activities of visitors.

Coral Sea Islands

Official name Coral Sea Islands Territory
Form of government External territory of Australia
Capital None; administered from Canberra
Area 3 sq km (1.2 sq miles)
Time zone GMT + 10 hours
Population No permanent population
Climate Tropical
Map reference Page 721

Costa Rica

Costa Rica lies on the Central American isthmus, between Nicaragua and Panama. Its rainforests and wildlife made it popular with tourists in the 1980s, but rising crime has recently reduced tourist interest. Like a number of other Central American countries it was historically influenced by the civilizations of the Maya and Inca, and the earliest human settlements go back 10,000 years. It was named by Christopher Columbus in 1502, *costa rica* meaning "rich coast," and from the 1570s it was a Spanish colony. It gained its independence in 1821 and became a republic in 1848.

Costa Rica is known for its high standards of education, long life expectancy, democratic and stable system of government, high per capita gross domestic product, and a relatively small divide between the rich and the poor. It abolished its national army in 1948. This portrait, however, underestimates the economic role played by US aid in recent times. With aid now reduced, Costa Rican governments have had to take austerity measures, and this has led to unrest.

Three ranges form the mountainous skeleton of the country. From the border of Nicaragua the northern Cordillera de Guanacaste descends to meet the Cordillera Central. Between the Cordillera Central and the southern

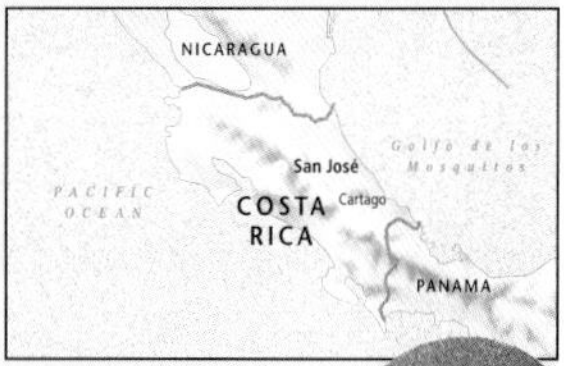

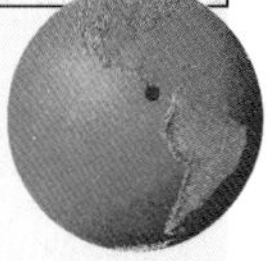

Costa Rica

Official name Republic of Costa Rica
Form of government Republic with single legislative body (Legislative Assembly)
Capital San José
Area 51,100 sq km (19,730 sq miles)
Time zone GMT – 6 hours
Population 3,674,490
Projected population 2005 4,083,884
Population density 71.9 per sq km (186.2 per sq mile)
Life expectancy 76
Infant mortality (per 1,000) 12.9
Official language Spanish
Other language English
Literacy rate 94.7%

(continues)

The Pacuare River running through rainforest in Costa Rica.

COSTA RICA *continued*

RELIGIONS Roman Catholic 95%, other 5%
ETHNIC GROUPS European and mixed indigenous–European 96%, African 2%, indigenous 1%, Chinese 1%
CURRENCY Costa Rican colón
ECONOMY Services 57%, agriculture 25%, industry 18%
GNP PER CAPITA US$2,610
CLIMATE Tropical, with wet season May to November
HIGHEST POINT Cerro Chirripó 3,819 m (12,530 ft)
MAP REFERENCE Page 838

Cordillera de Talamanca lies the temperate Meseta Central, the valley where the city of San José stands. The surrounding area is the main coffee-growing region, coffee production supporting more than 50 percent of the population.

The lowlands on the Caribbean and Pacific coasts are heavily forested and rich in wildlife. While the Pacific side is relatively dry, the Caribbean lowlands receive heavy rain. Both coasts have numerous mangrove swamps and white, sandy beaches. There are several volcanoes on the ranges, some of which are active. Cattle are raised in the dry northwest savanna region of Guanacaste.

Coffee is the country's largest export and along with bananas provides nearly half the country's export earnings. There are large bauxite deposits at Boruca, and aluminum smelting is a major industry. Minerals mined include small quantities of gold, silver, manganese, and mercury. Energy self-sufficiency is being pursued through the development of hydroelectric power.

Côte d'Ivoire

Côte d'Ivoire (Ivory Coast) is a west African country on the Gulf of Guinea. In the eighteenth century it was conquered by Baule people from Ghana. In 1893 it became a French colony, achieving independence in 1960. Since then, while retaining a close association with France, Côte d'Ivoire has been a more liberal and commercially oriented society than the socialist states established elsewhere in Africa in the 1960s. This, combined with political stability, has made it relatively prosperous. Under the 30-year leadership of Félix Houphouet-Boigny (who died in 1993) investment was secure, and most of this period saw sustained economic growth.

A sandy strip of land some 64 km (40 miles) wide runs along the shore of the Atlantic, broken by sandbars and lagoons around Abidjan. Coastal shipping has always had trouble on the west African coast where there is heavy surf and there are no natural harbors. French construction of the Vridi Canal, giving access to Abidjan through the sandbars to the sea, created a valuable deep-

Cloth being woven on hand looms in the Côte d'Ivoire.

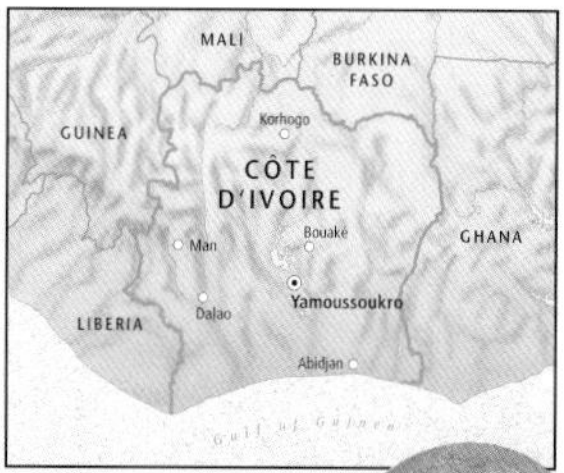

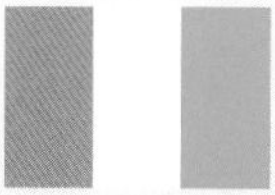

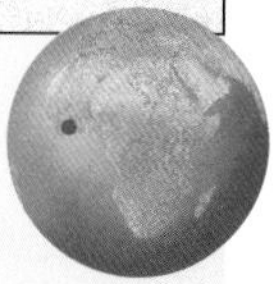

CÔTE D'IVOIRE

OFFICIAL NAME Republic of Côte d'Ivoire
FORM OF GOVERNMENT Republic with single legislative body (National Assembly)
CAPITAL Yamoussoukro
AREA 322,460 sq km (124,502 sq miles)
TIME ZONE GMT
POPULATION 15,818,068
PROJECTED POPULATION 2005 18,303,059
POPULATION DENSITY 49.1 per sq km (127.1 per sq mile)
LIFE EXPECTANCY 46.1
INFANT MORTALITY (PER 1,000) 94.2
OFFICIAL LANGUAGE French
OTHER LANGUAGES Indigenous languages, particularly Dioula
LITERACY RATE 39.4%
RELIGIONS Indigenous beliefs 63%, Muslim 25%, Christian 12%
ETHNIC GROUPS About 60 different indigenous groups: Baule 23%, Bete 18%, Senoufou 15%, other 44%
CURRENCY CFA (Communauté Financière Africaine) franc
ECONOMY Agriculture 70%, services 25%, industry 5%
GNP PER CAPITA US$660
CLIMATE Tropical, but drier in the north
HIGHEST POINT Mt Nimba 1,752 m (5,748 ft)
MAP REFERENCE Page 804

C

A traditional village of mud huts with thatched roofs, Côte d'Ivoire.

water port. From the coast the land rises gently, two rainy seasons and an equatorial climate providing a covering of rainforest further inland. There are three major national parks, with wildlife including elephant and pygmy hippopotamus.

Deforestation is a concern as hardwoods such as mahogany and ebony are felled. Growing in the place of native forest is plantation teak. Farther north the landscape changes to savanna grassland. Highlands are found in the northwest.

Côte d'Ivoire has varied mineral resources—petroleum, diamonds, manganese, bauxite, and copper—and is one of the world's main producers of coffee, cocoa beans, and palm oil. A large percentage of the population is engaged in farming, forestry, and livestock raising. Difficulties arise because of fluctuating coffee and cocoa prices but during the 1990s Côte d'Ivoire prospered, due mainly to the growth of new exports such as pineapples and rubber, trade and banking liberalization, and offshore oil and gas discoveries.

Croatia

Croatia wraps around the northern and western extremities of Bosnia and Herzegovina, allowing its neighbor a tiny 20 km (12 mile) toehold south of its almost 600 km (375 mile) stretch of coastline on the Adriatic Sea. It also shares borders with Slovenia to the northwest, Hungary to the northeast, and Yugoslavia to the east. The state of Croatia emerged in the ninth century AD, peopled by Slavic immigrants from present-day Ukraine. In 1091 it was invaded by Hungary with which it remained united until 1526 when most of the country came under the rule of the Ottoman Turks. In 1699 the Turks were driven out by the Austrian Hapsburgs. Once again, Croatia came under Hungarian rule, but with its own monarchy. In 1867 Croatia became part of the Austro-Hungarian Empire. In 1918 it declared its independence and joined with its neighboring states to form the Kingdom of Serbs, Croats, and Slovenes—the precursor of the state of Yugoslavia. Serbian domination of the new country provoked agitation by Croation separatists, and this led, in 1939, to Croatia's being declared a self-governing region within Yugoslavia. During the Second World War, the invading Axis powers proclaimed Croatia an independent state and installed a Fascist government intent on eliminating Serbs, Jews, and all political oppostion. At the war's end, Croatia once again became a republic in the reformed state of Yugoslavia. In 1991, after a referendum,

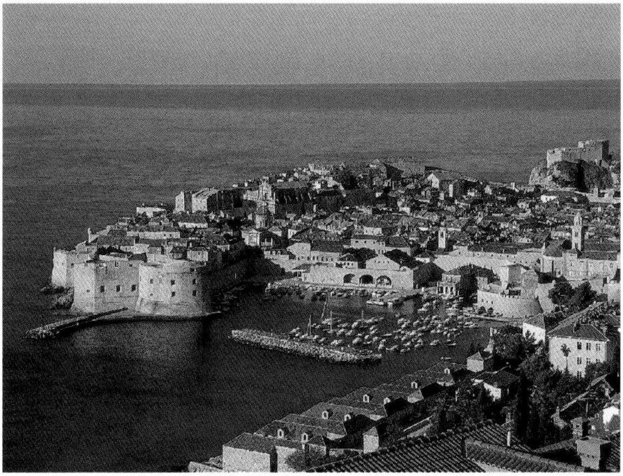

Dubrovnik Old Town, Croatia, is a fortress town.

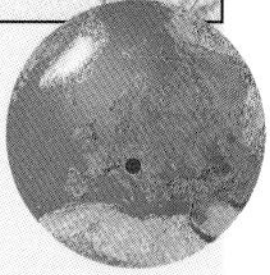

CROATIA

OFFICIAL NAME Republic of Croatia
FORM OF GOVERNMENT Republic with two legislative bodies (House of Districts and House of Assembly)
CAPITAL Zagreb
AREA 56,538 sq km (21,829 sq miles)
TIME ZONE GMT + 1 hour
POPULATION 4,676,865
PROJECTED POPULATION 2005 4,670,552
POPULATION DENSITY 82.7 per sq km (214.2 per sq mile)
LIFE EXPECTANCY 74
INFANT MORTALITY (PER 1,000) 7.8
OFFICIAL LANGUAGE Croatian
OTHER LANGUAGES Serbian, Italian, Hungarian, Czech, German
LITERACY RATE 97%
RELIGIONS Catholic 76.5%, Orthodox 11.1%, Slavic Muslim 1.2%, Protestant 0.4%, others 10.8%
ETHNIC GROUPS Croat 78%, Serb 12%, Muslim 0.9%, Hungarian 0.5%, Slovene 0.5%, others 8.1%
CURRENCY Kuna
ECONOMY Services 56%, industry 23%, agriculture 21%
GNP PER CAPITA US$3,250
CLIMATE Temperate; cold winters and warm summers inland, cooler and more temperate along coast
HIGHEST POINT Dinara 1,830 m (6,004 ft)
MAP REFERENCE Pages 778, 780

Croatia declared its independence and was then plunged into civil war as Croatian Serbs, supported by the Yugoslav army, sought to incorporate Croatia into a "Greater Serbia." The war ended officially in 1992, but hostilities between Serbs and Croats continued until 1995.

Along Croatia's spectacular Dalmatian coast are scattered about 600 small rocky islands, many of them former alpine peaks, isolated by rises in sea level. Further inland in the north, the Pannonian Plain, traversed by the Drava, Danube, and Sava Rivers, is a fertile region, centered around Zagreb, which is the hub of the country's agricultural production. A little more than one-fifth of the land is devoted to agriculture and about one-fifth of the population is directly involved in agricultural production. Cereal crops, fruit, and tobacco are widely grown and sheep are raised. Timber is a significant resource, and reserves of minerals, coal and iron are mined.

Civil and other regional wars in the 1990s have seriously impeded Croatia's transition to a market economy and cut industrial production. The tourist industry, once of great economic significance, has, since the early 1990s, largely ceased to exist. Much of the historic city of Dubrovnik on the southern Adriatic coast, once a major tourist center, was destroyed by shelling but it is being restored.

Dubrovnik Old Town is on the southern coast of Croatia.

Cuba

The largest island in the Caribbean, Cuba is the size of all the others combined. Led by Fidel Castro, it is the only communist state in the Americas, and despite internal and external pressures remains politically unchanged after 40 years. Cuba was visited by Columbus in 1492. It was at that time occupied by Arawak and Ciboney Indians. Under Spanish colonial rule sugar plantations worked by African slaves became the foundation of the island's economy—slavery only being abolished, under strong pressure from the Spanish government, in 1878. Gaining independence in 1898 but remaining under American tutelage until 1934, the country was run by a number of corrupt and gangster-ridden regimes until 1958, when Fidel Castro's army captured Havana. In 1976 the de facto monopoly of the Communist Party was formalized, with Castro, supported by his brother, making all decisions. Since the collapse of the Soviet system, on which Cuba had become economically dependent, times have been hard.

Cuba is only 193 km (120 miles) across at its widest point, but it stretches over 1,200 km (745 miles) from the Gulf of Mexico at its western extremity, to the Windward Passage between Cuba and Haiti in the east. In addition to the main island, the much smaller island of Isla de la Juventud lies off the southwest coast. Less mountainous than the other islands in the Greater Antilles group, Cuba nevertheless has three distinct ranges—the Oriental (Sierra Maestra), the Central, and the Occidental (Sierra de los Organos). These cover roughly 25 percent of the territory east to west. The remaining 75 percent of Cuba's surface area consists of lowlands and basins. On the more fertile soils sugar plantations, rice fields, coffee plantations, and tobacco fields are found; livestock is run on the central savanna. Cuba's irregular coastline is lined with mangroves, beaches, and coral reefs. Despite deforestation the island still has considerable areas of woodland, ranging from tropical near-jungle to pines growing in upland areas. Cuba has a mostly hot climate and also experiences heavy seasonal rainfall and periodic hurricanes.

Sugarcane remains the country's main cash crop, as it has for more than 100 years. Cuba is the world's third-largest sugar producer, and sugar represents almost 50 percent by value of the country's exports. Other crops are tobacco, rice, potatoes, tubers, citrus fruit, and coffee.

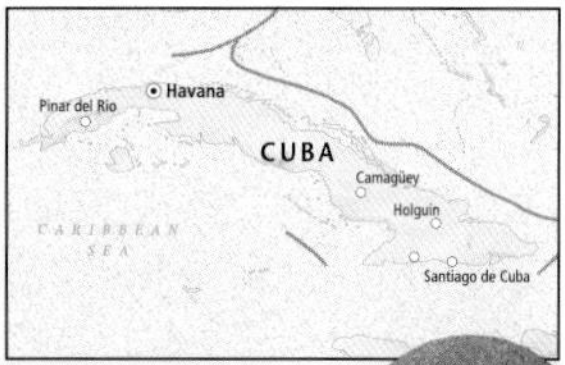

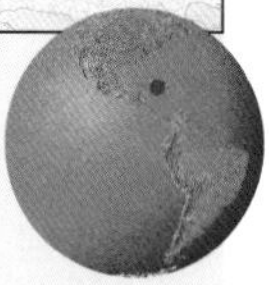

Cuba

Official name Republic of Cuba
Form of government Communist state with single legislative body (National Assembly of People's Power)
Capital Havana
Area 110,860 sq km (42,803 sq miles)
Time zone GMT – 5 hours
Population 11,088,829
Projected population 2005 11,313,934
Population density 100 per sq km (259 per sq mile)
Life expectancy 75.5
Infant mortality (per 1,000) 8.9
Official language Spanish
Literacy rate 95.4%
Religions Roman Catholic 40%, Protestant and African Spiritist 10%, non-religious 50%
Ethnic groups Mixed African–European 51%, European 37%, African 11%, Chinese 1%
Currency Cuban peso
Economy Services 48%, industry 29%, agriculture 23%
GNP per capita Est. US$766–3,035
Climate Tropical, moderated by trade winds; wet season May to October
Highest point Pico Turquino 1,974 m (6,476 ft)
Map reference Pages 838–39

An aerial view of Havana.

There are also extensive timber resources, including mahogany and cedar. Cuba has the world's fourth-largest nickel deposits, and production is rising as a result of a joint venture with a Canadian company.

Its situation as one of the world's few remaining communist states has left Cuba isolated and with few trading partners. In addition, because the government has been unwilling to hold multi-party elections, the country has been subject to a severe embargo imposed by the USA. Poor sugar harvests, insufficient funds to pay for fuel, and mounting deficits, have added to the country's difficulties in recent times.

However, recently the USA softened the embargo to allow more humanitarian aid. Tourism is also being encouraged, and the country is slowly opening to foreign investment. Recent trade talks in Rio de Janeiro between the European Union (EU) and Caribbean Community (CARICOM) saw Cuba's President, Fidel Castro, included in discussions. The talks centered on creating a free trade zone within these communities. Government subsidies on products are being reduced, and changes such as the legalization of self-employment, particularly in manufactured goods and handcrafts, show a commitment to improving the economy.

Cyprus

Cyprus takes its name from *kypros*, the Greek word for copper. It was an important metal 3,000 years ago, in classical times, and is still exported today. Occupied by a succession of Phoenicians, Greeks, and Romans, held from 1571 by the Turks and by the British from 1878, Cyprus today is politically a deeply divided island. The southern part forms the Republic of Cyprus proper, where most of the population lives. Since 1982 the northern part has consisted of an autonomous region calling itself the Turkish Republic of Northern Cyprus (see box).

Along the north coast runs the long limestone range of the Kyrenia Mountains. Just south of this range is the fertile Mesaoria Plain between Morphou and Ammochostos (Famagusta) where grapes, potatoes, citrus fruits, and cereals are grown, and the steeper land supports sheep, goats, and cattle. In the south is the broad, mineral-rich massif of Troödos from where the copper comes. This constitutes 50 percent of the country's total land area and is a good geological example of an ophiolite, a dome of mineral-rich sub-oceanic rocks. Both major rivers flow from this massif—the Pedieas to Ammochostos Bay (Famagusta Bay), the Karyoti to Morphou Bay. Nearly half the total area of Cyprus is arable and 20 percent of this is irrigated.

The gap between the economic fortunes of the two parts of Cyprus continues to grow wider. The agriculturally based Turkish north, severely disrupted by the events of 1974, has not recovered well, and has suffered considerably from inflation. It continues to produce some cereals, meat, fruits, and olives. The Greek Cypriot

A flourishing olive tree in Cyprus that is about 1,000 years old.

CYPRUS

OFFICIAL NAME (Greek/Turkish) Republic of Cyprus
FORM OF GOVERNMENT Two de facto republics each with single legislative body: House of Representatives in Greek area, Assembly of the Republic in Turkish area
CAPITAL Lefkosia (Nicosia)
AREA 9,250 sq km (3,571 sq miles)
TIME ZONE GMT + 2 hours
POPULATION 768,895
PROJECTED POPULATION 2005 816,812
POPULATION DENSITY 83.1 per sq km (215.2 per sq mile)
LIFE EXPECTANCY 77.1
INFANT MORTALITY (PER 1,000) 7.6
OFFICIAL LANGUAGES Greek, Turkish
OTHER LANGUAGE English
LITERACY RATE 94%
RELIGIONS Greek Orthodox 78%, Muslim 18%, other 4%
ETHNIC GROUPS Greek 78%, Turkish 18%, other 4%
CURRENCY Cypriot pound, Turkish lira
ECONOMY Services 67%, industry 19%, agriculture 14%
GNP PER CAPITA Est. > US$9,386
CLIMATE Temperate, with cool, wet winters and warm, dry summers
HIGHEST POINT Olympos 1,951 m (6,404 ft)
MAP REFERENCE Page 760

southern half of the island has prospered from a greater diversity of activities, including tourism, manufacturing, and the income from military installations, such as the British air base of Akrotiri near Limassol. Manufactured products include cigarettes, wine, clothing, footwear, and cement. Cyprus is currently attempting to join the European Union. Internet resources have been utilized to ensure the Turks have access to the dialogue with the EU; however, at this stage there has been little response and the Turks remain uncooperative.

The Cyprus question

What seems to be a national dispute between Greece and Turkey has religious roots. The early Christians Paul, Barnabas, and Mark all visited Cyprus, and the Cypriots were among the first to adopt Christianity. Later, the rise of Islam saw the island subjected to repeated Arab invasions between 644 and 975. From 1195 it was ruled by the family of Guy de Lusignan, to whom it was given after the Third Crusade, and in 1487 it passed into the hands of the Venetian Republic.

In 1571 rule by Venice was replaced by Turkish rule—the Turks massacring many Greeks before settling a large number of their own people on the island. With the decline of the Ottoman Empire in the nineteenth century an agreement was made in 1878 giving Britain the administration of Cyprus (it became a crown colony in 1925). Greek Cypriots soon began agitating for union with Greece. This was also supported by Greek Orthodox Church leaders, who argued that four-fifths of the population (the Greek Cypriots) wanted union with the "Mother Country." Riots occurred in Nicosia in 1931. After the Second World War this campaign for Greek union was renewed, the political situation on the island being complicated by a left-wing Greek Cypriot push for full independence.

Independence from Britain came in 1960, but violence soon flared. For 10 years the Greek majority and the Turkish minority struggled for control. In 1974 Turkey invaded and occupied 40 percent of the land in the north, expropriating and expelling 200,000 Greek Cypriots to the south. Nine years later Turkish Cypriots declared the northern third of the island a "Turkish Republic of Northern Cyprus," and although this is recognized only by Turkey, the region is effectively controlled by its own government and president. Along a buffer zone that separates the two regions, and divides Nicosia itself, some 2,000 UN troops costing more than US$100,000,000 per year continue to supervise an uneasy peace. There are ongoing discussions between the three parties to try and resolve the conflict. As yet little progress has been made.

Czech Republic

A landlocked country in central Europe, the Czech Republic was until 1993 linked politically to Slovakia, its neighbor to the southeast, from which it is separated by the Carpathian Mountains. The Czech Republic consists mainly of the ancient provinces of Bohemia in the west and Moravia in the east. Part of the province of Silesia is also within the Czech Republic, but most of it now forms a portion of Poland.

Czechoslovakia came into existence in 1918, with the collapse of the Austro-Hungarian Empire at the close of the First World War. The Czechs and the Slovaks had been under one rule since 1471, and since 1526, except for a brief revolt in 1618, had been under Austrian domination. Germany occupied Czech territory in 1939, establishing a protectorate of Bohemia-Moravia and setting up a separate state in Slovakia. In 1948 the communists came to power, and the country, once again united, came under Soviet influence. Nationalist fervor was never far below the surface and in 1968 caused a movement for democracy. The "Prague Spring," led by Alexander Dubcek, was put down by an invasion of Soviet forces. In 1989 a popular movement led to a transition to a democratic state. Tensions between Czechs and the minority Slovaks led to a peaceful separation of the two states on 1 January 1993.

Bohemia consists largely of gentle hills and plateaus. Low ranges of mountains surround the province to the north, west, and south and the central plateau is traversed by the Elbe and Vltava rivers, which merge and flow into

Strambeck nestles in the hills in Northern Moravia, Czech Republic.

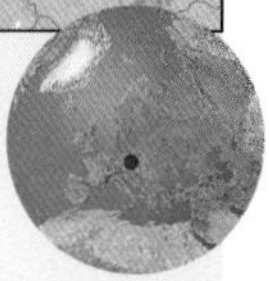

Czech Republic

Official name Czech Republic
Form of government Republic with two legislative bodies (Senate and Chamber of Deputies)
Capital Prague
Area 78,703 sq km (30,387 sq miles)
Time zone GMT + 1 hour
Population 10,280,513
Projected population 2005 10,394,294
Population density 130.6 per sq km (338.3 per sq mile)
Life expectancy 74.4
Infant mortality (per 1,000) 6.7
Official language Czech
Other language Slovak
Literacy rate 99%
Religions Roman Catholic 39.2%, Protestant 4.6%, Orthodox 3%, non-denominational 39.1%, other 13.4%
Ethnic groups Czech 94.4%, Slovak 3%, Polish 0.6%, German 0.5%, Gypsy 0.3%, Hungarian 0.2%, other 1%
Currency Koruna
Economy Industry 47%, services 45%, agriculture 8%
GNP per capita US$3,870
Climate Temperate, with cold winters and mild, wet summers
Highest point Mt Snezka 1,602 m (5,256 ft)
Map reference Pages 772–73

C

Germany. Most of the country's agriculture is centered on this river system, and much of its produce, which includes wheat, barley, and potatoes, is transported along these waterways.

Bohemia and Moravia are separated by a plateau known as the Moravian Heights. While Moravia is hillier than Bohemia, the center of the province, around Brno, consists of an extensive low plain. Winters are colder and rainfall is heavier in Moravia than in Bohemia.

Although not richly endowed with natural resources, reserves of black coal and iron ore have aided the development of iron and steelmaking as the country's major industries. Other important industries include clothing and car manufacture. Bohemian glass is famous and much sought after worldwide. Industrial production, however, has fallen in the 1990s as the country moves toward a free market economy. Tourism has made up for some of this fall-off.

The Bohemian city of Český Krumlov in the Czech Republic.

Czech conflict

The country formerly known as Czechoslovakia was at the center of successive conflicts in the twentieth century. It contains a volatile mixture of ethnic and political differences, and in the past fell victim to both German and Soviet totalitarian regimes. Hitler used the disaffection of the German minority in the Sudetenland as an excuse for invading Czechoslovakia in 1938. An insecure period of democracy after 1945 (marred by the expulsion of the still-resident German population) was followed by a communist takeover under Soviet auspices in 1948. In 1968 an effort to democratize the system led by Alexander Dubcek was crushed by Soviet tanks in August of that year. Along with other parts of East Europe it won independence from communist control in 1989, and now seeks EU membership—but these developments have been accompanied by the rise of ethnic separatism, and claims by one-time German citizens for restitution of property seized at the time of their expulsion after the Second World War. On 1 January 1993 the free-marketeering Czechs separated from the more statist Slovaks, and separate republics, reflecting different political traditions—the Czech "western," the Slovak "eastern"—came into existence. Under the presidency of the well-known playwright and (former) anti-communist dissident Vaclav Havel, a wholesale dismantling of state economic controls and structures then took place. However, the government which undertook these extensive reforms collapsed amid scandal and economic chaos at the end of 1997. Tensions with Slovakia continue, particularly as the Czech Republic gained control of a high number of resources, including military establishments, in the dissolution of the former Czechoslovakia.

View of Old Town Square from Town Hall tower, Prague, Czech Republic.

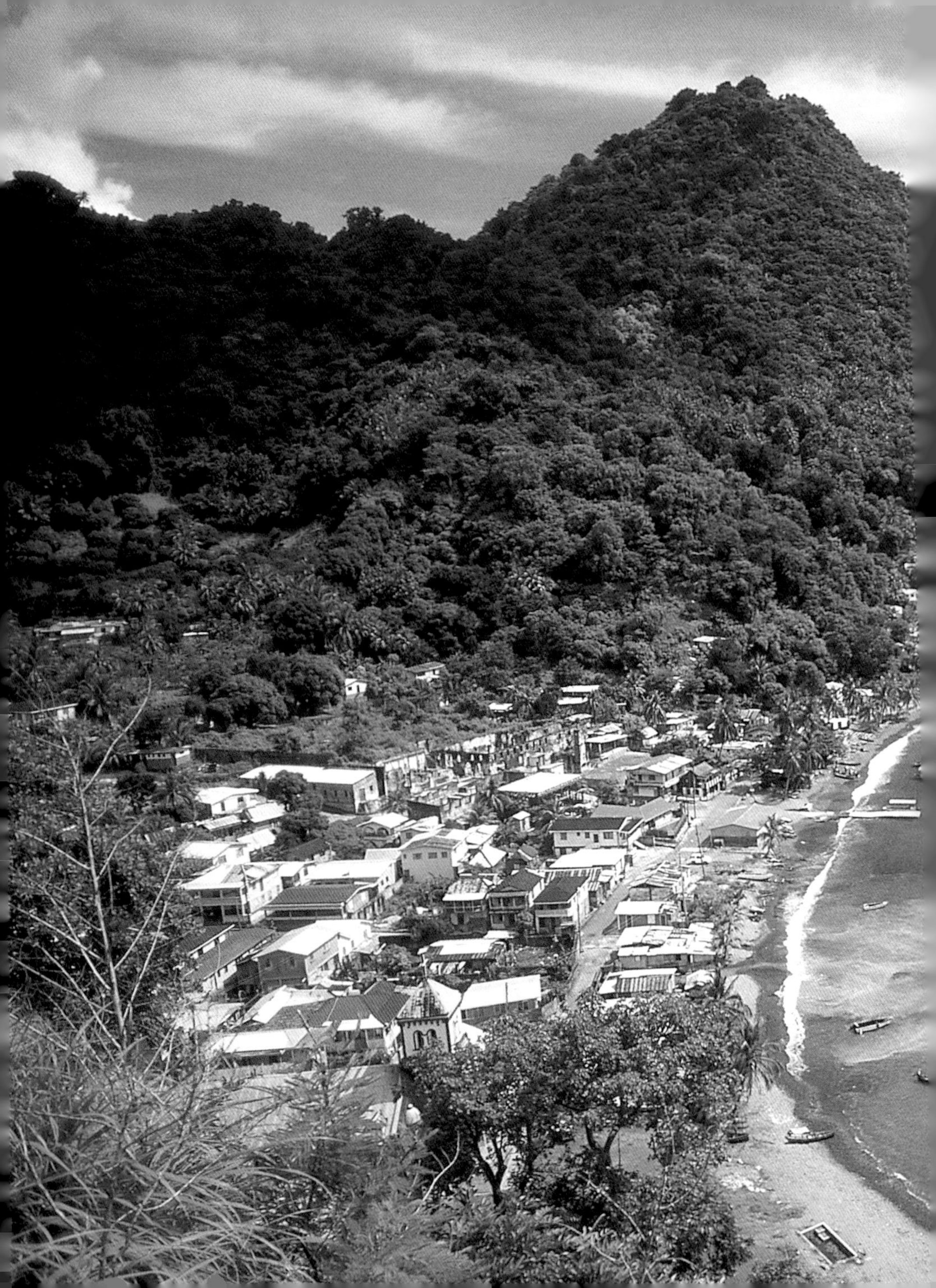

D

D

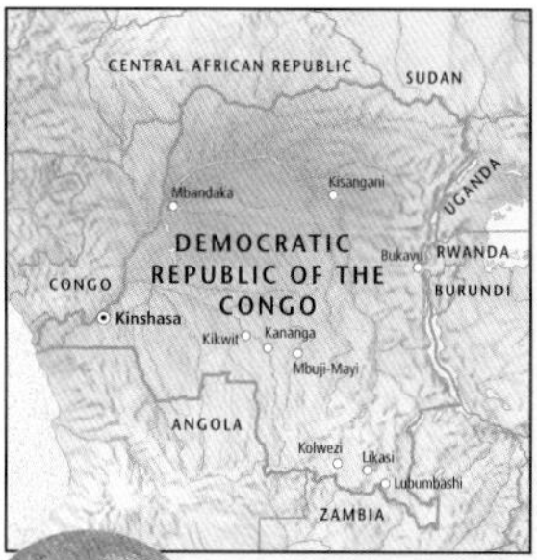

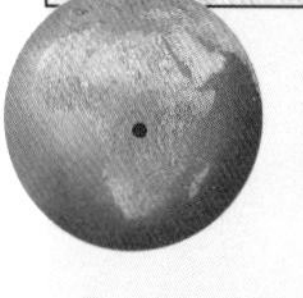

DEMOCRATIC REPUBLIC OF THE CONGO

OFFICIAL NAME Democratic Republic of the Congo
FORM OF GOVERNMENT Presidential rule
CAPITAL Kinshasa
AREA 2,345,410 sq km (905,563 sq miles)
TIME ZONE GMT + $\frac{1}{2}$ hour
POPULATION 50,481,305
PROJECTED POPULATION 2005 60,547,672
POPULATION DENSITY 21.5 per sq km (55.7 per sq mile)
LIFE EXPECTANCY 49.4
INFANT MORTALITY (PER 1,000) 99.5
OFFICIAL LANGUAGE French
OTHER LANGUAGES Lingala, Kingwana, Kikongo, Tshiluba
Literacy rate 76.4%
RELIGIONS Roman Catholic 50%, Protestant 20%, Kimbanguist 10%, Muslim 10%, other indigenous beliefs 10%
ETHNIC GROUPS More than 200 indigenous groups, mostly of Bantu origin: Kongo, Luba, Mongo, Mangbetu-Azande 51%; other 48%
CURRENCY New zaire
ECONOMY Agriculture 72%, services 15%, industry 13%
GNP PER CAPITA Not available
CLIMATE Tropical; wet season north of equator from April to October, wet season south of equator from November to March
HIGHEST POINT Mt Stanley 5,110 m (16,765 ft)
MAP REFERENCE Pages 808–809

Democratic Republic of the Congo

The Democratic Republic of the Congo (DRC) is the centerpiece of central Africa. It is the third-largest country on the continent after Algeria and Sudan and has one of the largest navigable rivers in the world. Historically occupied by the Kongo, Luba, Lunda, and Azande peoples, this enormous region fell into the hands of King Leopold of Belgium in 1885, who exploited it as a private domain. After international condemnation of his brutal rule, in 1908 it became a colony of Belgium. The country won its independence in 1960.

Since that time, 35 years of dictatorial mismanagement and corruption as a one-party state under the control of President Mobutu Sese Seko (who died in 1997) have brought the DRC to the point of collapse. War and disorder in neighboring Sudan, Rwanda, Burundi, and Angola have driven hundreds of thousands of refugees into the DRC. A military occupation of Kinshasa was successful in bringing the Mobutu regime to an end in 1997. The benefits of this transfer of power have yet to be seen.

Geographically the DRC is dominated by a single feature—the immense basin of the Congo River. The eastern rim of this basin is formed by the Mitumba Mountains (Monts Mitumbe) along the Rift Valley, and the volcanic Ruwenzori Range. In the far southeast Lake Mweru feeds into the Congo's main northward-flowing tributary, the Lualaba. Looping north and west in a great horseshoe, the Congo is joined on the borders of the Central African Republic by the Ubangi. After several cascades below Kinshasa the Congo empties into the Atlantic Ocean. The equatorial climate of the main river basin supports one of the world's most extensive rainforests, home to rare animals such as okapi and gorilla. The savanna grasslands of the east and south are home to giraffe, lion, antelope and rhinoceros.

Potentially one of Africa's richest countries, the DRC is currently one of its poorest. Most of its people try to survive the breakdown of civil society by subsistence farming and petty trade. Cash crops such as coffee, sugar, and palm oil continue to be produced, but a severe lack of infrastructure hampers trade. Hyperinflation, large government deficits, and falling mineral production mean that no end to the nation's economic difficulties is yet in sight.

Denmark

Denmark is both the smallest and the most southerly of the Scandinavian countries. Most of its land area consists of the Jutland Peninsula, which pushes northward from the northwestern tip of Germany. The North Sea washes Denmark's western coast, the Skagerrak Strait lies to the north separating it from the southern coast of Norway, and the Kattegat Strait separates it from the southwestern tip of Sweden. The Baltic Sea is to the east and within it, stretching almost as far as the southwestern tip of Sweden, is an archipelago of more than 400 islands. The largest of these islands is Sjaelland, on which is situated the Danish capital, Copenhagen.

Like the inhabitants of Sweden and Norway, modern Danes are descended from Viking invaders who from the fifth century AD moved northward into Scandinavia and then outward to other parts of western and eastern Europe. For much of its history, Denmark was the dominant country in Scandinavia. At the end of the fourteenth century, Norway and Sweden, as well as Iceland, were united under the Danish crown. The Swedes elected their own monarch 50 years later, but Norway continued to be part of Denmark for more than 400 years—until 1815, when the Congress of Vienna awarded it to Sweden in retaliation for Denmark having supported Napoleon Bonaparte. Despite its neutrality, Denmark was invaded by Germany during 1940. Liberated by British forces in 1945, Denmark joined the NATO alliance following the war, and

A model display at the tourist attraction Legoland, at Billund.

Denmark

Official name Kingdom of Denmark
Form of government Constitutional monarchy with one legislative body (Parliament)
Capital Copenhagen
Area 43,070 sq km (16,629 sq miles)
Time zone GMT + 1 hour
Population 5,356,845
Projected population 2005 5,432,898
Population density 124.4 per sq km (322.2 per sq mile)
Life expectancy 76.5
Infant mortality (per 1,000) 5.1
Official language Danish
Other languages Faroese, Greenlandic, German
Literacy rate 99%
Religions Evangelical Lutheran 91%, other Protestant and Roman Catholic 2%, other 7%
Ethnic groups Scandinavian, Eskimo, Faroese, German
Currency Danish krone
Economy Services 75%, industry 20%, agriculture 5%
GNP per capita US$29,890
Climate Temperate, with cold, wet winters and mild summers
Highest point Yding Skovhoj 173 m (568 ft)
Map reference Page 770

The Little Mermaid, Copenhagen.

is now a member of the European Union. Denmark is a constitutional monarchy, with an hereditary monarch. Its single-house parliament, which is headed by a prime minister, is elected every four years.

Almost the whole of Denmark is low-lying and its surface is covered in many places by rocky glacial debris, most prominently in the undulating mass of moraine that runs down the center of the Jutland Peninsula. This divides the peninsula into two distinct regions. To the west is a sandy landscape with extensive dunes and lagoons along the North Sea coast. To the east lies a loam plain, which extends across the islands of the archipelago, as far as the Baltic coast. This fertile region supports significant crops of barley, wheat, and sugar beet and a thriving livestock and dairying industry. Fishing, which is still a leading Danish industry, is based for the most part on the extensive, shallow lagoons that lie along the western coastline of Jutland.

As well as constituting a significant proportion of the country's exports, Denmark's agricultural and fishing produce also provide the raw materials for food processsing industries, which are a major source of employment. Other significant industries, for which

Chapel of the Cafés along the harbor in Copenhagen.

Denmark imports most of the raw materials are iron and metal working, machinery manufacturing, and furniture making. Despite having a relatively high unemployment rate during much of the 1990s, Denmark is a prosperous country and Danes generally enjoy a high standard of living. An extensive social security system means that serious poverty is comparatively rare.

Djibouti

One of the smallest African countries, Djibouti stands at the entrance to the Red Sea from the Gulf of Aden. This strategic location near the world's busiest shipping lanes has resulted in it being used as a base by European nations for a hundred years. After the construction of the Suez Canal, the British and French took an interest in Djibouti as a way of protecting their investment in the Canal route to Europe, the town of Djibouti becoming the capital of French Somaliland in 1892. Although Djibouti won independence in 1977, France continues to play a role in its affairs.

Since 1977 there has been a continuous political struggle between the majority Issa (who are Somali) and the minority Afar (also known as Danakil). Somalia, across the southeastern border, supports the Issa. Eritrea, to the north, supports the Afar, as does Ethiopia. Thus, both Issa and Afar have numerous external allies watching over their interests and inclined to interfere. The port of Djibouti

Men and their camels, Djibouti.

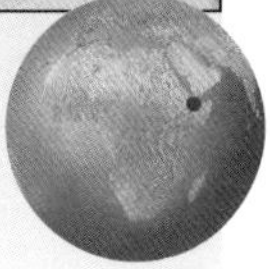

Djibouti

Official name Republic of Djibouti
Form of government Republic with single legislative body (Chamber of Deputies)
Capital Djibouti
Area 22,000 sq km (8,494 sq miles)
Time zone GMT + 3 hours
Population 447,439
Projected population 2005 516,114
Population density 20.3 per sq km (52.6 per sq mile)
Life expectancy 51.5
Infant mortality (per 1,000) 100.2
Official languages Arabic, French
Other languages Somali, Afar
Literacy rate 45%
Religions Muslim 94%, Christian 6%
Ethnic groups Somali 60%, Afar 35%, other (including French, Arab, Ethiopian, and Italian) 5%
Currency Djiboutian franc
Economy Services 75%, agriculture 14% industry 11%,
GNP per capita Not available (est. US$766–3,035)
Climate Semiarid; particularly hot on coast
Highest point Mousa Alli (Musa Āli Terara) 2,063 m (6,767 ft)
Map reference Page 807

An aerial view of the city of Djibouti, on the Gulf of Aden.

Street scene in Djibouti city.

is also the terminus of rail traffic for the vast landlocked hinterland of Ethiopia, a crucial matter for that state.

Djibouti is one of the hottest places on earth, little rain falls, and water is in exceptionally high demand. A subterranean river named the Ambouli is one essential source of water. Two-thirds of the population live in the capital city itself. Those who live elsewhere mostly inhabit the relatively fertile coastal strip along the Gulf of Tadjoura (Golfe de Tadjoura), avoiding the burning interior plateau and its volcanic wastes. Almost 90 percent of the interior terrain is desert, with a vegetation of scrub and desert thorns. Here, nomadic goat and camel herders eke out a living.

Djibouti's economy is that of a free trade zone providing essential services for the region. It has few natural resources (though geothermal energy is being developed, and natural gas has been found) and little industry, and its agricultural production mainly provides fruit and vegetables for domestic consumption. The services it renders are those of a transit port, of great value to Ethiopia and Somalia, and of an international depot and refueling center. Originally established by the French in the nineteenth century, the port is now being developed as a container facility.

Dominica

Fought over for years by the English and the French, the Caribbean island of Dominica was mainly occupied by the British after 1759. Locally it is known as the "nature island" because of its extensive forests and wildlife. It is unusual in still having a community of about 3,000 Carib Indians, whose fierce ancestors, protected by the forests in the interior, held off European colonization for 250 years. In the eighteenth century African slaves were brought to the island as labor and their descendants form the majority of the population today. Independence came to Dominica in 1978. Soon after, it was devastated by a series of hurricanes, while two coup attempts complicated its political life. Today it has free elections where power is contested between three parties in a stable democracy.

The most mountainous of the Lesser Antilles, Dominica is a volcanic island with fertile soils and the second largest boiling lake in the world. A high ridge forms the backbone of the island, from which several rivers flow to an indented coastline. There are many vents and hot springs. The rich volcanic soil supports dense tropical vegetation over 41 percent of Dominica's surface; only 9 percent of the land is arable. The climate is warm and humid, with a risk of hurricanes during the rainy season from June to October. During 1995 hurricanes ruined

Yacht club (left) Soufriére, southwest coast, Dominica.

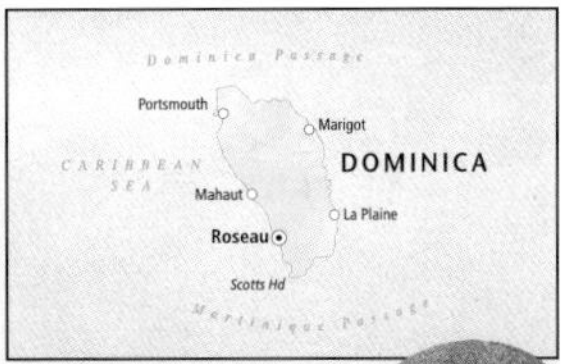

D

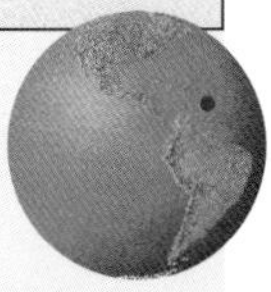

Official name Commonwealth of Dominica
Form of government Parliamentary state with single legislative body (House of Assembly)
Capital Roseau
Area 750 sq km (290 sq miles)
Time zone GMT – 4 hours
Population 64,881
Projected population 2005 60,761
Population density 86.5 per sq km (224 per sq mile)
Life expectancy 78
Infant mortality (per 1,000) 8.8
Official language English
Other language French Creole
Literacy rate 94%
Religions Roman Catholic 77%, Protestant 15%, other 6%, none 2%
Ethnic groups African 92%, mixed 6%, indigenous 1.5%, European 0.5%
Currency East Caribbean dollar
Economy Services 55%, agriculture 25%, industry 20%
GNP per capita US$2,990
Climate Tropical, moderated by trade winds
Highest point Morne Diablatins 1,447 m (4,747 ft)
Map reference Page 837

The coastal town of Soufrière, Dominica.

90 percent of the banana crop. The wildlife to be seen in the Morne Trois Pitons National Park is an important tourist attraction.

Dominica's only mineral resource is pumice and it has to import all its energy. There is hydroelectric potential in the rivers of the interior. Bananas, citrus fruits, and coconuts are the main cash crops—bananas accounting for 48 percent of exports, and coconut-based soaps 25 percent. Its other exports include bay oil and vegetables. The country has to import much of its food and is depending on the development of luxury tourism for economic growth. Ecotourism is increasing, with visitors coming to view rare indigenous birds and volcanic sulphur pools. The lack of an airport able to take jetliners makes the country less accessible than its neighbors for mass-market tourism.

Dominican Republic

The second largest Caribbean nation in both area and population, the Dominican Republic occupies the eastern two-thirds of the island of Hispaniola. The island was visited by Christopher Columbus in 1492 and in 1496 his brother founded the city of Santo Domingo on its southern coast—the oldest Spanish city in the Americas. It was first colonized by Spain but the development of its sugar industry resulted from a period of French control. The country won independence in 1844 and since that time it has been ruled by a series of dictators with only short intervals of democracy. A bitter civil war in 1965 brought the intervention of the USA, which has kept a watch on Dominican affairs since then. Civil unrest continues.

With a mountainous landscape, including the highest point in the West Indies, Pico Duarte, the Dominican Republic contains three considerable ranges—the Cordillera Septentrional in the north, the massive Cordillera Central, and the southern Sierra de Bahoruco. Between these ranges, and to the east, lie fertile valleys and lowlands. These include the Cibao Valley in the north, the Vega Real, and the coastal plains where sugar plantations are found. Because of the mountainous terrain there are wide variations in temperature and rainfall. Low-lying areas in the south and east support a dry savanna vegetation suitable for livestock raising. The Dominican Republic also has the lowest point in the West Indies—Lake Enriquillo, 44 m (144 ft) below sea level. The lake bisects the mountains in the southwest.

While still heavily dependent on its traditional agricultural base, in recent years the economy has been supplemented by industrial growth (making use of a vast hydroelectric potential), and a large increase in tourism. The Dominican Republic has good beaches, and a hotel capacity of 30,000 rooms, the highest in the Caribbean. Sugar is still the leading agricultural export, followed by coffee, cocoa, tobacco, and fruit. Nickel and gold mining are increasing in economic importance. Subsistence farming provides most of the rural population with its livelihood, the staple crops being rice and corn. State-owned sugar plantations provide another source of employment. Illegal narcotics also play a part in the economy; the country is a transshipment point for drugs bound for the USA.

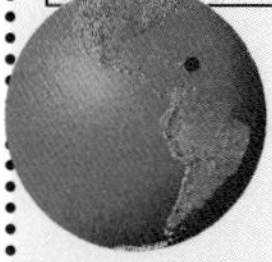

DOMINICAN REPUBLIC

OFFICIAL NAME Dominican Republic
FORM OF GOVERNMENT Republic with two legislative bodies (Senate and Chamber of Deputies)
CAPITAL Santo Domingo
AREA 48,730 sq km (18,815 sq miles)
TIME ZONE GMT – 4 hours
POPULATION 8,129,734
PROJECTED POPULATION 2005 8,936,667
POPULATION DENSITY 166.8 per sq km (432 per sq mile)
LIFE EXPECTANCY 70.1
INFANT MORTALITY (PER 1,000) 42.5
OFFICIAL LANGUAGE Spanish
OTHER LANGUAGE French Creole
LITERACY RATE 81.5%
RELIGIONS Roman Catholic 95%, other 5%
ETHNIC GROUPS Mixed African–European 73%, European 16%, African 11%
CURRENCY Peso
ECONOMY Agriculture 46%, services 38%, industry 16%
GNP PER CAPITA US$1,460
CLIMATE Tropical, with wet season May to November
HIGHEST POINT Pico Duarte 3,175 m (10,416 ft)
MAP REFERENCE Page 839

D

E

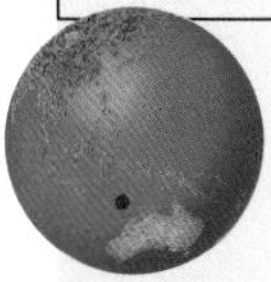

EAST TIMOR

CAPITAL Dili
TIME ZONE GMT + 9 hours
CLIMATE Tropical, with wet season December to March
MAP REFERENCE Page 734

East Timor

First settled by the Portuguese in 1520, the eastern part of the island of Timor was a prize sought after by various colonial powers. The Spanish arrived in 1522. The Dutch took over the western part of the island in 1613. While the Dutch and the Portuguese fought for control of East Timor, the British governed briefly, from 1812 to 1815; but ultimately, the Portuguese triumphed. Portuguese rule was established by treaties in 1860 and 1893. Portuguese sovereignty held sway for 300 years in East Timor, until 1975, when the political party Fretilin (the Revolutionary Front of Independent East Timor) declared independence from Portugal. This precipitated an immediate Indonesian invasion and the forcible incorporation of East Timor into Indonesia. Indonesia retained control of the territory despite United Nation concerns over the legality of the invasion.

The mountainous country has a dry climate with a moderate rainfall, and a wide variety of fauna including deer, monkeys and rare species. The north western sector is rich in sandalwood. Steep hillsides are terraced by rice paddies, and the lowlands are covered with scrub and grass, as well as coconut palms. The economy is based on agricultural produce, including coffee, copra, cotton, potatoes, rice, sandalwood, tobacco, wheat and wool. Pearls are also produced, and the small island of Kambing supports a fishing trade.

The capital of Dili suffers from environmental pressures. Originally surrounded by sandalwood forests and rich fertile plains, deforestation due to land clearing for agriculture, the need for firewood, and security concerns, has led to massive erosion. The rivers flowing past Dili have all but dried up because of irrigation.

Following the 1975 Indonesian invasion, there was considerable social unrest after the forced resettlement of thousands of East Timorese. Reports of human rights abuses, and falling health, education and living standards forced United Nations intervention in 1999. An agreement for a UN-conducted ballot on the future of East Timor was signed. The UN was to impart the information to the people, while security for the ballot was left under Indonesian control. However, several violent outbreaks by anti-autonomy militias led to a highly volatile situation. Many East Timorese fled prior to the ballot. In announcing the election results, the UN stated that 78 percent of the country had voted for independence. The militias immediately launched a campaign of violence, murdering civilians, destroying the infrastructure completely and forcing thousands to leave. The UN compounds were seized and the staff forced to flee, many into the forested foothills or West Timor. In September 1999 the East Timor International Force (INTERFET), a UN peacekeeping force led by Major General Peter Cosgrove, of the Australian Army, was deployed in East Timor. The role of the force was to aid humanitarian efforts, restore peace and protect the UN. As peace was gradually restored, the UN formed a Transitional Administration for East Timor (UNTAET). This team has the responsibility of guiding the country through its early years of independence, providing it with governance, humanitarian aid and emergency rehabilitation of the social and economic infrastructure. UNTAET communicates directly with East Timorese to ensure their participation in the administration. The task in 2000 was formidable, because the economy is shattered, millions are homeless and there was no special infrastructure left after the campaign of violence (see also *Indonesia*).

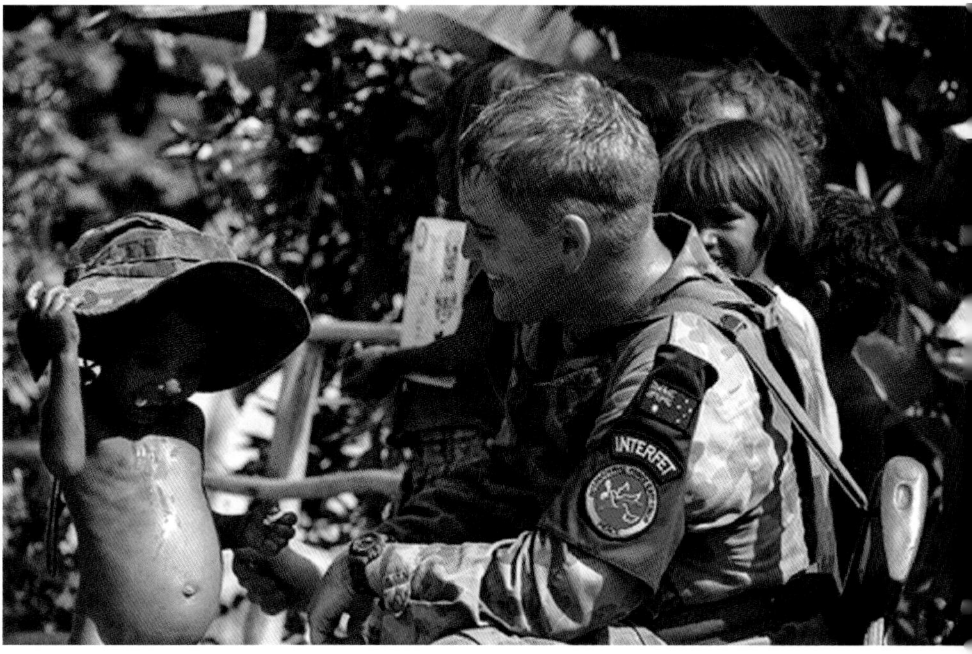

The hat of an Australian member of the INTERFET peacekeeping force intrigues a young East Timorese child.

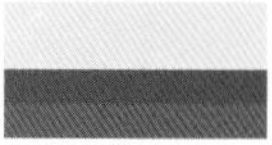

ECUADOR

OFFICIAL NAME Republic of Ecuador
FORM OF GOVERNMENT Republic with single legislative body (National Congress)
Capital Quito
AREA 283,560 sq km (109,483 sq miles)
TIME ZONE GMT – 5 hours
POPULATION 12,562,496
PROJECTED POPULATION 2005 13,837,829
POPULATION DENSITY 44.3 per sq km (114.7 per sq mile)
LIFE EXPECTANCY 72.2
INFANT MORTALITY (PER 1,000) 30.7
OFFICIAL LANGUAGE Spanish
OTHER LANGUAGES Indigenous languages, particularly Quechua
LITERACY RATE 89.6%
RELIGIONS Roman Catholic 95%, other 5%
ETHNIC GROUPS Indigenous–European 55%, indigenous 25%, Spanish 10%, African 10%
CURRENCY Sucre
ECONOMY Services 42%, agriculture 39%, industry 19%
GNP PER CAPITA US$1,390
CLIMATE Tropical on coast and plains, cooler in highlands
HIGHEST POINT Chimborazo 6,310 m (20,702 ft)
MAP REFERENCE Page 848

Ecuador

Ecuador is the smallest of the Andean republics, taking its name from the equator which divides it in half. Quito was briefly an Inca city before being conquered by the Spanish in the 1530s. The city is ringed by volcanoes, including Cotopaxi (5,896 m; 19,344 ft), the world's highest active volcano. The groups of Indians that form 25 percent of the population are pressing for recognition as distinct nationalities within the state.

Ecuador's agriculture is based on the coastal plains. Bananas, coffee, and cocoa are the main crops. Most production is on haciendas—huge estates established during the early years of Spanish occupation. Inland, among the Andes, are valleys where livestock is raised. The eastern slopes of the Andes give way to forested upland and the border with Peru. This region is so little known that hostilities between Peru and Ecuador in 1995 arose partly from uncertainty as to where the frontier should be. Petroleum and natural gas from this area are piped over the Andes to the Pacific port of Esmeraldas.

Ecuador grows more bananas than any other country in the world. Until overtaken by petroleum and natural gas, bananas were its biggest export earner, and access to markets in the USA and the EU is a continuing concern. The highland Indians survive through subsistence farming, growing maize and potatoes. Recent economic reforms have helped control inflation and increased foreign investment. Growth has been uneven, however,

Pigs for sale at the market at Otavalo.

The volcano Cotopaxi in Ecuador.

because manufacturing is handicapped by a shortage of electricity.

Ecuador owns the Galapagos Islands, home to many unique species of animal, such as the giant tortoise. These islands are a popular ecotourism destination, with visitor numbers limited to 40,000 a year so as to protect the fragile ecosystem.

A view of one of the Galapagos Islands, which are owned by Ecuador.

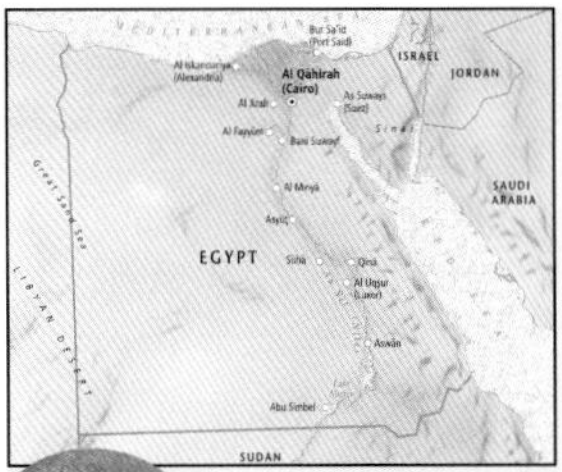

EGYPT

OFFICIAL NAME Arab Republic of Egypt
FORM OF GOVERNMENT Republic with two legislative bodies (Advisory Council and People's Assembly)
CAPITAL Al Qāhirah (Cairo)
AREA 1,001,450 sq km (386,660 sq miles)
TIME ZONE GMT + 2 hours
POPULATION 67,273,906
PROJECTED POPULATION 2005 74,635,910
POPULATION DENSITY 67.2 per sq km (174 per sq mile)
LIFE EXPECTANCY 62.4
INFANT MORTALITY (PER 1,000) 67.5
OFFICIAL LANGUAGE Arabic
OTHER LANGUAGES English, French, ethnic languages
LITERACY RATE 50.5%
RELIGIONS Muslim (mostly Sunni) 94%, other (including Coptic Christian) 6%
ETHNIC GROUPS Eastern Hamitic (Egyptian, Bedouin, and Berber) 95%; other (including Greek, Nubian, Armenian, Italian, and French) 5%
CURRENCY Egyptian pound
ECONOMY Services 55%, agriculture 34%, industry 11%
GDP PER CAPITA US$790
CLIMATE Mainly arid, with mild winters and hot, dry summers
HIGHEST POINT Jabal Kātrīnā 2,637 m (8,649 ft)
MAP REFERENCE Pages 802–803

Egypt

Egypt is sometimes known as "the gift of the Nile" (An Nīl) because the waters of this famous river have always been the lifeblood of the country. Every year, until the Aswan High Dam was built, the Nile would flood, spreading fertile silt across the floor of the valley. It was in the Nile Valley that Egyptian civilization began, 6,000 years ago, and the country was the first to have a society organized along political lines. The Great Pyramid itself, still one of the largest structures in the world, was built 5,000 years ago. Since then innumerable rulers and conquerors have come and gone—Persians, Greeks, and Romans being followed by the seventh-century conquests

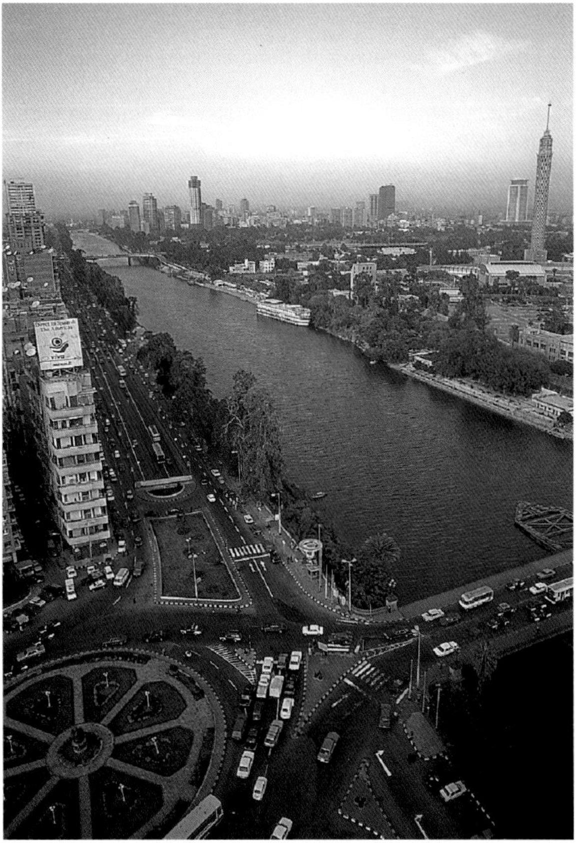

Cairo and the Nile at dusk.

of Mahomet's followers and the conversion of the region to Islam. During the nineteenth century, after the construction of the Suez Canal in 1869, Egypt came increasingly under the influence of the French and the British. Britain declared it a protectorate in 1914. It was not until 1953 that Egypt became an independent republic.

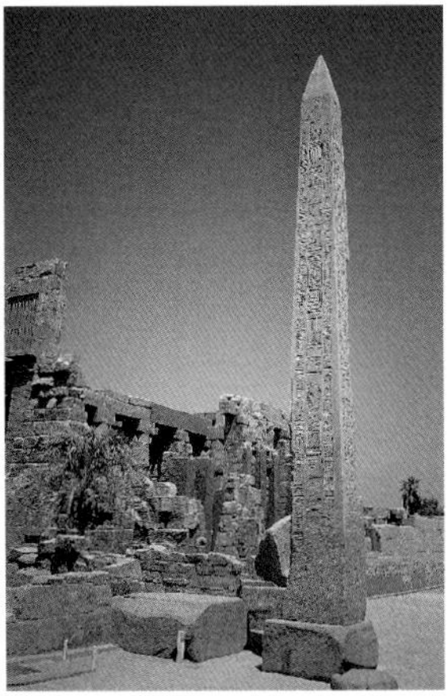

An obelisk, covered with hieroglyphs, among the ruins at Luxor.

Physical features and land use

Egypt is defined by the valley of the Nile and the spreading deserts on either side. The Nile rises at Lake Victoria, further south, and enters the country across the southern border, from Sudan. It first fills huge Lake Nasser, formed by the Aswan High Dam, which was completed in 1965. It then makes an eastward bend near Luxor before flowing steadily north. At Cairo the river fans out into a broad delta before entering the Mediterranean. The area north of Cairo is often known as Lower Egypt and the area south of Cairo as Upper Egypt.

Although the lands of the valley and the delta constitute only 3 percent of Egypt's total land area, this is where 99 percent of the people live and where nearly all agricultural activity takes place. West of the Nile, extending to the Libyan border, lies the Western (or Libyan) Desert. This arid limestone region consists of low valleys and scarps, and in the north contains a large area below sea level called the Qattara Depression. Scattered across the desert are isolated fertile oases where date palms grow. It is hoped to increase the agricultural production of these oases by using deep artesian bores.

Between the Nile and the Red Sea is the Eastern (or Arabian) Desert. Here, grasses, tamarisks, and mimosas grow, providing desert nomads with feed for their sheep,

Close-up of statues of Pharaohs at Abu Simbel.

St Catherine's Monastry, Sinai.

Statues of the pharaohs from the temple of Abu Simbel, saved from inundation by the Aswan High Dam in 1968 by being cut from the rock and reassembled on a cliff nearby

camels, and goats. Between the Gulf of Suez and the border with Israel is the almost uninhabited triangular limestone plateau of the Sinai Peninsula. Egypt's highest peak, Jabal Kātrīnā, is found in Sinai's mountainous south.

People and culture

While there are significant cultural differences between the 95 percent of the population who are Hamitic, and the Afro-Nubian peoples of the Upper Nile near Sudan, Egypt has a long tradition of ethnic and religious tolerance. In Cairo and Alexandria there have always been sizeable colonies of Greeks and Armenians, and although most Jews have now left for Israel, there is still a small Jewish community in Cairo. The small number of desert Bedouin divide into two main groups. In the southern part of the Eastern Desert live the Arabdah and Bisharin (Hamitic Beja), while Saadi and Murabatin (of Arab and Berber ancestry) are found throughout the Western Desert.

Ancient Egypt's art, architecture, pyramids and tombs are among the treasures of civilization. Evidence from tombs shows that even at the time of the first recorded dynasty, about 4400 BC, furniture inlaid with ivory and ebony was being made, along with alabaster vessels and fine work in copper and gold. In the pyramid-building period between 3700 BC and 2500 BC the Great Pyramid of Cheops was erected, a project thought to have occupied 100,000 men for 20 years. The pyramids were themselves immense tombs, containing chambers in which dead kings were buried, supplied with all they might need—food, clothing, and furniture—in the afterlife. It is not known when exactly Christianity began in Egypt, but it was very early, around AD 40. The new faith was readily accepted since the hope of a future life coincided with the views of the Egyptians themselves.

Today only about 6 percent of the people are Coptic Christians. The Copts claim to have received the gospel directly from St Mark, the first bishop of Alexandria. Their community has always valued education highly, and has contributed many figures to Egyptian public life. Over 90 percent of the population are Muslim, mainly Sunni.

With the rise of Islamic fundamentalism, the most bitter conflict within Egypt is between the modernizing political elite, and the fundamentalist Moslem Brotherhood. The latter is held responsible for terrorist activities. Arabic is the official language, but several other languages are used by ethnic minorities, from Hamito-Sudanic among the Nubians to the Berber-related language of the Siwah tribe east of the Qattara Depression.

Historic architecture in modern day Alexandria.

The Red Sea and the Sinai Desert.

E

Timeline Egypt

c.3600 BC Agriculture begins in alluvial soils deposited in the Nile Valley; irrigation used for growing fruit and vegetables

c.3100 BC King Menes founds first dynasty to rule nation; civilization begins with uniting of Upper and Lower regions in Nile Valley

c.2650 BC The first pyramids are built during a 500-year period of peace and prosperity under the Old Kingdom

1991 BC Egypt's power expands—King Amenemhet I and his successors conquer Nubia and trade with Syria and Palestine

1497–1426 BC King Thutmose III's reign marks height of Empire; buildings include Temple of Amon at Karnak (Al Karnak)

1153 BC Assassination of Ramses III; Egyptian power declines as a result of corruption and feuding between priests and kings

332 BC Egypt becomes part of Alexander the Great's empire; he builds the city of Alexandria on the Mediterranean coast

1869 Suez Canal completed, allowing quicker access to India and the Pacific

1882 British troops occupy Egypt

1914 Egypt made a protectorate of the United Kingdom

1922 Britain grants nominal independence

1940–42 German and Italian troops fight battles against Allied forces along the north coast of Egypt and in the Western Desert

1948–49 Egypt part of Arab League invasion of Israel after Palestine is partitioned into Arab and Jewish nations; Israel repels invasion

1953 Egypt becomes republ

Sunset over the River Nile.

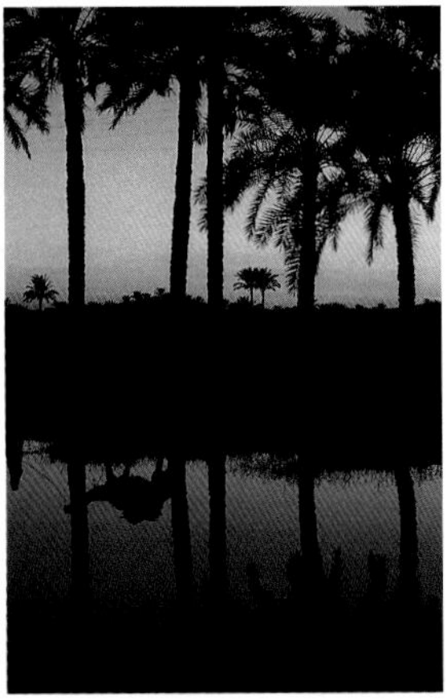

Economy and resources

Food crops have been grown in the fertile soils of the Nile floodplain and delta for many thousands of years. But a population of 67 million, increasing by over 1 million per year, is placing considerable pressure on Egypt's agricultural resources. In addition, salination of land below the High Aswan Dam, land lost to growing urbanization, and desertification as a result of wind-blown sand, are all reducing the amount of arable land. Today much of Egypt's food is imported.

In manufacturing, textiles are by far the largest industry, and include spinning, weaving, and the dyeing and printing of cotton, wool, silk, and synthetic-fiber materials. Along with finished textiles, raw cotton remains one of the main exports, only exceeded in value by petroleum. There are plans to restore the Suez Canal's earning capacity by deepening and widening it for modern shipping. Most large-scale industrial plants in Egypt remain state-owned, overstaffed, and over-regulated, in need of both technical improvements and investment. This hampers the country's economic performance and is a challenge to governmental efforts at reform.

31 BC Rome takes control of Egypt when Mark Antony and Cleopatra's navy is defeated by Octavian's fleet at Battle of Actium

AD 642 Egypt comes under the control of Muslim Arabs from the regions to the east

1517 Ottoman Turks defeat the Mamelukes (Turks, Mongols, and Circassians) and rule for the next 250 years

1798 Napoleon conquers Egypt and leaves French troops in control of the country

1801 British and Ottoman troops expel French occupation forces from Egypt

956 President Nasser 'st nationalizes Suez anal then closes it. ritain, France, and srael invade to reopen anal—UN intervenes

1960 Construction of the Aswan High Dam on the River Nile begins; it creates Lake Nasser, flooding several ancient sites

1967 Egypt and other Arab nations attack Israel but are defeated in "Six Day War"; Israel occupies the Gaza Strip and Sinai

1979 President Sadat ends hostilities with Israel and signs an agreement under which Sinai is returned to Egyptian control

1981 President Sadat assassinated and succeeded by Hosni Mubarak

1990 Egypt opposes Iraq's invasion of oil-rich Kuwait and sides with US and European allies in the Gulf War

1992 Cairo damaged in an earthquake which kills more than 500 people

E

El Salvador

El Salvador is the smallest, most densely populated country in Central America, and the only one without a coast on the Caribbean. It is in a seismic zone and has some 20 volcanoes, several of which are active. Once the home of the Pipil Indians and later a part of the Mexican Empire, the country won full independence in 1841 and established itself as the Republic of El Salvador in 1859. Over 100 years of civil strife and military rule followed.

From the 1880s about 75 percent of the land has been in the hands of 14 families, who farm huge plantations producing coffee, tobacco, and sugar. The potential for conflict between this landed oligarchy and the rural poor has been present since that time and in the 1970s left-wing disillusionment with the electoral process led to the formation of a number of guerrilla groups. Between 1979 and 1991 civil war raged, with the loss of 75,000 lives, and many people emigrated. The political and economic effects of this conflict are still evident.

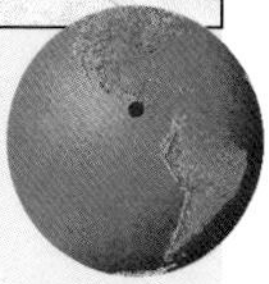

El Salvador

Official name Republic of El Salvador
Form of government Republic with single legislative body (Legislative Assembly)
Capital San Salvador
Area 21,040 sq km (8,123 sq miles)
Time zone GMT – 6 hours
Population 5,839,079
Projected population 2005 6,382,909
Population density 277.5 per sq km (718.7 per sq mile)

(continues)

EL SALVADOR *(continued)*

LIFE EXPECTANCY 70
INFANT MORTALITY (PER 1,000) 28.4
OFFICIAL LANGUAGE Spanish
OTHER LANGUAGE Nahua
LITERACY RATE 70.9%
RELIGIONS Roman Catholic 75%, Protestant and other 25%
ETHNIC GROUPS Mixed indigenous–European 94%, indigenous 5%, European 1%
CURRENCY Colón
ECONOMY Services 70%, industry 22%, agriculture 8%
GNP PER CAPITA US$1,610
CLIMATE Tropical, with wet season May to October; cooler in mountains
HIGHEST POINT Cerro El Pittal 2,730 m (8,957 ft)
MAP REFERENCE Page 838

Behind El Salvador's narrow Pacific coastal plain rises a volcanic range. Inland is a rich and fertile central plain, occupying 25 percent of the country's total land area. The urban and rural population in this area accounts for 60 percent of the country's total, and produces 90 percent of El Salvador's coffee and tobacco, along with most of its sugar and corn. Further inland still, along the frontier with Honduras, are mountain ranges. Once forested and unpopulated, they now draw poor farmers desperate for land.

El Salvador's economy has few strengths other than a large amount of cheap labor, which has encouraged the construction of factories assembling foreign goods. Damage to the economy from the civil war (mainly through guerrilla attacks on electrical installations) is estimated at over $2 billion and cotton and sugar cultivation declined significantly during the conflict. Coffee contributes about 90 percent of exports. Foreign aid remains important, much coming from the USA.

Manufacturing is based on food and beverage processing, while other industries are textiles, clothing, petroleum products, and cement. The civil war brought tourism to a standstill but peace has resulted in visitors returning to the Pacific beach resorts of El Salvador's Costa del Sol.

El Salvador contains about 20 volcanoes, some still active. Izalco Volcano, El Salvador, seen from lush forest.

Equatorial Guinea

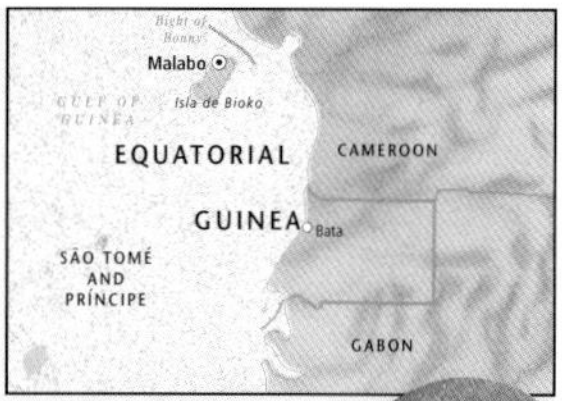

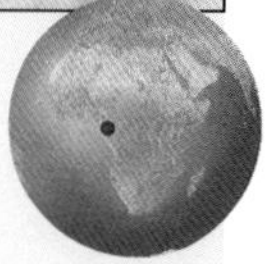

Equatorial Guinea consists of five islands in the Gulf of Guinea, plus the small mainland area of Río Muni that lies between Cameroon and Gabon. The largest of the islands, Bioco, was originally Portuguese, and was known for centuries as the slave depot and transshipment base of Fernando Po. The Spanish took over in 1778.

After gaining independence from Spain in 1968 Equatorial Guinea fell into the hands of Francisco Macias Nguema. A member of the Mongomo clan of the Fang tribe, his bloody and despotic rule lasted 11 years, after which he was overthrown and later executed. His nephew, also a Fang, continued to govern in much the same way, observers describing the one-candidate election in 1996 as meaningless. Equatorial Guinea illustrates the problems faced by tribal groups trying to adapt to democratic political arrangements.

The island of Bioco is mountainous and volcanic, with fertile soils. It has long supported cocoa on the lowland, and there are coffee plantations on the higher slopes which rise to Pico Basile. Rugged terrain and waterfalls are found in the southern half of the island. On the thinly populated area of mainland, mangrove swamps along the coast lead inland to dense tropical forests. Here, foreign companies have timber concessions, felling okoume and mahogany. In addition to timber, the country exports cocoa and coffee. In the years before independence, cocoa plantations on Bioco and the mainland provided Equatorial Guinea with the highest per capita income in West Africa. By the end of the Macias era, the state was in political and economic ruins and some 100,000 of the population had fled as refugees to neighboring countries. Most of those who remain in the country today are subsistence farmers growing yams, cassava, and bananas.

Equatorial Guinea has a variety of undeveloped mineral resources: titanium, iron ore, manganese, uranium, and alluvial gold. Recently oil exploration has been successful, and increased production of oil and natural gas is anticipated. Aid programs are currently in limbo, having been cut off because of gross government corruption and mismanagement.

Equatorial Guinea

Official name Republic of Equatorial Guinea
Form of government Republic with single legislative body (House of People's Representatives)
Capital Malabo
Area 28,050 sq km (10,830 sq miles)
Time zone GMT + 1 hour
Population 465,746
Projected population 2005 542,291
Population density 16.6 per sq km (43 per sq mile)
Life expectancy 54.4
Infant mortality (per 1,000) 91.2
Official language Spanish
Other languages Indigenous languages, including Fang, Bubi, Ibo; pidgin English
Literacy rate 77.8%
Religions Roman Catholic 85%, indigenous beliefs 15%
Ethnic groups Fang 80%, Bubi 15%, other 5%
Currency CFA (Communauté Financière Africaine) franc
Economy Agriculture 64%, services 24%, industry 12%
GNP per capita US$380
Climate Tropical; wetter on coast
Highest point Pico Basile 3,011 m (9,879 ft)
Map reference Page 805

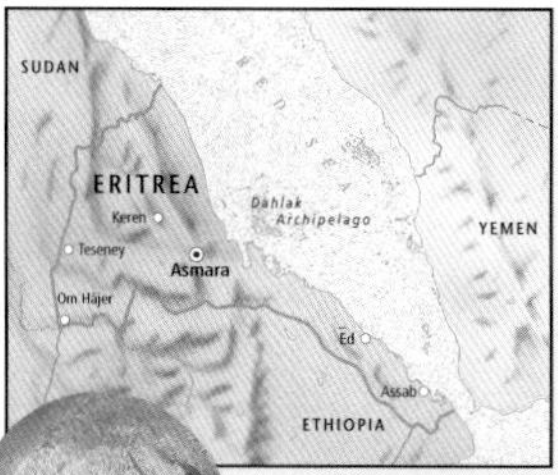

Eritrea

Official name State of Eritrea
Form of government Transitional government with single legislative body (Legislative Assembly)
Capital Asmara
Area 121,320 sq km (46,842 sq miles)
Time zone GMT + 3 hours
Population 3,984,723
Projected population 2005 4,958,211
Population density 32.8 per sq km (85 per sq mile)
Life expectancy 51
Infant mortality (per 1,000) 76.8
Official languages Tigrinya, Arabic
Other languages Tigré, other indigenous languages, English
Literacy rate 25%
Religions Muslim 50%, Christian (Coptic Christian, Roman Catholic, Protestant) 50%
Ethnic groups Tigrinya 50%, Tigré and Kunama 40%, Afar 4%, Saho (Red Sea coast dwellers) 3%, other 3%
Currency Ethiopian birr
Economy Agriculture 80%, industry and services 20%
GNP per capita Est. < US$465
Climate Hot and arid along coast, cooler and wetter in highlands; wet season June to September
Highest point Soira 3,018 m (9,899 ft)
Map reference Page 807

Eritrea

Eritrea was part of the Aksum Kingdom 2,000 years ago. In the fourth century AD Coptic Christianity was brought to the country, and a member of the Coptic Christian community, Issaias Ifawerki, is now its president. Italian influence in the region began in 1882, and despite the depredations of Mussolini between 1935 and 1941, Eritrea's modernization dates from those years. Italy introduced Western education and industry.

Forced to join Ethiopia in 1962, Eritrea began a 30-year war of independence, first against the Emperor and then against Ethiopia's Soviet-armed and financed Mengistu regime. Fighting from trenches dug from rock in the mountains, and in spite of inferior weapons, the Eritrean

Red rooftops in the capital city of Asmara.

troops hung on. Victory and separate nationhood were won in 1993. Since that year the country has shown unusual self-reliance and is now rebuilding itself.

Consisting of a hot dry desert strip along the Red Sea shore, Eritrea is dominated by rugged mountains in the north, and in the southeast by the arid coastal plain of the Danakil Desert. In and around this desert live the Afar, camel-keeping nomads. The country is bordered on the north by the Sudan, with whom it has uneasy relations, and on the south by Djibouti. Before independence, Eritrea provided Ethiopia's only access to the sea, other than through Djibouti. The prospect of being landlocked as a result of Eritrean secession—which is what happened—strengthened Ethiopian resolve during the war.

Poor and war-torn, with its roads and railways destroyed, Eritrea since 1993 has faced the task of reconstruction. Obligatory military service provides labor for public works. During the war trees were cut down by the enemy to deprive Eritrean soldiers of hiding places: these are being replanted by the thousand. In the long term, offshore oil deposits may prove important, but the population currently survives by subsistence farming, growing sorghum, lentils, vegetables, and maize. This is supplemented by food aid on which 75 percent of the people rely.

Rocky outcrop, Senafe.

The Eritrean monastery of Abune clings to the hillside at Libanos.

E

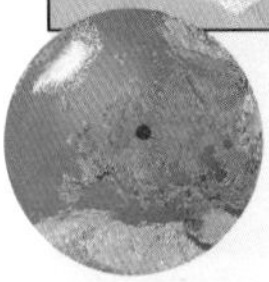

ESTONIA

OFFICIAL NAME Republic of Estonia
FORM OF GOVERNMENT Republic with single legislative body (Parliament)
CAPITAL Tallinn
AREA 45,100 sq km (17,413 sq miles)
TIME ZONE GMT + 3 hours
POPULATION 1,408,523
PROJECTED POPULATION 2005 1,357,949
POPULATION DENSITY 32.6 per sq km (84.5 per sq mile)
LIFE EXPECTANCY 68.7
INFANT MORTALITY (per 1,000) 13.8
OFFICIAL LANGUAGE Estonian
OTHER LANGUAGES Latvian, Lithuanian, Russian
LITERACY RATE 99%
RELIGIONS Evangelical Lutheran 96%; Eastern Orthodox and Baptist 4%
ETHNIC GROUPS Estonian 61.5%, Russian 30.3%, Ukrainian 3.2%, Belarusian 1.8%, Finnish 1.1%, other 2.1%
CURRENCY Kroon
ECONOMY Industry 42%, services 38%, agriculture 20%
GNP PER CAPITA US$2,860
CLIMATE Cool temperate; cold winters and mild summers
HIGHEST POINT Mt Munamagi 318 m (1,043 ft)
MAP REFERENCE Page 771

Estonia

Estonia, the smallest and least populous of the three Baltic countries, contains more than 1,500 lakes and its land area includes more than 800 islands in the Baltic Sea and the Gulf of Finland. The largest lake, Lake Peipus, is in the far east of the country and forms most of its border with Russia.

Russia has been the dominant power in Estonia's recent history and the large ethnic Russian minority bears witness to this. From the thirteenth until the eighteenth century the Estonians were ruled by outsiders, first the Germans and then the Swedes. In 1721 Russia assumed control and ruled the country for almost 200 years. Occupied by Germany during the First World War, Estonia declared its independence in 1918. This was achieved in 1920 when, after an armed struggle, Russia formally recognized the small country. However, during the Second World War Estonia was overrun first by the Russians and then by the Germans. In 1944 it was returned to the Soviets and remained part of the USSR until it once again declared itself independent in August 1991.

Most of Estonia is low-lying. Large areas of land are barren and stony, a legacy of the glaciers that once covered much of the landscape. Extensive woodlands supply raw materials for the important timber and woodworking industries. Engineering and textile manufacture are also significant. Little of the land is arable and the main agricultural industries are dairying and livestock raising, especially pig farming. Mineral resources are meager, though extensive deposits of shale are used in the production of gas and chemical products.

Compared with other former Soviet republics, the people of Estonia enjoy a high standard of living. The economy,

The medieval rooftops of Tallinn, the capital of Estonia, which is the country's main port.

after declining for some years following independence, has improved steadily as increasing trade with Western countries has shielded Estonia from some of the effects of the declining Russian economy.

Ethiopia

Ethiopia adopted Coptic Christianity in the fourth century AD. Despite strong Islamic influences, including a Muslim invasion in 1523, many people remain Christian today. Italy occupied the country between 1935 and 1941, but Ethiopia was never a colony. Under Emperor Haile Selassie it attempted to subjugate both the Somalis and the Eritreans. Haile Selassie was deposed in 1974 by a military coup; this triggered a civil war that exacerbated the effects of the famine in 1984. Always poor, Ethiopia is currently destitute—30 years of war and resulting famine are the legacy of the Marxist dictatorship of Mengistu Haile Mariam. His regime ended in 1991, when he was deposed.

The landscape is dominated by a mountainous volcanic plateau divided in two by the Rift Valley. The western highlands, with an average height of 2,700 m (8,800 ft), are the source of the Blue Nile, which spills out from Lake Tana to flow south and west, before flowing north into Sudan. East of the western highlands is the Danakil Desert, where a depression falls to 116 m (380 ft) below sea level. This is one of the hottest places on earth. In the highlands, however, the climate is moderate to warm, with frosts at night and occasional snow on the mountains. Ethiopia's war with neighbouring Somalia has left the southern section of the border in dispute.

The principal industries are state-owned food processing, textiles manufacture and chemical and metal production. Inefficiencies and overstaffing are widespread as a result of Mengistu's effort to establish a centrally controlled Soviet-model economy. The government intends to sell off some state-owned plants, but progress is slow.

Drought between 1981 and 1985, combined with agricultural mismanagement, resulted in a famine in which an estimated 1 million people died. Today, rural production accounts for half of gross domestic product and 80 percent of employment. Although Ethiopia still needs food aid there is a growing emphasis on aid in the form of credit for infrastructure development.

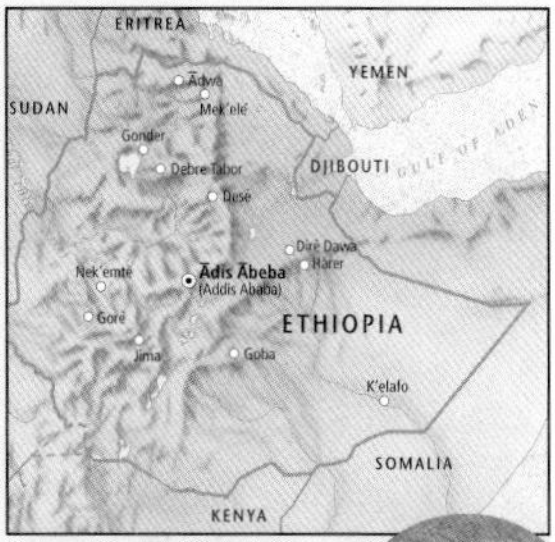

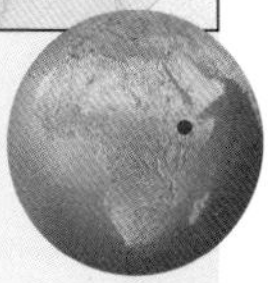

Ethiopia

Official name Federal Democratic Republic of Ethiopia
Form of government Federal republic with two legislative bodies (Federal Council and Council of People's Representatives)
Capital Ādis Ābeba (Addis Ababa)
Area 1,127,127 sq km (435,184 sq miles)
Time zone GMT + 3 hours
Population 59,690,383
Projected population 2005 67,831,860
Population density 53 per sq km (137.2 per sq mile)
Life expectancy 40.5
Infant mortality (per 1,000) 124.6
Official language Amharic
Other languages More than 100 indigenous languages, Arabic, English
Literacy rate 34.5%
Religions Ethiopian Orthodox 51%, Muslim 35%, animist 12%, other 2%
Ethnic groups Oromo 40%, Amhara and Tigrean 32%, Sidamo 9%, Shankella 6%, Somali 6%, Afar 4%, Gurage 2%, other 3%
Currency Birr
Economy Agriculture 80%, services 12%, industry 8%
GNP per capita US$100
Climate Tropical on lowlands, uplands more temperate; wet season April to September
Highest point Ras Dashen Terara 4,620 m (15,157 ft)
Map reference Pages 366–67

F

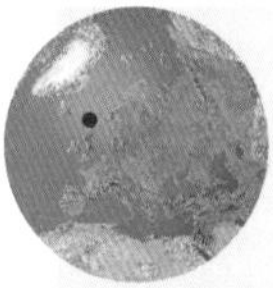

FAEROE ISLANDS

OFFICIAL NAME Faeroe Islands
FORM OF GOVERNMENT Self-governing overseas administrative division of Denmark
CAPITAL Torshavn
AREA 1,400 sq km (541 sq miles)
TIME ZONE GMT
POPULATION 41,059
LIFE EXPECTANCY 78.6
INFANT MORTALITY (PER 1,000) 10.3
LITERACY RATE Not available
CURRENCY Danish krone
ECONOMY Mainly fishing; some agriculture, light industry, and services
CLIMATE Mild winters, cool summers; foggy and windy
MAP REFERENCE Page 786

Faeroe Islands

The Faeroes are an archipelago of 22 islands in the north Atlantic Ocean, between Scotland and Iceland, eighteen of which are inhabited. Although they are part of Danish territory, the Faeroes have, since 1948, enjoyed a high degree of autonomy. They have their own parliament, which is elected for four-year terms.

In the eleventh century these islands came under Norwegian control, but when, in the fourteenth century, the crowns of Norway and Denmark combined, Denmark became the dominant power. Since 1709 the islands have been administered solely by Denmark.

The Faeroes, formed from volcanic lava, are rocky, with spectacular cliffs along the coasts. Sheep raising has been the economic mainstay, though recently fishing has supplanted it in importance. Despite international criticism, the Faeroese fishing companies maintain a vigorous whaling industry.

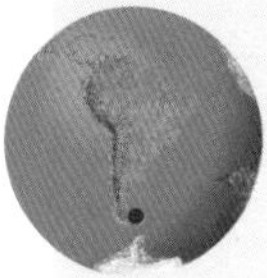

FALKLAND ISLANDS

OFFICIAL NAME Colony of the Falkland Islands
FORM OF GOVERNMENT Dependent territory of the UK
CAPITAL Stanley
AREA 12,170 sq km (4,699 sq miles)
TIME ZONE GMT – 4 hours
POPULATION 2,607 (1996)
CURRENCY Falkland Islands pound
ECONOMY Agriculture 95%, services and industry 5%
CLIMATE Cold, wet, and windy
MAP REFERENCE Page 858

Falkland Islands

The Falkland Islands are in the South Atlantic. They were named for Lord Falkland, a seventeenth-century British Navy official. Lying 772 km (480 miles) northeast of Cape Horn, they consist of a hilly archipelago where rain falls on average 180 days a year. The area is known for the diversity of bird life. East Falkland and West Falkland are the two main islands and there are about 200 islets.

Most people are employed in sheep farming. Efforts to establish a fishing industry have failed. Sovereignty of the islands is disputed between the United Kingdom and Argentina, which in 1982 invaded, unsuccessfully, in an assertion of its claim. The resulting conflict lasted for 3 months. However, with peace since re-established, the United Kingdom and Argentina launched a joint oil exploration program in 1995.

Fiji

Fiji consists of some 800 islands, 110 of them inhabited, located two-thirds of the way from Hawaii to New Zealand. On the air route from Australia to the USA, it is well served by flights, attracting many tourists. Originally inhabited by Melanesians, the islands were visited by Dutch explorers in 1643. From 1800 growing numbers of traders and Christian missionaries arrived. A period of intense tribal warfare ended when the paramount chief ceded sovereignty to Britain in 1874. In 1879, the British began bringing in Indian laborers for sugar production. When Fiji became independent in 1970, their descendants outnumbered the ethnic Fijians.

Racial divisions have caused tension and instability, as for many years the Indian immigrants were treated as second-class citizens, despite their vital role in the sugar industry. A coup in 1987, led by a Fijian army officer against a democratically elected government in which Indians were the majority, led to a new constitution in 1990 which was racially weighted to ensure permanent indigenous Fijian rule. Many Indian-Fijians emigrated as a result. In May 1999, the Indian leader of the Fijian Labor Party, Mahandra Chaudrey, was democratically elected Prime Minister. In May 2000, coup plotters, led by indigenous Fijian George Speight, took Chaudrey and other parliamentarians hostage, resulting in a declaration of martial law for a two year period by the military.

The Parliament House buildings in Suva.

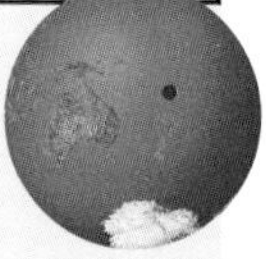

FIJI

OFFICIAL NAME Republic of Fiji
FORM OF GOVERNMENT Republic with two legislative bodies (Senate and House of Representatives)
CAPITAL Suva
AREA 18,270 sq km (7,054 sq miles)
TIME ZONE GMT + 12 hours
POPULATION 812,918
PROJECTED POPULATION 2005 877,594
POPULATION DENSITY 44.5 per sq km (115.2 per sq mile)
LIFE EXPECTANCY 66.6
INFANT MORTALITY (PER 1,000) 16.3
OFFICIAL LANGUAGE English
OTHER LANGUAGES Fijian, Hindustani
LITERACY RATE 91.3%
RELIGIONS Christian 52% (Methodist 37%, Roman Catholic 9%), Hindu 38%, Muslim 8%, other 2%
ETHNIC GROUPS Fijian 49%, Indian 46%, other (including European, other Pacific Islanders, Chinese) 5%
CURRENCY Fiji dollar
ECONOMY Agriculture 67%, services and industry 33%
GNP PER CAPITA US$2,440
CLIMATE Tropical, with wet season November to April
HIGHEST POINT Mt Tomanivi 1,323 m (4,341 ft)
MAP REFERENCE Pages 723, 727

The main islands are of volcanic origin. About 70 percent of the population live on the two biggest—Viti Levu and Vanua Levu. These have a sharp and rugged relief, rising to Mt Tomanivi on Viti Levu. The islands lie in a cyclone path (Cyclone Kina caused much damage in 1993) and trade winds bring heavy rain to their eastern sides. Dense tropical forest covers the higher slopes. Sugarcane is grown on the fertile coastal plains, sugar exports and tourism being Fiji's main sources of foreign exchange. About 250,000 tourists, many bound for resorts on the smaller coral atolls, visit the islands each year. Fiji has a variety of forest, mineral, and marine resources, and is one of the most developed of the Pacific island economies, producing (as well as sugar) copra, gold, silver, clothing, and timber.

Finland

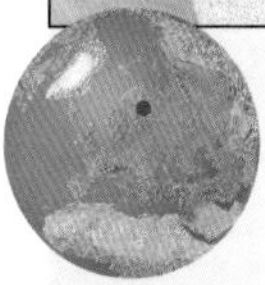

FINLAND

OFFICIAL NAME Republic of Finland
FORM OF GOVERNMENT Republic with single legislative body (Parliament)
CAPITAL Helsinki
AREA 337,030 sq km (130,127 sq miles)
TIME ZONE GMT + 1 hour
POPULATION 5,158,372
PROJECTED POPULATION 2005 5,178,305

Except for a small section of Norway which cuts it off from the Arctic Ocean, Finland is the most northerly country in continental Europe. As well as its northern boundary with Norway, Finland borders northern Sweden to the west and the Russian Federation in the east. In the south, the Gulf of Finland, the easternmost part of the Baltic Sea, separates it from Estonia, and on the west the Gulf of Bothnia, a northern inlet of the Baltic, sits between it and southern Sweden.

Modern Finland has its roots in a seventh century AD invasion by tribes from the Volga. They displaced the Lapps, Asiatic people who had lived in the area for centuries, and drove them north. Only about 2,500 Lapps, or Sami, who have their own culture and language, now survive in the north, tending reindeer herds. Viking incursions followed and in the twelfth century Swedes invaded Finland, bringing Christianity. Finland remained under Swedish control for the next 650 years, until 1809, when the Russians took over. Swedish influence is still evident in the country's significant Swedish-speaking minority, and the fact that some towns have both Finnish and Swedish names. A relatively benign Russian rule allowed considerable freedoms and encouraged a resurgence of the Finnish language, which had largely fallen into disuse. A more oppressive regime towards the end of the century fanned Finnish nationalism, and at the time of the Russian Revolution, in 1917, the country seized its independence.

Finland's harsh climate and the ruggedness of its northern regions means that most of its people live in the more moderate south. Much of the land consists of flat expanses of granite rock, the legacy of extensive glaciation. Remnants of an ancient mountain range, rising in places to more than 1,000 m (3,300 ft), exist in Lapland, the northern part of Finland. There are more than 60,000 substantial lakes throughout the country, mainly in the south, and tens of thousands of smaller ones. Forests, mainly of pine, birch, and spruce cover more than half the land area, contributing to the country's heavy reliance on timber-related industries, including wood processing, pulp, and papermaking.

Less than one-tenth of Finland's land is arable and agricultural production, which includes cereals, potatoes and sugar beet, is confined to the summer months, when the country is not snowbound.

In the 1980s living standards in Finland rose markedly, rivaling those of Sweden, although they fell back in the recession of the early 1990s. The country has an effective government-sponsored health system and the population is one of the most literate and highly educated in the world.

Population density 15.3 per sq km (39.6 per sq mile)
Life expectancy 77.3
Infant mortality (per 1,000) 3.8
Official languages Finnish, Swedish
Other languages Russian, Lapp
Literacy rate 99%
Religions Evangelical Lutheran 89%, Greek Orthodox 1%, none 9%, other 1%
Ethnic groups Finnish 93.6%, Swedish 6.2%, others (including Lapp, Gypsy, Tatar) 0.2%
Currency Markka
Economy Services 60%, industry 34%, agriculture 6%
GNP per capita US$20,580
Climate Mainly cold temperate, but polar in arctic regions
Highest point Haltiatunturi 1,328 m (4,357 ft)
Map reference Pages 768–69, 771

F

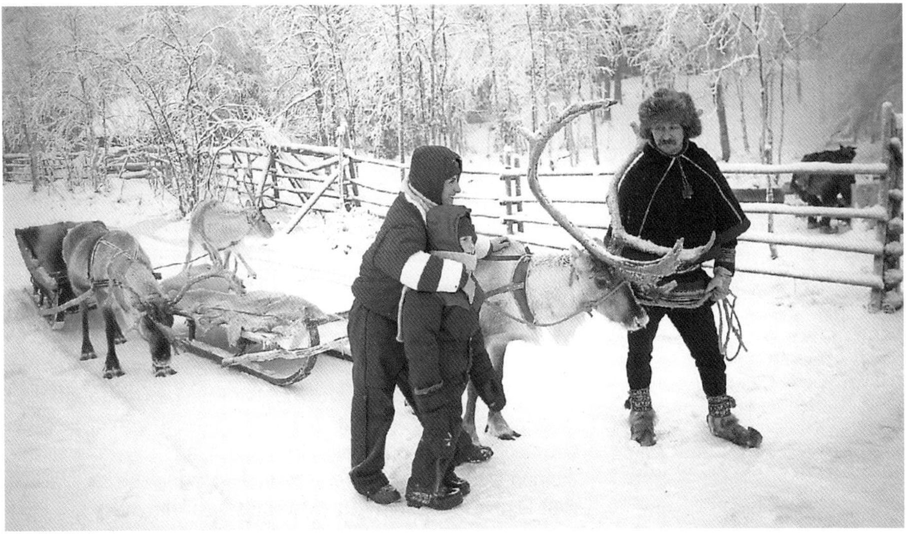

Sleds pulled by reindeer are a traditional but still widely used form of winter transport in Finland.

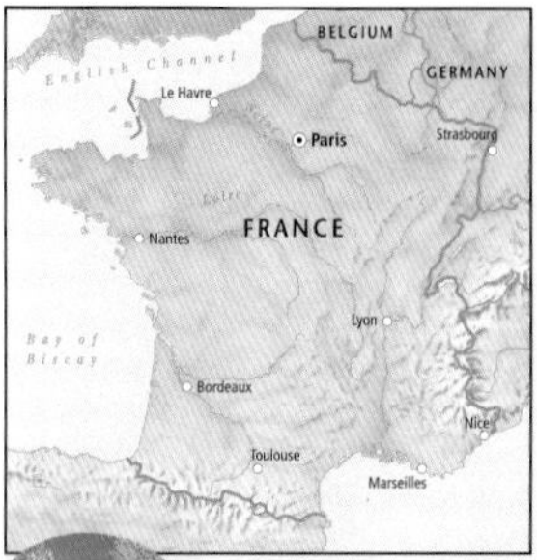

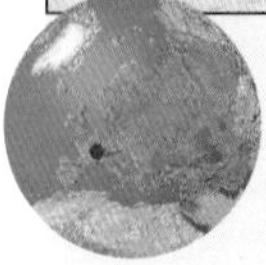

FRANCE

OFFICIAL NAME French Republic
FORM OF GOVERNMENT Republic with two legislative bodies (Senate and National Assembly)
CAPITAL Paris
AREA 547,030 sq km (211,208 sq miles)
TIME ZONE GMT + 1 hour
POPULATION 58,978,172
PROJECTED POPULATION 2005 59,624,720
POPULATION DENSITY 107.8 per sq km (279.2 per sq mile)
LIFE EXPECTANCY 78.6
INFANT MORTALITY (PER 1,000) 5.6
OFFICIAL LANGUAGE French
OTHER LANGUAGES Provençal, Breton, Alsatian, Corsican, Catalan, Basque, Flemish, German, Arabic
LITERACY RATE 99%
RELIGIONS Roman Catholic 90%, Protestant 2%, Jewish 1%, Muslim 1%, unaffiliated 6%
ETHNIC GROUPS French 95%; others, including Algerian, Portuguese, Moroccan, Italian, Spanish 5%
CURRENCY French franc
ECONOMY Services 73%, industry 20%, agriculture 7%
GNP PER CAPITA US$24,990
CLIMATE Temperate, with cool winters and mild summers; warmer on the Mediterranean coast
HIGHEST POINT Mont Blanc 4,807 m (15,771 ft)
MAP REFERENCE Pages 774–75

France

Situated at the west of continental Europe, France has three long stretches of coastline. To the north the English Channel separates it from the southern coast of England (the Channel Tunnel now links the two), to the west it faces the Bay of Biscay, and its southern shores are on the Mediterranean Sea. To the northeast and east, it shares borders with Belgium, Luxembourg, Germany, Switzerland, and Italy, and in the far southwest the Pyrenees Mountains separate it from Spain. Southeast of the mainland, in the Mediterranean, is the French island of Corsica.

History

A political entity roughly equivalent to the area of present-day France was first established in AD 843, when the Treaty of Verdun divided the enormous Frankish Empire, which had reached its high point under Charlemagne, between Charlemagne's three grandsons. These divisions corresponded approximately to what are now France, Germany, and Italy. Charles the Bald thus became king of Francia Occidentalis. His Carolingian Dynasty lasted only until 987, when territorial fighting between feudal lords led to the election of Hugh Capet, who controlled the region around Paris, as king. The Capetian Dynasty lasted for almost 350 years, during which time it consolidated its power and extended its territory. When, in 1328, the crown passed to Philip VI, the first of the Valois rulers, France was a great European power, although much of its present territory was in the hands of the English, who also laid claim to sovereignty over all of France. In 1338 there began a series of wars, which later became known as the Hundred Years War, and which, despite a major French defeat at Agincourt in 1415, led to the expulsion of the English from nearly all of France by the middle of the fifteenth century.

In the second half of the sixteenth century, France was wracked by religious wars between the Catholics and Protestants (Huguenots). These finally ended in 1598 with the accession of the first Bourbon king, the Protestant-turned-Catholic Henry of Navarre. Under the Bourbons, and especially under the 72-year reign of Louis XIV that ended in 1715, the monarchy reigned supreme and France acquired colonies in places as far afield as India, North America, and the Caribbean. Under royal patronage,

French literature, art, and music flourished and the royal court was the most opulent in Europe. During the eighteenth century, weak leadership and a series of debilitating wars led to the popular unrest that culminated in the French Revolution of 1789, which overthrew the monarchy but soon collapsed into a period of anarchy and savagery. The rise of Napoleon Bonaparte restored some stability, but his foreign military exploits led to his ultimate defeat at the Battle of Waterloo, in Belgium, in 1815.

Napoleon's defeat ushered in a period of political instability that saw first the restoration of the monarchy, which was twice overthrown in revolutions (1830 and 1848), then the installation of Napoleon's nephew, Louis-Napoleon, first as president of a republic and then as the Emperor Napoleon III. The defeat of France in the Franco-Prussian War of 1870–71 led to a new republic and a period of relative stability in which France acquired new colonies in Africa and Indochina.

During the first half of the twentieth century France suffered grievously in both world wars. In the trench warfare of the First World War, almost a million and a half

Regions

Alsace • Aquitaine • Auvergne
Basse-Normandie • Bourgogne
Bretagne • Centre
Champagne-Ardenne • Corse
Franche-Comté • Haute-Normandie
Île-de-France • Languedoc-Roussillon
Limousin • Lorraine
Midi-Pyrénées • Nord-Pas-de-Calais
Pays de la Loire • Picardie
Poitou-Charentes • Provence-Alpes-Côte d'Azur • Rhônes-Alpes

Overseas Territories

French Guiana • French Polynesia
French Southern and Arctic Lands
Guadeloupe • Martinique
Mayotte • New Caledonia
Réunion • St Pierre and Miquelon
Wallis and Futuna Islands

France's southern Alps.

La Roque Gageac on the Dordogne River.

Aerial of Chateau de Chenonceau, Loire Valley.

French lives were lost and the northwest of the country was devastated. In the Second World War northern France was occupied by German forces and the south was administered from Vichy by a pro-Nazi collaborationist government.

Political instability continued after the Second World War, as France unsuccessfully waged a war against insurgents in Indochina and as unrest in French-controlled Algeria threatened to bring down the government. In 1957 France's Second World War hero, Charles de Gaulle, was invited to assume power, under a constitution that greatly increased the powers of the president. This constitution has since undergone a number of revisions, the latest being in 1976. The French president, who controls defense and finance, is elected by universal suffrage for a seven-year term. There are two houses of parliament, elected at three- and five-year intervals.

Physical features and land use

Much of the French countryside is low-lying with almost two-thirds of its land at an elevation of less than

250 m (800 ft). These lowland regions stretch, interspersed with a number of hilly areas, from the Belgian and German borders, across the north to the rugged Breton Peninsula in the west, and inland to the Pyrenees in the southwest. Further east, along the Mediterranean coast and hemmed in by mountains, is the low-lying region of western Provence in the Rhône Delta. Except for the far northeast, which forms part of the Flanders Plain, most of these lowland areas comprise the basins of France's four main rivers and their tributaries. In the north, the Seine flows northwest, through Paris and the surrounding Île-de-France, to the English Channel; France's longest river, the Loire, flows north through the central region, then west-ward to the Atlantic Ocean; further south the Garonne, which rises in the Pyrenees, drains much of southwest France on its way to the Atlantic near Bordeaux; and in the east, the Rhône, rising in Switzerland, flows west to Lyon where, fed by the Saône from the north, it courses due south to the Mediterranean.

A cobbled street in St Paul de Vence

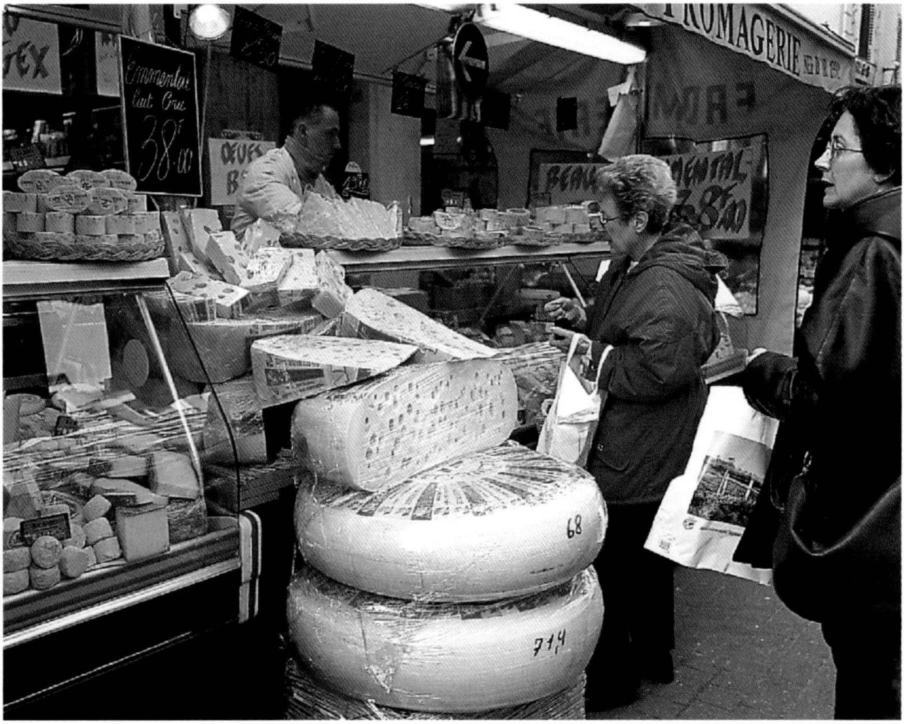

A cheese shop in Paris.

France Timeline

35,000 BP Neanderthal people living in caves, sometimes burying dead using decorated grave slabs

30,000–20,000 BP Cro-Magnon population in the southwest spreads out to northern and eastern regions

15,000–10,000 BP Cave paintings at sites such as Lascaux and Pech Merle depicting bulls, mammoths, horses, and humans

600 BC Greek merchants establish Massilia (later Marseilles) as a port on the Mediterranean coast

59–50 BC Roman legions led by Julius Caesar occupy the entire area of Gaul (France)

400 BC Franks and Visigoths move east into Gaul, defeating the Romans

AD 987 Hugh Capet becomes the first of the Capetian kings to rule all France

1309–77 The Papa moves from Rome Avignon in souther France

1337–1453 F and England fi Hundred Years despite Englis victories at Cr Agincourt the triumph

1848 Riots in Paris, with street fighting between the army and mobs of hungry, unemployed workers

1870–1 France loses Franco-Prussian War; Alsace and Lorraine ceded to Germany

1889 The Eiffel Tower, an iron structure designed by Gustave Alexandre Eiffel for the Exhibition of the same year, built in Paris

1914 First World War: Allies create the Wester Front in north France to stop German advance; deadlock lasts 31/2 years—1,357,800 Frenc casualties

1918 First World War ends with Treaty of Versailles under which Alsace and Lorraine are returned to France by Germany

F

French house with shingled roof and stairs.

In the center and south of the country, a vast central plateau, the Massif Central, covers almost a sixth of the total land area. Much of its landscape is rugged, characterized by granite outcrops, extinct volcanic peaks, and deep gorges. At its highest point, it reaches almost 1,900 m (6,000 ft). East of the Massif Central, separated from it by the Rhône Valley, are the Alps, which form the border with Italy and which, in the southeast corner of the country, extend to the coast. North of the Alps, the Jura, characterized by high limestone cliffs, separate France from Switzerland and further north, the heavily forested Vosges Mountains fringe the Rhine Valley near the German border. In the far southwest, the Pyrenees, which rival the Alps in rugged splendor, but which are less accessible, stand between France and Spain.

Industry, commerce, and agriculture

Second only to the USA as an exporter of agricultural produce, France produces a wide range of food, although most farms are relatively small. Over half the land area, mainly in the low-lying regions, is cultivated, the most abundant crops being wheat, maize, barley, and sugar beet. Vast areas, especially in the Burgundy and Champagne regions in the central north, around

1562–98 Wars of religion between Catholics and Huguenots (Protestants)

1643 Religious rsecution causes 00 Huguenots to flee, resulting in economic decline

1789 The storming of the Bastille by the Paris mob marks the start of the French Revolution

1792 First French Republic established; Louis XVI executed (1793)

1799 Napoleon Bonaparte siezes power; first as consul and later as Emperor of France

1814–15 Napoleon exiled to St Helena after losing Battle of Waterloo; monarchy restored under Louis XVIII

F

Start of Second War and quent German on of France to occupation is (1940)

1944 Allied troops reach Paris; General de Gaulle returns from exile in England to form a provisional government

1957 France joins other European nations in forming the European Common Market by signing the Treaty of Rome

1960 Rapid rise in immigration from ex-colonial territories in North Africa and the Caribbean brings concern over jobs

1960 France begins nuclear weapons testing program

1968 Student protests lead to a general strike over educational policies and political dissatisfaction; General de Gaulle resigns

1994 Railway tunnel under Channel to England in operation; idea first proposed in 1802 by Mathieu to Napoleon I

1995 Jacques Chirac becomes President; France accepts EC lifting of passport control

Bordeaux in the southwest and the Rhone Valley in the south, are devoted to viticulture. France is Europe's second largest wine producer.

After Germany, France is the largest industrial power in Europe, and until recently many of its industries were state-owned. Paris, Lille, Nantes, and Strasbourg in the north, Lyon and Grenoble in the center, and Marseilles and Toulouse in the south are among the major manufacturing centers. The main industries include steelmaking, car, aircraft, and weapons manufacture, oil refining, machine making, textiles, and chemicals.

Arc de Triomphe, Paris.

Les Gorges du Verdon, La Provence.

Mineral resources are not abundant, though there are reserves of iron ore, zinc, and uranium. Most of France's electricity is generated by state-owned nuclear plants.

On average, the French enjoy one of the highest standards of living in the world, but there are considerable disparities between rich and poor, with considerable wealth concentrated in an area around Paris and parts of southern France. The state heavily subsidizes health services, which are particularly stressed by a high level of smoking and alcohol-related disease.

FRENCH GUIANA

OFFICIAL NAME Department of Guiana
FORM OF GOVERNMENT Overseas department of France
CAPITAL Cayenne
AREA 91,000 sq km (35,135 sq miles)
TIME ZONE GMT – 3 hours
POPULATION 167,982
LIFE EXPECTANCY 76.6
INFANT MORTALITY (PER 1,000) 12.9
LITERACY RATE 83%
CURRENCY French franc
ECONOMY Services 61%, industry 21%, agriculture 18%
CLIMATE Tropical with two wet seasons (Dec and June)
MAP REFERENCE Page 850

French Guiana

Located along the northeast coast, French Guiana has a narrow coastal plain and a largely unpopulated, forested hinterland. Brazil lies across its southern and eastern borders. After the French Revolution one of the islands became the French penal colony of Devil's Island (Île du Diable). Now French Guiana is the site of the European Space Agency's rocket base. Sugarcane plantations influenced its development; today, cash crops such as bananas and sugarcane grow on the coast, and the main exports are fish and fish products. It depends on France for its economic viability.

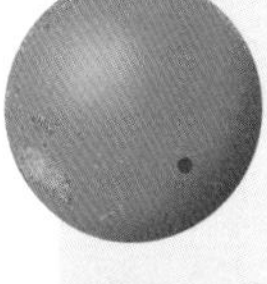

FRENCH POLYNESIA

OFFICIAL NAME Territory of French Polynesia
FORM OF GOVERNMENT Overseas territory of France
CAPITAL Papeete
AREA 4,167 sq km (1,609 sq miles)
TIME ZONE GMT – 10 hours
POPULATION 242,073
LIFE EXPECTANCY 72.3

French Polynesia

French Polynesia comprises five archipelagoes in the South Pacific, midway between Australia and South America, scattered over an area of ocean as large as Europe. They include the Society Islands (Archipel de la Société), the Marquesas (Îles Marquises), the Tubuai Islands, and the Tuamotus (Archipel des Tuamotu). The Polynesian inhabitants first settled the islands about 2,000 years ago. European contact dates from 1767. The conversion of the islanders to Christianity began in 1797 and after three years of armed resistance the chiefs of Tahiti accepted French colonial control in 1843. The islands send two deputies and a senator to the French Assembly in Paris, and since 1984 have had a local territorial assembly as well. Famous for providing the artist Gauguin with his best-known subjects, French Polynesia has been in the news more recently as a site for French nuclear testing on the atoll of Mururoa. This ceased in 1995. Large military expenditures over the preceding 30 years have provided the islands with employment, high wages, and improved infrastructure, and resulted in 70 percent of the population moving to live on Tahiti. Tourism now accounts for 20 percent of the gross domestic product. Cultured pearls are the main export.

Uninhabited Clipperton Island, a coral atoll in the Pacific Ocean west of Mexico, is administered by France from French Polynesia.

The peaks of Anau and Nunue and Bora Bora, French Polynesia.

Infant mortality (per 1,000) 13.6
Literacy rate Not available
Currency CFP (Comptoirs Français du Pacifique) franc
Economy Services 68%, industry 19%, agriculture 13%
Climate Tropical
Map reference Page 723

French Southern and Antarctic Lands

The French Southern and Antarctic Lands include Ile Amsterdam, Ile Saint-Paul, and Crozet and Kerguelen islands in the southern Indian Ocean. Mean annual temperatures range from 4°C to 10°C (39°F to 50°F) and the islands are wet and stormy. The main island of Kerguelen is mountainous (Mt Ross is 1,960 m; 6,430 ft), with an irregular coastline and deep fiords, and there are snowfields in the central area. Vegetation consists of coastal tussock grass and peaty uplands. Breeding colonies of seals and penguins are found in summer.

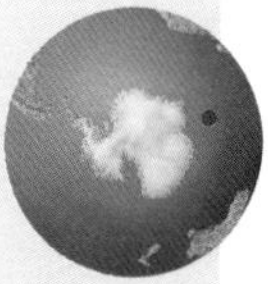

French Southern and Antarctic Lands

Official name Territory of the French Southern and Antarctic Lands
Form of government Overseas territory of France
Capital None; administered from Paris
Area 7,781 sq km (3,004 sq miles)
Time zone GMT + 3.5/5 hours
Population No permanent population
Economy None
Climate Cold and windy
Map reference Page 708 (E13)

G

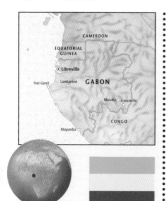

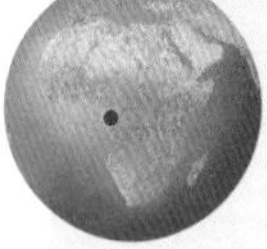

GABON

OFFICIAL NAME Gabonese Republic
FORM OF GOVERNMENT Republic with single legislative body (National Assembly)
CAPITAL Libreville
AREA 267,670 sq km (103,347 sq miles)
TIME ZONE GMT + 1 hour
POPULATION 1,225,853
PROJECTED POPULATION 2005 1,340,781
POPULATION DENSITY 4.6 per sq km (11.9 per sq mile)
LIFE EXPECTANCY 57
INFANT MORTALITY (PER 1,000) 83.1
OFFICIAL LANGUAGE French
OTHER LANGUAGES Indigenous languages (including Fang, Myene, Bateke, Bapounou/Eschira, Bandjabi)
LITERACY RATE 62.6%
RELIGIONS Christian 94%, Muslim 3%, other 3%
ETHNIC GROUPS Mainly Bantu tribes (including Fang, Eshira, Bapounou, Bateke) 92%, foreign Africans and Europeans 8%
CURRENCY CFA (Communauté Financière Africaine) franc
ECONOMY Agriculture 65%, industry and commerce 30%, services 5%
GNP PER CAPITA US$3,490
CLIMATE Tropical, with dry season mid-May to mid-September
HIGHEST POINT Mt Iboundji 1,575 m (5,167 ft)
MAP REFERENCE Page 808

Gabon

A slave station for the Portuguese after their arrival in 1483, Gabon was administered by France from 1842. After the French navy suppressed the still-continuing local slave trade, it released captives at a place on the coast which it named Libreville (Libertyville). Since Gabon achieved independence in 1966 France has continued to play a role in the country's politics and in its relatively prosperous oil-based economy.

The original inhabitants of this heavily forested equatorial country were probably Pygmy; today the main tribal group is the Fang. However, the 30-year rule of President El Hadj Omar Bongo (a Bateke who converted to Islam under Libyan influence in 1973) depended on a coalition that was designed to exclude the Fang from power. Widespread dissatisfaction with this state of affairs led to the introduction of a multi-party system in 1991. Whether or not this has allowed other ethnic groups a real voice in Gabonese politics is yet unclear.

Geographically, a coastal plain marked by sandbars and lagoons is interrupted by the estuary of the Ogooué River. The wooded basin of this large watercourse dominates Gabon, 60 percent of the country's land area being drained by its tributaries. These flow down from the African central plateau and the borders of Equatorial Guinea and Cameroon to the north, and from Congo to the east and south.

Before the development of oil and manganese in the early 1970s, valuable timbers were one of the country's main exports. These included Gabon mahogany, ebony, and walnut. Even today, as much as two-thirds of Gabon's total land area consists of untouched rainforest, but the completion in 1986 of the Trans-Gabon Railway from the port of Owendo to the interior town of Massoukou is likely to lead to further exploitation of timber resources.

Gabon has considerable mineral resources. It has about one-quarter of the world's known reserves of manganese, and is the world's fourth biggest manganese producer. France imports most of its uranium from Gabon. Oil currently accounts for 50 percent of gross domestic product. This figure, when combined with Gabon's small population, gives a distorted picture of the country's per capita earnings, disguising the fact that more than half the country's people still make their living by subsistence farming. A wide gap separates rural people from the urban élite and the country faces economic problems.

Gambia

Surrounded on nearly all sides by Senegal, Gambia is Africa's smallest independent state. Once a part of the Mali Empire, it became a British colony in 1816 and has been independent since 1965. Following independence it was governed for almost 30 years by Sir Dawda Jawara and the People's Progressive Party. A military coup displaced him in 1994. The country has been notably stable otherwise, though resentment of the dominant Mandinka exists among minority tribal groups such as the Fula and Wolof.

A subtropical climate and a sunny dry season has enabled Gambia to expand tourism but the conflict between tourist life and the main religion, Islam, has made this controversial. In 1982 Gambia joined its neighbor, Senegal, in a union named the Senegambian Federation. This proved unsuccessful and was dissolved in 1989.

The Gambia River and its estuary are navigable for some 200 km (125 miles), allowing ships of up to 3,000 tonnes to reach Georgetown. Consisting of a riverine plain running inland 275 km (170 miles) from the estuary, Gambia's countryside is low and undulating, the land beside the river varying from swamp to savanna. Although rice is grown in the swamps and on the river floodplain, not enough is produced to meet domestic needs. Millet, sorghum, and cassava are grown on higher ground. On the upper river, a dam provides irrigation.

Gambia has unmined deposits of minerals such as ilmenite, rutile, and zircon. The economy has a limited agricultural base, three-quarters of the population growing crops and raising livestock. Peanuts are the main cash crop, providing more than 75 percent of export earnings, and peanut processing is important industrially.

Fishing boats and fishermen at a beach in Gambia.

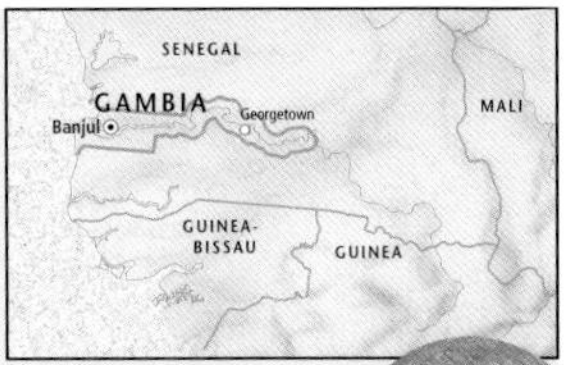

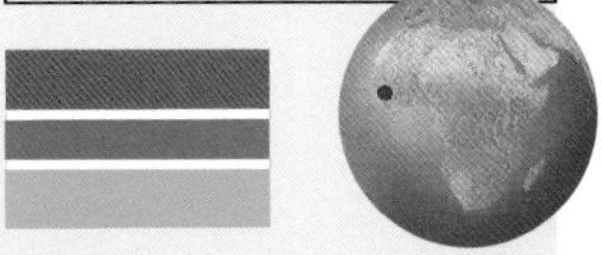

G

GAMBIA

OFFICIAL NAME Republic of the Gambia
FORM OF GOVERNMENT Republic with single legislative body (House of Representatives)
CAPITAL Banjul
Area 11,300 sq km (4,363 sq miles)
TIME ZONE GMT
POPULATION 1,336,320
PROJECTED POPULATION 2005 1,616,322
POPULATION DENSITY 118.2 per sq km (306.1 per sq mile)
LIFE EXPECTANCY 54.4
INFANT MORTALITY (PER 1,000) 75.3
OFFICIAL LANGUAGE English
OTHER LANGUAGES Indigenous languages (including Madinka, Wolof, Fula), Arabic
LITERACY RATE 37.2%
RELIGIONS Muslim 90%, Christian 9%, indigenous beliefs 1%
ETHNIC GROUPS Indigenous 99% (including Mandinka 42%, Fula 18%, Wolof 16%, Jola 10%, Serahuli 9%), non-Gambian 1%
CURRENCY Dalasi
ECONOMY Agriculture 75%; industry, commerce, and services 19%; government 6%
GNP PER CAPITA US$320
CLIMATE Tropical, with wet season June to November
HIGHEST POINT Unnamed location 53 m (174 ft)
MAP REFERENCE Page 804

Palm kernels are also exported. Because Banjul is the best harbor on the west African coast, much Senegalese produce passes through Gambia, and re-export forms one-third of economic activity.

Markets in Serekunda, Gambia.

Gaza Strip

Gaza Strip

Official name Gaza Strip (preferred Palestinian term, Gaza District)
Form of government Disputed by Israel and Palestinian National Authority; interim self-government administered by Palestinian Legislative Council
Capital Gaza
Area 360 sq km (139 sq miles)
Time zone GMT + 2 hours
Population 1,112,654
Life expectancy 73.4
Infant mortality (per 1,000) 22.9
Literacy rate Not available
Currency Israeli shekel
Economy Industry 44%, services 36%, agriculture 20%
Climate Temperate. Mild winters; warm, dry summers
Map reference Page 761

A disputed territory on the Mediterranean with a large permanent exile population of Palestinians, most of whom are descended from those who fled Israel in 1948. Egypt lies to the south and Israel surrounds it to the east and north. As with the West Bank, the Gaza Strip has been in Israeli hands since the Six Days War of 1967. Formally incorporated into Israel in 1973, it has eight Israeli settlements built since 1967. From when Israel assumed control, the Gaza Strip has been the scene of unrest and violence, the town of Gaza witnessing the Palestinian *intifada* ("uprising") in 1987–88. The accord reached between the Palestine Liberation Organization (PLO) and Israel in May 1994 gave self-rule to the Gaza Strip pending "final status" talks to take place in the future. The cycle of violence, involving Palestinian bombings in Israel and Israeli reprisals, made a resolution of the territory's status difficult to achieve.

As part of the 1994 peace deal, Palestine was given control of six centers in 1995. Elections were held in 1996 to select the Head of Executive Authority and Legislative Council, the intermediary governing force during the peace talks. Negotiations have continued, although violence still occurs throughout the Strip. The impact of the peace talks has been felt on the economy, with an increase in tourism in recent years.

Georgia

A mountainous country in the shadow of the Great Caucasus (Bol'shoy Kavkas), Georgia lies on the shore of the Black Sea between the Russian Federation and Turkey, and has borders with Armenia and Azerbaijan in the southeast. It has a long national history. The land of the Golden Fleece in Greek mythology (Colchis was today's Plain of Kolkhida) Georgia was conquered by Romans, Persians, Arabs, Tartars, and Turks, before falling to the Russians around 1800. Nevertheless, it maintains a strong culture, with a literary tradition based on a distinctive language and alphabet.

In 1991 Georgia rushed to proclaim its independence from the crumbling Soviet Union. Since then it has been chronically unstable, fighting off internal secessionist demands from both Abkhazia and South Ossetia. The town of Gori is the birthplace of Georgia's most famous son, Josef Stalin.

Georgia has four main areas: the Great Caucasus Range (Bol'shoy Kavkas) to the north which provides a natural boundary with Russia; the Black Sea plain in the west, including the subtropical Kholkida lowlands; the eastern end of the Lesser Caucasus (Malyy Kavkaz) to the south, whose peaks and plateaus extend into Turkey and Armenia; and a central plateau called the Kartalinian Plain, where the capital of T'bilisi stands, and which divides the northern and southern ranges. Further east, the Kura (Kür) River and its tributaries drain through a number of upland valleys toward Azerbaijan and the

An aerial view of a village in the Caucasus Mountains in Georgia.

Georgia

Official name Republic of Georgia
Form of government Republic with single legislative body (Parliament)
Capital T'bilisi
Area 69,700 sq km (26,911 sq miles)
Time zone GMT + 4 hours
Population 5,066,499
Projected population 2005 4,914,353
Population density 72.7 per sq km (188.3 per sq mile)
Life expectancy 64.6
Infant mortality (per 1,000) 52
Official language Georgian
Other languages Russian, Armenian, Azeri
Literacy rate 94.9%
Religions Christian Orthodox 75% (Georgian Orthodox 65%, Russian Orthodox 10%), Muslim 11%, Armenian Apostolic 8%, unknown 6%
Ethnic groups Georgian 70%, Armenian 8%, Russian 6.5%, Azeri 5.5%, Ossetian 3%, Abkhaz 2%, other 5%
Currency Lari
Economy Services 44%, industry 31%, agriculture 25%
GNP per capita US$440
Climate Temperate, with cool winters and hot, dry summers; subtropical on Black Sea coast
Highest point Gora Kazbek 5,047 m (16,558 ft)
Map reference Page 758

G

Fortress-like walls surrounding a church in Georgia.

Caspian Sea. The mountains contain extensive woodlands (nearly 40 percent of the country is forested) with broadleaf beech, oak, and chestnut at lower levels, and a sparse cover of birch on the higher slopes.

Georgia is an agricultural country, and its main industries are food processing and wine production. Collectivization had less impact on Georgia than elsewhere in the Soviet Union, so the recovery of its rural sector post-1991 has been fairly painless. Privately owned plots flourish, agriculture as a whole producing citrus fruits, tea (the main crop), grapes, tobacco, wheat, barley and vegetables, while perfumes are made from flowers and herbs. The Imeretia district has a flourishing silk industry. Other products from a small industrial sector include machinery, chemicals, and textiles. Manganese, copper, cobalt, and vanadium are mined. Tourism was once important, but has been damaged by civil strife. There are severe energy shortages. In the long term, hopes for Georgian economic progress hinge on re-establishing trade ties with Russia, and on international transportation (such as handling oil from Azerbaijan) through its Black Sea ports.

Germany

Landlocked, except for two stretches of coast along the North and Baltic Seas, Germany has land borders with nine countries. Poland is located to the east; the Czech Republic to the southeast; Austria and Switzerland to the south; France to the southwest; and Luxembourg, Belgium and the Netherlands to the west. Germany's coastlines are separated by the Jutland Peninsula, at the southern end of which Germany borders Denmark.

History

The area now occupied by Germany was roughly defined in the tenth century AD when Duke Conrad became king of the German-speaking eastern part of the Frankish Empire that had been established several centuries earlier. Under the Saxon King Otto I (AD 936–973), Germany's territory was extended. In 1273, however, the accession of the Austrian Rudolf of Hapsburg to the throne ushered in a long period of Austrian domination. The rise of Protestantism under Martin Luther during the sixteenth century flamed nationalist as well as religious passions and fuelled a peasants' revolt in 1524 that was savagely suppressed. More than a century of religious wars followed, climaxing in the Thirty Years War of 1618–48 in which, amid wholesale devastation, German states achieved the right to religious, if not political, autonomy.

Austria was weakened by the long years of war and this encouraged individual German states, such as Saxony, Hanover, and Prussia/Brandenburg to increase their power. Under the leadership of Frederick the Great during

The Alps in southern Germany.

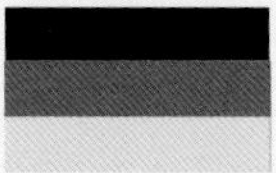

Germany

Official name Federal Republic of Germany
Form of government Federal republic with two legislative bodies (Federal Council and Federal Assembly)
Capital Berlin
Area 356,910 sq km (137,803 sq miles)
Time zone GMT + 1 hour
Population 82,087,361
Projected population 2005 81,860,165
Population density 230 per sq km (595.7 per sq mile)
Life expectancy 77.2
Infant mortality (per 1,000) 5.1
Official language German
Other languages Turkish, Italian, Greek, Dutch, Spanish, English
Literacy rate 99%
Religions Protestant 45%, Roman Catholic 37%, unaffiliated or other 18%
Ethnic groups German 95.1%, Turkish 2.3%, Italian 0.7%, Greek 0.4%, Polish 0.4%, other 1.1%
Currency Mark
Economy Services 53%, industry 41%, agriculture 6%
GNP per capita US$27,510
Climate Temperate, with cool, wet winters (colder in east and south) and mild summers
Highest point Zugspitze 2,962 m (9,718 ft)
Map reference Pages 772–73

STATES

Baden-Württemberg • Bavaria
Berlin • Brandenburg • Bremen
Hamburg • Hesse • Lower Saxony
Mecklenburg-West Pomerania
North Rhine-Westphalia • Rhineland-Palatinate • Saarland • Saxony
Saxony-Anhalt • Schleswig-Holstein
Thuringia (Thüringen)

G

Church and trees covered in snow, Bavaria.

the eighteenth century, Prussia developed into a major European power, gaining control of much of present-day Poland. At the end of the eighteenth century, Napoleon's armies overran both Austria and Prussia, but after Napoleon's defeat in 1815 Prussia became the dominant force in a German Confederation. This confederation, however, was still nominally under Austrian control. In 1866, under the leadership of Bismarck, the Prussians defeated the Austrian Hapsburgs, driving them out of Germany. Prussian victory in the Franco-Prussian War of 1870–71 consolidated Prussia as the leading European power and brought northern and southern Germany together to form a unified German Empire (Reich).

Germany's expansionist ambitions and its aggressive arms build-up during the last years of the nineteenth century led to international tensions that finally erupted in the First World War. Germany was to emerge from the war defeated and with its emperor, Kaiser Wilhelm, in exile. In 1919, the Weimar Republic, with a president and legislature elected by universal suffrage, was established. However, popular resentment was fanned by the loss of German territory and the harsh regime of reparations that were imposed by the Treaty of Versailles. This resentment was exacerbated by soaring inflation in the 1920s and the onset of depression at the end of the decade. In 1933 Adolf Hitler was elected chancellor as head of the National Socialist (Nazi) Party, promising to return the country to its former influence and power. He instituted a ruthlessly oppressive regime which persecuted Germany's Jewish population, and eventually plunged Europe into the Second World War when he invaded Poland in September 1939.

Café Central, Weihenstephan.

Neuschwanstein Castle in Bavaria, built by King Ludwig II toward the end of the nineteenth century.

At the end of the war a defeated and devastated Germany was divided into two principal zones, the western half administered by Britain, France, and the United States, and the eastern part under Soviet control. In 1949 this resulted in the creation of two separate states: the Federal Republic of Germany in the west, under a democratically elected government; and the Democratic Republic of Germany under a central, Soviet-dominated communist government in the east. Thus divided, the two Germanies became a focal point for Cold War tensions in Europe over the next 40 years. Control of the city of Berlin, in East German territory, was divided between the two countries. East Berlin was sealed off when communist authorities constructed a wall between the two parts of the city.

As the Soviet Union faltered in the late 1980s, waves of unrest in East Germany led to the collapse of its government and the reunification of the whole country in October 1990, with Berlin as its capital. In December,

Germany Timeline

35,000 BP Neanderthals, early humans named for the Neander Gorge near Düsseldorf, disappear from the fossil record

AD 10 The Romans, who rule much of what becomes Germany, are forced back to Rhine by the Germani, led by Arminius

AD 55 Caesar bridges the Rhine; Romans maintain a fleet on the river, developing it as a trade route and protective barrier

AD 800–14 Charlemagne, Holy Roman Emperor, sets up court at Aachen and briefly unifies the Germanic tribes

1241 The Hanseatic League, a union of northern towns, prospers through trade—rest of country divided and poor

1517 Luther's Protestant Reformation leads to a Peasants' Revolt in 1524

1618–48 Th Years War be Catholics an Protestants social and ec problems

1740–86 Frederick th Great of Pruss controls all German giving his own sta priority over othe German state

1939 Hitler annexes Austria, invades Poland; Britain, France declare war on Germany; Second World War ends 1945

1945 Germany partitioned into East and West, with the East run as a communist state by Russia and Berlin divided in two

1948 Russia withdraws from ruling council of occupying powers and blockades West Berlin; Allies airlift food and supplies to West Berlin

1949 The Federal Republic of West Germany is created

1950–55 With aid of development funds from US Marshall Plan, Germany's economic expansion becomes an "economic miracle"

1961 East Germany builds Berlin Wall to prevent East German citizens escaping to the more prosperous West Germany

1973 Federal Republic of Germany and German Democratic Republic achieve full UN membership

elections covering the entire country were held. Germany's political system is based on the 1949 West German constitution, which stipulates a parliament elected by universal suffrage for a four-year term with a president, elected by the parliament for a five-year term, as titular head of state.

Physical features and land use

The southern part of the country is generally mountainous and heavily forested. In the south-western region, east of the Rhine, which forms the border with France, is the vast expanse of rugged wooded peaks that constitute the Black Forest, an extension of Switzerland's Jura Mountains. Further east, the thickly wooded Bavarian Plateau rises out of the Danube Valley, leading to the spectacular peaks of the Alps along the border between Austria and Germany in the far southeast.

The central part of Germany is also a highland area, part of a chain of mountains and hills that extends from France as far east as the Carpathians. These, too, are heavily wooded, particularly in the more mountainous regions. The valleys are often fertile and undulating and extensively planted with crops and vines. The highest and most rugged peaks are found in the Harz Mountains in

A beech forest in Germany.

1862–71 Otto von Bismarck becomes the first Chancellor of a united Germany

1933 Adolf Hitler becomes Chancellor of Germany and supresses opposition, declaring Nazi Party the only legal party

1914–18 First World War: Germany joins Austria–Hungary and declares war on France and Russia but is defeated by Allies

1919 Formation of democratic Weimar Republic after German Emperor flees to Holland; republic lasts until late 1920s

1991 The Bundestag (German Parliament) reinstates Berlin as capital of Germany, replacing Bonn, the West German capital

1993 United Germany holds first free national elections since 1933

1995 Germany lifts passport regulations with six EU nations

9 Berlin Wall nolished; full ification with ast Germany proposed by ancellor Kohl

1990 East and West Germany sign a treaty formalizing unification of the separate states

1992 Main–Donau Canal links Main (a Rhine tributary) and Danube Rivers

1992–93 Neo-Nazi groups riot against immigration, claiming it to be the cause of unemployment among Germans

G

the north of these central uplands. In the northern part of the central uplands, where the country slopes toward the northern plain, there are areas of fertile soil that support crops such as wheat, barley, and sugar beet.

Northern Germany is an extensive lowland plain that covers about one-third of the country's area. Part of the North European Plain that stretches eastward into Russia, it is a region of fertile pasture and croplands, sandy heaths and stretches of marshland. A network of northward-flowing rivers, most notably the Elbe and its tributaries, drains this northern plain.

About one-third of German land is cultivated. Cereal crops are widely grown, as are hops for the German beers that are famous throughout the world. Vineyards are most widespread in the valleys of the Rhine and Mosel rivers. Cattle and pigs are the principal livestock and are concentrated mainly on the northern plain.

Mock-Tudor architecture, Fulda.

Industry, commerce, and culture

Manufacturing industry, centered largely in the Ruhr Valley but also in such cities as Frankfurt, Stuttgart, Munich, and Berlin, is the main strength of the German economy. Coal is the only mineral resource of which

Snow on bare branches and lighted ornate lamposts, Bavaria.

Germany has large reserves, although its importance has declined in recent decades as oil has replaced it as an industrial fuel. Iron and steel production support well-developed machine manufacturing and other metal industries. Cement, chemical, automobile, and electronic industries are also significant.

Unification has resulted in the juxtaposition of one of the world's most developed and efficient industrial economies with one that was mostly uncompetitive and outmoded in its methods and equipment. As a result, Germany has suffered considerable economic and social disruption because the more affluent western part of the country has had to subsidize attempts to improve conditions in the east. There is still a noticeable discrepancy between standards of living in east and west, and wages in the east are considerably lower. The move to a market economy in the former East Germany, with its emphasis on greater efficiency, has created high levels of unemployment. Under the former communist regime unemployment was virtually non-existent.

Munich Botanic Gardens.

Ghana

Ghana was once known as the Gold Coast. A well-known source of gold in West Africa for a thousand years, the nation's modern name comes from the Ghana Empire of the eighth to the twelfth centuries. The Ashanti people established themselves in the seventeenth century, selling slaves to Portuguese, British, Dutch and Danish traders. Under British control from 1874, Ghana became the first tropical African colony to win independence in 1956. Soon after this it became a Soviet-style one-party state.

A public voodoo ritual in eastern Ghana.

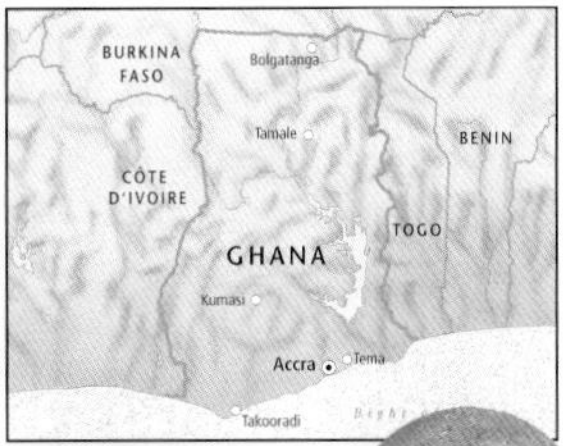

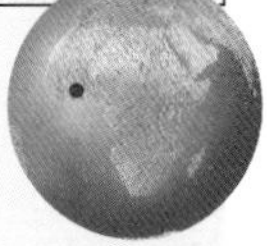

GHANA

OFFICIAL NAME Republic of Ghana
FORM OF GOVERNMENT Republic with single legislative body (Parliament)
CAPITAL Accra
AREA 238,540 sq km (92,100 sq miles)
TIME ZONE GMT
POPULATION 18,887,626
PROJECTED POPULATION 2005 21,128,132
POPULATION DENSITY 79.2 per sq km (205.1 per sq mile)
LIFE EXPECTANCY 57.1
INFANT MORTALITY (PER 1,000) 76.2
OFFICIAL LANGUAGE English
OTHER LANGUAGES Indigenous languages, including Akan, Mole-Dagbani, Ewe
LITERACY RATE 63.4%
RELIGIONS Indigenous beliefs 38%, Muslim 30%, Christian 24%, other 8%
ETHNIC GROUPS Indigenous 99.8% (including Akan 44%, Moshi-Dagomba 16%, Ewe 13%, Ga 8%), European and other 0.2%
CURRENCY Cedi
ECONOMY Agriculture 58%, services 31%, industry 11%
GNP PER CAPITA US$390
CLIMATE Tropical: warm and arid on southeast coast; hot and humid in southwest; hot and arid in north
HIGHEST POINT Mt Afadjato 880 m (2,887 ft)
MAP REFERENCE Page 804

The large, covered market in Kumasi, central Ghana.

After 1966, Ghana was wracked by military coups for 15 years before Flight-Lieutenant Jerry Rawlings took control in 1981. An election in 1996 returned Rawlings to power once more. Although government pressure is often brought to bear, vigorous political debate takes place in a relatively free media, and despite economic troubles Ghana still has twice the per capita output of the poorer countries in west Africa.

Geographically, the country is formed by the basin of the Volta Rivers. A large area flooded by the Akosombo Dam is now Lake Volta, the world's largest artificial lake. This provides hydroelectric power for smelting alumina into aluminum, and for use in the towns, mines, and industries of the Takoradi-Kumasi-Tema triangle. In the north there is savanna country. In earlier days the southern part of the country was covered by dense tropical forest. Much of this has been cleared for agriculture, especially for growing cocoa, which from 1924 until the present day has usually been the leading export.

Like other west African countries, Ghana has few natural harbors. Its coast consists mainly of mangrove swamps, with lagoons toward the mouth of the River Volta. The rivers are home to crocodile, manatee, and hippopotamus. The wildlife of the northern savanna includes lion, leopard, hyena, and antelope.

Ghana is well endowed with natural resources—gold, timber, industrial diamonds, bauxite, manganese, fish, and rubber. In 1995, largely as a result of increased gold, timber, and cocoa production, overall economic growth was about 5 percent. Although the economy is based on subsistence agriculture, Ghana is not self-sufficient in food. President Rawlings' efforts to reverse the statist policies of his predecessors continue, but face a number of obstacles. Public sector wage increases, and various peace-keeping missions, both internal and external, have strained the budget and led to inflationary deficit financing. Corruption is a continuing obstacle to growth.

Other factors have had an adverse economic impact. The recent drought has severely affected crops in the north and the low standard of living has worsened in some regions. Severe power failures in 1998 also affected the economy. However, the International Monetary Fund (IMF) helped to fund a three-phase economic restructuring. As a result, there has been an increase in funding for the country's economic infrastructure, although some small local companies have closed due to lack of foreign investment.

Gibraltar

Jutting into the Strait of Gibraltar at the southwest tip of Spain, Gibraltar sits at the entrance to the Mediterranean Sea. Spain's capture of Gibraltar in 1462 ended seven centuries of Moorish rule. Seized by the British and Dutch in 1704, it was ceded to Britain in 1713 and, despite subsequent Spanish attempts to take it back, it has remained in British hands ever since. Spain and Britain still dispute possession of "The Rock," and there is strong support for independence among the inhabitants. Gibraltar has its own elected parliament and is now virtually autonomous. Britain maintained a military garrison there until 1991, when it handed over control to the local regiment.

Gibraltar consists of a high rocky mountain, joined to the Spanish mainland by a sandy plain. Tourism, served by an airport on the peninsula, is an important contributor to Gibraltar's economy.

Gibraltar

Official name Gibraltar
Form of government Self-governing dependent territory of the United Kingdom
Capital Gibraltar
Area 6.5 sq km (2.5 sq miles)
Time zone GMT + 1 hour
Population 29,165
Life expectancy 78.7
Infant mortality (per 1,000) 8.4
Literacy rate Not available
Currency Gibraltar pound
Economy Financial services, tourism, manufacturing, horticulture
Climate Temperate; mild winters and warm summers
Map reference Page 776

Greece

Mainland Greece occupies the southernmost part of the Balkan Peninsula. The western shores of this peninsula are washed by the Ionian Sea, while on the east the Aegean Sea lies between it and Turkey. In the north, Greece shares borders with Albania, and to the northeast, with Macedonia and Bulgaria. In its far northeast corner there is a short border with Turkey. Dotted all over the Aegean Sea, and also in the Ionian Sea, are more than 1,500 Greek islands, only about one-tenth of which are inhabited. South of the mainland, in the Mediterranean Sea, is the large island of Crete.

It was in Crete that seeds of Greek civilization were sown. Here, for more than 2,000 years from about 3500 BC, grew and flourished the Minoan civilization, which, in about the sixteenth century BC spread to Mycenae, in the Peloponnese Peninsula. In the fifth century BC, Athens emerged as the center of Greek culture. It developed rich traditions in literature, theater, philosophy and politics which established the values on which most modern Western civilizations are based. In the fourth century BC,

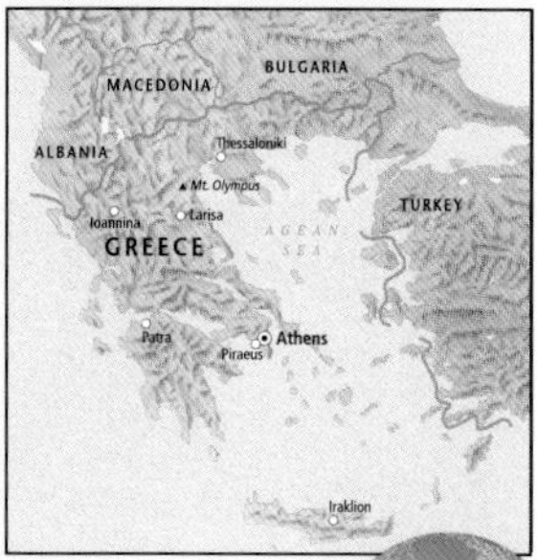

Greece

Official name Hellenic Republic
Form of government Republic with single legislative body (Chamber of Deputies)
Capital Athens
Area 131,940 sq km (50,942 sq miles)
Time zone GMT + 1 hour

(continues)

GREECE *continued*

POPULATION 10,707,135
PROJECTED POPULATION 2005 10,921,262
POPULATION DENSITY 81.2 per sq km (210.3 per sq mile)
LIFE EXPECTANCY 78.4
INFANT MORTALITY (PER 1,000) 7.1
OFFICIAL LANGUAGE Greek
OTHER LANGUAGES English, French
LITERACY RATE 96.7%
RELIGIONS Greek Orthodox 98%, Muslim 1.3%, other 0.7%
ETHNIC GROUPS Greek 98%, other 2%
CURRENCY Drachma
ECONOMY Services 56%, agriculture 25%, industry 19%
GNP PER CAPITA US$8,210
CLIMATE Temperate, with mild, wet winters and hot, dry summers
HIGHEST POINT Mt Olympus 2,917 m (9,570 ft)
MAP REFERENCE Page 771

under Alexander the Great, a vast Greek Empire spread across Asia as far as India and southward as far as Alexandria. Subsumed into the Roman Empire by the beginning of the second century BC, Greece eventually came under Byzantine rule, where it remained until the fall of Constantinople in AD 1204. Modern Greece dates back to 1832, when the country emerged from almost 400 years of Turkish domination and established a monarchy.

In 1941, Greece was overrun, in the face of fierce resistance, by German and Italian troops. It was liberated during 1944 by British and Greek forces, but almost immediately the country was plunged into civil war as monarchists and communists fought for supremacy. This destructive and debilitating struggle finally ended in 1949 with a victory by the monarchists. However, a military coup in 1967 resulted in the monarchy being expelled and a republic being established under an oppressive dictatorship. This regime fell in 1974 after an abortive attempt to invade Cyprus. In 1975, civilian government was restored and Greece became a democratic republic with a president elected for a five-year term, and a single-chamber parliament headed by a prime minister elected every four years.

Most of mainland Greece is mountainous, being dominated by the Pindos Mountains, an extension of the Dinaric Alps, that extend southeastward throughout the peninsula from the Albanian border. The mountains that

The city of Athens.

form Crete and the island of Rhodes, near the southwestern tip of Turkey, were once part of the same range. In the northeast the Rhodope Mountains form a natural border with Bulgaria. The only extensive low-lying areas are the northern plain, which extends from the Maritsa River on the Turkish border, across the northern Aegean region to the Greek province of Macedonia, and the plain of Thessaly in the central eastern mainland. Much of the Greek landscape, including that of many of the islands, is sparsely vegetated and has a rugged, rocky grandeur that, together with its warm climate, its beaches, and its rich historic heritage, attracts more than 10 million foreign visitors every year.

Despite its generally poor soils, Greece is heavily dependent on agriculture, which still employs about one-quarter of the workforce, largely on relatively small and inefficient farms. Wheat, olives, tobacco, and citrus and other fruits are among the main crops, and olives, particularly, are a major export item. Sheep and pigs are the principal livestock and are widely raised on the mainland and on Crete. Greece is almost self-sufficient in food production.

Not well endowed with mineral resources, Greece needs to import most of the raw materials for its industries, the majority of which are centered on Athens, though the area around Salonica in the northeast is also heavily industrialized. Food processing, based on local agricultural production, is important, as are textile manufacture and chemical processing. The tourist industry has helped the development of many local small-scale enterprises in such areas as ceramics, crafts, and textiles.

The dome of a church on the island of Thíra.

Village of Aperi, Karpathos Island.

Vegetable seller with donkey, Mykonos.

Agia Marina from Casto Steps, Leros.

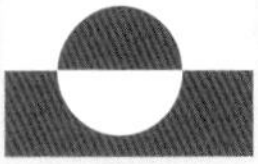

GREENLAND

OFFICIAL NAME Greenland
FORM OF GOVERNMENT Self-governing overseas administrative division of Denmark
CAPITAL Nuuk (Godthab)
AREA 2,175,600 sq km (839,999 sq miles)
TIME ZONE GMT – 1/4 hours
POPULATION 59,827
LIFE EXPECTANCY 70.1
INFANT MORTALITY (PER 1,000) 20.1
CURRENCY Danish krone
ECONOMY Fishing
CLIMATE Polar, with bitterly cold winters and cool to cold summers
MAP REFERENCE Page 821

Greenland

Greenland is nearly 50 times the size of its "mother country," Denmark, yet it has only 1 percent as much population. It is the biggest island in the world and about 85 percent of its land area is covered by an ice-cap with an average depth of 1,500 m (5,000 ft). Though there are a few sandy and clay plains in the ice-free areas of the island, settlement is confined to the rocky coasts.

It was named "Greenland" by the Viking Erik the Red during the tenth century, in the hope that the name would attract other Norsemen as settlers. The island became a Danish colony in 1721, an integral part of Denmark in 1973, and received full internal self-government in 1981. Most Greenlanders today are of mixed Inuit and Danish descent, and sometimes live uneasily between these two worlds. The social cost of this divide can be heavy; in the towns alcoholism, venereal disease, and suicide are high.

Greenland's economic prospects are somewhat limited in that it is now almost completely dependent on fishing and fish processing. These constitute 95 percent of all exports, and there is the added problem of falling catches of shrimp—in recent years the Arctic fishing industry has contracted. Though it has a certain amount of mineral resources, the last lead and zinc mine was closed in 1990. There is some ship building and also potential for the development of adventure tourism. One problem is the large role of the public sector, which accounts for two-thirds of total employment. About half of government revenue comes from Danish government grants.

Most of Greenland is covered by a thick ice cap. Ice floes are visible in the water surrounding the town of Narsaruaq.

Grenada

The state of Grenada consists of the island of Grenada, lying off the coast of Venezuela not far from Trinidad, and two small islands of the Southern Grenadines—Carriacou and Petite Martinique. The islands were visited by Columbus in 1498 but the original Carib Indian inhabitants fought off all invaders until French settlers arrived in the 1650s. Grenada then became a typical sugar-producing Caribbean island, with plantations worked by slaves brought from Africa. British since 1762, it has English as an official language, though some Grenadans still speak a French patois. It won independence in 1974 and in 1979 the country became communist after a bloodless coup. When the coup leader was murdered by fellow Marxists in 1983, the USA, with support from a number of other Caribbean countries, intervened to restore democratic elections. Since then power has been contested, and has alternated between several different political parties. Economic recovery from the events of 1983 has been slow.

Grenada is volcanic in origin and bisected by a mountain ridge. The coastal capital of St Georges is sheltered by hills.

G

GRENADA

OFFICIAL NAME Grenada
FORM OF GOVERNMENT Constitutional monarchy with two legislative houses (Senate and House of Representatives)
CAPITAL St Georges
AREA 340 sq km (131 sq miles)
TIME ZONE GMT – 4 hours
POPULATION 97,008
PROJECTED POPULATION 2005 104,434
POPULATION DENSITY 285.3 per sq km (738.9 per sq mile)
LIFE EXPECTANCY 71.6
INFANT MORTALITY (PER 1,000) 11.1
OFFICIAL LANGUAGE English
OTHER LANGUAGE French patois
LITERACY RATE 98%
RELIGIONS Roman Catholic 64%, Protestant (including Anglican, Seventh Day Adventist, Pentecostal) 27%, other 9%
ETHNIC GROUPS African 84%, mixed 12%, East Indian 3%, European 1%
CURRENCY East Caribbean dollar
ECONOMY Services 65%, agriculture 20%, industry 15%
GNP PER CAPITA US$2,980
CLIMATE Tropical, moderated by trade winds
HIGHEST POINT Mt Saint Catherine 840 m (2,756 ft)
MAP REFERENCE Page 837

The most southerly of the Windward Islands, the main island of Grenada is volcanic in origin and has fertile soils. A forested mountain ridge runs north–south, cut by rivers, and there are a number of lakes, including the Grand Etang at an elevation of 530 m (1,739 ft). The western coastline is precipitous; the southern coastal landscape of beaches is gentler and includes some natural harbors. In recent years the government has become interested in developing ecotourism, but the protection of key environmental sites remains a concern because large resort projects have resulted in serious beach erosion.

Grenada is known in the Caribbean as "the spice island," and is the world's leading producer of nutmeg and mace. Other exports include cocoa and bananas, but attempts to diversify the economy from an agricultural base have so far been unsuccessful. The farming practised by the rural population is mostly small scale, with the exception of a few cooperatives. The small manufacturing sector is based on food-processing and makes products such as chocolate, sugar, alcoholic beverages, and jam. Garments and furniture are also produced, mainly for export to Trinidad and Tobago. After the political crisis of 1979 to 1983 tourism largely ceased, but it is gradually recovering.

Guadeloupe

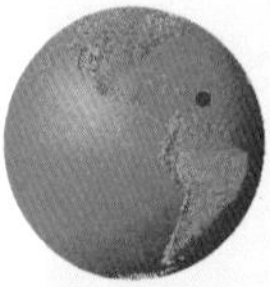

GUADELOUPE

OFFICIAL NAME Department of Guadeloupe
FORM OF GOVERNMENT Overseas department of France
CAPITAL Basse-Terre
AREA 1,780 sq km (687 sq miles)
TIME ZONE GMT – 4 hours
POPULATION 420,943
LIFE EXPECTANCY 78
INFANT MORTALITY (PER 1,000) 8.5
LITERACY RATE 90%
CURRENCY French franc
ECONOMY Services 65%, industry 20%, agriculture 15%
CLIMATE Subtropical, moderated by trade winds
MAP REFERENCE Page 837

Guadeloupe consists of seven Caribbean islands in the Lesser Antilles, to the southeast of Puerto Rico. The largest is the high, volcanic Basse-Terre (the active volcano of La Soufrière is the highest point in the Lesser Antilles) lying alongside the slightly smaller flat limestone island of Grande-Terre. A narrow sea channel separates the two. Arawak and Carib Indians were the original inhabitants. The first European settlers to arrive were the French, in 1635. Although there has been considerable agitation for independence, no vote in favor of it has succeeded, and the country is still governed by France—on which it is entirely dependent for subsidies and imported food. Tourism is important, most visitors coming from the USA. Sugar production is being phased out; bananas now supply about 50 percent of export earnings and the cultivation of other crops such as aubergines and flowers is being encouraged.

Guam

The largest and most southerly of the Mariana Islands in the northwest Pacific, Guam lies about 2,000 km (1,200 miles) due east of Manila in the Philippines. Originally settled by Malay-Filipino peoples around 1500 BC, Guam was mapped by Ferdinand Magellan in 1521, claimed by Spain from 1565, and administered by the USA from 1899 after Spain's defeat in the Spanish-American War. Of volcanic origin, Guam consists of a relatively flat coralline limestone plateau (the source of most fresh water), with steep coastal cliffs and narrow coastal plains in the north, low-rising hills in the center, and mountains in the south. About half of its population are Chamorro, of mixed Indonesian, Spanish, and Filipino descent. The island is of great strategic importance to the USA and about one-third of its land is occupied by American naval and air force facilities. This has resulted in a high standard of living, and there are concerns about the unemployment that is likely to follow the planned closing of four naval installations. As a Pacific tourist destination Guam is second only to Hawaii.

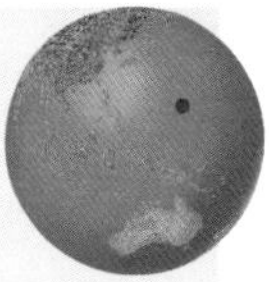

GUAM

OFFICIAL NAME Territory of Guam
FORM OF GOVERNMENT Organized, unincorporated territory of the USA
CAPITAL Agana
AREA 541 sq km (209 sq miles)
TIME ZONE GMT + 10 hours
POPULATION 167,590
LIFE EXPECTANCY 74.3
INFANT MORTALITY (PER 1,000) 15.2
LITERACY RATE 99%
CURRENCY US dollar
ECONOMY Services and tourism 54%, government 40%, other 6%
CLIMATE Tropical, moderated by trade winds; wet season July to October
MAP REFERENCE Page 724

Looking out over the city and bay, Guam.

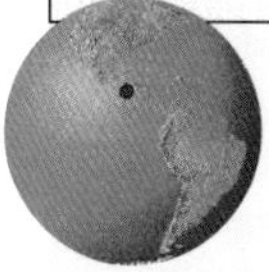

G

GUATEMALA

OFFICIAL NAME Republic of Guatemala
FORM OF GOVERNMENT Republic with single legislative body (Congress of the Republic)
CAPITAL Guatemala
AREA 108,890 sq km (42,042 sq miles)
TIME ZONE GMT – 6 hours
POPULATION 12,335,580
PROJECTED POPULATION 2005 14,423,051
POPULATION DENSITY 113.3 per sq km (293.4 per sq mile)
LIFE EXPECTANCY 66.5
INFANT MORTALITY (PER 1,000) 46.2
OFFICIAL LANGUAGE Spanish
OTHER LANGUAGES Indigenous languages
LITERACY RATE 55.7%
RELIGIONS Roman Catholic 75%, Protestant 25%; some traditional Mayan beliefs
ETHNIC GROUPS Mixed indigenous–European 56%, indigenous 44%
CURRENCY Quetzal
ECONOMY Agriculture 50%, services 38%, industry 12%
GNP PER CAPITA US$1,340
CLIMATE Tropical, but cooler in highlands
HIGHEST POINT Volcan Tajumulco 4,220 m (13,845 ft)
MAP REFERENCE Page 838

Guatemala

Guatemala lies just south of Mexico, and is the most populous of the Central American states. It was once part of the home of the Mayan civilization which reached its peak about AD 300–900. It has numerous volcanoes, including Tajumulco, which is the highest peak in Central America. In 1523 the region was overrun by Spanish conquistadors. As elsewhere in Central and South America, the newly arrived Spanish established large agricultural estates worked by Amerindian laborers, setting the social and economic pattern for 300 years. After becoming a republic in 1839, Guatemala has had a history of dictatorship, coups d'état, and guerrilla insurgency. Profound social divisions exist between the Amerindian majority, and an elite of mixed Spanish and Amerindian ancestry (called Ladinos) who run the government. Guatemala has had civilian rule since 1985. In 1996 a United Nations mediated accord was signed by President Alvaro Arzu and the members of the URNG guerrilla movement, which, it is hoped, will bring an end to 36 years of armed struggle.

Two large mountain ranges cross the heart of the country. In the north are the older and more eroded Altos Cuchumatanes. To the south the geologically younger Sierra Madre Range includes 33 volcanoes, of which three are still active. Soil enriched with volcanic ash washed

The Sunday market in Chichi, Guatemala.

down from the Sierra Madre has created a narrow but fertile plain on the Pacific coast. This has been used for agriculture on a commercial scale only since the 1950s, when malaria was first brought under control and access roads were built. Now cattle and cotton are more important than this region's traditional banana crop. On the lower mountain slopes, up to about 1,500 m (5,000 ft), most of the country's highest quality coffee is grown. In the north of Guatemala the highlands fall away to the large, flat, forested Peten Tableland, where many ancient Mayan ruins are found, and to the plains along the Gulf of Honduras.

Guatemala's economy is largely agricultural. Coffee is the main crop and chief export, other exports being sugar, bananas, cardamom, and beef. From the forests, now reduced to about 40 percent of the country's land area, come timber and chicle, the gum used for chewing gum. The country has few mineral or energy reserves, apart from small amounts of petroleum, and until recently guerrilla activity has hindered access to the wells. Industries include sugar refining, furniture, chemicals, metals, rubber, textiles and clothing, and tourism. Tourism, largely comprising visits to the Maya ruins, revived after the military activities of the 1980s, but fell into decline again in 1994 and 1995 following attacks on foreigners. From 1990 the economy has shown mild but consistent growth though, given the extreme disparity of wealth, the government faces many difficulties in implementing its program of modernization and the alleviation of poverty.

One of the ruined temples of Tikal, the great Mayan religious center.

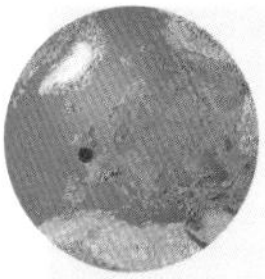

GUERNSEY

OFFICIAL NAME Bailiwick of Guernsey
FORM OF GOVERNMENT British crown dependency
CAPITAL St Peter Port
AREA 63 sq km (24 sq miles)
TIME ZONE GMT
POPULATION 65,386
LIFE EXPECTANCY 78.7
INFANT MORTALITY (PER 1,000) 8.4
LITERACY RATE Not available
CURRENCY Guernsey pound
ECONOMY Financial services, tourism, manufacturing, horticulture
CLIMATE Temperate; mild winters and cool summers
MAP REFERENCE Page 788

Guernsey

Guernsey, the second largest of the Channel Islands, lies in the English Channel, 50 km (30 miles) to the west of France. Though it is a British dependency, it is effectively self-governing, and administers all the other Channel Islands bar Jersey. Picturesque scenery, a gentle climate, and the relaxed lifestyle of its inhabitants make tourism an economic mainstay. Market gardening is also important and the island is famed for its distinctive cattle. Immigration is strictly controlled.

St Peter Port.

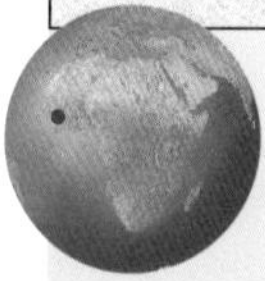

GUINEA

OFFICIAL NAME Republic of Guinea
FORM OF GOVERNMENT Republic with single legislative body (People's National Assembly)
CAPITAL Conakry
AREA 245,860 sq km (94,926 sq miles)

Guinea

Guinea is on the African Atlantic coast to the north of Sierra Leone and Liberia. A slave-trading center from the fifteenth century, it became the colony of French Guinea in 1890. After achieving independence in 1958 it was for 25 years a one-party Marxist dictatorship under Ahmed Sékou Touré. A member of the Malinke tribe, he centralized and nationalized, attempted to enforce the use of local languages in the place of French, and paid large numbers of state informers to monitor village and family life. Guinea now ranks last or near last on most international social development scales. The country's women face many disadvantages, including the practice of genital mutilation, which is widespread.

In the past 15 years governmental efforts at reform have led to a number of improvements, and in 1995 Guinea's first multi-party elections took place. The country has had to bear the additional burden of several hundred thousand refugees who have fled from the civil wars in Liberia and Sierra Leone although many are now returning home.

From mangrove swamps and lagoons along the coast, the land rises through densely forested foothills to the Fouta Djalon Highlands in the east. These highlands—from which the Gambia, Senegal, and Niger Rivers flow north and northeast—form a barrier between the coast and the grassland and savanna woodland of the Upper Niger Plains. Typical wildlife on the savanna includes lion and leopard, while crocodile and hippopotamus are found in the rivers.

The 80 percent of the workforce who live by agriculture are spread fairly evenly through the countryside. Those who live on the wet Atlantic coastal plain, much of which has been cleared for farming, cultivate bananas, palm oil, pineapples, and rice. Cattle are raised by nomadic herders in the interior.

Guinea possesses more than 25 percent of the world's reserves of high-grade bauxite, and three large bauxite mines contribute about 80 percent of the country's export revenue. Since it opened in 1984, the Aredor diamond mine has also been extremely profitable. Good soil and high yields give the country a prospect of self-sufficiency in food but the years of stifling state controls that were imposed by Touré have made market reforms difficult to implement, and infrastructures are few and much in need of modernizing. Corruption and harassment obstruct business growth. Aside from the bauxite industry, there is little foreign investment.

Children from rural Guinea.

Time zone GMT
Population 7,538,953
Projected population 2005 8,396,806
Population density 30.7 per sq km (79.5 per sq mile)
Life expectancy 46.5
Infant mortality (per 1,000) 126.3
Official language French
Other languages Indigenous languages
Literacy rate 34.8%
Religions Muslim 85%, Christian 8%, indigenous beliefs 7%
Ethnic groups Peuhl 40%, Malinke 30%, Soussou 20%, smaller tribes 10%
Currency Guinean franc
Economy Agriculture 80%, industry and commerce 11%, services 9%
GNP per capita US$550
Climate Tropical, with wet season May to November
Highest point Mt Nimba 1,752 m (5,748 ft)
Map reference Page 804

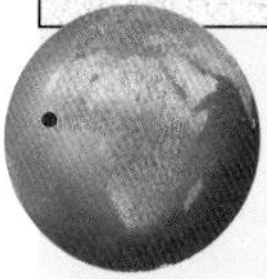

Guinea-Bissau

Official name Republic of Guinea-Bissau
Form of government Republic with single legislative body (National People's Assembly)
Capital Bissau
Area 36,120 sq km (13,946 sq miles)
Time zone GMT
Population 1,234,555
Projected population 2005 1,415,330
Population density 34.2 per sq km (88.5 per sq mile)
Life expectancy 49.6
Infant mortality (per 1,000) 109.5
Official language Portuguese
Other languages Indigenous languages
Literacy rate 53.9%
Religions Indigenous beliefs 65%, Muslim 30%, Christian 5%
Ethnic groups Indigenous 99% (incldding Balanta 30%, Fula 20%, Manjaca 14%, Mandinga 13%, Papel 7%), European and mixed 1%
Currency CFA (Communauté Financière Africaine) franc
Economy Agriculture 90%, industry and services 10%
GNP per capita US$250
Climate Tropical, with wet season June to November
Highest point Unnamed location in northeast 300 m (984 ft)
Map reference Page 804

Guinea-Bissau

Guinea-Bissau is a small west African state between Guinea and Senegal. A large part of the country consists of mangrove swamps, estuaries, and islands, and it is both poor and underdeveloped. After the French and British used the area as a slave-trading station in the seventeenth and eighteenth centuries, Portugal named it Portuguese Guinea and claimed it as a colony in 1879. Independence, achieved in 1974, came following 12 years of guerrilla war.

One-party rule plus attempted coups and assassinations marked the next 17 years. Moves toward multi-party democracy, designed to allow for ethnic divisons and inequalities, began in 1990. The contrast between the limited opportunities available to the 99 percent of the population which is African, and the privileges of the tiny Afro-Portuguese elite, is a major cause of tension. The existence of the opposition Democratic Front was made legal in 1991. Women face significant disadvantages and female genital mutilation is widespread.

Three main waterways—the Geba, Corubal, and Cacheu Rivers—mark the landscape. These wander across the plains toward broad estuaries and mangrove swamps on the coast. Here, the seasonal rainfall is especially heavy. Rice, the staple food, is grown on the floodplains and in the swamps, as well as on the offshore islands of the Arquipélago dos Bijagós, but not enough is produced to make the country self-sufficient. An area of upland savanna lies toward the border with Guinea in the southeast.

Mineral resources include phosphates, bauxite, and offshore oil but their development has been hampered by political instability, state controls, and (in the case of oil) disputes with Guinea and Senegal. Agriculture and fishing employ 90 percent of the workforce. Cashew nuts, peanuts, and palm kernels are the main exports. Economic reforms featuring monetary stability and private sector growth have been undertaken but progress is being hampered by the burden of foreign debt and the many cultural and institutional constraints.

Guyana

Guyana means "the land of many waters." In 1616 it was settled by the Dutch, who built dikes, reclaimed coastal land, and planted sugarcane. When the indigenous people refused to work in the sugar plantations, the Dutch, and later the British, imported slaves from Africa and indentured labor from India. The contrast between the communities descended from these two immigrant groups defines Guyanese political life. Beginning in 1953, and sharpened by independence in 1970, a struggle for dominance continues between the Afro-Guyanese and the numerically superior Indo-Guyanese. Some 95 percent of the people live on the coastal strip, and there is concern about flooding because of poor dike maintenance. The savannas, river valleys, and forested plateaus of the interior are largely unpopulated. There are, however, settlements of two neglected minorities in the forests—blacks descended from escaped slaves; and Carib, Warrau, and Arawak Amerindians.

Numerous rivers, including the country's main river, the Essequibo, flow down from the mountains in the west through tropical forests inhabited by a rich assortment of wildlife, including sloth, jaguar, tapir, and capybara. There is diamond dredging in many of the rivers, and in 1995 there was a major cyanide spill at the Omai gold mine near the Essequibo. The effects of mining activities on the wildlife is of major concern to conservationists.

The mining of high-quality bauxite and sugar production accounts for 80 percent of exports. Other resources include gold, diamonds, uranium, manganese, oil, copper, and molybdenum. Under successive governments, state ownership and government controls have stunted development and made adaptation to market fluctuations difficult. The bauxite industry remains a state monopoly. Recent deregulation has, however, shown benefits. Though weak infrastructure hampers tourist development, the spectacular scenery and wildlife of the interior is attracting visitors.

G

Guyana

Official name Cooperative Republic of Guyana
Form of government Republic with single legislative body (National Assembly)
Capital Georgetown
Area 214,970 sq km (83,000 sq miles)
Time zone GMT – 3 hours
Population 705,156
Projected population 2005 708,582
Population density 3.3 per sq km (8.5 per sq mile)
Life expectancy 61.8
Infant mortality (per 1,000) 48.6
Official language English
Other languages Amerindian languages, Hindi, Urdu
Literacy rate 97.9%
Religions Protestant 34%, Hindu 34%, Roman Catholic 18%, Muslim 9%, other 5%
Ethnic groups East Indian 51%, African and mixed indigenous–African 43%, indigenous 4%, European and Chinese 2%
Currency Guyana dollar
Economy Industry 44%, agriculture 34%, services 22%
GNP per capita US$590
Climate Tropical with two rainy seasons (May to mid-August, mid-November to mid-January)
Highest point Mt Roraima 2,810 m (9,219 ft)
Map reference Page 849

H

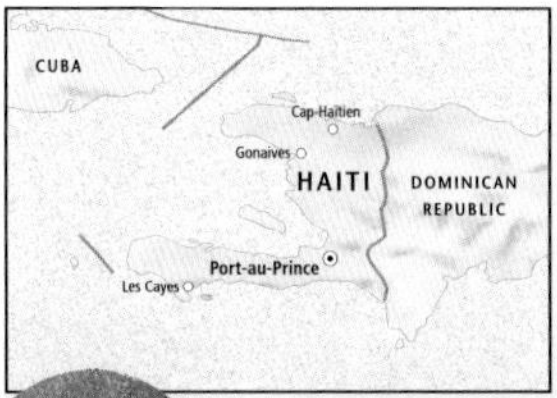

Haiti

Official name Republic of Haiti
Form of government Republic with two legislative bodies (Senate and Chamber of Deputies)
Capital Port-au-Prince
Area 27,750 sq km (10,714 sq miles)
Time zone GMT – 5 hours
Population 6,884,264
Projected population 2005 7,583,777
Population density 248.1 per sq km (642.6 per sq mile)
Life expectancy 51.7
Infant mortality (per 1,000) 97.6
Official language French
Other language French Creole
Literacy rate 44.1%
Religions Roman Catholic 80% (most of whom also practice Voodoo), Protestant 16% (Baptist 10%, Pentecostal 4%, Adventist 1%, other 1%), other 4%
Ethnic groups African 95%, mixed African–European 5%
Currency Gourd
Economy Agriculture 50%, services 44%, industry 6%
GNP per capita US$250
Climate Mainly tropical; semiarid in eastern mountains; wet seasons April to June and August to November
Highest point Pic de la Selle 2,680 m (8,792 ft)
Map reference Page 839

Haiti

Haiti lies in the Caribbean, east of Cuba. It is the western third of the island of Hispaniola, the Dominican Republic occupying the remainder. Visited by Columbus in 1492, it was used by the Spanish for sugarcane cultivation and was ceded to France in 1697. In the aftermath of the French Revolution it was the scene of a slave rebellion which led to the establishment, in 1804, of the world's first black republic. Since then the country has endured almost two centuries of instability, violence, dictatorship, military rule, and endemic poverty. Today, Haiti is the poorest country in the western hemisphere. Under the brutal regime of the Duvalier family, between 1957 and 1986, it became a police state enforced by a private militia called the Tontons Macoute. Recent years have seen faltering steps toward electoral democracy and modest civil service reforms, but political killings are still occurring under an apparently corrupt and ineffective judicial system.

Two peninsulas enclose the central plain of the Artibonite River, and the bight of the Golfe de la Gonâve beyond. Some 75 percent of Haiti's terrain is mountainous, the Massif du Nord providing the range which forms the northern peninsula, before extending east into the Dominican Republic where it becomes Hispaniola's Cordillera Central. The southern peninsula contains the Massif de la Hotte at its western end, and the Massif de la Selle in the east. The fertile lowland areas are densely populated, the largest of these being the Plaine du Nord. On the plains the major crop is sugarcane, while coffee plantations are found on the higher land. The majority of the population is engaged in subsistence farming, growing cassava, bananas, and corn. Haiti's environmental problems are severe: one-third of its soil is seriously eroded, and extensive deforestation has occurred in the course of charcoal production.

Haiti is without strategic resources and, during a period of economic sanctions imposed to put pressure on the government in 1991, it was forced to find clandestine sources of oil. In addition to sugar refining, light industry includes flour and and cement and the manufacture of textiles, shoes, and cooking utensils. The country's location, history, and culture proved attractive to tourists in the 1960s and 1970s, despite the repressive regime, but widespread crime has affected the industry in recent years.

Heard and McDonald Islands

Heard and McDonald islands are two bleak outposts in the Southern Ocean. Heard Island has the distinction of having the highest point in all Australian territory, being 2,750 m (9,021 ft). Classed as subantarctic islands, their mean annual sea level temperatures are between freezing and 3°C (37°F). They have ice caps, glaciers that descend to sea level, and furious gales. Vegetation consists of tussock grassland and small peaty fields. Seals and penguins breed ashore in summer.

Adélie penguin at Cape Bird, Antarctica

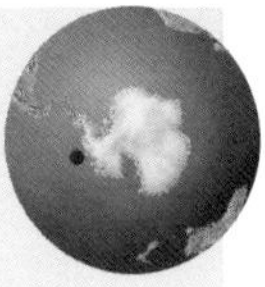

Heard and McDonald Islands

Official name Territory of Heard and McDonald Islands
Form of government External territory of Australia
Capital None; administered from Canberra
Area 412 sq km (159 sq miles)
Time zone GMT + 5 hours
Population No permanent population
Economy None
Climate Cold and windy
Map reference Page 708 (E14)

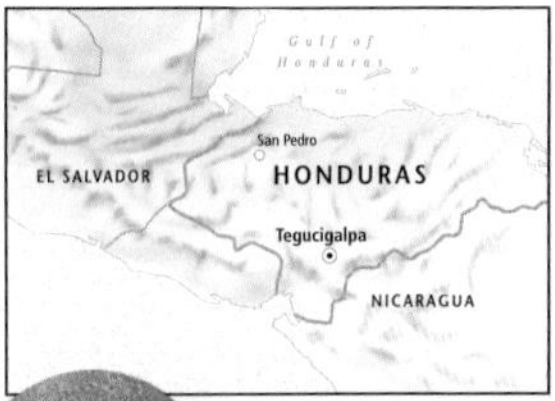

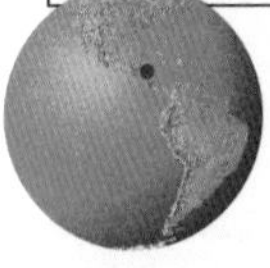

HONDURAS

OFFICIAL NAME Republic of Honduras
FORM OF GOVERNMENT Republic with single legislative body (National Congress)
CAPITAL Tegucigalpa
AREA 112,090 sq km (43,278 sq miles)
TIME ZONE GMT – 6 hours
POPULATION 5,997,327
PROJECTED POPULATION 2005 6,750,160
POPULATION DENSITY 53.5 per sq km (138.6 per sq mile)
LIFE EXPECTANCY 64.7
INFANT MORTALITY (PER 1,000) 40.8
OFFICIAL LANGUAGE Spanish
OTHER LANGUAGES Indigenous languages, English, Creole
LITERACY RATE 72%
RELIGIONS Roman Catholic 97%, Protestant 3%
ETHNIC GROUPS Mixed indigenous–European 90%, indigenous 7%, African 2%, European 1%
CURRENCY Lempira
ECONOMY Agriculture 60%, services 24%, industry 16%
GNP PER CAPITA US$600
CLIMATE Tropical on plains, cooler in mountains
HIGHEST POINT Cerro Las Minas 2,849 m (9,347 ft)
MAP REFERENCE Page 838

Honduras

Honduras is the second largest of the Central American countries. Its mountainous mass lies across the isthmus north of Nicaragua, with Guatemala to the west and El Salvador to the southwest. The Caribbean shoreline runs eastward from the Guatemalan border to the flat and almost uninhabited Mosquito Coast. In the west are the historic ruins of Copan, a site of the ancient Maya civilization which ended long before the Spaniards arrived in 1522. Gold first drew the Spanish to Honduras, and when they discovered it in the west, they founded the capital, Tegucigalpa, in 1524. The Honduran mountains are highly metalliferous and silver is still an important export.

Independent from Spain since 1821, the country has had decades of military rule with only the occasional elected government. The challenge for the present administration is to reduce the role of the military in political and economic life.

At least 75 percent of Honduras is mountainous. From the central highlands several river valleys run northwest to the coast, where the plains along the Caribbean shore broaden toward the east. The lower valleys have been reclaimed and the forests have been replaced by banana plantations. On the Pacific side there is a short stretch of coast in the Gulf of Fonseca. The adjacent lowlands are used for growing cotton. Rainforest in the northeast provides sanctuary for a great variety of wildlife.

The original "banana republic," Honduras was the world's leading exporter of the fruit during the 1920s and 1930s. Bananas still account for nearly a quarter of all exports but coffee is now the largest earner. The country depends heavily on the United States of America for trade: 53 percent of its exports and 50 percent of its imports are with the United States of America.

Most the workforce are farmers, many of them at a subsistence level: food staples are corn, beans, and rice. Small-scale manufactures include furniture, textiles, footwear, chemicals, and cement. Subject to an International Monetary Fund (IMF) restructuring program in the 1990s, Honduras has faced difficulties, with its already poor people subject to sharp tax rises. In 1998, Hurricane Mitch killed more than 9,000 people in Central America, and it devastated crops and left thousands homeless.

An aerial view of Tegucigalpa, the capital of Honduras.

Hungary

A landlocked, central European country, Hungary shares borders with Yugoslavia to the south, Croatia and Slovenia to the southwest, Austria to the west, Slovakia to the north, Ukraine to the northeast and Romania to the southeast. Modern Hungary had its beginnings in the eighth century AD, when the area was settled by the Magyars, nomadic tribes from the central Volga. Their kingdom thrived and expanded. In the sixteenth century the Turks seized the central part of Hungary and the northern and western sections of the country accepted Austrian Hapsburg rule rather than submit to Turkish domination. In 1699 the Turks were driven out and the entire country came under Hapsburg rule. Continuing unrest and the defeat of Austria by the Prussians in 1866 culminated in the establishment of Austria–Hungary as a dual monarchy in 1867. The defeat of Austria–Hungary in 1918 was followed by the establishment of the Hungarian nation, but with two-thirds of its former territory and almost 60 percent of its former

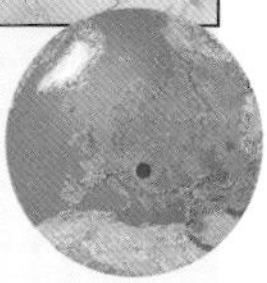

HUNGARY

OFFICIAL NAME Republic of Hungary
FORM OF GOVERNMENT Republic with single legislative body (National Assembly)
CAPITAL Budapest

(continues)

HUNGARY *(continued)*

AREA 93,030 sq km (35,919 sq miles)
TIME ZONE GMT + 1 hour
POPULATION 10,186,372
PROJECTED POPULATION 2005 10,084,830
POPULATION DENSITY 109.5 per sq km (283.6 per sq mile)
LIFE EXPECTANCY 71.2
INFANT MORTALITY (PER 1,000) 9.5
OFFICIAL LANGUAGE Hungarian
OTHER LANGUAGE Romany
LITERACY RATE 99%
RELIGIONS Roman Catholic 67.5%, Calvinist 20%, Lutheran 5%, other 7.5%
ETHNIC GROUPS Hungarian 89.9%, Gypsy 4%, German 2.6%, Serb 2%, Slovak 0.8%, Romanian 0.7%
CURRENCY Forint
ECONOMY Services 48%, industry 31%, agriculture 21%
GNP PER CAPITA US$4,120
CLIMATE Temperate; cold, wet winters and warm summers
HIGHEST POINT Mt Kekes 1,014 m (3,327 ft)
MAP REFERENCE Pages 773, 778, 780

population ceded to surrounding states. In the Second World War Hungary sided with Germany against the Soviet Union and was finally occupied by Soviet forces as they pushed southward in 1945. In 1948 communists, with Soviet support, again seized control, beginning 42 years of Soviet domination. A popular anti-communist uprising in 1956 was brutally suppressed by the Soviet Union. As the Soviet Union began to collapse a new constitution in 1989 set the scene for Hungary's first multi-party elections in 1990.

Hungary is drained by two southward-flowing rivers, the Danube and the Tisza. These two rivers traverse the Great Hungarian Plain, which occupies most of the eastern part of the country and more than half the total land area. West of the Danube a line of hills and mountains runs northeast from Lake Balaton, which covers an area of 370 sq km (140 sq miles), to the Slovakian border, where it joins the Carpathian Mountains. Northwest of these hills the Little Hungarian Plain extends to the westward-flowing Danube, which here separates Hungary from Slovakia. While most of the low-lying areas have long been cleared of trees, some of the forested areas still survive in the hills and mountains.

Most of the two plains areas are fertile agricultural country, although there are dry sandy expanses, as well as marshlands that are home to a rich variety of waterbirds. More than 70 percent of Hungary's agricultural land is devoted to crops, the most important of which are maize, wheat, sugar beet, and sunflowers. Of the rest, more than four-fifths are meadows and pasturelands and the rest are orchards and vineyards. Pigs and poultry are the most extensively farmed livestock.

Except for natural gas, bauxite, and lignite—a low quality coal that provides much of the country's energy—Hungary is poorly endowed with mineral resources. The country imports most of the raw materials for its now largely privatized industries, among which iron and steel production, and the manufacture of fertilizers, pharmaceuticals, and cement are prominent. Most of these industries are located in the north and are centered mainly around the capital, Budapest, and Miskolc, which is the second-largest city and is situated in the far northeast. Aluminum, using local bauxite, is manufactured north of Lake Balaton.

Hungarians enjoy a reasonable standard of living by the standards of former communist countries, though it still compares unfavorably with that in most Western countries. Pollution of air, soil, and water is a major problem and almost half the population lives in seriously affected areas.

Looking across the Danube from Buda to old city of Pest, Budapest, Hungary.

ICELAND

OFFICIAL NAME Republic of Iceland
FORM OF GOVERNMENT Republic with single legislative body (Parliament)
CAPITAL Reykjavík
AREA 103,000 sq km (39,768 sq miles)
TIME ZONE GMT
POPULATION 272,512
PROJECTED POPULATION 2005 281,653
POPULATION DENSITY 2.7 per sq km (6.9 per sq mile)
LIFE EXPECTANCY 79
INFANT MORTALITY (PER 1,000) 5.2
OFFICIAL LANGUAGE Icelandic
LITERACY RATE 99%
RELIGIONS Evangelical Lutheran 96%; other Protestant and Roman Catholic 3%; none 1%
ETHNIC GROUPS Icelandic 97%; others including Danish, American, British, Norwegian, German 3%
CURRENCY Króna
ECONOMY Services 61%, industry 35%, agriculture 4%
GNP PER CAPITA US$24,950
CLIMATE Cool temperate, with cool, windy winters and mild, wet summers
HIGHEST POINT Hvannadalshnukur 2,119 m (6,952 ft)
MAP REFERENCE Page 768

Iceland

True to its name, the island of Iceland, in the north Atlantic Ocean, has one-tenth of its total area covered in icefields and glaciers. The human occupation of this island, which lies just south of the Arctic Circle, dates back to the late ninth century AD when Norwegian Vikings settled there. In the thirteenth century the Icelanders submitted to Norwegian rule and a century and a half later, when the Norwegian and Danish monarchies were combined, they came under Danish control. In 1918 Iceland was granted its independence, but still owed allegiance to the Danish monarch. In 1944, as the result of a referendum, Iceland chose to become a republic. In 1972, because of its economic dependence on the surrounding seas, Iceland, without consultation with other nations, more than quadrupled the extent of its territorial waters from 12 to 50 nautical miles. Three years later it extended them to 200 nautical miles, a provocative move that brought condemnation, particularly from Britain, and gave rise to serious aggression at sea between Icelandic and British fishing vessels. Britain was later granted some degree of access to the disputed waters.

In addition to icefields and glaciers, Iceland's spectacularly rugged and volcanic landscape includes hot springs, sulphur beds, geysers, lava fields, deep rocky canyons, and plummeting waterfalls. There are numerous small freshwater lakes and 200 volcanoes, many of which are active. Earth tremors, and occasionally larger quakes, are a frequent occurrence.

The interior of the island consists mainly of an elevated plateau of basalt, interspersed with occasional high peaks. There are small areas of forest and very little arable land. In the north, however, there are extensive grasslands where a small number of sheep, cattle, and horses can graze. More than 90 percent of the population lives in towns and cities around the coast, mainly in the southwest corner near Reykjavík.

Deep-sea fishing is the backbone of Iceland's economy, with fish and associated products constituting more than two-thirds of the country's exports. Apart from fish processing, aluminum smelting from imported bauxite and cement manufacture are growing industries. All of Iceland's domestic and industrial electricity needs are met by locally generated power from hydroelectric or geothermal plants. About one in four Icelanders is employed in manufacturing and processing industries. Iceland attracts about 150,000 tourists a year, more than half its permanent population, making tourism an important income-earner.

The people of Iceland enjoy a very high standard of living. Their economy is robust but is susceptible to variations in international fish prices. The country's free health-care system has contributed to a life expectancy that is among the highest in the world.

India

India is the world's largest democracy, and one of the oldest and most successful in Asia. It is also the world's second most populous country, with a great variety of peoples, several major religious groupings, and 700 languages. In the 50 years since independence, in 1947, it has on the whole managed humanely and responsibly where other countries in the region have become totalitarian, or succumbed to military rule. There are major conflicts—there have been three wars with Pakistan alone. The dispute with Pakistan over Kashmir remains unresolved. The caste system produces endemic injustice. Millions live in desperate poverty. But Indians can change their government democratically by going to the polls, and the lot of most people has slowly but steadily improved. After a long period of state regulation of industry, barriers to outside investment, and a maze of protectionist controls, the country is opening its economy to the outside world. Population growth, however, at 2 percent on a base of almost a billion, tends to cancel out the nation's gains.

Physical features and land use

North to south, India can be divided into three main regions: the Himalayas and foothills; the Indo-Gangetic Plain; and the Deccan Plateau. From the northernmost border, the heavily glaciated terrain of the Himalayas—the world's highest mountains—cover 15 percent of the total surface area. The name itself comes from the Nepalese *him* ("snows") and *alya* ("home of"), the mountains being revered as the home of the gods. They rise to elevations of over 7,000 m (23,000 ft) in the Ladakh and Karakoram ranges. The western highlands towards the

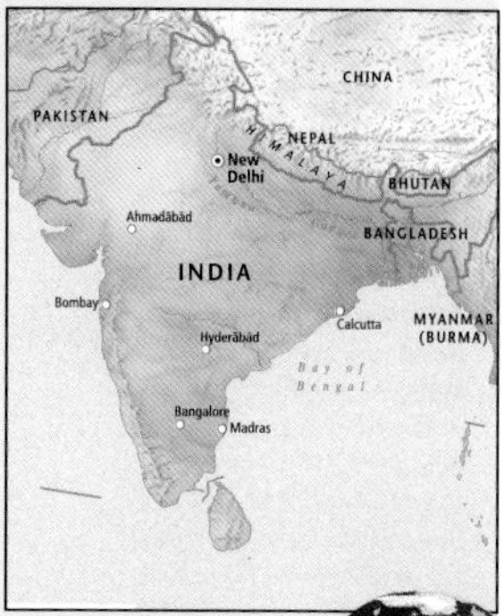

INDIA

OFFICIAL NAME Republic of India
FORM OF GOVERNMENT Federal republic with two legislative bodies (Council of States and People's Assembly)
CAPITAL New Delhi
AREA 3,287,590 sq km (1,269,338 sq miles)
TIME ZONE GMT + 5.5 hours
POPULATION Just over 1 billion
PROJECTED POPULATION 2005 1,096,929,474
POPULATION DENSITY 304.1 per sq km (787.7 per sq mile)
LIFE EXPECTANCY 63.4
INFANT MORTALITY (PER 1,000) 60.8
OFFICIAL LANGUAGES Hindi, Bengali, Telugu, Marathi, Tamil, Urdu, Gujarati, Malayalam, Kannada, Oriya, Punjabi,

(continues)

INDIA *continued*

Assamese, Kashmiri, Sindhi, Sanskrit, English
OTHER LANGUAGES Hindustani, about 700 indigenous languages
LITERACY RATE 51.2%
RELIGIONS Hindu 80%, Muslim 14%, Christian 2.4%, Sikh 2%, Buddhist 0.7%, Jain 0.5%, other 0.4%
ETHNIC GROUPS Indo-Aryan 72%, Dravidian 25%, Mongoloid and other 3%
CURRENCY Indian rupee
ECONOMY Agriculture 63%, services 26%, industry 11%
GNP PER CAPITA US$340
CLIMATE Tropical in south, temperate in north; monsoons June to September
HIGHEST POINT Kanchenjunga 8,598 m (28,208 ft)
MAP REFERENCE Pages 752–53, 754–55

STATES AND CAPITALS

ANDHRA PRADESH • Hyderabad
ARUNACHAL PRADESH • Itanagar
ASSAM • Dispur
BIHAR • Patna
GOA • Panaji
GUJARAT • Gandhinagar
HARYANA • Chandigarh
HIMACHAL PRADESH • Simla
JAMMU AND KASHMIR • Srinagar (summer) Jammu (winter)
KARNATAKA • Bangalore
KERALA • Trivandrum
MADHYA PRADESH • Bhopal
MAHARASHTRA • Mumbai (Bombay)
MANIPUR • Imphal
MEGHALAYA • Shillong
MIZORAM • Aizawi
NAGALAND • Kohima
ORISSA • Bhubaneswar
PUNJAB • Chandigarh
RAJASTAN • Jaipur
SIKKIM • Gangtok
TAMIL NADU • Madras
TRIPURA • Agartala
UTTAR PRADESH • Lucknow
WEST BENGAL • Calcutta

UNION TERRITORIES

ANDAMAN AND NICOBAR ISLANDS • Port Blair
CHANDIGARH • Chandigarh
DADRA AND NAGAR HAVELI • Silvassa
DAMAN AND DIU • Daman
DELHI • Delhi
LAKSHADWEEP • Kavaratti
PONDICHERRY • Pondicherry

Karakorams are harsh, dry, and inhabited only by small communities of herdspeople. At lower altitudes alpine meadows are grazed by the sheep of migratory pastoralists who arrive in the summer with their flocks. Lower still, rice terraces and orchards are found in the Vale of Kashmir.

The eastern highlands of northern Assam are markedly different. They are much wetter—this is where rhododendrons and magnolias grow wild and where terraced hills support buckwheat, barley, and rice. The climate of the high plateau of Meghalaya, separated from the Himalayas by the valley of the Brahmaputra, is damp and cool. On its southern flanks Cherrapunji has one of the world's highest rainfalls, averaging 10,798 mm (421.1 in) per year.

South of the northern mountains lie the *terai* or foothill plains; still further south the main plains region of India stretches from the western coastal lowlands, in a northern arc past the Thar Desert and down the Gangetic Plain to the mouth of the Hooghly on the Bay of Bengal. In the northwest—the Punjab and Haryana—farmers grow winter wheat, summer rice, cotton, and sugarcane, with sorghum in the drier areas. On the lowlands of the central part of Uttar Pradesh millet and sorghum are preferred to wheat and rice. Jute is cultivated where the Ganges enters the distributary system of the delta, while mangrove swamps line the marine margins of the delta itself.

The Thar Desert in the northwest contains a broad area of dunes in Rajasthan; southwest of this lie the cotton-growing lands of Gujarat, which includes the low peninsular plateau of Kathiawar between the Gulf of Khambhat and the Gulf of Khachchh, not far from the

The Taj Mahal.

Women washing clothes beside the Ganges in Varanasi.

Pakistan border. The Vindya Range east of the Gulf of Khambhat separates the Indo-Gangetic Plain from peninsular India and the Deccan Plateau. This plateau contains some of the world's oldest rocks, large tracts being covered with later basalt flows. The western edge of the plateau is defined by the mountain chain of the Western Ghats. At the foot of these mountains lies a coastal plain with coconut groves, fishing villages, ricefields, and tapioca plantations. On the plateau itself the main crops are millet and pulses.

History

Of India's various civilizations, the earliest developed in the Indus Valley (c.2600 BC) and in the Ganges Valley (c.1500 BC). At this time the subcontinent was mainly peopled by ethnic Dravidians. It is thought that the Indus civilization succumbed to an invasion of Sanskrit-speaking Aryan peoples who introduced the caste system, a scheme of social division that is fundamental in Indian life. Another important early civilization was the Maurya, which under Ashoka, who reigned from 273 to 232 BC, came to dominate the subcontinent. Later, a succession of Arab, Turkish, and Mongol influences led to the founding in 1526 of the Mogul Empire, which under Akbar (1542–1605) was extended throughout most of northern India and part of the Deccan. It was during the time of Mogul rule that the Taj Mahal was built by Shah Jahan.

Village, dam and rocky outcrop, Sravanbelagola, near Bangalore.

Timeline India

c.3500 BC First civilizations in Indus Valley (now Pakistan) —planting crops and domesticating sheep, cattle, and goats

2600 BC Dravidian peoples develop cities of Harappa and Mohenjo Daro in Indus Valley

1500 BC Aryan tribes from central Asia force Dravidians southward. Aryans plant wheat and barley, and introduce caste system

530 BC First invasion by Persians (Iranians) who sieze Gandhara (now Afghanistan) and parts of Punjab

c.500 BC Buddhism becomes widely accepted over the next 300 years but Hinduism eventually predominates

326 BC Alexander the Great invades India near the Indus River (now Pakistan) but is unable to sustain the colony when attacked

320 BC Maurya Dynasty (until c.185 BC) rules an empire covering almost all India from a base at Patna

300 AD Gupt begins. Sepa kingdoms all prosper with Gupta Empir 200 years

1740 East India Co (founded 1600) takes over Mogul land. Dutch, British establish ports at Madras, Bombay, Calcutta

1769 Severe famines in Bengal lead to rural depopulation for more than 20 years

1800 East India Co trades between Britain, Europe, China. India produces raw materials for British factories

1850 Failure of monsoon rains cau famines in norther India for more thar 30 years

1857 Indian Revolt against heavy taxes results in considerable loss of British and Indian lives. It is ruthlessly suppressed

1876 Q becom of India

Bamboo and terraced field.

The British effectively controlled India from 1805, during the nineteenth century introducing a civil service and a code of law which have profoundly shaped the nation since that time. With the coming of independence in 1947, the division between Hindus and Muslims resulted in the violent and tumultuous partition of the country into India and Pakistan. This first major division to split the country indicates that the most serious rifts within Indian society tend to be religious. In recent years the Sikhs of the Punjab have also been agitating for independence.

Economy

Once essentially rural, India's economy is now a mix of village farming, modern agriculture, handicrafts, a variety of modern industries, and innumerable support services. During the 1980s economic growth allowed a marked increase in real per capita private consumption. Since 1991 production, trade, and investment reforms have provided new opportunities for Indian business and some 200 million middleclass consumers. Among the nation's strengths is a home market of some 900 million, along with a workforce that includes many who are highly skilled, including those trained in high-tech areas such as computer programming. The textile sector is

1200 Delhi Sultanate brings Muslim rule to India, destroying many Hindu temples and instead building great mosques

1497 Vasco da Gama reaches trading port of Calicut; Portuguese later establish trading supremacy in Indian Ocean

1526 Babar conquers northern India, establishing Mogul Empire. Empire prospers for 200 years

1555 Emperor Akbar the Great, regarded as the greatest of the Moguls, subdues Rajput princes to control India

1632 Taj Mahal built at Agra by Emperor Shah Jehan in memory of his wife Mumtaz Mahal (completed 1643)

1880s Indian ...alist Movement ...pressure for an ... to British rule; ...olent attacks by extremists

1883 Commision into famine recommends building irrigation canals to supply water from Himalayas to grain-producing areas

1921 After more than 12 million deaths in 'flu epidemic of 1918–19 India's population surges; by 1921 it passes 250 million

1943 Severe food shortages in Bengal made worse by the army using scarce supplies results in loss of many lives

1947 India gains independence. Pakistan becomes a separate Muslim state (East and West). India takes over Kashmir

1965 Border war with Pakistan over Kashmir

1971 East Pakistan becomes independent country of Bangladesh; India's population reaches 500 million

1998 India tests nuclear weapons, followed by Pakistan; tension over Kashmir issue continues

1999 Population of India predicted to reach 1 billion

highly efficient. There has been a massive rise in foreign investment as the country has been opened up to foreign competition. The downside of this situation includes a sizable budget deficit along with high defense spending (including that for nuclear weapons) because of the continuing conflict with Pakistan. Other negative features include an absence of even elementary social services, poor roads, inadequate port facilities, and an antiquated telecommunications system.

Early in 2000, India's population passed the 1 billion mark. The Indian government celebrated this as an indication of numerical strength. To others, it is a sign that India is outstripping its resource base.

International trade, which began to expand in the late 1990s, has been affected by the undertaking of several nuclear tests. Fears of a nuclear war between India and Pakistan increased when Pakistan announced its plans for nuclear testing. The USA intervened and an International Test Ban Treaty has been developed, although neither the USA nor India has agreed to sign the non-proliferation accord. The influence of international pressure has resulted in India temporarily halting its nuclear testing program, although India's relations with the USA and several other trade markets remain tense.

Black and yellow-painted cow in a street in Bangalore.

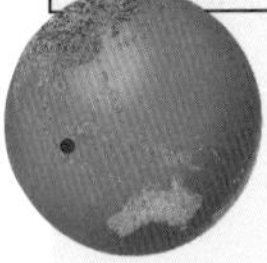

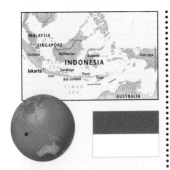

OFFICIAL NAME Republic of Indonesia
FORM OF GOVERNMENT Republic with single legislative body (House of Representatives)
CAPITAL Jakarta
AREA 1,919,440 sq km (741,096 sq miles)
TIME ZONE GMT + 7/9 hours
POPULATION 216,108,345
PROJECTED POPULATION 2005 234,875,553
POPULATION DENSITY 112.6 per sq km (291.6 per sq mile)
LIFE EXPECTANCY 62.9
INFANT MORTALITY (PER 1,000) 57.3
OFFICIAL LANGUAGE Bahasa Indonesia
OTHER LANGUAGES English, Dutch, indigenous languages
LITERACY RATE 83.2%
RELIGIONS Muslim 87%, Protestant 6%, Roman Catholic 3%, Hindu 2%, Buddhist 1%, other 1%
ETHNIC GROUPS Javanese 45%, Sundanese 14%, Madurese 7.5%, coastal Malays 7.5%, other 26%
CURRENCY Rupiah
ECONOMY Agriculture 54%, services 38%, industry 8%
GNP PER CAPITA US$980
CLIMATE Tropical, with wet season December to March (except in Moluccas where wet season is June to September)
HIGHEST POINT Puncak Jaya 5,030 m (16,502 ft)
MAP REFERENCE Pages 734–35, 736–37

Indonesia

Geologically, Indonesia is an active volcanic zone, but it was a political volcano which blew up in 1998. After 30 years of economic progress, during which a variety of political and ethnic conflicts were militarily contained, the collapse of the economy in 1998 triggered an outbreak of violent protest against the government. A change of leadership followed, and promises of new and more open elections. Nevertheless, long-suppressed class, ethnic, and religious conflicts have been unleashed, and a climate of political instability prevails. The national unity imposed on the numerous Indonesian islands has always been somewhat artificial. There are insurrectionary guerrilla groups such as Aceh Merdeka (Free Aceh) in north Sumatra, long at odds with Jakarta's urban elite.

The 13,677 islands of the world's largest archipelago (6,000 of them inhabited) rest on the platform of two continental shelves. The southern chain of islands, from Sumatra in the west to Timor in the southeast, and including Borneo to the north, form part of the Sunda shelf. This is a largely submerged extension of the Asian continent. Eastward, the northern Moluccas and New Guinea rest on the Sahul shelf, which is a northern extension of the Australian continent. Between the Asian and Australian ocean shelves, Sulawesi and the southern Moluccas form the island summits of suboceanic mountain ranges flanked by sea trenches that are 4,500 m (14,800 ft) deep.

All Indonesia's main islands are mountainous: this is an area of great crustal activity. Sumatra, Java, and the Lesser Sunda Islands (Nusa Tengara) form an arc containing 200 volcanoes, many of which are active—Krakatoa (Pulau Rakata) among them.

In Sumatra the Barisan Mountains run the length of the southwest-facing coast. Along with 10 active volcanoes there are a number of crater lakes, Lake Toba, at an altitude of 900 m (2,953 ft), being one of the more spectacular. Much of Sumatra was once forested but over-cutting of timber in the lowlands means that native forest is now virtually restricted to reserves and national parks. However, isolated mountain forests remain over wide areas. The heavily populated island of Java, next in the island chain, has a long range which contains 50 active volcanoes and 17 that are only recently dormant.

Throughout the archipelago many coasts are lined with mangrove swamps, notably in eastern Sumatra and southern Kalimantan. Several of the islands are of great beauty: tourism, not only to Bali, has been a major activity in recent years.

Indonesia's complex and varied population, and its four major religions—Islam, Hinduism, Christianity, and Buddhism—reflect the country's varied history. Hinduism was the first major religious influence 2,000 years ago, followed by Buddhism in the seventh century AD. Hindu-Buddhist religious authority began to decline with the collapse of the Majapahit Empire in the fourteenth century, and the arrival of Arab traders from the west gradually established Islam as the dominant religion.

Under Dutch colonial rule from 1608, the islands were from 1830 subject to a severe extractive regime known as the Culture System. This involved the forced cultivation of commercial crops for export and resulted in a distortion of the traditional economy. Indonesia fell to the Japanese in the Second World War. This additional colonial experience guaranteed that the Indonesians would expect independence after 1945 and not accept the return of the Dutch.

About one-tenth of Indonesia's land area is under permanent cultivation. The majority of the people live by agriculture, growing rice, maize, cassava, and sweet

Borobudur, the world's largest Buddhist monument, was built in the ninth century BC on the island of Java. Islam is the dominant religion in Indonesia today.

An Indonesian ceremonial mask.

Woman with stone bowls, Yogyakarta, Java.

Mist over Bandanaira, Maluku Islands.

potato. There are also extensive plantations producing rubber, palm oil, sugarcane, coffee, and tea. The last 30 years, however, have seen an intensive state-directed drive toward industrialization, based on diverse and abundant natural resources: oil, natural gas, timber, metals, and coal.

Foreign investment has played in important role in increased industrialization. Prosperity was initially tied to oil exports, but now the economy's growth depends on the continuing expansion of non-oil exports.

East Timor

East Timor, mainly Catholic after 300 years of Portuguese sovereignty, was declared independent of Portugal in 1975 by Fretelin (the Revolutionary Front of Independent East Timor). Indonesia immediately invaded East Timor, and retained control of the territory despite United Nations concerns about the legality of the invasion. Fretelin continued to fight for independence, while Indonesian troups bombed villages, carried out mass executions of suspected Fretelin sympathizers and forced the resettlement of thousands of East Timorese.

In 1999, reports of human rights abuses and falling health, education and living standards forced United Nations intervention. Agreement was reached for a UN-conducted ballot on the future of East Timor, during which the UN was to be responsible for communicating information to the people, while Indonesia was to be responsible for security arrangements. Anti-autonomy militia groups staged violent protests prior to the ballot, and many East Timorese fled.

UN-announced election results showed that 78% of the country had voted for independence. Anti-autonomy militias immediately launched an escalated campaign of violence, murdering civilians, seizing UN compounds, destroying the infrastructure completely and forcing thousands to flee, including UN staff. In September 1999 a UN peacekeeping force, the East Timor International Force (INTERFET), was deployed to aid humanitarian efforts, restore peace and protect UN peacekeepers. The UN also formed a Transitional Administration for East Timor (UNTAET), responsible for guiding the country through its early years of independence, providing governance, humanitarian aid and emergency rehabilitation of the social and economic infrastructure. UNTAET's brief was to communicate directly with East Timorese to ensure their participation in the new administration, which faces a daunting task in restoring a shattered economy and restoring the social infrastructure. (See also *East Timor*.)

Iran

Iran is one of the largest of the Persian Gulf states. It has borders with 10 other states in the region including Afghanistan, Pakistan, and Turkey. Now the home of the world's largest theocracy, and the main center for militant Shia Islam, Persia (as it was formerly known) has seen the rise and fall of a number of civilizations—Medes, Persians, Greeks, and Parthians. In the seventh century it was overrun by an invasion of Arabs who introduced Islam, a religion which under the Safavids in 1502 became the Shi'ite form of the faith which prevails today. Oil was discovered in 1908. From that time on Persia (retitled in the 1920s by a Shah who adopted the name Iran because it meant "Aryan") became of growing interest to the great powers, and the requirements of international oil companies began to figure in Iranian life.

After the Second World War the Iranians found the corrupt and despotic rule of Shah Reza Khan intolerable, and in 1979 he was overthrown in the first national revolution to be led by Islamic fundamentalists. This event has had profound effects and repercussions throughout the Muslim world. Iran's subsequent support for Islamic radicalism abroad soon produced strained relations with Central Asian, Middle Eastern, and North African nations, as well as the USA. More recently, Iran's economic difficulties and isolation have caused a general relaxation both in the domestic regime and in its external affairs.

A girl rides her donkey in one of the isolated mountain areas of Iran.

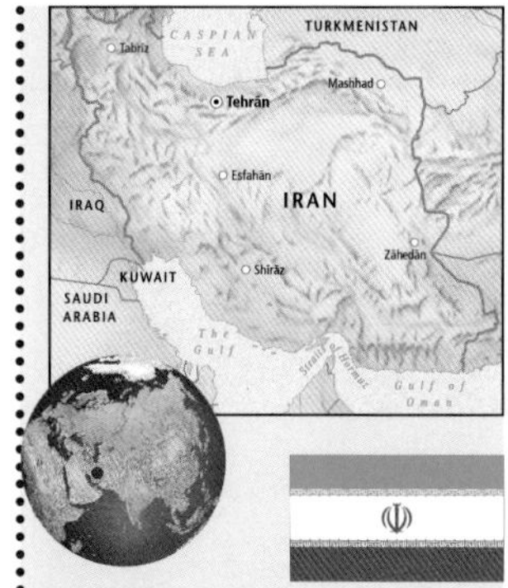

IRAN

OFFICIAL NAME Islamic Republic of Iran
FORM OF GOVERNMENT Theocratic republic with single legislative body (Islamic Consultative Assembly)
CAPITAL Tehrān
AREA 1,648,000 sq km (636,293 sq miles)
TIME ZONE GMT + 3.5 hours
POPULATION 70,351,549
PROJECTED POPULATION 2005 80,138,875
POPULATION DENSITY 42.7 per sq km (110.6 per sq mile)
LIFE EXPECTANCY 68.7
INFANT MORTALITY (PER 1,000) 47.0
OFFICIAL LANGUAGE Farsi (Persian)
OTHER LANGUAGES Turkic, Kurdish, Luri, Baloch, Arabic
LITERACY RATE 68.6%
RELIGIONS Shi'a Muslim 89%, Sunni Muslim 10%, other (including Zoroastrian, Jewish, Christian, and Baha'i) 1%
ETHNIC GROUPS Persian 51%, Azerbaijani 24%, Gilaki and Mazandarani 8%, Kurd 7%, Arab 3%, Lur 2%, Baloch 2%, Turkmen 2%, other 1%
CURRENCY Rial
ECONOMY Services 46%, agriculture 33%, industry 21%
GNP PER CAPITA Not available (c. US$766–3,035)
CLIMATE Mainly arid, temperate in far north; cold winters and hot summers
HIGHEST POINT Qolleh-ye Damavand 5,671 m (18,605 ft)
MAP REFERENCE Pages 756–57, 758

A portion of the facade of the Imam Mosque in Eşfahan, Iran.

The entire central region is dominated by a high, arid plateau (average elevation 1,200 m; 3,937 ft), most of it salt desert, containing the Dasht-e Lūt (Great Sand Desert) and the Dasht-e-Kavīr (Great Salt Desert). Mountain ranges surround the plateau: the volcanic Elburz Range (Reshteh-ye Kūhhā-ye Alborz) along the Caspian Sea; the Khorasan and Baluchestan Ranges in the east and southeast; and the Zagros Mountains (Kuhha-ye Zagros) inland from the Persian Gulf. The most productive parts of Iran, and the most heavily populated, lie on its periphery. In the north are the fisheries, tea gardens, and rice fields of the Caspian shore. In Khuzestan to the south there are sugar plantations and oilfields—a prime target of the Iraqis when they invaded in 1980 at the start of the eight-year Iran–Iraq War. Westward lie the wheatfields of Azarbaijan, while to the east are the fruit groves of the oases of Kavir in Kavir (Dasht-e Kavīr) and Lut in Lut Desert (Dasht-e Lūt).

Some 8 percent of Iran's land is arable, and 11 percent of it is forested, mostly in the provinces of Gilan and Mazandaran which border the Caspian Sea. The province of Tehran in the north is by far the most densely populated region supporting about 18 percent of the population.

In the years after 1945 Iran's economy became almost totally dependent on oil, and earnings from oil exports still provide 85 percent of its export revenue. But by the end of the war with Iraq (1980–88) production was half the level of 1979. This, combined with the general fall in oil prices, and a surge in imports that began in 1989, has left Iran in severe financial difficulties, and there has been a marked decline in general standards of living. Ideological considerations hamper effective reforms: there remains a continuing struggle over how to run a modern economy between the powerful religious leadership on the one hand, and reformist politicians on the other. The mullahs (the Islamic clergy) object to the government using borrowed money and are against the importation of "corrupt" Western technology.

Overall, the Iranian economy is a mix of centrally planned large-scale state enterprise; village agriculture producing wheat, barley, rice, sugar beet, tobacco, and pistachio nuts; and small-scale private trading and service ventures.

Iranian desert.

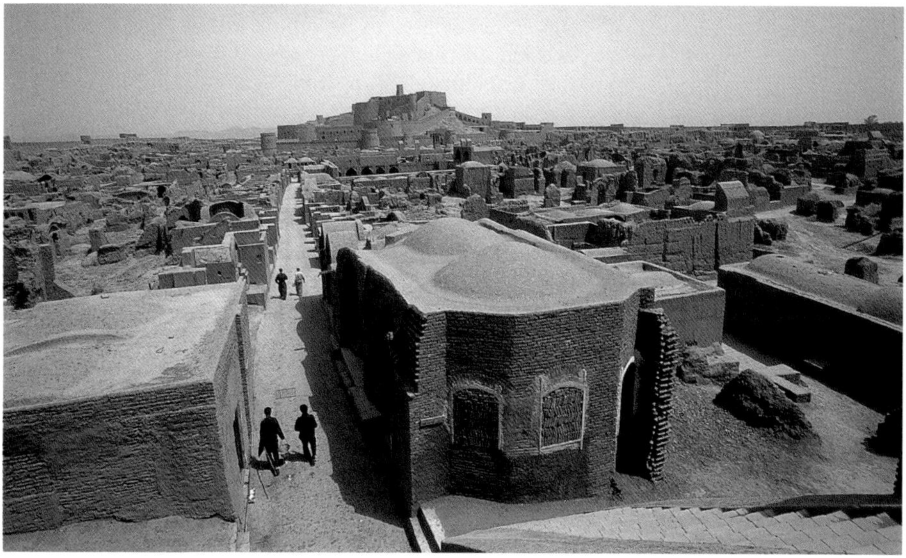

Arg-é-Bam Citadel.

IRAQ

OFFICIAL NAME Republic of Iraq
FORM OF GOVERNMENT Republic with single legislative body (National Assembly)
CAPITAL Baghdad
AREA 437,072 sq km (168,753 sq miles)
TIME ZONE GMT + 3 hours
POPULATION 23,871,623
PROJECTED POPULATION 2005 29,366,367
POPULATION DENSITY 54.6 per sq km (141.4 per sq mile)
LIFE EXPECTANCY 68.3
INFANT MORTALITY (PER 1,000) 52.5
OFFICIAL LANGUAGES Arabic, Kurdish
OTHER LANGUAGES Assyrian, Armenian
LITERACY RATE 56.8%
RELIGIONS Muslim 97% (Shi'a 60%–65%, Sunni 32%–37%), Christian or other 3%
ETHNIC GROUPS Arab 75%–80%, Kurdish 15%–20%, other (including Turkoman, Assyrian) 5%
CURRENCY Iraqi dinar
ECONOMY Services 48%, agriculture 30%, industry 22%
GNP PER CAPITA Est. US$766–3,035
CLIMATE Mainly arid, with cold winters and hot summers; winter snows in northern mountains
HIGHEST POINT Kuh-e Hajı Ebrahım 3,600 m (11,811 ft)
MAP REFERENCE Page 756

Iraq

If any country has the right to call itself the cradle of Western civilization it is Iraq. The first city states in the region date from nearly 3500 BC. The land "between the waters" of the Tigris and the Euphrates rivers (the meaning of the old name Mesopotamia) has seen many empires come and go. Babylon defeated its old rival Assyria here in 612 BC, and in the seventh century BC the territory was seized by the Persians; Baghdad became the greatest commercial and cultural center of the Muslim world. The Persians held Iraq until they were conquered by Alexander the Great in 334 BC. Part of the Ottoman Empire from 1534 to 1918, Iraq became independent in 1932.

Modern Iraq has been involved in two major conflicts in the space of 20 years: the First Gulf War with Iran, 1980–88, and the Second Gulf War when it invaded Kuwait, 1990–91.

After the days of the early Mesopotamian empires, the Arab peoples brought Islam to Iraq in the seventh century AD. Like Iran, Iraq has a majority of Shi'ite Muslims. Unlike Iran, the ruling elite in Iraq are Sunni Muslims who fear their own Shi'ites are secretly loyal to Iran. This underlies the tension within Iraqi society. The situation of the Kurds relates to an ethnic rather than a religious division. Distrusted and persecuted in every land in which they live (Turkey, Iran, Iraq, Syria, and Armenia), Iraq's Kurds were assaulted by Baghdad with chemical weapons in the 1980s.

In the far northeast Iraq shares part of the Zagros Mountains (Kūhhā-ye Zāgròs) with Iran. In the west its territory includes a piece of the Syrian Desert. The remainder of the country falls into two broad physiographic categories—the lowland desert to the west which makes up nearly 40 percent of the total land area; and the Tigris–Euphrates basin known formerly as Mesopotamia. Here the two rivers flow southeast roughly parallel, before meeting in a vast swamp on their way to the Gulf. In this swamp live communities of Marsh Arabs, Shi'ite Muslims targeted by the leadership in Baghdad after an attempted rebellion following the Second Gulf War. Most Iraqi agricultural activity takes place in the alluvial Tigris–Euphrates plain, where one-third of the farms are irrigated. Vegetables and cereals are the more important crops. In addition to the rice grown in warmer lowland areas, wheat and barley are cultivated in the temperate country near the Zagros Mountains. Exports have fallen sharply, but in better times Iraq's date crop met 80 percent of world demand.

Two wars, followed by international embargoes designed to force acceptance of UN inspection of weapons of mass destruction, have severely damaged the Iraqi economy. It was formerly dominated by the oil sector, but today oil exports are probably no more than 10 percent of their old level. Agricultural development has been hampered by labor shortages, salinization, and the dislocation caused by earlier land reform and collectivization programs. Living standards continue to deteriorate. Shortages are exacerbated by the government's spending of huge sums on both its army and internal security.

View across the rooftops of Sāmarrā', Iraq, to the River Tigris.

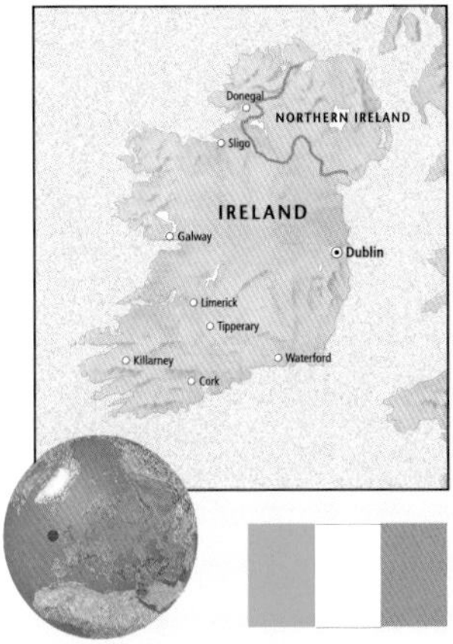

Ireland

Official name Ireland
Form of government Republic with two legislative bodies (Senate and House of Representatives)
Capital Dublin
Area 70,280 sq km (27,135 sq miles)
Time zone GMT
Population 3,632,944
Projected population 2005 3,727,595
Population density 51.7 per sq km (133.9 per sq mile)
Life expectancy 76.4
Infant mortality (per 1,000) 5.9
Official languages Irish Gaelic, English
Literacy rate 99%
Religions Roman Catholic 93%, Anglican 3%, other 4%
Ethnic groups Celtic 94%, English minority
Currency Irish pound
Economy Industry 54%, services 36%, agriculture 10%
GNP per capita US$14,710
Climate Temperate, with cool, wet winters and mild summers; wetter in the west
Highest point Carrauntoohil 1,041 m (3,415 ft)
Map reference Pages 787, 793

Ireland

Situated in the northern Atlantic Ocean and separated from the British mainland to the east by the Irish Sea, the Republic of Ireland covers more than three-quarters of the island of Ireland. The northeast corner comprises the six counties that form Northern Ireland, which is part of the United Kingdom. In the fourth century BC, Gaelic-speaking invaders conquered the island and established a Celtic civilization. Tradition has it that St Patrick brought Christianity to Ireland in AD 432, and to this day Catholicism remains the dominant religion. From the eighth century AD Viking raiders attacked the coasts and settled some coastal regions, but they were finally repulsed in 1014. During the twelfth century, the pope, Adrian IV, ceded the entire island to the English crown, but another five centuries were to pass before local opposition was finally subjugated.

From 1846 to 1851 disease destroyed the Irish staple crop, potatoes, leading to famine and more than a million deaths. Roughly half the population emigrated at this time, mainly to the USA.

Although the Irish were granted a degree of autonomy in the eighteenth century, opposition to British rule festered throughout the nineteenth century, leading to the unsuccessful Easter rebellion of 1916 and the eventual granting of home rule to most of the island, as the Irish Free State, in 1921. In 1949 the Republic of Ireland was declared and formal ties with the British crown were severed. Today Ireland is a parliamentary democracy, with

A cobbled shopping street in Dublin, Ireland.

a popularly elected president as head of state and two houses of parliament.

Most of the landscape consists of a low-lying limestone plain, with undulating hills and areas of fertile soils. Small lakes and peat bogs abound throughout the countryside. Mountain ranges run along much of the coast, creating, especially in the southwest, some of Europe's most spectacular coastal scenery. The most significant ranges are the Wicklow Mountains in the southeast and Macgillicuddy's Reeks in the far southwest. The Shannon, the country's longest river, rises in the Iron Mountains not far from the Northern Ireland border. It drains the central plain and flows through a number of Ireland's largest lakes.

Traditionally an agricultural country, Ireland now relies mainly on manufacturing and processing industries for its present, relatively healthy, economic strength. The country joined the European Community in 1973. Four in ten members of the population live in urban areas. Clothing, pharmaceuticals, and the manufacture of heavy machinery contribute largely to Ireland's export earnings and tourism is also significant. More than 3 million people visit Ireland every year. About one in eight workers is still involved in agriculture, mainly in livestock raising and dairying, but also in cultivating crops such as potatoes, barley, and wheat. The country has reserves of natural gas, oil and peat.

Crofts and a patchwork of fields on one of the Aran Islands in Ireland.

Emerald green grass and craggy hills with sheep and lamb on road .

The Troubles in Northern Ireland

Ever since Britain's granting of independence to the Irish Free State in 1921, Northern Ireland has been a troubled province, a place where terrorism and sectarian strife have been the norm. The arrangements for the government of Northern Ireland created bitter resentment among its minority Catholic population. Northern Ireland was then granted self-government, with its own parliament in Belfast, but maintaining strong links with the British government in London. The government ruled blatantly in favor of the Protestant majority, excluding Catholics from positions of authority or influence. Catholics moved in great numbers from the country to Belfast and other cities in order to find work, almost invariably in menial jobs in shipbuilding, textile, and other industries.

The Irish Republican Army (IRA), which had used guerrilla tactics against the British during Ireland's struggle for independence, became a threat to the stability of Northern Ireland, carrying out sporadic attacks on Protestant targets. When, in 1949, the Irish Free State, as Ireland was then called, left the British Commonwealth and became the Republic of Ireland, battle lines became marked. The IRA began to campaign aggressively for Northern Ireland to be

A unionist mural in Belfast, Northern Ireland.

absorbed into the republic and the breaking of ties with Britain, but for the next two decades it made little progress in the face of Northern Ireland's largely apathetic Catholic population.

However, as discrimination, especially in housing and employment, continued in Northern Ireland, Catholics grew increasingly militant, and in the late 1960s waged a widespread campaign for increased civil rights. Their demonstrations provoked some counter-demonstrations by militant Protestants and a 30-year period of violent sectarian clashes was launched. The situation was aggravated by the arrival of British troops, ostensibly to maintain the peace. They were soon perceived by the Catholics to be acting in the interests of the Protestants, especially after 1972, when they opened fire on Catholic demonstrators in Londonderry, killing 13 of them. In March 1972, in the wake of this incident, the British government suspended the parliament in Belfast and instituted direct rule for the province from London, a move that antagonized people on both sides of the struggle.

The desire of one section of the IRA to abandon violence led to a split in 1969. A wing of the IRA—the Provisionals, or Provos—consisting mainly of younger members, remained committed to terrorism and during the 1970s and 1980s carried out repeated bombings, murders, and kidnappings of both civilians and British army personnel, not only in Ireland, but also on the British mainland. Protestants in Northern Ireland responded in kind. From the early 1970s until the mid-1990s more than 3,000 people died in the conflict, and many more were wounded. The most prominent victim was Earl Mountbatten, who was assassinated in the Irish Republic in 1979. Northern Ireland towns and cities were divided into Catholic and Protestant zones, and an atmosphere of fear and distrust prevailed.

Any possibility of a negotiated peace was thwarted by the determination of successive British governments not to recognize or to have discussions with the IRA. This situation was changed in 1994, when the Provisional IRA suspended its terrorist campaign and talks, at first in secret, but later open, were held in London. The talks broke down in 1996 when the Provisional IRA revoked its cease-fire and continued its attacks. However, renewed efforts to reach a peace settlement continued, with the help of the USA. A major peace agreement tagged the Good Friday Accord, reached in 1998, included disarmament of the IRA and agreement on the establishment of a joint government. The interim government was suspended in early 2000 as neither Britain nor the IRA could be confident of meeting the May 2000 deadline for final implementation. The IRA is yet to begin disarmament, and disagreements over issues such as the nature of links between North Ireland and the Irish Republic, and the composition of the North Irish government, continue to vex the peace process.

Isle of Man

The Isle of Man is situated in the Irish Sea between the west coast of England and Northern Ireland, and just south of Galloway in Scotland. At its southern tip is a tiny uninhabited island, the Calf of Man, which is a nature reserve. Two regions of uplands in the center of the main island are divided by a valley extending from Douglas, on the east coast, to Peel, on the west.

The Isle of Man is a dependency of the British crown, but has its own legislature, legal system, and taxation system. Traditionally agriculture and fishing have been the island's main source of income, but it now depends mainly on tourism and financial and business services. Although English is the main language, the local Gaelic language—known as Manx—is still widely spoken and is taught in schools.

A seaside town on the Isle of Man.

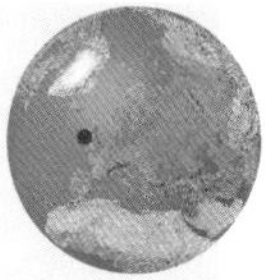

Isle of Man

Official name Isle of Man
Form of government British crown dependency
Capital Douglas
Area 588 sq km (227 sq miles)
Time zone GMT
Population 75,686
Life expectancy 77.8
Infant mortality (per 1,000) 2.5
Currency Manx pound
Economy Services 72%, industry 22%, transport and communication 6%
Climate Temperate; cool, wet winters and mild summers
Map reference Page 790

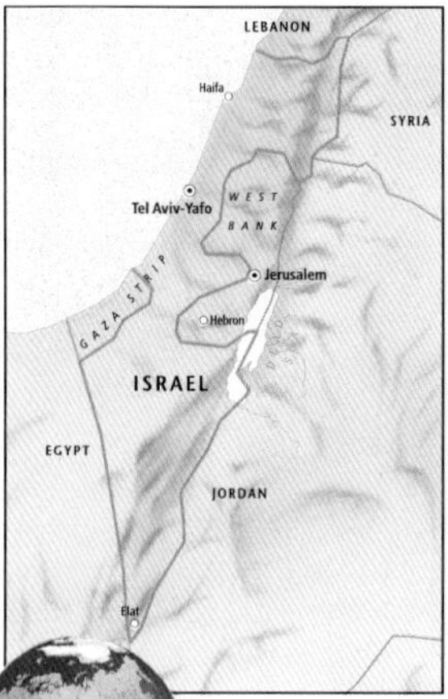

ISRAEL

OFFICIAL NAME State of Israel
FORM OF GOVERNMENT Republic with single legislative body (Knesset)
CAPITAL Jerusalem
AREA 20,770 sq km (8,019 sq miles)
TIME ZONE GMT + 2 hours
POPULATION 5,749,760
PROJECTED POPULATION 2005 6,303,057
POPULATION DENSITY 276.8 per sq km (717 per sq mile)
LIFE EXPECTANCY 78.6
INFANT MORTALITY (PER 1,000) 7.8
OFFICIAL LANGUAGES Hebrew, Arabic
Other languages English, French, German, Hungarian, Romanian, Russian, Spanish
LITERACY RATE 95%
RELIGIONS Jewish 82%, Muslim 14%, Druze 2%, Christian 2%
ETHNIC GROUPS Jewish 82%, Arab 17%, other 1%
CURRENCY Shekel
ECONOMY Services 75%, industry 21%, agriculture 4%
GNP PER CAPITA US$15,920
CLIMATE Temperate along coast, hot and dry in south and east
HIGHEST POINT Har Meron 1,208 m (3,963 ft)
MAP REFERENCE Page 761

Israel

Created as a Jewish homeland in 1948, Israel is a small country with an illustrious past that involves three of the world's great religions, and an uncertain future. For 50 years, through a succession of wars with hostile Arab neighbors, a secular, democratic political system has managed to constrain strong religious tendencies deeply rooted in the past. Key events in the Jewish history of the region are first, the occupation of the land by the 12 tribes of Israelites 4,000 years ago; second, the scattering (or "diaspora") of the one surviving tribe, the Jews, following a failed revolt against Rome in AD 138; third, the rise of Zionism in the nineteenth century advocating a Jewish homeland in Palestine as a solution to centuries of exile and persecution; fourth, the Holocaust, which reinforced arguments for territorial independence; and fifth, the proclamation of the State of Israel in May 1948, leading to the emigration of many Palestinian Arabs. Since then there has been continual strife between the new state and its neighbors. The subsequent seizure and occupation by Israel of additional territories (see entries for *Gaza Strip* and *West Bank*) has been bitterly resisted by their Arab inhabitants. This conflict has intensified as Jewish religious fundamentalists extend their settlements in contested areas.

Geographically, Israel consists of four main regions: the Mediterranean coastal plain of Sharon, irrigated by the Qishon, Soreq, and Sarida rivers; the rolling hills extending from Galilee in the north to Judea in the center; the Jordan–Red Sea section of the Rift Valley running

The wailing wall, Jerusalem.

north to south the full length of the eastern frontier from the Golan Heights to the Gulf of Aqaba; and the great southern wedge of desert plateau called the Negev (Ha Negev), which makes up about half of Israel's total land area. With irrigation, the Mediterranean coastal plain is fertile fruit-growing country. In the drier southern stretches its dunes have been stabilized with grass and tamarisk and reclaimed for pasture. The northern hill country around Galilee has good rainfall and a rich black soil weathered from basalt. Here and around Judea, pine, and eucalypt trees have been planted to fix the soil and hold the water. The Valley of Jezreel ('Emeq Yizre'el), lying between Galilee and Samaria to the south, has deep alluvial soils which are intensively tilled for market gardening. The Jordan–Western Negev Scheme—the most ambitious of Israel's various irrigation projects—diverts water from the upper Jordan and other sources through a series of culverts and canals south to the Negev. The desert is widely covered with blown sand and loess but tomatoes and grapes grow well when supplied with water.

The Old City of Jerusalem from the Mount of Olives.

Israel has the most industrialized economy in the region. Iron is smelted at Haifa and there are steel foundries at Acre. Chemical manufacturing takes place at Haifa and at plants by the Dead Sea. A national electricity grid provides power to widely dispersed towns where

Pilgrims outside the Church of the Holy Sepulchre in Jerusalem.

Israeli market, Jerusalem.

factories produce textiles, ceramics, and other products. In the Negev south of Beersheba new settlements mine oil, copper, and phosphates, the factories using potash and salt from the Dead Sea. Israel is largely self-sufficient in food production except for grains. Diamonds, high-technology equipment, and agricultural products are leading exports. About half the government's external debt is owed to the USA, its main source of aid. To earn foreign exchange the government has been targeting high-tech international market niches such as medical scanning equipment. Matters of continuing economic concern include the high level of unemployment following large-scale immigration from the former USSR, and the need to import strategically important raw materials.

Middle East Conflict

1964 Iran: Ayatollah Khomeini exiled for criticism of Shah's secular state.

1967 Israel: The Six Day War with Arab states. Israel seizes the Gaza Strip, Sinai, the Golan Heights, and the West Bank of the Jordan River.

1972 Iraq: Nationalization of Western-owned Iraq Petroleum Company.

1973 Egypt and Syria join in attack on Israel and fight 18-day war.

1978 Israel occupies southern Lebanon in response to Palestine Liberation Organization (PLO) attacks.

1979 Israel: Peace Treaty signed with Egypt. Iraq: Saddam Hussein takes over. Iran: Fall of the Shah. Ayatollah Khomeini returns from exile. Iran declared an Islamic Republic.

1980 Iraqi invasion starts Iran–Iraq War.

1981 Egypt: President Anwar Sadat, the first Arab leader to visit Israel, is assassinated.

1986 UN Security Council blames Iraq for war with Iran.

1987 Lebanon: Terry Waite, special envoy, arrives in Beirut to try to secure the release of western hostages and is himself captured.

1988 Iran: US naval ship shoots down Iranian airliner, 290 killed. Iran–Iraq War ends. Iraqi troops use chemical weapons on Kurds.

1990 Iran and Iraq resume diplomatic relations. Iraq invades and annexes Kuwait.

1991 Western allies liberate Kuwait. UN requires Iraq to accept weapons monitoring and to destroy weapons of mass destruction.

1993 Israel: PLO recognizes Israel in return for Palestinian autonomy in Gaza Strip and Jericho.

1994 Iraq recognizes Kuwaiti sovereignty.

1995 Israel: Palestinian autonomy extended to much of West Bank. Prime Minister Rabin assassinated.

1997 UN charges Iraqi officials with blocking weapons inspections. Iran: Mohammed Khatami, more liberal than his predecessors, becomes president.

1998 Iraq: Obstruction of UN weapons inspectors and fears of Iraq's biological weapons program leads to heavy bombing by US and UK.

1999 Wye River peace accord for the Gaza Strip is reached.

2000 Bombings in North Israel attributed to the Hamas sect (Palestinian Islamic Fundamentalists); however, peace talks with Palestine continue.

Italy

Situated in southern central Europe, the Italian mainland consists of a long peninsula that juts out into the Mediterranean Sea. Shaped roughly like a long, high-heeled boot, this land mass is bordered to the north by Switzerland and Austria, to the west by France, and to the east by Slovenia. At the southwestern tip of the peninsula, the narrow Strait of Messina separates the toe of the boot from the large Italian island of Sicily, while further west in the Mediterranean, separated from the mainland by the Tyrrhenian Sea and sitting just south of the French island of Corsica, is the island of Sardinia, also part of Italy. About 70 other small islands, scattered mainly around the coasts of Sicily and Sardinia and off the western coast of the mainland, make up the rest of present-day Italy. The peninsula's eastern coastline is washed by the waters of the Adriatic Sea, across which lies the coast of Croatia.

Fishing boats in the harbor of Camogli in Liguria, northern Italy.

ITALY

OFFICIAL NAME Italian Republic
FORM OF GOVERNMENT Republic with two legislative bodies (Senate and Chamber of Deputies)
CAPITAL Rome
AREA 301,230 sq km (116,305 sq miles)
TIME ZONE GMT + 1 hour
POPULATION 56,735,130
PROJECTED POPULATION 2005 56,253,452
POPULATION DENSITY 188.3 per sq km (487.7 per sq mile)
LIFE EXPECTANCY 78.5
INFANT MORTALITY (PER 1,000) 6.3
OFFICIAL LANGUAGE Italian
OTHER LANGUAGES German, French, Greek, Albanian
LITERACY RATE 98.1%
RELIGIONS Roman Catholic 98%, other 2%
ETHNIC GROUPS Italian, 94%; German–Italian, French–Italian, Slovene–Italian and Albanian–Italian communities 6%
CURRENCY Lira
ECONOMY Services 71%, industry 20%, agriculture 9%
GNP PER CAPITA US$19,020
CLIMATE Temperate; north has cool, wet winters and warm, dry summers; south has mild winters and hot, dry summers
HIGHEST POINT Mont Blanc 4,807 m (15,771 ft)
MAP REFERENCE Pages 778–79

I

Regions

Abruzzi • Basilicata • Calabria
Campania • Emilia-Romagna
Friuli-Venezia Giulia • Lazio
Liguria • Lombardy • Marche
Molise • Piedmont • Puglia
Sardinia • Sicily • Trentino-Alto
Adige • Tuscany • Umbria
Valle d'Aosta • Veneto

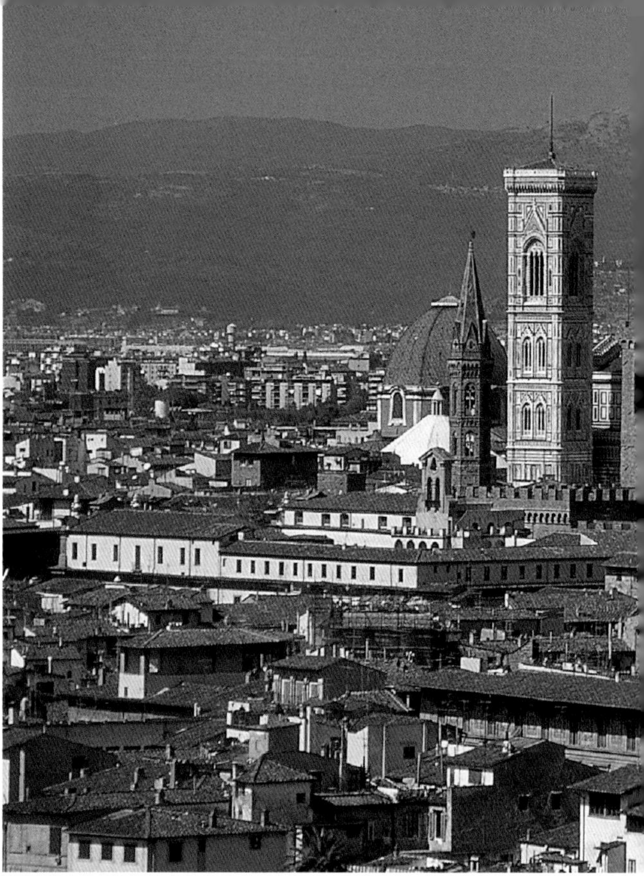

History

Italy's capital, Rome, situated in central western Italy, was for 800 years, from about 400 BC, the hub of the mighty Roman Empire. At the height of their powers in the first and second centuries AD the Romans controlled the whole of the Italian Peninsula and vast swathes of Europe. Their empire stretched as far as Britain in the north, the Iberian Peninsula in the west, into Egypt in North Africa and eastward as far as the Persian Gulf. Italy became Christianized after the conversion of the Roman Emperor Constantine in AD 313. The sacking of Rome by the Visigoths in AD 410 precipitated a series of subsequent invasions which resulted, over the centuries, in the fragmentation of Italy into a number of states ruled by different powers. For some time all of Italy came under the control of the eastern Roman Empire, based in Constantinople. The Franks, under Charlemagne, gained control of much of northern Italy at the end of the eighth

The rooftops of Florence, including the cathedral, seen from Piazzale Michelangelo.

Statue of Caesar, Rome.

Religious icon on the front of building, Rome.

century AD, and in the eleventh century the Normans invaded Sicily, which led to the creation of a kingdom based around the southern city of Naples.

In the later Middle Ages there emerged, in central and northern Italy, a number of powerful city-states, the most notable being Florence, Venice, Pisa and Genoa. From the fourteenth century, these states, especially Florence, promoted a great cultural revival which saw a blossoming of artistic, musical, literary, and scientific activity. This revival, which gradually spread through most of Europe, is now known as the Renaissance.

France, Spain, and Austria vied for the domination of different parts of Italy between the fifteenth and the eighteenth centuries. Most of Italy fell to Napoleon's armies in 1796–97, but after Napoleon's downfall in 1815 Italy was again fragmented, with Austria the dominant power in the north. A series of uprisings during the 1820s and 1830s gave rise to the movement known as the

Timeline Italy

900 BC Etruscan civilization founded between Arno and Tiber Rivers by people arriving from the east; lasts till c.200 BC

568 BC Langobardi (Lombards) seize much of northern Italy from Roman Empire

6TH CENTURY BC Under rule of Etruscan kings Rome grows from village to wealthy city

AD 79 Mt Vesuvius near Naples erupts, buries city of Pompeii in lava and ash, and Herculaneum under mud

476 Germanic leader Odoacer defeats last Roman Emperor; ends dominance of western sector of Roman Empire

800 Pope Le crowns Charlema Emperor of Rom

1814 Napoleon defeated by European powers; under Congress of Vienna most of Italy returns to Austrian rule

1858 French troops help Kingdom of Sardinia to push back Austrian troops, regaining most of northern Italy

1860 Garibaldi's redshirts regain contol of Sicily; eventually they take all southern Italy, including Naples

1861 King Victor Emmanuel announces Kingdom of Italy. To include entire peninsula except Rome, Venice, and San Marino

1908 Earthqua Messina, kills 120 people

Risorgimento (resurrection), which eventually led to the total unification of Italy and the installation of Victor Emmanuel II, the King of Sardinia, as King of Italy in 1861. During the next half-century Italy acquired a number of overseas territories, including Eritrea, part of Somalia, and some Greek islands.

Although officially allied to Germany, Italy at first remained neutral in the First World War and later joined the Allied side. In 1919 Benito Mussolini, a former socialist, founded the Fascist Party as a bulwark against communism. In 1922 he seized power, setting up a dictatorship. Embarking on a policy of foreign conquest, Italy invaded Ethiopia in 1935. Fascist Italy joined the side of Nazi Germany in the Second World War but in 1943 it was invaded by Allied troops and subsequently declared war on its former German ally. Dismissed from the Italian government, Mussolini was installed by Germany as head of a puppet government in northern Italy but he was captured and executed by partisans in 1945.

Rooftops and buildings of Siena.

After the war, Italy was stripped of its foreign territories. A referendum in 1946 resulted in the abolition of the monarchy and the establishment of a democratic republic. Since then, government in Italy has been wracked by instability as changing allegiances and

…tto the Great …ed Emperor of …oly Roman …e

c.1300 Renaissance begins. Interest flourishes in arts, sciences, and literature as well as philosophy, politics, and religion

1519 King Charles I of Spain becomes Holy Roman Emperor. Siezes much of Italy including Rome and Milan from France

1796 Napoleon Bonaparte invades north Italy, setting up independent republics. Interest in Italian independence grows

1000 Rise of city states such as Florence, Venice, Genoa, and Pisa which have strong commercial and cultural identities

1345 Black Death, or bubonic plague, kills more than one-quarter of the population

1663 Volcano Mt Etna erupts destroying much of the town of Catania, northeast of Sicily

1922 Mussolini becomes leader and the Fascist movement grows

1940 Italy's forces defeated in Eritrea, Ethiopia, and Greece; Mussolini overthrown, but reinstalled by Germans; Allies retake Italy (1943)

1960s Rapid postwar industrialization brings prosperity to northern cities but the south remains largely agricultural and poor

1980 Earthquake in southern Italy kills more than 4,500 and leaves 400,000 homeless

…5 Italy joins Allies …rst World War

1939 Start of Second World War; Italy enters on Germany's side nine months later, soon after the fall of France, in June 1940

1943 Allies invade Italy; Italian prime minister signs armistice with Allies; Italy declares war on Germany

1946 First free elections held since 1930s after Humbert III takes up the Italian throne; Italians vote to establish a Republic

coalitions have created a succession of short-lived governments. In 1993 a referendum approved a plan to simplify Italy's complex electoral system. Since 1994 three-quarters of the members of Italy's two houses of parliament have been elected by a simple majority of votes, while the rest are elected by proportional representation. The president, whose duties are largely ceremonial, is elected for a seven-year term. Both houses are elected for a maximum of five years.

Physical features and land use

Most of Italy is mountainous, with a central range, the Appenines, sweeping down the length of the peninsula and extending into Sicily, where the volcanic, and still active, peak of Mount Etna soars to a height of 3,323 m (10,902 ft) above sea level. Further north, near Naples, the active Mount Vesuvius offers evidence of the volcanic origins of Italy's mountains. The Appenines, which are rich in limestone, reach soaring heights of almost 3,000 m (10,000 ft) in the Gran Sasso Range, east of Rome. The slopes of the Appenines are covered with thin soils, which in some places provide reasonable pasture. In the valleys there are some extensive stretches of arable land. At the far northwestern tip of the Italian peninsula the Appenines

Aerial view of Positano.

One of the many palaces on the Grand Canal in Venice.

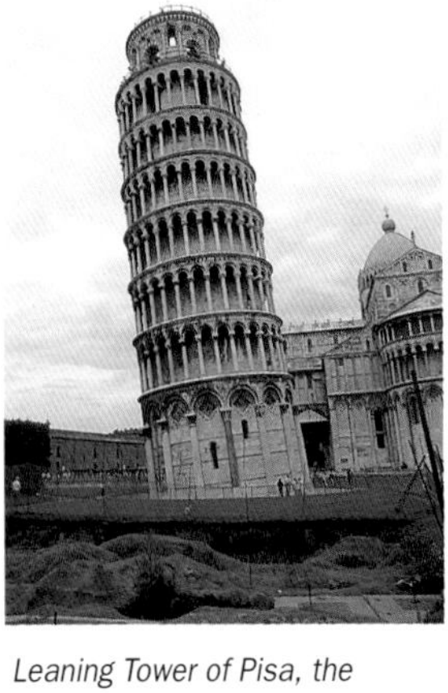

Leaning Tower of Pisa, the world's most famous campanile—about 55 m high with a 5 m lean.

merge with the Alps, which are generally higher than the Appenines and which arch right across the north of Italy, forming natural boundaries with the countries of Switzerland, Austria, and France. In the southern extremities of the Alps are a series of large, spectacular lakes, which include the much visited Lago Maggiore, Lago di Como, and Lago di Garda. These lakes and the rivers that feed into them are the source of the hydroelectricity which supplies about half the electricity needs of industrialized northern Italy.

In the northeast of the country, enclosed by the Alps to the north and the west and the Appenines to the south, and stretching in the east as far as the Adriatic coast, is the country's largest lowland region, known as the Plain of Lombardy. Drained by the River Po, which flows from west to east across the widest part of the country, this area is the most fertile, as well as the most heavily industrialized and populous part of Italy. About two-fifths of Italy's crops are grown here. Agriculture is also extensive on the coastal plains on each side of the Appenines. Farms are mainly small. Crops include potatoes, wheat, maize, olives, and other vegetables as well as a wide range of citrus and stone fruits. Italy produces more wine than any other country and there are extensive vineyards, most particularly in the Chianti region in Tuscany. Sheep, pigs, and cattle are the principal livestock.

Industry, commerce, and culture

Apart from marble in the south, for which it is famous, and some oil deposits in Sicily, Italy is not well endowed with mineral resources and imports most of the energy needed by its highly developed industrial sector. This is concentrated overwhelmingly in the north of the country—although Naples, Bari, and Taranto in the south and Rome in the center have a certain amount of heavy industry—and is based around such cities as Milan, Turin, and Genoa. The building of cars, aircraft, and other transport equipment are major industries, as are tool, textile, clothing, and chemical manufacture.

Italy's manufacturing sector, which was heavily subsidized by the state, developed largely in the half-century since the Second World War, before which the economy was based predominantly on agriculture. It now employs about a fifth of the country's workforce. Tourism is an important source of income, with about 30 million people visiting Italy every year.

There is a great divide in Italy between the high living standards of the industrialized, affluent north and the much lower living standards of the largely undeveloped south, especially in Calabria in the far south. In the south unemployment is chronically high, investment is hard to attract, poverty is widespread, and crime for many people offers the best means of survival.

Roman ruins, The Forum, Rome.

Ponte Vecchio on the Arno River, Florence.

I

J

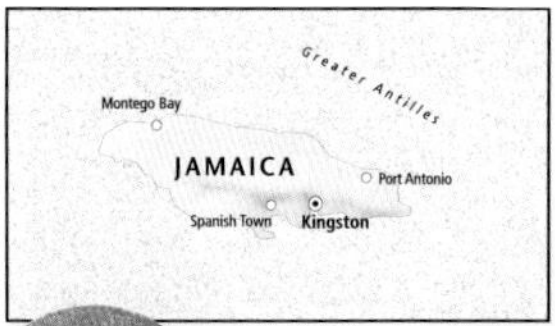

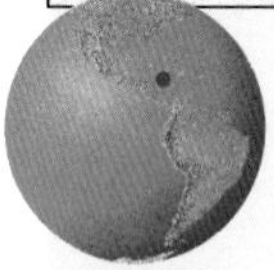

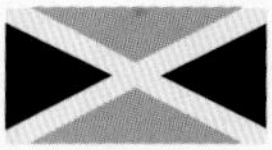

JAMAICA

OFFICIAL NAME Jamaica
FORM OF GOVERNMENT Constitutional monarchy with two legislative bodies (Senate and House of Representatives)
CAPITAL Kingston
AREA 10,990 sq km (4,243 sq miles)
TIME ZONE GMT – 5 hours
POPULATION 2,652,443
PROJECTED POPULATION 2005 2,763,836
POPULATION DENSITY 241.4 per sq km (625.2 per sq mile)
LIFE EXPECTANCY 75.6
INFANT MORTALITY (PER 1,000) 13.9
OFFICIAL LANGUAGE English
OTHER LANGUAGE Creole
LITERACY RATE 84.4%
RELIGIONS Protestant (mainly Anglican, Presbyterian–Congregational, Baptist, Methodist) 70%, Roman Catholic 7–8%, other including Rastafari 22–23%
ETHNIC GROUPS African 76.5%, mixed African–European 15%, East Indian and mixed African–East Indian 3%, European 3%, Chinese and mixed African–Chinese 1%, other 1.5%
CURRENCY Jamaican dollar
ECONOMY Services 63%, agriculture 25%, industry 12%
GNP PER CAPITA US$1,510
CLIMATE Tropical; cooler inland
HIGHEST POINT Blue Mountain Peak 2,256 m (7,402 ft)
MAP REFERENCE Page 839

J

Jamaica

The Caribbean island of Jamaica lies 144 km (98 miles) south of Cuba and southwest of Haiti. Mountainous in the interior, it is the most populous of the English-speaking Caribbean islands. Arawak Indians were its first inhabitants. Columbus visited in 1494 and a slave-based sugar producing plantation society was established by the British after they seized the island in 1655. It won independence from Britain in 1962. An important contributor to world music, Jamaica is the home of reggae, a style originating in Kingston's tough urban environment. Also from Jamaica come the Rastafarians, followers of the one-time Emperor of Ethiopia. In September 1988 Jamaica was devastated by the fiercest hurricane to strike the island this century, causing widespread loss of life and leaving 20 percent of the people homeless.

In the northwest of the island is a limestone area of steep ridges and isolated basins, pitted with sink-holes. This "cockpit country" once gave refuge to escaped slaves. In the east the land rises to become the densely forested Blue Mountains. In the west the River Black is navigable upstream for about 30 km (19 miles). Sugar plantations dominate the densely populated and extensively cultivated lowland coastal fringe. Seasonal rains fall most heavily on the northeastern mountain slopes—still covered in the rainforest once found all over the island. In the rainshadow of the mountains, the southern lowlands support only savanna scrub.

Bauxite has been mined since 1952. Most of it is exported as ore, and about one-fifth as alumina, making Jamaica the world's third-largest producer. This accounts for more than 50 percent of exports. Tourism and bauxite production are Jamaica's two main industries, and comprise almost two-thirds of foreign earnings. Other export industries include printing, textiles and food processing, along with rum distilling and sugar production. In agriculture, sugarcane and bananas are the main cash crops, along with coffee, cocoa, and fruit. In recent years the government has removed most price controls and privatized state enterprises. Unemployment remains high. Jamaica's medium-term prospects depend largely on its ability to attract foreign capital and limit speculation against the Jamaican dollar.

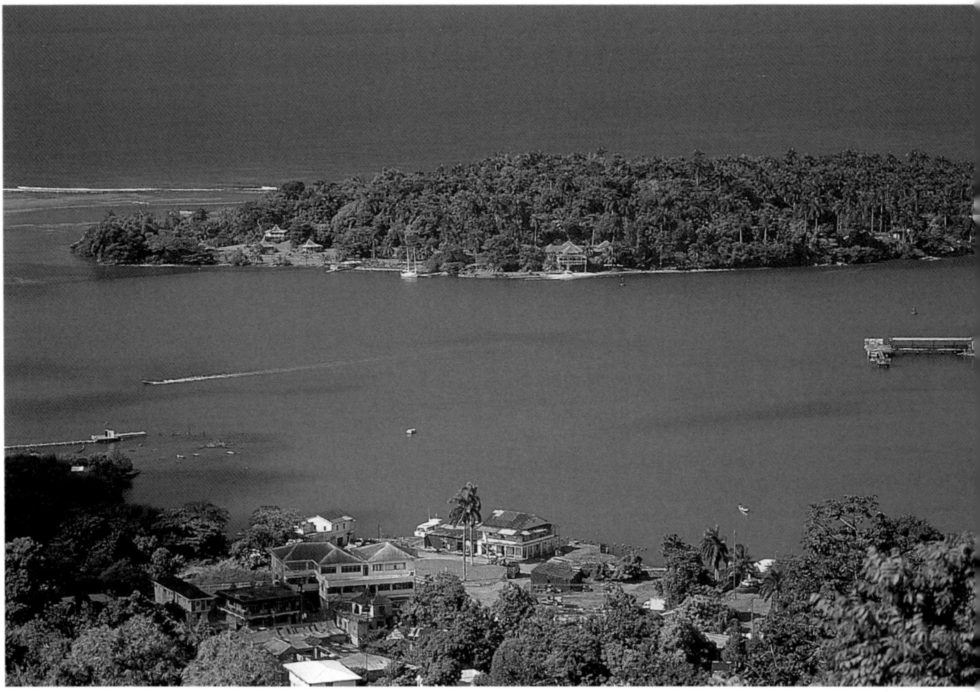

Port Antonio on the northeast coast of Jamaica.

Jan Mayen

The mountainous island of Jan Mayen lies in the Arctic Ocean about 900 km (560 miles) west of Norway. It is volcanic, with the mighty active Beerenberg volcano rising 2,400 m (7,874 ft) straight out of the surf. From its ice-cap some 15 glaciers descend into the sea. Once an important base for Arctic whaling, Jan Mayen's only resources today are rich fishing grounds. These were the subject of a long dispute with Greenland over fishing rights, and possible oil and gas deposits. Mediated by the International Court of Justice, the two parties reached a compromise on this issue in 1993. The island's birdlife is spectacular and includes millions of fulmar, petrel, kittiwake, little auk, guillemot, and puffin.

Jan Mayen

Official name Jan Mayen
Form of government Territory of Norway
Capital None
Area 373 sq km (144 sq miles)
Time zone GMT – 1 hour
Population No permanent population
Economy Radio and meteorological stations
Climate Polar: cold, windy, and foggy
Map reference Page 821

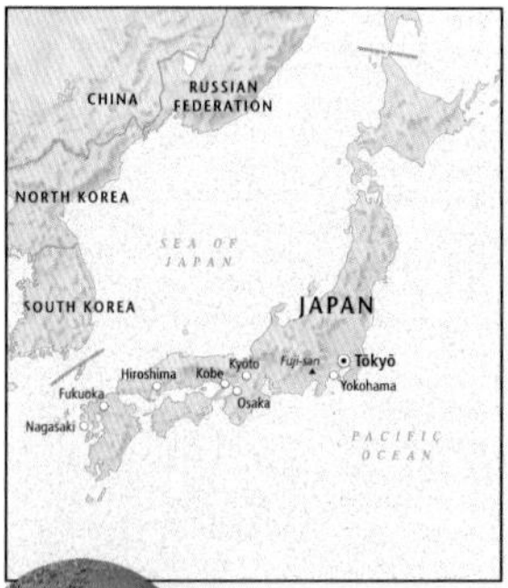

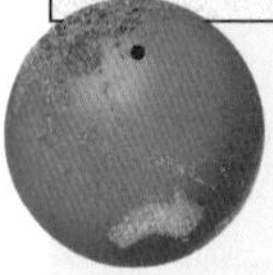

J

JAPAN

OFFICIAL NAME Japan
FORM OF GOVERNMENT Constitutional monarchy with two legislative bodies (House of Councillors and House of Representatives)
CAPITAL Tokyo
AREA 377,835 sq km (145,882 sq miles)
TIME ZONE GMT + 9 hours
POPULATION 126,182,077
PROJECTED POPULATION 2005 127,337,581
POPULATION DENSITY 334 per sq km (865 per sq mile)
LIFE EXPECTANCY 80.1
INFANT MORTALITY (PER 1,000) 4.1
OFFICIAL LANGUAGE Japanese
LITERACY RATE 99%
RELIGIONS Shinto and Buddhist 84%, other (including Christian 0.7%) 16%
ETHNIC GROUPS Japanese 99.4%, other (mostly Korean) 0.6%
CURRENCY Yen
ECONOMY Services 69%, industry 24%, agriculture 7%
GNP PER CAPITA US$39,640
CLIMATE Ranges from cold temperate in north to subtropical in south; wet season June to July
HIGHEST POINT Fuji-san (Mt Fuji) 3,776 m (12,388 ft)
MAP REFERENCE Pages 744–45

Japan

Mainly mountainous, with intensively cultivated coastal plains, the archipelago of Japan lies off the east Asian coast close to Korea and China. By the early 1990s it had become an industrial and trading colossus second only to the USA. But cracks in the country's apparently impregnable economic facade began to appear in 1998 as the yen slid steadily against the dollar. The nation's vast scientific and technological resources, its highly educated personnel, and its substantial trade surpluses, mean that it is better placed than most countries to cope with this and other problems.

History

First populated by migrants from mainland Asia, by the fifth century AD Japan was controlled by a number of clans. During the next 300 years several features of Chinese civilization were introduced, including Buddhism, Chinese script, and methods of administration, while cities modeled on those of the Tang Dynasty were built at Nara (AD 710) and Kyoto (AD 794). Centralized government, however, failed to eventuate and the clan basis of society prevailed. From the twelfth century until the rise of the Tokugawas power was held by rival groups of feudal lords, or shoguns, the emperor becoming a largely

A traditional house in rural Japan.

Man selling sweet potatoes, Todaiji Temple, Japan.

Woman in Japanese traditional dress.

symbolic figure. Lasting from 1192 to 1867, the shogun era fostered an ethical code known as bushido (the path of the warrior, or samurai) that stressed loyalty, frugality, and courage.

Until 1945 Japan remained unconquered. Two Mongol fleets sent to invade the country were destroyed by typhoons in 1274 and 1281, founding the legend of a kamikaze or "divine wind" sent to protect "the land of the Gods." From 1603 a form of semi-centralized feudal rule was imposed by the ruling shogunate, the Tokugawas. Under this family, some 250 daimyo (or "great names") ran their own estates watched by state inspectors and a network of spies. Western influence appeared briefly in 1542, when missionaries arrived from Macao bringing clocks, carpets, guns, and Christianity. The reaction of the Tokugawas was to close the door: from 1639 Japan's citizens were not allowed to travel abroad, and trading contacts were limited to a single Dutch settlement at Nagasaki.

This ended in 1853 when Commodore Perry of the US Navy brought a squadron of warships into Yokohama Harbor, demanding that the country's ports be opened to Western trade. The now weak Tokugawa shogunate collapsed, imperial rule was resumed under the Meiji Restoration, and within 50 years Japan had become westernized and a rising industrial force. Victories in wars with China (1894–95) and Russia (1904–05) led to the seizure of Taiwan and Korea. Expanding imperial ambitions led later to the invasion of China, and eventually, in 1941, to an attack on Hawaii and Japan's

Colorful alleyway full of shops.

Japan Timeline

4500 BC Islands of Japan inhabited by peoples from Asia. They are later known as Jomon after their pottery

c.1500 BC Rice is introduced from China and cultivated in the islands for the first time

660 BC Legendary leader Jimmu Tenno is Japan's first emperor and founds imperial dynasty which still holds office today

400 BC Wet rice-farming introduced from Korean Peninsula; intensive agriculture enables larger population to survive

AD 200 In the Yayoi period (until c.AD 700) rice is grown in irrigated fields and people live in villages protected by moats and wooden palisades

300 Large-scale immigration from the Asian continent until around 750 leads to a big increase in the population

550 Buddhism introduced from China

794 Japanese capital moves from Nara, the eastern end of the Tang Silk Road trade route, to Heian (later called Kyoto) until 1185

1281 Mongol conqueror Kublai Khan's invasion plans fail when his fleet is destroyed by a typhoon

1543 Portuguese sailors visit islands of southern Kyushu, making Europe aware of the wealth of the Japanese islands

1600 Honshu, Shikoku, and Kyushu united under the Tokugawa shogunate which rules for more than 250 years

1707 Mt Fuji, Japan's biggest volcano, erupts

1730 An earthquake on the island of Hokkaido causes the deaths of 137 000 people

1875 Population reaches more than 35 million; Tokyo 1 million by end of the century

1883 Tsunami kills 30,000 people. Three years later a tsunami occurs off Honshu and kills 28,000 people

1923 The Great Kanto earthquake, fires, and tsunamis destroy much of Tokyo-Yokohama and kill more than 140,000 people

1945 USA drops atomic bombs, destroying Hiroshima and Nagasaki. Second World War ends

1964 Shinkansen high-speed "bullet train" links Tokyo and Kyoto traveling at speeds of 210 km (130 miles) an hour

1994 Population of Tokyo-Yokohama exceeds 8 million

1995 Earthquake destroys much of Kobe city and kills 6,000 people

Red wooden arch in harbor, Japan.

entry into the Second World War. Allied victory in 1945 was followed by the introduction of a liberal, US-imposed democratic constitution which has since guided the nation's development.

Physical features and land use

Four large islands, so closely grouped that bridges and a tunnel now connect them, make up 98 percent of Japan's territory. They occupy a highly unstable zone on the earth's crust, and earthquakes and volcanic eruptions are frequent: 140,000 died in the 1923 earthquake which hit Yokohama and part of Tokyo; 6,000 died in the Kobe earthquake of January 1995. Folding and faulting has produced a mosaic of landforms throughout Japan, mountains and hills alternating with small basins and coastal plains. Inland there are several calderas and volcanic cones, the most famous being Fuji-san (3,776 m; 12,388 ft), the highest mountain in Japan, which last erupted in 1707.

Hokkaido, the northernmost of the main islands, is the most rural and traditional. Japan's biggest and most productive farming region, it has a climate similar to the US midwest—which may be why American advisors established wheat farming there in the 1860s. Hokkaido now produces more than half of Japan's cereal needs. Southwest of Hokkaido lies the island of Honshu, where the Japanese Alps provide spectacular scenery. The Kanto Plain where Tokyo stands is the largest of various small alluvial plains, their soils enriched by centuries of careful cultivation. Today the conurbation this plain supports is Japan's most heavily industrialized and densely populated region. From southwestern Honshu across the two southern islands of Shikoku and Kyushu a complex of mountain peaks and undulating uplands stretches down to the Ryukyu Islands (Nansei-Shotō), which includes Okinawa, before extending south toward Taiwan.

Small hut in front of Mt Fuji, Japan.

Economy

Japan's economy is notable for its government–industry cooperation, a motivated population with a strong work ethic, high educational levels and a mastery of high technology. These factors combined with a small defense allocation (1 percent of gross domestic product) have made it the second most powerful economy in the industrialized world. Japan is one of the world's largest and most advanced producers of steel and non-ferrous metallurgy, heavy electrical equipment, construction and

The Ginza district in Tokyo.

Taisetu Mountains, Japan.

J

Temple, Osaka.

mining equipment, motor vehicles and parts, communications and electronic equipment, machine tools, automated production systems, railroad rolling stock, ships, chemicals, textiles, and processed foods. Industry depends heavily on imported raw materials and fuel. The small agricultural sector is highly protected and subsidized; its crop yields are among the world's highest. Self-sufficient in rice, Japan imports about 50 percent of its other grain needs. After decades of spectacular growth, the late 1990s saw a marked contraction. The need for reconstruction remains evident, amid mounting fears of a banking crisis due to bad debts.

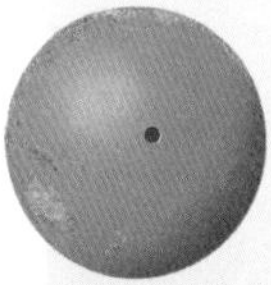

JARVIS ISLAND

OFFICIAL NAME Jarvis Island
FORM OF GOVERNMENT Unincorporated territory of the USA
CAPITAL None; administered from Washington DC
AREA 4.5 sq km (1.7 sq miles)
TIME ZONE GMT – 10 hours
POPULATION No permanent population
CLIMATE Hot, dry, and windy
MAP REFERENCE Page 725

Jarvis Island

An uninhabited island near the equator in the South Pacific, Jarvis Island lies about midway between Hawaii and the Cook Islands. A sandy coral islet with a fringing reef, it has a tropical climate with little rain and no fresh water. Guano deposits were worked until late in the nineteenth century, and Millersville settlement on the west of the island was used as a weather station from 1935 until the Second World War. Ground cover consists of sparse bunch grass, prostrate vines, and low-growing shrubs. The island is mainly a nesting place for seabirds and marine wildlife. Entry is by special-use permit only.

Jersey

Jersey, the largest and most populous of the Channel Islands, lies in the English Channel, 20 km (12 miles) from the west coast of the Cherbourg Peninsula in northern France. Said to be the sunniest part of the British Isles, it is noted for its superb beaches. These account for the booming tourist industry, which, along with financial services, has in recent years supplanted agriculture as the mainstay of the economy.

Jersey is a dependency of the British crown, but it has its own legislature and a tax regime that is entirely independent and whose low rates attract many foreign businesses. Jersey cattle are among the most important exports and flower cultivation is also a significant income earner.

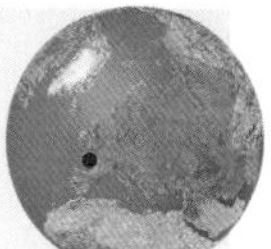

JERSEY

OFFICIAL NAME Bailiwick of Jersey
FORM OF GOVERNMENT British crown dependency
CAPITAL St Helier
AREA 117 sq km (45 sq miles)
TIME ZONE GMT
POPULATION 89,721
LIFE EXPECTANCY 78.8
INFANT MORTALITY (PER 1,000) 2.8
CURRENCY Jersey pound
ECONOMY Financial services, agriculture, tourism
CLIMATE Temperate; mild winters and cool summers
MAP REFERENCE Page 774

The Channel Islands

The Channel Islands lie in the English Channel between 15 and 50 km (10 and 30 miles) off the coast of Normandy in northern France. As well as the two largest islands of Jersey and Guernsey, there are the smaller islands of Sark and Alderney and a number of even smaller islands. In all, the Channel Islands cover an area of only 200 sq km (80 sq miles).

Since the Norman invasion of England in 1066, these islands have been dependencies of the British crown and are the only part of the Duchy of Normandy to have been retained by Britain after 1204. During the Second World War they were the only region of Britain to be occupied by German troops.

Both Jersey and Guernsey have separate legislatures and their own taxation systems, independent of Britain. While English is the most widely spoken language, French is also common and it is the official language of the Jersey legislature. The majority of the place names on Jersey are French.

Especially during the summer, both English and French tourists flock to these islands, and tourism, along with financial services, is now the mainstay of the islands' economies. Tourism on Jersey employs a large number of Portuguese nationals. The residents of the Channel Islands enjoy a high standard of living, maintained in part by strictly enforced residential controls.

Mont Orgueil Castle, Gorey Harbor, Jersey.

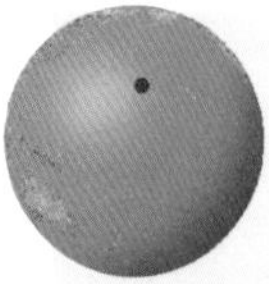

JOHNSTON ATOLL

OFFICIAL NAME Johnston Atoll
FORM OF GOVERNMENT Unincorporated territory of the USA
CAPITAL None; administered from Washington DC
AREA 2.8 sq km (1.1 sq miles)
TIME ZONE GMT – 10 hours
POPULATION No permanent population
ECONOMY US military base
CLIMATE Hot, dry, and windy
MAP REFERENCE Page 725

Johnston Atoll

This remote coral atoll consisting of two islets, Johnston Island and Sand Island, lies in the North Pacific about one-third of the way between Hawaii and the Marshall Islands. The atoll is 5 m (16 ft) above sea level at its highest point and has a dry tropical climate, northeast trade winds ensuring little seasonal temperature variation. Mined during the nineteenth century for its extensive guano deposits, the atoll is now home to approximately 1,200 US military personnel. It was formerly used as a nuclear weapons testing site. The territory is administered by the US Defense Nuclear Agency and managed cooperatively by the DNA and the Fish and Wildlife Service of the US Department of the Interior as part of the National Wildlife Refuge system.

JORDAN

OFFICIAL NAME Hashemite Kingdom of Jordan
FORM OF GOVERNMENT Constitutional monarchy with two legislative bodies (House of Notables and House of Representatives)
CAPITAL 'Ammān
AREA 89,213 sq km (34,445 sq miles)
TIME ZONE GMT + 2 hours
POPULATION 4,561,147
PROJECTED POPULATION 2005 5,403,895
POPULATION DENSITY 51.1 per sq km (132.3 per sq mile)
LIFE EXPECTANCY 73.1
INFANT MORTALITY (PER 1,000) 32.7

Jordan

The small Arab kingdom of Jordan, rich in historic associations and sites, lies between Saudi Arabia, Israel, and Syria, and also shares a border with Iraq. It has to deal with Israel on the one hand and with Israel's various Arab antagonists on the other, while accommodating huge numbers of refugees. After the Ottoman Turks were driven out during the First World War the British installed the Hashemite monarchy in 1921. In 1946 Jordan became independent, and King Hussein reigned from 1952 until his death in 1999.

Governing Jordan has not been easy, many problems being connected with the West Bank. In 1967 this area, containing both Jerusalem and much of Jordan's best land, was lost to Israel. With emigré Palestinians using Jordan as a base for guerrilla activities (they were expelled in 1970–71), through two Gulf Wars in which Jordan was sympathetic to its oil supplier Iraq, and with the recent expansion of Israeli settlements in the area, the West Bank became impossible to regain or to administer. In 1988 Jordan ceded it to the PLO.

The Red Sea–Jordan section of the Rift Valley forms the country's western border. It contains the Jordan River valley, the Dead Sea (the lowest point on the earth's surface, at 400 m/1,312 ft below sea level), the Sea of Galilee, and Wadī al Arabah. Parts of the Jordan Valley and the highlands east of the Rift Valley are irrigated, making arable farming possible. Crops include vegetables, olives, and fruit. Eighty percent of Jordan's land area is desert. In the north it merges with the Syrian Desert and in the south with the deserts of Saudi Arabia. Less than 0.5 percent of the country is forested, mainly in the east. Vegetation ranges from Mediterranean plants in the mountains to grass, sagebrush and shrubs in the steppe country.

Jordan has poor water, oil, and coal supplies. In the late 1970s and early 1980s it received Arab aid and the economy grew at more than 10 percent a year. In the late 1980s reductions in aid and in worker remittances slowed and imports outstripped exports. In 1991 the Second Gulf War overwhelmed the country. Worker remittances stopped, trade contracted, and further refugees arrived, straining resources. Recovery has been uneven. Poverty, debt, and unemployment are continuing problems.

Official language Arabic
Other language English
Literacy rate 85.5%
Religions Sunni Muslim 92%, Christian 8%
Ethnic groups Arab 98%, Circassian 1%, Armenian 1%
Currency Jordanian dinar
Economy Services 64%, industry 26%, agriculture 10%
GNP per capita US$1,510
Climate Mainly arid, but northwest temperate with cool, wet winters and hot, dry summers
Highest point Jabal Ramm 1,754 m (5,755 ft)
Map reference Page 761

J

One of the many rock-cut facades in the ancient city of Petra in Jordan.

KAZAKHSTAN

OFFICIAL NAME Republic of Kazakhstan
FORM OF GOVERNMENT Republic with two legislative bodies (Senate and Majilis)
CAPITAL Aqmola (Astana)
AREA 2,717,300 sq km (1,049,150 sq miles)
TIME ZONE GMT + 6 hours
POPULATION 16,824,825
PROJECTED POPULATION 2005 16,903,895
POPULATION DENSITY 6.2 per sq km (16 per sq mile)
LIFE EXPECTANCY 63.4
INFANT MORTALITY (PER 1,000) 58.8
OFFICIAL LANGUAGE Kazakh
OTHER LANGUAGE Russian
LITERACY RATE 97.5%
RELIGIONS Muslim 47%, Russian Orthodox 44%, Protestant 2%, other 7%
ETHNIC GROUPS Kazak 42%, Russian 37%, Ukrainian 5.3%, German 4.7%, Uzbek 2%, Tatar 2%, other 7%
CURRENCY Tenge
ECONOMY Services 43%, industry 31%, agriculture 26%
GNP PER CAPITA US$1,330
CLIMATE Mainly arid; cold winters and hot summers; cooler in north
HIGHEST POINT Khan Tängiri Shyngy 6,995 m (22,949 ft)
MAP REFERENCE Pages 758–59

K

Kazakhstan

With a land area nearly as large as India, Kazakhstan is an important member of the newly formed Commonwealth of Independent States (CIS). In earlier times, when it was a Soviet Republic, authorities used the region for testing nuclear weapons and for exiling ethnic minorities.

In the 1950s and 1960s when the Soviet "virgin lands" project was underway, vast tracts of pasture were plowed up and sown with wheat or given over to livestock production, and waters from rivers running into the Aral Sea were used in irrigation schemes. As a result, the sea shrank by 70 percent.

During the years of Soviet domination, high levels of immigration from Russia resulted in the Kazakhs being outnumbered. Outmigration of Russians since 1991 and the return of many expatriates has resulted in a Kazak majority once more, but ethnic tensions remain high.

Much of the country is tablelands—the eroded tableland of the east featuring shallow uplands, depressions, and lakes—and there are also several mountain ranges in the east including the Altai Range (Mongol Altayn Nuruu). Running from north to south, steppe country gives way to desert or semidesert, though irrigation schemes have made large areas productive between the Aral Sea and Lake Balkhash (Balqash Köli).

Three colorful folk dancers, Almaty, Kazakhstan.

With a climate marked by intense winter cold and extreme summer heat, rainfall is generally low. The lakes in the center of the country are saline, as are the marshes in the west, and in the central region there are few permanent rivers. The grassy steppes of the north are the most naturally fertile part of the country. Though the region has traditionally been associated with livestock rearing (Kazakhstan still supports up to 200,000 nomadic shepherds and herdsmen) the agricultural policies of the Soviet period converted much pasture to grain cultivation. By 1989 the country accounted for 20 percent of the entire cultivated area of the Soviet Union and 12 percent of its grain output.

Other crops grown include fruits, potatoes, vegetables, sugar beet, and cotton. High quality wool is produced, and Kazakhstan supplies meat to surrounding countries. Industry is based mainly on processing raw materials: fuel, metals, textiles, chemicals, and food. Products include rolled metals, agricultural machinery, plastics, clothing, footwear, paper, and cement. Well endowed with oil and gas reserves, the country also has deposits of coal, iron ore, bauxite, copper, nickel, tungsten, zinc, and silver. In addition, it holds 70 percent of CIS gold reserves. The government has been pursuing a moderate program of reform and privatization—investment incentives have been established, state controls have been lifted, and assets privatized. But government control of key industries remains extensive. Lack of pipeline transportation for oil export hinders a likely source of economic growth.

Environmental problems are extensive and severe. Radioactive or toxic chemical sites associated with weapons development are widespread. The drying up of the Aral Sea has left a crust of chemical pesticides which is periodically blown about in noxious dust storms.

Turkestan markets—fruit sellers with piles of melons behind them.

Dome of the Khodja Ahmed Yasavi Mausoleum in Turkestan, Kazakhstan.

Fortress-like entrance to Khodja Ahmed Yasavi mausoleum in the town of Turkestan.

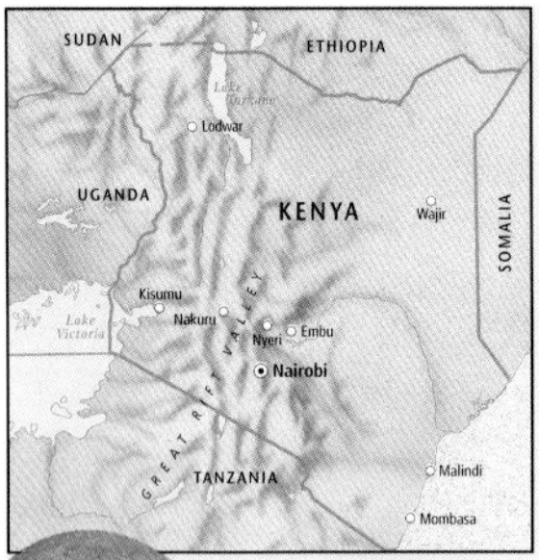

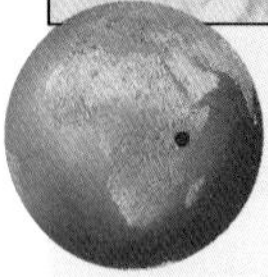

KENYA

OFFICIAL NAME Republic of Kenya
FORM OF GOVERNMENT Republic with single legislative body (National Assembly)
CAPITAL Nairobi
AREA 582,650 sq km (224,961 sq miles)
TIME ZONE GMT + 3 hours
POPULATION 28,808,658
PROJECTED POPULATION 2005 31,156,521
POPULATION DENSITY 49.4 per sq km (128 per sq mile)
LIFE EXPECTANCY 47
INFANT MORTALITY (PER 1,000) 59.1
OFFICIAL LANGUAGES English, Swahili
OTHER LANGUAGES Indigenous languages
LITERACY RATE 77%
RELIGIONS Protestant 38%, Roman Catholic 28%, indigenous beliefs 26%, other 8%
ETHNIC GROUPS Kikuyu 22%, Luhya 14%, Luo 13%, Kalenjin 12%, Kamba 11%, Kisii 6%, Meru 6%, other 16% (including Asian, European, Arab 1%)
CURRENCY Kenya shilling
ECONOMY Agriculture 80%, services 12%, industry 8%
GNP PER CAPITA US$280
CLIMATE Coastal regions tropical, with wet seasons April to May and October to November; inland plateau cooler and drier
HIGHEST POINT Mt Kenya 5,199 m (17,057 ft)
MAP REFERENCE Pages 808-9

Kenya

Kenya, in east Africa, is where humankind may have originated: remains of humans and pre-humans found in the Olduvai Gorge go back several million years. By the tenth century AD Arabs had settled along the coast, and in the nineteenth century both Britain and Germany became interested in the region. In 1920 Kenya became a British colony, the pleasant climate in the highlands attracting English immigrants who displaced Kikuyu farmers and took their land.

After the Second World War, widespread resentment at this expropriation erupted in the violent Mau Mau rebellion which lasted eight years. Independence came in 1963. Since then, control of the state and its resources has been contested by political parties allied with particular tribes, the domination of the Kikuyu (in recent years under President Daniel Arap Moi) yielding to a trial of multi-party democracy in 1991.

The Kenya Highlands consist of a fertile plateau formed by volcanoes and lava flows. The highlands are divided in two by the Rift Valley, the Eastern Highlands falling away toward the densely populated plain near Lake Victoria, the Western Highlands descending to the valleys of the Tana and Galana Rivers as they cross the Nyika Plain to the north of Mombasa. The populous and fertile coastal belt is fringed by mangrove swamps, coral reefs, and groups of small islands. In the sparsely populated north toward Lake Turkana desert conditions prevail. Kenya's wildlife, consisting of the full range of African fauna, can be seen in the country's

Zebras in the Masai Mara National Reserve.

several large national parks, and has made it a leading destination for tourists for many years.

By African standards, Kenya has a stable and productive economy. It has a broad and highly successful agricultural base, with cash crops such as coffee and tea. It also has east Africa's largest and most diversified manufacturing sector, producing small-scale consumer goods such as plastics, furniture, batteries, textiles, and soap. But the country also has one of the world's highest rates of population growth: between 1988 and 2000 it is expected to experience an 82 percent increase in population, a figure exceeded only by Haiti.

This continuous increase in the number of its citizens is accompanied by deforestation, lack of drinking water, and infrastructural breakdown. Floods have destroyed roads, bridges, and telecommunications. Crime, including the murder of visitors and ethnic massacres, has caused a steep decline in tourist numbers.

A Masai woman in traditional dress.

Social weaver birds' nests hanging from an acacia tree, Kenya.

Kingman Reef

A barren triangular-shaped reef in the North Pacific, Kingman Reef is halfway between Hawaii and American Samoa. No more than 1 m (3 ft) above sea level, and awash most of the time, the reef is a maritime hazard. Although no economic activity takes place and the reef is uninhabited, the deep interior lagoon was used as a halfway station between Hawaii and American Samoa when Pan American Airways used flying boats in the Pacific in 1937 and 1938. While there is no land flora, the reef is rich in marine life. It is administered by the US Navy.

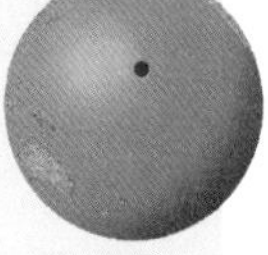

Kingman Reef

Official name Kingman Reef
Form of government Unincorporated territory of the USA
Capital None; administered from Washington DC
Area 1 sq km (0.4 sq miles)
Time zone GMT – 10 hours
Population No permanent population
Climate Tropical, moderated by sea breezes
Map reference Page 725

K

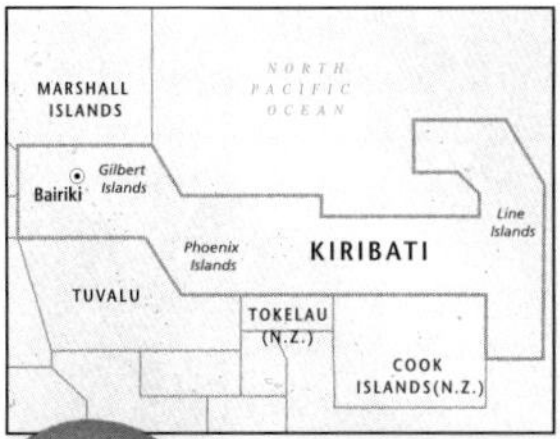

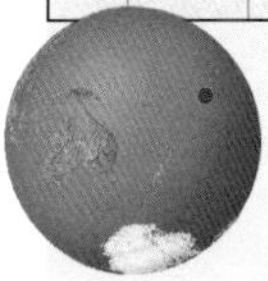

Kiribati

The Republic of Kiribati (pronounced Kiribass) consists of 33 scattered coral atolls in three separate groups in the mid-Pacific, plus the volcanic island, Banaba. The three groups are the 17 former Gilbert Islands in the west, the 8 Phoenix Islands, and the 8 Line Islands.

Banaba Island has provided the region with the most income. It is one of three great phosphate rock islands in the Pacific Ocean, the others being Nauru and Makatea. The people of Kiribati are Micronesian, though the Banabans pride themselves on being ethnically distinct.

Kiritimati Island (also known as Christmas Island), one of the Line Islands, was the site of the first British nuclear tests in the Pacific in 1957, but is now a favored location for tourist development. For Kiribati as a whole, it is difficult to see what else besides tourism can be developed as a national source of income—it is classified by the United Nations as a Least Developed Country. The phosphate deposits on Banaba had been exhausted by the time of independence in 1979. Copra (50 percent), seaweed (16 percent) and fish (15 percent) are now the main exports. A basic subsistence economy still flourishes, with small farms and gardens producing taro, breadfruit, and sweet potatoes. Kiribati imports little food but it depends heavily on foreign aid, largely from the UK and Japan. Aid has been 25 to 50 percent of gross domestic product in recent years.

Though Kiribati is a democracy, the political parties continue to be strongly influenced by a traditional chief

Huts on a coconut plantation.

Kiribati

Official name Republic of Kiribati
Form of government Republic with single legislative body (National Assembly)
Capital Bairiki
Area 717 sq km (277 sq miles)
Time zone GMT + 12/11 hours
Population 85,501
Projected population 2005 91,614
Population density 119.2 per sq km (308.67 per sq mile)
Life expectancy 62.9
Infant mortality (per 1,000) 48.2
Official language English
Other language Gilbertese
Literacy rate 90%
Religions Roman Catholic 52.5%, Protestant (Congregational) 41%, other (including Seventh-Day Adventist, Baha'i, Church of God, Mormon) 6.5%
Ethnic groups Predominantly Micronesian with small Polynesian and non-Pacific minorities
Currency Australian dollar
Economy Agriculture, copra production, fishing
GNP per capita US$920
Climate Tropical, moderated by trade winds
Highest point Unnamed location on Banaba Island 81 m (266 ft)
Map reference Page 725

system and have little formal organization. A major difficulty for Kiribati today is the problem of environmental degradation from the overpopulation of Tarawa, the island capital to which many Kiribati have migrated because of the lack of job opportunities elsewhere.

Kuwait

The Arab emirate of Kuwait lies in the northwest corner of the Persian Gulf, dwarfed by its neighbors Iraq, Iran, and Saudi Arabia. Beneath its surface lie huge oil reserves. It was settled by wandering Arab peoples in the eighteenth century. When Germany and Turkey were eyeing Kuwait possessively in the nineteenth century it formed a defensive alliance with Great Britain, becoming a British protectorate in 1914. In 1961, when it gained independence, Kuwait was claimed by Iraq.

A constitution was inaugurated by the al-Sabah ruling family in 1962. Whenever the National Assembly has been critical, however, it has been suspended. In 1990, despite Kuwait having lent millions of dollars to Iraq during the Iran–Iraq War of 1980–88, Iraq invaded. The Kuwaitis endured six months of brutality and the destruction of the city of Kuwait before a US-led international coalition expelled the Iraqis in 1991. During the occupation 400,000 residents fled the country—200,000 Palestinian migrant workers not being allowed to return as the Palestinian Liberation Organization had supported Iraq. The destruction of Kuwaiti oil wells by Iraq and deliberate oil-spills in the Gulf have caused environmental costs still difficult to assess.

Kuwait consists of an undulating sandy plateau which rises westward to an elevation of about 300 m (1,000 ft) on the Iraq–Saudi Arabia border. Along the border the plateau is cut to a depth of 45 m (150 ft) by the Wādī al Bāţin. In the northeast there are a few salt marshes and in the northwest is the Jal az-Zawr escarpment. Vegetation is limited to salt-tolerant plants along the coast, though in modern urban areas green spaces have been produced by irrigating imported soil. The territory of Kuwait also includes nine islands, of which Bubiyan is the largest.

Kuwait owns 10 percent of the world's proven crude oil reserves. Its petroleum sector currently accounts for

Kuwait

Official name State of Kuwait
Form of government Constitutional monarchy with single legislative body (National Assembly)
Capital Al Kuwayt (Kuwait)
Area 17,820 sq km (6,880 sq miles)
Time zone GMT + 3 hours
Population 1,991,115
Projected population 2005 2,436,509
Population density 111.7 per sq km (289.3 per sq mile)
Life expectancy 77.2
Infant mortality (per 1,000) 10.3
Official language Arabic
Other language English
Literacy rate 77.8%
Religions Muslim 85% (Sunni 45%, Shi'a 30%, other 10%), other (including Christian, Hindu, Parsi) 15%
Ethnic groups Kuwaiti 45%, other Arab 35%, South Asian 9%, Iranian 4%, other 7%
Currency Kuwaiti dinar
Economy Services 90%, industry 9%, agriculture 1%
GNP per capita US$17,390
Climate Arid, with cool winters and hot, humid summers
Highest point Unnamed location 306 m (1,004 ft)
Map reference Page 756

Kuwait City.

nearly half of gross domestic product, 90 percent of export revenues, and 70 percent of government income. With the exception of fish, Kuwait depends almost wholly on food imports, though hothouses and hydroponics produce some fruit and vegetables. About 75 percent of potable water must be distilled or imported. The shortage of water constrains industrial activities, which at present include petrochemical production, food processing, desalination, construction materials, and salt. The World Bank has urged the government to push ahead with privatization, including in the oil industry.

K

Kyrgyzstan

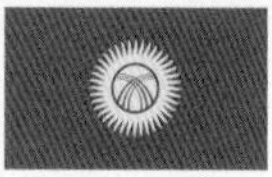

KYRGYZSTAN

OFFICIAL NAME Kyrgyz Republic

Kyrgyzstan is a small, mountainous, landlocked country in central Asia. China lies over the massive peaks of the Tian Shan Range along its southeast border, Kazakhstan is to the north, and Uzbekistan and Tajikistan are to the southwest. Not only is Kyrgyzstan the least urbanized of all the ex-Soviet republics, its population is growing faster in rural areas than in the towns. Native Kyrgyz are barely a majority and ethnic tension with Uzbeks and other nationals from nearby countries is a feature of everyday life. Fierce clashes between Kyrgyz and Uzbeks took place in the border city of Osh in 1990. Historically, the once nomadic Muslim Kyrgyz pastoralists are descended from refugees of Mongolian and Turkic origin who entered the region in the thirteenth century, escaping from Mongol invaders. For a while in the eighteenth century the region came under Manchu domination, then during the nineteenth century Russia began to colonize the country. Russian immigrants took the best land, settling in the low-lying, fertile areas. For years after the country's incorporation into the Soviet Union in the 1920s, resistance was carried out by local guerrilla groups called basmachi. Since independence in 1991, Kyrgyzstan has pursued liberal political and economic policies.

Geographically, Kyrgyzstan is dominated by the western end of the Tian Shan Range, which rises to Pik Pobedy (7,439 m; 24,406 ft) on the Chinese border. A large part of this mountain range is permanently snow-capped. The rest of the country is made up of a series of mountainous parallel ridges, separated by deep valleys and basins. The deep waters of Lake Ysyk-Köl are surrounded by snowy mountains in the northeast. The Fergana Valley, which is the main lowland region, lies in the southwest.

Much of the lower land is pasture for sheep, pigs, cattle, goats, horses, and yaks. Irrigated land is used to produce crops ranging from sugar beet and vegetables to rice, cotton, tobacco, grapes, and mulberry trees (for feeding silkworms). There are major salination problems caused mainly by the excessive irrigation of cotton.

Cotton, wool, and meat are the main agricultural products and exports: one of Kyrgyzstan's strengths is agricultural self-sufficiency. It has small quantities of coal, oil, gas, and the extensive snow-covered ranges ensure great hydropower potential. Energy policy aims at developing these resources in order to make the country less dependent on Russia. After the introduction of market reforms, and a program to control inflation, attention has turned to stimulating growth. This will not be easy: the economy is still dominated by the state and by the mentality of collective farming. Foreign aid plays a major role in the country's budget.

Form of government Republic with two legislative bodies (Assembly of People's Representatives and Legislative Assembly)
Capital Bishkek
Area 198,500 sq km (76,641 sq miles)
Time zone GMT + 6 hours
Population 4,546,055
Projected population 2005 4,829,120
Population density 22.9 per sq km (59.3 per sq mile)
Life expectancy 63.6
Infant mortality (per 1,000) 75.9
Official language Kyrghiz
Other language Russian
Literacy rate 97%
Religions Sunni Muslim 70%, Christian (predominantly Russian Orthodox) 30%
Ethnic groups Kyrghiz 52.5%, Russian 21.5%, Uzbek 13%, Ukrainian 2.5%, German 2.5%, other 8%
Currency Som
Economy Services 41%, agriculture 38%, industry 21%
GNP per capita US$700
Climate Subtropical in southwest, temperate in valleys, cold and snowy in mountains
Highest point Pik Pobedy 7,439 m (24,406 ft)
Map reference Page 759

Kyrgyz man cooking at a market in the town of Osh, Kyrgyzstan.

L

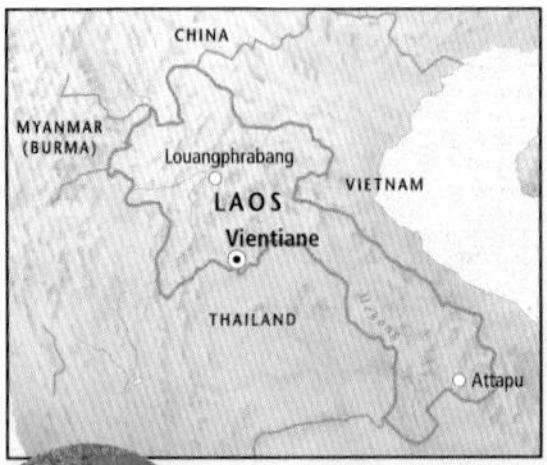

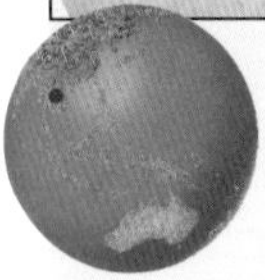

Laos

Laos is the only landlocked country in Southeast Asia. It also has one of the last official communist regimes, and is the poorest state in the region. Once the home of the fourteenth century kingdom of Lan Xang (the Million Elephant Kingdom), Laos became a French protectorate in 1893. Independent in 1953, it was fought over by royalists, communists, and conservatives from 1964 onward. It was used as a military supply route by the North Vietnamese during the Vietnam War and was heavily bombed with defoliants by the USA during the late 1960s. In 1975 it fell into the hands of the communist Pathet Lao who established a one-party state. Although the leadership has for economic reasons relaxed its doctrinal grip—the 1978 collectivization of agriculture was reversed in 1990—many hill-tribe people, such as the Hmong, remain alienated from the regime. Some continue guerrilla resistance, while others live in exile in Thailand. A new constitution in 1991 confirmed the monopoly of the communist Lao People's Revolutionary Party.

From the mountains in the northwest and the Plateau de Xiangkhoang, the country extends southeast, following the line of the Chaîne Anamitique Range. A number of rivers cross the country westward from this range to the Mekong River which forms the western border, among them the Banghiang, the Noi, and the Theun. The fertile Mekong floodplains in the west provide the only generally cultivable lowland. Despite deforestation and erosion, forest still covers 55 percent of the country.

The Laotian village of Luang Prabang from Chom Phet.

Laos

Official name Lao People's Democratic Republic
Form of government Communist state with single legislative body (National Assembly)
Capital Vientiane
Area 236,800 sq km (91,428 sq miles)
Time zone GMT + 7 hours
Population 5,407,453
Projected population 2005 6,337,670
Population density 22.8 per sq km (59 per sq mile)
Life expectancy 54.2
Infant mortality (per 1,000) 89.3
Official language Lao
Other languages French, English, indigenous languages
Literacy rate 55.8%
Religions Buddhist 60%, animist and other 40%
Ethnic groups Lao Loum (lowland) 68%, Lao Theung (upland) 22%, Lao Soung (highland) 9%, ethnic Vietnamese and Chinese 1%
Currency Kip
Economy Agriculture 80%, services and industry 20%
GNP per capita US$350
Climate Tropical monsoonal, with wet season May to October
Highest point Phou Bia 2,818 m (9,245 ft)
Map reference Pages 738–39

Most of the Laotian people are engaged in subsistence agriculture. In addition to the staple, rice, other crops grown include maize, vegetables, tobacco, coffee, and cotton. Opium poppies and cannabis are grown illegally: Laos is the world's third-largest opium producer.

The policy of privatization and decentralization that was adopted in 1986 has produced growth averaging an annual 7.5 percent since 1988. Textile and garment manufacture was established, as well as motorcycle assembly. The country's primitive infrastructure is a major handicap to growth. Laos has no railroads, its roads are inadequate, and its telecommunications severely limited. For the foreseeable future the economy will depend heavily on overseas aid.

Pha Bang Festival, Luang Prabang, Laos.

Latvia

Latvia lies between its sister Baltic republics of Estonia, to the north, and Lithuania, to the south, its coastline along the Baltic Sea indented by the Gulf of Riga. To the east and southeast respectively it shares borders with the Russian Federation and Belarus. Like Estonia and Lithuania, Latvia has for most of its history been controlled by foreign powers. For more than 1,000 years, its inhabitants, the Letts, have been ruled successively by Germans, Poles, Swedes, and finally Russians. In 1991 Latvia declared its independence from the Soviet Union.

The rooftops of a town in Latvia. More than two-thirds of the Latvian population are urbanized.

LATVIA

OFFICIAL NAME Republic of Latvia
FORM OF GOVERNMENT Republic with single legislative body (Parliament)
CAPITAL Riga
AREA 64,100 sq km (24,749 sq miles)
TIME ZONE GMT + 3 hours
POPULATION 2,353,874
PROJECTED POPULATION 2005 2,221,761
POPULATION DENSITY 36.7 per sq km (95.1 per sq mile)
LIFE EXPECTANCY 67.3
INFANT MORTALITY (PER 1,000) 17.2
OFFICIAL LANGUAGE Lettish
OTHER LANGUAGES Lithuanian, Russian
LITERACY RATE 99%

(continues)

LATVIA *(continued)*

RELIGIONS Mainly Lutheran with Russian Orthodox and Roman Catholic minorities
ETHNIC GROUPS Latvian 51.8%, Russian 33.8%, Belarusian 4.5%, Ukrainian 3.4%, Polish 2.3%, other 4.2%
CURRENCY Lats
ECONOMY Services 43%, industry 41%, agriculture 16%
GNP PER CAPITA US$2,270
CLIMATE Temperate. Cold, wet winters and mild summers
HIGHEST POINT Gaizinkalns 312 m (1,024 ft)
MAP REFERENCE Page 771

It is now a multi-party parliamentary democracy with an elected president as its head of state. Since independence, the Communist Party of Latvia has been banned.

The country is mostly flat with hillier land in the east. There are large areas of bogs and swamps and about 40 percent of the land is woodland or forest, in which oak and pine predominate. Small farms account for most agriculture, which is mainly dairy farming and cattle raising. Some grain and vegetable crops are also grown. Forestry and fishing, which were important in earlier times, have enjoyed a resurgence in recent years.

Latvia is the most heavily industrialized of the Baltic republics. It has few mineral resources and imports the raw materials needed for its industries —the manufacture of electrical goods, shipbuilding, and train and vehicle making. It relies on its former ruler for energy supplies and much of the Russian Federation's oil and gas exports pass through the Latvian port of Venspils. Air and water pollution from industrial wastes is a matter of concern.

Latvia's economy was severely affected in 1995 by bank failures and financial scandals and its dependence on Russia limits its development. Latvians have a reasonable standard of living, although discrepancies in wealth are marked.

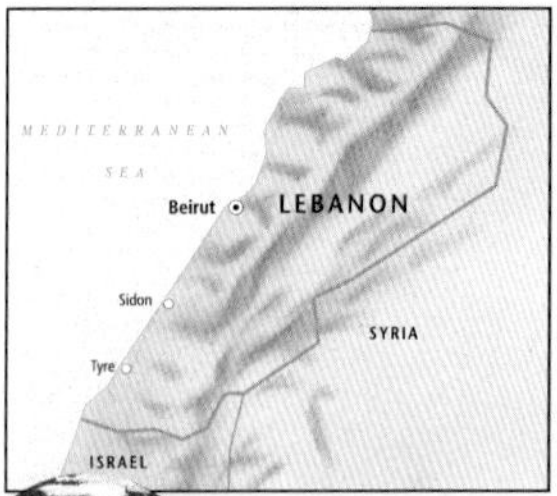

LEBANON

OFFICIAL NAME Republic of Lebanon
FORM OF GOVERNMENT Republic with single legislative body (National Assembly)

Lebanon

Lebanon, a small country on the eastern shore of the Mediterranean Sea, consists of the region that was once known as the Levant. It has a history that goes back at least 5,000 years. First settled by the Phoenicians around 3000 BC, it saw Alexander the Great (356–323 BC) conquer the Phoenician city of Tyre, and it later became part of the Roman Empire. Early in the seventh century AD Maronite Christians (named after Maro, a Syrian monk who was the sect's founder) settled in northern Lebanon; later, Druze Arabs, who are aligned with Shi'ite Islam, settled in the south of the country, and Sunni Muslims came to the coastal towns. From the eleventh to the thirteenth century the region was a center of confrontation between Western Christians and Muslims during the Crusades. It then became part of the Muslim Mameluke Empire. In 1516 the Ottoman Turks took control of the country, their rule

Byblos Harbor in Lebanon.

finally ending with conquest by the British and French during the First World War.

From 1920, following the withdrawal of Turkish forces, a French administration sought to balance the interests of the country's various religious groups. During this period Beirut, which already had a cosmopolitan air, took on a distinctly French flavor. The city became both a center of international commerce and a playground of the rich. The country gained independence in 1946. Deep and persistent tensions between Muslim and various non-Muslim sections of the population led to an outbreak of guerrilla war in 1975. For the next 15 years much of the country was devastated by civil war, and much of its urban infrastructure was destroyed.

From the narrow coastal plain along the Mediterranean, where crops are grown with the aid of irrigation, the land rises eastward to form the Lebanon Mountains (Jabal Lubnān). Running from north to south, these cover about 30 percent of Lebanon's land area. Between the harsh slopes of this range and the Anti-Lebanon Chain (Jabal ash Sharqī) that borders Syria, lies the fertile el Beqaa Valley which is another agricultural area. This is traversed by the River Litani on its journey south, before emptying into the Mediterranean Sea above Şūr (the ancient city of Tyre).

Decades of fighting have left the Lebanese economy in ruins. Tourism, which was once an important source of revenue, is beginning to revive with the rebuilding of the once-popular Corniche seafront area at Beirut. Since the decline of industry as a result of the war, agriculture has come to play a more important role: crops include apples, citrus fruits, bananas, carrots, grapes, tomatoes, and olives. Opium poppies and cannabis are illegally produced for export. Traditional areas of activity in the past were banking, food processing, textiles, cement, oil refining, and chemicals. The country now depends heavily on foreign aid.

CAPITAL Beirut
AREA 10,400 sq km (4,015 sq miles)
TIME ZONE GMT + 2 hours
POPULATION 3,562,699
PROJECTED POPULATION 2005 3,904,380
POPULATION DENSITY 342.5 per sq km (887 per sq mile)
LIFE EXPECTANCY 70.9
INFANT MORTALITY (PER 1,000) 30.5
OFFICIAL LANGUAGES Arabic, French
OTHER LANGUAGES Armenian, English
LITERACY RATE 92%
RELIGIONS Muslim 70%, Christian 30%
ETHNIC GROUPS Arab 95%, Armenian 4%, other 1%
CURRENCY Lebanese pound
ECONOMY Services 60%, industry 28%, agriculture 12%
GNP PER CAPITA US$2,660
CLIMATE Temperate, with short mild, wet winters and long, hot, dry summers. In winter rainfall in mountains often turns to snow
HIGHEST POINT Qurnat as Sawdā' 3,088 m (10,131 ft)
MAP REFERENCE Page 761

Beirut

With a population of only 6,000, Beirut was little more than a village in the year 1800. But the nineteenth century saw continuous commercial growth, and by 1850 its population had swelled to 15,000. An ominous development in 1860 also increased Beirut's population: in the nearby mountains there was a massacre of Christians by Druzes (an Islamic sect originating in Syria), with the result that large numbers of Christian refugees entered the city. During the second half of the century a variety of Western missionaries, both Catholic and Protestant, were active, and several major educational institutions (one becoming the highly regarded American University of Beirut) were founded.

In 1926 the Lebanese Republic was established, under French control, and as the city grew rapidly so did its social tensions. Under the terms of a French-brokered unwritten understanding in 1943, the Christians were able to dominate the Muslim population through a fixed 6:5 ratio of parliamentary seats. The Muslims bitterly resented this arrangement. After they had tried for three decades to change the situation, with a serious outbreak of violence between Christians and Muslims in 1958, full-scale civil war erupted in 1975 between numerous armed militias. On the Christian side the major groups consisted of Maronite Christians and Greek Orthodox, along with smaller numbers of Armenians, Greek Catholics, Protestants, and Roman Catholics. On the non-Christian side were the dominant Sunni Muslims, the minority Shi'ites, and the Druzes. As the war extended Beirut became first a divided city, then a city destroying itself. Lebanon had already been destabilized by a deluge of Palestinian refugees following the 1967 Arab–Israeli War, and by a further influx when the Palestinians in Jordan were expelled in 1970. The Palestinians used southern Lebanon as a base for attacks on Israel, and their militias behaved like an occupying army in the area. West Beirut was virtually destroyed in 1982 when Israel launched a full-scale assault on Palestinian Liberation Organization (PLO) bases in the city, action which led to the evacuation of PLO troops and leaders.

While some degree of order existed in East Beirut, West Beirut collapsed into endless anarchic battles between rival factions trying to settle scores. Hostage-taking became common, some captives being held for years on end. In 1986 West Beirut sought Syrian intervention to try to establish order; after a period of intensified fighting the major antagonists accepted the Ta'if Accord in 1989. Since then the level of internal conflict has declined. Syria remains a powerful influence in Lebanese affairs and its forces continue to occupy large areas. It is estimated that about 150,000 people died in the civil war.

Lesotho

Lesotho is a small landlocked country entirely surrounded by South Africa. Formerly the British Protectorate of Basutoland, it is the only country in the world where all the land is higher than 1,000 m (3,300 ft). About two-thirds of the terrain is mountainous, and at higher altitudes it often snows throughout the winter. As the head of a fragile constitutional monarchy, the king of Lesotho has no executive or legislative powers: traditionally, he could be elected or deposed by a majority vote of the College of Chiefs. Proposals to unite Lesotho with post-apartheid South Africa have been resisted by members of the population who feel an independent state will better defend their cultural heritage.

A high mountainous plateau declining from east to west, Lesotho's highest ridges were formed on basaltic lavas. Treeless, with steep valleys, the wet highlands are soft and boggy in summer and frozen in winter. Numerous river valleys and gorges dissect the plateau, among them the River Orange. To the northwest the border of the country is defined by the Caledon River. This is flanked by a 30 to 65 km (18 to 40 mile) strip of fertile land which supports most of Lesotho's farmers and provides the bulk of its agriculturally useful land. Subsistence crops include maize, sorghum, wheat, and beans. Sheep and goats are kept for wool and mohair on the high plateau.

Lesotho is without important natural resources other than water. Hopes are held for the future of a major hydroelectric facility, the Highlands Water Scheme, which

A village in the Maluti Mountains foothills.

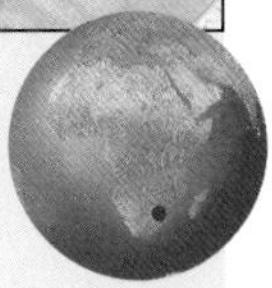

LESOTHO

OFFICIAL NAME Kingdom of Lesotho
FORM OF GOVERNMENT Constitutional monarchy with two legislative houses (Senate and National Assembly)
CAPITAL Maseru
AREA 30,350 sq km (11,718 sq miles)
TIME ZONE GMT + 2 hours
POPULATION 2,128,950
PROJECTED POPULATION 2005 2,327,735
POPULATION DENSITY 70.2 per sq km (181.8 per sq mile)
LIFE EXPECTANCY 53
INFANT MORTALITY (per 1,000) 77.6
OFFICIAL LANGUAGES Sesotho, English
OTHER LANGUAGES Zulu, Afrikaans, French, Xhosa
LITERACY RATE 70.5%
RELIGIONS Christian 80%, indigenous beliefs 20%
ETHNIC GROUPS Sotho 99.7%, European and Asian 0.3%
CURRENCY Loti
ECONOMY Agriculture 75%, services and industry 25%
GNP PER CAPITA US$770
CLIMATE Temperate, with cool, dry winters and hot, wet summers
HIGHEST POINT Thabana-Ntlenyana 3,482 m (11,424 ft)
MAP REFERENCE Page 811

will sell water to South Africa and become a major employer and revenue earner. The scheme will supply all of Lesotho's energy requirements. In scattered hamlets, cottage industry produces woven mohair rugs. Manufacturing based on farm products consists of milling, canning, and the preparation of leather and jute. Roughly 60 percent of Lesotho's male wage earners work across the border in South Africa, mostly as laborers in mines. The wages they send back provide some 45 percent of domestic income.

Liberia

Settled by freed slaves after 1822, and a republic since 1847, the west African state of Liberia has always been a socially divided country. The coastal settlements of ex-slaves from America formed an élite with a Christian faith and an American colonial lifestyle. They had little in common with the long-established tribal peoples of the interior. During the long rule of the coastal Americo-Liberian élite the country was politically stable. It also made economic progress, the activities of the Firestone Rubber Company turning Liberia into a major rubber producer.

This ended in 1980 with a coup led by Master Sergeant Samuel Doe (a Krahn). When Doe was ousted by forces led by members of the Gio tribe in 1990, civil war began. Massacres and atrocities have marked succeeding years; famine threatens several regions; some 750,000 refugees have fled the country; organized economic life is at a standstill; and the rule of law has ended.

Liberia has three major geographic regions. Like its neighbors, it has a narrow sandy coastal strip of lagoons and mangrove swamps. Inland from the Atlantic Ocean are rolling hills, covered in tropical rainforest, which rise to a plateau. This ascends to form a mountainous belt along the Guinean border. Most of the plateau region is grassland or forest—forests cover 39 percent of the land area. Only 1 percent of the country is arable.

Until the outbreak of civil war Liberia had been a producer and exporter of iron ore, rubber, timber, and coffee. Industries included rubber processing, food

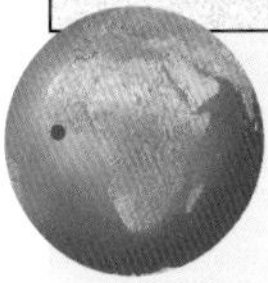

LIBERIA

OFFICIAL NAME Republic of Liberia
FORM OF GOVERNMENT Republic with single transitional legislative body (Transitional Legislative Assembly)
CAPITAL Monrovia
AREA 111,370 sq km (43,000 sq miles)
TIME ZONE GMT
POPULATION 2,923,725
PROJECTED POPULATION 2005 3,749,894
POPULATION DENSITY 26.3 per sq km (68 per sq mile)
LIFE EXPECTANCY 59.9
INFANT MORTALITY (PER 1,000) 100.6
OFFICIAL LANGUAGE English
OTHER LANGUAGES Indigenous languages
LITERACY RATE 39.5%
RELIGIONS Indigenous beliefs 70%, Muslim 20%, Christian 10%
ETHNIC GROUPS Indigenous tribes 95% (including Kpelle, Bassa, Gio, Kru, Grebo, Mano, Krahn, Gola, Gbandi, Loma, Kissi, Vai, Bella), Americo-

processing, construction materials, furniture making, palm oil processing, and diamond mining. Rice was the main staple, but some food was imported. The catch from coastal fisheries was supplemented by inland fish farms.

By the end of the 1990s war had destroyed much of the Liberian economy, especially the infrastructure in and around Monrovia. The business classes fled, taking with them their capital and expertise. With the collapse of the urban commercial part of the economy, many people have reverted to subsistence farming.

Liberian (descendants of repatriated slaves) 5%
CURRENCY Liberian dollar
ECONOMY Agriculture 70%, services 25%, industry 5%
GNP PER CAPITA US$487
CLIMATE Tropical, with wet season May to September
HIGHEST POINT Mt Wuteve 1,380 m (4,528 ft)
MAP REFERENCE Page 804

Libya

First settled by the Greeks, and once part of the empire of Alexander the Great, Libya was ruled by the Romans for 500 years. Tourists visiting the country today are shown the ruins of an impressive 2,000-year-old Roman theater at Leptis Magna. Later, in AD 642, the region was conquered by the Arabs, and later still became part of the Ottoman Empire. It was occupied by Italy in 1911, and the years 1938 to 1939 saw Mussolini bring in 30,000 Italians to farm the Jefra Plain. Libya became independent in 1951. Since 1969, when he seized power, it has been a one-party socialist state ruled dictatorially by Colonel Muammar al Gaddafi.

The arid Saharan Plateau takes up a vast 93 percent of Libya's land area. The great expanse of the Sahara gives way to a fertile coastal strip along the Mediterranean coast, where the majority of the population lives, though only 1 percent of the total land area is arable. Tripoli stands on the Jefra Plain, Libya's most productive farming area. Cereals, particularly barley, are the most important crop. Sorghum is grown in the Fezzan to the south; wheat, tobacco, and olives are produced in the north; dates and figs are cultivated at a few scattered oases in the desert. Predominantly low-lying, the desert terrain rises southward to Bikubiti in the Tibesti Range on the border with Chad. The country is without lakes or perennial rivers, and artesian wells supply nearly two-thirds of Libya's water requirements.

Oil provides almost all export earnings and about one-third of gross domestic product. Though Libya's per capita gross domestic product is usually Africa's highest, the

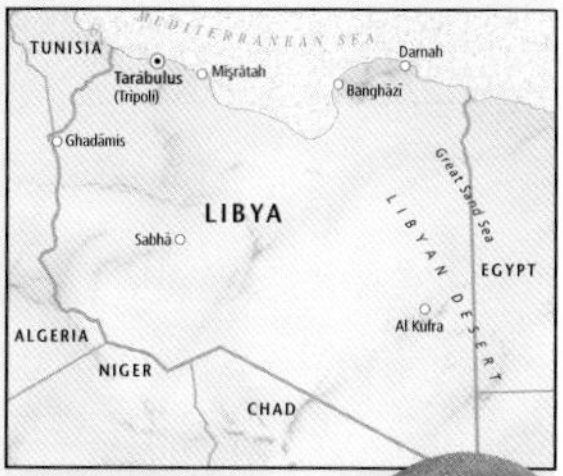

LIBYA

OFFICIAL NAME Socialist People's Libyan Arab Jamahiriya
FORM OF GOVERNMENT Republic with single legislative body (General People's Congress)
CAPITAL Tarābulus (Tripoli)
Area 1,759,540 sq km (679,358 sq miles)
TIME ZONE GMT + 2 hours
POPULATION 5,903,128
PROJECTED POPULATION 2005 7,315,326
POPULATION DENSITY 3.4 per sq km (8.8 per sq mile)
LIFE EXPECTANCY 65.8
INFANT MORTALITY (PER 1,000) 54.0
OFFICIAL LANGUAGE Arabic
OTHER LANGUAGES Italian, English
LITERACY RATE 75.0%
RELIGIONS Sunni Muslim 97%, other 3%

(continues)

L

LIBYA *(continued)*

ETHNIC GROUPS Berber and Arab 97%; other (including Greek, Maltese, Italian, Egyptian, Pakistani, Turkish, Indian, Tunisian) 3%
CURRENCY Libyan dinar
ECONOMY Services 51%, industry 32%, agriculture 17%
GNP PER CAPITA About US$766–3,035
Climate Mainly arid; temperate along coast
HIGHEST POINT Bikubiti 2,285 m (7,497 ft)
MAP REFERENCE Page 802

people suffer from periodic shortages of basic goods and foodstuffs caused by import restrictions and inefficient resource allocation.

The largely state-controlled industrial sector (almost all the oil companies were nationalized in 1973 and the state has a controlling interest in all new ventures) suffers from overstaffing and other constraints. However, oil revenues have enabled important state initiatives to be undertaken: the government has planted millions of trees, and the Great Manmade River Project, being built to bring water from large aquifers under the Sahara to the coastal cities.

Liechtenstein

This small central European country sits high in the Alps. To the west the Rhine River forms a border with Switzerland, with which Liechtenstein has political ties and whose currency it shares. Austria lies to the east and south. The country takes its name from the Austrian Liechtenstein family which, in 1699 and 1713, acquired two fiefdoms and formed them into the principality. It later came under French and then German influence. In 1866 it achieved independence, and two years later declared itself permanently neutral, a position it has since maintained. In all subsequent European wars, Liechtenstein has remained unmolested. Its head of state is an hereditary monarch who appoints a government on the recommendation of an elected parliament. Elections are held every four years and there is universal adult suffrage, although women have had the vote only since 1984.

The Rhine is the source of Liechtenstein's agricultural strength. Its floodplain has been drained and reclaimed for agricultural and pastoral use. The capital sits on a plateau overlooking the undulating expanses of the Rhine Valley. The slopes of the Rhatikon alpine range rise to impressive peaks in the south. From the southern highlands, the Samina River flows northward through the center of the country. Thick forests—of beech, maple, and ash—cover much of the mountain region.

The main agricultural industries are cattle, sheep, and pig raising, and some vegetables and cereal crops are

LIECHTENSTEIN

OFFICIAL NAME Principality of Liechtenstein
FORM OF GOVERNMENT Constitutional monarchy with single legislative house (Parliament)
CAPITAL Vaduz
AREA 160 sq km (62 sq miles)
TIME ZONE GMT + 1 hour
POPULATION 32,057
PROJECTED POPULATION 2005 33,981
POPULATION DENSITY 200.4 per sq km (519 per sq mile)
LIFE EXPECTANCY 78.1
INFANT MORTALITY (PER 1,000) 5.2
OFFICIAL LANGUAGE German
LITERACY RATE 99%
RELIGIONS Roman Catholic 87.3%, Protestant 8.3%, other 4.4%
ETHNIC GROUPS Alemannic 95%, Italian and other 5%
CURRENCY Swiss franc
ECONOMY Services 50%; industry, trade and building 48%; agriculture, fishing and forestry 2%

Modern village with onion-dome clock on valley hillside.

grown. There is little heavy industry but prominent among light industries are textile and ceramic goods and the manufacture of electronic equipment. There are no mineral resources, and Liechtenstein imports all its fuel and raw materials. A major source of revenue is the sale of postage stamps. More than half the country's residents are foreign nationals, largely attracted by the country's low rates of taxation and its banking laws, which ensure great secrecy.

GNP PER CAPITA US$33,000
CLIMATE Temperate, with cold, wet winters and mild, humid summers
HIGHEST POINT Grauspitz 2,599 m (8,527 ft)
MAP REFERENCE Page 772

Lithuania

The largest of the Baltic states, Lithuania has borders with Latvia to the north, Belarus to the east and southeast, Poland to the south, and the Russian Federation to the southwest. The Baltic Sea lies to its west. In the thirteenth century, Lithuania was united under a Christian king, in the sixteenth century it merged with Poland, then in 1795 it came under Russian control. Occupied by Germany in the First World War, Lithuania became independent in 1918. It became part of the Soviet Union in 1940 and was then invaded by Germany. When Soviet armies arrived in 1944, over 200,000 people, more than three-quarters of them Jews, had perished. In 1991 the country declared its independence from the Soviet Union. It is now a multi-party democracy with a president as head of state and a prime minister as head of government.

Most of Lithuania consists of a relatively fertile plain with extensive marshlands and forests. Many marshes

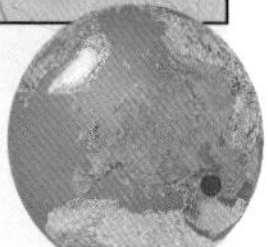

LITHUANIA

OFFICIAL NAME Republic of Lithuania
FORM OF GOVERNMENT Republic with single legislative body (Parliament)
CAPITAL Vilnius
AREA 65,200 sq km (25,174 sq miles)
TIME ZONE GMT + 3 hours
POPULATION 3,584,966
PROJECTED POPULATION 2005 3,526,180

(continues)

LITHUANIA *(continued)*

POPULATION DENSITY 55 per sq km (142.4 per sq mile)
LIFE EXPECTANCY 69
INFANT MORTALITY (PER 1,000) 14.7
OFFICIAL LANGUAGE Lithuanian
OTHER LANGUAGES Russian, Polish
LITERACY RATE 98.4%
RELIGIONS Roman Catholic 90%; Russian Orthodox, Muslim and Protestant minorities 10%
ETHNIC GROUPS Lithuanian 80.1%, Russian 8.6%, Polish 7.7%, Belarusian 1.5%, other 2.1%
CURRENCY Litas
ECONOMY Industry 42%, services 40%, agriculture 18%
GNP PER CAPITA US$1,900
CLIMATE Temperate. Cold winters and mild summers
HIGHEST POINT Mt Juozapine 292 m (958 ft)
MAP REFERENCE Pages 771, 773

have been reclaimed for growing cereal and vegetable crops. Sand dunes predominate along the Baltic coast and there is a range of hills dotted with more than 3,000 lakes in the southeast. Numerous rivers traverse the landscape.

Machine manufacturing, petroleum refining, shipbuilding, and food processing are some of Lithuania's key industries, but they have resulted in soil and groundwater contamination. The country has few natural resources and depends on Russia for oil and most of the raw materials needed for its industries. The main forms of agriculture are dairy farming and pig and cattle raising. Continuing dependence on Russia and a high rate of inflation are among factors that make Lithuania the least prosperous of the Baltic states.

Luxembourg

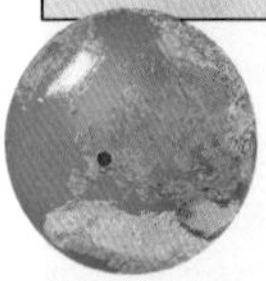

LUXEMBOURG

OFFICIAL NAME Grand Duchy of Luxembourg
FORM OF GOVERNMENT Constitutional monarchy with single legislative body (Chamber of Deputies)
CAPITAL Luxembourg
AREA 2,586 sq km (998 sq miles)
TIME ZONE GMT + 1 hour
POPULATION 429,080
PROJECTED POPULATION 2005 445,932
POPULATION DENSITY 165.9 per sq km (429.7 per sq mile)
LIFE EXPECTANCY 77.7
INFANT MORTALITY (PER 1,000) 5.0
OFFICIAL LANGUAGE Letzeburgish
OTHER LANGUAGES French, German
LITERACY RATE 99%
RELIGIONS Roman Catholic 97%, Protestant and Jewish 3%

The Grand Duchy of Luxembourg is one of the smallest countries in Europe. Situated in northern Europe, it shares borders with Belgium to the west and France to the south. Three connecting rivers—the Our, Sûre, and the Moselle —separate it from Germany to the east. Part of the Holy Roman Empire since the tenth century AD, Luxembourg became an independent duchy in 1354, one of hundreds of such states in medieval Europe. It is the only one to survive today as an independent nation. Throughout the intervening centuries, Luxembourg has come under Austrian, Spanish, French, and Dutch rule. In 1830 part of the duchy was taken over by Belgium when that country split from the Netherlands. Luxembourg separated from the Netherlands in 1890. Germany occupied Luxembourg during both world wars and annexed it in 1942. After the Second World War it became a founder member of NATO and in 1957 joined the European Economic Community. It has been a keen advocate of European cooperation and was the first country, in 1991, to ratify the Maastricht Treaty. Luxembourg is a constitutional monarchy, with the Grand Duke as head of state, and a prime minister as head of an elected 21-member Council of State.

The northern part of Luxembourg is called the Oesling. Covering about one-third of the country's total area, it is part of the densely forested Ardennes mountain range. Numerous river valleys dissect this northern region and deer and wild boar abound. It is a rugged, picturesque area but has poor soils. In contrast, the southern two-thirds, known as the Gutland or Bon Pays (meaning good land), consists of plains and undulating hills covered with rich soils and extensive pastureland.

Iron ore deposits in the south of the country contributed to the development of a thriving iron and steel industry. These deposits are now less abundant and industries such as food processing, chemical manufacturing and tyre making now rival steel in importance. A growing service sector, especially in banking, has become increasingly central to the country's prosperity. The Gutland area is still strongly agricultural. Wheat, barley, potatoes, and grapes are the principal crops and more than 5 million cattle and 6 million pigs are raised. The people of Luxembourg are among the most affluent in Europe. Unemployment is low and salaries, especially among urban workers, are high.

Ethnic groups Luxembourger (French and German) 70%; Portuguese, Belgian and Italian minorities 30%
Currency Luxembourg franc
Economy Services 77%, industry 19%, agriculture 4%
GNP per capita US$41,210
Climate Temperate, with cool winters and mild summers
Highest point Burgplatz 559 m (1,834 ft)
Map reference Page 775

Typical town in Luxembourg—two bridges cross the river, one of them an old stone footbridge with fortification.

M

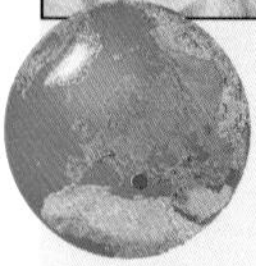

Macedonia

Official name Former Yugoslav Republic of Macedonia
Form of government Republic with single legislative body (Assembly)
Capital Skopje
Area 25,333 sq km (9,781 sq miles)
Time zone GMT + 1 hour
Population 2,022,604
Projected population 2005 2,086,849
Population density 79.8 per sq km (206.8 per sq mile)
Life expectancy 73.1
Infant mortality (per 1,000) 18.7
Official language Macedonian
Other languages Albanian, Turkish, Serbian, Croatian
Literacy rate 94.0%
Religions Eastern Orthodox 67%, Muslim 30%, other 3%
Ethnic groups Macedonian 65%, Albanian 22%, Turkish 4%, Serb 2%, Gypsy 3%, other 4%
Currency Denar
Economy Services and agriculture 60%; manufacturing and mining 40%
GNP per capita US$860
Climate Temperate, with cold winters and hot summers
Highest point Mt Korab 2,753 m (9,032 ft)
Map reference Pages 780–81, 782

Macedonia

This small, landlocked Balkan country in south-eastern Europe is bordered by Yugoslavia to the north, Bulgaria to the east, Greece to the south, and Albania to the west. During the third century BC Macedonia was the heart of the Greek Empire. It later became a Roman province, but from the fourth century AD it was invaded numerous times. In the fourteenth century it came under Ottoman control. As the Ottoman Empire declined in the nineteenth century, Bulgaria, Greece, and Serbia contended for control of Macedonia and by the First World War it had been divided between them. Present-day Macedonia is essentially the region that was in Serbian hands at the end of the First World War. Macedonia was then incorporated into the Kingdom of Serbs, Croats, and Slovenes, which in 1929 became the Republic of Yugoslavia. In 1946 it became an autonomous republic within Yugoslavia. In 1991 Macedonia withdrew from Yugoslavia and it is now a multi-party democracy, governed by a legislative body with 120 elected members and a directly elected president. Tensions with neighbors remain high. Macedonia is also the name of a Greek province, over which Greece claims the former Yugloslav state has territorial ambitions.

Macedonia is largely isolated from its neighbors by mountains. Mountain ranges separate it from Greece in the south and the Korab Mountains in the west lie along the Albanian border. Much of the country is a plateau more than 2,000 m (6,500 ft) above sea level. The River Vadar rises in the northwest. It flows north, almost to the

The town of Ohrid on the shore of Lake Ohrid in southwestern Macedonia.

Yugoslavian border, then continues on a southeasterly course through the center of the country and into Greece.

One-quarter of the land is used for agriculture. Crops include cereals, fruits, vegetables, and cotton, and sheep and cattle are raised extensively. The country is self-sufficient in food and, thanks to its coal resources, in energy. Manufacturing industries have suffered since independence, partly because of trade embargoes imposed by Greece. Macedonia is the least developed of the former Yugoslav republics and is suffering a decline in its standard of living.

Exterior of the Sveti Naum Monastery, Macedonia.

Madagascar

Larger than France, Madagascar is the world's fourth largest island. Located off the southeast coast of Africa, it contrasts sharply with the African mainland in its wildlife, people, culture, language, and history. In the center and the east live the Merina or Hova people who migrated to the island from the islands now known as Indonesia about 2,000 years ago. By the nineteenth century the Merinas, with their capital in Tanarive, ruled much of the country. In 1896 the island became a French colony. It won independence from France in 1960, following a bloody insurrection. From 1975 it was run as a one-party socialist state associated with the Soviet Union. Since 1991, following deepening poverty, riots, and mass demonstrations, there have been attempts to introduce multi-party democracy.

A street scene in Toliara, Madagascar.

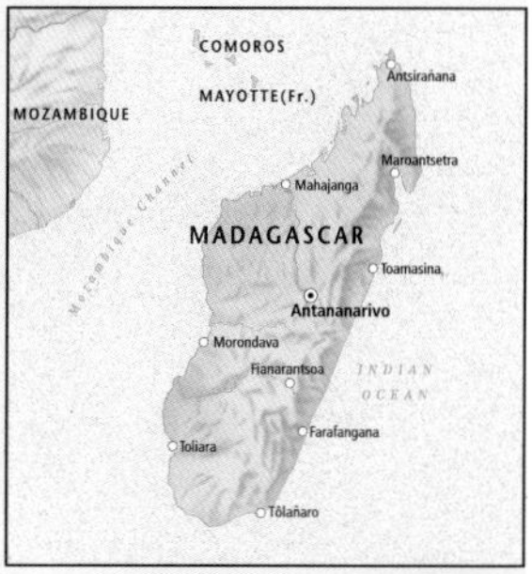

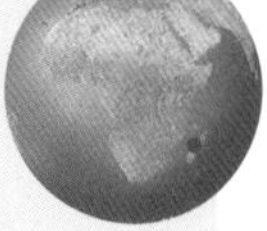

MADAGASCAR

OFFICIAL NAME Republic of Madagascar
FORM OF GOVERNMENT Republic with two legislative bodies (Senate and National Assembly)
CAPITAL Antanañarivo
AREA 587,040 sq km (226,656 sq miles)
TIME ZONE GMT + 3 hours
POPULATION 14,873,387
PROJECTED POPULATION 2005 17,558,869
POPULATION DENSITY 25.3 per sq km (65.5 per sq mile)
LIFE EXPECTANCY 53.2
INFANT MORTALITY (PER 1,000) 89.1
OFFICIAL LANGUAGES Malagasy, French
LITERACY RATE 83%

(continues)

M

MADAGASCAR *(continued)*

RELIGIONS Indigenous beliefs 52%, Christian 41%, Muslim 7%
ETHNIC GROUPS Chiefly Malayo-Indonesian inland (including Merina, Betsileo, Betsimisaraka) and mixed African, Arab, Malayo-Indonesian on coasts (including Tsimihety, Sakalava) 99%; other 1%
CURRENCY Malagasy franc
ECONOMY Agriculture 81%, services 13%, industry 6%
GNP PER CAPITA US$230
CLIMATE Tropical in coastal regions; temperate inland (wet season November to April); arid in south
HIGHEST POINT Maromokotro 2,876 m (9,436 ft)
MAP REFERENCE Page 812

To the east the land drops precipitously to the Indian Ocean through forests dissected by rushing streams. Inland lies the mountainous central plateau, accounting for 60 percent of the island's total area, and rising in several places above 2,500 m (8,200 ft). Various geological eras are represented in the island's rugged topography, which features steep faulting, volcanic outcrops, and deep-cut valleys. On the western slopes of the plateau the land falls away more gently to broad and fertile plains. In the central highlands both the landscape and agriculture have a south Asian character, rice farming being combined with raising cattle and pigs. Land usage is more African in style on the east coast and in the northern highlands, with fallow-farming of food crops such as cassava and maize, and the cultivation of coffee, sugar, and spices for export.

Separated from the African mainland for over 50 million years, Madagascar developed its own distinctive wildlife: three-quarters of the flora and fauna are found nowhere else. The island is known for its 28 species of lemur—dainty, large-eyed primates—and for the tenrec, a small, spiny, insect-eating mammal. Many of the island's 1,000 or so orchid species are endemic, and it is home to half the world's chameleon species.

Among the poorest countries in the world, Madagascar is not self-sufficient in food. The main staple is rice, but production is failing to keep pace with an annual population growth rate of around 3 percent. Additional problems derive from past government initiatives. When collective farming was introduced in 1975 it resulted in falling production and widespread resentment. Since 1993 corruption and political instability have accompanied economic confusion and a decay in the infrastructure.

Antananarivo, the capital of Madagascar.

Madeira

Madeira is the largest of a group of volcanic islands forming an autonomous region of Portugal. A tourist destination, they are situated 550 km (340 miles) from the coast of Morocco, and 900 km (560 miles) southwest of Lisbon. The two islands of Madeira and Porto Santo are inhabited but Desertas and Selvagens are not. Madeira is 55 km (34 miles) long and 19 km (12 miles) wide, has deep ravines and rugged mountains, contains the group's capital, Funchal, and rises to Pico Ruivo (1,862 m; 6,109 ft) in the middle of the island. It was once heavily forested, but settlers cleared the uplands for plantation use. Produce includes wine (madeira), sugar, and bananas.

Black and white mosaic-tiled town square surrounded by black-trimmed white buildings, Madeira.

MADEIRA

GOVERNMENT Autonomous region of Portugal
RELIGION Roman Catholic
OFFICIAL LANGUAGE Portuguese
MAJOR INDUSTRIES Sugar cane, fruit, fishing, agriculture, Madeira wine, wickerwork, embroidery, crafts, tourism
POPULATION 263,000
CAPITAL Funchal
CLIMATE Subtropical, Atlantic breezes in the summer, warm seas and winter sunshine
HIGHEST POINT Pico Ruivo de Santana 1,861m
MAP REFERENCE 798

Malawi

Malawi is a hilly and in places mountainous country at the southern end of Africa's Rift Valley, one-fifth of it consisting of Lake Malawi (Lake Nyasa). The lake contains 500 fish species which support a sizeable fishing industry. Most of the country's people are descended from the Bantu who settled the area centuries ago. Arab slave-trading was suppressed by the incoming British in 1887–89, and in 1907 the country became the British Protectorate of Nyasaland. Independence in 1964 put Dr Hastings Banda in charge and he ruled dictatorially for 30 years. Cumulative difficulties, including drought and crop failures, some 800,000 refugees from Mozambique, and resentment at the apparent assassination of political opponents, led to Dr Banda's removal and Malawi's first multi-party elections in 1994.

At the southern end of Lake Malawi (Lake Nyasa) the Shire River runs through a deep, swampy valley flanked

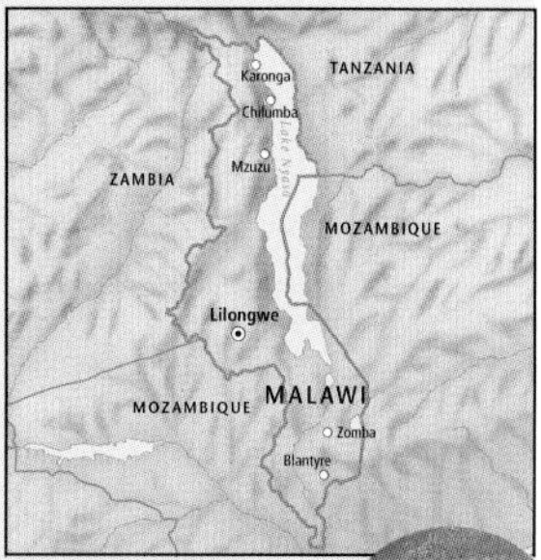

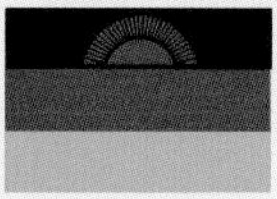

MALAWI

OFFICIAL NAME Republic of Malawi
FORM OF GOVERNMENT Republic with single legislative body (National Assembly)

continued

MALAWI *(continued)*

CAPITAL Lilongwe
AREA 118,480 sq km (45,745 sq miles)
TIME ZONE GMT + 2 hours
POPULATION 9,888,601
PROJECTED POPULATION 2005 10,469,217
POPULATION DENSITY 83.4 per sq km (216 per sq mile)
LIFE EXPECTANCY 33.7
INFANT MORTALITY (PER 1,000) 136.9
OFFICIAL LANGUAGES Chichewa, English
OTHER LANGUAGES Indigenous languages
LITERACY RATE 55.8%
RELIGIONS Protestant 55%, Roman Catholic 20%, Muslim 20%, indigenous beliefs 5%
ETHNIC GROUPS Indigenous tribes: Malavi (including Chewa, Nyanja, Tumbuke, Tonga) 58%, Lomwe 18%, Yao 13%, Ngoni 7%; Asian and European 4%
CURRENCY Kwacha
ECONOMY Agriculture 79%, services 16%, industry 5%
GNP PER CAPITA US$170
CLIMATE Tropical, with wet season November to April
HIGHEST POINT Mt Mulanje 3,001 m (9,846 ft)
MAP REFERENCE Page 809

by mountains to the east. Most of the population live in this southern region, growing maize as the main food crop and cultivating cash crops such as peanuts and sugarcane. The western central plateau rises northward to the Nyika Uplands, where rainfall is highest. In the Shire Highlands to the south, tea and tobacco are grown on large estates. Savanna grassland in the valleys gives way to open woodland, much of which has been cleared for cultivation. Wildlife is largely confined to reserves.

Agriculture provides more than 90 percent of exports. Reserves of bauxite and uranium exist, but not in commercially usable quantities. Hydroelectricity supplies only about 3 percent of total energy use—most needs are met from fuelwood, which is resulting in continued deforestation. The economy depends heavily on foreign aid.

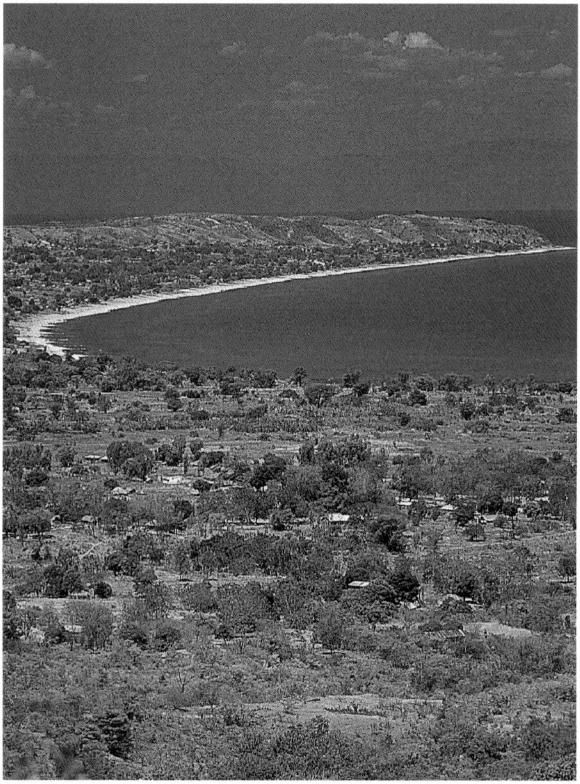

Lake Malawi (Lake Nyasa), near Chilumba, looking toward Mozambique.

Malaysia

Malaysia consists of the southern part of the Malay Peninsula, with Thailand to its north, plus Sarawak and Sabah in northern Borneo. Like Singapore, which lies at the southern tip of the Malay Peninsula, it has had an impressive record of economic growth in recent times.

In the fifteenth century a part of Malaysia was famous as the Kingdom of Malacca (now Melaka), a state that became powerful through its control of local sea routes and shipping. In 1414 the ruler of Malacca adopted Islam, which is the religion of Malaysia today. Seized by the Portuguese as a base for the spice trade in 1511, and held by the Dutch from 1641, Malacca was captured by the British in 1795. The British took control of Singapore in 1819 and in 1867 they established the Straits Settlements, which consisted of Penang Island (Pinang) in the northeast, Malacca, and Singapore, as a crown colony. During the Second World War Malaysia was occupied by the Japanese. In 1948 it received its independence from the British. A guerrilla war broke out, led by communists who were sympathetic to the Chinese Revolution. Following the defeat of this insurgency, after a four-year military campaign, the country evolved into the modern state it is today. Ethnic tensions exist, principally between the Malays, who are the most numerous, and the Chinese, who are considerably more prosperous. There were riots between the Malays and Chinese in 1969 with heavy loss of life. The many "affirmative action" provisions that are now in place to help Malays at the expense of Chinese and Indians are strongly resented by the latter groups. There

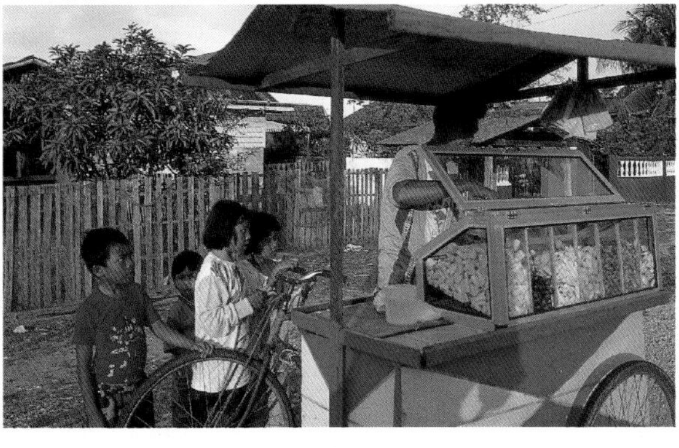

Street vendor with customers in Malaysia.

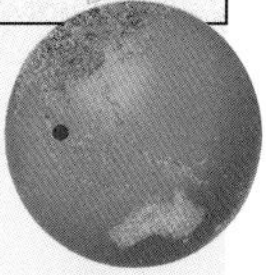

Malaysia

Official name Malaysia
Form of government Federal constitutional monarchy with two legislative bodies (Senate and House of Representatives)
Capital Kuala Lumpur
Area 329,750 sq km (127,316 sq miles)
Time zone GMT + 8 hours
Population 21,376,066
Projected population 2005 24,086,817
Population density 64.8 per sq km (167.8 per sq mile)
Life expectancy 70.7
Infant mortality (per 1,000) 21.7
Official language Malay (Bahasa Malaysia)
Other languages English, Chinese languages, Tamil
Literacy rate 83%
Religions Muslim 53%, Buddhist 17.5%, Confucian and Taoist 11.5%, Christian 8.5%, Hindu 7%, other 2.5%
Ethnic groups Malay 59%, Chinese 32%, Indian 9%
Currency Ringgit (Malaysian dollar)
Economy Agriculture 42%, services 39%, industry 19%
GNP per capita US$3,890
Climate Tropical, with northeast monsoon October to February and southwest monsoon May to September
Highest point Gunung Kinabalu 4,101 m (13,453 ft)
Map reference Pages 736–37

Houses straddling polluted waterway.

M

are also a number of unresolved territorial disputes with neighboring states—Sabah in Borneo, for example, being claimed by the Philippines.

Fold mountains aligned on a north-south axis dominate the Malay Peninsula. There are seven or eight distinct chains of mountains, often with exposed granite cores. Climbing to 2,189 m (7,181 ft) at Gunung Tahan, the main range divides the narrow eastern coastal belt from the fertile alluvial plains in the west. To the south lies poorly drained lowland, marked by isolated hills, some of which rise to over 1,060 m (3,500 ft). Several smaller rivers have also contributed to the margin of lowland around the peninsular coasts.

About 2,000 km (1,250 miles) east of the Malay Peninsula, northern Borneo has a mangrove-fringed coastal plain about 65 km (40 miles) wide, rising behind to hill country averaging 300 m (1,000 ft) in height. This ascends through various secondary ranges to the mountainous main interior range. The granite peak of Gunung Kinabalu, the highest mountain in Southeast Asia, rises from the northern end of this range in Sabah, towering above Kinabalu National Park. Dense rainforest in Sarawak and Sabah support a great diversity of plants and animals.

With a mixture of private enterprise and public management, the Malaysian economy averaged 9 percent annual growth from 1988 to 1995. Poverty is being substantially reduced and real wages are rising. New light industries including electronics are playing an important role in this development: Malaysia is the world's biggest producer of disk drives. Heavy industry has also grown:

Rice paddies in east Malaysia.

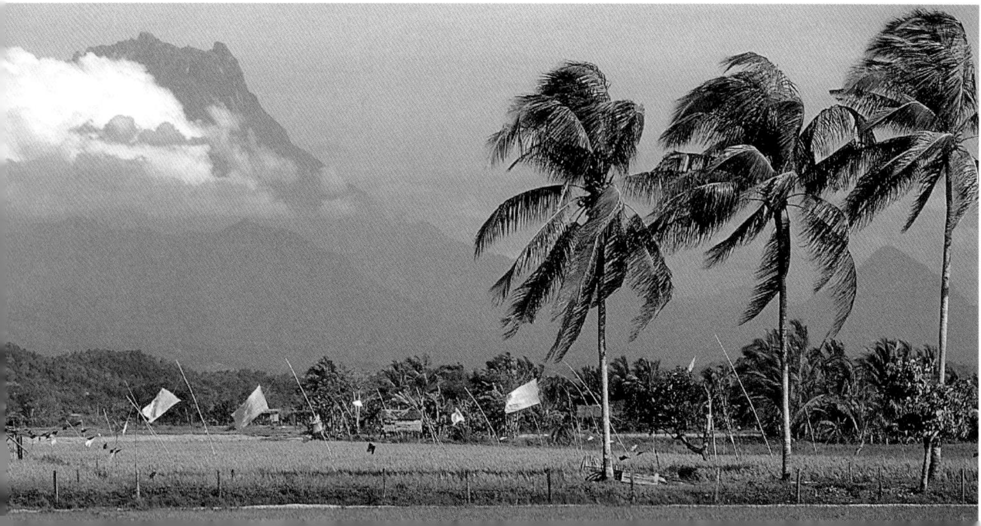

Malaysia's "national car", the Proton, is now being exported. The traditional mainstays of the economy, however, remain rice, rubber, palm oil, and tin—Malaysia being the world's biggest producer of palm oil and tin. Rice is a problem. Subsistence farming has regularly failed to ensure self-sufficiency in food, and rice production does not meet demand. The main industries on the peninsula are rubber and palm oil processing and manufacturing, light industry, electronics, tin mining, smelting, logging, and timber processing. The main activities on Sabah and Sarawak are logging, petroleum production, and the processing of agricultural products. Malaysia exports more tropical timber than any other country, and the tribal people of Sarawak have been campaigning against the scale of logging on their land.

The Asian economic downturn in 1998 saw a depreciation of the Malaysian currency and a marked slowing of the economy. Prime Minister Mahatir bin Muhammad introduced capital controls to protect currency. He also reduced interest rates, and funding was given to combat Kuala Lumpur's rising unemployment rate. Mahatir was re-elected in 1999, although the Islamic fundamentalists gained 27 seats after political unrest leading up to the elections in which Former Deputy Prime Minister Anwhar Ibrahmin was imprisoned on charges of corruption. Increased government spending on infrastructure has lead to an increase in industrial production and a small rise in Gross Domestic Product.

Malaysia suffers from environmental concerns caused by deforestation and the application of pesticides in rubber and palm oil plantations. Studies indicate that heavy use of these pesticides, particularly paraquat, are having detrimental affects on the fauna as well as on the human population, and these issues will need to be addressed in the future.

Father and son preparing to enter the mosque in Kangar.

M

Muslim school in Perlis, Maylaysia.

Sam Poh Tong Temple, Ipoh.

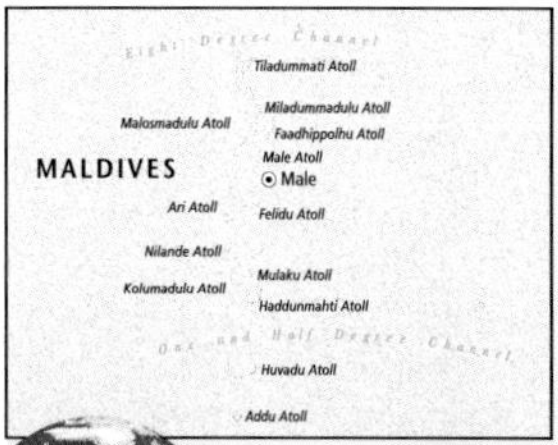

MALDIVES

OFFICIAL NAME Republic of the Maldives
FORM OF GOVERNMENT Republic with single legislative body (Citizens Council)
CAPITAL Male
AREA 300 sq km (116 sq miles)
TIME ZONE GMT + 5 hours
POPULATION 300,220
PROJECTED POPULATION 2005 364,147
POPULATION DENSITY 1,000.7 per sq km (2,591.8 per sq mile)
LIFE EXPECTANCY 68.3
INFANT MORTALITY (PER 1,000) 38.1
OFFICIAL LANGUAGE Divehi
OTHER LANGUAGES Arabic, English, Hindi
LITERACY RATE 93%
RELIGIONS Predominantly Sunni Muslim
ETHNIC GROUPS Sinhalese, Dravidian, Arab, African
CURRENCY Rufiyaa
ECONOMY Tourism, fishing, manufacturing
GNP PER CAPITA US$990
CLIMATE Tropical, with wet season May to August
HIGHEST POINT Unnamed location on Wilingili 24 m (79 ft)
MAP REFERENCE Page 752

M

Maldives

The Maldive Archipelago consists of an 800 km (500 mile) string of nearly 2,000 islands and atolls (202 of them inhabited) southwest of India's southern tip, Cape Comorin. Made up of tiny islets ringed by white sands and clear blue lagoons, they have recently been developed as tourist resorts and receive up to 300,000 visitors each year. Long ago, their first visitors were probably Dravidians from southern India, in around 400 BC. Centuries later, the islands seem to have been taken over by people from Sri Lanka—Divehi, the national language, is a form of Sinhalese. In 1153 the king of the Maldives ordered his subjects to adopt Islam in place of Buddhism: today the people are mainly Sunni Muslims and there are 689 mosques. For the next 800 years the islands were ruled as a Muslim sultanate, though there was a brief period, between 1558 and 1573, of Portuguese control from Goa. The British established a protectorate in 1887, the islands achieved independence in 1965, and the sultan was deposed in 1968. Since then government has been in the hands of a small group of influential families, and by 1995 the president then in office, a wealthy businessman, had survived three attempted coups. Younger political contenders who have tasted democracy abroad are pressing for a more open regime.

The atolls of the Maldives are coral reefs which have grown up around the peaks of a submerged volcanic mountain range. None of them rise more than 1.8 m (6 ft) above sea level. There is concern that if the Greenhouse Effect causes a rise in sea levels, some may be submerged. Adequate rainfall supports a variety of tropical vegetation, and palm and breadfruit trees occur naturally.

Food crops include coconuts, bananas, mangoes, sweet potatoes, and spices. Agriculture is constrained by the small amount of cultivable land, and most staple foods must be imported. In the lagoons and the open sea fish are plentiful. Bonito and tuna are leading exports, fishing being the second leading growth sector of the economy. Manufacturing, consisting mainly of garment production, boat building, and handicrafts, accounts for 15 percent of gross domestic product. Since the 1980s tourism has been the leading growth sector, and now accounts for more than 60 percent of foreign exchange receipts. At present more than 90 percent of tax revenue comes from import duties and tourism-related taxes.

One of the many palm-fringed beaches in the Maldives.

M

Mali

Mali is a landlocked west African country, watered by the River Niger in the south and with vast stretches of the Sahara Desert lying to the north. It derives its name from the Malinke or Mandingo people whose empire flourished between the eighth and fourteenth centuries. Later it was a center of trade and Islamic scholarship, based on the city of Timbuktu (now Tombouctou). At the end of the nineteenth century it became a colony of French West Africa, achieving independence in 1960. For the next 30 years the country was ruled by either civilian or military dictators. Demonstrations in 1991 in which about 100 people died were followed by the overthrow of the regime, and free elections were held for the first time in 1992.

There is a major ethnic division between the black African majority in the south, and the minority of Arab Tuareg nomads in the north. Violent Tuareg guerrilla activity in northern Mali ended with a peace pact in 1995.

Mali's flat landscape consists mainly of plains and sandstone plateaus. The need for water is the main concern. The northern and virtually rainless Saharan

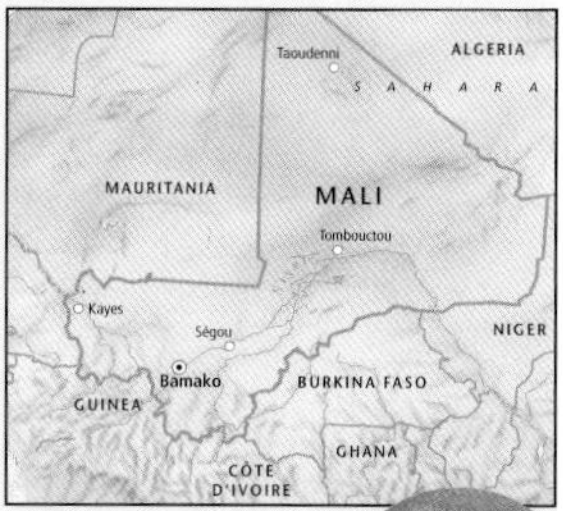

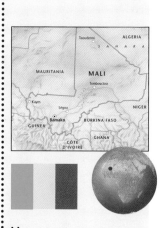

MALI

OFFICIAL NAME Republic of Mali
FORM OF GOVERNMENT Republic with single legislative body (National Assembly)
CAPITAL Bamako
AREA 1,240,000 sq km (478,764 sq miles)
TIME ZONE GMT

(continues)

MALI *(continued)*

POPULATION 10,429,124
PROJECTED POPULATION 2005 12,536,227
POPULATION DENSITY 8.4 per sq km (21.8 per sq mile)
LIFE EXPECTANCY 47.5
INFANT MORTALITY (PER 1,000) 119.4
OFFICIAL LANGUAGE French
OTHER LANGUAGES Bambara and other indigenous languages
LITERACY RATE 29.3%
RELIGIONS Muslim 90%, indigenous beliefs 9%, Christian 1%
ETHNIC GROUPS Mande 50%, Peul 17%, Voltaic 12%, Songhai 6%, Tuareg and Moor 10%, other 5%
CURRENCY CFA (Communauté Financière Africaine) franc
ECONOMY Agriculture 85%, services 13%, industry 2%
GNP PER CAPITA US$250
CLIMATE Subtropical in south and southwest; arid in north
HIGHEST POINT Hombori Tondo 1,155 m (3,789 ft)
MAP REFERENCE Pages 801, 804–05

plains are inhabited almost entirely by Tuareg nomads. The semiarid center—the Sahel—has in recent years suffered from devastating droughts. Such arable land as exists is found in the south, along the Senegal and Niger Rivers, the latter spreading out to form an inland delta before turning southward on its way to the border of Niger. These rivers provide water for stock and for irrigation. Rice is grown on irrigated land; millet, cotton, and peanuts grow elsewhere. Away from the rivers southern Mali is mostly savanna country where mahogany, kapok, and baobab trees grow, these being replaced further north by palms and scrub. Animal life includes lion, antelope, jackal, and hyena.

Some 80 percent of the labor force works in agriculture and fishing—dried fish is exported to Burkina Faso, Côte d'Ivoire, and Ghana. With 65 percent of its land either desert or semidesert, however, and industry limited mainly to a single gold mine, salt production, and small-scale textiles and shoes, Mali is extremely poor. As well as gold there are phosphates, uranium, bauxite, manganese, and copper but development is hampered by poor transport facilities and the fact that the country is landlocked. With expenditures almost double its revenues, Mali is a major recipient of foreign aid.

The city of Tombouctou, in Mali, following a dust storm.

Malta

The Republic of Malta consists of an archipelago of three inhabited islands—Malta, Gozo, and Comino—and three tiny uninhabited islands, which are little more than rocky outcrops. They are situated in the center of the Mediterranean Sea 93 km (58 miles) south of Sicily. Malta, the largest and most populous of the islands, contains the capital, Valletta, the country's fifth largest city, picturesquely situated on a promontory between two harbors, and the four larger cities of Birkirkara, Qormi, Hamrun, and Sliema. Successive civilizations have recognized the importance of Malta's position and the advantages of its many harbors. It was occupied successively by the Phoenicians, the Greeks, and the Romans. In the ninth century AD, when it was part of the Byzantine Empire, it was conquered by Arabs but fell two centuries later to Sicily and then, in 1282, to Spain. In 1530 the Spanish king gave Malta to the Knights of St John, a religious order, which built and fortified the town of Valletta and occupied the island of Malta until it was seized by Napoleon in 1798. Britain took the island in 1800 and held it until 1947, when the country was granted self-government as a parliamentary democracy. In 1964, Malta gained full independence. Relations with Britain and other Western nations have often been strained, largely because of Malta's close links with Libya in northern Africa.

The three inhabited islands are mostly flat—although the island of Malta is undulating in places—with spectacular rocky coastlines. There is little natural

One of Malta's old megalithic temples, built more than 5,000 years ago.

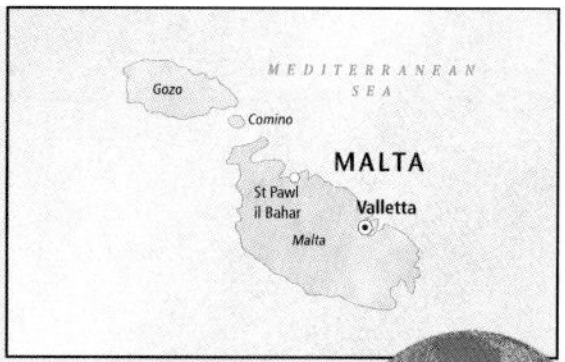

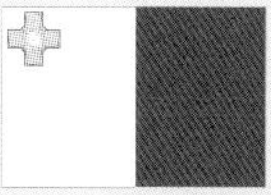

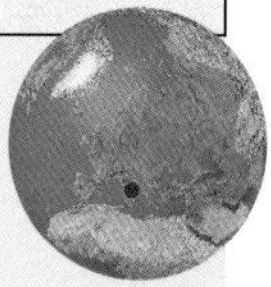

MALTA

OFFICIAL NAME Republic of Malta
FORM OF GOVERNMENT Republic with single legislative body (House of Representatives)
CAPITAL Valletta
AREA 320 sq km (124 sq miles)
TIME ZONE GMT + 1 hour
POPULATION 381,603
PROJECTED POPULATION 2005 389,772
POPULATION DENSITY 1,192.5 per sq km (3,088.6 per sq mile)
LIFE EXPECTANCY 77.8
INFANT MORTALITY (PER 1,000) 7.4
OFFICIAL LANGUAGES Maltese, English
LITERACY RATE 86%
RELIGIONS Roman Catholic 98%, other 2%
ETHNIC GROUPS Mixed Arab, Sicilian, French, Spanish, Italian and English
CURRENCY Maltese lira
ECONOMY Government 37%, services 30%, manufacturing 27%, construction 4%, agriculture 2%
GNP PER CAPITA US$7,200
CLIMATE Temperate, with mild, wet winters and hot, dry summers
HIGHEST POINT Dingli Cliffs 245 m (804 ft)
MAP REFERENCE Pages 801–02

vegetation and there are no forests or major rivers. Low rainfall, poor drainage, a limestone base and a hot climate all contribute to the paucity of the islands' shallow soils, which, however, support a range of cereal and vegetable crops as well as substantial vineyards.

Apart from limestone for building, Malta has virtually no mineral resources and is heavily dependent on imported materials. It has no natural sources of energy and produces only one-fifth of its population's food needs. Tourism is the mainstay of the economy. Every year about a million visitors, mainly from the United Kingdom, arrive to enjoy its beaches, its historic towns, and its rugged scenery. Ship repairs and clothing and textile manufacture are other significant industries. The average income is low by Western standards and Maltese residents are among the least affluent of Western Europeans.

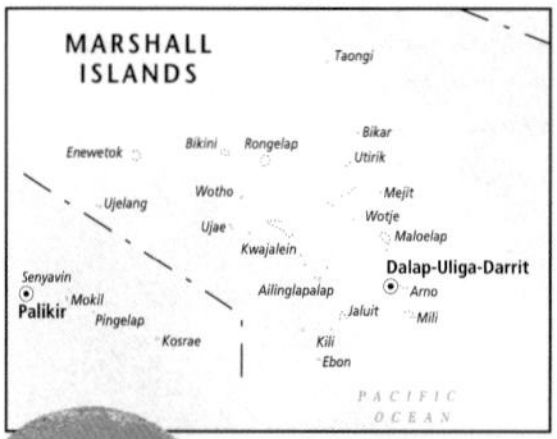

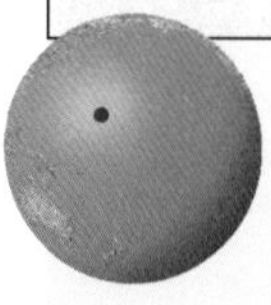

MARSHALL ISLANDS

OFFICIAL NAME Republic of the Marshall Islands
FORM OF GOVERNMENT Republic in free association with the USA; two legislative bodies (Parliament and Council of Chiefs)
CAPITAL Dalap-Uliga-Darrit
AREA 181 sq km (70 sq miles)
TIME ZONE GMT + 12 hours
POPULATION 65,507
PROJECTED POPULATION 2005 82,686
POPULATION DENSITY 361.9 per sq km (937.3 per sq mile)
LIFE EXPECTANCY 64.8
INFANT MORTALITY (PER 1,000) 43.4

Marshall Islands

A group of 31 coral atolls, 5 islands, and 1,152 islets, the Republic of the Marshall Islands is situated in the northern Pacific about halfway between Hawaii and Papua New Guinea. Settled around 2000 BC, the islands were visited by Spanish seafarers in 1529, and since 1874 have been successively under Spanish, German, Japanese, and US control. In 1986 they entered into a Compact of Free Association with the US. During the years after the Second World War the Marshalls became known as the location where the USA carried out nuclear bomb tests (on Bikini and Enewetak Atolls between 1946 and 1958). Claims for compensation by those affected or displaced by the tests have been settled in recent years, an award of US$40 million to 1,150 Marshall Islanders being made by the Nuclear Claims Tribunal in 1995. Clean-up work to remove residual radiation from Bikini Lagoon continues.

The terrain consists of low coral limestone and sand islands. Two archipelagoes of islands run roughly parallel northeast to southwest, the easternmost chain being a continuation of the Gilbert Islands of western Kiribati. Originating as coral reefs formed upon the rims of submerged volcanoes, each of the main islands encloses a lagoon. Bordering the cyclone belt, and nowhere higher than 10 m (30 ft) above sea level, they are vulnerable to storms and tidal waves. In June 1994 a tidal wave swept over the capital on Majuro Atoll.

On the outlying atolls a typical Pacific island subsistence economy survives, centered on agriculture and fishing. Small farms produce commercial crops such as coconuts, tomatoes, melons, and breadfruit, and a handful of cattle ranches supplies the domestic meat market. Industry consists of handicrafts, fish processing, and copra production, and the main exports are tuna, copra, and coconut oil products. About 10 percent of the population is employed in the tourist industry (visitors come from Japan and the USA), now the main source of foreign exchange. Imports are 11 times export rates, all fuel must be imported, and the country as a whole is heavily dependent on aid from the US plus income from the US leasing of Kwajalein Atoll for missile testing. With US grants due to be scaled back after 2001, every economic activity that can help the country stand on its own feet is being explored.

Official language English
Other languages Marshallese, Japanese
Literacy rate 93%
Religions Protestant 90%, Roman Catholic 9%, other 1%
Ethnic groups Micronesian 97%, other 3%
Currency US dollar
Economy Agriculture, fishing, tourism
GNP per capita Est. US$766–3,035
Climate Tropical, with wet season May to November
Highest point Unnamed location on Likiep 10 m (33 ft)
Map reference Pages 724–25

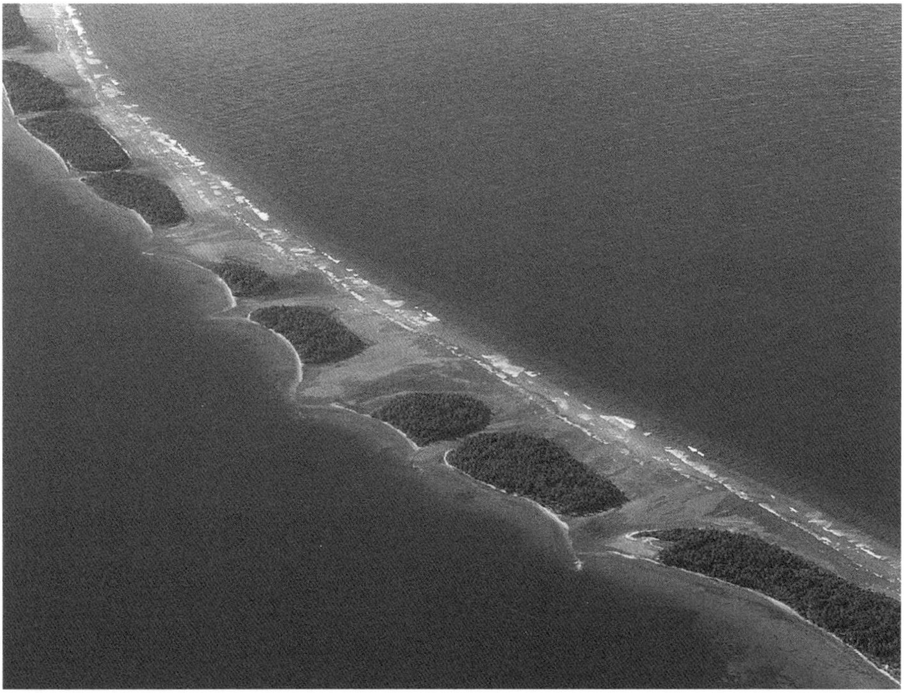

An aerial view of some of the Marshall Islands.

M

MARTINIQUE

OFFICIAL NAME Department of Martinique
FORM OF GOVERNMENT Overseas department of France
CAPITAL Fort-de-France
AREA 1,100 sq km (425 sq miles)
TIME ZONE GMT – 4 hours
POPULATION 411,539
LIFE EXPECTANCY 79.3
INFANT MORTALITY (PER 1,000) 6.8
LITERACY RATE 92.8%
CURRENCY French franc
ECONOMY Services 73%, industry 17%, agriculture 10%
CLIMATE Tropical, moderated by trade winds; wet season June to October
MAP REFERENCE Page 837

Martinique

Christopher Columbus described Martinique as "the most beautiful country in the world" when he laid eyes on it in 1493. This island in the eastern Caribbean was colonized by France in 1635 and has been French ever since. It consists of three groups of volcanic hills and the intervening lowlands, and is dominated by the dormant volcano Mt Pelée. Mt Pelée is famous for the eruption of 1902, when it killed all the inhabitants of the town of St-Pierre except one prisoner, who was saved by the thickness of his prison cell. The economy is based on sugarcane, bananas, tourism, and light industry, the export of bananas being of growing importance. Most sugarcane is used for making rum. The majority of the workforce is in the service sector and administration, tourism having become more important than agricultural exports as a source of foreign exchange.

The French Island of Martinique in the eastern Caribbean.

Mauritania

Most of Mauritania consists of the wastes of the western Sahara Desert. Islam in the region dates from the Almoravid Empire of the twelfth century. Later, it was conquered by Arab bidan or "white" Moors (Maure in French, meaning Moor), nomads who subjugated and enslaved the black Africans of the south, producing a people of mixed Arab and African descent known as harratin or "black" Moors. Deep social tensions between the dominant "white" Moors, the "black" Moors, and the subordinate 30 percent of black African farmers in the south lie at the heart of Mauritanian politics. Slavery in Mauritania was not officially abolished until 1970, and it is estimated that tens of thousands of harratin still live as slaves. France entered the region early in the nineteenth century and established a protectorate in 1903. Independence came in 1960.

Inland from the low-lying coastal plains of the Atlantic seaboard there are low plateaus—a tableland broken by occasional hills and scarps. The Saharan Desert to the north, which forms 47 percent of Mauritania's total land area, rises to the isolated peak of Kediet Ijill. In the southern third of the country there is just enough rain to support Sahelian thornbush and grasses. After rain, cattle herders drive their herds from the Senegal River through these grasslands, in good years the livestock outnumbering the general population five to one. During the 1980s the whole area suffered severely from drought and the nomadic population, which had numbered three-quarters of the national population, fell to less than one-third, many nomads abandoning rural life entirely for the towns.

Farmers near the Senegal River grow millet, sorghum, beans, peanuts, and rice, using the late-summer river floods for irrigation. A hydroelectric project on the river is intended to provide water for the irrigated cultivation of rice, cotton, and sugarcane, but drought has also driven many subsistence farmers from the land. Off the coast, cooled by the Canaries current, lie some of the richest fishing grounds in the world. Although about 100,000 tonnes of fish are landed annually, the potential catch is estimated at about 600,000 tonnes. Exploitation by foreign fishing boats threatens this source of revenue.

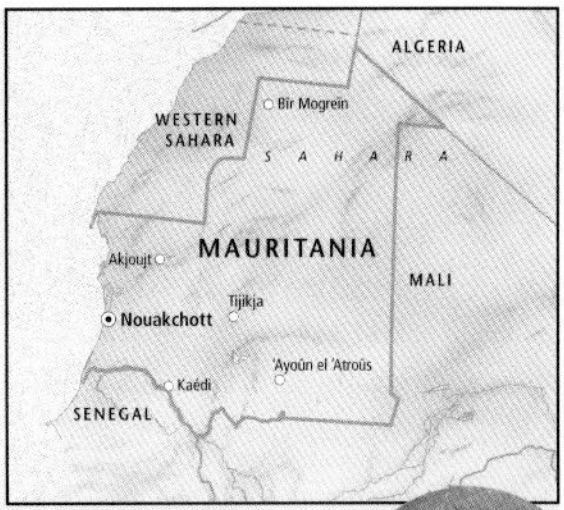

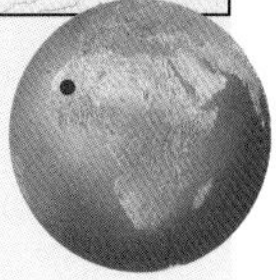

MAURITANIA

OFFICIAL NAME Islamic Republic of Mauritania
FORM OF GOVERNMENT Republic with two legislative bodies (Senate and National Assembly)
CAPITAL Nouakchott
AREA 1,030,700 sq km (397,953 sq miles)
TIME ZONE GMT
POPULATION 2,581,738
PROJECTED POPULATION 2005 3,088,823
POPULATION DENSITY 2.5 per sq km (6.5 per sq mile)
LIFE EXPECTANCY 50.5
INFANT MORTALITY (PER 1,000) 76.5
OFFICIAL LANGUAGES French, Hasaniya Arabic
OTHER LANGUAGES Indigenous languages, Arabic
LITERACY RATE 36.9%
RELIGIONS Muslim 99%, other 1%
ETHNIC GROUPS "Black" Moors 40%, "White" Moors 30%, African 30%
CURRENCY Ouguiya
ECONOMY Agriculture 70%, services 22%, industry 8%
GNP PER CAPITA US$460
CLIMATE Mainly arid, with wet season in far south (May to September)
HIGHEST POINT Kediet Ijill 915 m (3,002 ft)
MAP REFERENCE Pages 800, 804

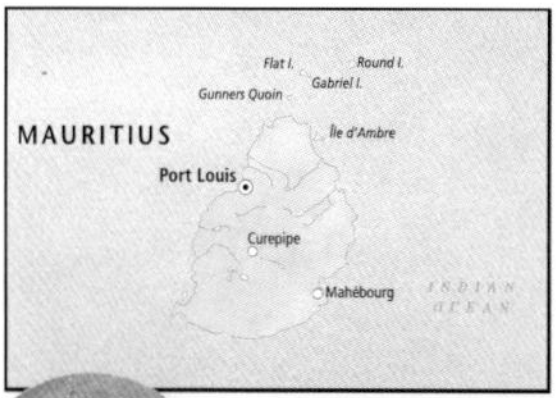

MAURITIUS

OFFICIAL NAME Republic of Mauritius
FORM OF GOVERNMENT Republic with single legislative body (Legislative Assembly)
CAPITAL Port Louis
AREA 1,860 sq km (718 sq miles)
TIME ZONE GMT + 4 hours
POPULATION 1,182,212
PROJECTED POPULATION 2005 1,265,011
POPULATION DENSITY 635.6 per sq km (1,646.2 per sq mile)
LIFE EXPECTANCY 71.1
INFANT MORTALITY (PER 1,000) 16.2
OFFICIAL LANGUAGE English
OTHER LANGUAGES Creole, French, Hindi, Urdu, Bojpoori, Hakka
LITERACY RATE 82.4%
RELIGIONS Hindu 52%, Roman Catholic 26%, Protestant 2.3%, Muslim 16.6%, other 3.1%
ETHNIC GROUPS Indo-Mauritian 68%, Creole 27%, Sino-Mauritian 3%, Franco-Mauritian 2%
CURRENCY Mauritian rupee
ECONOMY Services 51%, agriculture 27%, industry 22%
GNP PER CAPITA US$3,380
CLIMATE Tropical, moderated by trade winds
HIGHEST POINT Piton de la Petite Rivière Noire 828 m (2,717 ft)
MAP REFERENCE Pages 812, 813

Mauritius

Famous as the home of the now-extinct flightless bird, the dodo, the Republic of Mauritius consists of one large and several smaller islands 800 km (500 miles) east of Madagascar. Mauritius was uninhabited when visited by the Portuguese and the Dutch between the fifteenth and seventeenth centuries. It was first settled by the French, after 1715, who brought African slaves for the sugar plantations. In 1810 it was taken over by the British, who brought in numerous indentured laborers from India. These colonial origins produced two distinct communities, one Afro-French Creole (27 percent), the other English-speaking and Indian (73 percent), who compete for influence and power. Independence within the British Commonwealth was granted in 1968 and Mauritius became a republic in 1992. Despite occasional unrest, the country has a record of political stability and economic growth.

Fringed with coral reefs, the main island rises from coastal plains on its north and east to a plateau surrounded by rugged peaks—the remains of a giant volcano. Sugarcane is grown on 90 percent of the cultivated land, and accounts, with derivatives such as molasses, for 40 percent of export earnings. A by-product of the sugar industry, the cane-waste called bagasse, has been used to fuel power stations. Fast-flowing rivers descending from the plateau are used to produce hydroelectric power.

Industrial diversification (its textile and garment manufacture now accounts for 44 percent of export revenue) and the development of a tourist industry have enabled Mauritius to transcend the low income agricultural economy that existed at the time of independence.

Women agricultural workers walking beside a field of sugarcane.

Mayotte

Mayotte is a small island at the northern end of the Mozambique Channel, 34 km (21 miles) long, between Madagascar and the mainland. It is the easternmost of the four large islands of the Comoros group (a group first visited by European ships in the sixteenth century) and was the first to be ceded to France in 1841. When, in the 1974 referendum, the other islands chose to become the Republic of the Comoros, Mayotte decided to become a territorial collectivity of France. Volcanic in origin, Mayotte rises to 660 m (2,165 ft) at its highest point. The people are of African, Arab, and Madagascan descent. Agricultural products include coconuts, cocoa, and spices.

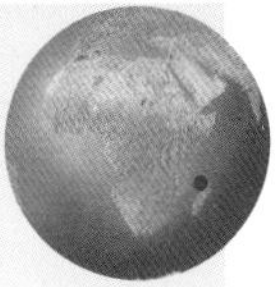

Mayotte

Official name Territorial Collectivity of Mayotte
Form of government Territorial collectivity of France
Capital Mamoudzou
Area 375 sq km (145 sq miles)
Time zone GMT + 3 hours
Population 112,863
Life expectancy 60
Infant mortality (per 1,000) 69.1
Currency French franc
Economy Mainly agriculture and fishing
Climate Tropical, with wet season November to May
Map reference Page 812

Melilla

Melilla is situated on the eastern coast of the Cap des Trois Fourches, a peninsula extending some 40 km (25 miles) into the Mediterranean Sea from the north coast of Morocco. Based on the site of an ancient city, which had been colonized by the Phoenicians and Romans, it fell to Spain in 1497. In 1912, the Sultan of Morocco signed a treaty with France making Morocco a French Protectorate. At the same time, the French, recognizing Spanish interests in the region, gave Spain several enclaves along the Moroccan coast. Two of these enclaves remain under the Spanish administration—Ceuta and Melilla.

In 1936 Melilla was the first Spanish state to rise in protest against the Popular Front government, an action which helped to precipitate the Spanish Civil War. When Morocco became independent in 1956, Spain retained Melilla as an enclave, and in 1995 the Spanish government approved statutes of autonomy for the city. It remains the site of a Spanish military base, and is the export point for iron ore from Morocco.

Melilla

Area 12 sq km (5 sq miles)
Population 58,000
Religions Roman Catholic 75%, Muslim 22%, other 3%
Map reference Page 796

Mexico

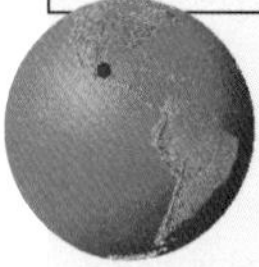

Mexico

Official name United Mexican States
Form of government Federal republic with two legislative chambers (Senate and Chamber of Deputies)
Capital Mexico City
Area 1,972,550 sq km (761,602 sq miles)
Time zone GMT – 6/8 hours
Population 100,294,036
Projected population 2005 110,573,561
Population density 50.8 per sq km (131.6 per sq mile)
Life expectancy 72
Infant mortality (per 1,000) 24.6
Official language Spanish
Other languages Indigenous languages
Literacy rate 89.2%
Religions Roman Catholic 93%, Protestant 4%, other 3%
Ethnic groups Mixed indigenous–European (mainly Spanish) 60%, indigenous 30%, European 9%, other 1%
Currency Mexican peso
Economy Services 57%, agriculture 23%, industry 20%
GNP per capita US$3,320
Climate Tropical in south and on coastal lowlands; cooler and drier in central plateau and mountains
Highest point Vol Citaltepetl (Pico de Orizaba) 5,700 m (18,701 ft)
Map reference Pages 840–41

The story of Mexico is the story of Central American civilization itself. For thousands of years people have lived in the central valley, and when the Spanish arrived under Cortés in 1519 the population of the Aztec Empire may have numbered 15 million. The pattern of settlement established by Spain in Mexico, with large estates worked by Indians, was followed in many other Central and South American countries. Although most Mexicans are Roman Catholics, the relation of Church and state has not always been easy, governments often viewing the Church's power as a challenge to their own. Mexico possesses major petroleum resources, is industrializing rapidly, and includes many traditional Indian cultures among its people, from the Tarahumara in the northwest to the Maya of Quintana Roo.

Physical features and land use

The northern and less-populated part of Mexico consists of the basin-and-range country of the Mesa Central. In this region desert scrub is the main plant cover, with grasses, shrubs, and succulents on higher ground. Cattle ranching is notable in this region. The land reaches heights of 2,400 m (7,900 ft) around Mexico City. South of the city three major peaks—Citlaltepetl, Popacatepetl, and Ixtaccihuatl—of the Sierra Volcanica Transversal reach elevations of around 5,500 m (18,000 ft). An active earthquake zone, this is the most densely settled part of the country.

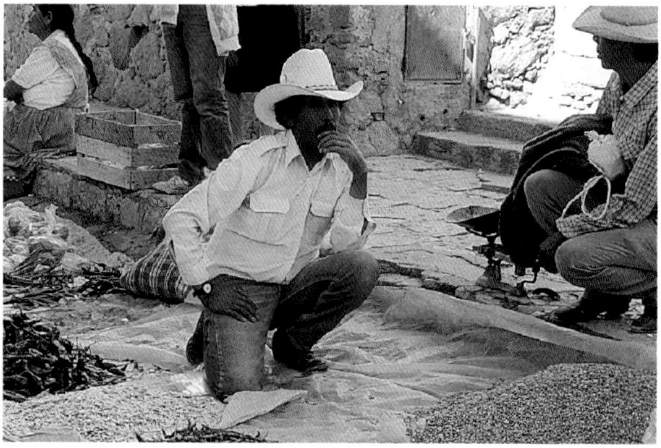

A market scene in Mexico.

East of the Mesa Central the land falls steeply from the Sierra Madre Oriental to a broad coastal plain on the Gulf of Mexico fringed with swamps, lagoons, and sandbars. Further south is the isthmus of Tehuantepec, a neck of rainforested land dividing the mountains of the Sierra del Sur from the highlands rising toward the Guatemalan border. The Yucatan Peninsula to the east is a limestone plain lying only a little above sea level, marked by natural wells and sinkholes. Petroleum discoveries in the 1970s in Tabasco and Campeche, in the northwest Yucatan, have made Mexico one of the world's biggest oil producers.

The Mesa Central ends just as abruptly on its western frontier, falling from the pine-forested heights of the Sierra Madre Occidental to a narrow coastal strip extending north to the Californian border. In the far northwest is the long narrow, dry, mountain-spined peninsula of Baja California.

The contrasts in altitude and latitude produce wide climatic variations, from the coasts, where temperatures are uniformly high, to the temperate land which prevails over much of the Mesa Central. Above 2,000 m (6,000 ft) lies what is known as the cold land, while on the higher slopes of the snow-capped volcanic cones is the frozen land where temperatures are usually below 10°C (50°F).

A woman washing radishes at the market.

M

The Mayan Pyramid of the Magician, Uxmal.

Children selling local art, Taxco, Guerrero.

Town of Taxco, Guerrero.

Avenue of the Dead, Teotihuacán, (religious centre of Toltec civilization.

M

People and culture

Most Mexicans are descendants of the Amerindian peoples who lived in the region at the time of the Spanish conquest, and of the Spanish colonists. The Aztecs were one of a number of developed cultures in the region. Their capital, Tenochtitlan, featured monumental architecture in the form of pyramids, and their society was strongly hierarchic, with slaves at the bottom and an emperor at the top. Art, sculpture, and poetry were advanced and they had a form of writing. Aztec religious practices involved the annual sacrifice (and eating) of large numbers of slaves, prisoners, and captives taken in war. The Maya in Yucatan were another major culture in the region but by the time the Spanish arrived the empire had already collapsed. Only their majestic stone monuments in the jungle remained, with settlements of corn-cultivating Mayan subsistence farmers nearby.

The Spanish brought Christianity and a system of large scale estates using poorly paid (or unpaid) Amerindian labor. Colonial control was exercised by a form of serfdom under which Amerindians paid either tribute or labor in return for conversion to Christianity. This system was abolished in 1829. In 1810 the independence struggle began, in 1822 Mexico declared itself a republic and in 1836 Spain formally recognized the country's independence. A century of political chaos climaxed with the violent Mexican Revolution of 1910 to 1921.

Since 1929 Mexico has been dominated by one party, the PRI, which has ruled until recently in a corporatist and authoritarian fashion. There is widespread dissatisfaction with the political process and with the unsolved 1994 murders of two high-profile reformers within the ruling party. A peasant revolt in Chiapas in 1994 dramatized the problem of rural poverty and the poor understanding of Mexico's urban élite of the world beyond the cities.

Traditional dancers perform at Pueblo, Mexico.

Micronesia

The Federated States of Micronesia consist of four states—Yap, Chuuk (Truk), Pohnpei, and Kosrae—made up of four island groups spread out across 3,200 km (2,000 miles) of ocean. Formerly known as the Caroline Islands, they are located in the northern Pacific about halfway between Australia and Japan. They are populated by Micronesian and Polynesian peoples divided into nine separate ethnic groups.

First settled around 1000 BC, the islands were visited by Spanish seafarers in 1565 and were annexed by Spain in 1874. In 1899 Spain sold them to Germany, and at the beginning of the First World War Japan took posession of them. After Japan's defeat in the Second World War, the USA took over the administration of the islands. US control ended in 1986 when the Federated States of Micronesia and the USA signed a 15-year Compact of Free Association. This granted internal self-government, the USA retaining responsibility for the country's defense.

During the course of the Second World War Chuuk was one of Japan's most important bases in the Pacific Ocean. Tourists now come to the island to scuba dive among the numerous wartime wrecks in the lagoon.

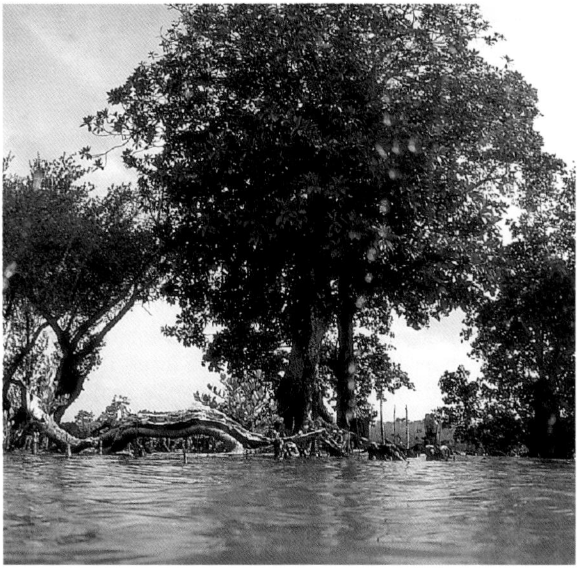

Mangroves in Micronesia.

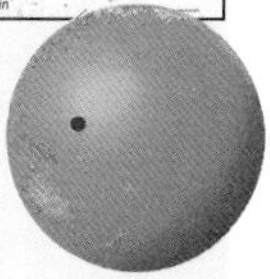

MICRONESIA

OFFICIAL NAME Federated States of Micronesia
FORM OF GOVERNMENT Federal Republic in free association with the USA; single legislative body (Congress)
CAPITAL Palikir
AREA 702 sq km (271 sq miles)
TIME ZONE GMT + 10 hours
POPULATION 131,500
PROJECTED POPULATION 2005 138,739
POPULATION DENSITY 187.3 per sq km (485.1 per sq mile)
LIFE EXPECTANCY 68.5
INFANT MORTALITY (PER 1,000) 34.0
OFFICIAL LANGUAGE English
OTHER LANGUAGES Micronesian languages
LITERACY RATE 90%
RELIGIONS Roman Catholic 50%, Protestant 47%, other and none 3%
ETHNIC GROUPS Micronesian and Polynesian
CURRENCY US dollar
ECONOMY Agriculture, fishing, services, textiles
GNP PER CAPITA Est. US$766–3,035
CLIMATE Tropical. Heavy rainfall year-round and occasional typhoons
HIGHEST POINT Totolom 791 m (2,595 ft)
MAP REFERENCE Page 724

The 607 widely scattered islands of Micronesia vary geologically from high and mountainous terrain to low coral atolls. Most of the islands are volcanic in origin, and the hot, rainy climate produces lush vegetation and tropical rainforest. Volcanic outcrops occur on Pohnpei, Kosrae, and Chuuk. Some of the atolls lack any surface water. Droughts occur frequently on Chuuk, often leading to water rationing. In 1992 emergency supplies of water had to be brought from Guam to Chuuk by the US Navy.

Subsistence fishing and farming occupies the majority of the population, with farmers growing tropical fruits and vegetables, coconuts, cassava (tapioca), sweet potatoes, and black pepper, and raising pigs and chickens. Fish, bananas, and black pepper are exported, and as a result of attempts at economic diversification a clothing industry has been developed.

Aside from deposits of high-grade phosphate the islands have few mineral resources. Imports exceed exports by a ratio of more than four to one, and the country as a whole depends heavily on financial aid from the USA. There is some potential for tourism—with their rich marine life the islands are a prime destination for scuba divers—but poor infrastructure and the country's remoteness hinder further development.

Midway Islands

MIDWAY ISLANDS

OFFICIAL NAME Midway Islands
FORM OF GOVERNMENT Unincorporated territory of the USA
CAPITAL None; administered from Washington DC
AREA 5.2 sq km (1.9 sq miles)
TIME ZONE GMT – 10 hours
POPULATION No permanent population
ECONOMY US military base
CLIMATE Tropical, moderated by sea breezes
MAP REFERENCE Page 725

The two Midway Islands constitute part of an atoll in the northern Pacific at the extreme western end of the Hawaiian chain, 1,931 km (1,200 miles) northwest of Hawaii. Their name derives from their position midway along the old shipping route from California to Japan.

The atoll is almost completely flat, and none of the land is higher than 4 m (13 ft) above sea level. During the Second World War it was the scene of a major battle between Japan and the USA, and today it is used as a naval airbase. It is also a wildlife refuge. The islands have no indigenous inhabitants and the population is confined to about 450 US military personnel and civilian contractors. They are serviced by the port of Sand Island, Johnston Atoll.

Moldova

Moldova is a small, landlocked country in southeastern Europe, near the northern shores of the Black Sea. To the west the Prut River separates Moldova from Romania. Otherwise, it is completely enclosed by Ukrainian territory. Bessarabia—the section between the Prut and Dniester rivers—which comprises almost all of present-day Moldova, was under Ottoman rule until 1812, when it passed to Russian control. With the collapse of the Russian Empire after the First World War, Bessarabia merged in 1918 with Romania, with which it is ethnically and linguistically almost identical. The part of Moldova east of the Dniester remained under Russian control. As a result of the Nazi–Soviet Pact of 1940 Romania was forced to cede Bessarabia. Most of it was combined with a narrow strip of the Ukraine east of the Dniester to form the new state of Moldova. The remaining parts were incorporated into Ukraine.

After the Second World War, Moldova became a Soviet republic and systematic attempts were made to suppress all links with Romania. Large numbers of ethnic Romanians were forcibly removed to other countries in the Soviet Union, and Russian and Ukrainian immigration was fostered. Independence came in 1991, as the Soviet Union crumbled, but tensions between the predominantly Russian population in the region lying to the east of the Dniester, who wished to declare a separate republic, and the ethnic Romanians, who sought closer ties, and even reunification with Romania, resulted in violent clashes. In 1992, a joint Russian–Moldovan peacekeeping force was instituted to help restore order, although ethnic tensions persist. In 1994 a constitution was adopted, defining the country as a democratic republic.

Most of the countryside of Moldova is low-lying but hilly steppe country. It is eroded by rivers and the landscape is cut by numerous deep valleys and gorges. Thick forests grow on many of the hillsides and most of the country is covered with thick, black, fertile soils. This fertile land, combined with a temperate climate, short winters and high summer rainfall, made Moldova one of the foremost producers of food in the former Soviet Union.

Agriculture remains the main element in the Moldovan economy. Vegetables, sunflower seeds, tobacco, wheat, and maize are the principal crops, as well as grapes, which contribute to a thriving winemaking industry.

MOLDOVA

OFFICIAL NAME Republic of Moldova
FORM OF GOVERNMENT Republic with single legislative body (Parliament)
CAPITAL Chisinau
AREA 33,700 sq km (13,012 sq miles)
TIME ZONE GMT + 3 hours
POPULATION 4,460,838
PROJECTED POPULATION 2005 4,522,745
POPULATION DENSITY 132.4 per sq km (342.9 per sq mile)
LIFE EXPECTANCY 64.4
INFANT MORTALITY (PER 1,000) 43.5
OFFICIAL LANGUAGE Moldovan
OTHER LANGUAGES Russian, Gagauz (Turkish dialect)
LITERACY RATE 98.9%
RELIGIONS Eastern Orthodox 98.5%, Jewish 1.5%
ETHNIC GROUPS Moldovan/Romanian 64.5%, Ukrainian 13.8%, Russian 13%, Gagauz 3.5%, Jewish 1.5%, Bulgarian 2%, other 1.7%
CURRENCY Leu
ECONOMY Services 46%, agriculture 34%, industry 20%
GNP PER CAPITA US$920
CLIMATE Temperate, with mild winters and warm summers
HIGHEST POINT Mt Balaneshty 430 m (1,411 ft)
MAP REFERENCE Page 780

M

The country has minimal reserves of mineral resources and depends upon Russian imports for all its oil, gas, and coal supplies. Electricity, too, is mainly imported and power shortages occur quite frequently. Industries include machine manufacturing and food processing.

Monaco

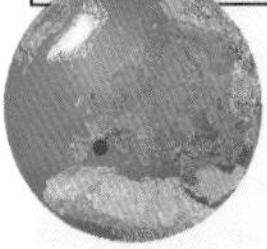

Monaco

Official name Principality of Monaco
Form of government Constitutional monarchy with single legislative body (National Council)
Capital Monaco
Area 1.9 sq km (0.7 sq miles)
Time zone GMT + 1 hour
Population 32,149
Projected population 2005 32,610
Population density 16,920.5 per sq km (43,824.1 per sq mile)
Life expectancy 78.6
Infant mortality (per 1,000) 6.5
Official language French
Other languages Italian, English, Monégasque
Literacy rate 99%
Religions Roman Catholic 95%, other 5%
Ethnic groups French 47%, Monégasque 16%, Italian 16%, other 21%
Currency French franc
Economy Tourism and services 90%, industry 10%
GNP per capita US$18,000
Climate Temperate, with mild, wet winters and hot, dry summers
Highest point Mt Agel 140 m (459 ft)
Map reference Page 775

Monaco, the world's smallest independent nation after the Vatican City, sits on the Mediterranean coast in the far southeast corner of France. Except for its coastline, it is completely surrounded by French territory. In the thirteenth century the Genoese built a fortress there and in 1297 members of the Grimaldi family of Genoa established themselves as rulers. Grimaldi princes retained control for almost 500 years, until 1792, when an uprising deposed the reigning prince and declared the state a republic. France annexed Monaco the following year, but in 1815, after the Congress of Vienna, it was placed under the protection of Sardinia. France annexed most of Monaco, including Menton, in 1848. In 1861, the Grimaldis were restored as rulers of less than half their former territory, governing under French protection. In 1911 democratic government was introduced by Prince Albert of Monaco. An 18-member National Council is elected every five years, but the head of government is selected by the monarch from a list drawn up by the French government. The present monarch, Prince Rainier

Monaco, looking out over the Mediterranean Sea.

III, is a descendant of the Grimaldis. He achieved fame in 1956 for his much-publicized marriage to the American film actress Grace Kelly.

Occupying the lower slopes of the Maritime Alps, Monaco is hilly and rugged. It is densely populated, mainly by foreign nationals. In the southwest is the industrial district of Fontvieille, which consists partly of land reclaimed from the sea. Further east is the old town of Monaco-Ville, where the royal palace is situated. La Condamine, the banking, commercial, and fashionable residential center, overlooks a sheltered harbor. Northeast of La Condamine is Monte Carlo, with its casino, luxury hotels, and apartment blocks.

Apart from pharmaceutical, food processing, and other light industries in Fontvieille, Monaco thrives on its attractions as a tourist haven. The major drawcard is the state-run casino, from which the citizens of Monaco are banned. Until 1962, Monaco's status as a tax haven attracted many wealthy French businesses. The people of Monaco still pay no income tax, but foreigners now do, though at quite favorable rates.

View of harbour, houses and hills behind Monaco.

Mongolia

The world's largest and most thinly populated landlocked country, Mongolia has a reputation for isolation. Its deserts, severe climate, and widely scattered population of nomadic pastoralists have tended to shut it off from modern life. Historically, however, it had its hour of glory. In the thirteenth century the Mongol tribes were united under Ghengis Khan (1162–1227), who then established the largest empire yet known, extending from eastern Europe to the Pacific and into northern India. The Mongol Empire collapsed in 1368, after which Mongolia (also known as Outer Mongolia to distinguish it from Inner Mongolia, one of China's Autonomous Regions) fell under Chinese control. Following the Russian Civil War (1918–22) the Chinese were expelled. Today, after 70 years within the Soviet system, the country is trying to remake itself in a more democratic mold.

Mongolia divides into two regions. In the northwest lie the Mongolian Altai Mountains (Mongol Altayn Nuruu), along with the Hangayn and Hentiyn Ranges. Here, high

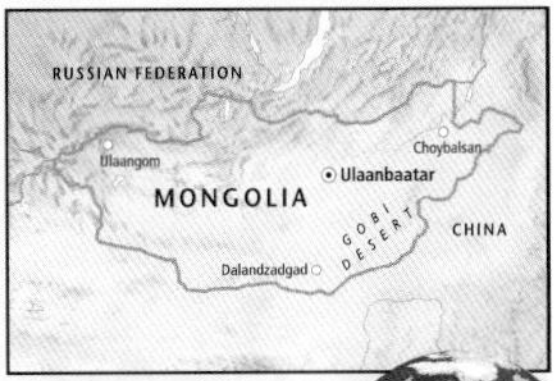

MONGOLIA

OFFICIAL NAME Mongolia
FORM OF GOVERNMENT Republic with single legislative body (State Great Hural)
CAPITAL Ulaanbaatar
AREA 1,565,000 sq km (604,247 sq miles)
TIME ZONE GMT + 8 hours
POPULATION 2,617,379
PROJECTED POPULATION 2005 2,834,466
POPULATION DENSITY 1.7 per sq km (4.4 per sq mile)

(continues)

MONGOLIA *(continued)*

LIFE EXPECTANCY 61.8
INFANT MORTALITY (PER 1,000) 64.6
OFFICIAL LANGUAGE Khalka Mongol
OTHER LANGUAGES Turkic, Russian, Chinese
LITERACY RATE 82.2%
RELIGIONS Predominantly Tibetan Buddhist with small Muslim minority
ETHNIC GROUPS Mongol 90%, Kazak 4%, Chinese 2%, Russian 2%, other 2%
CURRENCY Tugrik
ECONOMY Mainly agriculture with some industry
GNP PER CAPITA US$310
CLIMATE Cold and arid
HIGHEST POINT Tavan Bogd Uul 4,374 m (14,350 ft)
MAP REFERENCE Pages 784–85

mountains alternate with river valleys and lakes. Pastures support large herds of cattle and sheep, and wheat is cultivated. At the highest levels of the Altai in the northwest boreal forests cover the slopes. The second region is the southern half of the country. This is semidesert steppe changing further south to salt-pans, shallow depressions, and the arid stony wastes of the Gobi Desert.

While more people today live in towns than in the country, Mongolia remains a land of nomadic pastoralists. Herds of goats, sheep, yaks, camels, and horses still provide the base of the traditional economy, and Mongolia has the highest number of livestock per capita in the world. Cattle raising accounts for more than two-thirds of all production. Under the Soviets textiles and food processing were developed, and with aid from the USSR and Comecon mineral deposits such as copper, molybdenum, and coking coal were developed. Mongolia is the world's third biggest producer of fluorspar.

New laws have been passed regulating mining, banking, foreign investment, tourism, and economic planning. Mongolia continues to attract foreign aid, but suffers from the loss of Russian financial support. So far, foreign funds have not been found for the development of Mongolia's considerable oil and gas reserves.

A Mongolian musician playing a horsehair fiddle.

MONTSERRAT

OFFICIAL NAME Montserrat
FORM OF GOVERNMENT Dependent territory of the United Kingdom
CAPITAL Plymouth
AREA 100 sq km (39 sq miles)
TIME ZONE GMT – 4 hours
POPULATION 4,000 (after volcanic eruption led to evacuation; formerly 12,853)
LIFE EXPECTANCY 75.6
INFANT MORTALITY (PER 1,000) 12
CURRENCY EC dollar
ECONOMY Tourism, industry, agriculture
CLIMATE Tropical
MAP REFERENCE Page 837

Montserrat

Montserrat is a Caribbean island with seven active volcanoes. In 1995 deep ash from one of them destroyed numerous crops and forced the evacuation of the capital, Plymouth. Montserrat was colonized in 1632 by the British, who at first brought in Irish settlers. (Together with its lush green foliage, this is why it is locally known as "the Emerald Isle.") Later, the island's sugar plantations were worked by African slaves. It has been a self-governing UK dependent territory since 1960. Tourism provides a quarter of the national income, other support coming from the export of electronic components which are assembled on the island, plastic bags, clothing, rum, hot peppers, live plants, and cattle. Data processing facilities and offshore banking are available.

Mud and lava from the 1995 volcanic eruption on Montserrat.

Morocco

Morocco's earliest inhabitants were the Berbers, who still live in the country today. At one time under Carthaginian rule, and then a part of the Roman Empire, the Berbers were overrun by Arabs in the seventh century AD and converted to Islam. The country's name derives from the Arabic Maghreb-el-aksa ("the farthest west"), and because of the protective barrier of the Atlas Mountains, Morocco has always been less a part of the Arab world than the other north African states. Under political pressure from Spain and France during the nineteenth century, Morocco became a French protectorate in 1912. About 35 percent of the people live in the highlands and are Berber-speaking, while the Arab majority live in the lowlands.

Under the rule of King Hassan II since 1961, Morocco has followed generally pro-Western policies. The king's popularity at home owes a good deal to Morocco's disputed territorial claim to the phosphate-rich resources of Western Sahara across the southern border. A costly armed struggle with the Polisario Front guerrilla movement of Western Sahara led to a cease-fire in 1991, by which time 170,000 of the native-born Sahrawis of the region had become refugees in Algeria. Sovereignty is still unresolved.

More than one-third of Morocco is mountainous. Three parallel ranges of the Atlas Mountains run southwest to

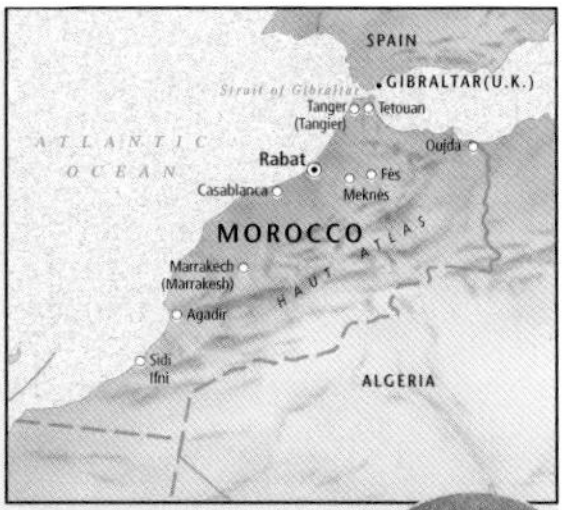

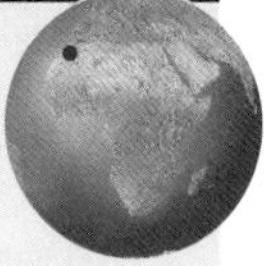

Morocco

Official name Kingdom of Morocco
Form of government Constitutional monarchy with single legislative body (Chamber of Representatives)
Capital Rabat
Area 446,550 sq km (172,413 sq miles)
Time zone GMT + 1 hour
Population 29,661,636
Projected population 2005 32,923,967
Population density 66.4 per sq km (172 per sq mile)
Life expectancy 68.9

(continues)

MOROCCO *(continued)*

INFANT MORTALITY (PER 1,000) 11.0
OFFICIAL LANGUAGE Arabic
OTHER LANGUAGES Berber languages, French
LITERACY RATE 42.1%
RELIGIONS Muslim 98.7%, Christian 1.1%, Jewish 0.2%
ETHNIC GROUPS Arab–Berber 99.1%, other 0.7%, Jewish 0.2%
CURRENCY Moroccan dirham
ECONOMY Agriculture 46%, services 30%, industry 24%
GNP PER CAPITA US$1,110
CLIMATE Temperate along northern coast, arid in south, cooler in mountains
HIGHEST POINT Jebel Toubkal 4,165 m (13,665 ft)
MAP REFERENCE Pages 800–01

northeast, where a plateau reaches toward the Algerian border. Most of the people living in the mountains are peasant cultivators and nomadic herders. Modern economic development is found mainly on the Atlantic plains and the plateaus—the fertile Moulouyan, Rharb, Sous, and High (Haut) Atlas plains constituting virtually all of Morocco's cultivable land. In the Rharb and Rif regions extensive areas are covered with cork oak, while on the northern slopes there are forests of evergreen oak and cedar. Wildlife includes Cuvier's gazelle, the Barbary macaque, and the mouflon (a wild sheep), while desert animals such as the fennec fox live in the south.

In 1995 Morocco suffered its worst drought in 30 years. This seriously affected agriculture, which produces about one-third of Morocco's exports and employs about half the workforce. Irrigation is essential over most of the country, the chief crops being barley and wheat, along with citrus fruit, potatoes, and other vegetables. Dates are grown in desert oases. The country's natural resources are still largely undeveloped. It has coal, iron ore, and zinc, along with the world's largest reserves of phosphates. Debt servicing, unemployment, the high rate of population increase, and the unresolved territorial claim to Western Sahara are all long-term problems.

M

A gold seller in Morocco.

The Medina in Fès.

Mozambique

Lying on the southeast coast of Africa facing Madagascar, Mozambique is divided in two by the Zambeze River. This division is also found in its social and political life: people in the north support the Renamo party, while south of the river they support Frelimo. Visited by Vasco da Gama in 1498 and colonized by Portuguese in search of gold, Mozambique remained a slave-trading center until the 1850s.

A long war of liberation against Portugal led to independence in 1975 and brought the Marxist Frelimo to power. Frelimo's one-party regime was then challenged by a guerrilla movement, Renamo, supported by South Africa. The ensuing civil war, aggravated by famine, led to nearly 1 million deaths. By 1989 Mozambique was the world's poorest country. That year Frelimo renounced Marxism. At multi-party elections in 1994 it won by a narrow majority.

A considerable amount of rain falls in the north: south of the Zambeze conditions are much drier. North of Maputo, the only natural harbor, is a wide coastal plain where there are coconut, sugar, and sisal plantations, and smallholders grow maize and peanuts. Inland, the terrain rises to the high veld.

Economically, Mozambique faces a huge task of reconstruction and the government is trying to redistribute to peasants large areas of land that were seized by the state. Agricultural output is only 75 percent of its 1981 level and grain is imported. Industry is operating at less than half capacity. There are substantial agricultural, hydropower and petroleum resources, and deposits of coal, copper and bauxite but these are largely undeveloped. Mozambique suffered a major humanitarian disaster in the summer of 2000, when floods devastated much of the country, destroying homes and crops. The international community sent aid in the form of air rescue vehicles and food, but the economic impact was severe and longlasting.

Cheetah stalking prey to feed her young cubs, Phinda Game Reserve.

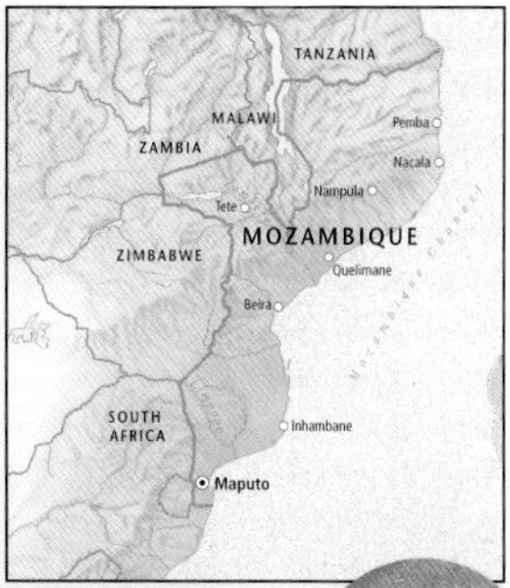

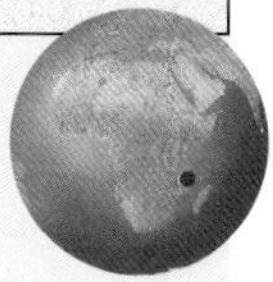

MOZAMBIQUE

OFFICIAL NAME Republic of Mozambique
FORM OF GOVERNMENT Republic with single legislative body (Assembly of the Republic)
CAPITAL Maputo
AREA 801,590 sq km (309,494 sq miles)
TIME ZONE GMT + 2 hours
POPULATION 19,124,335
PROJECTED POPULATION 2005 22,155,576
POPULATION DENSITY 23.9 per sq km (61.8 per sq mile)
LIFE EXPECTANCY 45.9
INFANT MORTALITY (PER 1,000) 117.6
OFFICIAL LANGUAGE Portuguese
OTHER LANGUAGES Indigenous languages
LITERACY RATE 39.5%
RELIGIONS Indigenous beliefs 55%, Christian 30%, Muslim 15%
ETHNIC GROUPS Indigenous tribes (including Shangaan, Chokwe, Manyika, Sena, Makua) 99.7%, other 0.3%
CURRENCY Metical
ECONOMY Agriculture 85%, services 8%, industry 7%
GNP PER CAPITA US$80
CLIMATE Mainly tropical: wet season December to March
HIGHEST POINT Monte Binga 2,436 m (7,992 ft)
MAP REFERENCE Pages 809, 811

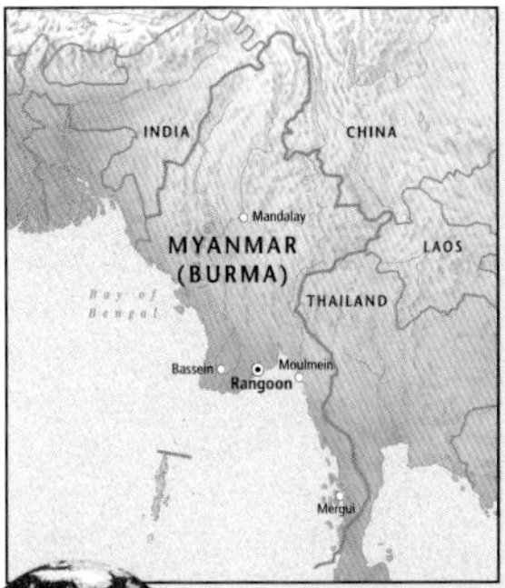

Myanmar

Official name Union of Myanmar (Burma)
Form of government Military regime; legislative body (People's Assembly) never convened since military takeover in 1988
Capital Yangon (Rangoon)
Area 678,500 sq km (261,969 sq miles)
Time zone GMT + 6.5 hours
Population 48,081,302
Projected population 2005 52,697,795
Population density 70.9 per sq km (183.6 per sq mile)
Life expectancy 54.7
Infant mortality (per 1,000) 76.3
Official language Burmese
Other languages Indigenous languages, English
Literacy rate 82.7%
Religions Buddhist 89%, Christian 4% (Baptist 3%, Roman Catholic 1%), Muslim 4%, other 3%
Ethnic groups Burman 68%, Shan 9%, Karen 7%, Rakhine 4%, Chinese 3%, Mon 2%, other 7%
Currency Kyat
Economy Agriculture 64%, services 27%, industry 9%
GNP per capita Est. < US$765
Climate Tropical monsoon; dry zone around Mandalay; moderate temperature on Shan Plateau
Highest point Hkakabo Razi 5,881 m (19,294 ft)
Map reference Pages 738, 741

M

Myanmar

Better known for the name of its Nobel Prize winning opposition leader Aung San Suu Kyi than for that of its prime minister, Myanmar is struggling to overcome 50 years of ethnic strife, one-party socialist government, and military rule. With an ancient literary tradition and style of script going back to the Mon civilization (third century BC), Myanmar was at various times ruled by the eleventh century Tibeto-Burman Dynasty of Anarutha the Great, by the Mongols under Khublai Khan (1287), and by the British, who incorporated the country into its Indian Empire in 1886.

After the country won independence in 1948, General Ne Win's Burmese Socialist Program Party abolished all private enterprise and private trade, nationalized industry, and placed the country under military control. Soon one of the region's richest countries had become an impoverished backwater. For decades, much of the government's energy and 35 percent of its budget has gone into trying to suppress ethnic insurgent movements led by Karens, Shans, Kachins, Mons, and others. To fund their resistance these groups grew opium poppies, a traditional crop, which has led to the country becoming the world's largest opium producer.

On the Bay of Bengal between Bangladesh and Thailand, Myanmar consists of central lowlands, where 75 percent of the people live, enclosed by mountains to the north, bordering China, and west, bordering India, and

Sunset over the Irrawaddy River and Buddhist temple ruins at Pagan.

the Shan Plateau to the east forming a frontier with Laos. The western mountains run southwest along the Indian border and form a series of forested ridges, ending in the Arakan Yoma Range (Pegu Yoma). From the mountains in the north the Irawaddy River flows south 2,100 km (1,300 miles), passing the old city of Mandalay and the capital of Yangon (Rangoon) on its way to the Andaman Sea. While the coast has a wet climate, the inner region, sheltered from the monsoon, has an annual rainfall of less than 1,000 mm (40 in). Here, in narrow valleys, small-scale irrigation supports such crops as rice, sugarcane, cotton, and jute.

Myanmar is rich in natural resources, having fertile soils and good fisheries, along with teak, gems, and natural gas and oil. Recently there has been some liberalization of the economy, notably of small scale enterprise. Twenty-five percent, however, remains under state control, the key industries—in energy, heavy industry, and foreign trade—being 20 military-run enterprises. A recent boom in trade with China has filled the north with Chinese goods and visitors. Economic weaknesses include a shortage of skilled labor, and of trained managers and technicians. Price controls mean that the economy is permeated by the black market. Published estimates of Myanmar's foreign trade are therefore greatly understated.

Fisherman on Inle Lake, a picturesque freshwater lake southeast of Mandalay.

The gold spire of Myanmar's most sacred temple, Shwe Dagon Pagoda, dominates the city of Rangoon.

N

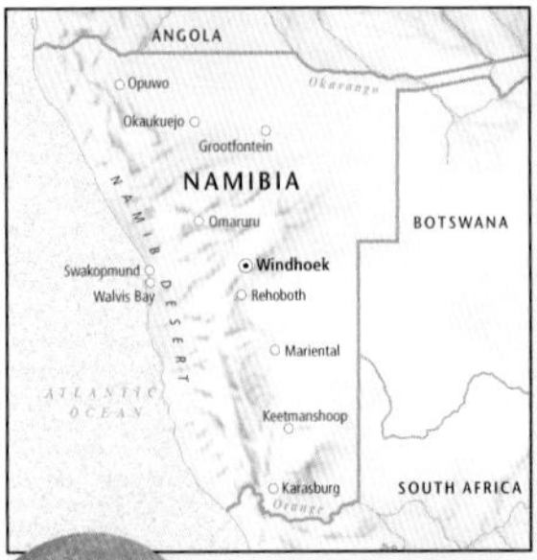

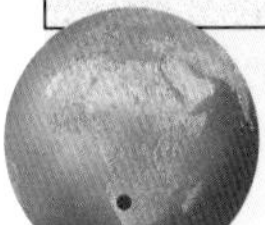

NAMIBIA

OFFICIAL NAME Republic of Namibia
FORM OF GOVERNMENT Republic with two legislative bodies (National Council and National Assembly)
CAPITAL Windhoek
AREA 825,418 sq km (318,694 sq miles)
TIME ZONE GMT + 2 hours
POPULATION 1,648,270
PROJECTED POPULATION 2005 1,798,625
POPULATION DENSITY 2 per sq km (5.2 per sq mile)
LIFE EXPECTANCY 41.3
INFANT MORTALITY (PER 1,000) 65.9
OFFICIAL LANGUAGE English
OTHER LANGUAGES Afrikaans, German, indigenous languages
LITERACY RATE 40%
RELIGIONS Christian 85% (Lutheran at least 50%, other Christian denominations 35%), indigenous beliefs 15%
ETHNIC GROUPS Indigenous tribes 86% (including Ovambo 50%, Kavangos 9%, Herero 7%, Damara 7%), mixed indigenous–European 7.4%, European 6.6%
CURRENCY Namibian dollar
ECONOMY Agriculture 60%, industry and commerce 19%, services 8%, government 7%, mining 6%
GNP PER CAPITA US$2,000
CLIMATE Mainly arid, with higher rainfall inland
HIGHEST POINT Brandberg 2,573 m (8,439 ft)
MAP REFERENCE Page 810

Namibia

A large, arid country in southwest Africa, Namibia was born of the European scramble for colonies in the nineteenth century. The German connection with the area (formerly South West Africa) began with the arrival of missionaries in the 1840s. Namibia was a German protectorate from 1884; the scene of a brutal German punitive action in 1904 in which the Herero were decimated and scattered; under South African control for many years; and endured 23 years of a bitter anti-colonial war that began in 1966. In 1989 an election gave the guerrilla movement SWAPO (the South West African People's Organization) victory at the polls, and in 1990 came independence.

The virtually uninhabited sand dunes of the Namib Desert fringe the country's south Atlantic coastline. A major escarpment inland separates the desert from a north–south range of mountains which includes the Tsaris Mountains, Aûas Mountains, and Mt Erongo. The interior plateau, which occupies the eastern part of the country, has an average elevation of 1,500 m (5,000 ft) and is covered with the dry scrub grassland typical of the Kalahari Desert. Largely rainless, the coast is often shrouded in fog. Here, welwitschia plants, some of them up to 2,000 years old, live by absorbing moisture from the fog that rolls in from the sea. Namibia's wildlife is typical of southern Africa, with Etosha National Park providing sanctuary for baboon, antelope, elephant, giraffe, zebra, and lion.

Namibia's natural resources include diamonds, copper, uranium (world's fifth largest producer), gold, lead

Sand storm in Sossus Vlei Naykluft National Park.

(world's second largest producer), tin, lithium, cadmium, zinc, vanadium, and natural gas, and there are thought to be deposits of oil, coal, and iron ore. Mining accounts for 25 percent of gross domestic product, this sector relying on the expertise of Namibia's small white population. More than half its African peoples depend on agriculture for a livelihood, working poor soils in an unfavorable climate. Livestock farmers produce beef and mutton. About half the country's food is imported, mainly from South Africa.

Nauru

Nauru is a tiny island in the Pacific 3,000 km (2,000 miles) northeast of Australia. It is the world's smallest republic and, because of the wealth of its phosphate deposits, Nauruans enjoy one of the highest per capita incomes in the Third World. This situation is coming to an end, however. By the year 2006 the phosphate is expected to run out, and it is not clear what the people will do then.

Although little is known of the original Polynesian inhabitants of the island, it was first visited by Europeans when a British ship stopped there in 1798. Clan warfare among the Polynesians became widespread in the 1870s, leading the Germans (who then controlled the Marshall Islands, and whose traders were active on Nauru) to incorporate it into their administration in 1888. Phosphate mining by both a German and a British company began in 1906. After the First World War the administration of Nauru passed to Australia and independence was granted in 1968. In 1970 Australia, New Zealand, and Great Britain relinquished their joint control of the phosphate industry to a Nauruan governmental agency, the Nauru Phosphate Corporation.

The island is a 20 sq km (8 sq mile) raised coral reef with a central plateau. This plateau consists of phosphate beds created by seabird droppings over many centuries. It is encircled by a fertile belt of semicultivated land where most of the people live. A ring road forms a continuous strip settlement around the coastal perimeter, where houses and other buildings occupy the only habitable land. After more than 90 years of phosphate mining, much of the rest of the island—in effect a largely worked-out quarry—has an aspect of lunar desolation. The climate is hot and humid, but because clouds sometimes miss the island, years can

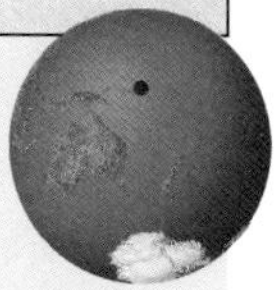

Nauru

Official name Republic of Nauru
Form of government Republic with single legislative body (Parliament)
Capital None; government offices in Yaren
Area 21 sq km (8.1 sq miles)
Time zone GMT + 12 hours
Population 10,605
Projected population 2005 11,118
Population density 505 per sq km (1,307.9 per sq mile)
Official language Nauruan
Other language English
Literacy rate 99%
Religions Protestant 66.7%, Roman Catholic 33.3%
Ethnic groups Nauruan 58%, other Pacific Islander 26%, Chinese 8%, European 8%
Currency Australian dollar
Economy Phosphate mining, financial services, coconut production
GNP per capita US$8,100
Climate Tropical, with wet season November to February
Highest point Unnamed location 61 m (200 ft)
Map reference Pages 724–25

pass without rainfall. What little vegetation there is consists of coconut palms, breadfruit trees, and scrub.

Phosphate is the country's only resource. About 80 percent of the island is now uninhabitable and uncultivable, and food, fuel, manufactured goods, building materials, and machinery are all imported. The diet of processed foods has led to widespread obesity, and one-third of the people suffer from non-insulin-dependent diabetes. Although many Nauruans live in traditional houses, they tend to spend their considerable incomes on luxury cars and electrical goods. Much phosphate income has been invested in trust funds to serve long-term needs, but not all the investments have been wise and since 1990 dividends have fallen sharply.

Navassa Island

NAVASSA ISLAND

OFFICIAL NAME Navassa Island
FORM OF GOVERNMENT Unincorporated territory of the United States
CAPITAL None
AREA 5.2 sq km (2 sq miles)
TIME ZONE GMT – 5 hours
POPULATION No permanent population
CLIMATE Tropical, moderated by sea breezes
MAP REFERENCE Page 839

Navassa Island is an uninhabited rocky outcrop in the Caribbean halfway between Cuba and Haiti. It is strategically located for the USA, since it is only 160 km (100 miles) south of the Guantanamo Bay (Bahía de Guantánamo) naval base. The island is administered by the US Coast Guard. The surface is mostly exposed rock but it has dense stands of fig-like trees, cacti, and enough grass to support herds of goats. Its principal resource is guano.

Nepal

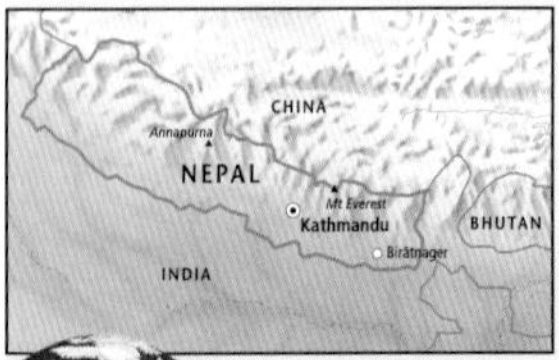

NEPAL

OFFICIAL NAME Kingdom of Nepal

The birthplace of the Buddha c. 568 BC, Nepal is a small landlocked kingdom on the southern slopes of the Himalayas. It is surrounded by India to the west, south, and east, and has a border with China (Tibet) to the north. Tourists coming to trek in the mountains and climb the peaks contribute to national income, but Nepal remains one of the world's poorest countries. Historically, it was influenced both by the Buddhist/Mongol culture of Tibet and by the Hindu/Indian culture of the subcontinent. The present royal family established its rule in 1769. During British colonial rule in India a British resident was installed to provide "guidance" in foreign affairs. In 1959 the country's first elections were held (the Nepali Congress party winning), but in 1960 the king suspended the constitution, and no further elections were held until 1992. In the late 1990s a parliamentary impasse existed: neither the Nepali Congress nor the United Marxist-Leninist (UML) parties had clear majorities enabling them to govern in their own right.

The mountainous heart of Nepal, consisting of the towering Himalayas (including the highest and third-highest peaks in the world, Mt Everest and Kanchenjunga) and the lower Siwalik Range to the south, forms three-quarters of the country. Three main river systems cut the Himalayas, the Karnali (feeding the Ganges), the Gandak, and the Kosi. Kathmandu stands among fruit trees and rice fields typical of Nepal's densely populated uplands. Further south, on the Terai/Ganges Plain, farming settlements grow rice, wheat, maize, sugarcane, and jute which are the country's economic maintstay.

Some 90 percent of Nepalis live by subsistence farming, and many do not live well: more than 40 percent of Nepal's citizens are undernourished. Most industry is concerned with the processing of jute, sugarcane, tobacco, and grain. Recently textile and carpet production has expanded and now provides 85 percent of foreign exchange earnings. The country has limitless hydropower resources. Electricity could be sold to Indian industry south of the border, and various schemes have been proposed, but the environmental considerations weigh against them. Restructuring is needed. International aid funds 62 percent of Nepal's development budget and 34 percent of total budgetary expenditure.

Mt Everest and surrounding peaks in Nepal.

FORM OF GOVERNMENT Constitutional monarchy with two legislative bodies (National Council and House of Representatives)
CAPITAL Kathmandu
AREA 140,800 sq km (54,363 sq miles)
TIME ZONE GMT + 5.5 hours
POPULATION 24,302,653
PROJECTED POPULATION 2005 28,172,635
POPULATION DENSITY 172.6 per sq km (447 per sq mile)
LIFE EXPECTANCY 58.4
INFANT MORTALITY (PER 1,000) 73.6
OFFICIAL LANGUAGE Nepali
OTHER LANGUAGES Indigenous languages
LITERACY RATE 27%
RELIGIONS Hindu 90%, Buddhist 5%, Muslim 3%, other 2%
ETHNIC GROUPS Newar, Indian, Tibetan, Gurung and many smaller minorities
CURRENCY Nepalese rupee
ECONOMY Agriculture 93%, services 6%, industry 1%
GNP PER CAPITA US$200
CLIMATE Subtropical in south, with wet season July to October; cold and snowy in north, wetter in east
HIGHEST POINT Mt Everest 8,848 m (29,028 ft)
MAP REFERENCE Pages 754–55

N

Orange house and countryside, Pokhara, Nepal.

NETHERLANDS

OFFICIAL NAME Kingdom of the Netherlands
FORM OF GOVERNMENT Constitutional monarchy with two legislative bodies (First Chamber and Second Chamber)
CAPITAL Amsterdam; The Hague is the seat of government
AREA 37,330 sq km (14,413 sq miles)
TIME ZONE GMT + 1 hour
POPULATION 15,807,641
PROJECTED POPULATION 2005 16,143,653
POPULATION DENSITY 423.5 per sq km (1,096.8 per sq mile)
LIFE EXPECTANCY 78.2
INFANT MORTALITY (PER 1,000) 5.1
OFFICIAL LANGUAGE Dutch
OTHER LANGUAGES Arabic, Turkish, English
LITERACY RATE 99%
RELIGIONS Roman Catholic 34%, Protestant 25%, Muslim 3%, other 2%, unaffiliated 36%
ETHNIC GROUPS Dutch 96%; Moroccan, Turkish, and other 4%
CURRENCY Netherlands guilder
ECONOMY Services 79%, industry 17%, agriculture 4%
GNP PER CAPITA US$24,000
CLIMATE Temperate, with cool winters and mild summers
HIGHEST POINT Mt Vaalserberg 321 m (1,053 ft)
MAP REFERENCE Page 772

OVERSEAS TERRITORIES

Aruba • Netherlands Antilles

Netherlands

Situated in northwestern Europe, with a western and northern coastline on the North Sea, the Netherlands is bordered by Germany to its east and Belgium to its south. About half the area of this low-lying nation is below sea level and the country is saved from inundation only by a series of coastal dikes and sand dunes, heavily planted with marram grass to prevent erosion, and a complex network of canals and waterways, into which excess water is pumped from low-lying areas and then carried to the rivers that flow to the coast. For centuries the Dutch have been engaged in battle with the sea, and have gradually reclaimed huge amounts of land from it. In the last century more than 3,000 sq km (1,000 sq miles) of land were added. The most spectacular reclamation was the Zuiderzee project that began in 1920 and was completed almost 50 years later.

In the first century BC the Germanic peoples of the Low Countries, which include present-day Belgium and Luxembourg, were colonized by Roman armies. From the fifth century AD the region came under the successive control of Frankish, Burgundian, Austrian, and finally, in the fifteenth century, Spanish rulers. In 1568, William of Orange, outraged by Spain's suppression of a spreading Protestant movement, led a revolt. In 1581 the seven northern provinces of the Low Countries declared their independence as the United Provinces of the Netherlands.

This set the scene for the consolidation and expansion of Dutch power throughout the seventeenth century. Trading posts and colonies were established in the East Indies (now Indonesia), the Caribbean (the Antilles), Africa, and South and North America. This period also saw the emergence of the Netherlands as a great maritime nation and a blossoming of Dutch art, literature, and scientific achievements.

The French, under Napoleon, invaded in 1794. After the defeat of France, the Congress of Vienna united the Netherlands, Belgium, and Luxembourg under a Dutch monarch in 1814. Belgium declared itself independent in 1831 and Luxembourg was granted autonomy in 1848. In 1848 a new constitution was introduced reducing the power of the monarch and investing greater authority in the Estates-General, as the parliament is still called. This laid the groundwork for the later emergence of a parliamentary democracy under a monarch with strictly formalized and limited powers.

The Netherlands remained neutral in the First World War and its neutrality was respected by both sides. In the Second World War it was overrun by Nazi forces in 1940. Its East Indies colonies were invaded by Japan. At the end of the war, the Netherlands began an armed conflict with rebel forces in its East Indies colony. It finally granted them independence, as the Republic of Indonesia, in 1949. Suriname, in South America, became independent in 1975, leaving the Antilles and Aruba as the Netherlands' only overseas territories.

After the Second World War the Netherlands joined the NATO alliance and became a founder member of the European Economic Community, later the European Union. In 1992 the Treaty on European Union, the Maastricht Treaty, was signed in the southern Dutch city of Maastricht.

Village street scene in Mersfoort, Holland.

Physical features and land use

Almost all of the Netherlands is flat and much of the landscape is covered by small farming plots, intensively cultivated and surrounded by ditches or canals. Dotting the landscape are windmills which for centuries have been used to drain the land. These are now largely picturesque as they have been supplanted by motor pumps. Much of this land is dedicated to horticulture, especially the growing of tulips and other bulb plants, often in tandem with vegetable produce.

Cattle farming and dairying, the country's main forms of agriculture, are strongest in the northwest, in the provinces of Nord Holland and Friesland, on either side of

Houses and houseboats along one of Amsterdam's canals.

One of the beautiful canals in Amsterdam, Holland.

the Ijsselmeer, the area of the Zuiderzee project. The Ijsselmeer is an expanse of fresh water, separated by a dike, 32 km (20 miles) long, from the salt water of the Waddenzee. This lies between the northwest coast and a succession of accumulations of sand, which are known as the West Frisian Islands.

Further south, near the coast, is a succession of densely populated urban areas that include Amsterdam and the other major Dutch cities, including Rotterdam, one of the world's largest ports. Just south of this urban conglomeration, the major rivers that flow into the Netherlands—among them the Rhine from Germany and the Schelde and the Meuse from Belgium—share a common delta area. The only relief from flat land is in the far southeast, where a range of hills rises in places to about 100 m (300 ft).

Industry and commerce

Concentrated in the heavily populated urban southwest, manufacturing industry employs about one in five members of the workforce. Food processing, chemical and electrical machinery manufacture, metal and engineering products, and petroleum refining are major industries. Natural gas is the country's principal natural resource, and there are extensive reserves in the north.

Most Dutch people enjoy an affluent lifestyle, although some groups of immigrants on the fringes of the cities live in conspicuous poverty. Social services are well developed and the country has one of the best state-funded health-care systems in the world.

Netherlands Antilles

NETHERLANDS ANTILLES

OFFICIAL NAME Netherlands Antilles
FORM OF GOVERNMENT Self-governing part of the Kingdom of the Netherlands
CAPITAL Willemstad
AREA 960 sq km (371 sq miles)
TIME ZONE GMT – 4 hours
POPULATION 215,139

The Netherlands Antilles consist of two very different island groups in two parts of the Caribbean. Curaçao and Bonaire are located off the coast of Venezuela, and while they may once have made money from the well-known orange liqueur, today 98 percent of their income comes from petroleum—either processed for products or for transshipment facilities. The other group, which lies east of the Virgin Islands, consists of the three islands of Saba, St Eustasius, and part of St Maarten. The people are largely of African and European descent, the original inhabitants having been killed in the sixteenth century by Spanish settlers. All told, the islands have a high per capita income and a well-developed infrastructure in comparison with others in the region. Nearly all consumer and capital goods are imported from the USA and Venezuela. Crops grown include aloes, sorghum, peanuts, vegetables, and tropical fruit, but poor soils and limited water make agriculture difficult.

Life expectancy 77.4
Infant mortality (per 1,000) 8.5
Currency Netherlands Antillean guilder
Economy Tourism, offshore finance
Climate Tropical, moderated by trade winds
Map reference Page 837

New Caledonia

New Caledonia is a group of islands 1,500 km (900 miles) off the northeast coast of Australia. Rich in minerals, and with more than 40 percent of the world's known nickel resources, it is France's largest overseas territory. First populated by indigenous Kanaks (who call the land Kanaky) around 4000 BC, the islands were visited by the Spanish in the sixteenth and seventeenth centuries, were named by Captain James Cook in 1774, and were used as a penal settlement by France between 1853 and 1897. By the end of the nineteenth century French settlers owned more than 90 percent of the land. Dissatisfaction with their situation led to violent resistance from the Kanaks during the 1970s and 1980s, but more recently they have come to accept French rule. The Kanaks now represent only 43 percent of the population, while 37 percent are of European descent. The main island, Grand Terre, consists of coastal plains with a mountainous interior. Only a small amount of land is suitable for cultivation. New Caledonia's prosperity is almost entirely dependent on nickel production, so the economy is at the mercy of varying world demand. Tourism from France, Japan, and Australia is also important.

New Caledonia

Official name Territory of New Caledonia and Dependencies
Form of government Overseas territory of France
Capital Nouméa
Area 19,060 sq km (7,359 sq miles)
Time zone GMT + 11 hours
Population 197,361
Life expectancy 75.4
Infant mortality (per 1,000) 12.2
Literacy rate 93.1%
Currency CFP (Comptoirs Français du Pacifique) franc
Economy Services 40%, agriculture 32%, industry 28%
Climate Tropical, moderated by trade winds
Map reference Pages 722, 727

An aerial view of Amadee Island, New Caledonia.

New Zealand

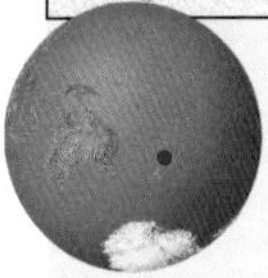

NEW ZEALAND

OFFICIAL NAME New Zealand/Aotearoa
FORM OF GOVERNMENT Constitutional monarchy with single legislative body (House of Representatives)
CAPITAL Wellington
AREA 268,680 sq km (103,737 sq miles)
TIME ZONE GMT + 12 hours
POPULATION 3,662,265
PROJECTED POPULATION 2005 3,868,442
POPULATION DENSITY 13.6 per sq km (35.3 per sq mile)
LIFE EXPECTANCY 77.8
INFANT MORTALITY (PER 1,000) 6.2
OFFICIAL LANGUAGE English
OTHER LANGUAGE Maori
LITERACY RATE 99%
RELIGIONS Anglican 17.5%, Roman Catholic 13%, Presbyterian 13%, other Christian 17%, other 2.5%, unaffiliated 37%
ETHNIC GROUPS European 71.7%, Maori 14.5%, other (including Samoan, Tongan, Cook Islander, Asian) 13.8%
CURRENCY New Zealand dollar
ECONOMY Services 70%, industry 20%, agriculture 10%
GNP PER CAPITA US$14,340
CLIMATE Temperate: warmer in north, colder in south and wetter in west
HIGHEST POINT Mt Cook 3,764 m (12,349 ft)
MAP REFERENCE Pages 718–19

OVERSEAS TERRITORIES

Cook Islands • Niue • Tokelau

New Zealand's unique physical and human geography is shaped by three main factors: its geological youth, its isolated location, and its environmental fragility. Mountainous, partly volcanic, and situated about 1,600 km (1,000 miles) southeast of Australia, New Zealand is the biggest of the island groups of Oceania. It consists of three main islands, The North and South Islands—which are separated by Cook Strait—and Stewart Island, several smaller islands, and three small territories in the Pacific. The country's temperate climate has wide regional variations, the northern part of the North Island being subtropical, while in the southern extremity of the South Island, winter snow is common. *Aotearoa*, meaning 'land of the long white cloud', is the traditional Maori name for New Zealand.

New Zealand has a liberal and progressive political history, pioneering votes for women in 1893, introducing a welfare state including a health service in 1938, and having a creditable record in ethnic relations. New Zealand's record as a progressive leader in the field of democratic rights for women was highlighted in 1999, when it became the first country in the world to have two women contest each other for the country's top political position, that of Prime Minister.

In terms of human population, it is a relatively young country. The first people to arrive in the country were the Polynesian ancestors of the Maori around 1,000 years ago.

The kea, the world's only alpine parrot, is widespread on the South Island of New Zealand.

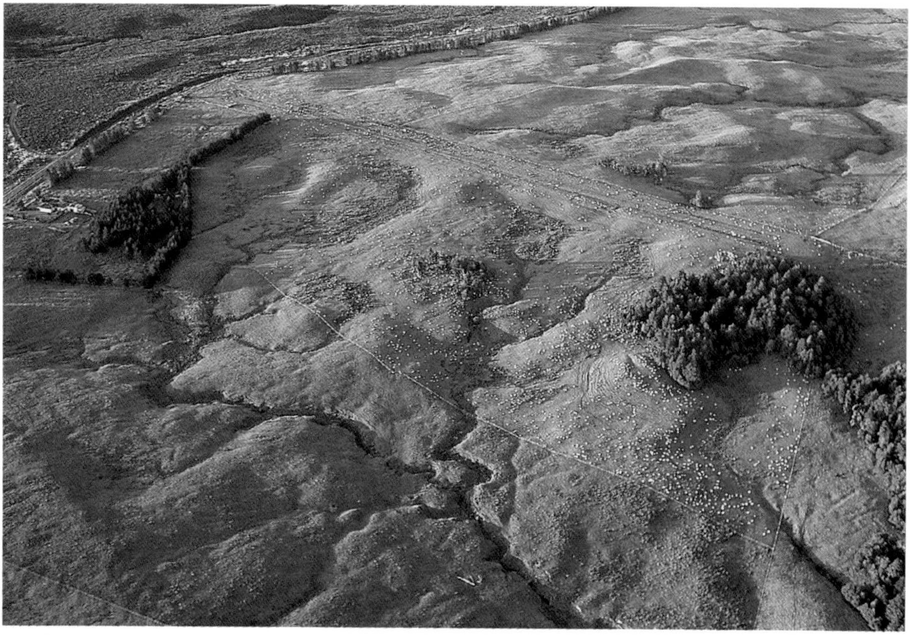

A sheep farm on New Zealand's North Island.

N

During the subsequent years of constant occupation, the Maori people (*tangata whenua*, or 'people of the land') have developed a distinctive modern Polynesian culture. The people of the early Maori communities were skilled in canoe building, ocean navigation, fighting, hunting, fishing, gardening and crafts, and they had a system of social and political relationships that suited their subsistence economy. *Pa*—fortified villages with pallisades, ditches and embankments—emerged, where economic expansion was possible. Maori language developed in this new environment.

In 1642 the Dutch explorer Abel Tasman was probably the first European to sight the islands, and in 1769 Captain James Cook was the first European to land. Cook estimated the Maori population as 150,000, with most people living on the North Island. A period of settlement by whalers and sealers, and of Maori tribal warfare using modern firearms, followed. By 1840 there were an estimated 2,000 Europeans in New Zealand, and Maori were beginning to express growing concern over the alienation of land, a concern that lay in part behind their entry into treaty negotiations with the British Crown in 1840. Maori chiefs ceded sovereignty to the British Crown and the Treaty of Waitangi was signed in 1840. After this

Sunset at Mt Taranaki, North Island.

N

date systematic and mostly peaceful colonization took place until the discovery of gold in Otago in 1861, followed by the Marlborough and West Coast rushes in 1867-68. These events generated a second major influx of Europeans, either directly from the United Kingdom or from Victoria in Australia. By this time, conflicts over land between settlers and Maori, especially in the North Island, had given rise to outright war. When hostilities ceased in 1872, extensive areas of Maori land were confiscated, surveyed, and settled. Large areas were also sold by their Maori owners, a process facilitated and expedited by the Maori Land Court established in 1865. The colonial authorities followed a policy of 'pacification' and 'assimilation', effected through Maori representation in parliaments, the extension of various forms of civil authority over Maori, the construction of roads and railways, and the continued purchase by the Crown of Maori land. The Maori people became progressively marginalized, both economically and geographically, while many succumbed to the ravages of introduced diseases. In recent years claims for compensation to Maori have become a major political issue.

The survival of Maori as a people and as a society is in itself a great achievement. The 1970s and 1980s were years of Maori protest and cultural renaissance, when long-held grievances against the Crown were made visible through land marches and demonstrations. In 1975 the

Waitangi Tribunal was established to hear land claims. Commenced in the 1980s, *Kohanga reo* projects, an initiative to teach young children Maori, have revived Maori language and culture for new generations. The population, which fell to 45,594 in 1901, is now about 600,000 out of a total population of about 3.5 million.

Geologically, New Zealand is a young country. The Southern Alps in the South Island emerged from the sea in the past 10 to 15 million years, while the volcanic action that shaped much of North Island occurred between 1 and 4 million years ago. The comparatively low ranges in North Island are formed from folded sedimentary rocks with higher volcanic peaks. Overlaying these rocks in the center of the North Island is a plateau of lava, pumice, and volcanic tuff. Minor earthquakes are common, and there are many areas of volcanic and geothermal activity on the North Island. Three volcanoes dominate the central plateau (Ruapehu being the most active) while Lake Taupo, the country's largest natural lake, occupies an ancient crater. In the South Island the Southern Alps form a northeast–southwest oriented ice-capped central massif with Mt Cook at its center. Glaciers descend the flanks of this massif and on the rainy western side forested slopes fall steeply to the sea. On the east, broad outwash fans lead

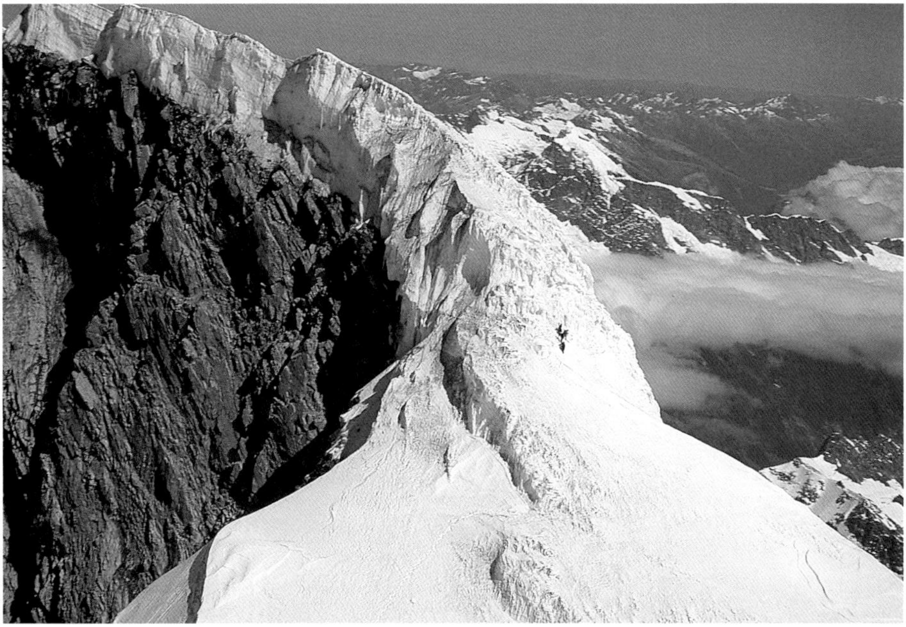

Climbers on the Chandolier at the top of Linda Glacier on the South Island.

to the much drier, treeless lowlands of the Canterbury Plains. The rugged, forested coastline of the South Island's far southwest, deeply indented with fiords, comprises Fiordland, the country's largest national park.

Few landscapes have been as transformed by humans as New Zealand's. Since European settlement began in 1840 more than 80 species of mammal, bird and fish have been introduced into the country, along with 1,800 species of plants. Already much changed by centuries of Maori occupation, the effect of introduced species—combined with widespread land clearance for farming and forestry—has been the total transformation of the landscape in most areas.

From 1850 to 1950 vast areas of forest in the North Island were cleared, leaving steep, bare hills which were sown with grass for grazing sheep. Erosion is now a serious problem in many areas. Rich pastures produced by year-round rain made agriculture the original foundation of the economy. The export of frozen mutton to Britain began in 1882, and New Zealand is still one of the world's main exporters of wool, cheese, butter, and meat. This produce goes to Australia, the USA, Japan and other parts of Asia. Since 1984 successive governments have sought

Sheep farm on the Canterbury Plains with the Alps in the background, South Island.

Parliament buildings including the Beehive, Wellington.

to reorient the largely agrarian economy toward a more industrialized, open economy that can compete globally.

Politically and economically, New Zealanders have become increasingly aware of their place in the South Pacific. Where immigrants had previously come mostly from Britain, from the mid-1970s there has been an influx of migrants from Southeast Asia and the Pacific Islands. Auckland has absorbed a large number of migrants and now has the biggest Polynesian population of any city in the world. The changed role of Britain when it entered the European Economic Community in the 1970s caused a rethinking of New Zealand's future, both political and economic. Inflation grew through the 1970s and as unemployment rose, many New Zealanders sought work across the Tasman Sea in Australia. By 1984, New Zealand was more culturally diverse than before, but its economy was in crisis. Consequently, in 1984 a new reforming Labour government attempted to sacrifice some equity in the cause of economic growth and greater efficiency. Drastic neo-liberal financial deregulation and fiscal reform were introduced. The economic reform, including partial dismantling of the welfare state, was controversial. In recent years there has been a burst of entrepreneurial innovation, in agricultural products, processing and marketing. The beneficiaries of these new developments patronize boutique vineyards, enjoy the latest cuisine, and are able to take skiing holidays. The less favored are aware of reduced levels of free health care and the diminished power of the unions.

At a time of extreme economic and cultural division, New Zealanders are showing a strong attachment to their environment, and recreation and sport enjoy mass appeal. Most New Zealanders oppose nuclear testing in the Pacific, and since 1985, nuclear warships have been banned from entering New Zealand waters. This anti-nuclear stance shows that the people of New Zealand are prepared to stand alone in order to define and defend their own culture.

New Zealand has limited petroleum resources, though it produces natural gas—almost a third of which is used to make synthetic petrol. There are large reserves of coal. The most important source of domestic energy is hydroelectric power, easily generated because of the favorable rainfall and terrain. This has allowed the development of aluminum production using imported

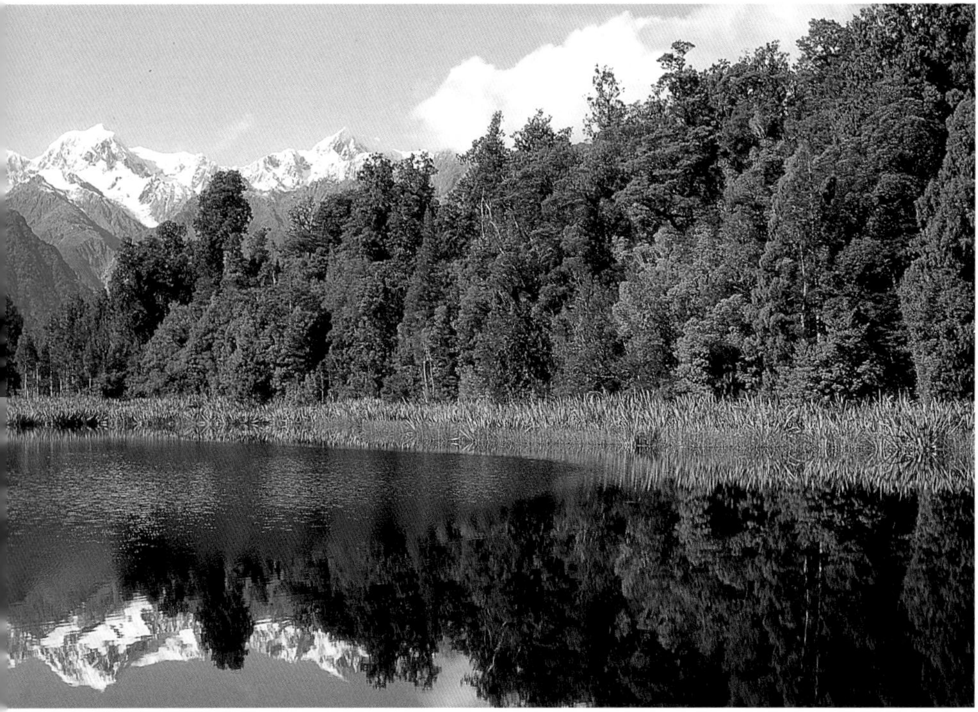

Forests edging Lake Matheson in southern New Zealand.

bauxite. In recent years, new products have been developed for new international markets. One of these is kiwifruit, the main fresh fruit export in 1996; new varieties of high-quality apples are currently a leading export. A minor feature of the rural scene only 20 years ago, vineyards are now widespread, Marlborough, Hawke's Bay, and Gisborne being the main wine-producing regions. Forest products play a vital economic role. Radiata pine, the main commercial timber, is grown in vast state pine forests. Cutting rights to parts of these have been sold and the industry as a whole is widely privatized. New Zealand's varied scenery, combining quiet harbors and sunlit beaches, with volcanoes, lakes, alpine snowfields, and fiords, draws more than 1.5 million visitors per year. As a dollar-earner tourism is second only to primary industry.

Isolation has had its advantages, helping to some extent to distance the country from the external conflicts and threats experienced by many other nations, and protecting the land from overpopulation. Its very remoteness is now proving an economic drawcard by attracting tourists to its unique environment.

Dairy farm framed by the Alps.

imeline ew ealand

c.AD 900 Polynesians reach New Zealand islands and settle, founding Aotearoa—land of the long white cloud

c.1500–1600 Maori build many pa, earthwork forts, to protect communities, and settle Chatham Islands

c.1500–1600 Moas, large flightless birds, hunted to extinction; Maori live off seals, fish, root fern, and cultivate kumera, taro

1642–43 Abel Tasman explores coasts of the islands for Dutch East India Co. Does not land and recommends no action be taken

1769 Captain James Cook sails around both islands and claims them for Britain; Maori population 100,000

1791 Traders from Sydney begin sealing and whaling, some settling in Bay of Islands

1835 Britain establishes a protectorate over New Zealand

1840 Treaty of Waitangi gives Britain sovereignty over New Zealand and Maori sovereignty over their lands

1852 European population 28,000, including 15,000 colonists brought in by New Zealand Co (founded 1838)

1853 New Zealand granted self-government; first provincial superintendents and councils are elected

1860 Maori Wars between Maori and British over land; Maori resistance worn down after defeat at Te Ranga

1860 Gold rush in Otago brings European and Asian immigrants; another rush occurs in Canterbury in 1864

1881 Refrigeration allows export of dairy produce and meat to European markets, helping to overcome economic depression

1900 Maori population down to 40,000 due to disease and warfare; European population about 1 million

1914 New Zealand troops join Australians in support of Allies; in 1915 they help establish ANZAC legend in landings at Gallipoli

1931 Country's worst earthquake hits Hawke's Bay, killing more than 250 people and devastating cities of Napier and Hastings

1939–45 New Zealand supports Allies in Europe, also raising a Third Division to aid US forces in the Pacific and defend their own country

1950s Postwar boom leads to migration from rural areas to the cities by Maori

1975 Maori protests culminate in a Land March from the far north to Wellington

1985 David Lange's Labour Government bans nuclear-powered and nuclear-missile carrying ships from New Zealand ports

Nicaragua

The largest republic in the Central American isthmus, Nicaragua is also the least populated. The western half, including Lake Nicaragua, the largest lake in Central America, was settled by the Spanish in the sixteenth century, and the Caribbean shore was for two centuries the British protectorate of Mosquito Coast (Costa de Miskitos). Becoming independent from Spain in 1821, Nicaragua then experienced much instability. The 45-year right-wing rule of the Somoza family ended in 1979, being overthrown by the Marxist Sandinistas. Their left-wing rule provoked a US-backed insurgency known as the "contras." In free elections held in 1996 a right-of-center party defeated the Sandinistas. In rural areas, however, violence continues.

Nicaragua's broad plain on the Caribbean side leads to a coastal region of lagoons, beaches, and river deltas. Rainfall here is heavy and the tropical wildlife includes crocodile and jaguar. Inland, toward the east, there are mountain ranges broken by basins and fertile valleys. In the west and south a broad depression containing Lakes Managua and Nicaragua runs from the Gulf of Fonseca, on the Pacific Coast, to the mouth of the San Juan del Norte River, on the Caribbean. Before the Panama Canal was built this was an important route across the isthmus.

NICARAGUA

OFFICIAL NAME Republic of Nicaragua
FORM OF GOVERNMENT Republic with single legislative body (National Assembly)
CAPITAL Managua
AREA 129,494 sq km (49,998 sq miles)
TIME ZONE GMT – 6 hours
POPULATION 4,717,132
PROJECTED POPULATION 2005 5,521,705
POPULATION DENSITY 36.4 per sq km (94.3 per sq mile)
LIFE EXPECTANCY 67.1
INFANT MORTALITY (PER 1,000) 40.5
OFFICIAL LANGUAGE Spanish
OTHER LANGUAGES Indigenous languages, English
LITERACY RATE 65.3%
RELIGIONS Roman Catholic 95%, Protestant 5%
ETHNIC GROUPS Mixed indigenous–European 69%, European 17%, African 9%, indigenous 5%
CURRENCY Córdoba
ECONOMY Agriculture 47%, services 37%, industry 16%
GNP PER CAPITA US$380
CLIMATE Tropical in lowlands, cooler in highlands; wet season May to January
HIGHEST POINT Pico Mogoton 2,107 m (6,913 ft)
MAP REFERENCE Page 838

Thatched house on the island of Omotepe, with the volcano of Concepción in the background.

This is a region of cotton growing. Overlooking the lakes are 40 volcanoes, among them the active Momotombo. An earthquake destroyed most of Managua in 1972.

Nicaragua is still reorganizing its economy—at one point under the Sandinistas inflation reached 3,000 percent. Large-scale confiscation of estates took place under the Sandinistas but the peasants to whom land was given have not always been able to live off their allotments, and some land has been resold. Coffee and cotton are the major export crops. Staples grown by the many subsistence farmers include maize, rice, and beans. Mineral production is led by silver and gold, followed by tungsten, lead, and zinc. Falling prices for most of Nicaragua's export commodities, the loss of aid, and the impact of IMF policies reduced the nation's income in 1993 to close to Haiti's—the poorest in the Americas. There is a huge foreign debt. Conditions peculiar to Nicaragua include Sandinista "land reforms" in which luxury properties were seized and given to the movement's leaders and "privatized" state operations that are union-controlled. More than 50 percent of agricultural and industrial firms are state-owned.

Fruit sellers outside blue and aqua door in city of Granada.

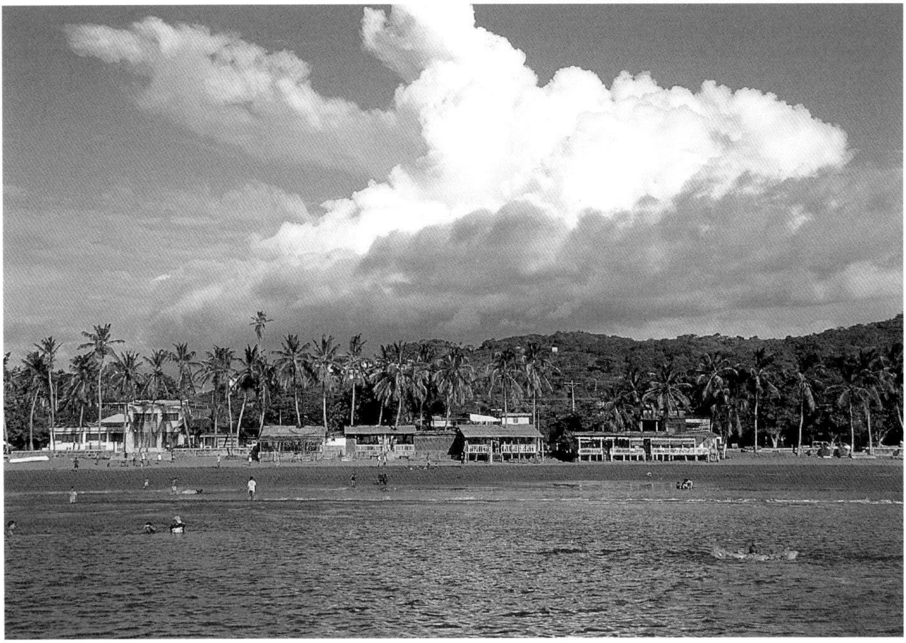

The port of San Juan del Sur on the west coast of Nicaragua.

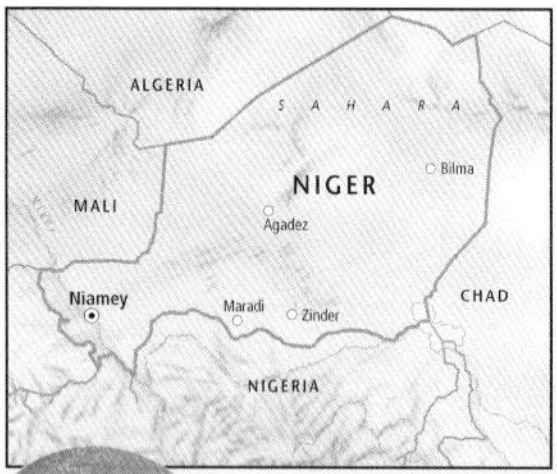

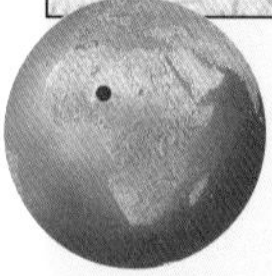

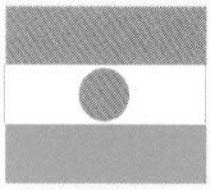

NIGER

OFFICIAL NAME Republic of Niger
FORM OF GOVERNMENT Republic with single legislative body (National Assembly)
CAPITAL Niamey
AREA 1,267,000 sq km (489,189 sq miles)
TIME ZONE GMT + 1 hour
POPULATION 9,962,242
PROJECTED POPULATION 2005 11,864,407
POPULATION DENSITY 7.9 per sq km (20.5 per sq mile)
LIFE EXPECTANCY 42
INFANT MORTALITY (PER 1,000) 112.8
OFFICIAL LANGUAGE French
OTHER LANGUAGES Hausa, Djerma, Fulani
LITERACY RATE 13.1%
RELIGIONS Muslim 80%, Christian and indigenous beliefs 20%
ETHNIC GROUPS Hausa 56%, Djerma 22%, Fula 8.5%, Tuareg 8%, Beri Beri 4.3%, other (including 4,000 French expatriates) 1.2%
CURRENCY CFA (Communauté Financière Africaine) franc
ECONOMY Agriculture 87%, services 10%, industry 3%
GNP PER CAPITA US$220
CLIMATE Mainly arid; tropical in south, with wet season June to October
HIGHEST POINT Mt Gréboun 1,994 m (6,540 ft)
MAP REFERENCE Pages 801–02, 805

Niger

Niger is two-thirds desert, which may seem strange for a country that is named after a great river (the name "Niger" comes from the Tuareg word *n'eghirren*, for flowing water), but the River Niger only cuts across the extreme southwest of this large, landlocked country. Elsewhere, there is an arid landscape of stony basins, drifting sands, and a northern highland that forms part of the mountain chain stretching from Algeria to Chad.

The home of the Sokoto Empire of the Fulani in the nineteenth century, the region became part of French West Africa in 1922, and received independence in 1960. Then followed three decades of dictatorial civilian and military rule. Despite the holding of multi-party elections in 1993, continuing unrest caused by Tuareg rebels in the north and power struggles within the government led to the reimposition of military rule in 1996.

Niger's central geographic feature is the Massif de l'Aïr. In these mountains, which rise out of the Saharan plains to jagged peaks up to 1,900 m (6,230 ft) high, there is sometimes sufficient rain for thorny scrub to grow. Formerly nomads grazed their camels, horses, cattle, and goats in this area, but devastating droughts in 1973 and 1983 destroyed their livelihood. To the east and west of the Massif de l'Aïr are the Saharan Desert plains of Ténéré du Tafassasset and the Western Talk. Sand and sandy soil cover most of the desert plains to the north and east, an area which is virtually rainless and, aside from small numbers of people living at the occasional palm-fringed

Women drawing water from a deep well in Niger.

oasis, uninhabited. Plant life includes kapok and baobab trees. Buffalo, antelope, lion, hippopotamus, and crocodile are found in Niger but their survival today is more a matter of chance than good management.

With its gross domestic product growth barely matching the growth of its population, Niger is one of the most impoverished countries in Africa. More than 95 percent of its people earn a living from farming and trading. Where the Niger River crosses the country in the far southwest there are fertile arable soils: crops include yams, cassava, and maize, and rice in areas where the river floods. On the drier land toward Lake Chad (Lac Tchad) millet and sorghum are grown. The drought that has affected extensive areas of the Sahel has reduced Niger from self-sufficiency to being an importer of food. Tin and tungsten are mined, and there are reserves of iron ore, manganese, and molybdenum. During the 1970s, when prices were high, uranium became the main source of revenue, and it continues to be the country's most valuable export. Between 1983 and 1990, however, revenues fell by 50 percent. At present the government of Niger relies on aid for both operating expenses and for public investment.

Wooded countryside turned to desert in Niger as a result of drought.

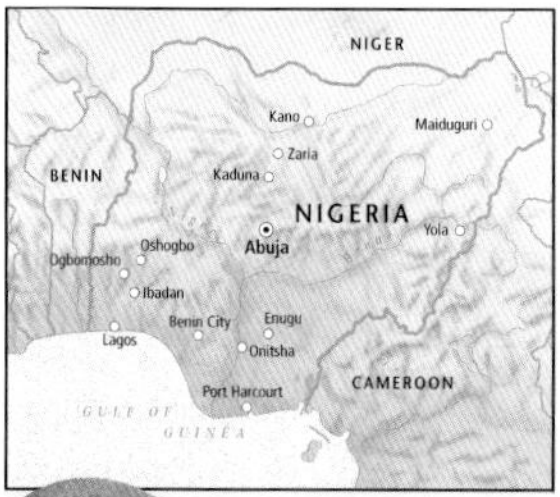

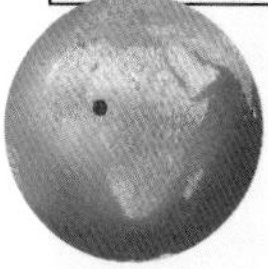

NIGERIA

OFFICIAL NAME Federal Republic of Nigeria
FORM OF GOVERNMENT Military regime
CAPITAL Abuja
AREA 923,770 sq km (356,668 sq miles)
TIME ZONE GMT + 1 hour
POPULATION 113,828,587
PROJECTED POPULATION 2005 133,974,486
POPULATION DENSITY 123.2 per sq km (319 per sq mile)
LIFE EXPECTANCY 53.3
INFANT MORTALITY (PER 1,000) 89.5
OFFICIAL LANGUAGES English
OTHER LANGUAGES French, Hausa, Yoruba, Ibo, Fulani
LITERACY RATE 55.6%
RELIGIONS Muslim 50%, Christian 40%, indigenous beliefs 10%
ETHNIC GROUPS About 250 indigenous groups: the largest of which are Hausa, Fulani, Yoruba, Ibo 68%; Kanuri, Edo, Tiv, Ibidio, Nupe 25%; other 7%
CURRENCY Naira
ECONOMY Services 51%, agriculture 45%, industry 4%
GNP PER CAPITA US$260
CLIMATE Tropical in south, with wet season April to October; arid in north
HIGHEST POINT Chappal Waddi 2,419 m (7,936 ft)
MAP REFERENCE Page 805

Nigeria

With the continent's largest population, huge oil revenues, and a territory that is four times the size of the United Kingdom, Nigeria is one of Africa's most important nations. It also ranks as one of the most corrupt countries in the world, and a place where tensions between the main tribal groups are close to breaking point.

Such tensions are not new to the region: regional and ethnic conflict go back to the days of Nigeria's ancient city-states. The life of the Yoruba people centered on the city of Ife, while the Hausa kingdom was in the north. The kingdom of Benin, well known for its portrait bronzes of past rulers, was in the west, and a number of communities of Ibo lived in the southeast. Bringing all these peoples together to form a single nation has proved difficult: since independence, in 1960, there has been a series of military dictatorships, and only 10 years of elected government. An unsuccessful attempt to secede by the Ibo in 1967 (who set up an independent state named Biafra) failed in 1970, following a bitter civil war in which thousands of people died. Today, an uneasy peace prevails under military rule.

Physical features and land use

Nigeria's coast on the west African Gulf of Guinea consists of long, sandy beaches, and mangrove swamps where its rivers flow into the sea. The mouth of the Niger forms an immense delta, threaded with thousands of creeks and lagoons, with Port Harcourt on one of the main channels. Upstream it divides, the Benue (Bénoué) River leading east into Cameroon, the Niger heading northwest toward Benin. These two large rivers provide transport, by boat, for cargo and people. High rainfall on the coast and in the river valleys enables yams, cassava, maize, and vegetables to be grown and on floodland alongside the rivers rice is cultivated.

In the rainy forested belt to the north the hills gradually rise to the semiarid central savanna plateau, and then to the Jos Plateau, reaching 1,780 m (5,840 ft) at Share Hill. Up the Benue (Bénoué) River to the east the land rises to the wooded slopes of the Adamaoua Massif and the Cameroon highlands. From these hill-slope areas come such products as cocoa, rubber, hardwoods, and palm oil. North of the Jos Plateau the savanna becomes dry, in many places degenerating into arid Sahelian scrub, where

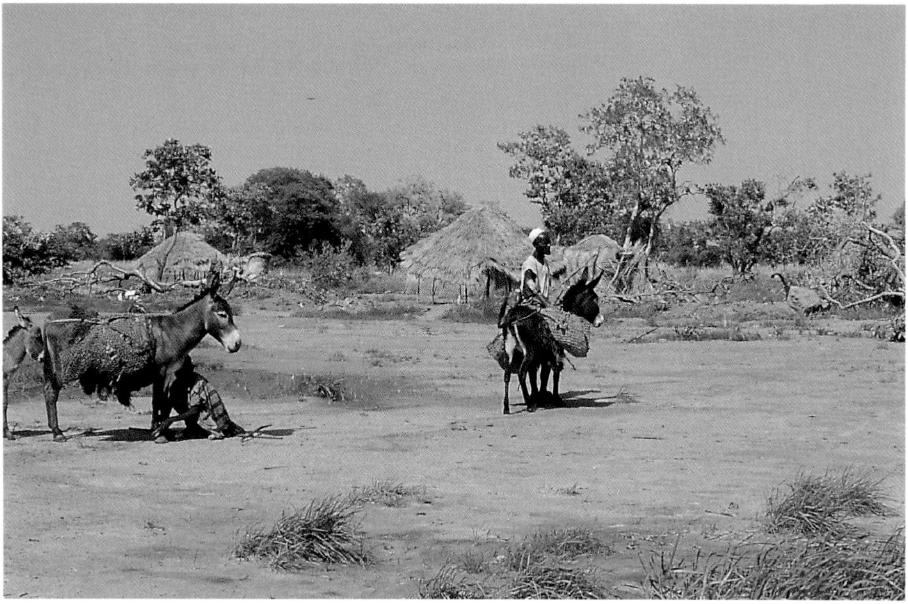

Donkeys are used to transport produce in a village.

N

both herds and herders have difficulty surviving. Around Lake Chad (Lac Tchad) the typical vegetation is hardy acacia and doum palms.

The river systems of the Niger and the Benue (Bénoué) drain 60 percent of Nigeria's total land area. Though much reduced by clearing for cultivation, the Nigerian rainforests still produce mahogany and iriko. Wildlife includes elephant, chimpanzee, and the red river hog.

People and culture

In addition to the Yoruba, Fulani, Hausa, and Ibo, Nigeria has 245 much smaller ethnic groups. Not only are they divided along lines of ethnicity, language, and regional dialect, there is also a major religious division. The north of the country is largely Islamic (the religion of the Hausa and Fulani) while the south is for the most part Christian, combined with indigenous African beliefs. Outbreaks of communal violence in the north sometimes occur as a result of clashes between Islamic fundamentalists and missionary Christians. Despite widespread Christian proselytizing there is evidence that Islamic influence is gradually growing in the south.

A grazing herd of springbok.

Although 54 percent of the labor force works in agriculture, and many rural people are subsistence farmers, Nigerians have also lived in cities for centuries. This contrasts with many other parts of Africa. Long before European commercial expansion into the region, places such as Benin, Kano, Ibadan, and Ife were administrative and trading centers with sizeable populations. As in other parts of west Africa, women in the non-Islamic Nigerian cultures play a prominent role in commercial life.

Economy and resources

Nigeria is rich in natural resources and these are the basis of its economic strength. They include tin, columbite, iron ore, coal, limestone, lead, zinc, and natural gas. By far the most important, however, is oil: Nigeria is OPEC's fourth largest producer, with oil providing 80 percent of government revenue and 90 percent of export earnings overall. This has led to what many consider over-dependence on a single commodity. In addition it has provided a limitless source of independent wealth for the political élite.

Agricultural production has failed to keep pace with population growth, and Nigeria is now a food importer. There are fundamental imbalances in the economy that result in chronic inflation and a steadily depreciating currency. Investors are wary because of political instability and corruption at the highest levels of government. Domestic and international debts prevent an agreement with the IMF on debt relief.

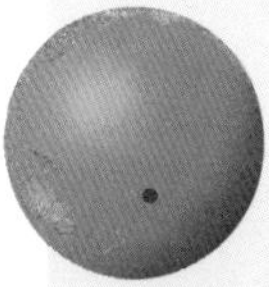

NIUE

OFFICIAL NAME Niue
FORM OF GOVERNMENT Self-governing territory in free association with New Zealand
CAPITAL Alofi
AREA 260 sq km (100 sq miles)
TIME ZONE GMT – 11 hours

Niue

Niue is one of the world's biggest coral atolls, lying about 700 km (400 miles) east of Tonga in the South Pacific. The terrain consists of a central limestone plateau with steep cliffs around the coast; the highest point is 68 m (223 ft). The economy is heavily dependent on aid from the New Zealand government. Most of the inhabitants live by subsistence farming. Light industry consists of processing passionfruit, lime oil, honey, and coconut cream. The sale of postage stamps and tourism are also a source of foreign currency. Remittances from family members living overseas supplement domestic income: lack of employment opportunities on the island means that five out of six of the people of Niue live and work in New Zealand.

Clear blue waters form an inlet on the South Pacific island of Niue.

POPULATION 2,321 (1994)
CURRENCY New Zealand dollar
ECONOMY Agriculture, industry (food processing, coconuts), services
CLIMATE Tropical, moderated by trade winds
MAP REFERENCE Pages 718, 722

Norfolk Island

Some 1,400 km (850 miles) east of Australia, Norfolk Island is inhabited by descendants of the famous mutineers from HMS Bounty. Of volcanic origin, the island was uninhabited when discovered by Captain James Cook in 1774. After serving as a penal settlement in Australia's early history it became a refuge for the entire population of the Pitcairn Islands' Bounty mutiny survivors, who were resettled there in 1856. (Some later returned to live on Pitcairn Island.) About one third of the current population still has links with the Pitcairn Islands' Bounty survivors. The present inhabitants speak a mixture of nineteenth century English, Gaelic, and Old Tahitian. They enjoy a degree of autonomy and have rejected proposals to become a part of the Australian state.

While there is no income tax, the government raises revenue from customs duty, liquor sales, a public works levy, financial institutions levy, and departure fees. Tourism is the main activity, the island receiving around 30,000 visitors each year. To preserve the unique environment on the island, tourist numbers are strictly controlled through the Immigration office. Transport is

N

NORFOLK ISLAND

OFFICIAL NAME Territory of Norfolk Island
FORM OF GOVERNMENT External territory of Australia
CAPITAL Kingston
AREA 35 sq km (14 sq miles)
TIME ZONE GMT + 11.5 hours
POPULATION 2,756 (1995)
CURRENCY Australian dollar
ECONOMY Tourism, agriculture
CLIMATE Subtropical
MAP REFERENCE Pages 719, 722

Historic colonial buildings and ruins on Norfolk Island.

also controlled, with no public transport system in place and hire vehicles, which are available on the island, help to limit the amount of traffic. Visitor permits must be obtained to travel to Norfolk Island, and immigration is also strictly controlled.

North Korea

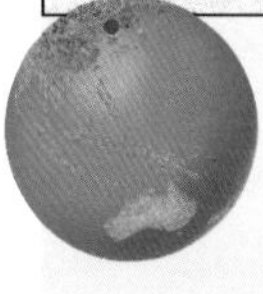

NORTH KOREA

OFFICIAL NAME Democratic People's Republic of Korea
FORM OF GOVERNMENT Communist state with single legislative body (Supreme People's Assembly)
CAPITAL P'yongyang
AREA 120,540 sq km (46,540 sq miles)
TIME ZONE GMT + 9 hours

North Korea occupies the northern half of the Korean Peninsula. It is separated from South Korea along the ceasefire line that was established at the end of the Korean War (1950–53), roughly along the 38th parallel. After a period as an independent kingdom in the tenth century AD, control of Korea was disputed for hundreds of years between China and Japan, the latter seizing it as a colony in 1910. Following the Second World War it became a separate communist state and after the Korean War it developed into a rigidly closed totalitarian state system. The 50-year-long personal rule of Kim Il Sung ("Great Leader") passed by hereditary succession to his son Kim Jong Il ("Dear Leader") in 1994. The people of North Korea are classed by the state into three quasi-castes: loyal, wavering, and hostile. Membership of a caste determines whether an individual receives either education or employment. Citizens are subject to arbitrary arrest and execution for criticizing the Korean leaders or listening to foreign broadcasts. Unceasing political indoctrination takes place through the media, the workplace, the military, mass spectacles, and cultural events.

Mountains and rugged hills occupy most of the Korean Peninsula, and dominate its northern half. In the northeast the volcanic peak of Mt Paektu is surrounded by the Kaema Plateau. High forested mountains, cut by river gorges, lie along the border with Manchuria, northeast China. Other mountain chains extend north to south along the east coast. The Yalu River valley in the northwest marks the Korean–Chinese border, while to the southwest the fertile Chaeryŏng and Pyongyang plains are the main areas for agricultural activity. The principal crop is rice, followed by millet and other grains. Fruit and vegetables are grown, and also oilseed rape, flax, and cotton.

The North Korean economy is run according to the Stalinist model. More than 90 percent of operations are controlled by the state, agriculture is totally collectivized, and state-owned industry produces 95 percent of all manufactured goods. Despite over 50 years of complete control by the state, the country is still not self-sufficient in food. The industrial sector produces military weapons, chemicals, minerals (including coal, magnesite, iron ore, graphite, copper, zinc, lead, and precious metals), along with a number of food products and textiles.

During the late 1990s the economy was in crisis: power supplies were unreliable and food shortages were causing famine in the countryside. Flooding in 1995 damaged harvests and led North Korea to seek foreign aid for the first time in decades; aid donors were muted in their response, demanding proof that aid had been properly distributed. North Korea continues to fall farther and farther behind South Korean development and living standards.

POPULATION 22,337,878
PROJECTED POPULATION 2005 23,348,444
POPULATION DENSITY 185.3 per sq km (480 per sq mile)
LIFE EXPECTANCY 67.5
INFANT MORTALITY (PER 1,000) 35.0
OFFICIAL LANGUAGE Korean
LITERACY RATE 95%
RELIGIONS Buddhist and Confucian 51%, traditional beliefs 45%, Christian 4%
ETHNIC GROUPS Korean 100%
CURRENCY Won
ECONOMY Services and industry 64%, agriculture 36%
GNP PER CAPITA Est. US$7,940
CLIMATE Temperate, with cold, snowy winters and warm, wet summers
HIGHEST POINT Mt Paektu 2,744 m (9,003 ft)
MAP REFERENCE Page 744

Northern Mariana Islands

These islands are located in the North Pacific about three-quarters of the way between Hawaii and the Philippines. Unlike the nearby Caroline Islands, the Northern Marianas chose not to seek independence in 1987, preferring to remain part of the USA. There are 14 main islands including Saipan, Rota, and Tinian. The southern islands are limestone with level terraces and fringing coral reefs; the northern islands are volcanic, with active volcanoes on Pagan and Agrihan. There is little seasonal

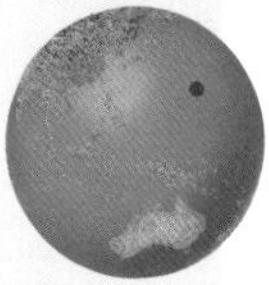

NORTHERN MARIANA ISLANDS

OFFICIAL NAME Commonwealth of the Northern Mariana Islands
FORM OF GOVERNMENT Territory of the USA; commonwealth in political union with the USA
CAPITAL Saipan

(continues)

NORTHERN MARIANA ISLANDS *(continued)*

AREA 477 sq km (184 sq miles)
TIME ZONE GMT + 10 hours
POPULATION 69,343
LIFE EXPECTANCY 76
INFANT MORTALITY (PER 1,000) 6.5
CURRENCY US dollar
ECONOMY Tourism, industry, agriculture
CLIMATE Tropical, moderated by trade winds
MAP REFERENCE Page 724

variation in the tropical marine climate, as the temperature is moderated by northeast trade winds. The people of the islands belong to a variety of ethnic groups and include Chamorros (mixed Indonesian, Spanish, and Filipino), Micronesians, Japanese, Chinese, and Koreans. The economy is substantially supported by the USA. Tourism is a fast-growing source of income, employing increasing numbers of the workforce and bringing in most revenue. Cattle ranches produce beef, and small farms produce coconuts, breadfruit, tomatoes, and melons. Industry consists of handicrafts, light manufacturing, and garment production.

Norway

Norway's long, narrow landmass wraps around the western part of Sweden and the north of Finland and shares a land border with the northwest tip of the Russian Federation. Its rugged western coastline is washed by the North Sea in the south and the Norwegian Sea further north. Its northern tip juts into the Arctic Ocean, making it the most northerly part of Europe. To the south the Skagerrak Strait separates it from the northern tip of Denmark. Like the Swedes and Danes, modern Norwegians are descendents of the Vikings, Teutonic peoples who settled the area and who, from the ninth to the eleventh centuries AD, raided and conquered lands to the north, east, and west. In the fourteenth century, Denmark, Sweden, and Norway came under Danish rule. Although Sweden became independent in the sixteenth century, Norwegians remained subject to the Danes. In 1815, at the end of the Napoleonic Wars, in which Denmark sided with France, control of Norway was transferred to the Swedish crown. The modern Norwegian state dates from 1905, when the country declared its independence. Norway remained neutral in the First World War and was not attacked. However, Nazi forces invaded in 1940 and, despite spirited resistance, subdued the country. Norway joined the NATO alliance in 1949, and in the early 1990s attempted to join the European Union, a move that was thwarted when the option was defeated at a referendum. Norway is a parliamentary democracy with a monarch as the titular head of state.

N

NORWAY

OFFICIAL NAME Kingdom of Norway
FORM OF GOVERNMENT Constitutional monarchy with single legislative body (Parliament)
CAPITAL Oslo
AREA 324,220 sq km (125,181 sq miles)
TIME ZONE GMT + 1 hour
POPULATION 4,438,547
PROJECTED POPULATION 2005 4,523,798
POPULATION DENSITY 13.7 per sq km (35.5 per sq mile)
LIFE EXPECTANCY 78.4

Norway's more than 21,000 km (13,000 miles) of coast is punctuated by deep fiords. Most of the country consists of mountains with deep valleys formed by ancient glaciers. There are also vast areas of high plateaus. More than one-quarter of the land surface is forested, mainly with conifers, and there are many lakes. The population is centered in the lowlands on the southern coasts and in the southeast. Only a tiny proportion of the land area is suitable for cultivation and agriculture is limited mainly to areas around lakes.

Norway has large oil and gas reserves in the North Sea and produces more oil and gas than any other European country. Its electricity, produced mainly from hydroelectric plants, is used largely to power industry. Key industries include pulp and paper manufacture, shipbuilding, and aluminum production. Fishing and fish farming are also major industries and farmed salmon is a major export.

INFANT MORTALITY (PER 1,000) 5.0
OFFICIAL LANGUAGE Norwegian
OTHER LANGUAGES Lapp, Finnish
LITERACY RATE 99%
RELIGIONS Evangelical Lutheran 94%; Baptist, Pentecostalist, Methodist and Roman Catholic 6%
ETHNIC GROUPS Germanic (Nordic, Alpine, Baltic) 97%, others include Lapp minority 3%
CURRENCY Norwegian krone
ECONOMY Services 61%, industry 36%, agriculture 3%
GNP PER CAPITA US$31,250
CLIMATE Cold in north and inland, temperate and wet on coast
HIGHEST POINT Glittertind 2,472 m (8,110 ft)
MAP REFERENCE Pages 768–69, 770

OVERSEAS TERRITORIES

Bouvet Island • Jan Mayen • Peter Island • Svalbard

Houses built along the banks of a small fiord in Norway.

N

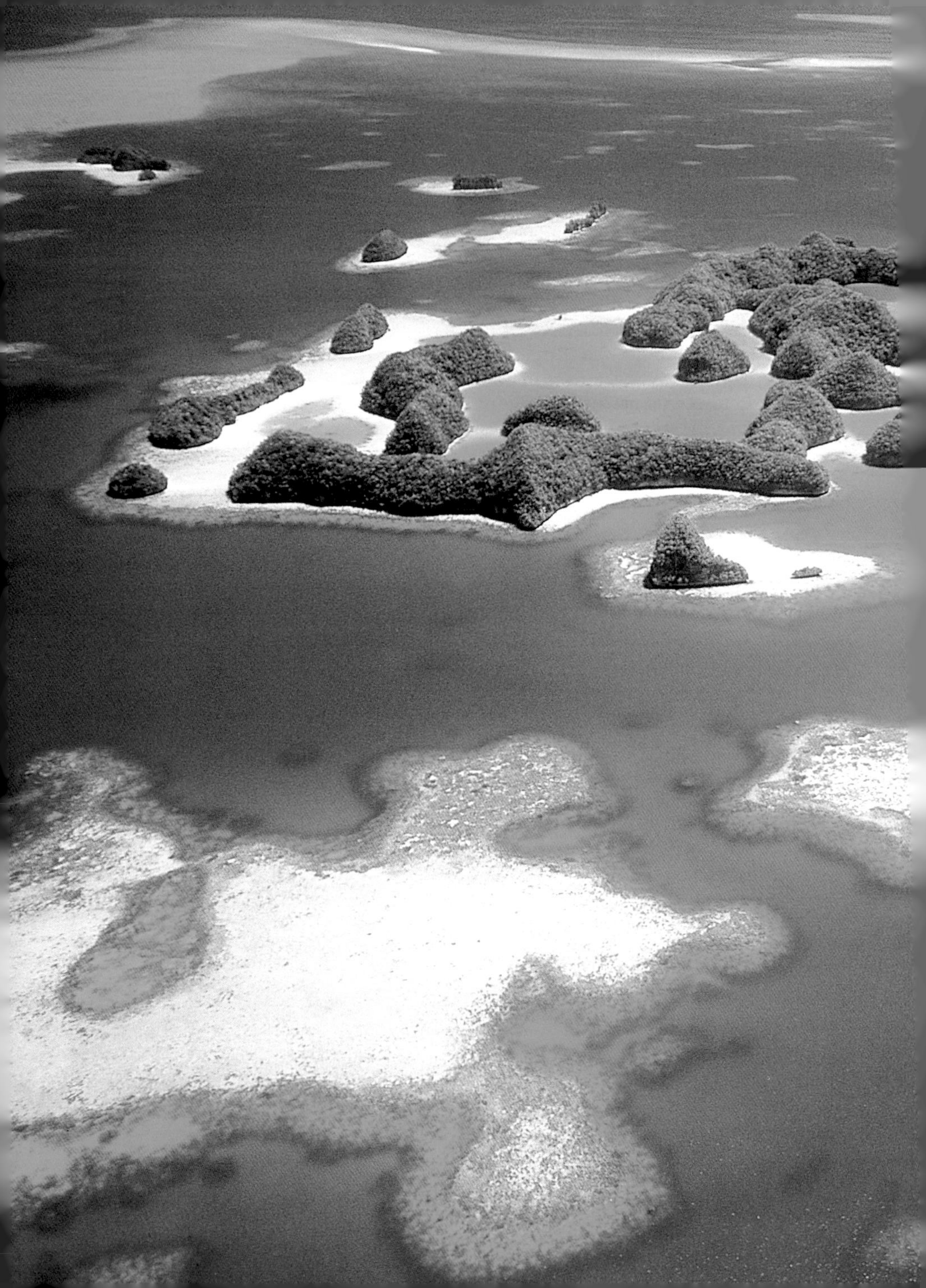

0,P

Oman

Official name Sultanate of Oman
Form of government Monarchy with advisory Consultative Council
Capital Muscat
Area 212,460 sq km (82,031 sq miles)
Time zone GMT + 4 hours
Population 2,446,645
Projected population 2005 2,999,546
Population density 11.5 per sq km (29.8 per sq mile)
Life expectancy 71.3
Infant mortality (per 1,000) 24.7
Official language Arabic
Other languages English, Baluchu, Urdu
Literacy rate 35%
Religions Ibadhi Muslim 75%, Sunni Muslim, Shi'a Muslim and Hindu 25%
Ethnic groups Mainly Arab with Baluchi, Indian, Pakistani, Sri Lankan, Bangladeshi, African minorities
Currency Omani rial
Economy Agriculture 50%, services 28%, industry 22%
GNP per capita US$4,820
Climate Mainly hot and arid; light rains in south June to September
Highest point Jabal Ash Shām 3,019 m (10,199 ft)
Map reference Pages 756–7

Oman

Oman is the second largest country in the Arabian Peninsula. Standing on the peninsula's eastern corner, it looks across the Arabian Sea toward Baluchistan and India—in fact Baluchis form a small but significant part of the population. A small, separate, and highly strategic piece of Oman's territory is the tip of the Musandam Peninsula, commanding the entrance to the Strait of Hormuz. The Omani capital of Muscat was a trading center for hundreds of years, dhows sailing to India in one direction and down the African coast to Zanzibar in the other. Zanzibar itself was an Omani conquest, and in the 1960s, when it became part of Tanzania, many Arab Zanzibaris came to Oman. From 1798 Oman had strong ties with the British, and it became a British protectorate. Full independence came in 1971. Sultan Qabus Ibn Sa'id rules his country as an absolute monarch, advised by a *majlis alshura* (consultative council), but in the late 1990s the country was moving towards constitutional government. In the late 1960s Oman faced a leftist rebellion in the western province of Dhofur, encouraged and supported by the People's Republic of Yemen across the border. This was defeated in 1975. Since then, with the country enjoying the prosperity of its oil and natural gas (huge additional reserves were discovered in 1991), peace has reigned.

In the north the limestone Hajar Mountains overlook the fertile coastal plain of al-Batinah. Most of Oman's

The Gubra Bowl in Oman.

population lives along the alluvial al-Batinah strip, where date gardens stretch for more than 250 km (155 miles). The Jabal Akhdar ridge is the highest part of the Hajar Range, rising to 3,107 m (10,193 ft). Soils in the upland region are poor: herders use the area for running camels, sheep, and goats. Wadis cutting the Jabal Akhdar ridge, underground canals, and wells provide a certain amount of irrigation. North of the Ẓufār (Dhofar) uplands in the southwest the desert meets the sandy wastes of the Saudi Arabian Ar Rub' al Khāli (or "Empty Quarter").

Rural Omanis live by subsistence agriculture, growing dates, limes, bananas, alfalfa, and vegetables. Pastoralists keep camels, cattle, sheep, and goats. The smaller urban population, however, including a considerable number of guest workers, depends on imported food. The national economy as a whole is dominated by the oil industry, where petroleum accounts for nearly 90 percent of export earnings, about 75 percent of government revenues, and roughly 40 percent of gross domestic product. Oman has proved oil reserves of 4 billion barrels, which are equal to 20 year's supply at the present rate of extraction.

A village in the Oman mountains, surrounded by terraced cultivation.

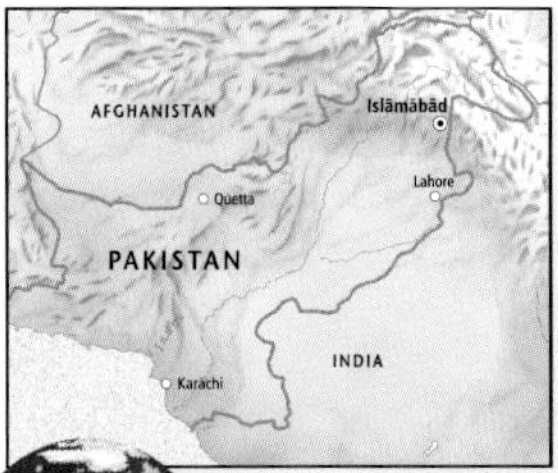

PAKISTAN

OFFICIAL NAME Islamic Republic of Pakistan
FORM OF GOVERNMENT Republic with two legislative bodies (Senate and National Assembly)
CAPITAL Islāmābād
AREA 803,940 sq km (310,401 sq miles)
TIME ZONE GMT + 5 hours
POPULATION 138,123,359
PROJECTED POPULATION 2005 156,135,833
POPULATION DENSITY 171.8 per sq km (445 per sq mile)
LIFE EXPECTANCY 59.4
INFANT MORTALITY (PER 1,000) 91.9
OFFICIAL LANGUAGES Urdu, English
OTHER LANGUAGES Punjabi, Sindhi, Urdu, Pashto, Baluchi, Brahvi
LITERACY RATE 37.1%
RELIGIONS Muslim 97% (Sunni 77%, Shi'a 20%), other (Christian, Hindu) 3%
ETHNIC GROUPS Punjabi 60%, Sindhi 14%, Pashtun (Pathan) 9%, other (Baloch and Mohajir) 17%
CURRENCY Pakistani rupee
ECONOMY Agriculture 50%, services 38%, industry 12%
GNP PER CAPITA US$460
CLIMATE Mainly arid; temperate in northwest, cold and snowy in mountains
HIGHEST POINT K2 8,611 m (28,251 ft)
MAP REFERENCE Page 757

Pakistan

Pakistan occupies the valley of the Indus and its tributaries in the northwest of the Indian subcontinent. Its most sensitive political frontiers are with India to the east and Afghanistan to the west. It has shorter borders with Iran and China.

Forming a part of India until 1947, Pakistan shares a history of early civilizations, migrations, and invasions—farmers in the Indus Valley were already using elaborate irrigation works by the second millennium BC. At the time of partition in 1947, Pakistan was two widely separated territories (West and East Pakistan). A dispute over Kashmir has poisoned relations with India since that time. In 1971 East Pakistan achieved independence as Bangladesh. In that year the populist leader Ali Bhutto assumed power in Pakistan, and in 1973 announced a program of "Islamic socialism" under which banks, insurance companies, heavy industry, and even education were nationalized. Since 1977, when he was overthrown by General Zia ul-Haq (and subsequently executed), military and civilian rule have alternated, accompanied by varying degrees of violence and disorder.

Although 97 percent of Pakistan's population is Muslim, there is a wide range of ethnic groupings, languages, and conflicts. The main linguistic separation is between Iranian languages such as Baluchi and Pashto, and the Indo-Aryan languages of Punjabi, Sindhi, and Urdu. Each of Pakistan's minorities has its own particular concerns. In the northwest of the country the Pathans want to join their kin over the Afghan frontier. The Urdu-speaking Mohajirs migrated in their millions from India at the time of partition and make up the majority of the population in Karachi and Hyderabad. They resent Punjabi domination and the rule of the old land-owning elite.

The whole of Pakistan is drained by the Indus River. Rising in the Great Highlands of the north it flows southwest, joined by tributaries such as the Jhelum, Chenab, Beas, Ravi, and Sutlej, and forms a fertile and densely populated floodplain in the east of the country before spilling into the Arabian Sea. The waters of this basin feed into one of the largest irrigation systems in the world, the total area being 13 million hectares (32 million acres). Two constructions, one at Tarbela on the Indus, and the other at Mangla on the Jhelum, are among the world's biggest earth- and rock-filled dams. West of the Indus Delta is an ascending landscape of alternating ridges and arid basins, some containing salt marshes like the Hamun-i-Mashkel. In the extreme northwest are the Great Highlands, with the Khyber Pass on the frontier with Afghanistan to the west and the spectacular peaks of the Karakoram and Pamirs to the east. Along with Nanga Parbat, these include the second highest mountain in the world—K2, Mt Godwin Austen (8,611 m; 28,251 ft) on the border of Tibet.

Irrigation agriculture combined with the new plant varieties that were introduced as part of the "green revolution" during the 1970s produces abundant cotton, wheat, rice, and sugarcane. Fruit and vegetables are also grown widely, while opium poppies and cannabis are illegally cultivated to supply the international drug trade. Despite the fact that approximately half the population work on the land, agriculture now accounts for less than a quarter of the national income.

Karachi is a considerable manufacturing center for the production of textiles, as is Lahore. Other industries produce a wide variety of petroleum products, construction materials, foodstuffs, and paper products. The country has large reserves of unused minerals: copper, bauxite, phosphates, and manganese. However, Pakistan also faces a range of problems. The country's economy is dependent on the highly competitive textile sector, there is a chronic trade deficit and debt burden, and much of the nation's revenue goes into funding massive defense spending on items such as nuclear weaponry and the army.

Conflict with India has led to threats of nuclear testing, despite international concern. The UN and USA have called on Pakistan to sign the Non-Proliferation Test Ban Treaty to prevent a nuclear war with India. Pakistan also has internal conflict as fundamentalists protest over increasing foreign trade.

Villagers on a suspension bridge in northern Pakistan.

The road between Quetta in Pakistan and the border with Iran.

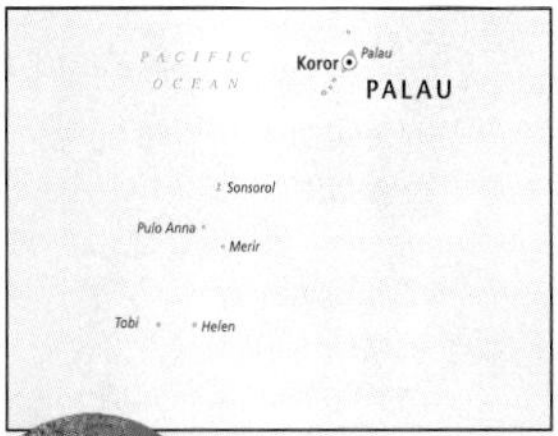

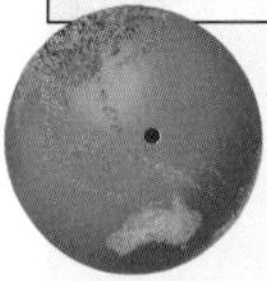

Palau

Palau consists of several groups of islands in the northwest Pacific, about 750 km (450 miles) east of the Philippine island of Mindanao. The westernmost of the Micronesian Caroline chain, and settled by Southeast Asian migrants from about 1000 BC, the islands have in the past 100 years been successively occupied and controlled by Spain, Germany, Japan, and the USA. After Spain's defeat in the 1898 Spanish–American War they were sold to Germany. Japan seized and held the islands from the outbreak of the First World War until the Second World War, when they were fought over by Japanese and US forces. In 1978, Palau rejected incorporation into the neighboring Federated States of Micronesia (a union of the rest of the Caroline Islands); in 1981 it adopted a constitution banning nuclear weapons and military bases in the area; and in 1982 it entered into a Compact of Free Association with the USA which contained military provisions in conflict with its constitution. After a lengthy political stalemate, in 1993 voters approved the Compact, which provides US$500 million in aid over 15 years in exchange for the right of the USA to maintain military facilities. In 1994 Palau became the 185th member of the UN, and in 1995 it joined the South Pacific Forum.

Palau, an archipelago of six separate groups of islands, consists of 26 islands and over 300 islets. The terrain varies from the mountainous main island of Babelthuap to low coral islands usually fringed by reefs. Natural resources consist of forests, minerals (including gold), marine products, and deep-seabed minerals. The rural people live by subsistence agriculture, growing coconuts, cassava, and sweet potatoes (though the rugged terrain of the larger islands makes farming difficult), and by fishing. Industries include tourism, craft items made from shell, wood, and pearls, and some commercial fishing. Exports include trochus shell, tuna, copra, and handicrafts. The government is the main employer, and relies heavily on aid from the USA. As a result, the population has a per capita income twice that of the Philippines.

Palau

Official name Republic of Palau
Form of government Republic in free association with the USA; two legislative bodies (Senate and House of Delegates)
Capital Koror
Area 458 sq km (177 sq miles)
Time zone GMT + 9 hours
Population 17,797
Projected population 2005 19,075
Population density 38.9 per sq km (100.7 per sq mile)
Life expectancy 71
Infant mortality (per 1,000) 25.1
Official languages Palauan, English
Other languages Sonsoral, Angaur, Japanese, Tobi
Literacy rate 99%
Religions Roman Catholic 40%, indigenous Modekngei religion 27%, Protestant 25%, other 8%
Ethnic groups Palauan (mixed Polynesian, Melanesian, Malayan) 83%, Filipino 10%, other 7%
Currency US dollar
Economy Government, agriculture, fishing, tourism
GNP per capita US$5,000
Climate Tropical, with wet season May to November
Highest point Mt Ngerchelchauus 242 m (794 ft)
Map reference Page 724

P

Some of the islands of Palau, seen from the air.

Palmyra Atoll

A privately owned uninhabited atoll in the northern Pacific, Palmyra Atoll lies about halfway between Hawaii and Samoa. At no point more than 2 m (6 ft) above sea level, the atoll consists of about 50 islets covered with dense vegetation, coconut palms, and balsa-like trees that grow up to 30 m (100 ft) tall. A number of roads and causeways were built during the Second World War, but they are now overgrown and unserviceable, as is the airstrip. In 1990 a Hawaiian property developer took out a 75-year lease from its owners, the Fullard-Leo brothers. There are plans to turn the atoll into a "get away from it all" tourist complex.

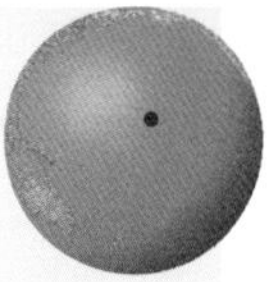

PALMYRA ATOLL

OFFICIAL NAME Palmyra Atoll
FORM OF GOVERNMENT Incorporated territory of the USA
CAPITAL None; administered from Washington DC
AREA 12 sq km (4.6 sq miles)
TIME ZONE GMT – 10 hours
POPULATION No permanent population
CLIMATE Tropical
MAP REFERENCE Page 725

Panama

Panama joins two oceans and two continents. With Costa Rica to the west and Colombia to the east, it forms a narrow neck of land connecting Central to South America, while the Panama Canal links the Atlantic Ocean to the Pacific. The first proposal for a canal was made by the Spanish in the early sixteenth century. Later, at the time of the Californian Gold Rush, the USA began to press for action. In 1881 work began on a design prepared by de Lesseps, who was the builder of the Suez Canal, but malaria and yellow fever killed so many workers on the project that it had to be abandoned. Control of these diseases was one of the achievements of the later American builders, who eventually completed the canal in 1914.

Part of Colombia until 1903, Panama has been closely linked with the USA since the construction of the canal gave the latter rights over a 16 km (10 mile) wide Canal Zone. These rights were legislated to run out in the year 2000. A major upheaval took place in Panama during 1989 when the USA invaded and removed the country's self-proclaimed "maximum leader" General Manuel Noriega in order that he face drug charges in Miami. Electoral democracy was restored in the country, and Noriega was jailed, but the laundering of large amounts of drug money in association with cartels in neighboring Colombia continues to be a problem.

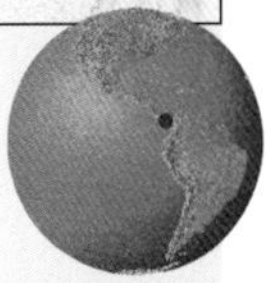

PANAMA

OFFICIAL NAME Republic of Panama
FORM OF GOVERNMENT Republic with single legislative body (Legislative Assembly)
CAPITAL Panama
AREA 78,200 sq km (30,193 sq miles)
TIME ZONE GMT – 5 hours
POPULATION 2,778,526
PROJECTED POPULATION 2005 3,030,173
POPULATION DENSITY 35.5 per sq km (92 per sq mile)
LIFE EXPECTANCY 74.7
INFANT MORTALITY (PER 1,000) 23.4
OFFICIAL LANGUAGE Spanish
OTHER LANGUAGE English
LITERACY RATE 90.5%
RELIGIONS Roman Catholic 85%, Protestant 15%

(continues)

P

PANAMA *(continued)*

ETHNIC GROUPS Mixed indigenous–European 70%, African 14%, European 10%, indigenous 6%
CURRENCY Balboa
ECONOMY Services 60%, agriculture 27%, industry 13%
GNP PER CAPITA US$2,750
CLIMATE Tropical, with long wet season May to January
HIGHEST POINT Volcán Barú 3,475 m (11,401 ft)
MAP REFERENCE Page 839

A ship heading east through the Gatun locks on the Panama Canal.

P

The 3,000 m (9,850 ft) tall mountains of the Serrania de Tabasara (Cordillera Central) run west of the canal along the isthmus, and are separated from the southern Peninsula de Azuera by a long stretch of plain. East of the canal two more ranges of mountains form arcs running parallel to the Pacific and Caribbean coasts. Most of the country, however, including 750 offshore islands, lies below 700 m (2,300 ft) and swelters in tropical heat and high humidity. Rainforests are extensive, and those of the Darien National Park, with their abundant wildlife, are among the wildest areas left in the whole of the Americas. Most Panamanians live within 20 km (12 miles) of the Canal Zone, a quarter of them in the capital itself.

Panama's economy is based on services, and is heavily weighted toward banking, commerce, and tourism. The country has the largest open-registry merchant fleet in the world. Along with the export of bananas (43 percent of total exports) and shrimp (11 percent), plus income derived from the USA's military installation, Panama has the highest standard of living in Central America. However, the country's commercial debt is also one of the highest in the world in per capita terms, and during the mid-1990s the country experienced an economic slowdown. Despite the presence of a degree of nationalist fervor, with the termination of the US Canal Zone, approximately 75 percent of Panamanians now favor a continuing US presence in the country to help preserve stability.

In preparation for the handover from USA to Panama, the country employed a team of top international architects, including USA architect Frank Gerhy, to help develop a revitalization plan. A master plan for the 16 km wide Canal Strip includes: the transformation of the abandoned military bases into apartments and hotels; development of infrastructure, including building a bridge over the canal; preservation of an historic Spanish fort; a focus on ecotourism; and research into tropical biodiversity. The objective of the plan is to capitalize on the tourist potential of the Canal Strip, and capture the tourist market of the 300 cruise ships that pass through the Canal each year. Gerhy has coined the tag "Tourism, Conservation, Research" to describe the plan, which also includes capital works on the Canal itself, such as docking facilities for the cruise ships.

Papua New Guinea

Papua New Guinea consists of the eastern half of the large island of New Guinea, the 600 or so smaller islands of the Bismarck Archipelago, and Bougainville. It lies north of northeastern Australia, just south of the equator. The largely rural population of "mainland" Papua New Guinea is made up of hundreds of distinct tribal groups, speaking more than 750 different languages. They can be broadly divided into the lowlanders of the coast and the more isolated highlanders of the mountainous interior. The main island was named New Guinea in 1545 by a Spanish explorer who thought its people resembled those of the African Guinea coast. During the last two centuries, the Netherlands, Germany, Japan, and Australia have controlled parts of it at different times. The western half—West Irian (Irian Jaya)—is now part of Indonesia; the eastern half, most recently administered by Australia, became fully independent as Papua New Guinea in 1975. Australia's relationship remains close, and it contributes 20 percent of the state budget.

A cordillera of rugged mountains runs down the main island. Covered with tropical forest, these mountains have an average elevation between 2,500 m and 4,600 m (8,000 ft and 15,000 ft). In high and isolated valleys there are settlements where people live by cultivating traditional garden crops such as sweet potato, sugar cane, bananas, maize, and cassava. Pigs are raised, but are eaten mainly at ceremonies for status and ritual purposes. Taro is a staple food of the villagers in the lowlands, where yams and sago are also grown. Soils are mostly heavily leached, and fertile only in lowland areas and upland basins. On the southwestern coast the Fly River forms a vast swampy delta plain, one of

The New Ireland coast, Papua New Guinea.

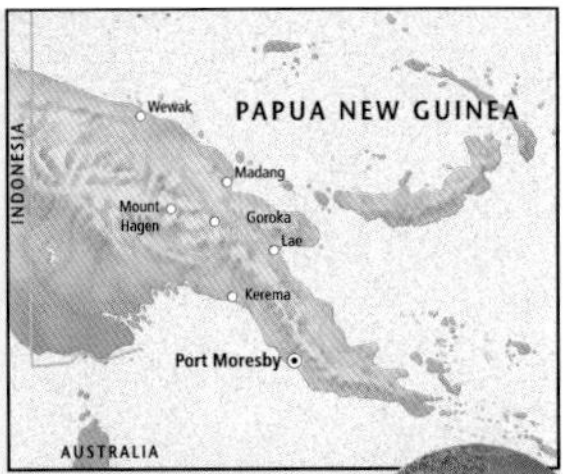

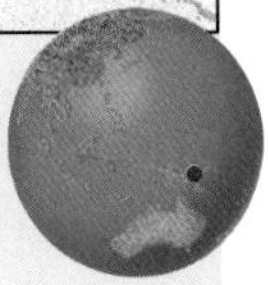

Papua New Guinea

Official name Independent State of Papua New Guinea
Form of government Constitutional monarchy with single legislative body (National Parliament or House of Assembly)
Capital Port Moresby
Area 461,690 sq km (178,258 sq miles)
Time zone GMT + 10 hours
Population 4,705,126
Projected population 2005 5,363,582
Population density 10.2 per sq km (26.4 per sq mile)
Life expectancy 58.5
Infant mortality (per 1,000) 55.6
Official languages English, Pidgin, Motu
Other languages About 750 indigenous languages
Literacy rate 71.2%
Religions Protestant 44% (including Lutheran 16%; Presbyterian, Methodist, London Missionary Society 8%; Anglican 5%; Evangelical Alliance 4%; other sects 11%), indigenous beliefs 34%, Roman Catholic 22%
Ethnic groups New Guinea Papuan 84%; Polynesian, Chinese, European and other 16%
Currency Kina
Economy Agriculture 64%, services and industry 36%
GNP per capita US$1,160
Climate Tropical, with wet season December to March
Highest point Mt Wilhelm 4,509 m (14,793 ft)
Map reference Page 726

A young girl in traditional dress and face paint in Papua New Guinea.

the world's biggest wetlands. The other major islands further east (New Ireland, New Britain, Manus, and Bougainville) are mainly of volcanic origin and are generally ringed by coral reefs. Three-quarters of the land area of Papua New Guinea is covered with dense rainforest.

The country has a variety of natural resources but rugged terrain and high infrastructural costs make their extraction difficult. Much travel is only possible by air. While most people live by subsistence agriculture, copper and gold account for about 60 percent of export earnings. The main cash crops are coffee, cocoa, coconuts, palm kernels, tea, and rubber. Timber from the forests is also important. The government is looking to petroleum and mineral exports to drive its program of economic development, but there are social and political obstacles to be overcome. Corruption is endemic, tribal and criminal violence are high, and what was once the world's biggest copper mine—Panguna on Bougainville—has been closed for years. The Bougainville people are culturally kin to the people of the Solomons and strongly resent their domination by Papua New Guinea. Grievances over their share of the mine's earnings and compensation have become a demand for independence.

Paracel Islands

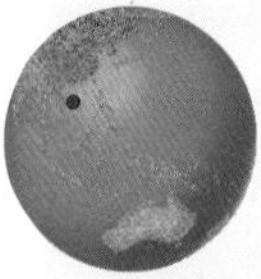

PARACEL ISLANDS

OFFICIAL NAME Paracel Islands
FORM OF GOVERNMENT Disputed territory occupied by China, but claimed by Taiwan and Vietnam
CAPITAL None
AREA Not available
TIME ZONE GMT + 8 hours
POPULATION No permanent population; Chinese garrisons
CLIMATE Tropical. Prone to typhoons
MAP REFERENCE Page 739

Situated in the South China Sea, the Paracel Islands are a collection of coral atolls about one-third of the way from central Vietnam to the northern Philippines. The Chinese have garrisoned the islands and have built port facilities and an airport on Woody Island. They are the center of a regional dispute because oil and natural gas are thought to exist within their territorial waters.

The complex political history of the Islands has contributed to the current conflict. During the Vietnam war, Hanoi was receiving aid from China, and although Saigon still proclaimed ownership of the Islands, Hanoi made no statements about Chinese activity in the Paracels, and effectively allowed China to gain control. Saigon was still issuing Decrees of Administration until its defeat in 1974. It is now widely felt that although Vietnam's claim may be valid, its silence during the war had forfeited any claim. Taiwan also claims the Islands as heir to legitimate Chinese accords.

Paraguay

A small landlocked country, Paraguay was originally the home of the Guaraní Indians. It was settled by the Spaniards in 1537 who hoped to use the Guaraní as laborers on their big estates. The strong influence of the Jesuits, however, largely prevented the exploitation of the indigenous people by settlers that occurred elsewhere in South America under Spanish Catholic rule, and a socially benign intermix took place. Today, 95 percent of the population are of combined Indian and Spanish descent.

Fully independent since 1813, Paraguay is best known in modern times for the severe regime imposed by General Stroessner between 1954 and 1989. Assuming power after a period of chronic upheaval—six presidents in six years and revolts that had left thousands dead—he brought economic and political stability, and greatly improved the national infrastructure. This was at the price of considerable repression, and the huge hydroelectric projects that were built on the Paraná River incurred sizeable foreign debts.

Across the plains, and south of Asunción, the Paraná becomes a highway to the sea. Paraguay has around 3,100 km (1,900 miles) of navigable waterways, the most important being the Paraguay River, which bisects the country north to south. To the west of Paraguay are the marshy, insect-infested plains of the Gran Chaco, but as the land rises toward the Bolivian border the Chaco changes to semidesert scrub. East of the river the land rises to a plateau forested with tropical hardwoods.

The economy of Paraguay has long been based on agriculture, and large numbers of people still live by means of subsistence farming. Cattle raising and the production of meat products remain the leading agricultural activity but cash crops such as cotton, soybeans, and timber are of increasing importance as a source of export income. Moreover, Paraguay's excess electricity capacity enables it to export power to Brazil.

The informal sector of the economy is also important. Small enterprises and street vendors flourish by importing and re-exporting consumer goods such as electronic devices, alcoholic beverages, and perfumes. While tourism is poorly developed, day-trippers pour in from Brazil and Argentina to buy these goods.

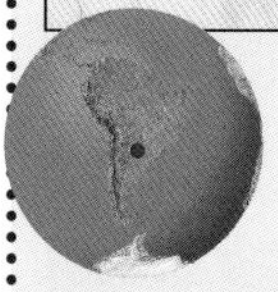

PARAGUAY

OFFICIAL NAME Republic of Paraguay
FORM OF GOVERNMENT Republic with two legislative bodies (Senate and Chamber of Deputies)
CAPITAL Asunción
AREA 406,750 sq km (157,046 sq miles)
TIME ZONE GMT – 4 hours
POPULATION 5,434,095
PROJECTED POPULATION 2005 6,340,163
POPULATION DENSITY 13.4 per sq km (34.7 per sq mile)
LIFE EXPECTANCY 72.4
INFANT MORTALITY (PER 1,000) 36.4
OFFICIAL LANGUAGE Spanish
OTHER LANGUAGE Guaraní
LITERACY RATE 91.9%
RELIGIONS Roman Catholic 90%; other (including Mennonite, Baptist and Anglican) 10%
ETHNIC GROUPS Mixed indigenous–European 95%; indigenous, European, Asian, African 5%
CURRENCY Guaraní
ECONOMY Agriculture 49%, services 30%, industry 21%
GNP PER CAPITA US$1,690
CLIMATE Subtropical; wet in east, semiarid in west
HIGHEST POINT Cerro San Rafael 850 m (2,789 ft)
MAP REFERENCE Pages 853, 856–7

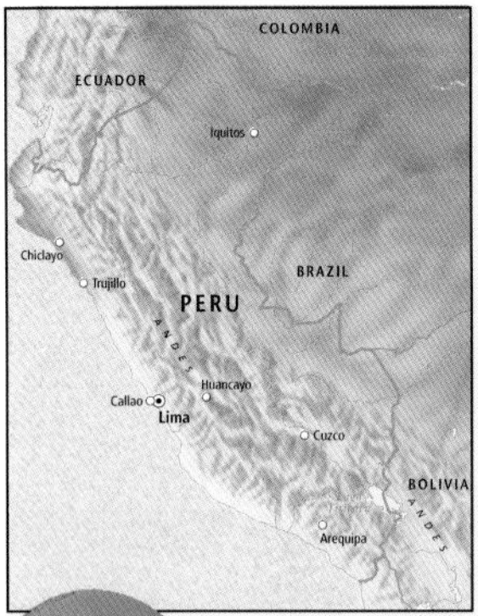

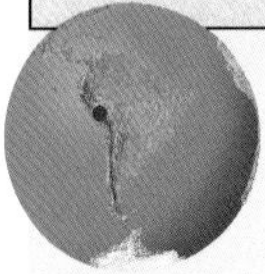

PERU

OFFICIAL NAME Republic of Peru
FORM OF GOVERNMENT Republic with single legislative body (Congress)
CAPITAL Lima
AREA 1,285,220 sq km (496,223 sq miles)
TIME ZONE GMT – 5 hours
POPULATION 26,625,121
PROJECTED POPULATION 2005 29,658,649
POPULATION DENSITY 20.7 per sq km (53.7 per sq mile)
LIFE EXPECTANCY 70.4
INFANT MORTALITY (PER 1,000) 41.4
OFFICIAL LANGUAGES Spanish, Quechua
OTHER LANGUAGE Aymara
LITERACY RATE 88.3%
RELIGIONS Roman Catholic 90%; others, including Anglican and Methodist 10%
ETHNIC GROUPS Indigenous 45%, mixed indigenous–European 37%, European 15%; others (mainly African, Japanese, Chinese) 3%
CURRENCY Nuevo sol
ECONOMY Services 53%, agriculture 35%, industry 12%
GNP PER CAPITA US$2,310
CLIMATE Tropical in east, arid along coast, cold on high mountains
HIGHEST POINT Nev. Huascarán 6,768 m (22,204 ft)
MAP REFERENCE Pages 848, 852–3

Peru

Humans have been living in Peru for about 10,000 years. By 3,000 years ago Peruvian civilization had emerged, with irrigation, agriculture, fine pottery, and expertly woven textiles. The Incas, one of the many tribes that inhabited the highlands of Peru, established a great empire in the thirteenth century that extended from Ecuador south to central Chile. Accomplished engineers, the Incas built an extensive network of roads and bridges, and many fine cities. The most famous of these is Machu Picchu, high above the Urubamba Valley. The Spanish came to Peru in 1532, lured by stories of a "kingdom of gold" and rapidly destroyed Inca civilization.

Recently Peru has experienced serious political trouble. Deep social divisions gave rise in 1980 to the movement known as *Sendero Luminoso*, or Shining Path, a Maoist guerrilla group. By 1990 its activities had resulted in the loss of 23,000 lives—most of them members of its own constituency, the Indians and mixed Spanish–Indians of the Andes—along with damage to the economy in the order of US$20 billion. In recent years there has been greater stability.

Some 40 percent of Peru's population live on its arid coastal plain, which merges in the south with the rainless Atacama Desert of northern Chile. Numerous rivers crossing the plain from the Andes have made fertile valleys where cotton, rice, and sugarcane are grown. Inland, in the valleys of two high ranges of the Andean Sierra, the western and the eastern Cordilleras, about 50 percent of the people live, most of them Indians practicing subsistence agriculture. East of the Andes the land falls away into the almost uninhabited region of the Amazon Basin. Here, the Ucayali and Marañón Rivers flow through rainforest to Iquitos, the most inland navigable port on the Amazon River.

Peru's economy depends heavily on copper and petroleum exports. Agriculture is limited by the lack of arable land. Fishing for anchovies and sardines has been historically important in the cool Humboldt current offshore, but periodic warming of the ocean from the El Niño effect reduces the catch, as has occurred several times in recent years. In 1992 it fell by 30 percent.

The ruins of Machu Picchu are an incomparable spectacle for tourists, but poor facilities and guerrilla activities have discouraged visitors. Battered by hyprinflation, which reached 7,480 percent in 1990, Peru has recently undergone a series of economic reforms guided by the IMF and the World Bank. By 1995 inflation had been reduced to 11percent, while growth in gross domestic product for that year was about 7 percent.

A rural settlement near Cuzco, Peru.

Peter 1 Island

One of the Antarctic maritime islands, Peter 1 Island lies off the continent near the Venable Ice Shelf. It was named by a captain in the Imperial Russian Navy, Thaddeus von Bellingshausen in honor of the founder of the Russian Navy when von Bellingshausen led exploratory expeditions in 1819–21.

Though slightly moderated by the sea, the climate is basically that of the adjacent continent and the temperature rises above freezing only for short periods in summer. In winter the island is entirely surrounded by pack ice.

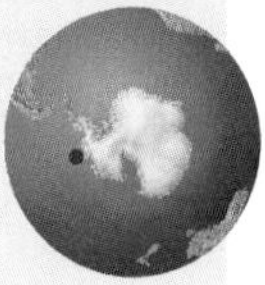

Peter 1 Island

Official name Peter 1 Island
Form of government Dependent territory of Norway
Capital None; administered from Oslo
Area 180 sq km (70 sq miles)
Time zone GMT – 6 hours
Population No permanent population
Economy None
Climate Cold and windy
Map reference Page 862

Philippines

The islands of the Philippines present a combination that is unique in Asia. The people are Malayo-Polynesian; the majority of the population is Roman Catholic; English is the only common language in a country that has 87 native tongues; nearly four centuries of Spanish colonialism have left a flavor of Latin America; and 100 years of US influence (following the Spanish–American War in 1898) mean that the Philippines is also somewhat Americanized.

Long ago, and before the Spaniard explorer Ferdinand Magellan arrived from across the Pacific on his round-the-world voyage in 1521, Islam had reached the southern island of Mindanao. It is still the religion of a substantial minority in that part of the country. The Spanish then imposed whatever unity the archipelago can be said to have (there are 7,107 islands), building haciendas and

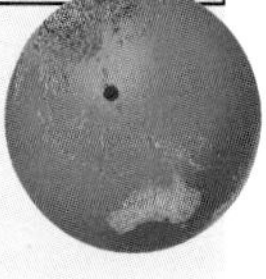

Philippines

Official name Republic of the Philippines
Form of government Republic with two legislative bodies (Senate and House of Representatives)

(continues)

PHILIPPINES *(continued)*

CAPITAL Manila
AREA 300,000 sq km (115,830 sq miles)
TIME ZONE GMT + 8 hours
POPULATION 79,345,812
PROJECTED POPULATION 2005 89,055,628
POPULATION DENSITY 264.5 per sq km (685 per sq mile)
LIFE EXPECTANCY 66.6
INFANT MORTALITY (PER 1,000) 33.9
OFFICIAL LANGUAGES Filipino, English
OTHER LANGUAGES About 87 indigenous languages
LITERACY RATE 94.4%
RELIGIONS Roman Catholic 83%, Protestant 9%, Muslim 5%, Buddhist and other 3%
ETHNIC GROUPS Malay 95.5%, Chinese 1.5%, other 3%
CURRENCY Philippine peso
ECONOMY Services 48%, agriculture 42%, industry 10%
GNP PER CAPITA US$1,050
CLIMATE Tropical, with wet season June to November
HIGHEST POINT Mt Apo 2,954 m (9,692 ft)
MAP REFERENCE Page 740

P

A coral reef in the Philippines.

sugar plantations on its main islands. Administered by the USA from 1898, the Philippines was occupied by the Japanese during the Second World War, was governed by the corrupt and authoritarian Marcos regime from 1965 to 1986, and faced a wide range of insurgencies during the last half of the twentieth century. The first insurgents were communist; more recently they have been members of the Islamic Moro National Liberation Front.

There are three main island groupings within the archipelago of the Philippines: the Luzon group, the Visayan group, and the Mindanao and Sulu Islands. Luzon to the north and Mindanao to the south are the two biggest islands and together they constitute two-thirds of the country's total land area.

Common to all of the main islands is a ruggedly mountainous and volcanic topography with narrow coastal belts, a north–south alignment of upland ridges, and rivers that drain toward the north. Lying to the north of Manila Bay, and stretching to the shores of the Lingayan Gulf, is Luzon's heavily populated central plain. This is an important rice-producing area. Beyond hills to the northeast lies the fertile valley of the Cagayan River. Irrigated rice terraces, constructed by the Igorot people, rise tier upon tier up the mountain slopes of northern Luzon. The peninsulas of southeastern Luzon contain a number of volcanoes. The highest peak in the Philippines, Mt Apo (2,954 m; 9,692 ft), is on Mindanao.

Government investment and a range of tax concessions have been used to encourage industrial development. Mixing agriculture and light industry, the Philippine economy has been growing at a steady rate in recent years, without approaching the dynamic performance of other countries in the region.

While rice is the Philippines' main food crop, maize is the staple on the islands of Cebu, Leyte, and Negros, reflecting the country's old connection with Spanish America.

The country is well supplied with mineral resources and nickel, tin, copper, zinc and lead are processed in smelting and refining works. The Philippines is also the world's biggest supplier of refractory chrome, and the second biggest user of geothermal power after the USA. Foreign investment turned sluggish as a consequence of the 1998 regional economic slowdown. Persistent weaknesses in the economy include a rudimentary infrastructure, power failures due to inadequate generating capacity, low domestic savings rates, and a foreign debt of US$45 billion.

Pitcairn Islands

The Pitcairn Islands are located in the southern Pacific about midway between Peru and New Zealand. They have a rugged volcanic formation, cliffs along a rocky coast, and a tropical, hot, and humid climate. The islands are the United Kingdom's most isolated dependency. Uninhabited when they were discovered by Europeans, they were used as a refuge by the mutineers from HMS *Bounty* in 1790, some of whose descendants still live there speaking a dialect that is part-Tahitian, part-English. They exist by fishing and subsistence farming. The fertile valley soils produce fruits and vegetables including citrus, sugarcane, watermelons, bananas, yams, and beans. Barter is an important economic activity. The main source of revenue is the sale of postage stamps and handicrafts to passing ships.

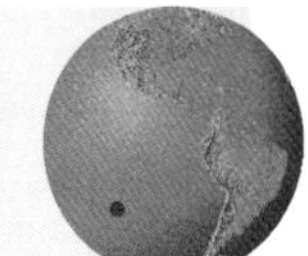

Pitcairn Islands

Official name Pitcairn, Henderson, Ducie, and Oeno Islands
Form of government Dependent territory of the United Kingdom
Capital Adamstown
Area 47 sq km (18 sq miles)
Time zone GMT – 8.5 hours
Population 54 (1995)
Currency New Zealand dollar
Economy Fishing, agriculture, services
Climate Tropical, with rainy season from November to March
Map reference Page 723

Poland

Situated in northern central Europe, Poland has a northern coastline on the Baltic Sea and land borders with seven countries. To the west, the Oder River forms part of the border with Germany, while to the southwest the Sudeten Mountains separate it from the Czech Republic. The Carpathian Mountains form a natural boundary with Slovakia in the south. Ukraine and Belarus lie to the east, Lithuania is to the northeast and a part of the Russian Federation is adjacent to the northern coastline.

In the seventh and eighth centuries AD, Slavic peoples from the south—known as Polanie, or plain-dwellers—occupied most of Poland. In the tenth century their king was converted to Christianity, beginning a Catholic tradition that has survived to the present, despite attempts to suppress it by post-war communist governments. Over the next two centuries, invaders from Prussia divided up the country, which was reunited in the fourteenth century. Poland retained its independence and at times extended its power during the next two centuries, but again came under Prussian and Austrian control in the late eighteenth century. The nation regained its independence in 1918 with the defeat of Austria–Germany in the First World War. Early in the Second World War, Poland was

Poland

Official name Republic of Poland
Form of government Republic with two legislative bodies (Senate and Parliament or Sejm)
Capital Warsaw
Area 312,683 sq km (120,727 sq miles)
Time zone GMT + 1 hour
Population 38,608,929
Projected population 2005 39,257,669
Population density 123.5 per sq km (319.8 per sq mile)
Life expectancy 73.1

(continues)

P

POLAND *(continued)*

INFANT MORTALITY (PER 1,000) 12.8
OFFICIAL LANGUAGE Polish
LITERACY RATE 99%
RELIGIONS Roman Catholic 95%; others include Eastern Orthodox, Protestant 5%
Ethnic groups Polish 97.6%, German 1.3%, Ukrainian 0.6%, Belarusian 0.5%
CURRENCY Zloty
ECONOMY Services 40%, industry 32%, agriculture 28%
GNP PER CAPITA US$2,790
CLIMATE Temperate, with cold winters and warm, wet summers
HIGHEST POINT Rysy 2,499 m (8,199 ft)
MAP REFERENCE Page 773

overrun by Germany and then Russia, which divided the country between them until June 1941, when the Germans took full control. After the war Poland's borders shifted to the west, as part of what was formerly Germany was ceded to Poland, and as the Soviets were given control of substantial territories in the east. Under these arrangements Poland suffered a net loss of both territory and population. From then until 1989 Poland was effectively a vassal state of the Soviet Union.

Growing civil unrest during the 1980s focused on a series of strikes in a range of industries, organized by the trade union Solidarity. In 1989 the besieged government capitulated and allowed Solidarity to contest the government elections, which it won decisively. The first entirely free elections were held in 1991. Poland is now a democratic republic with a directly elected president and a multi-party system.

Except for the mountain ranges in the south and southwest, most of Poland is low-lying, forming part of the North European Plain. The landscape is drained by numerous rivers, the most significant of which is the Vistula, which rises in the Carpathian Mountains and flows through the center of the country, through Warsaw, and to the Baltic Sea near the industrial city of Gdansk. Most of this plain is fertile, covered with rich loess soil which supports a range of cereal and vegetable crops, in which Poland is almost self-sufficient, and livestock, the most important of which are cattle and pigs. In the northeast the country is more undulating, and much of northern Poland is dotted with extensive lakes. Towards

The rooftops of Gdansk in northern Poland, a major port and birthplace of the trade union Solidarity.

P

the Baltic coast a range of hills, known as the Baltic Heights, slope down to a sandy coastal plain.

Agriculture, which once employed more than half of Poland's workforce, still accounts for just over a quarter of it. The post-war years saw a rapid expansion of heavy industries, which now include shipbuilding, based in Gdansk, and steel and cement manufacture, based around the mining centers in the south. Many industrial activities rely on Poland's rich coal reserves, and coal is used to generate more than half the country's electricity. Reliance on this form of fuel has resulted in serious air pollution and acid rain. Other mineral resources include natural gas, iron ore, and salt, on which important chemical industries are based.

Poland has been more successful than many former communist states in converting to a privatized economy. While many Poles have prospered from a growing number of entrepreneurial activities, others, however, have seen their incomes seriously lowered. Unemployment remains comparatively high.

Winter snow scene in a forest, Sopot, Gdansk.

Portugal

Situated at the western edge of the Iberian Peninsula, Portugal is shaped somewhat like a long, narrow rectangle. It has a long Atlantic coastline bordering its western edge, and a much shorter one at its southern extremity. Spain surrounds it on the other two sides. From the second century BC until the fifth century AD, Portugal was part of the Roman Empire. As the empire collapsed the territory suffered a series of invasions—by Germanic tribes, Visigoths, and, in the eighth century, by Muslim Moors from northern Africa. The Moors were finally expelled by Christian invaders from Burgundy during the twelfth century and a Burgundian line of monarchs was established. An abortive Castilian attempt to seize the crown in the fourteenth century saw a new dynasty installed under John of Aviz, who reigned as John I. His son, Prince Henry the Navigator, encouraged widespread exploration and the establishment of a vast empire, with colonies in Africa, South America, India, and Southeast Asia. The invasion of Portugal by the Spanish in 1581 heralded the decline in Portugal's influence. A French

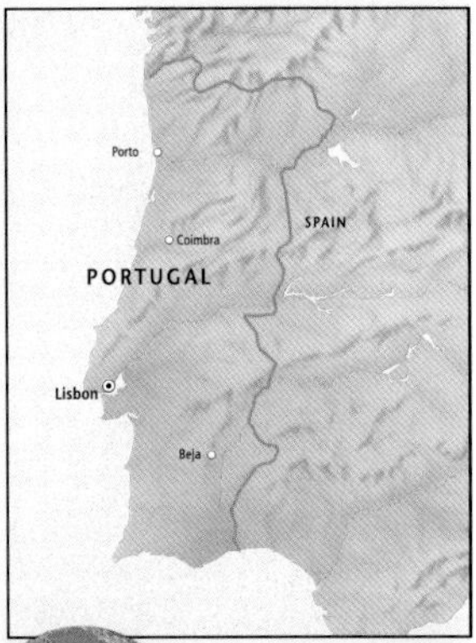

PORTUGAL

OFFICIAL NAME Portuguese Republic
FORM OF GOVERNMENT Republic with single legislative body (Assembly of the Republic)

(continues)

PORTUGAL *(continued)*

CAPITAL Lisbon
AREA 92,080 sq km (35,552 sq miles)
TIME ZONE GMT + 1 hour
POPULATION 9,918,040
PROJECTED POPULATION 2005 9,792,757
POPULATION DENSITY 107.7 per sq km (279 per sq mile)
LIFE EXPECTANCY 75.9
INFANT MORTALITY (per 1,000) 6.7
OFFICIAL LANGUAGE Portuguese
LITERACY RATE 89.6%
RELIGIONS Roman Catholic 97%, Protestant 1%, other 2%
ETHNIC GROUPS Portuguese 98%, African immigrants from former colonies 2%
CURRENCY Escudo
ECONOMY Services 61%, industry 26%, agriculture 13%
GNP PER CAPITA US$9,740
Climate Temperate; cool and rainy in north, warm and dry in south
HIGHEST POINT Ponta de Pico in the Azores 2,351 m (7,713 ft); Serra de Estrela on the mainland, 1,993 m (6,539 ft)
MAP REFERENCE Page 776

Farm buildings at the foot of Mt Giestoso in Minho Province.

invasion in 1807 was reversed three years later when the British expelled the invaders in 1811.

During the nineteenth century widespread poverty and growing resentment at the power of the monarchy culminated in the 1910 revolution, in which the monarchy was overthrown. An army coup in 1926 installed Olivier Salazar as a right-wing dictator. He remained in power until 1968, but his successor, Marcello Caetano, was overthrown by a left-wing army coup in 1974, which eventually led to democratic elections in 1976. Portugal is now a democratic republic, with a popularly elected president as head of state.

Portugal is divided fairly evenly into its wetter northern and more arid southern regions by the River Tagus. This river flows west into the country from Spain and then takes a southwesterly course toward the Atlantic, entering it at Lisbon. Highland forested areas dominate the north. The highest mountains are in the far north, especially in the east. Here, the landscape is characterized by high plateaus, punctuated by deep gorges and river valleys, which gradually descend to the western coastal plain. In these mountains are thick forests of both conifers and deciduous trees. South of the Douro River the landscape becomes less rugged and the slopes more gentle until they reach the plain around the Tagus. South of the Tagus, the country is mainly flat or undulating. In the Tagus Valley and further south are forests of cork oaks, the bark of which is used to produce wine corks. In the Algarve, in the far south, a range of hills runs across the country from the Spanish border to its southwestern tip.

Portugal has two self-governing regions in the Atlantic: the nine volcanic islands that constitute the Azores and the volcanic archipelago of two inhabited and two groups of uninhabited islets that make up Madeira. In 1987, Portugal signed a treaty to return its last territory, Macau, to China in 1999.

By western European standards Portugal is still a highly rural society, with agriculture and fishing still employing a significant number of the country's workforce. Many farms, especially the smaller ones that predominate in the north, continue to use traditional methods. Cereals and vegetables are widely cultivated, and wine production, especially port wine from the Douro Valley, is the major agricultural activity. Manufacturing is growing in importance, much of it concerned with processing the country's agricultural products. Paper and cork manufacture, and texiles and footwear, are among

P

the significant industries. Tourism, especially in the warm, southern Algarve region, has greatly expanded in recent years, leading to rapid building development and considerable attendant environmental degradation.

Puerto Rico

Puerto Rico is a large Caribbean island east of the Dominican Republic. Ceded by Spain to the USA in 1898, its citizens enjoy a number of privileges as a result of their American connection (for example, Puerto Ricans have full US citizenship, pay no federal taxes, and have free access to the US). In 1993 the population once more voted to continue their self-governing commonwealth status and forgo becoming either the 51st state of the USA or independent. Mountainous, with a narrow coastal plain, the little flat ground available for agriculture is used for growing sugarcane, coffee, bananas, and tobacco. Today, Puerto Rico's economy is essentially modern and industrialized. Tax relief and cheap labor have brought many businesses to the island and tourism is growing. Industries include petrochemicals, pharmaceuticals (the island produces over 90 percent of all US tranquillizers), and electronics. The standard of living in Puerto Rico is the highest in Latin America (outside the island tax havens), and is rising.

The oceanfront in old San Juan.

Puerto Rico

Official name Commonwealth of Puerto Rico
Form of government Commonwealth associated with the United States
Capital San Juan
Area 9,104 sq km (3,515 sq miles)
Time zone GMT – 4 hours
Population 3,890,353
Life expectancy 75.2
Infant mortality (per 1,000) 10.5
Literacy rate 87.8%
Currency US dollar
Economy Government 22%, manufacturing 17%, trade 20%, construction 6%, communications and transportation 5%, other 30%
Climate Tropical, moderated by sea breezes
Map reference Page 837

P

CAFE

Q,R

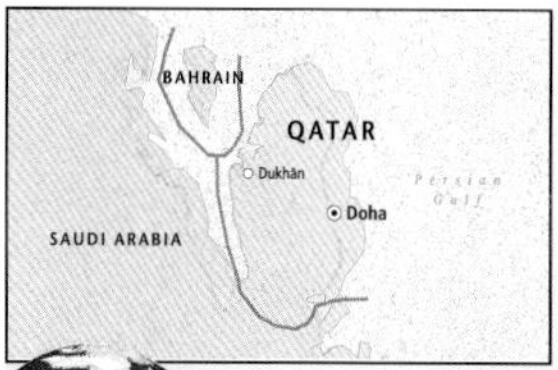

FACT FILE

OFFICIAL NAME State of Qatar
FORM OF GOVERNMENT Monarchy with Advisory Consultative Council
CAPITAL Ad Dawhah (Doha)
AREA 11,000 sq km (4,247 sq miles)
TIME ZONE GMT + 3 hours
POPULATION 723,542
PROJECTED POPULATION 2005 874,179
POPULATION DENSITY 65.8 per sq km (170.4 per sq mile)
LIFE EXPECTANCY 74.2
INFANT MORTALITY (PER 1,000) 17.3
OFFICIAL LANGUAGE Arabic
OTHER LANGUAGE English
LITERACY RATE 78.9%
RELIGIONS Muslim 95%, other 5%
ETHNIC GROUPS Arab 40%, Pakistani 18%, Indian 18%, Iranian 10%, other 14%
CURRENCY Qatari rial
ECONOMY Services 50%, industry (particularly oil production and refining) 48%, agriculture 2%
GNP PER CAPITA US$11,600
CLIMATE Hot and arid; humid in summer
HIGHEST POINT Qurayn Aba al Bawl 103 m (338 ft)
MAP REFERENCE Page 756

Qatar

Qatar is a small, wealthy emirate in the Persian Gulf. In 1971 it chose not to join the neighboring United Arab Emirates as a member state, but to go it alone. Recently it has continued to act with independence, signing a security pact with the USA in 1995 involving the stationing of 2,000 US troops, while simultaneously challenging the Gulf Cooperation Council's policy on Iraq. The peninsula it occupies, projecting north from the southern shore of the Persian Gulf near Bahrain, consists of flat and semiarid desert. Most of its population are guest workers from the Indian subcontinent, Iran, and north Africa.

Qatar was ruled for centuries by the Khalifah dynasty. A rift in dynastic affairs opened in 1783, war with Bahrain followed in 1867, and then the British intervened to set up a separate emirate under the al-Thani family. Qatar became a full British protectorate in 1916. At this time it was occupied by nomadic Bedouin wandering the peninsula with their herds of goats and camels. Oil production, which commenced in 1949, changed everything and now almost 90 percent of the people live in the capital city of Doha or its suburbs. The northern parts of Qatar are dotted with abandoned villages.

A bloodless palace coup in 1995 saw the present emir displace his father, a move that was accepted without fuss. The emir of Qatar rules as an absolute monarch, he occupies the office of prime minister and he appoints his own cabinet. He is advised by a partially elected 30-member *majlis al-shura* (consultative council). From time to time there are calls for democratic reforms from prominent citizens.

The Qatar Peninsula is mainly low-lying except for a few hills in the west of the country at Jabal Dukhān (the Dukhan Heights) and some low cliffs in the northeast. Sandy desert, salt flats, and barren plains cut by shallow wadis (creek beds) occupy 95 percent of its land area. There is little rainfall aside from occasional winter showers. As a result of the shortage of fresh water Qatar is dependent on large-scale desalinization facilities. Summers are usually hot and humid; winter nights can be cool and chilly. Drought-resistant plant life is mainly found in the south. However, by tapping ground-water supplies, Qatar is now able to cultivate most of its own vegetables.

Crude oil production and refining is by far the most important industry. Oil accounts for more than 30 percent of gross domestic product, about 75 percent of export earnings, and 70 percent of government revenues. Reserves of 3.3 billion barrels should ensure continued output at present levels for at least another 25 years. Oil has given Qatar a per capita gross domestic product that is comparable to some of the leading western European industrial economies. Long-term goals include the development of offshore wells and economic diversification.

Doha trading dhow, Qatar.

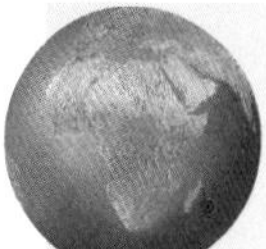

RÉUNION

OFFICIAL NAME Department of Réunion
FORM OF GOVERNMENT Overseas department of France
CAPITAL Saint-Denis
AREA 2,510 sq km (969 sq miles)
TIME ZONE GMT + 4 hours
POPULATION 717,723
LIFE EXPECTANCY 75.7
INFANT MORTALITY (PER 1,000) 6.9
LITERACY RATE 78.6%
CURRENCY French franc
ECONOMY Services 49%, agriculture 30%, industry 21%
CLIMATE Tropical; cool and dry May to November, hot and rainy November to April
MAP REFERENCE Page 813

Réunion

Réunion is the largest of the Mascarene Islands which lie southwest of Mauritius and east of Madagascar. A fertile plain surrounds Réunion's rugged and mountainous interior. One of two volcanic peaks, Piton des Neiges rises to 3,069 m (10,069 ft) and is sporadically active. Plentiful rainfall comes with the winter trade winds. On the intensively cultivated lowlands there are large sugarcane plantations which provide 75 percent of exports and are the island's only significant industry. Vanilla, perfume oils, and tea also produce revenue, while vegetables and maize are grown for local consumption. Tourism is growing, but unemployment is high. The population is divided over continued association with France, which uses Réunion as its main military base in the area.

The small, uninhabited islands of Bassas da India, Europa, Glorieuses, Île Juan de Nova, and Tromelin are associated dependencies.

A bay and a small village in Réunion.

Romania

Except for its Black Sea coast, Romania is land-locked—by Ukraine to the north, Moldova to the northeast, Hungary to the west, Yugoslavia to the southwest, and Bulgaria to the south. From the sixth century AD the country was often invaded. From the ninth to the eleventh centuries Magyars occupied part of Transylvania and between the fourteenth and sixteenth centuries Walachia, Moldova, and Transylvania formed part of the Ottoman Empire. At the end of the First World War, Bessarabia—most of present-day Moldova—Transylvania and Bukovina were restored to Romania. Much of this land was lost during the Second World War when Romania, which sided with Nazi Germany, came under Soviet control. During Ceausescu's oppressive regime, beginning in 1967, Romania distanced itself from the Soviets. In 1989 a popular uprising saw Ceausescu arrested and executed. Romania is now ruled by an elected parliament headed by a president.

The Carpathian Mountains curve through the center of the country, dividing the timbered uplands of Transylvania from the Danube Plain. The southern part of the range, the Transylvanian Alps, contains the highest peaks

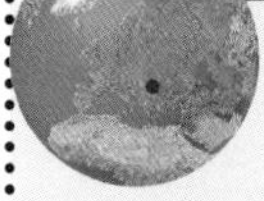

Romania

Official name Romania
Form of government Republic with two legislative bodies (Senate and House of Deputies)
Capital Bucharest
Area 237,500 sq km (91,699 sq miles)
Time zone GMT + 2 hours
Population 22,334,312
Projected population 2005 22,304,366
Population density 94 per sq km (243.5 per sq mile)
Life expectancy 70.8
Infant mortality (per 1,000) 18.1
Official language Romanian
Other languages Hungarian, German
Literacy rate 96.9%
Religions Romanian Orthodox 87%, Roman Catholic 5%, Protestant 5%, other 3%
Ethnic groups Romanian 89.1%, Hungarian 8.9%, other 2%
Currency Leu
Economy Industry 38%, services 34%, agriculture 28%
GNP per capita US$1,480
Climate Temperate; cold winters and warm, wet summers; cooler in Carpathian Mountains
Highest point Moldoveanu 2,544 m (8,346 ft)
Map reference Page 780

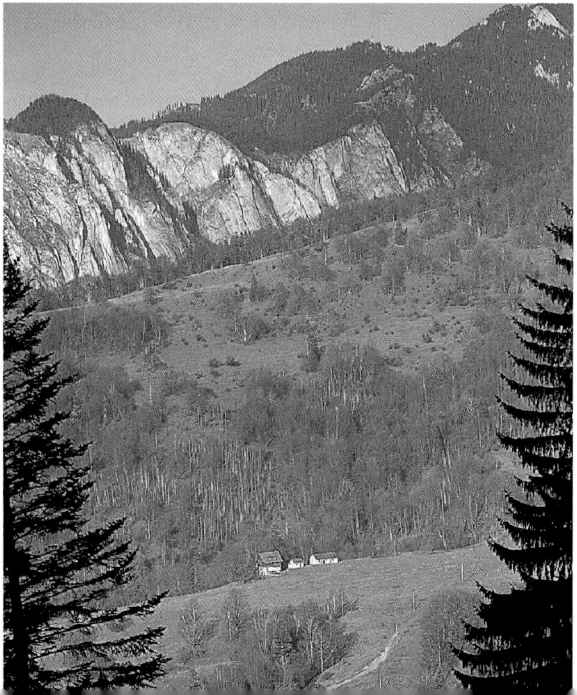

The Transylvanian Alps.

and the most rugged scenery. The fertile eastern plain is crossed by many tributaries of the Danube. To the east, around the Danube Delta, the landscape is marshy and dotted with numerous lakes and lagoons.

There has been a shift toward heavy industries since the 1970s but agriculture is still economically important. Maize, wheat, vegetables, and grapes for wine are the main crops and sheep and pigs the main livestock. Romania is rich in coal, natural gas, iron ore, and petroleum. Most of the raw materials for the country's industries are imported. Prominent industries include chemical and metal processing and machine manufacturing. Lumbering has depleted much of the country's forest and industry has caused widespread pollution. Moves to a market economy have been slow and Romania's standard of living remains relatively low.

RUSSIAN FEDERATION

R

OFFICIAL NAME Russian Federation
FORM OF GOVERNMENT Federal republic with two legislative bodies (Federation Council and State Duma)
CAPITAL Moscow
AREA 17,075,200 sq km (6,592,735 sq miles)
TIME ZONE GMT + 3–12 hours
POPULATION 146,393,569
PROJECTED POPULATION 2005 144,263,571
POPULATION DENSITY 8.6 per sq km (22.3 per sq mile)
LIFE EXPECTANCY 65.1
INFANT MORTALITY (PER 1,000) 23.0
OFFICIAL LANGUAGE Russian
OTHER LANGUAGES More than 100 minority languages
LITERACY RATE 98.7%

Russian Federation

Sprawling across the easternmost part of northern Europe and occupying the whole of northern Asia, the Russian Federation, often called simply Russia, is the largest country in the world—it is almost twice the size of the United States—and it has the sixth largest population. Its 21 republics cover three-quarters of the area of what was for almost 70 years (until it collapsed in 1991) the Union of Soviet Socialist Republics.

The Russian Federation has coastlines along the Arctic Ocean in the north and along the Pacific Ocean in the east. Its southeastern coastline is on the Sea of Japan, and north of this the Kamchatka Peninsula encloses the Sea of Okhotsk. In its far southwestern corner there is a short stretch of coast along the Caspian Sea; a little further north, it briefly borders the Black Sea; and in the northwest, near St Petersburg, it touches on the eastern tip of the Gulf of Finland. Its mainland has borders with 12 other countries. In the far southeast it borders the northeast tip of North Korea. In the south it borders China in two places: to the east and the west of its long border with Mongolia. The western half of its southern border is with the former Soviet republic of Kazakhstan. To the west of the Caspian Sea are Azerbaijan and Georgia, and north of the Black Sea are Ukraine, Belarus, Latvia, and Estonia. Northeast of the Gulf of Finland is a border with Finland and at its very northwest tip the Russian Federation borders on a tiny part of Norway. Further west, tucked in between Lithuania and Poland, and with a coast on the Baltic Sea, is another small area of Russian territory, centered on the coastal city of Kaliningrad.

History

Until the sixth century AD, almost all of what is now Russia was inhabited only by nomadic tribes of Finnic and Slavic origin. In the sixth century peoples from what are now Iran and Turkey settled the part of southwestern Russia between the Carpathian Mountains and the Volga River, establishing a capital on the Caspian Sea. They in turn were overrun by Viking invaders and traders who spread southward along river routes from the Baltic Sea. One tradition has it that modern Russia dates back to the establishment of a dynasty by the Viking Rurik at Novgorod in AD 862. Soon after, however, the center of power moved farther southwest, to Kiev in present-day Ukraine, and a unified confederation, known as Kievan Rus, emerged. In the tenth century the leader Vladimir was converted to Christianity. Over the next two centuries a Russian culture, based on the traditions of Orthodox Christianity, developed, but in the thirteenth century Kievan Rus fell to invaders from Mongolia and the confederation broke down into a number of dukedoms, under Mongol domination. The Muscovite dukes emerged as the most powerful, mainly through their role as tribute collectors for the Mongols. Opposition to Mongol rule gathered strength during the fourteenth century and in the fifteenth century the Muscovite Duke Ivan III finally expelled the Mongols. His grandson, Ivan IV, known as "The Terrible," was the first to declare himself "Tsar of all the Russians." Under his oppressive rule, which lasted from

RELIGIONS Russian Orthodox 27%; Muslim, Jewish, Roman Catholic and other minorities 73%

ETHNIC GROUPS Russian 81.5%, Tatar 3.8%, Ukrainian 3%, Chuvash 1.2%, Bashkir 0.9%, Belarusian 0.8%, Moldovan 0.7%, other 8.1%

CURRENCY Ruble

ECONOMY Industry 27%, agriculture 15%, education and culture 11%, other 47%

GNP PER CAPITA US$2,240

CLIMATE Warm and dry in far south; cold temperate (long, cold winters and short, mild summers) in most inland areas; polar in far north

HIGHEST POINT Mt Elbrus 5,633 m (18,481 ft)

MAP REFERENCE Pages 783, 784–5

R

Shoppers in Arbat Street, a prosperous part of Moscow.

Fishing through a hole in the ice, using large nets, in Siberia.

St Petersburg, once the capital of Russia, seen from across the misty Neva River.

1533 to 1584, the power of princes and landowners (known as "boyars") was broken and the Muscovite state spread eastward across the Urals and into what is now Siberia.

After Ivan's death, a series of internal disputes culminated in Polish invasion in 1609 and, after the ousting of the Poles in 1612, the emergence of the first Romanov tsar, Mikhail, in 1613. Under his grandson, Peter I (known as "The Great"), who ruled from 1696 to 1725, the country was renamed "Russia," and a new capital was established at St Petersburg. Territories along the Baltic were acquired from Sweden, and western European ideas, technology, and styles of dress and other fashions were embraced. During the eighteenth and nineteenth centuries Russia extended its borders south and east into Asia.

The defeat of Napoleon's invading armies in 1812 confirmed Russia's status as a great power, but the country remained socially and industrially backward in comparison with Western Europe. A feudal system, under which peasants were bonded to landlords, remained until 1861, when the leader Tsar Alexander II abolished serfdom. Alexander's political and social reforms earned him powerful enemies and led to his assassination in 1881. The oppressive rule of his successor, Alexander III, spawned the formation of the Marxist Russian Social Democratic Party in 1898, under the leadership of Vladimir Ilich Ulyanov, who called himself Lenin. Civil unrest intensified following Russia's defeat in its war with Japan in 1904–05, forcing Tsar Nicholas II to establish a parliament, known as the Duma, elected by a very limited suffrage, and to institute some civil liberty reforms.

These reforms, however, failed to stem the revolutionary tide, which was further strengthened by the reverses and heavy loss of life in the First World War. In February 1917, rioting and strikes broke out in the capital, St Petersburg, there was a massive defection of Russian troops, and Tsar Nicholas II abdicated, leading to the decisive revolution of October 1917, in which the All-Russian Communist Party emerged as the ruling force, with Lenin as dictatorial leader. Four years of civil war ensued, until the communists fully took control. In December 1922, Russia, with Moscow as capital, became the dominant power in the newly formed Union of Soviet Socialist Republics, having seized Georgia, Armenia, and Azerbaijan and established its ascendancy in Ukraine and central Asia.

Following Lenin's death in 1924, there was a bitter factional struggle for power. By 1929 Josef Stalin was the undisputed leader and remained in power until he died in 1953. Under his regime, agriculture was collectivized, industry was expanded, and brutal labor camps were established in Siberia for those suspected of espousing dissident ideas. Political rivals and enemies, whether real or imagined, were routinely eliminated in a series of ruthless purges. In one purge in 1929–30, hundreds of thousands of peasants who opposed farm collectivization were either murdered or sent away to remote, desolate parts of the country. Farm collectivization led to immense agricultural disruption and resulted in famine in the early 1930s in which many thousands of people died.

Russia, and the rest of the Soviet Union, suffered terribly during the Second World War. At first allied with Germany, the Soviet Union, in 1939 and 1940, seized territory in Poland and Romania, and annexed the Baltic republics of Estonia, Latvia, and Lithuania. In 1941, Hitler's troops suddenly invaded the Soviet Union, and in the occupation and struggles that ensued in the following four years, an estimated 20 million Soviet citizens were killed.

At the end of the war, the regions that were occupied by Soviet forces—most of Eastern Europe—came under Soviet domination. This gave rise to a 40-year period of international tension as the Soviet Union and the United States assumed the mantles of mutually distrustful, competing superpowers, each building up an arsenal of ever more potentially destructive nuclear weapons. During the premiership of Stalin's successor, Nikita Khrushchev, the Soviet Union and its satellites entered into a defense treaty, the Warsaw Pact, to oppose the Western NATO alliance. Nuclear war seemed a real danger in 1962, when a Soviet

The gilded domes and turrets of Pushkin Palace in Moscow.

R

A group of Russian women at a festival wearing traditional costume.

attempt to place nuclear weapons on Cuba was met by a United States blockade. Khrushchev's humiliating back-down in this crisis, as well as a serious rift between Russia and communist China, led to his being removed from office the next year and his replacement by Leonid Brezhnev.

The Brezhnev era lasted until 1982 and during this time, Soviet–Western relations fluctuated. Periods of relaxation, which became known as *détente*, alternated with times of renewed suspicion and hostility. Despite this, and despite the USSR's invasions of Czechoslovakia in 1968 and Afghanistan in December 1979, genuine agreements about nuclear arms reduction were achieved. During the brief premierships of Brezhnev's two immediate successors, East–West relations soured again. However, in 1985, the accession to the leadership of Mikhail Gorbachev led to an era of greater trust as well as to a less dictatorial and more open style of political leadership, and the first tentative moves toward a loosening of government controls over the economy. The terms *glasnost*, meaning "openness" and *perestroika*, meaning "restructuring" were used widely at this time, in reference to Gorbachev's reforms.

Growing social unrest, deteriorating economic conditions, and a resurgence of nationalism in a number of Soviet republics created immense strains in the Soviet Union. An attempted coup by communist conservatives took place in 1991 but was put down, largely through the heroic opposition of Boris Yeltsin, who emerged as the de facto leader of the country, enjoying wide-spread popular support.

Against Gorbachev's wishes, the Soviet Union was officially dissolved in December 1991 and replaced by the Commonwealth of Independent States. Gorbachev then resigned as president and Yeltsin assumed control. Yeltsin's leadership was confirmed in a national referendum that was held in 1993 and, despite a poor economic situation and widespread hardship, as well as serious misgivings about his health, Yeltsin was re-elected president in 1996. In the parliamentary, or Duma, elections, however, conservative nationalists, some of them stridently anti-Western, received widespread support.

A new constitution, adopted in 1993, established a two-chambered Federal Assembly, headed by a prime minister, who is appointed by the president. The president is popularly elected for a five-year term and has considerable powers, including the right to dissolve parliament.

Yeltsin continued to suffer poor health and his lack of action and increasingly intransigent behaviour led to a decline in support. He stepped down in December 1999. Alexander Putin, a former KGB staffer, was appointed to act in Yeltsin's role and was subsequently confirmed as president early in 2000. After Yeltsin's inaction in Chechnya, Putin's decision to continue fighting in the Chechnyan capital of Grozny, under the control of rebels, led to widespread public support.

Despite the change of leadership, the economy continued to suffer greatly. The International Monetary Fund (IMF) commenced a program of providing funding, as well as advice on economic reforms such as the corporatization of government structures. However some regions continue to suffer shortages, particularly energy cuts. The regions of Kamchatka and Petropavlovsk were given UN emergency humanitarian aid after energy cuts caused several deaths.

A river winding through fertile farming country.

Russia Timeline

20,000 BP Huts made from mammoth bones covered in animal skins at Mezhirich in Ukraine region

4000 BC Horses domesticated on the steppes, first mainly as draft animals but later (2000 BC) as fast transport in warfare

AD 300 Spread of peoples including Huns, Goths, and Magyars into forests west of the Ural Mountains

AD 770 Germanic traders and soldiers from Baltic move into Volga region previously occupied by Finnic and Slavic groups

AD 830 Scandinavian merchants establish new base in the Volga region, close to present-day Ryazan

AD 882 Scandinavia groups capture Kiev Russia takes its nam from Kievan Rus, terr given by Slavic group to the Black Sea are

1773–74 The Peasants Revolt sweeps across Russia from the Urals to the Volga but is put down by troops

1812 Napoleon's invasion of Russia defeated. Most of the 500,000 French forces die or are captured

1890 Migration of large numbers of people from eastern Russia to Siberia and Asia lasts for around 10 years

1891 Construction of the Trans-Siberian Railroad from Moscow to Vladivostok begins. Not completed until 1916

1914 Germany declares war on Russia and for three years Russia sides with Allies

1917 Revolution puts Bolsheviks in power after storming of the Winter Palace, at St Petersburg

1918 Tsar Nicholas II and family are shot, allegedly at the hands of the Bolsheviks; Moscow again capital of Russia

1918-20 Communists victorious in a civil war with the anti-communist White Russians

1924 Stalin leader of one of four factions that run party

1928 First Five- Plan introduce further centralize economy and incre industrial agricultural produc

Conflict between the so-called 'center and the regions' is causing ongoing economic and political damage. Although it is widely felt that of the 89 constituent regions, those such as Chechnya, Tatarstan, Bashkorlostan and Dagestan who are either openly declaring independence or moving towards it, are in the minority, and the breakup of the Russian Federation is not an immediate concern.

Physical features and land use

Stretching all the way from the Arctic Ocean in the north to the border with Kazakhstan in the south, the Ural Mountains separate European Russia in the west from the vast Siberian Plain to the east. European Russia, where most of the population lives and where the bulk of Russian industry and agriculture is located, consists mainly of a huge fertile plain, the East Europe Plain, which has an average elevation of 170 m (550 ft) but rises to a maximum of 400 m (1,300 ft). In the far southwest, the Caucasus Mountains form a natural boundary with Georgia and Azerbaijan, and there are upland areas in the far north near the border with Finland. In the western part of the plain are the Valdai Hills, in which the Volga and Dnieper Rivers have their source.

ussia becomes Mongol Empire e 1400s, ng the 's boundaries c, Baltic and

1318 Mongols appoint Yuri of Moscow Crown Prince; he makes Moscow an important center and later the capital of Russia

1547 Ivan IV, known as "the Terrible," is crowned Tsar and takes the title for all Russia

1613 Romanovs become the Tsarist family, ruling until the murder of Nicholas II in 1918

1697 First recorded eruption of Klyuchevskaya Volcano in Kamchatka, Siberia

1703 Peter the Great opens Russia to Western ideas. Builds St Petersburg on the Baltic Sea, making it the capital in 1712

1725 Catherine the Great becomes Empress. Encourages Western ideas in arts and education. Most Russians impoverished

.929 Stalin becomes ited leader rules USSR more than 20 years

1935 Great Purge by Stalin's secret police takes many lives; millions starve in a famine partly caused by farm collectivization

1941 Russia sides with Allies in Second World War after Germany invades USSR and is defeated in the Battle of Stalingrad (1943)

1956 Bezymianny Volcano in Kamchatka, Siberia, erupts leaving ash 50 cm (20 in) deep 10 km (6 miles) from volcano

1985 Gorbachev heads Communist Party; pursues policies of *perestroika* (economic restructuring) and *glasnost* (openness)

1986 Chernobyl nuclear reactor in Ukraine explodes; cancers from radiation kill up to 40,000 worldwide

1991 USSR ceases to exist. Replaced by the Commonwealth of Independent States. Russia retains the control of most resources. Chechnya declares independence from the Russian Federation.

1993 Yeltsin dissolves parliament after a failed coup attempt. New constitution in place.

1994 Fighting in Chechnya begins

Most of Russia's agriculture is concentrated in the south of the plain, as the harsh climates further north are not conducive to the growing of crops or to the raising of livestock. Less than one-tenth of Russia is under cultivation. Cereals are the main crops, although in most years the country produces only about half the grain it requires. The rest has to be imported. Livestock raising, most commonly cattle and dairy farming, is also based mainly in the west.

To the east of the Ural Mountains, the Siberian Plain is largely desolate, treeless, and flat. Central Siberia, to the east of the Yenisey River, is a region of plateaus that range from between 450 and 900 m (1,500 and 3,000 ft) in height and rise in the south to a series of mountain ranges that border Mongolia and China. Lowlands flank these plateaus to the north and east. East of the Lena River the country rises again toward the rugged and mountainous east coast. South of the Bering Sea, the Kamchatka Peninsula and the Kuril Islands form part of the Pacific "Ring of Fire." This is an area of considerable geothermal activity and there are about 30 active volcanoes.

The landscape of northern Russia is mainly arctic tundra—a treeless expanse which remains frozen throughout the year. Tundra vegetation consists of sedges, grasses, mosses, lichens, and ground-hugging plants. Further south, and in the southwest, the landscape varies between tracts of semidesert and expanses of forest, largely conifers, known as the taiga.

Industry, commerce, and culture

Russia, and especially Siberia, has abundant mineral resources. These contributed greatly to the country's rapid transformation during the Soviet period from a predominantly agricultural economy to one that was heavily industrialized. These mineral resources underpin the federation's present reliance on heavy industry and provide important mining exports. They include coal, petroleum, natural gas, iron ore, bauxite, copper, lead, zinc, and gold and other precious metals. Steelmaking, the manufacture of agricultural machinery, chemicals, textiles, and food processing are among the principal industries, centered on such large cities to the west of the Urals as Moscow, St Petersburg, Novgorod, and Volgograd, but also in a number of cities in Siberia such as Yekaterinburg and Novosibirsk.

The country's move toward a market economy has been fraught with difficulties and has been accompanied by a marked increase in social and financial inequalities as a new class of rich entrepreneurs has emerged. The majority of Russians live in relative poverty, victims of steeply rising prices and severe shortages of food and other basic consumer items. Corruption and crime have also increased significantly and a number of the leaders of organized crime are among the richest citizens in the nation. These conditions were aggravated by a virtual collapse of the Russian economy in 1998 and continuing political uncertainty based on serious doubts, unallayed by official reassurances, about the capacity of the president, Boris Yeltsin, who suffers chronic ill health. There are strong movements within the country for a return to centralized control of the economy and for a more aggressive nationalistic approach to relations with the West.

Russia has contributed much to literature, music, and the performing arts, especially in the nineteenth century. Writers such as Turgenev prepared the way for other giants of literature like Tolstoy and Dostoyevsky. Among composers, Tchaikovsky and Stravinsky established Russia's place in musical history. The Imperial Russian Ballet was founded in 1735, and Russian ballet has become internationally renowned for its choreography and dancers like Pavlova and Nureyev.

The Commonwealth of Independent States

The Commonwealth of Independent States is a loose confederation of twelve former Soviet republics that was formed after the breakdown of the Soviet Union in 1991. The idea for the formation of the commonwealth was agreed to at a meeting of Russian president Boris Yeltsin and the presidents of Belarus and Ukraine in Minsk, in Belarus, in early December 1991 and was ratified at Alma-Ata in Kazakhstan by 11 of the former Soviet republics on 21 December. Georgia and the three Baltic states of Estonia, Latvia, and Lithuania declined to join, although Georgia has since become a member. Not surprisingly, Russia assumed the status of dominant member of the group, taking control of all former Soviet embassies and consulates and occupying the former Soviet Union's seat on the United Nations Security Council. Minsk was designated as the administrative center of the new commonwealth, which was much more an alliance than a state entity. According to the agreement, the political independence of each state was guaranteed in return for a commitment to certain forms of economic and defence cooperation.

The commonwealth remains a tenuous confederation and there are many areas of dispute between its constituent members. There is a natural suspicion that the Russian Federation seeks to impose its political will on the other members, and this was in no way diminished in 1996 when the Russian parliament, or Duma, passed a non-binding resolution in favor of reinstating the former Soviet Union. Difficult economic conditions throughout the former Soviet Union have led to increasing support, especially in Belarus, for a return to the previous status quo.

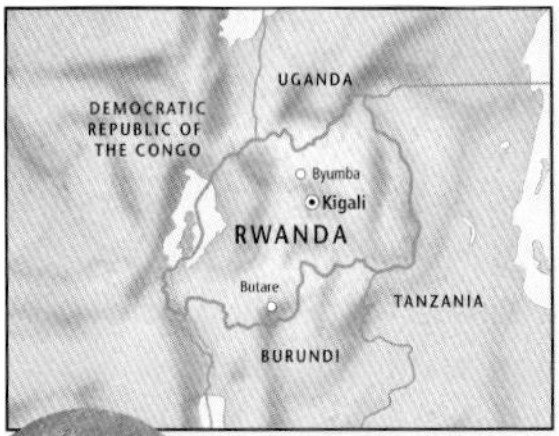

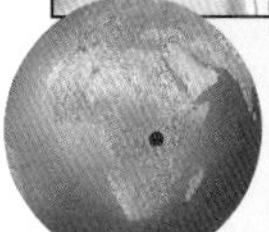

Rwanda

Official name Republic of Rwanda
Form of government Republic with transitional legislative body (National Assembly)
Capital Kigali
Area 26,340 sq km (10,170 sq miles)
Time zone GMT + 2 hours
Population 8,154,933
Projected population 2005 9,135,398
Population density 309.6 per sq km (801.9 per sq mile)
Life expectancy 41.3
Infant mortality (per 1,000) 112.9
Official languages French, Kinyarwanda
Other language Kiswahili
Literacy rate 59.2%
Religions Roman Catholic 65%, Protestant 9%, Muslim 1%, indigenous beliefs and other 25%
Ethnic groups Hutu 80%, Tutsi 19%, Twa (Pygmy) 1%
Currency Rwandan franc
Economy Agriculture 93%, services 5%, industry 2%
GNP per capita US$180
Climate Tropical, with two wet seasons (October to December and March to May)
Highest point Karisimbi 4,507 m (14,783 ft)
Map reference Page 809

Rwanda

A small landlocked country in central Africa, Rwanda shares much of its social history with Burundi, across its southern border. In the fifteenth and sixteenth centuries a tall cattle-herding people, named Tutsi, probably from Sudan, came to the region and formed a small feudal aristocracy that dominated the more numerous Hutu farmers who had settled in the area some time before them. Since then, the Hutu people have endured the situation with resentment. In recent times, beginning with a Hutu revolt in 1959 (independence from Belgium coming in 1962), there have been decades of ethnic strife and intermittent violence, with hundreds of thousands of deaths occurring on both sides. This culminated in the massacre of half a million Tutsi (and also some moderate Hutu) by Hutu in 1994, waves of refugees spilling out into the Democratic Republic of Congo, Burundi, Tanzania, and Uganda. An uneasy peace followed.

Rwanda is the most densely populated country in Africa. Almost 30 percent of the land is arable, steep slopes are intensively cultivated, and terracing and contour plowing are used in order to keep erosion to a minimum. Lake Kivu and a part of the southward-flowing Ruzizi River form the western boundary of the country. From here the land rises steeply to the mountains, part of the Rift Valley, which constitute the Nile–Congo divide. To the north are the mountains, and several volcanoes, of the

The endangered mountain gorilla still survives in the highlands of Rwanda.

Mufumbiro Range. These include one of the last refuges of the mountain gorilla. From the heights of the eastern rim of the Rift Valley a plateau slopes eastward toward the Tanzanian border, the River Kagera marshes, and a number of lakes.

During peacetime, Rwanda's production of coffee and tea constituted 80 to 90 percent of total exports. Pyrethrum and sugarcane are other cash crops, cassava, maize, bananas, sorghum, and vegetables being crops grown for food. In keeping with their status as one-time nomadic herders, the Tutsi people keep cattle. The Hutu generally keep sheep and goats. Arable land is overused and deforestation and soil erosion are widespread. Natural resources include gold, tin, tungsten, and natural gas, but they are undeveloped because of infrastructure and transport difficulties. Political and ethnic disorders have affected the economy which suffers from infrastructural damage, lack of maintenance, looting, and the widespread destruction of property and crops. Recovery of production to earlier levels will take time.

A crater lake in Volcanoes National Park.

S

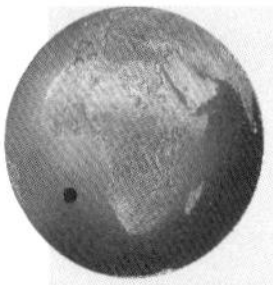

St Helena

Official name St Helena
Form of government Dependent territory of the United Kingdom
Capital Jamestown
Area 410 sq km (158 sq miles)
Time zone GMT
Population 7,145
Life expectancy 75.9
Infant mortality (per 1,000) 28
Literacy rate 97.3%
Currency St Helenian pound
Economy Mainly fishing and agriculture
Climate Tropical, moderated by trade winds
Map reference Page 813

St Helena

The island of St Helena lies about 1,950 km (1,200 miles) off the west coast of Africa. Together with Tristan da Cunha and Ascension Island, it is a British crown colony, and is Britain's main dependency in the South Atlantic. The crater rim of an extinct volcano, St Helena is marked by gorges and valleys, has many freshwater springs, and rises to an elevation of 824 m (2,703 ft).

Discovered by the Portuguese in 1502 and first visited by the English in 1588, St Helena was granted to the British East India Company in 1659. It was Napoleon's place of exile from 1815 to 1821. Today, the island's main activities are fishing, livestock raising, and the sale of handicrafts, but it depends on aid from the United Kingdom. Tristan da Cunha, 2,000 km (1,243 miles) to the south, has a farming community. Ascension Island, a military base and communications center, has no resident population.

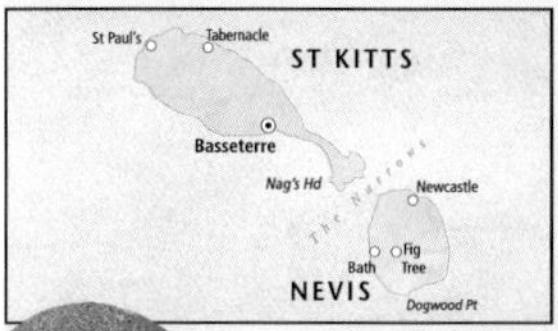

S

St Kitts

Official name Federation of St Kitts and Nevis
Form of government Constitutional monarchy with single legislative body (House of Assembly)
Capital Basseterre
Area 269 sq km (104 sq miles)
Time zone GMT – 4 hours
Population 42,838
Projected population 2005 46,750
Population density 159.2 per sq km (412.3 per sq mile)
Life expectancy 67.9

St Kitts and Nevis

St Kitts and Nevis is a federation of two Caribbean islands in the Leeward Islands group. Each is well-watered and has a mountain of volcanic origin rising to about 1,000 m (3,300 ft). Once inhabited by Carib and Arawak Indians, St Kitts and Nevis were, in 1623 and 1628, the first West Indian islands to be colonized by Britain. Ownership of the islands was disputed with the French until 1783. In 1983 the country became fully independent from Britain.

African slaves were imported as labor for sugar and cotton plantations, this ceasing with the abolition of slavery in 1834. Most islanders today are descended from former slaves. The growing and processing of sugarcane remains important, though falling prices have hurt local industry in recent years. The government intends to revitalize this sector. Tourism and export-oriented manufacturing are of growing significance, in addition to manufactured products including machinery, food, electronics, clothing, footwear, and beverages. The main cash crops are sugarcane on St Kitts, cotton and coconuts on Nevis. Staple foods include rice, yams, vegetables, and bananas, but most food is imported.

Nevis claims it is starved of funds by its partner and is dissatisfied with its place in the federation. In 1996 Nevis announced its intention of seeking independence from St Kitts. Nevis had the constitutional right to secede if two-thirds of the elected legislators approved and two-thirds of voters endorsed it through a referendum. However, the proposal did not go the vote, and Nevis remains part of the federation. Foreign investment has increased dramatically, as the federation does not have taxes, is open to offshore banking and is utilised for asset protection by many of the world's largest banking corporations. The increase in foreign investment has encouraged a rapid increase in tourism.

St Lucia

An island in the Caribbean, St Lucia is one of the prettiest of the Windward Group of the Lesser Antilles. Tropical beaches and typical Caribbean towns like Soufrière have long drawn tourists to the island, who also come to see its varied plant and animal life. Once inhabited by Arawak and Carib Indians, St Lucia was wrangled over between France and Britain before finally being ceded to Britain in 1814. As elsewhere in the Caribbean, African slaves were imported to work sugar plantations until slavery was abolished in 1834. Most of the population are descended from slaves, though some are from South Asia. Internally self-governing from 1967, St Lucia has been fully independent since 1979.

The main features of the island are its forested mountains stretching north to south, cut by river valleys, and rising to Mt Gimie. In the southwest lies the Qualibou, an area with 18 lava domes and 7 craters. In the west, marking the entrance to Jalousie Plantation harbor, are the spectacular twin Pitons, two peaks rising steeply from the sea to a height of about 800 m (2,625 ft). The climate is tropical, with annual rainfall varying from 1,500 mm (59 in) in the lowlands to 3,500 mm (137 in) in the mountainous areas.

While not poor, St Lucia still depends heavily on bananas (60 percent of export income), a crop which is easily ruined by hurricanes and disease. Bananas are

Infant mortality (per 1,000) 17.4
Official language English
Other Language English Creole
Literacy rate 90%
Religions Anglican 36%, Methodist 32.5%, Roman Catholic 11%, Pentecostal 5.5%, Baptist 4%, other 11%
Ethnic groups African 94.5%, mixed African–European 3%, European 1%, other 1.5%
Currency East Caribbean dollar
Economy Services 69%, industry and agriculture 31%
GNP per capita US$5,170
Climate Tropical, moderated by sea breezes
Highest point Mt Misery 1,156 m (3,793 ft)
Map reference Page 837

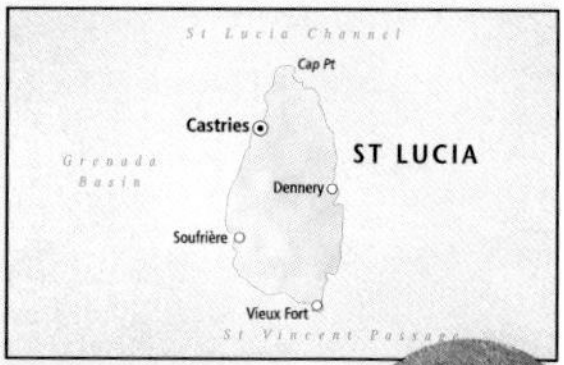

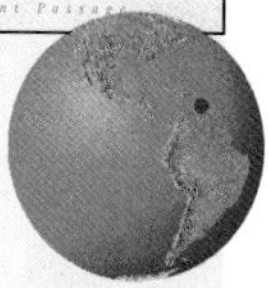

St Lucia

Official name St Lucia
Form of government Constitutional monarchy with two legislative bodies (Senate and House of Assembly)
Capital Castries
Area 620 sq km (239 sq miles)
Time zone GMT – 4 hours
Population 154,020
Projected population 2005 164,413
Population density 248.4 per sq km (643.4 per sq mile)
Life expectancy 71.8
Infant mortality (per 1,000) 16.6
Official language English
Other language French Creole
Literacy rate 82%
Religions Roman Catholic 90%, Protestant 7%, Anglican 3%

(continues)

ST LUCIA *(continued)*

ETHNIC GROUPS African 90.5%, mixed 5.5%, East Indian 3%, European 1%
CURRENCY East Caribbean dollar
ECONOMY Services 65%, agriculture 26%, industry 9%
GNP PER CAPITA US$3,370
CLIMATE Tropical, moderated by trade winds; wet season May to August, dry season January to April
HIGHEST POINT Mt Gimie 950 m (3,117 ft)
MAP REFERENCE Page 837

also a source of political tension: in recent years the USA has pushed for the abolition of the preferential treatment the EU accords banana imports from the Caribbean. The people of St Lucia have strongly objected to this. Other agricultural exports are coconuts, coconut oil, and cocoa. Clothing is the second largest export, and the free port of Vieux Fort has attracted modern light industry. Grande Cul de Sac Bay in the south is one of the deepest tanker ports in the region and is used for the transshipment of oil.

The spires of the Pitons on the southwest coast of St Lucia.

St Pierre and Miquelon

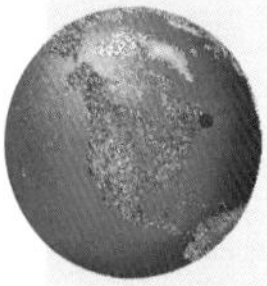

S

ST PIERRE AND MIQUELON

OFFICIAL NAME Territorial collectivity of St Pierre and Miquelon
FORM OF GOVERNMENT Territorial collectivity of France
CAPITAL St-Pierre
AREA 242 sq km (93 sq miles)
TIME ZONE GMT – 4 hours
POPULATION 6,966
LIFE EXPECTANCY 77.1
INFANT MORTALITY (PER 1,000) 8.1
LITERACY RATE 99%
CURRENCY French franc
ECONOMY Mainly fishing and fish processing
CLIMATE Cold, wet, and foggy
MAP REFERENCE Page 827

St Pierre and Miquelon are islands in the North Atlantic Ocean, south of Newfoundland. They are cold and wet and have little vegetation. Surrounded by some of the world's richest fishing grounds, the islands were settled by French fishermen in the seventeenth century. Since then the inhabitants have earned a living from fishing and by servicing the foreign trawler fleets that operate off the coast. A dispute between Canada and France over fishing and mineral rights was settled in 1992. Since the French subsidize the islands, and their economy has been declining, the authorities are now trying to diversify by developing port facilities and encouraging tourism.

St Vincent and the Grenadines

The mountainous, volcanic Caribbean island of St Vincent has 89 percent of the country's total land area and 95 percent of the population, the rest consisting of the islands of the Northern Grenadines—Bequia, Mustique, Canouan, and Union. St Vincent was visited by Columbus in 1498 but the fierce resistance of the Amerindian Caribs meant that settlement was slow. A long dispute with France (the French often being supported by the Caribs) finally led to it becoming a British colony in 1783. As St Vincent and the Grenadines the country became self-governing in 1969 and independent in 1979.

St Vincent is dominated by a north–south spur of densely forested mountains, cut east to west by numerous short, fast-running rivers and streams. In the north, volcanic Mt Soufrière is still very active. It caused serious damage in 1891 and in 1902 it killed 2,000 people. The 1979 eruption, which was followed by a hurricane the next year, devastated agriculture and caused a major setback in tourism.

The Northern Grenadines are coralline islets, extending south of St Vincent, some of them with picturesque names such as All Awash Island and The Pillories. The tropical climate is moderated by steady trade winds.

Agriculture, led by banana production, is the foundation of the country's economy, most of it small-scale or subsistence farming on the lower mountain slopes or terraces. Other crops exported include arrowroot starch used to make medicines, and paper for computer printers. Tourism is of growing importance, with visitors drawn to the clear, clean waters of Mustique and Bequia. Attempts to develop various industries have so far had little success: unemployment stands at about 35 to 40 percent.

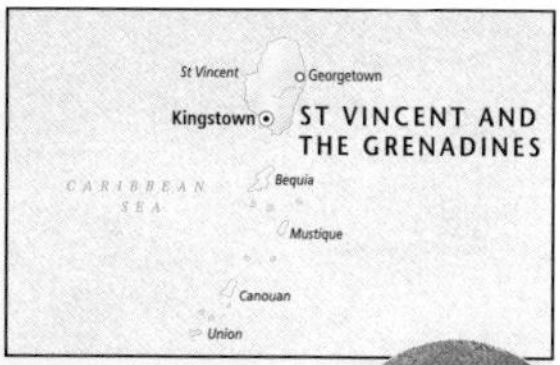

St Vincent and the Grenadines

Official name St Vincent and the Grenadines
Form of government Constitutional monarchy with single legislative body (House of Assembly)
Capital Kingstown
Area 340 sq km (131 sq miles)
Time zone GMT – 4 hours
Population 120,519
Projected population 2005 125,501
Population density 354.5 per sq km (918 per sq mile)
Life expectancy 73.8
Infant mortality (per 1,000) 15.2
Official language English
Other language French Creole
Literacy rate 82%
Religions Anglican 42%, Methodist 21%, Roman Catholic 12%, other 25%
Ethnic groups African 82%, mixed 14%, European, East Indian, indigenous 4%
Currency East Caribbean dollar
Economy Agriculture 50%, services 30%, industry 20%
GNP per capita US$2,280
Climate Tropical, with wet season May to November
Highest point Mt Soufrière 1,234 m (4,048 ft)
Map reference Page 837

Kingstown Harbor on the island of St Vincent.

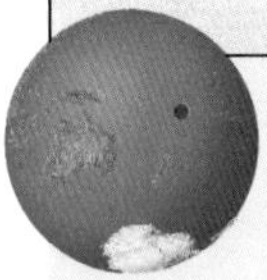

Samoa

The Samoan islands lie in the South Pacific about midway between Hawaii and New Zealand. Consisting of the two big islands of Savai'i and Upolu, plus seven small islands and a number of islets, Samoa is a larger island group with a much greater population than American Samoa, which lies further east, but has a more uncertain economic future.

Believed to have been originally settled by Tongans around 1000 BC, the islands of Samoa were first visited by Europeans when the French explorer Louis Antoine de Bougainville arrived in 1766. A mission was established in 1835 by the London Missionary Society. In the late nineteenth century control of the islands was contested by three colonial powers—Britain, Germany, and the USA—Germany taking control for a short period from 1899. After the First World War the islands were administered by New Zealand. In 1962 Samoa regained its full independence and signed a friendship treaty with New Zealand.

Samoa is a society in which chiefly rank plays an important part, *matai* (men who head extended families) having a good deal more power, prestige, and authority than commoners. This system has delayed the introduction of full democracy. In 1991 the first direct elections under a universal franchise were held but only *matai* were allowed to be candidates.

The larger islands of Samoa are volcanic, Savai'i experiencing major eruptions in 1902 and 1911. The interiors of Savai'i and Upolu are broadly similar; their mountainous central regions are densely forested and cut by a number of fast-flowing rivers. Major streams include the Sili and Faleata on Savai'i, and the Vaisigano on Upolu. Narrow coastal plains lie between the highlands and the sea; coral reefs lie offshore. Other than arable land (19 percent), the only natural resources are hardwood forests and fish. Yams, breadfruit, banana, and papaya are grown for food, and cocoa, taro, and coconuts (for oil, copra, and cream) are cultivated for export.

With assistance from the United Nations, fishing has also become a significant export industry. Reforestation programs have been introduced with the aim of keeping timber exports at a sustainable level. Power for industry—a Japanese automobile parts factory opened in 1991—is mainly provided by hydroelectricity.

SAMOA

OFFICIAL NAME Independent State of Samoa
FORM OF GOVERNMENT Constitutional monarchy with single legislative body (Legislative Assembly)
CAPITAL Apia
AREA 2,860 sq km (1,104 sq miles)
TIME ZONE GMT – 11 hours
POPULATION 229,979
PROJECTED POPULATION 2005 261,857
POPULATION DENSITY 80.4 per sq km (208.2 per sq mile)
LIFE EXPECTANCY 69.8
INFANT MORTALITY (PER 1,000) 30.5
OFFICIAL LANGUAGES Samoan, English
LITERACY RATE 98%
RELIGIONS Christian 99.7% (50% associated with London Missionary Society), other 0.3%
ETHNIC GROUPS Samoan 92.6%, mixed Polynesian–European 7%, European 0.4%
CURRENCY Tala
ECONOMY Agriculture 65%, services and tourism 30%, industry 5%
GNP PER CAPITA US$1,120
CLIMATE Tropical, wet season from December to April followed by a cooler dry season from May to November
HIGHEST POINT Mauga Silisili 1,858 m (6,092 ft)
MAP REFERENCE Pages 722, 727

The economy depends heavily on remittances from Samoans working overseas and on foreign aid to support a level of imports that significantly exceeds export earnings. Tourism has become the most important growth industry. Many of the more than 50,000 visitors per year come to see the house that was once lived in by the Scottish writer Robert Louis Stevenson. It is now the official residence of the Samoan Head of State.

San Marino

This state is completely surrounded by Italian territory. Most of the tiny state of San Marino is situated on the slopes of Mount Titano in the Appenine Mountains, 20 km (12 miles) inland from the city of Rimini on the Adriatic coast of northern Italy.

The republic takes its name from St Marinus who, so legend has it, arrived there with a group of followers in the fourth century AD and established an independent settlement. This makes it arguably the world's oldest surviving republic. Records of its existence can be traced back to the twelfth century. It became one of the many mini-states on the Italian peninsula and was accorded papal recognition in 1631.

The Sanmarinesi, as its inhabitants are known, offered refuge to Giuseppe Garibaldi when he passed through in

A Samoan church with a Mediterranean influence.

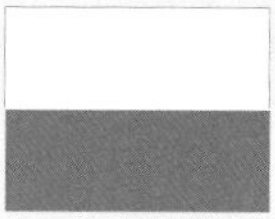

San Marino

Official name Republic of San Marino
Form of government Republic with single legislative body (Great and General Council)
Capital San Marino
Area 60 sq km (23 sq miles)
Time zone GMT + 1 hour
Population 25,061
Projected population 2005 25,864
Population density 417.7 per sq km (1,081.81 per sq mile)
Life expectancy 81.5
Infant mortality (per 1,000) 5.4
Official language Italian
Literacy rate 99%
Religions Roman Catholic 95%, other 5%
Ethnic groups Sanmarinesi 87.1%, Italian 12.4%, other 0.5%
Currency Italian lira
Economy Services 58%, industry 40%, agriculture 2%
GNP per capita US$15,000
Climate Temperate, with mild winters and warm summers
Highest point Monte Titano 739 m (2,425 ft)
Map reference Page 778

S

1849, pursued by his enemies. However, when the newly unified state of Italy was declared in 1861 the Sanmarinesi declined to join. San Marino fought with Italy in the First World War. In the Second World War it began by supporting Fascist Italy but later changed sides and was invaded by Germany. San Marino is a democratic republic with elections held every five years.

This picturesque little country is centered on the fortified medieval town of San Marino, where most of the population lives. On the lower slopes, beneath the rugged limestone peak, are thick forests, expanses of pastureland and a string of ancient villages. Almost one-fifth of the land is used for agriculture. Cereals, olives, and vines are cultivated and sheep and goats are raised. A wide range of cheeses and wine are its principal agricultural products.

Since 1862 San Marino has had a friendship and co-operation treaty with Italy. It also shares the Italian currency and enjoys a standard of living that is roughly equivalent to that of its neighbor. About one in five of Sanmarinesi workers are in the tourism industry, which caters for more than 2 million visitors each year, although many do not stay overnight.

Winemaking, textiles, and ceramics are significant industries. Even more significant is the sale of the country's distinctive postage stamps, which are sought by collectors and account for up to 10 percent of the country's revenues.

São Tomé and Príncipe

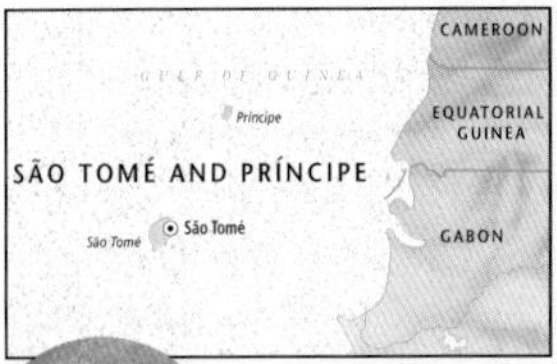

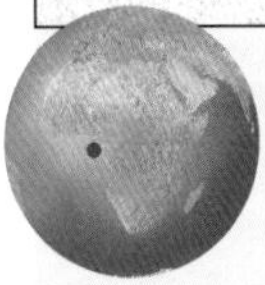

São Tomé and Príncipe

Official name Democratic Republic of São Tomé and Príncipe

São Tomé and Príncipe are two islands lying off the coast of Gabon in the Gulf of Guinea. They were occupied in the 1520s by the Portuguese, who used slaves as laborers on the sugar plantations. The population now consists mainly of the Afro-Portuguese descendants of these first immigrants, plus contract laborers brought from Mozambique and Cape Verde to work on cocoa plantations in the nineteenth century. Following independence in 1975, a one-party Marxist regime was imposed. For a time the islands were allied to the Soviet bloc and Russian and Cuban military advisors were brought in. At a referendum in 1990, however, 72 percent of the people voted in favor of democratic government. Now the main concern of the government is to rebuild the country's relationship with

Portugal and to secure beneficial working relationships with the EU and the USA.

An extinct volcano, São Tomé is the largest and most populous of the two main islands, some 440 km (273 miles) off the coast of Gabon. Low lying in the northeast and the southwest, it rises to Pico de São Tomé in the volcanic highlands. The island of Príncipe lies about 150 km (100 miles) to the northeast. As well as the two main islands there are also a number of rocky islets—Caroco, Pedras, Tinhosas, and Rõlas. On both São Tomé and Príncipe, streams drain to the sea from mountainous interiors, up to 70 percent of which are densely forested. The climate is hot and humid, moderated to a certain extent by the cold Benguela current that flows up Africa's western shore.

Following independence in 1975 the cocoa plantations that formed the foundation of the country's economy deteriorated as a result of mismanagement aggravated by drought. By 1987 the production of cocoa had fallen to 3,500 tonnes from an annual output of 9,000 tonnes prior to 1975. While there has been some economic recovery in recent years, São Tomé and Príncipe have had serious balance of payments problems. During the 1980s agriculture diversified into palm oil, pepper, and coffee but since then production has faltered. Deforestation and soil erosion are an increasing cause for concern. Today, São Tomé imports 90 percent of its food, all its fuel and most manufactured goods.

FORM OF GOVERNMENT Republic with single legislative body (National People's Assembly)
CAPITAL São Tomé
AREA 960 sq km (371 sq miles)
TIME ZONE GMT
POPULATION 154,878
PROJECTED POPULATION 2005 187,394
POPULATION DENSITY 161.3 per sq km (417.8 per sq mile)
LIFE EXPECTANCY 64.7
INFANT MORTALITY (PER 1,000) 52.9
OFFICIAL LANGUAGE Portuguese
OTHER LANGUAGES Various creoles
LITERACY RATE 67%
RELIGIONS Roman Catholic 80%, Protestant and other 20%
ETHNIC GROUPS Predominantly mixed African–Portuguese, with various African minorities
CURRENCY Dobra
ECONOMY Mainly agriculture and fishing
GNP PER CAPITA US$350
CLIMATE Tropical, with wet season October to May
HIGHEST POINT Pico de São Tomé 2,024 m (6,640 ft)
MAP REFERENCE Pages 805, 813

Saudi Arabia

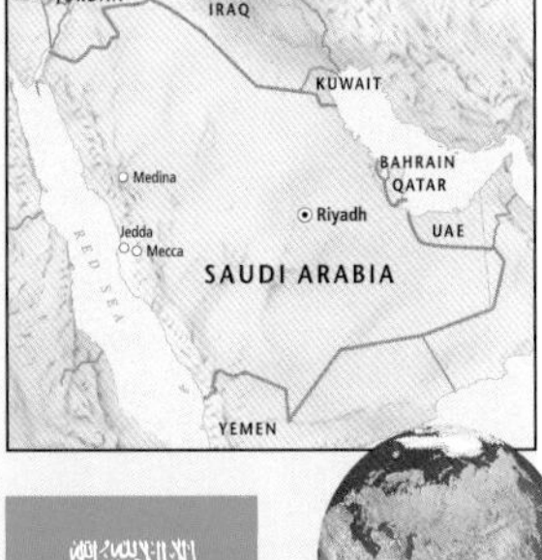

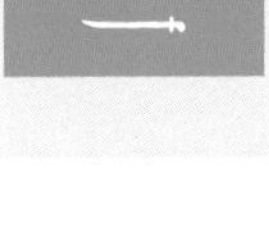

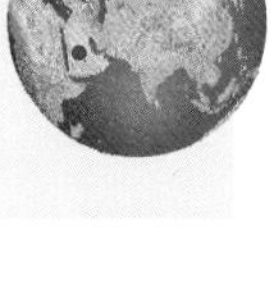

Saudi Arabia occupies most of the Arabian Peninsula and covers an area about the size of western Europe. With one-quarter of the world's petroleum reserves, it supplies several major industrial nations with oil. Its role as the custodian of Islam's most holy places, Mecca (Makkah) and Medina (Al Madīnah), is equally important. Aloof from international affairs for many years, the Saudis braced themselves to fight off Iraq (which they had earlier supported) in 1990–91. The 500,000 western troops who entered the country (considered a profanation of Muslim land) were seen by the Saudis as both necessary and unwelcome. The war highlighted tensions in a society

SAUDI ARABIA

OFFICIAL NAME Kingdom of Saudi Arabia
FORM OF GOVERNMENT Monarchy with advisory Consultative Council
CAPITAL Ar Riyad (Riyadh)
AREA 1,960,582 sq km (756,981 sq miles)
TIME ZONE GMT + 3 hours
POPULATION 21,504,613
PROJECTED POPULATION 2005 26,336,476
POPULATION DENSITY 11 per sq km (28.4 per sq mile)
LIFE EXPECTANCY 70.6
INFANT MORTALITY (PER 1,000) 38.8
OFFICIAL LANGUAGE Arabic
OTHER LANGUAGE English
LITERACY RATE 61.8%
RELIGIONS Sunni Muslim 85%, Shi'a Muslim 15%
ETHNIC GROUPS Arab 90%, mixed African–Asian 10%
CURRENCY Saudi riyal
ECONOMY Agriculture 49%, services 37%, industry 14%
GNP PER CAPITA US$7,040
CLIMATE Mainly hot and arid; some areas rainless for years
HIGHEST POINT Jabal Sawda 3,133 m (10,279 ft)
MAP REFERENCE Pages 756–7

which politically is largely feudal (192 people were beheaded in 1995), yet because of its oil cannot escape the modern world.

Mecca was Muhammad's birthplace (c.570) and Medina the place where Islam was born. In the eighteenth century a severe branch of Islam was adopted by the Sa'ud Bedouin —the Wahhabi Movement—and this, with its austere criminal code, was established by the Saudis throughout their lands early this century. During the 1930s most Saudis were still living traditional desert lives, but this changed when oil was found near Riyadh in 1937. The spending for which the royal family was known in the 1960s and 1970s ended with the drop in oil prices of the 1980s. This is now starting to have social effects. People who were content to live under absolute monarchic rule with prodigious benefits may now be questioning the balance of power. Per capita income fell from $17,000 in 1981 to $10,000 in 1995.

Paralleling the Red Sea, a range of mountains extends northwest to southeast, rising to 3,133 m (10,279 ft) at Jabal Sawdā in the southwest, Saudi Arabia's highest peak. The Asir Highlands in this southwestern corner is the only region with reliable rainfall. Benefiting from the monsoon, the slopes are terraced to grow grain and fruit trees. Further east, separated from the mountains by a wide stretch of basaltic lava, is the high central desert plateau of Najd. The eastern border of this region is a vast arc of sandy desert, broadening into the two dune-wastes of Arabia: An Nafūd in the north, and Ar Rub' al Khāli, or "Empty Quarter" to the south—the world's largest expanse of sand. Some Bedouin nomads still live here as traders and herdsmen. Over 95 percent of Saudi Arabia is arid or semiarid desert.

Petroleum accounts for 75 percent of budget revenue, 35 percent of gross domestic product, and 90 percent of export earnings. Saudi Arabia has the largest reserves of petroleum in the world (26 percent of the proven total), is the largest exporter of petroleum, and backs this up with world-class associated industries. For more than a decade, however, expenditures have outstripped income. To compensate, the government plans to restrain public spending and encourage non-oil exports. As many as 4 million foreign workers are employed. The 2 million pilgrims who come to visit Mecca each year also contribute to national income.

Saudis at a market wearing traditional dress.

Senegal

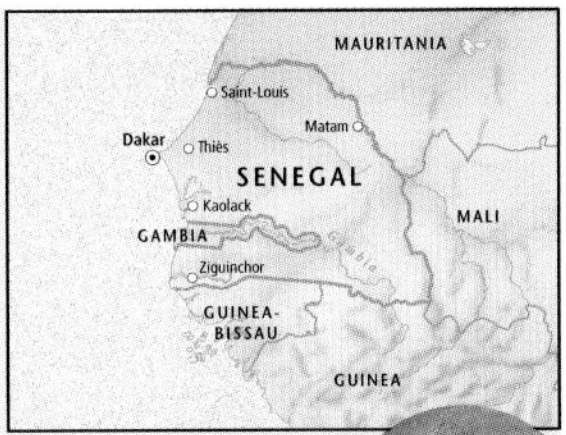

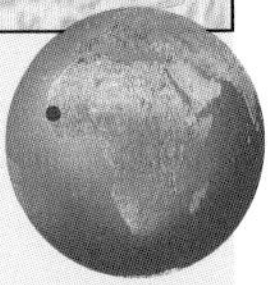

Dakar, the capital of Senegal, lies on the westernmost point of west Africa and in the seventeenth and eighteenth centuries it was a major slave-trading base. French colonial control of Senegal was established during the suppression of the slave trade in the nineteenth century. As the administrative center of the huge region of French West Africa, an effective road network was established in Dakar, plus extensive port facilities and a large civil service.

Independence from France came in 1960. Despite being a de facto one-party state for the next ten years, Senegal avoided military and dictatorial rule, and has recently liberalized its economic and political life. The country's most serious problem is continuing armed revolt in the oil-rich southern province of Casamance, south of Gambia, a region that differs ethnically, economically, and geographically from the north.

Senegal is split by the near-enclave of Gambia and the Gambia River. To the north the land is drier, with sand dunes along the coast. Inland there are plains, savanna, and semidesert, where Fulani cattle-herders eke out an existence. South of Dakar and Cape Vert it is wetter and more fertile, with coastal mangrove swamps and forest inland. Sorghum is grown in the rainier areas of savanna bushland, while south of Gambia rice is cultivated on the floodplain of the Casamance River—the most fertile part of the country.

Peanuts have long been the foundation of Senegal's economy and are grown on half the cultivated land.

Women removing small fish from a fishing net in Senegal.

SENEGAL

OFFICIAL NAME Republic of Senegal
FORM OF GOVERNMENT Republic with single legislative body (National Assembly)
CAPITAL Dakar
AREA 196,190 sq km (75,749 sq miles)
TIME ZONE GMT
POPULATION 9,051,930
PROJECTED POPULATION 2005 12,235,259
POPULATION DENSITY 51.2 per sq km (132.6 per sq mile)
LIFE EXPECTANCY 57.8
INFANT MORTALITY (PER 1,000) 59.8
OFFICIAL LANGUAGE French
OTHER LANGUAGES Wolof, Pulaar, Diola, Mandingo
LITERACY RATE 32.1%
RELIGIONS Muslim 92%, indigenous beliefs 6%, Christian 2% (mainly Roman Catholic)
ETHNIC GROUPS Wolof 36%, Fulani 17%, Serer 17%, Toucouleur 9%, Diola 9%, Mandingo 9%, European and Lebanese 1%, other 2%
CURRENCY CFA (Communauté Financière Africaine) franc
ECONOMY Agriculture 81%, services 13%, industry 6%
GNP PER CAPITA US$600
CLIMATE Tropical, with wet season June to October
HIGHEST POINT Unnamed location in southeast 581 m (1,906 ft)
MAP REFERENCE Page 804

S

Efforts are being made to diversify, and sugarcane, millet, cotton, and rice are now cultivated. Other than the recently developed oil fields in Casamance, with the promise of more lying offshore, natural resources are few. Though its arrangements are democratic, Senegal's ruling party has been in power since the 1950s, creating a network of patronage through the civil service, the judiciary, and the state-owned industries. Senegal receives a considerable amount of foreign aid.

Seychelles

The Seychelles are a group of 4 large and 36 small granite islands, plus a scattering of about 65 coralline islands, in the Indian Ocean northeast of Madagascar. Some 98 percent of the population live on the four main islands, the great majority on tropical and mountainous Mahé. Uninhabited when occupied by the French in 1742, the Seychelles were ceded to the British at the time of the Napoleonic Wars, and became a crown colony in 1903. After independence in 1976 the islands were ruled for 15

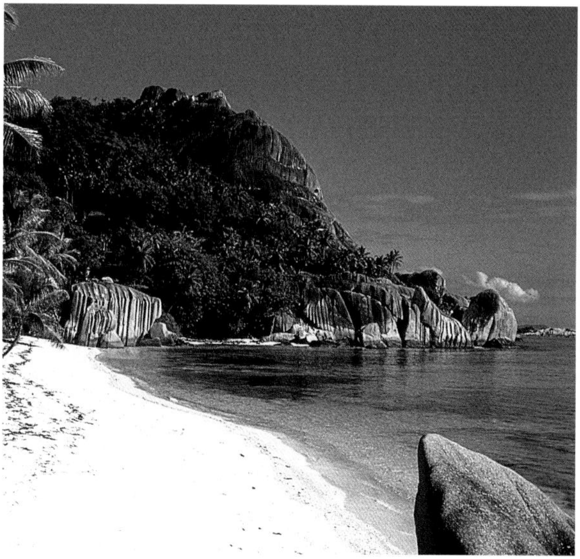

La Digue Island, the Seychelles

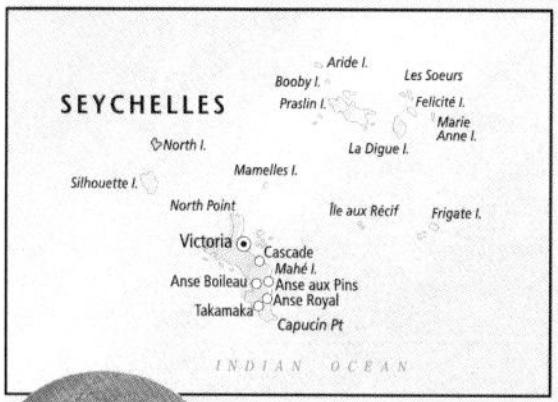

Seychelles

Official name Republic of Seychelles
Form of government Republic with single legislative body (People's Assembly)
Capital Victoria
Area 455 sq km (176 sq miles)
Time zone GMT + 4 hours
Population 79,164
Projected population 2005 82,044
Population density 174 per sq km (450 per sq mile)
Life expectancy 71
Infant mortality (per 1,000) 16.5
Official languages English, French, Creole
Literacy rate 88%
Religions Roman Catholic 90%, Anglican 8%, other 2%
Ethnic groups Seychellois (mixture of Asian, African, European) 93.8%, Malagasy 3.1%, Chinese 1.6%, British 1.5%
Currency Seychelles rupee
Economy Services 80%, agriculture 10%, industry 10%
GNP per capita US$6,620

Looking toward Silhouette Island in the Seychelles.

years as a one-party socialist state, North Korean military advisors being hired to guard against attempted coups. The first open elections were held in 1993 and the previous government party won a new term in office.

The granite islands consist of a mountainous central spine—sometimes consisting of bare, eroded rock—surrounded by a flat coastal strip with dense tropical vegetation. In the areas cleared for farming, vanilla, tobacco, tea, cinnamon and coconuts (for copra) are grown for export, along with food crops such as cassava, sweet potatoes, and bananas. Most food, however, is imported. The outer coralline islands are flat, waterless, and sparsely inhabited, having a total population of only 400. Short droughts periodically occur; though catchments collect some rainwater, there are no natural sources of supply. The Seychelles lie outside the cyclone belt, which is important for an economy depending on tourism.

The island's only natural resources are fish, copra, and cinnamon trees, which in earlier times provided a bare subsistence. Since independence in 1976, however, with the vigorous promotion of the tourist industry, per capita output has increased sevenfold. In recent years foreign investment has been encouraged in order to upgrade hotels and other services. Visitors find many attractions—the unique wildlife includes a rare giant land turtle and the colorful green sea turtle found on the coral reefs. The country's vulnerability in relying so heavily on tourism was shown during the Gulf War, when visitor numbers dropped sharply. The government is moving to reduce over-dependence on this sector by promoting farming, fishing, and small-scale manufacturing, including furniture-making, coconut-fiber rope-making, printing, and the re-export of petroleum products.

CLIMATE Tropical, with wet season December to May

HIGHEST POINT Morne Seychellois 905 m (2,969 ft)

MAP REFERENCE Pages 812–13

The Seychelles nut tree (Coco de Mer) is widespread on those islands .

S

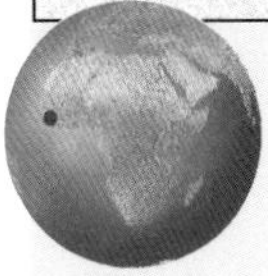

Sierra Leone

Official name Republic of Sierra Leone
Form of government Republic with single legislative body (House of Representatives)
Capital Freetown
Area 71,740 sq km (27,699 sq miles)
Time zone GMT
Population 5,296,651
Projected population 2005 6,415,757
Population density 73.8 per sq km (191.1 per sq mile)
Life expectancy 49.1
Infant mortality (per 1,000) 126.2
Official language English
Other languages Krio, Mende, Temne
Literacy rate 30.3%
Religions Muslim 60%, indigenous beliefs 30%, Christian 10%
Ethnic groups 13 indigenous tribes 99%, other 1%
Currency Leone
Economy Agriculture 70%, services 17%, industry 13%
GNP per capita US$180
Climate Tropical, with wet season April to November
Highest point Loma Mansa 1,948 m (6,391 ft)
Map reference Page 804

S

Sierra Leone

Sierra Leone's capital, Freetown, was so named when the British government settled freed slaves there in 1787. Once the freed-slave settlers became a ruling class over the Africans already living in the country, deep social divisions opened. Many settlers, and foreign missionaries, were killed in a war with the indigenous Mende in 1898.

Once a British crown colony, and independent from 1961, Sierra Leone's recent history has been marked by military coups, ethnic factionalism, and violence. Since 1992, civil war has raged in the east and the south, thousands of lives have been lost, and thousands of farms have been abandoned in the country's main grain growing areas. Liberian troops have been involved, and Libyan weapons. Child soldiers have been used by both sides.

Unlike most of west Africa, Sierra Leone is mountainous near the sea. These mountains are volcanic, and run south-east of Freetown on the Atlantic forming a thickly wooded peninsula (the Sierra Leone, or Lion Range). The peninsula interrupts a swampy coastal plain, stretching north and south, dominated by mangrove forests. The rolling savanna uplands to the north are known as the Bolilands. Inland, to the northeast, the land rises to the Loma Mountains and the Tingi Hills. Rainfall on the coast is extremely high. The soils are heavily leached and weathered.

Subsistence farming dominates the agricultural sector, which employs about two-thirds of the population. Rice is the staple food crop and along with palm oil it is produced throughout Sierra Leone, except in the drier north. There, in the savanna, peanuts and cattle herding predominate. The country has substantial mineral resources, and the mining of diamonds, bauxite, and rutile or titanium ore provides essential hard currency.

The economy virtually reached a standstill in 1999 because infrastructure collapsed through neglect, and both the mining and agricultural sectors were disrupted by civil war. With Algerian troops acting as monitors, in late 1999 the UN recommended increasing the forces to assist in disarming the combatants. The UN Mission UNAMSIL retained 11,000 people on service in early 2000; however, violence continues. Of primary concern are the thousands of displaced people, to whom the distribution of humanitarian aid is difficult because of the violence. The situation slowly improved since the extra UN force was introduced.

Singapore

A muddy, mangrove-swampy islet nobody wanted in 1819, Singapore is now a leading Asian city-state with one of the highest standards of living in the world. This was achieved without any resources beyond the skills and commitment of its citizens and the economic vision of its leadership. Standing at the southern extremity of the Malay Peninsula, Singapore was established as a free-trading port and settlement early in the nineteenth century by the English colonial administrator Sir Stamford Raffles. Without customs tariffs or other restrictions it drew numbers of Chinese immigrants, and after the opening of the Suez Canal played a leading role in the growing trade in Malaysian rubber and tin.

After the Second World War, during which it was occupied by the Japanese, it reverted to its former status as a British crown colony. In 1963 it became part of Malaysia, but, after two years, tensions between Chinese Singapore and the Malay leadership in Kuala Lumpur led Malaysia to force the island to go it alone. Under Lee Kuan Yew, prime minister for 31 years until 1990, a strategy of high-tech industrialization enabled the economy to grow at a rate of 7 percent a year. However, freedom of speech is constrained, political debate limited, and both public behavior and private life (chewing gum is forbidden, and vandalism punished by caning) are watched closely.

Singapore Island is largely low-lying, with a hilly center. With limited natural freshwater resources, water is brought from the Malaysian mainland nearby. Reservoirs on high ground hold water for the city's use. Urban development has accelerated deforestation and swamp and land reclamation: 5 percent of the land is forested, and 4

A view of Singapore's central business district.

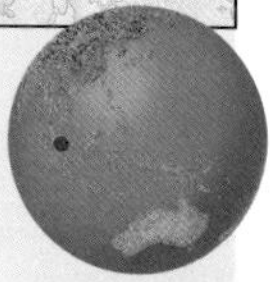

SINGAPORE

OFFICIAL NAME Republic of Singapore
FORM OF GOVERNMENT Republic with single legislative body (Parliament)
CAPITAL Singapore
AREA 633 sq km (244 sq miles)
TIME ZONE GMT + 8 hours
POPULATION 3,531,600
PROJECTED POPULATION 2005 3,725,838
POPULATION DENSITY 5,579.1 per sq km (14,449.8 per sq mile)
LIFE EXPECTANCY 78.8
INFANT MORTALITY (PER 1,000) 3.8
OFFICIAL LANGUAGES Malay, Chinese, Tamil, English
LITERACY RATE 91%
RELIGIONS Buddhist and Taoist 56%, Muslim 15%, Christian 19%, Hindu 5%, other 5%
ETHNIC GROUPS Chinese 76.5%, Malay 15%, Indian 6.5%, other 2%
CURRENCY Singapore dollar
ECONOMY Services 70%, industry 29%, agriculture 1%
GNP PER CAPITA US$26,730
CLIMATE Tropical
HIGHEST POINT Bukit Timah 162 m (531 ft)
MAP REFERENCE Page 736

Modern architecture, Singapore.

percent is arable. In addition to the main island of Singapore there are 57 smaller islands lying within its territorial waters, many of them in the Strait of Singapore, which opens from the busy seaway of the Strait of Malacca. Between the main island and the Malaysian mainland is the narrow channel of the Johore Strait. A causeway across this strait links Malaysia to Singapore.

While the foundation of its economic growth was the export of manufactured goods, the government has in recent years promoted Singapore as a financial services and banking center, using the latest information technology. In 1995 this sector led economic growth. Singapore is a world leader in biotechnology. Rising labor costs threaten the country's competitiveness today, but its government hopes to offset this by increasing productivity and improving infrastructure. Despite the reduced growth rate accompanying the Asian economic downturn in 1998 there are plans for major infrastructural development: an additional stage for Changi International Airport, extensions to the mass rapid transit system, and a deep-tunnel sewerage project to dispose of wastes. In applied technology, per capita output, investment, and industrial harmony, Singapore possesses many of the attributes of a large modern country.

Slovakia

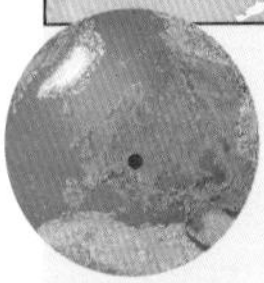

SLOVAKIA

OFFICIAL NAME Slovak Republic
FORM OF GOVERNMENT Republic with single legislative body (National Parliament)
CAPITAL Bratislava
AREA 48,845 sq km (18,859 sq miles)
TIME ZONE GMT + 1 hour

This small central European country is bordered by Poland to the north, the Czech Republic to the northwest, Austria to the west, Hungary to the south, and Ukraine to the east. It is the smaller, less populous, and less industrially developed part of the former state of Czechoslovakia, which split peacefully in 1993 to form the two separate nations of Slovakia and the Czech Republic.

Ethnically distinct from their former compatriots, the Slovaks had lived for ten centuries under continuous Hungarian domination when, in 1918, they merged with the Czechs to form a new, independent nation. At the beginning of the Second World War, Czechoslovakia was invaded by Germany and the Germans installed a pro-Fascist government in Slovakia. Soviet troops restored the pre-war status quo in 1945 and communists seized power in 1948, making the country effectively a Soviet satellite. In 1968 Soviet forces invaded to put down an attempt

The city of Trenčín in Slovakia.

to establish democracy under the leadership of Czechoslovakia's First Secretary, Alexander Dubcek, a Slovak. Twenty-one years later a revival of nationalism and a weakened Soviet Union led to a successful declaration of independence and the establishment of democratic government. Since its separation from the Czech Republic, Slovakia has been governed by a single-chamber parliament, whose 150 members, or deputies, are elected for a four-year term.

Except for lowland areas in the south and southeast, most of the country is mountainous, with extensive forests and tracts of pastureland. In the north of the country the high Carpathian Mountains extend along the Polish border, and further south, the Tatra Mountains, an offshoot of the Carpathians and the Slovakian Ore Mountains, run parallel across the center of the country. Ski resorts in the Tatra Mountains attract large numbers of tourists. The Danube, which forms part of the border with Hungary, flows through an extensive fertile plain. Here, and in the lowland area further to the east, most of Slovakia's agriculture, which employs more than one-tenth of the workforce, is centered. Wheat and potatoes are the principal crops, and sheep, cattle, and pigs are widely raised.

Slovakia is poorly endowed with mineral resources. There are significant deposits of lignite, but most is poor in quality. Industries, which employ about one in three workers, are centered on the cities of Bratislava in the southwest and Kosice in the southeast. Significant industries are iron and steelmaking, and car and clothing manufacture. The move from a centrally controlled to a privatized market economy has proceeded fitfully, and the country has suffered economically from the loss of subsidies that it used to receive from the Czech Republic.

POPULATION 5,396,193
PROJECTED POPULATION 2005 5,509,202
POPULATION DENSITY 110.5 per sq km (286.2 per sq mile)
LIFE EXPECTANCY 73.5
INFANT MORTALITY (PER 1,000) 9.5
OFFICIAL LANGUAGE Slovak
OTHER LANGUAGE Hungarian
LITERACY RATE 99%
RELIGIONS Roman Catholic 60.3%, Protestant 8.4%, Orthodox 4.1%, other 27.2%
ETHNIC GROUPS Slovak 85.7%, Hungarian 10.7%, others include Gypsy, Czech 3.6%
CURRENCY Koruna
ECONOMY Services 44%, industry 44%, agriculture 12%
GNP PER CAPITA US$2,950
CLIMATE Temperate, with cold winters and warm, wet summers
HIGHEST POINT Gerlachovka 2,655 m (8,711 ft)
MAP REFERENCE Page 773

Colorful houses in a Slovakian village.

Farms nestled among rolling hills, Slovakia.

S

Slovenia

Official name Republic of Slovenia
Form of government Republic with two legislative bodies (National Assembly and National Council)
Capital Ljubljana
Area 20,256 sq km (7,821 sq miles)
Time zone GMT + 1 hour
Population 1,970,570
Projected population 2005 1,977,517
Population density 97.3 per sq km (252 per sq mile)
Life expectancy 75.4
Infant mortality (per 1,000) 5.3
Official language Slovenian
Other languages Serbian, Croatian
Literacy rate 96%
Religions Roman Catholic 96%, Muslim 1%, other 3%
Ethnic groups Slovene 91%, Croatian 3%, Serbian 2%, Muslim 1%, other 3%
Currency Tolar
Economy Services 52%, industry 46%, agriculture 2%
GNP per capita US$2,950
Climate Temperate, with colder winters and hotter summers inland
Highest point Mt Triglav 2,864 m (9,396 ft)
Map reference Page 778

Slovenia

This former Yugoslav republic shares borders with Italy to the west, Austria to the north, Hungary to the east, and Croatia to the south. The port of Koper on Slovenia's short coastline on the Gulf of Venice is an important transit point for products from Austria and much of central Europe. First settled by Slavic peoples in the sixth century AD, Slovenia became a Hungarian province in the eleventh century. Austria gained control of the region in the sixteenth century, and Slovenia was later absorbed into the Austro-Hungarian Empire. At the end of the First World War it became part of the Kingdom of the Croats, Serbs, and Slovenes, which in 1929 became Yugoslavia. Like the rest of Yugoslavia, it was occupied by Axis powers during the Second World War. In 1991 it became the first Yugoslav republic to declare its independence. This prompted a military response from the Yugoslav army, which, however, withdrew its forces after a ten-day conflict. According to its constitution of 1991, Slovenia is a democratic republic with a directly elected president and prime minister as head of the government.

Slovenia is mountainous, with the highest and most spectacular regions in the Slovenian Alps near the border with Austria in the northwest. Almost half the land is densely forested. There are areas of lowland in the west near the coast and much of the center and east of the country consists of undulating plains. The most fertile region is in the east, where the Drava River flows southward across the Pannonian Plain into Croatia.

Slovenia's tourist industry, based on its alpine scenery and its coastal beaches, remains important, although it has been adversely affected by conflicts in the region. Almost half the workforce is employed in mining and manufacturing industries. Metallurgy and heavy machine manufacture, including trucks and cars, are prominent among these. Textile manufacture is also widespread. The main mineral resource is coal and there are large mercury deposits in the northwest. Dairy farming and pig raising are the main agricultural activities. Slovenia's nuclear power plant, which supplies one-third of the country's electricity, is a cause of some international tension, especially with Austria.

Lake Bled in Slovenia.

Solomon Islands

The Solomon Islands lie in the western Pacific, northeast of Australia. Inhabited by Melanesian people since about 1000 BC, they consist of two chains of islands running southeast of Bougainville. They were named by the Spanish navigator Alvaro de Mendana, who visited them in 1568 and thought he had found "the riches of Solomon." Twenty years later he returned and established a small, short-lived colony on the Santa Cruz Islands. Outside contacts were few in the ensuing centuries. In the 1870s and 1880s labor recruiters called "blackbirders" were busy inveigling islanders into working on Australian sugar plantations and their unsavory activities led Britain to establish a protectorate over the Southern Solomons in 1893.

In the Second World War the Solomons were occupied by the Japanese. The battle for Guadalcanal saw fierce fighting between Japanese and US forces, the islands overall being the scene of several major Allied naval and

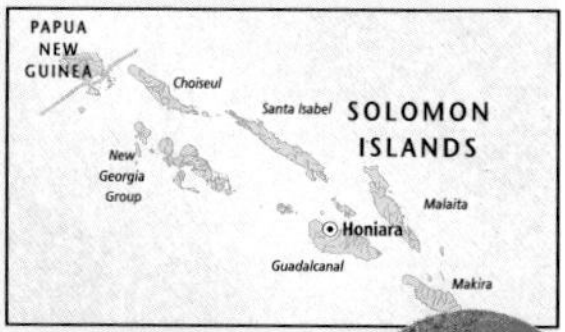

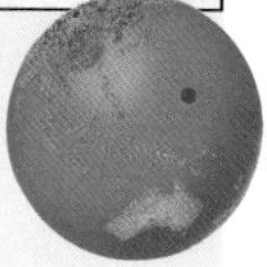

SOLOMON ISLANDS

OFFICIAL NAME Solomon Islands
FORM OF GOVERNMENT Constitutional monarchy with single legislative body (National Parliament)
CAPITAL Honiara
AREA 28,450 sq km (10,985 sq miles)
TIME ZONE GMT + 11 hours
POPULATION 455,429
PROJECTED POPULATION 2005 544,573

(continues)

SOLOMON ISLANDS *(continued)*

POPULATION DENSITY 16 per sq km (41.4 per sq mile)
LIFE EXPECTANCY 72.1
INFANT MORTALITY (PER 1,000) 23.0
OFFICIAL LANGUAGE English
OTHER LANGUAGES Pidgin, indigenous languages
LITERACY RATE 62%
RELIGIONS Protestant 77% (including Anglican 34%, Baptist 17%, United 11%, Seventh-Day Adventist 10%), Roman Catholic 19%, indigenous beliefs 4%
ETHNIC GROUPS Melanesian 93%, Polynesian 4%, Micronesian 1.5%, European 0.8%, other 0.7%
CURRENCY Soloman Islands dollar
ECONOMY Agriculture 85%, services 10%, industry 5%
GNP PER CAPITA US$910
CLIMATE Tropical, most rain falling November to April
HIGHEST POINT Mt Makarakomburu 2,447 m (8,126 ft)
MAP REFERENCE Pages 726–7

military victories. In recent years relations with Papua New Guinea have been strained because of the Solomon Islands' support for secessionists on Bougainville and the rebels of the Bougainville Revolutionary Army. Although Bougainville is geographically and ethnically a part of the Solomon Islands group, it has been treated politically as a part of Papua New Guinea for over one hundred years.

In geological terms, the islands represent a part of the submerged outermost crustal fold of the ancient Australian continent. Their interiors are rugged and mountainous. The six main islands—Guadalcanal, Malaita, New Georgia, Makira (formerly San Cristobal), Santa Isabel, and Choiseul—are all of volcanic origin, and have densely forested ranges with steep-sided river valleys. Around the coasts are narrow plains where most of the population live as subsistence farmers growing beans, coconuts, palm kernels, rice, potatoes, and vegetables. Palm oil, cocoa and copra are leading agricultural exports, and tuna fish is the single biggest earner. Forestry provides an important industry but the unsustainable level of timber extraction is an environmental concern. The islands are rich in undeveloped mineral resources such as lead, zinc, nickel, gold, bauxite, and phosphate—significant phosphate deposits are being mined on Bellona Island. The government is nearly insolvent and depends on foreign aid.

Coastal village with WWII pontoons, Solomon Islands.

S

Somalia

Somalia, a coastal state on the Horn of Africa, is in one respect unlike any other African country. It is the only place where the whole population feels that they are "one people"—Somali—and because of this ethnic homogeneity it has the makings of a nation state. Briefly under the control of Egypt from 1875, the region became a British protectorate in 1885. In 1889 Italy took control of the eastern coast, and from then on the country was divided into two: British Somaliland in the north and Italian Somaliland in the south and east. It has been independent since 1960.

The history of the people of Somalia since independence has been one of repression (under the Soviet-aligned Siyad Barre), military adventure (the invasion of the Ethiopian Ogaden), and civil war. When in 1992 an estimated 2,000 people a day were dying from war and starvation, the United Nations intervened, but its troops were unable to stop the military and civil unrest and withdrew. Anarchy and banditry now prevail. In the absence of any central authority, and without a functioning government in Muqdisho, the northern area once known as British Somaliland seceded and proclaimed itself an independent state. Centered on the city of Hargeysa, it calls itself the Somaliland Republic. It has not been recognised internationally.

Along the northern shore facing the Gulf of Aden lies the semiarid Guban coastal plain. Behind this is a range of

A group of Somali villagers.

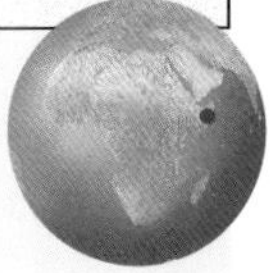

SOMALIA

OFFICIAL NAME Somali Democratic Republic
FORM OF GOVERNMENT Republic; no effective central government exists at the present time
CAPITAL Muqdisho (Mogadishu)
AREA 637,660 sq km (246,200 sq miles)
TIME ZONE GMT + 3 hours
POPULATION 7,140,643
PROJECTED POPULATION 2005 8,795,258
POPULATION DENSITY 11.2 per sq km (29 per sq mile)
LIFE EXPECTANCY 46.2
INFANT MORTALITY (PER 1,000) 125.8
OFFICIAL LANGUAGE Somali
OTHER LANGUAGES Arabic, Italian, English
LITERACY RATE 24%
RELIGIONS Sunni Muslim with tiny Christian minority
ETHNIC GROUPS Somali 85%, remainder mainly Bantu with small Arab, Asian, and European minorities 15%
CURRENCY Somali shilling
ECONOMY Agriculture 76%, services 16%, industry 8%
GNP PER CAPITA Est. < US$765
CLIMATE Mainly hot and arid, with higher rainfall in the south
HIGHEST POINT Mt Shimbiris 2,416 m (7,927 ft)
MAP REFERENCE Page 807

mountains, the Ogo Highlands, running eastward from Ethiopia to the point of the Horn itself. South of the highlands is the Haud Plateau, and beyond this the land slopes toward the Indian Ocean. Much of Somalia has semidesert thornbush and dry savanna cover. Only in the better watered south is there enough rainfall to support meager forests and grassland. Arable farming takes place between the Rivers Jubba and Shabeelle in the south. The Shabeelle, blocked by dunes, provides water for irrigation. Bananas from this area are a major export, mainly to Italy. Rival clans fight over this important resource; some plantation work is done by women and children in slave-labor conditions guarded by armed militia.

Nomadic pastoralists form much of the population in the north. Searching for grass and water, they wander with their herds across the state boundaries between southern Djibouti, the Ogaden, and northeast Kenya. Livestock accounts for 40 percent of gross domestic product and 65 percent of export earnings. In the south, in addition to the export crop of bananas, food crops of sugar, sorghum, and maize are grown. A small industrial sector is based on the processing of food products, but the prevailing disorder has caused many facilities to be closed.

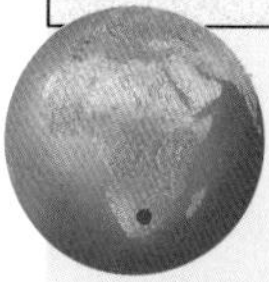

SOUTH AFRICA

OFFICIAL NAME Republic of South Africa
FORM OF GOVERNMENT Republic with two legislative bodies (Senate and National Assembly)
CAPITAL Pretoria (administrative); Cape Town (legislative); Bloemfontein (judicial)

South Africa

Occupying the southernmost tip of the African continent, South Africa comprises a central plateau or veld, bordered to the south and east by the Drakensberg Mountains and to the north by the countries of Namibia, Botswana, Zimbabwe and Mozambique. The Independent State of Lesotho is contained within South Africa's borders. European settlement in the seventeenth century culminated in white minority rule, and a controversial policy of racial segregation called apartheid was officially implemented in 1948. After 50 years of deepening crisis and international isolation as a result of its racial policies, South Africa changed course in 1990, held democratic elections in 1994, and under a new government rejoined the international community. Always the economic powerhouse of southern Africa, it is now free from sanctions and able to renew normal trading relations. The abandonment of apartheid, and the freeing of long-term

An elephant browsing in Kruger National Park, Southern Natal.

political prisoner (and later president) Nelson Mandela, have had an uplifting effect on national morale and provided a chance for a fresh start. Problems currently facing the nation include discrepancies between the educational level and skills of blacks and whites; vastly different income levels; increasing unemployment; high urban crime rates; and the ongoing conflict between Zulu groups and the ruling party, the African National Congress.

Physical features and land use

South Africa has three main geographic regions. First, there is the vast African plateau of the interior. This slopes gradually north and west to form part of the semiarid and sparsely populated Kalahari basin, while to the east it rises to elevations of 2,000 m (6,500 ft). Second, the Great Escarpment, varying in height, structure, and steepness, forms a rim around the entire plateau from the mountains of the Transvaal Drakensberg in the northeast to Namibia in the northwest. Its highest peaks are in the Drakensberg along the Lesotho border. The third region consists of the narrow, fertile strips of land along the peripheral coastal plains.

Agricultural products include maize (a staple for many African farmers); apples, pears, stone fruit, grapes, and wine from Eastern Cape Province; wheat from Western

AREA 1,219,912 sq km (471,008 sq miles)
TIME ZONE GMT + 2 hours
POPULATION 43,426,386
PROJECTED POPULATION 2005 46,220,919
POPULATION DENSITY 35.6 per sq km (92.2 per sq mile)
LIFE EXPECTANCY 54.8
INFANT MORTALITY (PER 1,000) 52
OFFICIAL LANGUAGES Afrikaans, English, Ndebele, Pedi, Sotho, Swazi, Tsonga, Tswana, Venda, Xhosa, Zulu
OTHER LANGUAGES Indigenous languages, Hindi, Urdu, Gujarati, Tamil
LITERACY RATE 81.4%
RELIGIONS Christian (most Europeans and people of mixed origin and about 60% of Africans) 68%, Hindu (60% of Indians) 2%, Muslim 2%, indigenous beliefs 28%
ETHNIC GROUPS Indigenous 75.2%, European 13.6%, mixed 8.6%, Indian 2.6%
CURRENCY Rand
ECONOMY Services 62%, industry 24%, agriculture 14%
GNP PER CAPITA US$3,160
CLIMATE Mainly semiarid; subtropical on southeast coast
HIGHEST POINT Thabana-Ntlenyana 3,482 m (11,424 ft)
MAP REFERENCE Pages 810–11

PROVINCES

Eastern Cape • Free State • Gauteng • KwaZulu-Natal • Mpumalanga • Northern Province • Northern Cape • North West • Western Cape

Giraffe and crocodile in Kruger National Park.

S

The Hex River Pass.

Cape Province; and sugarcane from coastal KwaZulu-Natal. On the grasslands of the plateau large-scale pastoralism produces wool, mohair, skins, and meat. South Africa is geologically ancient—only a few superficial strata are less than 600 million years old. In the 1880s rocks of the Witwatersrand were found to contain gold and diamonds, and since then gold and diamond mining has been the basis of South Africa's national wealth.

Along the west coast, north of Cape Town, the cold Benguela current inhibits rainfall, producing the desert of the Namib. In the northeast there is dry savanna bushland. On the Mozambique border the best-known of South Africa's eight wildlife reserves, Kruger National Park, contains lions, leopards, giraffes, elephants, and hippopotamuses.

People and culture

First inhabited by San, or bushmen, southern Africa was in the fifteenth century occupied by a wave of cattle-keeping, grain-growing Bantu peoples from the north—their modern descendants being groups such as the Xhosa and the Zulu. Then in 1652 and 1688 two groups of

Cape Dutch-style house, Tulbagh.

The seaside town of Muizenberg.

Village in the foothills of Drakensberg Mountains.

settlers arrived from Europe—the first Dutch, the second French Huguenot, both firmly Protestant in their faith—and established a colony in the south at Cape Town. They became known as Boers (farmers) and later as Afrikaners (after their language, Afrikaans). The British established themselves on the Cape in 1806. Over the years, a population of mixed Afro-European descent emerged who became known as "Cape Coloreds." In the nineteenth century laborers from India were brought in by the British, creating yet another large and distinct ethnic community. There are also a small number of Malays.

After 1948, under the ruling Afrikaners, apartheid (apartness) laws were drafted defining how each community should associate, where each should live, whether they could intermarry, and what work they could do. The entire population was to be organized in a hierarchy of privilege, with whites at the top and blacks at the bottom. Africans were to be confined to a series of internal Black States called "homelands," which were in practice mere labor pools, since the only way people could find employment was by leaving home and traveling to the South African mines. The impracticality, unreality, and injustice of the system aroused widespread international condemnation. The misery it created led to ongoing violent resistance.

Royal Natal National Park ranger's Cape Dutch-style house with Drakensberg Mountains behind.

Economy and resources

Although both the Bantu and the first Europeans to colonize South Africa were farming people, and agriculture formed the foundation of the economy for hundreds of years, during the nineteenth century gold and diamonds were the attractions that drew a new wave

Highrise buildings in Pretoria.

South Africa Timeline

3 MYA Cave-dwelling Australopithecines in what is now Cape Province and Gauteng, kill animals for meat and eat plants

120,000 BP "Modern" humans inhabit cave near Port Elizabeth; they eat shellfish, tortoises, and birds' eggs

25,000 BP Rock paintings on shelters show ceremonial dancers and animals, like antelope, which were hunted for food

c.2000 BC Kalahari San (bushmen) inhabit the Kalahari Desert herding animals

4–500 AD Bantu people arrive from East Africa to find grazing for sheep and cattle and to plant crops. Displace Khoisan hunter-gatherers

c.1000 Urban centers established; bone and ivory crafts; products traded between groups

1100 Diff language emerge, s Xhosa anc

1488 First Po vessels arri Cape of Gc

c.1800 Zulu nation founded in today's KwaZulu-Natal, forcing Shoshangane clan into Swaziland and Mzilikazi clan into Zimbabwe

1836–38 10,000 Boer settlers unhappy with British rule in Cape set out on Great Trek to seek new land in Natal and Orange River areas

1860 Laborers from India are imported by Natal farmers to work on farms and plantations

1870 Gold rush in the Kimberley area and discovery of diamonds transform the economic base from agriculture to mining

1880–81 British fail to bring Boer republics (Orange Free State, Transvaal) into federation—British defeat in First Boer War

1899 Gold-n industry emp 110,000 wo almost 100, African labor

1899–1902 defeat the Bc (Afrikaners) ir Boer War

Rhinos in Kruger National Park.

of settlers. Today, gold and precious stones still make up half the country's total exports, and over the last 100 years almost half the world's gold has come from South African mines. Other important minerals include asbestos, nickel, vanadium, and uranium (which can sometimes be found in old gold mines). In addition, South Africa is the world's largest producer of manganese, platinum, and chromium.

Energy conservation is a vital concern to the country as no petroleum deposits have yet been found. During the long period of South Africa's isolation and of trade boycotts, the state corporation Sasol extracted oil from coal. Though this is a expensive process, extensive deposits of coal make this a feasible supplementary supply. Many white South Africans enjoy a standard of living that is equal to the highest in the world. The challenge for the government in the next century will be to provide the circumstances and conditions in which less privileged social groups can have a share of the wealth. This will not be an easy task: at present there are jobs for less than 5 percent of the 300,000 workers who enter the labor force each year.

1615 British ent at Table ay lasts only a few years

1652 Dutch East India Co. garrison at site of Cape Town supplies Dutch fleet; settlers granted land at Liesbeek River in 1657

1657 First slaves brought to the Cape from India, Indonesia, and West Africa as agricultural labor and to act as herders

1713 Khoikhoi pastoralists displaced by "trekboer" settlers in search of grazing land; numerous San people die of smallpox

1795–1802 British occupy Cape, a vital trade route supply post prior to opening of Suez Canal; more British settlers arrive

African Congress nded by black interested in political

1931 South Africa granted independence by Britain as a member of the Commonwealth

1948 National Party passes law restricting parliamentary representation to whites; "apartheid" official in 1950

1961 South Africa leaves Commonwealth and becomes a Republic, without asking non-whites

1962 Nelson Mandela and other leading members of the ANC are imprisoned

1976 Black African protest over compulsory Afrikaans language lessons results in violence and the loss of 600 lives

1990 Mandela freed; apartheid abolished (1991); population 37 million (76% black, 13% white, 9% mixed race, 2% Asian)

1994 Mandela elected president in first non-racial general election—pronounces the new South Africa a "Rainbow Republic"

1999 Tabo Mbeki succeeds Mandela as President

South Georgia and South Sandwich Islands

South Georgia is a barren island in the South Atlantic 1,300 km (800 miles) southeast of the Falklands. Annexed by Captain Cook in 1775, the harbor of Grytviken was long used as a whaling base. Until the 1940s it had a population of up to 800 employed in the whaling industry. Its wildlife is now attracting increasing numbers of ecotourists.

The South Sandwich Islands are six uninhabited volcanic cones to the southeast of South Georgia.

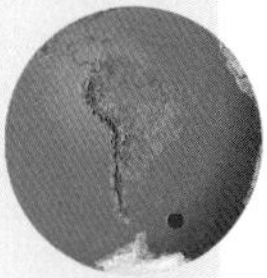

South Georgia and the South Sandwich Islands

Official name South Georgia and the South Sandwich Islands
Form of government Dependent territory of the UK
Capital None; Grytviken is garrison town
Area 4,066 sq km (1,570 sq miles)
Time zone GMT – 4 hours
Population No permanent population
Economy Military base and biological station only
Climate Cold, wet, and windy
Map reference Pages 859, 862

S

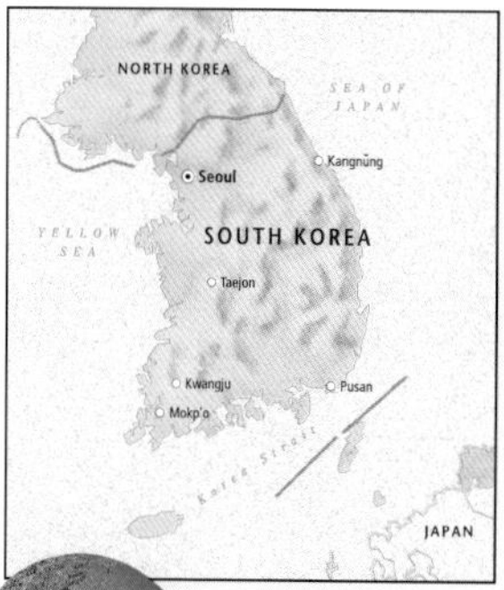

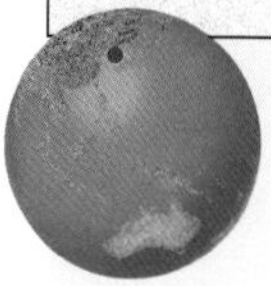

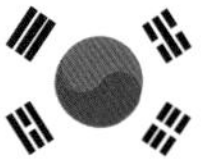

South Korea

Official name Republic of Korea
Form of government Republic with single legislative body (National Assembly)
Capital Seoul
Area 98,480 sq km (38,023 sq miles)
Time zone GMT + 9 hours
Population 46,884,800
Projected population 2005 49,489,750
Population density 476.1 per sq km (1,223.1 per sq mile)
Life expectancy 74.3
Infant mortality (per 1,000) 7.6
Official language Korean
Other language English
Literacy rate 97.9%
Religions Christianity 21%, Buddhism 24%, Confucianism 1.5%, other 1%, no religion 52.5%
Ethnic groups Korean 99.9%, Chinese 0.1%
Currency Won
Economy Services 55%, industry 27%, agriculture 18%
GNP per capita US$9,700
Climate Temperate, with cold winters and hot, wet summers
Highest point Halla-san 1,950 m (6,398 ft)
Map reference Page 744

South Korea

South Korea occupies the southern half of the Korean Peninsula. The border between South and North Korea consists of the ceasefire line established at the end of the Korean War (1950–53), roughly corresponding to the original pre-1950 border at the 38th parallel. The kingdom of Korea was dominated by either China or Japan for many centuries and finally annexed by Japan in 1910. After Japan's defeat at the end of the Second World War, Korea was divided between a northern Soviet zone of influence, and a southern zone under US control. These zones soon became separate political entities. In 1950 communist North Korea invaded South Korea, and though the war ended in a stalemate in 1953, bitter hostility between north and south endures to the present day, with covert operations continuing.

In the 40-year period following 1953, both Koreas diverged socially, politically, and economically. South Korea, after a few years under the authoritarian rule of its first president, established constitutional liberalism in the Second Republic of 1960. From then until his assassination in 1979 it was under the elected presidency of General Park Chung Hee, who laid the basis for the economic success of the modern South Korean state with a combination of state planning and free-market incentives.

While questionable practices flourished at the top (two former presidents have been jailed) the country achieved a remarkable record of growth. Only 30 years ago its standard of living was much the same as the poorer countries of Africa. Today its gross domestic product per

Rural scenery in South Korea.

capita is nine times India's, fourteen times North Korea's, and on a par with some economies of the European Union. Regionally, its technological and scientific prowess is second only to Japan's.

A broad avenue for public recreation in Seoul.

More than 80 percent of South Korea's terrain is mountainous. Along the eastern side of the country the Tabaek-Sanmaek Mountains descend north to southwest. The Han and Naktong Rivers drain from these mountains through low-lying plains—the Han to the northwest, the Naktong to the south. Densely populated and intensively farmed, these plains cover 15 percent of South Korea's total land area. Rice, a staple crop in which the country is almost self-sufficient, is grown on family-owned farms. Other food crops include barley and fruit such as apples, grapes, peaches, nectarines, and plums. Silk and tobacco are produced for the export market. About two-thirds of South Korea is forested. As many as 3,000 small islands lie off the west and south coasts, including Cheju which has South Korea's highest peak, the extinct volcano Halla-san at 1,950 m (6,398 ft).

There is little at the high-tech end of modern industry that South Korea does not manufacture and sell. It produces electronic equipment, machinery, ships, and automobiles. Textiles, an early item in its drive for export success, remain significant, along with clothing, food processing, chemicals, and steel. Real gross domestic product grew by an average 10 percent from 1986 to 1991, then tapered off. With the downturn in the Asian economies in 1998 the economy shrank for the first time in years, but the country won IMF praise for acting promptly in order to wipe out billions in bad bank loans and purge companies that were unviable.

Spain

Official name Kingdom of Spain
Form of government Constitutional monarchy with two legislative bodies (Senate and Congress of Deputies)
Capital Madrid
Area 504,750 sq km (194,884 sq miles)
Time zone GMT + 1 hour
Population 39,167,744
Projected population 2005 39,334,191
Population density 77.6 per sq km (201 per sq mile)
Life expectancy 77.7
Infant mortality (per 1,000) 6.4
Official language Spanish (Castillian)
Other languages Catalan, Galician, Basque
Literacy rate 97.1%
Religions Roman Catholic 99%, other 1%
Ethnic groups Ethnically homogenous, but divided into the following cultural/linguistic groups: Spanish 73%, Catalan 17%, Galician 7%, Basque 2%, Gypsy 1%
Currency Peseta
Economy Services 68%, industry 21%, agriculture 11%
GNP per capita US$13,580
Climate Temperate, with mild, wet winters and hot, dry summers; cooler and wetter in northwest
Highest point Mulhacén 3,478 m (11,411 ft)
Map reference Pages 776–7

Spain

Spain occupies the bulk of the Iberian Peninsula at the southwestern tip of Europe. It shares land borders with Portugal to the west, France to the north, and the tiny principality of Andorra, perched high in the Pyrenees on the border with France. To the west and south, Spain has short stretches of coastline along the Atlantic Ocean and to the north, a long coast on the Bay of Biscay. Its southern tip is separated from Morocco by the Strait of Gibraltar and its southeastern and eastern coastlines are on the western edge of the Mediterranean Sea.

The Iberian Peninsula had already experienced a long history of human habitation when, at the end of the third century BC, the Romans subdued the Celts, Iberians, and

Fertile countryside in Catalonia.

Basques who lived there. The region remained a Roman colony until the Visigoths invaded early in the fifth century AD. Over the next three centuries the region became Christianized, but in AD 711 an invasion from Morocco in the south established what would become a flourishing Islamic civilization that lasted for six centuries. In the ninth century Christian invaders from the north gained control of Catalonia in the northeast, thus beginning a process of slow reconquest that would, by the early thirteenth century, see the Moors only retaining control of Granada in the south.

The marriage of Ferdinand II of Aragon and Isabella I of Castile in 1469 brought together the two most powerful states on the peninsula, and in 1492, when the Moors were finally expelled from Granada, Spain became a unified country under Catholic rule. Thus began a century of Spanish exploration and conquest in which Spain acquired colonies in Central and South America, as well as the Philippines in Southeast Asia. The Spanish also conquered a large part of Western Europe, including Portugal, the Netherlands, Austria, and part of Italy.

REGIONS

Andalusia • Aragon • Asturias
Baleares • Basque Country
Canary Islands • Cantabria
Castilla-La Mancha • Castilla Y León
Catalonia • Ceuta and Melilla
Extremadura • Galicia • La Rioja
Madrid • Murcia • Navarra
Valencia

A small farm in the province of Navarra.

Storks are among the many bird species found in southern Spain.

The beginning of Spain's decline from being a dominant power in the world to a state of secondary importance can be traced to 1588, when Philip II sent his mighty armada of 130 ships in an abortive attempt to invade Protestant England. This defeat by the English spelled the end of Spain's maritime dominance. By 1714 Spain had lost all its European possessions and by 1826 it had been forced to surrender all its American colonies except Cuba and Puerto Rico.

French revolutionary forces invaded Spain in 1794. They were defeated in 1814 and the Spanish Bourbon monarchy was restored. During the nineteenth and much of the twentieth century Spain has been destabilized by political turmoil and a series of military revolts and wars. Quarrels about the succession to the crown led to the removal of Isabella II from the throne in 1868, the declaration of a republic in 1873, and a military uprising in 1874 that restored the monarchy. In 1898 Spain and the United States fought a war at the end of which a defeated Spain was forced to cede its colonies of Cuba, Puerto Rico, and the Philippines to its adversary.

Spain remained neutral in both world wars, but was wracked by a bitter civil war from 1936 to 1939. Universal adult suffrage was introduced in 1931 and in 1936 the election of a Republican government with socialist leanings prompted an army officer, Francisco Franco, to

The Ramblas in Barcelona.

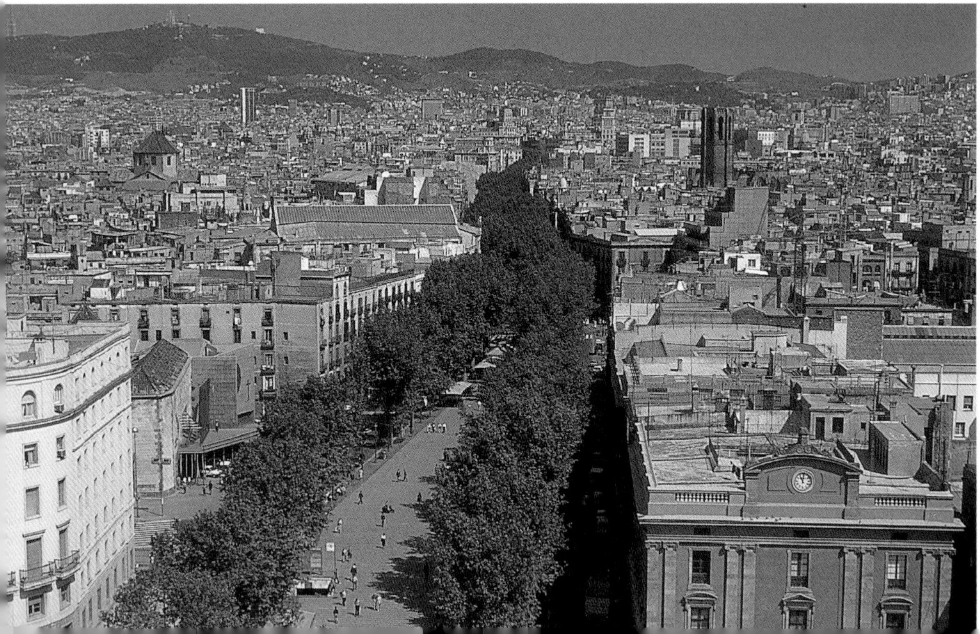

lead a revolt against the government. With the support of right-wing Spanish forces and of Fascist Italy and Nazi Germany, and after the loss of 750,000 Spanish lives, Franco's forces were eventually victorious and Franco was installed as head of state. His dictatorial regime lasted until his death in 1975. Almost immediately the monarchy was restored and in June 1977 the first parliamentary elections since 1936 were held. In December 1978 a referendum approved a new constitution in which Spain was declared a parliamentary democracy with a monarch as head of state. There are two houses of parliament, both elected by universal adult suffrage for maximum terms of four years.

Historic narrow street.

Physical features and land use

More than half Spain's land area is occupied by a central plateau, the Meseta. It has an average elevation of 700 m (2,300 ft). Much of the Meseta is harsh and barren. It is surrounded by mountain ranges to the north, northeast, south, and southwest, and is traversed by a low mountain range, the Sistema Central. The plateau is drained by three rivers—the Douro to the north of the Sistema Central, and the Tagus and Guadiana to its south—all of these rivers flow westward to the Atlantic.

Spanish countryside.

In the far northeast of the country, between the Sistema Ibérico, a range that fringes the Meseta on the northeast and the Pyrenees to the north, is an extensive lowland area through which the Ebro River, which rises in the Basque country, flows south to the Mediterranean. In the southwest of Spain, beyond the Sierra Morena Range at the Meseta's southwestern edge, the Guadalquivir River

Ocean headland, Ibiza.

Pasta shop, Barcelona.

Spain Timeline

780,000 BP Stone tools used by hominids in northern Spain; classified as Homo heidelbergensis

280,000 BP Caves inhabited by Homo Sapiens at Atapuerca, Burgos, northern Spain, as well as Torralba and Ambrona

10,000 BC Images of bison painted on the walls of a deep cave at Altamira, northern Spain, probably used for ceremonies

5500 BC Sheep and wheat used by early farmers along the western Mediterranean

3200 BC Larger communities develop around southern and southwestern Spain and Portugal, such as Los Millares, Almeria

3000 BC Iberian people, including Gauls and Basques, move in from the north to found towns on Iberian Peninsula

1000 BC P traders fro Mediterrar to colonize and easter of Spain

400 BC Cartha of North Afri over much c

1516 King Charles I, grandson of Ferdinand and Isabella, is first Hapsburg to rule Spain; becomes Holy Roman Emperor in 1519

1556 Charles's son becomes King Philip II; height of Spanish Empire in Americas, Europe, and Africa

1808 French invade Spain; Spanish resistance grows, French expelled in Peninsular War (1814)

1820 Spanish troops refuse to sail to reconquer American colonies; revolt spreads, crushed with help of French troops

1860 Population begins to decline for almost a century due to emigration

1931 King Alfor flees after el show preferenc republic; Spain a democracy- political di

Catholic priest talking with a man.

drains another extensive low-lying region. In the far southeast is a coastal range, the Sistema Pinibético, which contains the snow-covered peaks of the Sierra Nevada, including the country's highest mountain, Mulhacén.

About one-tenth of Spain is heavily forested. Most of the forests are in the north and northwest, where the weather is wetter and more humid than in the center and south. Beech and oak predominate. Despite the fact that much of the country is arid and covered with low-growing scrub and water is a scarce resource, crops are widely grown. The most productive areas are in the north of the country, especially in the valley of the Ebro. There are significant crops of cereals, vegetables, fruits, and olives.

Spain is one of Europe's main producers of wine and there are 1.5 million hectares (3.7 million acres) of vineyards, mainly in the south and east. About one-fifth of Spain is pastureland, though cattle and dairying are largely confined to the north and pig farming to the southwest. Sheep are widespread on the Meseta, while goats graze in many of the more barren regions.

Industry and commerce

Although Spain has a wide range of mineral resources, it is not rich in any of them and imports the oil and gas defeat of ns in the ic War, y becomes Roman

AD 711 Moors invade from North Africa bringing Muslim religion and building palaces and mosques

1469 Marriage of Ferdinand of Aragon and Isabella of Castile brings together both kingdoms—almost all of modern Spain

AD 476 Romans rename peninsula ania; lose control o Germanic tribes who occupy whole territory by 573

962–1212 Christian push back Moors; Moors confined to Granada

1492 Columbus sails on first voyage in the service of Ferdinand and Isabella; Spanish take last Moorish stronghold, Granada

1960s Rapid industrialization, pansion of economy nd growth in tourist resort development along Mediterranean

1973 Basque separatists (ETA) assassinate Prime Minister Carrero Blanco in Madrid

1976 Government under Prime Minister Suarez liberalizes politics, permits new parties to participate in elections (1977)

1986 Prime Minister González embarks on more economic development; Spain joins European Community (EC)

3 Spanish Civil torious ists under enter Madrid

1970 Population grows following industrialization. More than 1 million immigrants in 10 years, almost half illegal

1975 On the death of Franco, Spain adopts political reform agenda despite accession of Juan Carlos (grandson of Alfonso XIII) as king

1980 The 2.5 million Basque people of northern Spain are granted limited autonomy

1995 Population more than 39 million; Spain lifts passport controls with EC nations

needed to fuel its industries. These industries are concentrated towards the north, mainly around the major cities of Madrid and Barcelona. Spain is a major manufacturer of motor vehicles and a number of multinational companies have car manufacturing plants in parts of northern and central Spain. Steelmaking and shipbuilding are among the most significant heavy industries. There are important shipyards at Barcelona, on the Mediterranean coast, La Coruña in the far northwest, and Cadiz in the southwest. Chemical manufacture and fishing are also major industries. Spain has one of the world's largest fishing fleets, although its activities have been curtailed in recent years by European Union restrictions in response to serious fish stock depletions. About one in ten of Spain's workers are employed in the tourist industry.

While Spain is still a predominantly Catholic country, the influence of the Church has waned in recent years. This is reflected in the fact that Spain has one of the lowest birth-rates in Europe, even though divorce is still relatively rare. Although most Spaniards enjoy a reasonably high standard of living, unemployment during the 1990s has been alarmingly high.

Red motorbike and bar.

S

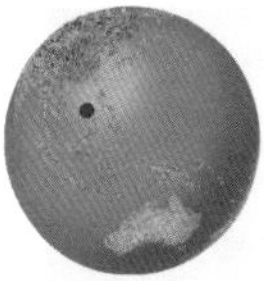

SPRATLY ISLANDS

OFFICIAL NAME Spratly Islands
FORM OF GOVERNMENT Disputed territory claimed by China, Taiwan, Vietnam, Malaysia, and the Philippines
CAPITAL None
AREA 5 sq km (1.9 sq miles)
TIME ZONE GMT + 8 hours
POPULATION No permanent population
CLIMATE Tropical. Prone to typhoons
MAP REFERENCE Page 739

Spratly Islands

The Spratly Islands consist of a collection of reefs, islands, and atolls scattered across a large area of the South China Sea, about two-thirds of the way from southern Vietnam to the southern Philippines. Brunei has made Louisa Reef an exclusive economic zone, but has not publicly claimed the island. The islands are subject to territorial disputes because of their proximity to oil- and gas-producing sedimentary basins.

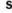

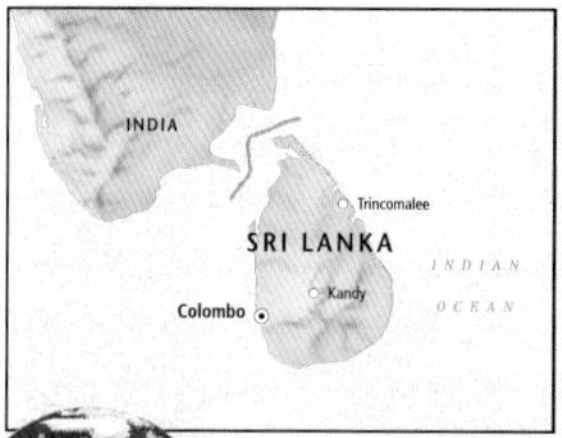

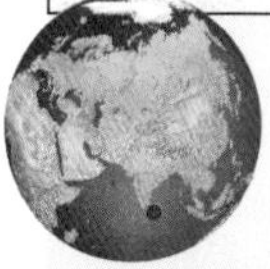

SRI LANKA

OFFICIAL NAME Democratic Socialist Republic of Sri Lanka
FORM OF GOVERNMENT Republic with single legislative body (Parliament)
CAPITAL Colombo
AREA 65,610 sq km (25,332 sq miles)
TIME ZONE GMT + 5.5 hours
POPULATION 19,144,875
PROJECTED POPULATION 2005 20,418,172
POPULATION DENSITY 291.8 per sq km (755.8 per sq mile)
LIFE EXPECTANCY 72.7
INFANT MORTALITY (PER 1,000) 16.1
OFFICIAL LANGUAGE Sinhala
OTHER LANGUAGES Tamil, English
LITERACY RATE 90.1%
RELIGIONS Buddhist 69%, Hindu 15%, Christian 8%, Muslim 8%

Sri Lanka

Sri Lanka is a large, scenically dramatic island off India's southeast coast, and was known as Ceylon until 1972. It has a mountainous center, and a string of coral islets called "Adam's Bridge" link it to India in the northwest. Over the last 50 years the country has suffered intermittent strife. For over 1,000 years a minority of Hindu Tamils in the north and a majority of Sinhalese elsewhere have lived side by side. From the sixteenth century successive European nations—the Portuguese, the Dutch, and the British—visited and left their ethnic mark. Britain controlled the whole island from 1815, and brought in large numbers of additional Tamil plantation workers from south India later that century.

When Sri Lanka gained its independence in 1948 the majority Sinhalese stripped 800,000 Tamils of citizenship and the right to vote, and made Sinhala the country's sole official language. From then on there was civil unrest and from 1983 there has been civil war. The Tamil demand for an autonomous northern state has been complicated by separate leftist insurrections by radical Sinhalese seeking to overthrow the government. Sri Lanka has a large number of political parties and movements on the left (including one that is officially Trotskyist) which have added intransigence to its political life. Civil war and insurgencies have taken at least 50,000 lives.

With high mountains, intermontane plateaus, and steep river gorges, the rugged terrain of the central uplands dominates the island. Much of this higher ground is used for growing tea on large plantations. Falling away to the southwest, the terrain declines toward the sandy coastal lowlands where coconuts are grown (Sri Lanka is the world's fifth-largest producer). Rubber is the third important plantation crop. Overall, 37 percent of the country supports tropical vegetation and open woodland. Though reduced by deforestation, rainforest still covers the wettest areas. The fertile, rice-growing northern plains are bordered to the southeast by the Mahaweli River.

Among Sri Lanka's mineral resources are a variety of precious and semi-precious stones including sapphire, ruby, tourmaline, and topaz. Also mined are graphite, mineral sands, and phosphates. About 43 percent of the workforce is engaged in agriculture, the main subsistence crop being rice—although production falls considerably short of the country's requirements. Fruit, vegetables, and spices are grown as staples and for export and Sri Lanka is one of the world's main exporters of tea. But today industry, dominated by the manufacture of clothing and expanding in special Export Processing Zones, has overtaken agriculture as the principal source of export earnings. The uncertain economic climate created by civil strife continues to cloud the nation's prospects, deterring tourists and discouraging foreign investment.

ETHNIC GROUPS Sinhalese 74%, Tamil 18%, Sri Lankan Moor 7%, other 1%
CURRENCY Sri Lankan rupee
ECONOMY Services 45%, agriculture 43%, industry 12%
GNP PER CAPITA US$700
CLIMATE Tropical; southwest wetter with most rain falling April to June and October to November; northeast drier with most rain falling December to February
HIGHEST POINT Mt Pidurutalagala 2,524 m (8,281 ft)
MAP REFERENCE Page 752–3

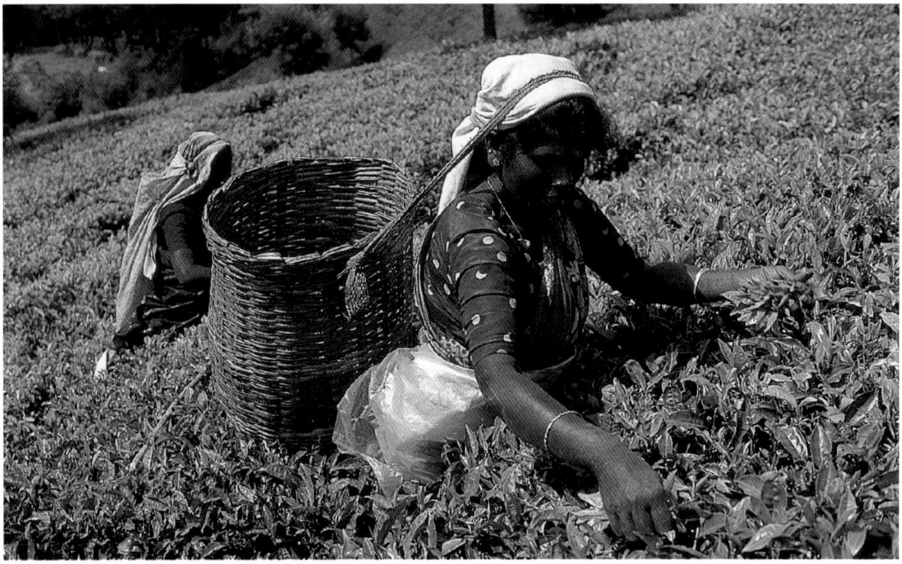

Tea-pickers on a tea estate in the highlands of Sri Lanka.

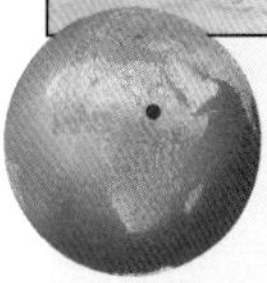

Sudan

Official name Republic of the Sudan
Form of government Military regime with single transitional legislative body (Provisional National Assembly)
Capital Al Kharṭūm (Khartoum)
Area 2,505,810 sq km (967,493 sq miles)
Time zone GMT + 2 hours
Population 34,475,690
Projected population 2005 40,899,171
Population density 13.8 per sq km (35.7 per sq mile)
Life expectancy 56.4
Infant mortality (per 1,000) 70.9
Official language Arabic
Other languages Nubian, Ta Bedawie, English, indigenous languages
Literacy rate 44.8%
Religions Sunni Muslim 70%, indigenous beliefs 25%, Christian 5%
Ethnic groups African 52%, Arab 39%, Beja 6%, other 3%
Currency Sudanese pound
Economy Agriculture 65%, services 31%, industry 4%
GNP per capita US$423
Climate North mainly arid; south tropical, with wet season April to October
Highest point Mt Kinyeti 3,187 m (10,456 ft)
Map reference Pages 802–3, 806–7

S

Sudan

South of Egypt, Sudan is Africa's largest country, and the pathway to the headwaters of the Nile (An Nīl). It is also one of Africa's most divided countries. Known in Ancient Egypt as Nubia, its northern region came under Islamic Arab control in the fourteenth century, and Egyptian and British rule in the nineteenth. With some 570 distinct ethnic groups and over 100 languages, it has been difficult to form Sudan into a modern state.

Since achieving independence from Egypt and Britain in 1956, Sudan has seen military rule, coups, and civil conflict for all but 10 of the next 40 years. The main cause is the determination of the Muslim north to impose Arab and Islamic values on the varied African, animist, and Christian peoples of the south. Strict *sharia* (Muslim) law has been proclaimed but is widely ignored. At present the government is conducting a "war of annihilation" against the 1.5 million Nuba people. Over half a million people have died in the past 12 years, the miseries of the ethnic Africans being compounded by famine, displacement, and the enslavement of women and children. One task of relief workers has been to purchase the freedom of slaves.

In northern Sudan the rocky Sahara Desert stretches westward to become a waste of sand dunes, the land rising to 3,071 m (10,075 ft) at the Darfur Massif toward the

Omourman Mahdi's tomb.

Crowds gather to watch Dervish dancing, Sudan.

border with Chad. In the east the Red Sea Mountains rise 2,000 m (6,500 ft) above a narrow coastal plain. Most people live near the south–north flowing Nile (An Nīl), a river that divides into two streams at Khartoum. From here the source of the Blue Nile (Al Bahr al Azraq) can be traced southeast to the Ethiopian border and Lake Tana. The White Nile (Al Bahr al Abyad) runs southwards into the vast marshland of the Sudd (where dense, floating vegetation makes navigation difficult), then further upstream to Uganda and its headwaters in Lake Albert.

About two-thirds of Sudan's workforce are farmers. There is a heavy emphasis on growing cotton, at the expense of food crops, as it accounts for 24 percent of export revenue. Food crops include sorghum (the staple) along with millet, wheat, barley, and peanuts. Declining rainfall and huge displacements of the rural population as a result of war have played havoc with production in recent years. The socialist government is resisting reform: in 1990 the IMF declared Sudan noncooperative because of nonpayment of debts. At present aid comes mainly from Iran. Natural resources include copper, chromium ore, zinc, tungsten, mica, silver, and gold. Some gold is mined.

Crumbling pyramids in the desert at Merouë in the Sudan.

S

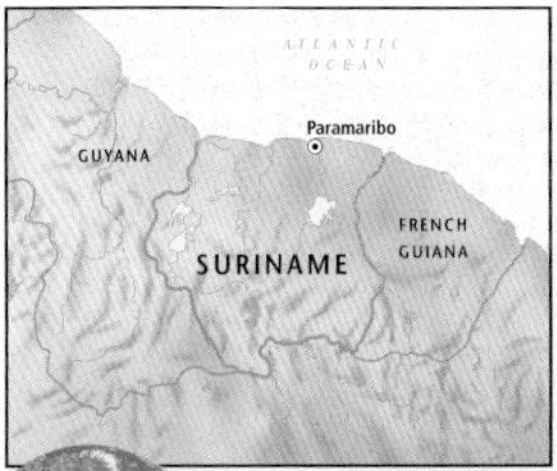

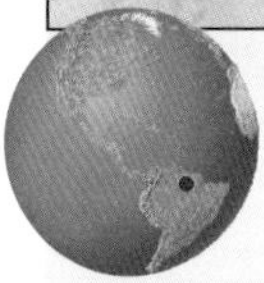

SURINAME

OFFICIAL NAME Republic of Suriname
FORM OF GOVERNMENT Republic with single legislative body (National Assembly)
CAPITAL Paramaribo
AREA 163,270 sq km (63,038 sq miles)
TIME ZONE GMT – 3 hours
POPULATION 431,156
PROJECTED POPULATION 2005 445,506
POPULATION DENSITY 2.6 per sq km (6.7 per sq mile)
LIFE EXPECTANCY 70.9
INFANT MORTALITY (per 1,000) 26.5
OFFICIAL LANGUAGE Dutch
OTHER LANGUAGES English, Sranang Tongo (Surinamese), Hindi, Javanese, Chinese
LITERACY RATE 92.7%
RELIGIONS Hindu 27.4%, Muslim 19.6%, Roman Catholic 22.8%, Protestant 25.2%, indigenous 5%
ETHNIC GROUPS Hindustani (East Indian) 37%, mixed European–African 31%, Javanese 15%, African 10%, Amerindian 3%, Chinese 2%, European 1%, other 1%
CURRENCY Suriname guilder
GNP PER CAPITA US$880
CLIMATE Tropical: hot and wet year-round
HIGHEST POINT Julianatop 1,230 m (4,035 ft)
MAP REFERENCE Page 850

Suriname

Formerly known as Dutch Guiana, Suriname is a small country on the northeastern coast of South America. In 1667 two colonial powers exchanged territory: the Dutch gave the British New Amsterdam, which became New York. In return the British gave Suriname to the Dutch. From the Low Countries the new proprietors brought their dike-building skills to reclaim a narrow coastal strip, and soon sugar plantations took the place of marshes and mangrove swamps. At first African slaves were imported to do the work; later labor was brought from India, China, and Java, and these three immigrant groups have determined both the ethnic composition of the country and its political fate.

Since 1954 Suriname has had the status of an equal partner in the "Tripartite Kingdom of the Netherlands." This has benefited those who have fled the continual military coups and civil disturbance in Suriname, using their Dutch citizenship to enter the Netherlands in large numbers. As was the case in nearby Guyana, escaped African slaves established isolated settlements in the hinterland. Guerrilla uprisings in both 1986 and 1994 have made the descendants of these people an urban political force.

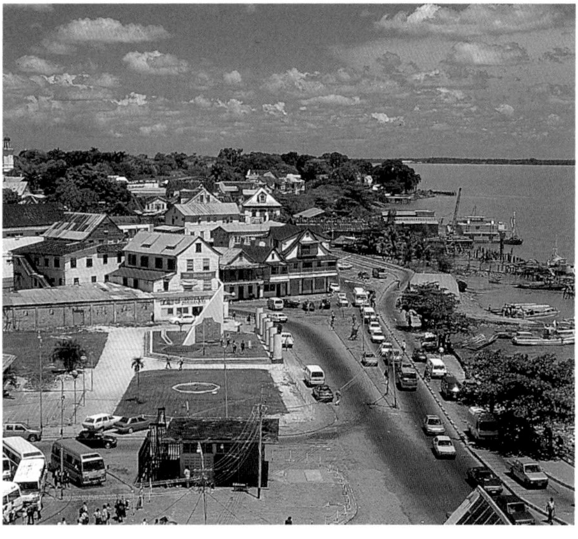

View of Paramaribo and harbor, Surinam.

Inland of the cultivated coastal strip lies a zone of sandy savanna, and south of this a vast area of dense forest begins (92 percent of the nation's total land area). Suriname has the world's highest ratio of forested country and it is still virtually untouched as timber is not among the nation's exports. The forests stretch inland to the Guiana Highlands, which are an extension of the Tumucumaque mountain range in northeastern Brazil. Over time, weathered soils have been washed from the uplands down to the alluvial valleys below, providing the foundation of the thriving bauxite industry.

Bauxite accounts for 15 percent of Suriname's gross domestic product and more than 65 percent of export earnings. Other exports include shrimp, fish, rice, bananas, citrus fruits, and coconuts. For most people rice is the staple food, supplemented by tropical fruits and vegetables.

Both ethnic conflict and economic crises have damaged the country's prospects for some years, although the campaign by guerrillas against the urban political elite seems for the present to have faded. Inflation was running at 600 percent in 1994. The resumption of economic aid by the Netherlands has led to a greater confidence in Suriname's economy, but substantial progress is unlikely without major economic reform.

A civic building in Paramaribo, Suriname.

Svalbard

Situated in the Arctic Ocean about 650 km (400 miles) north of Norway, Svalbard consists of nine bleak, rocky, and icy islands. From Viking times until the sixteenth century, these islands remained unknown. Recently they have served as a base for Arctic explorers. Svalbard's coal reserves have been mined by a number of nations, under Norway's supervision. Now, only Norway and Russia mine the much depleted deposits.

Vegetation on the islands is restricted to mosses, lichens, and a few hardy, low-growing plants. There is an expanding tourist industry. Visitors are attracted mainly by the many migratory birds that come to the islands.

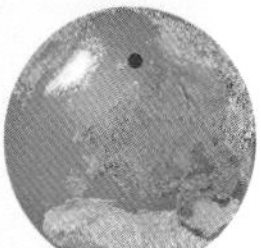

SVALBARD

OFFICIAL NAME Svalbard
FORM OF GOVERNMENT Territory of Norway
CAPITAL Longyearbyen
AREA 62,049 sq km (23,957 sq miles)
TIME ZONE GMT + 1 hour
POPULATION 2,864 (1996)
LIFE EXPECTANCY Not available
CURRENCY Norwegian krone
ECONOMY Mainly coal mining, some tourism
CLIMATE Polar, moderated by Gulf Stream ocean current; cold winters and cool summers
MAP REFERENCE Page 784

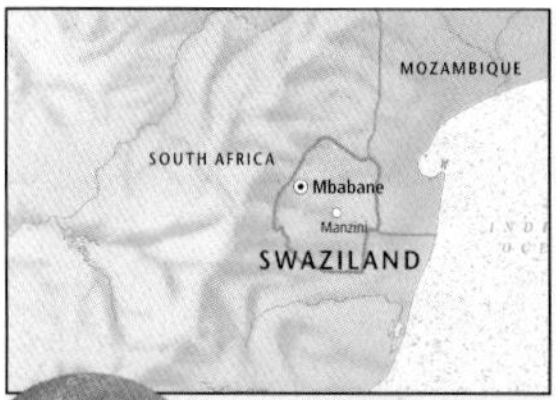

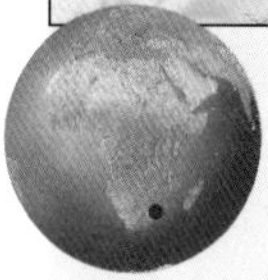

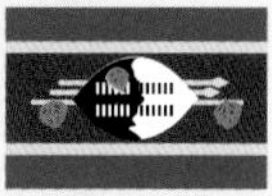

SWAZILAND

OFFICIAL NAME Kingdom of Swaziland
FORM OF GOVERNMENT Monarchy with two legislative bodies (Senate and House of Assembly)
CAPITAL Mbabane
AREA 17,360 sq km (6,703 sq miles)
TIME ZONE GMT + 2 hours
POPULATION 985,335
PROJECTED POPULATION 2005 1,101,082
POPULATION DENSITY 56.8 per sq km (147 per sq mile)
LIFE EXPECTANCY 57.3
INFANT MORTALITY (PER 1,000) 101.9
OFFICIAL LANGUAGES English, Swazi
OTHER LANGUAGES Indigenous languages
LITERACY RATE 75.2%
RELIGIONS Christian 60%, indigenous beliefs 40%
ETHNIC GROUPS Indigenous 97%, European 3%
CURRENCY Lilangeni
ECONOMY Agriculture 60%, industry and services 40%
GNP PER CAPITA US$1,170
CLIMATE Temperate, with wet season November to March
HIGHEST POINT Emlembe Peak 1,862 m (6,109 ft)
MAP REFERENCE Page 811

Swaziland

Swaziland is a tiny landlocked kingdom almost surrounded by South Africa. Across its eastern border it is about 130 km (80 miles) from the Indian Ocean and the Mozambique port of Maputo. Enjoying relative stability and prosperity, popular among South African tourists for its wildlife reserves, mountain scenery, and casinos, the kingdom's hereditary Bantu monarchy is now being pressed to modernize and accept constitutional reforms including democracy and political opposition.

The country owes its autonomy to events in the mid-nineteenth century. The Swazi were then facing Zulu expansion, as well as pressure from Boer farmers. They sought and received British protection, and from 1906 Swaziland was administered by the high commissioner for Basutoland (now Lesotho), Bechuanaland (now Botswana), and Swaziland. Full independence came in 1968.

The landscape descends in three steps from west to east. The high veld in the west is mountainous with a temperate climate, and supports grasslands, and plantations of pine and eucalyptus. Mixed farming takes place in the middle veld, the most populous area, where the black Swazi subsistence farmers grow maize, sorghum, and peanuts. Cash crops such as sugarcane, citrus fruits, and tobacco are produced by white-run agribusinesses and by Swazi on resettlement schemes. Livestock are raised on the low veld.

Swaziland's economy is relatively diversified and buoyant: during the 1980s it grew at a rate of 4.5 percent a year. Relaxed investment rules have ensured a supply of development capital, and project aid has been forthcoming from a number of donors. Sugar and forestry products are the main earners of hard currency, and are produced by white residents on large plantations. The country has small deposits of gold and diamonds. Mining was once important, but is now in decline. The high-grade iron ore deposits were depleted by 1978 and health concerns have cut the demand for asbestos. Remittances from workers in South Africa provide up to 20 percent of household income. The main threat to the Swazi way of life comes from land pressure due to high population growth. Family planning is being promoted; however, environmental issues, such as a lack of potable water and over-grazing are starting to affect the population.

In the late 1990s, Swaziland invited South Africa to negotiate on several territories that had previously been part of the kingdom, or that held large populations of Swazis. Political unrest between the trade unions and the government has caused several strikes, which have had a negative economic impact. However, the unrest has mostly been peaceful, barring the bombing of the Deputy Prime Minister's offices in the late in the 1990s.

A typical kraal *(village) in Swaziland.*

Sweden

The fourth largest country in Europe, Sweden shares the Scandinavian Peninsula with Norway, which sits between it and the North Atlantic Ocean. To the northeast Sweden shares a border with Finland, and its eastern coastline is separated from the west coast of Finland by the Gulf of Bothnia. Its southern shores are washed by the Baltic Sea, and south of the land border with Norway the Kattegat Strait divides it from the northern tip of Denmark. Close to Sweden's southeast tip are Gotland and Öland, the largest of many islands dotted around the Swedish coastline.

By the seventh century AD, Teutonic tribes from the south had occupied much of central Sweden, and between the ninth and the eleventh centuries Swedes took part in Viking raids deep into Russia and south to the Black Sea. Over the following five centuries Sweden and Denmark vied for Scandinavian supremacy. Both Sweden and Norway came under the Danish crown in 1397, but 50 years later the Swedes rebelled and elected their own king. The accession to the Swedish throne in 1523 of Gustav I ended Danish claims to all but the south of Sweden. During the next 200 years Sweden became one of the most powerful states in Europe, annexing parts of Estonia, Finland, and Poland, driving the Danes out of southern

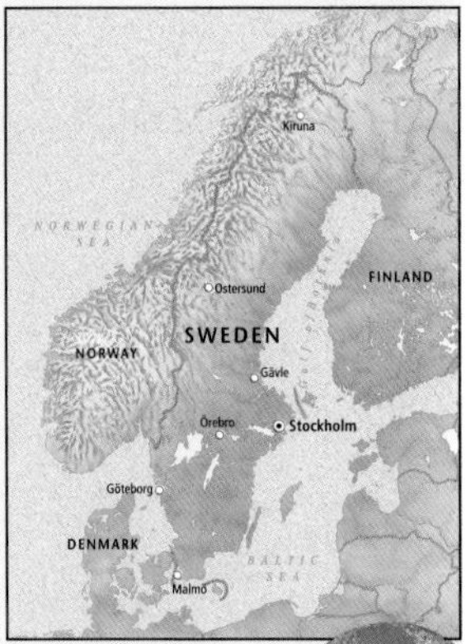

SWEDEN

OFFICIAL NAME Kingdom of Sweden
FORM OF GOVERNMENT Constitutional monarchy with single legislative body (Parliament, Riksdag)
CAPITAL Stockholm

(continues)

SWEDEN *(continued)*

AREA 449,964 sq km (173,731 sq miles)
TIME ZONE GMT + 1 hour
POPULATION 8,911,296
PROJECTED POPULATION 2005 9,051,287
POPULATION DENSITY 19.8 per sq km (51.3 per sq mile)
LIFE EXPECTANCY 79.3
INFANT MORTALITY (PER 1,000) 3.9
OFFICIAL LANGUAGE Swedish
OTHER LANGUAGES Lapp, Finnish
LITERACY RATE 99%
RELIGIONS Evangelical Lutheran 94%, Roman Catholic 1.5%, Pentecostal 1%, other 3.5%
ETHNIC GROUPS Swedish 91%, others include Lapp, Finnish, Yugoslav, Danish, Norwegian, Greek, Turkish 9%
CURRENCY Swedish krona
ECONOMY Services 69%, industry 28%, agriculture 3%
GNP PER CAPITA US$23,750
CLIMATE Temperate in the south, with cold winters and mild summers; subpolar in the north, with severe winters
HIGHEST POINT Kebnekaise 2,111 m (6,926 ft)
MAP REFERENCE Pages 768–9

PROVINCES

Älvsborg • Blekinge • Gävleborg
Göteborg and Bohus • Gotland
Halland • Jämtland • Jönköping
Kalmar • Kopparberg
Kristianstad • Kronoberg
Malmöhus • Norrbotten • Örebro
Östergötland • Skaraborg
Södermanland • Stockholm
Uppsala • Värmland •
Västerbotten • Västernorrland
Västmanland

Sweden, and playing a crucial role in curbing Hapsburg expansion in northern Europe. At the beginning of the eighteenth century, however, a coalition of Russia, Poland, and Denmark forced Sweden to relinquish its Baltic possessions.

At the end of the Napoleonic wars, in 1815, Norway was ceded to Sweden, a union that lasted until 1905. In the mid-nineteenth century the beginnings of parliamentary democracy were introduced in Sweden with the establishment of a two-chamber parliament, although suffrage was limited largely to landowners and industrialists. Universal adult suffrage was introduced in 1919.

Sweden remained neutral in both the First and the Second World Wars. Following the Second World War it tried unsuccessfully to form a military alliance with Denmark and Norway. When these nations joined NATO Sweden did not follow, fearing closer ties with the West might damage its relations with the Soviet Union, and give it an excuse to absorb Finland into the Soviet bloc. Since then, although maintaining a high level of defence preparedness, it has kept its distance from NATO and maintained its reputation for neutrality, for playing an active role in international affairs, and as a negotiator in international disputes.

During the 1960s and early 1970s, Sweden's Social Democrats, who had laid the foundations of a welfare state since 1932, held the majority of seats in the Riksdag and were able to govern alone. They then inaugurated the more radical socialist policies that came to define modern

Early summer foliage in a birch and pine forest.

Rows of holiday chalets and small boats in Sweden.

Swedish politics. Welfare services were extended, and "the Swedish Way" was seen by socialists as a model for the rest of Europe. After 1982 Olof Palme's government introduced what it called a middle way between capitalism and communism, with annual levies on profits and wages which went into "wage-earner funds" used to buy stock in private firms for the benefit of labor. Palme was assassinated in mysterious circumstances in Stockholm in 1986. By then the economic costs of the welfare state were becoming evident. The country had almost zero economic growth, and was becoming less competitive in world markets.

From the late 1970s domestic policy discussion has been less along socialist/capitalist lines and more concerned with ecological issues. Sweden has taken the lead in a number of environmental debates, and has been the venue of influential conferences devoted to such matters as global warming and greenhouse gases. An application for EC membership was lodged in 1992. In 1995 the country was admitted to the European Union. Sweden is a constitutional monarchy with a single-chamber parliament that is elected every three years.

Fresh cover of snow on cars and houses, Göteborg.

Physical features and land use

Northeastern Sweden is a region of low plateaus that drop away to a coastal plain along the Gulf of Bothnia, but rise to the Kjólen Mountains along the Norwegian border. Most of the country's more than 95,000 lakes are in this mountainous region. Shaped by ancient glaciers, many of the lakes are in the upper valleys of the numerous rivers that flow east to the Gulf of Bothnia. They are the source of most of Sweden's hydroelectricity, which is gradually replacing nuclear energy as the main means of power generation. The mountains are heavily forested. Despite extensive land clearing for agriculture in the south, well over half the country remains forested, with spruce, pine and birch among the most prominent trees.

Central Sweden is a lowland area that stretches between Stockholm in the east and the country's second largest city, Göteborg, in the southwest. Four large lakes—the only remnants of a strait that once joined the Baltic to the Kattegat Strait—cover much of this region, the most heavily populated part of the country. The rich soils around these lakes support much of Sweden's agriculture produce, which includes cereals and vegetables and fodder crops for herds of cattle. Dairy farming is the main form of agriculture, and Sweden is self-sufficient in dairy products.

South of the lakes is a low, largely infertile plateau and further south, stretching to the tip of the peninsula and across to the island of Gotland, is a rich plain—the most intensively cultivated part of the country. Significant areas of woodland still survive here, dotted between stretches of farming and grazing land.

Although it lacks oil and coal reserves, Sweden is rich in mineral resources, most of which are concentrated in the northeast. These include iron ore, zinc, lead, copper, and silver, and almost one-sixth of the world's known reserves of uranium.

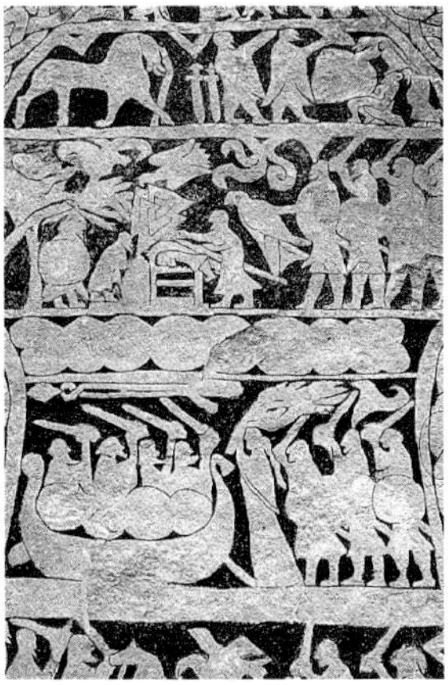

Viking headstone, Gotland.

Industry, commerce, and culture

Sweden's vast forests are the basis for timber and paper manufacturing industries that form almost one-fifth of the country's exports. Machines, cars, trucks, aircraft, and chemical and electrical goods and communication equipment are among the chief manufacturing industries, based in the central region and Malmö in the southwest.

Apart from the Saami people (Lapps) in the far north of the country, Sweden is ethnically and culturally quite homogeneous. Despite there being a relatively high rate of unemployment, its citizens enjoy one of the highest standards of living in Europe and an extensive range of government-provided social services. Sweden also boasts one of Europe's highest rates of female participation throughout its workforce.

Stockholm, capital and busy port, is on the east coast.

S

Scandinavia

Today the term Scandinavia is often understood to refer only to Norway and Sweden, which both occupy the Scandinavian Peninsula, and the more southerly peninsula and islands that make up Denmark. Many people, however, would also include Finland, Iceland, and the Faeroe Islands, which are possessions of Denmark. These countries are also collectively referred to as the Nordic countries, or Norden.

Culturally, geographically, and geologically, the countries of Scandinavia have much in common and the whole region forms a distinctive part of Europe. All of them lie close to the Arctic Circle and share a cold, moist, and often harsh climate, which is mitigated in parts of Scandinavia by the effect of the Gulf Stream. All five countries have a high degree of ethnic and religious homogeneity. Lutheran is the overwhelmingly predominant religion in every country of Scandinavia. The languages of four of the countries are closely related, but Finnish is entirely different and is more closely related to the Estonian language. Historical links are also very strong and during the fifteenth century the countries were united under Danish rule. For five centuries, until 1809, Finland was under Swedish control and Swedish was the language of its ruling classes. For almost a century, until 1905, Norway was ruled by Sweden, and Iceland only gained its independence as late as 1944, after almost five and half centuries of Danish rule and domination.

Greenland has, since the early eighteenth century, been part of Denmark. Situated to the west of Iceland, it is ethnically distinct and geographically closer to North America. Although it was granted home rule in 1979 Greenland's inhabitants are still Danish citizens and Denmark still controls its foreign affairs.

Despite climatic difficulties, Scandinavian economies have traditionally depended on agriculture and fishing. The improvements in agricultural techniques and technologies that flowed from the Industrial Revolution were slow to be implemented in Scandinavia and until late in the nineteenth century the region remained economically stagnant. In recent years, however, there have been significant technological innovations and increasing industrialization and Scandinavians now enjoy some of the highest standards of living in Europe.

Ålesund on the west coast of Norway.

Switzerland

A landlocked country in central Europe, Switzerland shares borders with Italy to its south and southeast, France to its west, Germany to its north, and Austria and Liechtenstein to its east. This small nation has enjoyed a generally peaceful independence for more than 450 years, despite the conflicts that have often raged around it. Modern Switzerland dates back to the late thirteenth century when three German districts, or cantons, combined to form a federation. A century later, other cantons had joined the federation, which survived as a unit, despite linguistic differences and often intense and violent conflicts between Catholics and emerging Protestant groups. Although part of the Holy Roman Empire, and effectively under Hapsburg domination, the Swiss cantons remained neutral during the Thirty Years War of 1618–48, at the end of which they were formally granted independence. In 1798 French revolutionary armies invaded Switzerland and declared it to be a centralized Helvetic Republic, named after Helvetia, the Roman province that had existed there in ancient times. In 1815, after the defeat of Napoleon, the Congress of Vienna declared Switzerland to be independent once more, as well as permanently neutral, and added two more cantons—Valais and the previously separate republic of Geneva.

The country has maintained this military neutrality ever since and its stance has been respected by its neighbors throughout numerous conflicts, including the First and Second World Wars. Religious tensions flared briefly in

An alpine vegetable farm in Switzerland.

Switzerland

Official name Swiss Confederation
Form of government Federal republic with two legislative bodies (Council of States and National Council)
Capital Bern
Area 41,290 sq km (15,942 sq miles)
Time zone GMT + 1 hour
Population 7,275,467
Projected population 2005 7,351,686
Population density 176.2 per sq km (456.4 per sq mile)
Life expectancy 79
Infant mortality (per 1,000) 4.9
Official languages German, French, Italian
Other languages Spanish, Romansch
Literacy rate 99%
Religions Roman Catholic 48%, Protestant 44%, other 8%
Ethnic groups German 65%, French 18%, Italian 10%, Romansch 1%, other 6%
Currency Swiss franc
Economy Services 64%, industry 30%, agriculture 6%
GNP per capita US$40,630
Climate Temperate, varying with altitude; generally cold winters and warm, wet summers
Highest point Dufourspitze 4,634 m (15,203 ft)
Map reference Pages 722, 775, 778

1847, when the Catholic cantons seceded. The following year, however, a new constitution, inspired by that of the United States, re-established the former federation and defined Switzerland as a republic with a strong central government but with considerable powers still vested in individual cantons. In 1874 a new constitution was adopted which essentially confirmed this division of power. Switzerland's central government, which controls foreign policy, railway and postal services, and the mint, consists of an elected bicameral parliament, with a president, elected by the parliament for a one-year term. Women were granted the vote only in 1971.

Physical features and land use

Mountains dominate the Swiss landscape making it Europe's most mountainous country. They cover seven-tenths of the land area. The rest of the country consists of an elevated central plateau on which the majority of the population lives and which is the center of the country's agricultural, industrial, and economic activity. This area is bordered by a number of large lakes and drained by the River Aare, which rises in Lake Neuchâtel and flows northward into the Rhine, which constitutes Switzerland's border with Germany and part of Austria. Lake Neuchâtel is overlooked by the lightly wooded Jura Mountains,

A valley in Switzerland with vineyards.

which separate Switzerland from France. More than half of Switzerland is covered by the peaks and glaciers of the Alps, which sweep across the south of the country. The most spectacular sections are in the Pennine Alps along the southwestern frontier with Italy. Both the Rhône and the Rhine rivers rise in this alpine region and drain it in opposite directions, flowing respectively through the two largest lakes in the country, which are Lake Geneva in the far southwest, and Lake Constance in the far northeast.

About one-quarter of Switzerland consists of forests, which are found mainly in the valleys and on the lower slopes. Cypresses and figs are prominent among the tree species. About one-tenth of the land is arable. Crop cultivation is concentrated in the area immediately to the east and southeast of the Jura and in the valleys of the Rhône and Rhine rivers. Wheat, potatoes, and sugar beet are the main crops. The principal agricultural activity is dairy farming, although pig raising is also significant. Switzerland produces less than half its food needs.

Switzerland is not well endowed with mineral resources. Most of its electricity is generated by hydropower, but a significant amount is provided by the country's five nuclear power plants. A sixth nuclear plant was planned but was cancelled in the aftermath of the Chernobyl disaster in Ukraine in 1986.

The Jungfrau Mountain in Switzerland's Bernese Oberland.

Industry, commerce, and culture

Switzerland has for centuries been a world leader in the production of precision instruments such as clocks and watches. Other industries which are vital to the country's prosperity include heavy engineering, textile manufacture, clothing, chemicals and food processing. Swiss chocolate, sought after the world over because of its high quality, is also a major contributor to the national economy. Tourism, centered mainly on the Alps, attracts more than 12 million visitors annually.

Banking is highly developed and is one of the country's key industries. Switzerland attracts almost half the world's foreign investment capital and is the base of numerous multinational companies.

Although the country is divided geographically among its predominantly German-, Italian- and French-speaking populations, Switzerland is now a unified nation and its people have a strong sense of common purpose. This is attributable in large measure to Switzerland's status as one of the world's most stable and prosperous countries, with a very high per capita income.

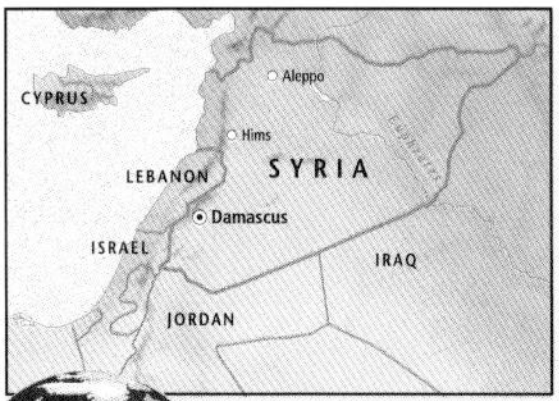

Syria

Syria is in the eastern Mediterranean, with Iraq and Turkey to the east and north and Lebanon, Israel and Jordan to the west and south. Throughout history it has played a key role in the region. Over the years Egyptians, Hittites, Persians, Greeks, and Romans came and went. Converted to Islam when overrun by the Arabs in 634, the Syrians' capital Damascus became a major center during the Umayyad Dynasty. Crusaders seized much of Syria in the twelfth century, but were ousted by the Kurdish general Saladin. Under French control from 1920, Syria became independent in 1946. After various military coups and counter-coups the Ba'ath Party seized power in 1963, and from 1971 party leader Hafez al-Assad has ruled Syria with an iron fist. A member of the minority Alawite religious sect, he has faced resistance from other Muslims, notably the Sunni majority. But in 1992 when the Sunni Moslem Brotherhood rose against Damascus their revolt was crushed, with up to 20,000 deaths. Following the Second Gulf War in 1991 Syria received huge amounts of aid as a result of its unexpected support for the coalition against Iraq.

Syria

Official name Syrian Arab Republic
Form of government Republic with single legislative body (People's Council)
Capital Damascus (Dimashq)
Area 185,180 sq km (71,498 sq miles)
Time zone GMT + 2 hours
Population 17,213,871
Projected population 2005 20,530,413
Population density 93 per sq km (240.8 per sq mile)
Life expectancy 68.1
Infant mortality (per 1,000) 36.4
Official language Arabic
Other languages Kurdish, French, Armenian, Aramaic, Circassian
Literacy rate 69.8%
Religions Sunni Muslim 74%, other Muslim sects 16%, Christian 10%; tiny Jewish communities
Ethnic groups Arab 90%; Kurdish, Armenian and other 10%
Currency Syrian pound
Economy Services 63%, agriculture 22%, industry 15%
GNP per capita US$1,120
Climate Temperate, with mild, wet winters and dry, hot summers; arid in interior
Highest point Jabal ash Shaykh 2,814 m (9,232 ft)
Map reference Pages 736, 761

Syria's Mediterranean coast, well-watered from subterranean sources, is one of the country's most fertile, intensively farmed, and densely populated regions. Inland is the Ghab Depression, a rift valley flanked by two mountain ranges. To the south, the Heights of Hermon rise above the eastern slopes of the Anti-Lebanon Range (Jabal ash Sharqī). Snowmelt from the range provides water for Damascus. Inland lies the Syrian Desert (Bādiyat ash Shām), crossed by the Euphrates River (Firat Nehri). Oil was discovered along the Euphrates in the 1980s. Power from the Euphrates barrage produces 70 percent of Syria's electricity.

Under the socialist Ba'ath Party most industry is government controlled. The main industries are textiles, food processing, beverages, tobacco, phosphate rock mining, petroleum, and cement. Oil, textiles, cotton, and agricultural produce are the main exports. The country has many weak government-owned firms and low productivity. Oil production has begun to decline and unemployment is expected to rise as the more than 60 percent of the population that is under 20 years old enters the labor force. Syria's Gulf War aid windfall of $5 billion has been spent.

Krac des Chevaliers in Syria, a French Crusader castle built in the twelfth century.

T

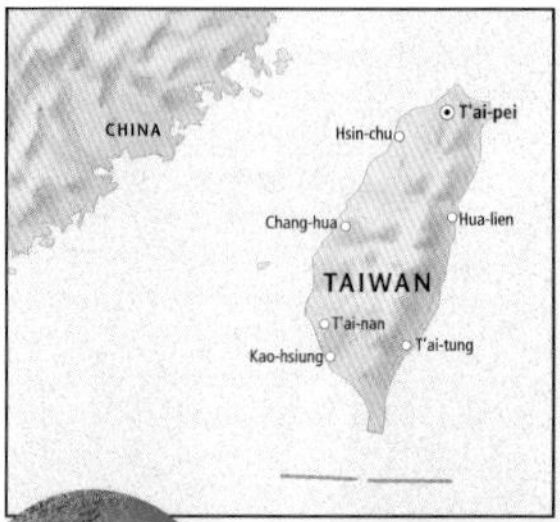

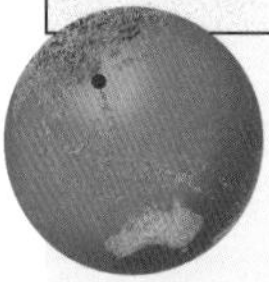

Taiwan

Taiwan is a large island off the coast of China which, with support from the USA, has acted as a de facto independent country for the past 50 years. This is strongly opposed by China, which from the seventeenth century controlled the island and made it a Chinese province in the 1880s. However, Beijing has not had effective control of Taiwan for 100 years. It was ceded to Japan in 1895 (after Japanese victory in the Sino-Japanese War). From 1949 until the present it has been under the Nationalist Kuomintang (KMT), who after being driven from mainland China by the communists in 1949 used Taiwan as their last refuge. Ruling dictatorially over the Taiwanese until 1987, the KMT turned the country into a political, military, and economic fortress.

Seated in the UN as the official representative of China for two decades, Taiwan was displaced in 1971, and still has a marginal status in the international community. Today, after democratic elections, multiple parties are represented in the National Assembly, and both the president and the prime minister are native-born Taiwanese.

High mountains extending the length of the island occupy the central and eastern parts of Taiwan. The mountains of the Central Range, or Taiwan Shan, are the top of a submerged mountain chain, and rise steeply up from the east coast. Lush vegetation is found through much of the interior—the poor commercial quality of most of the timber having preserved it as forest cover. Rising to altitudes of more than 3,000 m (10,000 ft), the lower slopes support evergreens such as camphor and Chinese cork oak, while further up pine, larch, and cedar dominate.

A Taiwanese family in Taipei.

A commercial street in Taipei.

TAIWAN

OFFICIAL NAME Republic of China
FORM OF GOVERNMENT Republic with two legislative bodies (National Assembly and Legislative Yuan)
CAPITAL T'ai-pei (Taipei)
AREA 35,980 sq km (13,892 sq miles)
TIME ZONE GMT + 8 hours
POPULATION 22,113,250
PROJECTED POPULATION 2005 23,325,314
POPULATION DENSITY 614.6 per sq km (1,591.8 per sq mile)
LIFE EXPECTANCY 77.5
INFANT MORTALITY (PER 1,000) 6.0
OFFICIAL LANGUAGE Mandarin Chinese
OTHER LANGUAGES Taiwanese, Hakka languages
RELIGIONS Buddhist, Confucian, and Taoist 93%; Christian 4.5%; other 2.5%
ETHNIC GROUPS Taiwanese 84%, mainland Chinese 14%, indigenous 2%
CURRENCY New Taiwain dollar
ECONOMY Services 49%, industry 30%, agriculture 21%
GNP PER CAPITA US$10,500
CLIMATE Tropical, with wet season May to September
HIGHEST POINT Yu Shan 3,997 m (13,113 ft)
MAP REFERENCE Page 742

Rice is grown on the well-watered lowlands of the western coastal plain. Other crops include sugarcane, sweet potatoes, tea, bananas, pineapples, and peanuts.

Economically, agriculture is now of less importance than Taiwan's thriving industrial sector. The country as a whole demonstrated an almost unprecedented growth rate of 9 percent annually for three decades until 1996. During this period it was successively the world's biggest producer of television sets, watches, personal computers, and track shoes. Among Taiwan's strengths are its highly educated workforce, many US-trained, with an inside knowledge of the US market. Today the leading exports are electrical machinery, electronic products, textiles, footwear, foodstuffs, and plywood and wood products. With huge dollar reserves, Taiwan has become a major investor in China, Malaysia, and Vietnam. The Asian economic downturn in 1998 has had a steadying effect, but Taiwan is better situated than most to weather the storm. Political relations with China remain cool.

School children in alleyway, Taiwan.

Tajikistan

Tajikistan lies between Uzbekistan, Afghanistan, and China on the western slope of the Pamirs. It also shares borders with Kyrgyzstan to the north and Pakistan to the south. The country is an irregular shape because it was carved out of the Soviet Republic of Uzbekistan on Stalin's orders in 1929. This was intended to deal with Tajik resistance to the Soviet regime, but because it left the two Tajik centers of Samarqand and Bukhoro in Uzbekistan, it merely added another grievance. The Tajiks are Persian–Iranian both culturally and linguistically, not Turkic–Mongol like many other peoples of Central Asia. Immigration of both Uzbeks and Russians during the Soviet era caused further resentment. Since independence in 1991 ethnic hostility has resulted in a state of near civil war. Tens of thousands have been killed and thousands more have fled to Afghanistan and Kyrgyzstan. Fighting between government and opposition forces goes on, marked by random violence and banditry.

A long finger of territory in the north contains the only fertile agricultural region. This is the western end of the Fergana Valley through which the Syrdar'ya drains

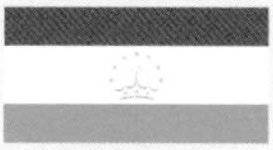

TAJIKISTAN

OFFICIAL NAME Republic of Tajikistan
FORM OF GOVERNMENT Republic with single legislative body (Supreme Assembly)
CAPITAL Dushanbe
AREA 143,100 sq km (55,251 sq miles)
TIME ZONE GMT + 6 hours
POPULATION 6,102,854
PROJECTED POPULATION 2005 6,719,665
POPULATION DENSITY 42.6 per sq km (110.3 per sq mile)
LIFE EXPECTANCY 64.3

(continues)

TAJIKISTAN *(continued)*

INFANT MORTALITY (PER 1,000) 114.8
OFFICIAL LANGUAGE Tajik
OTHER LANGUAGE Russian
LITERACY RATE 96.7%
RELIGIONS Sunni Muslim 80%, Shi'a Muslim 5%, other (including Russian Orthodox) 15%
ETHNIC GROUPS Tajik 65%, Uzbek 25%, Russian 3.5%, other 6.5%
CURRENCY Tajik ruble
ECONOMY Agriculture 43%, services 35%, industry 22%
GNP PER CAPITA US$340
CLIMATE Mild winters and hot summers in valleys and on plains, drier and much colder in mountains
HIGHEST POINT Pik imeni Ismail Samani 7,495 m (24,590 ft)
MAP REFERENCE Page 759

northwest toward the Aral Sea. Cotton is the chief crop, though cereals and fruit are also grown. The region has seen the overuse of pesticides on cotton, and the drying up of the distant Aral Sea has been aggravated by water taken for irrigation. Between this valley and one to the south drained by the Vakhsh stand the Turkestan and Gissar Ranges. This substantial physical divide also corresponds to the political divide between the Uzbek communists in the north and the Islamic secularists in the south. Most of eastern Tajikistan consists of the Pamirs, a part of the Tien Shan Range of western China.

Tajikistan has the second-lowest per capita gross domestic product of any former USSR republic, the fastest growing population, and a low standard of living. Agriculture is the most important sector and cotton the main crop. The country has limited mineral resources, including silver, gold, uranium, and tungsten. Hydropower provides energy for the manufacture of aluminum, cotton textiles and clothing, and for food processing. The economy is weak from years of conflict. Subsidies once provided by the USSR are gone, along with markets—Russia once bought Tajik uranium for its weapons program. Basic subsistence for many people depends on foreign aid. Social instability, plus the continuation in power of politicians and officials from the Soviet era, has hindered economic reforms.

A yurt in the Pamir region of Tajikistan.

T

Tanzania

With Africa's highest mountain (Kilimanjaro), and Serengeti National Park, Tanzania is well known to the outside world. It also the home of some of East Africa's most ancient human remains, those found at Olduvai Gorge dating back 2 million years. From the eighth century AD onward, the country's coastal region was subject to Islamic influence from Arab traders who dealt in slaves and ivory. In the nineteenth century both British and German settlers arrived.

Tanzania won independence from England in 1961, becoming a de facto one-party state under Julius Nyerere, whose version of African socialism prevailed until he retired in 1985. Opposition parties were allowed in 1992. An uprising by pro-Tanzanian forces violently incorporated the Muslim island of Zanzibar in 1964: unreconciled Islamic interests on the island represent a potential flashpoint.

From the coast, Tanzania stretches across a plateau averaging about 1,000 m (3,000 ft) to the Rift Valley Lakes of Malawi (Lake Nyasa) and Tanganyika. The eastern Rift Valley, with the alkaline Lake Natron, and Lakes Eyasi and Manyara, divides the Northern Highlands. These are dominated by Mt Kilimanjaro near the Kenyan border. The Southern Highlands overlook Lake Malawi (Lake Nyasa). Semiarid conditions in the north and tsetse fly in the west–central areas mean that people mainly live on the country's margins. Attempts to farm the savanna woodland have failed.

Though repressive, Nyerere's government achieved relatively high levels of education and welfare, but the economy languished as a result of falling commodity prices abroad and inefficient and corrupt state corporations at home. Over 80 percent of the workforce live off the land, producing cash crops such as coffee, tea, sisal, cotton, and pyrethrum, along with food crops of maize, wheat, cassava, and bananas. Since 1985 there has been some liberalization of the market, along with an effort to boost tourism and a substantial increase in gold production. Reforms have increased private sector growth and investment.

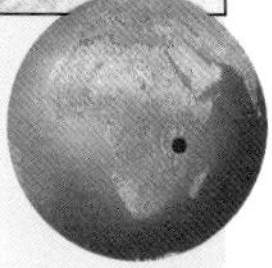

TANZANIA

OFFICIAL NAME United Republic of Tanzania
FORM OF GOVERNMENT Republic with single legislative body (National Assembly)
CAPITAL Dodoma
AREA 945,090 sq km (364,899 sq miles)
TIME ZONE GMT + 3 hours
POPULATION 31,270,820
PROJECTED POPULATION 2005 35,686,963
POPULATION DENSITY 33.1 per sq km (85.7 per sq mile)
LIFE EXPECTANCY 46.2
INFANT MORTALITY (PER 1,000) 95.3
OFFICIAL LANGUAGES Swahili, English
OTHER LANGUAGES Arabic, indigenous languages
LITERACY RATE 66.8%
RELIGIONS Mainland: Christian 45%, Muslim 35%, indigenous beliefs 20%; Zanzibar: Muslim 99%, other 1%
ETHNIC GROUPS Indigenous 99%, other 1%
CURRENCY Tanzanian shilling
ECONOMY Agriculture 85%, services 10%, industry 5%
GNP PER CAPITA US$120
CLIMATE Mainly tropical; hot and humid along coast, drier inland, cooler in mountains
HIGHEST POINT Mt Kilimanjaro 5,895 m (19,340 ft)
MAP REFERENCE Page 809

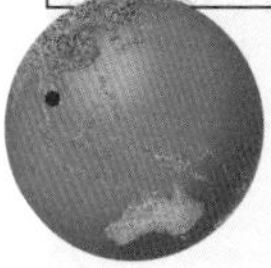

THAILAND

OFFICIAL NAME Kingdom of Thailand
FORM OF GOVERNMENT Constitutional monarchy with two legislative bodies (Senate and House of Representatives)
CAPITAL Bangkok
AREA 514,000 sq km (198,455 sq miles)
TIME ZONE GMT + 7 hours
POPULATION 60,609,046
PROJECTED POPULATION 2005 63,794,047
POPULATION DENSITY 117.9 per sq km (305.4 per sq mile)
LIFE EXPECTANCY 69.2
INFANT MORTALITY (PER 1,000) 29.5
OFFICIAL LANGUAGE Thai
OTHER LANGUAGES Chinese, Malay, English
LITERACY RATE 93.5%
RELIGIONS Buddhist 95%, Muslim 3.8%, Christian 0.5%, Hindu 0.1%, other 0.6%
ETHNIC GROUPS Thai 75%, Chinese 14%, other 11%
CURRENCY Baht
ECONOMY Agriculture 70%, services 24%, industry 6%
GNP PER CAPITA US$2,740
CLIMATE Tropical, with wet season June to October, cool season November to February, hot season March to May
HIGHEST POINT Doi Inthanon 2,590 m (8,497 ft)
MAP REFERENCE Pages 738–9

Thailand

Lying between Burma, Laos, and Cambodia, Thailand has a system of "semi-democracy" that has somehow preserved it from the misfortunes of its neighbors. Known as Siam until 1939, it was the home of the Buddhist kingdom of Ayutthaya from the fourteenth to the eighteenth century, during which time the monarch came to be regarded as a sort of god-king, and a bureaucratic administration system was developed. The Chakkri Dynasty was founded in 1782 at Bangkok, and in the late nineteenth century its representatives ushered Siam into the modern age: treaties with the West were signed, slavery abolished, and study abroad encouraged. The king acquiesced in a bloodless coup which set up a constitutional monarchy in 1932. Since then civilian and military governments have alternated, climaxing in the events of 1992, when violent demonstrations against another general taking over the government led the king to intervene, and the constitution was amended. The prime minister now has to be an elected member of parliament. The military, however, still plays an important part in both political and industrial life.

Thailand can be divided into four regions. To the north there are forested mountain ranges which are the southernmost extension of the Himalayas. The rich intermontane valleys of the Rivers Ping, Yom, Wang, and Nan support intensive agriculture and the forests produce teak and other valuable timbers. The forests provide a home for many hill tribes who live by the shifting cultivation of dry rice and opium poppies. In the northeast lies the Khorat Plateau, a region of poor soils sparsely vegetated with savanna woodlands where crops of rice and

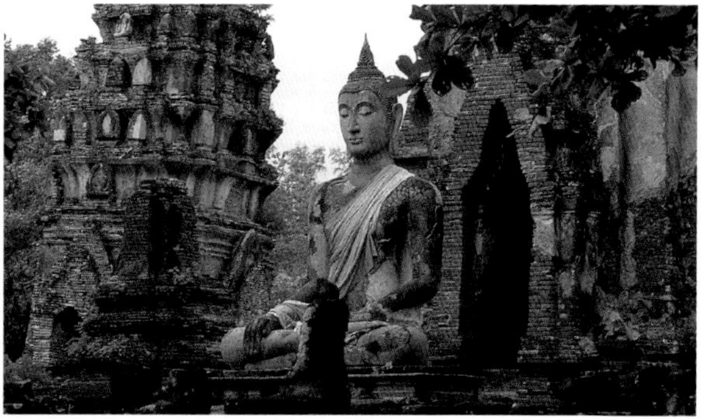

Ruins of a Thai Buddhist temple.

cassava are grown. The third region is the central plains—Thailand's rice bowl—with vistas of rice fields, canals, rivers, and villages on stilts. The mountainous southern provinces on the Malay Peninsula are dominated by tropical rainforest. The hills produce tin ore and plantation rubber and the picturesque islands off the west coast draw tourists.

Agriculture is still the main employer, although its economic importance is declining. Rice is the principal crop and Thailand is still one of the world's leading exporters. Other crops include sugar, maize, rubber, manioc, pineapples, and seafoods. Mineral resources include tin ore, lead, tungsten, lignite, gypsum, tantalum, fluorite, and gemstones. Thailand is the world's second largest producer of tungsten, and the third largest tin producer. Tourism is the largest single source of foreign exchange, the development of resorts on the coast along the Andaman Sea having been a major success.

The development of urban manufacturing industry, involving the export of high-technology goods, has been the most significant feature of the economy in recent years. This and the development of the service sector have fueled a growth rate of 9 percent since 1989. Thailand's domestic savings rate of 35 percent is a leading source of capital, but the country has also received substantial investment from overseas. Beginning in 1997, Thailand was the first country in the region to be affected by a range of problems associated with the Asian economic downturn—a falling currency, rising inflation, and unemployment heading toward 2 million.

Two hill tribe women from the mountains of northern Thailand.

Landscape near Chiang Mai.

T

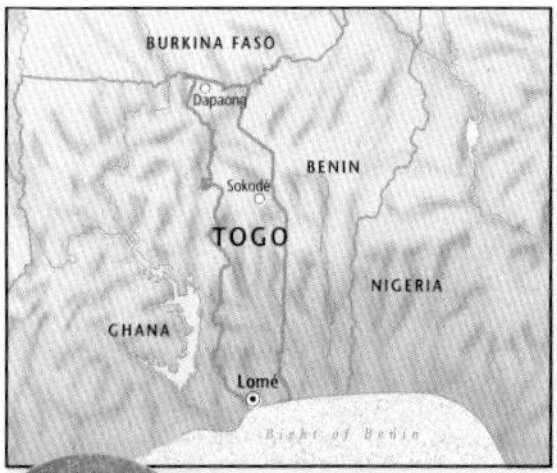

Togo

Togo is a small west African country squeezed between Ghana and Benin. It was colonized by Germany in 1884, later becoming French Togoland. It became independent in 1960. A deep social division exists between the Kabye people in the north and the majority Ewe of the south. The Ewe are generally better educated, and live in the more developed part of the country, but have no say in government. This is run by Africa's longest serving president, General Eyadema, a Kabye who has held this position since his coup in 1967. The first multi-party elections took place in 1993.

Most people live on the coast and the adjacent plains. Inland a mountain chain crosses the country north to south. The far northwest is mainly granite tableland. Roads connect the northern savanna with the railhead of Blitta, and the phosphate mining area with its port of Kpeme. The River Oti crosses in the northwest between Burkina Faso and Ghana; the River Mono drains south into the Gulf of Guinea. About a quarter of the land is arable. The most fertile land—28 percent of the country—is forested; here slash-and-burn cultivation occurs.

Togo depends on subsistence agriculture. Food crops include yams, cassava, maize, beans, rice, and sorghum. The main export crops are coffee, cocoa, and cotton, which together generate about 30 percent of earnings. Cattle, sheep, and pigs are raised in the north. The annual fish catch is about 14,000 tonnes. Togo is normally self-sufficient in food, though drought has recently cut productivity, and the deforestation caused by slash-and-burn agriculture is causing concern. Phosphate mining is the most important industrial activity.

Traditional houses in Togo.

Togo

Official name Republic of Togo
Form of government Republic with single legislative body (National Assembly)
Capital Lomé
Area 56,790 sq km (21,927 sq miles)
Time zone GMT
Population 5,081,413
Projected population 2005 6,254,894
Population density 89.5 per sq km (231.8 per sq mile)
Life expectancy 59.3
Infant mortality (per 1,000) 77.6
Official language French
Other languages Ewe, Mina, Dagomba, Kabye
Literacy rate 50.4%
Religions Indigenous beliefs 70%, Christian 20%, Muslim 10%
Ethnic groups Indigenous (Ewe, Mina, and Kabye largest of 37 tribes) 99%, European and Syrian–Lebanese 1%
Currency CFA (Communauté Financière Africaine) franc
Economy Agriculture 68%, services 28%, industry 4%
GNP per capita US$310
Climate Tropical, with wet seasons Mar to July and Oct to Nov; semiarid in north, with wet season Apr to July
Highest point Pic Baumann 986 m (3,235 ft)
Map reference Page 804

Tokelau

Tokelau is a small group of islands in the South Pacific about midway between Hawaii and New Zealand. The islands consist of low coral atolls, that are no higher than 5 m (16 ft) above sea level, enclosing large lagoons. Lying in the Pacific typhoon belt (a cyclone in 1990 wrecked much of Tokelau's infrastructure), they have a tropical climate moderated by trade winds. There are limited natural resources, subsistence farmers growing coconuts, breadfruit, papaya, and bananas. Small-scale industry produces copra, woodwork, plaited craft goods, stamps, and coins. A tuna cannery is expected to help the economy, and it is hoped that a catamaran link between the atolls will boost tourism. Aid from New Zealand is the main source of revenue and money remitted by relatives in New Zealand is a vital source of domestic income

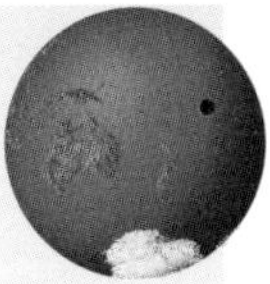

TOKELAU

OFFICIAL NAME Tokelau
FORM OF GOVERNMENT Territory of New Zealand
CAPITAL None; administrative center on each atoll
AREA 10 sq km (3.9 sq miles)
TIME ZONE GMT – 11 hours
POPULATION 1,503 (1995)
CURRENCY New Zealand dollar
ECONOMY Agriculture, industry
CLIMATE Tropical, moderated by trade winds April to November
MAP REFERENCE Page 725

Tonga

The Polynesian kingdom of Tonga consists of an archipelago of 170 islands (36 of them inhabited) north-east of New Zealand in the South Pacific. Samoa lies to the north and Fiji to the west. Inhabited since about 1000 B.C, they were named the "Friendly Isles" by Captain James Cook when he visited them in the 1770s. When Wesleyan missionaries arrived in the 1820s the people quickly began to adopt Christianity. In 1900, after Germany made colonial moves toward the islands, the King of Tonga signed a Treaty of Friendship and Protection with Britain.

Tonga was never fully colonized, and its people see themselves and their royal family as unique in the Pacific. A monarchy in which the king and a small group of hereditary nobles have a permanent majority in the Legislative Assembly, Tonga is now experiencing demands for a more democratic form of government. Although politicians of the newly established Pro-Democracy Movement have been harrassed for sedition and defamation there are signs the king may be ready for change: in 1995 he announced that it would only be a matter of time before a fully elected government was created.

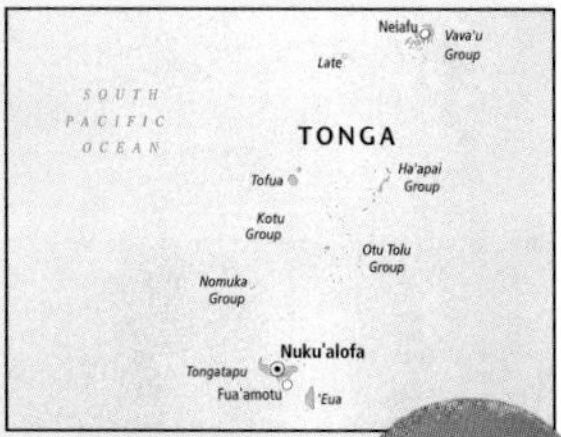

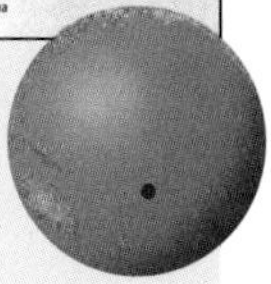

TONGA

OFFICIAL NAME Kingdom of Tonga
FORM OF GOVERNMENT Constitutional monarchy with single legislative body (Legislative Assembly)
CAPITAL Nuku'alofa
AREA 748 sq km (289 sq miles)
TIME ZONE GMT + 12 hours
POPULATION 109,082
PROJECTED POPULATION 2005 114,386
POPULATION DENSITY 145.8 per sq km (377.6 per sq mile)

(continues)

TONGA *(continued)*

LIFE EXPECTANCY 69.8
INFANT MORTALITY (PER 1,000) 37.9
OFFICIAL LANGUAGES Tongan, English
RELIGIONS Protestant 60% (including Free Wesleyan 43%, other 17%), Roman Catholic 16%, Mormon 12%, other 12%
ETHNIC GROUPS Polynesian 98%, European 2%
CURRENCY Pa'anga
ECONOMY Agriculture 70%, industry and services 30%
GNP PER CAPITA US$1,630
CLIMATE Tropical, moderated by trade winds; wettest period December to March
HIGHEST POINT Mt Kao 1,033 m (3,389 ft)
MAP REFERENCE Pages 722, 727

North to south Tonga's three main groups of islands are Vava'u, Ha'apai, and Tongatapu, the archipelago dividing into two parallel belts of islands. In the east there are low, fertile coralline-limestone formations. In the west the terrain is higher and volcanic, with the island of Kao, north of Tofua, rising to 1,033 m (3,389 ft). Mountainous landscapes of volcanic rock are found on the Vava'u group and one island in the Ha'apai group. In 1995 a new volcanic island which had emerged from the sea was discovered in the Ha'apai group. About 25 percent of Tonga's land area is arable, but surface water is rare on the coral islands.

Most of the people of Tonga live by subsistence farming, the main food crops being yams, taro, and cassava. Two-thirds of exports come from coconuts, bananas, and vanilla beans, other cash crops being pumpkin, fruits and vegetables, cocoa, coffee, ginger, and black pepper. Despite the high level of agricultural activity a good deal of food has to be imported, most of it coming from New Zealand. In the early 1990s the economy continued to grow, largely because of a rise in pumpkin exports, increased foreign aid, and a number of construction projects. Tourism is now the main source of hard currency earnings, but Tonga remains dependent on sizeable aid funds, plus remittances from its many citizens who live and work in New Zealand, Australia, and the United States.

An aerial view of Smi Island and its fringing reef, Tonga.

Trinidad and Tobago

Trinidad is a square-shaped Caribbean island at the south end of the Windward Island chain, only 11 km (7 miles) off the coast of Venezuela. Along with Tobago it is the most prosperous island in the West Indies, oil and asphalt forming the basis of its wealth. It was visited by Columbus in 1498 and then held by the Spanish for three centuries before becoming a British possession after it was seized in 1797. The island's sugar plantations were initially worked by African slaves, and then after the abolition of slavery in 1834 East Indian and Chinese labor was imported. Today, in rural districts, some villages are mainly Afro-Trinidadian, some mainly Asian. Since gaining independence in 1962, Trinidad has been vexed by racial and ethnic complications, notably "Black Power" in 1970 and an attempted coup by black Muslim extremists in 1990. In 1995 the first prime minister from the Asian community was sworn in.

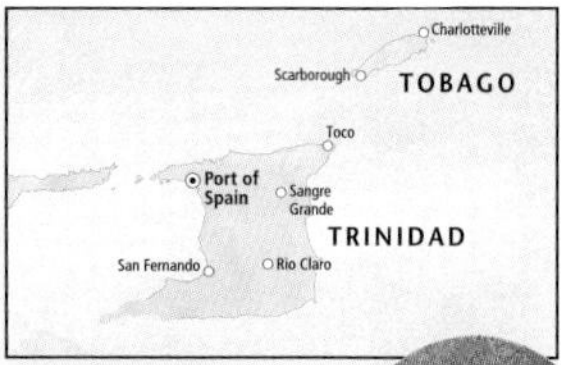

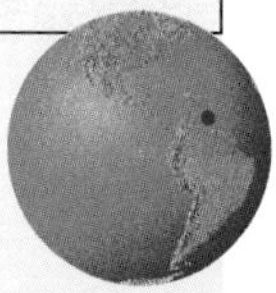

Trinidad and Tobago

Official name Republic of Trinidad and Tobago
Form of government Republic with two legislative bodies (Senate and House of Representatives)
Capital Port of Spain
Area 5,130 sq km (1,981 sq miles)
Time zone GMT – 4 hours
Population 1,102,096
Projected population 2005 1,032,684
Population density 214.8 per sq km (556.3 per sq mile)
Life expectancy 70.7
Infant mortality (per 1,000) 18.6
Official language English
Other languages Hindi, French, Spanish
Literacy rate 97.9%
Religions Roman Catholic 32%, Hindu 24.5%, Anglican 14.5%, other Protestant 14%, Muslim 6%, other 9%
Ethnic groups African 43%, East Indian 40%, mixed 14%, European 1%, Chinese 1%, other 1%
Currency Trinidad and Tobago dollar
Economy Services 73%, industry 15%, agriculture 12%
GNP per capita US$3,770
Climate Tropical, with wet season June to December
Highest point El Cerro del Aripo 940 m (3,084 ft)
Map reference Page 837

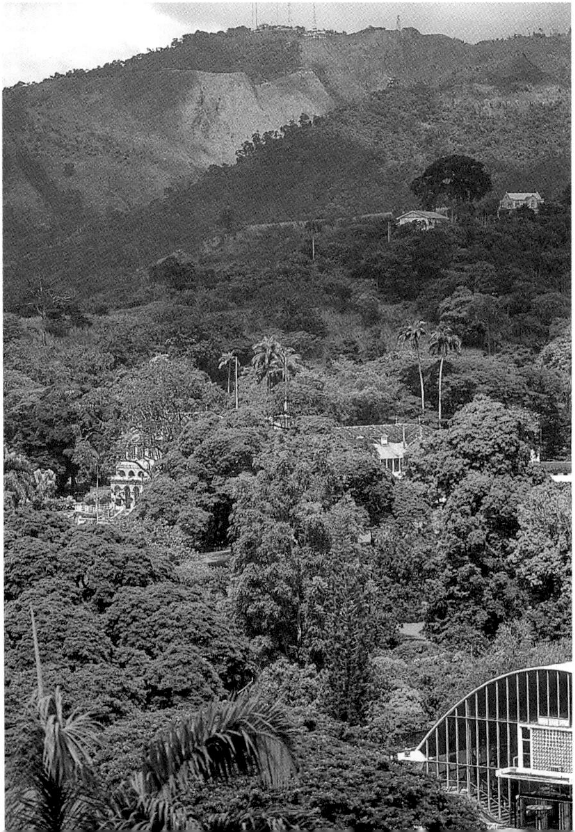

Houses in rainforest—looking across Queens Hall (foreground) and President's house, Port of Spain.

T

Las Cuevas Bay on the north coast of Trinidad.

Unlike the Caribbean islands to the north, Trinidad is geologically an extension of South America across the Gulf of Paria. It is traversed by three mountain ranges (northern, central and southern) with El Cerro del Aripo in the Northern Range, and is drained by the Caroni, Ortoire and Oropuche Rivers. The Caroni Swamp is notable for the immense variety of its butterflies. The rest of the island is mostly low-lying, fringed with mangrove swamps.

Tobago Island is a detached piece of the Northern Range, with volcanic uplands, that lies 34 km (21 miles) to the northeast of Trinidad. Tourism is concentrated on Tobago, which is renowned for its wildlife.

The strength of Trinidad's economy is its oil sector, and its large petroleum reserves. But living standards have fallen since the boom years of 1973 to 1982 and the country's prospects depend to a great extent on the success of efforts toward diversification and on economic reforms. The floating of the exchange rate, capital market liberalization, and the partial privatization of such state operations as the main airline are among recent government initiatives.

A view of one of Tobago's many bays.

Tunisia

Tunisia has a long history. Located in north Africa, across from Sicily, it was founded by Phoenician sailors 3,000 years ago, became famous as the Carthage of Queen Dido, and fell to the Romans in 146 BC. Arab conquest brought Islam to the region in the seventh century AD.

In modern times control of Tunisia was disputed by Italy, England, and France before it became a French protectorate in 1883. Ruled since independence in 1956 as a de facto one-party state, Tunisia held its first multi-party elections in 1994 (the government claiming 99.9 percent of the vote). Tunisia is a relatively prosperous country, strongly influenced by French and European culture, with a record of modest but steady economic growth. While Islamic fundamentalism is on the rise, women are treated with greater equality in Tunisia than elsewhere in the Arab world.

The eastern end of the Atlas Mountains juts across the border from Algeria in the north. A mountainous plateau called the Dorsale extends northeast, sloping down to the coastal plains. Parallel to the Mediterranean Sea in the extreme northwest, the Kroumirie Mountains, covered with cork oaks, shelter the fertile valley of the Majardah River as it flows down from the Dorsale. Harnessed for hydroelectric power, this enters the sea near Tūnis across broad alluvial lowlands used for growing a wide variety of crops, some extensively irrigated: wheat and barley, olives, sugar beet, citrus fruits, grapes, and vegetables. South of the mountains a dry expanse of plateau-steppe gives way to a series of salt lakes, the largest, Shaţţ al Jarīd, extending halfway across the country. The large remaining area to the south is desert.

Tunisia has a diverse economy. Agriculture is the main employer, but in recent years it has declined in importance as an revenue earner relative to mineral and petroleum exports. Most industrial production is based on agricultural and mining products. Real growth averaged 4.2 percent from 1991 to 1995, with moderate inflation. Growth in tourism has been a key factor. Since the 1960s Tunisia has been a popular destination for European tourists, drawn by winter sunshine, beaches, and Roman remains. In recent times there have been almost 2 million visitors per year, with tourism employing 200,000 people, but the activities of Islamic militants have had a dampening effect.

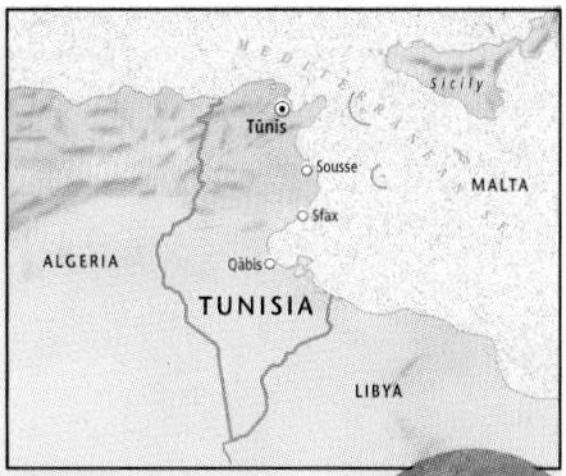

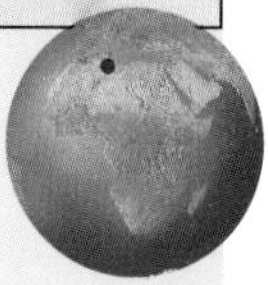

TUNISIA

OFFICIAL NAME Republic of Tunisia
FORM OF GOVERNMENT Republic with single legislative body (Chamber of Deputies)
CAPITAL Tunis
AREA 163,610 sq km (63,170 sq miles)
TIME ZONE GMT + 1 hour
POPULATION 9,513,603
PROJECTED POPULATION 2005 10,302,595
POPULATION DENSITY 58.5 per sq km (151.5 per sq mile)
LIFE EXPECTANCY 73.4
INFANT MORTALITY (PER 1,000) 31.4
OFFICIAL LANGUAGE Arabic
OTHER LANGUAGE French
LITERACY RATE 65.2%
RELIGIONS Muslim 98%, Christian 1%, Jewish 1%
ETHNIC GROUPS Arab–Berber 98%, European 1%, Jewish 1%
CURRENCY Dinar
ECONOMY Agriculture 48%, services 42%, industry 10%
GNP PER CAPITA US$1,820
CLIMATE Temperate in north, with mild, rainy winters and hot, dry summers; desert in south
HIGHEST POINT Jabal ash Sha'nabī 1,544 m (5,065 ft)
MAP REFERENCE Page 801

TURKEY

OFFICIAL NAME Republic of Turkey
FORM OF GOVERNMENT Republic with single legislative body (Grand National Assembly of Turkey)
CAPITAL Ankara
AREA 780,580 sq km (301,382 sq miles)
TIME ZONE GMT + 2 hours
POPULATION 65,597,383
PROJECTED POPULATION 2005 71,662,725
POPULATION DENSITY 84 per sq km (217.6 per sq mile)
LIFE EXPECTANCY 73.3
INFANT MORTALITY (PER 1,000) 35.8
OFFICIAL LANGUAGE Turkish
OTHER LANGUAGES Kurdish, Arabic
LITERACY RATE 81.6%
RELIGIONS Muslim 99.8% (mostly Sunni), other 0.2%
ETHNIC GROUPS Turkish 80%, Kurdish 20%
CURRENCY Turkish lira
ECONOMY Agriculture 50%, services 35%, industry 15%
GNP PER CAPITA US$2,780
CLIMATE Temperate, with mild, wet winters and hot, dry summers; arid in the interior
HIGHEST POINT Agri Dagi (Mt Ararat) 5,166 m (16,949 ft)
MAP REFERENCE Page 760

Turkey

Asia Minor, a large mountainous plateau lying between the Black Sea and the Mediterranean, forms the main part of Turkey. A much smaller part, European Turkey or Thrace, lies across the narrow straits of the Bosphorus and the Dardanelles. Early in the twentieth century Turkey's leader Kemal Ataturk (1881–1938) attempted to create a modern Islamic state that was willing and able to be a part of Europe. At the end of the twentieth century, with Islamic fundamentalism a growing internal force and no end in sight to the repression of the Kurds, his legacy is uncertain. Full integration with Europe still seems remote. Two long-running sources of conflict remain unresolved—Cyprus and the Turkish Kurds. Turkey has occupied the Muslim north of Cyprus since 1974, but their claim is unrecognized internationally. The Kurds in southeastern Turkey are demanding an independent homeland. Opposed by the State, this conflict has resulted in an estimated 19,000 deaths so far.

Historically, Asia Minor or Anatolia was the stage on which some famous scenes have been enacted. The legendary city of Troy stood on the shore of the Aegean. Ephesus and its ruins can still be visited today. Astride the Bosphorus, Constantinople (now Istanbul) was the capital of the Byzantine Empire from the fourth century AD until it fell to the Seljuk Turks in 1071. Later, during the height of its expansion in the sixteenth century, the Empire of the Ottoman Turks spread throughout the Middle East and North Africa, carrying Islam through the Balkans to Vienna. From this time the Ottoman Empire steadily declined (becoming known as "the sick man of Europe") until it was finally dismembered at the end of the First World War. The boundaries of the present Turkish state were set in 1923.

European Turkey has fertile rolling plains surrounded by low mountains. The main feature of the Asian provinces is the largely semiarid Central Anatolian Plateau (1,000 to 2,000 m; 3,300 to 6,600 ft) much of which is used for grazing sheep. On its southern flank the three main ranges of the Taurus Mountains lie inland from the Mediterranean coast. In addition to timber, the uplands provide summer grazing for the flocks of the plateau. The Pontic Mountains stretching west to east along the Black Sea boundary of the plateau are more densely wooded, and have fertile plains. A number of other ranges further east culminate in the volcanic cone of Ağri Daği (Mt Ararat) (5,166 m; 16,949 ft). Important minerals found in the thinly populated eastern regions include chrome, copper, oil, and gold. Tobacco and figs are grown in two fertile valleys that lead westward down from the plateau to the Aegean Sea. Cotton is produced on the deltaic plain near the southern city of Adana.

The Turkish economy combines modern industry and commerce with village agriculture and crafts. Though still of importance, agriculture has been overtaken by manufacturing. A busy industrial sector produces textiles, processed foods, steel, petroleum, construction materials, lumber, and paper, while coal, chromite, and copper are mined. Energy for industry comes in part from oil that is imported, but also from domestic coal and from the country's abundant hydroelectric power.

During the 1980s growth averaged more than 7 percent a year. In 1994 an outbreak of triple-digit inflation led to a period during which public debt, money supply, and the current account deficit were simultaneously out of control. Severe austerity measures and structural reforms were required in order to correct the situation. Shifting political coalitions and economic instability present a challenge for Turkey today.

Efeso archaeological site.

Stone dwellings in the Göreme Valley in the Cappadocia Region.

T

TURKMENISTAN

OFFICIAL NAME Republic of Turkmenistan
FORM OF GOVERNMENT Republic with single legislative body (Parliament)
CAPITAL Ashgabat
AREA 488,100 sq km (188,455 sq miles)
TIME ZONE GMT + 5 hours
POPULATION 4,366,383
PROJECTED POPULATION 2005 4,791,263
POPULATION DENSITY 9 per sq km (23.3 per sq mile)
LIFE EXPECTANCY 61.1
INFANT MORTALITY (PER 1,000) 73.1
OFFICIAL LANGUAGE Turkmen
OTHER LANGUAGES Russian, Uzbek
LITERACY RATE 97.7%
RELIGIONS Muslim 87%, Eastern Orthodox 11%, other 2%
ETHNIC GROUPS Turkmen 73.3%, Russian 9.8%, Uzbek 9%, Kazak 2%, other 5.9%
CURRENCY Manat
ECONOMY Agriculture 44%, services 36%, industry 20%
GNP PER CAPITA US$920
CLIMATE Mainly arid, with cold winters and hot summers
HIGHEST POINT Ayrybaba 3,139 m (10,298 ft)
MAP REFERENCE Page 758

Turkmenistan

Turkmenistan is in southern Central Asia. From the Caspian Sea it stretches east to Afghanistan, and borders Iran to the south, Kazakhstan and Uzbekistan lie to the north. The Turkmen are probably descended from the same tribes as the Seljuk and Ottoman Turks who conquered what is now Turkey in the eleventh century. Russia annexed Turkmenistan in 1884 and began colonizing it in 1906. In 1924 it became the Turkmen Soviet Socialist Republic. Fierce local resistance to Sovietization continued into the 1930s and there were mass arrests of cultural and religious leaders. Turkmenistan declared its independence in 1991 but little has changed politically.

It remains a one-party state and the first secretary of the former Communist Party is now the president, elected with a 99.5 percent share of the vote. The chief difference is that the government can now seek outside capital to develop the country's vast natural gas reserves, and looks to Muslim countries rather than Russia for support.

More than 90 percent of the country is arid, the greater part of it being the Kara Kum Desert. Most of the Kara Kum is made up of the plains of the Krasnovodskoye Plato, but 10 percent consists of huge sand dunes. In the east the Amu Darya River forms part of the Afghanistan border. This river once fed the Aral Sea but from the 1950s much of its water was diverted into the Kara Kum Canal which crosses two-thirds of the country westward to Kizyl-Arvat (Gyzlarbat). This provided irrigation for cotton, but also helped dry up the Aral Sea. To the west of the plateau the land falls to the Caspian shore.

Turkmenistan is poor, despite its natural gas and oil reserves. Half its irrigated land is planted in cotton but industrial development has been limited. Apart from Astrakhan rugs and food processing, industry is largely confined to mining sulfur and salt, and to natural gas production. Through 1995 inflation soared, and falling production saw the budget shift from a surplus to a deficit.

Since independence in 1991 there have been few changes in economic policy, leading to growing poverty and a shortage of basic foods. Cotton and grain harvests were disastrous in 1996 and desertification remains a serious problem. The economic outlook is bleak.

Melon sellers at a market in Turkmenistan.

Turks and Caicos Islands

The Turks and Caicos Islands are a large group of 30 islands, 8 of them inhabited, north of Hispaniola which lies in the Greater Antilles. They are composed of low, flat, scrub-covered limestone, with areas of marsh and swamp. There is little land for agriculture, though cassava, maize, citrus fruits, and beans are grown on Caicos by subsistence farmers.

Today, the islands' economy is mainly based on tourism, fishing, and offshore financial services. Nearly all consumer and capital goods are imported. The islands have been British since 1766, and a crown colony since 1973. Their colonial legacy is shared with many of the small islands in the Caribbean (see box on page 644.)

Turks and Caicos

Official name Turks and Caicos Islands
Form of government Dependent territory of the United Kingdom
Capital Grand Turk
Area 430 sq km (166 sq miles)
Time zone GMT – 5 hours
Population 15,192
Life expectancy 75.5
Infant mortality (per 1,000) 12.4
Currency US dollar
Economy Fishing, tourism, agriculture
Climate Tropical, moderated by trade winds
Map reference Page 839

The Caribbean's colonial legacy

The Caribbean contains many small island states and a significant number of dependencies. This diversity in status is the legacy of centuries of engagement with colonial powers. After Columbus discovered the area at the end of the fifteenth century, Spain took possession of many islands, but Great Britain, France and the Netherlands also claimed, fought over and exploited the Caribbean. From the end of the fifteenth century to the middle of the eighteenth century the indigenous people were nearly wiped out and replaced by a much larger population of Europeans and African slaves, imported to work in the sugar, tobacco and coffee plantations that dominated the local economies. The Caribbean has long served as an important trading route between North and South Americas and to Europe and the East.

The result is a diversity of economic, social and political interests. Some islands have retained their colonial status while others chose independence. The mixture of races (Carib, African and European) and cultures has created national identities marked by different peoples, languages, customs and political systems.

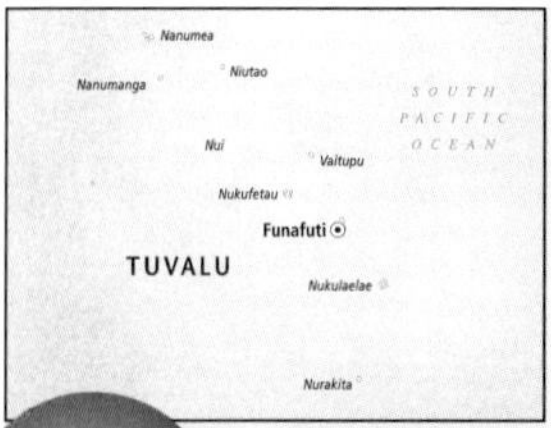

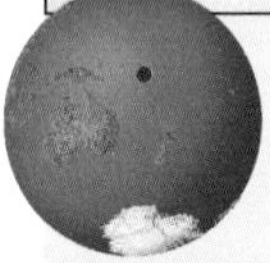

TUVALU

OFFICIAL NAME Tuvalu
FORM OF GOVERNMENT Constitutional monarchy with single legislative body (Parliament)
CAPITAL Funafuti
AREA 26 sq km (10 sq miles)
TIME ZONE GMT + 12 hours
POPULATION 10,588
PROJECTED POPULATION 2005 11,485
POPULATION DENSITY 407.2 per sq km (1,054.6 per sq mile)
LIFE EXPECTANCY 64.2

Tuvalu

Tuvalu is a tiny Pacific island state with the world's smallest economy. It consists of five coral atolls and four reef islands, none more than 5 m (15 ft) above sea level, about midway between Hawaii and Australia. Formerly known as the Ellice Islands (and once part of the British colony of the Gilbert and Ellice Islands), they were first populated by Polynesian migrants from Samoa and Tonga some time in the fourteenth century—the language used today is a Polynesian-Samoan dialect. Though sighted by the Spanish in the sixteenth century, further European contact did not take place until the eighteenth century; it was not until 1826 that the whole group was finally discovered and mapped. In the 1860s labor recruiters known as "blackbirders" became active, either inveigling or abducting islanders for work on Fijian and Australian sugar plantations (the population fell from 20,000 in 1850 to 3,000 in 1880).

The abuses of the labor trade led the British government to annex the islands as a protectorate in 1892. Though brought together as a single administrative unit, the Micronesian Gilbertese and the Polynesian Tuvaluans were not comfortable with this arrangement, and in 1978 Tuvalu became an independent state closely linked with Britain.

Tuvalu's chain of coral islands is 579 km (360 miles) long, consisting north to south of the islands of Nanumea, Niutao, Nanumanga, Nui, Vaitupu, Nukufetau, Funafuti (the capital), Nukulaelae, and Niulakita. There are no streams or rivers, and groundwater is not drinkable. All water needs must be met by catchment systems with storage facilities. The soil is of poor quality, subsistence farming supporting 70 percent of the population. The limited range of food crops such as taro must be grown in special pits dug out of the coral. Although the islands support no export crop other than coconuts, the area of the maritime Exclusive Economic Zone is 1.2 million sq km (500,000 sq miles). The rich fishing grounds within this zone are a source of revenue from license fees paid by fishing fleets from Taiwan, Korea, and the USA. Too small, remote, and lacking in amenities to be able to establish a tourist industry, government revenues come mainly from the sale of stamps and coins and from remittances: large numbers of Tuvalu men live and work abroad, some as seamen and others mining phosphate on Nauru.

The value of imports exceeds exports by 200 to 1. Substantial income is generated by an international trust fund established in 1987 by Australia, New Zealand, and the United Kingdom, which is also supported by Japan and South Korea. In 1998, the country began negotiations with a Canadian corporation for the sale of its Internet domain, .TV, as this would allow companies to utilize this rather than .COM. However, the $50 million deal collapsed after the company reneged on two payments. Negotiations with other companies are now underway. The expected value of the deal would revolutionize the economy for the tiny population of 10,000 people, and the government has developed plans for improvements to infrastructure and quality of life pending the closure of the deal.

INFANT MORTALITY (PER 1,000) 25.5
OFFICIAL LANGUAGES Tuvaluan, English
LITERACY RATE 95%
RELIGIONS Church of Tuvalu (Congregationalist) 97%, Seventh-Day Adventist 1.4%, Baha'i 1%, other 0.6%
ETHNIC GROUPS Polynesian 97%, other 3%
CURRENCY Tuvaluan dollar, Australian dollar
ECONOMY Agriculture and fishing 70%, services 28%, industry 2%
GNP PER CAPITA US$400
CLIMATE Tropical, moderated by trade winds
HIGHEST POINT Unnamed location on Niulakita 4.6 m (15 ft)
MAP REFERENCE Page 725

U,V

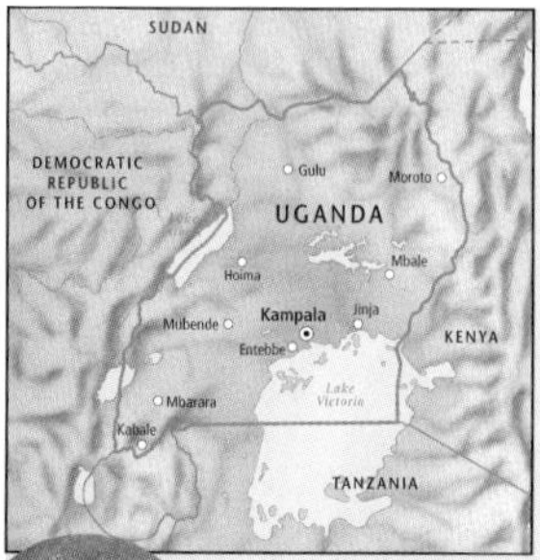

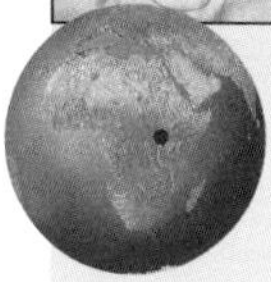

UGANDA

OFFICIAL NAME Republic of Uganda
FORM OF GOVERNMENT Republic with single legislative body (National Assembly)
CAPITAL Kampala
AREA 236,040 sq km (91,135 sq miles)
TIME ZONE GMT + 3 hours
POPULATION 21,470,864
PROJECTED POPULATION 2005 24,157,273
POPULATION DENSITY 91 per sq km (235.6 per sq mile)
LIFE EXPECTANCY 38.6
INFANT MORTALITY (PER 1,000) 96.5
OFFICIAL LANGUAGE English
OTHER LANGUAGES Luganda, Swahili, Bantu and Nilotic languages
LITERACY RATE 61.1%
RELIGIONS Roman Catholic 33%, Protestant 33%, indigenous beliefs 18%, Muslim 16%
ETHNIC GROUPS Indigenous tribal groups 99% (mainly Ganda, Teso, Nkole, Nyoro, Soga), other 1%
CURRENCY Ugandan shilling
ECONOMY Agriculture 86%, services 10%, industry 4%
GNP PER CAPITA US$240
CLIMATE Tropical, with two wet seasons March to May and September to November; semiarid in northeast
HIGHEST POINT Mt Stanley 5,110 m (16,765 ft)
MAP REFERENCE Page 806

Uganda

Extending north from Africa's largest body of water, Lake Victoria, the east African state of Uganda is a country of lakes and marshland. With a mild climate and varied resources—from fertile soil to freshwater fish to copper—it was once called "the pearl of Africa." After independence in 1962, however, its people suffered two decades of civil war, military coups, atrocities, and massacres, the worst period being the ten years under Idi Amin. It is estimated that between 1966 and Yoweri Museveni's takeover in 1986 more than half a million Ugandan inhabitants were killed.

The Museveni regime has overseen a return to peace and prosperity. Because the tribal basis of the old political parties was a cause of conflict, the government banned overt political activity, while inviting participation in a "one-party/no-party" policy of national unity. Multi-party elections in 1994 returned Museveni to power, but this taste of democracy created expectations of greater local autonomy. Some people are demanding the restoration of the region's traditional kingdoms.

Uganda's lake system is the source of the Nile. The pattern of lakes originates in the tilting and faulting of the Rift Valley, with the Ruwenzori Range on the western side of the country and the extinct volcano of Mt Elgon to

The Ruwenzoris in western Uganda, Africa's highest range of mountains.

the east. North of the lakes lies a savanna of trees and grassland, where farmers grow millet and sorghum for food, with cotton and tobacco as cash crops. Certain areas where cattle herding is impossible because of tsetse fly have been designated wildlife parks. Desert nomads live in arid Karamoja further north. Coffee, tea, and sugarcane are grown in the south, which is the most fertile region and has the highest rainfall. This is the most densely settled part of the country, and is where the industrial center of Jinja is located, not far from Kampala, near the large Owen Falls hydroelectric plant.

Agriculture is the basis of the economy, with coffee the main export. Since 1986 the government has been engaged in raising producer prices for export crops, increasing prices for petroleum products (all oil must be imported), and raising civil service wages. Railways are being rebuilt. With the return of prosperity and public order, Indo-Ugandan entrepreneurs (expelled by the Obote and Amin regimes) are beginning to return from exile. The mining of gold and cobalt in the Ruwenzori region is also expected to resume.

Ukraine

Ukraine, formerly part of the USSR, has a southern coastline on the Black Sea and on the almost landlocked Sea of Azov. Surrounding it are seven other countries. From southeast across its northern border to southwest, they are the Russian Federation, Belarus, Poland, Slovakia, Hungary, Romania, and Moldova. The Ukrainian capital, Kiev, has existed since the ninth century AD, when a Viking tribe established a center there. A century later it was a powerful force in eastern Europe. It was overrun by Mongols in the thirteenth century and then came under Polish control. In the seventeenth century the eastern part of Ukraine fell to the Russians, who eventually absorbed the whole of the country into their empire. Despite attempts to establish a separate state after the 1917 Revolution, invading Soviet armies subdued Ukraine in 1920. During the 1930s more than 3 million Ukrainians perished in a famine and another 6 million died in the Nazi occupation during the Second World War. After the war, part of western Ukraine that was under Polish

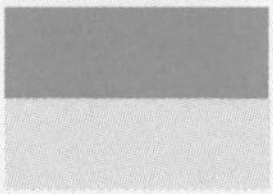

U

Ukraine

Official name Ukraine
Form of government Republic with single legislative body (Supreme Council)
Capital Kiev
Area 603,700 sq km (233,089 sq miles)
Time zone GMT + 3 hours

(continueds)

UKRAINE *(continued)*

POPULATION 49,811,174
PROJECTED POPULATION 2005 48,308,739
POPULATION DENSITY 82.5 per sq km (213.7 per sq mile)
LIFE EXPECTANCY 65.9
INFANT MORTALITY (PER 1,000) 21.7
OFFICIAL LANGUAGE Ukrainian
OTHER LANGUAGES Russian, Romanian, Hungarian, Polish
LITERACY RATE 98.8%
RELIGIONS Predominantly Christian (Ukrainian Orthodox, Ukrainian Autocephalus Orthodox, Roman Catholic); small Protestant, Jewish and Muslim minorities
ETHNIC GROUPS Ukrainian 73%, Russian 22%, other 5%
CURRENCY Hryvna
ECONOMY Services 46%, industry 33%, agriculture 21%
GNP PER CAPITA US$1,630
CLIMATE Temperate, with cold winters and mild summers; warmer on Black Sea coast
HIGHEST POINT Hora Hoverla 2,061 m (6,762 ft)
MAP REFERENCE Pages 773, 782

U

occupation was returned, as was the Crimea, and Ukraine assumed its present boundaries, under Soviet domination.

Ukraine declared its independence in 1991 as the Soviet Union began to break up, although it still retains close ties with Russia. It is now a democratic republic, with a directly elected president as head of state.

Formerly referred to as "the granary of the Soviet Union," most of Ukraine consists of fertile black-soil plains that produce an abundance of wheat and other cereal grains as well as vegetables, fruits, and fodder crops. However, much of the country's agricultural output remains affected by the widespread contamination caused by the nuclear accident at Chernobyl, near the Belarus border, in 1986.

There are mountainous areas in the southwest, where the Carpathian Mountains sweep down from Poland, and in the Crimean Peninsula in the far south. The Dnieper River flows through the heart of the country and empties into the Black Sea. In its northern plain there are large stretches of marshland and many forest-rimmed lakes. In the south, bordering the Black Sea, much of the landscape is a semiarid, treeless plain.

Coal is Ukraine's most abundant and heavily exploited mineral resource. There are also significant reserves of natural gas, uranium, and oil, though the latter remains largely unexploited. Steel production, machine building, engineering, and chemical processing are the main industries. In the post-Soviet era, the Ukrainian economy has suffered periods of extremely high inflation and growth has been hampered by a largely conservative legislature that has resisted many attempts at reform. There is widespread poverty, exacerbated by a declining healthcare system.

Yalta and the crowded promenade on the Sea of Azov, Ukraine.

United Arab Emirates

People in the seven small principalities that form the United Arab Emirates lived for centuries as seagoing traders on the shores of the Persian Gulf. When piracy became a nuisance in 1820, Britain entered into truces with the local emirs to end attacks on shipping, and established a protectorate in the region. Soon the principalities were known as the Trucial States. In 1971 they became independent and formed the federation of sheikdoms now known as the United Arab Emirates (UAE). They are situated along the southern coast of the Persian Gulf between the Qatar Peninsula to the west and the Straits of Hormuz, and share borders with Qatar, Saudi Arabia, and Oman.

Abu Dhabi is more than six times the size of all the other states put together, has the biggest population, and is the main oil producer. In the form of federal funds, it contributes to development projects in the poorer states. The port in Dubai is one of the world's largest maritime facilities, and has attracted companies from 58 countries active in the petroleum industry, trading, and financial services. A major economic contribution has been made by expatriates who flocked to the country during the 1970s' oil boom—only 20 percent of UAE citizens are native born. Whether this workforce can now be 'Emiratized' is a concern, as is the growth of Islamic fundamentalism among the young. In world affairs the UAE is a force for moderation in the Arab world. It maintains close links with the United Kingdom and the United States of America.

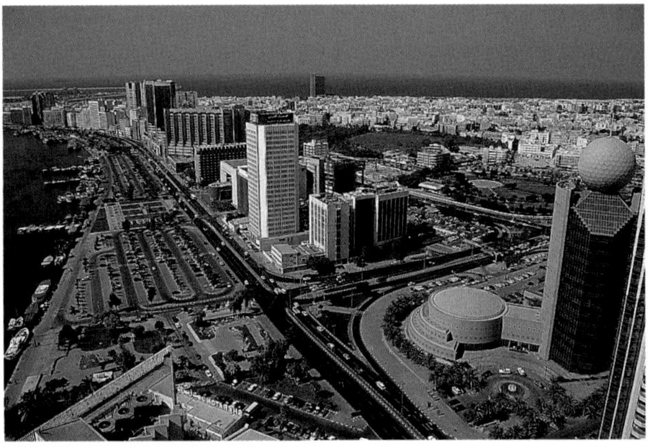

Aerial view of Dubai, United Arab Emirates.

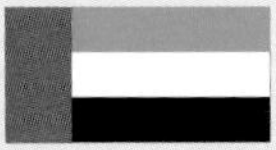

UNITED ARAB EMIRATES

OFFICIAL NAME United Arab Emirates
FORM OF GOVERNMENT Federation of Emirates with one advisory body (Federal National Council)
CAPITAL Abu Dhabi
AREA 75,581 sq km (29,182 sq miles)
TIME ZONE GMT + 4 hours
POPULATION 2,344,402
PROJECTED POPULATION 2005 2,610,901
POPULATION DENSITY 31 per sq km (80.3 per sq mile)
LIFE EXPECTANCY 75.2
Infant mortality (per 1,000) 14.1
OFFICIAL LANGUAGE Arabic
OTHER LANGUAGES English, Farsi (Persian), Hindi, Urdu
LITERACY RATE 78.6%
RELIGIONS Muslim 96% (Shia 16%); Christian, Hindu, other 4%
ETHNIC GROUPS Emiri 19%, other Arab and Iranian 23%, South Asian 50%, other expatriates 8% (only 20% of population are citizens)
CURRENCY Emirian dirham
ECONOMY Services 57%, industry 38%, agriculture 5%
GNP PER CAPITA US$17,400
CLIMATE Mainly arid; cooler in eastern mountains
HIGHEST POINT Jabal Yibir 1,527 m (5,010 ft)
MAP REFERENCE Pages 756–7

Jumeura Mosque (in a new suburb of Dubai), United Arab Emirates.

The Gulf coast features saline marshes merging inland with barren desert plains. In the east there is a range of steep mountains. These are an extension of Oman's Hajar Mountains, running northward along the Musandam Peninsula. The sheikhdom of Al-Fujayrah looks out from this peninsula onto the Gulf of Oman, and contains the only highland expanse. Less than 1.2 percent of UAE land is arable, and most vegetation is sparse and scrubby. Virtually all agricultural activity is found in the emirates of Sharjah, Ras al-Khaimana, Ajman, and Fujairah, where oasis date palms grow. Government incentives, however, plus irrigation works, have increased the number of farmers fourfold in recent years. While much food is imported, self-sufficiency in wheat was a target for the year 2000.

Once an impoverished region of small desert sheikhdoms, the UAE has since 1973 been transformed into a modern state with a high standard of living. Oil and gas production is the largest economic sector, accounting for 89 percent of export revenue. Though in the short term the fortunes of the economy fluctuate with the price of gas and oil, at the present level of production oil reserves should last more than 100 years. Increased privatization is being encouraged by the government, and service industries are being developed. Although the UAE is much stronger economically than most of the Gulf states, a number of weaknesses remain. While the largest solar-powered water-production plant in the Gulf region is at Taweela, industrial development is likely to be limited by the fact that water will always be in short supply. There is a lack of skilled labor. Most raw materials and foodstuffs have to be imported.

Stone house and enclosure in recently abandoned village

U

United Kingdom

Lying just north of the westernmost edge of continental Europe, the United Kingdom consists of the large island of Great Britain, the far northeast corner of the island of Ireland, which sits across the Irish Sea to the west, and several hundred small islands scattered around the British coast. The United Kingdom is separated by the English Channel from the north coast of France which, at its nearest point, is no more than 32 km (20 miles) away, and a rail tunnel under the Channel now links England and France. England, in the south and southwest, occupies the greatest part of the island. Scotland is to the north, and Wales in the west juts out into the Irish Sea. The eastern coast of Great Britain faces the North Sea; its western coastline is on the Atlantic Ocean and the Irish Sea.

History

Thanks partly to the natural protection offered by surrounding waters, but also to its maritime supremacy in certain periods of history and to a degree of good fortune in others, Britain is unique among major European nations in that it has escaped foreign invasion for almost 1,000 years. When William, Duke of Normandy led his successful invasion in 1066, this was the culmination of a long series of incursions that the island kingdom had suffered since the first invasion—the Romans in the first century AD.

Within 60 years of their arrival in Britain in A.D. 55, the Romans had established control over England and Wales and later introduced Christianity. When they finally withdrew at the beginning of the fifth century, the Britons

The Cuckmere River meanders through pastureland in England.

UNITED KINGDOM

OFFICIAL NAME United Kingdom of Great Britain and Northern Ireland
FORM OF GOVERNMENT Constitutional monarchy with two legislative houses (House of Lords and House of Commons)
CAPITAL London
AREA 244,820 sq km (94,525 sq miles)
TIME ZONE GMT
POPULATION 57,832,824
PROJECTED POPULATION 2005 58,135,972
POPULATION DENSITY 236.2 per sq km (611.8 per sq mile)
LIFE EXPECTANCY 77.6
INFANT MORTALITY (PER 1,000) 5.8
OFFICIAL LANGUAGE English
OTHER LANGUAGES Welsh, Scots Gaelic; Chinese, Gujarati, Bengali, Punjabi, Urdu, Hindi, Arabic, Turkish, Greek, Spanish
LITERACY RATE 99%
RELIGIONS Anglican 63%, Roman Catholic 14%, Presbyterian 4%, Methodist 3%, Muslim 3%, other 13%
ETHNIC GROUPS English 81.5%, Scottish 9.6%, Irish 2.4%, Welsh 1.9%, Northern Irish 1.8%, other 2.8%
CURRENCY Pound sterling
ECONOMY Services 78%, industry 20%, agriculture 2%
GNP PER CAPITA US$18,700
CLIMATE Temperate, with cool winters and mild summers; generally wetter and warmer in the west; cooler in the north
HIGHEST POINT Ben Nevis 1,343 m (4,406 ft)
MAP REFERENCE Pages 786–7

U

Constituent Countries
England • London
Scotland • Edinburgh

Constituent Region
Northern Ireland • Belfast

Principality
Wales • Cardiff

Overseas Territories
Anguilla
Bermuda
British Indian Ocean Territory
British Virgin Islands
Cayman Islands
Falkland Islands
Gibraltar
Guernsey
Isle of Man
Jersey
Montserrat
Pitcairn Islands
St Helena
South Georgia and the South Sandwich Islands
Turks and Caicos Islands

eventually fell prey to Germanic tribes from Scandinavia and the Low Countries. By the eighth century most of Britain, except the far west and the north, had succumbed and the country was divided into a number of Anglo-Saxon kingdoms.

Viking attacks from Norway and Denmark occurred during the course of the eighth and ninth centuries, with Danish invaders controlling much of north and northeast England by the late ninth century. United under the kings of Wessex by the middle of the tenth century, England again fell to Danish control early in the eleventh century. When Edward the Confessor came to the throne in 1042, he presided over a unified, but fractious, kingdom. On his death in 1066, both his brother-in-law, Harold, and his cousin, William of Normandy, claimed the throne. William was victorious at the Battle of Hastings and was crowned on Christmas Day 1066.

The feudal system of government developed by William gave significant power to the nobles. Under Henry II, the first Plantagenet king, power became more centralized in the crown. This, and increasing civil unrest during the reign of John, led to a revolt by nobles, who in 1215 forced the king to sign the Magna Carta, a document limiting royal power and enshrining basic civil rights. This in turn led to the development of a more consultative style of government, and, by the late thirteenth century, to the establishment of a House of Commons with powers to raise taxes.

Heathland on the rugged Pembrokeshire coast of Wales.

Under Edward I (1272–1307) Wales was brought under English control, much of Ireland was subjugated, and a portion of Scotland was conquered. In 1314, however, at the Battle of Bannockburn, the English were driven out of Scotland. Between 1338 and 1453, in a series of devastating wars, known as the Hundred Years War, England lost all its French territories. This led to a further 30 years of civil war, known as the Wars of the Roses, which culminated in the accession to the throne of Henry VII, the first of the Tudor monarchs, in 1485.

The Tudor dynasty lasted until 1603, and during this time, especially during the reign of Elizabeth I (1558–1603), England became a leading power in the world, enjoying a golden age in which colonies were established in North America, British navigators sailed to remote corners of the globe, and there was a notable flowering of English theatre. During the reign of Elizabeth's father, Henry VIII, Protestantism, in the form of the Church of England, had been established in England.

When Elizabeth died without an heir, James VI of Scotland, the first Stuart king, succeeded her, combining the two kingdoms and reigning as James I of England. Attempts by his son, Charles I, to curb the powers of parliament led to the outbreak of civil war in 1642. With the victory of the parliamentary armies, led by Oliver Cromwell, in 1646, the monarchy was abolished and a commonwealth, virtually a military dictatorship, set up

Ebbw Valley British Steel tinplate mill in the town of Ebbw Vale, south Wales.

The Giant's Causeway, a promontory of hexagonal basalt columns, in County Antrim, Northern Ireland.

Rental houseboats and marina, Lower Heyford.

A tile-hung house in a village in southern England

under Cromwell. The commonwealth did not long survive the death of Cromwell and in 1660 Charles II was installed as king. When, however, his brother, the Catholic James II, attempted to restore Catholic domination, he was ousted and his Protestant daughter, Mary, and her Dutch husband, William of Orange, accepted the crown in 1689. In the same year, parliament enacted legislation barring Catholics from the throne. In 1690, at the Battle of the Boyne, their armies defeated a Catholic uprising in Ireland. In 1707 an Act of Union, between the Scottish and English parliaments, formally joined the two countries. Scottish rebellions against British rule were finally put down in 1746, when Charles Edward Stuart (Bonnie Prince Charlie) was defeated in the Battle of Culloden.

Under the Hanoverian monarchs, the first of whom, George I, accepted the throne in 1814 as King of Great Britain and Ireland, greater power devolved to the parliament. In 1721, Sir Hugh Walpole became the first prime minister to head a ministry that exercised executive power with the sanction of parliament. The eighteenth century, too, was a period of great expansion of British power that saw the acquisitions of British colonies in India and Canada and the exploration and colonization of Australia. A major setback was the loss of the American colonies in 1776. The military defeat of Irish rebels in 1798 led to an Act of Union that formally joined the two countries in 1801. Defeat of Bonaparte at Waterloo in 1815 confirmed Britain as the world's leading power.

The nineteenth century was a time of further expansion and consolidation of Britain's influence and power. By the

Polegate windmill, East Sussex.

end of Queen Victoria's 64-year reign in 1901, Britain's colonies extended throughout much of the world, including large parts of Africa, although by then Australia, New Zealand, and Canada had gained their independence and demands for Irish independence were growing. During the century a number of Reform Bills brought in significant democratic reforms and the Industrial Revolution resulted in increasing industrialization, urban growth, and a slowly rising standard of living.

Three-quarters of a million British soldiers were killed during the First World War, which also left the country considerably weakened economically. This situation was exacerbated by the Great Depression. After a protracted and bitter struggle, Ireland, with the exception of the provinces of Northern Ireland, became independent in 1922 and British troops faced growing unrest in India and in parts of the Middle East. Following the Second World War, in which British cities, especially London, were subjected to sustained German bombardment from the air, Britain endured almost a decade of austerity.

India gained its independence in 1947, and in 1956 Britain suffered a humiliating defeat in its armed attempt to prevent Egypt's nationalization of the Suez Canal. In 1982, Britain was again at war, this time against Argentina, which attempted to seize the Falkland Islands. In a two-week conflict, Britain repulsed the Argentines with the loss of 255 British lives. In recent years, bitter

Thatched cottage by the sea, Cornwall, England.

Scotney Castle in Kent, southeastern England.

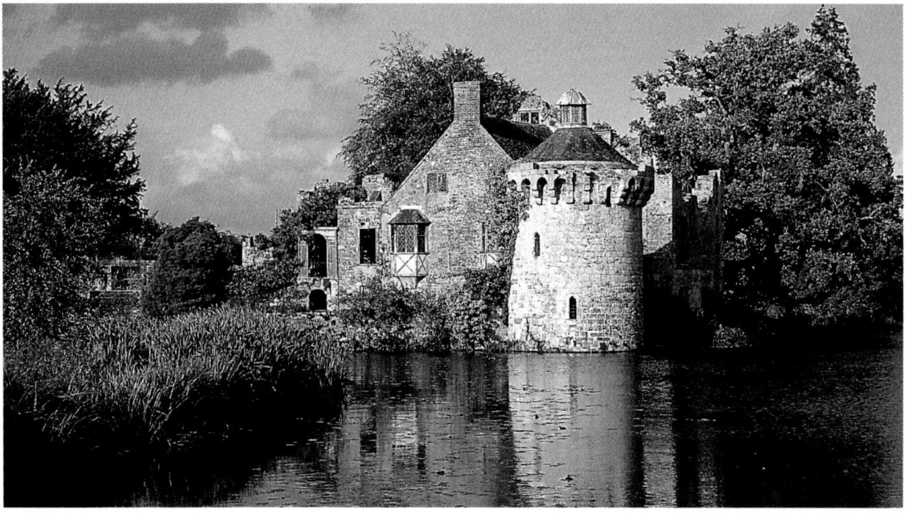

U

Timeline United Kingdom

200,000 BC Hominids living in southeastern Britain use stone tools and hunt animals

12,000 BC Paleolithic hunters carve mammal bones at Cresswell Crags, Derbyshire; one shows a dancing man, others, animal heads

4000 BC Tribes from various parts of Europe arrive; they farm and live in villages, burying their dead in earth mounds

3300 bc Construction of a large stone circle begins: Stonehenge completed 1800 BC

43 BC–AD 446 Roman occupation of Britain brings wealth, military skills, and Christianity; Hadrian's Wall built AD 120

AD 410 Anglo-Saxons settle in south England destroying remains of Roman culture; later, Danish Vikings settle in north and east

1066 Norm invasion. William Domesday Bo assesses Britair wealth and estimat population abo 2 milli

1825 World's first public railway opens between Stockton and Darlington, starting a worldwide boom in railway construction

1837 Queen Victoria crowned. Rule lasts until 1901, coincides with period of great wealth and growth of British Empire

1845–46 Potato crop failure causes Great Famine in Ireland; millions die or emigrate to England, USA, Canada, Australia

1901 The population of Britain reaches 42 million after rapid population growth in the second half of the nineteenth century

1914–18 First Wor War against Germar causes the loss more than 900,00 British Empire live

1920 Northe separates fron of Ireland anc part of th Kingdom; the I State (southerr is set up

Alfriston Clergy House, Sussex. Built in the fourteenth century, it was the First National Trust house, bought in 1896.

violence between Catholics and Protestants in Northern Ireland has been a major preoccupation of British governments. Since 1995, however, there have been developments, including the intervention of the United States, that augur well for a peaceful resolution of this conflict.

Britain, as a member of the European Union and a signatory of the Maastricht Treaty, is a significant force in Europe as it moves closer to political and economic integration. It is one of the world's most stable multi-party democracies, in spite of ongoing debate about the role and viability of the monarchy and of its unelected, and largely hereditary, upper house of parliament, the House of Lords, which is in the process of reform. Power resides in the House of Commons, which is elected by universal adult suffrage for terms of five years.

Physical features and land use

The United Kingdom has a considerable variety of landscapes, ranging from craggy mountain ranges and tranquil upland lakes in the north, to gently rolling hills and green plains that are characteristic of the south and the southeast.

Scotland is the most mountainous part of the country. Mainland Scotland has three main regions: the Highlands

ation
nillion after
apidly as a
re
ming

closure of
land forces
ople off the
using
s and rural
ation

1500 Little ice age of cold winters and wet summers (which continues until 1700) causes crop failures across the country

1536 Parliament formally makes Wales part of English territory

1664–66 Great Plague kills more than 75,000 of London's population of around 450,000, then spreads to other parts of the country

1707 Act of Union between England and Scotland creates United Kingdom of Great Britain

1750 Use of iron grows rapidly; machines for spinning and weaving invented in late 1700s, accelerating Industrial Revolution

1801 Act of Union extended to join Ireland to United Kingdom

1930s Unemployment rises to 3 million; some relief provided by economic progress in manufacturing industries

1939–45 Cities across Britain bombed during Second World War— widespread damage and the loss of thousands of lives

1945 Churchill loses election to Labour Party's Attlee who begins a program of reconstruction, reform, and nationalization

1957 Extensive postwar migration from Commonwealth regions such as Pakistan, India, and West Indies

1967 Britain fails to join the EC; membership not achieved until 1973; sterling devalued

1975 Offshore North Sea oilfields begin operation, boosting the UK economy; Britain becomes self-sufficient in oil

1994 Passenger train services through the fixed-link railway tunnel under the English Channel link France and the UK

in the north, the Southern Uplands near the border with England, and in between the flatter, though often hilly, Central Lowlands. It also has several groups of offshore islands: the Shetlands in the far north, the Orkneys, off the northeastern tip of the mainland, and the Inner and Outer Hebrides off the northwestern coast. The most rugged country is in the north, where two granite ranges, the North West Highlands and the Grampians, dominate the scene. In the northwest the mountains are cut by deep glaciated valleys and the coastline is rocky and deeply indented. South and east of the Great Glen, which contains the famous Loch Ness, are the Grampians, where Britain's highest peaks are found. Here, the country is generally less harsh, and there are stretches of sheep-grazing land and forested slopes where there are herds of deer. East of the Grampians is a rich agricultural lowland area that stretches in an arc from near Inverness around to Aberdeen.

Scotland's two largest cities, Glasgow and Edinburgh, lie in the Central Lowlands, the most populous region and Scotland's industrial heart. The Central Lowlands contain several ranges of undulating hills and are drained by the eastward-flowing Tay and Forth rivers and the westward-flowing Clyde. The area east of Edinburgh is prime

Edinburgh Castle, Scotland.

Church ruins, Scotland.

country, both for stock raising and crop cultivation. The Southern Uplands, gentler and less lofty than their northern counterparts, are characterized by hills, moorlands, and picturesque valleys, and in the valley of the Tweed and its tributaries are large areas of sheltered farmland. The Cheviot Hills in the south form a natural border with England.

Beginning just south of the Cheviot Hills, and running southward as far as north Derbyshire, are the Pennine Mountains, a predominantly limestone range of hills, plateaus, expanses of moorlands, and soft, green valleys, which are often referred to as the Dales. West of the Pennines, and separated from it by the valley of the Eden, are the Cumbrian Mountains, a region of craggy peaks with many lakes. This is England's famous Lake District.

The European Union

On 1 January 1999 eleven European countries adopted a new and common currency—the euro. This momentous step marked the climax of a movement for closer European integration which had begun in 1957. In March of that year Belgium, France, the Federal Republic of Germany, Italy, Luxembourg, and the Netherlands signed a treaty which proposed the gradual integration of their economies in the European Economic Community (EEC or EC). They planned to gradually eliminate restrictive quotas and import duties between member nations in order to allow the free movement of persons and capital within their common boundaries. It was hoped that the larger market that resulted would promote greater productivity and higher standards of living for all.

The success of the Community led to a number of additional countries seeking membership. Others, however, objected to the surrender of sovereignty that was entailed: at first Britain, along with the Scandinavian nations, Switzerland, Austria, and Portugal, formed their own free-trade area (known as the outer seven) instead. Nor were the policies of the EEC uniformly successful: the Common Agricultural Policy, for example, led to the overproduction of butter, wine, and sugar in member countries. However, although national referenda on membership and treaty ratification have not been without a degree of controversy, most of the countries in Europe have now decided that the benefits of being a member of the EEC outweigh the costs, and by 1997 all of the following states belonged: Austria, Belgium, Denmark, Finland, France, Germany, Greece, Ireland, Italy, Luxembourg, the Netherlands, Portugal, Spain, Sweden, and the UK.

With the ratification of the Maastricht Treaty, which prepared the way for monetary union and the euro, the EEC and its associated bodies became formally known as the European Union (EU). An important feature of monetary union has been the establishment of an independent Euro-pean Central Bank (ECB). This bank has as its main goal "price stability," a term meaning inflation of less than 2 percent per year. At present the UK, Denmark, and Sweden have decided not to adopt the euro, while Greece is unable to satisfy the economic criteria for monetary union and the new currency.

To the east of the Pennines are the elevated expanses of the North York Moors.

South of the Pennines, beginning around the fertile valleys of the Trent and Avon rivers, the countryside becomes flatter and gently undulating, reaching its lowest point in the marshy fen country north of Cambridge. Numerous ranges of hills provide relief from the generally rolling countryside. The most notable hills are the Cotswolds, in the central southwest, where England's longest river, the Thames, begins its course eastward across the country, passing through London, and out to the North Sea.

Wales, which juts out into the Irish Sea to the west of England, is more mountainous, its center dominated by the Cambrian Mountains, in which the Severn, Britain's second longest river, rises. Mount Snowdon, situated in Snowdonia, a large national park in northern Wales, rises to 1,085 m (3,559 ft) and is the highest peak in England and Wales.

Northern Ireland is flat for the most part, but to the north of Belfast is the Antrim Plateau, whose basalt cliffs provide some of the country's most arresting coastal scenery.

Giant's Ring, a prehistoric enclosure, includes a Stone Age burial site under the dolmen, Belfast, Northern Ireland.

Industry, commerce, agriculture, and culture

Crop cultivation in Britain is concentrated mainly in the east and southeast of the country. Wheat is the principal crop, though potatoes and fruits are widely cultivated. Pasturelands are more common in the west and southwest, where sheep and cattle raising and dairy farming predominate. Although the United Kingdom exports much of its produce, it still imports about one-third of its food needs.

The United Kingdom has traditionally used coal for its energy resources, and there are still adequate reserves. However, the replacement of most coal-fired power stations with gas-powered facilities in recent years has resulted in the near closure of the coalmining industry. The country also has a number of nuclear power stations, which are a continuing subject of controversy. Oil and gas reserves in the North Sea are a major source of revenue, and have helped to make the country self-sufficient in energy.

Manufacturing was once the mainstay of the British economy, with a large proportion of heavy industry centered on industrial cities in the Midlands such as Birmingham, Manchester, and Liverpool. Food processing, machinery, and textile manufacture are still among the

Loch Ness and Urquart Castle, Scotland.

principal manufacturing industries. Motor vehicle and aircraft manufacture are long-established core industries, although much of the motor vehicle industry is now owned by foreign companies. Most of the raw materials needed to supply Britain's industries have to be imported from other countries.

White horse in the lee of an old watchtower on a bleak day on the Isle of Skye, Scotland.

Apart from the ethnic and cultural minorities found in Wales and Scotland, Britain's population is relatively homogeneous. Since the 1950s, however, large numbers of immigrants from former British colonies in the Caribbean, Asia (especially India and Pakistan), and Africa have changed the racial composition, most notably in inner city areas, where the majority of ethnic minorities have congregated. Despite certain tensions, these immigrants are now generally accepted as an integral, if still relatively disadvantaged, part of British society. Britain's economy is one of the most developed in Western Europe and its people enjoy a high standard of living, although there are considerable variations in levels of affluence. Universal free school education and health systems are maintained by the state, although some social services and the value of pensions, including those for the elderly, have been sharply cut back in recent years.

Seven Sisters with houses, East Sussex.

U

United States of America

In the United States of America a variety of peoples, united by a shared belief in social and economic freedom, have built the most prosperous and powerful nation on Earth. Abundant resources, a climate and soils ensuring plentiful food supplies, and an open society rewarding individual energy and initiative, were all advantages from the beginning. In addition, huge oceans on both eastern and western coasts isolated America from the troubles of Europe and Asia, and its relations with Mexico to the south and Canada to the north were generally benign. Starting with these favorable conditions, and guided by the ideals of democracy and freedom, the United States of America—in this respect unique among nations—successfully invented itself according to its own political and social ideals.

The most serious danger to its existence was self-inflicted. From 1861 to 1865 the US was wracked by a civil war in which the implications of universal human liberty were played out in a struggle between slave-owners in the south of the country and slave-liberators in the north, but the nation survived. Later, in the face of widespread domestic opposition, the US entered the First World War in 1917, its military strength leading to Germany's defeat. Even more decisive was its role in the Second World War between 1941 and 1945, in alliance with Great Britain and the Soviet Union, when its industrial power and military might ensured victory over both Germany and Japan.

Changing colors in northern Maine.

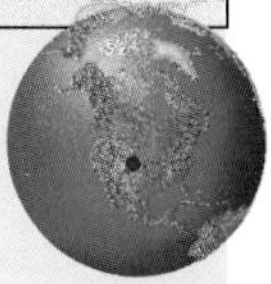

UNITED STATES OF AMERICA

OFFICIAL NAME United States of America
FORM OF GOVERNMENT Federal republic with two legislative bodies (Senate and House of Representatives)
CAPITAL Washington DC
AREA 9,372,610 sq km (3,618,765 sq miles)
TIME ZONE GMT – 5/11 hours
POPULATION 272,639,608
PROJECTED POPULATION 2005 286,291,020
POPULATION DENSITY 29.1 per sq km (75.4 per sq mile)
LIFE EXPECTANCY 76.2
INFANT MORTALITY (PER 1,000) 6.3
OFFICIAL LANGUAGE English
OTHER LANGUAGES Spanish, German, French, Italian, Chinese, indigenous languages
LITERACY RATE 99%
RELIGIONS Protestant 56%, Roman Catholic 28%, Jewish 2%, other 4%, none 10%
ETHNIC GROUPS European 83.5%, African 12.5%, Asian 3%, Native American 1%
CURRENCY US dollar
ECONOMY Services 79%, industry 18%, agriculture 3%
GNP PER CAPITA US$26,980
CLIMATE Varied: eastern states are temperate, with warm summers and snowy winters in north and subtropical conditions in south; southwest is arid and semiarid; west coast is temperate but warmer in California and wetter in the Pacific Northwest; Hawaii is mainly tropical; Alaska is mainly polar but cooler and wetter on south coast
HIGHEST POINT Mt McKinley 6,194 m (20,321 ft)
MAP REFERENCE Pages 828–9, 830–31, 832–3, 834–5, 836

STATES AND CAPITALS

ALABAMA • Montgomery
ALASKA • Juneau
ARIZONA • Phoenix
ARKANSAS • Little Rock
CALIFORNIA • Sacramento
COLORADO • Denver
CONNECTICUT • Hartford
DELAWARE • Dover
DISTRICT OF COLUMBIA • Washington DC
FLORIDA • Tallahassee
GEORGIA • Atlanta
HAWAII • Honolulu
IDAHO • Boise
ILLINOIS • Springfield
INDIANA • Indianapolis
IOWA • Des Moines
KANSAS • Topeka
KENTUCKY • Frankfort
LOUISIANA • Baton Rouge
MAINE • Augusta
MARYLAND • Annapolis
MASSACHUSETTS • Boston
MICHIGAN • Lansing
MINNESOTA • St Paul
MISSISSIPPI • Jackson
MISSOURI • Jefferson City
MONTANA • Helena
NEBRASKA • Lincoln
NEVADA • Carson City
NEW HAMPSHIRE • Concord
NEW JERSEY • Trenton
NEW MEXICO • Santa Fe
NEW YORK • Albany
NORTH CAROLINA • Raleigh
NORTH DAKOTA • Bismarck
OHIO • Columbus
OKLAHOMA • Oklahoma City
OREGON • Salem
PENNSYLVANIA • Harrisburg
RHODE ISLAND • Providence
SOUTH CAROLINA • Columbia
SOUTH DAKOTA • Pierre
TENNESSEE • Nashville
TEXAS • Austin
UTAH • Salt Lake City
VERMONT • Montpelier
VIRGINIA • Richmond
WASHINGTON • Olympia
WEST VIRGINIA • Charleston
WISCONSIN • Madison
WYOMING • Cheyenne

After 1945, challenged for superpower supremacy by the Soviets, it engaged in a protracted trial of strength known as the Cold War. This ended in 1989 with the collapse of the USSR and its communist allies, leaving America stronger politically and economically than ever before.

The economy, already the most powerful, diverse, and technologically advanced in the world, continues to grow. But US prosperity is combined with a variety of problems: drug addiction; crime; long-term unemployment for some sectors of the population; racial tensions; air and water pollution in some areas from automotive and industrial wastes; traffic congestion approaching "gridlock" in major cities; and rising medical costs. All these side-effects appear to be the price of modernity on the American model. It is a price that most other developed countries have been prepared to pay, however, in order to establish high-tech, high-energy industrial societies.

Physical features and land use

Mainland United States can be divided into three major physical regions. The eastern part consists of the range of the Appalachian Mountains and the coastal plain that runs along the Atlantic Ocean. The broad basin of the Mississippi and Missouri Rivers comprises the central section. The western region is composed of mountain ranges, desert landscapes, and the land along the Pacific coast. In addition, there are two outlying sections of the country—Alaska and Hawaii.

In eastern North America the Appalachians, a band of sedimentary mountains and plateaus that are still widely forested, extend from northern Alabama to the Gulf of St Lawrence. They consist of a number of parallel ranges, including the Blue Ridge Mountains in Virginia and the Great Smoky Mountains along the North Carolina–Tennessee border. For a long time these ranges constituted a barrier to inland settlement. In New York State the valley of the Mohawk River divides the mountains of the Appalachians from the Adirondacks, which are a southern extension of the ancient granite mass of the Canadian Shield. Traveling up this valley, from east to west, the early settlers were able to find a way through the range that led on to the land bordering the Great Lakes and the Ohio country beyond.

The original vegetation on these mountains was broadleaf deciduous forest of oak, ash, beech, and maple, grading into yellow birch, hemlock, and pine toward the north. During the eighteenth and nineteenth centuries much of this forest area was cleared for farming, but declining agriculture in New England and the abandonment of farmland has brought widespread regeneration of tree growth. Flying across eastern America, much of the landscape still gives the impression of continuous woodland.

The coastal plain to the southeast through the Carolinas and Georgia is generally low-lying, and includes many areas of swamp. Nearly 1,700 km (more than 1,000 miles) of barrier islands and sandbars run parallel to the shore and are popular seaside resort areas for the inland population, despite being exposed to occasional hurricanes.

To the west of the Appalachian Range lies the enormous continental drainage basin of the Mississippi–Missouri system. This basin is about 2,500 km (1,500 miles) wide, extending south from the Canadian border to the Gulf of Mexico. At its northern limit there are the hills along Lake Superior, a vestige of the Canadian Shield. What are called the Central Lowlands of this drainage basin are bounded on the east by the low plateaus of Kentucky and Tennessee. To the west of the Mississippi lie vast areas planted in wheat, and eventually grasslands, as the Great Plains reach 1,500 km (900 miles) across to the foothills of the Rocky Mountains.

Once the home of such tribes as the Mandan, the Omaha, and the Kansa Indians (settled farmers near the Missouri River), and the nomadic Blackfoot, Crow, and Arapaho further west, most of the plains had been taken by incoming ranchers and farmers by the end of the nineteenth century. Former range land was planted in wheat and maize. These crops were hugely productive at first, but overcropping and dry years led to severe soil deterioration in the first decades of the twentieth century. This reached a climax in the disasters of the 1930s, when a large part of the region became a "dustbowl." Although diversification of grain crops, contour plowing, and widespread irrigation have helped to restore agricultural productivity, some areas are still highly sensitive to climatic variation, especially where the original terrain was semidesert. Combined with fluctuations in grain prices, agriculture remains a risky business in a region where much of the land is marginal.

The mountain ranges of the western Cordillera, as it extends south from Canada, are divided by a number of high plateaus and deep valleys. There are two main systems, to the west and the east. The northern and central Rocky Mountains are the eastern arm facing out

Overseas Territories

American Samoa
Baker and Howland Islands
Guam
Jarvis Island
Johnston Atoll
Kingman Reef
Midway Islands
Navassa Island
Northern Mariana Islands
Palmyra Atoll
Puerto Rico
Virgin Islands of the US
Wake Island

One of California's large and numerous vineyards

Devils Tower—the remainder of the magma core of an ancient volcano, Wyoming.

across the Great Plains, with the Grand Tetons forming spectacular ridges in Wyoming. The southern Rockies of Colorado and New Mexico—the remains of an ancient granite plateau—are also weathered into a series of striking peaks. In Colorado there are more than 1,000 mountains of 3,000 m (10,000 ft) or more. As with the mountains on the east of the continent, the Rockies were a major obstacle for westward-heading settlers. One major route lay through the Wyoming Basin, a rangeland where bison once grazed, and where yesterday's pioneer trails have become interstate highways.

On the lower slopes of the Rockies grow a mixture of piñon pines and juniper scrub, with ponderosa pine, spruce, and fir at higher altitudes. Wildlife includes elk, deer, moose, mountain sheep, bear, and a variety of smaller animals. National Parks such as Yellowstone and Grand Teton provide an opportunity to see these animals in dramatic natural settings, and draw millions of visitors to the region every year.

High plateaus, rocky ranges, and desert basins extend westward across the states of Utah, Arizona, and Nevada, seamed in many places by vast, abrupt canyons, of which the Grand Canyon of the Colorado River is the most spectacular. On the Pacific side of these plateaus is the western branch of the cordillera. This forms a chain of

Great Basin National Park, Nevada.

mountains consisting of the Sierra Nevada in the south and the Cascade Range to the north. Stretching from Washington through Oregon to Lassen Peak in California, the Cascades include several large volcanoes, Mt Saint Helens erupting violently in 1980. The Sierra Nevada faces out over the fertile Central Valley of California, with its fruit and vegetable growing, viticulture, cotton, other crops, and livestock. In the early days long dry summers made farming difficult in the Central Valley. Meltwater from the snows of the Sierra Nevada, much of it diverted in lengthy canals, now provides summer irrigation.

Juneau, in Alaska, lies on the Inside Passage, a marine waterway that runs through the vast Tongass National Forest.

Beyond the Central Valley on its western side rise the comparatively low Coast Ranges, running parallel to the Pacific shore all the way from the Mexican border to Canada. Together, the Coast Ranges, the Cascades, and the Sierra Nevada, all serve to keep precipitation away from the interior plateaus and create its arid landscape. East of the Cascade Range in the Pacific Northwest lies the Columbia Basin. Here, the meltwaters of ancient glaciers have cut deep gorges in the land. In western Washington the most spectacular trees consist of Douglas fir, western hemlock, and Sitka spruce, some almost as tall as the giant redwoods of northern California. The wealth of the US northwest was originally based on timber from the huge conifers that covered the Cascade Range.

The two non-contiguous parts of the US have very different physical landscapes. The expansive state of Alaska is a mixture of massive glaciated mountains and broad river valleys, with a vegetation cover that varies from dense forest to sparse tundra. For much of the year,

The Grand Canyon, Arizona.

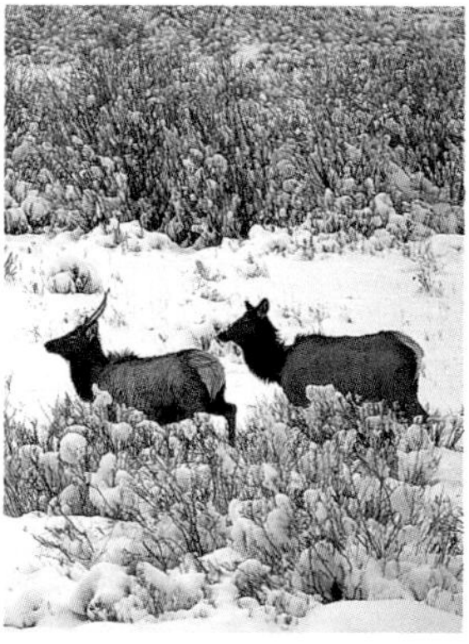

Wapiti (American Elk) in snow, Colorado.

Undulating farming country in Idaho.

large areas of Alaska are covered in snow. The Hawaiian islands mostly consist of the tops of prominent volcanoes which protrude above the sea, with a host of distinctive plants nurtured by the tropical climate.

History and settlement

The first peoples to settle North America probably crossed from Siberia to Alaska during the ice ages between 10,000 and 30,000 years ago. It is thought they became the ancestors of the many Indian tribes living in North America when the first Europeans arrived. Their cultures varied widely, from the Iroquois who lived in bark lodges in the east, to the cliff-dwelling Pueblo peoples of the west, to the salmon-fishing and whale-hunting Northwest Coast Indians of Washington State and British Columbia, who lived in large timber houses. Plains Indians such as the Sioux or the Comanche are sometimes depicted hunting bison on horseback, but this was only possible after horses had been introduced by incoming European settlers from the fifteenth century onward.

The oldest authenticated European settlement in North America was made by Norse Vikings at the northern tip of the island of Newfoundland about AD 1000, but it was occupied for only a short time. The first successful English settlement was at Jamestown, Virginia, in 1607.

Sunset on Junipers, Canyonlands National Park, Utah.

Not long after this a party of religious dissenters, the so-called Pilgrim Fathers, arrived in 1620 to found the first of the New England colonies at Plymouth. Joined by other migrants later, this became part of the large colony in Massachusetts Bay.

A Dutch colony on Manhattan Island (founded in 1624) was captured by the British in 1664, who changed its name from New Amsterdam to New York. The Quaker William Penn founded one of the more successful of the early English colonies in 1682. Part of Pennsylvania later split off to become Delaware; North and South Carolina were established in 1663; and Georgia, originally designed as a philanthropic alternative to a debtor's prison, in 1732. The defeat of the French, which ended the Seven Years War in 1763, brought huge territorial accessions to England: all of France's Canadian territories, the land west of the Mississippi River, plus Louisiana and Florida. The settlers throughout these areas became directly subject to the British Crown, and when London sought to recoup the huge expenses of the war (about £101,500,500) by imposing taxes. The cry of "No taxation without representation" was raised in Boston, and resistance to England began. When the American War of Independence broke out in 1776 George Washington commanded the troops, and when it was won and the first elections were held in 1788 he became the inaugural president. In the aftermath, tens of thousands of "loyalists" moved north to Canada.

The British government had forbidden west-ward expansion beyond the mountains of the Appalachians. After independence, however, this took place with a rush. Indian tribes were quickly dispossessed from the area and exiled, their land taken for farms, and throughout the nineteenth century there was a series of wars in the region to crush resistance. The last armed Indian defiance collapsed with the Ghost Dance Uprising of 1890. But by far the most serious crisis for the new nation was the American Civil War of 1861 to 1865. This was both a clash of ideals (liberty versus servitude) and of ways of life (the industrializing, modern north versus the old agrarian south). Led by the eloquent commonsense of Abraham Lincoln, the northern forces of the Union defeated the southern armies of the Confederacy, but the legacy of bitterness lasted for many decades.

Meanwhile, westward expansion proceeded apace. Pioneers followed trails explored by men such as Lewis and Clark. Railroads spanned the continent, coal and iron

Rugged countryside of Yosemite.

Navajo Indians in Monument Valley, Arizona.

Crater lakes in Oregon.

U

The temple and square of Salt Lake City, Utah.

were discovered and used, and new cities such as Pittsburgh and Chicago grew up in the interior. European migrants pouring in through the ports of Boston, Philadelphia, and New York substantially changed the nation's ethnic composition. Manufacturing cities, which were big markets in their own right, developed along the shores of the Great Lakes, while the mechanized farming of the Midwestern "corn belt" turned it into the granary of much of the Western world.

The history of California differed from that of the rest of the country in many ways, in that it was a part of Spanish conquest rather than of English settlement. The small, semi-nomadic hunting and seed-gathering Indian cultures of the area were little affected by the spread northward of Spanish forts and missions from New Spain (Mexico) in the 1760s. But by the middle of the nineteenth century pressures from land-hungry pioneers moving in from the eastern states were irresistible: by the end of the century the whole of the southwest, including Texas, had been either ceded, purchased, or annexed. Since then the Pacific Coast economy has passed through various stages, from gold-prospecting and lumbering, through agriculture, the expansion of the aircraft industry after the Second World War, to the highest of high-tech today in Silicon Valley south of San Francisco Bay.

Once independence was established by the beginning of the nineteenth century, the US kept Europe at arm's length, and the Monroe Doctrine warned Europe that the representatives of the old empires—Spanish, Portuguese, and

Three pinnacles in Monument Valley Arizona.

British—were not to intervene in the Americas any more. Isolationism was the other side of this doctrine: the US had no wish to be entangled in Europe's troubles. But as the US developed into a major global power this disengagement was no longer possible. In two world wars in the twentieth century American military intervention was decisive, and with the onset of the Cold War, designed to contain the Soviet Union after 1945, it was prepared to intervene wherever it saw the need. However, subsequent action in Korea from 1950 to 1953, and in Vietnam from 1964 to 1975, both with heavy loss of US lives, has made the nation less enthusiastic about overseas military commitments, and the risks and casualties of policing trouble spots (Haiti, Somalia, the Persian Gulf) are often unpopular at home. Generally the American mood is inward-looking, more concerned with domestic than with foreign affairs.

Township and skislope, Aspen.

People and culture

The US is a prosperous, industrial, capitalistic democracy, in which anyone with training and skills who is prepared to assimilate can usually find a place. It is the most open multicultural society on earth, which is the main reason why there are so many people from other countries wanting to live here. In addition to its huge numbers of legal immigrants (the US still has the highest legal immigration level of any country in the world) illegal entry is estimated to bring in up to one million people a year.

Flat Iron Building, New York City.

The descendants of the original Native American inhabitants are a small but not insignificant element of the population. People arriving from overseas were at first mainly English, and with those of Scots and Irish descent dominated all other arrivals from the other side of the Atlantic until the middle of the nineteenth century. During this period the only other major ethnic group to arrive were African slaves imported to work the plantations in the South. After the Civil War, however, mass immigration was encouraged, and a flood of migrants arrived from Italy, Scandinavia, Germany, the Balkans, and various troubled parts of Eastern Europe, including Russia. Many were Jews fleeing poverty and pogroms. In the 60 years up until 1920, 30 million people arrived, radically changing the ethnic composition of the country. Although there were national concentrations in specific neighborhoods (such as Littlc Italy in New York) the ideal of assimilation ensured that by the middle of the twentieth century most new arrivals, or their children, had come to share the benefits of other citizens. More

Mardi Gras, New Orleans.

Timeline United States of America

35,000–12,000 BP Modern humans *Homo sapiens sapiens* migrate to North America across Bering Strait land bridge and spread south

13,000 BP Settlements appear from south of Canadian border to Mexico; stone spearpoints in use in New Mexico

3500 BC Native Americans hunt bison; by 2500 BC squash, goosefoot, and sunflowers (seeds used as winter food) cultivated

1000 BC The Adena in eastern North America build ceremonial mounds; agriculture established in southwest

300 BC Hohokam, Mogollon, and Anasazi people inhabit the south and southwest; Anasazi build villages at Chaco, New Mexico

200 BC Hopewell culture takes over from Adena; Hopewell become first farmers in eastern North America (until AD 500)

AD 700 St… period in … Native Am… Hopi, Zuni… tribes live built main…

790 Vikin… coasts of North Am… next 100 … forming se… Greenland…

1776 USA founded, with American colonies adopting Declaration of Independence. Population 3 million

1804 Lewis and Clark explore the Missouri River then cross Rocky Mts and reach the Pacific near mouth of Columbia River

1805 The Louisiana Purchase acquires a large area of south from France, almost doubling the land area of the USA

1848 Califo… rush. Withi… 90,000 peo… San Francis… east, and o… travel to di…

1861–6… between… (Confede… northe… states; all sla… in Confeder…

Lettuce pickers, Salinas, California.

River and patchwork paddocks, Central Valley, California.

recently there has been an influx of Japanese, Chinese, Filipinos, Cubans, Vienamese, Koreans, and large numbers of Mexicans and Central Americans. In some places, Puerto Rican, Cuban, and Mexican groups provide a strongly Hispanic cultural orientation.

One group of long-term residents did not enjoy full participation in American life. These were the African-Americans descended from the slaves, who became increasingly concentrated in the cities. Long after the Civil War, systematic discrimination barred them from jobs, and from equal access to housing, commercial premises, public facilities, and education—even forcing them to sit at the back of the bus in the old slave states. As a result of agitation and affirmative action, the second half of the twentieth century saw the legal rights of African-Americans secured. What remains, however, are inequalities which law alone seems unable to resolve. In the cities, many African-Americans remain part of an underclass plagued by unemployment, drug addiction, crime, and unstable family life.

Economy and resources

The US economy is the largest among the industrial nations, possessing an invaluable combination of skilled

1492 Columbus reaches America while searching for route to Orient; later, French and English establish fur trading posts in Canada

1539 Hernando de Soto reaches Florida and travels up the Mississippi; following year Coronado explores southwest

1584 Sir Walter Raleigh claims Virginia for England, but no permanent settlement created until founding of Jamestown in 1607

1619 First slaves shipped from West Africa to USA

1869 World's first transcontinental railroad is completed when the Union Pacific line and Central Pacific line link up

1908 Ford launches Model T, a mass market automobile. It transforms US industry and economy; 15.5 million sold in 19 years

1917 USA enters First World War on the side of Allies

1920 More Americans now living in industrial cities than on the land; women are given the vote in all elections

1929 Wall Street Crash ruins many investors and affects industry and farming; millions lose jobs in the Depression

1936 Boulder Dam on Colorado River completed impounding Lake Mead; renamed Hoover Dam (1947)

1941 USA joins Allies in Second World War after Japan bombs Pearl Harbor; war ends 1945 after USA drops atomic bombs on Japan

1969 Apollo 11 mission opens a new chapter in space exploration by landing three astronauts on Moon

1992 Hurricane Andrew strikes Florida and Louisiana causing $25 billion damage and the loss of more than 50 lives

and unskilled labor and natural resources. Internationally, it is the most powerful, diverse, and scientifically advanced. With the early application of both research and technology, agriculture developed into a highly mechanized industry for food production and processing, with a distinct zonal pattern across the country. Dairy farming predominates in a broad belt from New England to Minnesota. Further west, where the climate is drier, wheat is grown. The corn (maize) belt, highly productive land which was once prairie and forest, consists of the maize-growing eastern and central states from Ohio to Nebraska. Maize is mainly used for feeding to cattle and pigs. In the warmer southern states where cotton and tobacco were grown—the old "cotton belt"—a variety of other crops are now also cultivated, from vegetables to fruit and peanuts. There has been a strong tendency for farming to move from small to large-scale operations and from labor-intensive to mechanized. Although agriculture's share of gross domestic product is only 2 percent, the US remains a leading producer of meat, dairy foods, soy beans, maize, oats, wheat, barley, cotton, sugar, and forest products.

Despite 20 years of strong competition from Japan and various other Asian economies, the giant US economy

Chinatown, San Francisco.

Golden Gate Bridge, San Francisco.

U

The famous Empire State Building in New York City.

remained resurgent throughout the 1990s. One reason for its success may be the greater flexibility of US capitalist enterprise when compared with either Asia or Western Europe. A labor market responsive to changing demands is another factor, and over the last 20 years there has been a huge shift in employment from manufacturing to services. US unemployment remains today one of the lowest in all the major industrialized states. But the main reason for the health of the economy is probably its dynamic technological inventiveness. In every field, US firms are at or near the frontier of technological advance. This is especially so in computers, medical equipment, and aerospace. The advantages of this onrush of technology are obvious. But there are major social costs as well. A so-called two-tier labor market has evolved in which those at the bottom lack enough skills and education to compete, failing to get pay rises, health insurance cover, and other benefits.

Despite the economy's basic good health, marked by low inflation and low unemployment, debate continues on how a number of its continuing problems should be addressed. These include low rates of saving, inadequate investment in infrastructure, the rising medical costs of an ageing population, large budget and trade deficits, and the stagnation of family income in the lower economic groups.

Crater of Haleakala Volcano on Maui—world's largest dormant volcano, Hawaii, United States of America.

Uruguay

Uruguay, the second-smallest country in South America, lies northeast of Argentina on the estuary of the River Plate (Río de la Plata). Controlled for 150 years alternately by the Portuguese and the Spanish, Uruguay finally gained independence in 1828, after which came 40 years of civil war. When peace was secured, waves of immigrants flocked to Uruguay from Spain and Italy, the cattle industry and meat exports expanded, investment poured in, and the country prospered. It may even have prospered too much: many benefits and welfare provisions were introduced in the days of prosperity which in poorer times have proved difficult to pay for. An urban guerrilla movement known as the Tupamaros paralyzed the cities during the 1960s, provoking a repressive military crackdown and dictatorship. Democracy was restored in 1984.

Most of Uruguay is temperate and mild: it never snows and frosts are rare, though the *pampero*, a wind coming off the pampas to the south, can be cold and violent. Most of the country is covered with rich grasslands, a continuation of the Argentine pampas, where cattle and sheep are raised. Although 90 percent of Uruguay's land is suitable for cultivation, only around 10 percent is currently used for agriculture, but this is enough to ensure that the country is largely self-sufficient in food. Uruguay's main river is the Negro, flowing east–west across the center of the country. On either side of the

View across rooftops of Uruguayan city to sea.

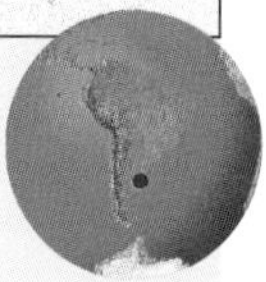

Uruguay

Official name Eastern Republic of Uruguay
Form of government Republic with two legislative bodies (Senate and Chamber of Deputies)
Capital Montevideo
Area 176,220 sq km (68,038 sq miles)
Time zone GMT – 3 hours
Population 3,308,583
Projected population 2005 3,458,798
Population density 18.8 per sq km (48.7 per sq mile)
Life expectancy 75.8
Infant mortality (per 1,000) 13.5
Official language Spanish
Literacy rate 97.1%
Religions Roman Catholic 66%, Protestant 2%, Jewish 2%, unaffiliated 30%
Ethnic groups European 88%, mixed indigenous–European 8%, African 4%
Currency Uruguayan peso
Economy Services 67%, industry 18%, agriculture 15%
GNP per capita US$5,170
Climate Temperate, with warm summers and mild winters
Highest point Cerro Catedral 513 m (1,683 ft)
Map reference Page 857

Negro the land rises to a plateau that marks the southern limits of the Brazilian Highlands. Water from the uplands feeds down the Negro into a large artificial lake, Lake Rincón del Bonete, which is used for hydroelectric power.

Uruguay's rural economy is based on sheep and cattle raising, and its industries are mainly based on animal products: meat processing, leather, and wool and textile manufacturing. The country is the second largest wool exporter in the world. But Uruguay is not rich in other resources: it has no petroleum or minerals except for agate, amethyst, gold deposits, and small quantities of iron ore. It is entirely dependent on imported oil. The ample supplies of hydroelectricity that are available help to offset this disadvantage, and only governmental regulatory constraints prevent industrial expansion.

Uruguay is at present undergoing a program of modernization, the most prominent issue being the privatization of the extremely large state sector (25 percent of the country's employees are currently civil servants) inherited from its more prosperous past. Tourism is booming, consisting mainly of visitors to Montevideo.

Uzbekistan

UZBEKISTAN

OFFICIAL NAME Republic of Uzbekistan
FORM OF GOVERNMENT Republic with single legislative body (Supreme Assembly)
CAPITAL Toshkent (Tashkent)
AREA 447,400 sq km (172,741 sq miles)

Uzbekistan stretches from the shrinking Aral Sea to the heights of the western Pamirs. Its main frontiers are with Kazakhstan to the north and Turkmenistan to the south. The Uzbek people are of Turkic origin and seem to have taken their name from the Mongol Öz Beg Khan (AD 1313–40), who may also have converted them to Islam. In the fifteenth century they moved south into their present land. The Muslim cities of Samarqand and Bukhoro are in Uzbekistan, Bukhoro being a major religious center. Muslims unable to visit Mecca can become *hajis* by visiting Bukhoro seven times instead. In the former USSR the territory was the Uzbek Soviet Socialist Republic, Uzbek leaders suffering much during Stalin's purges. In 1991 Uzbekistan became independent and is today ruled by the old communist elite as a de facto one-party state. The most populous of the Central Asian republics, Uzbekistan also has the greatest variety of ethnic groups. This is often a source of conflict. The

Turkish-speaking Uzbeks clash with the Farsi-speaking Tajiks, and the Meskhetian Turks (deported from Georgia to Central Asia by Stalin) clash with the Uzbeks in the Fergana Valley. Hundreds died during fighting between the latter groups in 1989 and 1990.

The middle region of Uzbekistan consists of the desert plains of the Kyzyl Kum (Peski Kyzylkum). While some of this area supports herders with cattle and sheep, it is today more important for its oil and gas reserves. To the west is the river delta formed where the Syrdar'ya (Oxus) enters the Aral Sea, while the Ustyurt Plateau lies in the extreme northwest. East of the Kyzyl Kum, beyond the capital of Toshkent and the Chatkal Mountains, is a spur jutting into Kyrgyzstan. This contains a large part of the fertile Fergana Basin. Uzbekistan is the world's fourth-largest cotton producer, and the Fergana Valley bears the environmental scars of the fertilizers and pesticides which helped to bring this about.

Although it grows large quantities of cotton, Uzbekistan is unable to produce enough grain for its own needs, importing it from Russia, Kazakhstan, and the United States. A rethinking of the Soviet-style economy has yet to take place.

As well as one of the world's largest gold mines, at Murantau, Uzbekistan has large deposits of natural gas, petroleum, coal, and uranium. Gas is currently used domestically, but it could become a major export. After 1991 the government tried to strengthen the economy with subsidies and tight price controls. Inflation rose to 1,500 percent at one point and in 1995 food rationing had to be introduced. At present, efforts are being made to tighten monetary policies, expand privatization, and to reduce the state's role in the economy, but so far there have been few serious structural changes.

Seventeen-century Tila Kala Marasa, Samarqand, Uzbekistan.

Time zone GMT + 6 hours
Population 24,102,473
Projected population 2005 26,111,101
Population density 53.9 per sq km (139.6 per sq mile)
Life expectancy 63.9
Infant mortality (per 1,000) 71.6
Official language Uzbek
Other languages Russian, Tajik
Literacy rate 97.2%
Religions Muslim 88% (mostly Sunnis), Eastern Orthodox 9%, other 3%
Ethnic groups Uzbek 71.5%, Russian 8.3%, Tajik 4.7%, Kazak 4%, Tatar 2.5%, other 9%
Currency Som
Economy Agriculture 43%, services 35%, industry 22%
GNP per capita US$970
Climate Mainly arid, with cold winters and long, hot summers
Highest point Adelunga Toghi 4,299 m (14,105 ft)
Map reference Pages 758–9

View from Ayaz Kala of remains of ancient fortifications (settlement behind), Uzbekistan.

U

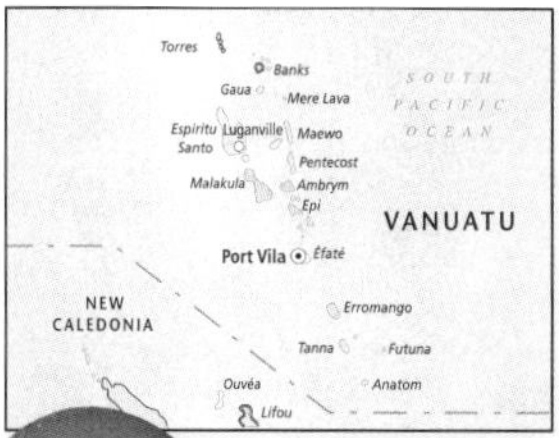

VANUATU

OFFICIAL NAME Republic of Vanuatu
FORM OF GOVERNMENT Republic with single legislative body (Parliament)
CAPITAL Port Vila
AREA 14,760 sq km (5,699 sq miles)
TIME ZONE GMT + 11 hours
POPULATION 189,036
PROJECTED POPULATION 2005 211,781
POPULATION DENSITY 12.8 per sq km (33.1 per sq mile)
LIFE EXPECTANCY 61.4
INFANT MORTALITY (PER 1,000) 59.6
OFFICIAL LANGUAGES English, French
OTHER LANGUAGE Bislama, 105 indigenous languages
LITERACY RATE 64%
RELIGIONS Presbyterian 36.7%, Anglican 15%, Catholic 15%, indigenous beliefs 7.6%, Seventh-Day Adventist 6.2%, Church of Christ 3.8%, other 15.7%
ETHNIC GROUPS Melanesian 94%, French 4%, other (including Vietnamese, Chinese, Pacific Islanders) 2%
CURRENCY Vatu
ECONOMY Agriculture 75%, services 22%, industry 3%
GNP PER CAPITA US$1,200
CLIMATE Tropical, moderated by trade winds
HIGHEST POINT Mt Tabwemasana 1,879 m (6,158 ft)
MAP REFERENCE Pages 722, 727

Vanuatu

Vanuatu is an archipelago in the South Pacific consisting of 13 large islands and 70 islets. Part of Melanesia, it lies northeast of New Caledonia and west of Fiji. Inhabited since 5000 BC, it was first visited by Europeans when the Portuguese arrived in 1606. After Captain Cook explored the islands in 1774 he named them the New Hebrides, and they were jointly administered by France and Britain from 1887.

In the late 1800s labor recruiters inveigled and sometimes kidnapped islanders for work on sugar plantations in Australia and Fiji. Aside from this, the islands remained isolated until the Second World War, when Espíritu Santo and Port Vila became major United States military bases in the Pacific. In 1980 the archipelago became independent under the name Vanuatu. Since then, after surviving a secession attempt by a Francophone movement on the island of Espíritu Santo, the country has had a volatile but mostly democratic political life. Vanuatu is populated almost entirely by ethnic Melanesians speaking 105 distinct languages—the world's highest per capita density of language forms. The lingua franca is a form of pidgin known as Bislama.

Most of the islands are mountainous and volcanic in origin, with coral beaches and offshore reefs. The interior is forested, with limited land for coastal cultivation. Some 75 percent of the people live by subsistence farming, growing taro, yams, sweet potatoes, bananas, and cassava for food, as well as cash crops such as coconuts, cocoa, and coffee. Fishing is also important. Unlike most South Pacific islands, beef raising is of economic significance, livestock numbering some 130,000 head of cattle. Meat canning is an industry. Frozen beef and fish are exported. Other exports include copra, shells, coffee, and cocoa. Mineral deposits are negligible.

Recently the government has emphasized tourist development (tourism is now the second largest earner of foreign exchange after copra), offshore banking, and foreign investment, advertising Vanuatu's potential as a finance center and tax haven. There is a "flag of convenience" shipping registry of some 60 ships from 20 countries. Vanuatu is one of many low-lying islands in the Pacific that are currently facing the threat of rising sea levels due to the impact of global greenhouse warming.

Fruit and vegetables for sale at Port Vila Market, Vanuatu.

Vatican City

Occupying a hill in the city of Rome on the western bank of the Tiber, and including as well the pope's residence at Castel Gandolfo, southeast of Rome, and ten churches throughout Rome, Vatican City is the world's smallest state, and probably its most homogeneous. Its population is 100 percent Catholic, and it is the home of the pope, the spiritual head of the Roman Catholic Church, and several hundred clergy and Catholic lay people, all employees of the Vatican.

Vatican City is all that remains of the former Papal States, which from the fourteenth to the nineteenth centuries expanded from a palace on the present site to cover an area of almost 45,000 sq km (17,000 sq miles). During the *Risorgimento* (resurrection), which resulted in the unification of Italy in the 1860s, most of this area was absorbed into the new Italian state. From 1870 until 1929, neither the Church nor the successive Italian governments recognized each other's sovereignty over the area, which

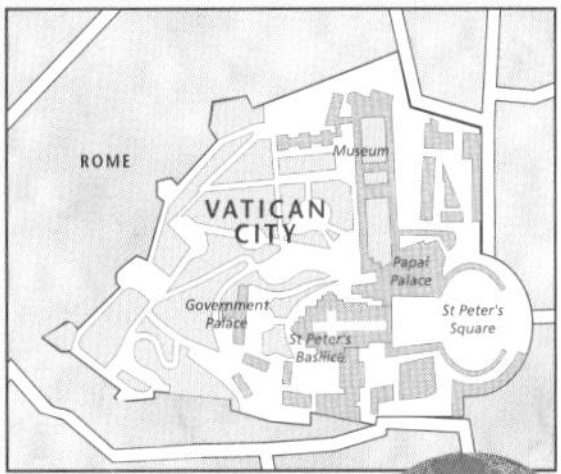

Vatican City

Official name Vatican City State (Holy See)
Form of government Monarchical–sacerdotal state with single legislative body (Pontifical Commission)
Capital Vatican City

(continues)

VATICAN CITY *(continued)*

AREA 0.44 sq km (0.16 sq miles)
TIME ZONE GMT + 1 hour
POPULATION 1,000
POPULATION DENSITY 2,272.7 per sq km (5,886.3 per sq mile)
OFFICIAL LANGUAGES Italian, Latin
RELIGION Roman Catholic
ETHNIC GROUPS Predominantly Italian; some Swiss
CURRENCY Vatican lira
ECONOMY Services 100%
CLIMATE Temperate, with mild winters and hot summers
HIGHEST POINT Unnamed location 75 m (246 ft)
MAP REFERENCE Page 779

the Church refused to relinquish to the state. In 1929, however, Pope Leo XI and Mussolini concluded an agreement—the Lateran Treaty—under which the independence of the Vatican City State, and the pope's temporal sovereignty over it, was recognized in return for the Church's recognition of the kingdom of Italy. Under this treaty, Catholicism was also recognized as the state religion of Italy. This provision, along with a number of other privileges enjoyed by the Church in Italy, was removed under a subsequent Church–state agreement, known as a "concordat," signed in 1984. Vatican City, which now has diplomatic relations with more than 100 countries, has the pope as head of state, while responsibility

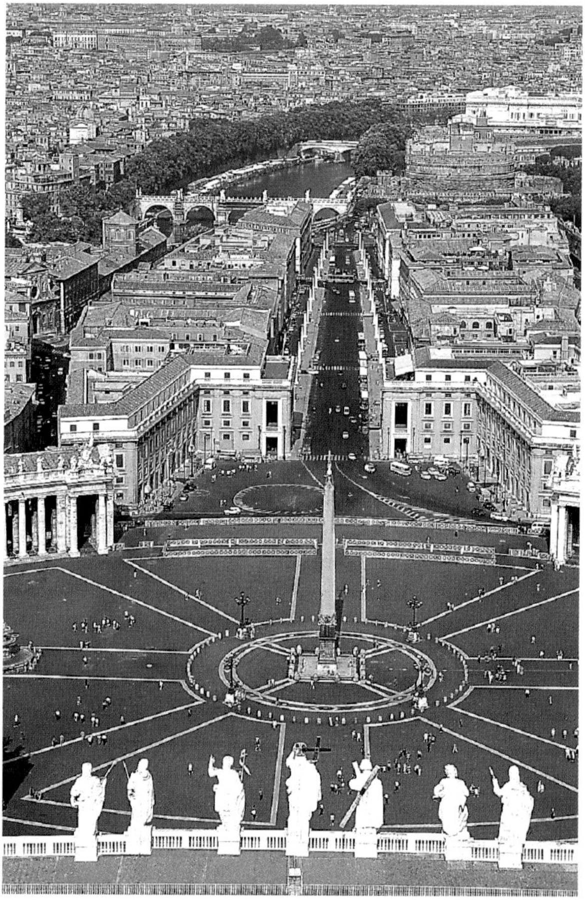

St Peter's Square in Vatican City, from the roof of the Basilica.

for administration of the area is vested in a Commission of Cardinals. The roles of secretary of state, chief of staff, and foreign minister are filled by senior members of the clergy.

Surrounded by medieval walls, Vatican City contains the huge St Peter's Basilica, built between 1506 and 1626 by a number of architects, including Michelangelo and Bernini. Pilgrims come to visit the Basilica in vast numbers throughout the year, but particularly to celebrate Christmas and Easter. Visitors also come to see the richly endowed Vatican Museums, which include the renowned Sistine Chapel (the personal chapel of the popes) in the Vatican Palace. Parklands cover most of Vatican City.

Vatican City has its own radio station, publishes a daily newspaper, and issues its own stamps and coins. It also has an army—the 100-strong Swiss Guard—which is responsible for maintaining security. Vatican state finances depend on voluntary contributions, interest on extensive investments, and on the income derived from millions of tourists.

Venezuela

Venezuela is on the north coast of South America. When the first Spaniards arrived in 1499 they named it "New Venice" because the Indian stilt houses built in the water of Lake Maracaibo reminded them of the Italian city. The famous liberator Simon Bolivar was a Venezuelan general, the military campaign he led resulting in the country becoming independent in 1821. For the next century Venezuela's economy was largely based on agriculture, but in the 1920s it took a new direction with the development of a petroleum industry. In the last 80 years great wealth (unevenly shared) followed by industrialization have produced one of Latin America's most urbanized societies. Out of every 20 Venezuelans, 17 are city-dwellers, and migration from the countryside has left much of the interior depopulated.

Confident that its oil revenues would never end, the Venezuelan government expanded the economic role of the state, even buying hotels. Falling oil prices in the early 1980s produced a fiscal crisis, and in 1991 a program of cutbacks and austerity measures triggered street riots in

VENEZUELA

OFFICIAL NAME Republic of Venezuela
FORM OF GOVERNMENT Federal republic with two legislative bodies (Senate and Chamber of Deputies)
CAPITAL Caracas
AREA 912,050 sq km (352,142 sq miles)
TIME ZONE GMT – 4 hours

(continues)

VENEZUELA *(continued)*

POPULATION 23,203,466
PROJECTED POPULATION 2005 25,504,115
POPULATION DENSITY 25.4 per sq km (65.8 per sq mile)
LIFE EXPECTANCY 73
INFANT MORTALITY (PER 1,000) 26.5
OFFICIAL LANGUAGE Spanish
OTHER LANGUAGES Indigenous languages
LITERACY RATE 91%
RELIGIONS Roman Catholic 96%, Protestant 2%, other 2%
ETHNIC GROUPS Mixed indigenous–European 67%, European 21%, African 10%, indigenous 2%
CURRENCY Bolívar
ECONOMY Services 63%, industry 25%, agriculture 12%
GNP PER CAPITA US$3,020
CLIMATE Tropical, with dry season December–April; cooler in highlands
HIGHEST POINT Pico Bolívar 5,007 m (16,427 ft)
MAP REFERENCE Pages 848–9

which hundreds died. Two attempted coups took place during 1992. Since that time there has been a concerted effort to achieve economic diversification and to cut back the state sector.

The hot lowlands surrounding Lake Maracaibo in the far northwest comprise one of the areas of greatest population density. In this region abundant electricity from oil-fired generators provides power for light industry: food processing, pharmaceuticals, electrical equipment, and machinery. A spur of the northern Andes divides the Maracaibo Basin from the drainage system of the Orinoco to the east. Here are the lowland plains of the Llanos, savanna country used for cattle grazing. Much of the Llanos floods during the summer rains, especially in the west, though it is dry for the rest of the year. To the south is the vast granite plateau of the Guiana Highlands, and the highest waterfall in the world—the Angel Falls (979 m; 3,212 ft).

Despite fluctuations in oil prices, petroleum continues to provide over 70 percent of Venezuela's export earnings and 45 percent of government revenue. Other minerals exported include iron ore, gold, and diamonds. The main cash crops are coffee, sugarcane, and tobacco; food crops include bananas, sorghum, and maize. Only 5 percent of arable land is cultivated, and agriculture supplies little more than 70 percent of the country's needs. During the 1990s, economic reforms proposed by the IMF have been resisted as "economic totalitarianism" by the populist president, who has responded to economic rationalism by defending exchange controls and other regulatory measures.

Hatcha Falls, Venezuela.

Vietnam

Vietnam is located on the eastern side of the Indochinese Peninsula. A long, narrow strip of country lying between two major river systems, Vietnam bears the scars of one of the longest and most devastating wars of the second half of the twentieth century. Historically, it was for more than a thousand years under Chinese domination, achieving a degree of independence in AD 939. Christian missionary activity began in the seventeenth century and it was a French colony from 1883. During the Second World War a communist-led resistance movement fought the Japanese, and later fought the returning French, defeating them decisively in 1954. The country was divided into two mutually hostile regimes, with a communist government in the north and a French- and later US-backed government in the south. The north initiated 20 years of insurgency and then full-scale war (the north backed by the USSR, the south by the USA with at one stage 500,000 troops), eventually winning in 1975 and establishing the Socialist Republic of Vietnam.

About 66 percent of Vietnam's land area is dominated by the heavily forested terrain of the Annam Highlands (or Chaîne Annamitique). The crest of this range mostly follows the western border with Laos in the north and Cambodia to the south. At either end of the country are intensively cultivated and densely populated river deltas—the Red River Delta in the north, which is also fed by waters from the valley of the Da, and the Mekong Delta in the south. Both are major rice-growing areas. Rice is the main staple and export crop, Vietnam being the world's third-largest exporter. Other food crops include sweet

Vietnamese farmers working in the rice fields.

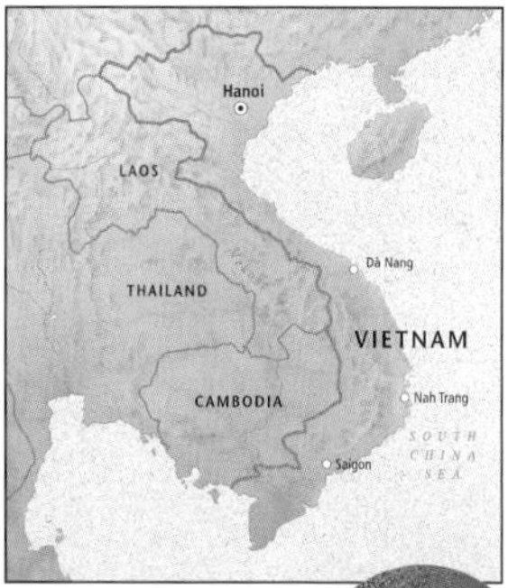

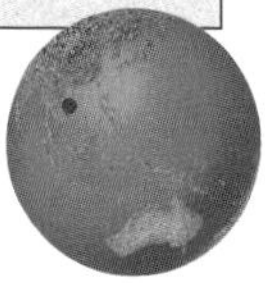

Vietnam

Official name Socialist Republic of Vietnam
Form of government Communist state with single legislative body (National Assembly)
Capital Hanoi
Area 329,560 sq km (127,243 sq miles)
Time zone GMT + 7 hours
Population 77,311,210
Projected population 2005 83,441,920
Population density 234.6 per sq km (607.6 per sq mile)
Life expectancy 68.1
Infant mortality (per 1,000) 34.8
Official language Vietnamese
Other languages French, Chinese, English, Khmer, indigenous languages
Literacy rate 64%
Religions Buddhist 60%, Roman Catholic 7%, Taoist, Islam and indigenous beliefs 33%
Ethnic groups Vietnamese 85%–90%, Chinese 3%, other 7–12%
Currency Dong
Economy Agriculture 65%, industry and services 35%
GNP per capita US$240
Climate Tropical in south, subtropical in north; wet season May to October
Highest point Fan Si Pan 3,143 m (10,312 ft)
Map reference Page 739

Vietnamese shrine.

Seaside village and mountain at Halong Bay.

A fisherman casting his net from a basket boat.

potato and cassava. On the mountain slopes of the Annam Highlands tea, coffee, and rubber plantations have been established. Most mineral resources are located in the north and include anthracite and lignite. Coal is the main export item and is the principal energy source.

After ten years during which a typical communist command economy was imposed, along with collectivized agriculture, the government changed direction. In 1986 the more liberal *doi moi* (renovation) policy was introduced. Investment was welcomed from outside, and during the period 1990 to 1995 real growth averaged more than 8 percent annually. Foreign capital contributed to a boom in commercial construction, and there was strong growth in services and industrial output. Crude oil remains the country's largest single export, now amounting to a quarter of exports overall, slightly more than manufactures. But progress is handicapped by a continuing strong commitment to state direction and bureaucratic controls. Banking reform is needed and administrative and legal barriers delay investment. There is no evidence of a relaxation of the political grip of the Communist Party to match the attempted economic liberalization: in 1991 open anti-communist dissent was made a criminal offence.

Sunset on rice fields, Vietnam.

Indochina

The term Indochina indicates that cultural influences from India and China are intermingled throughout this region. Also once known as French Indochina, it consists of the three states of Vietnam, Laos, and Cambodia, all of which were formerly associated with France in a political group known as the French Union. Despite the fact that the French exercised political control over their countries from the late nineteenth century, the Vietnamese, Cambodian, and Laotian royal houses continued to exercise wide authority. The Japanese occupied Indochina during the Second World War, but interfered little in the existing colonial arrangements; only after 1945 did the military turmoil begin which was to convulse the region.

In 1945, following the withdrawal of the Japanese, the Vietnamese communist nationalist leader Ho Chi Minh proclaimed the Democratic Republic of Vietnam. The returning French attempted to hold their colonial possession together, but soon the protracted guerrilla struggle that became known as the First Indochina War broke out. The forces in the North received support from the Chinese. In 1954 after the siege of Dien Bien Phu, a ceasefire was agreed to by both France and China. This resulted in two independent states: North Vietnam and South Vietnam, which were divided by the 17th parallel.

During the 1960s the attempt of North Vietnamese forces to infiltrate and subvert the south led to the Second Indochina War, also know as the Vietnam War. This period saw increasing United States military involvement in the defense of South Vietnam. The United States gave strong support to the South Vietnamese government and in 1961 the US commenced sending military advisers.

The US actively entered the Viernam War in 1964. Fighting continued until the Paris ceasefire of 1973, and Saigon was ultimately captured by the North Vietnmese in 1975.

Between 1954 and 1975 about 1,000,000 North Vietnamese soliders, 200,000 South Vietnamese soldiers and 500,000 civilians were killed. Between 1961 and 1975 about 56,500 US soldiers were killed. In 1976 the Socialist Republic of Vietnam was established. This period also saw the rise and fall of the Khmer Rouge regime in Cambodia, and was followed by a Vietnamese invasion of Cambodia in 1978. Before withdrawing from Cambodia, Vietnam installed in power the Communist Khmer People's Revolutionary Party (now the Cambodian People's Party) whose domination of the political system, reinforced by a violent coup in 1997, is a source of widespread discontent.

Today several boundary disputes exist between the three countries of Indochina. In addition to Vietnam's claims to various islands in the South China Sea, sections of the boundary between Cambodia and Vietnam are in dispute, and the maritime boundary between these countries is not defined. A boundary dispute also exists between Laos and Thailand.

Women at a market in Hanoi.

Indochina conflicts

1946 Vietnam: Return of French after Second World War. Outbreak of First Indochina War.

1954 Vietnam: Defeat of French at Dien Bien Phu. Division of Vietnam into North supported by USSR and South supported by USA.

1960 Vietnam: Communists in South initiate guerrilla war as Viet Cong.

1961 Vietnam: USA sends "military advisers" to South Vietnam to fight Viet Cong.

1964 US Congress approves war with Vietnam. US bombs Vietnamese sanctuaries in Laos, plus Ho Chi Minh Trail—north–south supply route.

1965 Vietnam: Arrival of first US combat troops. Start of intense US bombing of North which continues until 1968.

1970 Right-wing coup in Cambodia deposes Prince Sihanouk. In exile Sihanouk forms movement backed by communist Khmer Rouge.

1974 Cambodia: Sihanouk and Khmer Rouge capture Phnom Penh. Thousands die as revolutionary programs were enforced.

1975 Vietnam: Fall of Saigon. North Vietnamese and Viet Cong take power in South. Laos: Communist Pathet Lao seize power.

1976 Cambodia: Sihanouk resigns—all the power held by Pol Pot, leader of the Khmer Rouge.

1978 Vietnam invades Cambodia.

1979 Vietnam captures Phnom Penh. Pol Pot flees, and is held responsible for more than 2 million deaths.

1989 Vietnamese troops leave Cambodia.

1991 Cambodia: Sihanouk again head of state. Flight of Khmer Rouge officials.

1992 Vietnam: Foreign investment permitted; Communist Party monopoly unchanged.

1993 Cambodia: UN-supervized elections. Departure of UN peace mission.

1995 Normalization of the US–Vietnam diplomatic relations.

1997 Cambodia: Violent coup restores power to communists under Hun Sen.

1998 Cambodia: Pol Pot dies.

Marble Mountain, Da Nang, Vietnam.

Virgin Islands of the United States

The Virgin Islands of the United States consist of 68 hilly volcanic islands east of Puerto Rico in the Caribbean. They are on a key shipping lane and were bought from Denmark by the United States of America in 1917 to protect the approaches to the Panama Canal.

They contain, on St Croix, one of the world's largest oil refineries but tourism is still the main economic activity, accounting for over 70 percent of the island's gross domestic product and 70 percent of employment. Manufacturing includes textiles, pharmaceuticals, electronics, and watch assembly. Business and financial services are also of growing importance. Agriculture is limited, most food being imported.

Virgin Islands of the United States

Official name Virgin Islands of the United States
Form of government Unincorporated territory of the United States
Capital Charlotte Amalie
Area 352 sq km (136 sq miles)
Time zone GMT + 7 hours
Population 119,555
Life expectancy 78.5
Infant mortality (per 1,000) 9.4
Currency US dollar
Economy Tourism, light industry, agriculture
Climate Subtropical; wet season May to November
Map reference Page 837

The Virgin Islands of the United States.

V

W

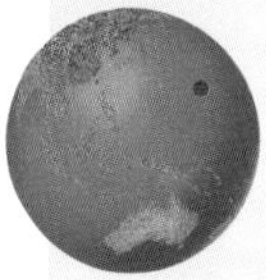

Wake Island

Official name Wake Island
Form of government Unincorporated territory of the USA
Capital None; administered from Washington DC
Area 6.5 sq km (2.5 sq miles)
Time zone GMT – 10 hours
Population No permanent population
Economy US military base
Climate Tropical
Map reference Page 724

Wake Island

Wake Island is located in the North Pacific about two-thirds of the way between Hawaii and the Northern Mariana Islands. It consists of three tiny coral islets linked by causeways around a lagoon. The islets are built on fragments of the rim of an extinct underwater volcano, the lagoon being the former crater. With no indigenous inhabitants or economic activity, the 300 or so US military personnel stationed on Wake Island provide help in the case of emergency landings by aircraft on transpacific flights.

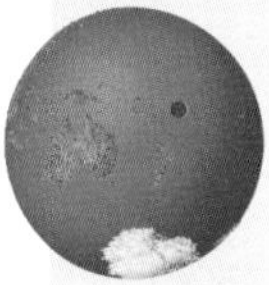

Wallis and Futuna Islands

Official name Territory of the Wallis and Futuna Islands
Form of government Overseas territory of France
Capital Mata Utu
Area 274 sq km (106 sq miles)
Time zone GMT + 12 hours
Population 15,129
Currency CFP (Comptoirs Français du Pacifique) franc
Economy Agriculture, fishing
Climate Tropical, with wet season November to April
Map reference Page 725

Wallis and Futuna Islands

This group comprises three main islands—Futuna, Alofi and Wallis (Uvea)—and 20 islets, located west of Samoa and northeast of Fiji. They are of volcanic origin, with low hills rising to 765 m (2,510 ft) at Mt Singavi. All the main islands have fringing reefs. In the hot wet season from November to April 2,500–3,000 mm (100–120 in) of rain may fall. This rain, combined with deforestation (timber is used locally for fuel), has eroded the terrain of Futuna. The people live by subsistence farming. Exports are negligible and French aid is essential to the islands. First settled perhaps 2,000 years ago, and visited by the Dutch in 1616, the islands became a French protectorate in 1886. In a referendum on independence in 1959 they chose to become a French Overseas Territory. There is no independence movement.

The problems of coral bleaching

Coral reefs constitute one of the Earth's great diverse ecosystems. They are made of limestone formed by millions of tiny marine animals and can only live in tropical seas within a narrow range of physical and chemical conditions. Coral reefs generally form only when winter water temperatures exceed 18°C (64°F) and when light levels are high. Coral is found in the rock record in the form of fossils dating back to the Paleozoic Era. However, although coral has survived this long, it is not immune to the impact of human activities.

In recent years scientists have become interested in the apparent link between the death of large tracts of coral in the Pacific and Caribbean regions and global warming. The greenhouse effect—a result of changes in the amounts of carbon dioxide and other gases in the atmosphere since the industrial revolution—is the cause of global warming. Satellite data from the US National Oceanographic and Atmospheric Administration show a warming trend in sea-surface temperatures since 1982.

In some areas, such as along the Great Barrier Reef in Australia, a combination of higher than usual summer temperatures and the run-off from floods (which reduces salinity) appears to be damaging the coral. As the essential conditions required for the maintenance of a healthy reef system are disrupted, the coral formations turn white.

What will happen to coral reefs in the future? Are the bleaching episodes observed in recent years in so many tropical areas really due to global warming or are there other causes? Predictions that ocean surface temperatures in the tropics may rise by up to 5°C (41°F) in the twenty-first century are no longer considered fantasy. If this happens, it could greatly disturb even resilient ecosystems, such as coral reefs, and reduce the Earth's biodiversity as well as the ability of societies to live and work in these areas.

W

WEST BANK

OFFICIAL NAME West Bank
FORM OF GOVERNMENT Disputed by Israel and Palestinian National Authority; interim self-government administered by Palestinian Legislative Council
CAPITAL Jerusalem
AREA 5,860 sq km (2,263 sq miles)
TIME ZONE GMT + 2 hours
POPULATION 1,611,109
LIFE EXPECTANCY 72.8
INFANCY MORTALITY (PER 1,000) 25.2
CURRENCY Israeli shekel, Jordanian dinar
ECONOMY Industry 45%, services 34%, agriculture 21%
CLIMATE Temperate, with cool to mild winters and warm to hot summers
MAP REFERENCE Page 761

West Bank

Under a 1947 UN agreement this area on the west bank of the Jordan River was to become Palestinian when the State of Israel was formed. After the 1967 Six Day War Israel had control of a larger area than originally proposed. The building of Israeli settlements since then has been bitterly resented by the more than 95 percent Palestinian Arab population. The area depends on remittances from workers in Israel. Lack of jobs has also led to many working in the Gulf States. But the *intifada* in 1988 reduced the numbers working in Israel, and many West Bank workers were sent home following Palestinian support for Iraq during the Gulf War. Unemployment is about 30 percent. Under a 1993–95 Israeli–PLO declaration certain powers were to be transferred to a Palestinian Legislative Council, but ongoing Palestinian bombings in Israel, Israeli reprisals, and persistent Israeli settlement construction, make a speedy end to strife unlikely.

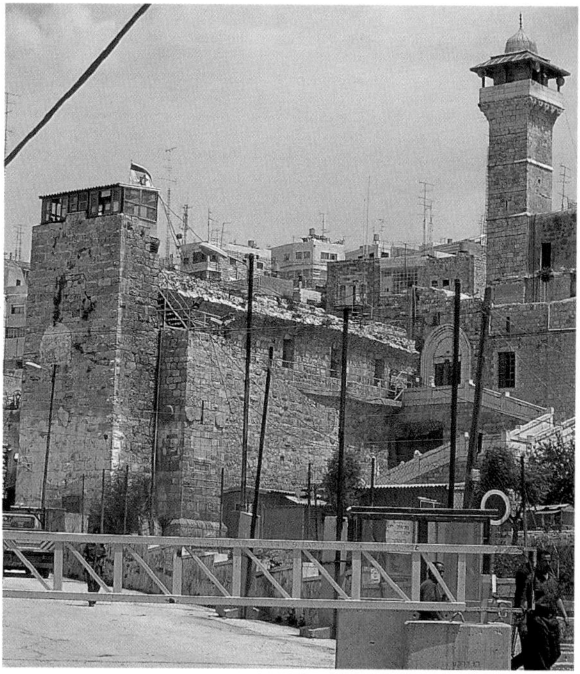

Area of confrontation between Jews and Palestinians in Hebron.

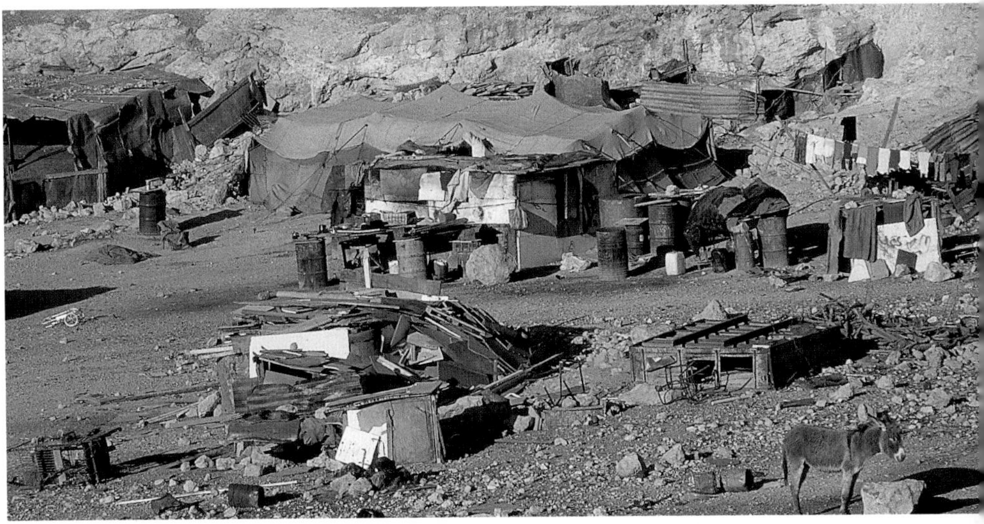

A semi-permanent home on the West Bank, an area still in dispute.

Western Sahara

Western Sahara is a former Spanish possession. South of Morocco (and more than half the size of Morocco itself) it consists of the desert country lying between Mauritania and the Atlantic coast. The terrain is largely flat, with large areas of rock and sand, rising to low mountains in the northeast and the south. Possessing the world's largest known deposits of phosphate rock, it is a contested region of uncertain sovereignty, though since 1975 it has been occupied and administered by Morocco. Most of the indigenous people are Sahrawis, a mixture of Berber and Arab. Since 1983 a war has been waged on their behalf by the Polisario Front (Popular Front for the Liberation of the Saguia el Hamra and Rio de Oro) and by 1991 more than 170,000 Sahrawi refugees had fled the country and were living in camps in Algeria. Guerrilla activities continue, despite a United Nations-monitored ceasefire in 1991. Trade and other activities are controlled by the Moroccan government and most food for the urban population must be imported. Western Sahara's standard of living is well below that of Morocco.

Western Sahara

Official name Western Sahara
Form of government Territory disputed by Morocco and Polisario Front independence movement
Capital None
Area 266,000 sq km (102,703 sq miles)
Time zone GMT
Population 239,333
Life expectancy 49.1
Infant mortality (per 1,000) 136.7
Currency Moroccan dirham
Economy Agriculture 50%; fishing 25%, mining 25%
Climate Mainly hot and arid
Map reference Page 800

W

Y,Z

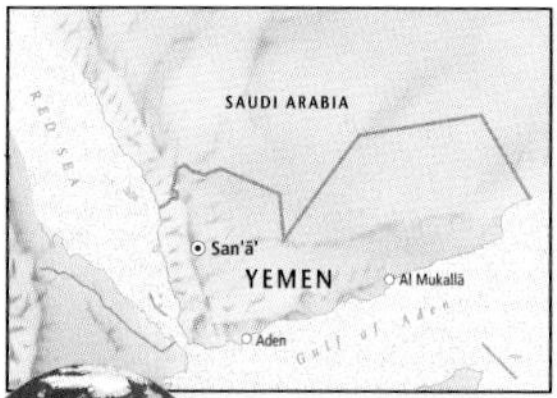

YEMEN

OFFICIAL NAME Republic of Yemen
FORM OF GOVERNMENT Republic with single legislative body (House of Representatives)
CAPITAL Şan'ā
AREA 527,970 sq km (203,849 sq miles)
TIME ZONE GMT + 3 hours
POPULATION 16,942,230
PROJECTED POPULATION 2005 20,806,931
POPULATION DENSITY 32.1 per sq km (83.1 per sq mile)
LIFE EXPECTANCY 60
INFANT MORTALITY (PER 1,000) 69.8
OFFICIAL LANGUAGE Arabic
OTHER LANGUAGE English
LITERACY RATE 41.1%
RELIGIONS Muslim: predominantly Sunni in the south, Shi'ite majority in the north
ETHNIC GROUPS Predominantly Arab; small mixed African–Arab and Indian minorities
CURRENCY Yemeni rial
ECONOMY Agriculture 63%, services 26%, industry 11%
GNP PER CAPITA US$260
CLIMATE Mainly arid; humid in southwest and cooler in western highlands; drier in east
HIGHEST POINT Jabal an-Nabi Shu'ayb 3,760 m (12,336 ft)
MAP REFERENCE Page 756

Y

Yemen

The Republic of Yemen occupies the southwestern corner of the Arabian Peninsula. Although its people have been Muslim for centuries it has deeply divided political allegiances and was two separate countries until 1990. North Yemen became independent of the Ottoman Empire in 1918, and in 1962 the Yemen Arab Republic (YAR) was proclaimed. The politics of the YAR tended to be both conservative and Islamic.

South Yemen came under British influence in 1839 and Aden became a vital port on the sea route to India. In 1967 the British withdrew from the region, and in 1969 the People's Democratic Republic of Yemen was proclaimed—the only Marxist state in the Arab world.

Since independence both north and south were mutually hostile but a turning point came with the Soviet collapse in 1989. Having lost USSR support, South Yemen sought political union with the YAR. In 1990 the two countries became the Republic of Yemen. In 1994 an assassination attempt on a northern politician led to civil war and the south's attempted secession. An uneasy peace prevails.

The narrow Red Sea coastal plain of Tihāma, extending south from Saudi Arabia, is generally barren: here, cotton-growing predominates. From the coast the land rises steeply to a comparatively fertile and well-cultivated

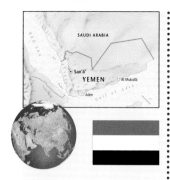

A Yemeni desert town.

interior. Around Şan'ā vines are cultivated and a variety of fruit crops are grown. The mountains overlooking Şan'ā rise to Jabal an-Nabi Shu'ayb, the highest point on the Arabian Peninsula. From these heights a number of rivers drain east toward the Ar Rub' al Khālī (Empty Quarter) where they disappear into the sands. Along the coast of the Gulf of Aden a sandy plain rises inland to the rugged Yemen Plateau, which to the north slopes down to the uninhabited wastes of the Rub al-Khali. In this region 10 percent of the mainly rural population is nomadic.

Despite having oil and gas reserves, Yemen is weak economically. In the Gulf War of 1990–91 Yemen supported Iraq. As punishment, Saudi Arabia and Kuwait expelled hundreds of thousands of Yemeni workers. Their remittances ceased and they became a huge burden on the economy. The government then abandoned agricultural subsidies and farmers stopped growing food and export crops. Instead they planted a shrub called qat—a stimulant used by Yemenis that has no export value.

High inflation and political conflicts make it difficult to implement long-range economic policies and reforms.

Women herd goats outside a small village near Dhamār in the Central Highlands of Yemen.

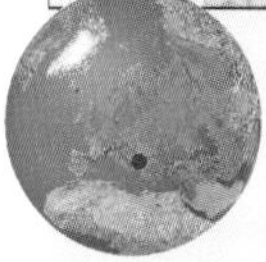

YUGOSLAVIA

OFFICIAL NAME Federal Republic of Yugoslavia
FORM OF GOVERNMENT Federal republic with two legislative bodies (Chamber of Republics and Chamber of Citizens)
CAPITAL Belgrade
AREA 102,350 sq km (39,517 sq miles)
TIME ZONE GMT + 1 hour
POPULATION 10,526,478
PROJECTED POPULATION 2005 10,626,538
POPULATION DENSITY 102.8 per sq km (266.2 per sq mile)
LIFE EXPECTANCY 73.5
INFANT MORTALITY (PER 1,000) 16.5
OFFICIAL LANGUAGE Serbian
OTHER LANGUAGE Albanian
LITERACY RATE 93%
RELIGIONS Eastern Orthodox 65%, Muslim 19%, Roman Catholic 4%, Protestant 1%, other 11%
ETHNIC GROUPS Serbian 63%, Albanian 14%, Montenegrin 6%, Hungarian 4%, other 13%
CURRENCY Yugoslav dinar
ECONOMY Services and agriculture 60%, industry 40%
GNP PER CAPITA US$1,500
CLIMATE Temperate, with cold winters and hot summers
HIGHEST POINT Daravica 2,656 m (8,714 ft)
MAP REFERENCE Page 780

Yugoslavia

At its southwestern edge, the "rump" republic of Yugoslavia has a toehold on the Adriatic Sea. Otherwise it is landlocked, sharing borders with seven countries. Moving from the west around to south clockwise, these are Bosnia and Herzegovina, Croatia, Hungary, Romania, Bulgaria, Macedonia, and Albania. Yugoslavia now comprises the republics of Serbia and Montenegro—all that remains of the former federation of Yugoslavia after four of its six constituent republics seceded in the early 1990s. Yugoslavia came into existence in December 1918 as a combination of formerly separate Balkan states, most of which had been under Austro-Hungarian control. Serbia had become independent in 1878, bringing to an end five centuries of almost continuous Ottoman rule.

The new country was originally called the Kingdom of Serbs, Croats, and Slovenes, but in 1929 the name Yugoslavia was adopted. During the Second World War Yugoslavia was invaded by Germany and the country was further devastated by civil war. More than a million Yugoslavs perished during this time. At the end of the war, a communist government, led by a Croat, Josip Broz, better known as Marshal Tito, came to power, but remained independent of the Soviet Union. After Tito died in 1980 ethnic tensions began to assert themselves, and in 1991 Croatia and Slovenia seceded, leading to four years of bitter ethnic-based conflict between Serbia and its neighbors. Ethnic conflict still simmers. A constitution adopted in 1992 decreed that democratic elections for the presidency and for two houses of parliament be held every five years.

In 1999, Serbia forced most of the population of the southern province of Kosovo—Muslim Albanians—to leave. Conflict continued between guerrilla forces of the Kosovo Liberation Army (KLO) and Serb forces as a meeting of NATO nations decided to launch air strikes against major administrative and industrial targets in Serbia. Most of the NATO strikes were aimed at bridges and buildings in the Serb capital of Belgrade, with strikes also affecting the Serb city of Novi Sad and the Kosovo capital of Pristina. Russia, which opposed the NATO air strikes, held talks with Serb President Slobodan Milosevic, as well as US President Clinton, in an attempt to resolve the conflict. After eleven weeks of bombing, Serbia capitulated and a UN peacekeeping force moved into Kosovo. The thousands of refugees from the bombings began to return, and evidence of mass killings and other atrocities were uncovered. The lack of infrastructure made emergency aid for the refugees difficult. However, ongoing unrest lead to a renewed need for a peacekeeping force in early 2000, and sporadic violence is ongoing.

Serbia and Montenegro are largely mountainous. The heavily forested Balkan Mountains, with their rocky peaks, separate Serbia from Bulgaria and Romania and stretch across much of southern and central Serbia and into Bosnia and Herzegovina. Much of Montenegro, in the southwest, is covered by the bare limestone ridges of the Dinaric Alps, which run from Slovenia south into Albania. In the north of the country, and covering most of the province of Vojvodina, is the fertile Pannonian Plain. A number of rivers, including the Sava, the Tisza and the Danube traverse this plain, which extends northwest into Croatia and Hungary.

Agricultural produce is centered on the northern plain, which supports substantial crops of wheat, maize, and vegetables as well as livestock and poultry. Agriculture in Montenegro is based mainly on the raising of sheep and goats. Yugoslavia has considerable reserves of coal and petroleum and is largely self-sufficient in fuel. Most of these resources are in the northern province of Vojvodina and the troubled southern region of Kosovo. Mining and heavy machine manufacture are major contributors to the country's economy, which, however, remains seriously destabilized by years of warfare and the consequent disruption of trade links.

An old stone bridge spans a river in Montenegro, Yugoslavia.

The Balkans

The Balkans is the collective name for the eleven countries that occupy the Balkan Peninsula, the easternmost of the three peninsulas that jut southward into the Mediterranean Sea. It comprises the countries of Greece, Bulgaria, Romania, Moldova, Albania, Macedonia, Yugoslavia, Bosnia and Herzegovina, Croatia, and Slovenia. The word Balkan emerged in the nineteenth century. It was the Turkish name for a mountain range in Bulgaria and at first was applied to the land that lay to the south of this range. At various times since, it has had different meanings. Since the First World War, which was sparked by the assassination of the heir to the Austro-Hungarian Empire in Sarajevo, in Bosnia, the region has often been referred to as "the powder keg of Europe," and has had strong connotations of violence and ethnic conflict. In more recent times that phrase has acquired new significance and the term Balkan is increasingly used to refer specifically to those countries that formerly constituted the state of Yugoslavia.

The present troubles in the Balkans can be traced back to the reawakening of long-dormant nationalist sentiments as the formerly powerful Turkish Empire declined during the nineteenth century. This led to the formation of a number of nation states, some of which were, until the end of the First World War, under Austro-Hungarian domination. Many of these states were formed with scant regard to the ethnic, religious, or linguistic homogeneity of their populations. Thus significant populations of Muslim Albanians were incorporated into predominantly Christian Serbia and Macedonia and large numbers of Serbs, the most widely dispersed of the Balkan peoples, lived in Croatia and Bosnia, which is now called Bosnia and Herzegovina.

The explosive potential of this situation was largely contained after the formation of the federated state of Yugoslavia, in which Serbians were dominant, and during the Second World War, in which all Balkan countries suffered grievously. Ethnic tensions remained suppressed during the regime of the strong communist leader Marshal Tito after the Second World War. During this period, Cold War politics dominated Europe, and Yugoslavia adopted relatively liberal socialist policies independently of the Soviet Union. Albania and Romania also pursued their own, albeit more oppressive, socialist agendas, but like Yugoslavia, refused to bow to Soviet domination. Greece remained non-communist, but only after a bitter civil war, which saw the communists finally defeated in 1949.

The death of Tito in 1980 and the later disintegration of communist regimes in Eastern Europe set the scene for the breakdown of Yugoslavia into its component republics. A series of civil wars followed, as Serb minorities in Croatia and Bosnia and Herzegovina fought, with Serbian support, for the extension of Serbian territories. An uneasy truce was brokered in 1995, only after the deployment of United Nations forces. In 1998, the simmering residual resentment by the ethnic Albanians in the southern Yugoslav province of Kosovo erupted again into bloody warfare and led to brutal massacres by the Yugoslav forces.

Zambia

Zambia is a landlocked country in south-central Africa. It stretches from Victoria Falls in the south to Lake Tanganyika in the north, and is one of the world's major copper producers. Ancestral branches of the Zambian Tonga first entered the area in the eighth century AD, but other African groups now living there are more recent arrivals—the Ngoni and Kololo came as fugitives from Zulu aggression in 1835. Formerly a British colony, and once known as Northern Rhodesia, Zambia became independent in 1964. From that year it was ruled for more than a quarter of a century by President Kaunda, who nationalized commerce and industry and built a one-party socialist state. In 1991, economic decline and political agitation led to Zambia's first free elections. Kaunda was defeated, but recovery from his economic and political legacy may take time.

A wide expanse of high plateau broken by scattered mountains and valleys, Zambia is drained by the Zambeze in the west and south, where the river forms a boundary with Zimbabwe and Namibia. Below Victoria Falls the Zambeze is dammed at the Kariba Gorge to form one of the largest artificial lakes in the world, Lake Kariba. Power from the Lake Kariba hydroelectric station is shared with Zimbabwe. Another major river, the Luangwa, runs southwest from the Malawi border down a broad rift valley to join the Zambeze at the frontier of Mozambique.

Compared with its neighbors, Zambia has a high ratio of urban dwellers who are dependent on the rural sector for food. Commercial farming of maize in the central districts, and other food crops such as sorghum and rice, is proving insufficient to meet their needs. This situation has been aggravated both by drought and the phasing out of agricultural subsidies.

Zambia is dependent on copper production, which accounts for over 80 percent of export earnings. Production is down, however, and so are world copper prices, which is intensifying the difficulties caused by high inflation and shrinking internal food supplies. In the post-Kaunda years there has been some attempt at privatization and budgetary reform, but this has produced little improvement. In 1995 four of Zambia's 20 banks failed. Most export earnings go toward paying off the 7 billion dollar external debt—itself a product to some extent of bureaucratic misuse of funds.

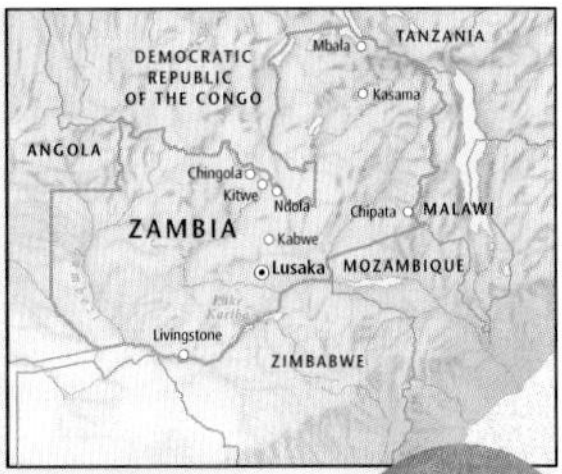

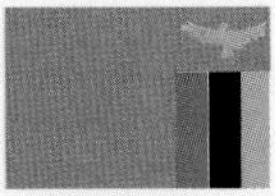

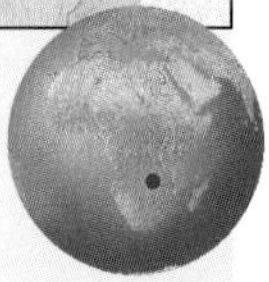

ZAMBIA

OFFICIAL NAME Republic of Zambia
FORM OF GOVERNMENT Republic with single legislative body (National Assembly)
CAPITAL Lusaka
AREA 752,610 sq km (290,583 sq miles)
TIME ZONE GMT + 2 hours
POPULATION 9,663,535
PROJECTED POPULATION 2005 10,972,136
POPULATION DENSITY 12.8 per sq km (33.1 per sq mile)
LIFE EXPECTANCY 37
INFANT MORTALITY (PER 1,000) 91.9
OFFICIAL LANGUAGE English
OTHER LANGUAGES About 70 indigenous languages including Bemba, Kaonda, Lozi, Lunda, Luvale, Nyanja, Tonga
LITERACY RATE 76.6%
RELIGIONS Protestant 84%, Hindu 35%, Roman Catholic 26%, other including Muslim, indigenous beliefs 5%
ETHNIC GROUPS Indigenous 98.7%, European 1.1%, other 0.2%
CURRENCY Kwacha
ECONOMY Agriculture 82%, services 10%, industry 8%
GNP PER CAPITA US$400
CLIMATE Tropical, with three seasons: cool and dry May to August, hot and dry August to November, wet December to April
HIGHEST POINT Mafinga Hills 2,301 m (7,549 ft)
MAP REFERENCE Pages 808–9, 810–11

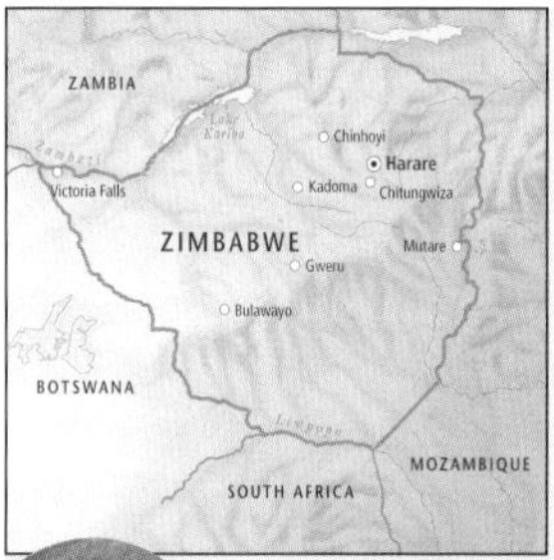

ZIMBABWE

OFFICIAL NAME Republic of Zimbabwe
FORM OF GOVERNMENT Republic with single legislative body (Parliament)
CAPITAL Harare
AREA 390,580 sq km (150,803 sq miles)
TIME ZONE GMT + 2 hours
POPULATION 11,163,160
PROJECTED POPULATION 2005 11,703,270
POPULATION DENSITY 28.6 per sq km (74 per sq mile)
LIFE EXPECTANCY 58
INFANT MORTALITY (per 1,000) 61.2
OFFICIAL LANGUAGE English
OTHER LANGUAGES Shona, Ndebele
LITERACY RATE 84.7%
RELIGIONS Mixed Christian–indigenous beliefs 50%, Christian 25%, indigenous beliefs 24%, Muslim and other 1%
ETHNIC GROUPS Indigenous 98% (Shona 71%, Ndebele 16%, other 11%), European 1%, other 1%
CURRENCY Zimbabwean dollar
ECONOMY Agriculture 65%, services 29%, industry 6%
GNP PER CAPITA US$540
CLIMATE Tropical, moderated by altitude; wet season November to March
HIGHEST POINT Inyangani 2,592 m (8,504 ft)
MAP REFERENCE Page 811

Zimbabwean dancers.

Zimbabwe

Landlocked Zimbabwe lies south of Zambia. Zimbabwe means "house of the chief" in Shona and refers to the Great Ruins, built by Bantu peoples in the country's south and thought to date from the ninth century AD. The country's two main tribes, the minority Ndebele (popularly known as Matabele) and the majority Shona, arrived as nineteenth-century fugitives from the warlike expansion of the Zulus under King Shaka.

British settlement began in the 1890s, and there were 280,000 whites in the country in 1965 when their leader, Ian Smith, declared independence from the UK. African guerrilla action to overthrow Smith led to black majority rule in 1980. Since then the government has been led by Robert Mugabe, a Shona. Though he renounced Marxism–Leninism in 1991, and market reforms are on the agenda, during the 1990s Zimbabwe has edged closer to being a de facto one-party state.

Some 25 percent of the country consists of a broad mountainous ridge known as the high veld, which crosses the country southwest to northeast. On the northeastern Mozambique border this climbs to the peak of Inyangani. The rolling plateaus of the middle veld fall gently away north and south of this central upland, reaching the riverine low veld regions near the Limpopo River in the south and the Zambeze in the north. On the northern border the Zambeze plunges over Victoria Falls into a number of gorges. The Falls is Zimbabwe's principal tourist attraction. Almost 40 percent of electricity needs are met by hydroelectric power, much of it from the Kariba Dam facility shared with Zambia.

Zimbabwe's near self-sufficiency in food is a by-product of the trade boycotts and economic isolation imposed on the white minority regime of Ian Smith after 1965. This forced both agriculture and manufacturing to diversify. African farms are still mainly small-scale subsistence operations, growing maize, cassava, and wheat. Large-scale white-owned enterprises produce most of the cash crops such as tobacco, cotton, and sugarcane, and earn much of agriculture's 35 percent share of national export revenue. Zimbabwe's mineral resources include coal, chromium, asbestos, gold, nickel, copper, iron, vanadium, lithium, tin, and platinum. Mining employs only 5 percent of the workforce, but minerals and metals account for about 40 percent of exports.

African wildlife

Nowhere on earth is there anything to equal the variety of African wildlife, much of it still to be seen in a natural setting. There are 90 species of hoofed mammal alone, including a huge variety of antelope, from the giant eland to the swift impala. Africa has the world's fastest animal, the cheetah, and also the world's largest land animal, the African elephant. In the giraffe it has the tallest animal in the world, while Africa's chimpanzees and gorillas represent families of primates closer to *Homo sapiens* than any others.

The future welfare of African wildlife is a major international concern. Today, many animals only survive in the many national parks throughout the continent, the oldest and best-known being Kruger National Park in South Africa. Kenya's parks include the 20,000 sq km (8,000 sq mile) expanse of Tsavo, one of the biggest. Tanzania's Serengeti National Park has unrivaled herds of antelope and the migratory movements of wildebeest amid lions, leopards, and other predators—not to mention crocodiles in the rivers—provide a glimpse of life on the grasslands of east Africa as it has been for thousands of years.

Only one large African mammal is known to have become extinct in historical times: this is an antelope called the blaubok. However, there were also so few white rhinoceros at the end of the nineteenth century that they were thought to be extinct. Then a few were discovered in the South African province of Natal, and as a result of careful protection in South African national parks their numbers had grown to 6,375 by 1994. Outside South Africa very few white rhinoceros have survived: there may be no more than 80 in Kenya. A number of other animals are endangered, including the critically endangered mountain gorillas found in the Democratic Republic of the Congo, Uganda, and Rwanda.

In the early twentieth century, professional hunters from Europe and America depleted numbers of animals such as lion, rhino, and buffalo. Today, the main threat comes from Africans themselves. Pastoral people kill wildlife because antelope compete for grassland with their cattle. Many mountain gorillas died during the civil wars in Rwanda in the 1990s. Most killing in Kenya and Tanzania is done by poachers seeking decorative skins, ivory, and rhino horn. A 2 kg (4 lb) rhino horn sells for up to US$122,000 in Asia, where in a powdered form it is valued as an aphrodisiac. It is estimated that in the last two decades 40,000 rhinos have been killed for their horns.

The management of wild animal populations is not easy. After policies designed to ensure the survival of elephants were followed in Tsavo National Park, herds grew until there are now too many elephants for the land to support. This is damaging the habitat of other native species.

LUNA
MERCURIUS
VENUS
QUATUOR ELEMENTAE
IGNIS
AER
AQUA
TERRA
NOVA TOTIUS TERRARUM ORBIS GE
Ulterius Septentrionem versus America omnino est incognita sitne aqua vel terra hoc loco incertum est
plurimi tam ex rerum circumstantijs, conjectant Americam ab hac parte Septentrionali mari succinctam
AMERICA
Anno Domini 1492 a Christopho ro Columbo nomine Regis Castel: le primum detecta, et ab Americo Vesputio nomen sortita 1499.
ZONA TEMPERATA ZONA TORRIDA ZONA TEMPERATA ZONA FRIGIDA
FRIGIDA ZONA
AMERICA SEPTEN TRIONALIS
Anian Regnum
Quivira Regnum
NOVA FRANCIA
Tropicus Cancri
Ilhas de Ladrones
MAR DEL
Linea Aequinoctialis
Insulae Salomonis
ZUR
Nova Guinea
Tropicus Capricorni
PACIFICUM
MARE
Fretum Magelanicum
AMERICA SEPTENTRIONALIS
MA
TERRA AU
STRALI
GAL
MURUS BABYLONIS
COLOSSUS
PYRAMIDES
S E P
P L A N
M IR AB IL

Part 4
Maps

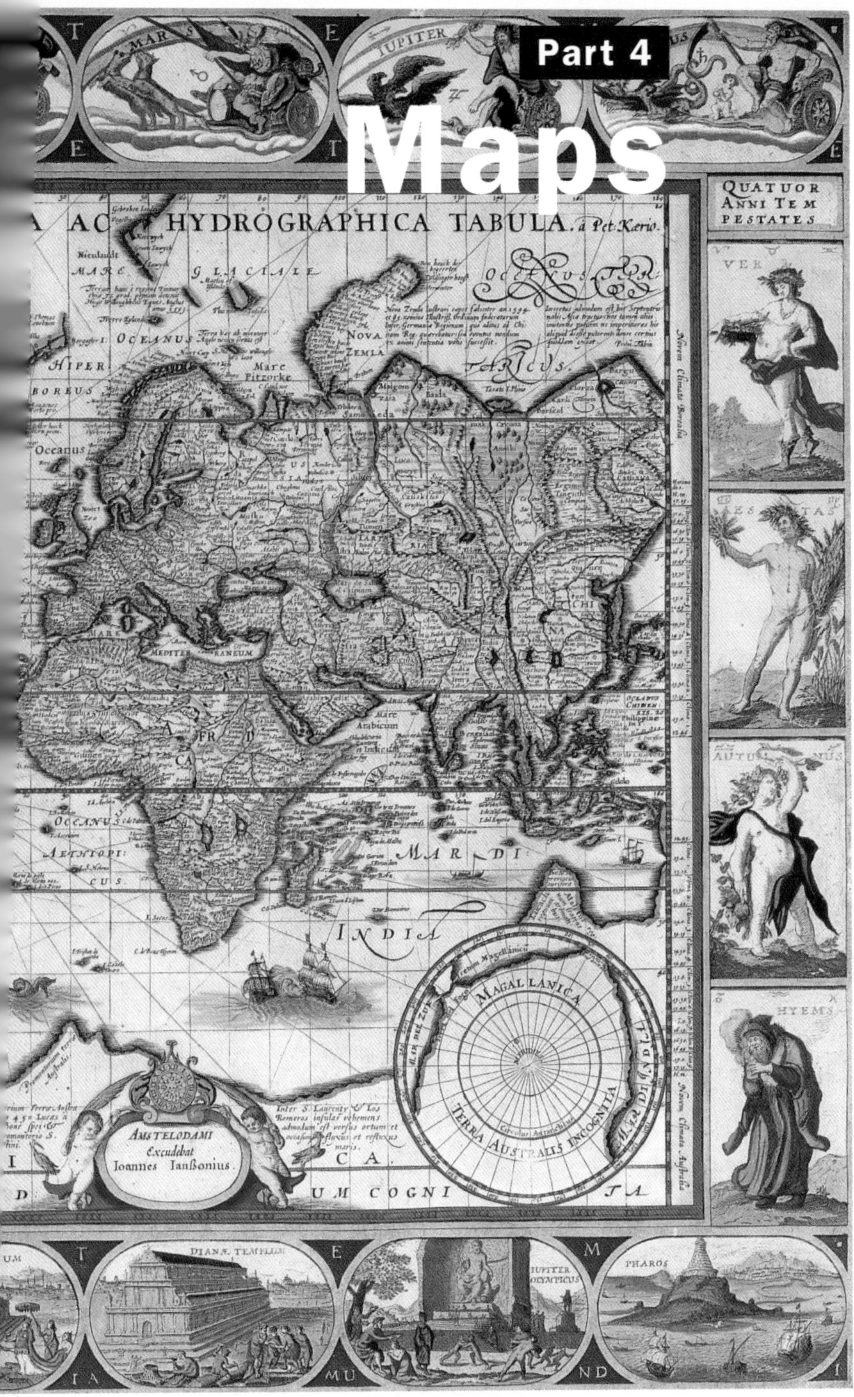
MARS
IUPITER
A AC HYDROGRAPHICA TABULA. à Pet. Kerio.
QUATUOR ANNI TEM PESTATES
VER
AUTU NUS
HYEMS
MARE GLACIALE
OCEANUS
NOVA ZEMLA
HIPER BOREUS
Oceanus
Mare Pitzorke
MARE MEDITER RANEUM
Mare Arabicum
OCEANUS
AETHIOPI CUS
MAR DI
INDIA
MAGAL LANICA
TERRA AUSTRALIS INCOGNITA
AMSTELODAMI Excudebat Ioannes Ianßonius.
UM COGNI TA
DIANÆ TEMPLUM
IUPITER OLYMPICUS
PHAROS

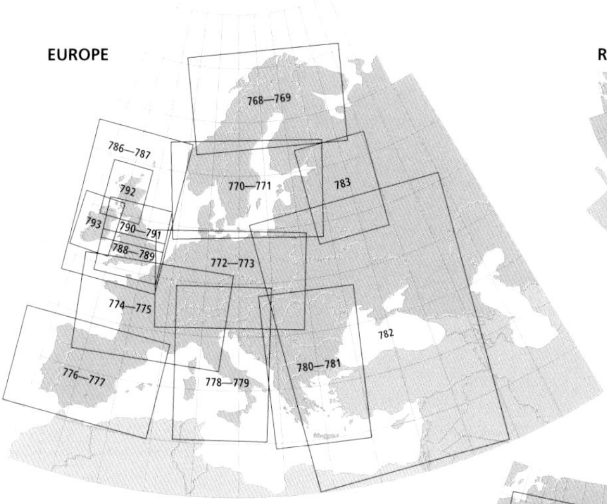
EUROPE
768—769
786—787
770—771
783
792
793
790—791
788—789
772—773
774—775
782
776—777
778—779
780—781

RUSSIAN FEDERATION
784—785

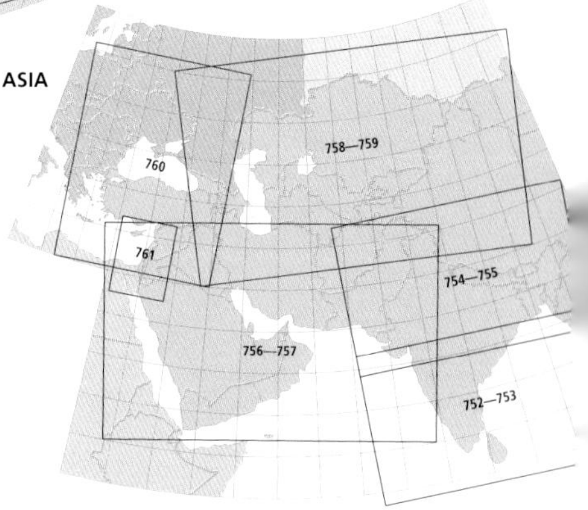
ASIA
758—759
760
761
754—755
756—757
752—753

OTHER MAPS

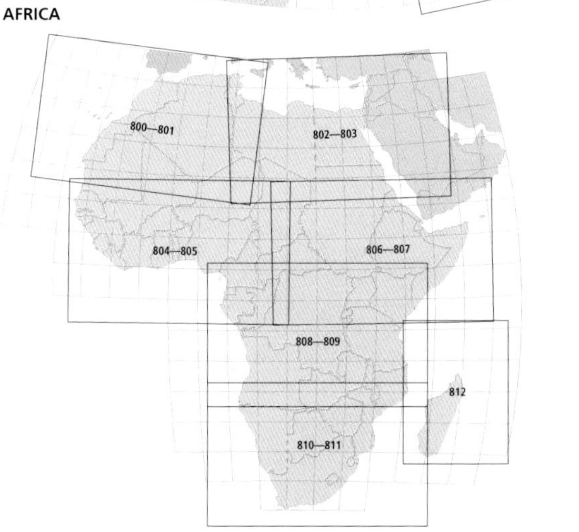
AFRICA
800—801
802—803
804—805
806—807
808—809
812
810—811

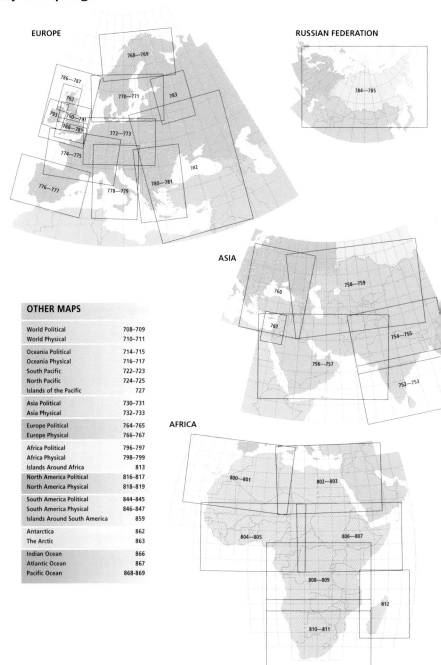

CANADA
820—821
SIA
748—749
746—747
744—745
750—751
742
743
NORTH AMERICA
822—823
824—825
826—827
828—829
830—831
836
832—833
834—835
CENTRAL AMERICA
840—841
838—839
837
HEAST ASIA
741
738—739
740
736—737
734—735
726
720—721
SOUTH AMERICA
848—849
850—851
852—853
854—855
856—857
858
NEW ZEALAND
718—719

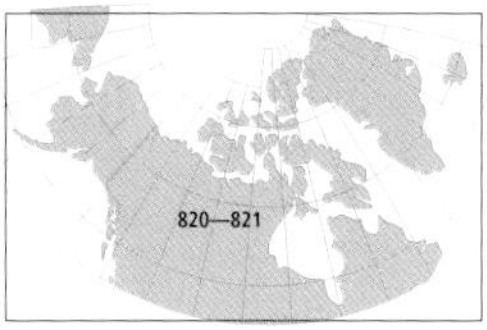

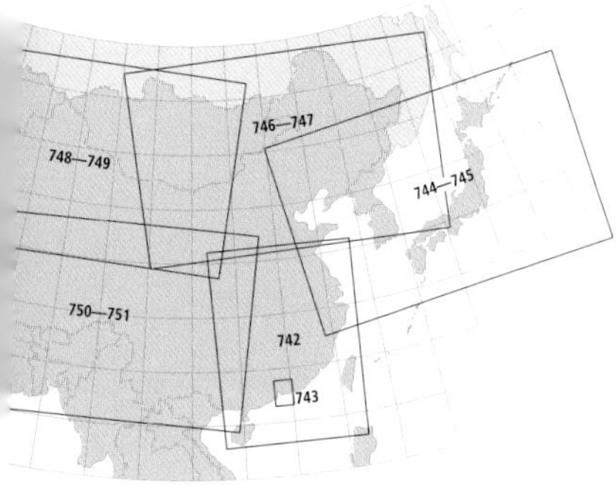

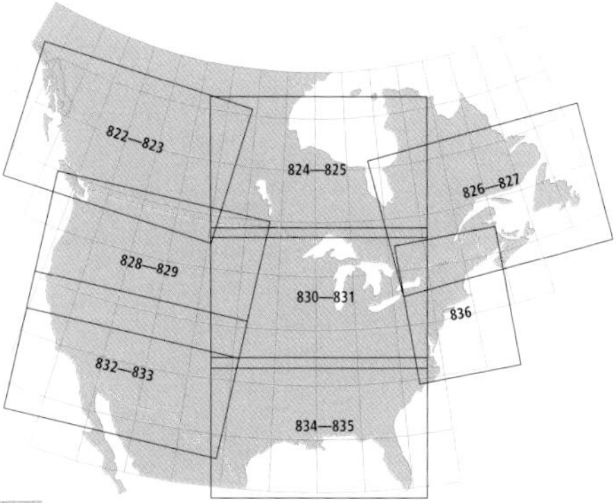

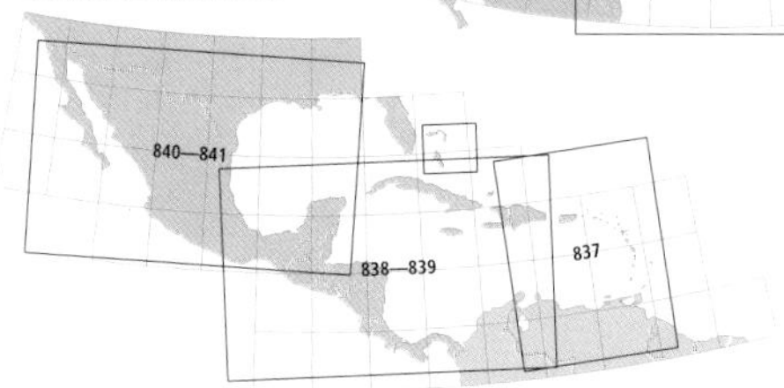

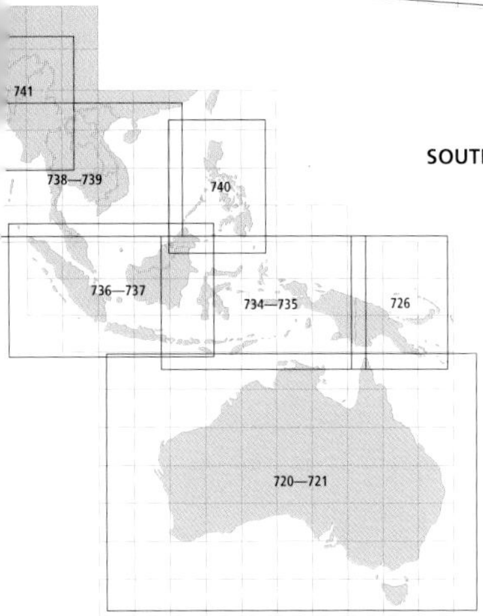

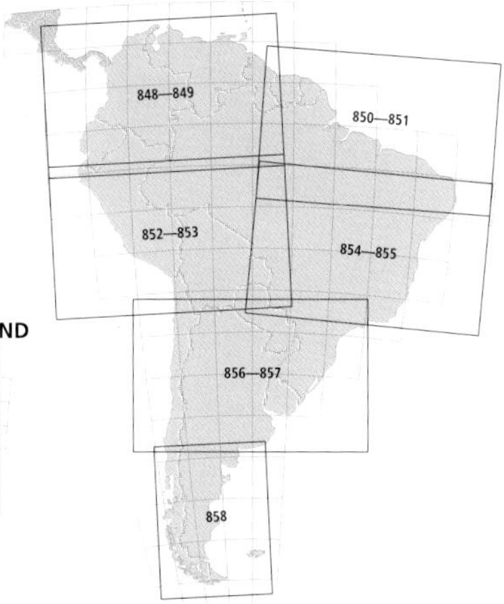

A
B
C
D
E
F
G
H
0°
20°
40°
60°
80°
100°
120°
140°
70°
60°
50°
40°
30°
20°
10°
0°
1
2
3
4
5
6
7
8
9
10
11
12
13
14
15
SVALBARD (Nor.)
ARCTIC OCEAN
Novaya Zemlya
JAN MAYEN (Nor.)
BARENTS SEA
Arctic Circle
ICELAND
SWEDEN
FINLAND
FAEROE IS (Den.)
NORWAY
Oslo
Helsinki
Tallinn
ESTONIA
Stockholm
Riga
LATVIA
RUSSIAN FEDERATION
Moskva
UNITED KINGDOM
DENMARK
København
LITHUANIA
Vilnius
Minsk
BELARUS
ISLE OF MAN (U.K.)
Dublin
IRELAND
Amsterdam
NETH.
Berlin
POLAND
Warszawa
London
BELG.
Bruxelles
Luxembourg
LUX.
GERMANY
Praha
CZECH REP.
SLOVAKIA
Bratislava
UKRAINE
Kyyiv
CHANNEL ISLANDS (U.K.)
Paris
Bern
LIECH.
Wien
AUST.
Budapest
MOLDOVA
Chişinău
SWITZ.
SLOV.
HUNG.
ROMANIA
CROAT.
Ljubljana
Zagreb
B.-H.
Beograd
Bucureşti
FRANCE
Sarajevo
YUG.
Sofiya
BULGARIA
MACE.
Skopje
ANDORRA
Madrid
PORTUGAL
SPAIN
Lisboa
Roma
Tiranë
ALBANIA
ITALY
GREECE
Athina
Ankara
TURKEY
GEORGIA
T'bilisi
ARM.
AZER.
Bakı
Yerevan
Ashgabat
TURKMENISTAN
UZBEKISTAN
Toshkent
KYRGYZSTAN
Bishkek
Dushanbe
TAJIKISTAN
Astana
KAZAKHSTAN
Ulaanbaatar
MONGOLIA
Beijing
P'yŏngyang
NORTH KOREA
Sŏul
SOUTH KOREA
JAPAN
Tōkyō
OKH
GIBRALTAR (U.K.)
Madeira (Port.)
Rabat
MOROCCO
Islas Canarias (Sp.)
Alger
Tūnis
TUNISIA
MALTA
Valletta
Tarābulus
Lefkosia
CYPRUS
SYRIA
LEBANON
Dimashq
Bayrūt
JORDAN
ISRAEL
Yerushalayim
'Ammān
IRAQ
Baghdād
Tehrān
IRAN
Kābol
AFGHANISTAN
Islāmābād
CHINA
ALGERIA
LIBYA
EGYPT
Al Qāhirah
Al Kuwayt
KUWAIT
BAHRAIN
Al Manāmah
Ad Dawhah
QATAR
Abū Zaby
U.A.E.
Ar Riyāḑ
Masqaţ
SAUDI ARABIA
OMAN
PAKISTAN
New Delhi
NEPAL
Kathmandu
BHUTAN
Thimphu
BANGLADESH
Dhaka
INDIA
T'ai-pei
TAIWAN
W. SAHARA
Tropic of Cancer
MAURITANIA
Nouakchott
MALI
NIGER
CHAD
SUDAN
Asmara
ERITREA
YEMEN
Şan'ā'
Al Kharţūm
ARABIAN SEA
Suquţrá (Yemen)
Bay of Bengal
MYANMAR
Yangon
LAOS
Hà Nôi
Viangchan
VIETNAM
THAILAND
Krung Thep
CAMBODIA
Phnum Pénh
PHILIPPINES
Manila
GUAM (U.S.A.)
SENEGAL
Dakar
GAMBIA
GUINEA-BISSAU
GUINEA
Conakry
SIERRA LEONE
Freetown
LIBERIA
Monrovia
Bamako
Niamey
Ouagadougou
BURKINA
NIGERIA
Abuja
BENIN
TOGO
GHANA
CÔTE D'IVOIRE
Yamoussoukro
Accra
Lomé
Porto-Novo
Malalabo
EQ. GUINEA
CAMEROON
Yaoundé
Ndjamena
C.A.R.
Bangui
ETHIOPIA
Ādis Ābeba
Djibouti
DJIBOUTI
SOMALIA
Muqdisho
SRI LANKA
Colombo
MALDIVES
Male
MALAYSIA
Kuala Lumpur
SINGAPORE
Bandar Seri Begawan
BRUNEI
Koror
PALAU
Equator
SÃO TOMÉ & PRÍNCIPE
GABON
Libreville
DEM. REP. OF THE CONGO
UGANDA
Kampala
KENYA
Kigali
RWANDA
Nairobi
Bujumbura
BURUNDI
CONGO
Brazzaville
Kinshasa
TANZANIA
Dodoma
Victoria
SEYCHELLES
Chagos Archipelago
BRITISH INDIAN OCEAN TERRITORY (U.K.)
INDONESIA
Jakarta
CHRISTMAS ISLAND (Aust.)
EAST TIMOR
PAPUA N
Port Mo
ASCENSION ISLAND (ST HELENA)
Luanda
ANGOLA
ZAMBIA
Lusaka
MALAWI
Lilongwe
Moroni
COMOROS
MAYOTTE (Fr.)
COCOS (KEELING) ISLANDS (Aust.)
ASHMORE & CARTIER ISLANDS ISLANDS (Aust.)
ST HELENA (U.K.)
Harare
ZIMBABWE
MOZAMBIQUE
Antananarivo
MADAGASCAR
MAURITIUS
Port Louis
RÉUNION (Fr.)
INDIAN OCEAN
NAMIBIA
Windhoek
BOTSWANA
Gaborone
Tropic of Capricorn
Pretoria
Maputo
Mbabane
SWAZILAND
Bloemfontein
Maseru
LESOTHO
SOUTH AFRICA
Cape Town
AUSTRALIA
TRISTAN DA CUNHA (U.K.)
Île Amsterdam (Fr.)
FRENCH SOUTHERN & ANTARCTIC ISLANDS (Fr.)
Prince Edward Is (S. Africa)
Îles Crozet (Fr.)
Îles de Kerguélen (Fr.)
Tasmania
SOUTH ATLANTIC OCEAN
HEARD & McDONALD ISLANDS (Aust.)
BOUVET ISLAND (Nor.)
SOUTHERN OCEAN
ANTARCTICA
Antarctic Circle
J

GREENLAND (KALAALLIT NUNAAT) (Den.)
BEAUFORT SEA
Banks Island
Baffin Bay
Victoria Island
Baffin Island
CHUKCHI SEA
Bering Strait
Davis Strait
Arctic Circle
U.S.A.
ICELAND
Reykjavík
CANADA
Hudson Bay
BERING SEA
Gulf of Alaska
Aleutian Islands
NORTH ATLANTIC OCEAN
Newfoundland
Ottawa
ST PIERRE AND MIQUELON (Fr.)
UNITED STATES OF AMERICA
Washington D.C.
Azores (Port.)
PACIFIC OCEAN
BERMUDA (U.K.)
Isla Guadalupe (Mex.)
Gulf of Mexico
BAHAMAS
Nassau
MIDWAY ISLANDS (U.S.A.)
MEXICO
La Habana
Tropic of Cancer
CUBA
Hawaiian Islands (U.S.A.)
México
Kingston
HAITI
DOMINICAN REPUBLIC
Santo Domingo
JAMAICA
BELIZE
Belmopan
Islas Revillagigedo (Mex.)
ST KITTS & NEVIS
ANTIGUA & BARBUDA
CAPE VERDE
JOHNSTON ATOLL (U.S.A.)
Guatemala
GUATEMALA
EL SALVADOR
San Salvador
HONDURAS
Tegucigalpa
NICARAGUA
Managua
San José
COSTA RICA
ST VINCENT & THE GRENADINES
DOMINICA
ST LUCIA
BARBADOS
GRENADA
TRINIDAD & TOBAGO
Port of Spain
Praia
PANAMA
Panamá
Caracas
VENEZUELA
Georgetown
Paramaribo
FRENCH GUIANA (Fr.)
Dalap-Uliga-Darrit
KINGMAN REEF (U.S.A.)
PALMYRA ATOLL (U.S.A.)
Bogotá
COLOMBIA
Bairiki
BAKER AND HOWLAND ISLANDS (U.S.A.)
JARVIS ISLAND (U.S.A.)
Islas Galápagos (Ecu.)
Quito
ECUADOR
Equator
KIRIBATI
Funafuti
TOKELAU (N.Z.)
TUVALU
PERU
BRAZIL
WALLIS & FUTUNA (Fr.)
SAMOA
Apia
AMERICAN SAMOA (U.S.A.)
Îles Marquises
Lima
FIJI
Suva
TONGA
NIUE (N.Z.)
COOK ISLANDS (N.Z.)
Nuku'alofa
Archipel de la Société
Tahiti
Îles Tuamotu
La Paz
BOLIVIA
Sucre
Brasília
Trindade (Brazil)
Tropic of Capricorn
FRENCH POLYNESIA (Fr.)
PITCAIRN IS. (U.K.)
Isla de Pascua (Chile)
Sala y Gómez (Chile)
PARAGUAY
Asunción
Kermadec Is (N.Z.)
Archipiélago Juan Fernández (Chile)
ARGENTINA
URUGUAY
Santiago
Buenos Aires
Montevideo
CHILE
Chatham Is (N.Z.)
SOUTH ATLANTIC OCEAN
Bounty Is (N.Z.)
Antipodes Is (N.Z.)
FALKLAND ISLANDS (U.K.)
SOUTH GEORGIA & SOUTH SANDWICH ISLANDS (U.K.)
Cabo de Hornos
South Shetland Islands (U.K.)
South Orkney Islands (U.K.)
BELLINGSHAUSEN SEA
Antarctic Peninsula
Antarctic Circle
0 1500 3000 4000 kilometers
0 1000 2000 miles

Spitsbergen
Greenland (Kalaallit Nunaat)
Severnaya Zemlya
ARCTIC OCEAN
GREENLAND SEA
Novaya Zemlya
KARSKOYE MORE
MORE LAPTEVYKH
Nordkapp
BARENTS SEA
NORWEGIAN SEA
Arctic Circle
Iceland
Scandinavia
Gulf of Bothnia
Onezhskoye Ozero
Ladozhskoye Ozero
North European Plain
Ural'skiy Khrebet
Ob'
Zapando Sibirskaya Ravnina
Yenisey
Sredne-Sibirskoye Ploskogor'ye
Lena
British Isles
NORTH SEA
BALTIC SEA
Volga
Dnepr
Rhine
Carpathian Mts
SEA OF AZOV
ARAL SEA
Balqash Köli
Ozero Baykal
Stanovoy Khrebet
OKH
Bay of Biscay
ALPS
Pyrenees
Iberian Peninsula
Balkan Pen.
Gora El'brus 5641 m
BLACK SEA
CASPIAN SEA
Syrdar'ya
Amu Darya
Gobi
SEA OF JAPAN
Honsh
Strait of Gibraltar
MEDITERRANEAN SEA
ATLAS MTS
Euphrates
Tigris
Dasht-e Kavir
Hindu Kush
Kunlun Shan
HIMALAYA
Mt Everest 8848 m
Huang
YELLOW SEA
EAST CHINA SEA
Kyūshū
Tropic of Cancer
SAHARA
Libyan Des.
L. Nasser
Nile
RED SEA
An Nafūd Desert
Arabian Peninsula
Thar Desert
Ganga (Ganges)
Chang
Nansei-shotō
Taiwan
Hainan
Luzon
SAHEL
Ar Rub' al Khālī
ARABIAN SEA
Deccan
Bay of Bengal
SOUTH CHINA SEA
PHILIPPINE SEA
Philippines
Lac Tchad (Lake Chad)
Gulf of Aden
Horn of Africa
ANDAMAN SEA
Lake Volta
Niger
Cape Comorin
Sri Lanka
Malay Peninsula
SULU SEA
Mindanao
Equator
Gulf of Guinea
Congo Basin
Lake Victoria
CELEBES SEA
MOLUCCA SEA
Borneo
Sumatera (Sumatra)
Sulawesi (Celebes)
BISMARCK SEA
Kilimanjaro 5895 m
Congo
L. Tanganyika
Great Rift Valley
JAVA SEA
BANDA SEA
New Guinea
ARAFURA SEA
TIMOR SEA
Mozambique Channel
Zambezi
Lake Kariba
St Helena
Madagascar
INDIAN OCEAN
Mauritius
Tropic of Capricorn
Limpopo
Kalahari Desert
Great Sandy Desert
Great Victoria Desert
Simpson Desert
Great Australian Bight
SOUTH ATLANTIC OCEAN
Îles Crozet
Îles de Kerguélen
Antarctic Circle

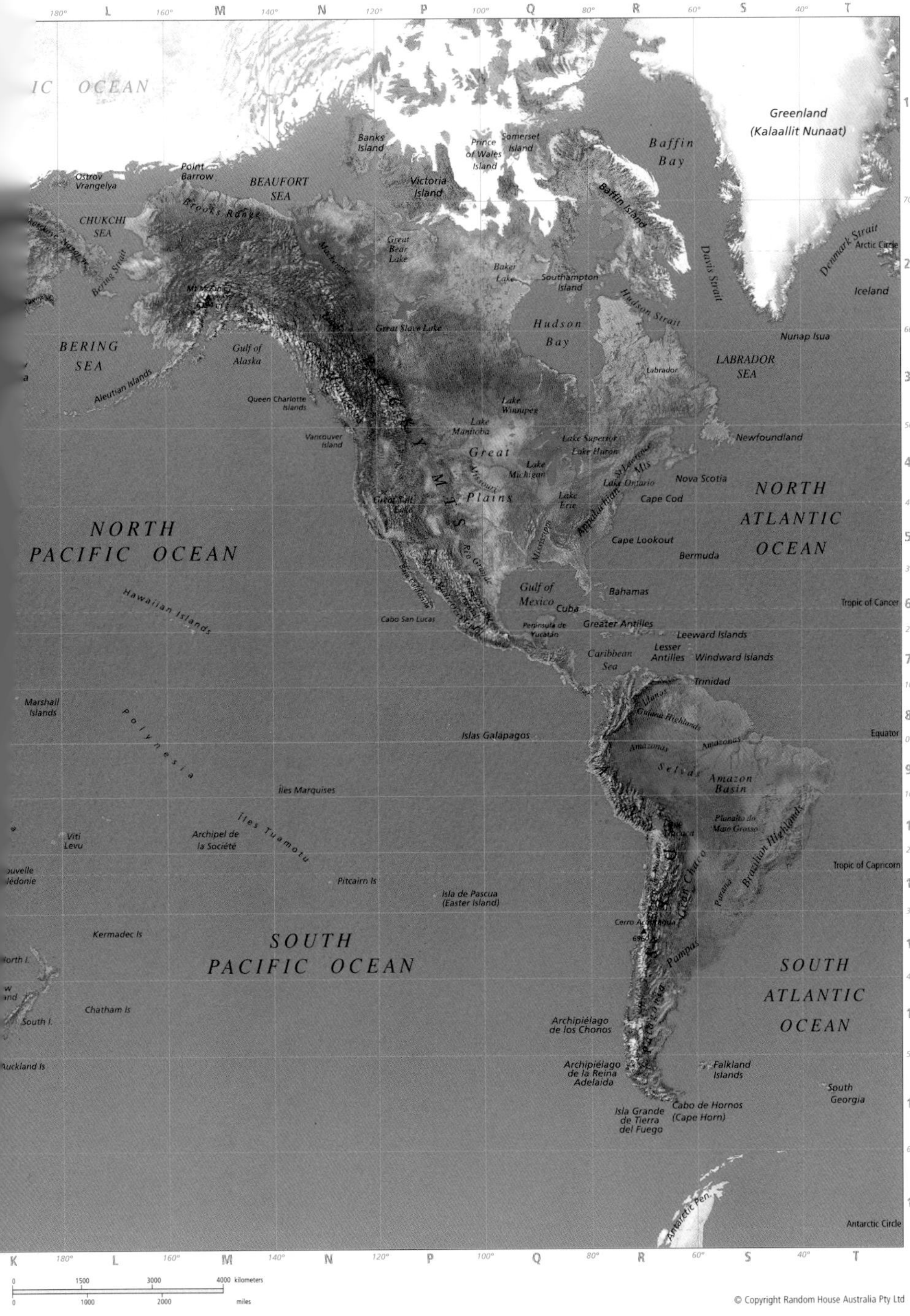
Greenland
(Kalaallit Nunaat)
Baffin Bay
Banks Island
Prince of Wales Island
Somerset Island
Victoria Island
Point Barrow
Ostrov Vrangelya
BEAUFORT SEA
CHUKCHI SEA
Brooks Range
Baffin Island
Davis Strait
Denmark Strait
Arctic Circle
Iceland
Great Bear Lake
Baker Lake
Southampton Island
Hudson Strait
Bering Strait
Hudson Bay
Great Slave Lake
Nunap Isua
BERING SEA
Gulf of Alaska
Aleutian Islands
Labrador
LABRADOR SEA
Queen Charlotte Islands
Lake Winnipeg
Lake Manitoba
Vancouver Island
Lake Superior
Lake Huron
Newfoundland
Great Plains
Lake Michigan
Lake Ontario
Nova Scotia
Great Salt Lake
Lake Erie
Cape Cod
NORTH ATLANTIC OCEAN
NORTH PACIFIC OCEAN
Appalachian Mts
Cape Lookout
Bermuda
Rio Grande
Gulf of Mexico
Bahamas
Hawaiian Islands
Cuba
Tropic of Cancer
Cabo San Lucas
Peninsula de Yucatán
Greater Antilles
Leeward Islands
Lesser Antilles
Caribbean Sea
Windward Islands
Trinidad
Marshall Islands
Polynesia
Guiana Highlands
Islas Galápagos
Equator
Amazonas
Selvas
Amazon Basin
Îles Marquises
Planalto do Mato Grosso
Brazilian Highlands
Îles Tuamotu
Archipel de la Société
Viti Levu
Tropic of Capricorn
Pitcairn Is
Gran Chaco
Isla de Pascua
(Easter Island)
Paraná
Cerro Aconcagua
Kermadec Is
SOUTH PACIFIC OCEAN
Pampas
SOUTH ATLANTIC OCEAN
Chatham Is
South I.
Archipiélago de los Chonos
Auckland Is
Archipiélago de la Reina Adelaida
Falkland Islands
South Georgia
Isla Grande de Tierra del Fuego
Cabo de Hornos
(Cape Horn)
Antarctic Pen.
Antarctic Circle
K L M N P Q R S T
180° 160° 140° 120° 100° 80° 60° 40°
70° 60° 50° 40° 30° 20° 10° 0° 10° 20° 30° 40° 50° 60°
1 2 3 4 5 6 7 8 9 10 11 12 13 14 15
0 1500 3000 4000 kilometers
0 1000 2000 miles

Oceania

BRUNEI
PHILIPPINES
MALAYSIA
CELEBES SEA
Sonsorol
Tobi
Helen
PALAU
Namoluk
Mortlock Is
Lukunor
Caroline Is
Nukuoro
MICRON
Kapingamarangi Atoll
Kot
Halmahera
Waigeo
Borneo
MOLUCCA SEA
Sulawesi (Celebes)
Yapen
Ninego Group
New Hanover
Admiralty Islands
PAPUA
New Ireland
Nuguria Is
Wewak
BISMARCK SEA
JAVA SEA
Buru
INDONESIA
BANDA SEA
Green Is
Buka
Madang
New Guinea
Mount Hagen
Goroka
NEW
New Britain
Bougainville
Lae
Jawa (Java)
FLORES SEA
Kep. Babar
Kep. Tanimbar
Kep. Aru
Dolak
Kerema
SOLOMON
GUINEA
Trobriand Is
Woodlark
Bali
Flores
EAST TIMOR
Timor
ARAFURA SEA
Port Moresby
SEA
Louisiade Arch.
Sumba
Roti
TIMOR SEA
Melville I.
Torres Strait
Wessel Is
Tagula
Rossel
ASHMORE AND CARTIER ISLANDS (Aust.)
Darwin
Joseph Bonaparte Gulf
Gulf of Carpentaria
CORAL
Katherine
Wyndham
CORAL SEA ISLANDS (Aust.)
Derby
Cairns
Halls Creek
NORTHERN
Broome
SEA
Tennant Creek
TERRITORY
Townsville
Whitsunday Group
Port Hedland
Karratha
Mount Isa
Mackay
QUEENSLAND
Tropic of Capricorn
Newman
Rockhampton
Alice Springs
Barcaldine
Gladstone
WESTERN
AUSTRALIA
Carnarvon
Maryborough
Fraser I.
Noosa Heads
Charleville
Meekatharra
AUSTRALIA
Toowoomba
Brisbane
Coober Pedy
Geraldton
Ballina
SOUTH AUSTRALIA
Grafton
Coffs Harbour
Bourke
Kalgoorlie-Boulder
Tamworth
Lord Howe (Aust.)
Port Macquarie
Perth
Broken Hill
Dubbo
Ceduna
Port Augusta
NEW SOUTH WALES
Whyalla
Port Pirie
Orange
Newcastle
Bunbury
Busselton
Esperance
Great Australian Bight
Bathurst
Sydney
Wollongong
Albany
Gawler
Port Lincoln
Adelaide
Murray Bridge
Wagga Wagga
Canberra
A.C.T.
Queanbeyan
Kangaroo I.
Albury
VICTORIA
TASM
Ballarat
Mount Gambier
Melbourne
Geelong
Warrnambool
Bass Strait
Furneaux Group
King I.
Flinders I.
Burnie
Devonport
Launceston
SEA
TASMANIA
Hobart
South Bruny I.
SOUTHERN OCEAN
A
B
C
D
E
120°
130°
140°
150°
0°
10°
20°
30°
40°
50°
1
2
3
4
5
6
7

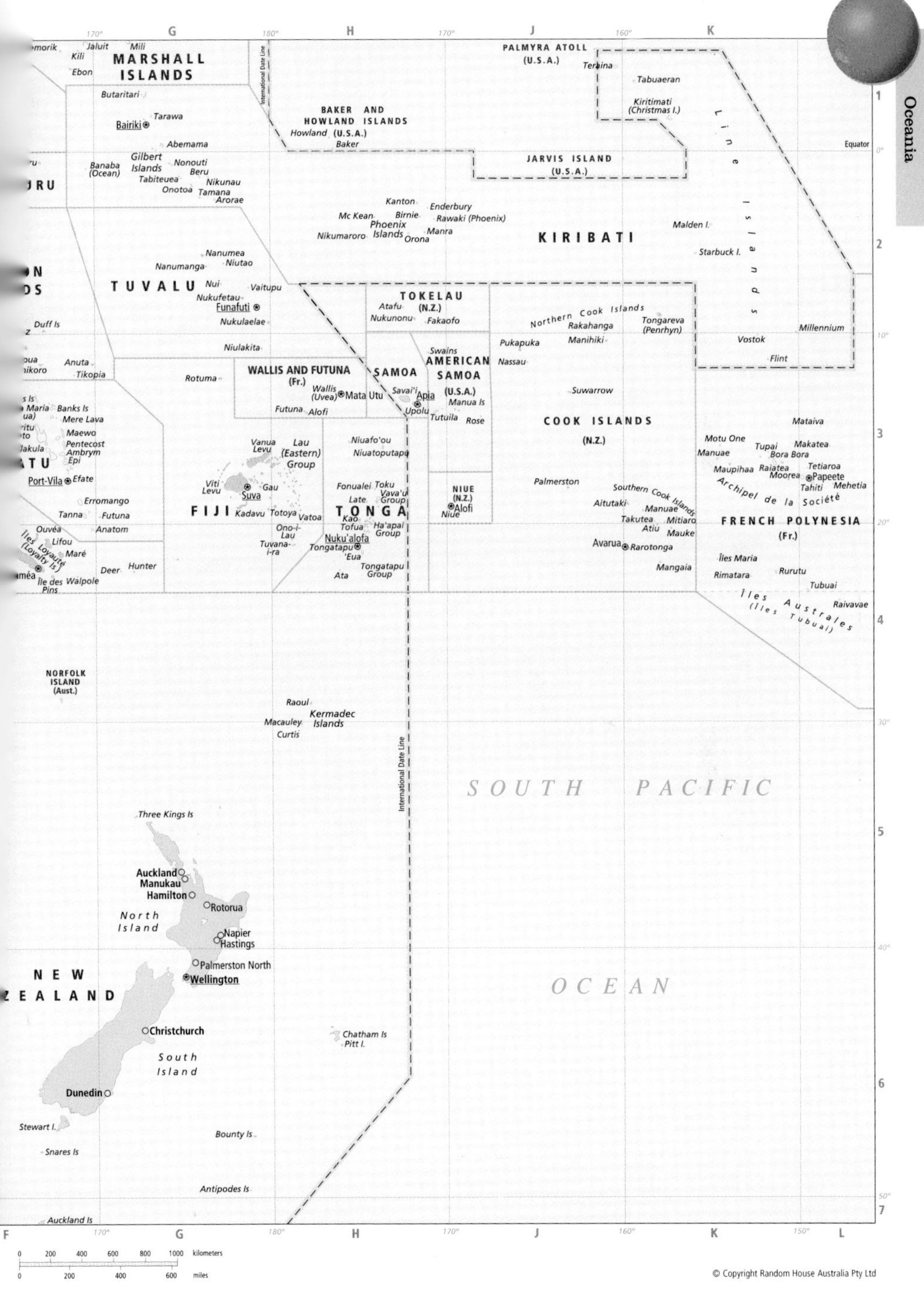
MARSHALL ISLANDS
Jaluit
Mili
Kili
Ebon
Butaritari
Tarawa
Bairiki
Abemama
Banaba (Ocean)
Gilbert Islands
Nonouti
Beru
Tabiteuea
Nikunau
Onotoa
Tamana
Arorae
International Date Line
BAKER AND HOWLAND ISLANDS
Howland (U.S.A.)
Baker
PALMYRA ATOLL (U.S.A.)
Teraina
Tabuaeran
Kiritimati (Christmas I.)
JARVIS ISLAND (U.S.A.)
Line Islands
Equator
Kanton
Enderbury
Mc Kean
Birnie
Rawaki (Phoenix)
Phoenix Islands
Manra
Nikumaroro
Orona
KIRIBATI
Malden I.
Starbuck I.
Nanumea
Niutao
Nanumanga
TUVALU
Nui
Vaitupu
Nukufetau
Funafuti
Nukulaelae
Niulakita
Duff Is
Anuta
Tikopia
Rotuma
TOKELAU (N.Z.)
Atafu
Nukunonu
Fakaofo
Northern Cook Islands
Rakahanga
Tongareva (Penrhyn)
Manihiki
Pukapuka
Nassau
Millennium
Vostok
Flint
Swains
AMERICAN SAMOA (U.S.A.)
WALLIS AND FUTUNA (Fr.)
Wallis (Uvea)
Mata Utu
SAMOA
Savai'i
Apia
Upolu
Manua Is
Tutuila
Rose
Futuna
Alofi
Suwarrow
COOK ISLANDS (N.Z.)
Mataiva
Banks Is
Mere Lava
Maewo
Pentecost
Ambrym
Epi
Port-Vila
Efate
Erromango
Tanna
Futuna
Anatom
Vanua Levu
Lau (Eastern) Group
Niuafo'ou
Niuatoputapu
Viti Levu
Suva
Gau
FIJI
Kadavu
Totoya
Vatoa
Fonualei
Toku
Late
Vava'u Group
TONGA
Kao
Tofua
Ha'apai Group
Ono-i-Lau
Tuvana-i-ra
Nuku'alofa
Tongatapu
'Eua
Ata
Tongatapu Group
NIUE (N.Z.)
Alofi
Niue
Palmerston
Motu One
Manuae
Tupai
Makatea
Bora Bora
Maupihaa
Raiatea
Tetiaroa
Moorea
Papeete
Tahiti
Mehetia
Archipel de la Société
Southern Cook Islands
Aitutaki
Manuae
Takutea
Mitiaro
Atiu
Mauke
FRENCH POLYNESIA (Fr.)
Avarua
Rarotonga
Mangaia
Îles Maria
Rimatara
Rurutu
Tubuai
Raivavae
Îles Australes (Îles Tubuai)
Ouvéa
Lifou
Îles Loyauté (Loyalty Is)
Maré
Île des Pins
Walpole
Deer
Hunter
NORFOLK ISLAND (Aust.)
Raoul
Kermadec Islands
Macauley
Curtis
SOUTH PACIFIC
OCEAN
Three Kings Is
Auckland
Manukau
Hamilton
Rotorua
North Island
Napier
Hastings
Palmerston North
Wellington
NEW ZEALAND
Christchurch
Chatham Is
Pitt I.
South Island
Dunedin
Stewart I.
Bounty Is
Snares Is
Antipodes Is
Auckland Is
F
G
H
J
K
L
170°
180°
160°
150°
0°
10°
20°
30°
40°
50°
1
2
3
4
5
6
7
0 200 400 600 800 1000 kilometers
0 200 400 600 miles

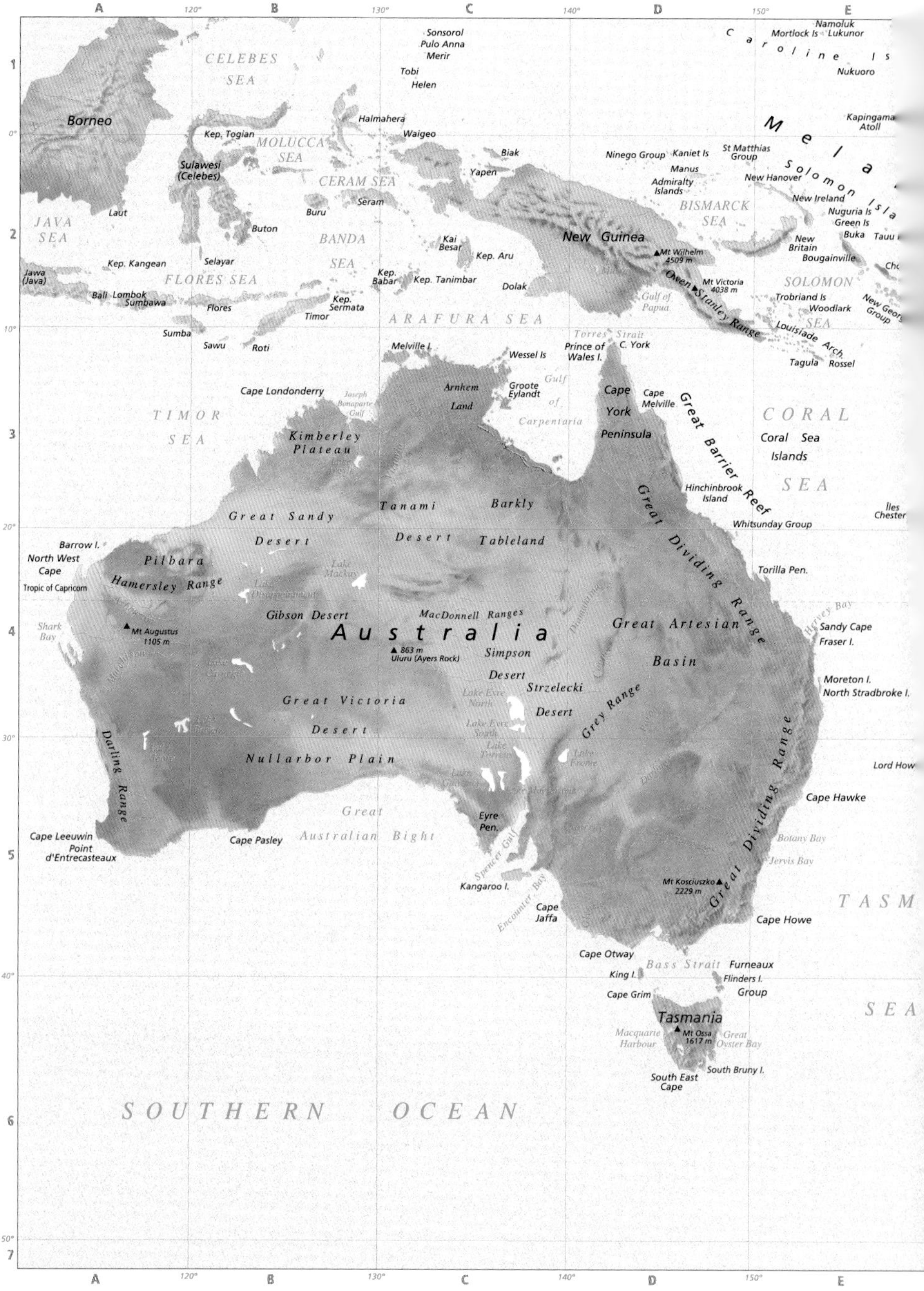
CELEBES SEA
Borneo
Kep. Togian
MOLUCCA SEA
Sulawesi (Celebes)
CERAM SEA
JAVA SEA
Laut
Buton
Seram
Buru
BANDA SEA
Kep. Kangean
Selayar
FLORES SEA
Jawa (Java)
Bali
Lombok
Sumbawa
Flores
Sumba
Sawu
Roti
Timor
Kep. Sermata
Kep. Babar
Kep. Tanimbar
Kai Besar
Kep. Aru
Dolak
Sonsorol
Pulo Anna
Merir
Tobi
Helen
Halmahera
Waigeo
Biak
Yapen
New Guinea
Mt Wilhelm 4509 m
Mt Victoria 4038 m
Owen Stanley Range
Gulf of Papua
Torres Strait
C. York
Prince of Wales I.
Wessel Is
ARAFURA SEA
Melville I.
Ninego Group
Kaniet Is
St Matthias Group
Manus
Admiralty Islands
New Hanover
BISMARCK SEA
New Ireland
Nuguria Is
Green Is
Buka
Tauu
New Britain
Bougainville
SOLOMON SEA
Trobriand Is
Woodlark
New Georgia Group
Louisiade Arch.
Tagula
Rossel
Caroline Is
Namoluk
Mortlock Is
Lukunor
Nukuoro
Kapingamarangi Atoll
Mela
Solomon Isla
CORAL SEA
Coral Sea Islands
Îles Chester
Cape Londonderry
Joseph Bonaparte Gulf
TIMOR SEA
Kimberley Plateau
Arnhem Land
Groote Eylandt
Gulf of Carpentaria
Cape York Peninsula
Cape Melville
Great Barrier Reef
Hinchinbrook Island
Whitsunday Group
Great Sandy Desert
Tanami Desert
Barkly Tableland
Great Dividing Range
Barrow I.
North West Cape
Tropic of Capricorn
Pilbara
Hamersley Range
Lake Mackay
Lake Disappointment
Torilla Pen.
Hervey Bay
Sandy Cape
Fraser I.
Shark Bay
Mt Augustus 1105 m
Gibson Desert
MacDonnell Ranges
Australia
863 m Uluru (Ayers Rock)
Simpson Desert
Great Artesian Basin
Lake Carnegie
Lake Eyre North
Lake Eyre South
Strzelecki Desert
Grey Range
Moreton I.
North Stradbroke I.
Great Victoria Desert
Darling Range
Lake Torrens
Lake Frome
Nullarbor Plain
Lord Howe
Cape Hawke
Great Australian Bight
Eyre Pen.
Spencer Gulf
Cape Leeuwin
Point d'Entrecasteaux
Cape Pasley
Botany Bay
Jervis Bay
Kangaroo I.
Encounter Bay
Mt Kosciuszko 2229 m
Cape Jaffa
Cape Howe
TASMAN SEA
Cape Otway
Bass Strait
Furneaux Group
Flinders I.
King I.
Cape Grim
Tasmania
Macquarie Harbour
Mt Ossa 1617 m
Great Oyster Bay
South Bruny I.
South East Cape
SOUTHERN OCEAN
A
B
C
D
E
1
2
3
4
5
6
7
0°
10°
20°
30°
40°
50°
120°
130°
140°
150°

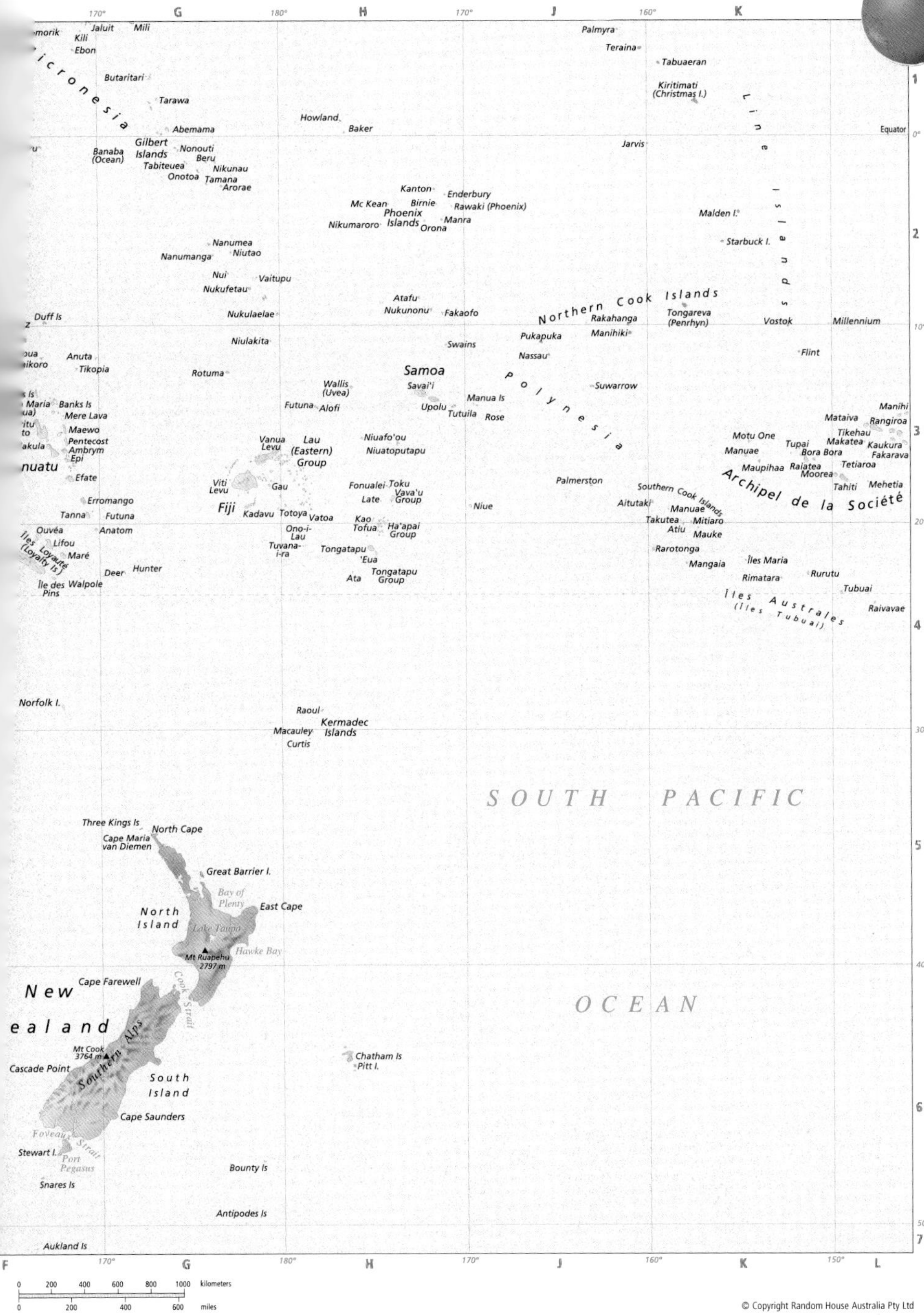
170°
G
180°
H
170°
J
160°
K
Jaluit
Mili
Kili
Ebon
Butaritari
Tarawa
Abemama
Gilbert Islands
Banaba (Ocean)
Nonouti
Beru
Tabiteuea
Nikunau
Onotoa
Tamana
Arorae
Howland
Baker
Palmyra
Teraina
Tabuaeran
Kiritimati (Christmas I.)
Line Islands
Jarvis
Equator
0°
1
Kanton
Enderbury
Mc Kean
Birnie
Rawaki (Phoenix)
Phoenix Islands
Manra
Nikumaroro
Orona
Malden I.
Starbuck I.
2
Nanumea
Niutao
Nanumanga
Nui
Vaitupu
Nukufetau
Nukulaelae
Atafu
Nukunonu
Fakaofo
Northern Cook Islands
Rakahanga
Tongareva (Penrhyn)
Manihiki
Pukapuka
Vostok
Millennium
10°
Duff Is
Anuta
Tikopia
Niulakita
Swains
Nassau
Flint
Rotuma
Samoa
Savai'i
Wallis (Uvea)
Polynesia
Suwarrow
Banks Is
Mere Lava
Futuna
Alofi
Upolu
Manua Is
Tutuila
Rose
Manihi
Mataiva
Rangiroa
Maewo
Pentecost
Ambrym
Epi
Vanua Levu
Lau (Eastern) Group
Niuafo'ou
Niuatoputapu
Motu One
Manuae
Tupai
Bora Bora
Makatea
Tikehau
Kaukura
Fakarava
3
Efate
Viti Levu
Gau
Fiji
Kadavu
Totoya
Vatoa
Fonualei
Toku
Late
Vava'u Group
Palmerston
Maupihaa
Raiatea
Moorea
Tetiaroa
Tahiti
Mehetia
Archipel de la Société
Erromango
Tanna
Futuna
Anatom
Niue
Aitutaki
Southern Cook Islands
Manuae
Takutea
Mitiaro
Atiu
Mauke
20°
Ouvéa
Lifou
Îles Loyauté (Loyalty Is)
Maré
Kao
Tofua
Ha'apai Group
Ono-i-Lau
Tuvana-i-ra
Tongatapu
'Eua
Rarotonga
Mangaia
Îles Maria
Rimatara
Rurutu
Tubuai
Deer
Hunter
Île des Pins
Walpole
Ata
Tongatapu Group
Îles Australes (Îles Tubuai)
Raivavae
4
Norfolk I.
Raoul
Kermadec Islands
Macauley
Curtis
30°
SOUTH PACIFIC
Three Kings Is
North Cape
Cape Maria van Diemen
5
Great Barrier I.
Bay of Plenty
East Cape
North Island
Lake Taupo
Hawke Bay
Mt Ruapehu 2797 m
40°
Cape Farewell
Cook Strait
New Zealand
OCEAN
Mt Cook 3764 m
Southern Alps
Chatham Is
Pitt I.
Cascade Point
South Island
6
Cape Saunders
Foveaux Strait
Stewart I.
Port Pegasus
Bounty Is
Snares Is
Antipodes Is
50°
Aukland Is
7
F
170°
G
180°
H
170°
J
160°
K
150°
L
0 200 400 600 800 1000 kilometers
0 200 400 600 miles

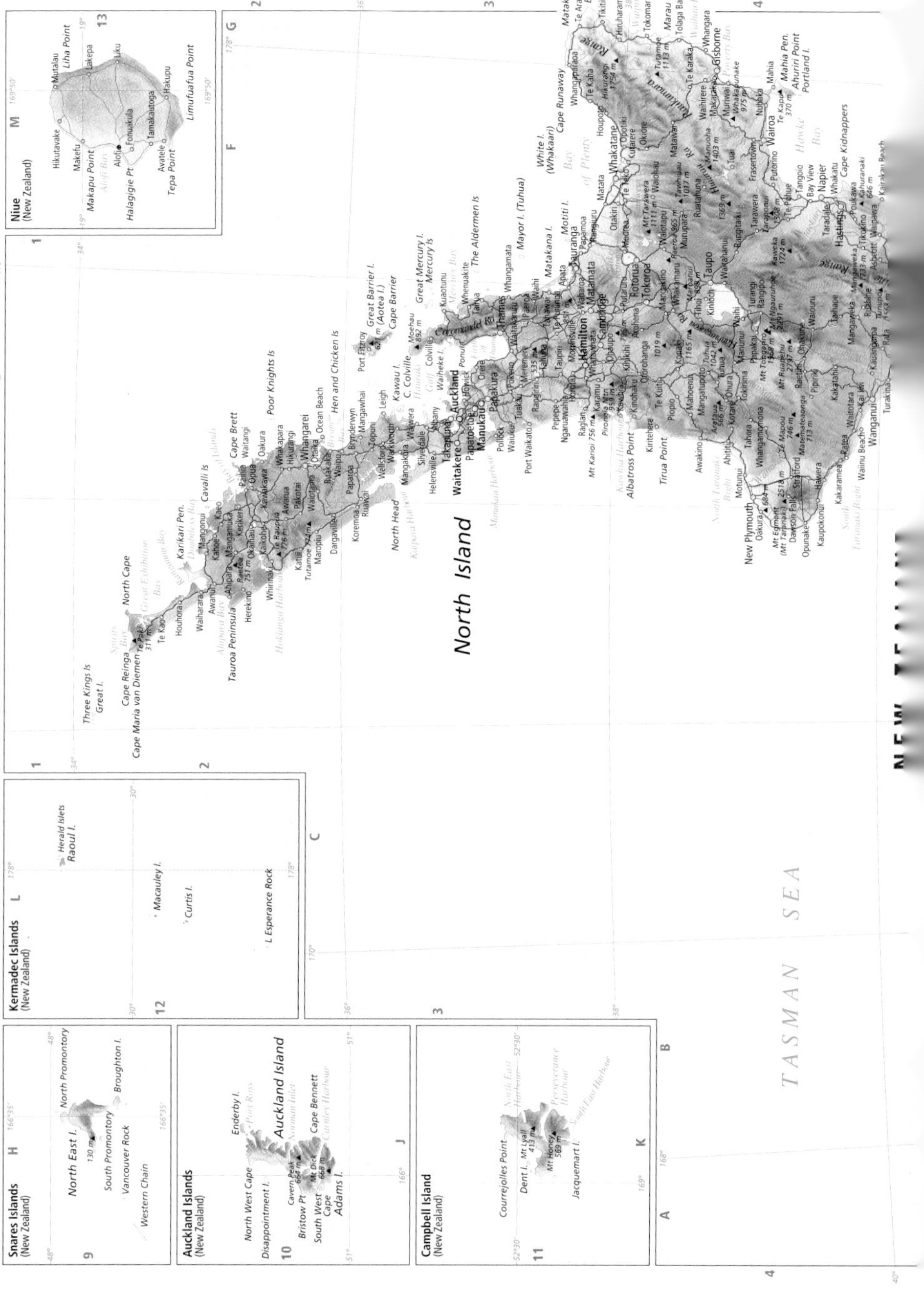
Niue
(New Zealand)
Kermadec Islands
(New Zealand)
Snares Islands
(New Zealand)
Auckland Islands
(New Zealand)
Campbell Island
(New Zealand)
North Island
TASMAN SEA
Auckland
Hamilton
Tauranga
Rotorua
Taupo
Gisborne
Napier
Hastings
New Plymouth
Wanganui
Whangarei
Cape Reinga
North Cape
Three Kings Is
Great Barrier I.
(Aotea I.)
Bay of Plenty
East Cape
Cape Kidnappers
Mt Egmont
(Mt Taranaki)
Mt Ruapehu
2797 m
Raoul I.
Macauley I.
Curtis I.
L'Esperance Rock
Auckland Island
Adams I.
Enderby I.
Disappointment I.
North East I.
Broughton I.
Western Chain
Dent I.
Jacquemart I.
Alofi
Lakepa
Liku
Hakupu
Avatele

South Island
SOUTH PACIFIC OCEAN
Stewart Island
Wellington
Lower Hutt
Nelson
Blenheim
Christchurch
Ashburton
Timaru
Oamaru
Dunedin
Invercargill
Greymouth
Westport
Hokitika
Kaikoura
Kaikoura Peninsula
Banks Peninsula
Otago Peninsula
Canterbury Plains
Canterbury Bight
Pegasus Bay
SOUTHERN ALPS
The Hunters Hills
Mt Cook 3764 m
Milford Sound
Cape Foulwind
Cape Campbell
Cape Palliser
Cape Providence
Puysegur Point
South Cape
Cascade Point
Bounty Islands
(New Zealand)
Western Group
Centre Group
Eastern Group
Antipodes Islands
(New Zealand)
Antipodes Island
Bollons I.
North Cape
Windward Is
Leeward I.
Albatross Point
Mt Galloway 366 m
Chatham Islands
(New Zealand)
Chatham I.
Pitt I.
The Sisters
Cape Young
C. Pattisson
Point Munning
Okawa Point
The Forty Fours
Point Durham
Cape Fournier
Cape L Eveque
Mangere I.
Rangatira I.
Pyramid I.
Kahuitara Point
0 50 100 150 200 kilometers
0 50 100 miles

Christmas Island
(Australia)
North West Pt
North East Pt
Flying Fish Cove
Murray Hill
359 m
Ross Hill
321 m
Egeria Pt
Smithson Bight
South Pt
Medwin Pt
Cocos (Keeling) Islands
(Australia)
Wreck Pt
North Keeling I.
INDIAN OCEAN
South Keeling Islands
Horsburgh I.
(Luar)
Direction I.
Home I.
Ujong Tanjong
Pulo Pandang
West I.
(Panjang)
South I.
(Atas)
Hibernia Reef
West Islet
Ashmore Reef
Middle Islet
East Islet
Cartier Islet
Ashmore Reef and Cartier Islet
(Australia)
734
Sawu
Roti
INDONESIA
TIMOR SEA
Ashmore Reef
Cartier I.
ASHMORE AND CARTIER ISLANDS
(Aust.)
Melville I.
Bathurst I.
Van Diemen Gulf
Beagle Gulf
Darwin
Palmerston
Berry Springs
Adelaide River
Pine Creek
Cape Ford
Joseph Bonaparte Gulf
Cape Londonderry
Admiralty Gulf
Kalumburu
Bigge I.
Bonaparte Archipelago
Wyndham
Kununurra
Timber Creek
Victoria River Wayside Inn
Lake Argyle Village
KIMBERLEY
Kupingarri
Top Springs
Cape Leveque
Lombadina
King Sound
King Leopold Ranges
Derby
Mt Broome
935 m
Kalkarindji
Broome
Roebuck Bay
Fitzroy Crossing
Halls Creek
NORTHERN TERRITORY
Lagrange
Tanami Desert
Eighty Mile Beach
Sandfire Roadhouse
Port Hedland
Pardoo Roadhouse
GREAT SANDY DESERT
Lake Gregory
Dampier
Roebourne
Marble Bar
Barrow I.
Karratha
PILBARA
Lake Mackay
Yuendumu
Exmouth Gulf
Onslow
Nullagine
Lake Dora
Lake Auld
North West Cape
Exmouth
Pannawonica
Nanutarra Roadhouse
Hamersley Range
Wittenoom
Mt Tom Price
1073 m
Tom Price
Paraburdoo
Mt Meharry
1253 m
Newman
Lake Disappointment
Lake Hopkins
Lake Neale
Lake Amadeus
Coral Bay
Gibson Desert
Minilya Roadhouse
Mt Augustus
1105 m
Yulara
Katatjuta (Mt Olga)
1066 m
Uluru (Ayers Rock)
863 m
Tropic of Capricorn
Lake MacLeod
Lake Carnegie
Boyd Lagoon
Mt Woodroffe
1435 m
Musgrave Ranges
Bernier I.
Dorre I.
Carnarvon
Shark Bay
Wiluna
Dirk Hartog I.
Denham
Lake Wells
GREAT VICTORIA DESERT
Steep Point
Overlander Roadhouse
Meekatharra
WESTERN AUSTRALIA
SOUTH AUSTRALIA
Lake Austin
Mount Magnet
Lake Noondie
Laverton
Kalbarri
Northampton
Leonora
Lake Carey
Jubilee Lake
INDIAN OCEAN
Houtman Abrolhos
Mullewa
Lake Barlee
Lake Minigwal
Geraldton
Dongara
Lake Ballard
Menzies
Lake Rebecca
Lake Moore
Wubin
Kalgoorlie-Boulder
Nullarbor Plain
Moora
Coolgardie
Kambalda
Wongan Hills
Southern Cross
Lake Lefroy
Lake Cowan
Madura
Eucla
Fowlers Bay
Goomalling
Merredin
Muchea
Northam
York
Balladonia
Perth
Kwinana
Rockingham
Mandurah
Hyden
Norseman
Lake Dundas
Twilight Cove
Great Australian Bight
Corrigin
Pinjarra
Narrogin
Lake King
Ravensthorpe
Collie
Wagin
Esperance
Cape Arid
Bunbury
Geographe Bay
Katanning
Busselton
Kojonup
Jerramungup
Archipelago of the Recherche
Margaret River
Bridgetown
Manjimup
Cape Leeuwin
Augusta
Mount Barker
Walpole
Albany
Denmark
Flinders Bay
SOUTHERN OCEAN
Macquarie Island
(Australia)
Hasselborough Bay
North Head
Anare Station
Buckles Bay
Langdon Pt
Mt Elder
371 m
Bauer Bay
Sandy Bay
Mt Waite
422 m
Mt Eitel 341 m
Victoria Pt
Sandell Bay
Mt Hamilton
433 m
Mt Fletcher
428 m
Mt Jeffryes 399 m
Caroline Cove
South West Pt
Hurd Pt
Heard Island and McDonald Islands
(Australia)
Anzac Peak
715 m
Corinthian Head
Laurens Pen.
Morgan I.
McDonald Islands
West Bay
Spit Pt
Mawson Peak
2745 m
Heard I.
Lambeth Bluff

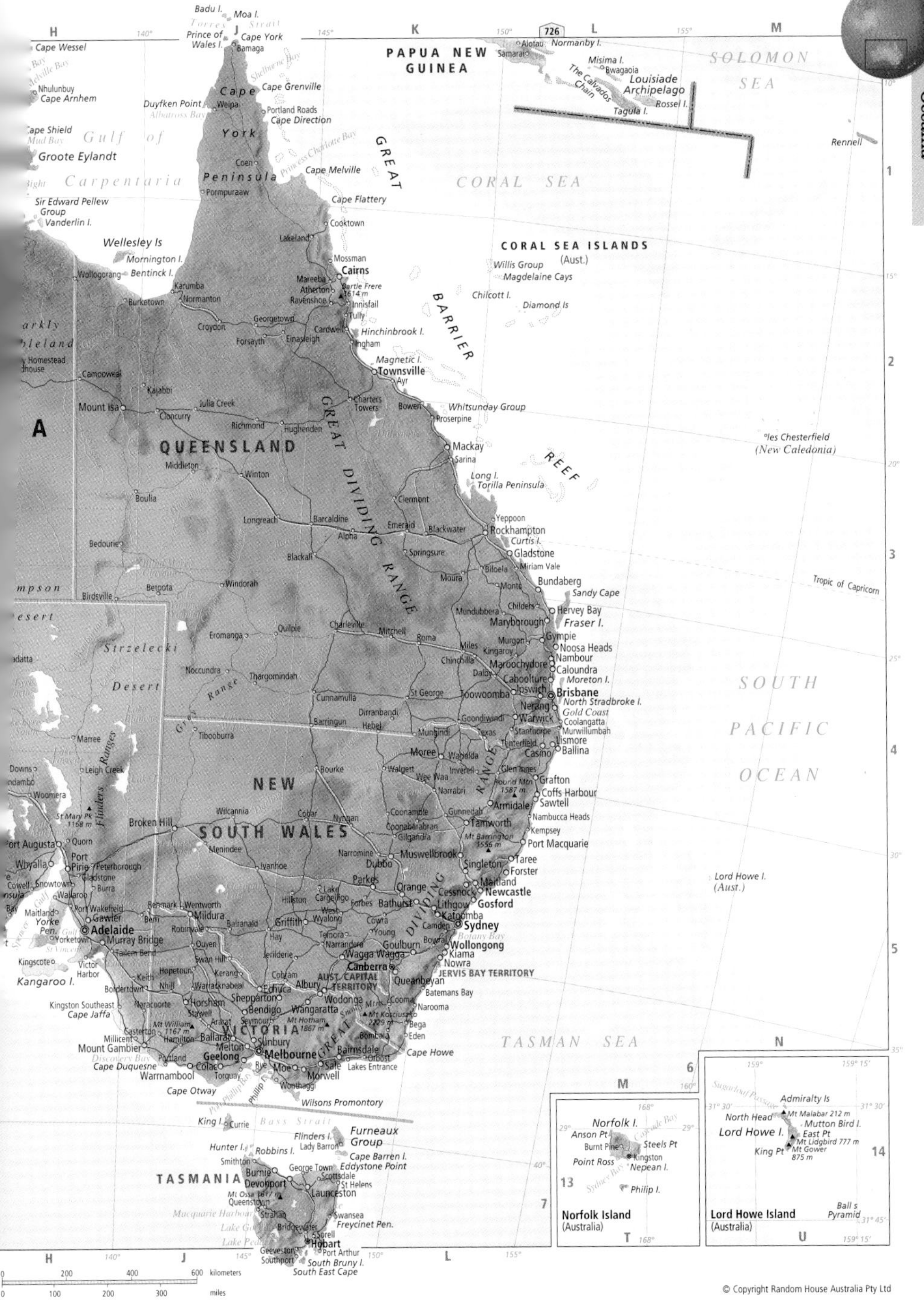
726
PAPUA NEW GUINEA
SOLOMON SEA
CORAL SEA
CORAL SEA ISLANDS (Aust.)
GREAT BARRIER REEF
SOUTH PACIFIC OCEAN
TASMAN SEA
Tropic of Capricorn
Gulf of Carpentaria
Torres Strait
Bass Strait
Badu I.
Moa I.
Prince of Wales I.
Cape York
Bamaga
Cape Wessel
Nhulunbuy
Cape Arnhem
Cape Grenville
Duyfken Point
Albatross Bay
Weipa
Portland Roads
Cape Direction
Cape York Peninsula
Cape Shield
Mud Bay
Groote Eylandt
Coen
Princess Charlotte Bay
Cape Melville
Pormpuraaw
Cape Flattery
Sir Edward Pellew Group
Vanderlin I.
Cooktown
Lakeland
Wellesley Is
Mornington I.
Bentinck I.
Wollogorang
Mossman
Cairns
Mareeba
Atherton
Bartle Frere 1614 m
Ravenshoe
Innisfail
Tully
Karumba
Normanton
Burketown
Georgetown
Croydon
Cardwell
Hinchinbrook I.
Einasleigh
Forsayth
Ingham
Magnetic I.
Townsville
Ayr
Alotau
Samarai
Normanby I.
Misima I.
Bwagaoia
Louisiade Archipelago
The Calvados Chain
Tagula I.
Rossel I.
Rennell
Willis Group
Magdelaine Cays
Chilcott I.
Diamond Is
Camooweal
Kajabbi
Mount Isa
Cloncurry
Julia Creek
Charters Towers
Bowen
Whitsunday Group
Proserpine
Richmond
Hughenden
QUEENSLAND
GREAT DIVIDING RANGE
Mackay
Sarina
Middleton
Winton
Long I.
Torilla Peninsula
Iles Chesterfield (New Caledonia)
Boulia
Clermont
Longreach
Barcaldine
Alpha
Emerald
Blackwater
Yeppoon
Rockhampton
Curtis I.
Gladstone
Bedourie
Springsure
Blackall
Biloela
Miriam Vale
Windorah
Betoota
Birdsville
Moura
Monto
Bundaberg
Sandy Cape
Childers
Hervey Bay
Fraser I.
Mundubbera
Maryborough
Quilpie
Charleville
Mitchell
Roma
Eromanga
Miles
Murgon
Kingaroy
Gympie
Noosa Heads
Nambour
Chinchilla
Maroochydore
Caloundra
Dalby
Caboolture
Moreton I.
Noccundra
Thargomindah
Ipswich
Brisbane
Toowoomba
North Stradbroke I.
St George
Cunnamulla
Nerang
Gold Coast
Warwick
Coolangatta
Murwillumbah
Dirranbandi
Hebel
Goondiwindi
Stanthorpe
Barringun
Mungindi
Texas
Tenterfield
Lismore
Tibooburra
Casino
Ballina
Moree
Warialda
Walgett
Wee Waa
Inverell
Glen Innes
Bourke
Round Mtn 1587 m
Grafton
NEW SOUTH WALES
Narrabri
Coffs Harbour
Sawtell
Armidale
Nambucca Heads
Wilcannia
Cobar
Nyngan
Coonamble
Gunnedah
Tamworth
Kempsey
Broken Hill
Coonabarabran
Gilgandra
Mt Barrington 1556 m
Port Macquarie
Menindee
Narromine
Dubbo
Muswellbrook
Singleton
Taree
Forster
Ivanhoe
Maitland
Newcastle
Parkes
Orange
Cessnock
Gosford
Lake Cargelligo
Forbes
Bathurst
Lithgow
Katoomba
Hillston
West Wyalong
Sydney
Botany Bay
Camden
Wollongong
Cowra
Young
Kiama
Nowra
Hay
Temora
Griffith
Narrandera
Goulburn
Bowral
Mildura
Wentworth
Renmark
Berri
Balranald
Robinvale
Wagga Wagga
Canberra
Ouyen
Swan Hill
Deniliquin
Jerilderie
Kerang
Cobram
Albury
AUST. CAPITAL TERRITORY
Queanbeyan
JERVIS BAY TERRITORY
Batemans Bay
Hopetoun
Nhill
Warracknabeal
Echuca
Shepparton
Wodonga
Cooma
Horsham
Stawell
Bendigo
Wangaratta
Mt Kosciuszko 2229 m
Narooma
Ararat
Seymour
Mt Hotham 1867 m
Bega
Mt William 1167 m
VICTORIA
Eden
Hamilton
Ballarat
Sunbury
Bombala
Casterton
Melton
Melbourne
Bairnsdale
Cape Howe
Millicent
Mount Gambier
Discovery Bay
Portland
Geelong
Colac
Moe
Sale
Orbost
Lakes Entrance
Cape Duquesne
Warrnambool
Torquay
Rye
Morwell
Wonthaggi
Port Phillip Bay
Cape Otway
Wilsons Promontory
Kingston Southeast
Cape Jaffa
Naracoorte
Bordertown
Keith
Victor Harbor
Kingscote
Kangaroo I.
Tailem Bend
Murray Bridge
Adelaide
Gawler
Yorketown
Yorke Pen.
Maitland
Port Wakefield
Kadina
Wallaroo
Cowell
Snowtown
Gladstone
Burra
Port Pirie
Peterborough
Whyalla
Port Augusta
Quorn
St Mary Pk 1168 m
Flinders Ranges
Woomera
Leigh Creek
Marree
Strzelecki Desert
Grey Range
King I.
Currie
Flinders I.
Furneaux Group
Lady Barron
Cape Barren I.
Hunter I.
Robbins I.
Smithton
Burnie
George Town
Eddystone Point
Scottsdale
TASMANIA
Devonport
St Helens
Mt Ossa 1617 m
Queenstown
Launceston
Macquarie Harbour
Strahan
Swansea
Freycinet Pen.
Bridgewater
Sorell
Hobart
Port Arthur
Geeveston
Southport
South Bruny I.
South East Cape
Lord Howe I. (Aust.)
Norfolk I.
Anson Pt
Burnt Pine
Steels Pt
Cascade Bay
Point Ross
Kingston
Nepean I.
Sydney Bay
Philip I.
Norfolk Island (Australia)
Admiralty Is
North Head
Mt Malabar 212 m
Mutton Bird I.
Lord Howe I.
East Pt
Mt Lidgbird 777 m
King Pt
Mt Gower 875 m
Ball's Pyramid
Lord Howe Island (Australia)
Sugarloaf Passage
0 200 400 600 kilometers
0 100 200 300 miles

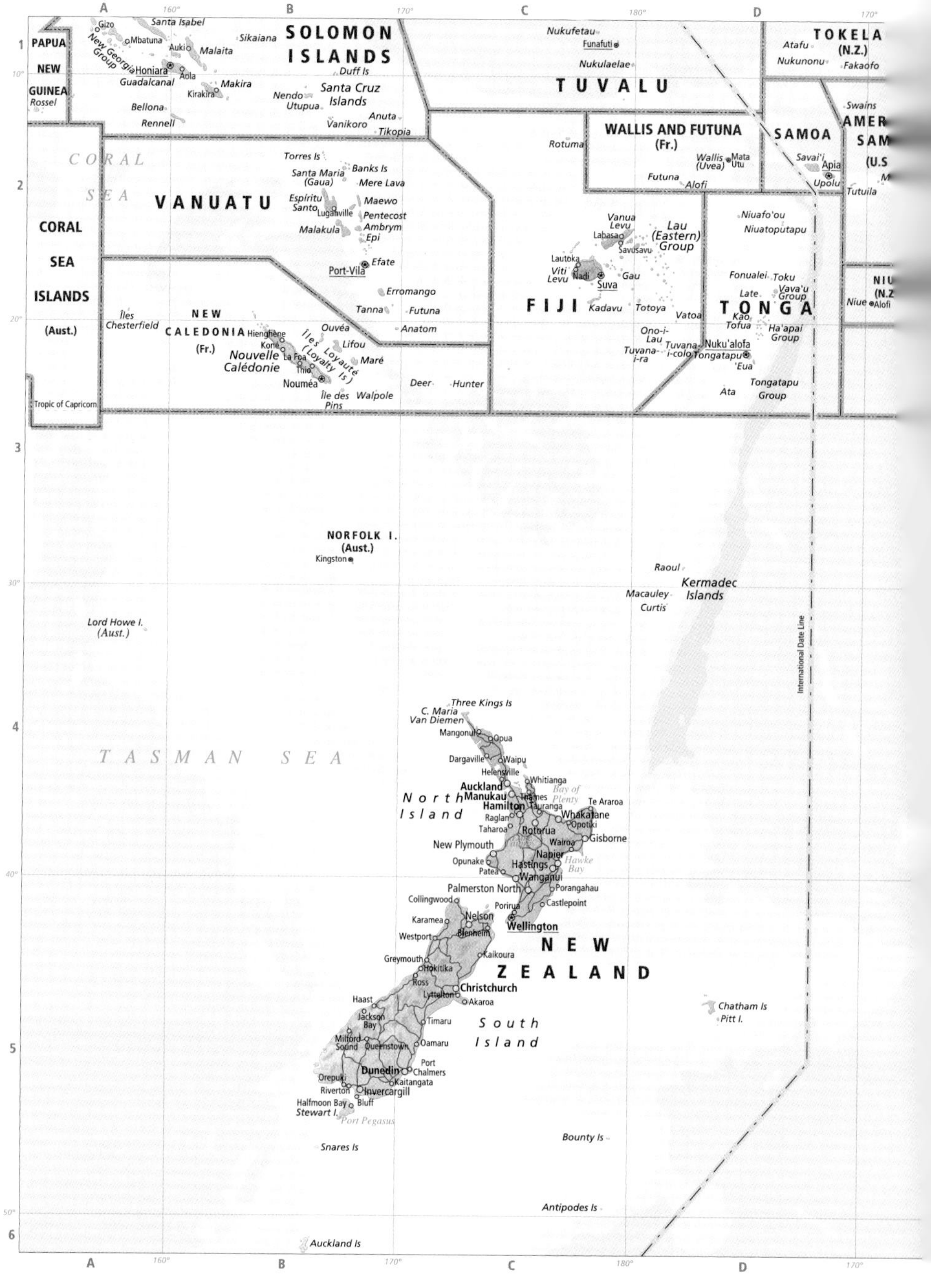
A
B
C
D
160°
170°
180°
170°
10°
20°
30°
40°
50°
1
2
3
4
5
6
PAPUA NEW GUINEA
Rossel
Gizo
Santa Isabel
Mbatuna
New Georgia Group
Aukio
Malaita
Honiara
Aola
Guadalcanal
Kirakira
Makira
Bellona
Rennell
Sikaiana
SOLOMON ISLANDS
Duff Is
Nendo
Utupua
Santa Cruz Islands
Anuta
Vanikoro
Tikopia
Nukufetau
Funafuti
Nukulaelae
TUVALU
TOKELA
(N.Z.)
Atafu
Nukunonu
Fakaofo
Swains
AMER
SAM
(U.S
WALLIS AND FUTUNA
(Fr.)
Rotuma
Wallis (Uvea)
Mata Utu
Futuna
Alofi
SAMOA
Savai'i
Apia
Upolu
Tutuila
CORAL SEA
VANUATU
Torres Is
Banks Is
Santa Maria (Gaua)
Mere Lava
Espíritu Santo
Luganville
Maewo
Pentecost
Malakula
Ambrym
Epi
Efate
Port-Vila
Erromango
Tanna
Futuna
Anatom
CORAL SEA ISLANDS
(Aust.)
Îles Chesterfield
NEW CALEDONIA
(Fr.)
Hienghène
Koné
La Foa
Thio
Nouvelle Calédonie
Nouméa
Îles Loyauté (Loyalty Is)
Ouvéa
Lifou
Maré
Île des Pins
Walpole
Deer
Hunter
Tropic of Capricorn
Vanua Levu
Labasa
Savusavu
Lau (Eastern) Group
Lautoka
Viti Levu
Nadi
Suva
Gau
FIJI
Kadavu
Totoya
Vatoa
Ono-i-Lau
Tuvana-i-ra
Tuvana-i-colo
Niuafo'ou
Niuatoputapu
Fonualei
Toku
Late
Vava'u Group
TONGA
Kao
Tofua
Ha'apai Group
Nuku'alofa
Tongatapu
'Eua
Tongatapu Group
Ata
NIU
(N.Z
Niue
Alofi
NORFOLK I.
(Aust.)
Kingston
Raoul
Macauley
Curtis
Kermadec Islands
Lord Howe I.
(Aust.)
International Date Line
TASMAN SEA
Three Kings Is
C. Maria Van Diemen
Mangonui
Opua
Dargaville
Waipu
Helensville
Whitianga
Auckland
Manukau
Thames
Bay of Plenty
North Island
Hamilton
Tauranga
Te Araroa
Whakatane
Raglan
Opotiki
Taharoa
Rotorua
New Plymouth
Wairoa
Gisborne
Napier
Opunake
Hastings
Hawke Bay
Patea
Wanganui
Palmerston North
Porangahau
Collingwood
Porirua
Castlepoint
Karamea
Nelson
Wellington
Westport
Blenheim
NEW ZEALAND
Greymouth
Kaikoura
Hokitika
Ross
Christchurch
Lyttelton
Akaroa
Haast
Jackson Bay
Timaru
South Island
Milford Sound
Queenstown
Oamaru
Port Chalmers
Dunedin
Orepuki
Kaitangata
Riverton
Invercargill
Halfmoon Bay
Bluff
Stewart I.
Port Pegasus
Chatham Is
Pitt I.
Snares Is
Bounty Is
Antipodes Is
Auckland Is

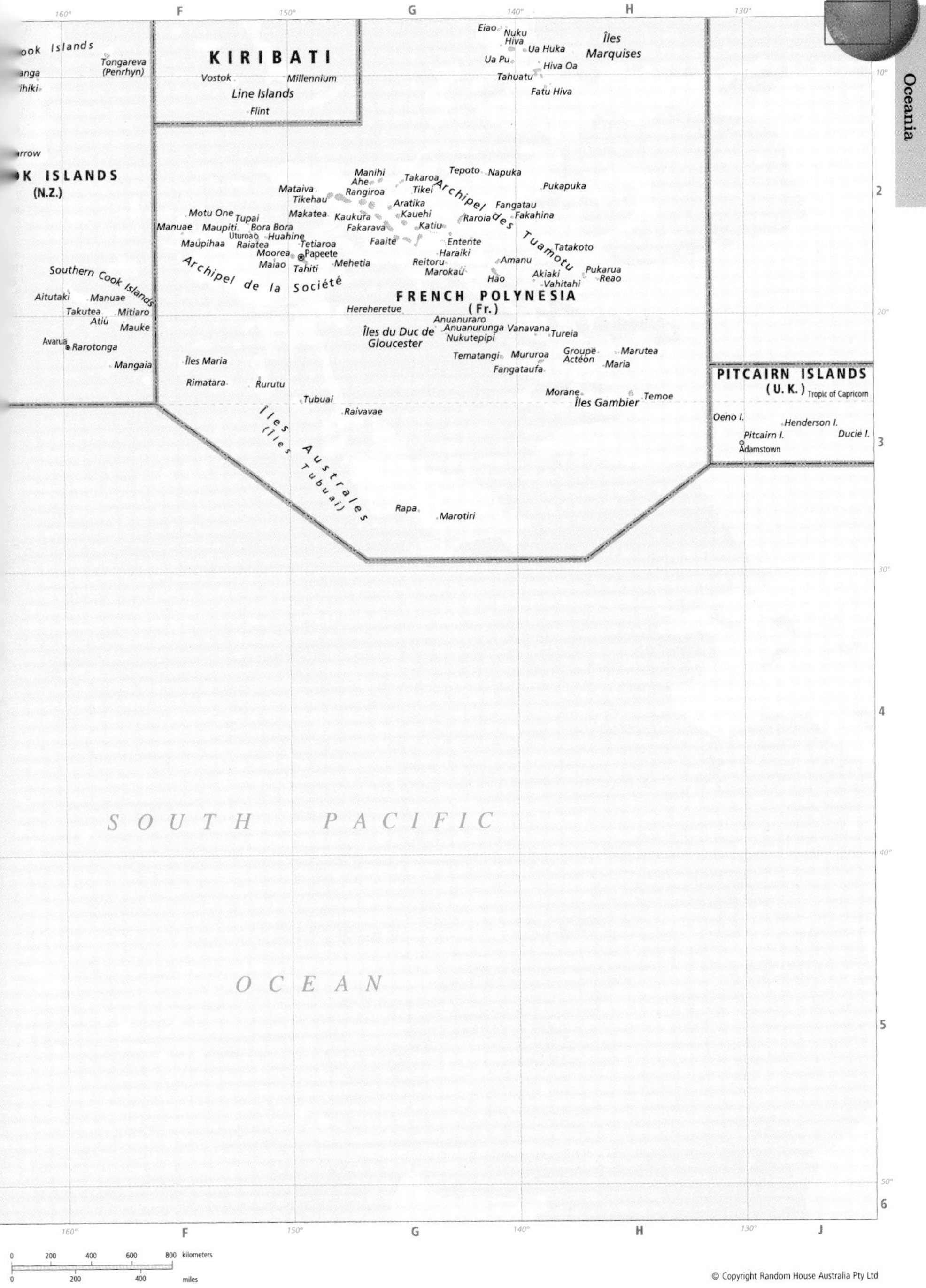
KIRIBATI
Tongareva (Penrhyn)
Vostok
Millennium
Line Islands
Flint
Eiao
Nuku Hiva
Ua Huka
Ua Pu
Hiva Oa
Tahuatu
Fatu Hiva
Îles Marquises
OK ISLANDS (N.Z.)
Manihi
Ahe
Rangiroa
Takaroa
Tikei
Tepoto
Napuka
Pukapuka
Mataiva
Tikehau
Makatea
Aratika
Kauehi
Kaukura
Fakarava
Katiu
Faaite
Fangatau
Fakahina
Raroia
Archipel des Tuamotu
Motu One
Tupai
Manuae
Maupiti
Bora Bora
Uturoa
Huahine
Maupihaa
Raiatea
Tetiaroa
Moorea
Papeete
Maiao
Tahiti
Mehetia
Entente
Haraiki
Reitoru
Marokau
Amanu
Hao
Tatakoto
Akiaki
Vahitahi
Pukarua
Reao
Archipel de la Société
Southern Cook Islands
Aitutaki
Manuae
Takutea
Mitiaro
Atiu
Mauke
Avarua
Rarotonga
Mangaia
FRENCH POLYNESIA (Fr.)
Hereheretue
Îles du Duc de Gloucester
Anuanuraro
Anuanurunga
Nukutepipi
Vanavana
Tureia
Tematangi
Mururoa
Fangataufa
Groupe Actéon
Marutea
Maria
Îles Maria
Rimatara
Rurutu
Tubuai
Raivavae
Morane
Îles Gambier
Temoe
PITCAIRN ISLANDS (U.K.)
Tropic of Capricorn
Oeno I.
Henderson I.
Pitcairn I.
Ducie I.
Adamstown
Îles Australes (Îles Tubuai)
Rapa
Marotiri
SOUTH PACIFIC OCEAN
160° 150° 140° 130°
F G H J
10° 20° 30° 40° 50°
2 3 4 5 6
0 200 400 600 800 kilometers
0 200 400 miles

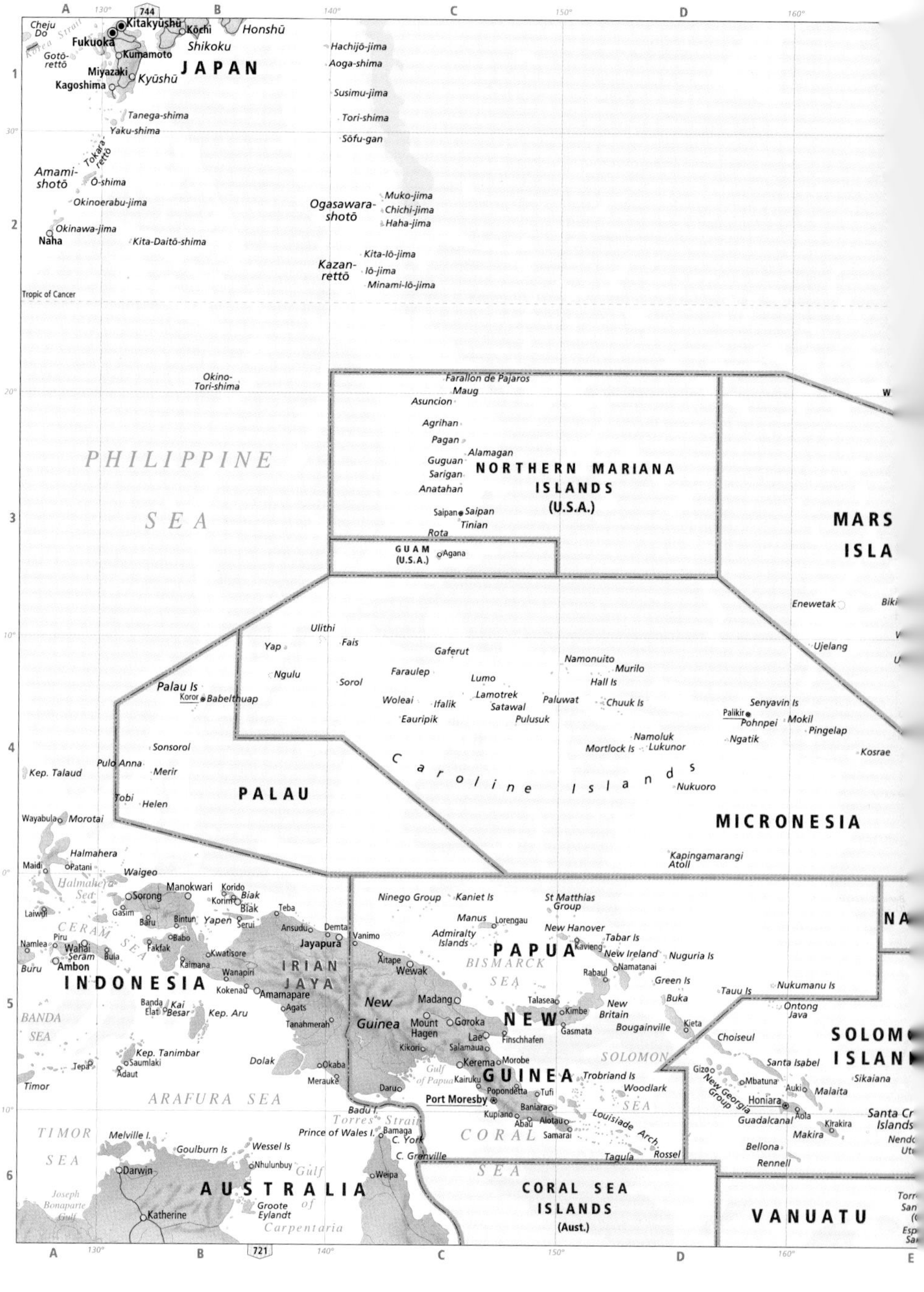

A
B
C
D
E
1
2
3
4
5
6
130°
140°
150°
160°
30°
20°
10°
0°
744
721
Cheju Do
Korea Strait
Kitakyūshū
Kōchi
Honshū
Fukuoka
Shikoku
Gotō-rettō
Kumamoto
JAPAN
Miyazaki
Kyūshū
Kagoshima
Tanega-shima
Yaku-shima
Tokara-rettō
Amami-shotō
Ō-shima
Okinoerabu-jima
Okinawa-jima
Naha
Kita-Daitō-shima
Hachijō-jima
Aoga-shima
Susimu-jima
Tori-shima
Sōfu-gan
Ogasawara-shotō
Muko-jima
Chichi-jima
Haha-jima
Kazan-rettō
Kita-Iō-jima
Iō-jima
Minami-Iō-jima
Tropic of Cancer
Okino-Tori-shima
PHILIPPINE SEA
Farallon de Pajaros
Maug
Asuncion
Agrihan
Pagan
Alamagan
Guguan
Sarigan
Anatahan
NORTHERN MARIANA ISLANDS (U.S.A.)
Saipan
Tinian
Rota
GUAM (U.S.A.)
Agana
MARS
ISLA
Enewetak
Biki
Ujelang
Ulithi
Yap
Fais
Gaferut
Namonuito
Murilo
Hall Is
Ngulu
Faraulep
Lumo
Sorol
Palau Is
Koror
Babelthuap
Woleai
Ifalik
Lamotrek
Satawal
Paluwat
Chuuk Is
Senyavin Is
Palikir
Pohnpei
Mokil
Pingelap
Eauripik
Pulusuk
Ngatik
Namoluk
Sonsorol
Mortlock Is
Lukunor
Kosrae
Pulo Anna
Merir
Kep. Talaud
Caroline Islands
Nukuoro
PALAU
Tobi
Helen
MICRONESIA
Wayabula
Morotai
Halmahera
Kapingamarangi Atoll
Maidi
Patani
Waigeo
Halmahera Sea
Manokwari
Korido
Sorong
Korim
Biak
Nienego Group
Kaniet Is
St Matthias Group
Laiwui
Gasim
Teba
Baru
Bintun
Yapen
Serui
Manus
Lorengau
Ansudu
Demta
CERAM SEA
Babo
Jayapura
Vanimo
Admiralty Islands
New Hanover
Tabar Is
Namlea
Piru
Wahai
Fakfak
Kavieng
Seram
Bula
Kwatisore
Aitape
PAPUA
New Ireland
Nuguria Is
Buru
Ambon
Kaimana
IRIAN JAYA
Wewak
BISMARCK SEA
Namatanai
INDONESIA
Wanapiri
Rabaul
Kokenau
Amamapare
Green Is
Tauu Is
Nukumanu Is
Banda Elat
Kai Besar
Agats
Madang
Talasea
Buka
New Guinea
Kimbe
New Britain
Ontong Java
BANDA SEA
Kep. Aru
Tanahmerah
Mount Hagen
Goroka
NEW
Gasmata
Bougainville
Kieta
Lae
Finschhafen
Choiseul
SOLOM
Kep. Tanimbar
Saumlaki
Tepa
Adaut
Dolak
Okaba
Kikori
Salamaua
SOLOMON
Kerema
Morobe
Gizo
Santa Isabel
ISLAN
Timor
Merauke
Gulf of Papua
Kairuku
GUINEA
Trobriand Is
Mbatuna
Sikaiana
New Georgia Group
Auki
Malaita
ARAFURA SEA
Daru
Popondetta
Tufi
Woodlark
Honiara
Port Moresby
Baniara
SEA
Badu I.
Torres Strait
Kupiano
Abau
Alotau
Louisiade Arch.
Guadalcanal
Aola
Santa Cr
Islands
TIMOR SEA
Melville I.
Prince of Wales I.
Bamaga
Samarai
Makira
Kirakira
Nendo
Goulburn Is
Wessel Is
C. York
CORAL
Bellona
Tagula
Rossel
Rennell
Nhulunbuy
Gulf
C. Grenville
SEA
Darwin
Weipa
AUSTRALIA
CORAL SEA ISLANDS (Aust.)
VANUATU
Joseph Bonaparte Gulf
Groote Eylandt
of Carpentaria
Katherine

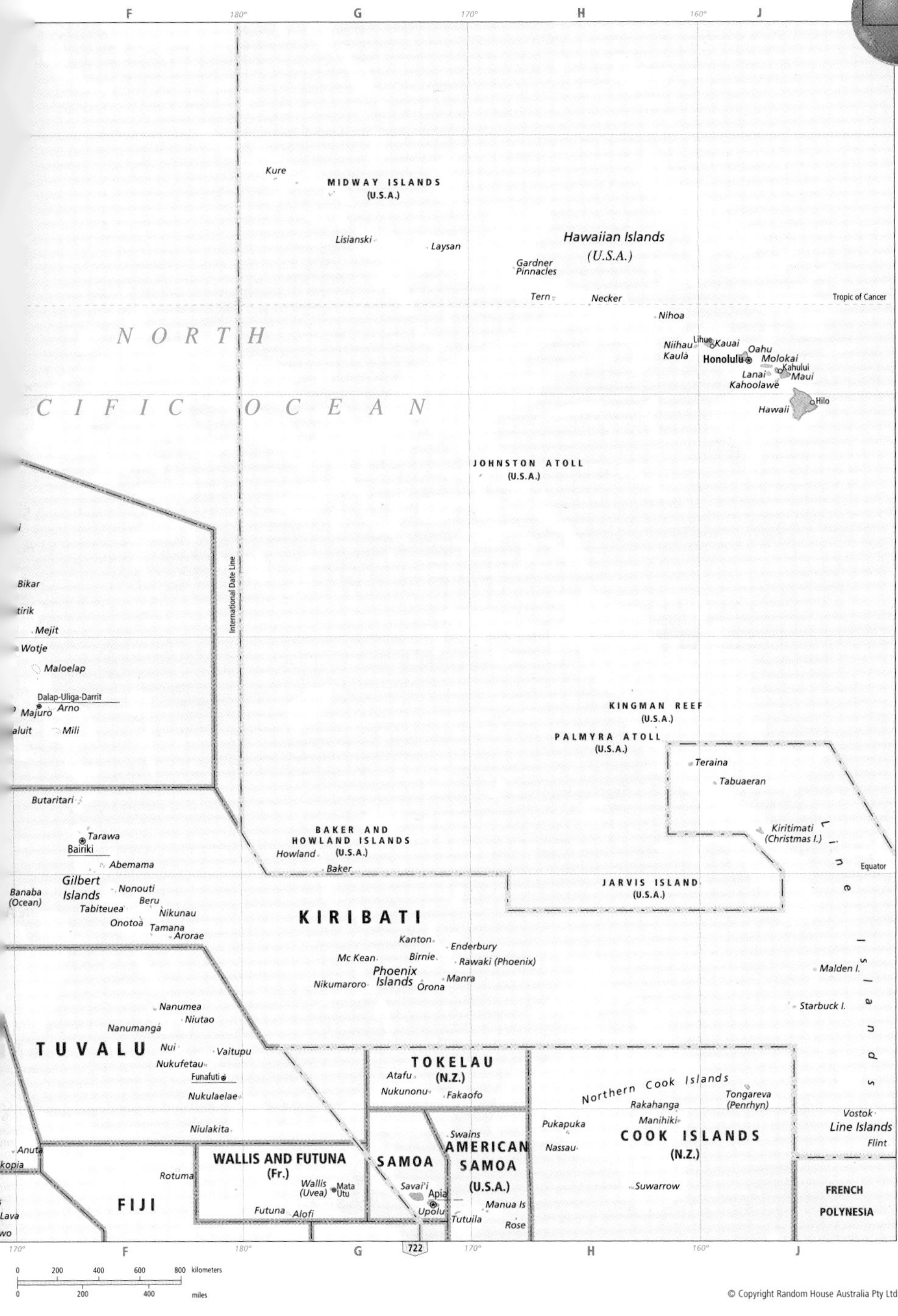
F
180°
G
170°
H
160°
J
1
30°
2
3
4
5
6
10°
20°
0°
Kure
MIDWAY ISLANDS
(U.S.A.)
Lisianski
Laysan
Hawaiian Islands
(U.S.A.)
Gardner Pinnacles
Tern
Necker
Tropic of Cancer
Nihoa
Niihau
Lihue
Kauai
Oahu
Kaula
Honolulu
Molokai
Kahului
Lanai
Maui
Kahoolawe
Hilo
Hawaii
NORTH
CIFIC OCEAN
JOHNSTON ATOLL
(U.S.A.)
International Date Line
Bikar
tirik
Mejit
Wotje
Maloelap
Dalap-Uliga-Darrit
Majuro
Arno
aluit
Mili
KINGMAN REEF
(U.S.A.)
PALMYRA ATOLL
(U.S.A.)
Teraina
Tabuaeran
Butaritari
Kiritimati
(Christmas I.)
Tarawa
Bairiki
BAKER AND HOWLAND ISLANDS
(U.S.A.)
Howland
Baker
Abemama
Equator
Gilbert Islands
Nonouti
Banaba
(Ocean)
Beru
Tabiteuea
Nikunau
Onotoa
Tamana
Arorae
JARVIS ISLAND
(U.S.A.)
KIRIBATI
Kanton
Enderbury
Birnie
Mc Kean
Rawaki (Phoenix)
Phoenix Islands
Nikumaroro
Orona
Manra
Malden I.
Line Islands
Starbuck I.
Nanumea
Niutao
Nanumanga
TUVALU
Nui
Vaitupu
Nukufetau
Funafuti
Nukulaelae
TOKELAU
(N.Z.)
Atafu
Nukunonu
Fakaofo
Northern Cook Islands
Tongareva
(Penrhyn)
Rakahanga
Manihiki
Vostok
Line Islands
Flint
Pukapuka
Nassau
COOK ISLANDS
(N.Z.)
Niulakita
Swains
Anuta
kopia
WALLIS AND FUTUNA
(Fr.)
SAMOA
AMERICAN SAMOA
(U.S.A.)
Rotuma
Wallis
(Uvea)
Mata Utu
Savai'i
Apia
Upolu
Suwarrow
FRENCH POLYNESIA
Lava
FIJI
Futuna
Alofi
Tutuila
Manua Is
Rose
ewo
170°
F
180°
G
170°
H
160°
J
0
200
400
600
800
kilometers
0
200
400
miles

Papua New Guinea

Oceania

PACIFIC OCEAN

Green Is
Nissan I.
C. Hanpan
Hanahan
Buka I.
Sohano
Kunua
Wakunai
Mt Balbi 2715 m
Torokina
Arawa
Kieta
Motupena Point
Panguna
Mt Takara 2219 m
Boku
Buin
Nukiki
Shortland I. (Alu)
Treasury Is
Mono I.
Vella Lavella
Kia
Santa Isabel

NORTH SOLOMONS
PAPUA NEW GUINEA
Bougainville I.
Aropa

SOLOMON ISLANDS
Choiseul
Sasamungga

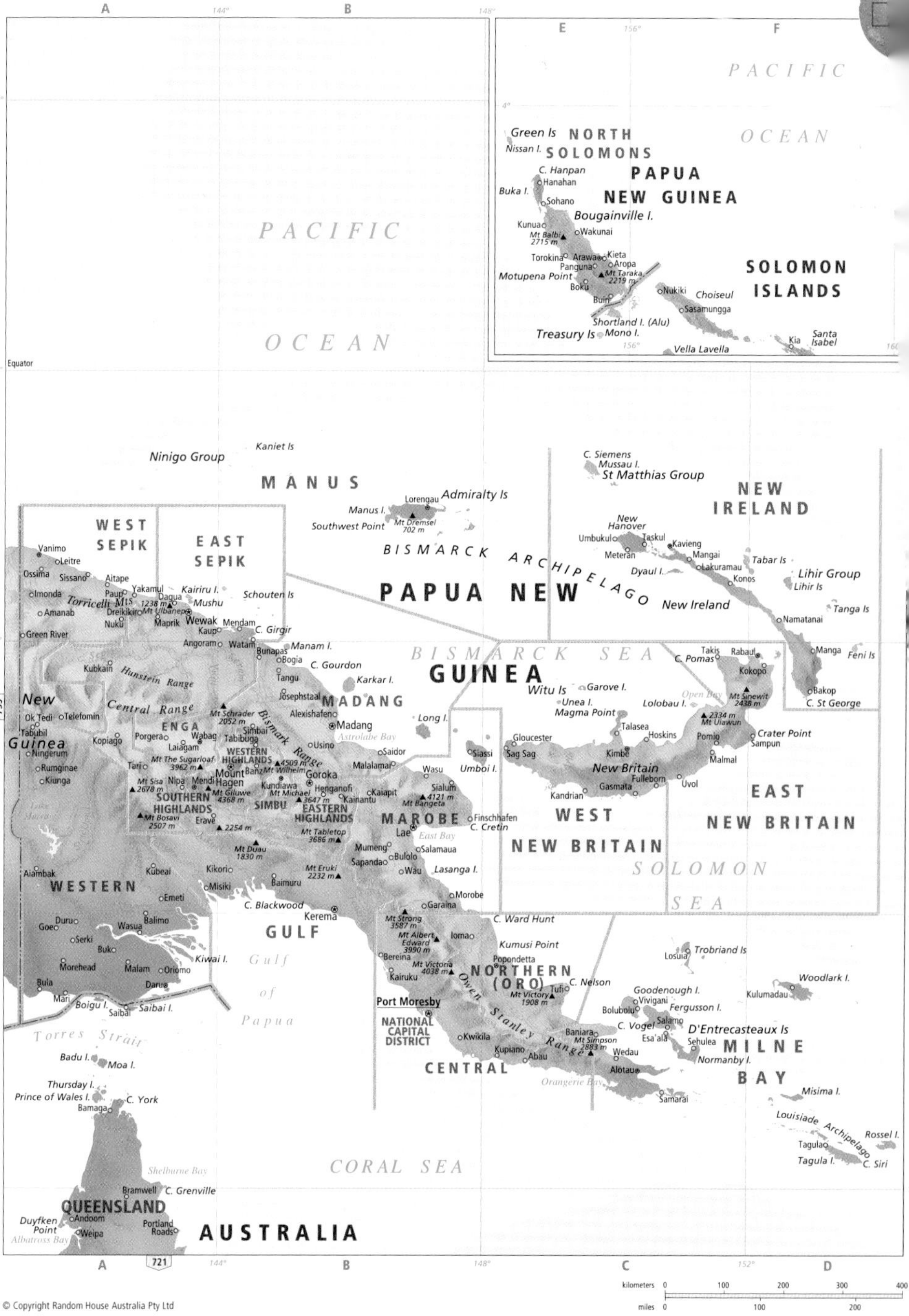

PACIFIC OCEAN

Equator

Kaniet Is
Ninigo Group
MANUS
Lorengau
Admiralty Is
Manus I.
Mt Dremsel 702 m
Southwest Point
BISMARCK ARCHIPELAGO
C. Siemens
Mussau I.
St Matthias Group
New Hanover
Umbukul
Taskul
Kavieng
Meteran
Mangai
Dyaul I.
Makuramau
Konos
NEW IRELAND
Tabar Is
Lihir Group
Lihir Is
New Ireland
Tanga Is
Namatanai

WEST SEPIK
Vanimo
Leitre
Ossima
Sissano
Aitape
Imonda
Paup
Yakamul
Kairiru I.
Schouten Is
Amanab
Drekikir
Ulupu
Mushu
Nuku
Wewak
Mendam
Angoram
Watam
C. Girgir
Manam I.

EAST SEPIK
Torricelli Mts
1238 m
Kaup

PAPUA NEW GUINEA

BISMARCK SEA
Takis
Pomas
Rabaul
Manga
Feni Is
Kokopo
Bakop
C. St George
Witu Is
Garove I.
Unea I.
Lolobau I.
Open Bay
Mt Sinewit 2438 m
Magma Point
Talasea
Hoskins
Pomio
Crater Point
Sampun
Gloucester
Sag Sag
Kimbe
Malmal
Gasmata
Fulleborn
Uvol

NEW GUINEA
New Guinea
Ok Tedi
Telefomin
Tabubil
Ningerum
Rumginae
Kiunga
Kubkain
Hunstein Range
Central Range
ENGA
Porgera
Wabag
Laiagam
Tari
Mt Sisa 2678 m
Nipa
Mendi
SOUTHERN HIGHLANDS
Mt Bosavi 2507 m
Erave
Obogia
Tangu
Karkar I.
Josephstaal
Alexishafen
MADANG
Madang
Astrolabe Bay
Usino
Saidor
Bismarck Range
Mt Schrader 2052 m
Simbai
Tabibuga
WESTERN HIGHLANDS
Mt The Sugarloaf 3962 m
Mount Hagen
Mt Wilhelm 4647 m
Mt Giluwe 4368 m
Kundiawa
Mt Michael
SIMBU
EASTERN HIGHLANDS
Henganofi
Kainantu
Goroka
Kaiapit
Mt Bangeta 4121 m
Long I.
Umboi I.
Siassi
Malalamai
Wasu
Sialum
Finschhafen
C. Cretin
WEST NEW BRITAIN
New Britain
EAST NEW BRITAIN
Kandrian
SOLOMON SEA

WESTERN
Alambak
Duru
Goe
Serki
Bula
Mari
Boigu I.
Saibai I.
Morehead
Malam
Oriomo
Daru
Kiwai I.
Balimo
Kubeal
Kikori
Emeti
Misiki
Baimuru
Kerema
GULF
Gulf of Papua
Mt Duau 1830 m
Mt Eruki 2232 m
Mt Tabletop 3686 m
MAROBE
Lae
East Bay
Salamaua
Mumeng
Bulolo
Wau
Lasanga I.
Morobe
Garaina
C. Blackwood
C. Ward Hunt

Torres Strait
Badu I.
Moa I.
Thursday I.
Prince of Wales I.
C. York
Bamaga

Mt Strong 3587 m
Iomao
Mt Victoria 4038 m
Mt Edward 2990 m
Bereina
Kairuku
NORTHERN (ORO)
Kumusi Point
Popondetta
Tufi
C. Nelson
Losuia
Trobriand Is
Woodlark I.
Kulumadau
Goodenough I.
Fergusson I.
Vivigani
Salamo
D'Entrecasteaux Is
Bolubolu
Baniara
Esa'ala
Sehulea
MILNE BAY
Misima I.
Normanby I.
Mt Victory 1908 m
Mt Albert Edward
Mt Simpson 2883 m
C. Vogel
Wedau
Port Moresby
NATIONAL CAPITAL DISTRICT
Kwikila
Kupiano
Abau
Alotau
CENTRAL
Owen Stanley Range
Orangerie Bay
Samarai
Louisiade Archipelago
Rossel I.
Tagula
Tagula I.
C. Siri

CORAL SEA

QUEENSLAND
Duyfken Point
Andoom
Weipa
Portland Roads
AUSTRALIA
Bramwell
C. Grenville
Albatross Bay
Shelburne Bay

kilometers 0 100 200 300 400
miles 0 100 200

© Copyright Random House Australia Pty Ltd

A B

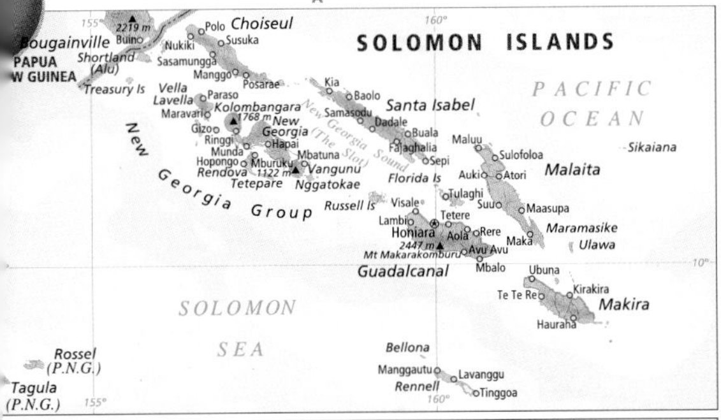
SOLOMON ISLANDS
Choiseul
Polo
Susuka
Bougainville
Buin
2219 m
PAPUA
NEW GUINEA
Nukiki
Shortland (Alu)
Sasamungga
Manggo
Treasury Is
Posarae
Kia
Baolo
Vella Lavella
Paraso
Kolombangara
Maravari
1768 m
New Georgia
Gizo
Ringgi
Hapai
Munda
Mburuku
Hopongo
Rendova
1122 m
Vangunu
Mbatuna
Tetepare
Nggatokae
New Georgia Group
New Georgia Sound (The Slot)
Samasodu
Santa Isabel
Dadale
Buala
Fajaghalia
Sepi
Florida Is
Maluu
Sulofoloa
Auki
Atori
Malaita
Sikaiana
Russell Is
Visale
Tulaghi
Suuo
Maasupa
Lambi
Tetere
Honiara
Aola
Rere
2447 m
Mt Makarakomburu
Avu Avu
Maka
Maramasike
Ulawa
Guadalcanal
Mbalo
Ubuna
Kirakira
Te Te Re
Makira
Hauraha
PACIFIC OCEAN
SOLOMON SEA
Rossel (P.N.G.)
Tagula (P.N.G.)
Bellona
Manggautu
Lavanggu
Rennell
Tinggoa
155°
160°
10°

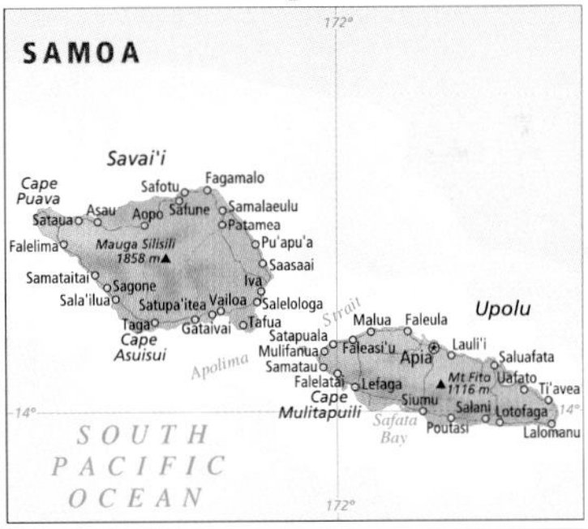
SAMOA
Savai'i
Cape Puava
Safotu
Fagamalo
Sataua
Asau
Aopo
Safune
Samalaeulu
Patamea
Falelima
Mauga Silisili 1858 m
Pu'apu'a
Saasaai
Samataitai
Sagone
Iva
Sala'ilua
Satupa'itea
Vailoa
Salelologa
Taga
Gataivai
Tafua
Cape Asuisui
Apolima Strait
Satapuala
Malua
Faleula
Upolu
Mulifanua
Faleasi'u
Apia
Lauli'i
Samatau
Saluafata
Falelatai
Lefaga
Mt Fito 1116 m
Uafato
Ti'avea
Cape Mulitapuili
Siumu
Salani
Lotofaga
Safata Bay
Poutasi
Lalomanu
SOUTH PACIFIC OCEAN
172°
14°

1

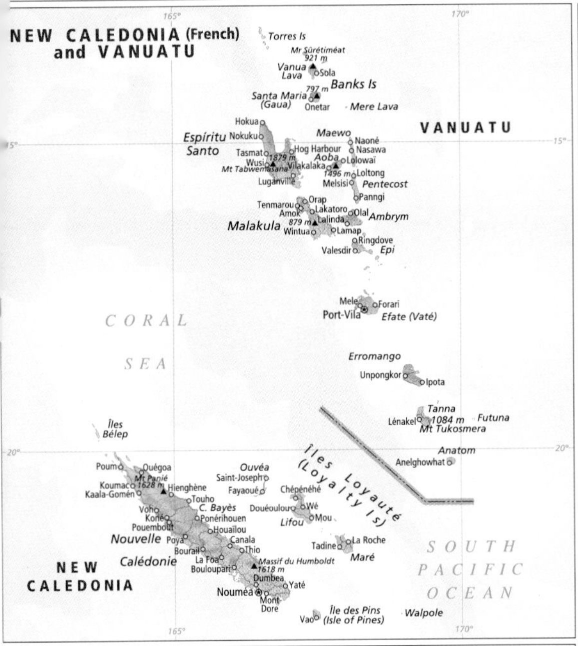
NEW CALEDONIA (French) and VANUATU
Torres Is
Mr Sûrétiméat 921 m
Vanua Lava
Sola
Banks Is
797 m
Santa Maria (Gaua)
Onetar
Mere Lava
Hokua
Espíritu Santo
Nokuku
Maewo
Naoné
Nasawa
VANUATU
Tasmat
1879 m
Hog Harbour
Aoba
Lolowai
Wusi
Mt Tabwemasana
Vilakalaka
1496 m
Loltong
Luganville
Melsisi
Pentecost
Panngi
Tenmarou
Orap
Lakatoro
Olal
Amok
Ambrym
879 m
Lalinda
Malakula
Wintua
Lamap
Ringdove
Valesdir
Epi
Mele
Forari
Port-Vila
Efate (Vaté)
CORAL SEA
Erromango
Unpongkor
Ipota
Tanna
Lénakel
1084 m
Mt Tukosmera
Futuna
Anatom
Anelghowhat
Îles Bélep
Poum
Ouégoa
Mt Panié
Koumac
1628 m
Hienghène
Kaala-Gomén
Touho
Voh
C. Bayès
Koné
Ponérihouen
Pouembout
Houaïlou
Nouvelle Calédonie
Poya
Canala
Bourail
La Foa
Thio
Boulouparis
Massif du Humboldt
1618 m
Dumbea
Yaté
Nouméa
Mont-Dore
NEW CALEDONIA
Ouvéa
Saint-Joseph
Fayaoué
Chépénéhé
Iles Loyauté (Loyalty Is)
Douéoulou
Wé
Lifou
Mou
Tadine
La Roche
Maré
SOUTH PACIFIC OCEAN
Île des Pins (Isle of Pines)
Vao
Walpole
165°
170°
15°
20°

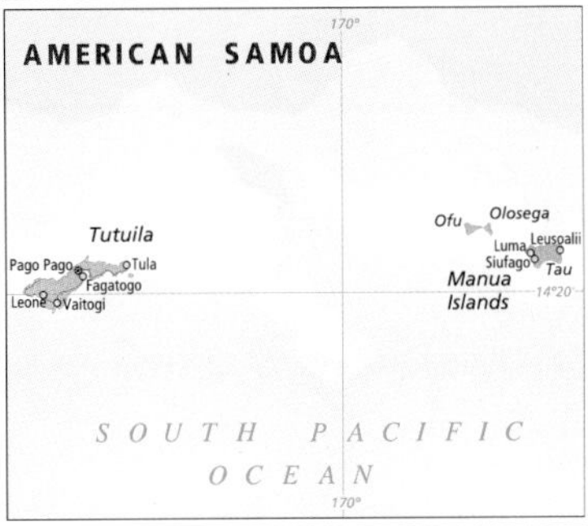
AMERICAN SAMOA
Tutuila
Pago Pago
Tula
Fagatogo
Leone
Vaitogi
Ofu
Olosega
Luma
Leusoalii
Siufago
Tau
Manua Islands
14°20'
SOUTH PACIFIC OCEAN
170°

2

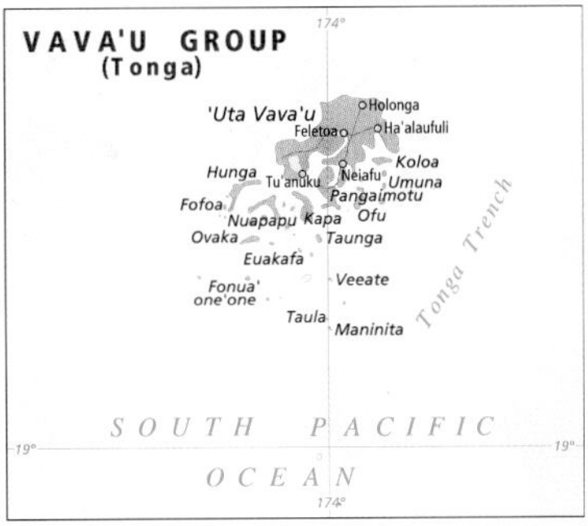
VAVA'U GROUP (Tonga)
'Uta Vava'u
Holonga
Feletoa
Ha'alaufuli
Hunga
Tu'anuku
Neiafu
Koloa
Umuna
Pangaimotu
Fofoa
Nuapapu
Kapa
Ofu
Ovaka
Taunga
Euakafa
Fonua' one'one
Veeate
Taula
Maninita
Tonga Trench
SOUTH PACIFIC OCEAN
174°
19°

3

FIJI
Cikobia
Vanua Levu
Udu Pt
Labasa
Natewa Bay
Nasorolevu 1032 m
Rabi
Buca
Yasawa Group
Yadua
Taveuni
Nabouwalu
Savusavu
Waiyevo
1241 m
Nanuku Passage
Naviti
Lau (Eastern) Group
Waya
Koro
Nasau
Lomaloma
Vanua Balavu
Ba
Rakiraki
Ovalau
Mago
Lautoka
Tomanivi 1323 m
Levuka
KORO SEA
Tuvuca
Viti Levu
Nadi
Vunindawa
Korovou
Nairai
Cicia
Lomawai
Suva
715 m
Gau
Nayau
Lakeba Passage
Sigatoka
Navua
Tubou
Lakeba
Beqa
Vatulele
Moala
Kadavu Passage
Ono
Totoya
Namuka-i-lau
Kadavu
Vunisea
Matuka
Kabara
Fulaga
SOUTH PACIFIC OCEAN
Vatoa
175°
180°
18°

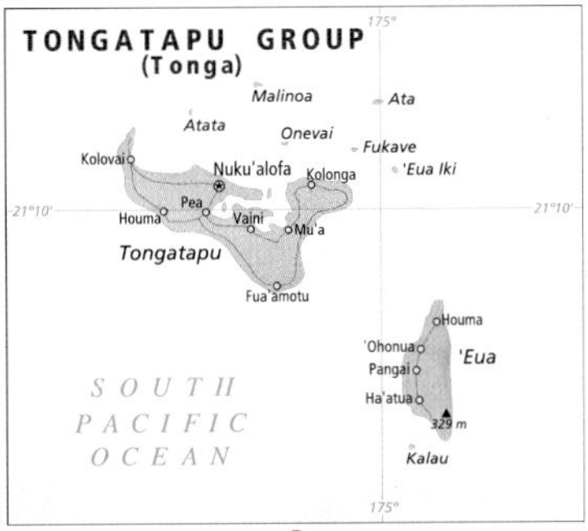
TONGATAPU GROUP (Tonga)
Malinoa
Ata
Atata
Onevai
Fukave
Kolovai
Nuku'alofa
Kolonga
'Eua Iki
Pea
Houma
Vaini
Mu'a
Tongatapu
Fua'amotu
Houma
'Ohonua
'Eua
Pangai
Ha'atua
329 m
Kalau
SOUTH PACIFIC OCEAN
175°
21°10'

4

A B

Asia and the Middle East

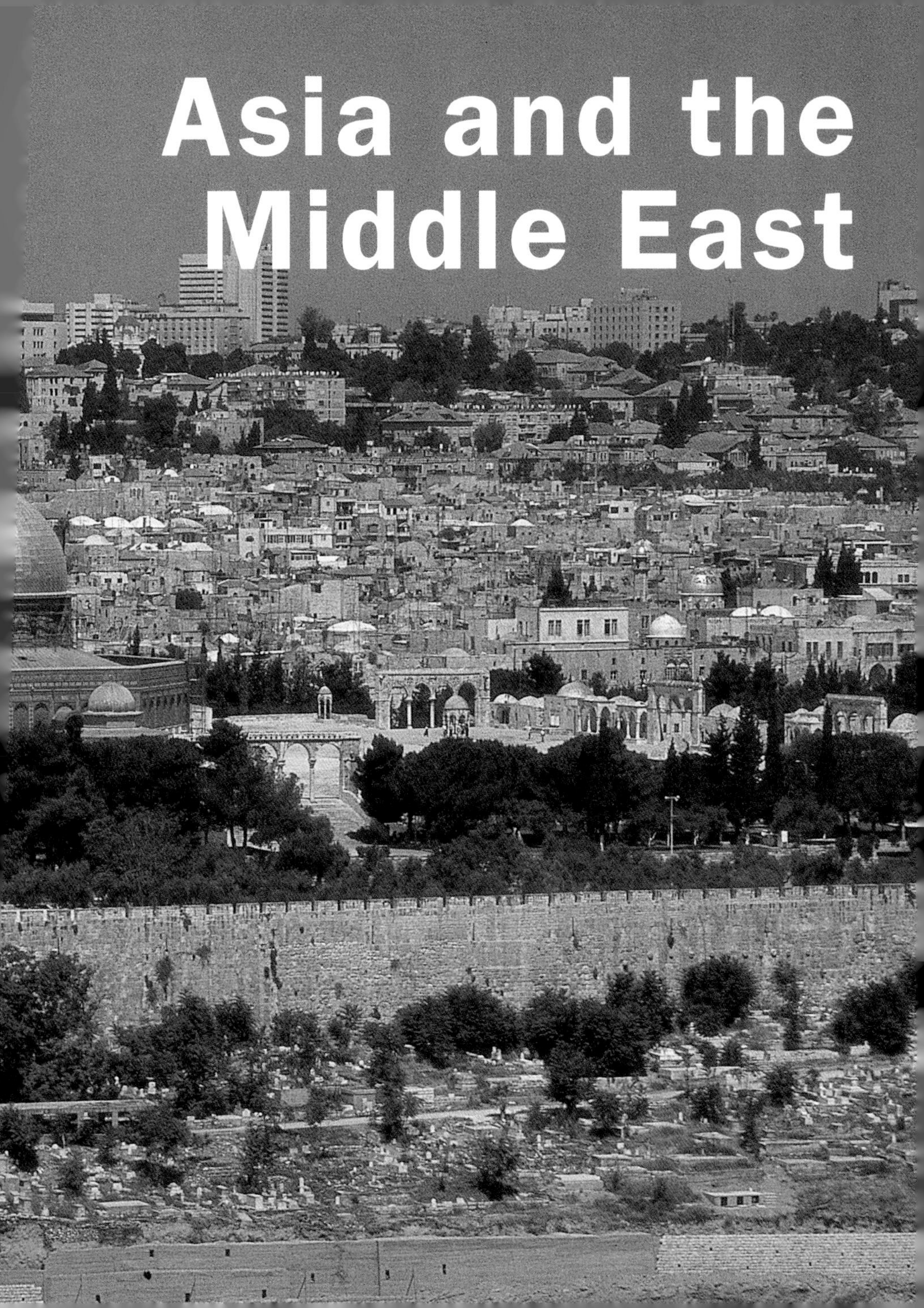

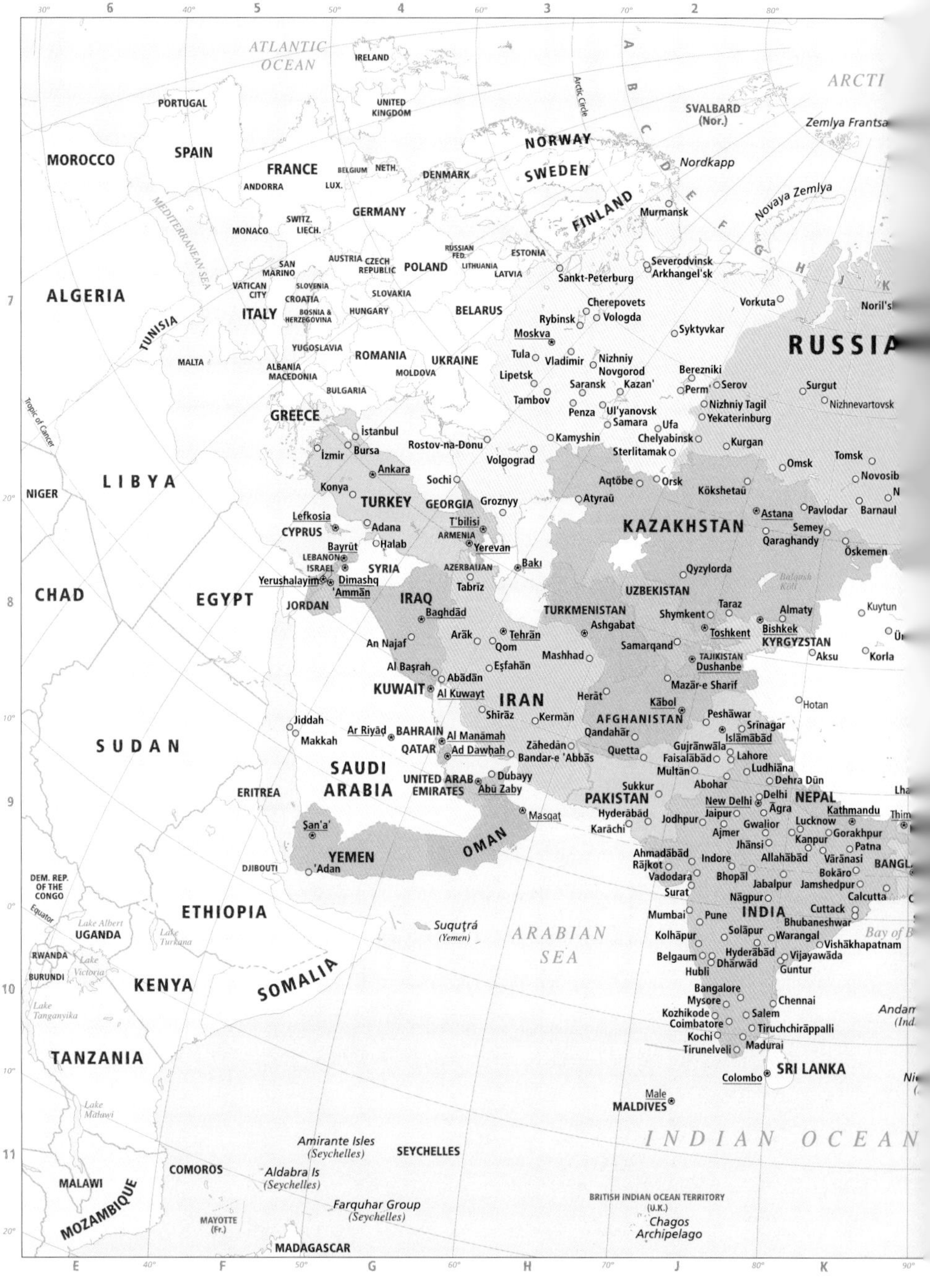
30°
6
40°
5
50°
4
60°
3
70°
2
80°
7
8
9
10
11
20°
10°
0°
10°
20°
E
40°
F
50°
G
60°
H
70°
J
80°
K
90°
A
B
C
D
E
F
G
H
J
K
ATLANTIC OCEAN
IRELAND
UNITED KINGDOM
PORTUGAL
SPAIN
MOROCCO
FRANCE
BELGIUM
NETH.
DENMARK
NORWAY
SWEDEN
FINLAND
ANDORRA
LUX.
GERMANY
SWITZ.
LIECH.
MONACO
MEDITERRANEAN SEA
Arctic Circle
SVALBARD (Nor.)
ARCTI
Zemlya Frantsa
Nordkapp
Novaya Zemlya
Murmansk
RUSSIAN FED.
ESTONIA
LITHUANIA
LATVIA
SAN MARINO
AUSTRIA
CZECH REPUBLIC
POLAND
VATICAN CITY
SLOVENIA
CROATIA
SLOVAKIA
ALGERIA
ITALY
BOSNIA & HERZEGOVINA
HUNGARY
BELARUS
TUNISIA
MALTA
YUGOSLAVIA
ALBANIA
MACEDONIA
ROMANIA
MOLDOVA
UKRAINE
BULGARIA
GREECE
Tropic of Cancer
Sankt-Peterburg
Severodvinsk
Arkhangel'sk
Cherepovets
Rybinsk
Vologda
Vorkuta
Noril'sk
Moskva
Syktyvkar
RUSSIA
Tula
Vladimir
Nizhniy Novgorod
Lipetsk
Saransk
Kazan'
Berezniki
Perm'
Serov
Surgut
Nizhnevartovsk
Tambov
Penza
Ul'yanovsk
Samara
Ufa
Nizhniy Tagil
Yekaterinburg
İstanbul
Bursa
İzmir
Rostov-na-Donu
Kamyshin
Chelyabinsk
Sterlitamak
Kurgan
Volgograd
Omsk
Tomsk
Novosib
LIBYA
Ankara
Sochi
Aqtöbe
Orsk
Kökshetaū
NIGER
Konya
TURKEY
GEORGIA
Groznyy
Atyraū
Astana
Pavlodar
Barnaul
Lefkosia
CYPRUS
Adana
T'bilisi
ARMENIA
KAZAKHSTAN
Semey
Qaraghandy
Öskemen
Bayrūt
LEBANON
ISRAEL
Ḥalab
Yerevan
SYRIA
AZERBAIJAN
Bakı
Qyzylorda
Yerushalayim
Dimashq
'Ammān
Tabrīz
Balqash Köli
UZBEKISTAN
CHAD
EGYPT
JORDAN
IRAQ
Baghdād
TURKMENISTAN
Taraz
Almaty
Kuytun
Shymkent
Ashgabat
Toshkent
Bishkek
KYRGYZSTAN
An Najaf
Arāk
Tehrān
Qom
Samarqand
Mashhad
TAJIKISTAN
Dushanbe
Aksu
Korla
Al Başrah
Eşfahān
Ābādān
Mazār-e Sharīf
KUWAIT
Al Kuwayt
IRAN
Herāt
Kābol
Hotan
Shīrāz
Kermān
AFGHANISTAN
Peshāwar
Jiddah
Makkah
Ar Riyāḑ
BAHRAIN
Al Manāmah
Qandahār
Srinagar
Islāmābād
SUDAN
QATAR
Ad Dawḩah
Zāhedān
Bandar-e 'Abbās
Quetta
Gujrānwāla
Faisalābād
Lahore
SAUDI ARABIA
Dubayy
UNITED ARAB EMIRATES
Abū Zaby
Multān
Ludhiāna
ERITREA
Sukkur
Abohar
Dehra Dūn
PAKISTAN
New Delhi
Delhi
NEPAL
Masqaṭ
Hyderābād
Jodhpur
Jaipur
Āgra
Kathmandu
Thim
Karāchi
Ajmer
Gwalior
Lucknow
Gorakhpur
Ṣan'ā'
Jhānsi
Kanpur
Patna
YEMEN
OMAN
Ahmadābād
Indore
Allahābād
Vārānasi
BANGL
DJIBOUTI
'Adan
Rājkot
Vadodara
Bhopāl
Bokāro
Jabalpur
Jamshedpur
DEM. REP. OF THE CONGO
Surat
Nāgpur
Calcutta
Equator
ETHIOPIA
Mumbai
Pune
INDIA
Cuttack
Bhubaneshwar
Lake Albert
UGANDA
Lake Turkana
Suquṭrā (Yemen)
ARABIAN SEA
Kolhāpur
Solāpur
Warangal
Bay of B
Vishākhapatnam
RWANDA
Lake Victoria
Belgaum
Hyderābād
Dhārwād
Vijayawāda
BURUNDI
KENYA
SOMALIA
Hubli
Guntur
Bangalore
Lake Tanganyika
Mysore
Chennai
Andam (Ind.
Kozhikode
Salem
Coimbatore
Tiruchchirāppalli
Kochi
Madurai
TANZANIA
Tirunelveli
SRI LANKA
Colombo
Male
MALDIVES
Lake Malawi
Amirante Isles (Seychelles)
SEYCHELLES
INDIAN OCEAN
COMOROS
Aldabra Is (Seychelles)
MALAWI
MOZAMBIQUE
Farquhar Group (Seychelles)
BRITISH INDIAN OCEAN TERRITORY (U.K.)
Chagos Archipelago
MAYOTTE (Fr.)
MADAGASCAR

St Lawrence I. (U.S.A.)
Ostrov Vrangelya
Anadyr'
BERING SEA
Aleutian Islands
MIDWAY ISLANDS (U.S.A.)
Tropic of Cancer
Magadan
Petropavlovsk-Kamchatskiy
OKHOTSKOYE MORE
Yakutsk
ATION
Ostrov Sakhalin
Kuril'skiye Ostrova
PACIFIC OCEAN
Komsomol'sk-na-Amure
Yuzhno-Sakhalinsk
Khabarovsk
Ozero Baykal
Blagoveshchensk
Asahikawa
Hokkaidō
Sapporo
Hakodate
Aomori
Akita
Chita
Jiamusi
Ulan-Ude
Qiqihar
Harbin
Jixi
Vladivostok
Mudanjiang
Changchun
Jilin
Ch'ŏngjin
Yamagata
Fukushima
Honshū
WAKE ISLAND (U.S.A.)
Ulaanbaatar
Siping
Liaoyuan
Fushun
Sea of Japan
Tōkyō
Yokohama
OLIA
Shenyang
Anshan
NORTH KOREA
P'yŏngyang
Kyōto
Ōsaka
Kōbe
Shikoku
Zhangjiakou
Dalian
Sŏul
Inch'ŏn
MARSHALL ISLANDS
Beijing
Tangshan
Tianjin
Pusan
Hiroshima
JAPAN
Shijiazhuang
Taegu
Kitakyūshū
Taiyuan
Jinan
SOUTH KOREA
Fukuoka
Kumamoto
Kyūshū
Kagoshima
Qingdao
Yuci
Xinxiang
Xintai
Zhengzhou
Kaifeng
Luoyang
Nantong
Nanjing
Shanghai
Xuchang
Xi'an
Hefei
Wuhu
Ningbo
Nansei-shotō (Japan)
NORTHERN MARIANA ISLANDS (U.S.A.)
Wuhan
Huangshi
Hangzhou
Wenzhou
Nanchong
Nanchang
Chongqing
Changsha
Fuzhou
T'ai-pei
Neijiang
Luzhou
Hengyang
T'ai-chung
Huaihua
Zunyi
Zixing
Chia-i
TAIWAN
GUAM (U.S.A.)
Guilin
Xiamen
Kao-hsiung
Shaoguan
Equator
Dali
Guangzhou
Dongguan
Liuzhou
Foshan
MICRONESIA
Nanning
Zhuhai
Juilong
Xianggang (Hong Kong)
Hà Nôi
Zhanjiang
Luzon
PHILIPPINES
Hai Phòng
Baguio
Hainan Dao
Angeles
Quezon City
LAOS
Manila
Lucena
Viangchan
SOUTH CHINA SEA
Mindoro
Đà Nang
Tacloban
THAILAND
Bago
Cebu
Bougainville
New Ireland
Negros
VIETNAM
PALAU
Cagayan de Oro
CAMBODIA
Palawan
Mindanao
Davao
New Britain
SOLOMON ISLANDS
Phnum Pénh
Zamboanga
PAPUA NEW GUINEA
Thanh Phô Hô Chí Minh
Gulf of Thailand
Kota Kinabalu
CELEBES SEA
Jayapura
Halmahera
Bandar Seri Begawan
BRUNEI
Manado
New Guinea
Kota Baharu
Kuala Terengganu
MALAYSIA
Ipoh
Kuala Lumpur
Kalimantan
Samarinda
Ambon
Seram
Seremban
Singapore
SINGAPORE
Balikpapan
Sulawesi
Pekanbaru
Pontianak
CORAL SEA ISLANDS (Aust.)
ARAFURA SEA
Padang
Jambi
Banjarmasin
INDONESIA
Sumatera
Palembang
Ujungpandang
Gulf of Carpentaria
Bandarlampung
Madura
Flores
EAST TIMOR
Melville I.
Semarang
Surabaya
Sumbawa
Jakarta
Jawa
Bali
Lombok
Bandung
Yogyakarta
Malang
Sumba
AUSTRALIA
kilometers
miles

ATLANTIC OCEAN
British Isles
Ireland
NORWEGIAN SEA
GREENLAND SEA
ARCTIC
Arctic Circle
Svalbard
Bay of Biscay
English Channel
Iberian Peninsula
Pyrenees
Strait of Gibraltar
Jebel Toubkal 4165 m
Atlas Mountains
Massif Central
Galdhøpiggen 2469 m
Scandinavia
Skagerrak
Gulf of Bothnia
BALTIC SEA
Nordkapp
Zemlya Frantsa-Iosifa
BARENTS SEA
Novaya Zemlya
Kol'skiy Poluostrov
Ostrov Kolguyev
Ostrov Vaygach
KARSKOYE MORE
Beloye More
Islas Baleares
Mont Blanc 4807 m
TYRRHENIAN SEA
Corse
Sardegna
MEDITERRANEAN SEA
Grand Erg Occidental
Appennino
ADRIATIC SEA
Dinara
North European Plain
Gydanskiy Poluostrov
Grand Erg Oriental
Sicilia
Hora Hoverla 2061 m
Carpathian Mts
Sredne-Russkaya Vozvyshennost'
Ural'skiy Khrebet (Ural Mountains)
SAHARA
IONIAN SEA
Stara Planina
Zapadno Sibirskaya Ravnina
Krym's'kyy Pivostriv (Crimean Peninsula)
BLACK SEA
Sea of Azov
Tropic of Cancer
Khalij Surt
AEGEAN SEA
Kriti
Anatolia
Toros Dağları
Anadolu Dağları
Bol'shoy Kavkaz
Gora El'brus 5641 m
Caspian Depression
CASPIAN SEA
Mughalzhar Tauy
Aral Sea
Mongol Altai
Libyan Desert
Cyprus
Agri Dagi (Mt Ararat) 5137 m
Plato Ustyurt
Tavan Bogd Uul 4374 m
Tibesti
Western Desert
Jabal ash Shaykh 2814 m
Sīnā'
Peski Kyzylkum
Balqash Köli
Nile
Bādiyat ash Shām (Syrian Desert)
Euphrates
Tigris
Reshteh-ye Kūhhā-ye Alborz (Elburz Mts)
Pic Pobedy 7439 m
Tian Shan
Eastern Desert
Al Hijāz
An Nafūd
Dasht-e Kavīr
Amu Darya
Pik Imeni Ismail Samani 7495 m
Lake Nasser
Iranian Plateau
Dasht-e Lūt
Kūhhā-ye Zāgros (Zagros Mountains)
Tarim Pendi
Hindu Kush
Kunlun
RED SEA
Arabian Peninsula
Persian Gulf
K2 8611 m
Sulaiman Range
Indus
Qingzang Gaoyuan (Plateau of Tibet)
Sutlej
HIMALAYA
Gulf of Oman
Indo-Gangetic Plain
Ar Rub'al Khālī
Thar Desert
Mt Everest 8848 m
Ganga (Ganges)
Rann of Kachchh
Vindhya Range
Sātpura Range
Ethiopian Highlands
Gulf of Aden
Deccan
Mouths of the Ganges
Equator
Lake Albert
Lake Turkana
Suquṭrá
ARABIAN SEA
Godavari
Western Ghats
Eastern Ghats
Bay of Bengal
Great Rift Valley
Lake Victoria
Kirinyaga (Mt Kenya) 5199 m
Lake Tanganyika
Kilimanjaro 5895 m
Palk Strait
Cape Comorin
Sri Lanka
INDIAN OCEAN
Maldives
Seychelles
Comoros
Madagascar
6
5
4
3
2
7
8
9
10
11
E
F
G
H
J
K
A
B
C
D
30°
40°
50°
60°
70°
80°
90°
20°
10°
0°

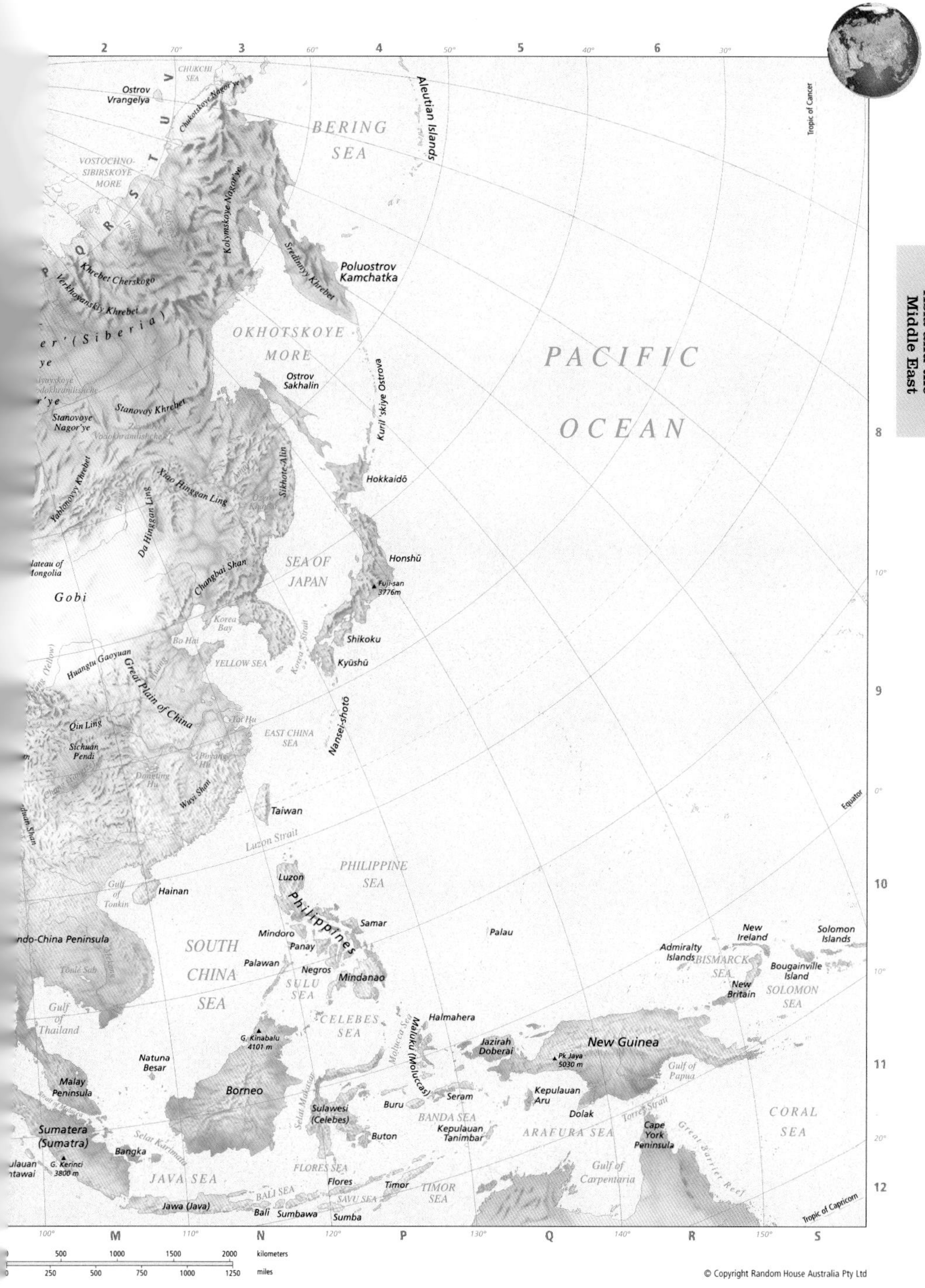

2
3
4
5
6
CHUKCHI SEA
Ostrov Vrangelya
Chukotskoye Nagor'ye
BERING SEA
Aleutian Islands
Tropic of Cancer
VOSTOCHNO-SIBIRSKOYE MORE
Kolymskoye Nagor'ye
Sredinnyy Khrebet
Poluostrov Kamchatka
Khrebet Cherskogo
Verkhoyanskiy Khrebet
(Siberia)
OKHOTSKOYE MORE
PACIFIC OCEAN
Ostrov Sakhalin
Kuril'skiye Ostrova
Stanovoy Khrebet
Stanovoye Nagor'ye
Xiao Hinggan Ling
Sikhote-Alin
Hokkaidō
Yablonovyy Khrebet
Da Hinggan Ling
Plateau of Mongolia
Gobi
Changbai Shan
SEA OF JAPAN
Honshū
Fuji-san 3776 m
Korea Bay
Bo Hai
Shikoku
Huangtu Gaoyuan
Great Plain of China
YELLOW SEA
Korea Strait
Kyūshū
Qin Ling
Tai Hu
EAST CHINA SEA
Nansei-shotō
Sichuan Pendi
Poyang Hu
Dongting Hu
Wuyi Shan
Taiwan
Equator
Luzon Strait
PHILIPPINE SEA
Luzon
Gulf of Tonkin
Hainan
Philippines
Samar
Mindoro
Palau
Indo-China Peninsula
SOUTH CHINA SEA
Panay
Palawan
Negros
Mindanao
SULU SEA
Tonlé Sab
Gulf of Thailand
CELEBES SEA
Molucca Sea
Maluku (Moluccas)
Halmahera
New Ireland
Solomon Islands
Admiralty Islands
BISMARCK SEA
Bougainville Island
New Britain
SOLOMON SEA
G. Kinabalu 4101 m
Jazirah Doberai
New Guinea
Pk Jaya 5030 m
Natuna Besar
Gulf of Papua
Malay Peninsula
Borneo
Kepulauan Aru
Buru
Seram
Sulawesi (Celebes)
Selat Makasar
BANDA SEA
Dolak
Torres Strait
CORAL SEA
Sumatera (Sumatra)
Buton
Kepulauan Tanimbar
ARAFURA SEA
Cape York Peninsula
Great Barrier Reef
Selat Karimata
Bangka
G. Kerinci 3800 m
JAVA SEA
FLORES SEA
Flores
Timor
TIMOR SEA
Gulf of Carpentaria
BALI SEA
SAVU SEA
Jawa (Java)
Bali
Sumbawa
Sumba
Tropic of Capricorn
8
9
10
11
12
M
N
P
Q
R
S
100°
110°
120°
130°
140°
150°
500
1000
1500
2000
kilometers
250
500
750
1000
1250
miles

A
B
C
D
116°
120°
124°
740
737
1
2
3
4
5
6
4°
0°
8°
12°
LABUAN
Victoria
Kuala Penyu
BRUNEI
Bandar Seri Begawan
Muara
Brunei Bay
Tg Baram
Lutong
Miri
Beaufort
Telupid
G. Trus Madi 2649 m
SABAH
Pinangah
Sukau
Lamag
Lahad Datu
Kunak
P. Timbun Mata
Tel. Darvel
Semporna
Tawau
Sapulut
Kalabakan
MALAYSIA
P. Sebatik
Tawitawi I.
Tapul Group
Sibutu I.
Sibutu Group
PHILIPPINES
Batulaki
Sarangani Is
Kep. Talaud
G. Mulu 2371 m
G. Harun 2160 m
Long Teru
Batu Niah
G. Murud 2438 m
Longbawan
G. Basakan 1372 m
P. Mandul
Sesayap
Tangung
Tarakan
Mantadau
SARAWAK
Peg. Iran
Long Murum
G. Bakayan 1599 m
Nyurang
Tanjungselor
KALIMANTAN
Tg Batu
P. Maratua
Tanjungredeb
Rumah Kulit
BORNEO
G. Kemal 2053 m
G. Guguang 2467 m
Longnawan
Barung
Tintang
Peg. Sambaliung
G. Liangpran 2240 m
TIMUR
Pelawanbesar
Pulai
G. Menyapa 2000 m
Peg. Muller
Sepasu
Tg Mangkalihat
Equator
Kembangjanggut
Longiram
Bontang
Purukcahu
KALIMANTAN
Samarinda
Kualakurun
Benangin
Muarapayang
G. Lumut 1233 m
Balikpapan
Pendang
TENGAH
G. Serempaka 1380 m
Tel. Adang
Palangkaraya
Kupangnunding
Tanahgrogot
Amuntai
Peg. Meratus
Jangeru
G. Besar 1892 m
Tel. Pamukan
Pulangpisau
KALIMANTAN
Rantau
SELATAN
Banjarmasin
Martapura
Peg.
Kotabaru
P. Sebuku
Pagatan
Kintap
Semaras
P. Laut
Selat Laut
Batakan
Tg Selatan
Tg Layar
Selat Makasar
JAVA SEA
Kep. Masalembu
CELEBES SEA
Tahuna
P. Sangihe
Ngalipaeng
P. Siau
Ulu
P. Tahulandang
P. Biaro
P. Bangka
Manado
Tondano
Tg Arus
G. Dako 2304 m
Tg Kandi
Bukaan
SULAWESI
UTARA
Tel. Amurang
Tolitoli
Tg Samia
P. Halm
Tinabogan
Peg. Paleleh
G. Ogoamas 2565 m
Tembito
G. Tentolomatinan 2207 m
Boroko
Kotamobagu
Tinombo
Marisa
Gorontalo
Bilungala
G. Bulawa 1970 m
Onggunoi
Tg Dampelas
Sigenti
Tg Manimbaya
Kasimbar
Tel. Tomini
Kep. Togian
Selat Walea
MOLUCCA SEA
Donggala
Tawaeli
Toboli
Parigi
Tg Api
Tg Batuhitam
Bunta
Teku
Palu
SULAWESI
Luwuk
Tg Santigi
Pakuli
Sedoa
Tel. Poso
G. Katoposa 2835 m
2400 m
G. Tumpu
Batui
Selat Peleng
P. Peleng
Uekuli
SULAWESI
(CELEBES)
Poso
2565 m
TENGAH
G. Tenamatua
Menanga
P. Mangole
Taripa
Teluk Tolo
Kep. Banggai
P. Taliabu
Auponhia
P. Sanana
Tg Waka
G. Kambuno 2950 m
Peg. Quarles
Wotu
G. Gandadiwata 3074 m
Mamuju
Tg Kai
Tg Bulupulu
Rantepao
Palopo
Tg Lasoni
Tg Palpetu
P. Buru
Bara
Namlea
G. Kapalatmada 2729 m
Tifu
Makale
3455 m
G. Rantekombola
Tg Tapaulama
Tel. Matarape
Peg. Mekongga
Majene
Tel. Mandar
Polewali
G. Mekongga 2790 m
P. Manui
SULAWESI
Siwa
Tel. Bone
Parepare
Danau Tempe
Singkang
Kendari
Watunea
P. Padamarang
Kolaka
Kolono
P. Wowoni
Watampone
SULAWESI
Tampo
Daule
SELATAN
TENGGARA
Raha
Tg Goram
Ujungpandang (Makassar)
Maros
Sinjai
Pising
P. Muna
P. Buton
2876 m
G. Lompobatang
P. Kabaena
Mawasangka
BAN
SE
Bira
Kep. Tukangbesi
Selat Selayar
Tg Pemali
P. Selayar
Benteng
P. Madura
Kep. Kangean
P. Tanahjampea
INDONES
P. Kalao
Asambi
P. Kalaotoa
P. Bonerate
Situbondo
BALI SEA
Bondowoso
Jawa (Java)
G. Raung 3332 m
Bali
FLORES SEA
Laliki
Arwala
Airpanas
P. Wetar
Hatpaas
Singaraja
G. Rinjani 3726 m
G. Tambora 2821 m
Tg Besi
Reo
P. Adonara
Kep. Alor
Selat Wetar
Lautem
Banyuwangi
Negara
BALI
G. Agung 3142 m
Sumbawa Besar
Dompu
Bima
P. Komodo
Labuhanbajo
Larantuka
Nebe
Lamakera
Kalabahi
Alor
Dili
Manatuto
Baukau
Denpasar
Mataram
Selong
Sumbawa
Raba
G. Ranakah 2382 m
Ruteng
G. Kelimutu 1200 m
Maumere
Kep. Solor
P. Pantar
Aileu
EAST TIMOR
2963 m
G. Tata Mailau
Vikeke
JAWA TIMUR
P. Nusa Penida
Lombok
Praya
Plampang
P. Rinca
Paga
Ende
Flores
Pantemakassar
Atambua
Suai
NUSA TENGGARA BARAT
Tg Sasar
NUSA TENGGARA TIMUR
Timor
Waingapu
SAVU SEA
G. Mutis 2427 m
Kefamenanu
Waikabubak
Sumba
G. Wanggamet 1225 m
Barate
Soe
Baing
P. Sawu
Kupang
Tg Ela
TIMOR SEA
Tg Pukuatu
Selat Roti
Nembrala
Roti
INDIAN OCEAN

E
132°
F
136°
G
140°
H
1
2
3
4
5
6
4°
0°
4°
8°
12°
Equator
PACIFIC
OCEAN
HALMAHERA
SEA
CERAM SEA
MALUKU
ARAFURA SEA
AUSTRALIA
IRIAN JAYA
WEST
SEPIK
EAST
SEPIK
WESTERN
New Guinea
PEG. VAN REES
Peg. Maoke
Peg. Jayawijaya
Torricelli Mts
P. Waigeo
Rabia
Selat Dampier
Warmandi
Koor
Mega
G. Kwoka
3000 m
Ambuaki
Kaironi
Mubrani
Sorong
Sajam
Manokwari
Tg Memori
Tg Manundi
P. Supiori
Korido
Korim
P. Biak
Biak
Tg Wararisbari
Tg Dadi
P. Salawati
Gasim
Germakolo
Rawas
Seget
G. Mebo
2940 m
Oransbari
Namber
P. Numfor
Selat Yapen
P. Yapen
Ransiki
P. Num
Atkri
Tamulol
Misool
Baru
Robooksibia
P. Rumberpon
Serui
Tel. Waropen
Tg Ranbausawa
P. Waar
Inanwatan
Tg Sabra
Tomu
Tel. Berau
Tel. Bintuni
Babo
Tel. Cenderawasih
Tg D'Urville
Teba
Pamdai
Sarmi
Maffin
Betaf
Ansudu
Kaptiau
Demta
Depapre
Jayapura
Vanimo
Leitre
Sissano
Ossima
Imonda
Aitape
Amanab
Wahai
Kokas
Tanisapata
Rufrufua
Fakfak
Siembra
Bula
Haya
Bemu
P. Seram
Kilwo
Urung
Tg Marsimang
P. Karas
Tel. Sebakor
Tg Tongerai
Mirobia
Kaimana
Tel. Kamrau
Kwatisore
Nabire
G. Dom
1430 m
Krau
G. Angemuk
3962 m
Wandai
Enarotali
G. Ubia
4234 m
Pk Jaya
5030 m
Tembagapura
Wamena
Pk Trikora
4730 m
Green River
Kubkain
Pk Yamin
4595 m
Pk Mandala
4700 m
Kep. Gorong
Tg Papisoi
P. Adi
Kep. Watubela
Aiduna
Wanapiri
Uta
Kokenau
Amamapare
Telefomin
Tabubil
Kep. Kai
Tg Borang
P. Kai Besar
P. Kai Kecil
Banda Elat
Dobo
Dosi
Tg Weduar
Tg Ngoni
Kep. Aru
Agats
Ningerum
Rumginae
Kiunga
Tanahmerah
Lake Murray
Damar
Tg Laru Mat
Tg Waarlangier
Tafermaar
Tg Ngabordamlu
Tg De Jongs
Mapi
Kep. Tanimbar
Watmuri
P. Yamdena
Batkes
Aiambak
Tepa
Latdalam
Saumlaki
Adaut
P. Dolak
Pembre
Kimaan
Okaba
Duru
Goe
Serki
Kep. Babar
Eliase
Kladar
Tg Vals
Wamal
P. Komoran
Kumbe
Merauke
Buk
Morehead
Bula
Mari
Boigu I.
Torres Strait
Badu I.
Moa I.
Thursday I.
Prince of Wales I.
Bamaga
Dundas Strait
C. Van Diemen
Cobourg Pen.
C. Cockburn
Wessel Is
Cape Wessel
Goulburn Is
Bathurst I.
Melville I.
C. Keith
Van Diemen Gulf
Beagle Gulf
C. Hotham
Darwin
Howard Island
Melville Bay
Nhulunbuy
0
100
200
300
400
kilometers
0
100
200
miles

726
720

738
A
B
C
96°
100°
104°
1
2
3
4
6
7
J
K
Nicobar Islands (India)
Little Nicobar
Great Nicobar
Bananga
Ko Lanta
Kantang
Songkhla
Hat Yai
THAILAND
Satun
Pattani
Yala
Narathiwat
Rangae
P. Langkawi
PERLIS
Kangar
Jitra
Alor Setar
KEDAH
Kota Baharu
Pasir Puteh
P. Redang
Sungai Petani
PINANG
George Town
P. Pinang (Penang)
Butterworth
G. Bintang 1862 m
Jeli
Macang
G. Noring 1889 m
Kuala Krai
KELANTAN
Kuala Terengganu
G. Camah 2171 m
G. Lawit 1519 m
PERAK
TERENGGANU
Taiping
Kuala Kangsar
G. Gagau
Kuala Dungun
Ipoh
G. Tahan 2187 m
1376 m
G. Mandi Angin 1459 m
MALAYSIA
Kampar
G. Batu Puteh 2131 m
Cukai
Bidor
Kuala Lipis
G. Benom 2107 m
G. Tapis 1512 m
Tg Gelang
Tg Beras Basah
G. Liang East 1933 m
Kuantan
Gambang
Raub
PAHANG
Maran
Pekan
SELANGOR
Karak
Temerloh
Kuala Selangor
Shah Alam
Kuala Lumpur
Kelang
KUALA LUMPUR
Seremban
NEGERI SEMBILAN
P. Tioman
Port Dickson
Segamat
Tg Resang
Tg Tuan
Tg Senebui
MELAKA
G. Ledang 1276 m
Labis
Jemaluang
Bagansiapiapi
Melaka
G. Belumut 1010 m
JOHOR
Muar
Ayer Hitam
P. Rupat
Batu Pahat
Kota Tinggi
Johor Baharu
Singapore
SINGAPORE
Dumai
P. Bengkalis
Pontian Kecil
Duri
P. Padang
P. Rangsang
P. Bintan
RIAU
P. Tebingtinggi
P. Rempang
Tandjungpinang
Buatan
P. Kundur
P. Galang
Pekanbaru
P. Mendol
Strait of Malacca
P. We
Sabang
P. Breueh
Banda Aceh
Sigli
Bireuen
Tg Jambuair
Lhokseumawe
Lhoksukon
Tangse
G. Geureudong 2855 m
Lhokkruet
Peureulak
Calang
Takengon
Langsa
U. Tamiang
G. Abongabong 2985 m
ACEH
G. Lembu 3077 m
Tel. Aru
Pangkalanbrandan
Blangkejeren
G. Bandahara 3012 m
Tg Raya
G. Leuser 3404 m
Belawan
Labuhanhaji
Binjai
Medan
G. Sibayak 2094 m
Tebingtinggi
Tapaktuan
Kabanjahe
Tanjungbalai
Tg Dewa
Pematangsiantar
P. Simeulue
Sinabang
Sidikalang
P. Samosir
Prapat
Tg Pertandangan
Labuhanbilik
Balige
Siborongborong
Barus
Tarutung
Kotapinang
P. Bangkaru
P. Tuangku
Tel. Tapanuli
Sibolga
SUMATERA UTARA
Langgapayung
Tg Dowi
P. Musala
Padangsidempuan
Lahewa
Gunungsitoli
P. Nias
Sirombu
G. Malea 2012 m
Pasirpengarayan
Telukdalam
Natal
Kotanopan
Panti
Bangkinang
SUMATERA (SUMATRA)
P. Pini
Airbangis
G. Ophir 2912 m
Equator
Sasak
P. Tanahmasa
Kep. Batu
Payakumbuh
Tembilahan
Tg Datuk
P. Sebangka
P. Lingga
Kep.
Kelume
Sambau
P. Tanahbala
Danau Maninjau
Bukittinggi
G. Marapi 2891 m
Japura
Rengat
P. Singkep
Danau Singkarak
Labu
Selat Siberut
Tg Sigep
Solok
Taluk
Seberida
Selat Berhala
Tg Jabung
Padang
Sungaidareh
Kagologolo
SUMATERA BARAT
Painan
Dusunmudo
JAMBI
INDIAN OCEAN
P. Siberut
Muarasiberut
G. Kerinci 3800 m
Muarabungo
Jambi
Tel. Kampar
Selat Mentawai
Sungaipenuh
Muntok
Selat Bungalaut
Siberimanua
Tapan
Danau Kerinci
Bangko
Bayunglincir
Pangkal
P. Sipura
Katiet
Pasapuat
G. Masurai 2935 m
P. Pagai Utara
Mukomuko
Surulangun
SUMATERA SELATAN
Sekayu
P. Pagai Selatan
Tg Beritarikap
P. Sanding
Peg. Barisan
Muaraaman
G. Daun 2467 m
Muarabeliti
Palembang
Perabumulih
Kayuagung
Ketaun
Lais
Kepahiang
Muaraenim
Umbulan
Gayohpecoh
Bengkulu
Lahat
G. Dempo 3159 m
Pagaralam
Baturaja
Tais
BENGKULU
Martapura
G. Patah 2817 m
Manna
Muaradua
Bintuhan
Kotabumi
G. Pesagi 2231 m
Gunung
Metro
Labuh
P. Enggano
Kayaapu
Krui
Kotaagung
LAMPUNG
Bandar
Tg Batuberagam
Bakauheni
Tg Rata
P. Tabuan
Balimbing
Krakatau
P. Panaitan
Tg Guhakolak
Tel. Pel
MALAYSIA
Selat Johor
Sembawang
P. Seletar
Woodlands
Yishun
Kranji Res.
Sarimbun Res.
Tg Punggol
Sungei Seletar Res.
P. Serangoon
P. Ubin
Punggol
Murai Res.
Serangoon Harbour
Bukit Panjang
Choa Chu Kang
Ang Mo Kio
Lower Peirce Res.
Upper Peirce Res.
Hougang
Pasir Ris
Changi
Poyan Res.
Changi Airport
Bukit Batok
Bishan
Serangoon
Jurong West
Tampines
SINGAPORE
Tengeh Res.
Bukit Timah
Bedok Res.
Jurong Town
Jurong East
Bukit Timah 162 m
Toa Payoh
Paya Lebar
1°20'
103°50'
Tuas
Jurong Industrial Estate
Clementi
Bedok
Katong
Geylang
Selat Jurong
P. Merlimau
Pasir Panjang
Tiong Bahru
Straits of Singapore
P. Pesek
P. Pesek Kechil
P. Seraya
Singapore
Telok Blangah
P. Ayer Chawan
P. Ayer Merbau
Tg Berlayar
P. Brani
P. Sakra
Sentosa
0 5 10 kilometers
0 5 miles
CHRISTMAS ISLAND (Aust.)

740
734
SOUTH CHINA SEA
JAVA SEA
BALI SEA
FLORES SEA
INDONESIA
MALAYSIA
BRUNEI
LABUAN
SABAH
SARAWAK
BORNEO
KALIMANTAN BARAT
KALIMANTAN TENGAH
KALIMANTAN TIMUR
KALIMANTAN SELATAN
SULAWESI (CELEBES)
SULAWESI TENGAH
SULAWESI SELATAN
JAWA (JAVA)
JAWA TENGAH
JAWA TIMUR
YOGYAKARTA
BALI
NUSA TENGGARA BARAT
NUSA TENGGARA TIMUR
P. Balambangan
P. Banggi
P. Malawali
P. Jambongan
Kudat
Langkon
Kanibongan
Tuaran
G. Kinabalu 4101 m
Kota Kinabalu
Lingkabau
Sandakan
Sukau
Kuala Penyu
Telupid
G. Trus Madi 2649 m
Beaufort
Lamag
Victoria
Muara
Bandar Seri Begawan
Pinangah
Lahad Datu
Tel. Darvel
Kunak
Sapulut
Kalabakan
Tawau
Semporna
P. Timbun Mata
Sibutu Group
Sibutu I.
Tawitawi I.
Tapul Group
Tg Baram
Lutong
Miri
G. Mulu 2371 m
G. Pagon 1850 m
G. Harun 2160 m
P. Sebatik
Long Teru
Batu Niah
Tg Payong
Longbawan
G. Murud 2438 m
G. Basakan 1372 m
P. Mandul
Tg Kidurong
Bintulu
Sesayap
Tangung
Tarakan
Mantadau
Tg Sirik
Mukah
Tatau
Long Murum
Nyurang
Peg. Iran
Tanjungselor
P. Bruit
Kejaman
G. Bakayan 1599 m
Sibu
Julau
Sarikei
Peg. Hose
Rumah Kulit
G. Kemal 2053 m
Tanjungredeb
Tg Batu
P. Maratua
Tg Datu
Tel. Datu
Sematan
Tg Sipang
Tg Po
Song
Kapit
Longnawan
G. Guguang 2467 m
Peg. Sambaliung
Barung
Tintang
Kuching
Saratok
Debak
Bau
Bandar Sri Aman (Simanggang)
Sambas
Pemangkat
G. Niut 1701 m
G. Lawit 1767 m
G. Kerihun 1980 m
G. Liangpran 2240 m
Peg. Muller
G. Menyapa 2000 m
Pelawanbesar
Pulai
Tg Mangkalihat
Tg Arus
G. Dako 2304 m
Tolitoli
Tinabogan
G. Ogoamas 2565 m
Singkawang
Putussibau
Sepasu
Ngabang
Sanggau
Tg Bangkai
Mempawah
Pontianak
Sintang
Tg Dampelas
Tinombo
Tg Manimbaya
Sigenti
Equator
Kasimbar
Kembangjanggut
Longiram
Bontang
Tg Putus
Kertamulia
G. Saran 1758 m
Nangapinoh
G. Raya 2278 m
Purukcahu
Samarinda
Teluk Tomini
Donggala
Tawaeli
Toboli
Parigi
P. Padangtikar
Telukbatang
Sukadana
Sandai
G. Sebayan 1377 m
Peg. Schwaner
Kualakurun
Benangin
Palu
Pakuli
Sedoa
Tel. Poso
P. Maya
Tel. Sukadana
Muarapayang
G. Lumut 1233 m
Balikpapan
Poso
Tentena
Kep. Karimata
Tumbangsamba
Pendang
Memala
Nangatayap
G. Serempaka 1380 m
Tel. Adang
Taripa
Tg Bawang
Ketapang
Kupangnunding
Tanahgrogot
Selat Karimata
Belitung
Tanjungpandan
Manggar
Dendang
Sukaraja
Pangkalanbuun
Palangkaraya
Sampit
Amuntai
Jangeru
G. Kambuno 2950 m
Mamuju
G. Gandadiwata 3074 m
Peg. Quarles
Wotu
Kendawangan
P. Bawal
P. Gelam
Tg Sambar
Kumai
Tel. Kumai
G. Besar 1892 m
Pulangpisau
Tel. Pamukan
Peg. Meratus
Tg Kai
Tg Bulupulu
Rantepao
Makale
G. Rantekombola 3455 m
Tg Keluang
Semuda
Rantau
Banjarmasin
Martapura
Tel. Sampit
Kotabaru
P. Sebuku
Tg Puting
Tg Malatayur
Pagatan
Kintap
Semaras
P. Laut
Polewali
Majene
Tel. Mandar
Siwa
Selat Makasar
Batakan
Tg Selatan
Selat Laut
Tg Layar
Parepare
Singkang
Danau Tempe
Tel. Bone
Watampone
Maros
Ujungpandang (Makassar)
G. Lompobatang 2876 m
Sinjai
Bira
Selat Selayar
P. Selayar
Benteng
Kep. Masalembu
Kep. Karimunjawa
P. Bawean
Pamanukan
Indramayu
Subang
Purwakarta
Bandung
Cirebon
Tg Bugel
Keling
G. Muria 1602 m
Jepara
Tg Benda
Kudus
Rembang
Tuban
Ketapang
P. Madura
Kep. Kangean
Pekalongan
Tegal
Blora
G. Careme 3078 m
Garut
G. Slamet 3418 m
Wonosobo
Semarang
Salatiga
Gresik
Bangkalan
Pamekasan
Surabaya
Ciamis
Purwokerto
Cilacap
Magelang
Surakarta (Solo)
Madiun
Selat Madura
Situbondo
Pasuruan
Probolinggo
Tel. Penanjung
Yogyakarta
Parangtritis
G. Lawu 3265 m
Ponorogo
G. Liman 2561 m
Kediri
Malang
G. Argopuro 3088 m
Bondowoso
Pacitan
Blitar
Kepanjen
G. Semeru 3676 m
Jember
G. Raung 3332 m
Banyuwangi
P. Nusa Barung
Bali
Singaraja
Negara
G. Agung 3142 m
Denpasar
P. Nusa Penida
G. Rinjani 3726 m
Mataram
Praya
Selong
Lombok
Sumbawa Besar
Plampang
Sumbawa
G. Tambora 2821 m
Dompu
Bima
Raba
P. Komodo
Labuhanbajo
Tg Besi
Reo
G. Ranakah 2382 m
Ruteng
P. Rinca
Flores
Tg Sasar
P. Tanahjampea
P. Kalao
Waingapu
Waikabubak
Sumba
G. Wanggamet 1225 m
Baing
108°
112°
116°
120°
E
F
G
H
1
2
3
4
5
0
100
200
300
400
kilometers
miles

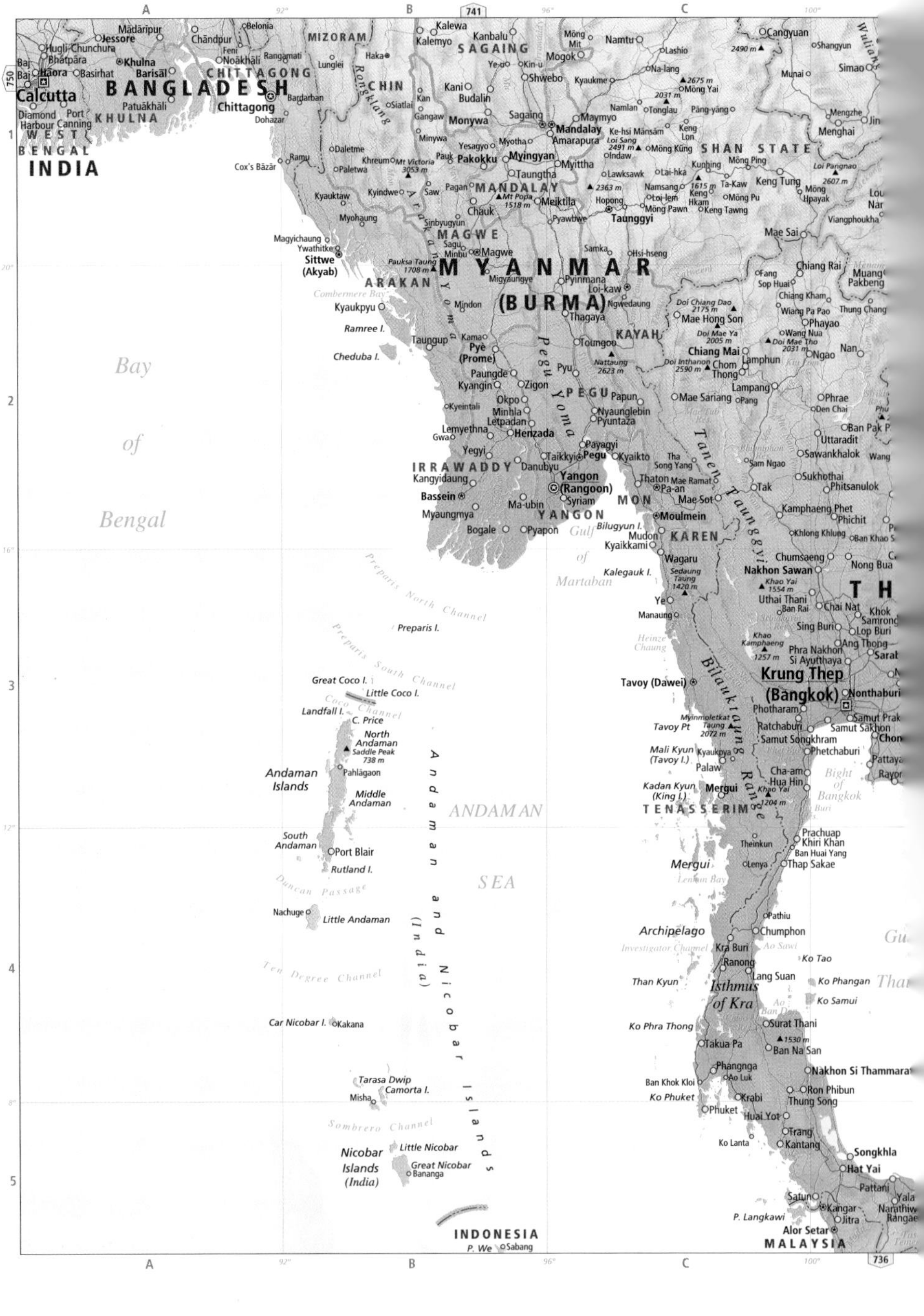
A
B
C
92°
96°
100°
741
750
736
1
2
3
4
5
BANGLADESH
Calcutta
Chittagong
CHITTAGONG
KHULNA
Khulna
Barisāl
Jessore
Mādārīpur
Chāndpur
Belonia
Feni
Noākhāli
Rangamati
Lunglei
Hugli-Chunchura
Bhatpāra
Hāora
Basirhat
Patuākhāli
Diamond Harbour
Port Canning
WEST BENGAL
INDIA
MIZORAM
CHIN
Haka
Siatlai
Bardarban
Dohazar
Cox's Bāzār
Ramu
Daletme
Paletwa
Khreum
Mt Victoria 3053 m
Kyauktaw
Myohaung
Magyichaung
Ywathitke
Sittwe (Akyab)
ARAKAN
Combermere Bay
Kyaukpyu
Ramree I.
Cheduba I.
SAGAING
Kalewa
Kalemyo
Kanbalu
Kin-u
Ye-u
Shwebo
Mogok
Mōng Mit
Namtu
Lashio
Na-lang
Kyaukme
Kani
Budalin
Monywa
Sagaing
Mandalay
Amarapura
Maymyo
Kan
Gangaw
Minywa
Yesagyo
Myotha
Pauk
Pakokku
Myingyan
Myittha
Taungtha
Saw
Kyindwe
Pagan
MANDALAY
Mt Popa 1518 m
Meiktila
Chauk
Sinbyugyun
MAGWE
Sagu
Minbu
Magwe
Pauksa Taung 1708 m
MYANMAR (BURMA)
Migyaungye
Pyinmana
Loi-kaw
Ngwedaung
Mindon
Thagaya
Kama
Taungup
Pye (Prome)
Toungoo
KAYAH
Nattaung 2623 m
Paungde
Kyangin
Zigon
Pyu
Pegu Yoma
PEGU
Okpo
Minhla
Letpadan
Kyeintali
Lemyethna
Gwa
Henzada
Papun
Nyaunglebin
Pyuntaza
Yegyi
Payagyi
Pegu
Taikkyi
Kyaikto
IRRAWADDY
Danubyu
Kangyidaung
Yangon (Rangoon)
Bassein
Syriam
Ma-ubin
Myaungmya
YANGON
Bogale
Pyapon
Gulf of Martaban
MON
Thaton
Pa-an
Moulmein
Bilugyun I.
Mudon
Kyaikkami
KAREN
Wagaru
Kalegauk I.
Sedaung Taung 1420 m
Ye
Manaung
Heinze Chaung
Tavoy (Dawei)
Tavoy Pt
Myinmoletkat Taung 2072 m
Mali Kyun (Tavoy I.)
Kyaukpya
Palaw
Kadan Kyun (King I.)
Mergui
TENASSERIM
Bilauktaung Range
Mergui Archipelago
Theinkun
Lenya
Investigator Channel
Kra Buri
Ranong
Than Kyun
Isthmus of Kra
Ko Phra Thong
Takua Pa
Phangnga
Ao Luk
Ban Khok Kloi
Ko Phuket
Phuket
Krabi
Huai Yot
Ko Lanta
Trang
Kantang
Satun
P. Langkawi
Kangar
Jitra
Alor Setar
MALAYSIA
Songkhla
Hat Yai
Pattani
Yala
Narathiwat
Rangae
Khao Yai 1204 m
SHAN STATE
Mōng Yai
Keng Lon
Ke-hsi Mānsām
Loi Sang 2491 m
Mōng Küng
Indaw
Lawksawk
Lai-hka
Namsang
Loi-lem
Hopong
Taunggyi
Mōng Pawn
Hkam
Keng Tawng
Mōng Pu
Kunhing
Mōng Ping
Ta-Kaw
Keng Tung
Mōng Hpayak
Loi Pangnao 2607 m
Tonglau
Pāng-yāng
Namlan
Samka
Hsi-hseng
Cangyuan
Shangyun
Simao
Munai
Mengzhe
Menghai
Jinghong
Mae Sai
Chiang Rai
Fang
Sop Huai
Chiang Kham
Wiang Pa Pao
Thung Chang
Phayao
Muang Pakbeng
Mae Hong Son
Doi Chiang Dao 2175 m
Doi Mae Ya 2005 m
Wang Nua
Doi Mae Tho 2031 m
Chiang Mai
Lamphun
Nan
Ngao
Doi Inthanon 2590 m
Chom Thong
Lampang
Mae Sariang
Pang
Phrae
Den Chai
Ban Pak Phun
Uttaradit
Tanen Taunggyi
Sawankhalok
Sam Ngao
Tha Song Yang
Mae Ramat
Sukhothai
Phitsanulok
Tak
Mae Sot
Kamphaeng Phet
Phichit
Khlong Khlung
Chumsaeng
Nakhon Sawan
Nong Bua
Khao Yai 1554 m
Uthai Thani
Ban Rai
Chai Nat
Khok Samrong
Lop Buri
Sing Buri
Ang Thong
Khao Kamphaeng 1257 m
Phra Nakhon Si Ayutthaya
Saraburi
Krung Thep (Bangkok)
Nonthaburi
Photharam
Samut Prakan
Ratchaburi
Samut Sakhon
Samut Songkhram
Phetchaburi
Cha-am
Hua Hin
Bight of Bangkok
Pattaya
Rayong
Chon Buri
Prachuap Khiri Khan
Ban Huai Yang
Thap Sakae
Pathiu
Chumphon
Lang Suan
Ko Tao
Ko Phangan
Ko Samui
Surat Thani
1530 m
Ban Na San
Nakhon Si Thammarat
Ron Phibun
Thung Song
Bay of Bengal
Preparis North Channel
Preparis I.
Preparis South Channel
Great Coco I.
Little Coco I.
Coco Channel
Landfall I.
C. Price
North Andaman
Saddle Peak 738 m
Andaman Islands
Pahlāgaon
Middle Andaman
South Andaman
Port Blair
Rutland I.
Duncan Passage
Nachuge
Little Andaman
Ten Degree Channel
Car Nicobar I.
Kakana
Tarasa Dwip
Camorta I.
Misha
Sombrero Channel
Nicobar Islands (India)
Little Nicobar
Great Nicobar
Bananga
Andaman and Nicobar Islands (India)
ANDAMAN SEA
INDONESIA
P. We
Sabang
TH

104°
E
108°
F
112°
G
116°
H
1
2
3
4
5
20°
16°
12°
8°
CHINA
GUANGXI
ZHUANGZU
ZIZHIQU
GUANGDONG
XIANGGANG
(HONG KONG)
Guangzhou
(Canton)
Foshan
Dongguan
Shenzhen
Jiulong
(Kowloon)
Xianggang (Hong Kong)
Macao
Zhuhai
Jiangmen
Zhaoqing
Shunde
Huizhou
Nanning
Beihai
Zhanjiang
Haikou
Maoming
Yangjiang
Yulin
Wuzhou
Qinzhou
HAINAN
Hainan
Dao
Sanya
Donghai Dao
Weizhou
Dao
Gulf
of
Tonkin
Hà Nội
(Hanoi)
Hải Phòng
Hồng Gai
Cẩm Phả
Nam Định
Ninh Bình
Thanh Hóa
Vinh
Hà Tĩnh
Đồng Hới
Đông Hà
Huế
Đà Nẵng
Hội An
Tam Kỳ
Quảng Ngãi
Kon Tum
Plây Cu
(Pleiku)
Qui Nho'n
Tuy Hòa
Buôn
Mê Thuột
Nha Trang
Ninh Hòa
Cam Lâm
(Cam Ranh)
Đà Lạt
Phan Rang
Phan Thiết
Biên Hòa
Thanh Phố Hồ Chí Minh
(Saigon)
Vũng Tàu
Mỹ Tho
Cần Thơ
Long Xuyên
Rạch Giá
Sóc Trăng
Bạc Liêu
Cà Mau
Mũi Cà Mau
Côn Sơn
Cù Lao So'n
Cù Lao Thu
VIETNAM
CAMBODIA
Phnum Pénh
(Phnom Penh)
Kâmpóng Cham
Kâmpóng Thum
Kâmpóng Chhnăng
Pouthisăt
Kâmpôt
Takêv
Svay Riĕng
Savannakhét
Muang Khammouan
Pakxé
Attapu
Saravan
Ubon
Ratchathani
Mukdahan
Nakhon
Phanom
Sakon
Nakhon
Chaîne Annamitique
Phnum Dângrek
XISHA QUNDAO
(Paracel Island)
(Sovereignty disputed)
SOUTH
CHINA
SEA
SPRATLY ISLANDS
(Sovereignty disputed)
MALAYSIA
Kota Kinabalu
Tuaran
Langkon
G. Kinabalu
4101 m
Redang
0
100
200
300
400
kilometers
0
100
200
miles

Asia and the Middle East

A
B
C
D
116°
120°
124°
128°
20°
16°
12°
8°
4°
1
2
3
4
5
6
Batan Is
Basco
Babuyan Is
Babuyan Channel
Mayraira Pt
Bangui
Palaui I.
C. Engaño
Abulog
Aparri
Bacarra
Laoag
Gonzaga
Agbulu
Batac
Mt Sicapoo 2048 m
Badoc
Alcala
Cabugao
Tuao
Vigan
Bangued
Tuguegarao
Narvacan
Tabuk
Lubuagan
Candon
Bontoc
Ilagan
Palanan Pt
Cervantes
Banaue
Cauayan
San Fernando
Santiago
Luzon
Mt Pulog 2934 m
Bauang
Bagabag
Bolinao
Baguio
Sierra Madre
Tarigtig Pt
Cabauyan I.
Lingayen Gulf
Agno
C. San Ildefonso
Lingayen
Dagupan
Villasis
San Carlos
Baler Bay
Baler
High Peak 2037 m
Tarlac
San Jose
Iba
Cabanatuan
Capas
Botolan
Angeles
Gapan
Dingalan Bay
Mt Pinatubo 1759 m
San Fernando
Malolos
Polillo Is
Olongapo
Quezon City
Infanta
Balanga
Bagac
Manila
Lamon Bay
Mariveles
Calagua Is
Santa Cruz
Muntinglupa
Labo
Calamba
Daet
Nasugbu
San Pablo
Mt Labo 1544 m
San Miguel Bay
Calatagan
Lipa
Lucena
Calauag
Tinambac
Yog Pt
Viga
Lubang Is
Batangas
Sipocot
Lagonoy
Catanduanes I.
Lobo
Tayabas Bay
Naga
Pili
Virac
Golo I.
Boac
Santa Cruz
Nabua
Lagonoy Gulf
C. Calavite
Calapan
Marinduque I.
San Andres
Tabaco
Batan I.
Paluan
Mt Halcon 2587 m
San Francisco
Rapu Rapu I.
Mamburao
Pinamalayan
Naujan
Legaspi
Mindoro
Donsol
Sorsogon
Sablayan
Bongabong
Burias I.
Bulan
Matnog
Mt Baco 2488 m
Romblon
Sibuyan I.
Ticao I.
Calintaan
Tablas I.
Catarman
San Jose
Bulalacao (San Pedro)
Mt Guitinguitin 2050 m
Masbate
Allen
Mt Capotoan 850 m
Busuanga
Busuanga I.
Mandaon
Masbate I.
Calbayog
Coron
Ilin I.
Baluad
Asid Gulf
Placer
Catbalogan
Taft
Semirara Is
Nabas
Pulanduta Pt
Biliran I.
Samar
Culion I.
Coron I.
Pucio Pt
Kalibo
VISAYAN SEA
Naval
Borongan
Roxas
Llorente
Nelyan Pt
Linapacan I.
Culasi
Daanbantayan
Carigara
Iloc I.
Tibiao
Sara
El Nido
Batas I.
Bugasong
Passi
San Remigio
Tacloban
Cuyo Is
Bantayan
Guiuan
Maytiguid I.
Panay
Cadiz
Ormoc
San Jose
Iloilo
Silay
Camotes Is
Leyte
Taytay
Leyte Gulf
Homonhon I.
Miagao
Bacolod
Danao
Baybay
Imuruan Bay
Boayan I.
Dumaran I.
Anini-y
San Carlos
Toledo
Mandaue
Sogod
Desolation Pt
Bacao
Bago
Cebu
Lapu-Lapu
Hilongos
Loreto
Caruray
Roxas
Panay Gulf
Negros
Maasin
Dinagat I.
Ulugan Bay
Cleopatra Needle 1593 m
Cebu
Pintuyan
Bacungan
Honda Bay
Kabankalan
Bohol
Siargao I.
Anepahan
Puerto Princesa
Sipalay
Cauayan
Dalaguete
Guindulman
Dapa
Long Pt
Panagtaran Pt
Hinoba-an
Tagbilaran
Surigao
Bucas Grande I.
Victoria Peak 1709 m
Palawan
Santander
L. Mainit
Quezon
Aborlan
Santa Catalina
Dumaguete
Camiguin I.
Cantilan
Rasa I.
Tolong Bay
Siquijor I.
Diuta Pt
Mt Hilonghilong 2012 m
Tandag
Palawan Passage
Island Bay
Siaton
Balingoan
Butuan
Mt Mantalingajan 2073 m
Balingasag
Bayugan
Brooke's Point
Dapitan
Salvacion
San Antonio Bay
Dipolog
El Salvador
Gingoog
Lianga
Rio Tuba
Oroquieta
Cagayan de Oro
Hinatuan
C. Buliluyan
Bugsuk I.
SULU SEA
Mt Jimenez
Iligan Bay
Lugait
Malaybalay
Sanco Pt
Pandanan I.
Sindangan
Mt Malindang 2425 m
Iligan
Bislig
Mindanao
Ozamiz
Panganuran
Liloy
Marawi
Kalatungan Mts 2865 m
Valencia
Balabac
Pagadian
Cateel
Balabac I.
Siocon
Ipil
Kabasalan
Monkayo
Baganga
Malabang
Kibawe
Tungawan
Margosatubig
Parang
Tagum
Caraga
P. Balambangan
P. Banggi
Sibuco
Midsayap
Mabini
Olutlanga I.
Cotabato
Mt Apo 2954 m
Samal I.
P. Malawali
Bolong
Pikit
Davao
Kudat
Tel. Paitan
Zamboanga
Sacol I.
Moro Gulf
Kidapawan
Mati
P. Jambongan
Lamitan
Linao Pt
Tacurong
Digos
Lamigan Pt
Isabela
Basilan I.
Lake Buluan
Langkon
Kanibongan
Maluso
1011 m
Lebak
Norala
Koronadal
Davao Gulf
Surallah
C. San Augustin
G. Kinabalu 4101 m
Tel. Labuk
Patikul
Tuaran
Jolo I.
Mt Matutum 2295 m
Malita
Lingkabau
Jolo
General Santos (Dadiangas)
Kota Kinabalu
SABAH
Sandakan
Kiamba
Tapul I.
Glan
Kuala Penyu
Telupid
Lamag
Sukau
Tapul Group
Beaufort
Sulu Archipelago
Batulaki
Victoria
G. Trus Madi 2649 m
Kinabatangan
Tawitawi I.
Siasi
Sarangani Is
Brunei Bay
Lahad Datu
Muara
MALAYSIA
Pinangah
Tel. Darvel
CELEBES
Bandar Seri Begawan
P. Timbun Mata
Sibutu I.
Kunak
BRUNEI
Kalabakan
Semporna
Sibutu Group
737
Geme
G. Harun 2160 m
Tawau
SEA
Kep. Talaud
Beo
G. Murud 2438 m
P. Sebatik
Longbawan
G. Basakan 1372 m
Mangaran
Sesayap
734
P. Mandul
INDONESIA
Tahuna
P. Sangihe
PHILIPPINE SEA
SOUTH CHINA SEA
PHILIPPINES
kilometers 0 100 200 300
miles 0 100 200

CHINA
XIZANG ZIZHIQU (TIBET)
Nyainqêntanglha Shan
BHUTAN
SIKKIM
INDIA
ARUNACHAL PRADESH
ASSAM
NĀGĀLAND
MEGHALAYA
MANIPUR
MIZORAM
TRIPURA
BANGLADESH
RAJSHAHI
DHAKA
KHULNA
CHITTAGONG
WEST BENGAL
MYANMAR (BURMA)
KACHIN STATE
SAGAING
CHIN
MANDALAY
MAGWE
SHAN STATE
ARAKAN
KAYAH
PEGU
IRRAWADDY
YANGON
MON
KAREN
THAILAND
LAOS
SICHUAN
YUNNAN
HENGDUAN SHAN
Mishmi Hills
Dafla Hills
Kumon Taungdan
Gangaw Taung
Mangin Taung
Letha Taung
Arakan Yoma
Pegu Yoma
Tanen Taunggyi
Shaluli Shan
Yun Ling
Nu Shan
Laobie Shan
Wuliang Shan
Mianmian Shan
Bay of Bengal
Gulf of Martaban
Preparis North Channel
Lhasa
Thimphu
Punākha
Dhaka (Dacca)
Calcutta
Chittagong
Shillong
Imphāl
Itānagar
Dibrugarh
Guwāhāti
Sylhet
Mandalay
Yangon (Rangoon)
Sittwe (Akyab)
Myitkyinā
Taunggyi
Moulmein
Bassein
Pegu
Chiang Mai
Dali
Lhasa
Kula Kangri 7554 m
Hkakabo Razi 5881 m
Mt Victoria 3053 m
Tropic of Cancer
0 100 200 300 400 kilometers
0 100 200 miles

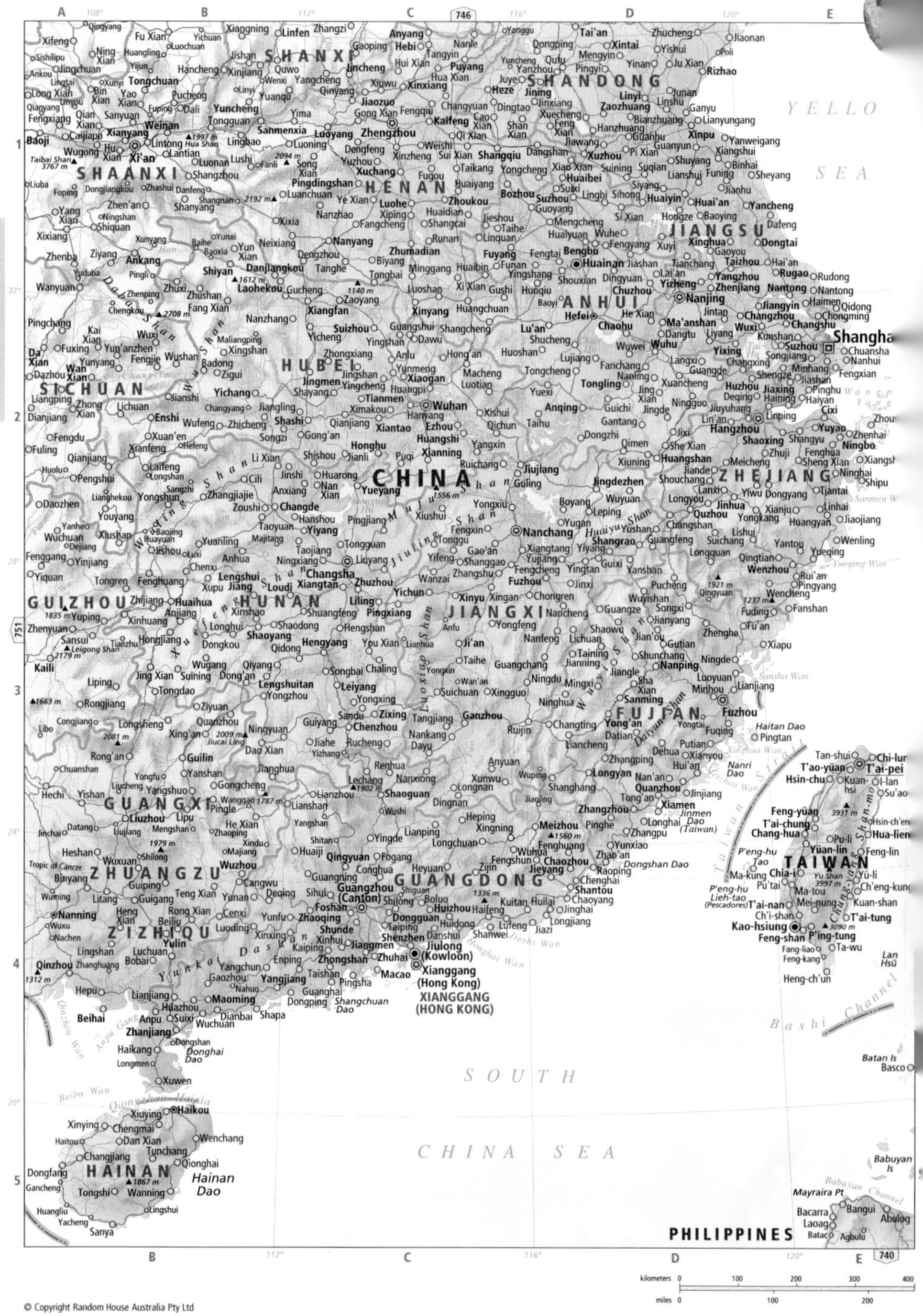
A
B
C
D
E
746
751
740
108°
112°
116°
120°
32°
28°
24°
20°
1
2
3
4
5
SHAANXI
SHANXI
HENAN
SHANDONG
JIANGSU
ANHUI
HUBEI
SICHUAN
CHINA
ZHEJIANG
GUIZHOU
HUNAN
JIANGXI
FUJIAN
GUANGXI
ZHUANGZU
ZIZHIQU
GUANGDONG
HAINAN
TAIWAN
PHILIPPINES
YELLOW SEA
SOUTH
CHINA SEA
Xi'an
Zhengzhou
Kaifeng
Luoyang
Jinan
Jining
Xuzhou
Lianyungang
Hefei
Nanjing
Wuhan
Changsha
Nanchang
Hangzhou
Shanghai
Ningbo
Wenzhou
Fuzhou
Xiamen
Guangzhou (Canton)
Shenzhen
Jiulong (Kowloon)
Xianggang (Hong Kong)
XIANGGANG (HONG KONG)
Macao
Zhuhai
Shantou
Guilin
Liuzhou
Nanning
Beihai
Zhanjiang
Haikou
Sanya
T'ai-pei
Kao-hsiung
T'ai-chung
Hainan Dao
Taiwan Strait
Bashi Channel
Babuyan Channel
Qiongzhou Haixia
Beibu Wan
Tropic of Cancer
kilometers 0 100 200 300 400
miles 0 100 200

Xianggang (Hong Kong) and Guangdong, China

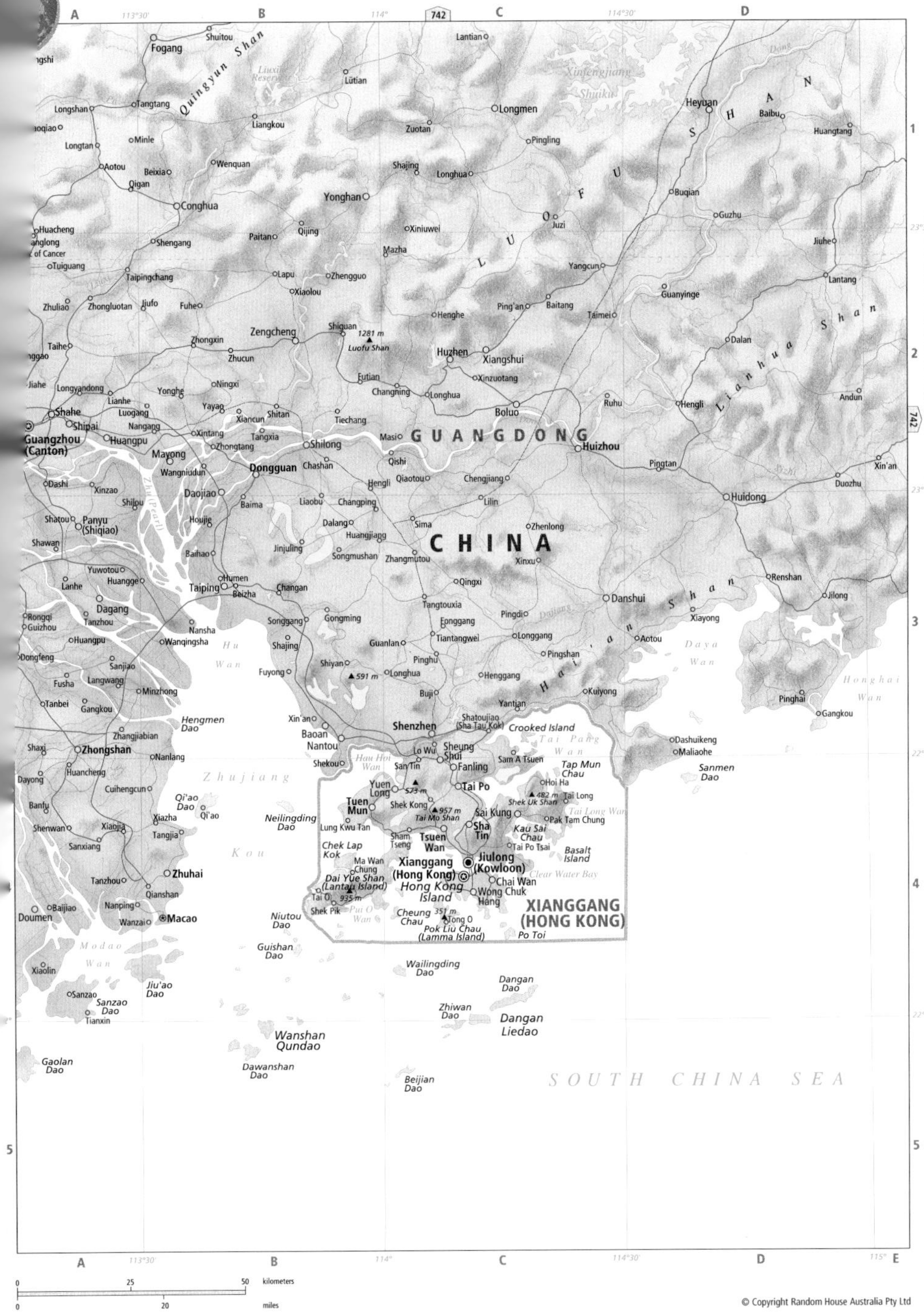
Asia and the Middle East
742
GUANGDONG
CHINA
XIANGGANG (HONG KONG)
Guangzhou (Canton)
Fogang
Shuitou
Qingyun Shan
Lantian
Liuxihe Reservoir
Lütian
Xinfengjiang Shuiku
Heyuan
Baibu
Huangtang
Longshan
Tangtang
Longmen
Liangkou
Zuotan
Pingling
Longtan
Minle
Aotou
Beixia
Wenquan
Shajing
Longhua
Qigan
Conghua
Yonghan
Buqian
Guzhu
Juzi
Huacheng
Shengang
Paitan
Qijing
Xiniuwei
Jiuhe
Tropic of Cancer
Tuiguang
Mazha
Yangcun
Lantang
Taipingchang
Lapu
Zhengguo
Guanyinge
Xiaolou
Zhuliao
Zhongluotan
Jiufo
Fuhe
Henghe
Ping'an
Baitang
Taimei
Lianhua Shan
Luofu Shan
Shiguan
1281 m
Zengcheng
Zhongxin
Taihe
Zhucun
Dalan
Huzhen
Xiangshui
Futian
Xinzuotang
Changning
Ningxi
Longyandong
Yonghe
Lianhe
Yayao
Luogang
Xiancun
Shitan
Tiechang
Ruhu
Hengli
Andun
Boluo
Shahe
Shipai
Nangang
Xintang
Huangpu
Tangxia
Zhongtang
Shilong
Masi
Huizhou
Mayong
Wangniudun
Dongguan
Chashan
Qishi
Pingtan
Xin'an
Qiaotou
Chengjiang
Duozhu
Dashi
Xinzao
Daojiao
Hengli
Huidong
Zhu (Pearl)
Shilou
Baima
Liaobu
Changping
Lilin
Shatou
Panyu (Shiqiao)
Houjie
Dalang
Sima
Zhenlong
Huangjiang
Shawan
Jinjiling
Songmushan
Zhangmutou
Baihao
Xinxu
Yuwotou
Huangge
Lanhe
Humen
Taiping
Beizha
Changan
Qingxi
Renshan
Dagang
Tangtouxia
Jilong
Danshui
Rongqi
Guizhou
Tanzhou
Nansha
Songgang
Gongming
Fenggang
Pingdi
Dajiang
Xiayong
Huangpu
Wanqingsha
Hu Wan
Shajing
Guanlan
Tiantangwei
Longgang
Aotou
Daya Wan
Dongfeng
Sanjiao
Pinghu
Pingshan
Fusha
Langwang
Shiyan
591 m
Longhua
Henggang
Honghai Wan
Minzhong
Fuyong
Haifeng Shan
Buji
Kuiyong
Tanbei
Gangkou
Yantian
Pinghai
Gangkou
Hengmen Dao
Xin'an
Shenzhen
Shatoujiao (Sha Tau Kok)
Crooked Island
Zhangjiabian
Baoan
Nantou
Tai Pang Wan
Dashuikeng
Shaxi
Zhongshan
Nanlang
Lo Wu
Sheung Shui
Sam A Tsuen
Maliaohe
Shekou
Hau Hoi Wan
San Tin
Fanling
Tap Mun Chau
Sanmen Dao
Huancheng
Zhujiang Kou
Yuen Long
573 m
Tai Po
Hoi Ha
Dayong
Cuihengcun
482 m
Shek Uk Shan
Tai Long
Qi'ao Dao
Qi'ao
Tuen Mun
Shek Kong
957 m
Tai Mo Shan
Sai Kung
Tai Long Wan
Banfu
Xiazha
Neilingding Dao
Lung Kwu Tan
Pak Tam Chung
Shenwan
Xiaojia
Tangjia
Sha Tin
Kau Sai Chau
Sanxiang
Chek Lap Kok
Sham Tseng
Tsuen Wan
Tai Po Tsai
Basalt Island
Ma Wan
Chung
Jiulong (Kowloon)
Xianggang (Hong Kong)
Dai Yue Shan (Lantau Island)
Hong Kong Island
Clear Water Bay
Chai Wan
Zhuhai
Tanzhou
Tai O
935 m
Wong Chuk Hang
Qianshan
Baijiao
Nanping
Shek Pik
Pui O Wan
Cheung Chau
351 m
Tong O
Doumen
Wanzai
Macao
Niutou Dao
Pok Liu Chau (Lamma Island)
Po Toi
Modao Wan
Guishan Dao
Wailingding Dao
Xiaolin
Dangan Dao
Jiu'ao Dao
Sanzao
Sanzao Dao
Zhiwan Dao
Dangan Liedao
Tianxin
Wanshan Qundao
Gaolan Dao
Dawanshan Dao
Beijian Dao
SOUTH CHINA SEA
A
B
C
D
E
1
2
3
4
5
113°30'
114°
114°30'
115°
23°30'
23°
22°30'
22°
0
25
50
kilometers
0
20
miles

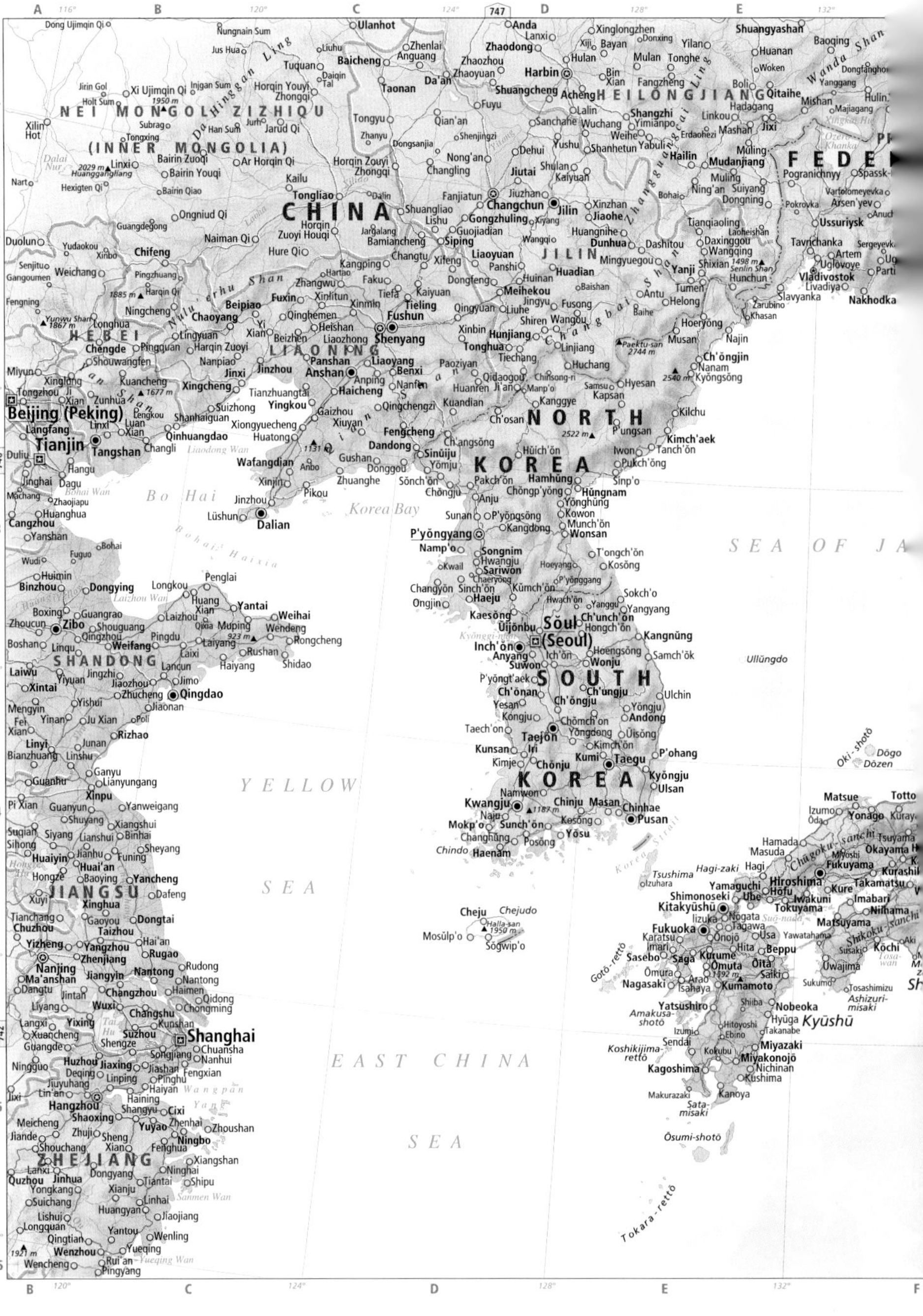
CHINA
NEI MONGOL ZIZHIQU
(INNER MONGOLIA)
HEILONGJIANG
JILIN
LIAONING
HEBEI
SHANDONG
JIANGSU
ZHEJIANG
NORTH KOREA
SOUTH KOREA
FEDE
Beijing (Peking)
Tianjin
Shanghai
Harbin
Changchun
Shenyang
Dalian
Qingdao
Nanjing
Hangzhou
P'yŏngyang
Sŏul (Seoul)
Inch'ŏn
Taejŏn
Taegu
Kwangju
Pusan
Vladivostok
Fukuoka
Kitakyūshū
Hiroshima
Kagoshima
Kumamoto
Nagasaki
Kyūshū
Bo Hai
Bohai Haixia
Korea Bay
Laizhou Wan
Liaodong Wan
YELLOW SEA
EAST CHINA SEA
SEA OF JA
Korea Strait
Tsushima
Cheju
Chejudo
Halla-san 1950 m
Ullŭngdo
Oki-shotō
Gotō-rettō
Ōsumi-shotō
Tokara-rettō
Amakusa-shotō
Koshikijima-rettō
Da Hinggan Ling
Changbai Shan
Paektu-san 2744 m
Wangpan Yang
Sanmen Wan
747
746
742
116°
120°
124°
128°
132°
44°
40°
36°
32°
28°
A
B
C
D
E
F
1
2
3
4
5
6

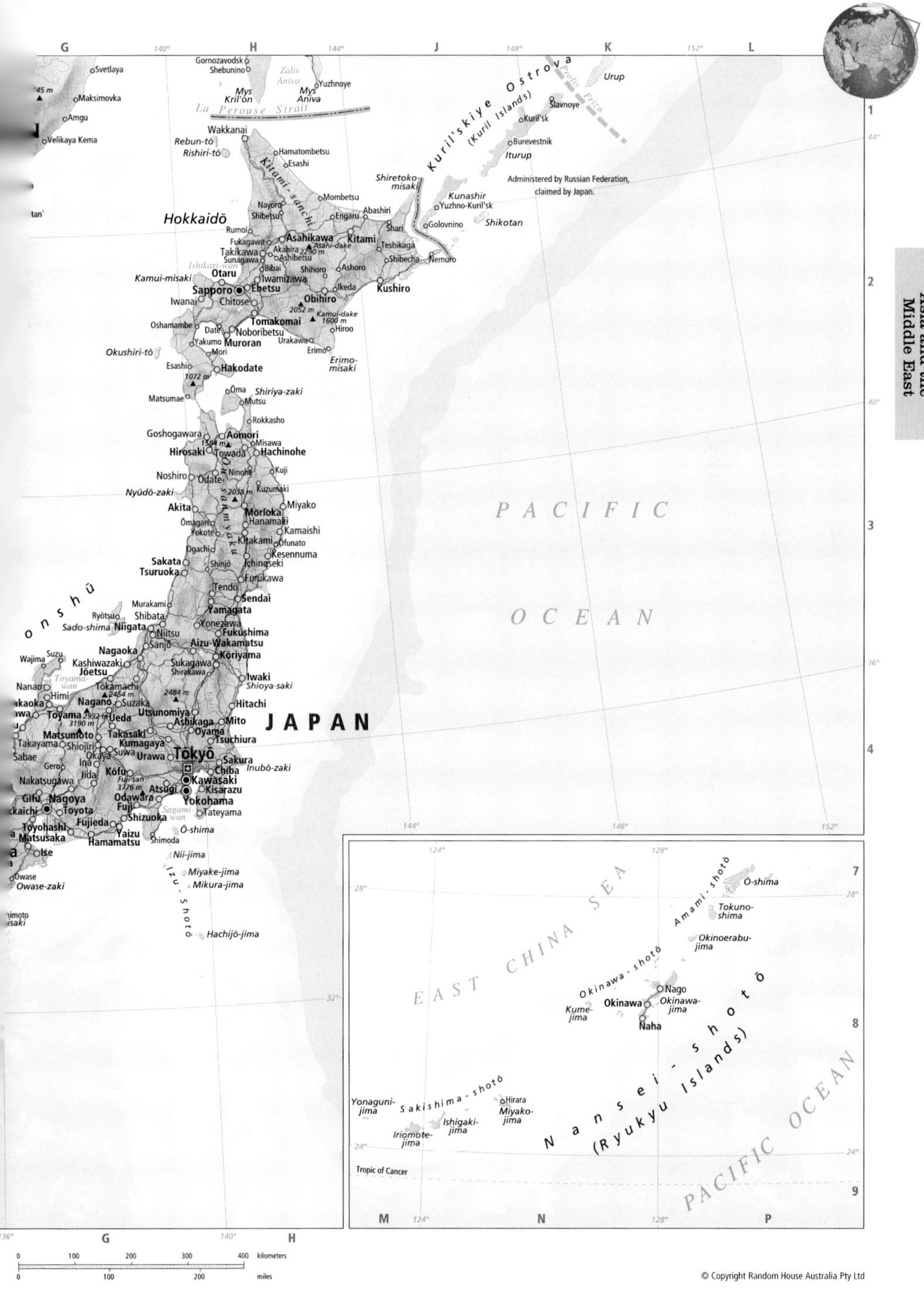
G
H
J
K
L
140°
144°
148°
152°
Svetlaya
Maksimovka
Amgu
Velikaya Kema
Gornozavodsk
Shebunino
Zaliv Aniva
Yuzhnoye
Mys Kril'on
Mys Aniva
La Perouse Strait
Kuril'skiye Ostrova
(Kuril Islands)
Proliv Friza
Urup
Slavnoye
Kuril'sk
Burevestnik
Iturup
Administered by Russian Federation, claimed by Japan.
Kunashir
Yuzhno-Kuril'sk
Golovnino
Shikotan
Shiretoko-misaki
Wakkanai
Rebun-tō
Rishiri-tō
Hamatombetsu
Esashi
Kitami-sanchi
Hokkaidō
Mombetsu
Nayoro
Shibetsu
Abashiri
Engaru
Shari
Rumoi
Fukagawa
Asahikawa
Asahi-dake
2290 m
Kitami
Teshikaga
Takikawa
Akabira
Ashibetsu
Sunagawa
Shibecha
Nemuro
Ishikari-wan
Bibai
Shihoro
Ashoro
Kamui-misaki
Otaru
Iwamizawa
Sapporo
Ebetsu
Ikeda
Kushiro
Iwanai
Chitose
Obihiro
2052 m
Kamui-dake
1600 m
Oshamambe
Date
Noboribetsu
Tomakomai
Hiroo
Yakumo
Muroran
Urakawa
Mori
Erimo
Okushiri-tō
Erimo-misaki
Esashi
1072 m
Hakodate
Matsumae
Ōma
Shiriya-zaki
Mutsu
Rokkasho
Goshogawara
Aomori
1584 m
Misawa
Hirosaki
Towada
Hachinohe
Noshiro
Ōdate
Ninohe
Kuji
Nyūdō-zaki
2038 m
Kuzumaki
Akita
Morioka
Miyako
Ōmagari
Hanamaki
Yokote
Kamaishi
Kitakami
Ōfunato
Ogachi
Kesennuma
Sakata
Shinjō
Ichinoseki
Tsuruoka
Furukawa
Tendō
Sendai
Murakami
Yamagata
Ryōtsu
Shibata
Yonezawa
Sado-shima
Niigata
Fukushima
Niitsu
Sanjō
Aizu-Wakamatsu
Honshū
Nagaoka
Kōriyama
Wajima
Suzu
Kashiwazaki
Sukagawa
Shirakawa
Jōetsu
Toyama-wan
Iwaki
Shioya-saki
Nanao
Tokamachi
Himi
2454 m
2484 m
Hitachi
Takaoka
Nagano
Suzaka
Toyama
2932 m
Ueda
Utsunomiya
Mito
3190 m
Ashikaga
JAPAN
Matsumoto
Takasaki
Oyama
Takayama
Shiojiri
Kumagaya
Tsuchiura
Sabae
Okaya
Suwa
Urawa
Tōkyō
Sakura
Gero
Ina
Chiba
Inubō-zaki
Iida
Kōfu
Kawasaki
Fuji-san
3776 m
Nakatsugawa
Atsugi
Kisarazu
Gifu
Odawara
Yokohama
Nagoya
Fuji
Sagami-wan
Tateyama
Yokkaichi
Toyota
Fujieda
Shizuoka
Toyohashi
Ō-shima
Matsusaka
Yaizu
Hamamatsu
Shimoda
Ise
Nii-jima
Owase
Owase-zaki
Miyake-jima
Mikura-jima
Izu-shotō
Hachijō-jima
PACIFIC OCEAN
1
2
3
4
44°
40°
36°
32°
136°
124°
128°
28°
24°
7
8
9
M
N
P
EAST CHINA SEA
Amami-shotō
Ō-shima
Tokuno-shima
Okinoerabu-jima
Okinawa-shotō
Nago
Kume-jima
Okinawa
Okinawa-jima
Naha
Nansei-shotō
(Ryukyu Islands)
Yonaguni-jima
Sakishima-shotō
Hirara
Miyako-jima
Ishigaki-jima
Iriomote-jima
Tropic of Cancer
PACIFIC OCEAN
0
100
200
300
400
kilometers
miles

785
749
751
742
RUSSIAN FEDERATION
MONGOLIA
RESPUBLIKA TYVA
USTʹ-ORDYNSKIY BURYATSKIY A.O.
IRKUTSKAYA OBLASTʹ
RESPUBLIKA BURYATIYA
AGINSKIY BURYATSKIY A.O.
HÖVSGÖL
DZAVHAN
BULGAN
SELENGE
ARHANGAY
TÖV
HENTIY
DORNOD
BAYANHONGOR
HANGAY
DUNDGOVĬ
SÜHBAATAR
DORNOGOVĬ
ÖMNÖGOVĬ
GOVĬ ALTAYN NURUU
Hangayn Nuruu
Hentiyn Nuruu
Gurvan Sayhan Uul
NEI MONGOL ZIZHIQU (INNER MONGOLIA)
NEI MONGOL
GANSU
NINGXIA HUIZU ZIZHIQU
QINGHAI
SHAANXI
SHANXI
HEBEI
CHINA
Badain Jaran Shamo
Yabrai Shan
Heli Shan
Lang Shan
Xiqing Shan
Khrebet Khamar-Daban
Primorskiy Khrebet
Khrebet Ulan-Burgasy
Malkhanskiy Khrebet
Yablonovyy Khrebet
Ozero Baykal (Lake Baikal)
Irkutsk
Ulan-Ude
Chita
Kyakhta
Sühbaatar
Darhan
Erdenet
Mörön
Uliastay
Tsetserleg
Bayanhongor
Arvayheer
Ulaanbaatar (Ulan Bator)
Nalayh
Mandalgovĭ
Öndörhaan
Choybalsan
Baruun-Urt
Saynshand
Dalandzadgad
Erenhot
Hohhot
Baotou
Linhe
Wuhai
Yinchuan
Shizuishan
Lanzhou
Xining
Wuwei
Jinchang
Zhangye
Datong
Zhangjiakou
Taiyuan
Shijiazhuang
Beijing (Peking)
Tianjin
Baoding
Yan'an
Changzhi
Linfen
Handan
Xingtai
Anyang

785
744
H
J
K
L
M
120°
124°
128°
132°
136°
2
3
4
5
6
48°
44°
40°
36°
AMURSKAYA
OBLAST'
KHABAROVSKIY KRAY
YEVREYSKAYA
AVTONOMNAYA
OBLAST'
PRIMORSKIY
KRAY
HEILONGJIANG
JILIN
LIAONING
NORTH
KOREA
SOUTH
KOREA
JAPAN
SEA OF JAPAN
YELLOW
SEA
Korea Bay
Bo Hai
Bohai Haixia
Liaodong Wan
Laizhou Wan
Magdagachi
Tygda
Ushumun
Sivaki
Ust'-Tygda
Fevral'sk
Lukachek
Ol'ginsk
Stoyba
Yashkino
Sofiysk
Norsko
Chagoyan
Shimanovsk
Duki
Ust'-Umal'ta
Boktor
Novogeorgiyevka
Novokiyevskiy Uval
Svobodnyy
Serysheva
Belogorsk
Romny
Chegdomyn
Komsomol'sk-na-Amure
Gurskoye
Vysokogornyy
Chekunda
Mogdy
Amursk
El'ban
Sogda
Bolon'
Innokent'yevka
Tyrma
Sel'gon
Troitskoye
Blagoveshchensk
Zavitinsk
Cheugda
Talakan
Litovko
Gora Tardoki-Yani 2078 m
Heihe
Raychikhinsk
Novobureyskiy
Ivankovtsy
Arkhara
Celny
Obluch'ye
Birobidzhan
Bira
Smidovich
Khabarovsk
Fuyuan
Pereyaslavka
Khor
Vyazemskiy
Gora Ko 2004 m
Bikin
Svetlaya
Maksimovka
Amgu
Pozharskoye
Novopokrovka
Dal'nerechensk
Velikaya Kema
Terney
Lesozavodsk
Plastun
Dal'negorsk
Rudnaya Pristan'
Spassk-Dal'niy
Kavalerovo
Arsen'yev
Anuchino
Ol'ga
Ussuriysk
Lazo
Valentin
Uglekamensk
Partizansk
Preobrazheniye
Nakhodka
Vladivostok
Artem
Uglovoye
Livadiya
Slavyanka
Zarubino
Khasan
Ozero Khanka
Pogranichnyy
Pokrovka
Mohe
Ershiwuzhan
Dzhalinda
Chador
Qiyahe
Yimuhe
Fukeshan
Yudi Shan 1054 m
Qiqian
Mangui
Alongshan
Niu'erhe
Shiwei
Derburo
Genhe
Keyihe
Yitulihe
Tulihe
Jiwen
Shangkuli
Xinzhangfang
Huder
Dayangshu
Hadat
Orqohan
Yakeshi
Mianduhe
Hailar
Onor
Bugt
Yadong
Chaor
Sugehe
Songling
Zalantun
Arun Qi
Gannan
Fuyu
Nianzishan
Qiqihar
Longjiang
Yushutun
Arxan
Bailang
Wuchagou
Solon
Jalaid Qi
Tailai
Qarsan
Guiler
Ulanhot
Zhenlai
Baicheng
Anguang
Taonan
Da'an
Tuquan
Horqin Youyi Zhongqi
Tongyu
Jarud Qi
Horqin Zuoyi Zhongqi
Ar Horqin Qi
Kailu
Tongliao
Zuoyi Houqi
Naiman Qi
Hure Qi
Kangping
Faku
Tieling
Fuxin
Beipiao
Chaoyang
Lingyuan
Shenyang
Fushun
Benxi
Liaoyang
Anshan
Panshan
Jinzhou
Jinxi
Yingkou
Xingcheng
Suizhong
Shanhaiguan
Qinhuangdao
Changli
Wafangdian
Dalian
Lüshun
Zhuanghe
Dandong
Sinŭiju
Penglai
Longkou
Yantai
Weihai
Wendeng
Rongcheng
Shidao
Rushan
Laiyang
Haiyang
Laizhou
Pingdu
Laixi
Weifang
Jimo
Qingdao
Jiaonan
Zhucheng
Jiaozhou
Nenjiang
Nehe
Bei'an
Laha
Kedong
Keshan
Tongbei
Hailun
Suileng
Baiquan
Mingshui
Lindian
Wangkui
Qing'an
Tieli
Suihua
Qinggang
Daqing
Longfeng
Anda
Lanxi
Xinglongzhen
Zhaodong
Bayan
Hulan
Harbin
Mulan
Bin Xian
Acheng
Shuangcheng
Zhaozhou
Zhaoyuan
Lalin
Wuchang
Shangzhi
Yimianpo
Weihe
Yabuli
Mudanjiang
Hailin
Ning'an
Dongning
Muling
Suiyang
Jixi
Mashan
Linkou
Boli
Qitaihe
Mishan
Hadagang
Huanan
Jiamusi
Shuangyashan
Baoqing
Fujin
Tongjiang
Luobei
Hegang
Yichun
Youhao
Jinshantun
Nancha
Xinqing
Jiayin
Sunwu
Xunhe
Yilan
Tonghe
Fangzheng
Hulin
Fuyu
Qian'an
Changling
Nong'an
Dehui
Changchun
Jiutai
Jilin
Jiaohe
Dunhua
Huadian
Gongzhuling
Siping
Liaoyuan
Meihekou
Panshi
Huinan
Antu
Helong
Yanji
Hunchun
Tumen
Hoeryŏng
Najin
Musan
Ch'ŏngjin
Kyŏngsŏng
Paektu-san 2744 m
Hyesan
Kilchu
Kimch'aek
Tanch'ŏn
Hamhŭng
Hŭngnam
Sinp'o
Kŭmya
Kowon
Munch'ŏn
Wonsan
Kosŏng
T'ongch'ŏn
P'yŏngyang
Namp'o
Songnim
Sariwon
Hwangju
Haeju
Kaesŏng
Sinch'ŏn
Ongjin
Sokch'o
Yangyang
Kangnŭng
Samch'ŏk
Ch'unch'ŏn
Hongch'ŏn
Ŭijŏngbu
Sŏul (Seoul)
Inch'ŏn
Anyang
Suwon
Wonju
Ch'ungju
Ulchin
Andong
Ch'ŏnan
Ch'ŏngju
Yŏngju
P'ohang
Taejŏn
Kumi
Taegu
Kyŏngju
Ulsan
Kunsan
Iri
Chŏnju
Kimje
Namwon
Ullŭngdo
Oki-shotō
Dōgo
Dōzen
Tottori
Maizuru
Matsue
Yonago
Himeji
Kobe
Okayama
Kakogawa
Hamada
Tsuyama
0 100 200 300 400 kilometers
0 100 200 miles

A
B
C
D
E
784
750
759
KAZAKHSTAN
KYRGYZSTAN
TAJIKISTAN
UZB.
AFGHANISTAN
PAKISTAN
RUS
JAMMU AND KASHMIR
AKSAI CHIN
XINJIANG UYGUR ZIZ
XIZANG ZIZHIQU (TIBET)
AQMOLA
PAVLODAR
QARAGHANDY
ALMATY
ZHAMBYL
SHYGHYS QAZAQSTAN
ALTAYSKIY KRAY
RESPUBLIKA ALTAY
Astana (Aqmola)
Pavlodar
Ekibastuz
Qaraghandy (Karaganda)
Temirtaū
Balqash
Semey
Öskemen
Rubtsovsk
Biysk
Gorno-Altaysk
Ayagūz
Taldygorghan (Taldykorgan)
Almaty
Bishkek
Taraz
Tokmak
Balykchy
Karakol
Naryn
Osh
Andijon
Jalal-Abad
Kashi (Kashgar)
Aksu
Kuqa
Korla
Ürümqi
Shihezi
Changji
Karamay
Kuytun
Yining
Hotan
Yecheng
Shache
Qiemo
Gilgit
Srinagar
Balqash Köli
Ysyk-Köl
Zaysan Köli
Alaköl
Qapshaghay Bögeni
Bosten Hu
Sarysik-Atyraū Qumy
Betpaqdala
Taūqum
Moyynqum
Khrebet Tarbagatay
Zhongghar Alataū Zhotasy
Qalba Zhotasy
Borohoro Shan
Junggar Pendi
Gurbantünggüt Shamo
Kyrgyz Ala-Too
Teskey Ala-Too
Tarim Pendi
TAKLIMAKAN SHAMO
TIAN SHAN
KUNLUN SHAN
KARAKORAM RANGE
Ladakh Range
Hoh Xil Shan
Kuruktag
Altun Shan
Pik Pobedy 7439 m
Khan Tängiri Shyngy 6995 m
Pik Dankova 5982 m
Muztagata 7546 m
Kongur Shan 7719 m
K2 8611 m
Nanga Parbat 8126 m
Saser Kangri 7672 m
Muztag 7723 m
Gora Belukha 4506 m
Aqsorang Biigi 1565 m
Pik imeni Ismail Samani 7495 m
Atyndagy Choku 7134 m
Bogda Feng 5445 m
Tarim
Yarkant
Hotan
Ili
Irtysh

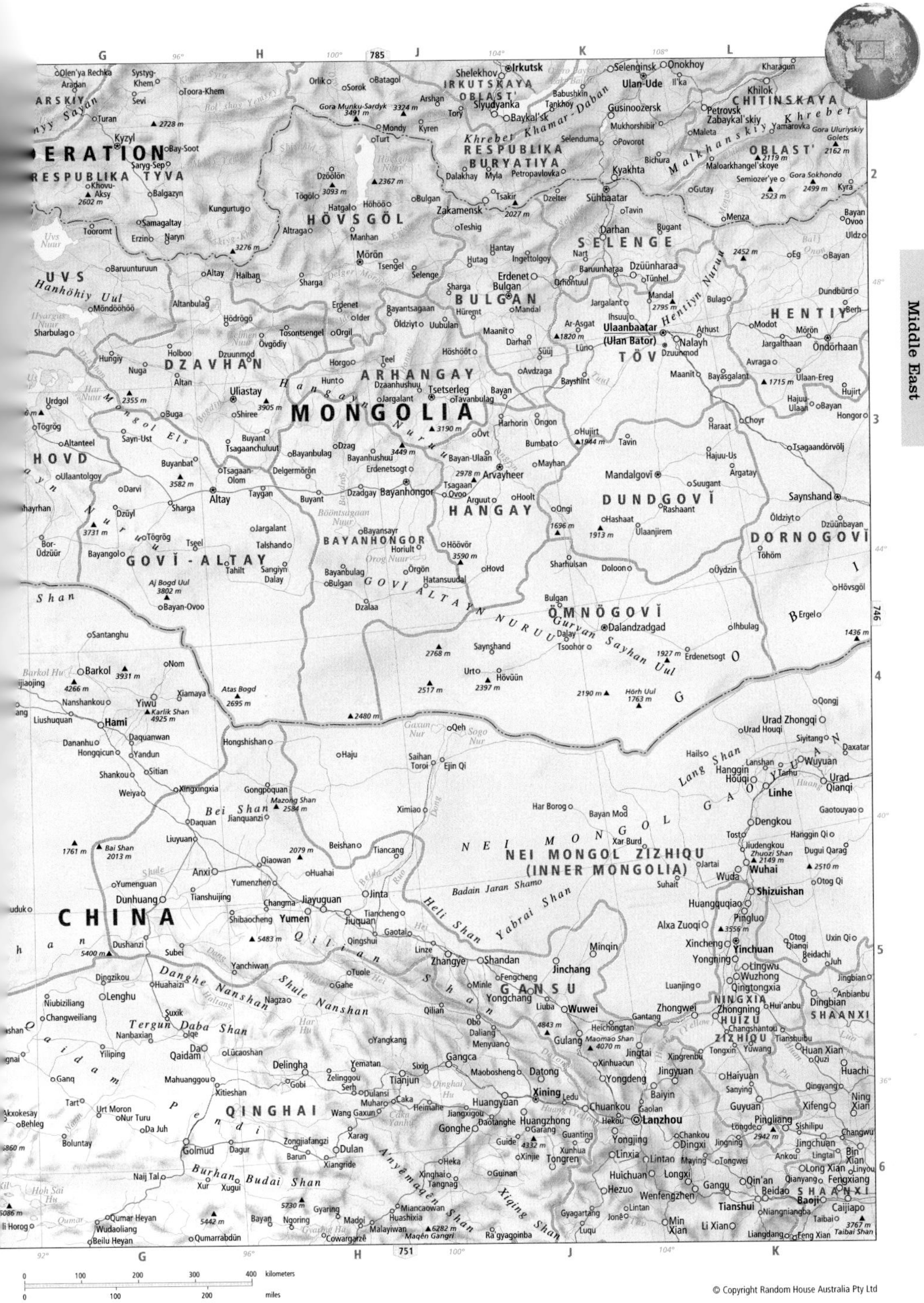
G
H
785
J
K
L
96°
100°
104°
108°
MONGOLIA
CHINA
RESPUBLIKA TYVA
IRKUTSKAYA OBLAST'
RESPUBLIKA BURYATIYA
CHITINSKAYA OBLAST'
HÖVSGÖL
SELENGE
BULGAN
HENTIY
TÖV
ARHANGAY
DZAVHAN
UVS
HOVD
GOVĬ-ALTAY
BAYANHONGOR
HANGAY
DUNDGOVĬ
DORNOGOVĬ
ÖMNÖGOVĬ
NEI MONGOL ZIZHIQU (INNER MONGOLIA)
GANSU
NINGXIA HUIZU ZIZHIQU
QINGHAI
SHAANXI
Irkutsk
Ulan-Ude
Ulaanbaatar (Ulan Bator)
Kyzyl
Uliastay
Tsetserleg
Altay
Bayanhongor
Arvayheer
Mandalgovĭ
Saynshand
Dalandzadgad
Erdenet
Bulgan
Mörön
Darhan
Sühbaatar
Kyakhta
Hami
Yiwu
Barkol
Jiayuguan
Yumen
Jiuquan
Dunhuang
Anxi
Zhangye
Jinchang
Wuwei
Xining
Lanzhou
Golmud
Delingha
Yinchuan
Shizuishan
Wuhai
Linhe
Tianshui
Baoji
Gobi
Badain Jaran Shamo
Qilian Shan
Bei Shan
Hangayn Nuruu
Govĭ Altayn Nuruu
Gurvan Sayhan Uul
Hentiyn Nuruu
Khrebet Khamar-Daban
Malkhanskiy Khrebet
Qaidam Pendi
Burhan Budai Shan
A'nyêmaqên Shan
Xiqing Shan
Lang Shan
Heli Shan
Yabrai Shan
Danghe Nanshan
Shule Nanshan
Tergun Daba Shan
Huang (Yellow) He
Uvs Nuur
Hövsgöl Nuur
5483 m
5400 m
4843 m
6282 m
746
751
92°
96°
100°
104°
G
H
J
K
2
3
4
5
6
40°
44°
48°
36°
0
100
200
300
400
kilometers
0
100
200
miles

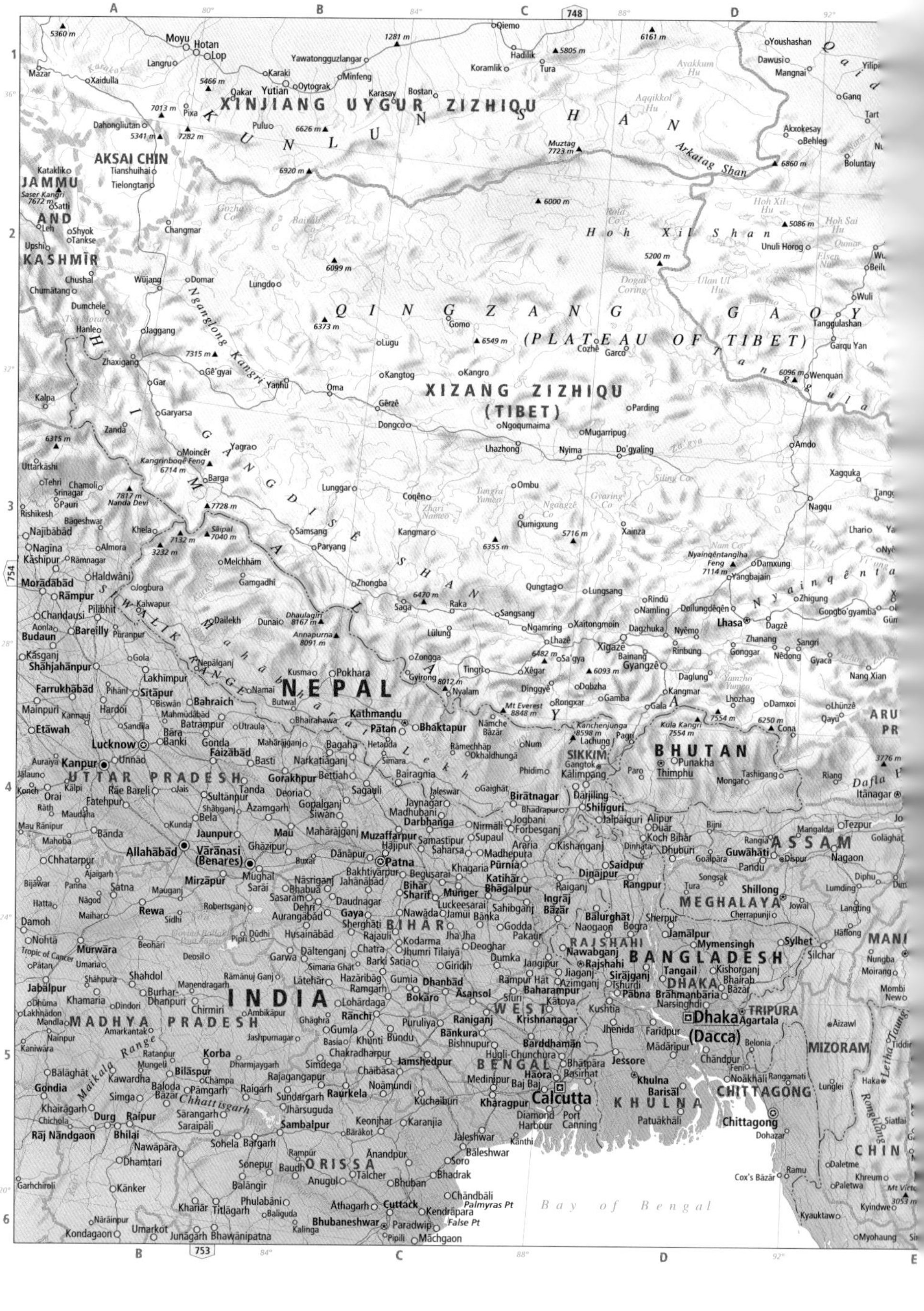

XINJIANG UYGUR ZIZHIQU
KUNLUN SHAN
AKSAI CHIN
JAMMU AND KASHMĪR
QINGZANG GAOYUAN (PLATEAU OF TIBET)
XIZANG ZIZHIQU (TIBET)
Hoh Xil Shan
Arkatag Shan
Tanggula Shan
Nyainqêntanglha Shan
GANGDISÊ SHAN
HIMALAYA
SIWALIK RANGE
Mahābhārat Lekh
NEPAL
SIKKIM
BHUTAN
ASSAM
MEGHALAYA
BANGLADESH
RAJSHAHI
DHAKA
KHULNA
CHITTAGONG
TRIPURA
MIZORAM
MANIPUR
UTTAR PRADESH
BIHAR
WEST BENGAL
INDIA
MADHYA PRADESH
ORISSA
Maikala Range
Chhattisgarh
Bay of Bengal
Palmyras Pt
False Pt
Moyu
Hotan
Lop
Yutian
Qiemo
Lhasa
Xigazê
Gyangzê
Nagqu
Amdo
Kathmandu
Pātan
Bhaktapur
Pokhara
Thimphu
Punakha
Gangtok
Dārjiling
Shiliguri
Lucknow
Kanpur
Allahābād
Vārānasi (Benares)
Patna
Gorakhpur
Muzaffarpur
Gaya
Rānchi
Jamshedpur
Calcutta
Hāora
Dhaka (Dacca)
Khulna
Chittagong
Shillong
Guwāhāti
Agartala
Aizawl
Cuttack
Bhubaneshwar
Raipur
Bhilai
Durg
Bilāspur
Sambalpur
Rourkela
Jabalpur
Rewa
Bareilly
Morādābād
Rāmpur
Shāhjahānpur
Mt Everest 8848 m
Kanchenjunga 8598 m
Kula Kangri 7554 m
Dhaulagiri 8167 m
Annapurna 8091 m
Nanda Devi 7817 m
Kangrinboqê Feng 6714 m
Nyainqêntanglha Feng 7114 m
Muztag 7723 m
Saser Kangri 7672 m
Tropic of Cancer
748
753
754

749

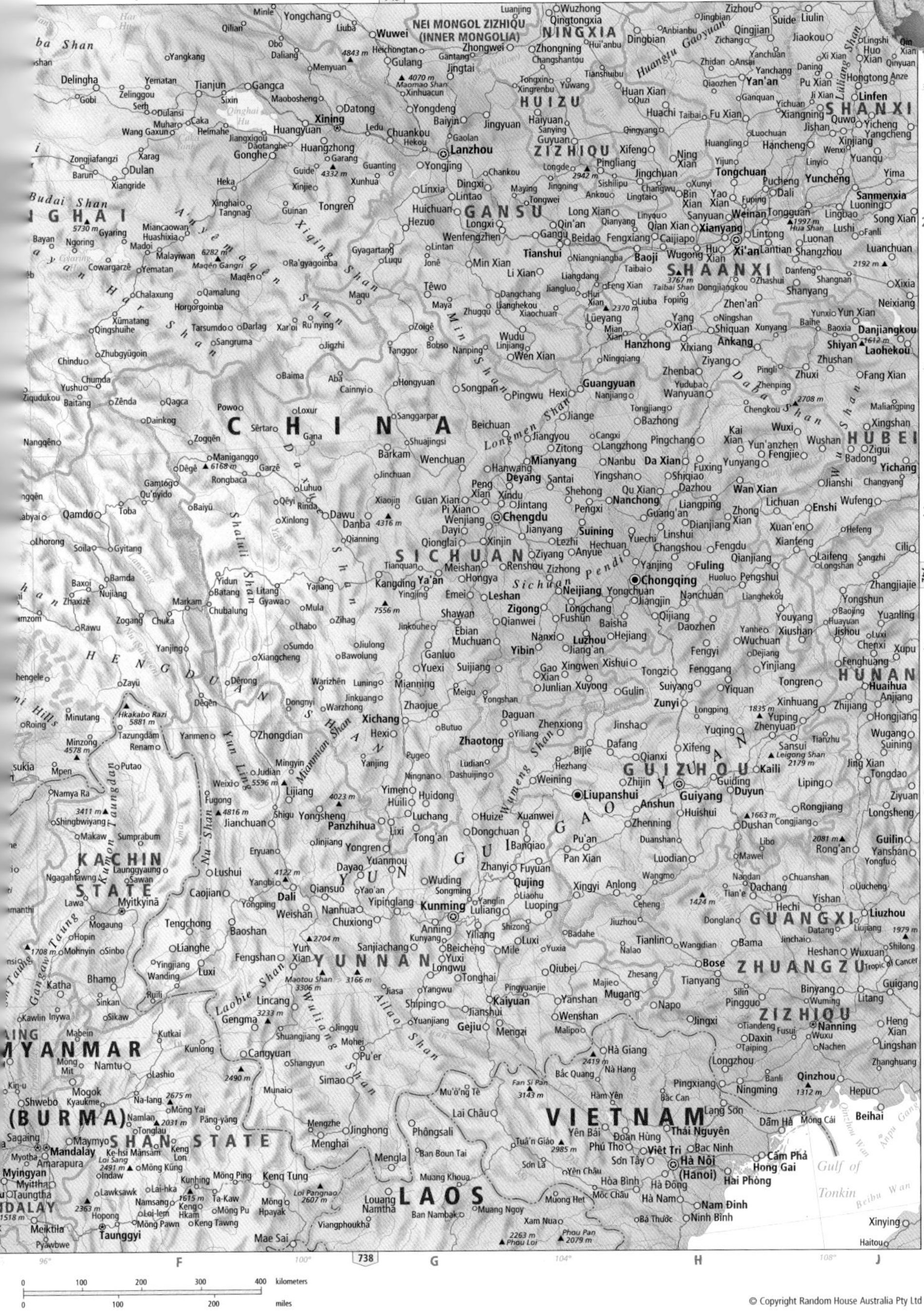

742

738

0 100 200 300 400 kilometers
0 100 200 miles

A
B
C
D
1
2
3
5
6
7
754
68°
72°
76°
20°
16°
12°
8°
4°
0°
GUJARĀT
Rānāvāv
Porbandar
Kutiyāna
Bāntva
Keshod
Jūnāgadh
Māngrol
Verāval
Kodinar
Diu
Delvāda
Una
Gir Hills
Kundla
Mahuva
Amreli
Pālitāna
Bhāvnagar
DAMĀN AND DIU
Gulf of Khambhāt
Bharūch
Rājpipla
Barwāni
Julwānia
MADHYA PRADESH
Sātpura Range
Khargon
Dediāpāda
Taloda
Shāhāda
Surat
Māndvi
Nandurbār
Shirpur
Burhānpur
Harisal
Multai
Pāndhurna
Bhusāwal
Gāwilgarh Hills
Paratwāda
Warud
Kāmthi
Achalpur
Nāgpur
Navsāri
Vyāra
Bilimora
Vānsada
Dhule
Jalgaon
Malkāpur
Akot
Amrāvati
Umrer
Valsād
Dharampur
Satāna
Pārola
Khāmgaon
Akola
Boris
Wardha
DAMĀN AND DIU
Damān
Mālegaon
Ajanta
Buldāna
Patūr
Kāranja
Deoli
Hinganghāt
Silvassa
Manmād
Ajanta Range
Mangrūl Pīr
Yavatmāl
Sātmāla Hills
Bhokardan
Dārwha
Warora
DĀDRA AND NAGAR HAVELI
Nāsik
Aurangābād
Wāshim
Karanji
Deolāli
Jālna
Pusad
Khandāla
Ādilābād
Kalamnūr
Bhiwandi
Thāne
Ulhāsnagar
MAHĀRĀSHTRA
Hadgaon
Gevrai
Parbhani
Nānded
Nirmal
Āsifābād
Mumbai (Bombay)
Kalyān
Amarnāth
Ahmadnagar
INDIA
Bīr
Bālāghāt Range
Parli
Jagtiāl
Pimpri-Chinchwad
Pune
Ahmadpur
Nizāmābād
Karīmnagar
Kirkee
Daund
Yermala
Lātūr
Udgīr
Deglūr
Sirsilla
Siddipet
Murud
Nira
Bārsi
Osmānābād
Bhor
Tembhurni
Tuljāpur
Budāda
Dāpoli
Bārāmati
Pandharpur
Homnābād
Bīdar
Zahīrābād
Sātāra
Mhāsvād
Sāngola
Solāpur
Chincholi
Secunderābād
Guhāgar
Akalkot
Sadāseopet
Hyderābād
Karād
Nagaj
Gulbarga
Dudhani
Vikārābād
Hatkamba
Sāngli
Seram
Korangal
Suriāpet
Ratnāgiri
Tikota
Bijāpur
Mahbūbnagar
ANDHRA
Kolhāpur
Miraj
Ichalkaranji
Hippargi
Shāhpur
Yādgīr
Rājāpur
Tālikota
Chikodi
Jamkhandi
Mudhol
Mālvan
Nipāni
Hukeri
Bāgalkot
Rāichūr
PRADESH
Sāvantvādi
Yargatti
Vengurla
Belgaum
Nargund
Kushtagi
Emmiganūru
Kurnool
Mārkāpur
Panaji
Dhārwād
Gadag-Betgeri
Sindhnūr
Ādoni
Nandyāl
Kanigiri
Marmagao
Dāndeli
Hubli
Hospet
Ālūr
Giddalūr
GOA
Guntakal
Allagadda
Kanduk
Kārwār
KARNĀTAKA
Bellary
Proddatūr
Hāveri
Rānībennur
Tādpatri
Ankola
Sirsi
Harihar
Kalyāndrug
Anantapur
Cuddapah
Kumta
Dāvangere
Hirekerūr
Pāvagada
Penukonda
Gūdūr
Bhatkal
Channagiri
Holalkere
Kadiri
Shimoga
Hiriyūr
Hindupur
Pālkonda Range
Bhadrāvati
Sira
Pileru
Coondapoor
Huliyār
Gauribidanūr
Madanapalle
Koppa
Chintāmani
Udipi
Kārkāl
Tiptūr
Tumkūr
Kolār
Chittoor
Chikmagalūr
Palmaner
Hassan
Bangalore
Gudiyattam
Mangalore
Bantvāl
Kolār Gold Fields
Vellore
Puttūr
Sakleshpur
Channapatna
Kānchipuram
Kushālnagar
Mandya
Malavalli
Kāsaragod
Krishnagiri
Jāvādi Hills
Mysore
Hosdrug
Nanjangūd
TAMIL
Tiruvannāmalai
Cannanore
PONDICHERRY
Mahe
Chāmrājnagar
NĀDU
Badagara
Udagamandalam
Salem
Attūr
Neyveli
Kozhikode (Calicut)
Nilgiri Hills
Erode
Nāmakkal
Perambalūr
Manjeri
Coonoor
Mettuppālaiyam
Turaiyūr
Coimbatore
Tiruppur
Tiruchchirāppalli
Ponnāni
Shoranūr
Pālghāt
Pollāchi
Kiranūr
Thanjāvūr
Trichūr
Vālpārai
Dindigul
Pudukkottai
KERALA
Munnār
Allinagaram
Nattam
Kāraikkudi
Angamāli
Cardamom Hills
Melūr
Kochi (Cochin)
Madurai
Sivaganga
Kottayam
Aruppukkottai
Tondi
Rājapālaiyam
Rāmanāthapuram
Alleppey
Sattūr
Kāyankulam
Kadaiyanallur
Sankarankovil
Punalūr
Vilātikkulam
Kollam (Quilon)
Tirunelveli
Tuticorin
Nedumangād
Palayankottai
Thiruvananthapuram (Trivandrum)
Melapalawam
Neyyāttinkara
Nāgercoil
Tisaiyānvilai
Cape Comorin
Kanniyākumāri
Gulf of Mannar
Mannar I.
Chilaw
Negombo
Colombo
Dehiwala-Mount Lavinia
Sri Jayawardanapura-Kotte
Moratuwa
Kalutara
ARABIAN SEA
Amindivi Is
Chetlat I.
Kiltān I.
Lakshadweep Is (Laccadive Is)
Kadamatt I.
LAKSHADWEEP
Agatti I.
Āndrott I.
Kavaratti I.
Suheli I.
Kalpeni I.
Cannanore Is
Nine Degree Channel
Minicoy I.
Eight Degree Channel
Tiladummati Atoll
MALDIVES
Miladummadulu Atoll
Malosmadulu Atoll
Faadhippolhu Atoll
Male Atoll
Male
Ari Atoll
INDIAN
Eight Degree Channel
Tiladummati Atoll
Miladummadulu Atoll
Malosmadulu Atoll
Faadhippolhu Atoll
MALDIVES
Male Atoll
Male
Ari Atoll
Felidu Atoll
Nilande Atoll
Mulaku Atoll
Kolumadulu Atoll
Haddunmahti Atoll
One and Half Degree Channel
Huvadu Atoll
Equator
Addu Atoll

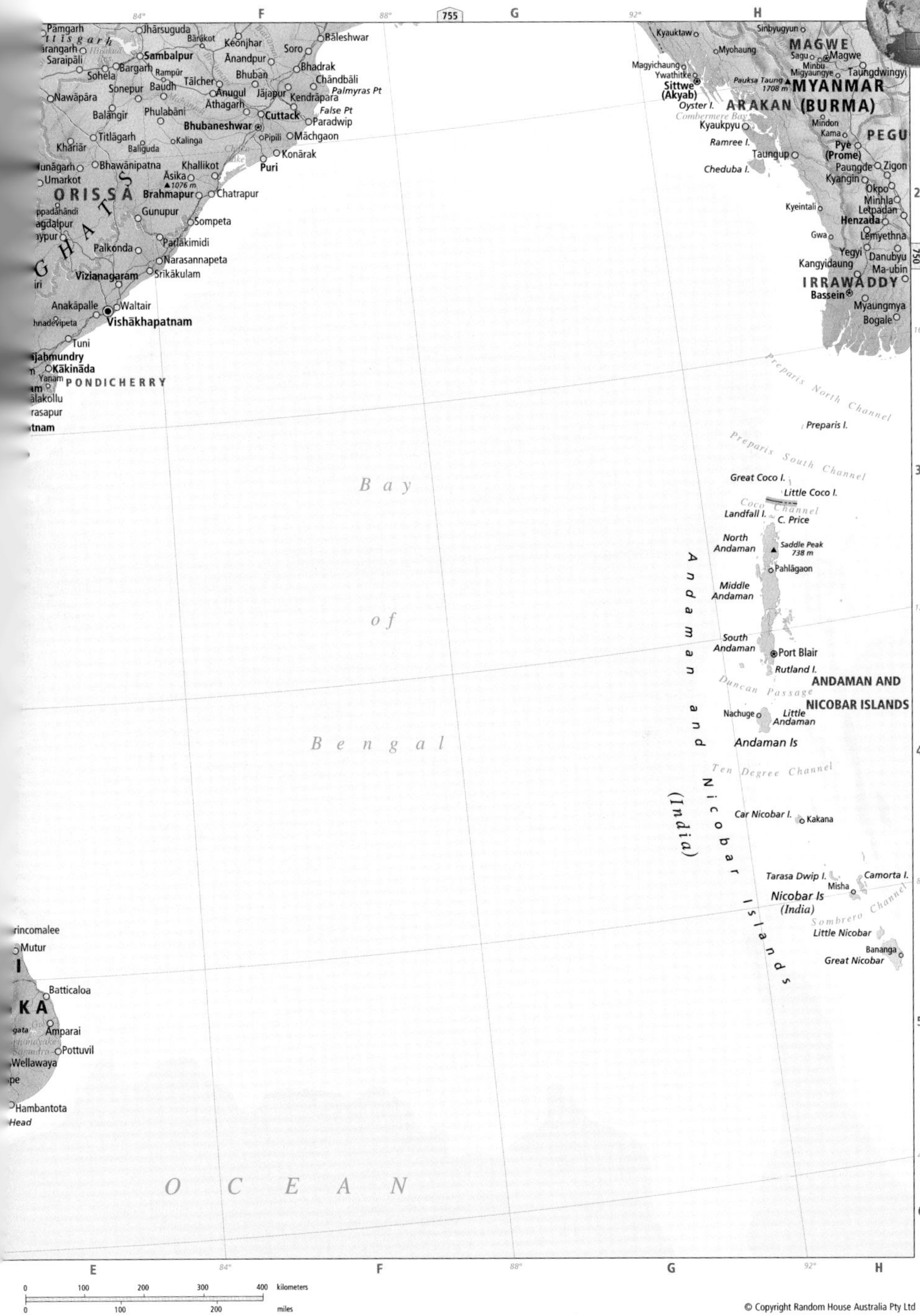
755
750
Bay of Bengal
OCEAN
ORISSA
GHATS
PONDICHERRY
MAGWE
MYANMAR (BURMA)
ARAKAN
PEGU
IRRAWADDY
ANDAMAN AND NICOBAR ISLANDS
Andaman and Nicobar Islands (India)
Andaman Is
Nicobar Is (India)
Pamgarh
Jhārsuguda
Bāleshwar
Keonjhar
Soro
Sambalpur
Ānandpur
Bhadrak
Saraipāli
Bargarh
Sohela
Rampūr
Sonepur
Bhuban
Chāndbāli
Baudh
Tālcher
Nawāpāra
Anugul
Jājapur
Kendrāpara
Palmyras Pt
Athagarh
Balāngir
Phulabāni
Cuttack
False Pt
Paradwip
Bhubaneshwar
Titlāgarh
Kalinga
Pipili
Māchgaon
Khariār
Baliguda
Konārak
Puri
Bhawānipatna
Khallikot
Umarkot
Āsika
1076 m
Brahmapur
Chatrapur
Gunupur
Sompeta
Parlakimidi
Palkonda
Narasannapeta
Vizianagaram
Srikākulam
Anakāpalle
Waltair
Vishākhapatnam
Tuni
Kākināda
Yanam
Trincomalee
Mutur
Batticaloa
Amparai
Pottuvil
Wellawaya
Hambantota
Head
Kyauktaw
Sinbyugyun
Myohaung
Sagu
Magwe
Minbu
Magyichaung
Ywathitke
Migyaungye
Taungdwingyi
Sittwe (Akyab)
Pauksa Taung
1708 m
Oyster I.
Combermere Bay
Kyaukpyu
Mindon
Kama
Ramree I.
Pye (Prome)
Taungup
Paungde
Zigon
Cheduba I.
Kyangin
Okpo
Minhla
Letpadan
Kyeintali
Henzada
Gwa
Lemyethna
Yegyi
Danubyu
Kangyidaung
Ma-ubin
Bassein
Myaungmya
Bogale
Preparis North Channel
Preparis I.
Preparis South Channel
Great Coco I.
Little Coco I.
Coco Channel
Landfall I.
C. Price
North Andaman
Saddle Peak
738 m
Pahlāgaon
Middle Andaman
South Andaman
Port Blair
Rutland I.
Duncan Passage
Nachuge
Little Andaman
Ten Degree Channel
Car Nicobar I.
Kakana
Tarasa Dwip I.
Camorta I.
Misha
Sombrero Channel
Little Nicobar
Bananga
Great Nicobar
84°
88°
92°
16°
12°
8°
4°
E
F
G
H
2
3
4
5
6
0
100
200
300
400
kilometers
miles

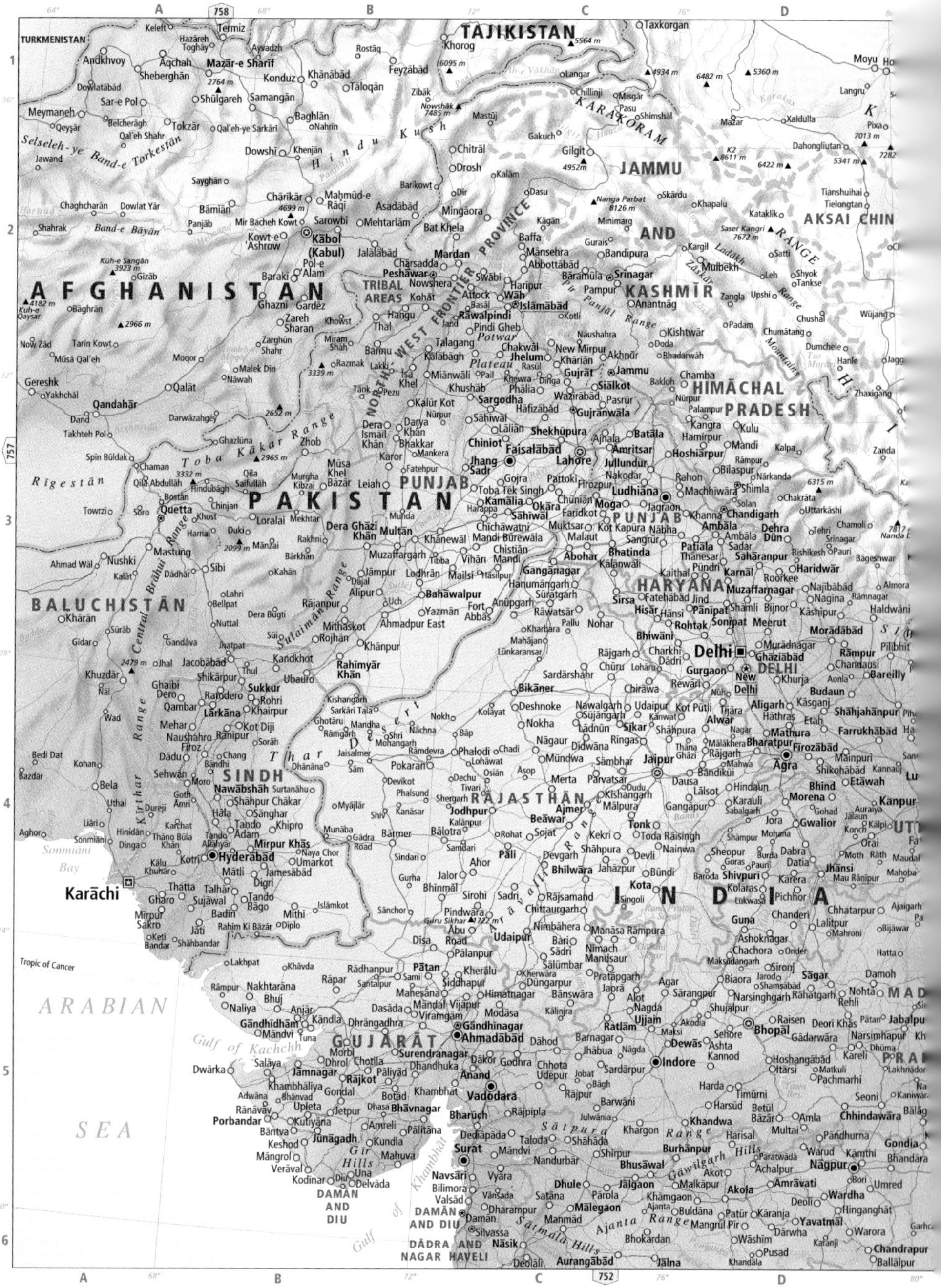

758
757
752
TURKMENISTAN
TAJIKISTAN
AFGHANISTAN
PAKISTAN
INDIA
JAMMU AND KASHMIR
AKSAI CHIN
HIMACHAL PRADESH
PUNJAB
HARYANA
DELHI
RAJASTHAN
GUJARAT
SINDH
BALUCHISTAN
NORTH-WEST FRONTIER PROVINCE
TRIBAL AREAS
DAMAN AND DIU
DADRA AND NAGAR HAVELI
ARABIAN SEA
Gulf of Kachchh
Gulf of Khambhat
Sonmiani Bay
Tropic of Cancer
Hindu Kush
KARAKORAM
Ladakh Range
Zaskar Range
Pir Panjal Range
Toba Kakar Range
Sulaiman Range
Central Brahui Range
Kirthar Range
Thar Desert
Aravalli Range
Satpura Range
Satmala Hills
Ajanta Range
Gir Hills
Rigestan
Potwar Plateau
Selseleh-ye Band-e Torkestan
K2 8611 m
Nanga Parbat 8126 m
Nowshak 7485 m
Saser Kangri 7672 m
Kabol (Kabul)
Islamabad
Rawalpindi
Peshawar
Lahore
Faisalabad
Multan
Quetta
Hyderabad
Karachi
Qandahar
Srinagar
Amritsar
Ludhiana
Chandigarh
Delhi
New Delhi
Jaipur
Agra
Jodhpur
Bikaner
Ahmadabad
Gandhinagar
Vadodara
Surat
Rajkot
Indore
Bhopal
Ujjain
Nagpur
Kanpur
Gwalior
Jhansi
Nasik
Aurangabad
Mazar-e Sharif

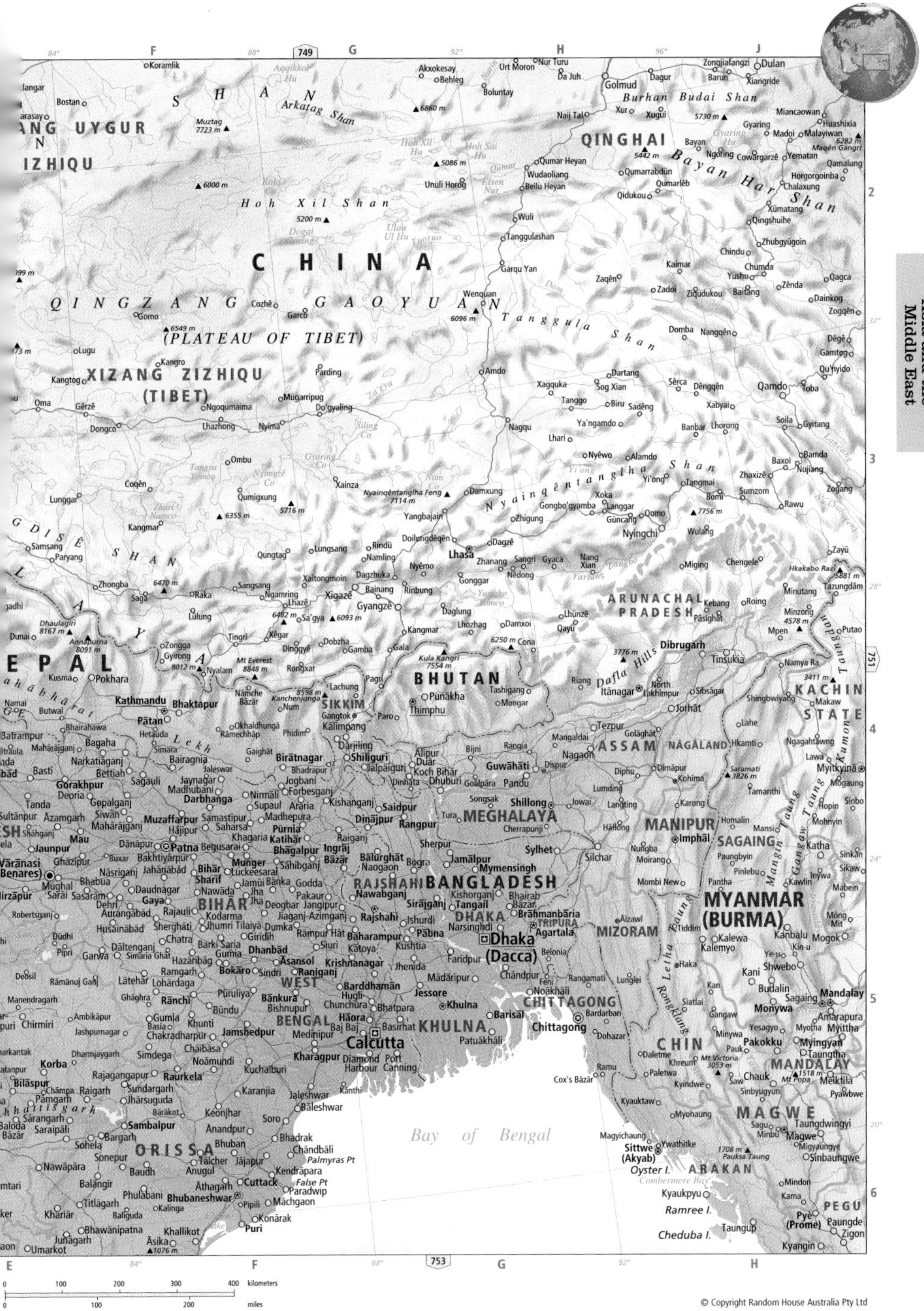
749
751
753
84°
88°
92°
96°
32°
28°
24°
20°
F
G
H
J
E
2
3
4
5
6
CHINA
QINGZANG GAOYUAN
(PLATEAU OF TIBET)
XIZANG ZIZHIQU
(TIBET)
QINGHAI
Hoh Xil Shan
Arkatag Shan
Burhan Budai Shan
Bayan Har Shan
Tanggula Shan
Nyainqêntanglha Shan
Nyainqêntanglha Feng 7114 m
Muztag 7723 m
Golmud
Lhasa
Xigazê
Gyangzê
Nagqu
Qamdo
Yushu
Dulan
Amdo
Wenquan
Tanggulashan
Nyingchi
Zayü
Arunachal Pradesh
BHUTAN
Thimphu
Punākha
SIKKIM
Gangtok
Kānchenjunga 8598 m
Mt Everest 8848 m
Annapurna 8091 m
Dhaulagiri 8167 m
Kula Kangri 7554 m
NEPAL
Kathmandu
Bhaktapur
Pātan
Pokhara
ASSAM
NĀGĀLAND
MANIPUR
MEGHALAYA
MIZORAM
TRIPURA
Guwāhāti
Shillong
Dispur
Imphāl
Kohima
Agartala
Dibrugarh
Itānagar
Dafla Hills
BANGLADESH
Dhaka
(Dacca)
RAJSHAHI
DHAKA
KHULNA
CHITTAGONG
Chittagong
Rājshāhi
Khulna
Barisāl
Sylhet
Mymensingh
Cox's Bāzār
BIHĀR
WEST BENGAL
ORISSA
Calcutta
Patna
Vārānasi
(Benares)
Gaya
Rānchi
Jamshedpur
Dhanbād
Bhubaneshwar
Cuttack
Puri
Sambalpur
Raurkela
Kharagpur
Hāora
Asansol
Bhāgalpur
Muzaffarpur
Darbhanga
Gorakhpur
Bilāspur
Korba
Shiliguri
Dārjiling
Birātnagar
Bay of Bengal
MYANMAR
(BURMA)
KACHIN STATE
SAGAING
CHIN
MANDALAY
MAGWE
ARAKAN
PEGU
Mandalay
Myitkyinā
Sittwe
(Akyab)
Oyster I.
Ramree I.
Cheduba I.
Kyaukpyu
Pye
(Prome)
Saramati 3826 m
Mt Victoria 3053 m
Mt Popa 1518 m
Hkakabo Razi 5881 m
0 100 200 300 400 kilometers
0 100 200 miles

A
B
C
D
E
F
760
758
802
807
CYPRUS
Lefkosia (Nicosia)
Lemesos (Limassol)
Larnaka
Ammochostos (Famagusta)
Ceasefire Line
Olympos 1951 m
Anamur
Anamur Burnu
Silifke
MEDITERRANEAN SEA
SYRIA
İskenderun
Antakya (Antioch)
Kilis
Halab (Aleppo)
Manbij
Akçakale
Al Lādhiqīyah (Latakia)
Ma'arrat an Nu'man
Jablah
Bāniyās
Ḩamāh
Ţarţus
Ţarābulus (Tripoli)
Ḩimş (Homs)
Ar Raqqah
Buḩayrat al Asad
Aş Şuwār
Dayr az Zawr
Al Mayādīn
Abū Kamāl
Al Qaryatayn
LEBANON
Bayrūt (Beirut)
Zaḩlah
An Nabk
Şaydā (Sidon)
Şūr (Tyre)
Dimashq (Damascus)
Sab' Ābār
At Tanf
ISRAEL
'Akko (Acre)
Ḩefa (Haifa)
Nawá
'Afula
As Suwaydā'
Dar'ā
Irbid
Tel Aviv-Yafo
Ashdod
'Ammān
1047 m
Jarash
Khān Yūnus
Gaza
Yerushalayim (Jerusalem)
Be'er Sheva' (Beersheba)
Al Karak
Aţ Ţafīlah
JORDAN
Ma'ān
Elat
Al 'Aqabah
Jabal Ramm 1754 m
Bādiyat ash Shām (Syrian Desert)
Ţurayf
Kāf
Al 'Īsāwīyah
Cizre
Al Qāmishlī
Al Ḩasakah
Dahūk
Al Mawşil (Mosul)
Arbīl
Rawāndūz
Kirkūk
As Sulaymānīyah
Ash Sharqāţ
Bayjī
Tikrīt
Ţūz Khurmātū
Kifrī
'Ānah
Sāmarrā'
Al Muqdādīyah
Ba'qūbah
Hīt
Ar Ramādī
Ḩabbānīyah
Baghdād
Ar Ruţbah
Baḩr al Milḩ
IRAQ
Karbalā'
Al Ḩillah
Al Kūt
An Najaf
Al Kūfah
Ad Dīwānīyah
Al 'Amārah
Qal'at Şāliḩ
As Samāwah
Ash Shaţrah
An Nāşirīyah
Sūq ash Shuyūkh
Al Başrah (Basra)
Al Buşayyah
Ash Shabakah
As Salmān
Badanah
'Ar'ar
Al 'Uwayqīlah
Al Jawf
Sakākah
Ẕahrat al Baţn
Rafḩā
KUWAIT
Al Jahrā'
Al Kuwayt (Kuwait)
Ḩawallī
Jazīrat Būbīyān
Jazīreh-ye Khārk (Khārg I.)
Ash Shu'bah
Ḩafar al Bāţin
Orūmīyeh (Urmia)
Benāb
Marāgheh
Mīāneh
Mīāndoāb
Mahābād
Heydarābād
Bandar-e Anzalī
Rasht
Tonekā
Zanjān
Qazvīn
Takāb
Saqqez
Dīvān Darreh
Abhar
Hashtgerd
Tākestān
Karaj
Marīvān
Sanandaj
Kabūdarāhang
Kāmyārān
Hamadān
Sāveh
Qom
Kermānshāh
Asadābād
Malāyer
Harsīn
Kerend
Borūjerd
Arāk
Delījān
Maḩallāt
Īlām
Kūhdasht
Dorūd
Khomeyn
Golpāyegān
Khorramābād
Mehrān
Andīmeshk
Dezfūl
Khomeynīshahr
Najafābād
Eşfahān
Shūsh
Shūshtar
Lālī
Masjed Soleymān
Shahr-e Kord
Ahvāz (Ahwaz)
Rāmhormoz
Behbahān
Bandar-e Khomeynī
Gonbardān
Kāzerūn
Borāzjān
Būshehr
Khvormūj
Kūh-hā-ye Zāgros
Persian Gulf
EGYPT
Al Iskandarīya (Alexandria)
Dumyāţ (Damietta)
Damanhūr
Būr Sa'īd (Port Said)
Al Ḩammām
Ţanţā
Al Manşūrah
Az Zaqāzīq
Al Ismā'īlīyah (Ismailia)
Al 'Arīsh
Al Jīzah
Al Qāhirah (Cairo)
Aş Şaff
As Suways (Suez)
An Nakhl
Al Fayyūm
1274 m
Bibā
Banī Suwayf
Maghāghah
Banī Mazār
Al Minyā
Mallawī
Dayrūţ
Manfalūţ
Asyūţ
Ra's Ghārib
Jabal Ghārib 1751 m
Abū Zanīmah
2637 m
Dhahab
Aţ Ţūr
Sharm ash Shaykh
Gulf of Suez
Gulf of Aqaba
Jamsah
Al Ghurdaqah
Jazīrat Shadwān
Ţahţā
Sūhāj
Qinā
Būr Safājah
Naj' Ḩammādī
Al Uqşur (Luxor)
Armant
Al Quşayr
Isnā
Idfū
Ar Radīsīya Baḩrī
Kawm Umbū
Darāw
Aswān
Marsá al 'Alam
1505 m Jabal Nuqruş
1977 m Jabal Ḩamāţah
Berenice
Foul Bay
Tropic of Cancer
Lake Nasser
Abū Sunbul (Abu Simbel)
Ḩaqi
Al Bi'r
2580 m Jabal al Lawz
Tabūk
Aş Şawrah
Jabal Dabbāgh 2350 m
Al Qalībah
Ḑubā
Taymā'
Al 'Ulā
Al Wajh
Al Ḩijāz
Umm Urūmah
Shaybārā
Ḩanak
Umm Lajj
Ra's Abū Madd
Ra's Banās
Ra's Barīdī
Yanbu' al Baḩr
Badr Ḩunayn
RED SEA
Al 'Uray'q
An Nafūd
At Taysīyah
Jabal Shammar
979 m
Al Jithāmīyah
Ḩā'il
Al Ajfar
Ḩafirat al 'Aydā
Ghazzālah
Ash Shurayf
Ḩulayfā'
Ad Dahnā'
An Nu'ayrīyah
Mish'āb
Ra's az Zawr
Al 'Uyūn
Buraydah
Ar Rubay'īyah
Al Bukayrīyah
Al Artāwīyah
Az Zilfī
Ar Rass
'Unayzah
Al Majma'ah
Nuqrah
Dukhnah
Al 'Uyūn
Al Ḩanākīyah
Al Madīnah (Medina)
Miskah
Nifī
Khuff
Shaqrā'
Al Musayjīd
Abū Rubayq
Al Qā'īyah
Ad Dawādimī
'Afīf
Ash Sha'rā'
Ad Dir'īyah
Ar Riyāḑ (Riyadh)
Al Kharj
Al Yamāmah
Ad Dilam
Ḩalabān
Al Ruwayḑah
Al Jubayl
Ra's Tannūrah
Az Ẓahrān (Dhahran)
Ad Dammām
Al Manāmah
BAHRAIN
Buqayq
Al Mubarraz
Al 'Uthmānīyah
Al Hufūf
Dukhān
QATAR
Ad Dawḩah (Doha)
Ḩaraḑ
SAUDI ARABIA
Mastūrah
Rābigh
Al Bi'ār
Al Qaḑīmah
Ad Dafinah
Al Muwayh
Ẕalim
'Urūq Subay'
Ḩalā'ib
Ras Hadarba
2216 m Jabal Asoteriba
Ra's Ḩāţibah
Khulayş
Dhahabān
'Usfān
Al Jumūm
'Ushayrah
Jiddah (Jedda)
Makkah (Mecca)
Ras Abu Shagara
Mastābah
Aţ Ţā'if
Turabah
Ras Oda
Al Kharfah
Laylá
Al Badī'
Al Biyāḑ
Qaşr Ḩamām
As Sulayyil
Ar Rub' al Khālī
Al Qa'āmīyāt
Al 'Aqīq
Al Līth
Ḩamdānah
Aẕ Ẕafir
Baljurashī
Qal'at Bīshah
Al 'Ulayyah
Tathlīth
Ad Dawqah
Rawḩah
Al Qunfudhah
Al Khawsh
An Nimāş
Khaybar
Ḩamḑah
Dirs
Bani Thawr
Al Birk
3133 m Jabal Sawdā'
Khamīs Mushayţ
Abhā
Ash Shuqayq
Ad Darb
Jazā'ir Farasān
Şabyā
Jīzān
Abū 'Arīsh
Ẓahrān
Najrān
Şa'dah
Sūq al Ghinān
Wuday'ah
Ḩaraḑ
Ḩūth
Khamr
Ḩajjah
Raydah
'Amrān
Az Zuhrah
Az Zaydīyah
Jabal an Nabī Shu'ayb 3760 m
Şan'ā'
Ma'rib
Bājil
Manākhah
Ramlat as Sab'atayn
Ḩaḑramawt
Al Ḩawţah
Shibām
Saywūn
YEMEN
Al Ḩudaydah
Al Marāwi'ah
Ḩarīb
Nuqūb
Bayḩān al Qişāb
Bayt al Faqīh
Dhamār
Al Fāzah
Zabīd
Yarīm
Al Ţawţah
'Atāq
Ḩabbān
Ḩays
Ibb
2513 m
Al Bayḑā'
Mawshij
3227 m
Ad Dāli'
Lawdar
Al Mukhā
Ta'izz
Māwiyah
Al Ḩumayshah
Dhubāb
Shaqrā'
Lahij
Zinjibār
At Turbah
Little Aden
Ash Shaykh 'Uthmān
'Adan (Aden)
Gulf of Aden
Balḩāf
Ash Shiḩr
Al Mukallā
Ra's al Kalb
Sayḩūt
Al Mahrah
Jabal Mahrāt
Damqawt
Al Ghayḑah
Mar'ayt
Sanāw
'Abd al Kūrī
Qulansiyah
Ra's Far
Bab el Mandeb
Dahlak Archipelago
Massawa Channel
NUBIAN Desert
Nubian Desert
SUDAN
Salālah
Dunqunāb
Muḩammad Qawl
Jabal Erba 2213 m
2259 m Jabal Oda
Abū Ḩamad
Būr Sūdān (Port Sudan)
Sallūm
Sawākin
Ash Shurayk
Al Bauga
Sinkāt
Erkowit
'Aţbara
Ad Dāmir
Ḩayyā
Ţawkar
Herbagat
Ras Kasar
Karora
2780 m
Shandī
Kabūshīyah
Derudeb
Algena
Nakfa
Abū Dulayq
Qawz Rajab
Aroma
Kassalā
ERITREA
Keren
Akordat
Massawa
Rufā'ah
Ḩalfā' al Jadīdah
Malawīya
Teseney
Wad Medanī
Khashm al Qirbah
Barentu
Asmara
Shuwak
Om Hājer
Ādī Ugrī
Dek'emhāre
3018 m
Soira
Mersa Fatma
Ādī Kwala
Ādī Keyih
Al Qaḑārif
Ādwa
Inda Silasē
Āksum
Ādīgrat
3291 m
Mesfinto
Ādī Ārk'ay
Ābiy Ādī
Wik'ro
4620 m
Āgula'i
Mek'elē
Ras Dashen Terara
Qallābāt
Metema
Gonder
Dabat
Āykel
Korem
Musa Ālī Terara 1200 m
2131 m
Jazīrat al Ḩanīsh al Kabīr
Ed
Beylul
Assab
Ad Damazin
Dangur
Gorgora
Ādīs Zemen
Werota
Debre Tabor
4193 m
Ābune Yosēf
Alamat'ā
K'obo
ETHIOPIA
Danakil Desert
Bambudi
Guba
3131 m
Bahir Dar
Guna Terara 4231 m
Weldiya
Serdo
Dangila
Tana Hāyk' (Lake Tana)
Injibara
Tendaho
Kurmuk
Bēlfodiyo
Burē
Mot'a
Desē
Kembolcha
DJIBOUTI
Khōr 'Angar
Tadjoura
1783 m
Yoboki
Djibouti
Blue Nile
Dinder
Atbara
Nile

G
H
J
K
L
60°
65°
70°
75°
758
754
752
2
3
4
5
6
30°
25°
20°
15°
55°
TURKMENISTAN
AFGHANISTAN
PAKISTAN
INDIA
OMAN
JAMMU AND KASHMĪR
ARABIAN SEA
Gulf of Oman
Gulf of Kachchh
Gulf of Khambhat
Sonmiani Bay
Gwatar Bay
Strait of Hormuz
Hindu Kush
Karakoram Range
Ladakh Range
Zāskār Mountains
Pīr Panjāl Range
Toba Kākar Range
Sulaimān Range
Kirthar Range
Siāhān Range
Central Makrān Range
Thar Desert
Rīgestān
Dasht-e Lūt
Dasht-e Mārgow
Gir Hills
Sātmāla Hills
Western Ghats
Al Hajar
Kavīr
Jazīrat Maşīrah
Khalīj Maşīrah
Ghubbat Şawqirah
Jiddat al Ḩarāsīs
Ra's al Ḩadd
Ra's al Madrakah
Ra's Naws
Jazā'ir Khurīyā Murīyā (Kuria Muria Is)
Laccadive Is
Suquṭrá (Socotra) (Yemen)
K2 8611 m
Nowshāk 7485 m
Nanga Parbat 8126 m
Saser Kangri 7672 m
Kūh-e Sangān 3923 m
Kūh-e Nāy Band 2992 m
Kūh-e Hazār 4420 m
Kūh-e Taftān 4042 m
Kūh-e Bazmān 3489 m
Guru Sikhar 1722 m
Jabal ash Shām 3019 m
Jabal Yibir 1527 m
2560 m
2488 m
2333 m
3007 m
2093 m
Mashhad
Bojnūrd
Qūchān
Neyshābūr
Sabzevār
Mary
Tejen
Bayramaly
Jolotan'
Mazār-e Sharīf
Konduz
Tāloqān
Kābol (Kabul)
Herāt
Qandahār
Ghaznī
Jalālābād
Bāmīān
Chārīkār
Farāh
Zāhedān
Zābol
Kermān
Bam
Khāsh
Īrānshahr
Chābahār
Gwādar
Turbat
Pasni
Ormāra
Karāchi
Hyderābād
Quetta
Sibi
Khārān
Nushki
Dalbandin
Khuzdār
Sukkur
Lārkāna
Jacobābād
Nawābshāh
Mīrpur Khās
Thatta
Badin
Peshāwar
Islāmābād
Rāwalpindi
Gilgit
Srīnagar
Jammu
Mardān
Lahore
Faisalābād
Multān
Bahāwalpur
Dera Ismāīl Khān
Dera Ghāzi Khān
Sargodha
Gujrānwāla
Sāhīwal
Rahīmyār Khān
Amritsar
Ludhiāna
Chandīgarh
Delhi
New Delhi
Ghāziābād
Meerut
Rohtak
Hisār
Bīkāner
Jaipur
Ajmer
Alwar
Jodhpur
Udaipur
Kota
Ahmadābād
Gāndhīnagar
Vadodara
Sūrat
Rājkot
Jāmnagar
Bhāvnagar
Porbandar
Jūnāgadh
Bhuj
Dwārka
Indore
Ujjain
Nāsik
Mumbai (Bombay)
Thāne
Pune
Ahmadnagar
Aurangābād
Dhule
Jalgaon
Kolhāpur
Sāngli
Belgaum
Panaji
Marmagao
Kārwār
Bhatkal
Masqaţ (Muscat)
Şūr
Şuḩār
Al Fujayrah
Al Khaşab
Ibrī
Nizwá
Ibrā'
Al Kāmil
Ḩaymā'
Ḩadbaram
Ḩāsik
Şadḩ
Mirbāţ
Dawwah
Khalūf
Jazīreh-ye Qeshm
Mīnāb
Kahnūj
Bīrjand
Ţabas
Kāshmar
Torbat-e Ḩeydarīyeh
Rafsanjān
Sīrjān
0 100 200 300 400 kilometers
0 100 200 miles

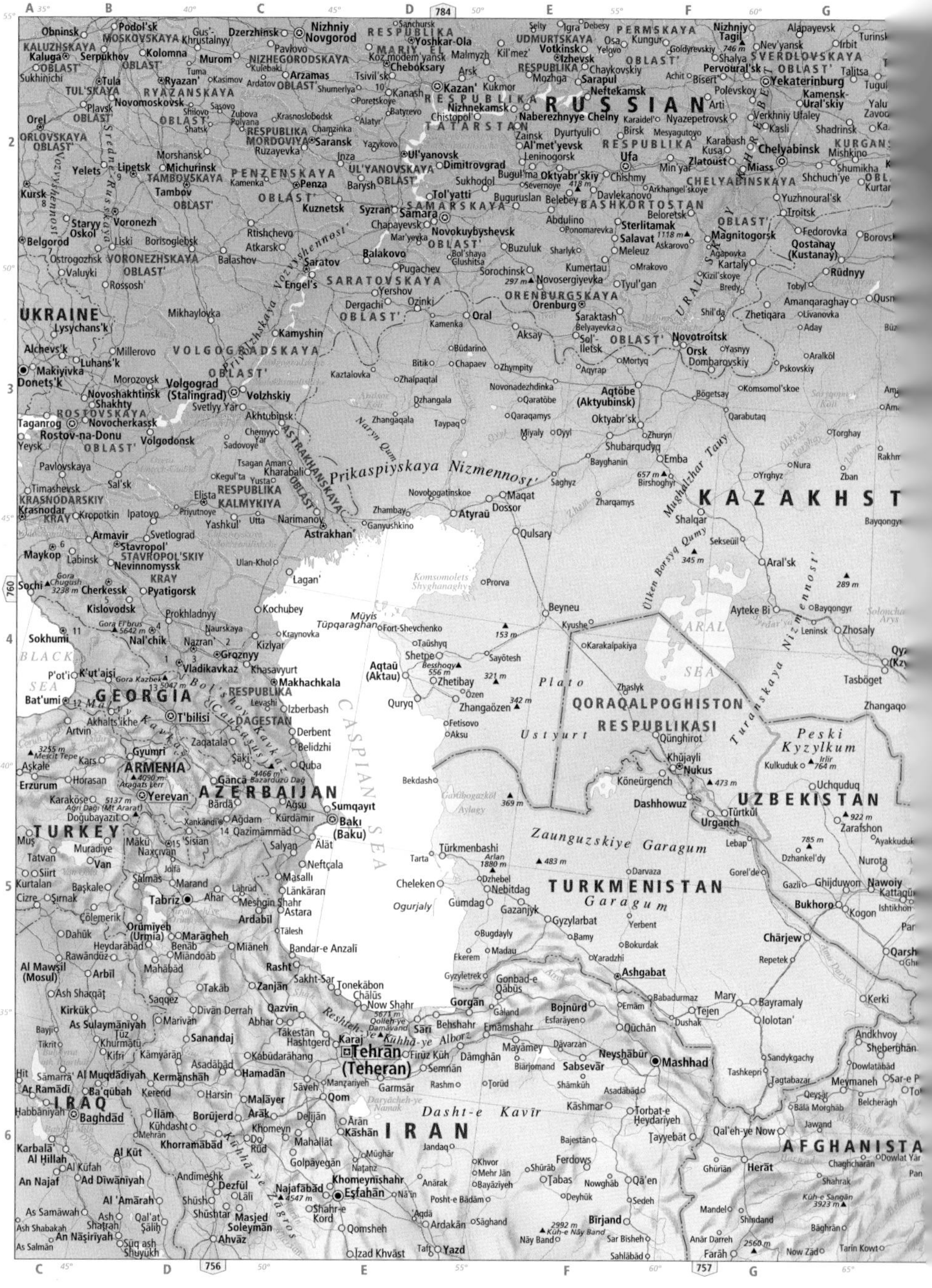
784
760
756
757
RUSSIAN
KAZAKHST
UKRAINE
GEORGIA
ARMENIA
AZERBAIJAN
TURKEY
IRAQ
IRAN
TURKMENISTAN
UZBEKISTAN
AFGHANISTA
QORAQALPOGHISTON RESPUBLIKASI
CASPIAN SEA
BLACK SEA
ARAL SEA
Prikaspiyskaya Nizmennost'
Plato Ustyurt
Zaunguzskiye Garagum
Garagum
Peski Kyzylkum
Dasht-e Kavīr
Mughalzhar Tauy
Ülken Borsyq Qumy
Turanskaya Nizmennost'
Nizhniy Novgorod
Kazan'
Samara
Saratov
Volgograd (Stalingrad)
Astrakhan'
Oral
Orenburg
Ufa
Chelyabinsk
Yekaterinburg
Aqtöbe (Aktyubinsk)
Atyraū
Aqtaū (Aktau)
Aral'sk
Nukus
Urganch
Dashhowuz
Türkmenbashi
Ashgabat
Mary
Chärjew
Bukhoro
Mashhad
Tehrān (Teheran)
Esfahān
Qom
Tabrīz
T'bilisi
Yerevan
Bakı (Baku)
Groznyy
Makhachkala
Rostov-na-Donu
Krasnodar
Stavropol'
Voronezh
Baghdād
Herāt

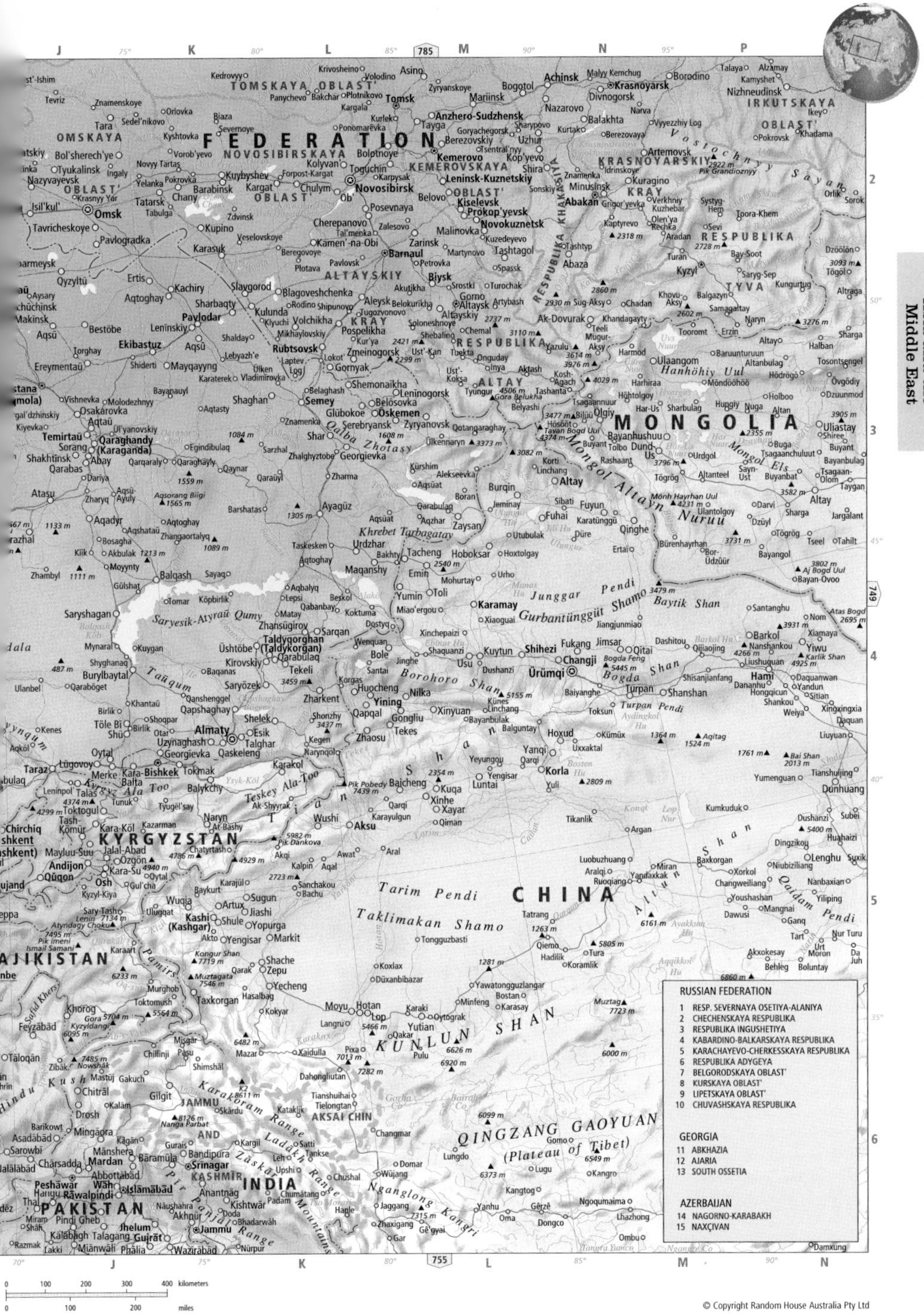
J
K
L
M
N
P
785
755
749
75°
80°
85°
90°
95°
70°
50°
45°
40°
35°
2
3
4
5
6
FEDERATION
TOMSKAYA OBLAST'
NOVOSIBIRSKAYA OBLAST'
OMSKAYA OBLAST'
KEMEROVSKAYA OBLAST'
ALTAYSKIY KRAY
KRASNOYARSKIY KRAY
IRKUTSKAYA OBLAST'
RESPUBLIKA KHAKASIYA
RESPUBLIKA TYVA
RESPUBLIKA ALTAY
Vostochnyy Sayan
MONGOLIA
Mongol Altayn Nuruu
Hanhöhiy Uul
CHINA
Junggar Pendi
Gurbantünggüt Shamo
Tarim Pendi
Taklimakan Shamo
Tian Shan
Bogda Shan
Borohoro Shan
Kunlun Shan
Altun Shan
Qaidam Pendi
QINGZANG GAOYUAN
(Plateau of Tibet)
Nganglong Kangri
KYRGYZSTAN
TAJIKISTAN
PAKISTAN
INDIA
JAMMU AND KASHMIR
AKSAI CHIN
Hindu Kush
Karakoram Range
Ladakh Range
Zaskar Mountains
Pir Panjal Range
Pamirs
Saryesik-Atyrau Qumy
Khrebet Tarbagatay
Qalba Zhotasy
Taūqum
Teskey Ala-Too
Kyrgyz Ala Too
Novosibirsk
Omsk
Tomsk
Barnaul
Kemerovo
Novokuznetsk
Krasnoyarsk
Abakan
Kyzyl
Pavlodar
Semey
Öskemen
Qaraghandy (Karaganda)
Almaty
Bishkek
Ürümqi
Karamay
Kashi (Kashgar)
Hotan
Aksu
Korla
Hami
Turpan
Srinagar
Islāmābād
Rawalpindi
Peshāwar
Jammu
Gilgit
K2 8611 m
Pik Pobedy 7439 m
Nanga Parbat 8126 m
RUSSIAN FEDERATION
1 RESP. SEVERNAYA OSETIYA-ALANIYA
2 CHECHENSKAYA RESPUBLIKA
3 RESPUBLIKA INGUSHETIYA
4 KABARDINO-BALKARSKAYA RESPUBLIKA
5 KARACHAYEVO-CHERKESSKAYA RESPUBLIKA
6 RESPUBLIKA ADYGEYA
7 BELGORODSKAYA OBLAST'
8 KURSKAYA OBLAST'
9 LIPETSKAYA OBLAST'
10 CHUVASHSKAYA RESPUBLIKA
GEORGIA
11 ABKHAZIA
12 AJARIA
13 SOUTH OSSETIA
AZERBAIJAN
14 NAGORNO-KARABAKH
15 NAXÇIVAN
0 100 200 300 400 kilometers
0 100 200 miles

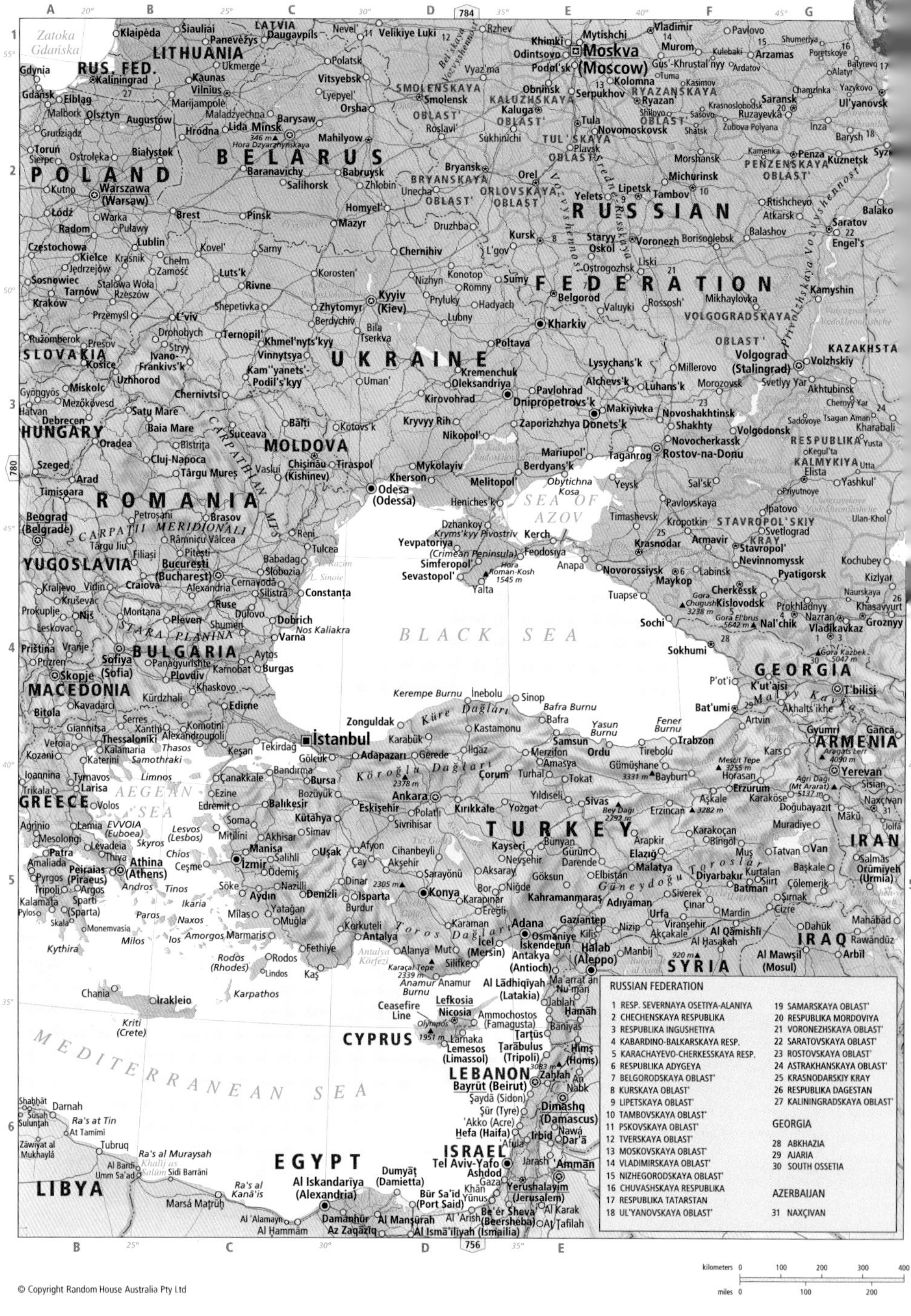
A
B
C
D
E
F
G
784
780
756
20°
25°
30°
35°
40°
45°
55°
50°
45°
40°
35°
Zatoka Gdańska
Klaipėda
Šiauliai
Panevėžys
LATVIA
Daugavpils
Nevel'
Velikiye Luki
Rzhev
Vladimir
Pavlovo
LITHUANIA
RUS. FED.
Kaliningrad
Gdynia
Gdańsk
Elbląg
Malbork
Olsztyn
Grudziądz
Kaunas
Vilnius
Ukmergė
Marijampolė
Augustów
Hrodna
Lida
Minsk
Maladzyechna
Barysaw
Polatsk
Vitsyebsk
Lyepyel'
Orsha
Mahilyow
Hora Dzyarzhynskaya
346 m
Khimki
Mytishchi
Odintsovo
Moskva
(Moscow)
Podol'sk
Kolomna
Obninsk
Serpukhov
Ryazan'
Kaluga
Tula
Novomoskovsk
Murom
Kulebaki
Arzamas
Ardatov
Gus'-Khrustal'nyy
Kasimov
Tuma
Sasovo
Shilovo
Shatsk
Saransk
Ruzayevka
Krasnoslobodsk
Zubova Polyana
Inza
Barysh
Shumerlya
Poretskoye
Batyrevo
Alatyr'
Chamzinka
Yazykovo
Ul'yanovsk
SMOLENSKAYA OBLAST'
Smolensk
KALUZHSKAYA OBLAST'
RYAZANSKAYA OBLAST
TUL'SKAYA OBLAST'
Vyaz'ma
Roslavl'
Sukhinichi
Plavsk
Bel'skaya Vozvyshennost'
Toruń
Sierpc
Ostrołęka
Białystok
POLAND
Kutno
Warszawa
(Warsaw)
Łódź
Warka
Radom
Puławy
Lublin
Częstochowa
Kielce
Kraśnik
Chełm
Jędrzejów
Zamość
Sosnowiec
Stalowa Wola
Tarnów
Rzeszów
Kraków
Przemyśl
BELARUS
Baranavichy
Babruysk
Salihorsk
Zhlobin
Brest
Pinsk
Homyel'
Mazyr
Bryansk
BRYANSKAYA OBLAST'
Unecha
ORLOVSKAYA OBLAST'
Orel
Yelets
Lipetsk
Tambov
Michurinsk
Morshansk
Kamenka
Penza
Kuznetsk
PENZENSKAYA OBLAST'
Syzran'
Rtishchevo
Atkarsk
Balashov
Saratov
Engel's
Balakovo
RUSSIAN FEDERATION
Kursk
Staryy Oskol
Voronezh
Borisoglebsk
Liski
Ostrogozhsk
Druzhba
L'gov
Srednerusskaya Vozvyshennost'
Privolzhskaya Vozvyshennost'
Kovel'
Sarny
Luts'k
Rivne
Korosten'
Chernihiv
Nizhyn
Konotop
Romny
Sumy
Pryluky
Hadyach
Lubny
Belgorod
Valuyki
Rossosh'
Mikhaylovka
Kamyshin
VOLGOGRADSKAYA OBLAST'
Kyyiv
(Kiev)
Zhytomyr
Berdychiv
Shepetivka
Bila Tserkva
L'viv
Drohobych
Ternopil'
Khmel'nyts'kyy
Vinnytsya
Stryy
Ivano-Frankivs'k
Ružomberok
Prešov
SLOVAKIA
Košice
Uzhhorod
Kharkiv
Poltava
UKRAINE
Kremenchuk
Oleksandriya
Uman'
Kam"yanets'-Podil's'kyy
Chernivtsi
Lysychans'k
Alchevs'k
Luhans'k
Millerovo
Morozovsk
Volgograd
(Stalingrad)
Volzhskiy
Svetlyy Yar
Akhtubinsk
KAZAKHSTAN
Gyöngyös
Miskolc
Mezőkövesd
Hatvan
Debrecen
HUNGARY
Satu Mare
Baia Mare
Oradea
Bistrița
Cluj-Napoca
Târgu Mureș
Suceava
Bălți
Kotovs'k
MOLDOVA
Chișinău
(Kishinev)
Tiraspol
Vaslui
Kirovohrad
Kryvyy Rih
Nikopol'
Dnipropetrovs'k
Pavlohrad
Zaporizhzhya
Donets'k
Makiyivka
Novoshakhtinsk
Shakhty
Novocherkassk
Rostov-na-Donu
Taganrog
Volgodonsk
Mariupol'
Berdyans'k
Chernyy Yar
Sadovoye
Tsagan Aman
Kharabali
RESPUBLIKA KALMYKIYA
Yusta
Kegul'ta
Utta
Elista
Szeged
Arad
Timișoara
ROMANIA
CARPATHIAN MTS
Mykolayiv
Kherson
Odesa
(Odessa)
Melitopol'
Obytichna Kosa
Heniches'k
SEA OF AZOV
Yeysk
Sal'sk
Yashkul'
Priyutnoye
Pavlovskaya
Timashevsk
Kropotkin
Ipatovo
Ulan-Khol
STAVROPOL'SKIY KRAY
Svetlograd
Beograd
(Belgrade)
Petroșani
Brașov
CARPAȚII MERIDIONALI
Râmnicu Vâlcea
Târgu Jiu
Pitești
Filiași
București
(Bucharest)
Reni
Tulcea
Babadag
Slobozia
L. Razim
L. Sinoie
Dzhankoy
Krymskyy Pivostriv
(Crimean Peninsula)
Yevpatoriya
Simferopol'
Sevastopol'
Feodosiya
Kerch
Hora Roman-Kosh
1545 m
Yalta
Anapa
Novorossiysk
Krasnodar
Armavir
Stavropol'
Nevinnomyssk
Kochubey
Labinsk
Maykop
Pyatigorsk
Kizlyar
YUGOSLAVIA
Kraljevo
Vidin
Craiova
Alexandria
Cernavodă
Silistra
Constanța
Kruševac
Prokuplje
Niš
Montana
Ruse
Dulovo
Dobrich
Leskovac
Pleven
Shumen
Varna
Nos Kaliakra
STARA PLANINA
Tuapse
Cherkessk
Gora Chugush
3238 m
Kislovodsk
Gora El'brus
5642 m
Nal'chik
Prokhladnyy
Nazran
Vladikavkaz
Groznyy
Naurskaya
Khasavyurt
Sochi
Sokhumi
BLACK SEA
Priština
Vranje
Prizren
Skopje
Sofiya
(Sofia)
BULGARIA
Panagyurishte
Plovdiv
Karnobat
Aytos
Burgas
Gora Kazbek
5047 m
GEORGIA
K'ut'aisi
T'bilisi
Malyy Kavkaz
P'ot'i
Bat'umi
Akhalts'ikhe
Artvin
MACEDONIA
Bitola
Kavadarci
Kărdzhali
Khaskovo
Edirne
Kerempe Burnu
İnebolu
Sinop
Bafra Burnu
Zonguldak
Küre Dağları
Kastamonu
Bafra
Yasun Burnu
Fener Burnu
Giannitsa
Serres
Xanthi
Komotini
Alexandroupoli
Thessaloniki
Kalamaria
Veroia
Thasos
Samothraki
Kozani
Katerini
Keșan
Tekirdağ
İstanbul
Karabük
Ilgaz
Samsun
Ordu
Tirebolu
Trabzon
Gyumri
Gäncä
ARMENIA
Kars
Aragats Lerr
4090 m
Yerevan
Gölcük
Adapazarı
Gerede
Köroğlu Dağları
2378 m
Merzifon
Amasya
Gümüşhane
Mescit Tepe
3255 m
Bayburt
Horasan
Ioannina
Tyrnavos
Larisa
Trikala
GREECE
Volos
AEGEAN SEA
Limnos
Çanakkale
Ezine
Edremit
Bandırma
Bursa
Bozüyük
Balıkesir
Soma
Kütahya
Ankara
Eskişehir
Polatlı
Sivrihisar
Kırıkkale
Çorum
Turhal
Tokat
Yozgat
Yıldızeli
Sivas
Bey Dağı
2792 m
Erzincan
3282 m
3331 m
Erzurum
Aşkale
Karaköse
Ağrı Dağı
(Mt Ararat)
5137 m
Sisian
Naxçıvan
Doğubayazıt
Mākū
Agrinio
Lamia
Mesolongi
Levadeia
Thiva
EVVOIA
(Euboea)
Skyros
Lesvos
(Lesbos)
Mitilini
Akhisar
Simav
TURKEY
Kayseri
Bünyan
Nevşehir
Gürün
Darende
Arapkir
Karakoçan
Bingöl
Elazığ
Muş
Tatvan
Van
Muradiye
Jolfa
IRAN
Patra
Amaliada
Pyrgos
Tripoli
Athina
(Athens)
Peiraias
(Piraeus)
Argos
Chios
Çeşme
İzmir
Manisa
Salihli
Ödemiş
Uşak
Afyon
Çay
Akşehir
Cihanbeyli
Sarayönü
Aksaray
Elbistan
Göksun
Malatya
Toroslar
Diyarbakır
Kurtalan
Siirt
Batman
Başkale
Salmās
Orūmīyeh
(Urmia)
Çölemerik
Kalamata
Sparti
(Sparta)
Pyloso
Skala
Monemvasia
Andros
Tinos
Ikaria
Paros
Naxos
Milos
Ios
Amorgos
Söke
Aydın
Nazilli
Denizli
Milas
Yatağan
Muğla
Marmaris
Dinar
2305 m
Isparta
Burdur
Konya
Karapınar
Ereğli
Niğde
Bor
Kahramanmaraş
Güneydoğu Toroslar
Adıyaman
Siverek
Çınar
Şırnak
Cizre
Kythira
Rodos
(Rhodes)
Lindos
Kaş
Fethiye
Korkuteli
Antalya
Antalya Körfezi
Alanya
Mut
Karaman
Toros Dağları
Adana
Osmaniye
İçel
(Mersin)
Silifke
Gaziantep
Kilis
Nizip
Urfa
Viranşehir
Akçakale
Mardin
Al Qāmishlī
Al Ḩasakah
920 m
Dahūk
Mahābād
Rawāndūz
IRAQ
Arbil
Al Mawşil
(Mosul)
İskenderun
Antakya
(Antioch)
Ḩalab
(Aleppo)
Manbij
Buḩayrat al Asad
SYRIA
Karaçal Tepe
2339 m
Anamur Burnu
Anamur
Karpathos
Chania
Irakleio
Kriti
(Crete)
Ceasefire Line
Lefkosia
Nicosia
Ammochostos
(Famagusta)
Olympos
1951 m
Larnaka
Lemesos
(Limassol)
CYPRUS
Al Lādhiqīyah
(Latakia)
Ma'arrat an Nu'man
Jablah
Ḩamāh
Bāniyās
Ţarţūs
Ḩimş
(Homs)
Ţarābulus
(Tripoli)
3083 m
LEBANON
Zaḩlah
An Nabk
Bayrūt (Beirut)
Şaydā (Sidon)
Şūr (Tyre)
Dimashq
(Damascus)
'Akko (Acre)
Ḩefa (Haifa)
'Afula
Irbid
Nawá
Dar'ā
ISRAEL
Tel Aviv-Yafo
Ashdod
Jarash
'Ammān
Gaza
Khān Yūnus
Yerushalayim
(Jerusalem)
Be'er Sheva'
(Beersheba)
Al Karak
Aţ Ţafīlah
MEDITERRANEAN SEA
Shaḩḩāt
Darnah
Sūsah
Sulunţah
Ra's at Tin
At Tamimi
Zāwiyat al Mukhaylá
Tubruq
LIBYA
Al Bardī
Umm Sa'ad
Ra's al Muraysah
Khalīj as Sallūm
Sidi Barrânî
Ra's al Kanā'is
Marsá Maţrūḩ
EGYPT
Al Iskandarīya
(Alexandria)
Dumyāţ
(Damietta)
Būr Sa'īd
(Port Said)
Al 'Arīsh
Al 'Alamayn
Al Ḩammām
Damanhūr
Az Zaqāzīq
Al Manşūrah
Al Ismā'īlīyah (Ismailia)
RUSSIAN FEDERATION
1 RESP. SEVERNAYA OSETIYA-ALANIYA
2 CHECHENSKAYA RESPUBLIKA
3 RESPUBLIKA INGUSHETIYA
4 KABARDINO-BALKARSKAYA RESP.
5 KARACHAYEVO-CHERKESSKAYA RESP.
6 RESPUBLIKA ADYGEYA
7 BELGORODSKAYA OBLAST'
8 KURSKAYA OBLAST'
9 LIPETSKAYA OBLAST'
10 TAMBOVSKAYA OBLAST'
11 PSKOVSKAYA OBLAST'
12 TVERSKAYA OBLAST'
13 MOSKOVSKAYA OBLAST'
14 VLADIMIRSKAYA OBLAST'
15 NIZHEGORODSKAYA OBLAST'
16 CHUVASHSKAYA RESPUBLIKA
17 RESPUBLIKA TATARSTAN
18 UL'YANOVSKAYA OBLAST'
19 SAMARSKAYA OBLAST'
20 RESPUBLIKA MORDOVIYA
21 VORONEZHSKAYA OBLAST'
22 SARATOVSKAYA OBLAST'
23 ROSTOVSKAYA OBLAST'
24 ASTRAKHANSKAYA OBLAST'
25 KRASNODARSKIY KRAY
26 RESPUBLIKA DAGESTAN
27 KALININGRADSKAYA OBLAST'
GEORGIA
28 ABKHAZIA
29 AJARIA
30 SOUTH OSSETIA
AZERBAIJAN
31 NAXÇIVAN
kilometers 0 100 200 300 400
miles 0 100 200

760
TURKEY
KARAMAN
İÇEL
ANTALYA
Alanya (Coracesium)
Ermenek
Mut
Mağara
Erdemli
Silifke
İncekum Burnu
Anamur
Bozyazı
Anamur Burnu
ADANA
HATAY
İskenderun
Antakya (Antioch)
Samandağı
HALAB
Halab (Aleppo)
IDLIB
Idlib
SYRIA
AR RAQQA
Ath Thawrah
AL LĀDHIQĪYAH
Al Lādhiqīyah (Latakia)
HAMĀH
Ḥamāh
TARṬŪS
Ṭarṭūs
Ḥimṣ (Homs)
HIMṢ
Tadmur (Palmyra)
Cape Andreas
Cape Plakoti
Cape Kormakitis
Kyrenia Range
Ceasefire Line
Cape Arnaoutis
Lefkosia (Nicosia)
Ammochostos (Famagusta)
Larnaka
Cape Greco
Troodos Mountains
Pafos
Lemesos (Limassol)
CYPRUS
Ṭarābulus (Tripoli)
Bayrūt (Beirut)
LEBANON
Zaḥlah
Ṣaydā (Sidon)
Ṣūr (Tyre)
DIMASHQ
Dimashq (Damascus)
Bādiyat ash Shām (Syrian Desert)
MEDITERRANEAN SEA
Hefa (Haifa)
'Akko (Acre)
Nahariyya
Nazerat (Nazareth)
Netanya
ISRAEL
Tel Aviv-Yafo
West Bank
Yerushalayim (Jerusalem)
Ashdod
Ashqelon
Gaza Strip
Gaza
Be'er Sheva' (Beersheba)
DAR'Ā
Dar'ā
AS SUWAYDĀ'
Irbid
Az Zarqā'
'Ammān
Al Mafraq
JORDAN
Al Karak
Aṭ Ṭafīlah
Ma'ān
Al 'Aqabah
Elat
HaNegev
Dumyāṭ (Damietta)
Būr Sa'īd (Port Said)
Al 'Arish
Al Ismā'īlīyah (Ismailia)
Al Qāhirah (Cairo)
Al Jīzah
As Suways (Suez)
Sīnā' (Sinai)
EGYPT
Jabal al Jalālah al Baḥrīyah
Jabal al Jalālah al Qiblīyah
Aṣ-Ṣaḥrā' ash Sharqīyah (Eastern Desert)
Gulf of Suez
Gulf of Aqaba
Jabal Katrīnā 2637 m
Jabal Mūsā (Mt Sinai)
Sharm ash Shaykh
Jazīrat Tirān
SAUDI ARABIA
Tabūk
Al Ḥismā
Wādī as Sirḥān
Ard aṣ Ṣawwān
Jabal ash Shifā
756
803
0 100 200 kilometers
0 50 100 miles

Asia and the Middle East

Europe and the Russian Federation

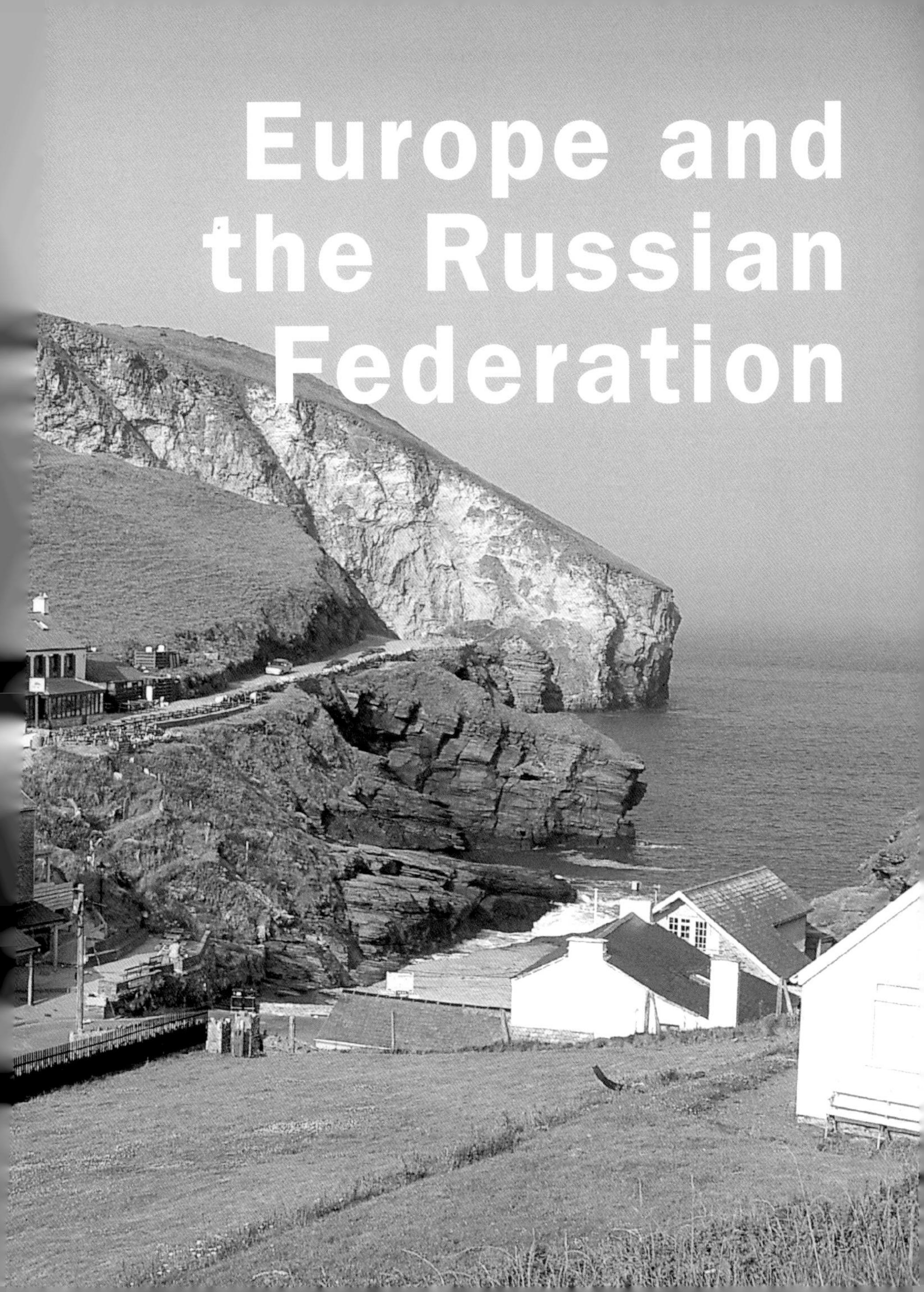

ARCTIC OCEAN
Arctic Circle
Hammer
Tromsø
Narvik
Kir
Bodø
Mo i Rana
Luleå
Skellefteå
Akureyri
Hafnarfjörður
Reykjavík
ICELAND
Seyðisfjörður
Höfn
Tórshavn
FAEROE ISLANDS (Den.)
Steinkjer
Trondheim
Kristiansund
Molde
SWEDEN
Umeå
Örnsköldsvik
Östersund
Härnösand
Sundsvall
Lillehammer
NORWAY
Hamar
Shetland Islands
Rockall (U.K.)
Bergen
Tamp
Hämee
Gävle
Ahvenanmaa (Åland)
Falun
Uppsala
Maariar
Orkney Islands
Drammen
Oslo
Skien
Karlstad
Västerås
Moss
Stavanger
Arendal
Örebro
Stockholm
UNITED KINGDOM
Inverness
SCOTLAND
Aberdeen
Kristiansand
Mariestad
Norrköping
Linköping
ATLANTIC OCEAN
Dundee
Glasgow
Edinburgh
N. IRELAND
Göteborg
Ålborg
Jönköping
Gotland
Belfast
Newcastle upon Tyne
NORTH SEA
DENMARK
Århus
Kalmar
Karlskrona
Liepāja
Galway
IRELAND
ISLE OF MAN (U.K.)
ENGLAND
Öland
Šiaul
Limerick
Dublin
Bradford
Leeds
Kingston upon Hull
Esbjerg
København
Helsingborg
Malmö
Odense
Klaipėda
Waterford
Manchester
Liverpool
Sheffield
Cork
Bornholm
Kaliningrad
RUSSIA FED.
Birmingham
Nottingham
Kiel
Gdańsk
WALES
Leicester
Coventry
Bremerhaven
Lübeck
Rostock
Koszalin
Elbląg
Swansea
Cardiff
Bristol
London
Groningen
NETHERLANDS
Amsterdam
Schwerin
Hamburg
Bremen
Szczecin
's-Gravenhage
Hannover
Berlin
Bydgoszcz
Toruń
Plymouth
Portsmouth
Brighton
Rotterdam
Essen
Münster
Poznań
POLAND
Antwerpen
Bruxelles
Dortmund
Magdeburg
CHANNEL IS (U.K.)
Lille
Köln
Düsseldorf
Leipzig
Kalisz
Warsz
Le Havre
Amiens
BELGIUM
Bonn
GERMANY
Dresden
Glogów
Łódź
Rado
Brest
Caen
Rouen
LUXEMBOURG
Luxembourg
Wiesbaden
Chemnitz
Wrocław
Kielce
Paris
Reims
Frankfurt am Main
Praha
Katowice
Rennes
Le Mans
Mannheim
Nürnberg
CZECH REPUBLIC
Ostrava
Kraków
Angers
Nancy
Karlsruhe
Orléans
Strasbourg
Stuttgart
Regensburg
Brno
Nantes
Tours
Freiburg im Breisgau
Augsburg
FRANCE
Dijon
Basel
Linz
Wien
SLOVAKIA
Košic
Zürich
München
Salzburg
Bratislava
Poitiers
Besançon
LIECHTENSTEIN
Limoges
Bern
Vaduz
AUSTRIA
Budapest
Debrecen
Miskol
Genève
SWITZERLAND
Innsbruck
A Coruña
Lyon
Graz
HUNGARY
Gijón
Bordeaux
Clermont-Ferrand
Bolzano
Trento
SLOVENIA
Maribor
Szeged
Vigo
Oviedo
Saint-Étienne
Ljubljana
Pécs
Arad
Ourense
Santander
Bilbao
Donostia-San Sebastián
Milano
Venezia
Trieste
Zagreb
Novi Sad
Braga
León
Vitoria-Gasteiz
Grenoble
Verona
Timișo
Porto
Torino
Padova
Rijeka
CROATIA
Bragança
Burgos
Toulouse
Genova
La Spezia
Bologna
Beograd
Coimbra
Viseu
Pamplona
Montpellier
Nîmes
BOSNIA AND HERZEGOVINA
Valladolid
Logroño
Nice
Monaco
MONACO
Rimini
Zadar
PORTUGAL
Salamanca
ANDORRA
Perpignan
Andorra la Vella
Marseille
San Marino
SAN MARINO
Sarajevo
YUGOSLAVIA
Santarém
Alcalá de Henares
Zaragoza
Pisa
Firenze
Lisboa
Madrid
Split
Mostar
Niš
Toledo
Barcelona
Corse
Perugia
Setúbal
Badajoz
Cuenca
Dubrovnik
Priština
Évora
Tarragona
Ajaccio
VATICAN CITY
Roma
Pescara
Podgorica
Beja
SPAIN
Castelló de la Plana
Kukës
Skop
Faro
Córdoba
Albacete
Valencia
Palma de Mallorca
Sassari
ITALY
Foggia
Tiranë
MACEDON
Huelva
Sevilla
Jaén
Napoli
Salerno
Bari
ALBANIA
Jeréz de la Frontera
Alicante
Islas Baleares
Sardegna
Taranto
Vlorë
Thessaloni
Cádiz
Málaga
Granada
Murcia
Lecce
GIBRALTAR (U.K.)
Almería
Cartagena
Cagliari
Cosenza
Ioannina
Ceuta (Sp.)
MEDITERRANEAN SEA
Catanzaro
GRE
Palermo
Messina
Melilla (Sp.)
Marsala
Reggio di Calabria
Patra
Catania
Siracusa
Tripoli
MOROCCO
Valletta
MALTA
ALGERIA
TUNISIA
A
B
C
D
E
F
3
4
5
6
7
8
9
10

J
K
L
M
N
40°
50° 70°
60°
70° 65°
80°
60°
Arctic Circle
RUSSIAN FEDERATION
KAZAKHSTAN
UZBEKISTAN
TURKMENISTAN
AFGHANISTAN
IRAN
IRAQ
TURKEY
SYRIA
CYPRUS
LEBANON
ISRAEL
JORDAN
SAUDI ARABIA
KUWAIT
OMAN
U.A.E.
GEORGIA
ARMENIA
AZERBAIJAN
BLACK SEA
CASPIAN SEA
Kolpashevo
Anzhero-Sudzhensk
Tomsk
Kemerovo
Nizhnevartovsk
Surgut
Leninsk-Kuznetskiy
Novosibirsk
Barnaul
Biysk
Nar'yan Mar
Inta
Igrim
Pechora
Nyagan'
Mezen'
Ukhta
Tatarsk
Rubtsovsk
Severodvinsk
Arkhangel'sk
Nazyvayevsk
Omsk
Ishim
Serov
Tyumen'
Syktyvkar
Solikamsk
Berezniki
Medvezh'yegorsk
Kotlas
Nizhniy Tagil
Kurgan
Yekaterinburg
Perm'
Kamensk-Ural'skiy
Pervoural'sk
Petrozavodsk
Vyatka
Chelyabinsk
Votkinsk
Zlatoust
Izhevsk
Sarapul
Vologda
Naberezhnyye Chelny
Cherepovets
Ufa
Magnitogorsk
Kostroma
Novgorod
Rybinsk
Yaroslavl'
Cheboksary
Kazan'
Al'met'yevsk
Sterlitamak
Ivanovo
Nizhniy Novgorod
Salavat
Tver'
Arzamas
Dimitrovgrad
Sergiyev Posad
Murom
Ul'yanovsk
Orsk
Velikiye Luki
Moskva
Samara
Orenburg
Tol'yatti
Kolomna
Saransk
Novokuybyshevsk
Obninsk
Ryazan'
Syzran'
Sol'-Iletsk
Penza
Smolensk
Kaluga
Tula
Novomoskovsk
Balakovo
Tambov
Saratov
Engel's
Bryansk
Lipetsk
Orel
Voronezh
Kursk
Chernihiv
Sumy
Belgorod
Volzhskiy
Kyyiv
Kharkiv
Volograd
Poltava
Kremenchuk
Luhans'k
Astrakhan'
Dniprodzerzhyns'k
Donets'k
Makiyivka
Kirovohrad
Taganrog
Rostov-na-Donu
Kryvyy Rih
Zaporizhzhya
Mariupol'
Bălţi
Mykolayiv
Melitopol'
Chişinău
Kherson
Stavropol'
Odesa
Armavir
Krasnodar
Cherkessk
Groznyy
Makhachkala
Simferopol'
Novorossiysk
Maykop
Nal'chik
Vladikavkaz
Brăila
Sevastopol'
Sochi
Constanţa
Varna
Burgas
Rodos
5
6
7
8
9
10
50°
80°
45°
70°
40°
35°
30°
60°
H
J
K
0
150
300
450
600
750
kilometers
miles

Arctic Circle
Iceland
Hekla
1491 m
Hvannadalshnúkur
2119 m
NORWEGIAN SEA
Vesterålen
Lofoten
Haltí
Kebnekaise
2111 m
Scandinavia
Faeroe Islands
Shetland Islands
Rockall
Galdhøpiggen
2469 m
Cape Wrath
Orkney Islands
Hebrides
ATLANTIC OCEAN
Ben Nevis
1343 m
Grampian Mountains
British Isles
Gotland
NORTH SEA
Skagerrak
Kattegat
Öland
BALTIC SEA
Jylland
IRISH SEA
Pennines
Carrauntoohil
1041 m
Mizen Head
Snowdon
1085 m
St George's Channel
CELTIC SEA
Bornholm
Ostfriesische Inseln
North
Harz
Land's End
English Channel
Strait of Dover
Channel Islands
Botrange 694 m
Ardennes
Erzgebirge
Sudety
Taunus
Praděd
1492 m
Gerlachovský Štit
2655 m
Vosges
Schwarzwald
Jura
Zugspitze
2962 m
Bay of Biscay
Cabo Fisterra
Matterhorn
4478 m
Monte Rosa
4634 m
Großglockner
3797 m
Massif Central
ALPS
Mont Blanc
4807 m
Dolomiti
Triglav
2863 m
Plain of Hungary
Cordillera Cantábrica
PYRENEES
Cévennes
Pico de Aneto
3404 m
Golfe du Lion
LIGURIAN SEA
APPENNINO
ADRIATIC SEA
Dinara
Iberian Peninsula
Corse
Korab
2764 m
Cabo de São Vicente
Sierra Morena
Golfo de Valencia
Islas Baleares
Menorca
Strait of Bonifacio
Golfo de Cádiz
Eivissa
Mallorca
Sardegna
Strait of Otranto
Pindos
Sierra Nevada
Mulhacén
3481 m
Strait of Gibraltar
MEDITERRANEAN SEA
TYRRHENIAN SEA
Golfo di Taranto
Monte Etna
3323 m
Sicilia
IONIAN SEA
Ionioi Nisoi
Strait of Sicily
Cap Bon
ATLAS MOUNTAINS
Jebel Toubkal
4165 m
Jabal ash Sha'nabī
1544 m
Malta
Shaṭṭ al Jarīd

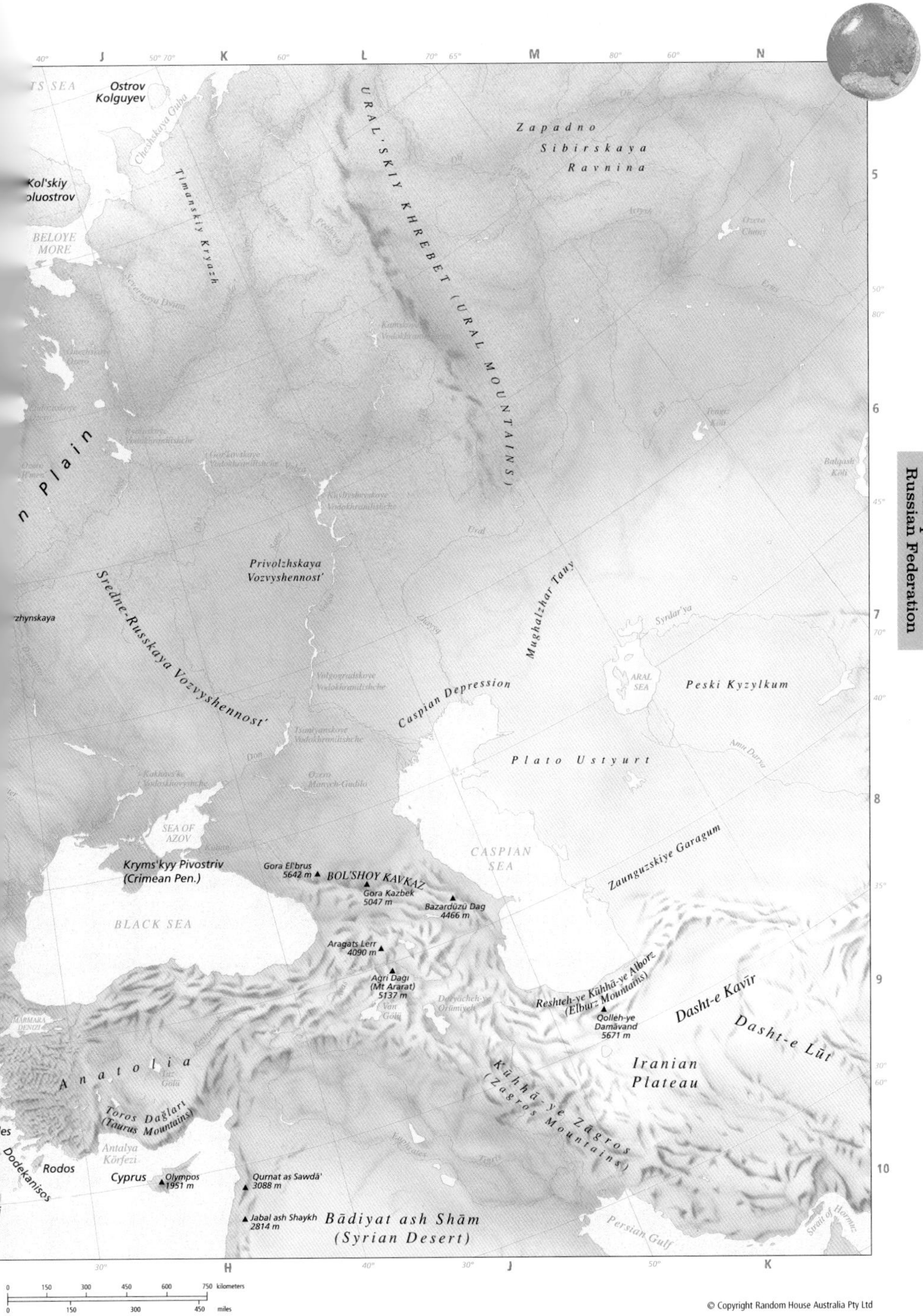
J
K
L
M
N
H
J
K
5
6
7
8
9
10
Ostrov Kolguyev
Cheshskaya Guba
Kol'skiy
oluostrov
BELOYE MORE
Timanskiy Kryazh
URAL'SKIY KHREBET (URAL MOUNTAINS)
Zapadno Sibirskaya Ravnina
n Plain
Privolzhskaya Vozvyshennost'
Sredne-Russkaya Vozvyshennost'
rzhynskaya
Mughalzhar Tauy
Syrdar'ya
ARAL SEA
Peski Kyzylkum
Caspian Depression
Plato Ustyurt
Amu Darya
SEA OF AZOV
Kryms'kyy Pivostriv (Crimean Pen.)
Gora El'brus 5642 m
BOL'SHOY KAVKAZ
Gora Kazbek 5047 m
Bazardüzü Dag 4466 m
CASPIAN SEA
Zaunguzskiye Garagum
BLACK SEA
Aragats Lerr 4090 m
Agri Dagı (Mt Ararat) 5137 m
Reshteh-ye Kūhhā-ye Alborz (Elburz Mountains)
Qolleh-ye Damāvand 5671 m
Dasht-e Kavīr
Dasht-e Lūt
Iranian Plateau
Anatolia
Kūhhā-ye Zāgros (Zagros Mountains)
Toros Dağları (Taurus Mountains)
Antalya Körfezi
Rodos
Dodekanisos
Cyprus
Olympos 1951 m
Qurnat as Sawdā' 3088 m
Jabal ash Shaykh 2814 m
Bādiyat ash Shām (Syrian Desert)
Persian Gulf
Strait of Hormuz
0 150 300 450 600 750 kilometers
0 150 300 450 miles

GREENLAND SEA
ATLANTIC OCEAN
ICELAND
Arctic Circle
Straumnes
Hornbjarg
Rifstangi
Fontur
Kópasker
Raufarhöfn
Bakkaflói
Bakkafjörður
Suðureyri
Ísafjörður
Unaðsdalur
Hraun
Siglufjörður
Ólafsfjörður
Húsavík
Hofsós
Dalvík
Grenivík
Kollumúli
Vopnafjörður
Bíldudalur
Vatneyri
Glama 920 m
Hólmavík
Húnaflói
Blönduós
Akureyri
Grímsstaðir
Borgarfjörður
Bjargtangar
Reykhólar
Bergsstaðir
Karlfell 1052 m
Seyðisfjörður
Breiðafjörður
Hvammstangi
Mýri
Herðubreið 1682 m
Egilsstaðir
Stykkishólmur
Búðardalur
Ódáðahraun
Fáskrúðsfjörður
Hellissandur
Breiðdalsvík
Búðir
Hofsjökull
Djúpivogur
Bárðarbunga 2000 m
1248 m
Borgarnes
Vatnajökull
Stokksnes
Faxaflói
Svianúkar 1719 m
Akranes
Höfn
Reykjavík
Laki 818 m
Hvannadalshnúkur 2119 m
Kálfafellsstaður
Sandgerði
Hafnarfjörður
Hekla 1491 m
Hafnir
Hella
Fagurhólsmýri
Grindavík
Þorlákshöfn
Hvolsvöllur
Mýrdalsjökull
Skógar
1450 m
Langholt
Dyrhólaey
Vík

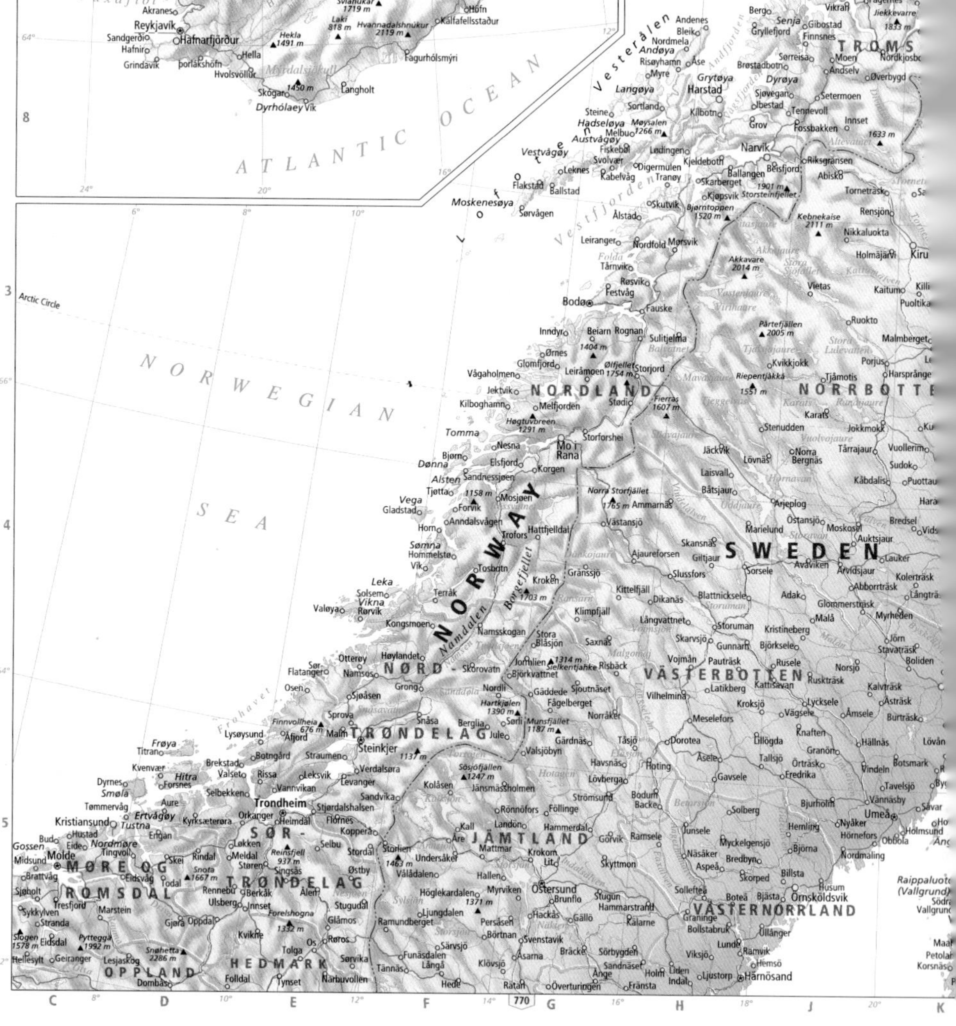
NORWEGIAN SEA
Arctic Circle
NORWAY
SWEDEN
NORDLAND
TROMS
NORRBOTTEN
VÄSTERBOTTEN
NORD-TRØNDELAG
SØR-TRØNDELAG
JÄMTLAND
VÄSTERNORRLAND
MØRE OG ROMSDAL
HEDMARK
OPPLAND
Vesterålen
Lofoten
Vestfjorden
Nordkvaløy
Vannareid
Vanna
Rebbenesøy
Ringvassøy
Mikkelvik
Reinøy
Tromvik
Skulgam
Olderviki
Kvaløy
Tromsø
Fagernes
Hillesøy
Vikran
Jiekkevarre 1833 m
Andenes
Bleik
Nordmela
Andøya
Bergo
Senja
Gibostad
Gryllefjord
Finnsnes
Risøyhamn
Åse
Brøstadbotn
Sørreisa
Moen
Nordkjosbotn
Myre
Andselv
Øverbygd
Grytøya
Harstad
Dyrøya
Langøya
Sjøvegan
Setermoen
Sortland
Ibestad
Tennevoll
Steine
Kilbotn
Grov
Innset
Hadseløya
Møysalen 1266 m
Fossbakken
Altevatnet
1633 m
Melbu
Austvågøy
Narvik
Fiskebøl
Lødingen
Riksgränsen
Vestvågøy
Svolvær
Kjeldebotn
Beisfjord
Abisko
Leknes
Digermulen
Ballangen
Kabelvåg
Tranøy
Skarberget
Torneträsk
1901 m
Flakstad
Ballstad
Kjøpsvik
Storsteinfjellet
Moskenesøya
Sørvågen
Skutvik
Bjørntoppen 1520 m
Kebnekaise 2111 m
Rensjön
Ålstad
Nikkaluokta
Leiranger
Nordfold
Mørsvik
Folda
Tårnvik
Akkajaure
Akkavare 2014 m
Holmajärvi
Kiruna
Røsvik
Festvåg
Vietas
Kaitum
Bodø
Fauske
Ruokto
Inndyr
Beiarn
Rognan
Sulitjelma
Pårtefjällen 2005 m
Malmberget
1404 m
Ørnes
Glomfjord
Ølfjellet 1754 m
Storjord
Kvikkjokk
Porjus
Vågaholmen
Leirāmoen
Riepentjåkkå 1551 m
Tjåmotis
Harsprånget
Jektvik
Stødi
Kilboghamn
Melfjorden
Fierras 1607 m
Karats
Høgtuvbreen 1291 m
Tomma
Storforshei
Stenudden
Jokkmokk
Nesna
Mo i Rana
Jäckvik
Norra Bergnäs
Tårrajaur
Vuollerim
Bjørn
Dønna
Elsfjord
Korgen
Lövnäs
Sudok
Alsten
Sandnessjøen
Laisvall
Kåbdalis
Puottaure
Tjøtta
1158 m
Mosjøen
Norra Storfjället 1765 m
Ammarnäs
Båtsjaur
Vega
Gladstad
Forvik
Anndalsvågen
Arjeplog
Västansjö
Bredsel
Horn
Trofors
Hattfjelldal
Mariehamn
Östansjö
Moskosel
Auktsjaur
Sømna
Hommelstø
Skansnäs
Giltjaur
Ajaureforsen
Vik
Tosbotn
Lauker
Avaviken
Arvidsjaur
Kolerträsk
Grånsjö
Slussfors
Sorsele
Leka
Krokén
Kittelfjäll
Abborrträsk
Solsem
Terråk
1703 m
Vikna
Rørvik
Dikanäs
Blattnicksele
Adak
Glommersträsk
Valøya
Klimpfjäll
Malå
Kongsmoen
Namdalen
Børgefjellet
Långvattnet
Myrheden
Namsskogen
Stora Blåsjön
Storuman
Kristineberg
Saxnäs
Skarvsjö
Gunnarn
Björksele
Stavaträsk
Jörn
Høylandet
Otterøy
Jormlien
1314 m
Sielkentjahke
Risbäck
Vojmån
Pauträsk
Rusele
Norsjö
Boliden
Sør-Flatanger
Namsos
Skorovatn
Björkvattnet
Ruskträsk
Osen
Grong
Nordli
Gäddede
Sjoutnäset
Vilhelmina
Latikberg
Kattisavan
Kalvträsk
Sjøåsen
Hartkjølen 1390 m
Fågelberget
Kroksjö
Lycksele
Åsträsk
Frohavet
Sprova
Sørli
Norråker
Meselefors
Vägsele
Åmsele
Burträsk
Finnvollheia 676 m
Snåsa
Munsfjället 1187 m
Frøya
Lysøysund
Åfjord
Malm
Berglia
Jule
Gärdnäs
Tåsjö
Dorotea
Lillögda
Knaften
Hällnäs
Lövånger
Titran
Steinkjer
1137 m
Valsjöbyn
Granön
Botngård
Straumen
Sösjöfjällen 1247 m
Tallsjö
Örträsk
Vindeln
Botsmark
Kvenvær
Brekstad
Verdalsøra
Havsnäs
Åsele
Hitra
Valset
Rissa
Leksvik
Hoting
Fredrika
Levanger
Lövberga
Gavsele
Dyrnes
Forsnes
Smøla
Selbekken
Vannvikan
Jänsmässholmen
Tavelsjö
Tømmervåg
Aure
Trondheim
Sandvika
Kolåsen
Strömsund
Bodum
Ertvågøy
Tustna
Stjørdalshalsen
Backe
Bjurholm
Vännäsby
Kristiansund
Kyrksæterøra
Orkanger
Heimdal
Flornes
Rönnöfors
Föllinge
Solberg
Umeå
Hustad
Ergan
Kopperå
Kall
Landön
Hammerdal
Nyåker
Sävar
Bud
Eide
Nordmøre
Løkken
Selbu
Åre
Görvik
Ramsele
Junsele
Hemling
Hörnefors
Obbola
Gossen
Tingvoll
Reinsfjell 937 m
Storlien
Mattmar
Krokom
Myckelgensjö
Björna
Midsund
Molde
Skei
Rindal
Meldal
Støren
Stordal
Undersåker
Lit
Skyttmon
Näsåker
Bredbyn
Nordmaling
Brattvåg
Eidsvåg
Todal
Snota 1667 m
Singsås
1463 m
Östby
Vålådalen
Hallen
Aspeå
Skorped
Billsta
Rappaluoto (Vallgrund)
Sjøholt
Rennebu
Berkåk
Ålen
Höglekardalen
Myrviken
Östersund
Brunflo
Stugun
Solleftea
Husum
Sykkylven
Tresfjord
Ulsberg
Innset
Stugudal
1371 m
Hammarstrand
Botea
Bjästa
Örnsköldsvik
Stranda
Marstein
Forelshogna
Sylsjön
Ljungdalen
Hackås
Gällö
Graninge
Gjøra
Oppdal
Glåmos
Ramundberget
Persåsen
Kälarne
Bollstabruk
Ullånger
Slogen 1578 m
Eidsdal
Pytteggja 1992 m
Kvikne
1332 m
Os
Røros
Börtnan
Svenstavik
Lunde
Ramvik
Hellesylt
Geiranger
Lesjaskog
Snøhetta 2286 m
Tolga
Sørvika
Funäsdalen
Särvsjö
Bräcke
Sörbygden
Viksjö
Hemsö
Tännäs
Långå
Klövsjö
Åsarna
Sandnäset
Holm
Ånge
Uden
Indal
Ljustorp
Härnösand
Dombås
Folldal
Tynset
Narbuvollen
Hede
Rätan
Överturingen
Fränsta
770

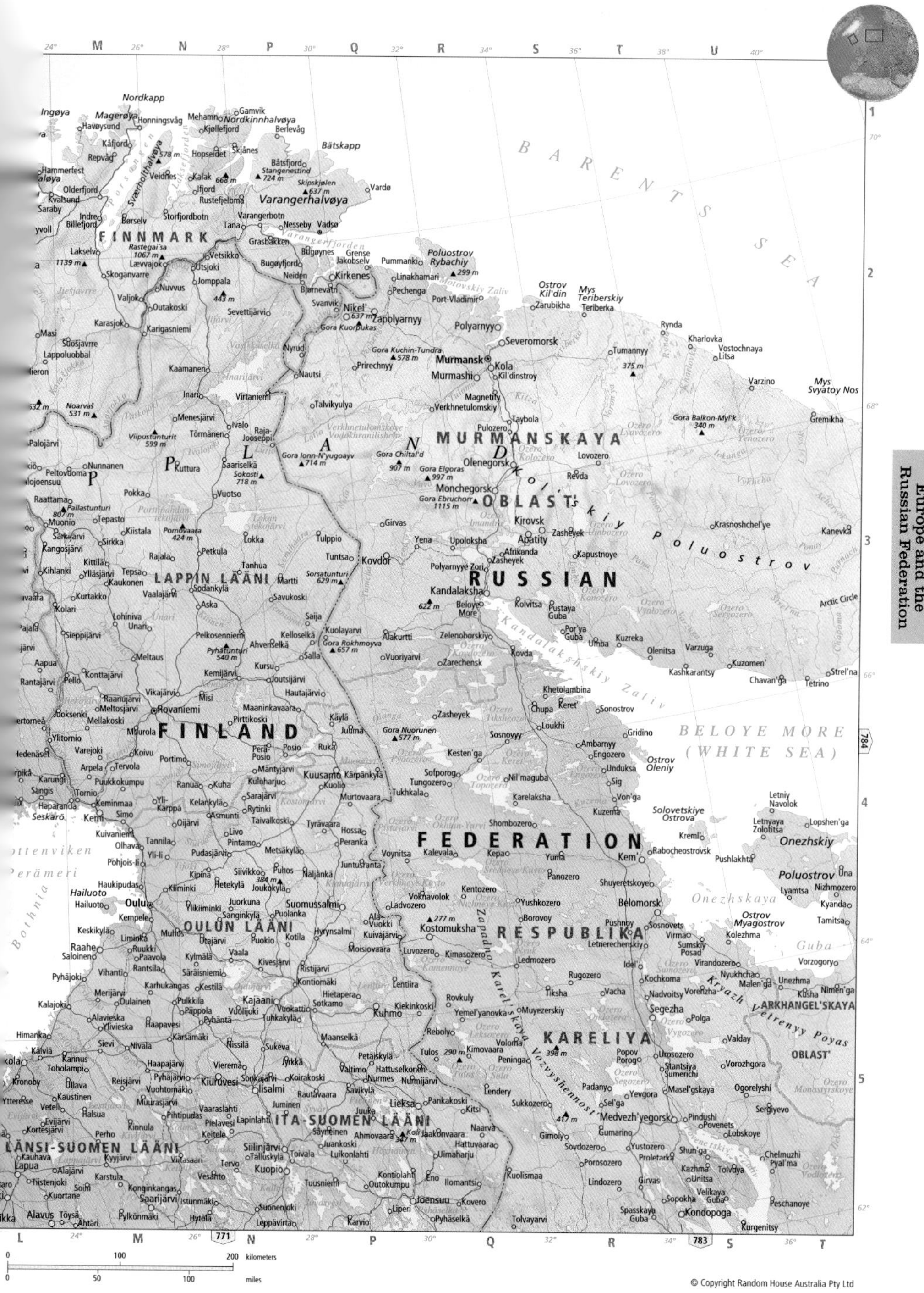
BARENTS SEA
BELOYE MORE (WHITE SEA)
FINNMARK
LAPPIN LÄÄNI
OULUN LÄÄNI
ITÄ-SUOMEN LÄÄNI
LÄNSI-SUOMEN LÄÄNI
FINLAND
LAPLAND
MURMANSKAYA OBLAST'
RUSSIAN FEDERATION
KARELIYA RESPUBLIKA
ARKHANGEL'SKAYA OBLAST'
Kol'skiy Poluostrov
Kandalakshskiy Zaliv
Zapadno-Karel'skaya Vozvyshennost'
Kryazh Vetrenyy Poyas
Onezhskaya Guba
Onezhskiy Poluostrov
Solovetskiye Ostrova
Ostrov Oleniy
Ostrov Myagostrov
Ostrov Kil'din
Mys Teriberskiy
Mys Svyatoy Nos
Poluostrov Rybachiy
Varangerhalvøya
Nordkinnhalvøya
Magerøya
Nordkapp
Båtskapp
Varangerfjorden
Motovskiy Zaliv
Arctic Circle
Bothnia
Perämeri
Ottenviken
Hailuoto
Murmansk
Kola
Severomorsk
Polyarnyy
Monchegorsk
Olenegorsk
Kirovsk
Apatity
Kandalaksha
Kovdor
Nikel'
Zapolyarnyy
Pechenga
Kirkenes
Vadsø
Vardø
Hammerfest
Tana
Karasjok
Inari
Ivalo
Sodankylä
Kemijärvi
Rovaniemi
Kemi
Tornio
Haparanda
Oulu
Raahe
Kajaani
Kuhmo
Kuusamo
Suomussalmi
Kostomuksha
Kem'
Belomorsk
Segezha
Medvezh'yegorsk
Kondopoga
Joensuu
Kuopio
Iisalmi
Lieksa
Kiuruvesi
Saarijärvi
Lapua
Alavus
Ähtäri
Kalajoki
Kokkola
Kemi
Loukhi
Chupa
Kovda
Umba
Lovozero
Revda
Teriberka
Gremikha
Varzino
Kanevka
Tetrino
Chavan'ga
Kuzomen'
Varzuga
Sosnovets
Pushnoy
Nyukhcha
Onega
Povenets
Pudozh
Gora Nuorunen 577 m
Gora Chiltal'd 907 m
Gora Elgoras 997 m
Gora Ebruchorr 1115 m
Gora Kuchin-Tundra 578 m
Gora Balkon-Myl'k 340 m
Pyhätunturi 540 m
Pallastunturi 807 m
Sokosti 718 m
Rastegai'sa 1067 m
Ozero Imandra
Ozero Umbozero
Ozero Lovozero
Ozero Kanozero
Ozero Topozero
Ozero Pyaozero
Ozero Segozero
Ozero Vygozero
Inarijärvi
Oulujärvi
Kilpisjärvi
24° 26° 28° 30° 32° 34° 36° 38° 40°
62° 64° 66° 68° 70°
M N P Q R S T U
L M N P Q R S T
1 2 3 4 5
771 783 784
0 100 200 kilometers
0 50 100 miles

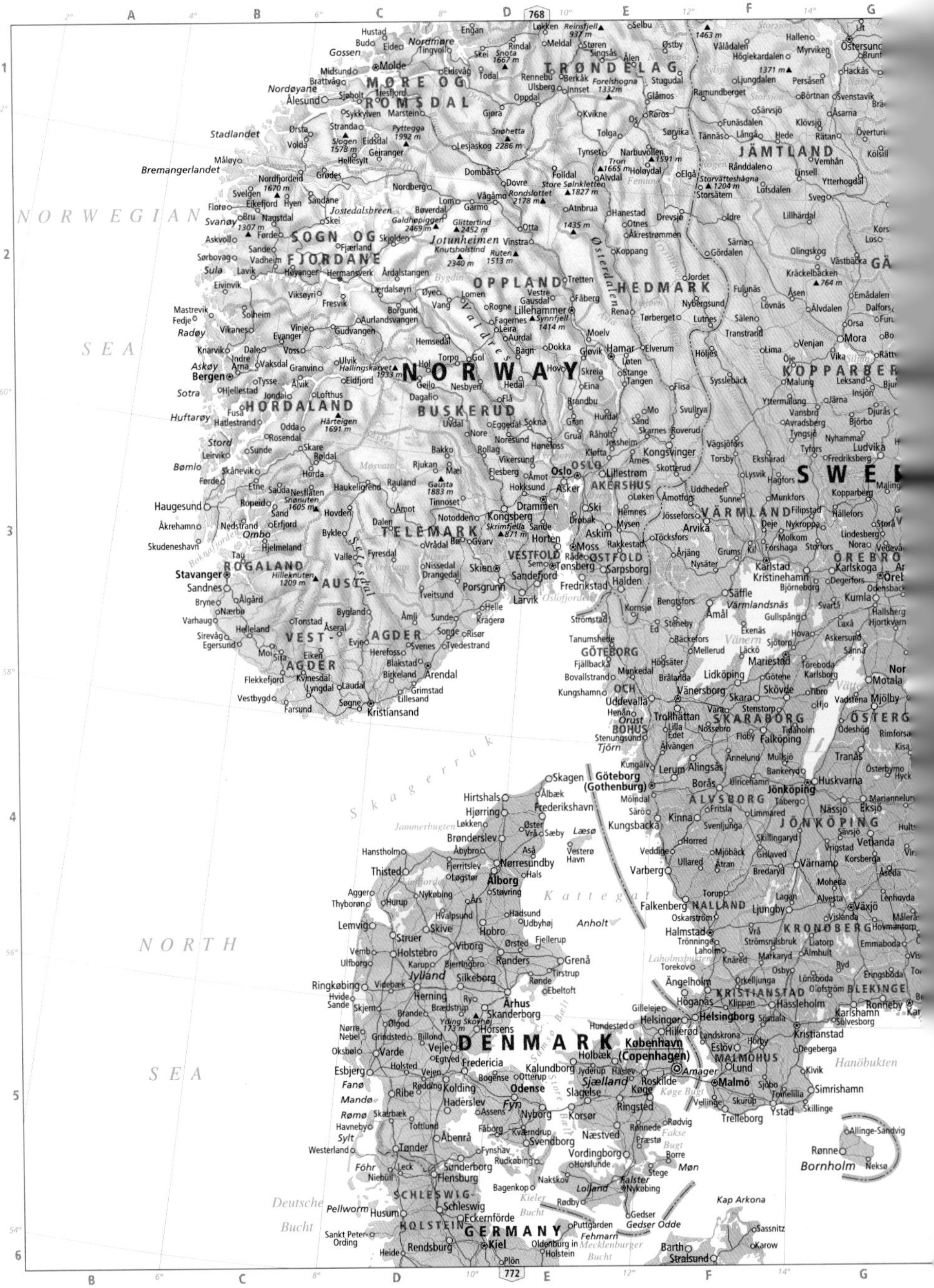
768
772
NORWEGIAN SEA
NORTH SEA
NORWAY
SWEDEN
DENMARK
GERMANY
MØRE OG ROMSDAL
TRØNDELAG
SOGN OG FJORDANE
OPPLAND
HEDMARK
HORDALAND
BUSKERUD
TELEMARK
ROGALAND
AUST-AGDER
VEST-AGDER
VESTFOLD
ØSTFOLD
AKERSHUS
OSLO
JÄMTLAND
KOPPARBERG
VÄRMLAND
ÖREBRO
SKARABORG
ÖSTERGÖTLAND
ÄLVSBORG
JÖNKÖPING
HALLAND
KRONOBERG
KRISTIANSTAD
BLEKINGE
MALMÖHUS
GÖTEBORG OCH BOHUS
SCHLESWIG-HOLSTEIN
Skagerrak
Kattegat
Jotunheimen
Jostedalsbreen
Oslo
Bergen
Stavanger
Kristiansand
Trondheim
Ålesund
Molde
Lillehammer
Hamar
Drammen
Skien
Larvik
Arendal
Göteborg (Gothenburg)
København (Copenhagen)
Malmö
Helsingborg
Ålborg
Århus
Odense
Esbjerg
Kiel
Flensburg
Bornholm
Jylland
Fyn
Sjælland
Lolland
Falster
Møn
Fehmarn
Anholt
Læsø
Vänern
Vättern
Galdhøpiggen 2469 m
Glittertind 2452 m
Snøhetta 2286 m
Hanöbukten
Kap Arkona
Deutsche Bucht
Kieler Bucht
Mecklenburger Bucht

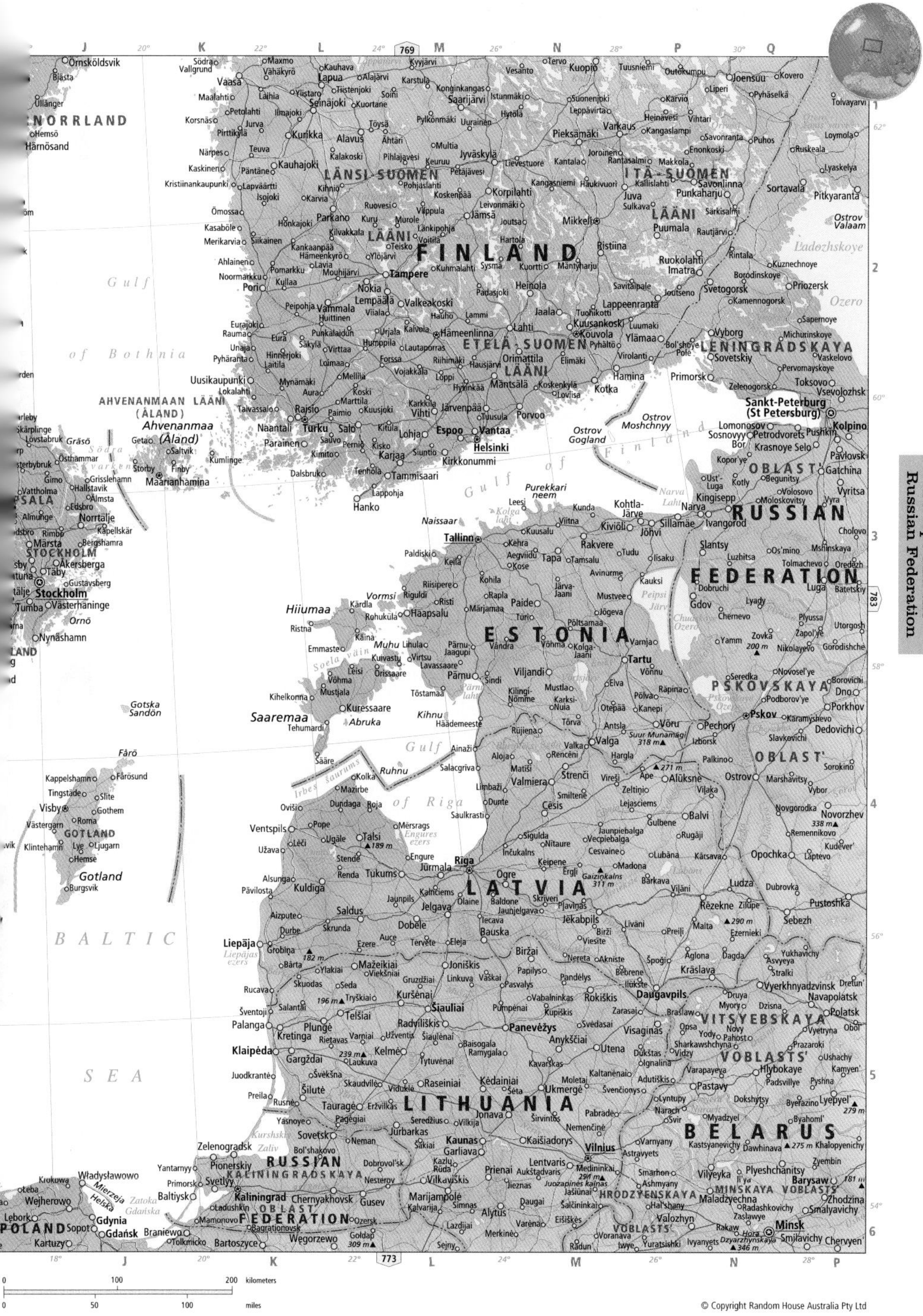
769
773
783
FINLAND
LÄNSI-SUOMEN LÄÄNI
ITÄ-SUOMEN LÄÄNI
ETELÄ-SUOMEN LÄÄNI
AHVENANMAAN LÄÄNI (ÅLAND)
Ahvenanmaa (Åland)
Gulf of Bothnia
Gulf of Finland
ESTONIA
LATVIA
LITHUANIA
BELARUS
RUSSIAN FEDERATION
LENINGRADSKAYA
OBLAST'
PSKOVSKAYA OBLAST'
VITSYEBSKAYA VOBLASTS'
MINSKAYA VOBLASTS'
HRODZYENSKAYA VOBLASTS'
RUSSIAN KALININGRADSKAYA OBLAST' FEDERATION
POLAND
STOCKHOLM
GOTLAND
Gotland
BALTIC SEA
Gulf of Riga
Hiiumaa
Saaremaa
Helsinki
Tallinn
Riga
Vilnius
Kaunas
Minsk
Tampere
Turku
Espoo
Vantaa
Sankt-Peterburg (St Petersburg)
Pskov
Tartu
Daugavpils
Klaipėda
Kaliningrad
Gdańsk
Gdynia
Stockholm
Liepāja
Ventspils
Šiauliai
Panevėžys
Ladozhskoye Ozero
Peipsi Järv
0 100 200 kilometers
0 50 100 miles

Europe and the Russian Federation

NORTH SEA
Deutsche Bucht
Waddeneilanden
Ostfriesische Inseln
NETHERLANDS
BELGIUM
FRANCE
GERMANY
SWITZERLAND
ITALY
LIECHTENSTEIN
NIEDERSACHSEN
SCHLESWIG-HOLSTEIN
MECKLENBURG-VORPOMMERN
SACHSEN-ANHALT
NORDRHEIN-WESTFALEN
HESSEN
THÜRINGEN
RHEINLAND-PFALZ
SAARLAND
BADEN-WÜRTTEMBERG
BAYERN
PICARDIE
CHAMPAGNE-ARDENNE
LORRAINE
ALSACE
BOURGOGNE
FRANCHE-COMTE
RHÔNE-ALPES
TIROL
VORARLBERG
TRENTINO-ALTO ADIGE
Amsterdam
's-Gravenhage (The Hague)
Rotterdam
Bruxelles (Brussels)
Antwerpen (Antwerp)
Luxembourg
Hamburg
Bremen
Hannover
Köln (Cologne)
Frankfurt am Main
Stuttgart
München (Munich)
Nürnberg
Strasbourg
Zürich
Bern
Genève (Geneva)
Lyon
Dijon
Metz
Nancy
Reims
Basel
Lausanne
Innsbruck
Bolzano
770
775

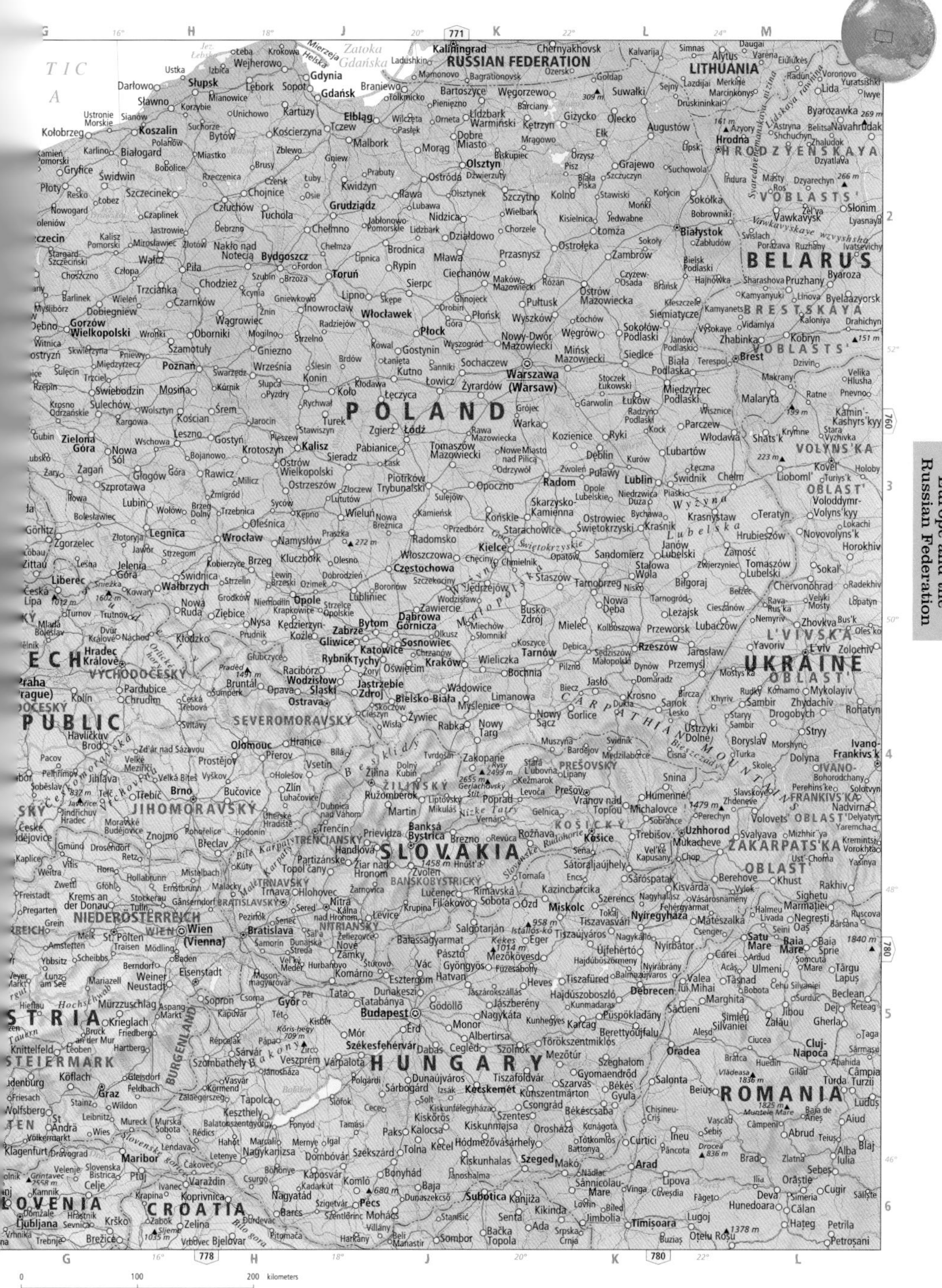
POLAND
RUSSIAN FEDERATION
LITHUANIA
BELARUS
UKRAINE
SLOVAKIA
HUNGARY
ROMANIA
CROATIA
SLOVENIA
Warszawa (Warsaw)
Budapest
Wien (Vienna)
Bratislava
Praha (Prague)
Kraków
Łódź
Gdańsk
Wrocław
Poznań
Lublin
Białystok
Brest
L'viv
Košice
Debrecen
CARPATHIAN MOUNTAINS
0 100 200 kilometers
0 50 100 miles

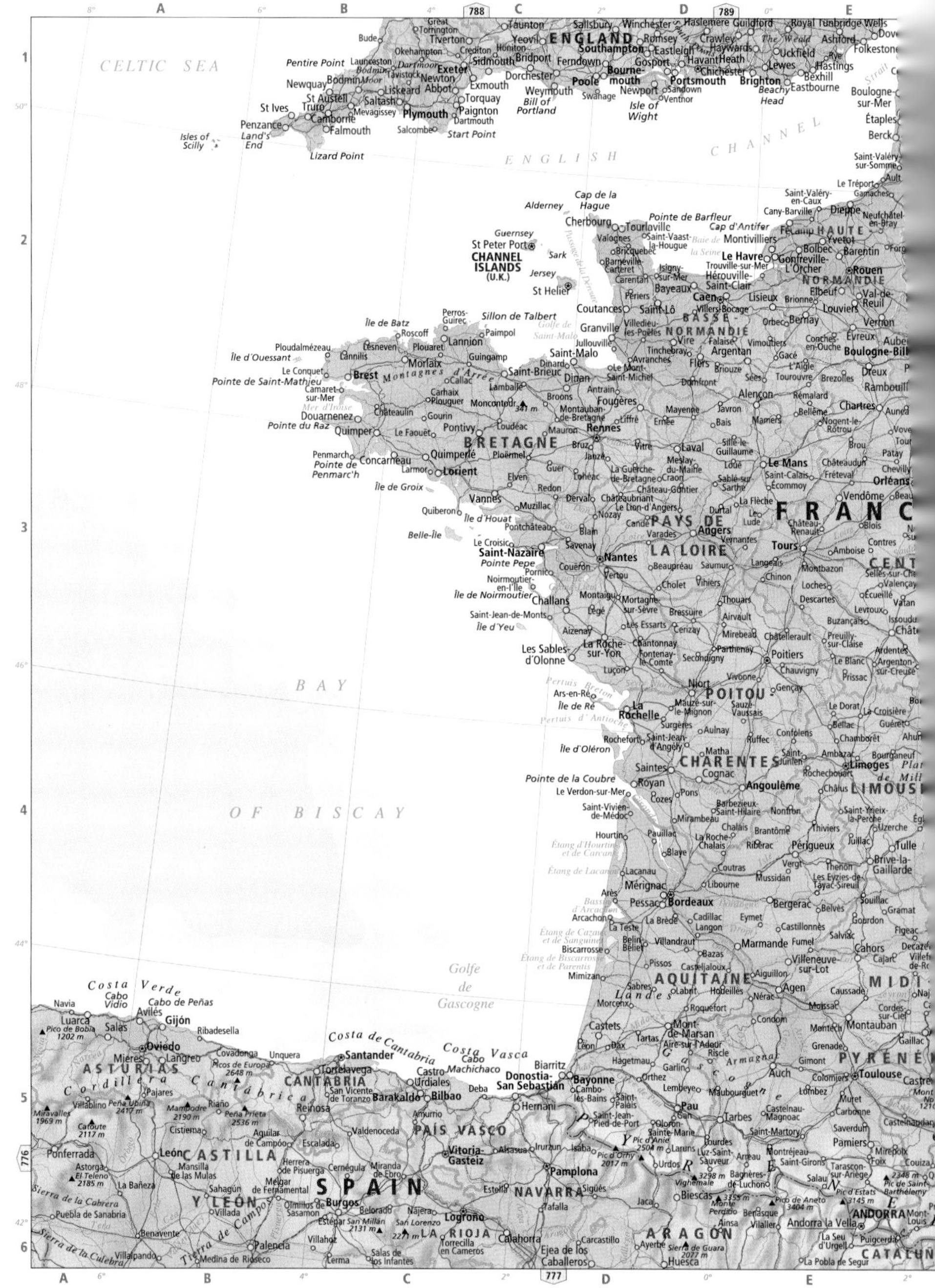
CELTIC SEA
ENGLISH CHANNEL
BAY OF BISCAY
Golfe de Gascogne
ENGLAND
CHANNEL ISLANDS (U.K.)
FRANCE
SPAIN
BRETAGNE
BASSE-NORMANDIE
HAUTE-NORMANDIE
PAYS DE LA LOIRE
POITOU-CHARENTES
AQUITAINE
LIMOUSIN
MIDI-PYRÉNÉES
ASTURIAS
CANTABRIA
PAÍS VASCO
NAVARRA
CASTILLA Y LEÓN
LA RIOJA
ARAGÓN
CATALUÑA
ANDORRA
Costa Verde
Costa de Cantabria
Costa Vasca
Cordillera Cantábrica
Isles of Scilly
Land's End
Lizard Point
Plymouth
Exeter
Southampton
Portsmouth
Brighton
Isle of Wight
Guernsey
Jersey
Alderney
St Peter Port
St Helier
Cherbourg
Caen
Le Havre
Rouen
Dieppe
Brest
Quimper
Lorient
Vannes
Saint-Brieuc
Saint-Malo
Rennes
Laval
Le Mans
Angers
Tours
Nantes
Saint-Nazaire
La Roche-sur-Yon
Niort
Poitiers
La Rochelle
Île de Ré
Île d'Oléron
Angoulême
Limoges
Périgueux
Bordeaux
Arcachon
Agen
Mont-de-Marsan
Bayonne
Biarritz
Pau
Tarbes
Toulouse
Auch
Montauban
Oviedo
Gijón
Santander
Bilbao
Donostia-San Sebastián
Vitoria-Gasteiz
Pamplona
Logroño
Burgos
León
Palencia
Huesca
Andorra la Vella
788
789
776
777

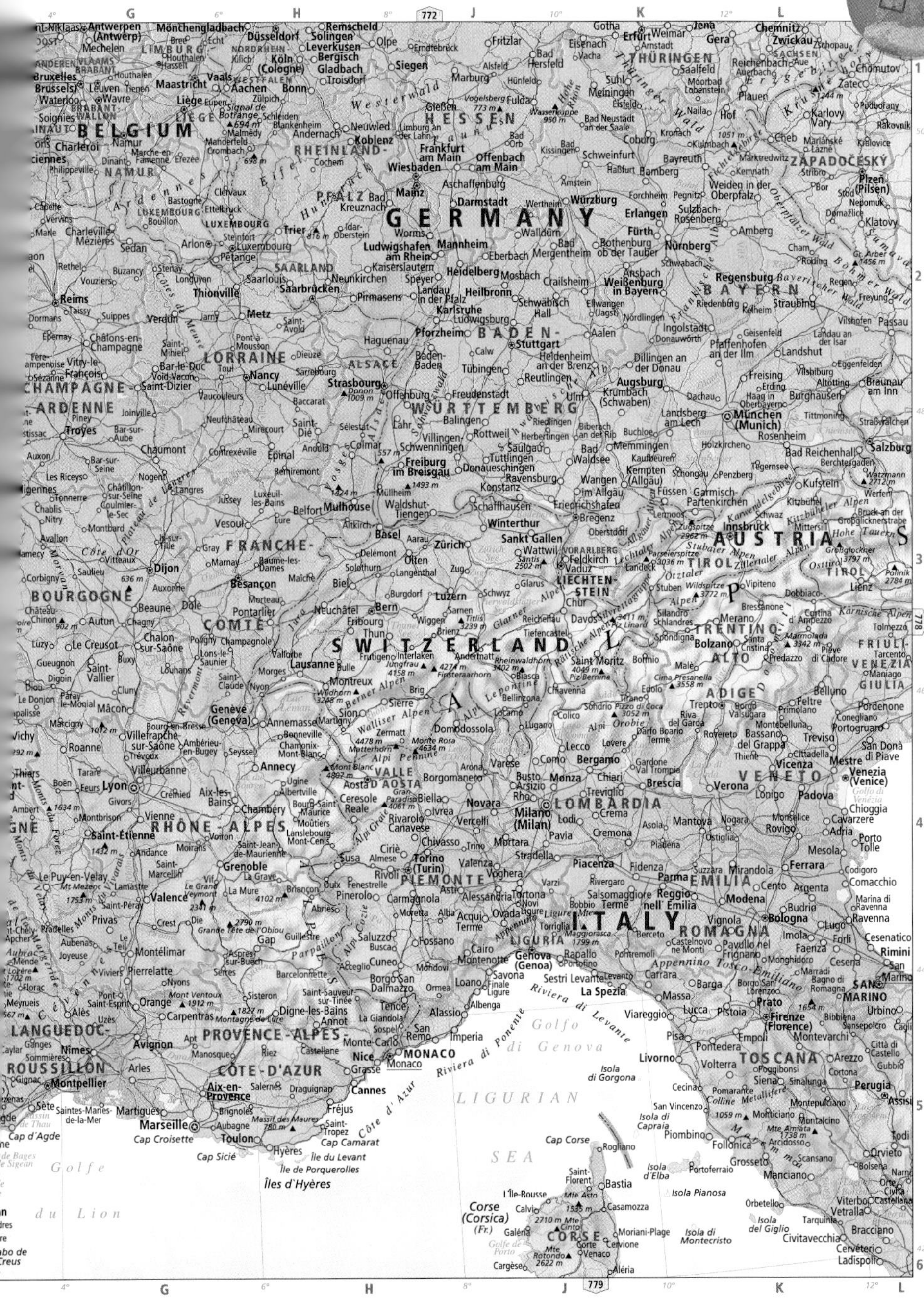

G
H
J
K
L
772
778
779
BELGIUM
GERMANY
SWITZERLAND
AUSTRIA
ITALY
LIECHTENSTEIN
MONACO
LUXEMBOURG
LIMBURG
BRABANT
NAMUR
HESSEN
THÜRINGEN
SACHSEN
RHEINLAND-PFALZ
SAARLAND
BADEN-WÜRTTEMBERG
BAYERN
ZÁPADOČESKÝ
LORRAINE
ALSACE
CHAMPAGNE-ARDENNE
FRANCHE-COMTÉ
BOURGOGNE
RHÔNE-ALPES
PROVENCE-ALPES-CÔTE-D'AZUR
LANGUEDOC-ROUSSILLON
TIROL
VORARLBERG
TRENTINO-ALTO ADIGE
FRIULI-VENEZIA GIULIA
VENETO
LOMBARDIA
PIEMONTE
VALLE D'AOSTA
LIGURIA
EMILIA-ROMAGNA
TOSCANA
SAN MARINO
CORSE
Corse (Corsica) (Fr.)
Antwerpen (Antwerp)
Bruxelles (Brussels)
Liège
Charleroi
Mönchengladbach
Düsseldorf
Köln (Cologne)
Bonn
Aachen
Koblenz
Wiesbaden
Mainz
Frankfurt am Main
Offenbach am Main
Darmstadt
Mannheim
Heidelberg
Saarbrücken
Karlsruhe
Stuttgart
Würzburg
Erlangen
Fürth
Nürnberg
Regensburg
Augsburg
München (Munich)
Salzburg
Innsbruck
Erfurt
Jena
Gera
Chemnitz
Zwickau
Plzeň (Pilsen)
Metz
Nancy
Strasbourg
Reims
Troyes
Dijon
Besançon
Mulhouse
Basel
Zürich
Bern
Luzern
Lausanne
Genève (Geneva)
Lyon
Grenoble
Saint-Étienne
Valence
Avignon
Nîmes
Montpellier
Marseille
Toulon
Nice
Cannes
Torino (Turin)
Milano (Milan)
Bergamo
Brescia
Verona
Vicenza
Padova
Venezia (Venice)
Trento
Bolzano
Genova (Genoa)
La Spezia
Parma
Modena
Bologna
Ferrara
Firenze (Florence)
Prato
Livorno
Pisa
Siena
Perugia
Bastia
Ajaccio
Golfe du Lion
Golfo di Genova
LIGURIAN SEA
Riviera di Ponente
Riviera di Levante
Côte d'Azur
Îles d'Hyères
Isola d'Elba
Isola di Capraia
Isola di Gorgona
Isola Pianosa
Isola di Montecristo
Isola del Giglio
Ardennes
Eifel
Westerwald
Taunus
Hunsrück
Schwarzwald
Schwäbische Alb
Thüringer Wald
Erzgebirge
Böhmer Wald
Vosges
Jura
Alpi Pennine
Berner Alpen
Walliser Alpen
Glarner Alpen
Alpi Lepontine
Alpi Graie
Alpi Cozie
Appennino Tosco-Emiliano
Massif des Maures
Mont Blanc 4807 m
Monte Rosa 4634 m
Matterhorn 4478 m
Grossglockner 3797 m
Zugspitze 2962 m

0 100 200 kilometers
0 50 100 miles

A
B
C
D
E
12°
10°
8°
6°
1
2
3
4
5
42°
40°
38°
36°
ATLANTIC
OCEAN
PORTUGAL
GALICIA
ASTURIAS
CASTILLA Y LE
EXTREMADURA
VIANA DO CASTELO
BRAGA
VILA REAL
BRAGANÇA
PORTO
AVEIRO
VISEU
GUARDA
COIMBRA
CASTELO BRANCO
LEIRIA
SANTARÉM
PORTALEGRE
LISBOA
SETÚBAL
ÉVORA
BEJA
FARO
GIBRALTAR (U.K.)
MOROCCO
Costa Verde
Cordillera Can
Sierra de la Cabrera
Sierra de la Culebra
Serra da Estrela
Sierra de Gredos
Sierra de San Pedro
Sierra de Aracena
Serranía de Ronda
Montes
Costa de la Luz
Golfo de Cádiz
Baía de Setúbal
Strait of Gibraltar
Punta da Estaca de Bares
Cabo Ortegal
Ortigueira
Cabo Prior
Ferrol
A Coruña
Malpica
Pontedeume
Betanzos
Carballo
Vimianzo
Cabo Touriñán
Cée
Fisterra
Cabo Fisterra
Santiago de Compostela
Ordes
Melide
Noia
Padrón
A Estrada
Lalín
Santa Eugenia
Vilagarcia de Arousa
Cerdedo
Chantada
Monforte
Illa de Ons
Pontevedra
Marín
Illas Cíes
Vigo
A Cañiza
Baiona
Tui
Ourense
Faro 1187 m
Avión 1151 m
A Guardia
Peneda 1373 m
Ponte da Barca
Viana do Castelo
Serra do Larouco 1525 m
Braga
Póvoa de Varzim
Guimarães
Porto
Penafiel
Vila Real
Marão 1415 m
Lamego
São João da Madeira
Montemuro 1381 m
Moimenta da Beira
Ovar
Aveiro
Albergaria-a-Velha
São Pedro do Sul
Viseu
Águeda
Mira
1075 m
Cabo Mondego
Figueira da Foz
Coimbra
Góis
Covilhã
Fundão
Penamacor
Pombal
Pontão
Cabeço Rainha 1084 m
Castelo Branco
Segura
Leiria
Fátima
Nazaré
Batalha
Caldas da Rainha
Tomar
Peniche
Rio Maior
Torres Novas
Abrantes
Cabo Carvoeiro
Óbidos
Santarém
Almeirim
Torres Vedras
Vila Franca de Xira
Coruche
Sintra
Cascais
Amadora
Lisboa (Lisbon)
Almada
Setúbal
Cabo Espichel
Vendas Novas
Montemor-o-Novo
Mora
Vimieiro
Arraiolos
Estremoz
Redondo
Ossa 653 m
Évora
Alcácer do Sal
Grândola 325 m
Torrão
Vidigueira
Portel
Mourão
Santiago do Cacém
Ferreira do Alentejo
Beja
Moura
Barrancos
Sines
Aljustrel
Serpa
Cercal
Santa Luzia
Castro Verde
Odemira
Mértola
Almodôvar
Odeceixe
Aljezur
Fóia 902 m
Mú 577 m
Alcoutim
Vila do Bispo
Portimão
Algarve
Castro Marim
Cabo de São Vicente
Sagres
Lagos
Loulé
Faro
Tavira
Ponta de Sagres
Cabo de Santa Maria
Viveiro
Xistral 1036 m
Mondoñedo
Ribadeo
Navia
Luarca
Cabo Vidio
Cabo de Peñas
Avilés
Gijón
Ribadesella
Vegadeo
Pico de Bobia 1201 m
Villalba
Baamonde
Meira
Guitiriz
Oviedo
Salas
Mieres
Langreo
Lugo
A Fonsagrada
Pajares
Peña Ubiña 2417 m
Mampodre 2190 m
Villablino
Sarriá
Becerreá
Miravalles 1969 m
Catoute 2117 m
Cistierna
Ponferrada
Astorga
León
Mansilla de las Mulas
Quiroga
El Teleno 2185 m
La Bañeza
Sahagún
Puebla de Trives
Cabeza de Manzaneda 1778 m
Villada
A Gudiña
Puebla de Sanabria
Benavente
Verín
Bragança
Villalpando
Rebordelo
Valpaços
Chaves
Boticas
Alcañices
Mirandela
Miranda do Douro
Zamora
Toro
Tordesillas
Tiedra
Fermoselle
Torre de Moncorvo
Mogadouro
Trabanca
Corrales
Fuentesaúco
Alaejos
Medina del Campo
Cañizal
Ledesma
Vitigudino
Marofa 976 m
Salamanca
Arévalo
Lumbrales
Barbadillo
Peñaranda de Bracamonte
Celorico da Beira
Pinhel
Boadilla
Vecinos
Fresno Alhándiga
Guarda
Vilar Formoso
Ciudad Rodrigo
El Cabaco
Guijuelo
Ibiza 2315 m
Serrota 2294 m
1730 m Peña de Francia
El Barco de Ávila
Piedrahita
Béjar
Almanzor 2592 m
Arenas de San Pedro
Plasencia
Jarandilla de la Vera
Moraleja
Coria
Navalmoral de la Mata
Alcántara
Bohonal
Jaraicejo
La Nava de Ricomalillo
Los Navalmorales
Valencia de Alcántara
Brozas
Aliseda
Cáceres
Trujillo
Guadalupe
Alpalhão
São Mamede 1027 m
Portalegre
Alburquerque
Alter do Chão
Zorita
Herrera del Duque
Miajadas
La Roca de la Sierra
Navalvillar de Pela
Talarrubias
Elvas
Badajoz
Mérida
Villanueva de la Serena
Olivenza
Almendralejo
Castuera
Cabeza del Buey
Almadén
Alor 610 m
Barcarrota
Santa Marta
Santa Eufemia
Zafra
Villanueva del Fresno
Campillo de Llerena
Fuente de Cantos
Llerena
Azuaga
Alcaracejos
Fuente Obejuna
Fregenal de la Sierra
Monesterio
Tentudía 1104 m
Espiel
Erillas 896 m
Rosal de la Frontera
Cortegana
Aracena
Cazalla de la Sierra
Córdoba
Sierra de Aracena 915 m
El Ronquillo
Lora del Río
Palma del Río
Puebla de Guzmán
Valverde del Camino
Carmona
Écija
Gibraleón
Huelva
Bollullos par del Condado
Sevilla
Alcalá de Guadaíra
Puente-Genil
Osuna
Estepa
Ayamonte
Mazagón
El Rocío
Utrera
Morón de la Frontera
Torre de la Higuera
Lebrija
Villamartín
Algodonales
Sanlúcar de Barrameda
Jeréz de la Frontera
Ronda
El Puerto de Santa María
Arcos de la Frontera
Ubrique
Marbella
Cádiz
San Fernando
Medina Sidonia
Jimena de la Frontera
Estepona
Chiclana de la Frontera
Vejer de la Frontera
La Línea de la Concepción
Barbate de Franco
Algeciras
Gibraltar
Punta Marroquí o de Tarifa
Tarifa
Punta Almina
Ceuta (Sp.)
Cap Spartel
Ksar es Sghir
Tanger (Tangier)
838 m
Tetouan (Tetuán)
Asilah

F
G
H
J
K
774
801
2°
0°
4°
42°
40°
38°
36°
1
2
3
4
5
FRANCE
MIDI-PYRÉNÉES
AQUITAINE
LANGUEDOC-
ROUSSILLON
PROVENCE-ALPES-CÔTE-D'AZUR
Landes
Gascogne
Armagnac
Languedoc
PYRENEES
ANDORRA
Andorra la Vella
CATALUÑA
ARAGÓN
NAVARRA
PAÍS VASCO
LA RIOJA
VALENCIA
CASTILLA LA MANCHA
MURCIA
SPAIN
Costa Vasca
Costa Brava
Costa Daurada
Costa del Azahar
Costa Blanca
Golfe du Lion
Golfo de Valencia
MEDITERRANEAN SEA
Islas Baleares (Balearic Islands)
ISLAS BALEARES
Mallorca
Menorca
Eivissa (Ibiza)
Formentera
Cabrera
ALGERIA
Alger (Algiers)
Toulouse
Montpellier
Marseille
Avignon
Nîmes
Perpignan
Narbonne
Carcassonne
Béziers
Agde
Cap d'Agde
Sète
Aix-en-Provence
Arles
Martigues
Aubagne
Cap Croisette
Millau
Albi
Montauban
Agen
Pau
Tarbes
Bayonne
Biarritz
Donostia-San Sebastián
Bilbao
Vitoria-Gasteiz
Pamplona
Logroño
Calahorra
Tudela
Tarazona
Soria
Zaragoza
Huesca
Lleida
Barcelona
L'Hospitalet de Llobregat
Badalona
Santa Coloma de Gramanet
Sabadell
Terrassa
Mataró
Girona
Figueres
Tarragona
Reus
Tortosa
Vinaròs
Benicarló
Castelló de la Plana
Sagunto
Valencia
Catarroja
Cullera
Gandía
Alzira
Xàtiva
Denia
Jávea
Cabo de la Nao
Alcoy
Benidorm
Villajoyosa
Alicante
Elche
Orihuela
Torrevieja
Murcia
Cartagena
Cabo de Palos
Mazarrón
Lorca
Águilas
Almería
Cabo de Gata
Granada
Guadix
Baza
Albacete
Cuenca
Teruel
Calatayud
Guadalajara
Alcalá de Henares
Palma de Mallorca
Manacor
Inca
Ciudadela
Mahón
Eivissa (Ibiza)
Sierra de Cuenca
Sierra Nevada
Mulhacén 3481 m
Pico de Aneto 3404 m
Dellys
Tizi Ouzou
Blida
Médéa
Chlef
Ténès
Cherchell
Mostaganem
Oran
Relizane
Tiaret
Mascara
Sig
Beni-Saf
'Aïn Temouchent
M'Sila
Isla del Alborán
Cap des Trois Fourches
0 100 200 kilometers
0 50 100 miles

780
772
773
775
GERMANY
CZECH REPUBLIC
SLOVAKIA
AUSTRIA
HUNGARY
SLOVENIA
CROATIA
BOSNIA AND HERZEGOVINA
SWITZERLAND
LIECHTENSTEIN
FRANCE
MONACO
SAN MARINO
ITALIA
ADRIATIC
LIGURIAN SEA
BAYERN
BADEN-WÜRTTEMBERG
TIROL
SALZBURG
KÄRNTEN
STEIERMARK
NIEDERÖSTERREICH
OBERÖSTERREICH
BURGENLAND
TRENTINO-ALTO ADIGE
FRIULI-VENEZIA GIULIA
VENETO
LOMBARDIA
PIEMONTE
VALLE D'AOSTA
LIGURIA
EMILIA ROMAGNA
TOSCANA
MARCHE
ALSACE
LORRAINE
FRANCHE-COMTÉ
Wien (Vienna)
Budapest
Zagreb
Ljubljana
Bratislava
Sarajevo
München (Munich)
Milano (Milan)
Venezia (Venice)
Genova (Genoa)
Firenze (Florence)

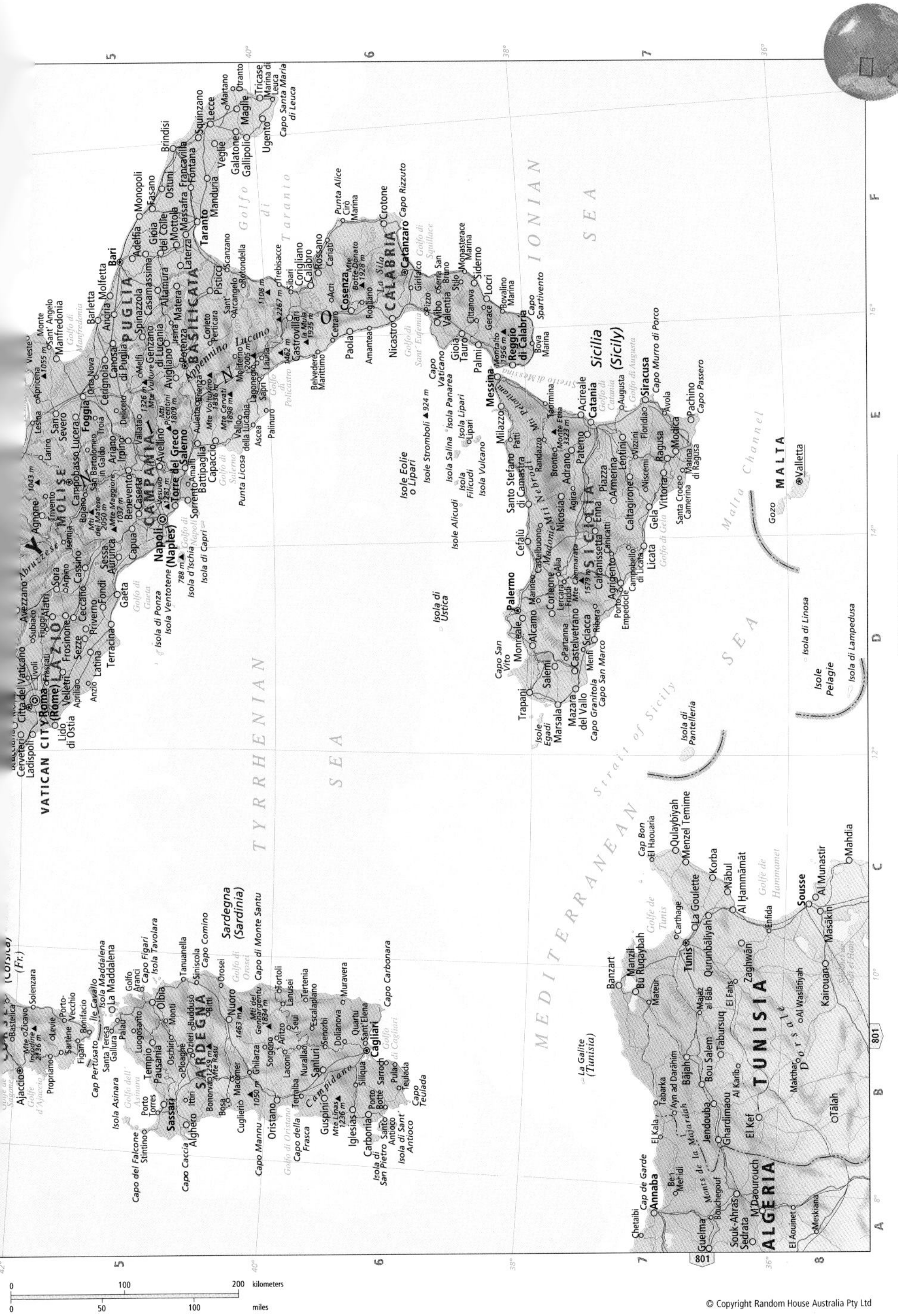
TYRRHENIAN SEA
IONIAN SEA
MEDITERRANEAN SEA
Strait of Sicily
Malta Channel
Golfo di Taranto
VATICAN CITY
Roma (Rome)
Napoli (Naples)
LAZIO
MOLISE
CAMPANIA
PUGLIA
BASILICATA
CALABRIA
SICILIA
Sicilia (Sicily)
SARDEGNA
Sardegna (Sardinia)
Corsica (Fr.)
MALTA
Valletta
Gozo
TUNISIA
ALGERIA
Tunis
Palermo
Messina
Catania
Cagliari
Bari
Taranto
Reggio di Calabria
Isole Eolie o Lipari
Isole Egadi
Isole Pelagie
Isola di Pantelleria
Isola di Lampedusa
Isola di Linosa
La Galite (Tunisia)
801
0 100 200 kilometers
0 50 100 miles

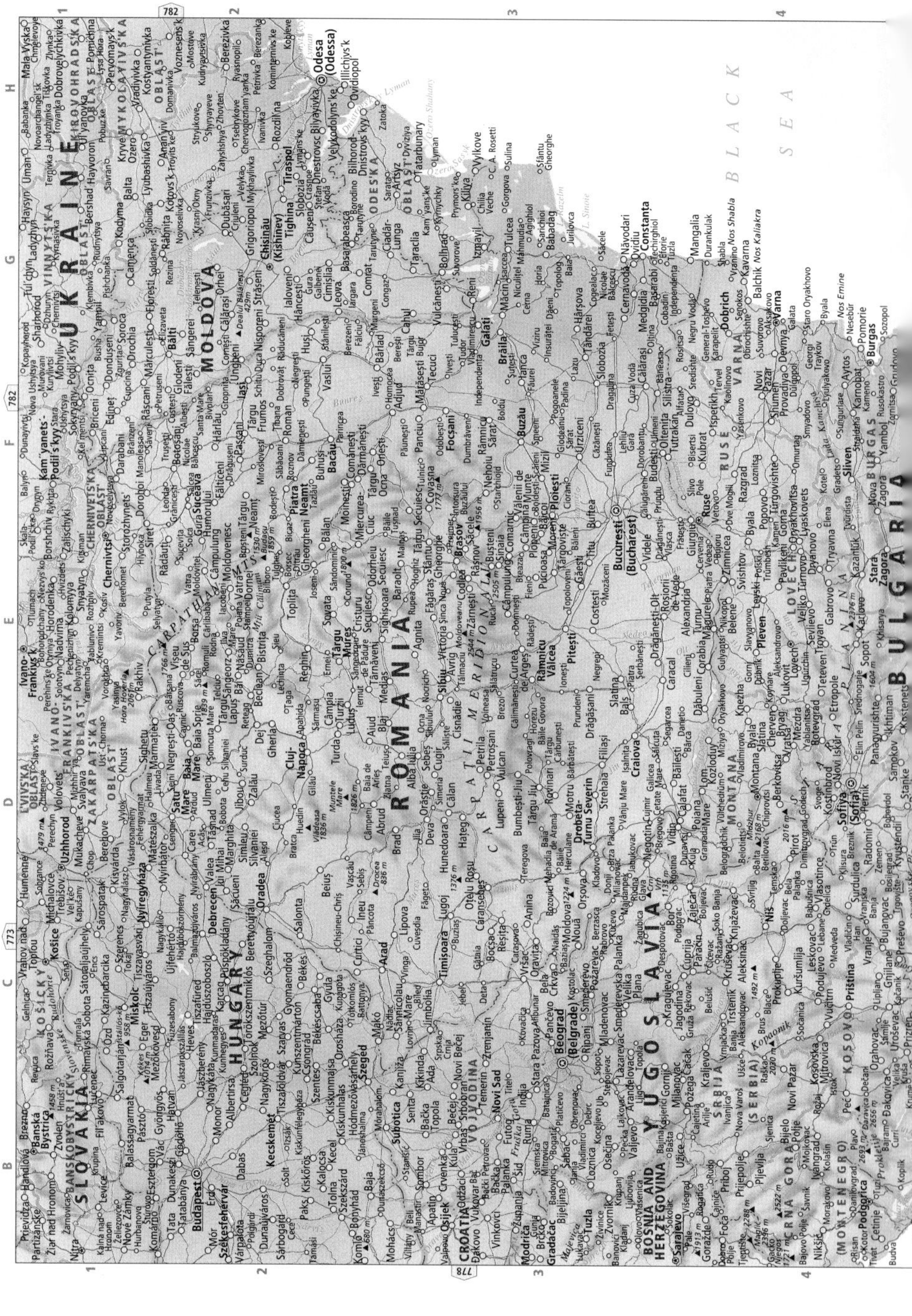
UKRAINE
MOLDOVA
ROMANIA
HUNGARY
SLOVAKIA
YUGOSLAVIA
BULGARIA
CROATIA
BOSNIA AND HERZEGOVINA
BLACK SEA
782
773
778

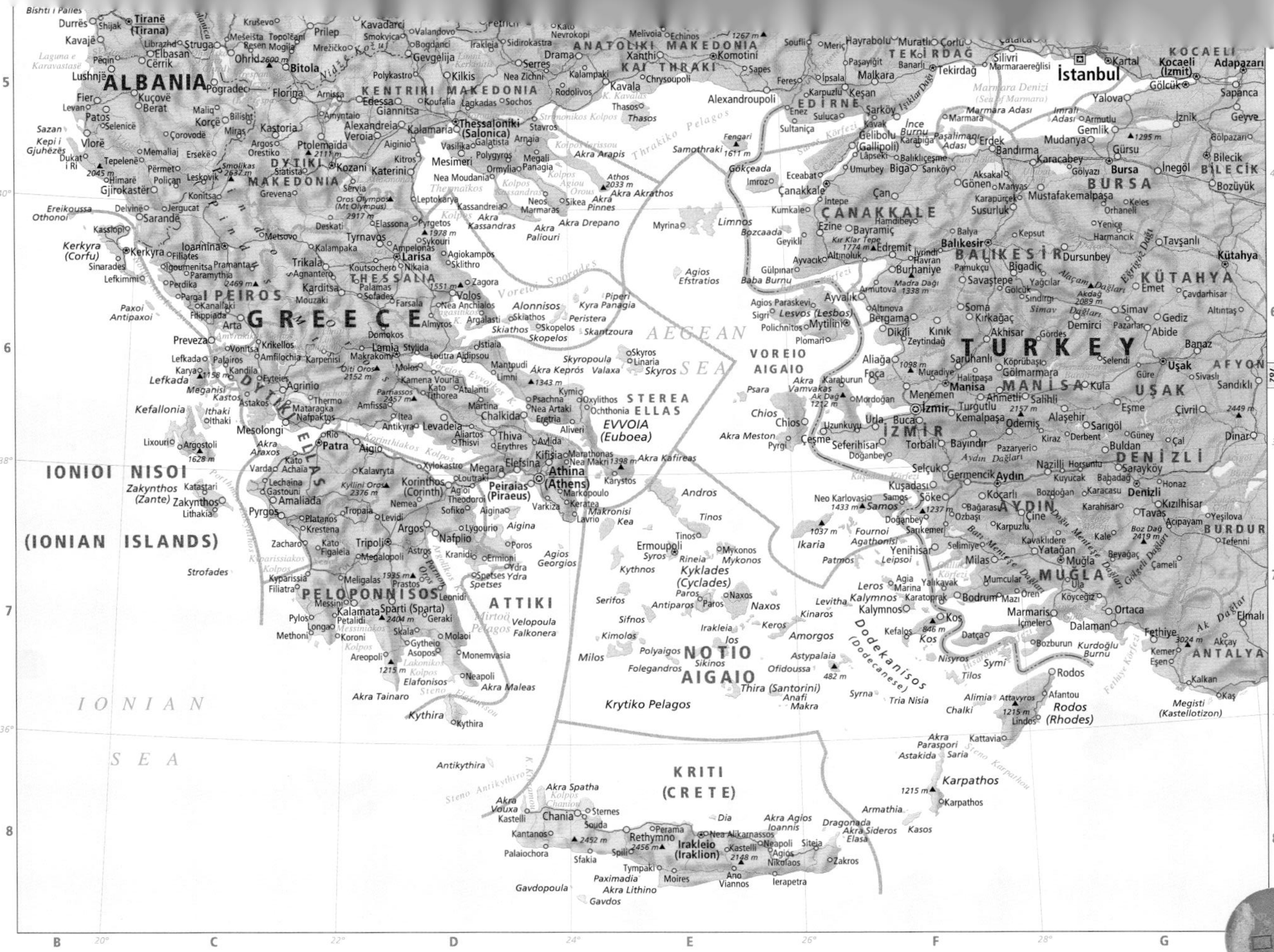

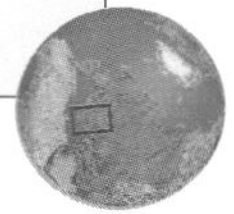

Europe and the Russian Federation

0 100 200 kilometers

0 50 100 miles

A B C D E F G
784
780
756
1 2 3 4 5 6
Zatoka Gdańska
LITHUANIA
RUS. FED.
Kaliningrad
LATVIA
Daugavpils
Klaipėda
Šiauliai
Panevėžys
Kaunas
Vilnius
Ukmergė
Marijampolė
Gdynia
Gdańsk
Elbląg
Malbork
Olsztyn
Augustów
Grudziądz
Toruń
Sierpc
Ostrołęka
Białystok
POLAND
Kutno
Warszawa (Warsaw)
Łódź
Warka
Radom
Puławy
Lublin
Częstochowa
Kielce
Kraśnik
Chełm
Jędrzejów
Zamość
Sosnowiec
Stalowa Wola
Tarnów
Rzeszów
Kraków
Przemyśl
Brest
Hrodna
Lida
Minsk
Maladzyechna
Barysaw
Hora Dzyarzhynskaya
346 m
BELARUS
Baranavichy
Salihorsk
Babruysk
Zhlobin
Mahilyow
Pinsk
Homyel'
Mazyr
Vitsyebsk
Polatsk
Lyepyel'
Orsha
Nevel'
Velikiye Luki
Rzhev
Vyaz'ma
SMOLENSKAYA
Smolensk
OBLAST'
Roslavl'
KALUZHSKAYA
Kaluga
OBLAST'
Sukhinichi
Bryansk
BRYANSKAYA
OBLAST'
Unecha
Druzhba
Orel
ORLOVSKAYA
OBLAST
Moskva (Moscow)
Khimki
Mytishchi
Odintsovo
Podol'sk
Obninsk
Serpukhov
Kolomna
Tula
Novomoskovsk
TUL'SKAYA
OBLAST'
Plavsk
Vladimir
Murom
Gus'-Khrustal'nyy
Tuma
Kasimov
RYAZANSKAYA
Ryazan'
Shilovo
Sasovo
OBLAST'
Shatsk
Pavlovo
Kulebaki
Arzamas
Ardatov
Shumerlya
Poretskoye
Batyrevo
Alatyr'
Chamzinka
Yazykovo
Krasnoslobodsk
Saransk
Ruzayevka
Ul'yanovsk
Zubova Polyana
Inza
Barysh
Kamenka
Penza
Kuznetsk
PENZENSKAYA
OBLAST'
Morshansk
Michurinsk
Tambov
Lipetsk
Yelets
RUSSIAN
FEDERATION
Rtishchevo
Atkarsk
Saratov
Engel's
Balakovo
Balashov
Borisoglebsk
Voronezh
Staryy Oskol
Kursk
L'gov
Liski
Ostrogozhsk
Belgorod
Valuyki
Rossosh'
Mikhaylovka
Kamyshin
VOLGOGRADSKAYA
OBLAST'
Volgograd (Stalingrad)
Volzhskiy
KAZAKHSTAN
Akhtubinsk
Svetlyy Yar
Chernyy Yar
Tsagan Aman
Sadovoye
Kharabali
RESPUBLIKA
Kegul'ta
KALMYKIYA
Elista
Utta
Yusta
Yashkul'
Priyutnoye
Ipatovo
Ulan-Khol
Privolzhskaya Vozvyshennost'
Srednerusskaya Vozvyshennost'
Chernihiv
Konotop
Romny
Nizhyn
Sumy
Pryluky
Hadyach
Lubny
Kharkiv
Poltava
Kyyiv (Kiev)
Zhytomyr
Berdychiv
Bila Tserkva
Korosten'
Shepetivka
Rivne
Luts'k
Kovel'
Sarny
L'viv
Drohobych
Stryy
Ternopil'
Khmel'nyts'kyy
Vinnytsya
Kam''yanets'-Podil's'kyy
Uman'
Ivano-Frankivs'k
Chernivtsi
UKRAINE
Kremenchuk
Oleksandriya
Kirovohrad
Dnipropetrovs'k
Pavlohrad
Kryvyy Rih
Nikopol'
Zaporizhzhya
Donets'k
Makiyivka
Lysychans'k
Alchevs'k
Luhans'k
Millerovo
Morozovsk
Novoshakhtinsk
Shakhty
Volgodonsk
Novocherkassk
Rostov-na-Donu
Taganrog
Mariupol'
Berdyans'k
Melitopol'
Mykolayiv
Kherson
Odesa (Odessa)
Heniches'k
Obytichna Kosa
SEA OF AZOV
Yeysk
Sal'sk
Pavlovskaya
Timashevsk
Kropotkin
STAVROPOL'SKIY
KRAY
Svetlograd
Stavropol'
Armavir
Krasnodar
Nevinnomyssk
Pyatigorsk
Kislovodsk
Cherkessk
Labinsk
Maykop
Novorossiysk
Anapa
Tuapse
Sochi
Gora Chugush 3238 m
Gora El'brus 5642 m
Nal'chik
Prokhladnyy
Nazran
Vladikavkaz
Groznyy
Khasavyurt
Kizlyar
Naurskaya
Kochubey
Sokhumi
Gora Kazbek 5047 m
Dzhankoy
Kryms'kyy Pivostriv (Crimean Peninsula)
Kerch
Feodosiya
Yevpatoriya
Simferopol'
Sevastopol'
Hora Roman-Kosh 1545 m
Yalta
BLACK SEA
Nos Kaliakra
MOLDOVA
Chişinău (Kishinev)
Tiraspol
Bălţi
Kotovs'k
Suceava
Vaslui
SLOVAKIA
Ružomberok
Prešov
Košice
Uzhhorod
Miskolc
Gyöngyös
Mezőkövesd
Hatvan
Debrecen
HUNGARY
Oradea
Szeged
Arad
Timişoara
Satu Mare
Baia Mare
Bistriţa
Cluj-Napoca
Târgu Mureş
ROMANIA
CARPATHIAN MTS
CARPAŢII MERIDIONALI
Braşov
Petroşani
Râmnicu Vâlcea
Târgu Jiu
Piteşti
Filiaşi
Bucureşti (Bucharest)
Craiova
Alexandria
Cernavodă
Constanţa
Slobozia
Silistra
Babadag
Tulcea
Reni
L. Razim
L. Sinoie
Beograd (Belgrade)
YUGOSLAVIA
Kraljevo
Vidin
Kruševac
Niš
Prokuplje
Leskovac
Priština
Vranje
Prizren
Montana
Pleven
Ruse
Dulovo
Dobrich
Varna
Shumen
STARA PLANINA
BULGARIA
Sofiya (Sofia)
Panagyurishte
Plovdiv
Karnobat
Aytos
Burgas
Khaskovo
Kŭrdzhali
Skopje
MACEDONIA
Bitola
Kavadarci
Edirne
Serres
Xanthi
Komotini
Alexandroupoli
Giannitsa
Thessaloniki
Kalamaria
Veroia
Kozani
Katerini
Thasos
Samothraki
Keşan
Tekirdağ
İstanbul
Gölcük
Adapazarı
Gerede
Karabük
Zonguldak
Keremepe Burnu
İnebolu
Sinop
Bafra Burnu
Bafra
Küre Dağları
Kastamonu
Ilgaz
Samsun
Yasun Burnu
Fener Burnu
Ordu
Tirebolu
Trabzon
Merzifon
Amasya
Tokat
Çorum
Turhal
Köroğlu Dağları
2378 m
Gümüşhane
Bayburt
3331 m
Mescit Tepe 3255 m
Horasan
Erzurum
Ağrı Dağı (Mt Ararat) 5137 m
Karaköse
Doğubayazıt
Gyumri
Gänca
ARMENIA
Aragats Lerr 4090 m
Yerevan
Sisian
Naxçıvan
Mākū
Jolfā
IRAN
Salmās
Orūmīyeh (Urmia)
GEORGIA
K'ut'aisi
T'bilisi
Malyy Kavkaz
P'ot'i
Bat'umi
Akhalts'ikhe
Artvin
Kars
Çanakkale
Bandırma
Bursa
Bozüyük
Eskişehir
Ankara
Polatlı
Sivrihisar
Kırıkkale
Yozgat
Yıldızeli
Sivas
Bey Dağı 2292 m
Erzincan
3282 m
Aşkale
Arapkir
Elazığ
Bingöl
Karakoçan
Muş
Tatvan
Van
Muradiye
TURKEY
Kayseri
Bünyan
Gürün
Darende
Nevşehir
Aksaray
Elbistan
Malatya
Toroslar
Diyarbakır
Kurtalan
Siirt
Batman
Başkale
Çölemerik
Güneydoğu Toroslar
Adıyaman
Siverek
Çınar
Şırnak
Cizre
Mardin
Urfa
Viranşehir
Akçakale
Nizip
Gaziantep
Kilis
Kahramanmaraş
Göksun
Niğde
Bor
Ereğli
Karapınar
Konya
Sarayönü
Akşehir
Cihanbeyli
Afyon
Çay
Uşak
Kütahya
Simav
Akhisar
Balıkesir
Edremit
Ezine
Soma
Manisa
Salihli
İzmir
Ödemiş
Çeşme
Mitilini
Lesvos (Lesbos)
Chios
Limnos
AEGEAN SEA
Skyros
EVVOIA (Euboea)
Söke
Aydın
Nazilli
Denizli
Dinar
2305 m
Isparta
Burdur
Yatağan
Muğla
Milas
Marmaris
Bodrum
Korkuteli
Antalya
Fethiye
Kaş
Antalya Körfezi
Alanya
Karaçal Tepe 2339 m
Mut
Silifke
Karaman
Toros Dağları
İçel (Mersin)
Adana
Osmaniye
İskenderun
Antakya (Antioch)
Ḥalab (Aleppo)
Manbij
Al Qāmishlī
Al Ḥasakah
SYRIA
920 m
Al Mawṣil (Mosul)
Arbīl
Dahūk
IRAQ
Rawāndūz
Mahābād
Anamur Burnu
Anamur
Al Lādhiqīyah (Latakia)
Jablah
Baniyās
Ṭarṭūs
Ḥamāh
Ḥimṣ (Homs)
Ṭarābulus (Tripoli)
3083 m
Zaḥlah
Nabk
LEBANON
Bayrūt (Beirut)
Ṣaydā (Sidon)
Ṣūr (Tyre)
Dimashq (Damascus)
'Akko (Acre)
Ḥefa (Haifa)
Irbid
Nawá
Dar'ā
'Afula
ISRAEL
Tel Aviv-Yafo
Jarash
'Ammān
Ashdod
Gaza
Yerushalayim (Jerusalem)
Khān Yūnus
Be'er Sheva (Beersheba)
Al Karak
Aṭ Ṭafīlah
Ceasefire Line
Lefkosia Nicosia
Ammochostos (Famagusta)
Olympos 1951 m
Larnaka
Lemesos (Limassol)
CYPRUS
Tynavos
Larisa
Trikala
Ioannina
GREECE
Volos
Lamia
Agrinio
Mesolongi
Levadeia
Thiva
Patra
Amaliada
Athina (Athens)
Peiraias (Piraeus)
Pyrgos
Tripoli
Argos
Kalamata
Sparti (Sparta)
Pyloso
Skala
Monemvasia
Andros
Tinos
Ikaria
Paros
Naxos
Milos
Ios
Amorgos
Kythira
Rodos (Rhodes)
Rodos
Lindos
Karpathos
Chania
Irakleio
Kriti (Crete)
MEDITERRANEAN SEA
Shaḥḥāt
Darnah
Sūsah
Sulunṭah
Ra's at Tin
At Tamimi
Zāwiyat al Mukhaylá
Tubruq
Ra's al Muraysah
Al Bardī
Khalīj as Sallūm
Umm Sa'ad
Sīdī Barrānī
LIBYA
Marsá Maṭrūḥ
Ra's al Kanā'is
EGYPT
Al Iskandarīya (Alexandria)
Dumyāṭ (Damietta)
Būr Sa'īd (Port Said)
Al 'Alamayn
Al Ḥammām
Damanhūr
Az Zaqāzīq
Al Manṣūrah
Al Ismā'īlīyah (Ismailia)
Al 'Arīsh
RUSSIAN FEDERATION
1 RESP. SEVERNAYA OSETIYA-ALANIYA
2 CHECHENSKAYA RESPUBLIKA
3 RESPUBLIKA INGUSHETIYA
4 KABARDINO-BALKARSKAYA RESP.
5 KARACHAYEVO-CHERKESSKAYA RESP.
6 RESPUBLIKA ADYGEYA
7 BELGORODSKAYA OBLAST'
8 KURSKAYA OBLAST'
9 LIPETSKAYA OBLAST'
10 TAMBOVSKAYA OBLAST'
11 PSKOVSKAYA OBLAST'
12 TVERSKAYA OBLAST'
13 MOSKOVSKAYA OBLAST'
14 VLADIMIRSKAYA OBLAST'
15 NIZHEGORODSKAYA OBLAST'
16 CHUVASHSKAYA RESPUBLIKA
17 RESPUBLIKA TATARSTAN
18 UL'YANOVSKAYA OBLAST'
19 SAMARSKAYA OBLAST'
20 RESPUBLIKA MORDOVIYA
21 VORONEZHSKAYA OBLAST'
22 SARATOVSKAYA OBLAST'
23 ROSTOVSKAYA OBLAST'
24 ASTRAKHANSKAYA OBLAST'
25 KRASNODARSKIY KRAY
26 RESPUBLIKA DAGESTAN
27 KALININGRADSKAYA OBLAST'
GEORGIA
28 ABKHAZIA
29 AJARIA
30 SOUTH OSSETIA
AZERBAIJAN
31 NAXÇIVAN
kilometers 0 100 200 300 400
miles 0 100 200

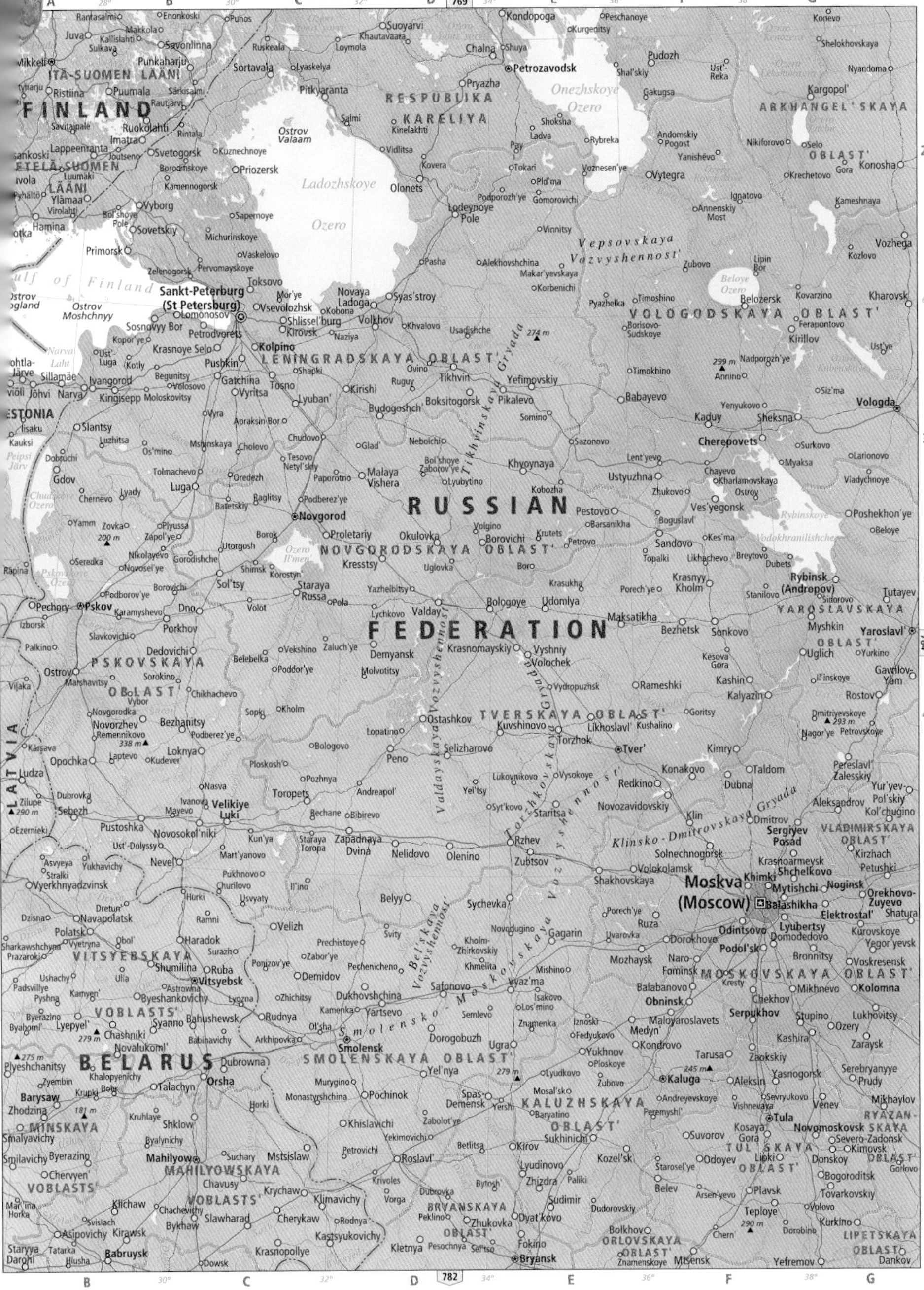
FINLAND
ITÄ-SUOMEN LÄÄNI
ETELÄ-SUOMEN LÄÄNI
RESPUBLIKA KARELIYA
ARKHANGEL'SKAYA OBLAST'
Onezhskoye Ozero
Ladozhskoye Ozero
Gulf of Finland
Sankt-Peterburg (St Petersburg)
Petrozavodsk
LENINGRADSKAYA OBLAST'
VOLOGODSKAYA OBLAST'
Vologda
Cherepovets
Vepsovskaya Vozvyshennost'
Tikhvinskaya Gryada
ESTONIA
RUSSIAN FEDERATION
Novgorod
NOVGORODSKAYA OBLAST'
Beloye Ozero
Rybinskoye Vodokhranilishche
Rybinsk (Andropov)
YAROSLAVSKAYA OBLAST'
Yaroslavl'
Pskov
PSKOVSKAYA OBLAST'
TVERSKAYA OBLAST'
Tver'
Valdayskaya Vozvyshennost'
LATVIA
Velikiye Luki
Klinsko-Dmitrovskaya Gryada
Moskva (Moscow)
MOSKOVSKAYA OBLAST'
VLADIMIRSKAYA OBLAST'
VITSYEBSKAYA VOBLASTS'
Vitsyebsk
Smolensk
SMOLENSKAYA OBLAST'
Smolensko-Moskovskaya Vozvyshennost'
BELARUS
MINSKAYA VOBLASTS'
MAHILYOWSKAYA VOBLASTS'
Mahilyow
KALUZHSKAYA OBLAST'
Kaluga
Tula
TUL'SKAYA OBLAST'
RYAZANSKAYA OBLAST'
BRYANSKAYA OBLAST'
Bryansk
ORLOVSKAYA OBLAST'
LIPETSKAYA OBLAST'
769
784
782
0 100 200 kilometers
0 50 100 miles

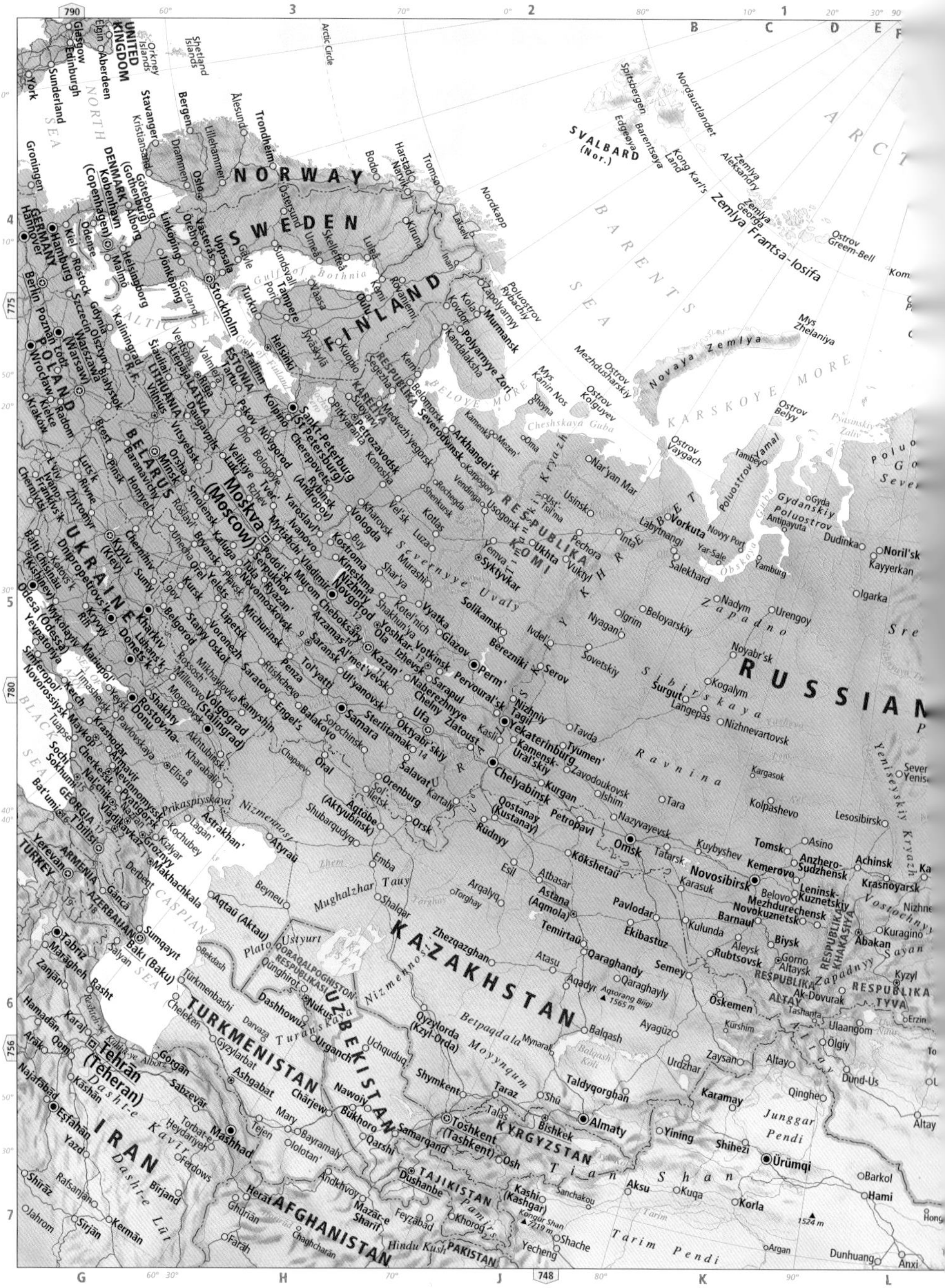
SVALBARD (Nor.)
Zemlya Frantsa-Iosifa
BARENTS SEA
Novaya Zemlya
KARSKOYE MORE
NORWAY
SWEDEN
FINLAND
ESTONIA
LATVIA
LITHUANIA
BELARUS
UKRAINE
POLAND
GERMANY
DENMARK
UNITED KINGDOM
NORTH SEA
BALTIC SEA
BLACK SEA
CASPIAN SEA
ARAL SEA
GEORGIA
ARMENIA
AZERBAIJAN
TURKEY
IRAN
AFGHANISTAN
PAKISTAN
TURKMENISTAN
UZBEKISTAN
TAJIKISTAN
KYRGYZSTAN
KAZAKHSTAN
RUSSIAN
RESPUBLIKA KOMI
RESPUBLIKA KARELIYA
Moskva (Moscow)
Sankt-Peterburg (St Petersburg)
Stockholm
Oslo
Helsinki
Tallinn
Riga
Vilnius
Minsk
Kyyiv (Kiev)
Warszawa (Warsaw)
Berlin
København (Copenhagen)
Tehrān (Teheran)
Baki (Baku)
T'bilisi
Yerevan
Ashgabat
Toshkent (Tashkent)
Bishkek
Dushanbe
Astana (Aqmola)
Almaty
Ürümqi
Novosibirsk
Omsk
Yekaterinburg
Chelyabinsk
Perm'
Kazan'
Samara
Volgograd (Stalingrad)
Rostov-na-Donu
Arkhangel'sk
Murmansk
Noril'sk
Zapadno Sibirskaya Ravnina
Kazakh Uplands
Tian Shan
Tarim Pendi
Junggar Pendi

1
2
3
820
4
5
6
7
M
749
N
P
744
Q
R
T
U
V
W
170°
180°
160°
80°
70°
60°
50°
40°
30°
110°
120°
130°
140°
150°
U.S.A.
Alaska Peninsula
Bristol Bay
Dillingham
Bethel
Togiak
Cape Newenham
Nunivak Island
Unimak Island
Seward Peninsula
Norton Sound
Nome
Kotlik
Scammon Bay
St Lawrence Island
Arctic Circle
Point Hope
Cape Lisburne
Wainwright
Bering Strait
CHUKCHI SEA
Ostrov Vrangelya
Ushakovskoye
Iul'tin
Chukotskiy Poluostrov
Mys Chukotskiy
Chukotskoye Nagor'ye
Ugol'nyye Kopi
Anadyr'
Gora Belaya 1359 m
Mys Shelagskiy
Pevek
Ostrov Ayon
Bilibino
Ostrova Medvezh'i
Cherskiy
Anadyrskoye Ploskogor'ye
1742 m
Koryakskoye Nagor'ye
Mys Olyutorskiy
BERING SEA
Aleutian Islands
Andreanof Islands
Rat Islands
Near Islands
Ostrov Beringa
Ostrov Mednyy
Komandorskiye Ostrova
Ostrov Karaginskiy
Mys Ozernoy
Ust'-Kamchatsk
Klyuchevskaya Sopka 4750 m
Sredinnyy Khrebet
Poluostrov Kamchatka
Kronotskiy Zaliv
Petropavlovsk-Kamchatskiy
Yelizovo
Mys Lopatka
Ostrov Paramushir
Ostrov Onekotan
Ostrov Shiashkotan
Ostrov Simushir
Ostrov Urup
Ostrov Iturup
Kuril'skiye Ostrova (Kuril Islands)
Administered by Russian Federation, claimed by Japan.
PACIFIC OCEAN
VOSTOCHNO-SIBIRSKOYE MORE
Novosibirskiye Ostrova
Ostrov Faddeyevskiy
Ostrov Novaya Sibir'
Ostrov Kotel'nyy
Ostrov Bol'shoy Lyakhovskiy
Mys Kovaskiy
Lyakhovskiye Ostrova
MORE LAPTEVYKH
Ostrov Bol'shoy Begichev
Yanskiy Zaliv
Yano-Indigirskaya Nizmennost'
Kolymskaya Nizmennost'
Deputatskiy
Tiksi
Khrebet Kular
Verkhoyanskiy Khrebet
Zhilinda
Siktyakh
2389 m
Verkhoyansk
Khonuu
Gora Pobeda 3147 m
Khrebet Cherskogo
Gora Volna 1585 m
Omsukchan
Ust'-Nera
2341 m
Susuman
Sinegor'ye
Kolymskoye Nagor'ye
Zaliv Shelikhova
Magadan
Mys Tolstoy
Poluostrov Koni
RESPUBLIKA SAKHA
Zhigansk
Orulgan
Udachnyy
Khrebet Suntar Khayata
Khandyga
Sangar
Okhotsk
OKHOTSKOYE MORE
(SEA OF OKHOTSK)
FEDERATION
Yakutsk
Nyurba
Mirnyy
Prilenskoye Plato
Olekminsk
Lensk
Khrebet Dzhugdzhur
Ayan
Mys Yelizavety
Okha
Shantarskiye Ostrova
Dikimdya
Aldan
Aldanskoye Nagor'ye
Chul'man
Gora Golets Skalistyy 2412 m
Stanovoy Khrebet
Nikolayevsk-na-Amure
Nogliki
Ostrov Sakhalin
Poronaysk
Mys Terpeniya
Bodaybo
Neryungri
Kirensk
Ust'-Ilim'sk
Ust'-Kut
Stanovoye Nagor'ye
Taksimo
Tynda
Zeya
Magdagachi
Skovorodino
Berezovyy
Komsomol'sk-na-Amure
1490 m
Chegdomyn
Shimanovsk
Belogorsk
Amursk
Vanino
Tatarskiy Proliv
Yuzhno-Sakhalinsk
Mys Aniva
Severobaykal'sk
Ozero Baykal (Lake Baikal)
Blagoveshchensk
Khabarovsk
Sikhote Alin'
Svetlaya
Usol'ye-Sibirskoye
RESPUBLIKA BURYATIYA
Chita
Ulan-Ude
Khilok
Sherlovaya Gora
Borzya
Obluch'ye
Bikin
Xiao Hinggan Ling
Wakkanai
Kitami
Hokkaidō
Asahikawa
Sapporo
Otaru
Muroran
JAPAN
Yakeshi
Nenjiang
Yichun
Hegang
Jiamusi
Dal'negorsk
Manzhouli
Hulun Nur
Qiqihar
Anda
Harbin
Jixi
Mudanjiang
Ussuriysk
Vladivostok
Kyra
Darhan
Erdenet
Choybalsan
Ulaanbaatar (Ulan Bator)
Kerulen (Herlen)
Baruun-Urt
MONGOLIA
Da Hinggan Ling
Baicheng
Changchun
Jilin
Ch'ŏngjin
SEA OF JAPAN
Hachinohe
Aomori
Morioka
Akita
Sendai
Honshū
Niigata
Toyama
Tokyo
Yokohama
Nagoya
Kyōto
Ōsaka
Kōchi
Shikoku
Hiroshima
Matsue
Arvayheer
Mandalgovi
Saynshand
Xi Ujimqin Qi
Tongliao
Fushun
Shenyang
Anshan
Kanggye
Hŭngnam
NORTH KOREA
Sinŭiju
P'yŏngyang
Erenhot
Dalandzadgad
Chifeng
Duolun
Bayan Har
Zhangjiakou
Beijing (Peking)
Tianjin
Dalian
Haeju
Sŏul (Seoul)
SOUTH KOREA
Andong
Taejŏn
Bohai Wan
Hohhot
Linhe
Baotou
Datong
CHINA
RUSSIAN FEDERATION
1 RESPUBLIKA DAGESTAN
2 RESPUBLIKA INGUSHETIYA
3 CHECHENSKAYA RESPUBLIKA
4 RESP. SEVERNAYA OSETIYA-ALANIYA
5 KABARDINO-BALKARSKAYA RESPUBLIKA
6 KARACHAYEVO-CHERKESSKAYA RESPUBLIKA
7 RESPUBLIKA ADYGEYA
8 RESPUBLIKA KALMYKIYA
9 RESPUBLIKA MORDOVIYA
10 CHUVASHSKAYA RESPUBLIKA
11 RESPUBLIKA TATARSTAN
12 RESPUBLIKA MARIY EL
13 UDMURTSKAYA RESPUBLIKA
14 RESPUBLIKA BASHKORTOSTAN
GEORGIA
15 ABKHAZIA
16 AJARIA
17 SOUTH OSSETIA
AZERBAIJAN
18 NAGORNO-KARABAKH
19 NAXÇIVAN
0 200 400 600 800 kilometers
0 200 400 miles

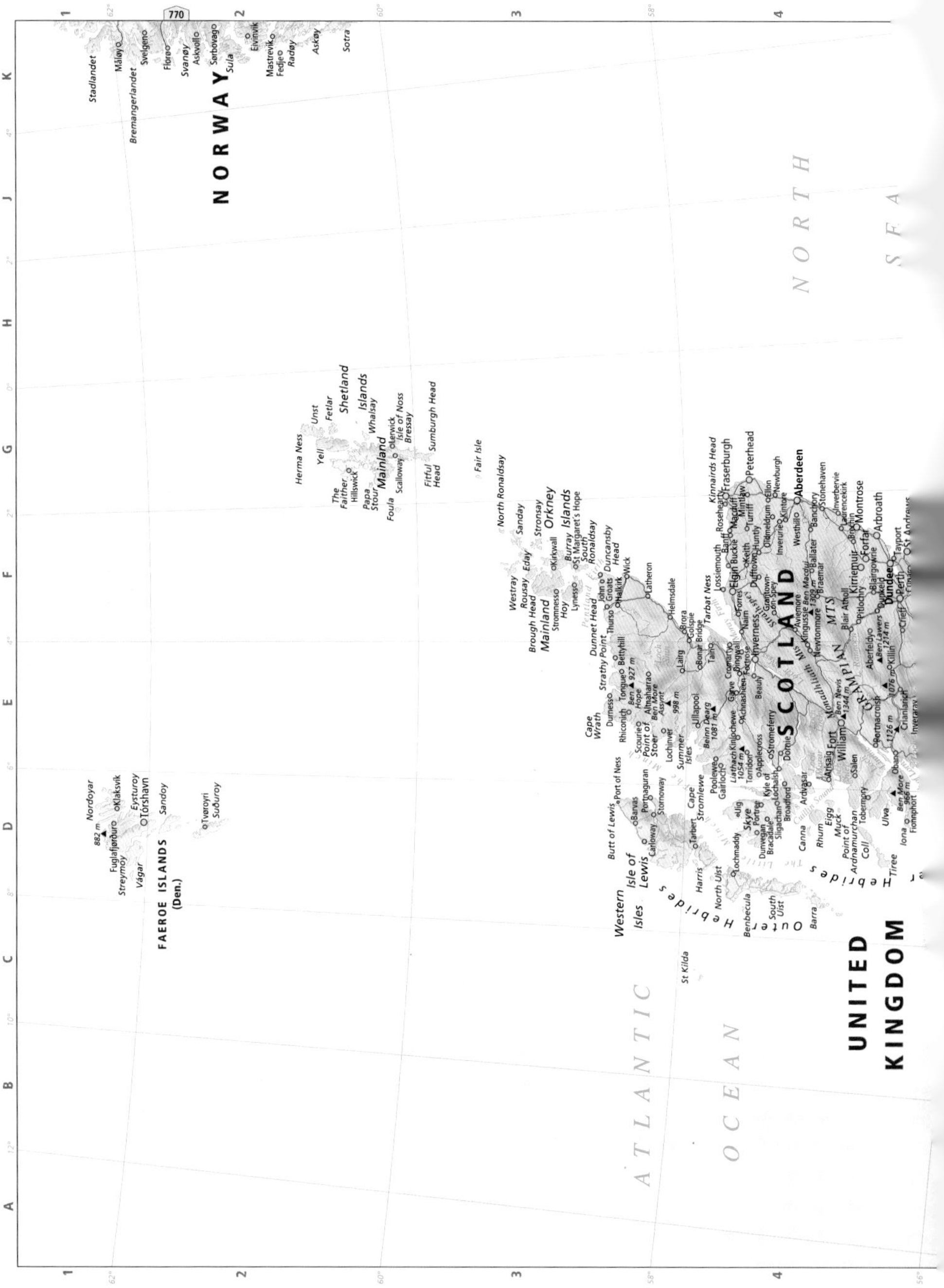
770
NORWAY
Stadlandet
Måløy
Bremangerlandet
Svelgen
Florø
Svanøy
Askvoll
Sørbøvåg
Sula
Eivinvik
Mastrevik
Fedje
Radøy
Askøy
Sotra
NORTH
SEA
Shetland Islands
Unst
Fetlar
Yell
Herma Ness
Whalsay
Lerwick
Isle of Noss
Bressay
Sumburgh Head
Mainland
The Faither
Hillswick
Papa Stour
Scalloway
Foula
Fitful Head
Fair Isle
North Ronaldsay
Sanday
Orkney Islands
Stronsay
Eday
Westray
Rousay
Kirkwall
Burray
St Margaret's Hope
South Ronaldsay
Duncansby Head
Brough Head
Mainland
Stromness
Hoy
Lyness
John o' Groats
Halkirk
Wick
Dunnet Head
Thurso
Latheron
Helmsdale
Brora
Golspie
Tarbat Ness
Lossiemouth
Kinnairds Head
Fraserburgh
Peterhead
Aberdeen
Stonehaven
Montrose
Arbroath
Dundee
Perth
St Andrews
SCOTLAND
GRAMPIAN MTS
Ben Nevis 1344 m
Fort William
Inverness
Cape Wrath
Strathy Point
Tongue
Bettyhill
Ben Hope 927 m
Durness
Lairg
Bonar Bridge
Tain
Ullapool
Lochinver
Summer Isles
Stornoway
Port of Ness
Butt of Lewis
Isle of Lewis
Western Isles
Harris
North Uist
Benbecula
South Uist
Barra
Outer Hebrides
Skye
Portree
Kyle of Lochalsh
Rhum
Eigg
Muck
Canna
Coll
Tiree
Tobermory
Ulva
Iona
Oban
Ben More 966 m
Crianlarich
Killin
Aberfeldy
Pitlochry
Blair Atholl
Kingussie
Aviemore
Newtonmore
Braemar
Ballater
Banchory
Forfar
Kirriemuir
Brechin
Huntly
Keith
Elgin
Buckie
Banff
Macduff
Nairn
Forres
Dingwall
Cromarty
St Kilda
FAEROE ISLANDS (Den.)
Nordoyar
Klaksvik
Eysturoy
Tórshavn
Sandoy
Tvøroyri
Suðuroy
Vágar
Streymoy
Fuglafjørður
882 m
ATLANTIC
OCEAN
UNITED KINGDOM

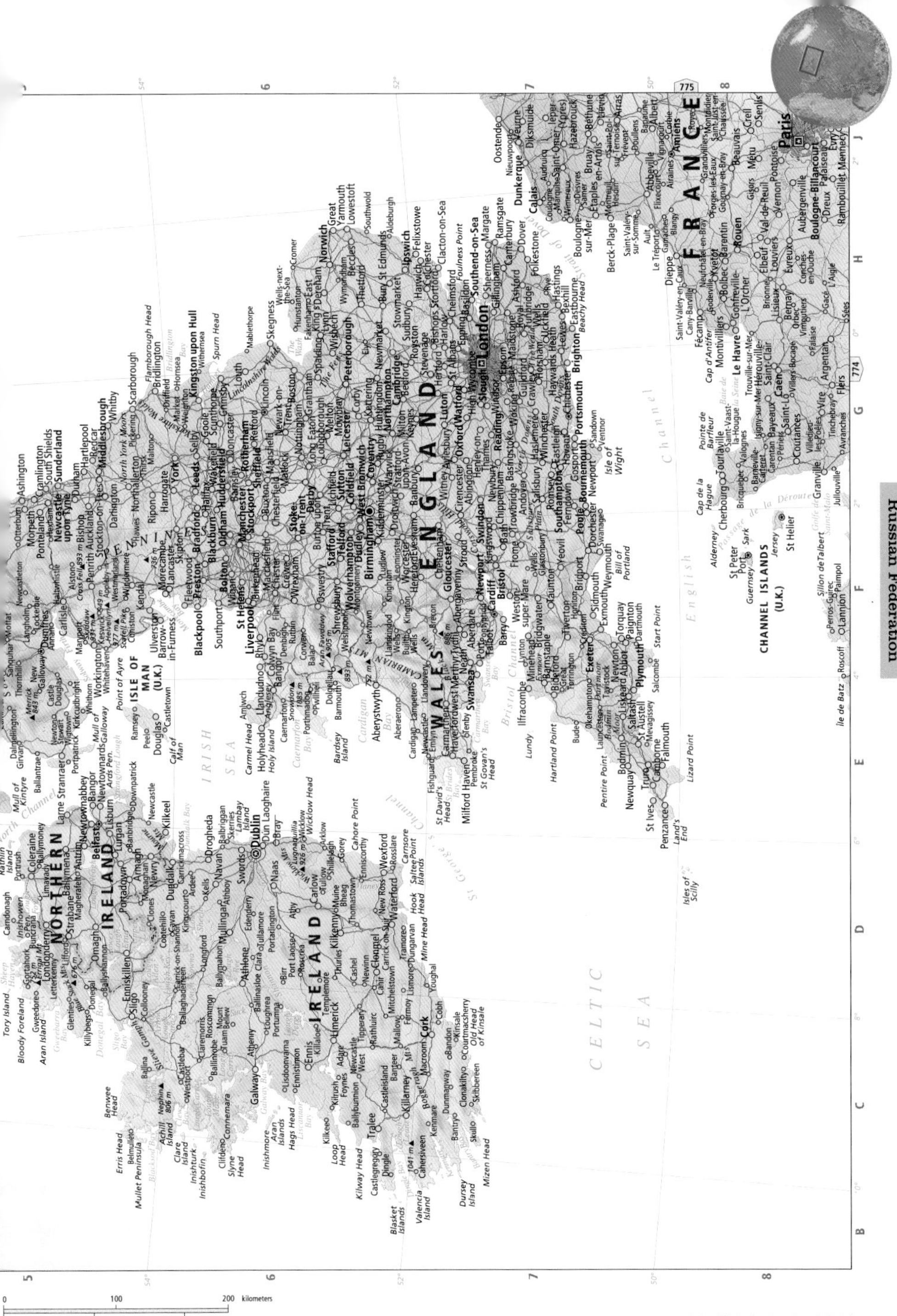
NORTHERN IRELAND
IRELAND
ENGLAND
WALES
FRANCE
ISLE OF MAN (U.K.)
CHANNEL ISLANDS (U.K.)
IRISH SEA
CELTIC SEA
English Channel
St George's Channel
Bristol Channel
North Channel
Strait of Dover
Cardigan Bay
Donegal Bay
Galway Bay
Dublin
Belfast
London
Paris
Birmingham
Cardiff
Cork
Galway
Limerick
Waterford
Wexford
Londonderry
Coleraine
Armagh
Newry
Dundalk
Drogheda
Sligo
Athlone
Kilkenny
Tralee
Killarney
Ennis
Liverpool
Manchester
Leeds
Sheffield
Bradford
York
Kingston upon Hull
Newcastle upon Tyne
Sunderland
Middlesbrough
Carlisle
Blackpool
Preston
Nottingham
Leicester
Coventry
Stoke-on-Trent
Derby
Norwich
Ipswich
Cambridge
Northampton
Peterborough
Oxford
Reading
Southampton
Portsmouth
Bournemouth
Brighton
Exeter
Plymouth
Bristol
Gloucester
Swansea
Newport
Swindon
Southend-on-Sea
Dover
Canterbury
Douglas
St Helier
St Peter Port
Calais
Dunkerque
Boulogne-sur-Mer
Amiens
Rouen
Le Havre
Caen
Cherbourg
Beauvais
Oostende
Isle of Wight
Isles of Scilly
Land's End
Lizard Point
Start Point
Flamborough Head
Spurn Head
Mizen Head
Malin Head
Wicklow Head
Carnsore Point
Jersey
Guernsey
Alderney
Sark
54°
52°
50°
0°
2°
4°
6°
8°
10°
B
C
D
E
F
G
H
J
5
6
7
8
774
775
0 50 100 miles
0 100 200 kilometers

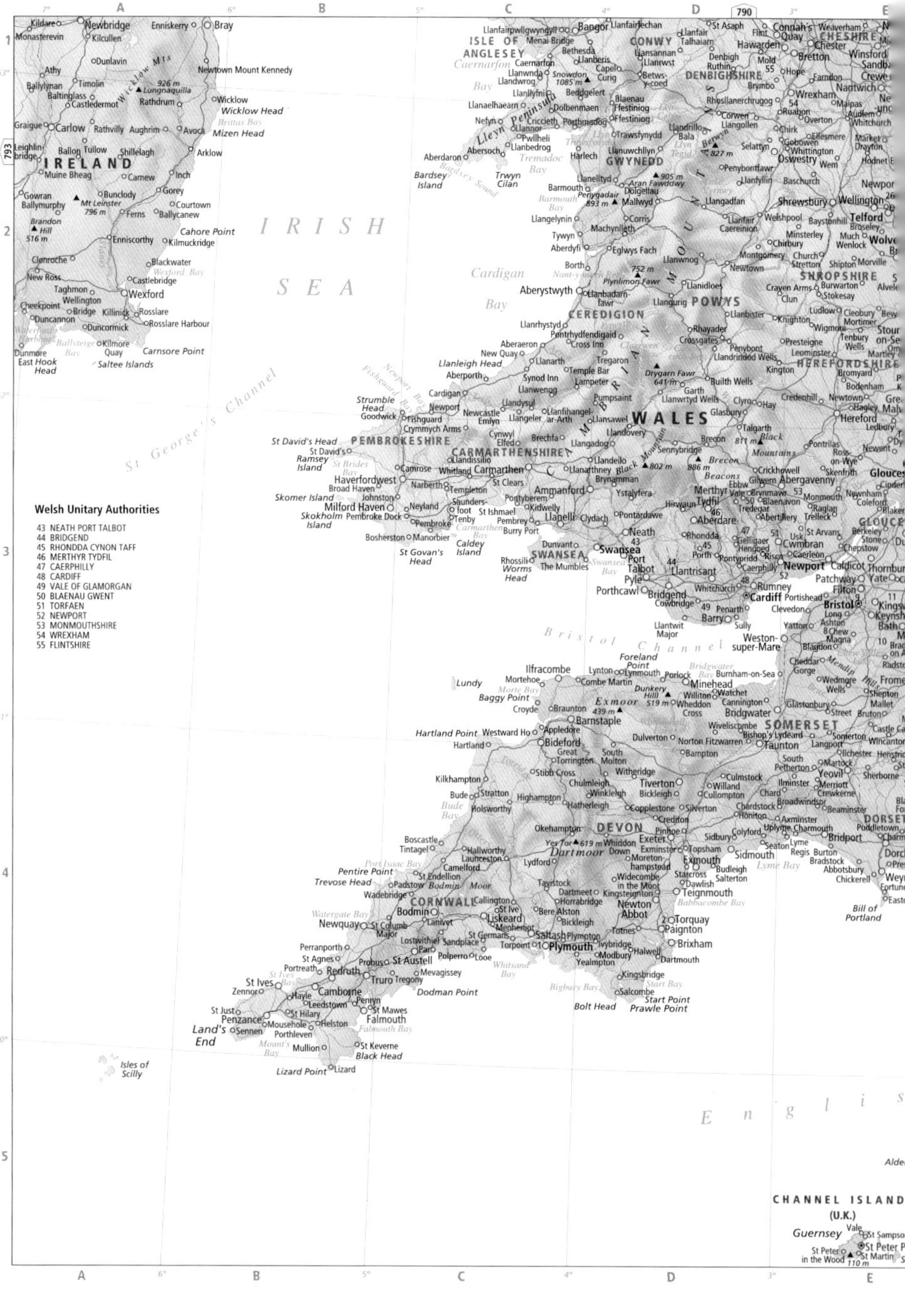
Welsh Unitary Authorities
43 NEATH PORT TALBOT
44 BRIDGEND
45 RHONDDA CYNON TAFF
46 MERTHYR TYDFIL
47 CAERPHILLY
48 CARDIFF
49 VALE OF GLAMORGAN
50 BLAENAU GWENT
51 TORFAEN
52 NEWPORT
53 MONMOUTHSHIRE
54 WREXHAM
55 FLINTSHIRE
IRELAND
WALES
IRISH SEA
St George's Channel
Bristol Channel
ISLE OF ANGLESEY
CONWY
DENBIGHSHIRE
GWYNEDD
POWYS
CEREDIGION
PEMBROKESHIRE
CARMARTHENSHIRE
SWANSEA
SHROPSHIRE
HEREFORDSHIRE
SOMERSET
DEVON
CORNWALL
DORSET
CHESHIRE
Cardigan Bay
CAMBRIAN MOUNTAINS
Exmoor
Dartmoor
Isles of Scilly
Land's End
Lizard Point
Lundy
CHANNEL ISLANDS (U.K.)
Guernsey
St Peter Port
Alderney
Sark
790
793

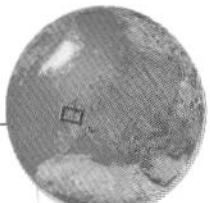

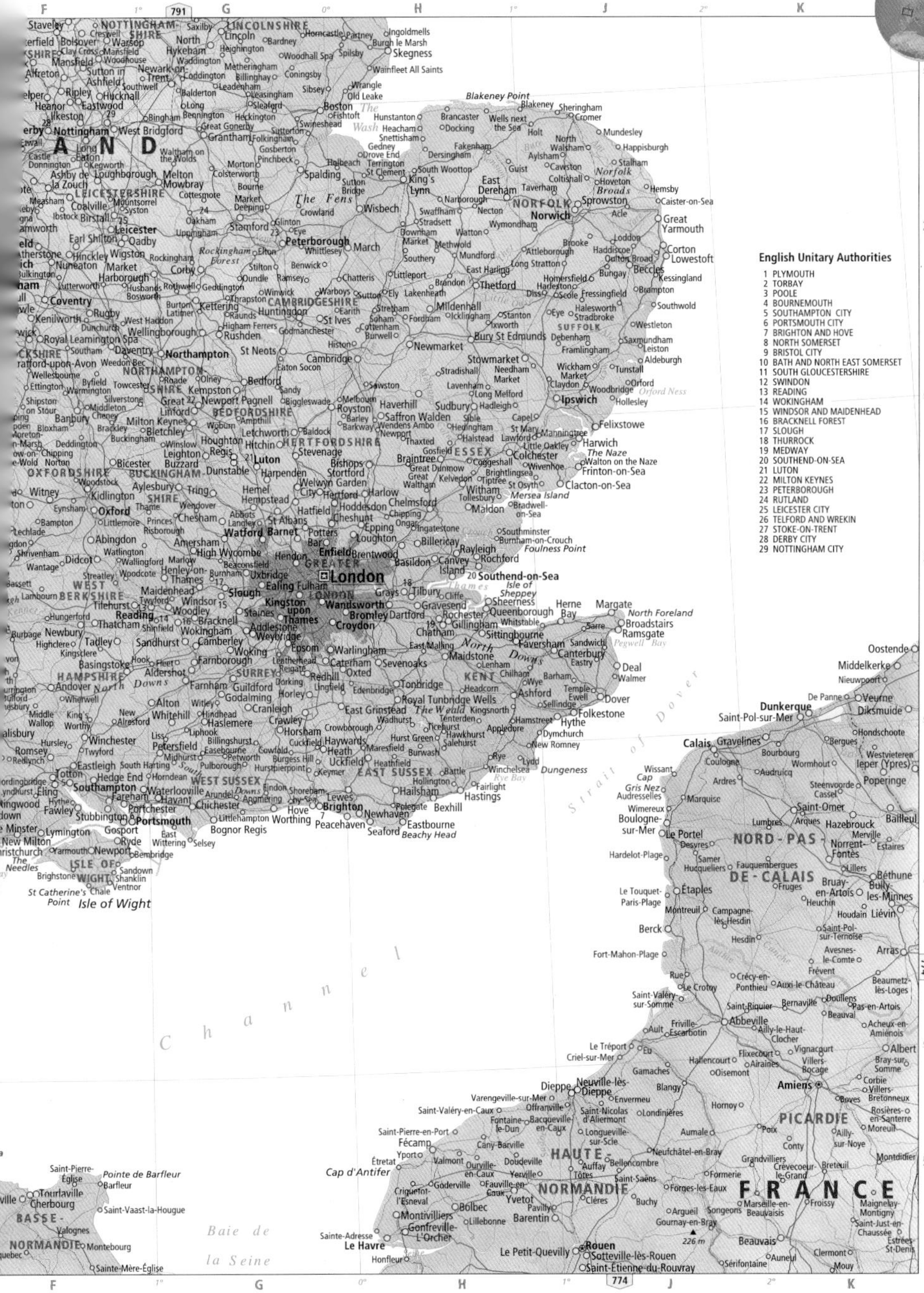

0 50 100 kilometers
0 25 50 miles

Europe and the Russian Federation

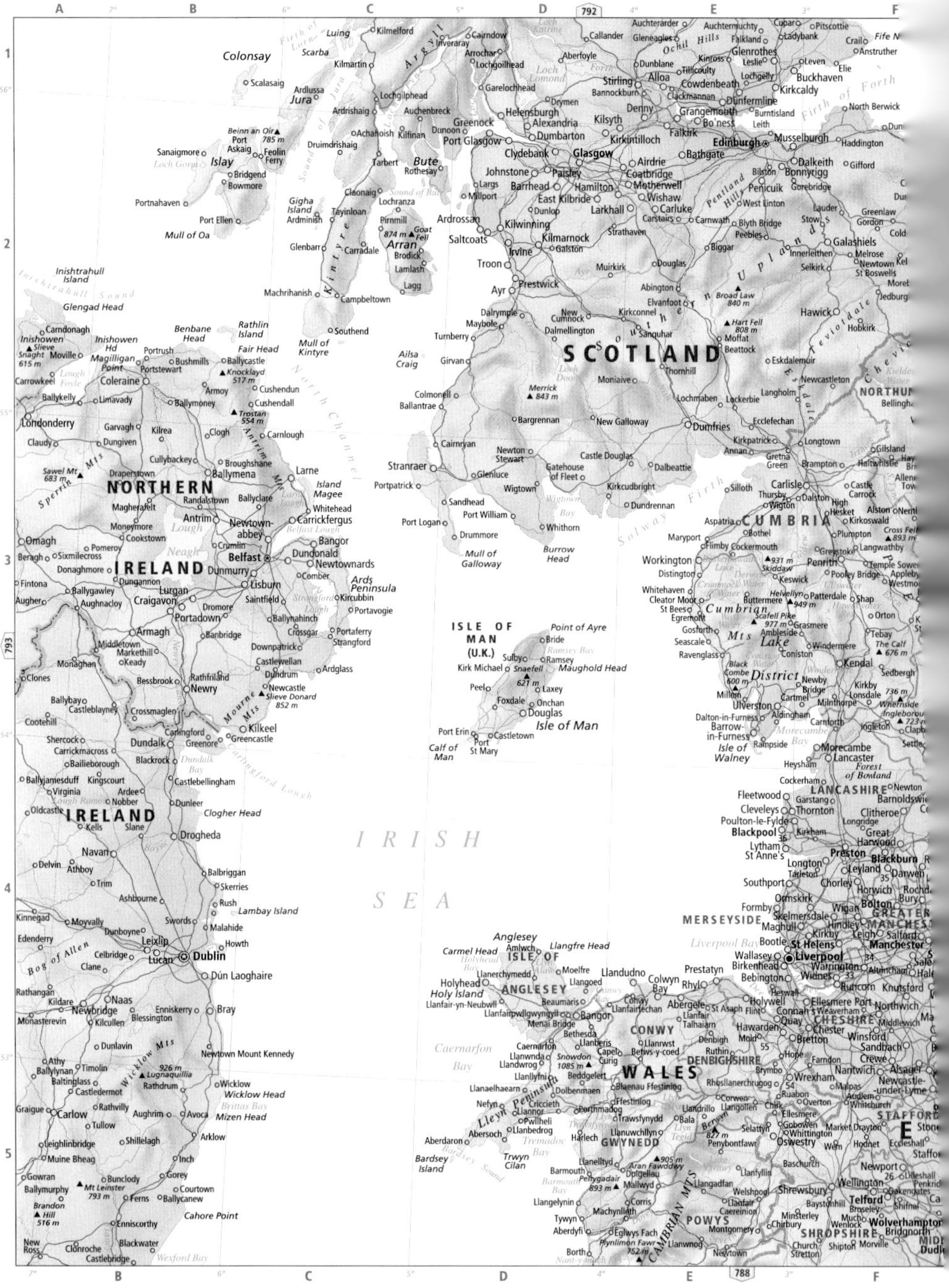

792
793
788
SCOTLAND
NORTHERN IRELAND
IRELAND
WALES
CUMBRIA
LANCASHIRE
MERSEYSIDE
GREATER MANCHESTER
CHESHIRE
DENBIGHSHIRE
CONWY
GWYNEDD
POWYS
SHROPSHIRE
ISLE OF ANGLESEY
ISLE OF MAN (U.K.)
IRISH SEA
North Channel
Solway Firth
Firth of Forth
Firth of Lorne
Sound of Jura
Liverpool Bay
Morecambe Bay
Cardigan Bay
Caernarfon Bay
Tremadoc Bay
Dundalk Bay
Carlingford Lough
Belfast Lough
Lough Neagh
Lough Foyle
Strangford Lough
Wexford Bay
Brittas Bay
Loch Lomond
Colonsay
Jura
Islay
Arran
Bute
Kintyre
Mull of Kintyre
Mull of Oa
Mull of Galloway
Ailsa Craig
Rathlin Island
Inishtrahull Island
Glengad Head
Fair Head
Benbane Head
Island Magee
Ards Peninsula
Lambay Island
Clogher Head
Wicklow Head
Mizen Head
Cahore Point
Point of Ayre
Maughold Head
Calf of Man
Isle of Walney
Anglesey
Holy Island
Carmel Head
Llangfre Head
Lleyn Peninsula
Bardsey Island
Trwyn Cilan
Southern Uplands
Cumbrian Mts
Lake District
Cambrian Mts
Mourne Mts
Antrim Mts
Sperrin Mts
Wicklow Mts
Bog of Allen
Forest of Bowland
Ochil Hills
Pentland Hills
Edinburgh
Glasgow
Stirling
Dumfries
Carlisle
Belfast
Dublin
Londonderry
Liverpool
Manchester
Preston
Blackpool
Lancaster
Kendal
Douglas
Ayr
Kilmarnock
Greenock
Paisley
Stranraer
Newry
Armagh
Dundalk
Drogheda
Bangor
Chester
Wrexham
Shrewsbury
Telford
Wolverhampton
Snowdon 1085 m
Scafell Pike 977 m
Helvellyn 949 m
Skiddaw 931 m
Merrick 843 m
Snaefell 621 m
Slieve Donard 852 m
Lugnaquillia 926 m
Goat Fell 874 m
Broad Law 840 m
Hart Fell 808 m
Trostan 554 m
Knocklayd 517 m
Aran Fawddwy 905 m
Cadair Idris 893 m
Plynlimon Fawr 752 m
Mt Leinster 793 m

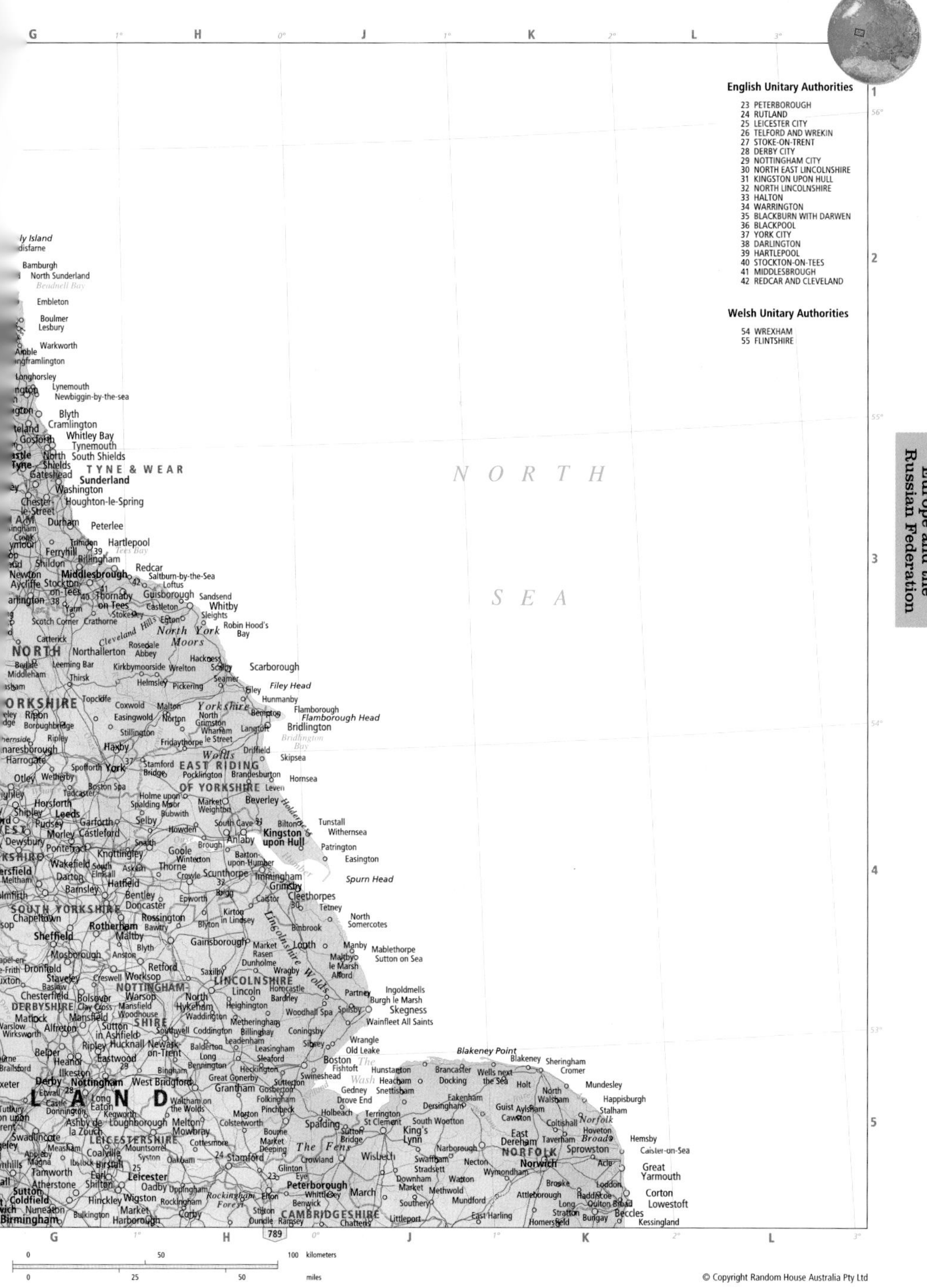
English Unitary Authorities
23 PETERBOROUGH
24 RUTLAND
25 LEICESTER CITY
26 TELFORD AND WREKIN
27 STOKE-ON-TRENT
28 DERBY CITY
29 NOTTINGHAM CITY
30 NORTH EAST LINCOLNSHIRE
31 KINGSTON UPON HULL
32 NORTH LINCOLNSHIRE
33 HALTON
34 WARRINGTON
35 BLACKBURN WITH DARWEN
36 BLACKPOOL
37 YORK CITY
38 DARLINGTON
39 HARTLEPOOL
40 STOCKTON-ON-TEES
41 MIDDLESBROUGH
42 REDCAR AND CLEVELAND
Welsh Unitary Authorities
54 WREXHAM
55 FLINTSHIRE
NORTH SEA
TYNE & WEAR
NORTH YORKSHIRE
EAST RIDING OF YORKSHIRE
SOUTH YORKSHIRE
LINCOLNSHIRE
NOTTINGHAMSHIRE
DERBYSHIRE
LEICESTERSHIRE
CAMBRIDGESHIRE
NORFOLK
Bamburgh
North Sunderland
Embleton
Boulmer
Lesbury
Warkworth
Amble
Longhorsley
Lynemouth
Newbiggin-by-the-sea
Blyth
Cramlington
Whitley Bay
Tynemouth
South Shields
Gosforth
Gateshead
Sunderland
Washington
Houghton-le-Spring
Durham
Peterlee
Hartlepool
Redcar
Saltburn-by-the-Sea
Loftus
Middlesbrough
Guisborough
Sandsend
Whitby
Robin Hood's Bay
North York Moors
Cleveland Hills
Northallerton
Scarborough
Filey Head
Filey
Hunmanby
Flamborough
Flamborough Head
Bridlington
Bridlington Bay
Skipsea
Hornsea
Driffield
York
Leeds
Beverley
Kingston upon Hull
Tunstall
Withernsea
Patrington
Easington
Spurn Head
Humber
Goole
Scunthorpe
Immingham
Grimsby
Cleethorpes
Tetney
North Somercotes
Doncaster
Rotherham
Sheffield
Gainsborough
Louth
Mablethorpe
Sutton on Sea
Lincolnshire Wolds
Lincoln
Ingoldmells
Burgh le Marsh
Skegness
Wainfleet All Saints
Wrangle
Old Leake
Boston
The Wash
Blakeney Point
Blakeney
Sheringham
Cromer
Mundesley
Happisburgh
Stalham
Hunstanton
Heacham
Wells next the Sea
King's Lynn
Norwich
Hemsby
Caister-on-Sea
Great Yarmouth
Corton
Lowestoft
Beccles
Kessingland
The Broads
The Fens
Spalding
Wisbech
Peterborough
March
Grantham
Nottingham
Derby
Leicester
Birmingham
Stamford
Oakham
Melton Mowbray
Loughborough
Rockingham Forest
Sutton Coldfield
Nuneaton
Hinckley
Market Harborough
G H J K L
0° 1° 2° 3°
1 2 3 4 5
54° 55° 56° 53°
789
0 50 100 kilometers
0 25 50 miles

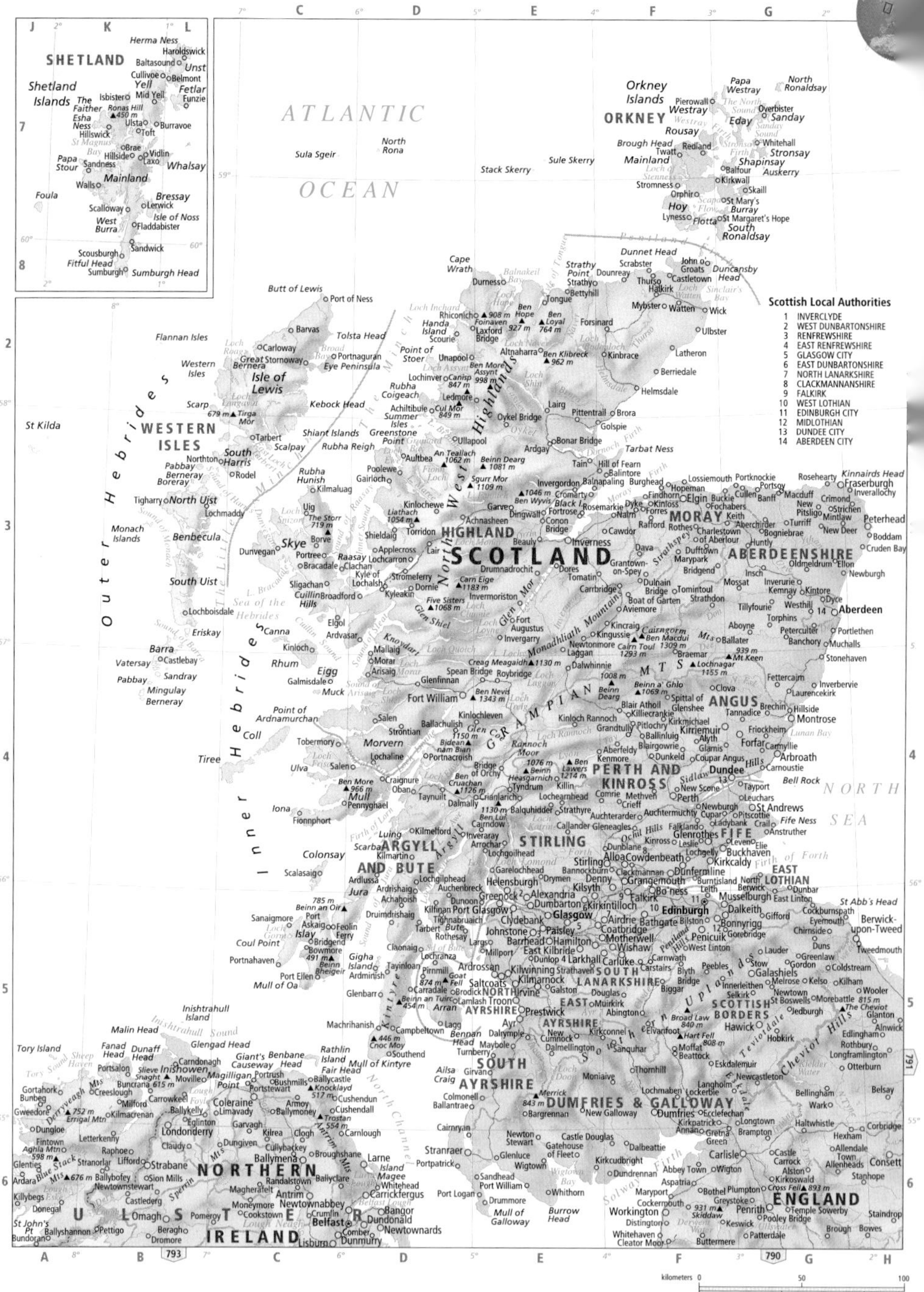
SHETLAND
Shetland Islands
Herma Ness
Haroldswick
Baltasound
Unst
Cullivoe
Belmont
Yell
Fetlar
Funzie
Isbister
Mid Yell
The Faither
Ronas Hill 450 m
Esha Ness
Ulsta
Burravoe
Hillswick
Toft
St Magnus Bay
Brae
Papa Stour
Hillside
Vidlin
Sandness
Laxo
Whalsay
Mainland
Walls
Foula
Bressay
Scalloway
Lerwick
Isle of Noss
West Burra
Fladdabister
Sandwick
Scousburgh
Fitful Head
Sumburgh
Sumburgh Head
ATLANTIC
OCEAN
Sula Sgeir
North Rona
Stack Skerry
Sule Skerry
Orkney Islands
ORKNEY
Papa Westray
North Ronaldsay
Pierowall
Westray
Overbister
Sanday
Eday
Rousay
Brough Head
Redland
Twatt
Whitehall
Stronsay
Mainland
Shapinsay
Auskerry
Balfour
Kirkwall
Stromness
Skaill
Orphir
Hoy
St Mary's
Burray
Lyness
Flotta
St Margaret's Hope
South Ronaldsay
Pentland Firth
Dunnet Head
John o' Groats
Duncansby Head
Scrabster
Thurso
Castletown
Halkirk
Wick
Cape Wrath
Durness
Strathy Point
Dounreay
Strathy
Bettyhill
Tongue
Ben Hope 927 m
Ben Loyal 764 m
Forsinard
Scottish Local Authorities
1 INVERCLYDE
2 WEST DUNBARTONSHIRE
3 RENFREWSHIRE
4 EAST RENFREWSHIRE
5 GLASGOW CITY
6 EAST DUNBARTONSHIRE
7 NORTH LANARKSHIRE
8 CLACKMANNANSHIRE
9 FALKIRK
10 WEST LOTHIAN
11 EDINBURGH CITY
12 MIDLOTHIAN
13 DUNDEE CITY
14 ABERDEEN CITY
Butt of Lewis
Port of Ness
Barvas
Tolsta Head
Flannan Isles
Carloway
Great Bernera
Stornoway
Portnaguran
Eye Peninsula
Western Isles
Isle of Lewis
Outer Hebrides
WESTERN ISLES
St Kilda
Scarp
Tirga Mor 679 m
Tarbert
Scalpay
South Harris
Northton
Pabbay
Berneray
Boreray
Rodel
North Uist
Lochmaddy
Tigharry
Monach Islands
Benbecula
South Uist
Lochboisdale
Eriskay
Barra
Castlebay
Vatersay
Sandray
Pabbay
Mingulay
Berneray
The Minch
The Little Minch
Sea of the Hebrides
Inner Hebrides
Skye
Dunvegan
Uig
The Storr 719 m
Portree
Raasay
Broadford
Cuillin Hills
Canna
Rhum
Eigg
Muck
Coll
Tiree
Mull
Ben More 966 m
Iona
Colonsay
Jura
Islay
Gigha Island
Kintyre
Mull of Kintyre
Campbeltown
HIGHLAND
SCOTLAND
North West Highlands
Ullapool
Inverness
Fort William
Ben Nevis 1343 m
Grampian Mts
Monadhliath Mountains
Cairngorm Mts
Ben Macdui 1309 m
MORAY
ABERDEENSHIRE
Aberdeen
Peterhead
Fraserburgh
Kinnairds Head
ANGUS
Dundee
Montrose
Arbroath
PERTH AND KINROSS
Perth
St Andrews
FIFE
STIRLING
Stirling
ARGYLL AND BUTE
Oban
Glasgow
Edinburgh
EAST LOTHIAN
Firth of Forth
NORTH SEA
Paisley
Greenock
Kilmarnock
NORTH AYRSHIRE
EAST AYRSHIRE
SOUTH AYRSHIRE
Ayr
Arran
SOUTH LANARKSHIRE
SCOTTISH BORDERS
Southern Uplands
Cheviot Hills
The Cheviot 815 m
DUMFRIES & GALLOWAY
Dumfries
Stranraer
Solway Firth
Carlisle
ENGLAND
Penrith
Workington
North Channel
NORTHERN IRELAND
ULSTER
IRELAND
Londonderry
Belfast
Larne
Antrim
Lough Neagh
Malin Head
Tory Island
Rathlin Island
kilometers 0 50 100
miles 0 25 50

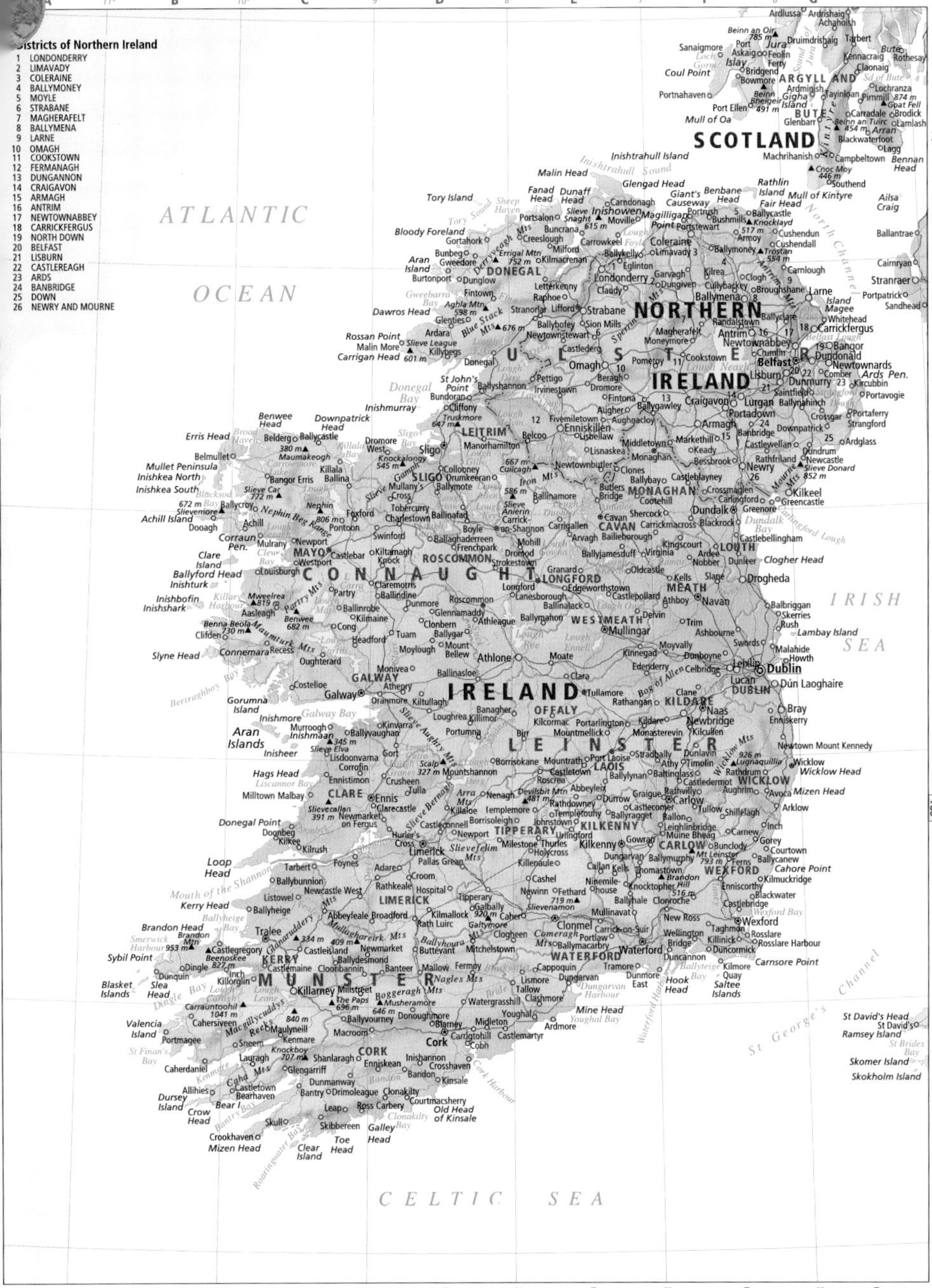

0 50 100 kilometers
0 25 50 miles

Europe and the Russian Federation

Africa

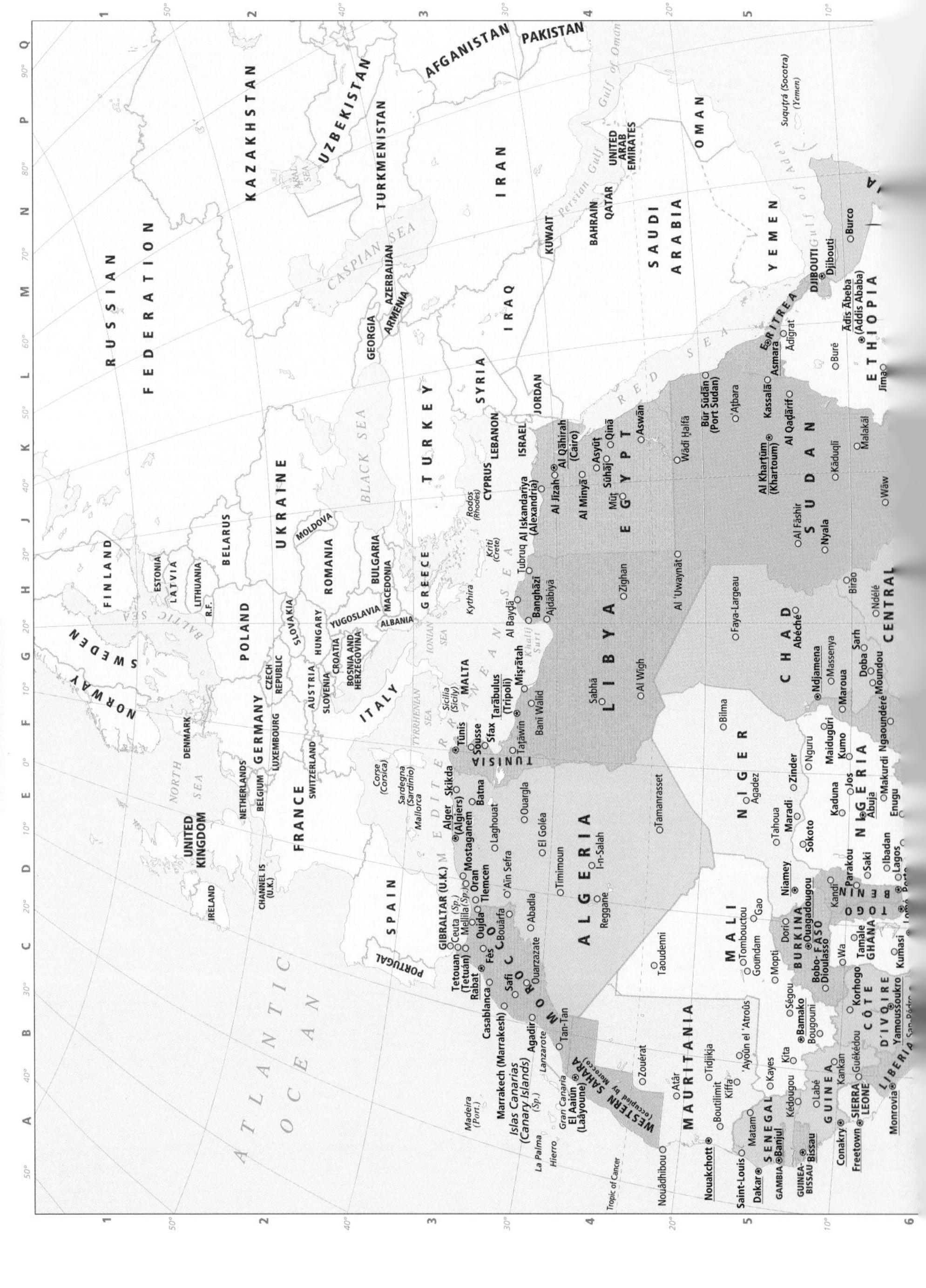
RUSSIAN FEDERATION
KAZAKHSTAN
UZBEKISTAN
TURKMENISTAN
AFGANISTAN
PAKISTAN
IRAN
IRAQ
KUWAIT
BAHRAIN
QATAR
UNITED ARAB EMIRATES
OMAN
SAUDI ARABIA
YEMEN
Suquţrá (Socotra) (Yemen)
Gulf of Oman
Persian Gulf
Gulf of Aden
CASPIAN SEA
ARAL SEA
GEORGIA
AZERBAIJAN
ARMENIA
SYRIA
JORDAN
ISRAEL
LEBANON
CYPRUS
TURKEY
BLACK SEA
UKRAINE
MOLDOVA
ROMANIA
BULGARIA
MACEDONIA
GREECE
ALBANIA
YUGOSLAVIA
BOSNIA AND HERZEGOVINA
CROATIA
SLOVENIA
HUNGARY
SLOVAKIA
AUSTRIA
CZECH REPUBLIC
POLAND
BELARUS
LITHUANIA
R.F.
LATVIA
ESTONIA
FINLAND
SWEDEN
NORWAY
BALTIC SEA
DENMARK
NORTH SEA
GERMANY
NETHERLANDS
BELGIUM
LUXEMBOURG
SWITZERLAND
FRANCE
ITALY
UNITED KINGDOM
IRELAND
CHANNEL IS (U.K.)
SPAIN
PORTUGAL
GIBRALTAR (U.K.)
Corse (Corsica)
Sardegna (Sardinia)
Mallorca
Sicilia (Sicily)
MALTA
Kriti (Crete)
Rodos (Rhodes)
Kythira
TYRRHENIAN SEA
IONIAN SEA
MEDITERRANEAN SEA
Khalij Surt
ATLANTIC OCEAN
Madeira (Port.)
Islas Canarias (Canary Islands) (Sp.)
La Palma
Hierro
Gran Canaria
Lanzarote
Tropic of Cancer
MOROCCO
Tetouan (Tetuán)
Rabat
Casablanca
Marrakech (Marrakesh)
Fès
Safi
Agadir
Ouarzazate
Oujda
Ceuta (Sp.)
Melilla (Sp.)
Bouârfa
ALGERIA
Alger (Algiers)
Oran
Mostaganem
Tlemcen
Skikda
Batna
Laghouat
Aïn Sefra
Abadla
Ouargla
El Goléa
Timimoun
Reggane
I-n-Salah
Tamanrasset
TUNISIA
Tūnis
Sousse
Sfax
Tatāwīn
LIBYA
Ţarābulus (Tripoli)
Mişrātah
Banī Walīd
Sabhā
Al Wīgh
Al Bayḑā'
Banghāzī
Ajdābiyā
Tubruq
Zīghan
Al 'Uwaynāt
EGYPT
Al Qāhirah (Cairo)
Al Iskandarīya (Alexandria)
Al Jīzah
Al Minyā
Asyūţ
Sūhāj
Qinā
Mūţ
Aswān
RED SEA
SUDAN
Wādī Ḩalfā
Būr Sūdān (Port Sudan)
'Aţbara
Al Kharţūm (Khartoum)
Kassalā
Al Qaḑārif
Al Fāshir
Nyala
Kādugli
Malakāl
Wāw
ERITREA
Asmara
Ādīgrat
DJIBOUTI
Djibouti
ETHIOPIA
Ādīs Ābeba (Addis Ababa)
Burē
Jīma
Burco
WESTERN SAHARA (occupied by Morocco)
El Aaiún (Laâyoune)
Tan-Tan
MAURITANIA
Nouakchott
Nouâdhibou
Atâr
Zouérat
Tidjikja
Boutilimit
Kiffa
'Ayoûn el 'Atroûs
SENEGAL
Dakar
Saint-Louis
Matam
Kédougou
GAMBIA
Banjul
GUINEA-BISSAU
Bissau
GUINEA
Conakry
Labé
Kankan
SIERRA LEONE
Freetown
LIBERIA
Monrovia
MALI
Kayes
Kita
Bamako
Bougouni
Ségou
Mopti
Tombouctou
Goundam
Gao
Taoudenni
BURKINA FASO
Ouagadougou
Bobo-Dioulasso
Dori
CÔTE D'IVOIRE
Korhogo
Yamoussoukro
GHANA
Tamale
Kumasi
Wa
TOGO
BENIN
Kandi
Parakou
NIGER
Niamey
Tahoua
Maradi
Zinder
Agadez
Bilma
Nguru
NIGERIA
Sokoto
Kaduna
Jos
Kano
Abuja
Makurdi
Enugu
Ibadan
Lagos
Saki
Maiduguri
Kumo
CHAD
Ndjamena
Faya-Largeau
Abéché
Massenya
Sarh
Doba
Moundou
Maroua
Ngaoundéré
Birao
Ndélé
CENTRAL

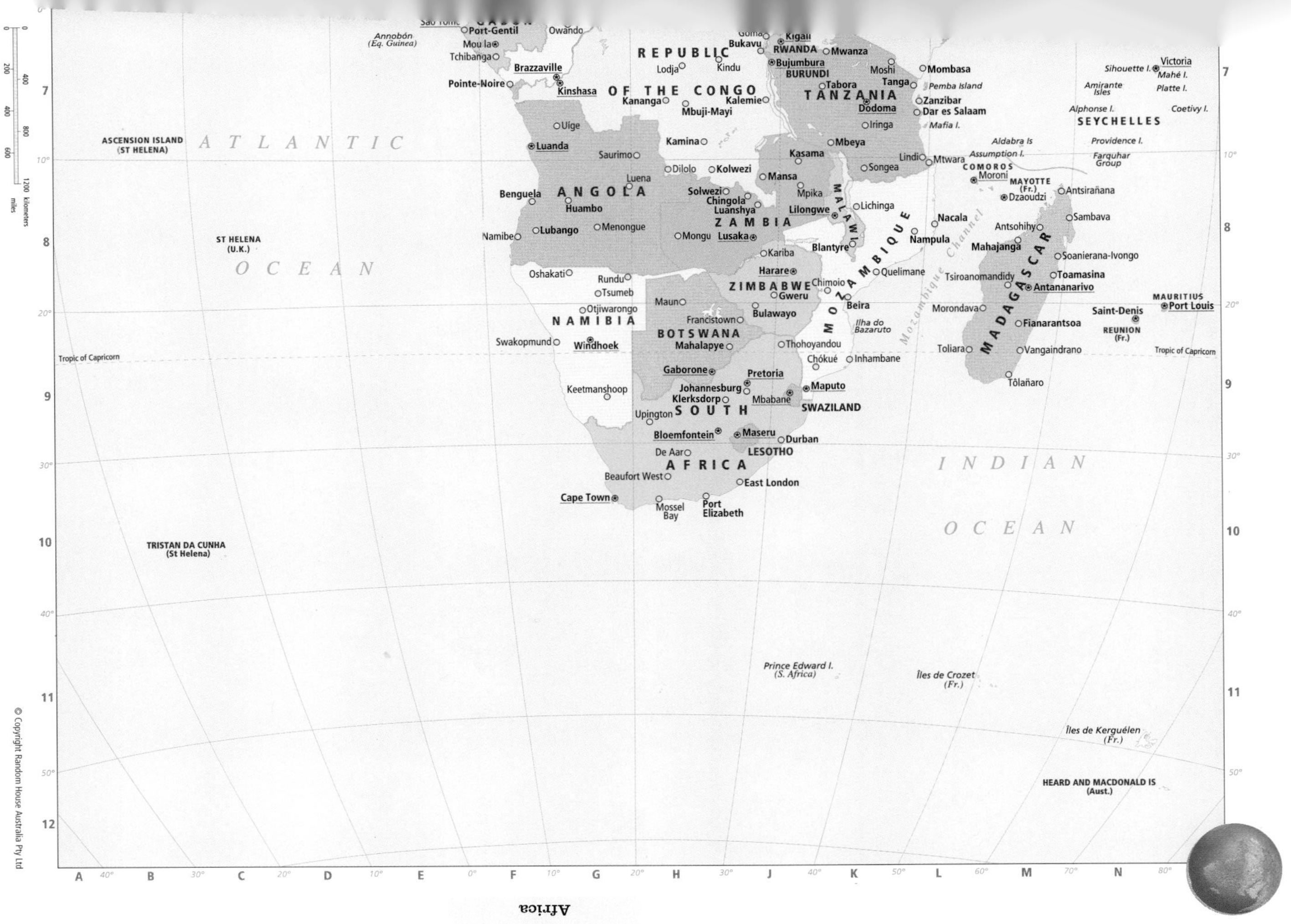
ATLANTIC OCEAN
INDIAN OCEAN
REPUBLIC OF THE CONGO
ANGOLA
ZAMBIA
NAMIBIA
BOTSWANA
ZIMBABWE
MOZAMBIQUE
MALAWI
TANZANIA
RWANDA
BURUNDI
SOUTH AFRICA
LESOTHO
SWAZILAND
MADAGASCAR
SEYCHELLES
COMOROS
MAYOTTE (Fr.)
MAURITIUS
REUNION (Fr.)
ASCENSION ISLAND (ST HELENA)
ST HELENA (U.K.)
TRISTAN DA CUNHA (St Helena)
Annobón (Eq. Guinea)
Prince Edward I. (S. Africa)
Îles de Crozet (Fr.)
Îles de Kerguélen (Fr.)
HEARD AND MACDONALD IS (Aust.)
Mozambique Channel
Tropic of Capricorn
Port-Gentil
Mou la
Tchibanga
Owando
Brazzaville
Pointe-Noire
Kinshasa
Kananga
Lodja
Kindu
Bukavu
Goma
Kigali
Bujumbura
Mwanza
Kalemie
Mbuji-Mayi
Kamina
Uíge
Luanda
Saurimo
Dilolo
Kolwezi
Luena
Benguela
Huambo
Lubango
Menongue
Namibe
Solwezi
Chingola
Luanshya
Mansa
Kasama
Mpika
Lilongwe
Lusaka
Mongu
Kariba
Lichinga
Blantyre
Harare
Gweru
Bulawayo
Chimoio
Beira
Quelimane
Nampula
Nacala
Oshakati
Rundu
Tsumeb
Otjiwarongo
Windhoek
Swakopmund
Keetmanshoop
Maun
Francistown
Mahalapye
Gaborone
Thohoyandou
Chókué
Inhambane
Ilha do Bazaruto
Pretoria
Johannesburg
Klerksdorp
Mbabane
Maputo
Upington
Bloemfontein
Maseru
Durban
De Aar
Beaufort West
East London
Cape Town
Mossel Bay
Port Elizabeth
Moshi
Tanga
Tabora
Dodoma
Iringa
Mbeya
Songea
Lindi
Mtwara
Mombasa
Pemba Island
Zanzibar
Dar es Salaam
Mafia I.
Aldabra Is
Assumption I.
Moroni
Dzaoudzi
Antsirañana
Sambava
Antsohihy
Mahajanga
Soanierana-Ivongo
Tsiroanomandidy
Toamasina
Antananarivo
Morondava
Fianarantsoa
Toliara
Vangaindrano
Tôlañaro
Saint-Denis
Port Louis
Sihouette I.
Victoria
Mahé I.
Platte I.
Amirante Isles
Alphonse I.
Coetivy I.
Providence I.
Farquhar Group
A B C D E F G H J K L M N
7 8 9 10 11 12
0 400 800 1200 kilometers
0 200 400 600 miles

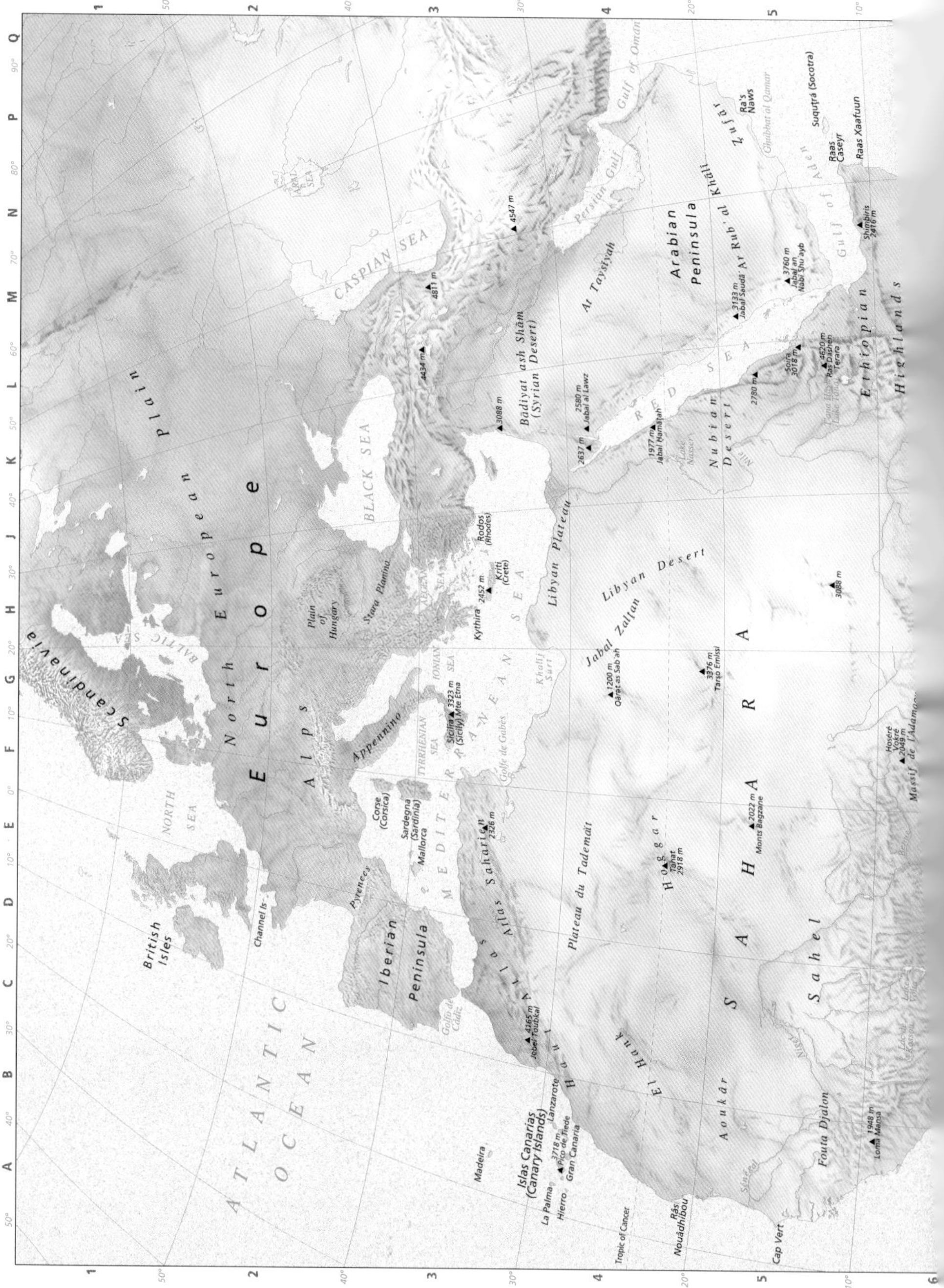
ATLANTIC OCEAN
British Isles
Channel Is.
NORTH SEA
Scandinavia
BALTIC SEA
North European Plain
Europe
Alps
Pyrenees
Iberian Peninsula
Golfo de Cádiz
Corse (Corsica)
Sardegna (Sardinia)
Mallorca
Appennino
TYRRHENIAN SEA
IONIAN SEA
Sicilia (Sicily)
3323 m Mte Etna
Plain of Hungary
Stara Planina
AEGEAN SEA
Kythira
2452 m
Kriti (Crete)
Rodos (Rhodes)
BLACK SEA
CASPIAN SEA
ARAL SEA
MEDITERRANEAN SEA
Golfe de Gabès
Khalīj Surt
Libyan Plateau
Libyan Desert
Jabal Zalṭan
1200 m Qārat as Sab'ah
Bādiyat ash Shām (Syrian Desert)
At Taysīyah
Arabian Peninsula
Ar Rub' al Khālī
Persian Gulf
Gulf of Oman
Ẓufār
Ra's Naws
Ghubbat al Qamar
Suquṭrā (Socotra)
Raas Caseyr
Raas Xaafuun
Gulf of Aden
Shimbiris 2416 m
RED SEA
2637 m
2580 m Jabal al Lawz
1977 m Jabal Ḩamāṭah
3088 m
4434 m
4811 m
4547 m
3133 m Jabal Sawdā'
3760 m Jabal an Nabī Shu'ayb
2780 m
Soira 3018 m
4620 m Ras Dashen Terara
Lake Nasser
Nubian Desert
Nile
Ethiopian Highlands
Atlas Saharien
2326 m
Haut Atlas
4165 m Jebel Toubkal
Plateau du Tademaït
Hoggar
Tahat 2918 m
2022 m Monts Bagzane
3376 m Tarso Emissi
3088 m
SAHARA
El Hank
Aoukâr
Sahel
Fouta Djalon
1948 m Loma Mansa
Niger
Sénégal
Massif de l'Adamaoua
Hosséré Vokré 2049 m
Madeira
Islas Canarias (Canary Islands)
Lanzarote
3718 m Pico de Teide
Gran Canaria
La Palma
Hierro
Tropic of Cancer
Râs Nouâdhibou
Cap Vert

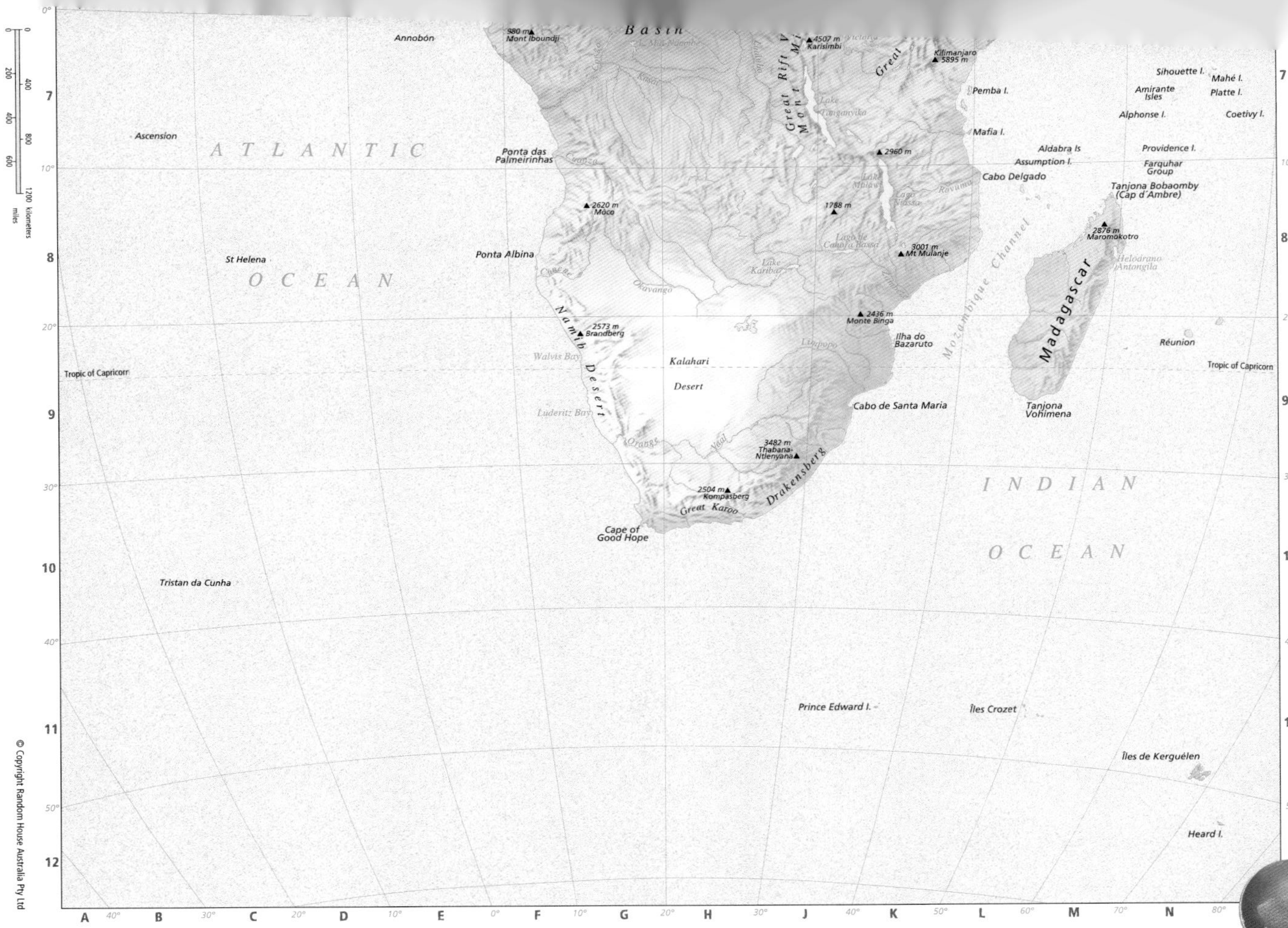
Annobón
Ascension
ATLANTIC OCEAN
St Helena
Tropic of Capricorn
Tristan da Cunha
Basin
980 m Mont Iboundji
Ponta das Palmeirinhas
Cuanza
2620 m Moco
Ponta Albina
Cunene
Okavango
Namib Desert
2573 m Brandberg
Walvis Bay
Luderitz Bay
Kalahari Desert
Orange
Vaal
2504 m Kompasberg
Great Karoo
Drakensberg
3482 m Thabana-Ntlenyana
Cape of Good Hope
Limpopo
Lake Kariba
Lago de Cahora Bassa
Zambezi
2436 m Monte Binga
Ilha do Bazaruto
Cabo de Santa Maria
3001 m Mt Mulanje
1788 m
Lake Malawi
Lago Niassa
Rovuma
2960 m
Lake Tanganyika
Great Rift Valley
4507 m Karisimbi
Kilimanjaro 5895 m
Great
Lualaba
Kasai
Pemba I.
Mafia I.
Cabo Delgado
Aldabra Is
Assumption I.
Mozambique Channel
Madagascar
2876 m Maromokotro
Tanjona Bobaomby (Cap d'Ambre)
Helodrano Antongila
Tanjona Vohimena
Sihouette I.
Mahé I.
Amirante Isles
Platte I.
Alphonse I.
Coetivy I.
Providence I.
Farquhar Group
Réunion
INDIAN OCEAN
Prince Edward I.
Îles Crozet
Îles de Kerguélen
Heard I.
0 200 400 600 miles
0 400 800 1200 kilometers
A B C D E F G H J K L M N
7 8 9 10 11 12

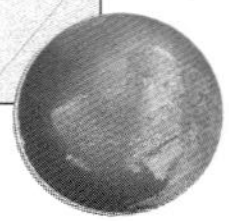

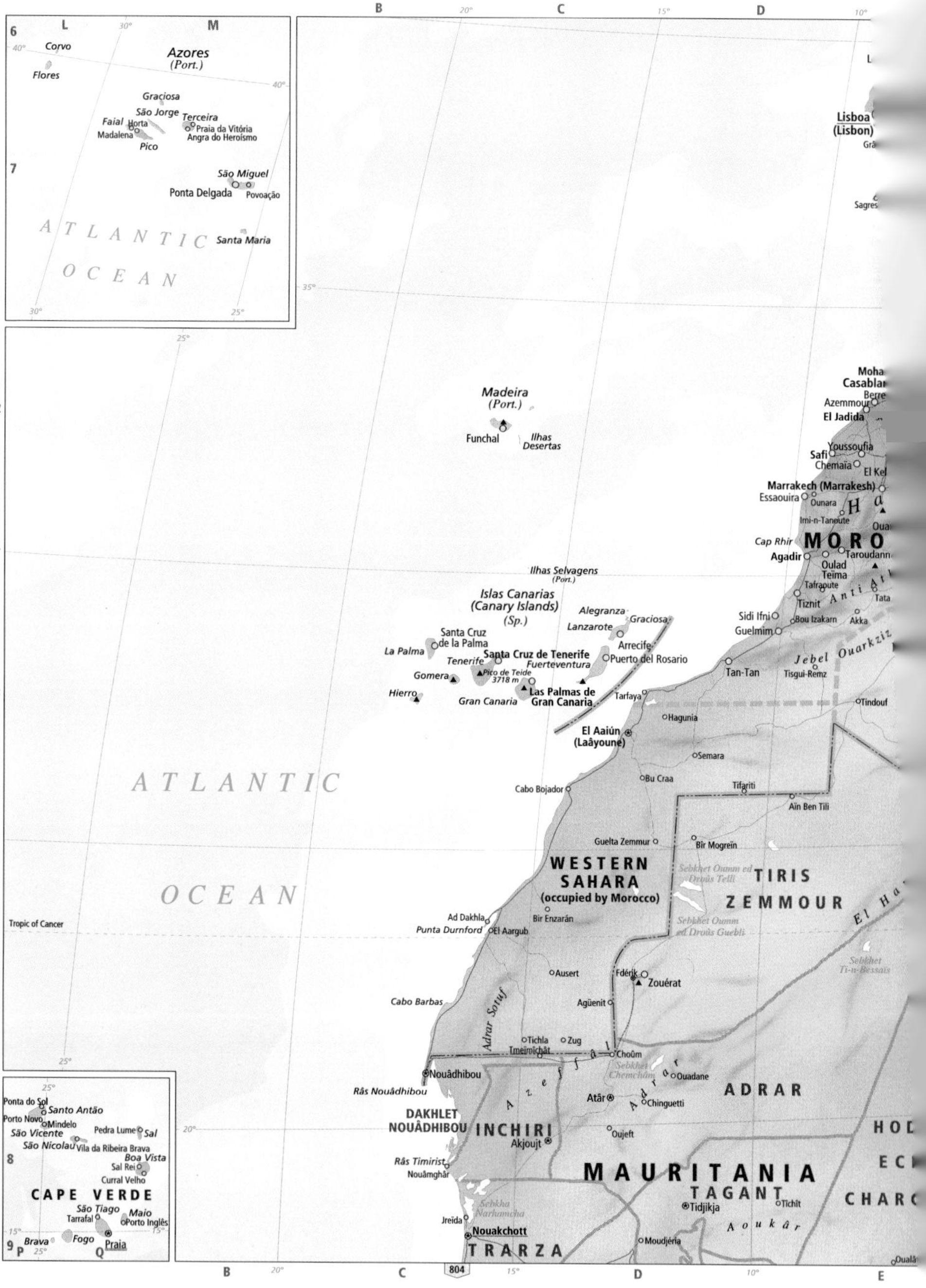
Azores
(Port.)
Corvo
Flores
Graciosa
São Jorge
Terceira
Faial
Horta
Madalena
Pico
Praia da Vitória
Angra do Heroísmo
São Miguel
Ponta Delgada
Povoação
Santa Maria
ATLANTIC
OCEAN
Madeira
(Port.)
Funchal
Ilhas
Desertas
Lisboa
(Lisbon)
Sagres
Ilhas Selvagens
(Port.)
Islas Canarias
(Canary Islands)
(Sp.)
Alegranza
Graciosa
Lanzarote
Arrecife
Puerto del Rosario
Santa Cruz
de la Palma
La Palma
Tenerife
Santa Cruz de Tenerife
Fuerteventura
Pico de Teide
3718 m
Gomera
Hierro
Gran Canaria
Las Palmas de
Gran Canaria
Azemmour
El Jadida
Youssoufia
Safi
Chemaïa
Marrakech (Marrakesh)
Essaouira
Ounara
Imi-n-Tanoute
Cap Rhir
MORO
Agadir
Taroudann
Oulad
Teïma
Tafraoute
Tiznit
Anti Atlas
Tata
Sidi Ifni
Bou Izakarn
Akka
Guelmim
Jebel Ouarkziz
Tan-Tan
Tisgui-Remz
Tarfaya
Tindouf
Hagunia
El Aaiún
(Laâyoune)
Semara
Bu Craa
Cabo Bojador
Tifariti
Aïn Ben Tili
ATLANTIC
Guelta Zemmur
Bir Mogreïn
WESTERN
SAHARA
(occupied by Morocco)
Sebkhet Oumm ed Droûs Telli
TIRIS
ZEMMOUR
OCEAN
Tropic of Cancer
Ad Dakhla
Bir Enzarán
Sebkhet Oumm ed Droûs Guebli
Punta Durnford
El Aargub
Sebkhet Ti-n-Bessaïs
Ausert
Fdérik
Zouérat
Cabo Barbas
Agüenit
Adrar Sotuf
Tichla
Zug
Tmeïmichât
Choûm
Nouâdhibou
Râs Nouâdhibou
Sebkhet Chemchâm
Ouadane
ADRAR
DAKHLET
NOUÂDHIBOU
Atâr
Chinguetti
INCHIRI
Akjoujt
Oujeft
Râs Timirist
Nouâmghâr
MAURITANIA
TAGANT
Tidjikja
Tîchît
Sebkha Narhamcha
Jreïda
Nouakchott
Aoukâr
Moudjéria
TRARZA
Ouâlâ
CHARC
Ponta do Sol
Santo Antão
Porto Novo
Mindelo
São Vicente
Pedra Lume
Sal
São Nicolau
Vila da Ribeira Brava
Boa Vista
Sal Rei
Curral Velho
CAPE VERDE
São Tiago
Maio
Tarrafal
Porto Inglês
Brava
Fogo
Praia
804

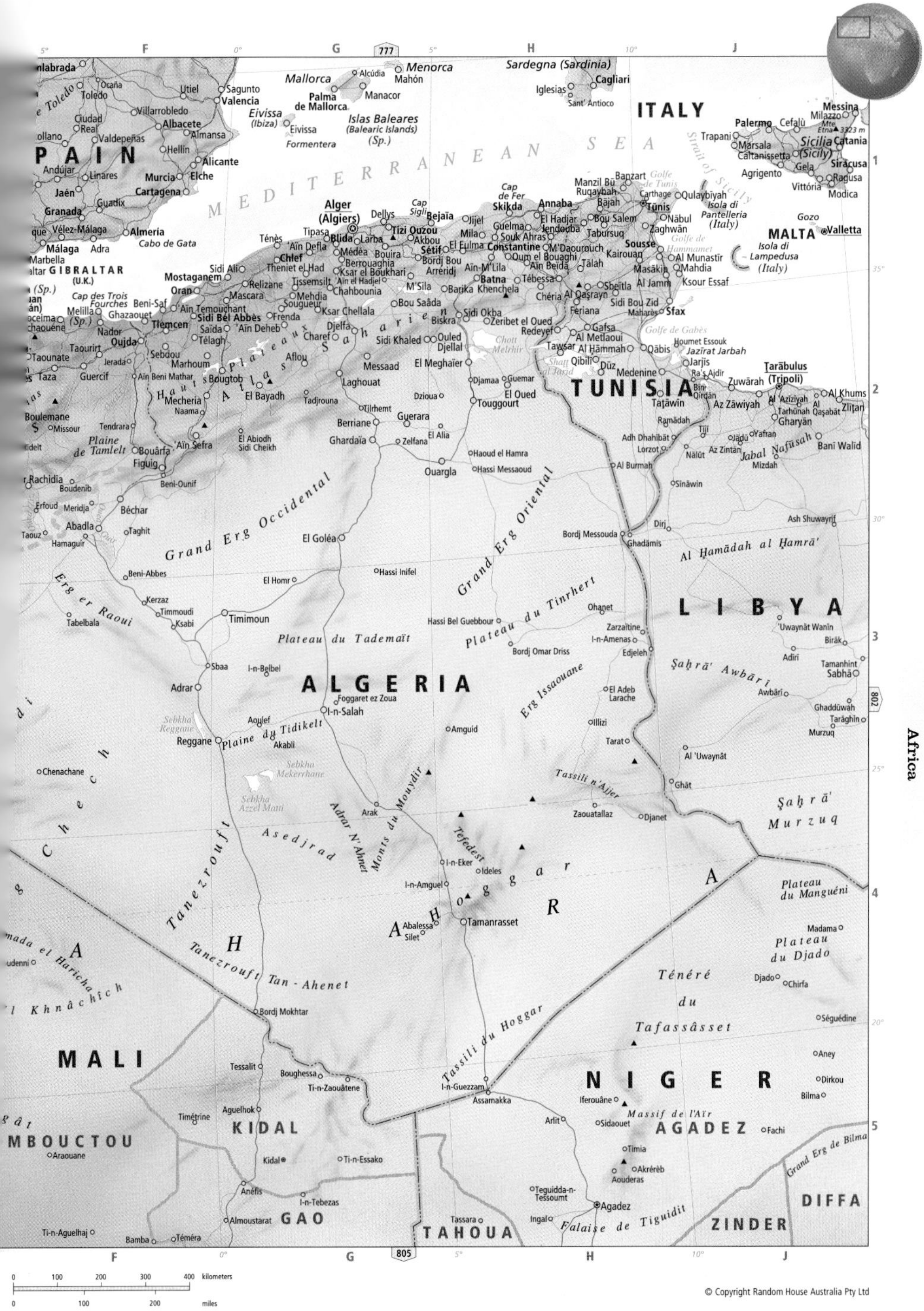

777
805
802
F
G
H
J
5°
0°
10°
35°
30°
25°
20°
1
2
3
4
5
Menorca
Alcúdia
Mahón
Mallorca
Palma de Mallorca
Manacor
Eivissa (Ibiza)
Eivissa
Formentera
Islas Baleares (Balearic Islands) (Sp.)
Sardegna (Sardinia)
Cagliari
Iglesias
Sant' Antioco
ITALY
Messina
Milazzo
Mte Etna
3323 m
Palermo
Cefalù
Trapani
Marsala
Caltanissetta
Sicilia (Sicily)
Catania
Agrigento
Gela
Siracusa
Ragusa
Vittória
Modica
Gozo
MALTA
Valletta
Isola di Pantelleria (Italy)
Isola di Lampedusa (Italy)
Strait of Sicily
MEDITERRANEAN SEA
PAIN
Toledo
Ocaña
Utiel
Sagunto
Valencia
Ciudad Real
Villarrobledo
Albacete
Valdepeñas
Almansa
Hellín
Alicante
Elche
Andújar
Linares
Murcia
Jaén
Cartagena
Guadix
Granada
Vélez-Málaga
Almería
Cabo de Gata
Málaga
Adra
Marbella
GIBRALTAR (U.K.)
Cap des Trois Fourches
Melilla (Sp.)
Beni-Saf
Ghazaouet
Nador
Oujda
Taourirt
Taounate
Jerada
Taza
Guercif
Aïn Beni Mathar
Boulemane
Missour
Tendrara
Plaine de Tamlelt
Bouârfa
Figuig
Beni-Ounif
Rachidia
Boudenib
Erfoud
Meridja
Béchar
Abadla
Taouz
Hamaguir
Taghit
Beni-Abbes
Erg er Raoui
Kerzaz
Timmoudi
Ksabi
Tabelbala
Timimoun
Sbaa
Adrar
Sebkha Reggane
Reggane
Chenachane
Alger (Algiers)
Cap Sigli
Dellys
Bejaïa
Jijel
Cap de Fer
Skikda
Annaba
Tipasa
Blida
Larba
Tizi Ouzou
Akbou
Ténès
Aïn Defla
Médéa
Bouira
Sétif
El Eulma
Mila
Constantine
Guelma
Souk Ahras
El Hadjar
Jendouba
Mostaganem
Sidi Ali
Chlef
Theniet el Had
Berrouaghia
Bordj Bou Arreridj
Aïn-M'Lila
Oum el Bouaghi
Aïn Beida
Relizane
Tissemsilt
Aïn el Hadjel
Ksar el Boukhari
M'Sila
Batna
Khenchela
Tébessa
Oran
Mascara
Mehdia
Chahbounia
Barika
Aïn Temouchant
Sidi Bel Abbès
Frenda
Sougueur
Bou Saâda
Tlemcen
Saïda
Aïn Deheb
Ksar Chellala
Djelfa
Biskra
Sidi Okba
Zeribet el Oued
Télagh
Charef
Sidi Khaled
Ouled Djellal
Chott Melrhir
Sebdou
Marhoum
Aflou
Messaad
El Meghaïer
Hauts Plateaux
Atlas Saharien
Bougtob
Mecheria
El Bayadh
Naama
Laghouat
Djamaa
Guemar
El Oued
Aïn Sefra
Tadjrouna
Dzioua
Touggourt
Tilrhemt
Berriane
Guerara
El Abiodh Sidi Cheikh
Ghardaïa
Zelfana
El Alia
Haoud el Hamra
Ouargla
Hassi Messaoud
Grand Erg Occidental
Grand Erg Oriental
El Goléa
Hassi Inifel
El Homr
Plateau du Tademaït
Plateau du Tinrhert
Hassi Bel Guebbour
Bordj Omar Driss
I-n-Belbel
ALGERIA
Foggaret ez Zoua
I-n-Salah
Aoulef
Plaine du Tidikelt
Akabli
Amguid
Sebkha Mekerrhane
Sebkha Azzel Matti
Erg Issaouane
Tassili n'Ajjer
Arak
Adrar N'Ahnet
Monts du Mouydir
Asedjrad
Tanezrouft
Tefedest
I-n-Eker
Ideles
I-n-Amguel
AHAGGAR
Tamanrasset
Abalessa
Silet
Tanezrouft Tan-Ahenet
Bordj Mokhtar
Tassili du Hoggar
I-n-Guezzam
Assamakka
Zaouatallaz
Djanet
El Adeb Larache
Illizi
Tarat
Ohanet
Zarzaïtine
I-n-Amenas
Edjeleh
Bordj Messouda
Ghadāmis
TUNISIA
Bizerte
Manzil Bū Ruqaybah
Bājah
Golfe de Tunis
Carthage
Tūnis
Qulaybīyah
Nābul
Bou Salem
Zaghwān
Tabursuq
Golfe de Hammamet
Sousse
Kairouan
Al Munastīr
Mahdia
M'Daourouch
Tālah
Masākin
Ksour Essaf
Al Jamm
Sbeïtla
Chéria
Al Qaşrayn
Sidi Bou Zid
Feriana
Mahārès
Sfax
Redeyef
Gafsa
Al Metlaoui
Golfe de Gabès
Houmet Essouk
Jazīrat Jarbah
Tawzar
Al Hāmmah
Qābis
Shatt al Jarīd
Qibilī
Dūz
Medenine
Jarjis
Ra's Ajdir
Bin Qirdān
Taţāwīn
Ramādah
Adh Dhahībāt
Lorzot
Al Burmah
Zuwārah
Ţarābulus (Tripoli)
Az Zāwiyah
Al 'Azīzīyah
Tarhūnah
Al Qaşabāt
Al Khums
Zlīţan
Gharyān
Yafran
Jādū
Tījī
Nālūt
Az Zintān
Jabal Nafūsah
Bani Walid
Mizdah
Sīnāwin
Dirj
Ash Shuwayrif
Al Hamādah al Hamrā'
LIBYA
'Uwaynāt Wanīn
Birāk
Adīrī
Tamanhint
Sabhā
Şaḩrā' Awbārī
Awbārī
Ghaddūwah
Tarāghin
Murzuq
Al 'Uwaynāt
Ghāt
Şaḩrā' Murzuq
Plateau du Manguéni
Madama
Plateau du Djado
Djado
Chirfa
Séguédine
Ténéré du Tafassâsset
Aney
Dirkou
Bilma
NIGER
Iferouâne
Massif de l'Aïr
Arlit
Sidaouet
AGADEZ
Fachi
Timia
Akréréb
Aouderas
Grand Erg de Bilma
DIFFA
Teguidda-n-Tessoumt
Agadez
Ingal
Falaise de Tiguidit
ZINDER
Tassara
TAHOUA
Hamada el Haricha
Khnâchîch
Chech
Oudenni
MALI
Tessalit
Boughessa
Ti-n-Zaouâtene
Aguelhok
Timétrine
KIDAL
MBOUCTOU
Araouane
Kidal
Ti-n-Essako
Anéfis
I-n-Tebezas
Almoustarat
GAO
Ti-n-Aguelhaj
Bamba
Téméra
0
100
200
300
400
kilometers
miles

Africa

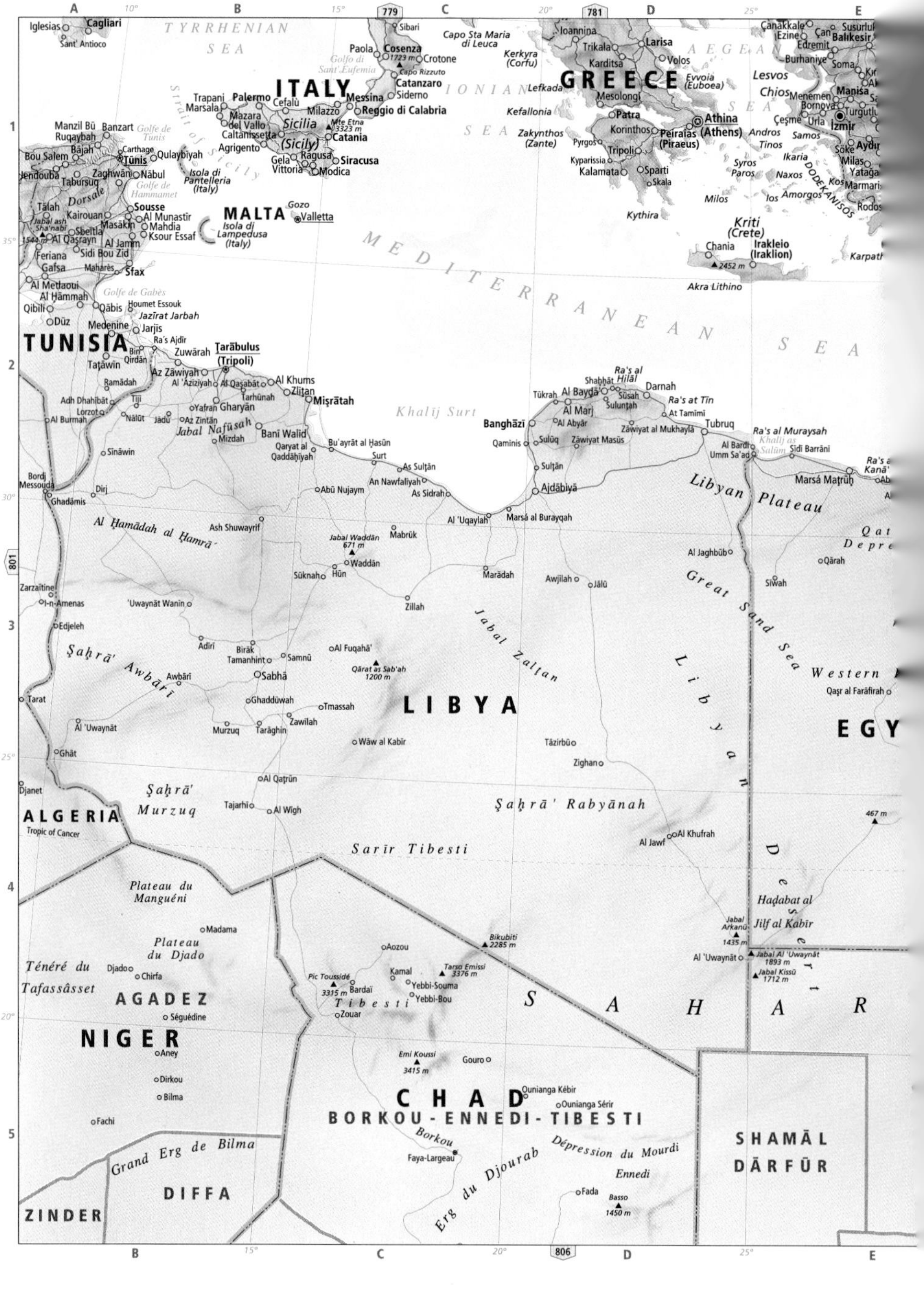
A
B
C
D
E
779
781
801
806
1
2
3
4
5
10°
15°
20°
25°
35°
30°
25°
20°
Iglesias
Cagliari
Sant' Antioco
TYRRHENIAN SEA
Sibari
Paola
Cosenza
1723 m
Crotone
Golfo di Sant' Eufemia
Capo Rizzuto
Catanzaro
Siderno
Capo Sta Maria di Leuca
Kerkyra (Corfu)
ITALY
Trapani
Palermo
Marsala
Cefalù
Mazara del Vallo
Messina
Milazzo
Reggio di Calabria
Sicilia (Sicily)
Caltanissetta
Mte Etna 3323 m
Catania
Agrigento
Gela
Ragusa
Siracusa
Vittoria
Modica
Strait of Sicily
IONIAN SEA
Manzil Bū Ruqaybah
Banzart
Golfe de Tunis
Bājah
Carthage
Tūnis
Qulaybiyah
Bou Salem
Jendouba
Zaghwān
Nābul
Taburşuq
Golfe de Hammamet
Isola di Pantelleria (Italy)
Dorsale
Tālah
Kairouan
Sousse
Al Munastīr
Jabal ash Sha'nabī 1544 m
Masākin
Mahdia
Sbeitla
Ksour Essaf
Al Qaşrayn
Al Jamm
Feriana
Sidi Bou Zid
Gafsa
Mahārès
Sfax
Al Metlaoui
Golfe de Gabès
Al Ḩammah
Qibili
Qābis
Houmet Essouk
Jazīrat Jarbah
Dūz
Medenine
Jarjis
TUNISIA
Ra's Ajdīr
Bin Qirdān
Zuwārah
Ţarābulus (Tripoli)
Taţāwīn
MALTA
Gozo
Valletta
Isola di Lampedusa (Italy)
Ioannina
Trikala
Larisa
Karditsa
Volos
AEGEAN SEA
Lefkada
GREECE
Evvoia (Euboea)
Mesolongi
Kefallonia
Patra
Athina (Athens)
Zakynthos (Zante)
Korinthos
Peiraias (Piraeus)
Pyrgos
Tripoli
Kyparissia
Kalamata
Sparti
Skala
Kythira
Andros
Tinos
Syros
Paros
Naxos
Ikaria
Milos
Ios
Amorgos
Samos
DODEKANISOS
Kriti (Crete)
Chania
Irakleio (Iraklion)
2452 m
Akra Lithino
Karpath
Çanakkale
Ezine
Çan
Balıkesir
Edremit
Burhaniye
Soma
Lesvos
Chios
Menemen
Manisa
Bornova
İzmir
Çeşme
Urla
Turgutlu
Söke
Aydın
Milas
Yatağa
Kos
Marmaris
Rodos
MEDITERRANEAN SEA
Az Zāwiyah
Ramādah
Al 'Azīzīyah
Al Qaşabāt
Al Khums
Adh Dhahībāt
Tiji
Tarhūnah
Zlīţan
Lorzot
Yafran
Gharyān
Mişrātah
Al Burmah
Nālūt
Jādū
Az Zintān
Jabal Nafūsah
Mizdah
Banī Walīd
Qaryat al Qaddāḩīyah
Bu'ayrāt al Ḩasūn
Sīnāwin
Surt
Khalīj Surt
As Sulţān
An Nawfalīyah
As Sidrah
Bordj Messouda
Ghadāmis
Dirj
Abū Nujaym
Al 'Uqaylah
Marsá al Burayqah
Ra's al Hilāl
Shaḩḩāt
Al Bayḑā'
Sūsah
Darnah
Ţūkrah
Al Marj
Suluntah
Ra's at Tīn
At Tamīmī
Banghāzī
Al Abyār
Zāwiyat al Mukhaylá
Ţubruq
Qamīnis
Sulūq
Zāwiyat Masūs
Ra's al Muraysah
Al Bardī
Khalīj as Sallūm
Umm Sa'ad
Sīdī Barrānī
Ra's al Kanā'is
Marsá Maţrūḩ
Sulţān
Ajdābiyā
Libyan Plateau
Al Ḩamādah al Ḩamrā'
Ash Shuwayrif
Jabal Waddān 671 m
Mabrūk
Waddān
Sūknah
Hūn
Marādah
Awjilah
Jālū
Al Jaghbūb
Qattara Depression
Qārah
Sīwah
Zarzaïtine
In-Amenas
'Uwaynāt Wanin
Zillah
Great Sand Sea
Edjeleh
Jabal Zalţan
Adīrī
Birāk
Tamanhint
Samnū
Al Fuqahā'
Şaḩrā' Awbārī
Awbārī
Sabhā
Qārat as Sab'ah 1200 m
Libyan Desert
Western Desert
Qaşr al Farāfirah
Tarat
Ghaddūwah
Tmassah
LIBYA
Al 'Uwaynāt
Murzuq
Zawīlah
Tarāghin
EGYPT
Ghāt
Wāw al Kabīr
Tāzirbū
Zighan
Djanet
Al Qaţrūn
Şaḩrā' Murzuq
Şaḩrā' Rabyānah
Tajarhī
Al Wīgh
ALGERIA
Tropic of Cancer
467 m
Al Jawf
Al Khufrah
Sarīr Tibesti
Plateau du Manguéni
Ḩaḑabat al Jilf al Kabīr
Madama
Jabal Arkanū 1435 m
Plateau du Djado
Bikubiti 2285 m
Aozou
Jabal Al 'Uwaynāt 1893 m
Al 'Uwaynāt
Ténéré du Tafassâsset
Djado
Chirfa
Kamal
Tarso Emissi 3376 m
Jabal Kissū 1712 m
Pic Toussidé 3315 m
Bardaï
Yebbi-Souma
Yebbi-Bou
AGADEZ
Tibesti
SAHARA
Séguédine
Zouar
NIGER
Aney
Emi Koussi 3415 m
Gouro
Dirkou
Ounianga Kébir
Bilma
CHAD
Ounianga Sérir
BORKOU-ENNEDI-TIBESTI
Fachi
Borkou
Dépression du Mourdi
SHAMĀL DĀRFŪR
Grand Erg de Bilma
Faya-Largeau
Erg du Djourab
Ennedi
DIFFA
Fada
Basso 1450 m
ZINDER

Africa

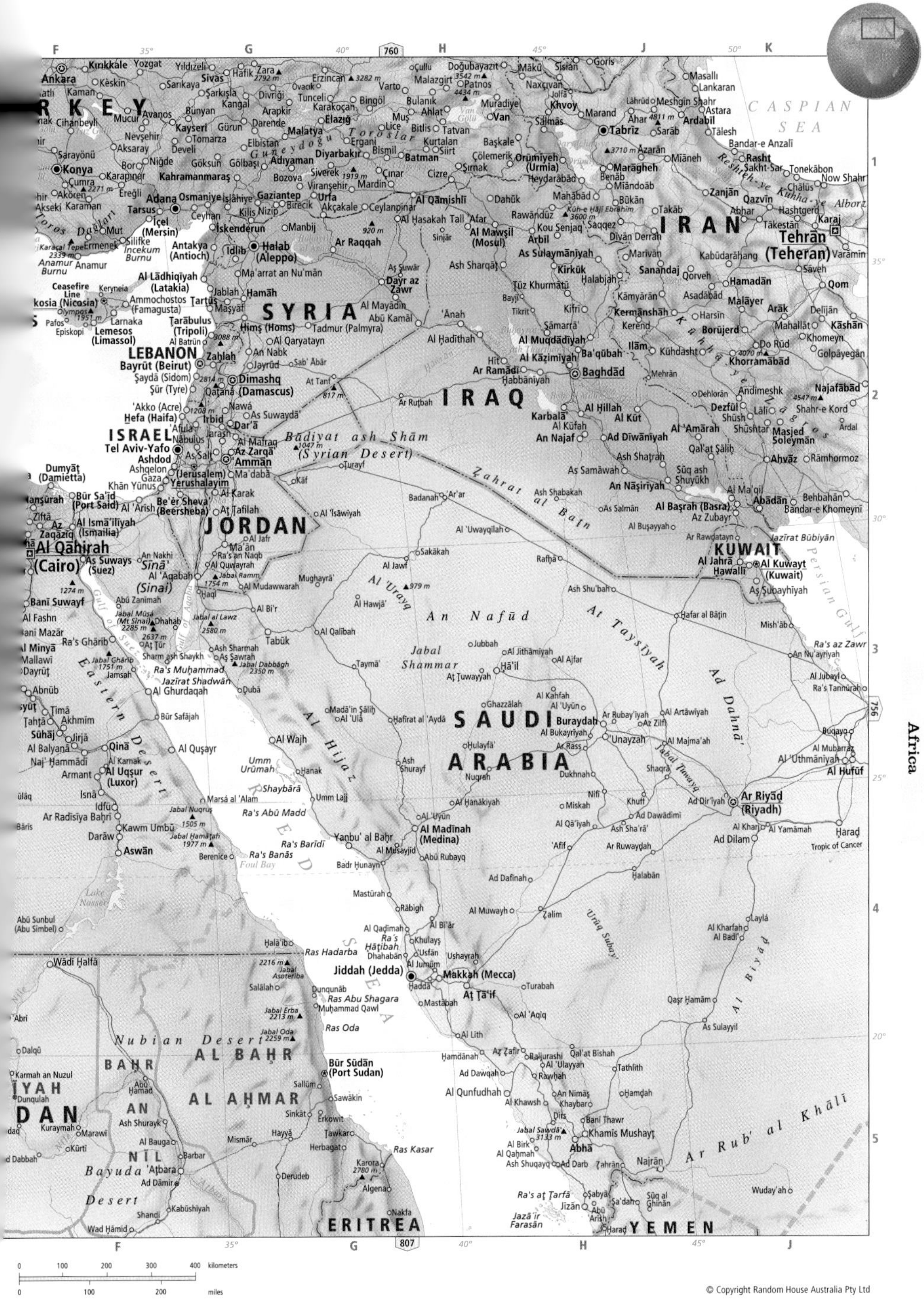
760
756
807
Africa
TURKEY
SYRIA
LEBANON
ISRAEL
JORDAN
IRAQ
IRAN
KUWAIT
SAUDI ARABIA
YEMEN
ERITREA
CASPIAN SEA
Persian Gulf
Red Sea
Gulf of Suez
Gulf of Aqaba
Ankara
Konya
Adana
Kayseri
Malatya
Diyarbakır
Van
Tabrīz
Rasht
Tehrān (Teheran)
Qom
Hamadān
Kermānshāh
Ahvāz
Al Mawṣil (Mosul)
Arbīl
Kirkūk
Baghdād
Karbalā'
An Najaf
Al Baṣrah (Basra)
Al Kuwayt (Kuwait)
Ḥalab (Aleppo)
Ḥimṣ (Homs)
Dimashq (Damascus)
Bayrūt (Beirut)
Tel Aviv-Yafo
Yerushalayim (Jerusalem)
'Ammān
Al Qāhirah (Cairo)
Būr Sa'īd (Port Said)
As Suways (Suez)
Al Uqṣur (Luxor)
Aswān
Ar Riyāḍ (Riyadh)
Al Madīnah (Medina)
Makkah (Mecca)
Jiddah (Jedda)
Aṭ Ṭā'if
Abhā
Būr Sūdān (Port Sudan)
Bādiyat ash Shām (Syrian Desert)
An Nafūd
Ad Dahnā'
Ar Rub' al Khālī
Al Ḥijāz
Nubian Desert
Eastern Desert
Sīnā' (Sinai)
Tropic of Cancer
0 100 200 300 400 kilometers
0 100 200 miles

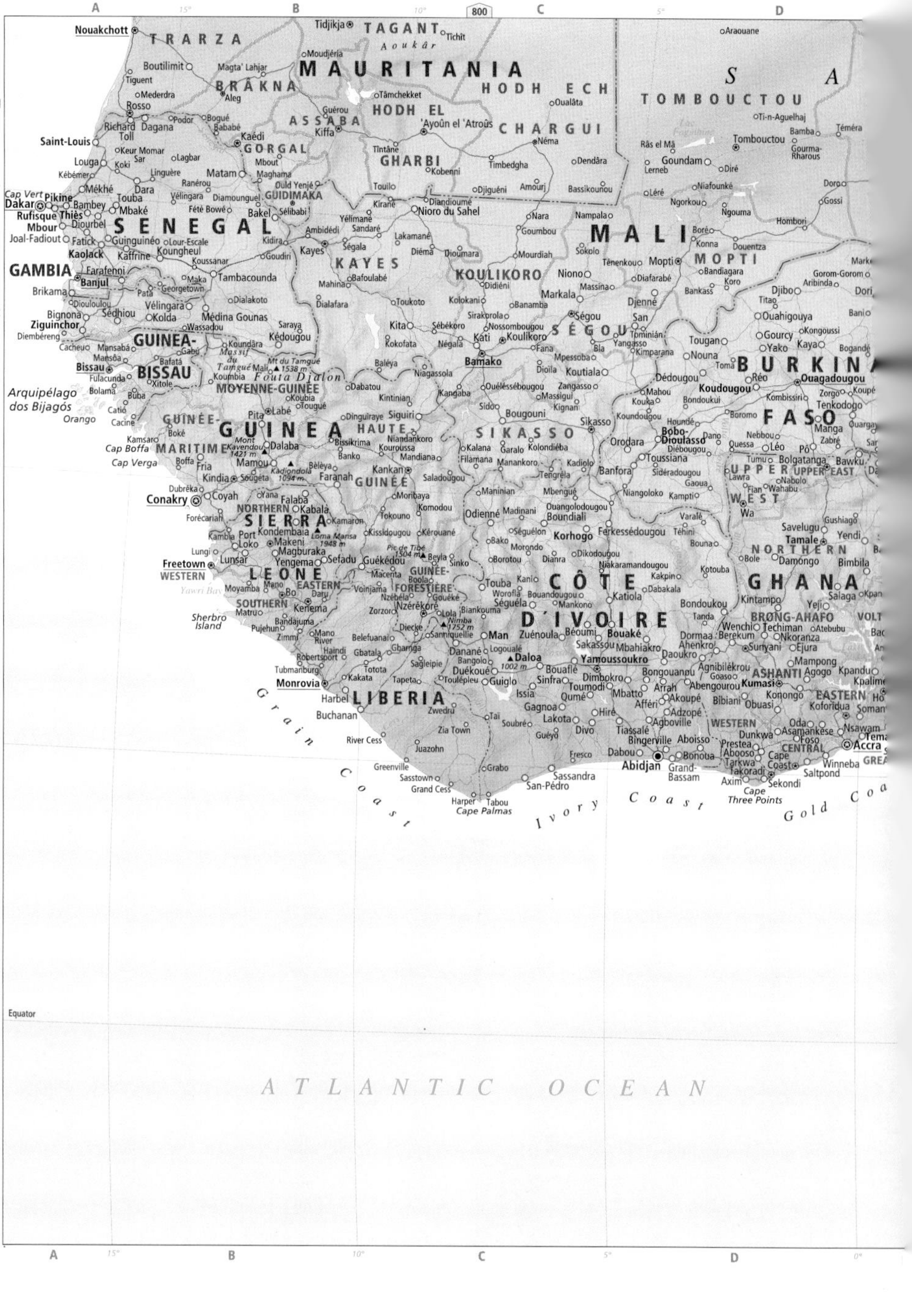
A
B
C
D
15°
10°
5°
0°
800
1
2
3
4
5
Nouakchott
TRARZA
Tidjikja
TAGANT
Tîchît
Aoukâr
Araouane
Boutilimit
Moudjéria
Magta' Lahjar
MAURITANIA
Tiguent
BRAKNA
Aleg
Mederdra
Rosso
Tâmchekket
HODH ECH
Oualâta
HODH EL
Guérou
ASSABA
Kiffa
'Ayoûn el 'Atroûs
CHARGUI
Néma
S
A
TOMBOUCTOU
Ti-n-Aguelhaj
Bamba
Téméra
Tombouctou
Gourma-Rharous
Rås el Må
Goundam
Lerneb
Diré
Richard Toll
Dagana
Podor
Bogué
Bababé
Kaédi
GORGAL
Saint-Louis
Keur Momar Sar
Louga
Koki
Lagbar
Kébémer
Linguère
Matam
Mbout
Maghama
Ould Yenjé
GUIDIMAKA
GHARBI
Kobenni
Tîntâne
Timbedgha
Dendâra
Touil
Djiguéni
Amourj
Bassikounou
Léré
Niafounké
Ngorkou
Ngouma
Doro
Gossi
Hombori
Cap Vert
Pikine
Dakar
Rufisque
Thiès
Mbour
Joal-Fadiout
Méckhé
Dara
Touba
Bambey
Diourbel
Mbaké
Vélingara
Diamounguel
Fété Bowé
Ranérou
Bakel
Sélibabi
Kiranè
Diandioumé
Nioro du Sahel
Yélimané
Sandaré
Nara
Nampala
Goumbou
SENEGAL
MALI
Fatick
Kaolack
Guinguinéo
Lour-Escale
Kaffrine
Koungheul
Koussanar
GAMBIA
Farafenni
Banjul
Brikama
Georgetown
Maka
Tambacounda
Ambidédi
Kidira
Kayes
Ségala
Goudiri
Lakamané
Diéma
Dioumara
Mourdiah
Sokolo
Boré
Konna
Douentza
MOPTI
Mopti
Ténenkou
Bandiagara
Koro
Diafarabé
KAYES
Mahina
Bafoulabé
KOULIKORO
Didiéni
Niono
Massina
Markala
Djenné
Bankass
Djibo
Titao
Gorom-Gorom
Aribinda
Dori
Bani
Diouloulou
Bignona
Ziguinchor
Diembéreng
Sédhiou
Vélingara
Kolda
Dialakoto
Médina Gounas
Wassadou
Dialafara
Toukoto
Kolokani
Banamba
Sirakorola
Ségou
San
Ouahigouya
Cacheu
Mansabá
Mansôa
GUINEA-BISSAU
Gabú
Bafatá
Bissau
Fulacunda
Bolama
Xitole
Búba
Catió
Cacine
Arquipélago dos Bijagós
Orango
Koundâra
Massif du Tamgué
Mt du Tamgué 1538 m
Mali
Saraya
Kédougou
Kita
Sébékoro
Nossombougou
Kati
Koulikoro
SÉGOU
Tominián
Yangasso
Kimparana
Bla
Fana
Tougan
Gourcy
Kongoussi
Yako
Kaya
Bogandé
Kokofata
Négala
Bamako
Baléya
Niagassola
Mpessoba
Dioïla
Koutiala
Nouna
Tomà
BURKINA
Ouagadougou
Koupéla
Koudougou
Réo
Kombissiri
Zorgo
Tenkodogo
Fouta Djalon
Koumbia
MOYENNE-GUINÉE
Koubia
Dabatou
Kintinian
Kangaba
Ouéléssébougou
Zangasso
Massigui
Kignan
Dédougou
Mahou
Kouka
Bondoukui
Pita
Labé
Tougué
GUINÉE-MARITIME
Boké
Kamsar
Cap Boffa
Cap Verga
Boffa
Fria
Dinguiraye
Siguiri
HAUTE-GUINÉE
GUINEA
Mont Kavendou 1421 m
Dalaba
Bissikrima
Niandankoro
Kouroussa
Mandiana
Banko
Sidoo
Bougouni
SIKASSO
Sikasso
Kalana
Garalo
Kolondiéba
Koundougou
Bobo-Dioulasso
Orodara
Houndé
Diébougou
Dano
Nebbou
Léo
Quessa
FASO
Manga
Zabré
Pô
Mamou
Kadiondola 1094 m
Bèlèya
Kindia
Souguéta
Faranah
Kankan
Saladougou
Filamana
Manankoro
Kadiolo
Tengréla
Banfora
Toussiana
Sidéradougou
Gaoua
Tumu
Bolgatanga
Bawku
UPPER WEST
UPPER EAST
Lawra
Nabolo
Wahabu
Fian
Wa
Dubréka
Conakry
Coyah
Yana
Falaba
Moribaya
Komodou
Maninian
Mbengué
Niangoloko
Kampti
NORTHERN
SIERRA
Kabala
Kamaron
Tokouno
Odienné
Madinani
Ouangolodougou
Boundiali
Varalé
Gushiago
Savelugu
Tamale
Yendi
Forécariah
Kambia
Port Loko
Kondembaia
Makeni
Loma Mansa 1948 m
Kissidougou
Kérouané
Séguélon
Korhogo
Ferkessédougou
Téhini
Bouna
Lungi
Freetown
WESTERN
Lunsar
Magburaka
Yengema
Sefadu
Guékédou
Pic de Tibé 1504 m
Beyla
Sinko
Bako
Morondo
Dikodougou
Borotou
Dianra
Niakaramandougou
Kotouba
Bole
Damongo
Bimbila
LEONE
EASTERN
Macenta
GUINÉE-FORESTIÈRE
Boola
Touba
Kani
CÔTE D'IVOIRE
Kakpin
Dabakala
GHANA
Salaga
Yawri Bay
Moyamba
Mano
Bo
Daru
Voinjama
Nzébéla
Gouéké
Woroflá
Bouandougou
Séguéla
Mankono
Katiola
Bondoukou
Kintampo
Yeji
SOUTHERN
Kenema
Matru
Zorzor
Nzérékoré
Lola
Biankouma
Tanda
BRONG-AHAFO
VOLTA
Sherbro Island
Pujehun
Bandajuma
Zimmi
Mano River
Belefuanai
Diecke
Nimba 1752 m
Sanniquellie
Man
Zuénoula
Béoumi
Bouaké
Dormaa
Berekum
Wenchi
Techiman
Atebubu
Nkoranza
Sunyani
Ejura
Sakassou
Mbahiakro
Ahenkro
Daoukro
Haindi
Robertsport
Gbatala
Gbarnga
Danané
Logoualé
Bangolo
Daloa 1002 m
Yamoussoukro
Mampong
Tubmanburg
Monrovia
Kakata
Totota
Tapeta
Saglepie
Duékoué
Toulépleu
Guiglo
Bouaflé
Sinfra
Dimbokro
Bongouanou
Agnibilékrou
Goaso
ASHANTI
Agogo
Kpandu
Kpalime
Kumasi
Abengourou
Konongo
EASTERN
Koforidua
Grain Coast
Harbel
LIBERIA
Buchanan
Zwedru
Issia
Gagnoa
Toumodi
Oumé
Mbatto
Arrah
Afféri
Akoupé
Bibiani
Obuasi
Adzopé
Taï
Soubré
Lakota
Hiré
Agboville
WESTERN
Dunkwa
Oda
Asamankese
Nsawam
Zia Town
Guéyo
Divo
Tiassalé
Bingerville
Aboisso
Prestea
Foso
River Cess
Juazohn
Fresco
Dabou
Abidjan
Bonoua
Aboso
CENTRAL
Cape Coast
Tarkwa
Takoradi
Winneba
Accra
Tema
Greenville
Grabo
Sassandra
Grand-Bassam
Axim
Sekondi
Saltpond
Sasstown
Grand Cess
San-Pédro
Harper
Tabou
Cape Palmas
Cape Three Points
Ivory Coast
Gold Coast
Equator
ATLANTIC OCEAN

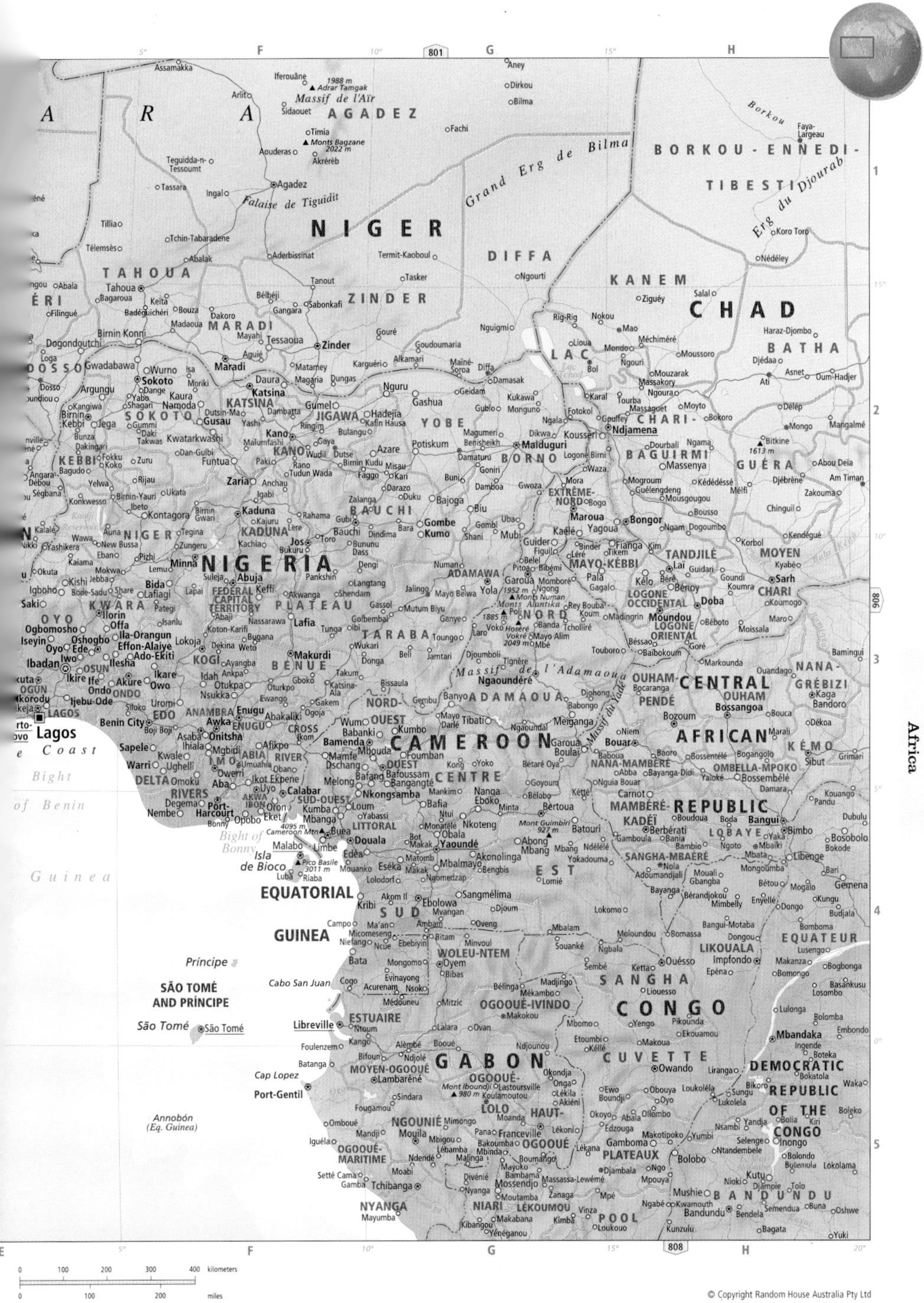
801
808
806
NIGER
NIGERIA
CHAD
CAMEROON
CENTRAL AFRICAN REPUBLIC
CONGO
GABON
EQUATORIAL GUINEA
SÃO TOMÉ AND PRÍNCIPE
DEMOCRATIC REPUBLIC OF THE CONGO
AGADEZ
TAHOUA
ZINDER
MARADI
DIFFA
DOSSO
KANEM
LAC
BATHA
BORKOU-ENNEDI-TIBESTI
CHARI-BAGUIRMI
GUÉRA
MAYO-KÉBBI
TANDJILÉ
MOYEN CHARI
LOGONE OCCIDENTAL
LOGONE ORIENTAL
SOKOTO
KATSINA
KANO
JIGAWA
YOBE
BORNO
KEBBI
ZAMFARA
KADUNA
BAUCHI
NIGER
KWARA
OYO
OGUN
OSUN
ONDO
EKITI
KOGI
FEDERAL CAPITAL TERRITORY
PLATEAU
TARABA
ADAMAWA
BENUE
EDO
ENUGU
ANAMBRA
IMO
ABIA
CROSS RIVER
AKWA IBOM
RIVERS
DELTA
LAGOS
EXTRÊME-NORD
NORD
ADAMAOUA
NORD-OUEST
OUEST
CENTRE
SUD-OUEST
LITTORAL
EST
SUD
WOLEU-NTEM
ESTUAIRE
MOYEN-OGOOUÉ
OGOOUÉ-IVINDO
OGOOUÉ-LOLO
HAUT-OGOOUÉ
NGOUNIÉ
OGOOUÉ-MARITIME
NYANGA
NIARI
LÉKOUMOU
POOL
PLATEAUX
CUVETTE
SANGHA
LIKOUALA
EQUATEUR
BANDUNDU
SANGHA-MBAÉRÉ
LOBAYE
OMBELLA-MPOKO
NANA-MAMBÉRÉ
MAMBÉRÉ-KADÉÏ
OUHAM-PENDÉ
OUHAM
KÉMO
NANA-GRÉBIZI
Niamey
Abuja
Lagos
Ndjamena
Yaoundé
Malabo
Libreville
Bangui
São Tomé
Porto-Novo
Massif de l'Aïr
1988 m Adrar Tamgak
Monts Bagzane 2022 m
Grand Erg de Bilma
Falaise de Tiguidit
Erg du Djourab
Borkou
Massif de l'Adamaoua
Massif du Yadé
4095 m Cameroon Mtn
Pico Basile 3011 m
Mont Ibounji 980 m
Mont Gumbiri 927 m
Monts Atlantika 1885 m
Hosséré Vokré 2049 m
Monts Numan 1952 m
1613 m
Lac Tchad
Bight of Benin
Bight of Bonny
Gulf of Guinea
Coast
Isla de Bioco
Príncipe
São Tomé
Cabo San Juan
Cap Lopez
Port-Gentil
Annobón (Eq. Guinea)
Kano
Kaduna
Zaria
Sokoto
Katsina
Maiduguri
Ibadan
Ogbomosho
Ilorin
Benin City
Enugu
Onitsha
Port-Harcourt
Calabar
Jos
Makurdi
Lokoja
Douala
Bamenda
Garoua
Maroua
Ngaoundéré
Moundou
Sarh
Agadez
Zinder
Maradi
Tahoua
Bouar
Berbérati
Ouésso
Franceville
Lambaréné
0 100 200 300 400 kilometers
0 100 200 miles

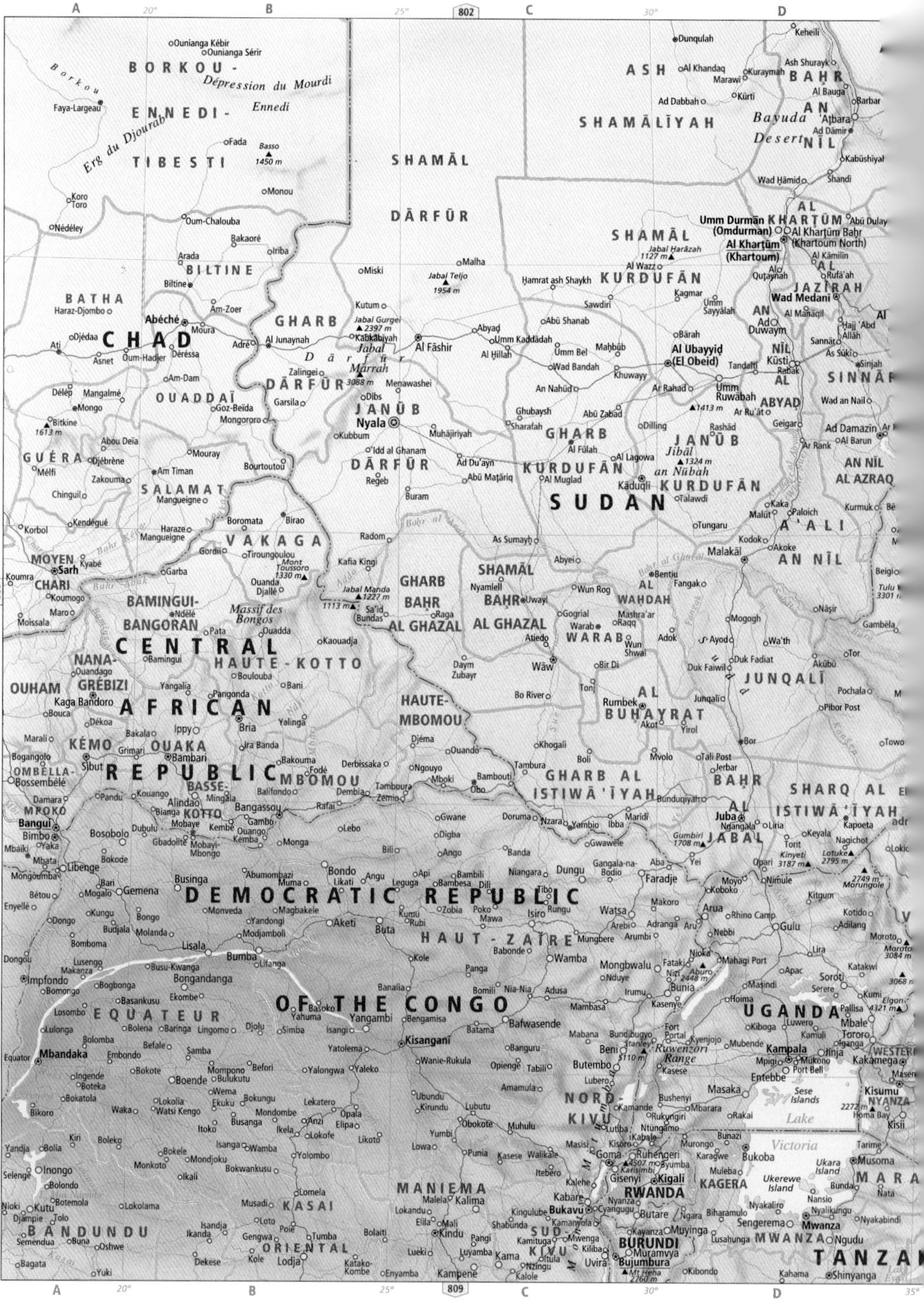
802
805
809
CHAD
SUDAN
CENTRAL AFRICAN REPUBLIC
DEMOCRATIC REPUBLIC OF THE CONGO
UGANDA
RWANDA
BURUNDI
BORKOU-ENNEDI-TIBESTI
BILTINE
BATHA
OUADDAÏ
GUÉRA
SALAMAT
MOYEN CHARI
VAKAGA
BAMINGUI-BANGORAN
HAUTE-KOTTO
NANA-GRÉBIZI
OUHAM
KÉMO
OUAKA
OMBELLA-MPOKO
BASSE-KOTTO
MBOMOU
HAUTE-MBOMOU
SHAMĀL DĀRFŪR
GHARB DĀRFŪR
JANŪB DĀRFŪR
ASH SHAMĀLĪYAH
AL KHARṬŪM
SHAMĀL KURDUFĀN
GHARB KURDUFĀN
JANŪB KURDUFĀN
AL JAZĪRAH
SINNĀR
AN NĪL AL AZRAQ
A'ALI AN NĪL
SHAMĀL BAḤR AL GHAZAL
GHARB BAḤR AL GHAZAL
WARAB
AL WAḤDAH
JUNQALĪ
AL BUḤAYRAT
GHARB AL ISTIWĀ'ĪYAH
SHARQ AL ISTIWĀ'ĪYAH
BAḤR AL JABAL
HAUT-ZAÏRE
EQUATEUR
NORD-KIVU
SUD-KIVU
MANIEMA
KASAI ORIENTAL
BANDUNDU
KAGERA
MWANZA
Umm Durmān (Omdurman)
Al Kharṭūm (Khartoum)
Al Kharṭūm Baḥr (Khartoum North)
Wad Medanī
Al Ubayyiḍ (El Obeid)
Nyala
Al Fāshir
Malakāl
Wāw
Juba
Abéché
Sarh
Bangui
Kisangani
Mbandaka
Kampala
Kigali
Bujumbura
Bukavu
Goma
Mwanza
Jabal Marrah 3088 m
Lake Victoria
Bayuda Desert
Massif des Bongos
Ruwenzori Range
Dépression du Mourdi
Erg du Djourab
A
B
C
D
20°
25°
30°
35°
1
2
3
4
5
15°
10°
5°
0°

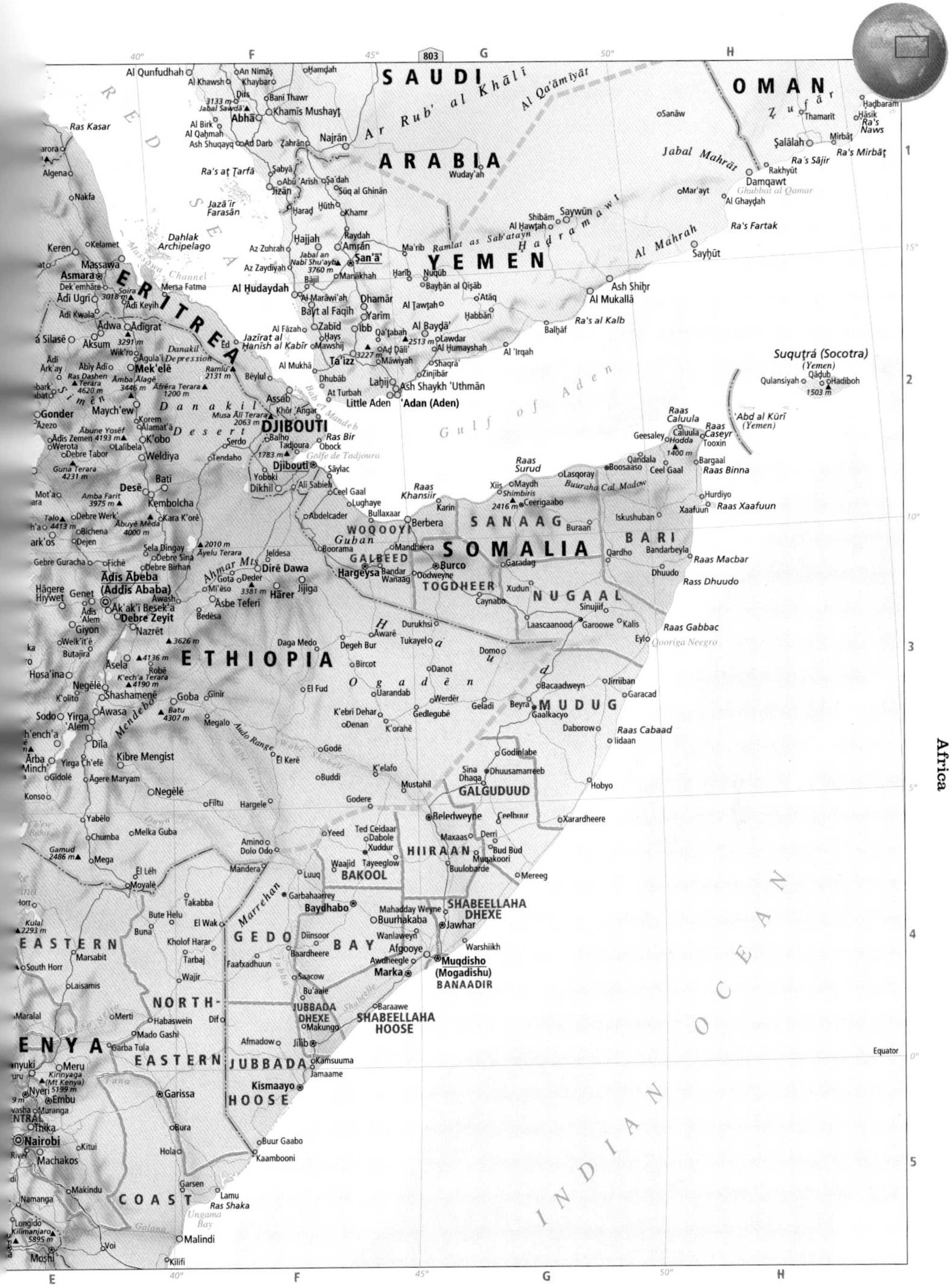

0 100 200 300 400 kilometers

0 100 200 miles

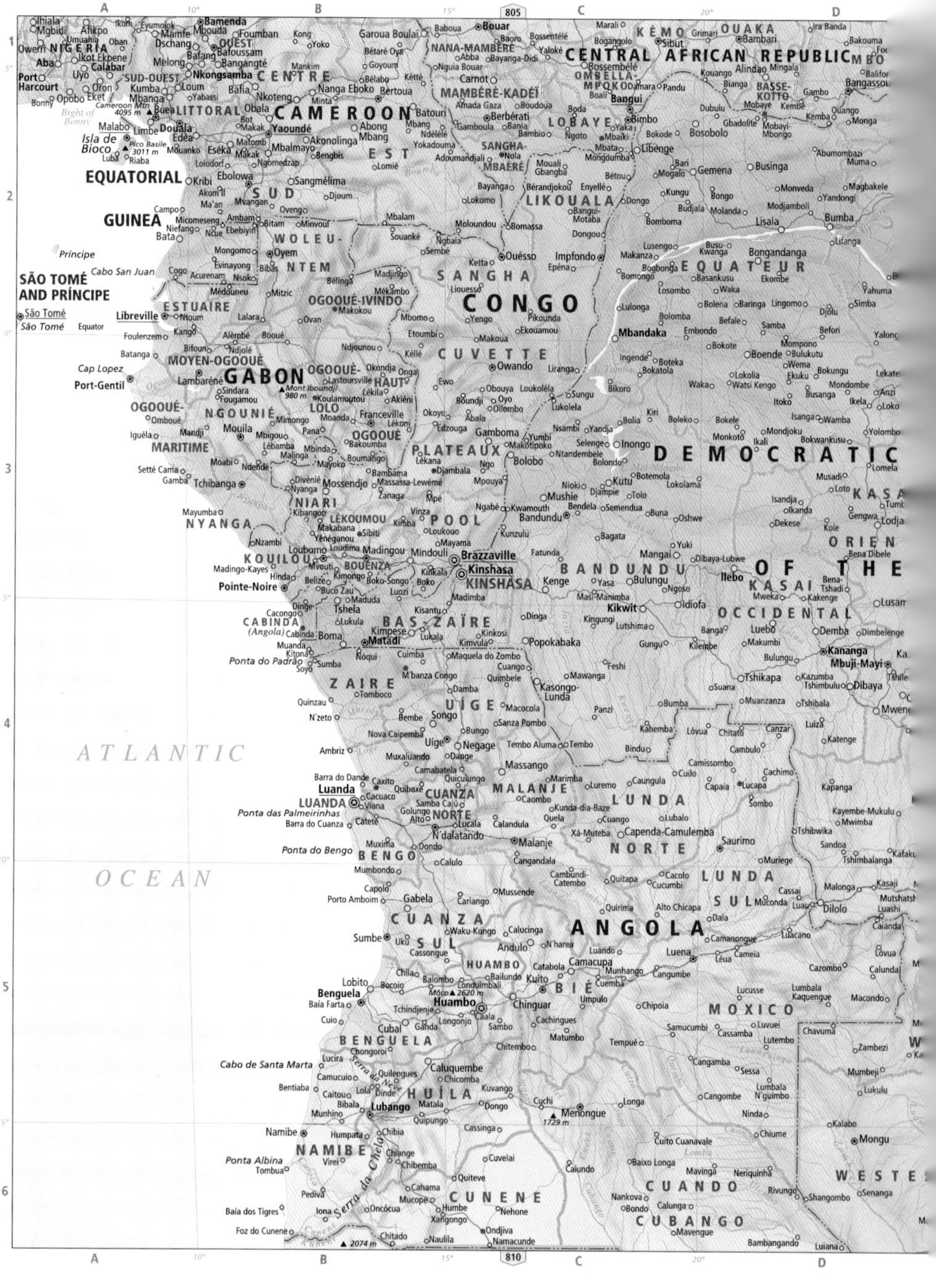

805
810
A
B
C
D
NIGERIA
CAMEROON
CENTRAL AFRICAN REPUBLIC
EQUATORIAL GUINEA
SÃO TOMÉ AND PRÍNCIPE
GABON
CONGO
DEMOCRATIC
OF THE
ANGOLA
CABINDA (Angola)
ATLANTIC
OCEAN
Yaoundé
Douala
Malabo
Libreville
Port-Gentil
Pointe-Noire
Brazzaville
Kinshasa
Bangui
Mbandaka
Kikwit
Kananga
Mbuji-Mayi
Luanda
Benguela
Huambo
Lubango
Namibe
Malanje
Saurimo
Luena
Kuito
Menongue
Matadi
Cabinda
São Tomé
Príncipe
Equator
Isla de Bioco
Cameroon Mtn 4095 m
Pico Basile 3011 m
Mont Iboundji 980 m
Mòco 2620 m
1729 m
2074 m
Bight of Bonny
Cap Lopez
Cabo San Juan
Cabo de Santa Marta
Ponta Albina
Ponta do Padrão
Ponta das Palmeirinhas
Ponta do Bengo
Baía dos Tigres
Foz do Cunene
Serra da Neve
Serra da Chela
LITTORAL
SUD-OUEST
OUEST
CENTRE
EST
SUD
ESTUAIRE
WOLEU-NTEM
OGOOUÉ-IVINDO
MOYEN-OGOOUÉ
OGOOUÉ-HAUT-LOLO
NGOUNIÉ
OGOOUÉ-MARITIME
NYANGA
NIARI
LÉKOUMOU
KOUILOU
BOUENZA
POOL
PLATEAUX
CUVETTE
SANGHA
LIKOUALA
LOBAYE
SANGHA-MBAÉRÉ
MAMBÉRÉ-KADÉÏ
NANA-MAMBÉRÉ
OMBELLA-MPOKO
KÉMO
OUAKA
BASSE-KOTTO
EQUATEUR
BANDUNDU
KINSHASA
BAS-ZAÏRE
KASAI OCCIDENTAL
KASAI ORIENTAL
ZAIRE
UÍGE
CUANZA NORTE
BENGO
MALANJE
LUNDA NORTE
LUNDA SUL
CUANZA SUL
HUAMBO
BIÉ
BENGUELA
HUÍLA
NAMIBE
CUNENE
CUANDO CUBANGO
MOXICO
WESTERN

806

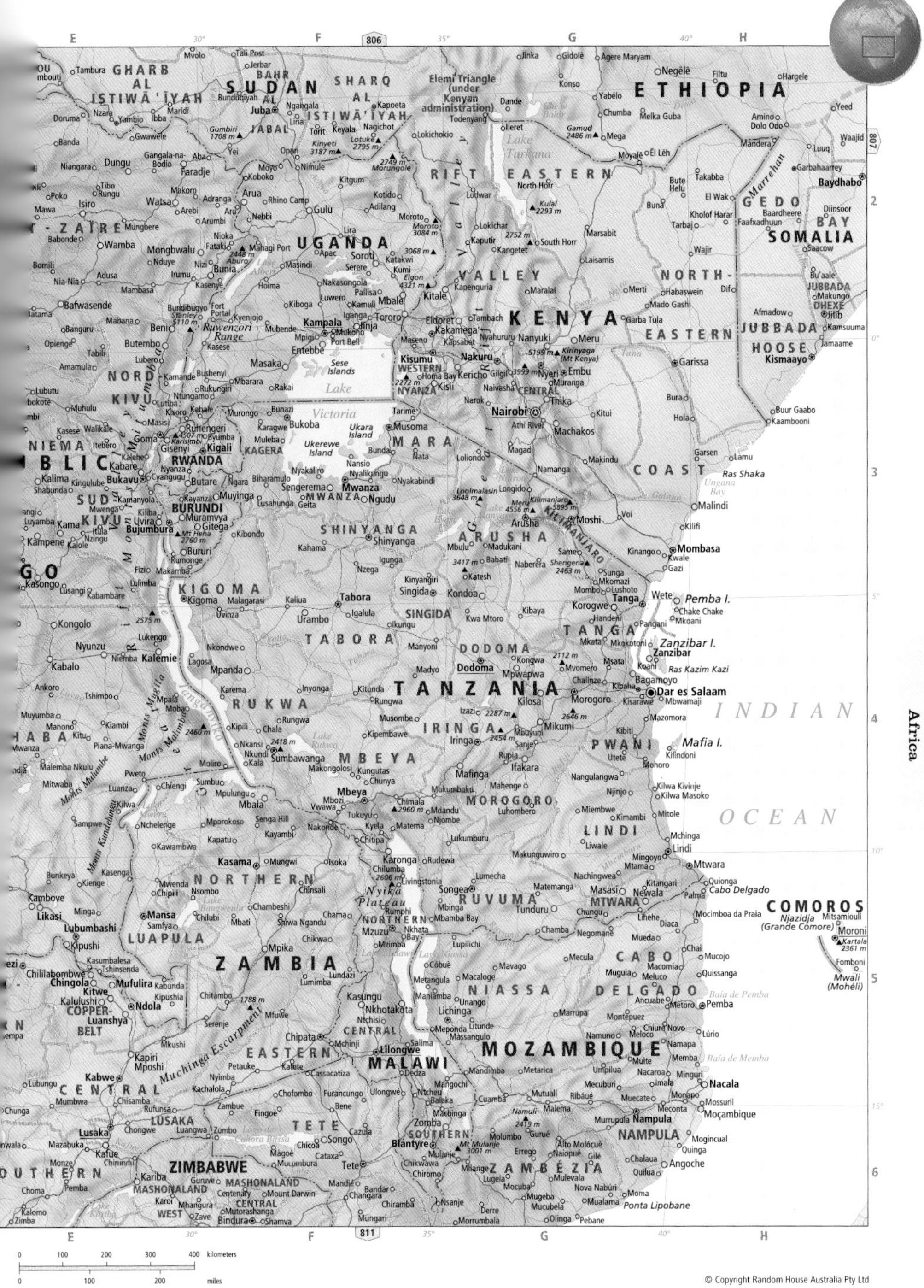

807

Africa

811

E 30° F 35° G 40° H

SUDAN

GHARB AL ISTIWĀ'ĪYAH
SHARQ AL ISTIWĀ'ĪYAH
BAHR AL JABAL

Elemi Triangle (under Kenyan administration)

ETHIOPIA

GEDO
JUBBADA DHEXE
JUBBADA HOOSE

SOMALIA

UGANDA

RIFT
Lake Turkana
EASTERN

KENYA

VALLEY

NORTH-EASTERN

NORD KIVU
ZAĪRE
NIEMA
BLIC
SUD KIVU
GO

WESTERN
NYANZA
CENTRAL
COAST

Lake Victoria

MARA

Nairobi

Mombasa

RWANDA
Kigali
KAGERA

BURUNDI
Bujumbura

KIGOMA

SHINYANGA
ARUSHA
KILIMANJARO

Ras Shaka
Ungwa Bay

TABORA
SINGIDA
DODOMA
TANGA

Zanzibar I.

INDIAN

Dodoma
TANZANIA

Dar es Salaam

RUKWA
IRINGA
PWANI
Mafia I.

OCEAN

MBEYA
MOROGORO
LINDI

Lindi

NORTHERN

RUVUMA
MTWARA

Mtwara

COMOROS
Njazidja (Grande Comore)
Moroni

ZAMBIA

LUAPULA
CENTRAL
NIASSA
CABO DELGADO

COPPERBELT
Mwali (Mohéli)

LUSAKA
EASTERN
MALAWI

MOZAMBIQUE

NAMPULA
Nampula
Nacala

CENTRAL

ZIMBABWE
MASHONALAND
MASHONALAND WEST
TETE
SOUTHERN
Blantyre
ZAMBÉZIA

A
B
C
D
808
10°
15°
20°
5°
1
2
3
4
5
6
ANGOLA
HUÍLA
NAMIBE
CUNENE
MOXICO
CUANDO
CUBANGO
Caluquembe
Chicomba
Lubango
Namibe
Tombua
Menongue
Cuito Cuanavale
Cabo de Santa Marta
Ponta Albina
Baía dos Tigres
Foz do Cunene
OHANGWENA
OSHANA
OMUSATI
OSHIKOTO
OKAVANGO
KUNENE
OTJOZONDJUPA
NAMIBIA
OMAHEKE
ERONGO
KHOMAS
HARDAP
KARAS
Oshakati
Ondangwa
Rundu
Tsumeb
Grootfontein
Otjiwarongo
Okahandja
Windhoek
Swakopmund
Walvis Bay
Rehoboth
Mariental
Keetmanshoop
Lüderitz
Rosh Pinah
Oranjemund
Cape Fria
Rocky Pt
Palgrave Pt
Dolphin Head
Diaz Pt
Cape Dernberg
Namib Desert
Tropic of Capricorn
ATLANTIC OCEAN
BOTSWANA
NGAMIL
GHANZI
KGALAGADI
Kalahari Desert
Maun
Ghanzi
Tshabong
NORTHERN CAPE
SOUTH AFRICA
WESTERN CAPE
Upington
Springbok
Port Nolloth
Alexander Bay
Wreck Point
Cape Columbine
Vredenburg
Saldanha
Malmesbury
Atlantis
Bellville
Cape Town
Nyanga
Paarl
Stellenbosch
Worcester
Strand
Swellendam
Hermanus
Cape of Good Hope
Danger Pt
Quoin Pt
Cape Agulhas
Mossel Bay
George
Knysna
Oudtshoorn
Beaufort West
Graaff-Reinet
Cape George
Cape Seal

E 30° F 809 35° G 40° H

MOZAMBIQUE
MALAWI
ZIMBABWE
MADAGASCAR
LESOTHO
SWAZILAND

NIASSA
EASTERN
CENTRAL
LUSAKA
SOUTHERN
TETE
NAMPULA
ZAMBÉZIA
MANICA
SOFALA
MASHONALAND CENTRAL
MASHONALAND WEST
MASHONALAND EAST
MANICALAND
MIDLANDS
MATABELELAND NORTH
MASVINGO
MATABELELAND SOUTH
NORTH EAST
INHAMBANE
GAZA
MAPUTO
NORTHERN PROVINCE
MPUMALANGA
GAUTENG
KWAZULU-NATAL
TOLIARA

Mkushi
Kapiri Mposhi
Kabwe
Mumbwa
Chisamba
Rufunsa
Lusaka
Chongwe
Luangwa
Zambue
Zumbo
Mazabuka
Monze
Kafue
Chirundu
Pemba
Kariba
Karoi
Mhangura
Guruve
Centenary
Mount Darwin
Chinhoyi
Zave
Bindura
Shamva
Mutoko
Murewa
Concession
Harare
Chitungwiza
Chegutu
Marondera
Chakari
Gokwe
Kadoma
Empress Mine
Msuna
Kamativi
Binga
Maamba
Lupane
Nkayi
Kwekwe
Redcliff
Gweru
Chivhu
Mvuma
Lalapansi
Shurugwi
Gutu
Inyathi
Fort Rixon
Mashava
Masvingo
Bulawayo
Nyamandhlovu
Ngamo
Plumtree
Esigodini
Mbalabala
Zvishavane
Filabusi
Ngundu
Bikita
Zaka
Chiredzi
Kezi
Gwanda
West Nicholson
Mbizi
Mwenezi
Francistown
Sebina
Mmadinare
Serule
Selebi Phikwe
Bobonong
Sefophe
Tuli
Mazunga
Beitbridge
Messina
Sango
Chicualacuala
Machaila
Pafuri
Alldays
Thohoyandou
Vivo
Mara
Louis Trichardt
Giyani
Tom Burke
Soekmekaar
Ellisras
Pietersburg
Tzaneen
Phalaborwa
Lebowakgomo
Thabazimbi
Nylstroom
Warmbad
Marble Hall
Tshokwane
Newington
Siyabuswa
Sun City
Pretoria
Mamelodi
Tembisa
Soweto
Johannesburg
Germiston
Heidelburg
Bethal
Evaton
Vereeniging
Vanderbijlpark
Klerksdorp
Sasolburg
Standerton
Ermelo
Barberton
Nelspruit
Mbabane
Mhlume
Manzini
Siteki
Big Bend
Hlatikulu
Lavumisa
Piet Retief
Volksrust
Kroonstad
Welkom
Virginia
Bethlehem
Harrismith
Madadeni
Newcastle
Vryheid
Ozizweni
Dundee
Ulundi
Phuthaditjhaba
Ladysmith
Empangeni
Richards Bay
Estcourt
Greytown
Sundumbili
Stanger
Lejoge
Maseru
Teyateyaneng
Mokhotlong
Roma
Mafeteng
Thabana-Ntlenyana 3482 m
Pietermaritzburg
Kwa Mashu
Umlazi
Durban
Isipingo
Mohale's Hoek
Quthing
Umzinto
Amanzimtoti
Scottburgh
Kokstad
Marburg
Port Shepstone
Uvongo
Barkly East
Elliot
Tsolo
Port St Johns
Umtata
Coffee Bay
Queenstown
Butterworth
King William's Town
Stutterheim
Bisho
East London
Mdantsane
Zwelitsha
Grahamstown
Port Alfred

Chipata
Mchinji
Lilongwe
Salima
Petauke
Katete
Nyimba
Kachalola
Cassacatiza
Chofombo
Fingoè
Furancungo
Ulongwè
Bene
Dedza
Ntcheu
Balaka
Mangochi
Machinga
Cazula
Songo
Cahora Bassa
Chicoa
Magoé
Mucumbura
Cataxa
Tete
Zomba
Chiradzulu
Blantyre
Mulanje
Mt Mulanje 3001 m
Chikwawa
Milange
Mandié
Bandar
Changara
Chiromo
Nsanje
Chiramba
Mungari
Guro
Nhamalábue
Vila de Sena
Caia
Catandica
Maringuè
Nyanga
Inyangani 2592 m
Serra da Gorongosa 1862 m
Rusape
Wedza
Gorongosa
Inhaminga
Mutare
Chimoio
Buhera
Cashel
Chimanimani
Monte Binga 2436 m
Chipinge
Dombe
Espungabera
Hacufera
Chitobe
Massangulo
Mandimba
Metarica
Maúa
Cuamba
Mutuali
Namuli 2419 m
Gurué
Malema
Molumbo
Erreqo
Alto Molócuè
Naiopué
Gilé
Mulevala
Lugela
Mugeba
Mocuba
Mucubela
Derre
Morrumbala
Namacurra
Olinga
Nova Nabúri
Mualama
Pebane
Namidobe
Quelimane
Mopeia
Marromeu
Chinde
Ponta Timbue
Nhamatanda
Dondo
Beira
Buzi
Sofala
Divinhe
Machanga
Nova Mambone
Bartolomeu Dias
Jofane
Ilha do Bazaruto
Massangena
Mabote
Vilanculos
Mapinhane
Nhachengue
Chigubo
Mapai
Funhalouro
Ponta da Barra Falsa
Massinga
Morrumbene
Homoine
Panda
Ponta da Barra
Inhambane
Mabalane
Massingir
Chókwè
Mapulanguene
Inharrime
Quissico
Macia
Chidenguele
Xai-Xai
Magude
Moamba
Matola
Marracuene
Maputo
Cabo de Santa Maria
Bela Vista
Catuane
Ubombo
Lake St Lucia

Namuno
Namapa
Muite
Memba
Baía de Memba
Umpilua
Nacaroa
Minguri
Mecuburi
Nacala
Mogovolas
Mossuril
Meconta
Muecate
Ribáuè
Murrupula
Nampula
Moçambique
Mogincual
Quinga
Chalaua
Quilua
Angoche
Moma
Ponta Lipobane

Mozambique Channel
Bassas da India (Réunion)
Île Europa (Réunion)
INDIAN OCEAN

Tambohorano
Maintirano
Reharaka
Masoarivo
Belo Tsiribihina
Tanjona Tsiribihina
Morondava
Andranopasy
Manja
Morombe
Tanjona Ankaboa
Ankazoabo
1348 m
Mahaboboka
Manombo Atsimo
Sakaraha
Toliara
Andranovory
Tongobory
Betioky
Soamanonga
Fotadrevo
Ejeda
Itampolo
Ampanihy
Androka
Beloha
Tanjona Vohimena

15° 20° 25° 30° 35°

1 2 3 812 4 5 6

Africa

E 30° F 35° G 40° H 45° J

0 100 200 300 400 kilometers
0 100 200 miles

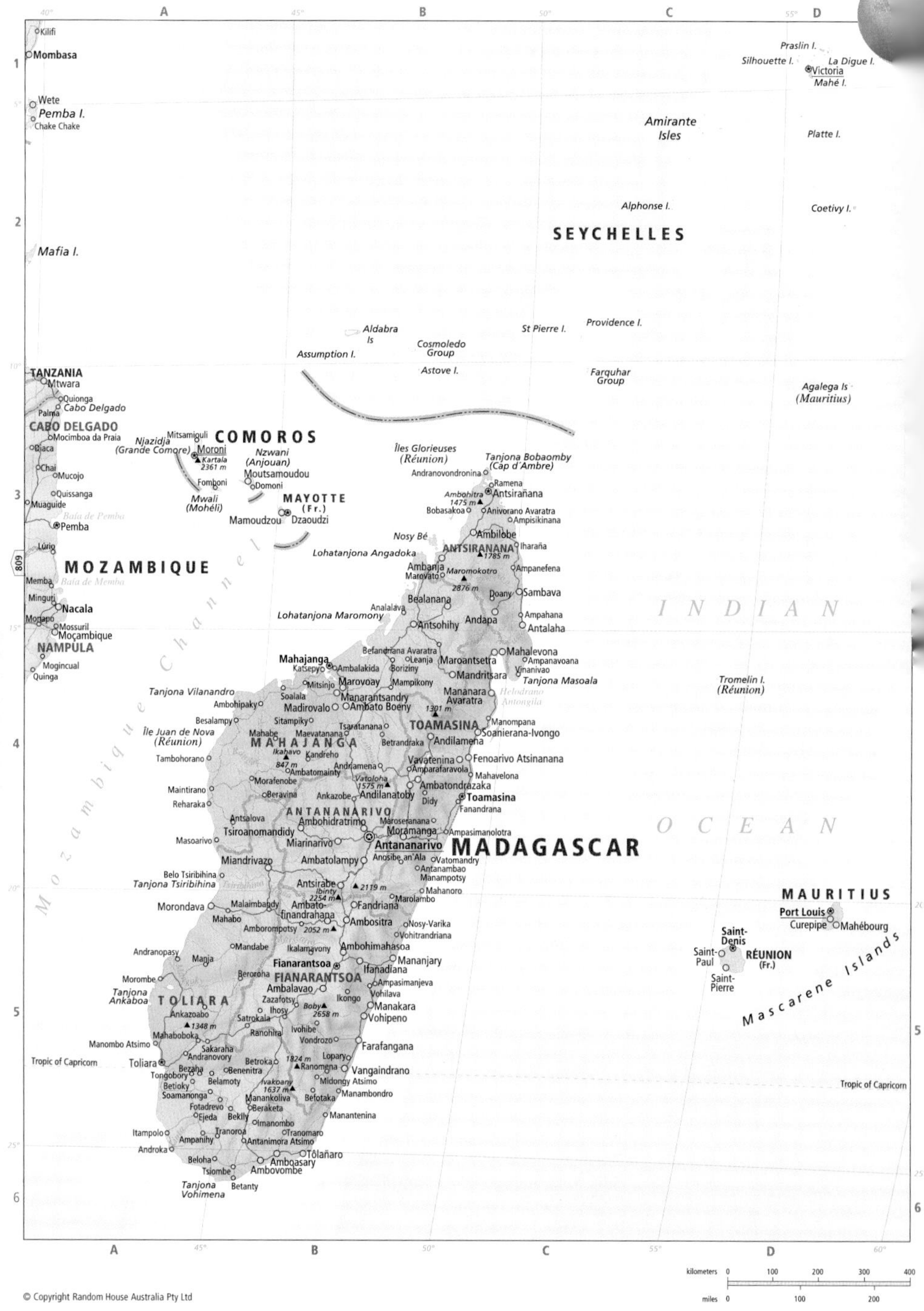

A
B
C
D
40°
45°
50°
55°
60°
10°
15°
20°
25°
1
2
3
4
5
6
Kilifi
Mombasa
Wete
Pemba I.
Chake Chake
Mafia I.
Praslin I.
Silhouette I.
La Digue I.
Victoria
Mahé I.
Amirante Isles
Platte I.
Alphonse I.
Coetivy I.
SEYCHELLES
Aldabra Is
Assumption I.
Cosmoledo Group
Astove I.
St Pierre I.
Providence I.
Farquhar Group
Agalega Is (Mauritius)
TANZANIA
Mtwara
Quionga
Cabo Delgado
Palma
CABO DELGADO
Mocimboa da Praia
Diaca
Chai
Mucojo
Quissanga
Muaguide
Baía de Pemba
Pemba
Lúrio
MOZAMBIQUE
809
Memba
Baía de Memba
Mingurí
Nacala
Mogapo
Mossuril
Moçambique
NAMPULA
Mogincual
Quinga
COMOROS
Mitsamiouli
Njazidja (Grande Comore)
Moroni
Kartala 2361 m
Fomboni
Mwali (Mohéli)
Nzwani (Anjouan)
Moutsamoudou
Domoni
MAYOTTE (Fr.)
Mamoudzou
Dzaoudzi
Mozambique Channel
Îles Glorieuses (Réunion)
Tanjona Bobaomby (Cap d'Ambre)
Andranovondronina
Ramena
Ambohitra 1475 m
Antsirañana
Bobasakoa
Anivorano Avaratra
Ampisikinana
Nosy Bé
Ambilobe
Lohatanjona Angadoka
ANTSIRANANA
1785 m
Iharaña
Ambanja
Marovato
Maromokotro 2876 m
Ampanefena
Doany
Sambava
Bealanana
Analalava
Lohatanjona Maromony
Andapa
Ampahana
Antalaha
Antsohihy
Befandriana Avaratra
Mahalevona
Mahajanga
Katsepy
Ambalakida
Leanja
Boriziny
Maroantsetra
Ampanavoana
Vinanivao
Mandritsara
Tanjona Masoala
Mitsinjo
Marovoay
Mampikony
Tanjona Vilanandro
Soalala
Manarantsandry
Mananara Avaratra
Helodrano Antongila
Ambohipaky
Madirovalo
Ambato Boeny
1301 m
Besalampy
Sitampiky
Tsaratanana
TOAMASINA
Manompana
Île Juan de Nova (Réunion)
Mahabe
Maevatanana
Betandraka
Andilamena
Soanierana-Ivongo
MAHAJANGA
Tambohorano
Ikahavo 847 m
Kandreho
Vavatenina
Fenoarivo Atsinanana
Ambatomainty
Andriamena
Amparafaravola
Mahavelona
Morafenobe
Vatoloha 1575 m
Ambatondrazaka
Maintirano
Beravina
Ankazobe
Andilanatoby
Didy
Toamasina
Reharaka
Fanandrana
ANTANANARIVO
Antsalova
Ambohidratrimo
Maroseranana
Tsiroanomandidy
Moramanga
Ampasimanolotra
Masoarivo
Miarinarivo
Antananarivo
MADAGASCAR
Miandrivazo
Ambatolampy
Anosibe an'Ala
Vatomandry
Antanambao Manampotsy
Belo Tsiribihina
Tanjona Tsiribihina
Antsirabe
Ibity 2254 m
2119 m
Mahanoro
Marolambo
Morondava
Malaimbandy
Ambatofinandrahana
Fandriana
Mahabo
Amborompotsy
2052 m
Ambositra
Nosy-Varika
Vohitrandriana
Andranopasy
Mandabe
Ikalamavony
Ambohimahasoa
Manja
Fianarantsoa
Mananjary
Morombe
Beroroha
FIANARANTSOA
Ifanadiana
Tanjona Ankaboa
TOLIARA
Ambalavao
Ampasimanjeva
Vohilava
Zazafotsy
Ikongo
Ankazoabo
Ihosy
Boby 2658 m
Manakara
Vohipeno
1348 m
Satrokala
Mahaboboka
Ranohira
Ivohibe
Vondrozo
Manombo Atsimo
Sakaraha
Andranovory
Farafangana
Tropic of Capricorn
Toliara
Betroka
1824 m
Ranomena
Lopary
Vangaindrano
Bezaha
Benenitra
Tongobory
Betioky
Belamoty
Ivakoany 1637 m
Midongy Atsimo
Soamanonga
Manankoliva
Befotaka
Manambondro
Fotadrevo
Ejeda
Bekily
Beraketa
Imanombo
Manantenina
Itampolo
Ampanihy
Tranoroa
Tranomaro
Androka
Antanimora Atsimo
Beloha
Tôlañaro
Tsiombe
Ambosary
Ambovombe
Tanjona Vohimena
Betany
INDIAN
OCEAN
MAURITIUS
Port Louis
Curepipe
Mahébourg
Saint-Denis
Saint-Paul
RÉUNION (Fr.)
Saint-Pierre
Mascarene Islands
Tromelin I. (Réunion)
kilometers 0 100 200 300 400
miles 0 100 200

A B C

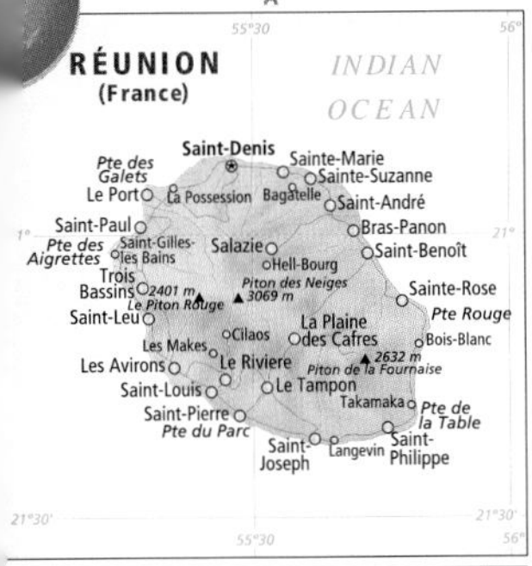
RÉUNION
(France)
INDIAN
OCEAN
Saint-Denis
Sainte-Marie
Sainte-Suzanne
Pte des Galets
Le Port
La Possession
Bagatelle
Saint-André
Saint-Paul
Bras-Panon
Saint-Gilles-les Bains
Pte des Aigrettes
Salazie
Saint-Benoît
Hell-Bourg
Trois Bassins
2401 m
Le Piton Rouge
Piton des Neiges 3069 m
Sainte-Rose
Pte Rouge
Saint-Leu
La Plaine des Cafres
Cilaos
Les Makes
Bois-Blanc
Les Avirons
Le Riviere
2632 m
Piton de la Fournaise
Saint-Louis
Le Tampon
Takamaka
Saint-Pierre
Pte de la Table
Pte du Parc
Saint Joseph
Langevin
Saint-Philippe

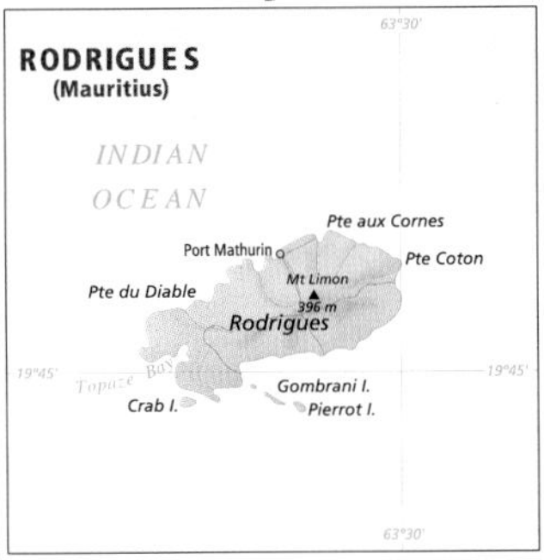
RODRIGUES
(Mauritius)
INDIAN
OCEAN
Pte aux Cornes
Port Mathurin
Pte Coton
Pte du Diable
Mt Limon
396 m
Rodrigues
Topaze Bay
Crab I.
Gombrani I.
Pierrot I.

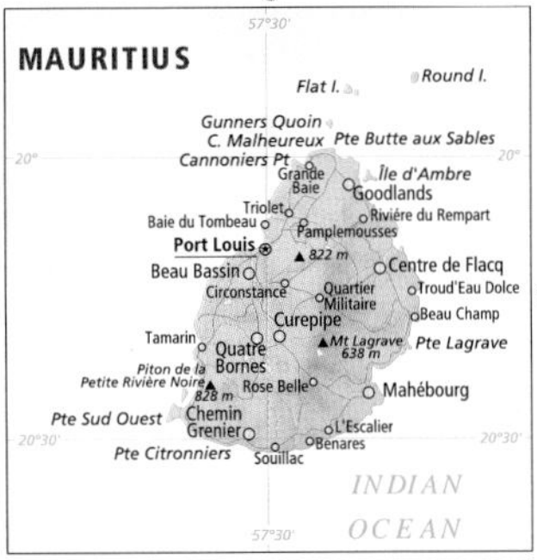
MAURITIUS
Flat I.
Round I.
Gunners Quoin
C. Malheureux
Pte Butte aux Sables
Cannoniers Pt
Grande Baie
Île d'Ambre
Goodlands
Triolet
Rivière du Rempart
Baie du Tombeau
Pamplemousses
Port Louis
822 m
Beau Bassin
Centre de Flacq
Circonstance
Quartier Militaire
Troud'Eau Dolce
Beau Champ
Curepipe
Tamarin
Quatre Bornes
Mt Lagrave 638 m
Pte Lagrave
Piton de la Petite Rivière Noire
828 m
Rose Belle
Mahébourg
Pte Sud Ouest
Chemin Grenier
L'Escalier
Benares
Pte Citronniers
Souillac
INDIAN
OCEAN

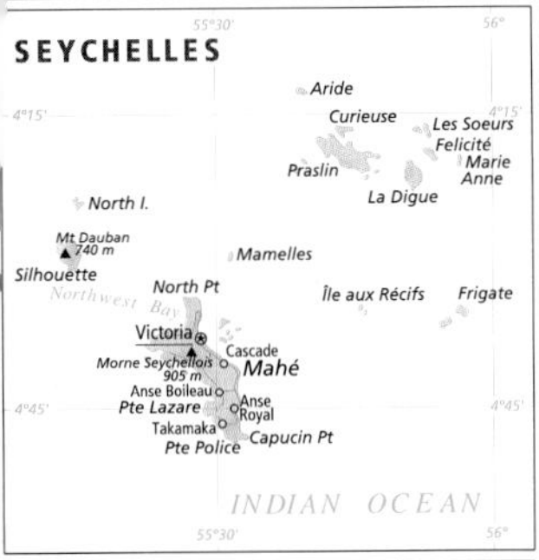
SEYCHELLES
Aride
Curieuse
Les Soeurs
Félicité
Marie Anne
Praslin
La Digue
North I.
Mt Dauban 740 m
Silhouette
Mamelles
North Pt
Northwest Bay
Île aux Récifs
Frigate
Victoria
Cascade
Morne Seychellois 905 m
Mahé
Anse Boileau
Pte Lazare
Anse Royal
Takamaka
Capucin Pt
Pte Police
INDIAN OCEAN

SOCOTRA
(Yemen)
ARABIAN
SEA
Ghubbat Qarmah
Ra's Ḥūlāf
Qulansiyah
Hadiboh
Ar Rak
Ra's Shū'ab
773 m
Qāḍub
1503 m
Hajhir
Ra's Qaṭānan
Suquṭrá (Socotra)
'Abd al Kūrī
Samḥah
Darsah
Al Ikhwān (The Brothers)
INDIAN
OCEAN

TRISTAN DA CUNHA
(St Helena)
Edinburgh
Rookery Pt
Queen Mary's Peak
2060 m
Sandy Pt
Anchorstock Pt
Tristan da Cunha
ATLANTIC
OCEAN
Seal Bay
Stonyhill Pt
West Pt
Inaccessible I.
561 m
East Pt
Stoltenhoff I.
Middle I.
Nightingale I.

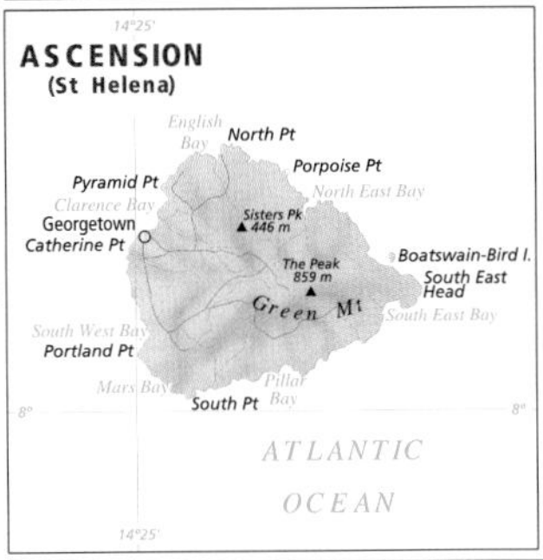
ASCENSION
(St Helena)
English Bay
North Pt
Porpoise Pt
Pyramid Pt
Clarence Bay
North East Bay
Georgetown
Catherine Pt
Sisters Pk 446 m
Boatswain-Bird I.
The Peak 859 m
South East Head
Green Mt
South West Bay
South East Bay
Portland Pt
Mars Bay
Pillar Bay
South Pt
ATLANTIC
OCEAN

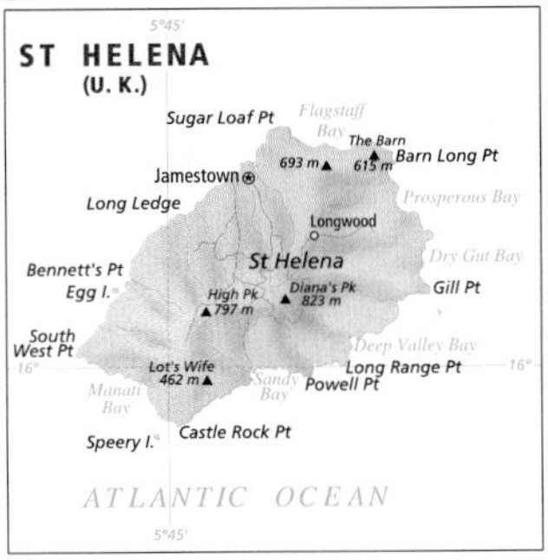
ST HELENA
(U. K.)
Sugar Loaf Pt
Flagstaff Bay
The Barn
Jamestown
693 m
615 m
Barn Long Pt
Long Ledge
Prosperous Bay
Longwood
Bennett's Pt
St Helena
Dry Gut Bay
Egg I.
High Pk 797 m
Diana's Pk 823 m
Gill Pt
South West Pt
Deep Valley Bay
Lot's Wife 462 m
Long Range Pt
Manati Bay
Sandy Bay
Powell Pt
Castle Rock Pt
Speery I.
ATLANTIC OCEAN

MADEIRA
(Portugal)
Porto Santo
517 m
Ilhéu de Ferro
Porto Santo
Ilhéu de Baixo
Porto Moniz
São Vicente
Santana
Pto do Pargo
1862 m
Faial
Calheta
Pico Ruivo de Santana
Pta de São Lourenço
Machico
Madeira
Ribeira Brava
Santa Cruz
Câmara de Lobos
Funchal
Deserta Grande
ATLANTIC
OCEAN
Ilhas Desertas
Ilhéu do Bugio

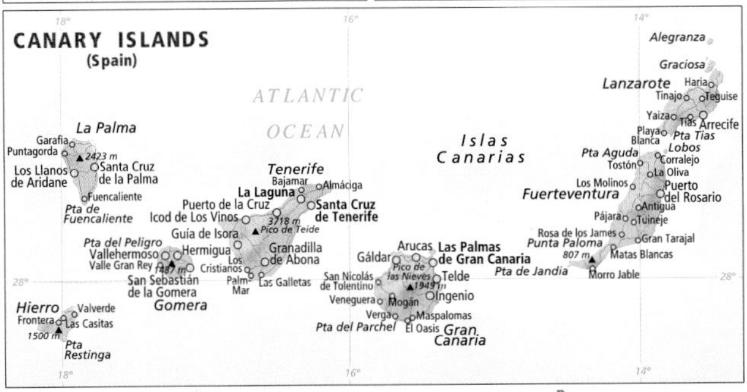
CANARY ISLANDS
(Spain)
Alegranza
Graciosa
Lanzarote
Haria
Tinajo
Teguise
ATLANTIC
OCEAN
Yaiza
Tías
Arrecife
La Palma
Playa Blanca
Pta Tías
Garafia
Puntagorda
Islas Canarias
Lobos
2423 m
Pta Aguda
Corralejo
Los Llanos de Aridane
Santa Cruz de la Palma
Tenerife
Tostón
La Oliva
Bajamar
Almáciga
Los Molinos
Puerto del Rosario
Fuencaliente
La Laguna
Fuerteventura
Pta de Fuencaliente
Puerto de la Cruz
Santa Cruz de Tenerife
Antigua
Icod de Los Vinos
3718 m
Pico de Teide
Pájara
Tuineje
Guía de Isora
Rosa de los James
Gran Tarajal
Pta del Peligro
Hermigua
Granadilla de Abona
Punta Paloma
Vallehermoso
Arucas
Las Palmas de Gran Canaria
807 m
Matas Blancas
Valle Gran Rey
1487 m
Los Cristianos
Gáldar
Pico de las Nieves
Telde
Pta de Jandia
Morro Jable
San Sebastián de la Gomera
Palm-Mar
Las Galletas
San Nicolás de Tolentino
1949 m
Ingenio
Gomera
Veneguera
Mogán
Hierro
Valverde
Vergá
Maspalomas
Frontera
Las Casitas
Pta del Parchel
El Oasis
Gran Canaria
1500 m
Pta Restinga

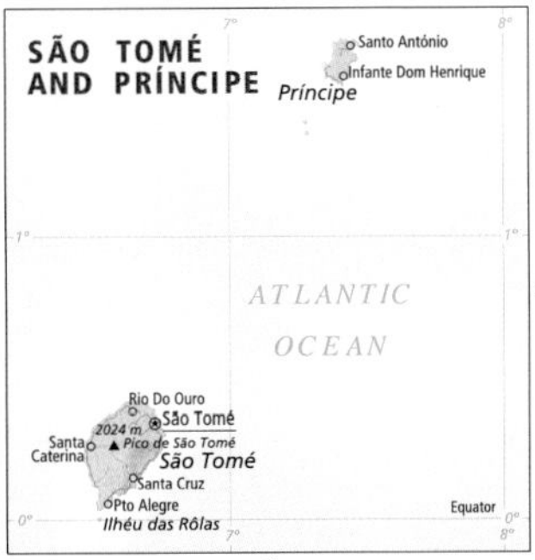
SÃO TOMÉ AND PRÍNCIPE
Santo António
Infante Dom Henrique
Príncipe
ATLANTIC
OCEAN
Rio Do Ouro
São Tomé
2024 m
Pico de São Tomé
Santa Caterina
São Tomé
Santa Cruz
Pto Alegre
Equator
Ilhéu das Rôlas

A B C

Africa

North and
Central
America

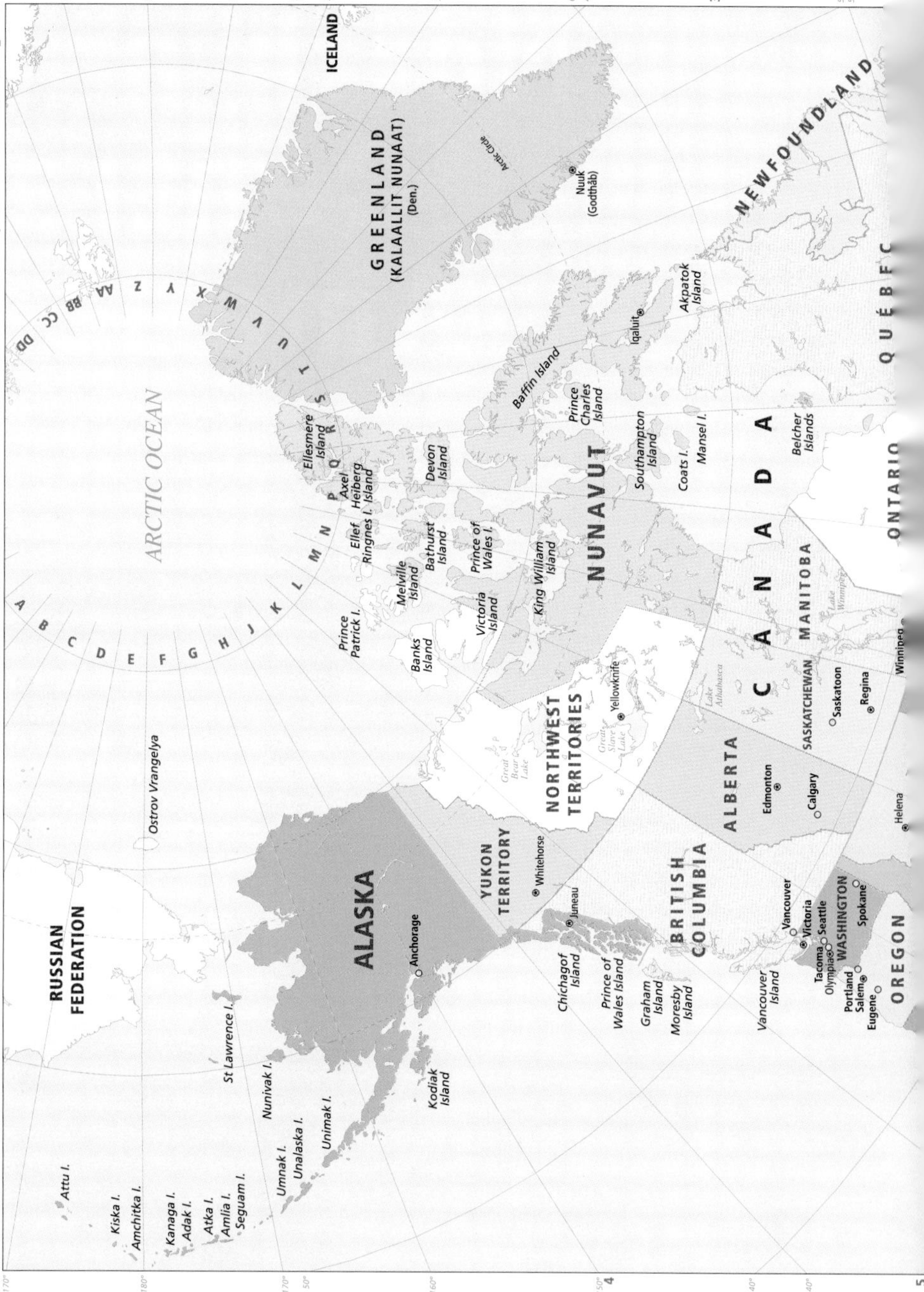
ARCTIC OCEAN
ICELAND
GREENLAND (KALAALLIT NUNAAT) (Den.)
Nuuk (Godthåb)
Arctic Circle
NEWFOUNDLAND
QUÉBEC
ONTARIO
CANADA
NUNAVUT
MANITOBA
SASKATCHEWAN
ALBERTA
NORTHWEST TERRITORIES
YUKON TERRITORY
BRITISH COLUMBIA
WASHINGTON
OREGON
ALASKA
RUSSIAN FEDERATION
Ostrov Vrangelya
Ellesmere Island
Axel Heiberg Island
Devon Island
Baffin Island
Prince Charles Island
Iqaluit
Akpatok Island
Southampton Island
Coats I.
Mansel I.
Belcher Islands
Ellef Ringnes I.
Bathurst Island
Prince of Wales I.
Melville Island
Prince Patrick I.
Victoria Island
King William Island
Banks Island
Yellowknife
Great Slave Lake
Great Bear Lake
Lake Athabasca
Lake Winnipeg
Winnipeg
Saskatoon
Regina
Edmonton
Calgary
Helena
Whitehorse
Juneau
Anchorage
Vancouver
Victoria
Seattle
Tacoma
Olympia
Spokane
Portland
Salem
Eugene
Chichagof Island
Prince of Wales Island
Graham Island
Moresby Island
Vancouver Island
St Lawrence I.
Nunivak I.
Kodiak Island
Unimak I.
Unalaska I.
Umnak I.
Attu I.
Kiska I.
Amchitka I.
Kanaga I.
Adak I.
Atka I.
Amlia I.
Seguam I.

North and Central America

PACIFIC OCEAN

ATLANTIC OCEAN

CARIBBEAN SEA

UNITED STATES OF AMERICA

CALIFORNIA
NEVADA
UTAH
ARIZONA
COLORADO
NEW MEXICO
NEBRASKA
KANSAS
OKLAHOMA
TEXAS
IOWA
MISSOURI
ARKANSAS
LOUISIANA
MISSISSIPPI
ALABAMA
ILLINOIS
INDIANA
OHIO
KENTUCKY
TENNESSEE
GEORGIA
FLORIDA
SOUTH CAROLINA
NORTH CAROLINA
VIRGINIA
W.VIRGINIA
PENNSYLVANIA
NEW YORK
NEW JERSEY
DELAWARE
MARYLAND
CONNECTICUT
RHODE ISLAND
MASSACHUSETTS
HAMPSHIRE

San Jose
Modesto
Fresno
Bakersfield
Las Vegas
Anaheim
Long Beach
Los Angeles
San Diego
Mexicali
Ensenada
Salt Lake City
Cheyenne
Denver
Pueblo
Phoenix
Mesa
Tucson
Santa Fe
Albuquerque
Amarillo
Lubbock
El Paso
Lincoln
Des Moines
Davenport
Topeka
Oklahoma City
Jefferson City
Fort Worth
Dallas
Shreveport
Austin
San Antonio
Houston
Corpus Christi
Madison
Milwaukee
Chicago
Springfield
St Louis
Little Rock
Memphis
Nashville
Jackson
Baton Rouge
New Orleans
Mobile
Montgomery
Birmingham
Atlanta
Columbus
Chattanooga
Tallahassee
Jacksonville
Orlando
Tampa
St Petersburg
Fort Lauderdale
Miami
Savannah
Charleston
Columbia
Charlotte
Raleigh
Virginia Beach
Richmond
Washington D.C.
Annapolis
Dover
Harrisburg
Trenton
New York
Hartford
Providence
Boston
Concord
Montpelier
Albany
Buffalo
Lansing
Detroit
Indianapolis
Louisville
Frankfort
Toronto
Hamilton
Ontario
Erie

MEXICO

Hermosillo
Chihuahua
La Paz
Nuevo Laredo
Monterrey
Matamoros
San Luis Potosí
Tampico
Guadalajara
Léon
Querétaro
Morelia
México
Cuernavaca
Puebla de Zaragoza
Acapulco
Coatzacoalcos
Tuxtla Gutiérrez
Campeche
Mérida

Isla Guadalupe (Mex.)
Islas Revillagigedo (Mex.)
Islas Galápagos (Ecu.)

BELIZE
Belmopan
GUATEMALA
Guatemala
HONDURAS
Tegucigalpa
San Salvador
EL SALVADOR
NICARAGUA
Managua
COSTA RICA
San José
PANAMA
Panamá
Isla de Coiba

BERMUDA (U.K.)
BAHAMAS
Nassau
CUBA
La Habana (Havana)
Pinar del Rio
Matanzas
Cienfuegos
Bayamo
Santiago de Cuba
CAYMAN ISLANDS (U.K.)
JAMAICA
Kingston
TURKS AND CAICOS ISLANDS (U.K.)
HAITI
Port-au-Prince
DOMINICAN REPUBLIC
Santo Domingo
PUERTO RICO (U.S.A.)
VIRGIN ISLANDS (U.S.A.)
VIRGIN ISLANDS (U.K.)
ANGUILLA (U.K.)
ANTIGUA AND BARBUDA
St Johns
Basseterre
ST KITTS AND NEVIS
MONTSERRAT (U.K.)
GUADELOUPE (Fr.)
DOMINICA
Roseau
MARTINIQUE (Fr.)
ST LUCIA
Castries
BARBADOS
Bridgetown
ST VINCENT AND THE GRENADINES
GRENADA
St George's
TRINIDAD AND TOBAGO
Port of Spain
ARUBA (Neth.)
NETHERLANDS ANTILLES (Neth.)

VENEZUELA
GUYANA
COLOMBIA
ECUADOR
PERU
BRAZIL

Tropic of Cancer
Equator

0 150 300 450 600 750 kilometers
0 150 300 450 miles

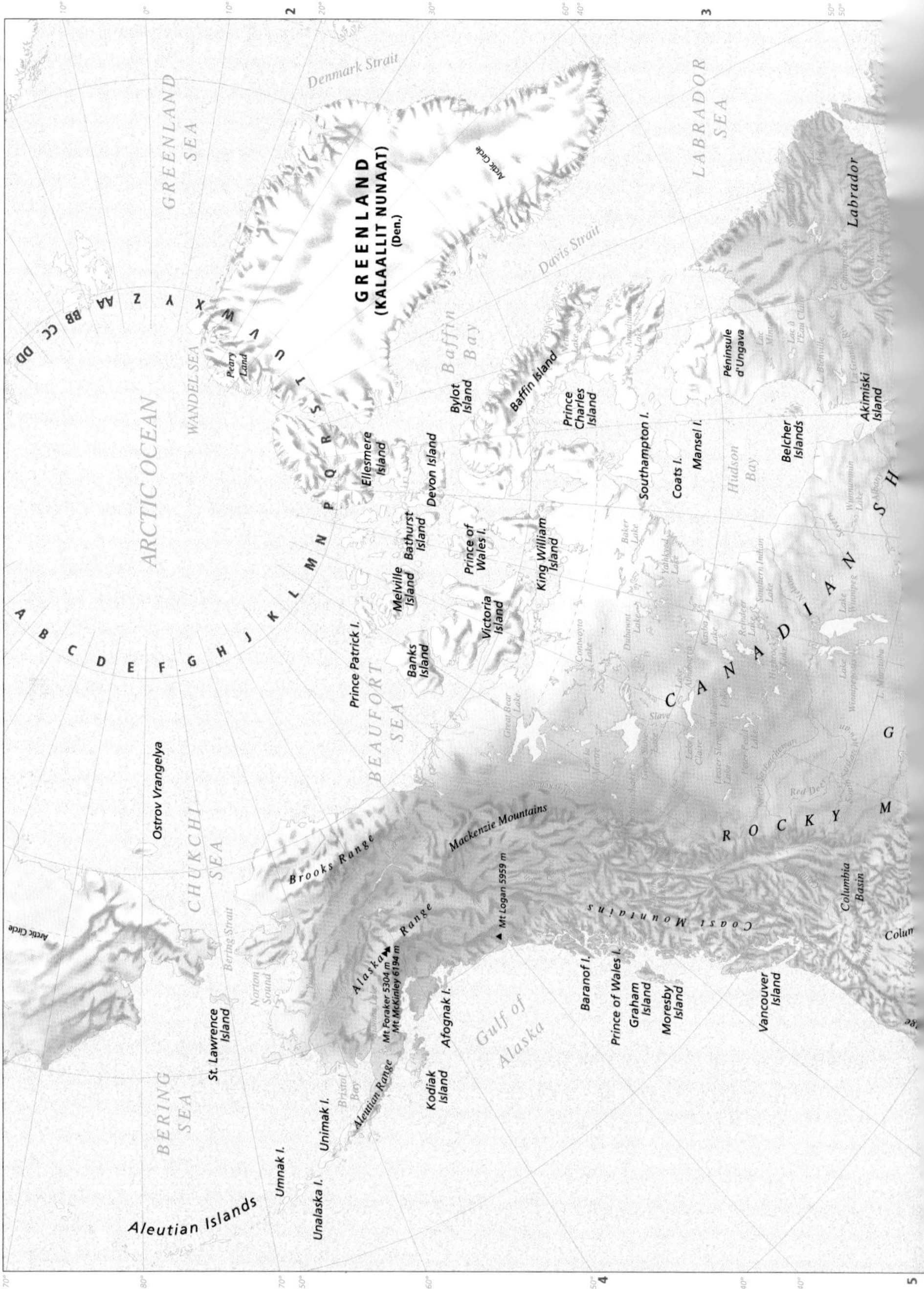
ARCTIC OCEAN
GREENLAND SEA
WANDEL SEA
Denmark Strait
GREENLAND
(KALAALLIT NUNAAT)
(Den.)
Arctic Circle
Peary Land
Davis Strait
LABRADOR SEA
Baffin Bay
Baffin Island
Bylot Island
Prince Charles Island
Ellesmere Island
Devon Island
Bathurst Island
Prince of Wales I.
Melville Island
King William Island
Victoria Island
Banks Island
Prince Patrick I.
Southampton I.
Coats I.
Mansel I.
Hudson Bay
Belcher Islands
Akimiski Island
Péninsule d'Ungava
Labrador
BEAUFORT SEA
CHUKCHI SEA
Ostrov Vrangelya
Bering Strait
Brooks Range
Mackenzie Mountains
Mt Logan 5959 m
Alaska Range
Mt Foraker 5304 m
Mt McKinley 6194 m
Coast Mountains
ROCKY M
CANADIAN SH
Columbia Basin
Norton Sound
St. Lawrence Island
BERING SEA
Bristol Bay
Aleutian Range
Unimak I.
Umnak I.
Unalaska I.
Aleutian Islands
Kodiak Island
Afognak I.
Gulf of Alaska
Baranof I.
Prince of Wales I.
Graham Island
Moresby Island
Vancouver Island
Great Bear Lake
Slave
Lake Athabasca
Baker Lake
Lake Winnipeg

Great Basin
Death Valley
Mojave Desert
Grand Canyon
Colorado Plateau
AINS
Plains
Lakes
APPALACHIAN MOU
Gulf of Maine
Isla Guadalupe
Tropic of Cancer
Baja California
Golfo de California
Sierra Madre Occidental
Sierra Madre Oriental
Bermuda
ATLANTIC OCEAN
Florida
Gulf of Mexico
Islas Revillagigedo
Cuba
Península de Yucatán
Vol. Popocatépetl 5452 m
Pico Turquino 2005 m
Hispaniola
Pico Duarte 3175 m
Co de Punta 1338 m
Puerto Rico
Barbuda
Antigua
St Kitts
Nevis
Guadeloupe
Dominica
Lesser Antilles
Golfo de Honduras
Victoria Peak 1120 m
Blue Mountain Peak 2256 m
Vol. Tajumulco 4220 m
Cerro Las Minas 2849 m
Cerro El Pital 2730 m
Pico Mogotón 2107 m
CARIBBEAN SEA
Clipperton I.
Aruba
Bonaire
Tobago
Pico Cristóbal Colón 5775 m
Cerro Chirripó 3819 m
Trinidad
PACIFIC OCEAN
Pico Bolívar 5007 m
Mte Roraima 2810 m
Cordillera Oriental
Equator
Islas Galápagos
Chimborazo 6310 m
M
N
P
Q
R
S
5
6
7
8
9
0 150 300 450 600 750 kilometers
0 150 300 450 miles

North and Central America

GREENLAND (KALAALLIT NUNAAT) (Den.)
ICELAND
JAN MAYEN (Nor.)
NEWFOUNDLAND
QUÉBEC
ONTARIO
NITOBA
NAVUT
ADA
NEW BRUNSWICK
NOVA SCOTIA
PRINCE EDWARD ISLAND
ST PIERRE AND MIQUELON (Fr.)
Labrador
ATLANTIC OCEAN
LABRADOR SEA
GREENLAND SEA
Denmark Strait
Davis Strait
Baffin Bay
Hudson Bay
Hudson Strait
Foxe Basin
Foxe Channel
Ungava Bay
James Bay
Gulf of St Lawrence
Cabot Strait
Lancaster Sd
Jones Sd
Gulf of Boothia
Cumberland Sound
Frobisher Bay
Nares Strait
Kane Basin
Smith Sd
Lincoln Sea
Arctic Circle
Baffin Island
Ellesmere Island
Devon Island
Axel Heiberg Island
Somerset Island
Southampton Island
Coats I.
Mansel I.
Nottingham I.
Salisbury I.
Resolution I.
Akpatok I.
Bylot I.
Coburg I.
Philpots I.
Graham I.
Belcher Is
Ottawa Is
Akimiski I.
Ile d'Anticosti
Cape Breton I.
Boothia Peninsula
Melville Pen.
Brodeur Pen.
Foxe Pen.
Meta Incognita Pen.
Cumberland Pen.
Hall Pen.
Henry Kater Pen.
Péninsule d'Ungava
Torngat Mts
Laurentian Mts
Long Range Mts
Knud Rasmussen Land
Kong Frederik VIII Land
Kong Christian X Land
Kong Christian IX Land
Kong Frederik IX Land
Kong Frederik VI Kyst
Peary Land
Nares Land
Milne Land
Kap Morris Jesup
Kap Eiler Rasmussen
Kap Bridgman
Kap York
Kap Seddon
Kap Parry
Kap Vedel
Kap Gustav Holm
Kangikajik
Shannon Ø
Store Koldewey
Île de France
Kap Marie Valdemar
Norske Øer
Hovgaard Ø
Traill Ø
Daneborg
Ittoqqortoormiit
Mestersvig
Petermanns Bjerg 2939 m
Gunnbjørn Fjeld 3700 m
Mont Forel 3360 m
J.A.D. Jensen Nunatakker 1680 m
2935 m
Qaanaaq (Thule)
Siorapaluk
Savissivik
Kullorsuaq
Nuussuaq
Tasiusaq
Upernavik
Maarmorilik
Illorsuito
Uummannaq
Qeqertarsuaq (Disko)
Qeqertarsuaq
Ataa
Ilulissat
Qasigiannguit (Christianshåb)
Kangaatsiaq
Kangerlussuaq
Sisimiut
Maniitsoq
Atammiko
Kapisillit
Nuuk (Godthåb)
Qeqertarsuatsiaat
Paamiut
Narsarsuaq
Kangilinnguit (Ivittuut)
Qaqortoq
Nanortalik
Nunap Isua
Timmiarmiut
Kangeq
Ammassalik
Tasiilaq
Sermiligaaq
Reykjavík
Hafnarfjörður
Stykkishólmur
Blönduós
Akureyri
Raufarhöfn
Fontur
Seyðisfjörður
Höfn
Fagurhólsmýri
Vík
Alert
Alert Pt
Eureka
Grise Fiord
Resolute
Arctic Bay
Pond Inlet
Clyde River
Igloolik
Hall Beach
Gjoa Haven
Pelly Bay
Repulse Bay
Coral Harbour
Rankin Inlet
Whale Cove
Arviat
Baker Lake
Pangnirtung
Iqaluit
Kimmirut
Cape Dorset
Kangeeak Pt
C. Sherard
C. Crauford
C. Baffin
C. Adair
C. Raper
C. Dyer
C. Mercy
C. Wilson
C. Dominion
C. Dobbs
C. Low
C. Jones
C. Chidley
C. Harrison
C. Churchill
C. Tatnam
C. Henrietta Maria
C. Ray
C. St. Mary's
Prince Charles I.
Salluit
Ivujivik
Kangiqsujuaq
Quaqtaq
Killiniq
Kangirsuk
Akulivik
Puvirnituq
Kangiqsualujjuaq
Kuujjuaq
Inukjuak
Sanikiluaq
Kuujjuaraapik
Chisasibi
Eastmain
Waskaganish
Mistassini
Chibougamau
Matagami
Miquelon
Dolbeau
Jonquière
Chicoutimi
Forestville
Rimouski
Sept-Îles
Havre-St-Pierre
Natashquan
Gaspé
La Martre
Bonaventure
Bathurst
Moncton
Grand Falls
Charlottetown
Sydney
Canso
Schefferville
Esker
Churchill Falls
Happy Valley-Goose Bay
Twin Falls
Labrador City
Wabush
Pitaga
Gagnon
Waco
Hebron
Cod I.
Okak Is
Nain
Davis Inlet
Hopedale
Cartwright
Port Hope Simpson
Red Bay
St Anthony
La Scie
Wesleyville
Bonavista
Port aux Choix
Springdale
Grand Falls-Windsor
St John's
Stephenville
Channel-Port aux Basques
Burgeo
Grand Bank
Churchill
York Factory
Gillam
Shamattawa
Fort Severn
Winisk
Peawanuck
Webequie
Summer Beaver
Attawapiskat
Ogoki
Lansdowne House
Pickle Lake
Moosonee
Moose Factory
Island Lake
Deer Lake
Pikangikum
South Bay
Manigotagan
Norway House
Warren Landing

K 824 L M 826 N

0 200 400 600 800 kilometers
0 200 400 miles

YUKON TERRITORY
ALASKA
U. S. A.
BRITISH COLUMBIA
COAST MOUNTAINS
ROCKY
PACIFIC OCEAN
Whitehorse
Robinson
Carcross
Jakes Corner
Johnsons Crossing
Teslin
St Elias Mts
Mt Hay 2704 m
Mt Fairweather 4663 m
Skagway
Atlin
Nakina
Mt Murray 2162 m
Logan Mountains
Watson Lake
Fort Liard
Coal River
Liard River
Cassiar
Good Hope Lake
Cassiar Mountains
Stikine Plateau
Meszah Peak 2164 m
Dease Lake
King Mtn 2408 m
Muncho Lake
Toad River
Mt Roosevelt 2972 m
Summit Lake
Fort Nelson
Mt Sylvia 2942 m
Elfin Cove
Hoonah
Hawk Inlet
Juneau
Douglas
Chichagof Island
Admiralty Island
Telegraph Creek
Iskut
Prophet River
Sitka Pt
Sitka
Baranof
Kake
Mt Ratz 3136 m
Mt Will 2515 m
Mt Cushing 2469 m
Truch
Baranof Island
Petersburg
Bob Quinn Lake
Skeena Mountains
Ware
2896 m Great Snow Mt
Sikanni Chief
Chatham Strait
Wrangell
Pink Mountain
Omineca Mountains
Alexander Archipelago
Sustut Peak 2469 m
Wonowon
Prince of Wales Island
Craig
Stewart
Fort St John
Hudson's Hope
Ketchikan
Chetwynd
Hazelton
New Hazelton
MacKenzie
Moricetown
2755 m Seven Sisters Peaks
Smithers
Telkwa
Mcleod Lake
Babine Lake
Dixon Entrance
C. Knox
Terrace
Prince Rupert
Masset
Houston
Forestdale
Fort St James
Porcher I.
Graham Island
Kitimat
Burns Lake
Fraser Lake
Engen
Summit Lake
Queen Charlotte Islands
Queen Charlotte Mts
Queen Charlotte
Sandspit
Hecate Strait
Pitt I.
Francois Lake
Lily Lake
Vanderhoof
Prince George
Giscome
Upper Fraser
Sinclair Mills
Ootsa Lake
Kemano
Banks I.
Red Rock
Dome Creek
Crescent Spur
Hixon
Strathnaver
Fawnie Nose 1926 m
Princess Royal I.
Lyell I.
Kitimat Ranges
Nazko
Wells
Barkerville
Quesnel
Kersley
Moresby Island
Aristazabel I.
Kunghit I.
Bella Coola
Mt Saugstad 2908 m
Marguerite
Soda Creek
Redstone
Williams Lake
Queen Charlotte Sound
Tatla Lake
Hanceville
Springhouse
Lac la Hache
Big Creek
Calvert I.
100 Mile House
Dog Creek
Mt Tatlow 3065 m
Mt Waddlington 4016 m
Mt Queen Bess 3313 m
Pacific Ranges
Clinton
C. Scott
Port Hardy
Sointula
Gold Bridge
Pavilion
Cache Creek
Quatsino
Lillooet
Ashcroft
Savona
Kamloops
Port Alice
Kelsey Bay
Sayward
Brem River
Pemberton
Mount Currie
Spences Bridge
C. Cook
Mt Tinniswood 2606 m
Kyuquot Sound
Zeballos
Campbell River
Lytton
Whistler
Merritt
Gold River
Powell River
Mt Garibaldi 2678 m
Courtenay
Comox
Brackendale
Nootka I.
Nootka
Vancouver Island
Irvines Landing
Squamish
2385 m
Boston Bar
Estevan Point
Strait of Georgia
Britannia Beach
Yale
Sechelt
Princeton
Flores I.
Tofino
Port Alberni
Vancouver
Burnaby
Hope
Nanaimo
White Rock
Langley
Chilliwack
Ucluelet
Ladysmith
Abbotsford
Barkley Sound
Blaine
Glacier
C. Beale
Duncan
Ferndale
Mt Baker 3285 m
Clo-oose
Sidney
Bellingham
Acme
Port Renfrew
Victoria
Anacortes
Hamilton
C. Flattery
Sooke
Sedro Woolley
Rockport
Neah Bay
Strait of Juan de Fuca
Oak Harbor
Oso
Mt Logan 2733 m
Sappho
Joyce
Port Angeles
Sequim
Forks
Marysville
WA
Winthrop
Carlton
Clearwater
Summerland
820
828

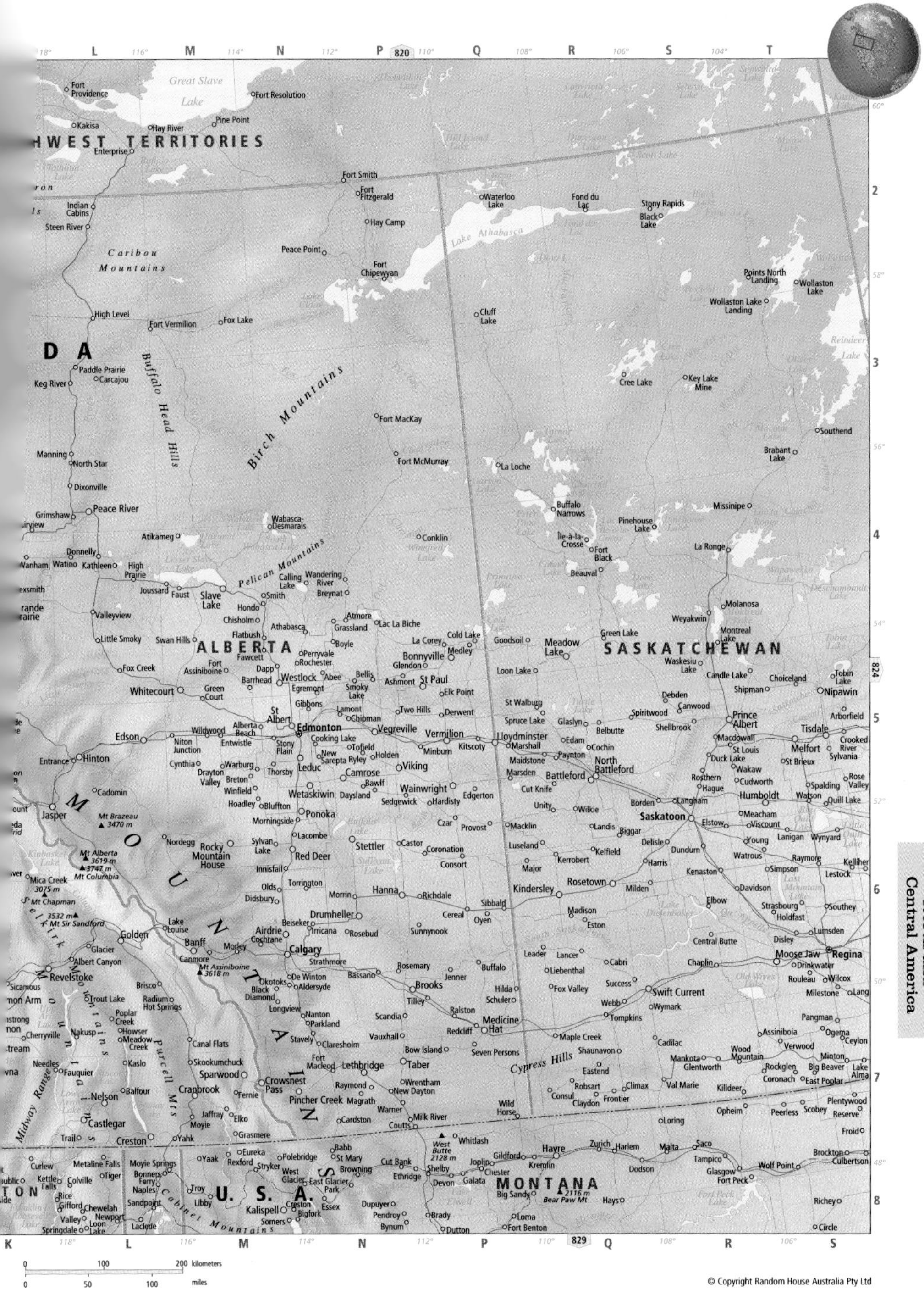
118° L 116° M 114° N 112° P 820 110° Q 108° R 106° S 104° T
NORTHWEST TERRITORIES
Great Slave Lake
Fort Providence
Fort Resolution
Kakisa
Hay River
Pine Point
Enterprise
Tathlina Lake
Buffalo Lake
Fort Smith
Fort Fitzgerald
Indian Cabins
Steen River
Hay Camp
Peace Point
Fort Chipewyan
Lake Claire
Caribou Mountains
Waterloo Lake
Fond du Lac
Stony Rapids
Black Lake
Lake Athabasca
Points North Landing
Wollaston Lake
Wollaston Lake Landing
Hill Island Lake
Scott Lake
Tazin Lake
Selwyn Lake
Labyrinth Lake
Snowbird Lake
Kasba Lake
Cluff Lake
High Level
Fort Vermilion
Fox Lake
CANADA
Paddle Prairie
Carcajou
Keg River
Buffalo Head Hills
Birch Mountains
Reindeer Lake
Cree Lake
Key Lake Mine
Fort MacKay
Fort McMurray
Southend
Brabant Lake
Manning
North Star
Dixonville
La Loche
Peter Pond Lake
Buffalo Narrows
Churchill Lake
Grimshaw
Peace River
Missinipe
Wabasca-Desmarais
Atikameg
Conklin
Winefred Lake
Pinehouse Lake
Île-à-la-Crosse
Fort Black
La Ronge
Lesser Slave Lake
Pelican Mountains
Donnelly
Watino
Kathleen
High Prairie
Joussard
Faust
Slave Lake
Calling Lake
Wandering River
Smith
Breynat
Beauval
Primrose Lake
Wapawekka Lake
Deschambault Lake
Valleyview
Hondo
Chisholm
Atmore
Lac La Biche
Athabasca
Grassland
Flatbush
Weyakwin
Molanosa
Montreal Lake
Green Lake
Little Smoky
Swan Hills
ALBERTA
Boyle
Perryvale
Rochester
La Corey
Cold Lake
Goodsoil
Meadow Lake
SASKATCHEWAN
Fawcett
Fort Assiniboine
Dapp
Bonnyville
Glendon
Medley
Waskesiu Lake
Fox Creek
Barrhead
Westlock
Abee
Bellis
Ashmont
St Paul
Loon Lake
Candle Lake
Choiceland
Tobin Lake
Whitecourt
Green Court
Egremont
Smoky Lake
Elk Point
Shipman
Nipawin
Debden
Canwood
Gibbons
Lamont
Two Hills
Derwent
St Walburg
St Albert
Chipman
Spruce Lake
Spiritwood
Prince Albert
Arborfield
Edson
Wildwood
Alberta Beach
Edmonton
Vegreville
Vermilion
Lloydminster
Glaslyn
Belbutte
Shellbrook
Tisdale
Niton Junction
Entwistle
Stony Plain
Cooking Lake
Tofield
Minburn
Kitscoty
Marshall
Edam
Cochin
Macdowall
Melfort
Crooked River
Entrance
Hinton
Cynthia
Warburg
New Sarepta
Ryley
Holden
Maidstone
Paynton
North Battleford
St Louis
Duck Lake
St Brieux
Sylvania
Drayton Valley
Breton
Thorsby
Leduc
Camrose
Viking
Marsden
Battleford
Wakaw
Rosthern
Cudworth
Rose Valley
Cadomin
Winfield
Wetaskiwin
Daysland
Bawlf
Wainwright
Cut Knife
Hague
Humboldt
Spalding
Watson
Quill Lake
Jasper
Mt Brazeau 3470 m
Hoadley
Bluffton
Ponoka
Sedgewick
Hardisty
Edgerton
Unity
Wilkie
Borden
Langham
Saskatoon
Meacham
Viscount
Elstow
Morningside
Czar
Provost
Macklin
Landis
Biggar
Lanigan
Wynyard
Nordegg
Rocky Mountain House
Sylvan Lake
Lacombe
Stettler
Castor
Luseland
Delisle
Young
Mt Alberta 3619 m
3747 m
Mt Columbia
Red Deer
Coronation
Consort
Kerrobert
Kelfield
Dundurn
Watrous
Raymore
Kelliher
Mica Creek
3075 m
Mt Chapman
Innisfail
Major
Harris
Simpson
Lestock
Kenaston
Torrington
Olds
Morrin
Hanna
Richdale
Kindersley
Rosetown
Milden
Davidson
Didsbury
Drumheller
Sibbald
Madison
Elbow
Strasbourg
Southey
3532 m
Mt Sir Sandford
Selkirk Mountains
Golden
Lake Louise
Beiseker
Irricana
Rosebud
Sunnynook
Cereal
Oyen
Eston
Holdfast
Lumsden
Glacier
Banff
Airdrie
Cochrane
Morley
Calgary
Central Butte
Disley
Albert Canyon
Canmore
Mt Assiniboine 3618 m
Strathmore
Rosemary
Leader
Lancer
Cabri
Chaplin
Moose Jaw
Drinkwater
Regina
Revelstoke
Brisco
De Winton
Okotoks
Aldersyde
Bassano
Jenner
Buffalo
Liebenthal
Success
Rouleau
Wilcox
Sicamous
Trout Lake
Radium Hot Springs
Black Diamond
Brooks
Tilley
Hilda
Schuler
Fox Valley
Swift Current
Milestone
Lang
Poplar Creek
Longview
Nanton
Scandia
Ralston
Webb
Wymark
Pangman
Nakusp
Howser
Meadow Creek
Parkland
Redcliff
Medicine Hat
Tompkins
Assiniboia
Ogema
Cherryville
Purcell Mts
Canal Flats
Stavely
Claresholm
Vauxhall
Bow Island
Seven Persons
Maple Creek
Cadillac
Verwood
Ceylon
Needles
Kaslo
Skookumchuck
Fort Macleod
Lethbridge
Taber
Cypress Hills
Shaunavon
Mankota
Wood Mountain
Glentworth
Rockglen
Minton
Lake Alma
Fauquier
Sparwood
Crowsnest Pass
Wrentham
New Dayton
Eastend
Coronach
East Poplar
Nelson
Balfour
Cranbrook
Fernie
Pincher Creek
Raymond
Magrath
Robsart
Consul
Claydon
Climax
Frontier
Val Marie
Killdeer
Midway Range
Castlegar
Jaffray
Elko
Warner
Wild Horse
Opheim
Peerless
Scobey
Plentywood
Reserve
Moyie
Cardston
Coutts
Milk River
Loring
Froid
Trail
Creston
Yahk
Grasmere
West Butte 2128 m
Whitlash
Eureka
Babb
Havre
Zurich
Harlem
Malta
Saco
Brockton
Culbertson
Curlew
Metaline Falls
Moyie Springs
Yaak
Rexford
Polebridge
St Mary
Cut Bank
Joplin
Gildford
Kremlin
Tampico
Wolf Point
Kettle Falls
Colville
Tiger
Bonners Ferry
Stryker
West Glacier
Browning
East Glacier Park
Shelby
Chester
Dodson
Glasgow
Fort Peck
Ethridge
Devon
Galata
MONTANA
Naples
Troy
Libby
U. S. A.
Big Sandy
2116 m Bear Paw Mt
Hays
Fort Peck Lake
Rice
Gifford
Chewelah
Sandpoint
Kalispell
Creston
Essex
Dupuyer
Richey
Valley
Newport
Bigfork
Pendroy
Brady
Loma
Springdale
Loon Lake
Laclede
Somers
Bynum
Dutton
Fort Benton
Circle
Cabinet Mountains
K 118° L 116° M 114° N 112° P 110° 829 Q 108° R 106° S
2 3 4 5 6 7 8
60° 58° 56° 54° 52° 50° 48°
824
0 100 200 kilometers
0 50 100 miles

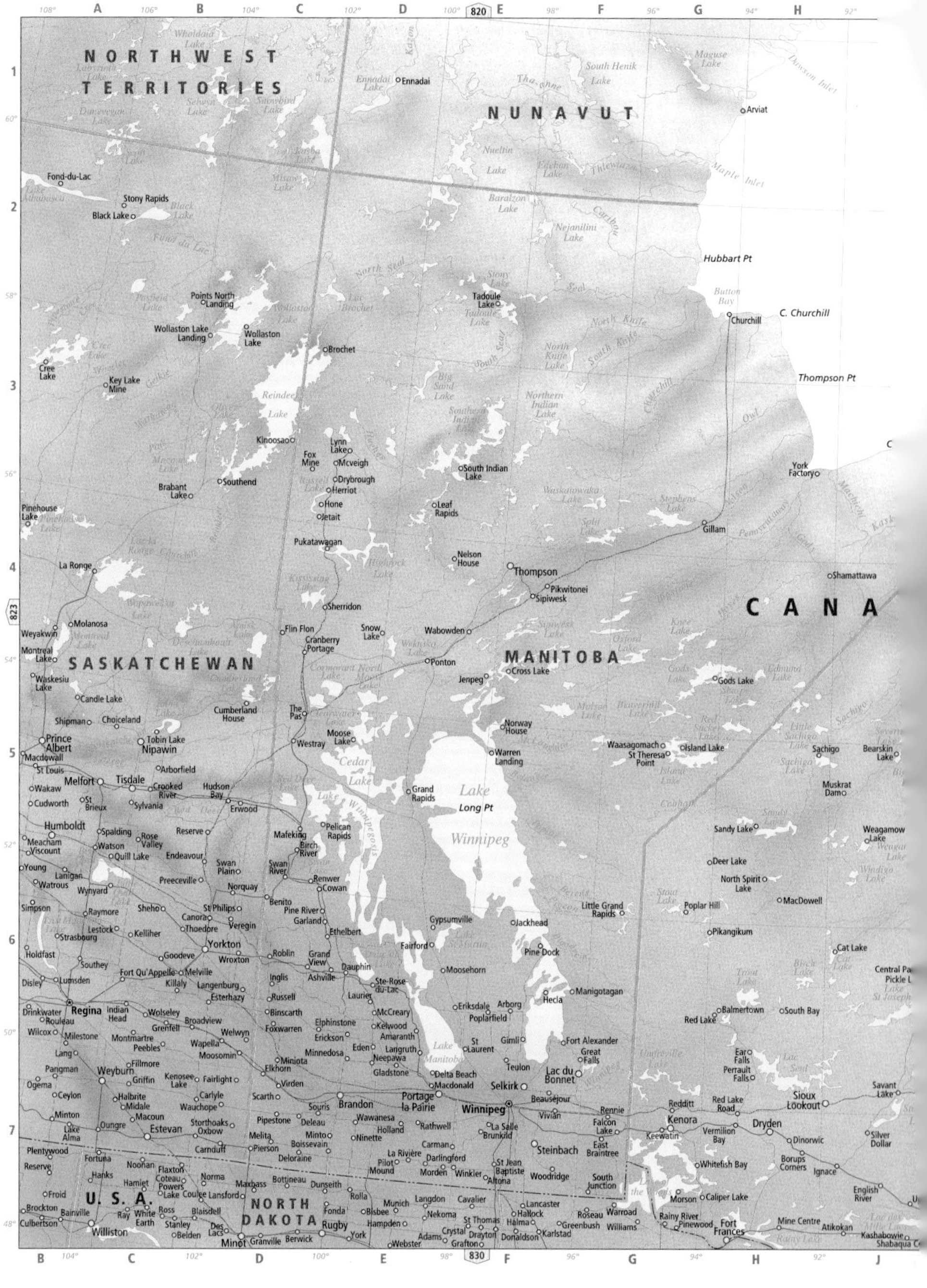

North and Central America

NORTHWEST TERRITORIES
NUNAVUT
SASKATCHEWAN
MANITOBA
CANA
U. S. A.
NORTH DAKOTA
Ennadai
Arviat
Fond-du-Lac
Stony Rapids
Black Lake
Hubbart Pt
Points North Landing
Wollaston Lake Landing
Wollaston Lake
Tadoule Lake
Churchill
C. Churchill
Brochet
Cree Lake
Key Lake Mine
Thompson Pt
Kinoosao
Lynn Lake
Fox Mine
Mcveigh
South Indian Lake
York Factory
Southend
Drybrough
Herriot
Brabant Lake
Hone
Jetait
Leaf Rapids
Pinehouse Lake
Gillam
Pukatawagan
Nelson House
La Ronge
Thompson
Shamattawa
Pikwitonei
Sipiwesk
Sherridon
Molanosa
Weyakwin
Flin Flon
Snow Lake
Wabowden
Cranberry Portage
Montreal Lake
Ponton
Waskesiu Lake
Jenpeg
Cross Lake
Gods Lake
Candle Lake
Cumberland House
The Pas
Shipman
Choiceland
Norway House
Moose Lake
Prince Albert
Tobin Lake
Nipawin
Westray
Warren Landing
Waasagomach
Island Lake
St Theresa Point
Sachigo
Bearskin Lake
Macdowall
St Louis
Arborfield
Wakaw
Melfort
Tisdale
Crooked River
Hudson Bay
Grand Rapids
Long Pt
Muskrat Dam
Cudworth
St Brieux
Sylvania
Erwood
Lake Winnipeg
Humboldt
Spalding
Rose Valley
Reserve
Mafeking
Pelican Rapids
Sandy Lake
Weagamow Lake
Meacham
Viscount
Watson
Quill Lake
Endeavour
Birch River
Young
Lanigan
Swan Plain
Swan River
Deer Lake
Watrous
Preeceville
Renwer
Cowan
North Spirit Lake
Wynyard
Norquay
Benito
Simpson
Raymore
Sheho
St Philips
Pine River
Little Grand Rapids
Poplar Hill
MacDowell
Lestock
Kelliher
Canora
Thoedore
Veregin
Garland
Ethelbert
Gypsumville
Jackhead
Strasbourg
Yorkton
Pikangikum
Holdfast
Goodeve
Wroxton
Roblin
Grand View
Fairford
Pine Dock
Cat Lake
Southey
Fort Qu'Appelle
Melville
Dauphin
Moosehorn
Disley
Lumsden
Killaly
Langenburg
Inglis
Ashville
Ste-Rose-du-Lac
Manigotagan
Central Pa
Pickle L
Esterhazy
Russell
Laurier
Drinkwater
Regina
Indian Head
Wolseley
Binscarth
McCreary
Eriksdale
Arborg
Hecla
Rouleau
Broadview
Poplarfield
Balmertown
South Bay
Wilcox
Milestone
Grenfell
Foxwarren
Elphinstone
Kelwood
Red Lake
Montmartre
Welwyn
Erickson
Amaranth
Lang
Peebles
Wapella
Eden
Langruth
St Laurent
Gimli
Fort Alexander
Moosomin
Minnedosa
Neepawa
Great Falls
Ear Falls
Fillmore
Miniota
Lake Manitoba
Pangman
Weyburn
Elkhorn
Gladstone
Teulon
Perrault Falls
Griffin
Kenosee Lake
Fairlight
Delta Beach
Lac du Bonnet
Ogema
Virden
Macdonald
Selkirk
Savant Lake
Ceylon
Halbrite
Carlyle
Scarth
Brandon
Portage la Prairie
Beausejour
Reddit
Red Lake Road
Sioux Lookout
Midale
Wauchope
Souris
Winnipeg
Rennie
Minton
Macoun
Storthoaks
Pipestone
Wawanesa
Vivian
Kenora
Dryden
Lake Alma
Oungre
Estevan
Oxbow
Deleau
Holland
Rathwell
La Salle
Falcon Lake
Melita
Minto
Ninette
Brunkild
Keewatin
Vermilion Bay
Dinorwic
Silver Dollar
Carnduff
Pierson
Boissevain
Carman
Steinbach
East Braintree
Plentywood
Fortuna
Deloraine
La Rivière
Darlingford
Reserve
Noonan
Flaxton
Pilot Mound
Morden
Winkler
St Jean Baptiste
Woodridge
Whitefish Bay
Borups Corners
Ignace
Hanks
Coteau
Norma
Altona
South Junction
Hamlet
Powers Lake
Maxbass
Bottineau
Dunseith
Froid
Coulee
Lansford
Rolla
English River
Munich
Langdon
Cavalier
Lancaster
Morson
Caliper Lake
Brockton
Bainville
Ray
White Earth
Ross
Blaisdell
Fonda
Bisbee
Nekoma
Hallock
Roseau
Warroad
Rainy River
Pinewood
Culbertson
Williston
Stanley
Des Lacs
Minot
Rugby
Hampden
St Thomas
Halma
Greenbush
Williams
Fort Frances
Mine Centre
Atikokan
Kashabowie
Shabaqua C
Belden
Granville
Berwick
York
Crystal
Drayton
Donaldson
Karlstad
Adams
Webster
Grafton
Cedar Lake
Reindeer Lake
820
823
830

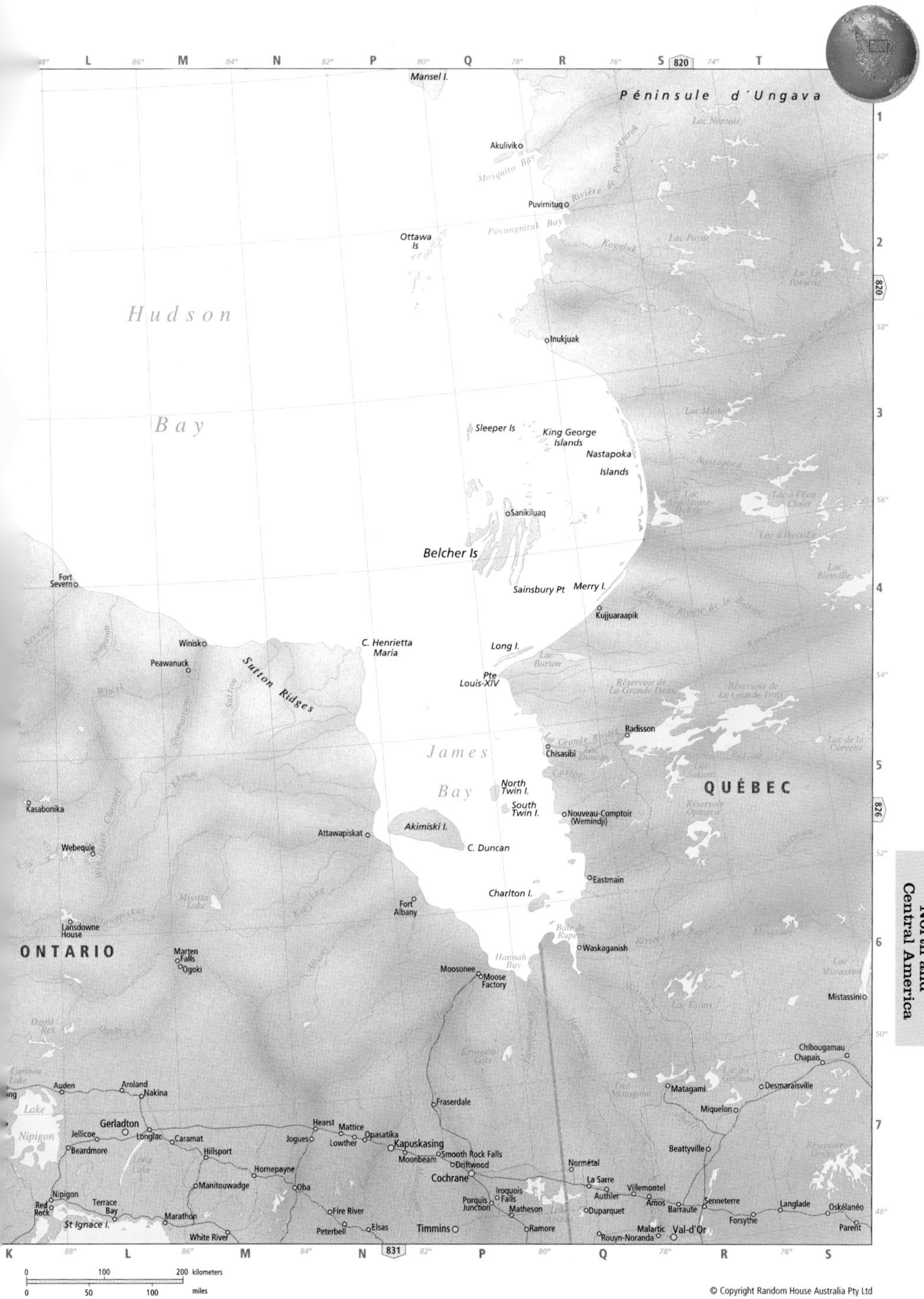

Péninsule d'Ungava
Mansel I.
Akulivik
Mosquito Bay
Puvirnituq
Povungnituk Bay
Rivière de Povungnituk
Kogaluk
Lac Payne
Ottawa Is
Hudson
Bay
Inukjuak
Lac Minto
Sleeper Is
King George Islands
Nastapoka Islands
Nastapoca
Sanikiluaq
Belcher Is
Lac Guillaume-Delisle
Lac à l'Eau Claire
Lac d'Iberville
Fort Severn
Sainsbury Pt
Merry I.
Kujjuaraapik
Grande Rivière de la Baleine
Winisk
Peawanuck
Sutton Ridges
C. Henrietta Maria
Long I.
Lac Burton
Pte Louis-XIV
Réservoir de La Grande Deux
Réservoir de La Grande Trois
Radisson
La Grande Rivière
Chisasibi
James
Bay
North Twin I.
South Twin I.
QUÉBEC
Kasabonika
Nouveau-Comptoir (Wemindji)
Akimiski I.
Attawapiskat
C. Duncan
Webequie
Eastmain
Charlton I.
Fort Albany
Lansdowne House
ONTARIO
Marten Falls
Ogoki
Baie de Rupert
Waskaganish
Hannah Bay
Moosonee
Moose Factory
Mistassini
Lac Mistassini
Lac Evans
Chibougamau
Chapais
Auden
Aroland
Nakina
Matagami
Desmaraisville
Fraserdale
Lake Nipigon
Miquelon
Gerladton
Jellicoe
Longlac
Caramat
Hearst
Mattice
Opasatika
Jogues
Lowther
Kapuskasing
Beardmore
Hillsport
Moonbeam
Smooth Rock Falls
Driftwood
Beattyville
Hornepayne
Normétal
Cochrane
La Sarre
Manitouwadge
Oba
Villemontel
Nipigon
Red Rock
Terrace Bay
Iroquois Falls
Porquis Junction
Authier
Amos
Senneterre
Fire River
Matheson
Duparquet
Barraute
Langlade
Oskélanéo
St Ignace I.
Marathon
Forsythe
Peterbell
Elsas
Timmins
Ramore
Malartic
Val-d'Or
Parent
White River
Rouyn-Noranda
820
826
831
0 100 200 kilometers
0 50 100 miles

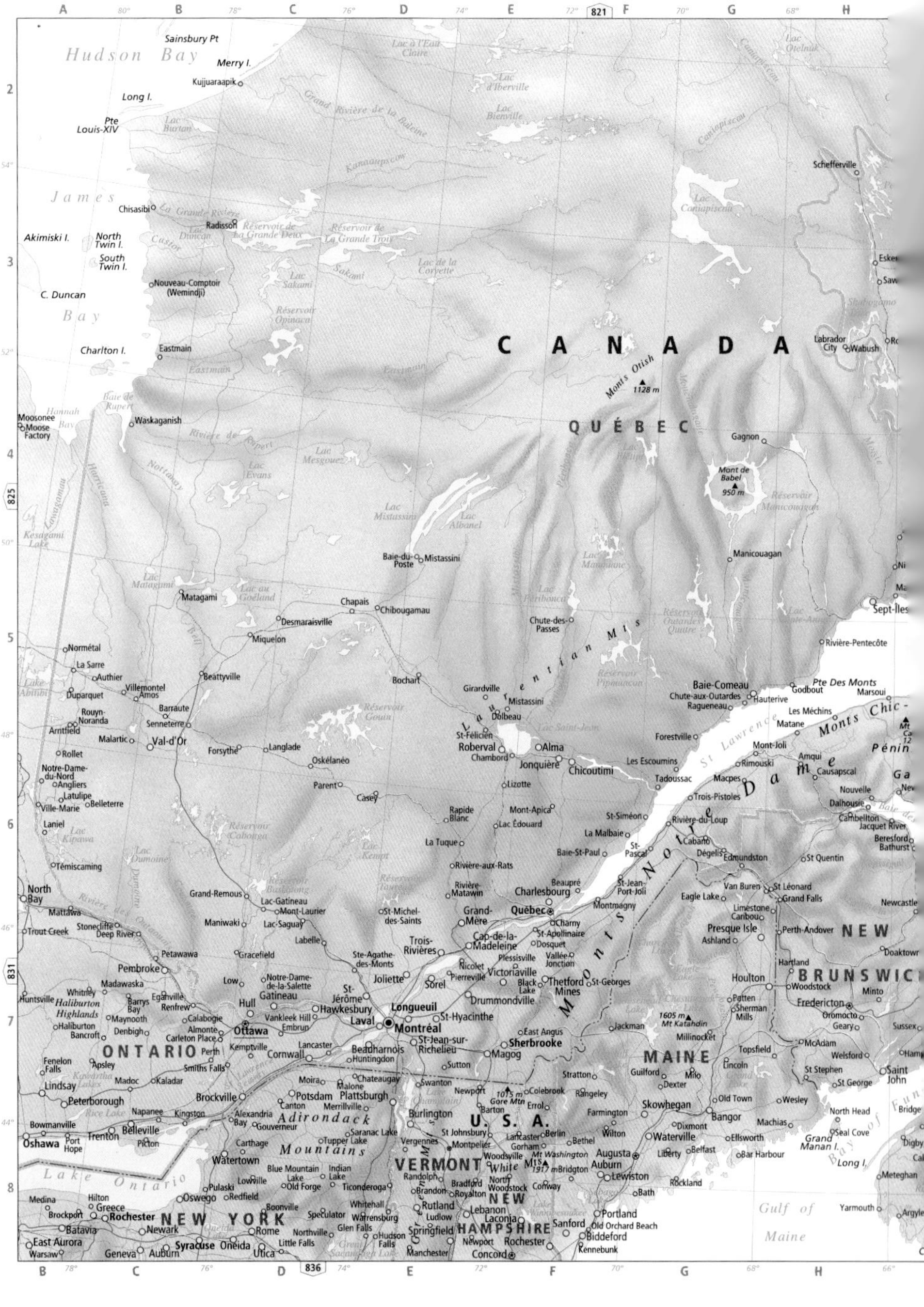

A
B
C
D
E
F
G
H
80°
78°
76°
74°
72°
70°
68°
66°
821
825
831
836
2
3
4
5
6
7
8
54°
52°
50°
48°
46°
44°
Hudson Bay
Sainsbury Pt
Merry I.
Kujjuaraapik
Long I.
Pte Louis-XIV
James Bay
Chisasibi
Radisson
Akimiski I.
North Twin I.
South Twin I.
Nouveau-Comptoir (Wemindji)
C. Duncan
Charlton I.
Eastmain
Moosonee
Moose Factory
Waskaganish
CANADA
QUÉBEC
Monts Otish
1128 m
Gagnon
Mont de Babel
950 m
Schefferville
Labrador City
Wabush
Manicouagan
Baie-du-Poste
Mistassini
Matagami
Chapais
Chibougamau
Desmaraisville
Miquelon
Chute-des-Passes
Laurentian Mts
Sept-Îles
Rivière-Pentecôte
Normétal
La Sarre
Authier
Villemontel
Amos
Duparquet
Beattyville
Bochart
Girardville
Mistassini
Dolbeau
Baie-Comeau
Chute-aux-Outardes
Ragueneau
Hauterive
Godbout
Pte Des Monts
Marsoui
Les Méchins
Matane
Monts Chic-Chocs
Rouyn-Noranda
Arntfield
Barraute
Senneterre
Malartic
Val-d'Or
Forsythe
Langlade
St-Félicien
Roberval
Chambord
Alma
Jonquière
Chicoutimi
Lac Saint-Jean
Forestville
St Lawrence
Mont-Joli
Rimouski
Amqui
Causapscal
Rollet
Oskélanéo
Notre-Dame-du-Nord
Angliers
Latulipe
Belleterre
Ville-Marie
Parent
Casey
Lizotte
Les Escoumins
Tadoussac
Macpes
Trois-Pistoles
Nouvelle
Dalhousie
Campbellton
Jacquet River
Laniel
Rapide Blanc
Mont-Apica
Lac Édouard
St-Siméon
Rivière-du-Loup
La Malbaie
La Tuque
Cabano
Dégelis
Edmundston
St Quentin
Beresford
Bathurst
Témiscaming
Baie-St-Paul
St-Pascal
Rivière-aux-Rats
Notre Dame
Beaupré
Charlesbourg
St-Jean-Port-Joli
Montmagny
Van Buren
St Léonard
Grand Falls
North Bay
Grand-Remous
Lac-Gatineau
Mont-Laurier
St-Michel-des-Saints
Rivière-Matawin
Grand-Mère
Québec
Charny
Eagle Lake
Limestone
Caribou
Newcastle
Mattawa
Trout Creek
Stonecliffe
Deep River
Maniwaki
Lac-Saguay
Trois-Rivières
Cap-de-la-Madeleine
St-Apollinaire
Dosquet
Presque Isle
Ashland
Perth-Andover
NEW BRUNSWICK
Petawawa
Gracefield
Labelle
Ste-Agathe-des-Monts
Plessisville
Vallée-Jonction
Nicolet
Pierreville
Victoriaville
Doaktown
Pembroke
Madawaska
Low
Notre-Dame-de-la-Salette
Joliette
Sorel
Black Lake
Thetford Mines
St-Georges
Monts Notre Dame
Hartland
Houlton
Woodstock
Minto
Huntsville
Whitney
Haliburton Highlands
Barrys Bay
Eganville
Renfrew
Hull
Gatineau
St-Jérôme
Hawkesbury
Longueuil
Drummondville
Patten
Sherman Mills
Fredericton
Oromocto
Maynooth
Haliburton
Bancroft
Denbigh
Calabogie
Ottawa
Vankleek Hill
Embrun
Laval
Montréal
St-Hyacinthe
East Angus
Sherbrooke
Jackman
1605 m Mt Katahdin
Millinocket
Geary
Sussex
Carleton Place
Almonte
ONTARIO
Perth
Kemptville
Cornwall
Lancaster
Beauharnois
Huntingdon
St-Jean-sur-Richelieu
Magog
MAINE
Topsfield
McAdam
Welsford
Fenelon Falls
Apsley
Smiths Falls
Sutton
Lincoln
St Stephen
Saint John
St George
Lindsay
Madoc
Kaladar
Brockville
Moira
Malone
Chateaugay
Swanton
Newport
Colebrook
1015 m Gore Mtn
Stratton
Rangeley
Guilford
Milo
Dexter
Peterborough
Potsdam
Canton
Plattsburgh
Merrillville
Barton
Errol
Skowhegan
Old Town
Wesley
North Head
Bridgetown
Bowmanville
Napanee
Kingston
Alexandria Bay
Gouverneur
Adirondack Mountains
Burlington
U.S.A.
Farmington
Bangor
Machias
Oshawa
Port Hope
Trenton
Belleville
Picton
Saranac Lake
St Johnsbury
Lancaster
Berlin
Wilton
Dixmont
Seal Cove
Grand Manan I.
Bay of Fundy
Digby
Carthage
Tupper Lake
Vergennes
Montpelier
Gorham
Bethel
Augusta
Waterville
Ellsworth
Watertown
Woodsville
Mt Washington
White Mts
1917 m
Bridgton
Auburn
Liberty
Belfast
Bar Harbour
Long I.
Lake Ontario
Blue Mountain Lake
Indian Lake
Lowville
VERMONT
Randolph
Bradford
North Woodstock
Conway
Lewiston
Rockland
Meteghan
Pulaski
Old Forge
Ticonderoga
Brandon
Royalton
NEW HAMPSHIRE
Bath
Medina
Hilton
Greece
Oswego
Redfield
Whitehall
Rutland
Ludlow
Lebanon
Laconia
Portland
Gulf of Maine
Yarmouth
Argyle
Brockport
Rochester
NEW YORK
Boonville
Speculator
Warrensburg
Green Mts
Old Orchard Beach
Batavia
Newark
Rome
Northville
Glen Falls
Hudson Falls
Springfield
Sanford
Biddeford
East Aurora
Warsaw
Geneva
Auburn
Syracuse
Oneida
Utica
Little Falls
Manchester
Newport
Rochester
Concord
Kennebunk

North and Central America

LABRADOR SEA
Tunungayualok Island
Davis Inlet
Hopedale
C. Makkovik
C. Harrison
C. Turley
Mt Benedict 829 m
Holton
Groswater Bay
C. Porcupine
Grady Harbour
Cartwright
Separation Point
Batteau
Comfort Bight
Labrador
Lake Melville
Happy Valley - Goose Bay
Mealy Mts
Square Islands
Port Hope Simpson
Table Head
Belle Isle
Red Bay
C. Bauld
L'Anse aux Meadows
Blanc-Sablon
Rivière-St-Paul
Forteaux
Strait of Belle Isle
St Anthony
Main Brook
Hare Bay
St-Augustin
Brig Bay
Groais I.
Grey Is
St John I.
Northern
Englee
Bell I.
Port aux Choix
Mutton Bay
Hawkes Bay
Williamsport
Horse Is
Daniel's Harbour
Peninsula
Long Range Mts
White Bay
C. St John
La Scie
Baie Verte
Westport
Notre Dame Bay
Fogo
Fogo I.
Baie-Johan Beetz
Havre-St-Pierre
Natashquan
Kegaska
Pointe-Parent
Gethsémani
Sally's Cove
Rocky Harbour
Hampden
Gros Morne 806 m
Springdale
Musgrave Harbour
Cape Freels
Gander Bay
Wesleyville
Île d'Anticosti
Mt St Gregory 674 m
Deer Lake
Grand Falls-Windsor
Badger
Gander
Bonavista Bay
Bonavista
Chicotte
Pte de l'Est
Corner Brook
Grand Lake
Buchans
Gambo
Glover I.
Red Indian Lake
Summerville
Lourdes
Lewis Hills 815 m
Stephenville
Newfoundland
Musgravetown
Grates Cove
Cape St George
Victoria Lake
Clarenville
Meelpaeg Lake
Middle Ridge
Goobies
Trinity Bay
Conception Bay
Pouch Cove
Gulf of St Lawrence
St George's Bay
St Alban's
Milltown
Carbonear
St John's
Bay Roberts
Mount Pearl
C. Anguille
Avalon Peninsula
Bay Bulls
Harbour Breton
Placentia
C. Ray
Channel-Port aux Basques
Rose Blanche
Burgeo
Hermitage Bay
Fortune Bay
Garnish
Marystown
Placentia Bay
Ferryland
Grand-Entrée
Cap aux Meules
Îles de la Madelaine
Havre-Aubert
Miquelon
Grand Bank
Fortune
ST PIERRE AND MIQUELON (Fr.)
St Pierre
St Lawrence
Branch
C. St Mary's
St Mary's Bay
Trepassey
Cape Race
Cape Pine
Cabot Strait
North Cape
PRINCE EDWARD ISLAND
Cape North
Ingonish
Chéticamp
Summerside
St Peters
East Pt
Elmira
Charlottetown
Montague
Cape Tormentine
Margaree Forks
Inverness
Port Hood
New Waterford
Glace Bay
Sydney
Whycocomagh
Cape George
Main-à-Dieu
Bras d'Or Lake
Cape Breton Island
Amherst
Oxford
Tatamagouche
New Glasgow
Port Hawkesbury
Fourchu
Isle Madam
Stellarton
Monastery
Arichat
Truro
Bolyston
Aspen
Canso
Tor Bay
Windsor
NOVA SCOTIA
Musquodoboit Harbour
Sheet Harbour
Halifax
Dartmouth
Sambro
Lunenburg
ATLANTIC OCEAN
0 100 200 kilometers
0 50 100 miles

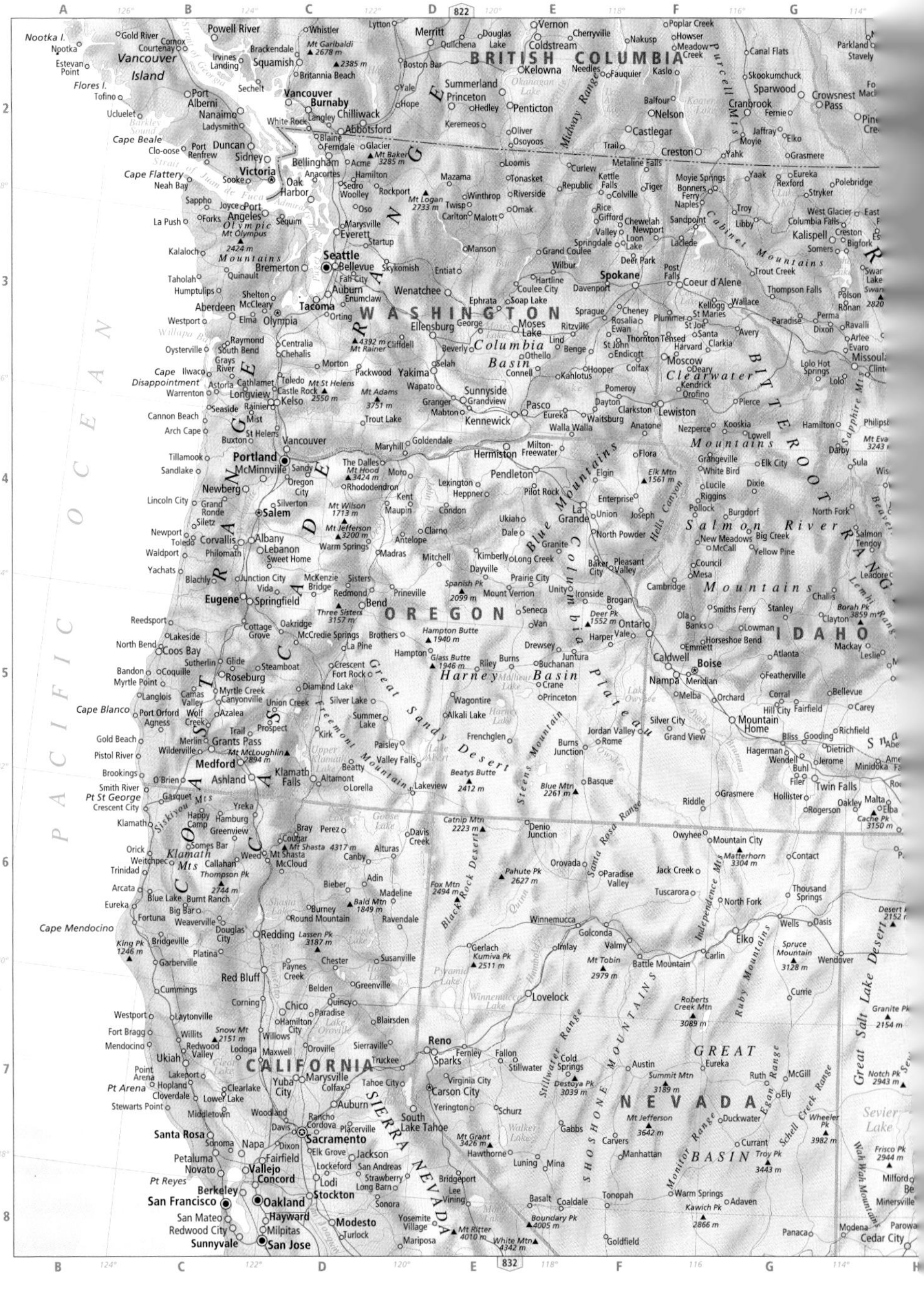

North and Central America

A B C D E F G
822
832
BRITISH COLUMBIA
WASHINGTON
OREGON
IDAHO
CALIFORNIA
NEVADA
PACIFIC OCEAN
Vancouver Island
Nootka I.
Flores I.
Gold River
Comox
Courtenay
Powell River
Whistler
Lytton
Merritt
Douglas Lake
Quilchena
Vernon
Cherryville
Coldstream
Kelowna
Nakusp
Poplar Creek
Howser
Meadow Creek
Canal Flats
Parkland
Stavely
Nootka
Estevan Point
Tofino
Ucluelet
Port Alberni
Nanaimo
Ladysmith
Duncan
Sidney
Victoria
Sooke
Cape Beale
Clo-oose
Port Renfrew
Cape Flattery
Neah Bay
Irvines Landing
Brackendale
Squamish
Sechelt
Britannia Beach
Mt Garibaldi 2678 m
2385 m
Vancouver
Burnaby
White Rock
Langley
Chilliwack
Abbotsford
Boston Bar
Yale
Hope
Summerland
Princeton
Hedley
Penticton
Keremeos
Oliver
Osoyoos
Needles
Fauquier
Kaslo
Balfour
Nelson
Castlegar
Trail
Creston
Skookumchuck
Sparwood
Cranbrook
Fernie
Crowsnest Pass
Jaffray
Moyie
Yahk
Elko
Grasmere
Purcell Mts
Midway Range
Blaine
Ferndale
Glacier
Mt Baker 3285 m
Bellingham
Acme
Anacortes
Hamilton
Oak Harbor
Sedro Woolley
Rockport
Mazama
Mt Logan 2733 m
Twisp
Winthrop
Carlton
Malott
Omak
Loomis
Tonasket
Riverside
Curlew
Republic
Metaline Falls
Kettle Falls
Colville
Tiger
Moyie Springs
Bonners Ferry
Naples
Yaak
Eureka
Rexford
Stryker
Polebridge
Troy
Libby
West Glacier
Columbia Falls
Kalispell
Creston
Bigfork
Somers
Sappho
Joyce
Port Angeles
Forks
La Push
Sequim
Olympic Mountains
Mt Olympus 2424 m
Marysville
Everett
Startup
Oso
Kalaloch
Seattle
Bellevue
Bremerton
Skykomish
Fall City
Auburn
Enumclaw
Quinault
Taholah
Humptulips
Shelton
McCleary
Aberdeen
Elma
Olympia
Tacoma
Orting
Westport
Raymond
South Bend
Oysterville
Grays River
Cape Disappointment
Ilwaco
Astoria
Warrenton
Cathlamet
Longview
Toledo
Castle Rock
Kelso
Centralia
Chehalis
Morton
Mt Rainier 4392 m
Cliffdell
Packwood
Mt St Helens 2550 m
Mt Adams 3751 m
Trout Lake
Entiat
Wenatchee
Manson
Grand Coulee
Wilbur
Hartline
Coulee City
Ephrata
Soap Lake
George
Ellensburg
Moses Lake
Ritzville
Sprague
Cheney
Spokane
Davenport
Deer Park
Springdale
Loon Lake
Chewelah
Gifford
Rice
Valley
Newport
Sandpoint
Laclede
Post Falls
Coeur d'Alene
Kellogg
Wallace
St Maries
Plummer
St Joe
Santa
Tensed
Harvard
Clarkia
Avery
Thompson Falls
Trout Creek
Plains
Paradise
Perma
Dixon
Ravalli
Arlee
Evaro
Missoula
Clinton
Lolo
Lolo Hot Springs
Columbia Basin
Beverly
Othello
Lind
Benge
St John
Rosalia
Ewan
Thornton
Endicott
Colfax
Moscow
Deary
Kendrick
Orofino
Pierce
Clearwater
Selah
Yakima
Wapato
Granger
Mabton
Sunnyside
Grandview
Connell
Kahlotus
Hooper
Pomeroy
Dayton
Waitsburg
Walla Walla
Pasco
Kennewick
Eureka
Clarkston
Lewiston
Anatone
Nezperce
Kooskia
Lowell
Hamilton
Darby
Sula
Seaside
Rainier
Mist
Cannon Beach
Arch Cape
St Helens
Buxton
Vancouver
Portland
Tillamook
Sandlake
McMinnville
Sandy
Oregon City
Newberg
Lincoln City
Grand Ronde
Silverton
Salem
Siletz
Newport
Toledo
Corvallis
Albany
Lebanon
Sweet Home
Waldport
Philomath
Yachats
Blachly
Junction City
Vida
Eugene
Springfield
Maryhill
Goldendale
The Dalles
Mt Hood 3424 m
Moro
Rhododendron
Kent
Maupin
Mt Wilson 1713 m
Mt Jefferson 3200 m
Warm Springs
Antelope
Madras
Clarno
Condon
Lexington
Heppner
Milton-Freewater
Hermiston
Pendleton
Pilot Rock
Elgin
Enterprise
La Grande
Union
Joseph
Ukiah
Dale
Granite
North Powder
Baker City
Pleasant Valley
Kimberly
Long Creek
Dayville
Prairie City
Unity
Ironside
Brogan
Mitchell
Prineville
Sisters
McKenzie Bridge
Redmond
Bend
Spanish Pk 2099 m
Mount Vernon
Seneca
Three Sisters 3157 m
Hampton Butte 1940 m
Deer Pk 1552 m
Ontario
Vale
Harper
Van
Drewsey
Juntura
Riley
Burns
Buchanan
Crane
Princeton
Hampton
Glass Butte 1946 m
Harney Basin
Malheur Lake
Blue Mountains
Columbia Plateau
Hells Canyon
Elk Mtn 1561 m
Flora
Grangeville
White Bird
Lucile
Riggins
Pollock
Burgdorf
Dixie
Elk City
North Fork
Salmon River Mountains
New Meadows
McCall
Big Creek
Yellow Pine
Council
Mesa
Cambridge
Salmon
Tendoy
Leadore
Challis
Borah Pk 3859 m
Clayton
Stanley
Smiths Ferry
Ola
Banks
Lowman
Horseshoe Bend
Emmett
Caldwell
Boise
Nampa
Meridian
Mackay
Leslie
Atlanta
Featherville
Melba
Orchard
Corral
Bellevue
Carey
Hill City
Fairfield
Silver City
Grand View
Mountain Home
Bliss
Gooding
Richfield
Hagerman
Wendell
Dietrich
Jerome
Buhl
Filer
Twin Falls
Minidoka
Hollister
Oakley
Malta
Elba
Rogerson
Cache Pk 3150 m
Bitterroot Range
Lemhi Range
Sapphire Mts
Cabinet Mountains
Reedsport
Lakeside
North Bend
Coos Bay
Bandon
Coquille
Myrtle Point
Sutherlin
Glide
Roseburg
Steamboat
Myrtle Creek
Canyonville
Langlois
Camas Valley
Cape Blanco
Port Orford
Agness
Wolf Creek
Azalea
Gold Beach
Pistol River
Brookings
Smith River
Pt St George
Crescent City
Klamath
Merlin
Grants Pass
Wilderville
Trail
Prospect
Medford
Ashland
O'Brien
Gasquet
Mt McLoughlin 2894 m
Klamath Falls
Altamont
Lorella
Cottage Grove
Oakridge
McCredie Springs
La Pine
Crescent
Fort Rock
Diamond Lake
Union Creek
Silver Lake
Summer Lake
Kirk
Paisley
Valley Falls
Beatty
Lakeview
Beatys Butte 2412 m
Frenchglen
Burns Junction
Rome
Jordan Valley
Basque
Blue Mtn 2261 m
Wagontire
Alkali Lake
Brothers
Great Sandy Desert
Fremont Mountains
Steens Mountain
Cascade Range
Coast Ranges
Siskiyou Mts
Klamath Mts
Riddle
Grasmere
Yreka
Happy Camp
Hamburg
Greenview
Somes Bar
Orick
Weitchpec
Trinidad
Callahan
Thompson Pk 2744 m
Weed
Mt Shasta 4317 m
McCloud
Bray
Cougar
Perez
Canby
Alturas
Davis Creek
Goose Lake
Catnip Mtn 2223 m
Denio Junction
Santa Rosa Range
Orovada
Paradise Valley
Jack Creek
Owyhee
Mountain City
Matterhorn 3304 m
Contact
Tuscarora
North Fork
Thousand Springs
Wells
Oasis
Elko
Spruce Mountain 3128 m
Wendover
Carlin
Pahute Pk 2627 m
Fox Mtn 2494 m
Black Rock Desert
Winnemucca
Golconda
Valmy
Battle Mountain
Imlay
Mt Tobin 2979 m
Gerlach
Kumiva Pk 2511 m
Pyramid Lake
Winnemucca Lake
Lovelock
Roberts Creek Mtn 3089 m
Currie
Ruby Mountains
Independence Mts
Great Salt Lake Desert
Granite Pk 2154 m
Desert Pk 2152 m
Arcata
Eureka
Fortuna
Blue Lake
Burnt Ranch
Big Bar
Weaverville
Douglas City
Redding
Lassen Pk 3187 m
Bieber
Adin
Madeline
Bald Mtn 1849 m
Burney
Round Mountain
Ravendale
Cape Mendocino
King Pk 1246 m
Bridgeville
Garberville
Platina
Red Bluff
Paynes Creek
Chester
Susanville
Greenville
Belden
Quincy
Cummings
Corning
Chico
Paradise
Hamilton City
Blairsden
Westport
Laytonville
Fort Bragg
Willits
Mendocino
Snow Mtn 2151 m
Redwood Valley
Willows
Lodoga
Maxwell
Oroville
Sierraville
Ukiah
Point Arena
Lakeport
Pt Arena
Hopland
Cloverdale
Clearlake
Lower Lake
Stewarts Point
Middletown
Woodland
Yuba City
Marysville
Colfax
Truckee
Tahoe City
Auburn
Reno
Sparks
Fernley
Fallon
Stillwater
Virginia City
Carson City
Yerington
Schurz
South Lake Tahoe
Cold Springs
Destoya Pk 3039 m
Austin
Eureka
Summit Mtn 3189 m
Ruth
McGill
Ely
Notch Pk 2943 m
Santa Rosa
Sonoma
Napa
Davis
Rancho Cordova
Placerville
Sacramento
Dixon
Elk Grove
Jackson
Petaluma
Fairfield
Novato
Vallejo
Concord
Lockeford
San Andreas
Pt Reyes
Berkeley
Lodi
Strawberry
Long Barn
San Francisco
Oakland
Stockton
Sonora
San Mateo
Hayward
Redwood City
Milpitas
Sunnyvale
San Jose
Modesto
Turlock
Yosemite Village
Mariposa
Mt Ritter 4010 m
White Mtn 4342 m
Mt Grant 3426 m
Hawthorne
Gabbs
Luning
Mina
Bridgeport
Lee Vining
Basalt
Coaldale
Boundary Pk 4005 m
Tonopah
Goldfield
Mt Jefferson 3642 m
Carvers
Manhattan
Warm Springs
Kawich Pk 2866 m
Adaven
Duckwater
Currant
Troy Pk 3443 m
Wheeler Pk 3982 m
Sevier Lake
Frisco Pk 2944 m
Milford
Minersville
Modena
Panaca
Cedar City
Stillwater Range
Shoshone Mountains
Monitor Range
Egan Range
Schell Creek Range
Wah Wah Mountains
Great Basin
Sierra Nevada

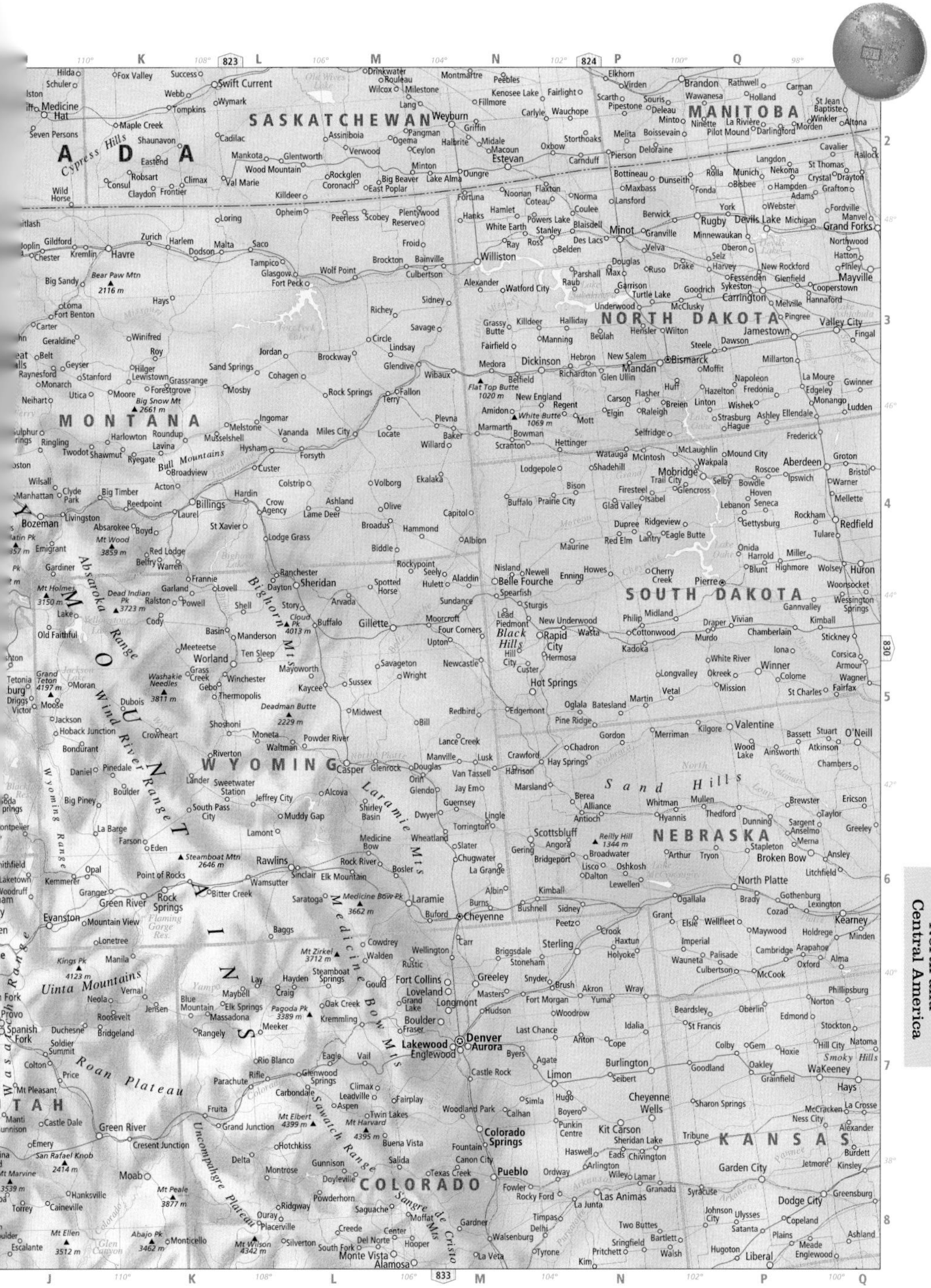

0 100 200 kilometers
0 50 100 miles

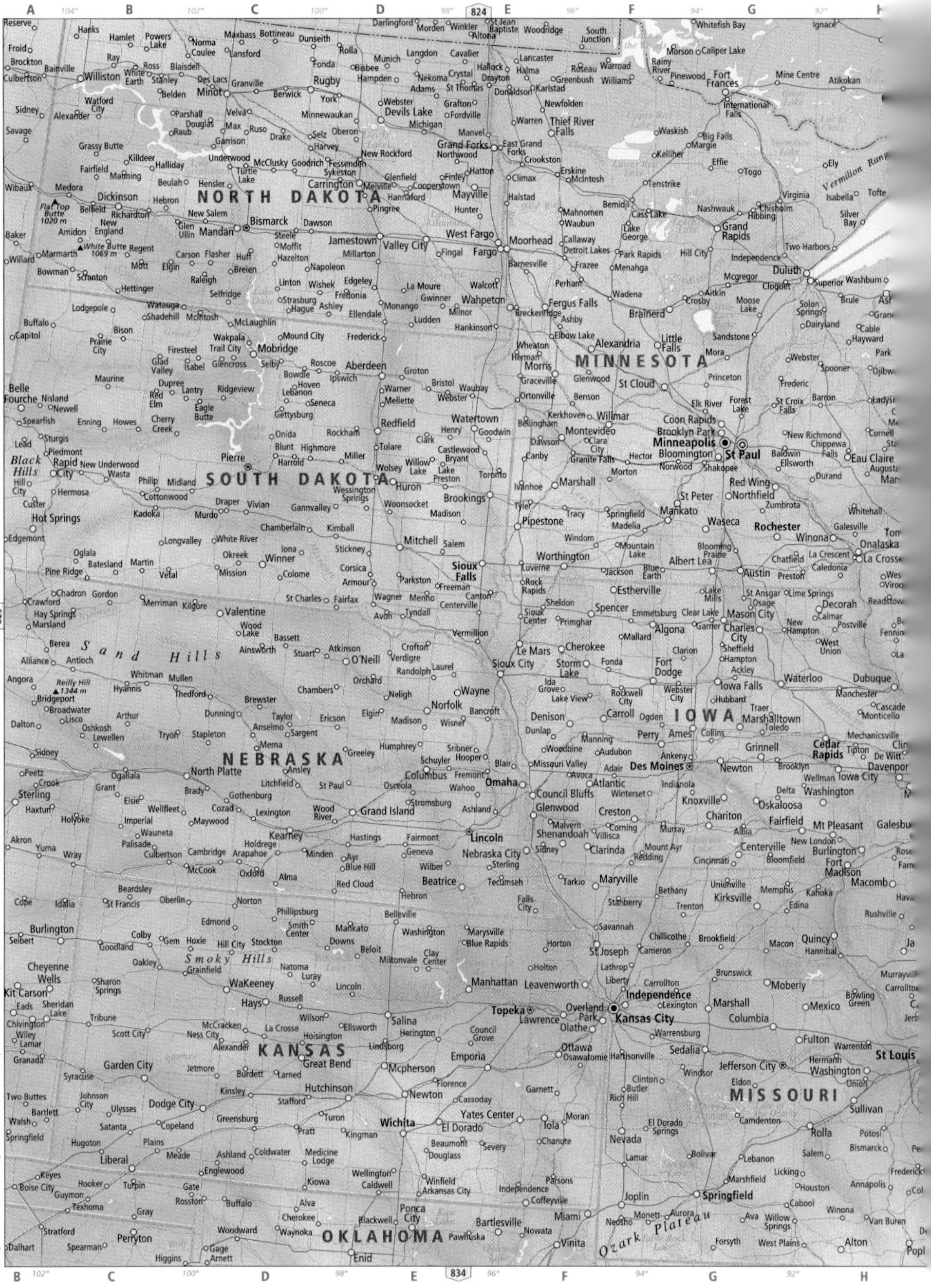
A B C D E F G H
104° 102° 100° 98° 96° 94° 92°
1 2 3 4 5 6 7
48° 46° 44° 42° 40° 38° 36°
824
829
834
NORTH DAKOTA
SOUTH DAKOTA
NEBRASKA
KANSAS
OKLAHOMA
MINNESOTA
IOWA
MISSOURI
Sand Hills
Smoky Hills
Ozark Plateau
Black Hills
Vermilion Range
Flat Top Butte 1020 m
White Butte 1069 m
Reilly Hill 1344 m
Bismarck
Pierre
Lincoln
Topeka
Des Moines
Jefferson City
St Paul
Minneapolis
Kansas City
Omaha
Sioux Falls
Fargo
Grand Forks
Duluth
Wichita
Springfield
St Louis

825

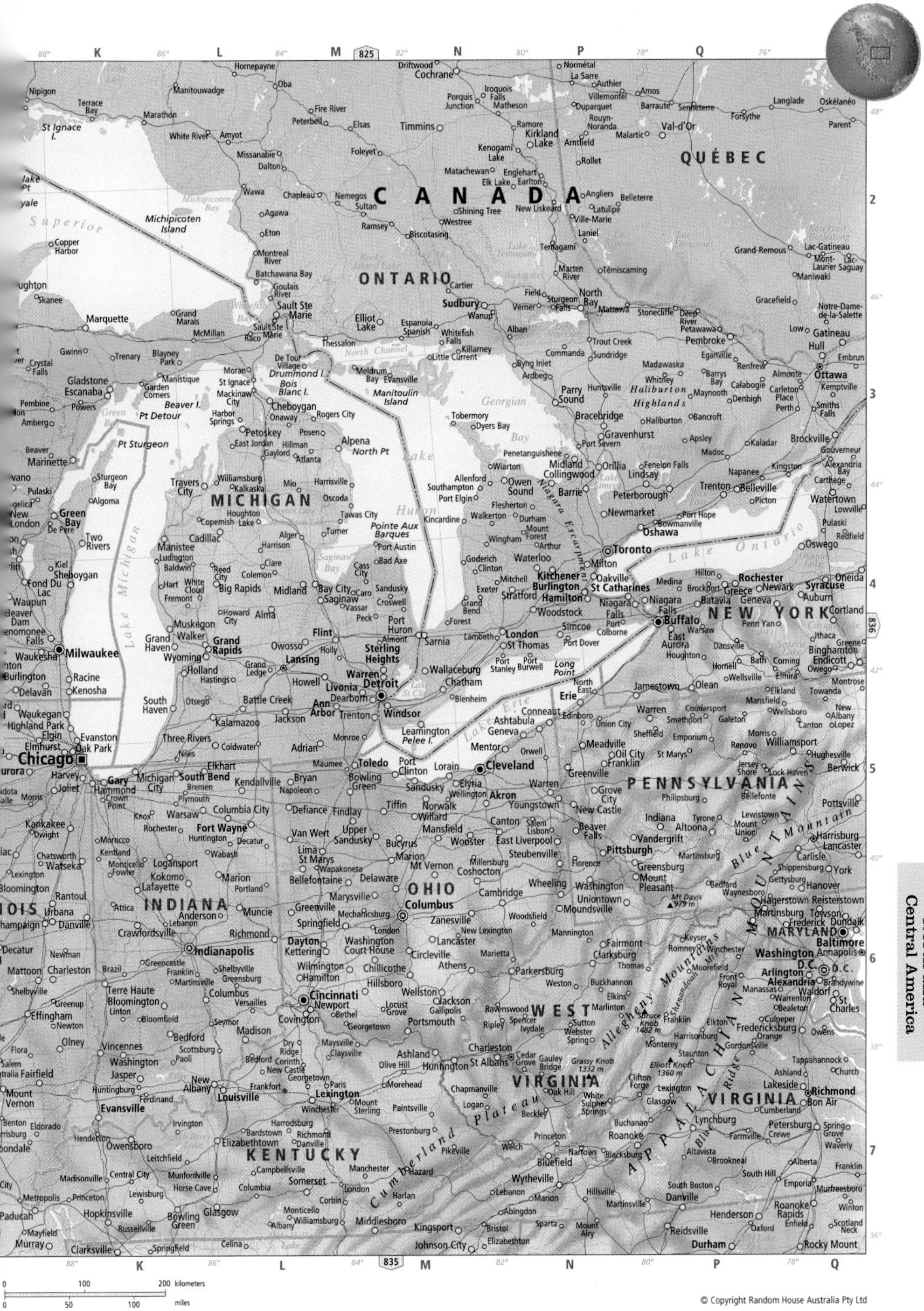
CANADA
ONTARIO
QUÉBEC
MICHIGAN
NEW YORK
PENNSYLVANIA
OHIO
INDIANA
KENTUCKY
WEST VIRGINIA
VIRGINIA
MARYLAND
Lake Superior
Lake Michigan
Lake Huron
Georgian Bay
Lake Erie
Lake Ontario
North Channel
Saginaw Bay
Niagara Escarpment
APPALACHIAN MOUNTAINS
Allegheny Mountains
Blue Mountain
Blue Ridge
Cumberland Plateau
Shenandoah Mts
Haliburton Highlands
Michipicoten Island
Manitoulin Island
Drummond I.
Bois Blanc I.
Beaver I.
Pelee I.
Long Point
Pointe Aux Barques
Pt Sturgeon
Pt Detour
North Pt
Mt Davis 979 m
Spruce Knob 1482 m
Grassy Knob 1332 m
Elliott Knob 1360 m
Ottawa
Toronto
Sudbury
Sault Ste Marie
Timmins
Kirkland Lake
North Bay
Kingston
Hamilton
London
Windsor
Kitchener
Detroit
Lansing
Grand Rapids
Flint
Chicago
Milwaukee
Toledo
Cleveland
Buffalo
Rochester
Syracuse
Erie
Pittsburgh
Columbus
Cincinnati
Dayton
Indianapolis
Fort Wayne
Louisville
Lexington
Charleston
Harrisburg
Baltimore
Washington D.C.
Richmond
Lynchburg
Roanoke
North and Central America

835

836

0 100 200 kilometers
0 50 100 miles

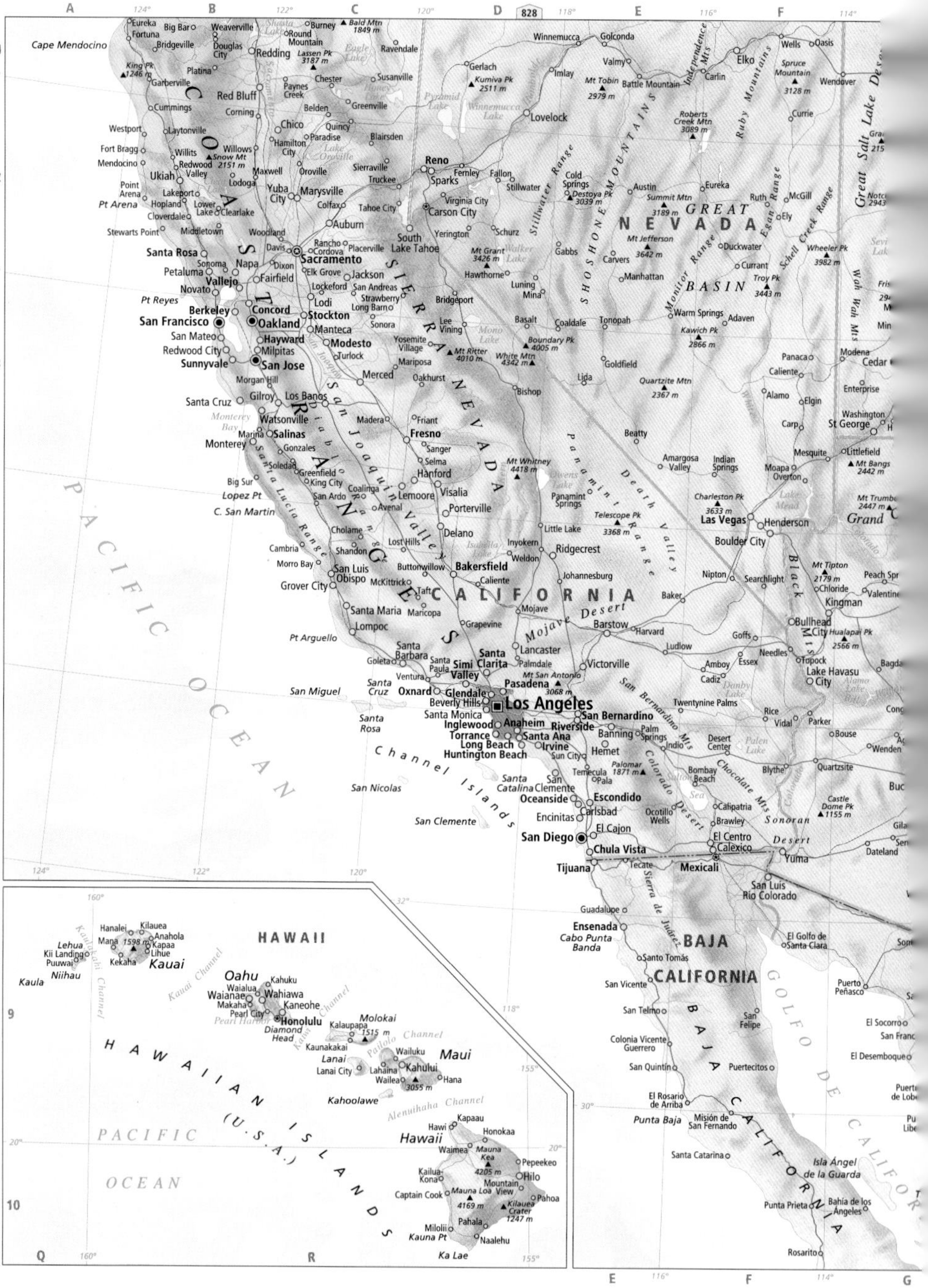

North and Central America

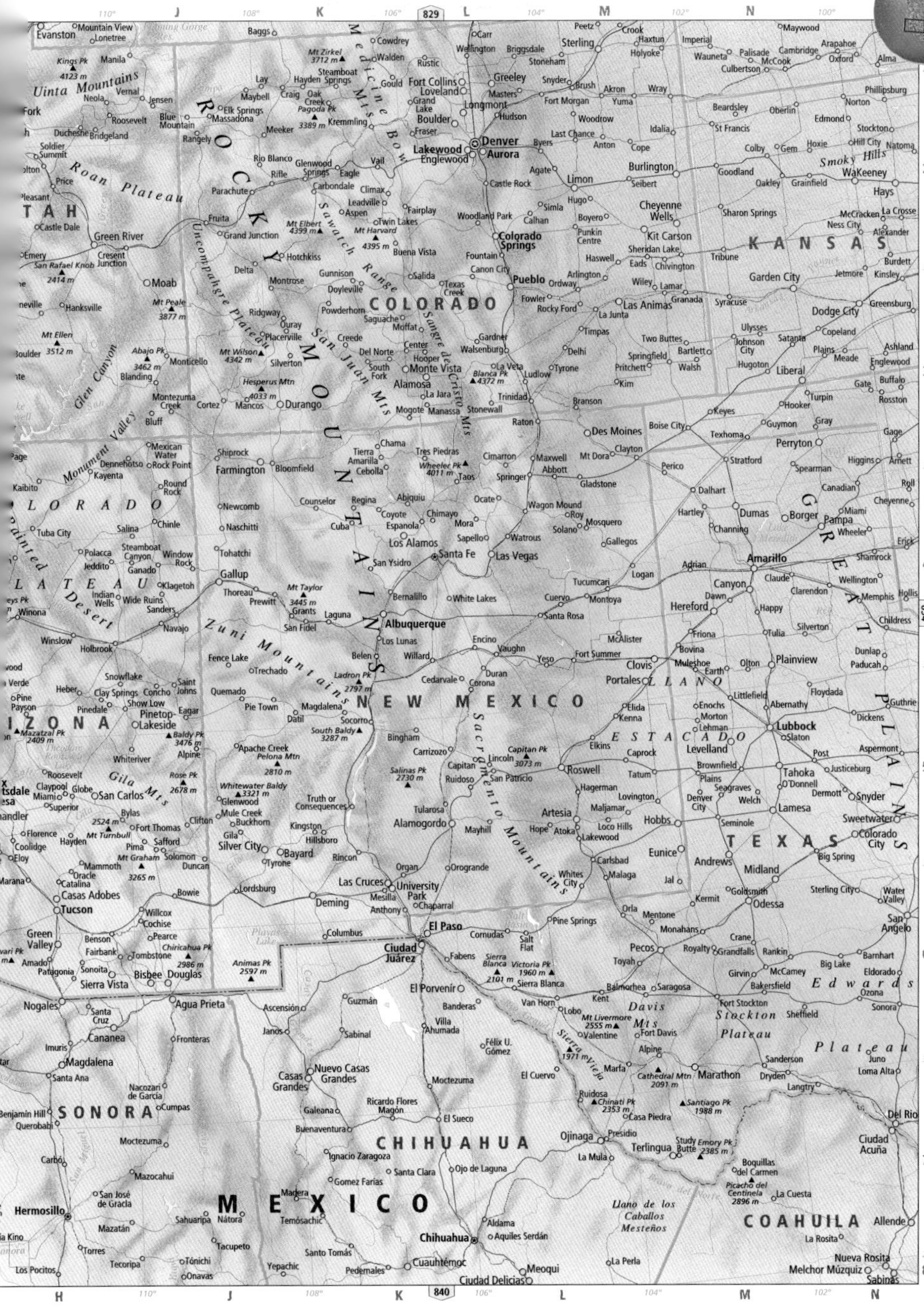

110° J 108° K 106° 829 L 104° M 102° N 100°
H 110° J 108° K 840 106° L 104° M 102° N
2
3
4
5
6
7
8
834
40°
38°
36°
34°
32°
30°
28°
ROCKY MOUNTAINS
COLORADO
NEW MEXICO
TEXAS
KANSAS
ARIZONA
UTAH
MEXICO
CHIHUAHUA
SONORA
COAHUILA
GREAT PLAINS
LLANO ESTACADO
Uinta Mountains
Roan Plateau
Uncompahgre Plateau
Sawatch Range
Sangre de Cristo Mts
San Juan Mts
Medicine Bow Mts
Zuni Mountains
Sacramento Mountains
Gila Mts
Glen Canyon
Monument Valley
Painted Desert
Colorado Plateau
Smoky Hills
Davis Mts
Edwards Plateau
Stockton Plateau
Sierra Vieja
Llano de los Caballos Mesteños
Denver
Aurora
Lakewood
Englewood
Boulder
Longmont
Fort Collins
Loveland
Greeley
Colorado Springs
Pueblo
Grand Junction
Durango
Alamosa
Monte Vista
Trinidad
Limon
Burlington
Sterling
Farmington
Gallup
Santa Fe
Los Alamos
Las Vegas
Albuquerque
Socorro
Roswell
Carlsbad
Hobbs
Clovis
Alamogordo
Las Cruces
Deming
Silver City
Tucumcari
Raton
Amarillo
Lubbock
Midland
Odessa
El Paso
Ciudad Juárez
Pecos
San Angelo
Del Rio
Tucson
Nogales
Hermosillo
Chihuahua
Ciudad Delicias
Ojinaga
Garden City
Dodge City
Liberal
Hays
WaKeeney
Moab
Green River
Mt Elbert 4399 m
Mt Harvard 4395 m
Mt Wilson 4342 m
Blanca Pk 4372 m
Wheeler Pk 4011 m
Mt Taylor 3445 m
Sierra Blanca 3658 m
Capitan Pk 3073 m
Guadalupe Pk
Emory Pk 2385 m
Mt Livermore 2555 m
Kings Pk 4123 m
North and Central America

0 100 200 kilometers
0 50 100 miles

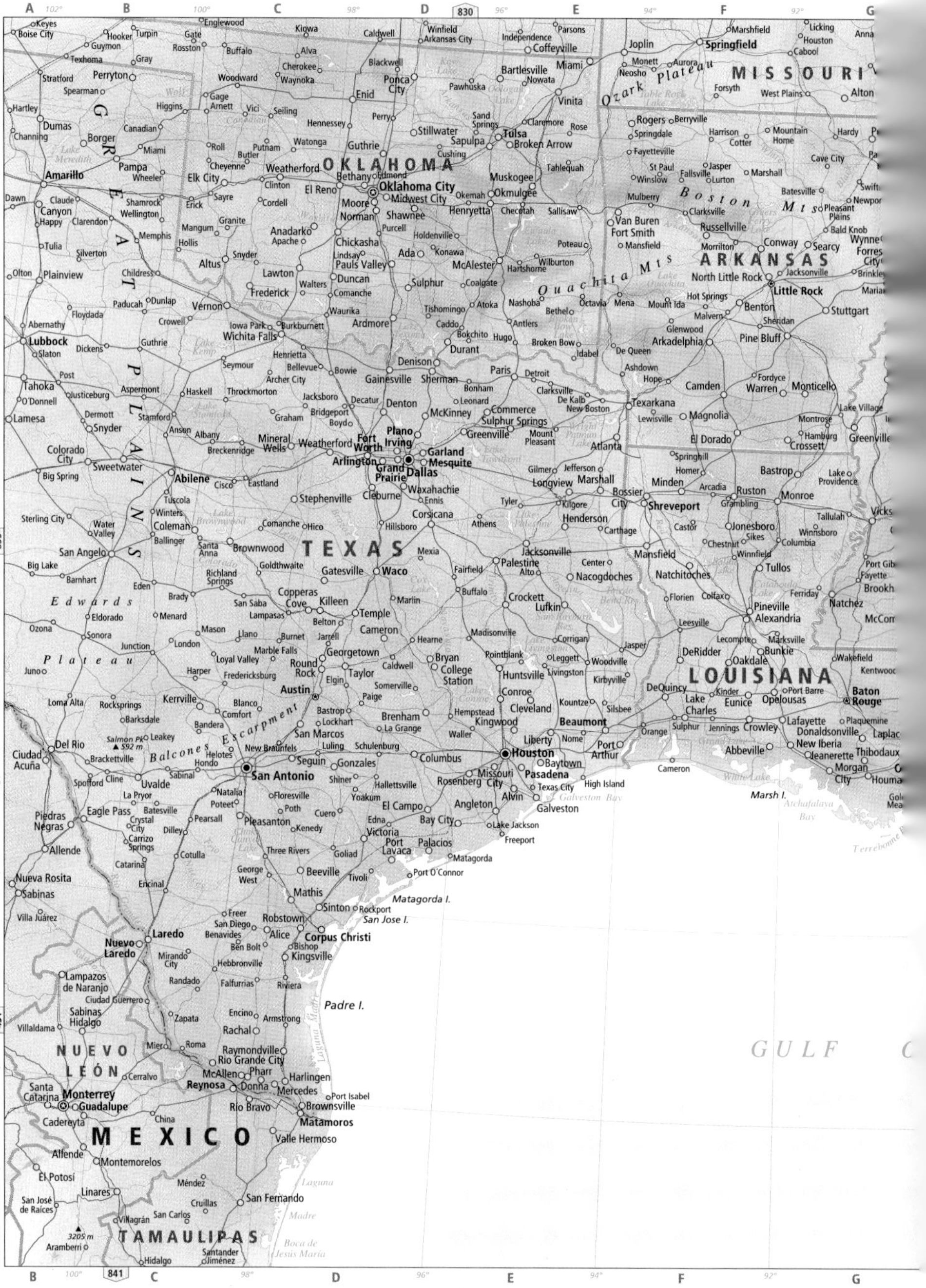
OKLAHOMA
TEXAS
ARKANSAS
LOUISIANA
MISSOURI
MEXICO
NUEVO LEÓN
TAMAULIPAS
GULF
GREAT PLAINS
Edwards Plateau
Balcones Escarpment
Ozark Plateau
Boston Mts
Ouachita Mts
Padre I.
Matagorda I.
San Jose I.
Marsh I.
Oklahoma City
Tulsa
Amarillo
Lubbock
Wichita Falls
Abilene
Fort Worth
Dallas
Arlington
Waco
Austin
San Antonio
Houston
Galveston
Beaumont
Corpus Christi
Laredo
Nuevo Laredo
Brownsville
Matamoros
Monterrey
Shreveport
Little Rock
Fort Smith
Springfield
Joplin
Texarkana
Lake Charles
Baton Rouge
Alexandria
Del Rio
San Angelo
Tyler
Killeen
Temple
Bryan
College Station
Victoria
McAllen
Harlingen
Reynosa
Kingsville
Port Arthur
Lafayette
Monroe
Norman
Lawton
Enid
Muskogee
830
833
431
841
GULF

831

836

0 100 200 kilometers
0 50 100 miles

A B C D 826 E 70° F 68° G

1

Lac Kipawa · Témiscaming · Mattawa · Stonecliffe · Deep River · Pembroke · Petawawa · Renfrew · Whitney · Madawaska · Bancroft · Haliburton Highlands · Minden · Haliburton · Apsley · Fenelon Falls · Lindsay · Peterborough · Port Hope · Bowmanville

Réservoir Cabonga · Grand-Remous · Mont-Laurier · Maniwaki · Gracefield · Low · Gatineau · Hull · Ottawa · Kemptville · Smiths Falls · Perth · Cornwall

La Tuque · Rivière-aux-Rats · Charlesbourg · Québec · Trois-Rivières · Drummondville · Sorel · Longueuil · Montréal · Sherbrooke · Magog

Baie-St-Paul · Edmundston · NEW BRUNSWICK · Fredericton · Houlton · MAINE · Bangor · Augusta · Portland

QUÉBEC · **CANADA** · **ONTARIO**

2

NEW YORK · Rochester · Syracuse · Utica · Albany · **VERMONT** · **NEW HAMPSHIRE** · Concord · Manchester · **MASSACHUSETTS** · Boston · Worcester · Springfield · Hartford · **CONNECTICUT** · **RHODE ISLAND** · Providence · New Haven · Bridgeport · Stamford · Yonkers · **New York** · Newark · Elizabeth · Trenton · Philadelphia · Camden · **NEW JERSEY** · **PENNSYLVANIA** · Scranton · Wilkes Barre · Allentown · Reading · Harrisburg · York · Lancaster · Baltimore · Annapolis · **MARYLAND** · **Washington D.C.** · Alexandria · Arlington · **DELAWARE** · Dover · **VIRGINIA** · Richmond · Petersburg · Newport News · Norfolk · Virginia Beach · Chesapeake · **NORTH CAROLINA** · Rocky Mount · Wilson · Goldsboro · Kinston · New Bern

Lake Ontario · *Lake Erie* · *APPALACHIAN MTS* · *ATLANTIC OCEAN* · *Gulf of Maine* · *Cape Cod* · *Long Island* · *Chesapeake Bay* · *Hatteras I.* · *Cape Lookout*

kilometers 0 100 200
miles 0 50 100

© Copyright Random House Australia Pty Ltd

North and Central America

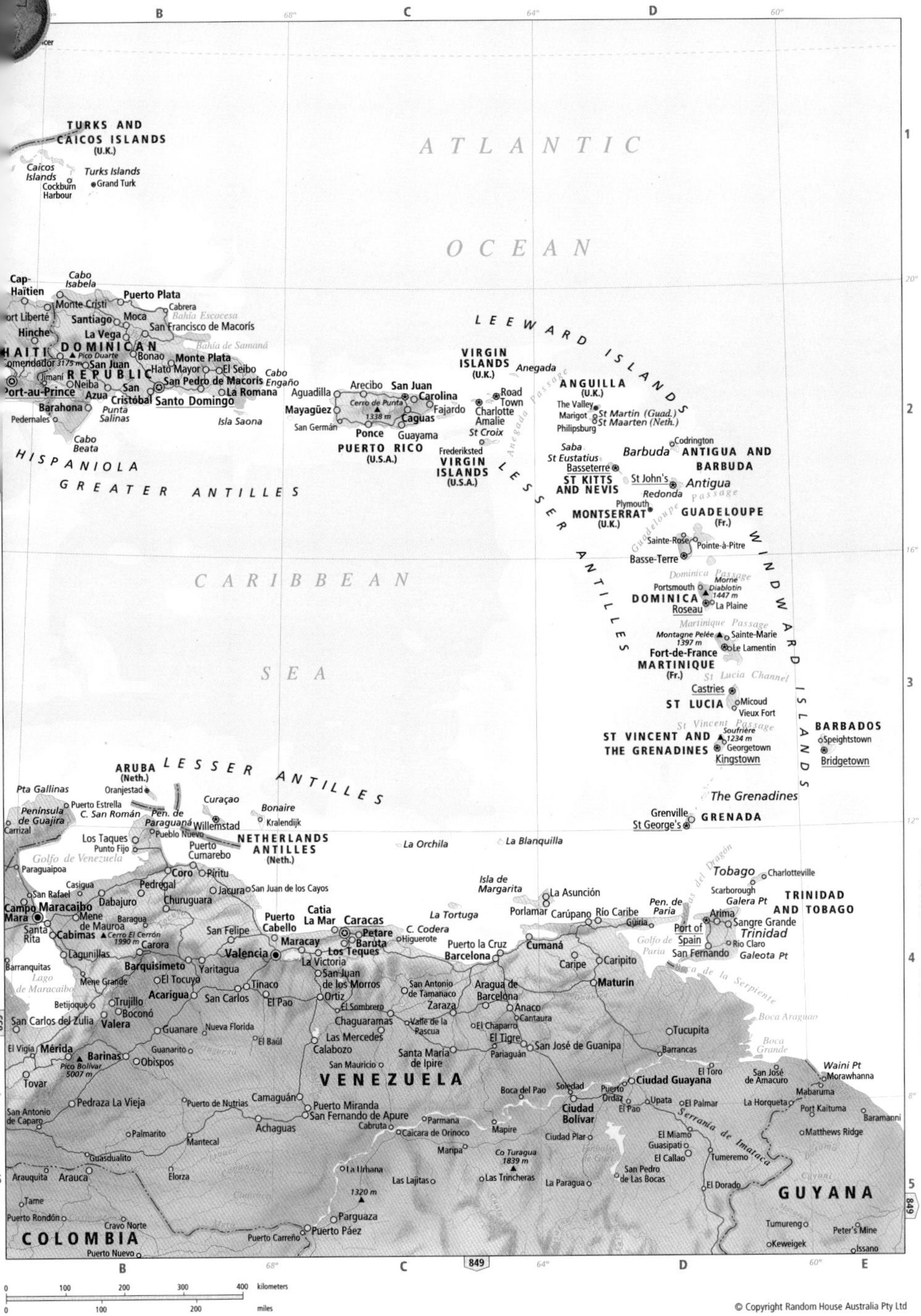
B
68°
C
64°
D
60°
E
1
2
3
4
5
ATLANTIC
OCEAN
CARIBBEAN
SEA
TURKS AND CAICOS ISLANDS (U.K.)
Caicos Islands
Turks Islands
Grand Turk
Cockburn Harbour
20°
16°
12°
8°
Cap-Haïtien
Cabo Isabela
Puerto Plata
Monte Cristi
Cabrera
Bahía Escocesa
Fort Liberté
Santiago
Moca
San Francisco de Macorís
Hinche
La Vega
Bahía de Samaná
HAITI
DOMINICAN REPUBLIC
Pico Duarte 3175 m
Bonao
Monte Plata
Comendador
San Juan
Hato Mayor
El Seibo
Cabo Engaño
Elías Piña
Neiba
San Pedro de Macorís
Port-au-Prince
Azua
San Cristóbal
Santo Domingo
La Romana
Barahona
Punta Salinas
Isla Saona
Pedernales
Cabo Beata
HISPANIOLA
GREATER ANTILLES
Aguadilla
Arecibo
San Juan
Carolina
Mayagüez
Cerro de Punta 1338 m
Fajardo
San Germán
Caguas
Ponce
Guayama
PUERTO RICO (U.S.A.)
VIRGIN ISLANDS (U.K.)
Anegada
Road Town
Charlotte Amalie
St Croix
Frederiksted
VIRGIN ISLANDS (U.S.A.)
Anegada Passage
LEEWARD ISLANDS
ANGUILLA (U.K.)
The Valley
Marigot
St Martin (Guad.)
St Maarten (Neth.)
Philipsburg
Saba
St Eustatius
Codrington
Barbuda
ANTIGUA AND BARBUDA
Basseterre
ST KITTS AND NEVIS
St John's
Antigua
Redonda
Plymouth
MONTSERRAT (U.K.)
Guadeloupe Passage
GUADELOUPE (Fr.)
LESSER ANTILLES
Sainte-Rose
Pointe-à-Pitre
Basse-Terre
Dominica Passage
Portsmouth
Morne Diablotin 1447 m
DOMINICA
Roseau
La Plaine
Martinique Passage
Montagne Pelée 1397 m
Sainte-Marie
Le Lamentin
Fort-de-France
MARTINIQUE (Fr.)
St Lucia Channel
Castries
ST LUCIA
Micoud
Vieux Fort
St Vincent Passage
Soufrière 1234 m
Georgetown
ST VINCENT AND THE GRENADINES
Kingstown
WINDWARD ISLANDS
BARBADOS
Speightstown
Bridgetown
The Grenadines
Grenville
St George's
GRENADA
ARUBA (Neth.)
Oranjestad
LESSER ANTILLES
Curaçao
Willemstad
Bonaire
Kralendijk
NETHERLANDS ANTILLES (Neth.)
Pta Gallinas
Puerto Estrella
C. San Román
Península de Guajira
Pen. de Paraguaná
Carrizal
Pueblo Nuevo
Los Taques
Punto Fijo
Puerto Cumarebo
La Orchila
La Blanquilla
Golfo de Venezuela
Paraguaipoa
Coro
Píritu
Casigua
Pedregal
Jacura
San Juan de los Cayos
San Rafael
Dabajuro
Churuguara
Campo Mara
Maracaibo
Mene de Mauroa
Baragua
Santa Rita
Cabimas
Cerro El Cerrón 1990 m
Carora
San Felipe
Puerto Cabello
Catia La Mar
Caracas
Petare
Barúta
C. Codera
Higuerote
Isla de Margarita
La Asunción
La Tortuga
Porlamar
Carúpano
Río Caribe
Pen. de Paria
Güiria
Tobago
Charlotteville
Scarborough
Galera Pt
TRINIDAD AND TOBAGO
Arima
Sangre Grande
Port of Spain
Trinidad
Golfo de Paria
Rio Claro
San Fernando
Galeota Pt
Lagunillas
Maracay
Valencia
Los Teques
Puerto la Cruz
Barcelona
Cumaná
Caripe
Caripito
Bachaquero
Barranquitas
Lago de Maracaibo
Barquisimeto
Yaritagua
La Victoria
San Juan de los Morros
Mene Grande
El Tocuyo
Tinaco
San Antonio de Tamanaco
Aragua de Barcelona
Maturín
Boca de la Serpiente
Betijoque
Trujillo
Acarigua
San Carlos
El Pao
Ortiz
El Sombrero
Zaraza
Anaco
Cantaura
Boconó
San Carlos del Zulia
Valera
Guanare
Nueva Florida
Chaguaramas
Valle de la Pascua
El Chaparro
Tucupita
Boca Araguao
El Vigía
Mérida
Guanarito
El Baúl
Las Mercedes
El Tigre
San José de Guanipa
Barinas
Calabozo
Santa María de Ipire
Pariaguán
Barrancas
Boca Grande
Pico Bolívar 5007 m
Obispos
San Mauricio
Tovar
VENEZUELA
El Toro
San José de Amacuro
Waini Pt
Morawhanna
Boca del Pao
Soledad
Puerto Ordaz
Ciudad Guayana
Mabaruma
Pedraza La Vieja
Puerto de Nutrias
Camaguán
Puerto Miranda
Ciudad Bolívar
Upata
El Palmar
La Horqueta
Port Kaituma
San Antonio de Caparo
San Fernando de Apure
El Pao
Serranía de Imataca
Baramanni
Achaguas
Cabruta
Parmana
Caicara de Orinoco
Mapire
Ciudad Piar
El Miamo
Matthews Ridge
Palmarito
Mantecal
Maripa
Guasipati
Guasdualito
Co Turagua 1839 m
El Callao
Tumeremo
La Urbana
Las Lajitas
Las Trincheras
La Paragua
San Pedro de Las Bocas
Arauquita
Arauca
Elorza
El Dorado
GUYANA
1320 m
Tame
Puerto Rondón
Cravo Norte
Parguaza
Tumureng
Peter's Mine
COLOMBIA
Puerto Carreño
Puerto Páez
Keweigek
Issano
Puerto Nuevo
839
849
0 100 200 300 400 kilometers
0 100 200 miles

North and Central America

GULF OF MEXICO
Bahía de Campeche
VERACRUZ
MEXICO
OAXACA
Istmo de Tehuantepec
TABASCO
CHIAPAS
CAMPECHE
YUCATÁN
QUINTANA ROO
Península de Yucatán
Meseta de Zohlaguna
BELIZE
GUATEMALA
HONDURAS
EL SALVADOR
NICARAGUA
COSTA RICA
Golfo de Tehuantepec
Golfo de Honduras
PACIFIC OCEAN
Yucatán Channel
Cabo Catoche
Cabo San Antonio
Isla Cozumel
Turneffe I.
Islas de la Bahía
Sierra Madre de Chiapas
Sierra de Miahuatlán
Lago de Nicaragua
Golfo de Fonseca
Golfo de Nicoya
Punta Cosigüina
Cabo Santa Elena
Cabo Blanco
Cabo Rojo
Punta Roca Partida
Punta Herrero
Tampico
Ciudad Madero
Poza Rica de Hidalgo
Jalapa Enríquez
Veracruz
Puebla de Zaragoza
Orizaba
Córdoba
Oaxaca de Juárez
Coatzacoalcos
Minatitlán
Villahermosa
Tuxtla Gutiérrez
Campeche
Mérida
Cancún
Chetumal
Belmopan
Belize
Guatemala
San Salvador
Nueva San Salvador (Santa Tecla)
Santa Ana
San Miguel
Tegucigalpa
San Pedro Sula
La Ceiba
Managua
León
Granada
San José
Alajuela
Puntarenas
Liberia
Quezaltenango
Tapachula
BAHAMAS
Grand Bahama
Freeport
Abaco
Marsh Harbour
Northwest Providence Channel
Northeast Providence Channel
New Providence
Nassau
Eleuthera Island
Andros Island
Cat Island
Great Exuma Island
George Town
Long Island
Rum Cay
San Salvador

100 200 300 400 kilometers

100 200 miles

North and Central America

837

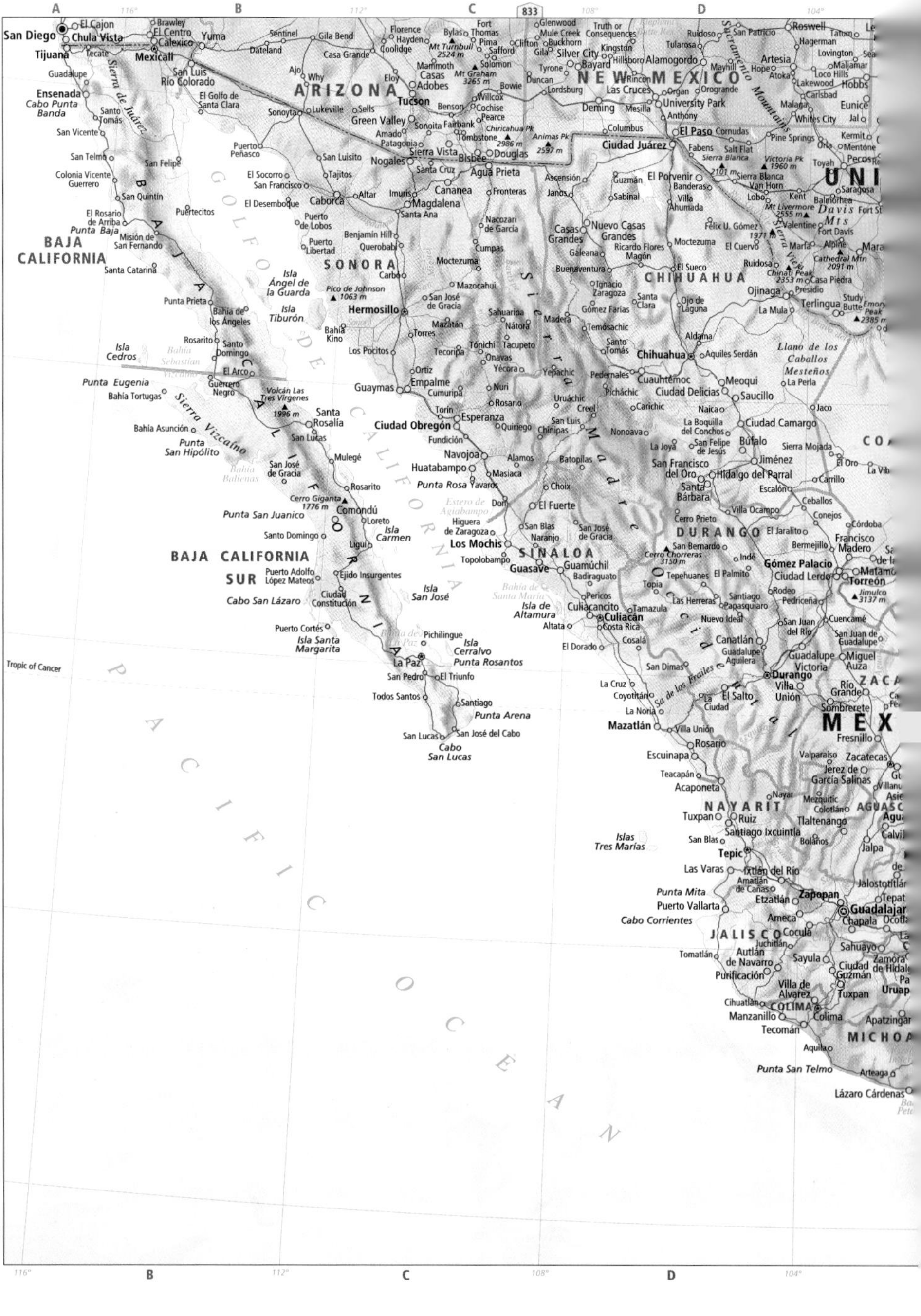
833
ARIZONA
NEW MEXICO
BAJA CALIFORNIA
BAJA CALIFORNIA SUR
SONORA
CHIHUAHUA
SINALOA
DURANGO
NAYARIT
JALISCO
COLIMA
GOLFO DE CALIFORNIA
PACIFIC OCEAN
Sierra Madre Occidental
Sierra de Juárez
Sierra Vizcaíno
Tropic of Cancer
San Diego
Chula Vista
Tijuana
Mexicali
Yuma
Ensenada
Tucson
Hermosillo
Guaymas
Ciudad Obregón
Los Mochis
Culiacán
Mazatlán
La Paz
Chihuahua
Ciudad Juárez
El Paso
Durango
Torreón
Gómez Palacio
Tepic
Guadalajara
Zapopan
Puerto Vallarta
Manzanillo
Colima
Isla Cedros
Isla Tiburón
Isla Ángel de la Guarda
Islas Tres Marías
Cabo San Lucas
Cabo Corrientes
Punta Eugenia

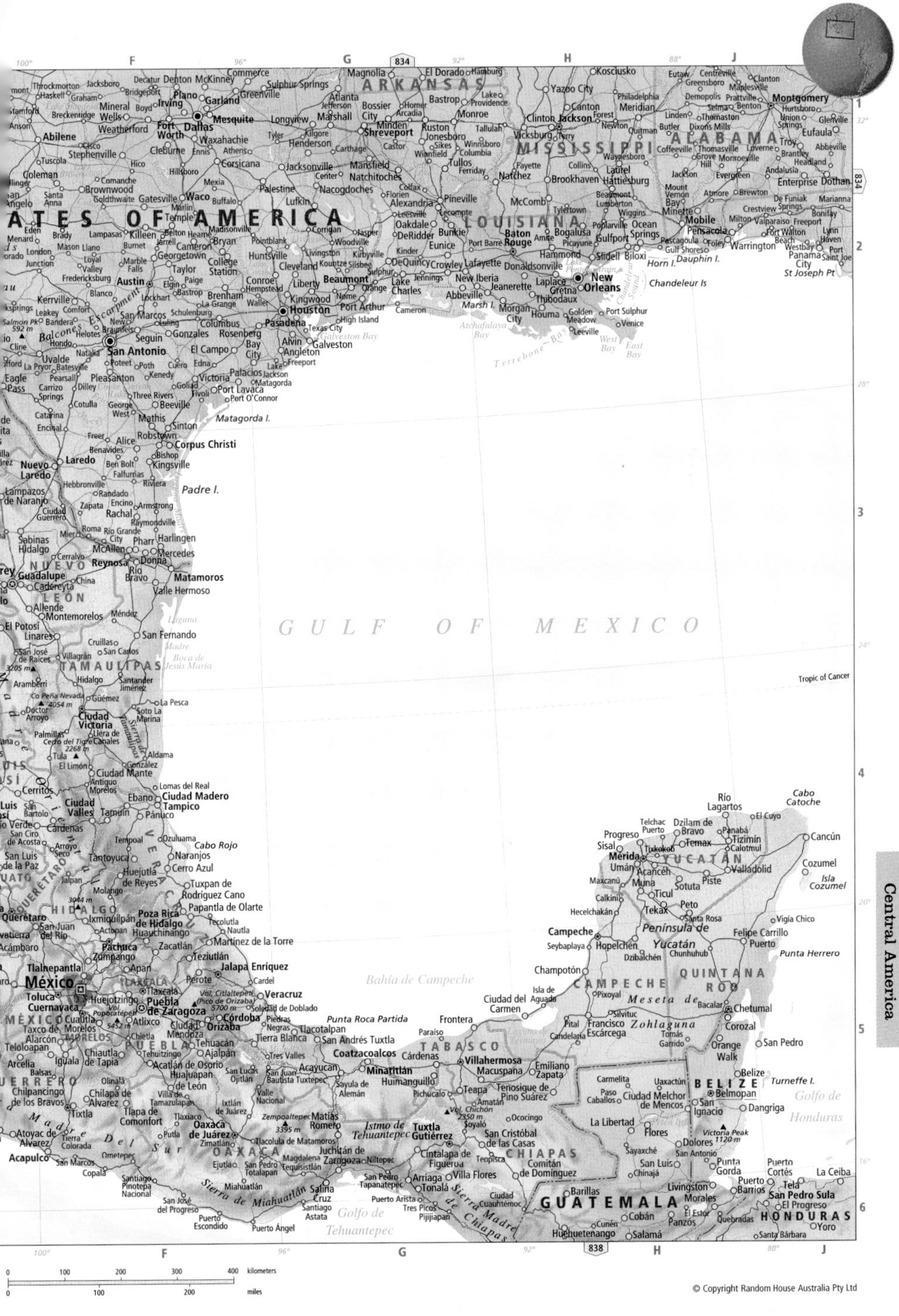
834
ARKANSAS
MISSISSIPPI
ALABAMA
LOUISIANA
ATES OF AMERICA
Dallas
Fort Worth
Mesquite
Plano
Irving
Garland
Abilene
Waco
Shreveport
Jackson
Montgomery
Baton Rouge
New Orleans
Mobile
Pensacola
Houston
Pasadena
Galveston
Beaumont
Austin
San Antonio
Corpus Christi
Laredo
Nuevo Laredo
Matamoros
Reynosa
Guadalupe
NUEVO LEÓN
TAMAULIPAS
Ciudad Victoria
Ciudad Madero
Tampico
VERACRUZ
HIDALGO
Querétaro
México
Puebla de Zaragoza
Veracruz
Jalapa Enríquez
Oaxaca de Juárez
Acapulco
OAXACA
GUERRERO
MORELOS
PUEBLA
TABASCO
Villahermosa
CHIAPAS
Tuxtla Gutiérrez
CAMPECHE
Campeche
YUCATÁN
Mérida
QUINTANA ROO
Chetumal
Cancún
Cozumel
BELIZE
Belmopan
GUATEMALA
HONDURAS
GULF OF MEXICO
Bahía de Campeche
Golfo de Tehuantepec
Golfo de Honduras
Península de Yucatán
Tropic of Cancer
Padre I.
Matagorda I.
Chandeleur Is
838
F
G
H
J
100°
96°
92°
88°
0 100 200 300 400 kilometers
0 100 200 miles

South America

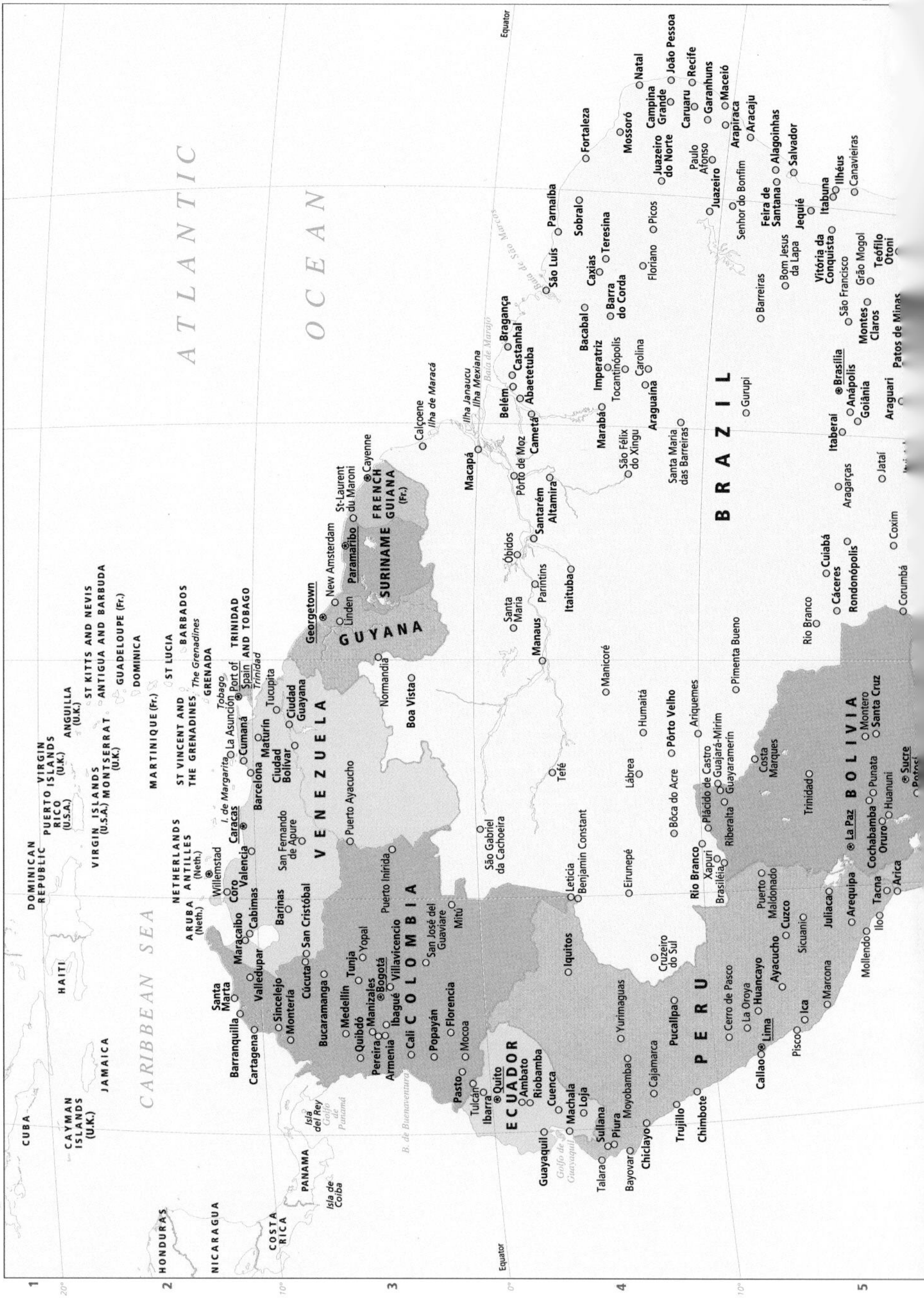
ATLANTIC OCEAN
CARIBBEAN SEA
BRAZIL
VENEZUELA
COLOMBIA
ECUADOR
PERU
BOLIVIA
GUYANA
SURINAME
FRENCH GUIANA (Fr.)
CUBA
HAITI
DOMINICAN REPUBLIC
JAMAICA
CAYMAN ISLANDS (U.K.)
PUERTO RICO (U.S.A.)
VIRGIN ISLANDS (U.K.)
VIRGIN ISLANDS (U.S.A.)
ANGUILLA (U.K.)
ST KITTS AND NEVIS
ANTIGUA AND BARBUDA
MONTSERRAT (U.K.)
GUADELOUPE (Fr.)
DOMINICA
MARTINIQUE (Fr.)
ST LUCIA
BARBADOS
ST VINCENT AND THE GRENADINES
GRENADA
TRINIDAD AND TOBAGO
NETHERLANDS ANTILLES (Neth.)
ARUBA (Neth.)
HONDURAS
NICARAGUA
COSTA RICA
PANAMA
Equator
Caracas
Bogotá
Quito
Lima
La Paz
Sucre
Brasília
Georgetown
Paramaribo
Cayenne
Port of Spain
Maracaibo
Valencia
Barquisimeto
Ciudad Bolívar
Ciudad Guayana
Medellín
Cali
Barranquilla
Cartagena
Guayaquil
Cuenca
Iquitos
Arequipa
Cuzco
Trujillo
Chiclayo
Piura
Cochabamba
Santa Cruz
Manaus
Belém
Macapá
Santarém
São Luís
Fortaleza
Natal
João Pessoa
Recife
Maceió
Aracaju
Salvador
Teresina
Porto Velho
Rio Branco
Boa Vista
Cuiabá
Goiânia
Anápolis
Imperatriz
Marabá
Parnaíba
Mossoró
Campina Grande
Juazeiro do Norte
Feira de Santana
Vitória da Conquista
Montes Claros
Teófilo Otoni
Corumbá
Trinidad
Oruro
Potosí
Arica
Tacna
Ilo
Mollendo

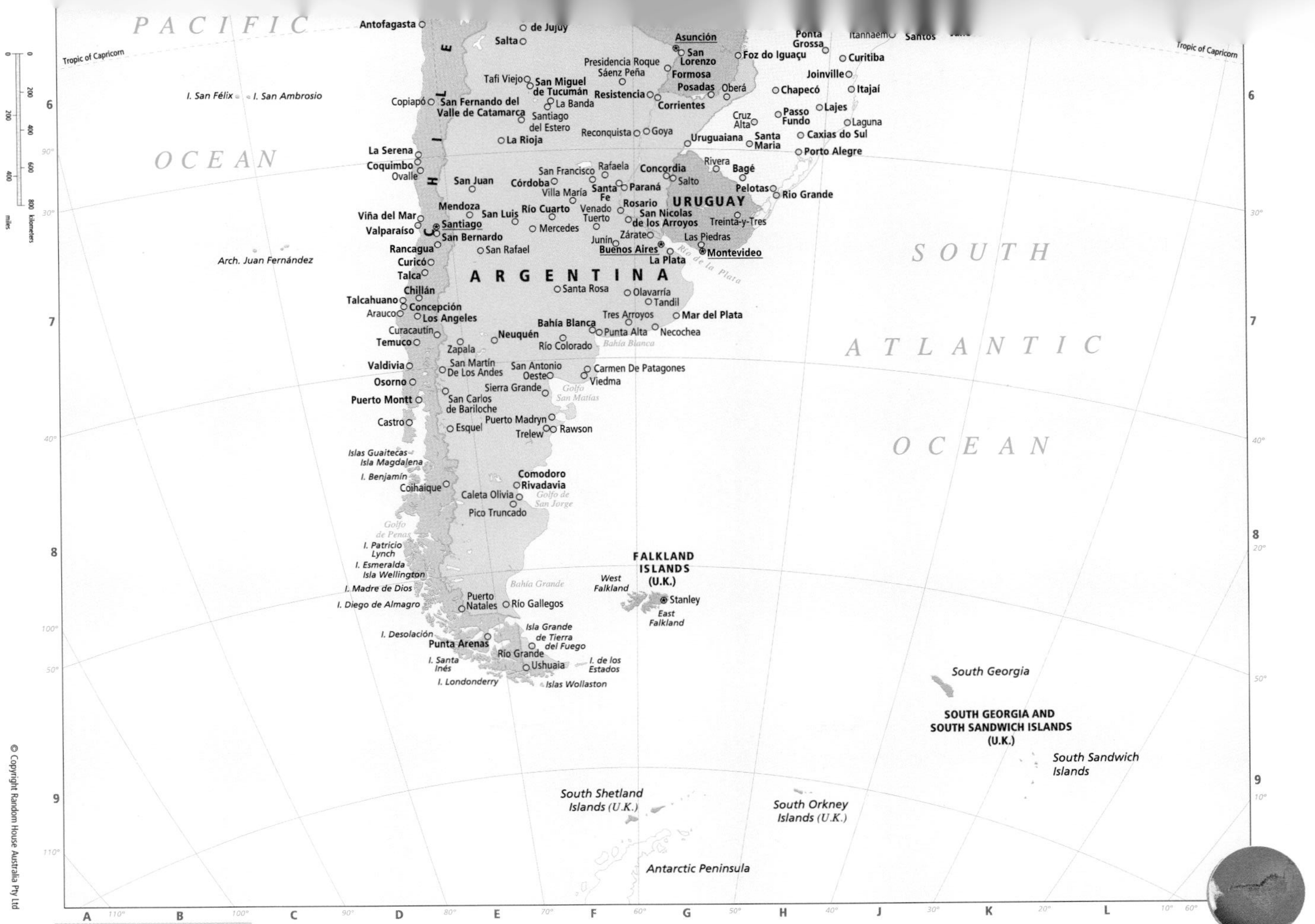
PACIFIC OCEAN
SOUTH ATLANTIC OCEAN
Tropic of Capricorn
ARGENTINA
CHILE
URUGUAY
Antofagasta
Salta
de Jujuy
Asunción
San Lorenzo
Formosa
Posadas
Oberá
Foz do Iguaçu
Ponta Grossa
Curitiba
Joinville
Itajaí
Chapecó
Lajes
Passo Fundo
Laguna
Caxias do Sul
Porto Alegre
Santa Maria
Cruz Alta
Uruguaiana
Presidencia Roque Sáenz Peña
Resistencia
Corrientes
Tafí Viejo
San Miguel de Tucumán
La Banda
Santiago del Estero
Copiapó
San Fernando del Valle de Catamarca
La Rioja
Reconquista
Goya
I. San Félix
I. San Ambrosio
La Serena
Coquimbo
Ovalle
San Juan
Córdoba
San Francisco
Rafaela
Villa María
Santa Fe
Paraná
Concordia
Salto
Rivera
Bagé
Pelotas
Rio Grande
Mendoza
San Luis
Río Cuarto
Venado Tuerto
Rosario
San Nicolas de los Arroyos
Treinta-y-Tres
Viña del Mar
Valparaíso
Santiago
San Bernardo
Mercedes
Zárate
Las Piedras
Junín
Buenos Aires
Montevideo
La Plata
Río de la Plata
Rancagua
San Rafael
Arch. Juan Fernández
Curicó
Talca
Santa Rosa
Olavarría
Tandil
Chillán
Talcahuano
Concepción
Arauco
Los Angeles
Tres Arroyos
Mar del Plata
Bahía Blanca
Punta Alta
Necochea
Curacautín
Neuquén
Temuco
Zapala
Río Colorado
Bahía Blanca
Valdivia
San Martín De Los Andes
San Antonio Oeste
Carmen De Patagones
Viedma
Osorno
Sierra Grande
Golfo San Matías
Puerto Montt
San Carlos de Bariloche
Puerto Madryn
Castro
Esquel
Trelew
Rawson
Islas Guaitecas
Isla Magdalena
I. Benjamín
Comodoro Rivadavia
Coihaique
Caleta Olivia
Golfo de San Jorge
Pico Truncado
Golfo de Penas
I. Patricio Lynch
I. Esmeralda
Isla Wellington
FALKLAND ISLANDS (U.K.)
West Falkland
East Falkland
Stanley
Bahía Grande
I. Madre de Dios
I. Diego de Almagro
Puerto Natales
Río Gallegos
I. Desolación
Punta Arenas
Isla Grande de Tierra del Fuego
Río Grande
I. Santa Inés
Ushuaia
I. de los Estados
I. Londonderry
Islas Wollaston
South Georgia
SOUTH GEORGIA AND SOUTH SANDWICH ISLANDS (U.K.)
South Sandwich Islands
South Shetland Islands (U.K.)
South Orkney Islands (U.K.)
Antarctic Peninsula
0 200 400 600 800 kilometers
0 200 400 miles

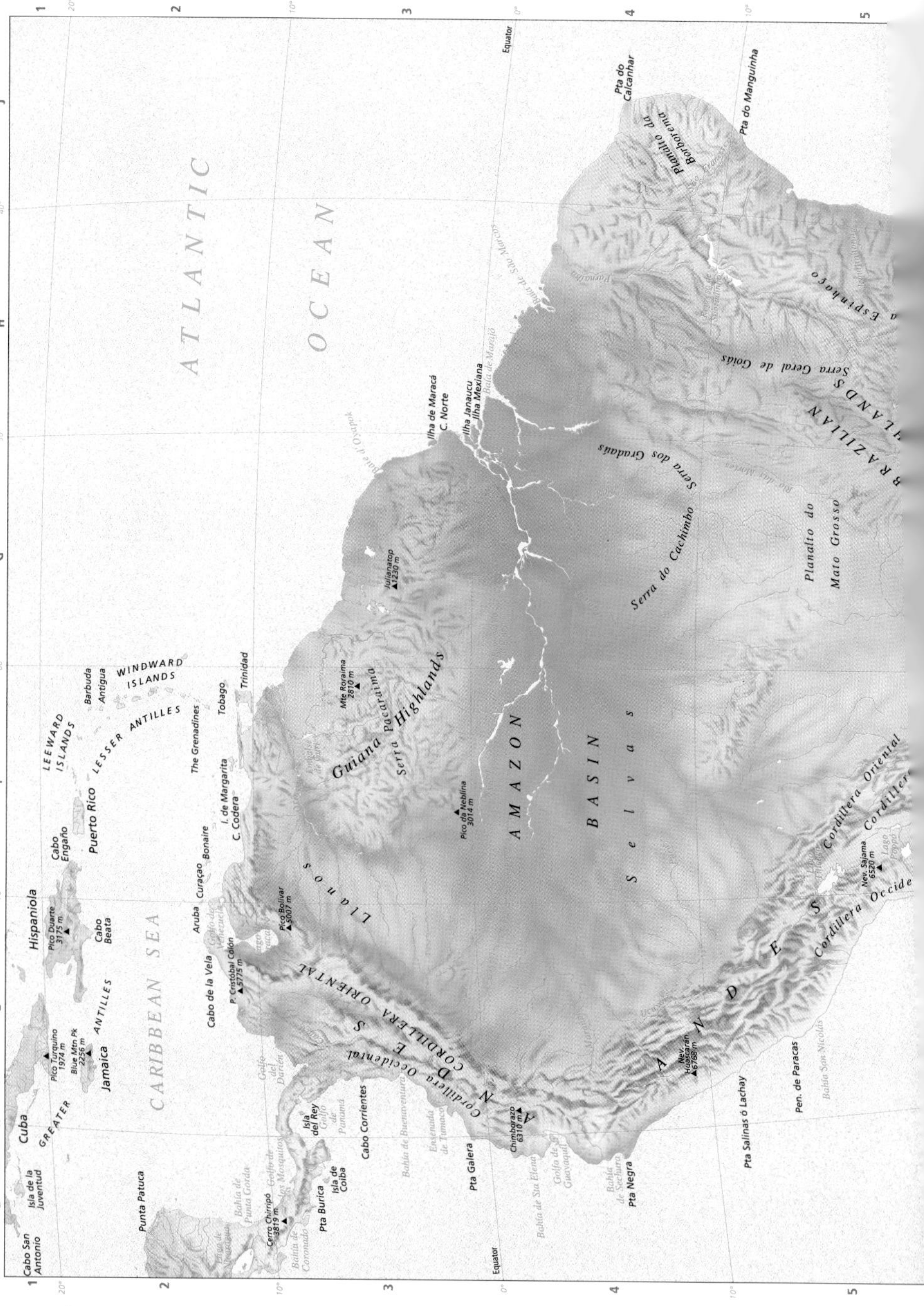
ATLANTIC OCEAN
CARIBBEAN SEA
Cuba
Isla de la Juventud
Cabo San Antonio
GREATER ANTILLES
Jamaica
Blue Mtn Pk 2256 m
Pico Turquino 1974 m
Hispaniola
Pico Duarte 3175 m
Cabo Beata
Cabo Engaño
Puerto Rico
LEEWARD ISLANDS
LESSER ANTILLES
WINDWARD ISLANDS
Barbuda
Antigua
The Grenadines
Tobago
Trinidad
Aruba
Curaçao
Bonaire
I. de Margarita
C. Codera
Cabo de la Vela
P. Cristóbal Colón 5775 m
Pico Bolívar 5007 m
Llanos
Guiana Highlands
Serra Pacaraima
Mte Roraima 2810 m
Julianatop 1230 m
Pico da Neblina 3014 m
AMAZON BASIN
Selvas
Ilha de Maracá
C. Norte
Ilha Janaucu
Ilha Mexiana
Serra dos Gradaús
Serra do Cachimbo
Planalto do Mato Grosso
Serra Geral de Goiás
BRAZILIAN HIGHLANDS
Planalto da Borborema
Pta do Calcanhar
Pta do Manguinha
Equator
CORDILLERA ORIENTAL
Cordillera Occidental
ANDES
Cordillera Oriental
Cordillera Occidental
Nev. Sajama 6520 m
Lago Poopó
Nev. Huascarán 6768 m
Chimborazo 6310 m
Punta Patuca
Cerro Chirripó 3819 m
Pta Burica
Isla de Coiba
Isla del Rey
Golfo de Panamá
Golfo del Darién
Cabo Corrientes
Bahía de Buenaventura
Ensenada de Tumaco
Pta Galera
Golfo de Guayaquil
Bahía de Sta Elena
Bahía de Sechura
Pta Negra
Pta Salinas ó Lachay
Pen. de Paracas
Bahía San Nicolás
D
E
F
G
H
J
1
2
3
4
5
20°
10°
0°
80°
70°
60°
50°
40°

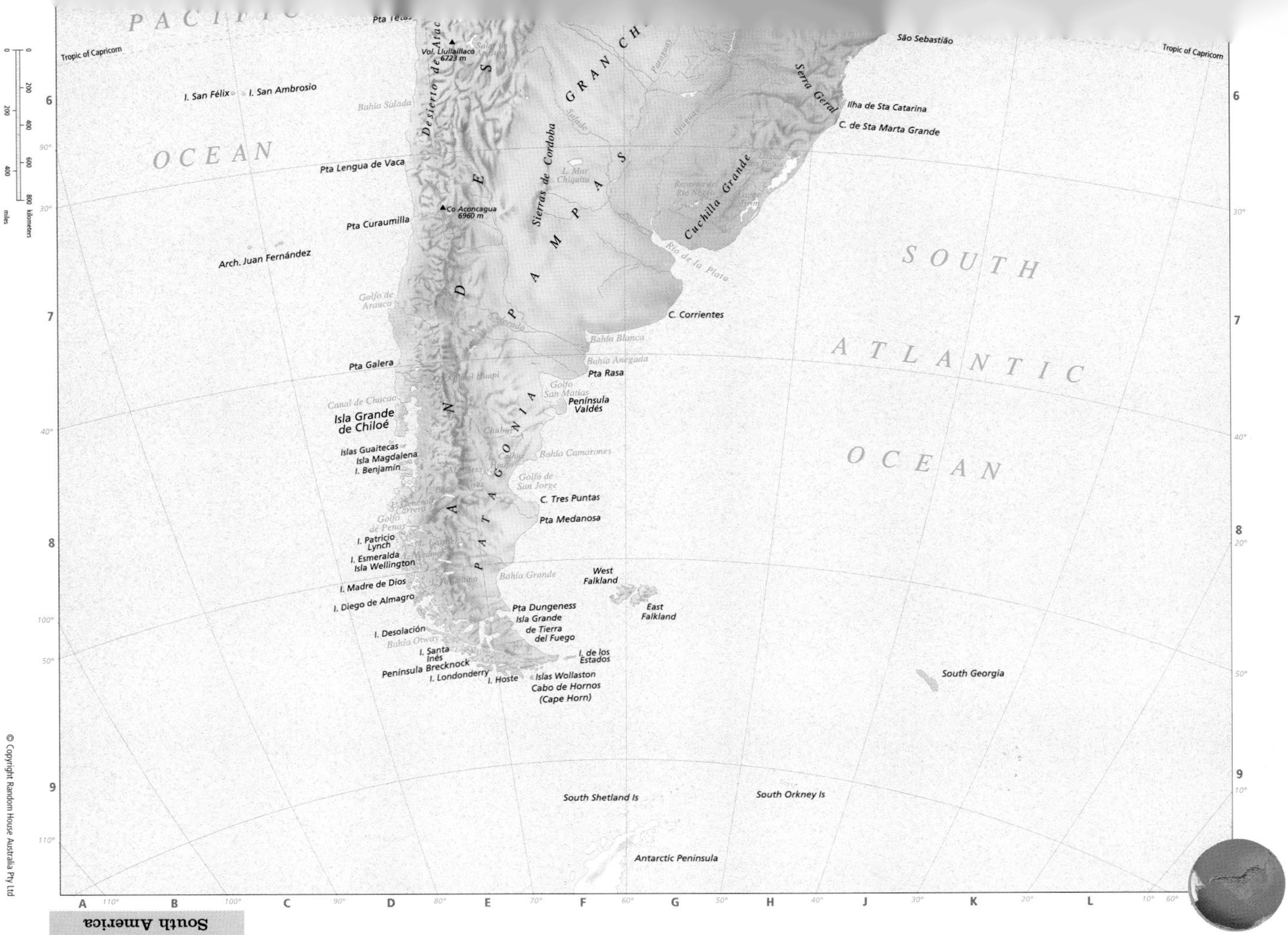
PACIFIC OCEAN
SOUTH ATLANTIC OCEAN
Tropic of Capricorn
I. San Félix
I. San Ambrosio
Bahía Salada
Pta Lengua de Vaca
Pta Curaumilla
Arch. Juan Fernández
Vol. Llullaillaco 6723 m
Co Aconcagua 6960 m
Desierto de Atac
ANDES
GRAN CH
PAMPAS
Sierras de Cordoba
L. Mar Chiquita
Salado
Uruguay
Paraguay
Serra Geral
São Sebastião
Ilha de Sta Catarina
C. de Sta Marta Grande
Cuchilla Grande
Río de la Plata
C. Corrientes
Colorado
Bahía Blanca
Bahía Anegada
Pta Rasa
Golfo San Matías
Península Valdés
Golfo de Arauco
Pta Galera
Canal de Chacao
Isla Grande de Chiloé
Islas Guaitecas
Isla Magdalena
I. Benjamín
PATAGONIA
Chubut
Bahía Camarones
Golfo de San Jorge
C. Tres Puntas
Pta Medanosa
Golfo de Penas
I. Patricio Lynch
I. Esmeralda
Isla Wellington
I. Madre de Dios
I. Diego de Almagro
Bahía Grande
West Falkland
East Falkland
Pta Dungeness
Isla Grande de Tierra del Fuego
I. Desolación
Bahía Otway
I. Santa Inés
Península Brecknock
I. Londonderry
I. Hoste
Islas Wollaston
Cabo de Hornos (Cape Horn)
I. de los Estados
South Georgia
South Shetland Is
South Orkney Is
Antarctic Peninsula
A B C D E F G H J K L
6 7 8 9
0 200 400 600 800 kilometers
0 200 400 miles

South America

A
B
C
D
839
852
1
2
3
4
5
CARIBBEAN SEA
PACIFIC
OCEAN
NICARAGUA
COSTA RICA
PANAMA
COLOMBIA
ECUADOR
PERU
ANDES
Santo Domingo
Laguna de Perlas
Juigalpa
Acoyapa
Bluefields
Punta Gorda
Bahía de Punta Gorda
San Carlos
San Juan del Norte
Vol. Miravalles 2028 m
Río Frío
Altamira
Guápiles
Puerto Jesús
Alajuela
Heredia
Puerto Limón
Puntarenas
Cartago
San José
Bribri
Parrita
Cerro Chirripó 3819 m
B. de Coronado
Dominical
Ciudad Cortés
Volcán Barú 3475 m
Volcán
Boquete
La Concepción
David
Península de Osa
Puerto Armuelles
Pta Burica
Golfo de Chiriquí
Isla de Coiba
Golfo de los Mosquitos
Santa Catalina
Cordillera Central
Penonomé
Antón
Coclé del Norte
Portobelo
El Porvenir
Colón
Palenque
Panamá
San Miguelito
La Chorrera
Chimán
Arch. de San Blás
Ailigandí
Golfo de San Blás
Isla del Rey
San Miguel
I. San José
Golfo de Panamá
La Palma
Yaviza
El Real
Garachiné
Jaqué
Tolé
San Francisco
Aguadulce
Santiago
Parita
Soná
Atalaya
Chitré
Río de Jesús
Las Tablas
Golfo de Montijo
Península de Azuero
Pedasí
Pta Mala
Isla de Cébaco
Tonosí
Pta Mariato
Golfo del Darién
Golfo de Urabá
Serr. del Darién
Puerto Obaldía
Acandí
Turbo
Chigorodó
Palo de las Letras
Riosucio
Jurado
Cupica
Golfo de Cupica
Pta Logos
El Valle
Nuquí
Cabo Corrientes
Quibdó
Serr. de Baudó
Istmina
Bajo Baudó
Pta Charambirá
Buenaventura
B. de Buenaventura
Naya
Pta Coco
Guapi
Mosquera
Ensenada de Tumaco
Tumaco
Barbacoas
B. de Ancón de Sardinas
San Lorenzo
Valdez
Esmeraldas
Punta Galera
Muisné
Cabo de San Francisco
Rosa Zárate
Cabo de
Ríohacha
Santa Marta
Barranquilla
Puerto Colombia
Baranoa
Soledad
Ciénaga
Sabanalarga
P. Cristóbal Colón 5775 m
Barrancas
Villanueva
Cartagena
Turbaco
Pivijay
Valledupar
Fundación
Arjona
Calamar
Sierra de Perijá
El Carmen de Bolívar
El Difícil
Augustin Codazzi
Golfo de Morrosquillo
Tolú
Plato
Sincelejo
Sincé
Chiriguaná
Mompós
La Jagua de Ibirico
Lorica
Magangué
El Banco
Puerto Rey
Cereté
Sahagún
Montería
Sucre
Tamalameque
La Gloria
Planeta Rica
Ayapel
Tierralta
Caucasia
Ocaña
Simití
Sardinata
Cáchira
Cúcuta
Serr. de Abibe
Serr. de San Jerónimo
Cáceres
Zaragoza
Pamplona
3960 m Paramillo
Ituango
Barrancabermeja
Bucaramanga
Dabeiba
Yarumal
Amalfi
Segovia
Zapatoca
Floridablanca
Antioquia
San Gil
Anzá
Cisneros
Puerto Berrío
Socorro
Bello
Medellín
Itagüí
Envigado
Cocorná
Vélez
Belén
Barbosa
Bolívar
Santa Bárbara
Sonsón
Chiquinquirá
Duitama
Sogamoso
Andes
Aguadas
La Dorada
Tunja
Salamina
Honda
Ubaté
Manizales
Líbano
Chocontá
Armero
Zipaquirá
Pereira
Nev. del Ruiz 5399 m
Facatativá
Cartago
Armenia
Soacha
Bogotá
Ibagué
Fusagasugá
Sevilla
Agua de Dios
4560 m
Villavicencio
Tuluá
Saldaña
Puerto López
Cerro Nevado
Buga
Chaparral
San Martín
Yumbo
Natagaima
Granada
Pavón
Cali
Palmira
Colombia
Puerto Tejada
Aipe
Baraya
Chafurray
5750 m
Nev. de Huila
Neiva
Santander
Campoalegre
Puerto La C
San Jos
Co Munchique 3012 m
Popayán
Gigante
La Plata
Volcán Puracé 4646 m
Garzón
Altamira
San Vicente del Caguán
Calamar
Cordillera Occidental
Cordillera Oriental
Serr. de la Macarena
Pitalito
Florencia
La Unión
La Cruz
Sotomayor
El Diviso
Sandoná
Pasto
Nev. de Cumbal 4764 m
Túquerres
Mocoa
Tulcán
Ipiales
San Gabriel
Puerto Asís
Tres Esquinas
Santa Rita
Mesa de Iguaje
Cerro Cumare 720 m
Macujer
Otavalo
Ibarra
Volcán Cayambe 5790 m
Cayambe
Lago Agrio
Hacha
La Tagua
Puerto Leguízamo
Cuyabeno
Equator
Santo Domingo de los Colorados
Quito
5704 m
Vol. Antisana
Puerto Francisco de Orellana
Machachi
Baeza
Vol. Cotopaxi 5897 m
Co Maine Hanari 860 m
La Chorrera
B. de Caráquez
Bahía de Caráquez
Chone
B. de Manta
Rocafuerte
Quevedo
Latacunga
Tena
Pantoja
Manta
Montecristi
Portoviejo
Santa Ana
Zapotal
Ambato
Jipijapa
Balzar
Chimborazo 6310 m
Puyo
Villano
Arica
Santa María
Paján
Guaranda
Babahoyo
Riobamba
El Encanto
Santa Lucía
Vol. Sangay 5230 m
B. de Sta Elena
Ayuy
Montalvo
Río Tigre
Salinas
Guayaquil
Durán
Alausí
Macas
Santa Elena
Santa Clotilde
Playas
Naranjal
Cañar
Azogues
Morona
Puerto Tunigrama
Andoas
Golfo de Guayaquil
Isla Puná
Cuenca
Gualaceo
Machala
Girón
Cord. del Cóndor
Intuto
Mazán
Francisco de Orellana
Zarumilla
Santa Rosa
Tumbes
Zorritos
Saraguro
Piñas
Puerto Pardo
Santa María de Nanay
Iquitos
Zamora
Canoas
Máncora
Catacocha
Loja
Tamshiyacu
Omaguas
Lobitos
Talara
Macará
Cariamanga
Borja
Concordia
Nauta
Pta Pariñas
Suyo
Las Lomas
Orellana
Barranca
Negritos
Sullana
La Huaca
Tambo Grande
Paita
Piura
Chulucanas
Requena
Palmeiras do Javari
Catacaos
Castilla
San Ignacio
Cahuapanas
Lagunas
82°
78°
74°
10°
6°
2°

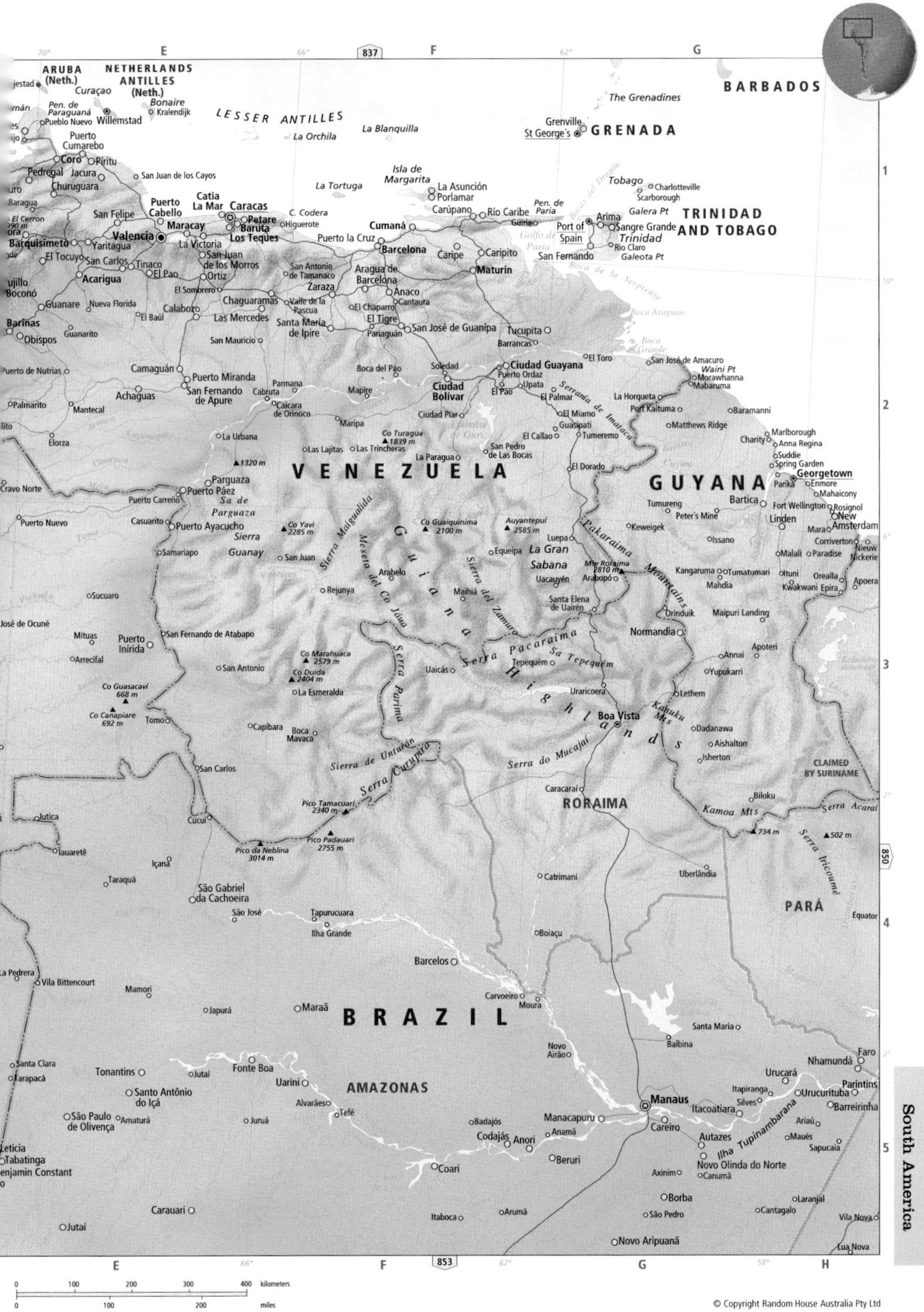
70° E 66° 837 F 62° G
ARUBA (Neth.)
NETHERLANDS ANTILLES (Neth.)
Oranjestad
Curaçao
Bonaire
Kralendijk
Pen. de Paraguaná
Pueblo Nuevo
Willemstad
LESSER ANTILLES
La Orchila
La Blanquilla
The Grenadines
BARBADOS
Grenville
St George's
GRENADA
Puerto Cumarebo
Coro
Píritu
Pedregal
Jacura
Churuguara
San Juan de los Cayos
Isla de Margarita
La Asunción
Porlamar
La Tortuga
Tobago
Charlotteville
Scarborough
Baragua
El Cerron
Barquisimeto
Puerto Cabello
Catia La Mar
Caracas
Petare
Baruta
Los Teques
C. Codera
Higuerote
San Felipe
Maracay
Valencia
La Victoria
Yaritagua
El Tocuyo
San Carlos
Tinaco
El Pao
San Juan de los Morros
Ortiz
Cumaná
Carúpano
Río Caribe
Güiria
Pen. de Paria
Port of Spain
Arima
Sangre Grande
Galera Pt
TRINIDAD AND TOBAGO
Trinidad
Rio Claro
Golfo de Paria
San Fernando
Galeota Pt
Puerto la Cruz
Barcelona
Caripe
Caripito
Maturín
Boca de la Serpiente
Boconó
Acarigua
Guanare
Nueva Florida
El Sombrero
Calabozo
El Baúl
San Antonio de Tamanaco
Zaraza
Aragua de Barcelona
Anaco
Cantaura
Chaguaramas
Valle de la Pascua
El Chaparro
El Tigre
Las Mercedes
Santa María de Ipire
Pariaguán
San José de Guanipa
Tucupita
Barrancas
Boca Araguao
Boca Grande
Barinas
Obispos
Guanarito
San Mauricio
El Toro
San José de Amacuro
Waini Pt
Morawhanna
Mabaruma
Puerto de Nutrias
Camaguán
Puerto Miranda
San Fernando de Apure
Achaguas
Parmana
Cabruta
Caicara de Orinoco
Mapire
Boca del Pao
Soledad
Ciudad Bolívar
Ciudad Guayana
Puerto Ordaz
El Pao
Upata
El Palmar
Serrania de Imataca
La Horqueta
Port Kaituma
Baramanni
Palmarito
Mantecal
Maripa
Ciudad Piar
Embalse de Guri
El Miamo
Guasipati
El Callao
Tumeremo
Matthews Ridge
Marlborough
Charity
Anna Regina
Elorza
La Urbana
Las Lajitas
Las Trincheras
Co Turagua 1839 m
La Paragua
San Pedro de Las Bocas
El Dorado
Suddie
Spring Garden
Georgetown
1320 m
VENEZUELA
GUYANA
Cravo Norte
Parguaza
Puerto Páez
Puerto Carreño
Sa de Parguaza
Parika
Enmore
Mahaicony
Bartica
Fort Wellington
Rosignol
New Amsterdam
Linden
Tumureng
Peter's Mine
Puerto Nuevo
Casuarito
Puerto Ayacucho
Sierra Guanay
Co Yavi 2285 m
Sierra Maigualida
Co Guaiquinima 2100 m
Auyantepui 2585 m
Luepa
Pakaraima Mountains
Keweigek
Issano
Mara
Corriverton
Nieuw Nickerie
Samariapo
San Juan
Meseta del Co Jáua
Guiana Highlands
Sierra del Zamuro
Equeipa
La Gran Sabana
Mte Roraima 2810 m
Arabopó
Uacauyén
Kangaruma
Tumatumari
Malali
Paradise
Ituni
Orealla
Apoera
Mahdia
Kwakwani
Epira
Sucuaro
Arabelo
Rejunya
Maihiá
Santa Elena de Uairén
Orinduik
Maipuri Landing
San José de Ocuné
Mituas
Puerto Inírida
San Fernando de Atabapo
Normandia
Arrecifal
Co Marahuaca 2579 m
Co Duida 2404 m
San Antonio
La Esmeralda
Serra Parima
Uaicás
Serra Pacaraima
Tepequém
Sa Tepequém
Apoteri
Annai
Yupukarri
Co Guasacaví 668 m
Co Canapiare 692 m
Tomo
Capibara
Boca Mavaca
Uraricoera
Boa Vista
Kanuku Mts
Lethem
Dadanawa
Aishalton
Isherton
Sierra de Unturán
Serra Curupira
Serra do Mucajaí
CLAIMED BY SURINAME
San Carlos
Caracaraí
RORAIMA
Biloku
Pico Tamacuarí 2340 m
Kamoa Mts
Serra Acaraí
Jutica
Mitú
Cucuí
Pico da Neblina 3014 m
Pico Padauari 2755 m
734 m
502 m
Serra Iricoumé
Iauareté
Içana
Taraquá
São Gabriel da Cachoeira
Catrimani
Uberlândia
850
PARÁ
São José
Tapurucuara
Ilha Grande
Boiaçu
Equator
Barcelos
La Pedrera
Vila Bittencourt
Mamori
Carvoeiro
Moura
Japurá
Maraã
BRAZIL
Santa Maria
Balbina
Novo Airão
Faro
Nhamundá
Santa Clara
Tarapacá
Tonantins
Jutaí
Fonte Boa
Uarini
AMAZONAS
Urucará
Parintins
Itapiranga
Silves
Urucurituba
Santo Antônio do Içá
Alvarães
Tefé
Manaus
Itacoatiara
Barreirinha
São Paulo de Olivença
Amaturá
Juruá
Badajós
Manacapuru
Careiro
Ariaú
Codajás
Anori
Anamã
Autazes
Maués
Ilha Tupinambarana
Sapucaia
Leticia
Tabatinga
Benjamin Constant
Coari
Beruri
Novo Olinda do Norte
Axinim
Canumã
Borba
Laranjal
Carauari
Itaboca
Arumã
São Pedro
Cantagalo
Vila Nova
Jutaí
Novo Aripuanã
Lua Nova
70° E 66° F 853 62° G 58° H
1 2 3 4 5
10° 6° 2°
0 100 200 300 400 kilometers
0 100 200 miles

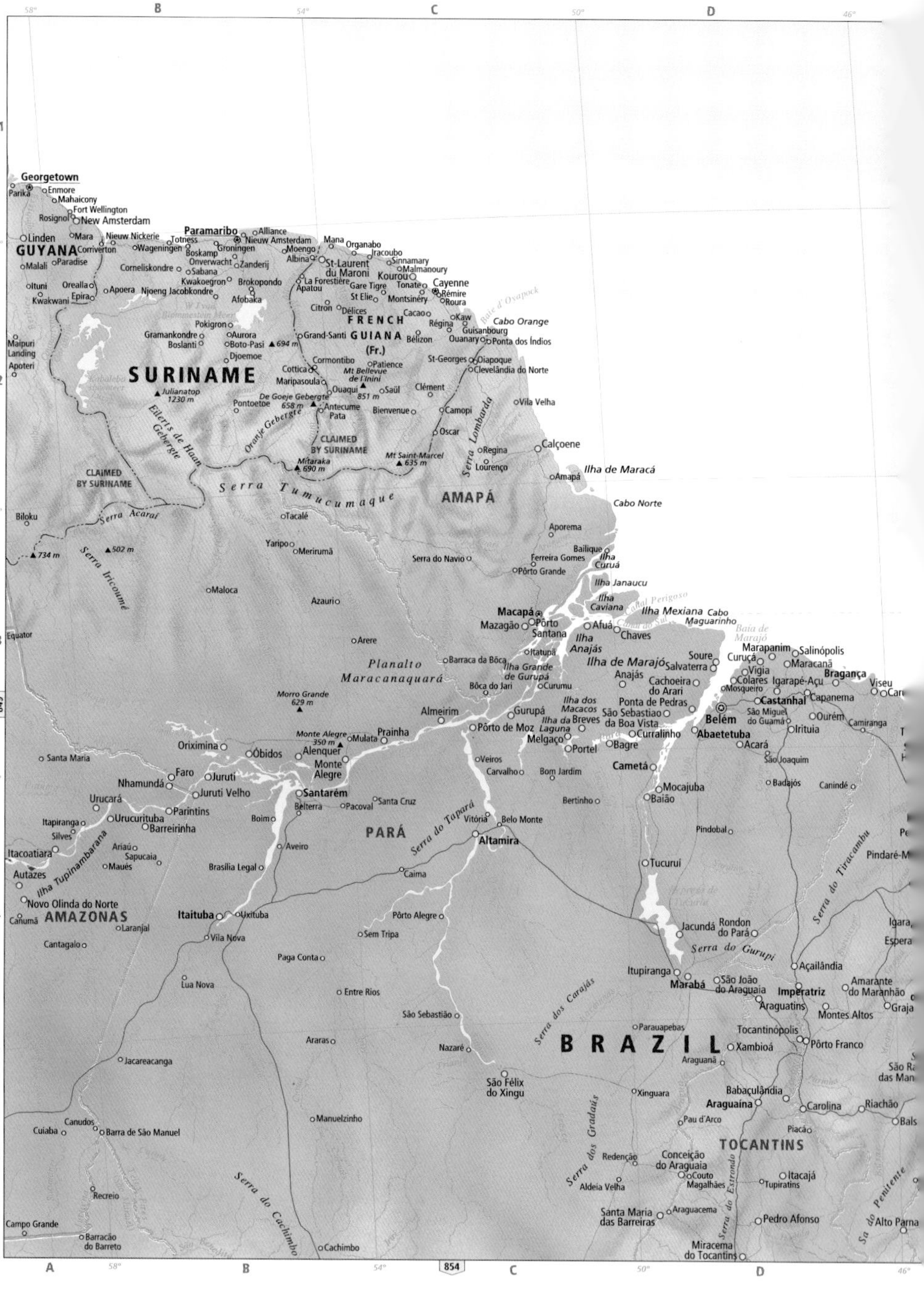

B
C
D
1
2
3
4
5
A
58°
54°
50°
46°
6°
2°
Georgetown
Parika
Enmore
Mahaicony
Fort Wellington
Rosignol
New Amsterdam
Linden
Mara
Nieuw Nickerie
Totness
Paramaribo
Alliance
Nieuw Amsterdam
GUYANA
Corriverton
Wageningen
Boskamp
Groningen
Moengo
Mana
Organabo
Iracoubo
Malali
Paradise
Onverwacht
Zanderij
Albina
St-Laurent du Maroni
Sinnamary
Malmanoury
Corneliskondre
Sabana
Kourou
Ituni
Orealla
Apoera
Njoeng Jacobkondre
Kwakoegron
Brokopondo
La Forestière
Apatou
Gare Tigre
Tonate
Cayenne
Rémire
Roura
Kwakwani
Epira
Afobaka
St Elie
Montsinéry
Citron
Délices
Cacao
FRENCH GUIANA (Fr.)
Pokigron
Régina
Kaw
Cabo Orange
Guisanbourg
Gramankondre
Aurora
Grand-Santi
Bélizon
Ouanary
Ponta dos Índios
Boslanti
Boto-Pasi
694 m
Maipuri Landing
Apoteri
Djoemoe
Cormontibo
Patience
St-Georges
Diapoque
SURINAME
Cottica
Maripasoula
Mt Bellevue de l'Inini
Clevelândia do Norte
Ouaqui
851 m
Saül
Clément
Julianatop 1230 m
De Goeje Gebergte 658 m
Pontoetoe
Antecume Pata
Bienvenue
Camopi
Vila Velha
Eilerts de Haan Gebergte
Oranje Gebergte
CLAIMED BY SURINAME
Oscar
Serra Lombarda
Regina
Calçoene
Mitaraka 690 m
Mt Saint-Marcel 635 m
Lourenço
Ilha de Maracá
CLAIMED BY SURINAME
Amapá
Serra Tumucumaque
AMAPÁ
Cabo Norte
Biloku
Serra Acaraí
Tacalé
Aporema
Yaripo
Merirumã
734 m
502 m
Serra Iricoumé
Bailique
Serra do Navio
Ferreira Gomes
Ilha Curuá
Pôrto Grande
Maloca
Ilha Janaucu
Azauri
Macapá
Ilha Caviana
Ilha Mexiana
Cabo Maguarinho
Mazagão
Pôrto Santana
Afuá
Chaves
Equator
Arere
Ilha Anajás
Baía de Marajó
Marapanim
Salinópolis
Itatupã
Soure
Curuçá
Maracanã
Planalto Maracanaquará
Barraca da Bôca
Ilha Grande de Gurupá
Ilha de Marajó
Salvaterra
Vigia
Anajás
Cachoeira do Arari
Colares
Igarapé-Açu
Bragança
Viseu
Bôca do Jari
Curumu
Mosqueiro
Castanhal
Capanema
Morro Grande 629 m
Ilha dos Macacos
Ponta de Pedras
849
Almeirim
Gurupá
Breves
São Sebastião da Boa Vista
Belém
São Miguel do Guamá
Ourém
Camiranga
Monte Alegre 350 m
Mulata
Prainha
Pôrto de Moz
Ilha da Laguna
Curralinho
Abaetetuba
Irituia
Oriximina
Óbidos
Alenquer
Melgaço
Portel
Bagre
Acará
Santa Maria
Veiros
São Joaquim
Faro
Monte Alegre
Carvalho
Bom Jardim
Cametá
Nhamundá
Juruti
Santarém
Badajós
Canindé
Urucará
Juruti Velho
Mocajuba
Belterra
Santa Cruz
Bertinho
Baião
Parintins
Pacoval
Itapiranga
Urucurituba
Boim
Vitória
Belo Monte
Silves
Barreirinha
Serra do Tapará
Pindobal
Ariaú
PARÁ
Altamira
Itacoatiara
Sapucaia
Aveiro
Ilha Tupinambarana
Maués
Tucuruí
Pindaré-M
Autazes
Brasília Legal
Caima
Serra do Tiracambu
Novo Olinda do Norte
Itaituba
Uxituba
Pôrto Alegre
Jacundá
Rondon do Pará
Canumã
AMAZONAS
Laranjal
Igara
Vila Nova
Sem Tripa
Espera
Cantagalo
Serra do Gurupi
Paga Conta
Itupiranga
Açailândia
Marabá
São João do Araguaia
Lua Nova
Entre Rios
Imperatriz
Amarante do Maranhão
Araguatins
São Sebastião
Montes Altos
Graja
Serra dos Carajás
Parauapebas
Tocantinópolis
Araras
Nazaré
BRAZIL
Xambioá
Pôrto Franco
Jacareacanga
Araguanã
São Félix do Xingu
Xinguara
Babaçulândia
Araguaína
Carolina
Riachão
Manuelzinho
Canudos
Pau d'Arco
Cuiaba
Barra de São Manuel
Piacá
TOCANTINS
Serra dos Gradaús
Redenção
Conceição do Araguaia
Couto Magalhães
Itacajá
Tupiratins
Aldeia Velha
Serra do Estrondo
Serra do Penitente
Recreio
Serra do Cachimbo
Santa Maria das Barreiras
Araguacema
Campo Grande
Pedro Afonso
Alto Parna
Barracão do Barreto
Cachimbo
Miracema do Tocantins
854

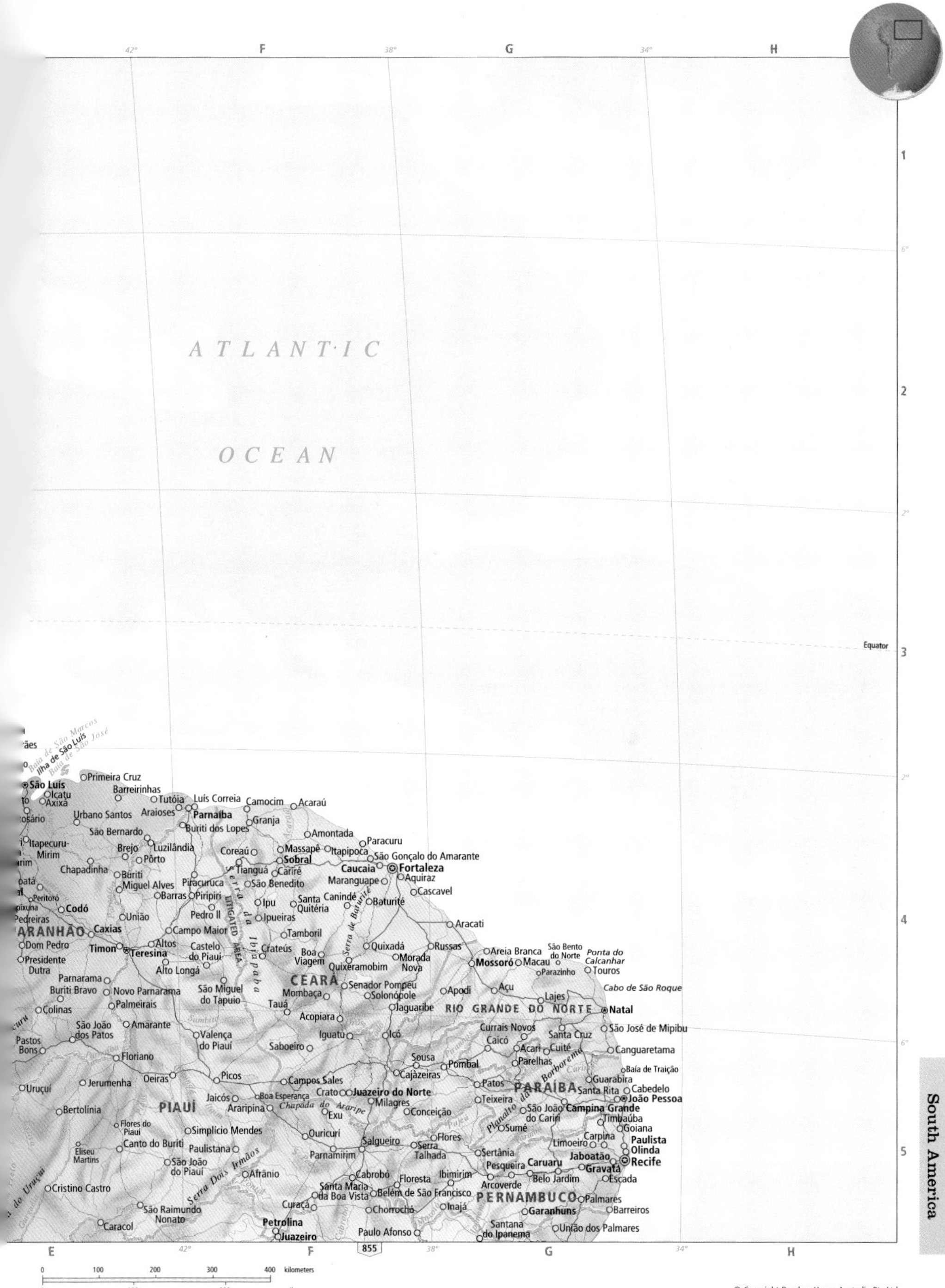

855

South America

42° F 38° G 34° H
1
ATLANTIC
2
OCEAN
6°
2°
Equator
3
2°
Baía de São Marcos
Ilha de São Luís
Baía de São José
...ães
São Luís
Primeira Cruz
Icatu
Axixá
Barreirinhas
Tutóia
Luís Correia
Camocim
Acaraú
...osário
Urbano Santos
Araioses
Parnaíba
Granja
Buriti dos Lopes
São Bernardo
Amontada
Paracuru
Itapecuru-Mirim
Brejo
Luzilândia
Coreaú
Massapê
Itapipoca
São Gonçalo do Amarante
...rim
Pôrto
Sobral
Caucaia
Fortaleza
Chapadinha
Buriti
Tianguá
Cariré
Maranguape
Aquiraz
...oatá
Miguel Alves
Piracuruca
São Benedito
Cascavel
Peritoró
Barras
Piripiri
Serra da Ibiapaba
Ipu
Santa Quitéria
Canindé
Baturité
...pixuna
Codó
Serra de Baturité
Pedreiras
União
Pedro II
Ipueiras
LITIGATED AREA
Aracati
...ARANHÃO
Caxias
Campo Maior
Tamboril
4
Dom Pedro
Timon
Altos
Castelo do Piauí
Crateús
Boa Viagem
Quixadá
Russas
Areia Branca
São Bento do Norte
Ponta do Calcanhar
Presidente Dutra
Teresina
Alto Longá
Quixeramobim
Morada Nova
Mossoró
Macau
Parazinho
Touros
Parnarama
CEARÁ
Senador Pompeu
Apodi
Açu
Cabo de São Roque
Buriti Bravo
Novo Parnarama
São Miguel do Tapuio
Mombaça
Solonópole
Lajes
Palmeirais
Tauá
Jaguaribe
RIO GRANDE DO NORTE
Natal
Colinas
Acopiara
São João dos Patos
Amarante
Valença do Piauí
Iguatu
Icó
Currais Novos
Santa Cruz
São José de Mipibu
Pastos Bons
Saboeiro
Caicó
Acari
Cuité
Canguaretama
6°
Floriano
Sousa
Pombal
Parelhas
Cajàzeiras
Serra da Borborema
Baía de Traição
Uruçuí
Jerumenha
Oeiras
Picos
Campos Sales
Patos
PARAÍBA
Guarabira
Santa Rita
Cabedelo
Jaicós
Boa Esperança
Crato
Juazeiro do Norte
Teixeira
João Pessoa
PIAUÍ
Araripina
Chapada do Araripe
Milagres
São João do Cariri
Campina Grande
Bertolínia
Exu
Conceição
Planalto da Borborema
Timbaúba
Flores do Piauí
Simplício Mendes
Ouricurí
Sumé
Goiana
Paulista
Carpina
Limoeiro
Olinda
Eliseu Martins
Canto do Buriti
Paulistana
Salgueiro
Flores
Serra Talhada
Sertânia
Jaboatão
Serra Dois Irmãos
Parnamirim
Caruaru
Recife
São João do Piauí
Pesqueira
Gravatá
Afrânio
Cabrobó
Floresta
Ibimirim
Belo Jardim
Escada
Cristino Castro
Santa Maria da Boa Vista
Belém de São Francisco
Arcoverde
Serra do Uruçuí
Curaçá
Inajá
PERNAMBUCO
Palmares
São Raimundo Nonato
Chorrochó
Garanhuns
Barreiros
Caracol
Petrolina
Santana do Ipanema
União dos Palmares
Juazeiro
Paulo Afonso
E 42° F 855 38° G 34° H
0 100 200 300 400 kilometers
0 100 200 miles

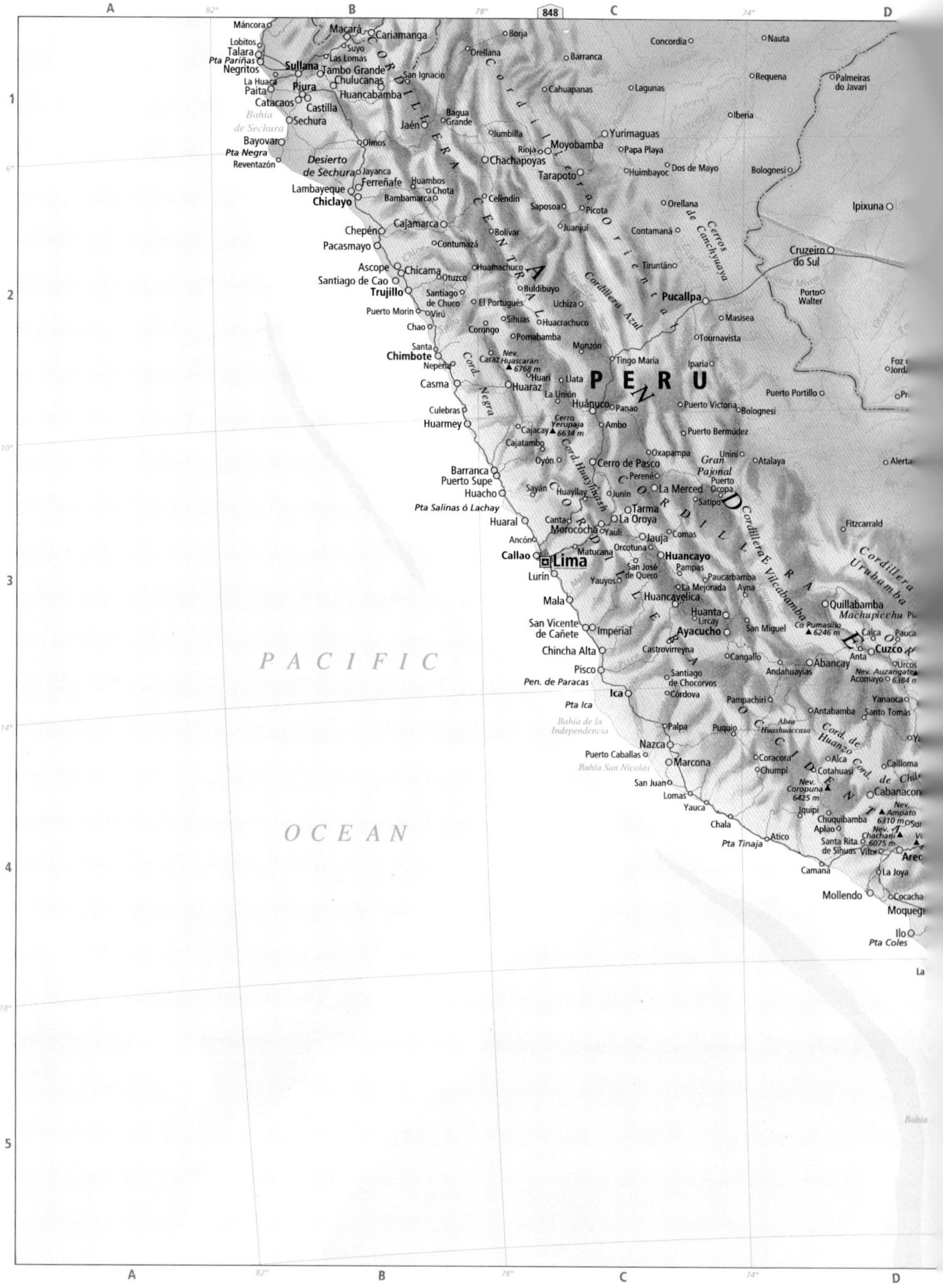
A
B
C
D
82°
78°
74°
848
1
2
3
4
5
6°
10°
14°
18°
Máncora
Lobitos
Talara
Pta Pariñas
Negritos
La Huaca
Paita
Sullana
Piura
Catacaos
Castilla
Bahía de Sechura
Sechura
Bayovar
Pta Negra
Reventazón
Macará
Cariamanga
Suyo
Las Lomas
Tambo Grande
Chulucanas
Huancabamba
San Ignacio
Jaén
Bagua Grande
Olmos
Desierto de Sechura
Jayanca
Ferreñafe
Lambayeque
Chiclayo
Huambos
Chota
Bambamarca
Celendín
Cajamarca
Chepén
Pacasmayo
Contumazá
Bolívar
Ascope
Chicama
Santiago de Cao
Otuzco
Trujillo
Santiago de Chuco
Puerto Morin
Virú
Chao
Santa
Chimbote
Nepeña
Casma
Culebras
Huarmey
Borja
Orellana
Barranca
Cahuapanas
Lagunas
Concordia
Nauta
Requena
Palmeiras do Javari
Iberia
Yurimaguas
Papa Playa
Jumbilla
Rioja
Moyobamba
Chachapoyas
Tarapoto
Huimbayoc
Dos de Mayo
Bolognesi
Saposoa
Picota
Juanjuí
Orellana
Contamaná
Cerros de Canchyuaya
Ipixuna
Cruzeiro do Sul
Porto Walter
Tiruntáno
Cordillera Central
Cordillera Oriental
Cordillera Azul
Huamachuco
Buldibuyo
El Portugués
Uchiza
Pucallpa
Masisea
Tournavista
Sihuas
Huacrachuco
Corongo
Pomabamba
Monzón
Caraz
Nev. Huascarán 6768 m
Huari
Llata
Huaraz
La Unión
Tingo María
Iparia
PERU
Cord. Negra
Huánuco
Panao
Ambo
Puerto Victoria
Bolognesi
Puerto Portillo
Puerto Bermúdez
Cerro Yerupaja 6634 m
Cajacay
Cajatambo
Oyón
Oxapampa
Unini
Atalaya
Gran Pajonal
Cerro de Pasco
Perené
Puerto Ocopa
La Merced
Satipo
Barranca
Puerto Supe
Huacho
Sayán
Huaylla
Junín
Cord. Huayhuash
Pta Salinas ó Lachay
Huaral
Canta
Tarma
La Oroya
Morococha
Yauli
Jauja
Comas
Ancón
Callao
Lima
Matucana
Orcotuna
Huancayo
San José de Quero
Pampas
Lurín
Yauyos
Paucarbamba
La Mejorada
Ayna
Huancavelica
Cordillera Occidental
Cordillera Vilcabamba
Cordillera Urubamba
Fitzcarrald
Quillabamba
Machupicchu
Mala
Huanta
Lircay
San Vicente de Cañete
Imperial
Ayacucho
San Miguel
Co Pumasillo 6246 m
Calca
Cuzco
Anta
Chincha Alta
Castrovirreyna
Cangallo
Andahuaylas
Abancay
Nev. Auzangate 6384 m
Acomayo
Urcos
Pisco
Pen. de Paracas
Santiago de Chocorvos
Córdova
Ica
Pta Ica
Pampachiri
Antabamba
Santo Tomás
Yanaoca
Bahía de la Independencia
Palpa
Puquio
Abra Huashuaccasa
Cord. de Huanzo
Cord. de Chila
Nazca
Puerto Caballas
Bahía San Nicolás
Marcona
Coracora
Chumpi
Alca
Cotahuasi
Caylloma
San Juan
Lomas
Nev. Coropuna 6425 m
Cabanaconde
Yauca
Iquipi
Chuquibamba
Nev. Ampato 6310 m
Chala
Aplao
Nev. Chachani 6075 m
Atico
Pta Tinaja
Santa Rita de Sihuas
Vitor
Camaná
La Joya
Mollendo
Cocachacra
Moquegua
Ilo
Pta Coles
PACIFIC
OCEAN

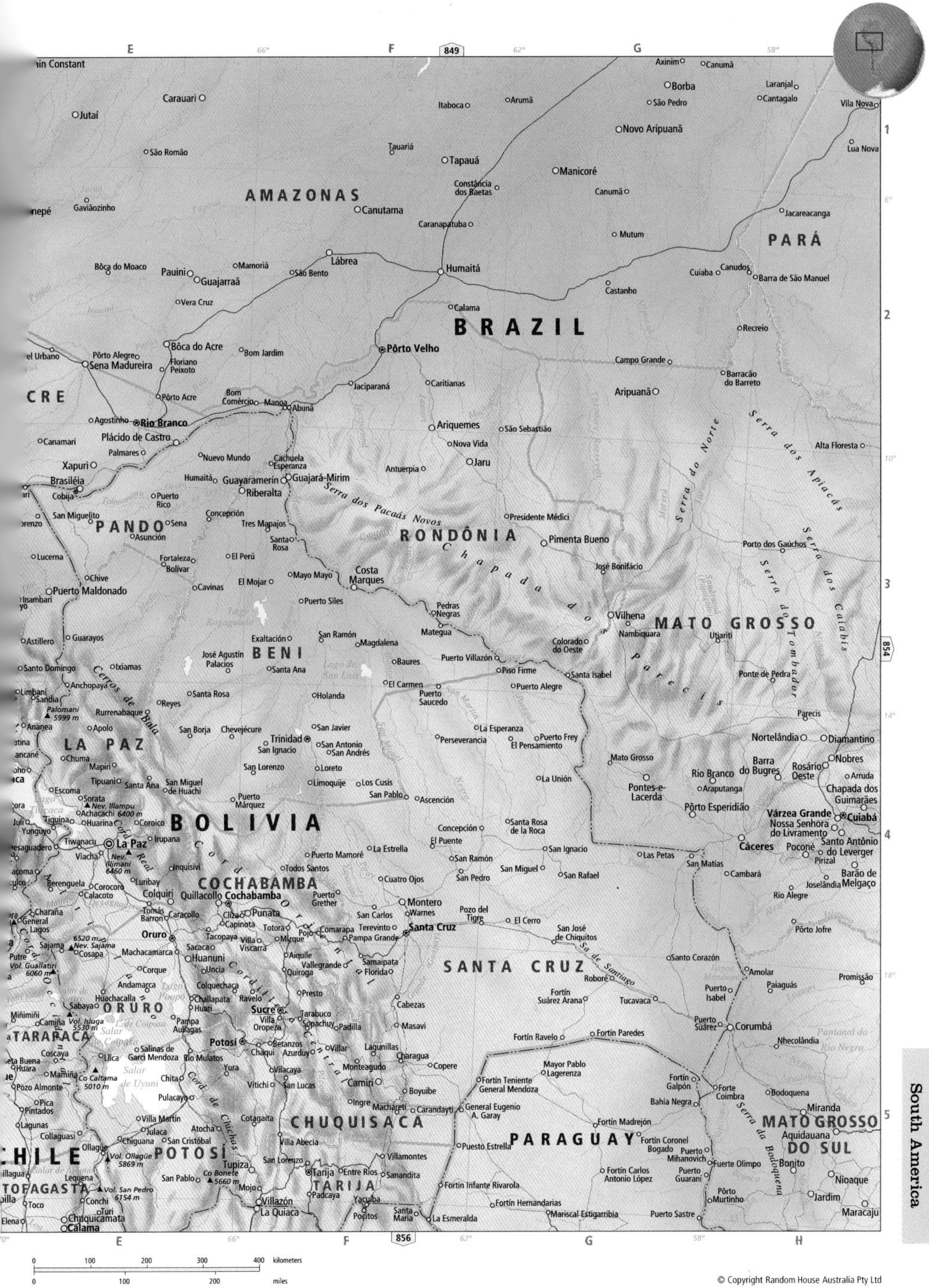

South America

AMAZONAS

PARÁ

B R A Z I L

CRE

Rio Branco

PANDO

RONDÔNIA

MATO GROSSO

BENI

LA PAZ

BOLIVIA

COCHABAMBA

SANTA CRUZ

ORURO

Sucre

Potosí

TARACACA

CHUQUISACA

PARAGUAY

MATO GROSSO DO SUL

POTOSÍ

HILE

TARIJA

TOFAGASTA

kilometers
0 100 200 300 400

miles
0 100 200

© Copyright Random House Australia Pty Ltd

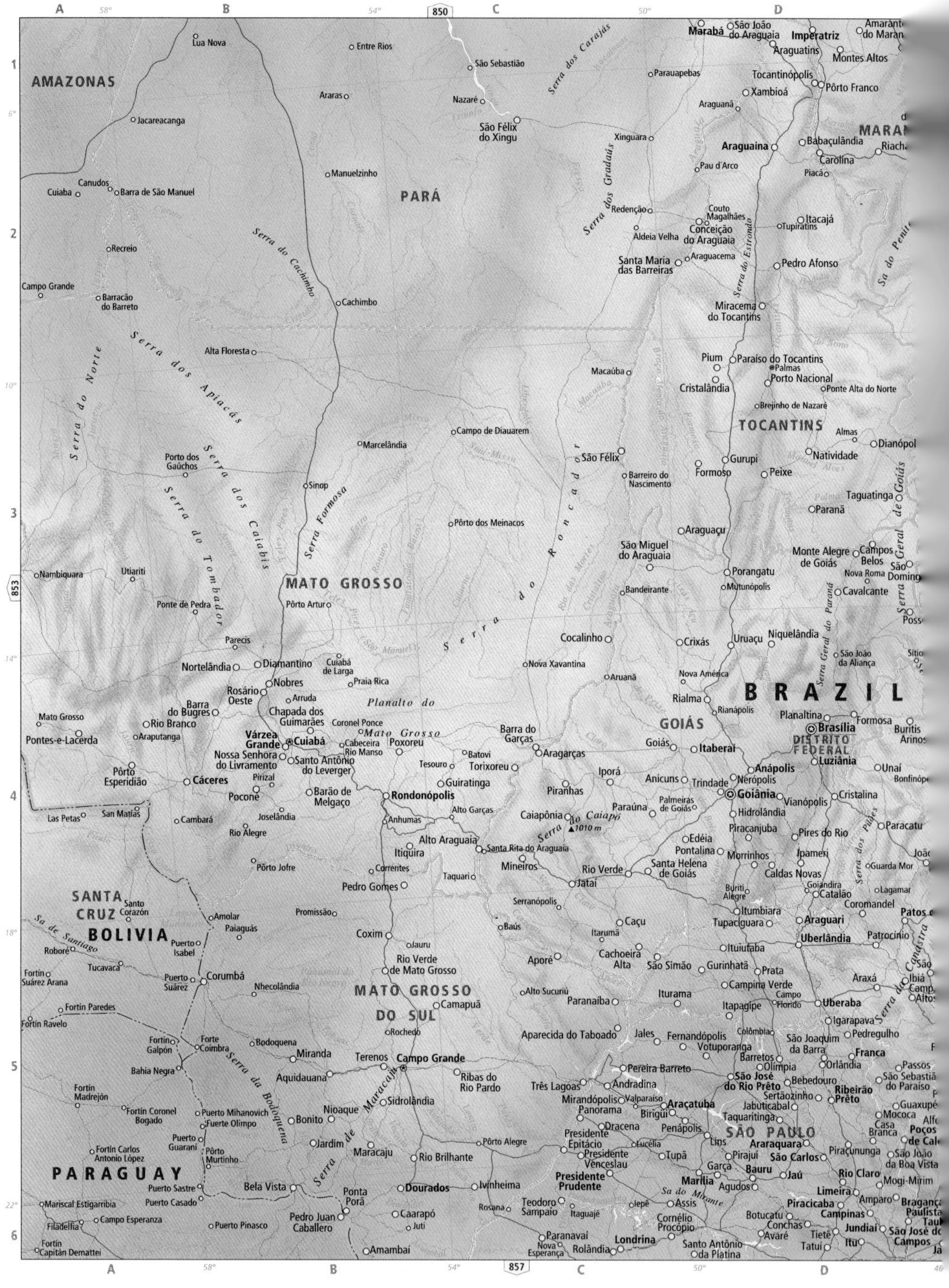
A
B
C
D
850
853
857
1
2
3
4
5
6
AMAZONAS
PARÁ
MATO GROSSO
MATO GROSSO DO SUL
TOCANTINS
GOIÁS
DISTRITO FEDERAL
SÃO PAULO
BRAZIL
BOLIVIA
PARAGUAY
SANTA CRUZ
Lua Nova
Entre Rios
São Sebastião
Serra dos Carajás
Marabá
São João do Araguaia
Imperatriz
Araguatins
Montes Altos
Parauapebas
Tocantinópolis
Pôrto Franco
Xambioá
Araras
Nazaré
Araguanã
Jacareacanga
São Félix do Xingu
Xinguara
Araguaína
Babaçulândia
Carolina
Piacá
Manuelzinho
Pau d'Arco
Serra dos Gradaús
Canudos
Cuiaba
Barra de São Manuel
Redenção
Couto Magalhães
Conceição do Araguaia
Aldeia Velha
Itacajá
Tupiratins
Recreio
Serra do Cachimbo
Santa Maria das Barreiras
Araguacema
Serra do Estrondo
Pedro Afonso
Campo Grande
Barracão do Barreto
Cachimbo
Miracema do Tocantins
Serra do Norte
Serra dos Apiacás
Alta Floresta
Pium
Paraíso do Tocantins
Palmas
Porto Nacional
Macaúba
Cristalândia
Ponte Alta do Norte
Brejinho de Nazaré
Campo de Diauarem
Marcelândia
Almas
Porto dos Gaúchos
Serra dos Caiabis
São Félix
Gurupi
Natividade
Formoso
Peixe
Barreiro do Nascimento
Sinop
Serra Formosa
Serra do Tombador
Taguatinga
Paranã
Pôrto dos Meinacos
Serra do Roncador
Araguaçu
São Miguel do Araguaia
Monte Alegre de Goiás
Campos Belos
Nova Roma
Nambiquara
Utiariti
Porangatu
Mutunópolis
Cavalcante
Bandeirante
Pôrto Artur
Ponte de Pedra
Cocalinho
Crixás
Uruaçu
Niquelândia
Serra Geral do Paraná
Parecis
Diamantino
Cuiabá de Larga
Nova Xavantina
São João da Aliança
Nortelândia
Nobres
Praia Rica
Aruanã
Nova América
Rosário Oeste
Arruda
Planalto do Mato Grosso
Rialma
Rianápolis
Barra do Bugres
Chapada dos Guimarães
Planaltina
Brasília
Formosa
Mato Grosso
Rio Branco
Coronel Ponce
Pontes-e-Lacerda
Araputanga
Várzea Grande
Cuiabá
Cabeceira Rio Manso
Poxoreu
Barra do Garças
Goiás
Itaberaí
Luziânia
Nossa Senhora do Livramento
Santo Antônio do Leverger
Batovi
Aragarças
Anápolis
Unaí
Tesouro
Torixoreu
Iporá
Anicuns
Trindade
Nerópolis
Pôrto Esperidião
Cáceres
Pirizal
Guiratinga
Piranhas
Goiânia
Vianópolis
Cristalina
Poconé
Barão de Melgaço
Rondonópolis
Palmeiras de Goiás
Paraúna
Hidrolândia
Las Petas
San Matías
Cambará
Joselândia
Alto Garças
Caiapônia
Serra do Caiapó
1010 m
Anhumas
Piracanjuba
Pires do Rio
Paracatu
Rio Alegre
Itiquira
Alto Araguaia
Santa Rita do Araguaia
Edéia
Pontalina
Morrinhos
Ipameri
Serra dos Pilões
Mineiros
Rio Verde
Santa Helena de Goiás
Caldas Novas
Guarda Mor
Pôrto Jofre
Correntes
Taquari
Jataí
Buriti Alegre
Goiandira
Catalão
Lagamar
Pedro Gomes
Serranópolis
Coromandel
Santo Corazón
Itumbiara
Amolar
Promissão
Caçu
Tupaciguara
Araguari
Sa de Santiago
Paiaguás
Baús
Itarumã
Uberlândia
Patrocínio
Puerto Isabel
Coxim
Jauru
Ituiutaba
Roboré
Cachoeira Alta
Aporé
São Simão
Gurinhatã
Prata
Fortín Suárez Arana
Tucavaca
Rio Verde de Mato Grosso
Araxá
Ibiá
Puerto Suárez
Corumbá
Nhecolândia
Iturama
Campina Verde
Campo Florido
Uberaba
Alto Sucuriú
Paranaíba
Itapagipe
Fortín Paredes
Camapuã
Igarapava
Fortín Ravelo
Rochedo
Colômbia
Pedregulho
Aparecida do Taboado
Jales
Fernandópolis
São Joaquim da Barra
Fortín Galpón
Forte Coimbra
Bodoquena
Votuporanga
Franca
Barretos
Serra da Bodoquena
Miranda
Terenos
Campo Grande
Olímpia
Orlândia
Bahia Negra
Ribas do Rio Pardo
Pereira Barreto
São José do Rio Prêto
Bebedouro
São Sebastião do Paraíso
Aquidauana
Três Lagoas
Andradina
Ribeirão Prêto
Fortín Madrejón
Sidrolândia
Mirandópolis
Valparaíso
Sertãozinho
Araçatuba
Jabuticabal
Serra de Maracaju
Birigui
Guaxupé
Fortín Coronel Bogado
Puerto Mihanovich
Nioaque
Panorama
Taquaritinga
Mococa
Fuerte Olimpo
Bonito
Dracena
Penápolis
Casa Branca
Poços de Caldas
Puerto Guaraní
Presidente Epitácio
Lins
Araraquara
Jardim
Pôrto Alegre
Lucélia
Piraçununga
Fortín Carlos Antonio López
Pôrto Murtinho
Maracaju
Presidente Venceslau
Tupã
Pirajuí
São Carlos
São João da Boa Vista
Rio Brilhante
Garça
Bauru
Jaú
Rio Claro
Presidente Prudente
Marília
Agudos
Mogi-Mirim
Limeira
Puerto Sastre
Bela Vista
Ponta Porã
Dourados
Ivinheima
Sa do Mirante
Amparo
Bragança Paulista
Mariscal Estigarribia
Puerto Casado
Teodoro Sampaio
Iepê
Assis
Piracicaba
Campinas
Rosana
Itaguajé
Cornélio Procópio
Botucatu
Conchas
Jundiaí
São José dos Campos
Filadelfia
Campo Esperanza
Puerto Pinasco
Pedro Juan Caballero
Caarapó
Juti
Avaré
Tietê
Tatuí
Itu
Campos
Fortín Capitán Demattei
Amambai
Paranavaí
Nova Esperança
Rolândia
Londrina
Santo Antônio da Platina
6°
10°
14°
18°
22°
58°
54°
50°
46°

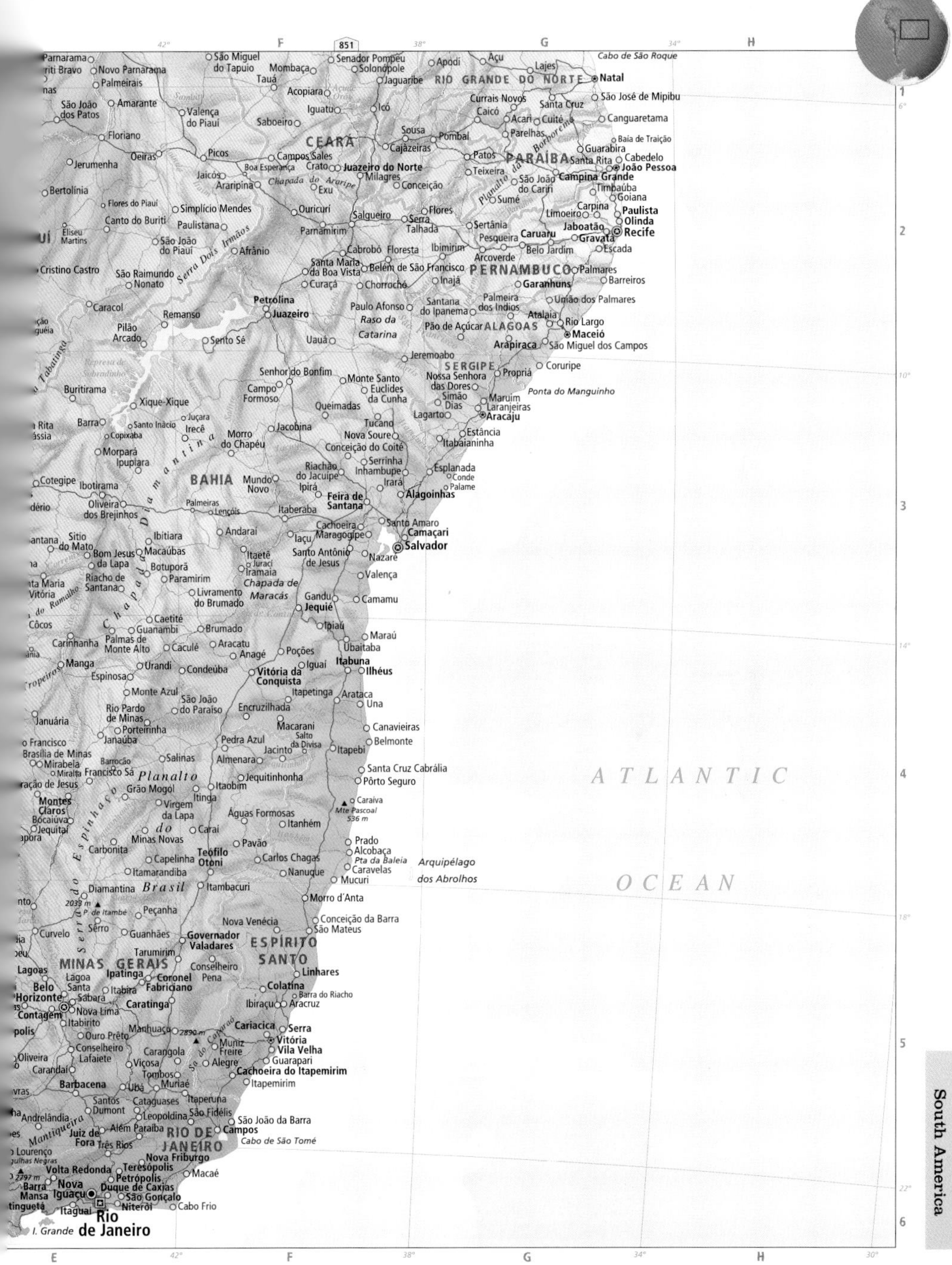

0 100 200 300 400 kilometers

0 100 200 miles

South America

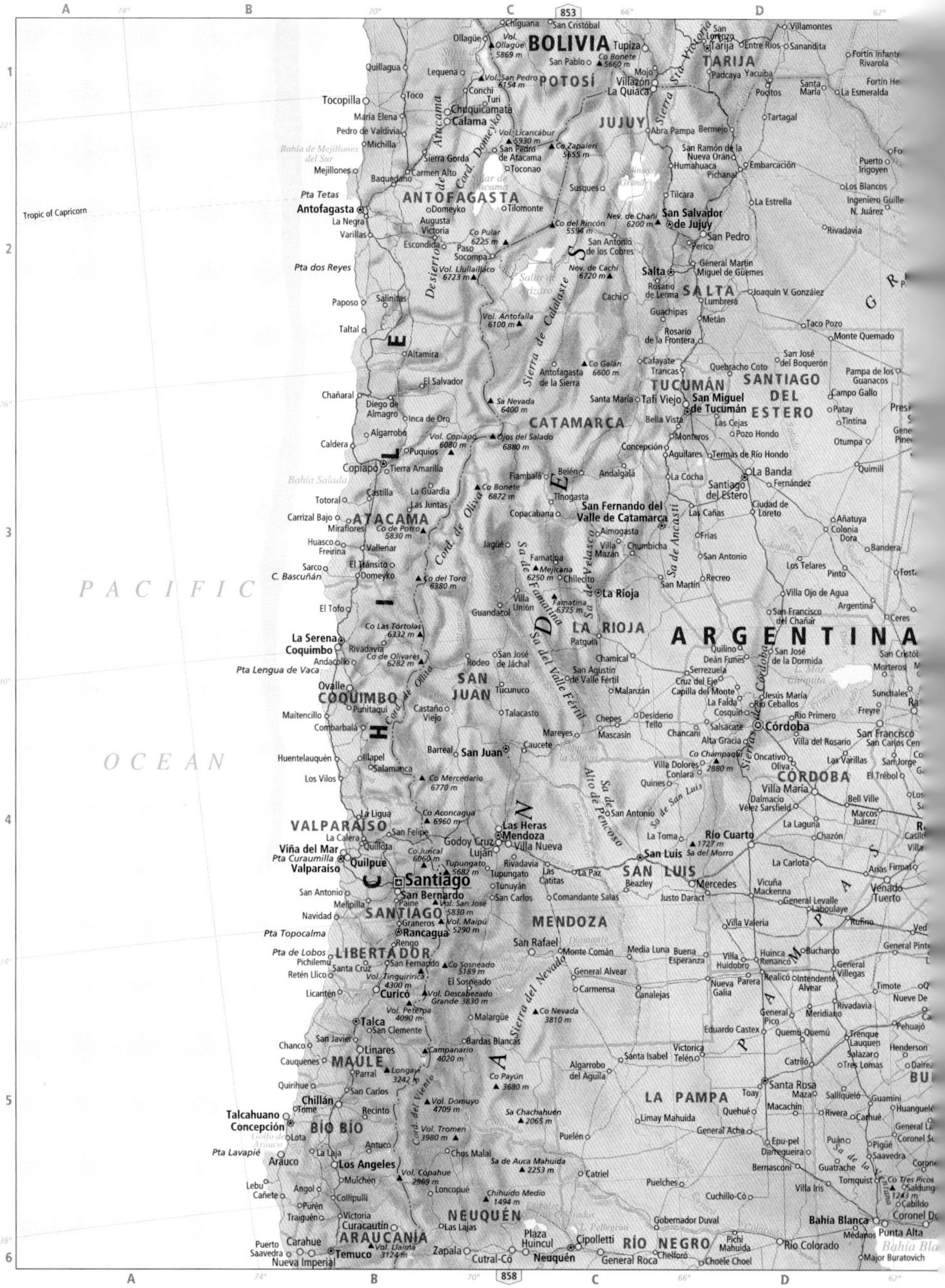
A
74°
B
70°
C
853
66°
D
62°
1
22°
2
26°
3
30°
4
34°
5
38°
6
858
Chiguana
San Cristóbal
Ollagüe
Vol. Ollagüe 5869 m
BOLIVIA
Tupiza
San Lorenzo
Tarija
Entre Ríos
Sanandita
Villamontes
Quillagua
Lequena
Vol. San Pedro 6154 m
San Pablo
Co Bonete 5660 m
POTOSÍ
Mojo
Villazón
La Quiaca
TARIJA
Padcaya
Yacuiba
Sierra Sta. Victoria
Santa María
La Esmeralda
Fortín Infante Rivarola
Tocopilla
Toco
Conchi
Turi
Chuquicamata
Calama
Pocitos
Tartagal
María Elena
Pedro de Valdivia
Michilla
Atacama
Cord. Domeyko
JUJUY
Vol. Licancábur 5930 m
San Pedro de Atacama
Co Zapaleri 5655 m
Abra Pampa
Bermejo
Bahía de Mejillones del Sur
Mejillones
Sierra Gorda
Carmen Alto
Baquedano
Toconao
Salar de Atacama
San Ramón de la Nueva Orán
Humahuaca
Embarcación
Pichanal
Puerto Irigoyen
Los Blancos
Ingeniero Guillermo N. Juárez
Pta Tetas
Antofagasta
ANTOFAGASTA
Domeyko
Tilomonte
Susques
Salinas Grandes
Tilcara
La Estrella
Tropic of Capricorn
La Negra
Varillas
Augusta Victoria
Co del Rincón 5594 m
Nev. de Chañi 6200 m
San Salvador de Jujuy
San Pedro
Rivadavia
Escondida
Co Pular 6225 m
Paso Socompa
San Antonio de los Cobres
Perico
Pta dos Reyes
Desierto de Atacama
Vol. Llullaillaco 6723 m
Nev. de Cachi 6720 m
Salta
General Martín Miguel de Güemes
Salar de Arizaro
Rosario de Lerma
SALTA
Joaquín V. González
Paposo
Salinitas
Cachi
Lumbrera
Guachipas
Metán
Taltal
Vol. Antofalla 6100 m
Sierra de Calalaste
Rosario de la Frontera
Taco Pozo
Monte Quemado
Altamira
Co Galán 6600 m
Cafayate
Trancas
Quebracho Coto
San José del Boquerón
Pampa de los Guanacos
El Salvador
Antofagasta de la Sierra
TUCUMÁN
SANTIAGO DEL ESTERO
Campo Gallo
Chañaral
Diego de Almagro
Sa Nevada 6400 m
Santa María
Tafí Viejo
San Miguel de Tucumán
Patay
Tintina
Inca de Oro
CATAMARCA
Bella Vista
Las Cejas
Algarrobo
Vol. Copiapó 6080 m
Ojos del Salado 6880 m
Monteros
Pozo Hondo
Otumpa
Caldera
Puquios
Concepción
Aguilares
Termas de Río Hondo
Copiapó
Tierra Amarilla
Quimilí
La Banda
Bahía Salada
Fiambalá
Belén
Andalgalá
La Cocha
Santiago del Estero
Fernández
La Guardia
Co Bonete 6872 m
Castilla
Tinogasta
Totoral
Las Juntas
San Fernando del Valle de Catamarca
Ciudad de Loreto
Carrizal Bajo
ATACAMA
Copacabana
Las Cañas
Añatuya
Miraflores
Co de Potro 5830 m
Cord. de Oliva
Aimogasta
Sa de Ancasti
Colonia Dora
Huasco
Freirina
Vallenar
Jagüé
Villa Mazán
Chumbicha
Frías
Bandera
Famatina
Sa de Velasco
San Antonio
Sarco
El Tránsito
Mejicana 6250 m
Chilecito
Los Telares
Pinto
C. Bascuñán
Domeyko
Co del Toro 6380 m
Sa de Famatina
Recreo
San Martín
PACIFIC
La Rioja
Villa Ojo de Agua
El Tofo
Villa Unión
Famatina 6375 m
Guandacol
San Francisco del Chañar
Argentina
Ceres
Co Las Tórtolas 6332 m
LA RIOJA
ARGENTINA
La Serena
Coquimbo
Patquía
Quilino
Rivadavia
San José de Jáchal
Deán Funes
San José de la Dormida
Andacollo
Co de Olivares 6282 m
Rodeo
Chamical
Serrezuela
Mar Chiquita
Pta Lengua de Vaca
SAN JUAN
San Agustín de Valle Fértil
Sa del Valle Fértil
Cruz del Eje
Morteros
Ovalle
COQUIMBO
Tucunuco
Malanzán
Capilla del Monte
Jesús María
Río Ceballos
Sunchales
Punitaqui
Castaño Viejo
Talacasto
La Falda
Cosquín
Sierras de Córdoba
Río Primero
Freyre
Maitencillo
Chepes
Desiderio Tello
Salsacate
Combarbalá
Mascasín
Chancaní
Córdoba
Mareyes
Alta Gracia
San Francisco
Villa del Rosario
Huentelauquén
Illapel
Barreal
San Juan
Caucete
Co Champaquí 2880 m
Oncativo
Oliva
Las Varillas
OCEAN
Salamanca
Co Mercedario 6770 m
Villa Dolores
Conlara
CÓRDOBA
El Trébol
Los Vilos
Quines
Villa María
Dalmacio Vélez Sarsfield
Bell Ville
La Ligua
Co Aconcagua 6960 m
Sa de Pencoso
Sa de San Luis
San Antonio
Marcos Juárez
VALPARAÍSO
Las Heras
Mendoza
La Laguna
La Calera
San Felipe
Godoy Cruz
Quillota
La Toma
Sa del Morro 1727 m
Río Cuarto
Chazón
Viña del Mar
Co Juncal 6060 m
Luján
Villa Nueva
Pta Curaumilla
Quilpué
Valparaíso
Tupungato 5682 m
Rivadavia
San Luis
La Carlota
Santiago
Tupungato
Las Catitas
La Paz
SAN LUIS
Arias
Venado Tuerto
San Antonio
San Bernardo
Tunuyán
Beazley
Mercedes
Vicuña Mackenna
Paine
Vol. San José 5830 m
San Carlos
Comandante Salas
Justo Daract
General Levalle
Melipilla
Navidad
SANTIAGO
Graneros
Vol. Maipú 5290 m
Laboulaye
Rancagua
MENDOZA
Villa Valeria
Rufino
Pta Topocalma
Rengo
San Rafael
Monte Comán
Media Luna
Buena Esperanza
Pta de Lobos
LIBERTADOR
Huinca Renancó
Bucharдо
General Pinto
Pichilemu
Santa Cruz
San Fernando
Co Sosneado 5189 m
Villa Huidobro
Retén Llico
Vol. Tinguiririca 4300 m
El Sosneado
General Alvear
Realicó
Intendente Alvear
General Villegas
Nueva Galia
Parera
Licantén
Curicó
Vol. Descabezado Grande 3830 m
Carmensa
Canalejas
Timote
Vol. Peteroa 4090 m
Sierra del Nevado
General Pico
Meridiano
Rivadavia
Talca
San Clemente
Malargüe
Co Nevada 3810 m
Eduardo Castex
Quemú-Quemú
Pehuajó
Chanco
San Javier
Bardas Blancas
Trenque Lauquen
Linares
Campanario 4020 m
Victorica
Telén
Salazar
Henderson
Cauquenes
MAULE
Santa Isabel
Algarrobo del Águila
Catriló
Tres Lomas
Parral
Longaví 3242 m
Co Payún 3680 m
Santa Rosa
Quirihue
San Carlos
Toay
Maza
Salliqueló
Guaminí
Chillán
Vol. Domuyo 4709 m
LA PAMPA
Quehué
Macachín
Rivera
Huanguelén
Talcahuano
Tomé
Recinto
Sa Chachahuén 2065 m
Carhué
Concepción
BÍO BÍO
Cord. del Viento
Limay Mahuida
General Acha
General La Madrid
Golfo de Arauco
Lota
Vol. Tromen 3980 m
Puelén
Epu-pel
Puán
Pigüé
Coronel Suárez
Pta Lavapié
Antuco
Chos Malal
Darregueira
Saavedra
Arauco
La Laja
Sa de Auca Mahuida 2253 m
Los Angeles
Bernasconi
Guatraché
Lebu
Cañete
Mulchén
Vol. Copahue 2969 m
Catriel
Puelches
Tornquist
Co Tres Picos 1243 m
Saldungaray
Angol
Collipulli
Loncopué
Chihuido Medio 1494 m
Villa Iris
Cabildo
Purén
Cuchillo-Có
Coronel Dorrego
Traiguén
Victoria
NEUQUÉN
Embalse Cerros Colorados
Gobernador Duval
Bahía Blanca
Curacautín
Las Lajas
Plaza Huincul
L. Pellegrini
Punta Alta
Médanos
Puerto Saavedra
Carahue
ARAUCANÍA
Zapala
Cipolletti
RÍO NEGRO
Pichi Mahuida
Río Colorado
Bahía Blanca
Temuco
Vol. Llaima 3124 m
Cutral-Có
Neuquén
General Roca
Chelforó
Choele Choel
Major Buratovich
Nueva Imperial

854

0 100 200 300 400 kilometers

0 100 200 miles

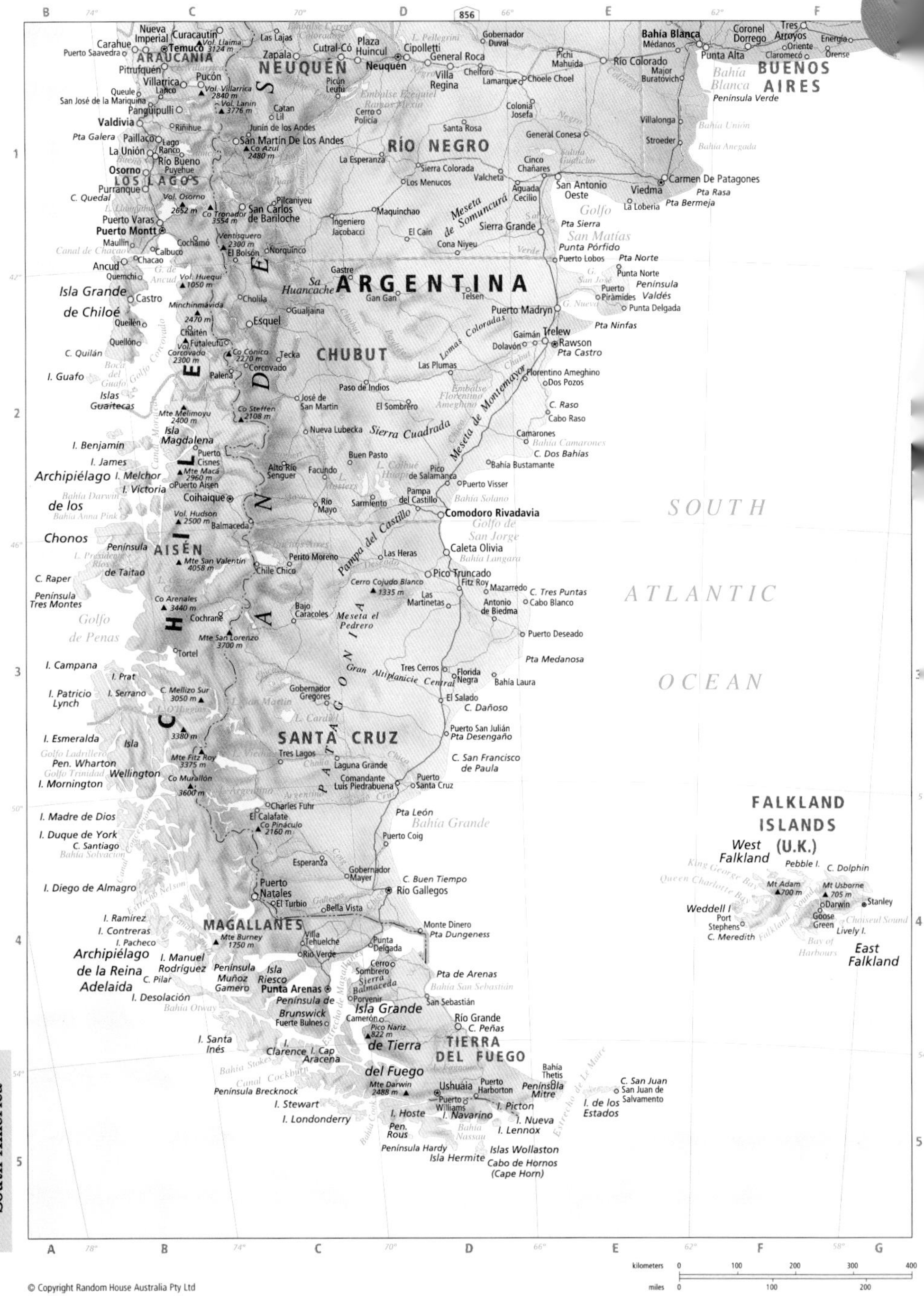

South America

ARGENTINA
CHILE
ANDES
PATAGONIA
NEUQUÉN
RÍO NEGRO
CHUBUT
SANTA CRUZ
TIERRA DEL FUEGO
BUENOS AIRES
ARAUCANIA
LOS LAGOS
AISÉN
MAGALLANES
SOUTH ATLANTIC OCEAN
FALKLAND ISLANDS (U.K.)
West Falkland
East Falkland
Isla Grande de Chiloé
Archipiélago de los Chonos
Archipiélago de la Reina Adelaida
Isla Grande de Tierra del Fuego
Golfo San Matías
Golfo de San Jorge
Golfo de Penas
Bahía Grande
Bahía Blanca
Península Valdés
Meseta de Somuncurá
Meseta de Montemayor
Sierra Cuadrada
Pampa del Castillo
Meseta el Pedrero
Gran Altiplanicie Central
Neuquén
Bahía Blanca
Carmen De Patagones
Viedma
San Carlos de Bariloche
Puerto Montt
Valdivia
Osorno
Temuco
Puerto Madryn
Trelew
Rawson
Comodoro Rividavia
Caleta Olivia
Puerto Deseado
Puerto San Julián
Puerto Santa Cruz
Río Gallegos
Punta Arenas
Puerto Natales
Coihaique
Ushuaia
Río Grande
Stanley
Cabo de Hornos (Cape Horn)
Islas Wollaston
I. de los Estados
kilometers 0 100 200 300 400
miles 0 100 200

A B C

GALÁPAGOS ISLANDS (Archipiélago de Colón) (Ecuador)

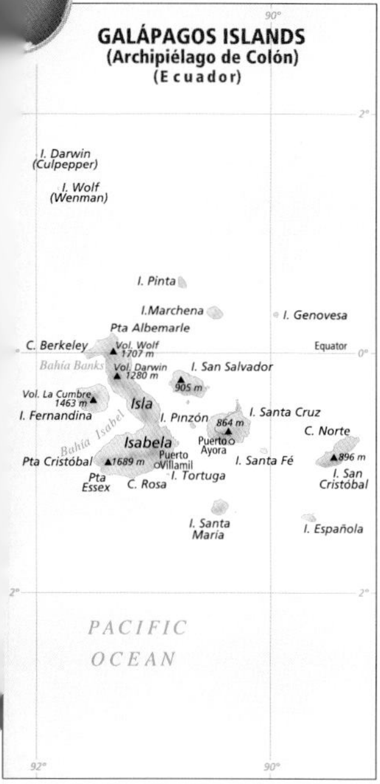

SAN ANDRÉS (Colombia)

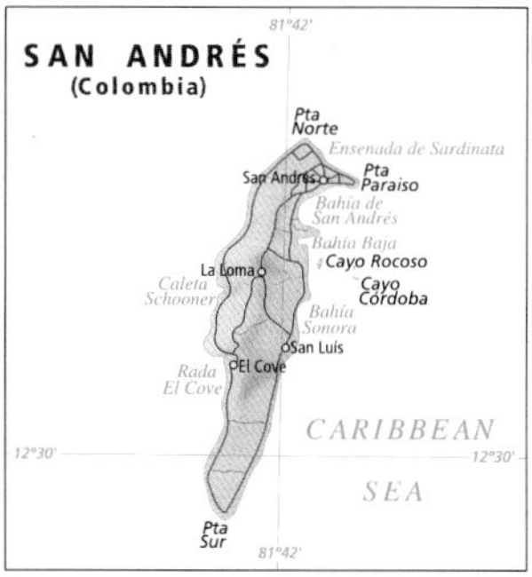

PROVIDENCIA (Colombia)

1

EASTER ISLAND (Chile)

RÓBINSON CRUSOE ISLAND (Archipiélago Juan Fernández) (Chile)

2

SOUTH GEORGIA (U.K.)

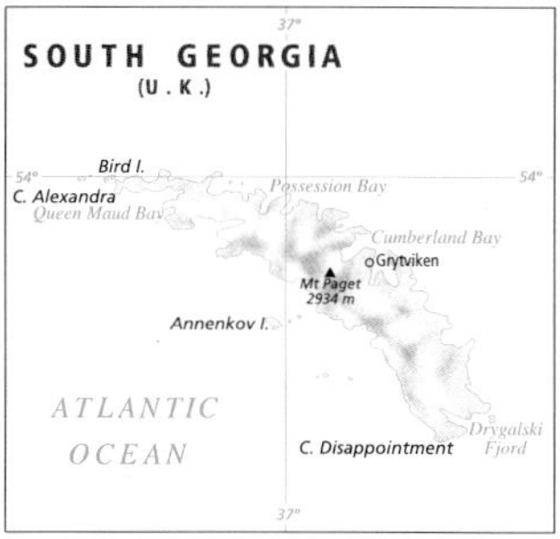

ARUBA (Netherlands)

CURAÇAO (Netherlands Antilles)

3

BONAIRE (Netherlands Antilles)

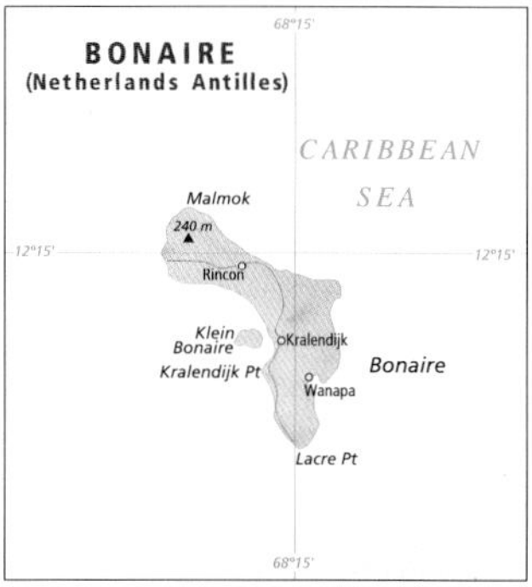

TOBAGO (Trinidad and Tobago)

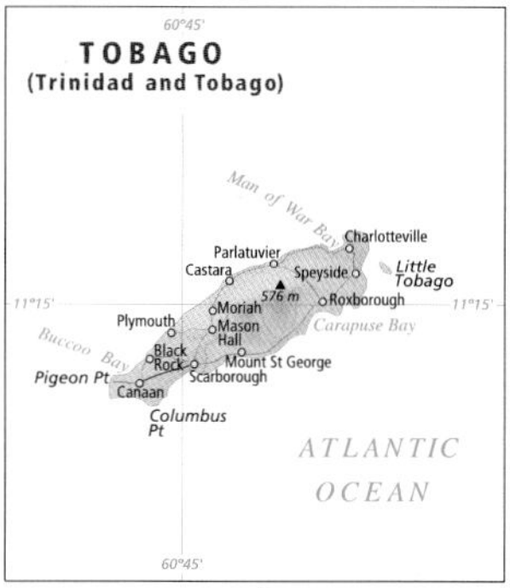

TRINIDAD (Trinidad and Tobago)

4

A B C

South America

Polar Regions

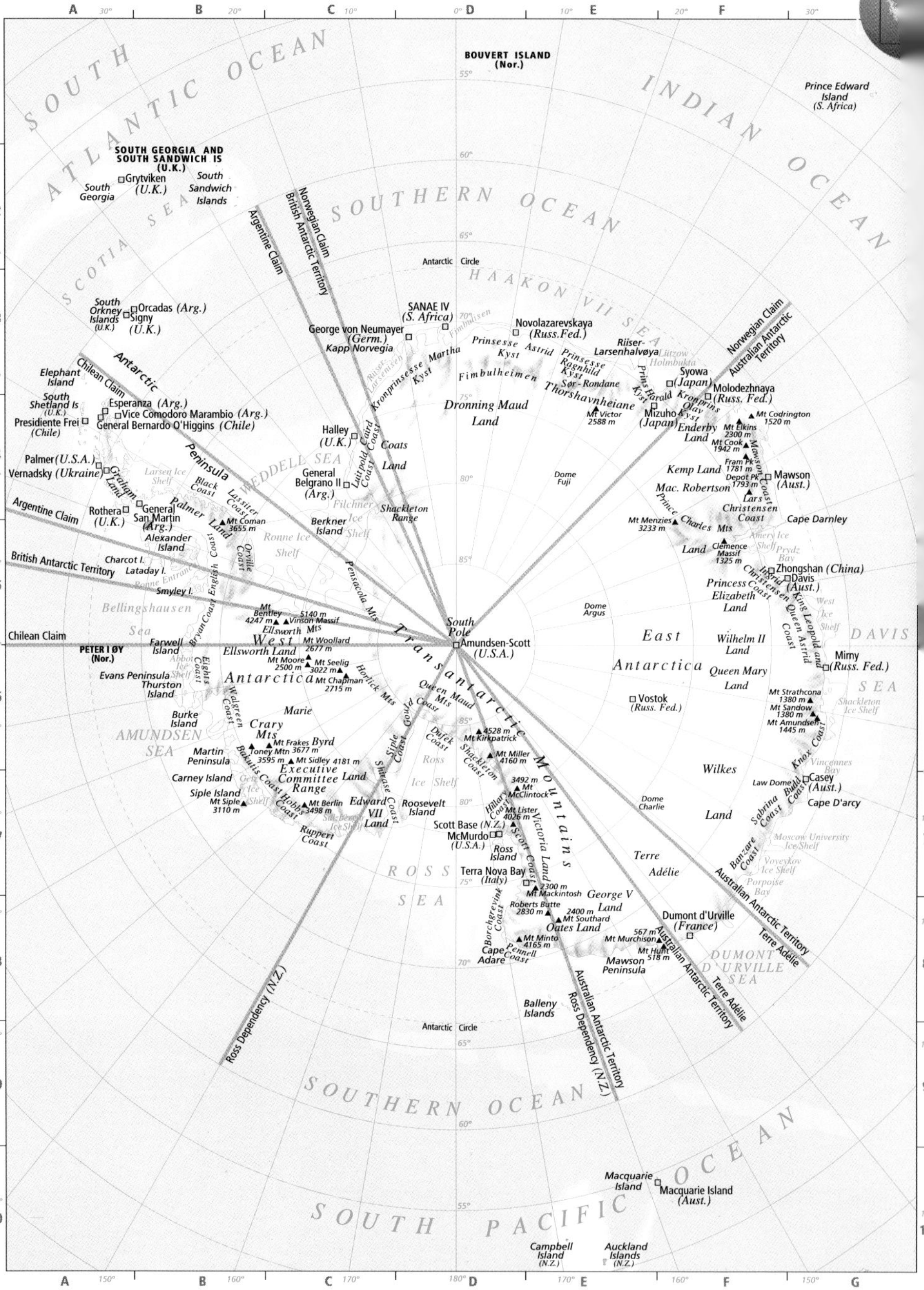

SOUTH ATLANTIC OCEAN
BOUVERT ISLAND (Nor.)
INDIAN OCEAN
Prince Edward Island (S. Africa)
SOUTH GEORGIA AND SOUTH SANDWICH IS (U.K.)
Grytviken (U.K.)
South Georgia
South Sandwich Islands
SCOTIA SEA
SOUTHERN OCEAN
Norwegian Claim
British Antarctic Territory
Argentine Claim
Antarctic Circle
HAAKON VII SEA
South Orkney Islands (U.K.)
Orcadas (Arg.)
Signy (U.K.)
SANAE IV (S. Africa)
George von Neumayer (Germ.)
Kapp Norvegia
Novolazarevskaya (Russ.Fed.)
Riiser-Larsenhalvøya
Norwegian Claim
Australian Antarctic Territory
Lützow Holmbukta
Fimbulisen
Prinsesse Astrid Kyst
Prinsesse Ragnhild Kyst
Sør-Rondane
Kronprinsesse Martha Kyst
Fimbulheimen
Thorshavnheiane
Riiser-Larsenisen
Syowa (Japan)
Molodezhnaya (Russ. Fed.)
Prins Harald Kyst
Kronprins Olav Kyst
Elephant Island
Chilean Claim
Antarctic Peninsula
South Shetland Is (U.K.)
Esperanza (Arg.)
Vice Comodoro Marambio (Arg.)
Presidente Frei (Chile)
General Bernardo O'Higgins (Chile)
Dronning Maud Land
Mt Victor 2588 m
Mizuho (Japan)
Mt Codrington 1520 m
Enderby Land
Mt Elkins 2300 m
Mt Cook 1942 m
Halley (U.K.)
Caird Coast
Coats Land
Luitpold Coast
WEDDELL SEA
Palmer (U.S.A.)
Vernadsky (Ukraine)
Graham Land
Larsen Ice Shelf
Black Coast
Lassiter Coast
General Belgrano II (Arg.)
Dome Fuji
Kemp Land
Fram Pk 1781 m
Mawson Coast
Mawson (Aust.)
Depot Pk 1793 m
Mac. Robertson Land
Lars Christensen Coast
Filchner Ice Shelf
Shackleton Range
Argentine Claim
Rothera (U.K.)
General San Martin (Arg.)
Palmer Land
Mt Coman 3655 m
Berkner Island
Alexander Island
Ronne Ice Shelf
Orville Coast
Prince Charles Mts
Mt Menzies 3233 m
Cape Darnley
Amery Ice Shelf
Clemence Massif 1325 m
Prydz Bay
British Antarctic Territory
Charcot I.
Lataday I.
Ronne Entrance
English Coast
Smyley I.
Pensacola Mts
Zhongshan (China)
Davis (Aust.)
Ingrid Christensen Coast
Princess Elizabeth Land
King Leopold and Queen Astrid Coast
West Ice Shelf
Bellingshausen Sea
Mt Bentley 4247 m
Vinson Massif 5140 m
Ellsworth Mts
South Pole
Amundsen-Scott (U.S.A.)
Dome Argus
DAVIS SEA
Chilean Claim
PETER I ØY (Nor.)
Farwell Island
Bryan Coast
West Antarctica
Ellsworth Land
Mt Woollard 2677 m
Mt Moore 2500 m
Mt Seelig 3022 m
Mt Chapman 2715 m
Transantarctic Mountains
East Antarctica
Wilhelm II Land
Mirny (Russ. Fed.)
Abbot Ice Shelf
Eights Coast
Evans Peninsula
Thurston Island
Horlick Mts
Queen Maud Mts
Queen Mary Land
Vostok (Russ. Fed.)
Mt Strathcona 1380 m
Mt Sandow 1380 m
Mt Amundsen 1445 m
Shackleton Ice Shelf
Burke Island
Walgreen Coast
Marie Byrd Land
Crary Mts
AMUNDSEN SEA
Mt Frakes 3677 m
Toney Mtn 3595 m
Mt Sidley 4181 m
Executive Committee Range
Siple Coast
Gould Coast
Dufek Coast
Mt Kirkpatrick 4528 m
Shackleton Coast
Mt Miller 4160 m
Knox Coast
Vincennes Bay
Martin Peninsula
Bakutis Coast
Carney Island
Getz Ice Shelf
Hobbs Coast
Siple Island
Mt Siple 3110 m
Mt Berlin 3498 m
Shirase Coast
Ross Ice Shelf
Mt McClintock 3492 m
Wilkes Land
Law Dome
Casey (Aust.)
Budd Coast
Cape D'arcy
Dome Charlie
Edward VII Land
Roosevelt Island
Sulzberger Ice Shelf
Ruppert Coast
Hillary Coast
Mt Lister 4026 m
Victoria Land
Sabrina Coast
Scott Base (N.Z.)
McMurdo (U.S.A.)
Ross Island
Scott Coast
Moscow University Ice Shelf
Terre Adélie
Banzare Coast
Voyeykov Ice Shelf
Porpoise Bay
ROSS SEA
Terra Nova Bay (Italy)
Mt Mackintosh 2300 m
George V Land
Roberts Butte 2830 m
Borchgrevink Coast
Mt Southard 2400 m
Oates Land
Dumont d'Urville (France)
Australian Antarctic Territory
Terre Adélie
Mt Minto 4165 m
Mt Murchison 567 m
Mt Hunt 518 m
Cape Adare
Pennell Coast
Mawson Peninsula
DUMONT D'URVILLE SEA
Ross Dependency (N.Z.)
Balleny Islands
Australian Antarctic Territory
Ross Dependency (N.Z.)
Terre Adélie
Australian Antarctic Territory
SOUTHERN OCEAN
Macquarie Island
Macquarie Island (Aust.)
SOUTH PACIFIC OCEAN
Campbell Island (N.Z.)
Auckland Islands (N.Z.)
0 400 800 1200 kilometers
0 200 400 600 miles

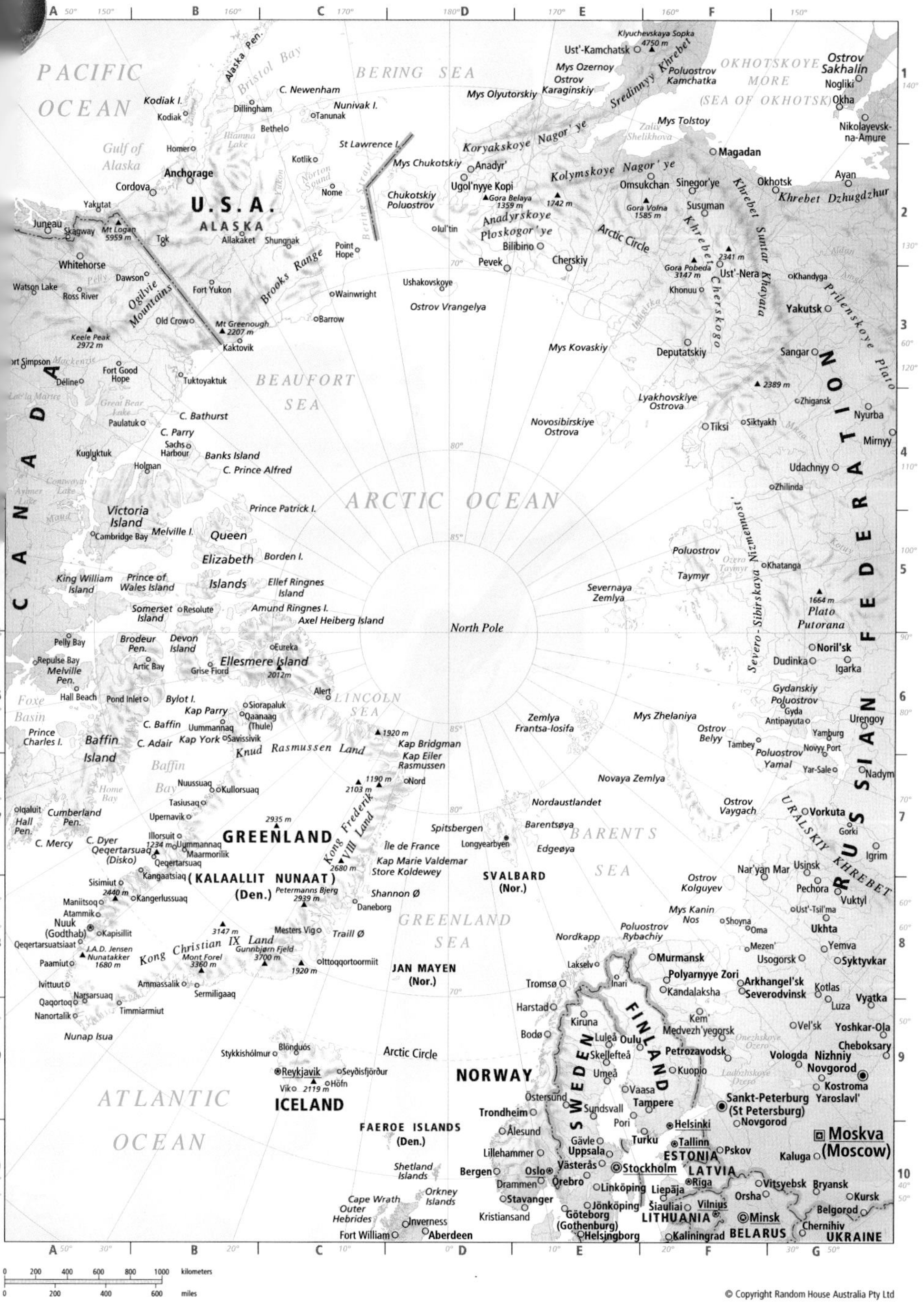
PACIFIC OCEAN
BERING SEA
OKHOTSKOYE MORE (SEA OF OKHOTSK)
Gulf of Alaska
Bristol Bay
Alaska Pen.
Kodiak I.
Kodiak
Dillingham
C. Newenham
Nunivak I.
Tanunak
Bethel
Iliamna Lake
Homer
Anchorage
Cordova
Kotlik
Norton Sound
Nome
St Lawrence I.
Bering Strait
U.S.A.
ALASKA
Yakutat
Juneau
Skagway
Mt Logan 5959 m
Tok
Allakaket
Shungnak
Point Hope
Brooks Range
Whitehorse
Dawson
Watson Lake
Ross River
Ogilvie Mountains
Fort Yukon
Wainwright
Barrow
Old Crow
Mt Greenough 2207 m
Kaktovik
Keele Peak 2972 m
Fort Simpson
Mackenzie
Fort Good Hope
Déline
Tuktoyaktuk
BEAUFORT SEA
Great Bear Lake
Paulatuk
C. Bathurst
C. Parry
Sachs Harbour
Banks Island
Kugluktuk
Holman
C. Prince Alfred
Victoria Island
Cambridge Bay
Melville I.
Prince Patrick I.
Queen Elizabeth Islands
Borden I.
King William Island
Prince of Wales Island
Ellef Ringnes Island
Somerset Island
Resolute
Amund Ringnes I.
Axel Heiberg Island
Pelly Bay
Brodeur Pen.
Devon Island
Eureka
Repulse Bay
Melville Pen.
Artic Bay
Grise Fiord
Ellesmere Island
2012 m
Alert
Hall Beach
Pond Inlet
Bylot I.
Foxe Basin
LINCOLN SEA
Siorapaluk
Qaanaag (Thule)
Kap Parry
C. Baffin
Uummannaq
Kap York
Savissivik
Prince Charles I.
Baffin Island
C. Adair
Knud Rasmussen Land
1920 m
Kap Bridgman
Kap Eiler Rasmussen
Baffin Bay
Nuussuaq
Kullorsuaq
1190 m
2103 m
Nord
Home Bay
Tasiusaq
Iqaluit
Cumberland Pen.
Hall Pen.
Upernavik
2935 m
Kong Frederik VIII Land
C. Mercy
C. Dyer
Qeqertarsuaq (Disko)
Illorsuit
1234 m
Uummannaq
Maarmorilik
Qeqertarsuaq
GREENLAND
Kangaatsiaq
(KALAALLIT NUNAAT) (Den.)
2680 m
Sisimiut
2440 m
Kangerlussuaq
Petermanns Bjerg 2939 m
Maniitsoq
Atammik
Nuuk (Godthab)
Kapisillit
3147 m
Qeqertarsuatsiaat
J.A.D. Jensen Nunatakker 1680 m
Kong Christian IX Land
Mont Forel 3360 m
Gunnbjørn Fjeld 3700 m
1920 m
Paamiut
Ammassalik
Sermiligaaq
Ivittuut
Narsarsuaq
Qaqortoq
Nanortalik
Timmiarmiut
Nunap Isua
Mesters Vig
Traill Ø
Ittoqqortoormiit
Daneborg
Shannon Ø
Île de France
Kap Marie Valdemar
Store Koldewey
GREENLAND SEA
JAN MAYEN (Nor.)
Stykkishólmur
Blönduós
Reykjavík
Seyðisfjörður
Vík
2119 m
Höfn
ICELAND
Arctic Circle
ATLANTIC OCEAN
FAEROE ISLANDS (Den.)
Shetland Islands
Orkney Islands
Cape Wrath
Outer Hebrides
Inverness
Fort William
Aberdeen
ARCTIC OCEAN
North Pole
Ushakovskoye
Ostrov Vrangelya
Chukotskiy Poluostrov
Mys Chukotskiy
Iul'tin
Anadyr'
Ugol'nyye Kopi
Gora Belaya 1359 m
Anadyrskoye Ploskogor'ye
Bilibino
Pevek
Cherskiy
Mys Olyutorskiy
Koryakskoye Nagor'ye
Ust'-Kamchatsk
Klyuchevskaya Sopka 4750 m
Mys Ozernoy
Ostrov Karaginskiy
Sredinnyy Khrebet
Poluostrov Kamchatka
Zaliv Shelikhova
Mys Tolstoy
Magadan
Kolymskoye Nagor'ye
1742 m
Omsukchan
Sinegor'ye
Gora Volna 1585 m
Susuman
Arctic Circle
Khrebet Cherskogo
Gora Pobeda 3147 m
2341 m
Ust'-Nera
Khonuu
Khrebet Suntar Khayata
Okhotsk
Khrebet Dzhugdzhur
Ayan
Ostrov Sakhalin
Nogliki
Okha
Nikolayevsk-na-Amure
Khandyga
Prilenskoye Plato
Yakutsk
Mys Kovaskiy
Deputatskiy
Sangar
2389 m
Lyakhovskiye Ostrova
Zhigansk
Novosibirskiye Ostrova
Tiksi
Siktyakh
Nyurba
Mirnyy
Udachnyy
Zhilinda
Poluostrov Taymyr
Ozero Taymyr
Khatanga
Severo-Sibirskaya Nizmennost'
Severnaya Zemlya
1664 m
Plato Putorana
Noril'sk
Dudinka
Igarka
RUSSIAN FEDERATION
Gydanskiy Poluostrov
Gyda
Antipayuta
Urengoy
Mys Zhelaniya
Ostrov Belyy
Tambey
Yamburg
Novyy Port
Poluostrov Yamal
Yar-Sale
Nadym
Zemlya Frantsa-Iosifa
Novaya Zemlya
Nordaustlandet
Ostrov Vaygach
Vorkuta
Uralskiy Khrebet
Gorki
Igrim
Spitsbergen
Barentsøya
Longyearbyen
Edgeøya
BARENTS SEA
SVALBARD (Nor.)
Nar'yan Mar
Usinsk
Ostrov Kolguyev
Pechora
Vuktyl
Ust'-Tsil'ma
Mys Kanin Nos
Shoyna
Oma
Ukhta
Nordkapp
Poluostrov Rybachiy
Mezen'
Yemva
Murmansk
Usogorsk
Syktyvkar
Lakselv
Inari
Polyarnyye Zori
Arkhangel'sk
Severodvinsk
Kandalaksha
Kotlas
Vyatka
Tromsø
Harstad
Luza
Kem'
Medvezh'yegorsk
Kiruna
Vel'sk
Yoshkar-Ola
Bodø
Luleå
Oulu
FINLAND
Onezhskoye Ozero
Petrozavodsk
Cheboksary
Vologda
Nizhniy Novgorod
Skellefteå
Kuopio
Ladozhskoye Ozero
Umeå
NORWAY
Vaasa
Kostroma
Yaroslavl'
Östersund
Tampere
Sankt-Peterburg (St Petersburg)
Sundsvall
SWEDEN
Pori
Trondheim
Novgorod
Ålesund
Helsinki
Moskva (Moscow)
Turku
Gävle
Tallinn
Pskov
Lillehammer
Uppsala
ESTONIA
Kaluga
Västerås
Bergen
Oslo
Stockholm
LATVIA
Drammen
Örebro
Riga
Vitsyebsk
Bryansk
Linköping
Liepāja
Orsha
Kursk
Stavanger
Jönköping
Šiauliai
Vilnius
Belgorod
Kristiansand
Göteborg (Gothenburg)
LITHUANIA
Minsk
Chernihiv
Helsingborg
Kaliningrad
BELARUS
UKRAINE
CANADA
0 200 400 600 800 1000 kilometers
0 200 400 600 miles

The Oceans

A B C D E F G H
30° 45° 60° 75° 90° 105° 120°
1 2 3 4 5 6 7 8
45° 30° 15° 0° 15° 30° 45°
Black Sea
Aral Sea
Caspian Sea
ASIA
Mediterranean Sea
Nile Fan
Yellow Sea
East China Sea
Persian Gulf
Red Sea
Tropic of Cancer
Indus Fan
Arabian Sea
Owen Fracture Zone
Arabian Basin
Bay of Bengal
Ganges Fan
South China Sea
South China Basin
Philippine Trench
Palawan Trough
Andaman Basin
AFRICA
Carlsberg Ridge
Chagos – Laccadive Plateau
Somali Basin
Sunda Shelf
Celebes Basin
Borneo
Equator
Chagos Trench
Sumatera
JAVA TRENCH
NINETY EAST RIDGE
Mid-Indian Basin
Investigator Ridge
Mascarene Plateau
INDIAN OCEAN
North Australian Basin
Mozambique Channel
Madagascar
Mascarene Plain
Mauritius Trench
Wharton Basin
Exmouth Plateau
Tropic of Capricorn
MID-INDIAN RIDGE
Madagascar Basin
AUSTRALIA
East Indian Ridge
Natal Basin
Madagascar Plateau
Perth Basin
Mozambique Plateau
Broken Ridge
Mozambique Fracture Zone
Indomed Fracture Zone
SOUTHWEST INDIAN RIDGE
Diamantina Fracture Zone
South Australian Basin
Agulhas Plateau
Fracture Zone
Crozet Basin
SOUTHEAST INDIAN RIDGE
Agulhas Basin
Crozet Plateau
Prince Edward
Kerguelen Plateau
SOUTHERN OCEAN
ENDERBY PLAIN
kilometers 0 1000 2000 3000
miles 0 500 1000 1500

A B C D E F G H J
90° 75° 60° 45° 30° 15° 0° 15°
1 2 3 4 5 6 7 8 9
Baffin Bay
Greenland
Jan Mayen Ridge
Iceland
Faeroe-Iceland Ridge
Hudson Bay
Northwest Atlantic Mid-Ocean Canyon
Imarssuak Seachannel
Reykjanes Ridge
Maury Seachannel
North Sea
Baltic Sea
NORTH AMERICA
Charlie-Gibbs Fracture Zone
Porcupine Plain
EUROPE
ATLANTIC OCEAN
Grand Banks of Newfoundland
Biscay Plain
Azores-Biscay Rise
Laurentian Fan
MID-ATLANTIC RIDGE
Oceanographer Fracture Zone
Strait of Gibraltar
Mediterranean Sea
Mediterranean Ridge
Blake Plateau
Hatteras Plain
Bermuda Rise
Atlantis Fracture Zone
Gulf of Mexico
Tropic of Cancer
Kane Fracture Zone
Cape Verde Basin
Peurto Rico Trench
Nares Plain
AFRICA
Cayman Trench
Beata Ridge
Aves Ridge
Caribbean Sea
Vema Fracture Zone
Gambia Plain
Middle America Trench
Demerara Plain
Doldrums Fracture Zone
Sierra Leone Basin
Romanche Fracture Zone
Guinea Basin
Amazon Fan
Equator
Carnegie Ridge
Ceara Plain
Chain Fracture Zone
Pernambuco Plain
Ascension Fracture Zone
SOUTH AMERICA
Peru-Chile Trench
Brazil Basin
Angola Basin
Nazca Ridge
Tropic of Capricorn
PACIFIC OCEAN
Rio Grande Rise
Walvis Ridge
Cape Basin
Agulhas Basin
Argentine Plain
Falkland Escarpment
Falkland Plateau
Humboldt Plain
South Georgia Ridge
South Sandwich Trench
ATLANTIC-INDIAN RIDGE
Drake Passage
0 1000 2000 3000 kilometers
0 500 1000 1500 miles

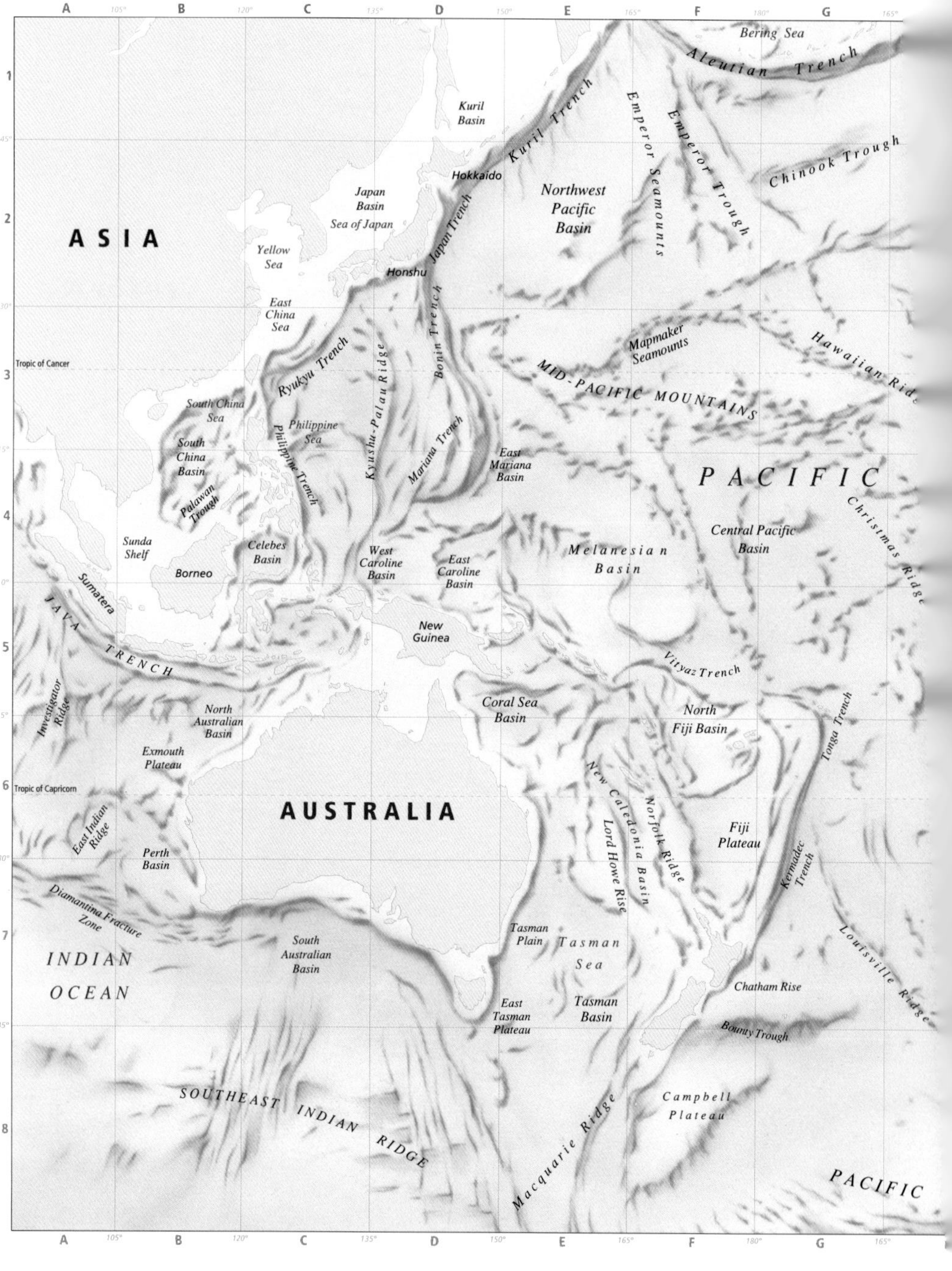

ASIA
AUSTRALIA
PACIFIC
INDIAN OCEAN
Bering Sea
Aleutian Trench
Kuril Basin
Kuril Trench
Emperor Seamounts
Emperor Trough
Chinook Trough
Hokkaido
Japan Basin
Sea of Japan
Northwest Pacific Basin
Japan Trench
Yellow Sea
Honshu
East China Sea
Bonin Trench
Mapmaker Seamounts
Hawaiian Ridge
Tropic of Cancer
Ryukyu Trench
Kyushu-Palau Ridge
MID-PACIFIC MOUNTAINS
South China Sea
Philippine Sea
Philippine Trench
Mariana Trench
South China Basin
East Mariana Basin
Palawan Trough
Christmas Ridge
Central Pacific Basin
Sunda Shelf
Celebes Basin
West Caroline Basin
East Caroline Basin
Melanesian Basin
Borneo
Sumatera
JAVA TRENCH
New Guinea
Vityaz Trench
Investigator Ridge
North Australian Basin
Coral Sea Basin
North Fiji Basin
Tonga Trench
Exmouth Plateau
Tropic of Capricorn
New Caledonia Basin
Norfolk Ridge
Lord Howe Rise
Fiji Plateau
East Indian Ridge
Perth Basin
Kermadec Trench
Diamantina Fracture Zone
Tasman Plain
Tasman Sea
Louisville Ridge
South Australian Basin
Chatham Rise
East Tasman Plateau
Tasman Basin
Bounty Trough
SOUTHEAST INDIAN RIDGE
Campbell Plateau
Macquarie Ridge
PACIFIC
A
B
C
D
E
F
G
1
2
3
4
5
6
7
8
105°
120°
135°
150°
165°
180°
165°
45°
30°
15°
0°
15°
30°
45°

ulf of Alaska
Tufts Plain
Patton Escarpment
racture Zone
eer Fracture Zone
racture Ridge
Cedros Trench
olokai Fracture Zone
Clarion Fracture Zone
CEAN
Clipperton Fracture Zone
Galapagos Fracture Zone
Marquesas Fracture Zone
Easter Fracture Zone
Challenger Fracture Zone
hwest cific asin
Agassiz Fracture Zone
Menard Fracture Zone
Eltanin Fracture Zone
Fracture Zone
TARCTIC RIDGE
EAST PACIFIC RISE
NORTH AMERICA
Gulf of Mexico
Mexico Basin
Middle America Trench
Cayman Trench
Guatemala Basin
Cocos Ridge
Panama Basin
Carnegie Ridge
Peru Basin
Galapagos Rise
Nazca Ridge
Chile Basin
Chile Rise
Southeast Pacific Basin
Humboldt Plain
Bellingshausen Plain
Blake Plateau
Hatteras Plain
Bermuda Rise
Puerto Rico Trench
Nares Plain
Beata Ridge
Aves Ridge
Caribbean Sea
Laurentian Fan
ATLANTIC OCEAN
Tropic of Cancer
SOUTH AMERICA
Peru-Chile Trench
Tropic of Capricorn
Argentine Plain
ATLANTIC OCEAN
Falkland Plateau
Drake Passage
J K L M N P Q
135° 120° 105° 90° 75° 60° 150°
45° 30° 15° 0° 15° 30° 45°
1 2 3 4 5 6 7 8
1000 2000 3000 kilometers
500 1000 1500 miles

Part 5

Gazetteer

Abbreviations Used on Maps

Arch. Archipelago, Archipel, Archipiélago, Arquipélago
Arg. Argentina
Arm. Armenia
Aust. Australia
Azer. Azerbaijan

B. Bay, Baía, Baie, Bahía
B.-H. Bosnia and Herzegovina
Belg. Belgium

C.A.R. Central African Republic
C. Cape, Cabo, Cap, Capo
Co Cerro
Col. Colombia
Cord. Cordillera
Croat. Croatia
Cuch. Cuchillo
Czech Rep. Czech Republic

D.C. District of Columbia
Dem. Rep. of the Congo Democratic Republic of the Congo
Den. Denmark

E. East
Ecu. Ecuador
Emb. Embalse
Eq. Guinea Equatorial Guinea
Est. Estrecho

Fr. France

G. Gora
G. Gulf, Golfe, Golfo, Gulfo
G. Gunung
Germ. Germany

Harb. Harbor
Hung. Hungary

I. Island, Île, Ilha, Isla, Isola
Is Islands, Îles, Ilhas, Islas

Jez. Jezioro

K. Kolpos
Kep. Kepulauan

L. Lake, Lac, Lacul, Lago, Limni, Loch
Liech. Liechtenstein
Lux. Luxembourg

Mace. Macedonia
Mex. Mexico
Mt Mount, Mont
Mte Monte
Mti Monti
Mtn Mountain
Mts Mountains, Monts

N. North
N.Z. New Zealand
Neth. Netherlands
Nev. Nevado
Nor. Norway

P. Pic, Pico
P. Pulau
P.N.G. Papua New Guinea
Peg. Pegunungan
Pen. Peninsula, Péninsula, Péninsule
Pk Peak
Pk Puncak
Port. Portugal
Pt Point
Pta Ponta, Punta
Pte Pointe
Pto Porto, Pôrto, Puerto

R. River
Ra. Range
Rep. Republic
Res. Reservoir
Russ. Fed. Russian Federation

S. San
S. South
S.A. South Africa
Sa Serra
Sd Sound
Serr. Serrania
Slov. Slovenia
Sp. Spain
St Saint
Sta Santa
Ste Sainte
Sto Santo
Switz. Switzerland

Tel. Teluk
Tg Tanjong

U. Ujung
U.A.E. United Arab Emirates
U.K. United Kingdom
U.S., U.S.A. United States of America

Vol. Volcán

W. West

Yug. Yugoslavia

Foreign Geographical Terms

Açude *(Portuguese)* reservoir
Adası *(Turkish)* island
Adrar *(Berber)* mountains
Agios *(Greek)* saint
Akra *(Greek)* cape, point
Alpen *(German)* Alps
Alpi *(Italian)* Alps
Alta *(Spanish)* upper
Altiplanicie *(Spanish)* high plain, plateau
-älven *(Swedish)* river
Ao *(Thai)* bay
Archipel *(French)* archipelago
Archipiélago *(Spanish)* archipelago
Arquipélago *(Portuguese)* archipelago
Avtonomnaya Oblast' *(Russian)* autonomous region
Avtonomnyy Okrug *(Russian)* autonomous area

Bab *(Arabic)* strait
Bælt *(Danish)* strait
Bahía *(Spanish)* bay
Baḩr, Bahr *(Arabic)* lake, river, sea
Baía *(Portuguese)* bay
Baie *(French)* bay
Barajı *(Turkish)* dam
Barragem *(Portuguese)* reservoir
Bassin *(French)* basin
Beinn, Ben *(Gaelic)* mountain
Bjerg *(Danish)* hill, mountain
Bôca *(Portuguese)* river mouth
Boca *(Spanish)* river mouth
Bocht *(Dutch)* bay
Bodden *(German)* bay
Bogazi *(Turkish)* strait
Bögeni *(Kazakh)* reservoir
-bre/en *(Norwegian)* glacier
Bucht *(German)* bay
Bugt, -bugten *(Danish)* bay
Buḩayrat *(Arabic)* lake
Bukit *(Malay)* mountain
-bukten *(Swedish)* bay
Burnu, Burun *(Turkish)* cape, point
Buuraha *(Somali)* hill/s, mountain/s

Cabo *(Portuguese, Spanish)* cape
Canal *(Spanish)* channel
Cap *(French)* cape
Capo *(Italian)* cape
Cerro/s *(Spanish)* hill/s, peak/s
Chaîne *(French)* mountain range
Chapada *(Portuguese)* hills, upland/s
Chhâk *(Cambodian)* bay
Chott *(Arabic)* marsh, salt lake
Cima *(Italian)* mountain
Ciudad *(Spanish)* city
Co *(Tibetan)* lake
Colline *(Italian)* hill/s
Cordillera *(Spanish)* mountain range, mountain chain
Côte *(French)* coast, slope
Cù Lao *(Vietnamese)* island
Cuchilla *(Spanish)* mountain range

Dağ/ı *(Turkish)* mountain
Dağlar/ı *(Turkish)* mountains
-dake *(Japanese)* peak
Danau *(Indonesian)* lake
Dao *(Chinese)* island
Đao *(Vietnamese)* island
Daryācheh *(Persian)* lake
Dasht *(Persian)* desert
Denizi *(Turkish)* sea
Desierto *(Spanish)* desert
Détroit *(French)* strait
Djebel *(Arabic)* mountain, mountain range

-elva *(Norwegian)* river
Embalse *(Spanish)* reservoir
Ensenada *(Spanish)* bay
Erg *(Arabic)* sand dunes
Estrecho *(Spanish)* strait
Étang *(French)* lagoon, lake
ezers *(Latvian)* lake

Falaise *(French)* cliff
Feng *(Chinese)* peak
Fjeld *(Danish)* mountain
-fjell *(Norwegian)* mountain
-fjord/en *(Danish, Norwegian, Swedish)* fiord

Gang *(Chinese)* harbor
Gaoyuan *(Chinese)* plateau
Garet *(Arabic)* hill
Gebergte *(Dutch)* mountain chain, mountain range
-gebirge *(German)* mountain range
Ghubbat *(Arabic)* bay
Gjiri *(Albanian)* bay
Golfe *(French)* gulf
Golfo *(Italian, Portuguese)* gulf
Gölü *(Turkish)* lake
Gora *(Russian)* mountain
Góry *(Polish)* mountains
Gross/er *(German)* big
Gryada *(Russian)* ridge
Guba *(Russian)* bay, gulf
Gulfo *(Spanish)* gulf
Gunung *(Indonesian, Malay)* mountain

Haixia *(Chinese)* strait
-halvøya *(Norwegian)* peninsula
Har *(Hebrew)* mountain
Haut, Haute *(French)* high
Hawr *(Arabic)* lake
Häyk' *(Amharic)* lake
Helodrano *(Malagasy)* bay
Hohe *(German)* height
Hora *(Belorussian, Czech)* mountain
-horn *(German)* peak
Hory *(Czech)* mountains
Hsü *(Chinese)* island, islet
Hu *(Chinese)* lake

Île/s *(French)* island/s
Ilha/s *(Portuguese)* island/s
Ilheu *(Portuguese)* islet
Isla/s *(Spanish)* island/s
Isola, Isole *(Italian)* island/s

Jabal *(Arabic)* mountain, mountain range
Jarv *(Estonian)* lake
-järvi *(Finnish)* lake
Jazīrat, Jaza'īr *(Arabic)* island/s
Jazireh *(Persian)* island
Jbel *(Arabic)* mountain
Jezioro *(Polish)* lake
-jima *(Japanese)* island
-joki *(Finnish)* river

Kalnas *(Lithuanian)* mountain
Kangri *(Tibetan)* mountain
Kap *(Danish, German)* cape
-kapp *(Norwegian)* cape
Kepi *(Albanian)* cape, point
Kepulauan *(Indonesian)* islands
Khalīj *(Arabic)* bay, gulf
Khao *(Thai)* peak
Khrebet *(Russian)* mountain range
Ko *(Thai)* island
Köli *(Kazakh)* lake
Kolpos *(Greek)* bay
Körfezi *(Turkish)* bay, gulf
Kray *(Russian)* territory
Kryazh *(Russian)* ridge
Kūh/hā *(Persian)* mountain/s
-kŭl *(Tajik)* lake
Kyst *(Danish)* coast
Kyun *(Burmese)* island

Lac *(French)* lake
Lacul *(Romanian)* lake
Lago *(Italian, Portuguese, Spanish)* lake
Lagoa *(Portuguese)* lagoon, lake
Laht *(Estonian)* bay
Lich *(Armenian)* lake
Liedao *(Chinese)* archipelago, islands
Limni *(Greek)* lake
Ling *(Chinese)* mountain range
Loch, Lough *(Gaelic)* lake
Lohatanjona *(Malagasy)* point
Loi *(Burmese)* mountain
Loma *(Spanish)* hill

Mae Nam *(Thai)* river
-man *(Korean)* bay
Mar *(Spanish)* lake, sea
Maşabb *(Arabic)* river mouth
Massif *(French)* mountains, upland
Meer, -meer *(Dutch)* lake, sea
Mesa *(Spanish)* tableland
Meseta *(Spanish)* plateau, tableland
-misaki *(Japanese)* cape, point
Mont/s *(French)* mountain/s
Montagne/s *(French)* mountain/s
Monte *(Italian, Portuguese, Spanish)* mountain
Montes *(Spanish)* mountain
Monti *(Italian)* mountain/s
More *(Russian)* sea
Morne *(French)* mountain
Morro *(Portuguese)* hill
Munţii *(Romanian)* mountains
Mys *(Russian)* cape, point

-nada *(Japanese)* gulf, sea
Nagor'ye *(Russian)* upland
Nevado *(Spanish)* snow-capped mountain
Nieuw *(Dutch)* new
Nisoi *(Greek)* islands
Nizmennost' *(Russian)* lowland
Nord *(French)* north
Norte *(Portuguese, Spanish)* north
Nos *(Bulgarian)* point
Nosy *(Malagasy)* island
Nur, Nuur *(Mongolian)* lake
Nuruu *(Mongolian)* mountain range

Ø, Øer *(Danish)* island/s
-ö, -ön *(Swedish)* island
Oblast' *(Russian)* province
Odde *(Danish)* cape, point
Oros *(Greek)* mountain
Ostrov/a *(Russian)* island/s
Oued *(Arabic)* river, watercourse
-øy, -øya *(Norwegian)* island
Ozero *(Russian)* lake

Pantanal *(Portuguese)* marsh, swamp
Pegunungan *(Indonesian)* island
Pelagos *(Greek)* sea
Pendi *(Chinese)* basin
Pertuis *(French)* strait
Phnum *(Cambodian)* mountain
Phou *(Laotian)* mountain
Pic *(French)* peak
Pico *(Spanish)* peak
Pik *(Russian)* peak
Piton *(French)* peak
Pivostriv *(Ukrainian)* peninsula
Piz, pizzo *(Italian)* peak
Planalto *(Portuguese)* plateau
Planina *(Bulgarian, Macedonian)* mountains
Plato *(Russian)* plateau
Ploskogor'ye *(Russian)* plateau, upland
Pointe *(French)* point
Poluostrov *(Russian)* peninsula
Ponta *(Portuguese)* point
Porthmos *(Greek)* strait
Porto, Pôrto *(Portuguese)* port
Proliv *(Russian)* strait
Puerto *(Spanish)* port
Pulau *(Indonesian, Malay)* island
Puncak *(Indonesian)* mountain
Punta *(Italian, Spanish)* point

Qārat *(Arabic)* hill
Qooriga *(Somali)* bay
Qundao *(Chinese)* archipelago, islands
Qurnat *(Arabic)* peak

Raas *(Somali)* cape, point
Ras, Ra's *(Arabic)* cape, point
Ravnina *(Russian)* plain
Represa *(Portuguese, Spanish)* reservoir
Réservoir *(French)* reservoir
Reshteh *(Persian)* mountain range
Respublika *(Russian)* republic
Respublikasi *(Uzbek)* republic
-retto *(Japanese)* island chain
Rio, Río *(Portuguese, Spanish)* river
Rivière *(French)* river
Rubha *(Gaelic)* cape, point
Rudohorie *(Slovak)* mountains

Sāgar/a *(Hindi)* lake
Şaḩrā' *(Arabic)* desert
-saki *(Japanese)* cape, point
Salar *(Spanish)* salt-flat, salt-pan
Salina/s *(Spanish)* salt-pan/s
Salto/s *(Portuguese, Spanish)* waterfall
-san *(Japanese, Korean)* mountain
San, Santa, Santo *(Spanish)* saint
-sanchi *(Japanese)* mountains
São *(Portuguese)* saint
Sarīr *(Arabic)* desert
Sebkha, Sebkhet *(Arabic)* salt-flat
See, -see *(German)* lake
Selat *(Indonesian)* strait
Serra *(Portuguese)* mountain range
Serranía *(Spanish)* mountain range
Shamo *(Chinese)* desert
Shan *(Chinese)* mountain/s
-shima *(Japanese)* island
-shotō *(Japanese)* islands
Shuiki *(Chinese)* reservoir
Sierra *(Spanish)* mountain range
Slieve *(Gaelic)* mountain
-spitze *(German)* peak
Steno *(Greek)* strait
Štít *(Slovak)* peak
Stretto *(Italian)* strait
Sud *(French)* south
Sul *(Portuguese)* south

Tanjona *(Malagasy)* cape
Tanjong *(Indonesian, Malay)* cape, point
Tao *(Chinese)* island
Tasek *(Malay)* lake
Tassili *(Berber)* plateau
Taungdan *(Burmese)* mountain range
Tekojärvi *(Finnish)* reservoir
Teluk *(Indonesian, Malay)* bay
Ténéré *(Berber)* desert
Tepe *(Turkish)* peak
Terara *(Amharic)* mountain
Tierra *(Spanish)* land
-to *(Japanese)* island

Ujung *(Indonesian)* cape, point
'Urūq *(Arabic)* dunes
Uul *(Mongolian)* mountain/s

väin *(Estonian)* channel, strait
-vatn *(Norwegian)* lake
-vesi *(Finnish)* lake, water
Voblasts' *(Belorussian)* province
Vodokhranilishche *(Russian)* reservoir
Vodoskhovyshche *(Ukrainian)* reservoir
Volcán *(Spanish)* volcano
Vozvyshennost' *(Russian)* plateau, upland
Vozyera *(Belorussian)* lake
Vrchovina *(Czech)* mountains

Wabē *(Amharic)* river, stream
Wādī *(Arabic)* watercourse
-wald *(German)* forest
Wan *(Chinese)* bay
-wan *(Japanese)* bay

Yam *(Hebrew)* lake, sea
Yang *(Chinese)* ocean
Yoma *(Burmese)* mountain range

-zaki *(Japanese)* cape, point
Zaliv *(Russian)* bay
Zangbo *(Tibetan)* river
Zatoka *(Polish)* bay, gulf
-zee *(Dutch)* sea
Zemlya *(Russian)* land
Zizhiqu *(Chinese)* autonomous region

Gazetteer

- The gazetteer contains the names shown on the continental and detailed regional maps at the end of each section.
- In the code given to locate a place, the **bold** number refers to the page on which the map is to be found, and the letter–number combination refers to the grid square formed by the lines of latitude and longitude on the map. Inset maps have their own letter–number combination.
- Where a name appears on more than one map, the gazetteer generally lists the largest scale map on which the name appears.
- Names that have a symbol (town or mountain peak) are given an area reference according to the location of the symbol. Names without a symbol are entered in the gazetteer according to the first letter of the name.
- Words in italics describe features in the gazetteer, e.g. *island*, *point* and *mountain peak*.
- All entries include the country or area in which the name is located.
- Features composed of a description and a proper name, e.g. Cape Hatteras, are positioned alphabetically by the proper name: Hatteras, Cape.
- Where a name contains a subordinate or alternative name in brackets on the map, the bracketed names are entered in the gazetteer with a cross-reference to the first name, eg. Peking *see* Beijing, China, **746** G5.
- Words abbreviated on the map, e.g. C. or I., are spelt out in the gazetteer. If the word is English, the description in italics is not included. For example, if I. (standing for island) is abbreviated on the map and spelt out in the gazetteer, *island* is not added. However, if Island is not in English, e.g. Isla, *island* is added.
- The location (ocean, area of a continent) is included before the area reference when a place is part of a country but not located within the country, e.g. Madeira, Portugal, Atlantic Ocean; and Ceuta, *enclave*, Spain, N.W. Africa.

A

A Cañiza, Spain, **776** C1
A Coruña, Spain, **776** C1
A Estrada, Spain, **776** C1
A Fonsagrada, Spain, **776** D1
A Guardia, Spain, **776** C2
A Gudiña, Spain, **776** D1
Aachen, Germany, **772** C3
Aalen, Germany, **772** E4
A'ali An Nīl, *state*, Sudan, **806** D2
Aapua, Sweden, **769** L3
Aarau, Switzerland, **775** J3
Aare, *river*, Switzerland, **775** J3
Aasleagh, Ireland, **793** C4
Aba, China, **751** G2
Aba, Democratic Republic of the Congo, **806** D4
Aba, Nigeria, **808** A1
Abacaxis, *river*, Brazil, **850** A4
Abaco, *island*, Bahamas, **838** F1
Ābādeh, Iran, **756** F2
Abadla, Algeria, **801** F2
Abaeté, *river*, Brazil, **854** D5
Abaetetuba, Brazil, **850** D3
Abag Qi, China, **746** F4
Abagaytuy, Russian Federation, **746** G2
Abaji, Nigeria, **805** F3
Abajo Peak, *mountain peak*, U.S.A., **833** J3
Abakaliki, Nigeria, **805** F3
Abakan, *river*, Russian Federation, **759** M2
Abakan, Russian Federation, **759** N2
Abala, Congo, **808** C3
Abala, Niger, **805** E2
Abalak, Niger, **805** E3/F1
Abalessa, Algeria, **801** G4
Abancay, Peru, **852** D3
Abarkūh, Iran, **756** F2
Abashiri, Japan, **745** J2
Abatskiy, Russian Federation, **759** J1
Abau, Papua New Guinea, **726** C5
Abay, Aqmola, Kazakhstan, **748** A2
Abay, Qaraghandy, Kazakhstan, **748** B2
Abaza, Russian Federation, **759** N2
Abba, Central African Republic, **808** C1
Abbeville, Alabama, U.S.A., **835** K4
Abbeville, France, **774** E1
Abbeville, Louisiana, U.S.A., **834** F5
Abbeville, South Carolina, U.S.A., **835** L2
Abbeyfeale, Ireland, **793** C5
Abbeyleix, Ireland, **793** E5
Abborrträsk, Sweden, **768** J4
Abbot Ice Shelf, Antarctica, **862** B6
Abbots Langley, England, U.K., **789** G3
Abbotsbury, England, U.K., **788** E4
Abbotsford, Canada, **822** H7
Abbott, U.S.A., **833** L3
Abbottābād, Pakistan, **754** C2
'Abd al Kūrī, *island*, Suquţrá (Socotra), Yemen, **813** B2
Abdelcader, Somalia, **807** F2
Abdulino, Russian Federation, **758** E2
Abéché, Chad, **806** B2
Abee, Canada, **823** N4
Abemama, *island*, Kiribati, **725** F4
Abengourou, Côte d'Ivoire, **804** D3
Åbenrå, Denmark, **770** D5
Abeokuta, Nigeria, **805** E3
Aberaeron, Wales, U.K., **788** C2
Aberchirder, Scotland, U.K., **792** G3
Aberdare, Wales, U.K., **788** D3
Aberdaron, Wales, U.K., **788** C2
Aberdeen, Idaho, U.S.A., **828** H5
Aberdeen, Mississippi, U.S.A., **835** H3
Aberdeen, Scotland, U.K., **792** G3
Aberdeen, South Africa, **810** D5
Aberdeen, South Dakota, U.S.A., **830** D3
Aberdeen, Washington, U.S.A., **828** C3
Aberdeen City, *local authority*, Scotland, U.K., **792** G3
Aberdeenshire, *local authority*, Scotland, U.K., **792** G3
Aberdyfi, Wales, U.K., **788** C2
Aberfeldy, Scotland, U.K., **792** F4
Aberfoyle, Scotland, U.K., **790** D1
Abergavenny, Wales, U.K., **788** E3
Abergele, Wales, U.K., **790** E4
Abernathy, U.S.A., **834** B3
Aberporth, Wales, U.K., **788** C2
Abersoch, Wales, U.K., **788** C2
Abert, Lake, U.S.A., **828** D5
Abertillery, Wales, U.K., **788** D3
Aberystwyth, Wales, U.K., **788** C2
Abhā, Saudi Arabia, **803** H5
Abhar, Iran, **758** D5
Abia, *state*, Nigeria, **805** F3
Abibe, Serranía de, *mountain range*, Colombia, **848** C2
Abide, Turkey, **781** G6
Abidjan, Côte d'Ivoire, **804** D3
Abilene, U.S.A., **834** C3
Abingdon, England, U.K., **789** F3
Abingdon, U.S.A., **831** N7
Abington, Scotland, U.K., **792** F5
Abiquiu, U.S.A., **833** K3
Abisko, Sweden, **768** J2
Abitibi, Lake, Canada, **825** Q7
Ābīy Ādī, Ethiopia, **807** E2
Abkhazia, *autonomous republic*, Georgia, **758** C4
Abnūb, Egypt, **803** F3
Abohar, India, **754** C3
Aboisso, Côte d'Ivoire, **804** D3
Abomey, Benin, **805** E3
Abong Mbang, Cameroon, **808** B2
Abongabong, Gunung, *mountain peak*, Indonesia, **736** B1
Abooso, Ghana, **804** D3
Aborlan, Philippines, **740** B4
Abou Deïa, Chad, **806** A2
Aboyne, Scotland, U.K., **792** G3
Abra Pampa, Argentina, **856** D2
Abra, *river*, Philippines, **740** C2
Abrantes, Portugal, **776** C3
Abrī, Sudan, **803** F4
Abriès, France, **775** H4
Abrolhos, Arquipélago dos, *islands*, Brazil, **855** F4
Abrud, Romania, **780** D2
Abruka, *island*, Estonia, **771** L3
Abruzzi, *autonomous region*, Italy, **779** D4
Absaroka Range, *mountain range*, U.S.A., **829** J4
Absarokee, U.S.A., **829** K4
Abu aḍ Ḍuhūr, Syria, **761** D2
Abū 'Arīsh, Saudi Arabia, **803** H5
Abu Dhabi *see* Abū Zaby, United Arab Emirates, **757** F4
Abū Dulayq, Sudan, **806** D1
Abū Durbah, Egypt, **761** B5
Abu Haggag, Egypt, **802** E2
Abū Ḥamad, Sudan, **803** F5
Abū Ḥammād, Egypt, **761** A4
Abū Kamāl, Syria, **803** H2
Abū Madd, Ra's, *point*, Saudi Arabia, **803** G4
Abū Maţāriq, Sudan, **806** C2
Abū Nujaym, Libya, **802** C2
Ābu Road, India, **754** C4
Abū Rubayq, Saudi Arabia, **803** G4
Abū Rudays, Egypt, **761** B5
Abū Rujmayn, Jabal, *mountain range*, Syria, **761** E2
Abu Shagara, Ras, *point*, Sudan, **803** G4
Abū Shanab, Sudan, **806** C2
Abu Simbel *see* Abū Sunbul, Egypt, **803** F4
Abū Sunbul (Abu Simbel), Egypt, **803** F4
Abū Zabad, Sudan, **806** C2
Abū Zaby (Abu Dhabi), United Arab Emirates, **757** F4
Abū Zanīmah, Egypt, **761** B5
Abu 'Ujaylah, Egypt, **761** C4
Abuja, Nigeria, **805** F3
Abulog, Philippines, **740** C2
Abumombazi, Democratic Republic of the Congo, **808** D2
Abunã, Brazil, **853** F2
Abunã, *river*, Bolivia/Brazil, **853** E2
Ābune Yosēf, *mountain peak*, Ethiopia, **807** E2
Aburo, *mountain peak*, Democratic Republic of the Congo, **806** D4
Ābuyē Mēda, *mountain peak*, Ethiopia, **807** E2
Åby, Sweden, **770** H3
Abyaḍ, Al Baḩr al (White Nile), *river*, Sudan, **806** D2
Abyaḍ, Sudan, **806** C2
Åbybro, Denmark, **770** D4
Abyei, Sudan, **806** C3
Åbyn, Sweden, **768** K4
Açailândia, Brazil, **850** D4
Acámbaro, Mexico, **841** E5
Acancéh, Mexico, **841** H4
Acandí, Colombia, **848** C2
Acaponeta, Mexico, **840** D4
Acapulco, Mexico, **841** F5
Acará, Brazil, **850** D3
Acará, *river*, Brazil, **850** D4
Acará-Mirim, *river*, Brazil, **850** D4
Acaraí, Serra, *mountain range*, Brazil, **850** B3
Acaraú, Brazil, **851** F4
Acaraú, *river*, Brazil, **851** F4
Acaray, Represa de, *reservoir*, Paraguay, **857** F2
Acari, Brazil, **851** G5
Acarigua, Venezuela, **849** E2
Acâş, Romania, **780** D2
Acatlán de Osorio, Mexico, **841** F5
Acayucan, Mexico, **841** G5
Acceglio, Italy, **778** A3
Accomac, U.S.A., **836** C6
Accra, Ghana, **804** D3
Aceh, *province*, Indonesia, **736** B1
Aceh, *river*, Indonesia, **736** A1
Achacachi, Bolivia, **853** E4
Achaguas, Venezuela, **849** E2
Achahoish, Scotland, U.K., **792** D5
Achalpur, India, **754** D5
Acheng, China, **747** J3
Acheryok, *river*, Russian Federation, **769** U3
Acheux-en-Amiénois, France, **789** K4
Achill, Ireland, **793** C4
Achill Island, Ireland, **793** B4
Achiltibuie, Scotland, U.K., **792** D2
Achinsk, Russian Federation, **784** L4
Achit, Russian Federation, **758** F1
Achnasheen, Scotland, U.K., **792** D3
Achwa, *river*, Uganda, **809** F2
Acigöl, *lake*, Turkey, **781** G7

Acıpayam, Turkey, **781** G7
Acireale, Sicilia, Italy, **779** E7
Ackley, U.S.A., **830** G4
Acklins Island, Bahamas, **839** G2
Acle, England, U.K., **789** J2
Acme, U.S.A., **828** C2
Acomayo, Peru, **852** D3
Aconcagua, Cerro, *mountain peak*, Argentina, **856** B4
Acopiara, Brazil, **851** F5
Acora, Peru, **853** E4
Acoyapa, Nicaragua, **838** D5
Acquasparta, Italy, **778** D4
Acqui Terme, Italy, **778** B3
Acre, *river*, Brazil, **853** E2
Acre *see* 'Akko, Israel, **761** C3
Acre, *state*, Brazil, **853** E2
Acri, Italy, **779** F6
Actéon, Groupe, *islands*, French Polynesia, **723** H3
Acton Point, New Zealand, **719** E5
Acton, U.S.A., **829** K4
Actopan, Mexico, **841** F4
Açu, Brazil, **851** G4
Acurenam, Equatorial Guinea, **808** B2
Ad Dabbah, Sudan, **803** F5
Ad Dafinah, Saudi Arabia, **803** H4
Ad Dahnā', *desert*, Saudi Arabia, **803** J3
Ad Dakhla, Western Sahara, **800** C4
Aḍ Ḍāli', Yemen, **756** D6
Ad Damazin, Sudan, **806** D2
Ad Dāmir, Sudan, **803** F5
Ad Dammām, Saudi Arabia, **756** F3
Ad Dāmūr, Lebanon, **761** C3
Ad Darb, Saudi Arabia, **803** H5
Ad Dawādimī, Saudi Arabia, **803** H4
Ad Dawḥah (Doha), Qatar, **756** F3
Ad Dawqah, Saudi Arabia, **803** H5
Ad Dilam, Saudi Arabia, **756** E4
Ad Dir'īyah, Saudi Arabia, **756** E4
Ad Dīwānīyah, Iraq, **803** H2
Ad Du'ayn, Sudan, **806** C2
Ad Duwaym, Sudan, **806** D2
Ada, U.S.A., **834** D2
Ada, Yugoslavia, **780** C3
Adair, Cape, Canada, **821** M2
Adair, U.S.A., **830** F5
Adaja, *river*, Spain, **776** E2
Adak, Sweden, **768** J4
Adak Island, Aleutian Islands, U.S.A., **816** F3
Adam, Mount, *mountain peak*, Falkland Islands, **858** F4
Adamaoua, Massif de l', *mountain range*, Cameroon, **805** G3
Adamaoua, *province*, Cameroon, **805** G3
Adamausa, *state*, Nigeria, **805** G3
Adamawa, *state*, Nigeria, **805** G3
Adams, Mount, *mountain peak*, New Zealand, **719** E5
Adams, Mount, *mountain peak*, U.S.A., **828** D3
Adams, U.S.A., **830** D1
Adams Island, Auckland Islands, New Zealand, **718** J10
Adams Lake, Canada, **823** K6
Adam's Peak, *mountain peak*, Sri Lanka, **752** E5
Adamstown, Pitcairn Islands, **723** J3
'Adan (Aden), Yemen, **756** E6
Adana, *province*, Turkey, **761** C1
Adana, Turkey, **760** E5
Adang, Teluk, *bay*, Indonesia, **737** G3
Adapazarı, Turkey, **760** D4
Adare, Cape, Antarctica, **862** D8
Adare, Ireland, **793** D5
Adaut, Indonesia, **735** E5
Adaven, U.S.A., **832** F2
Aday, Kazakhstan, **758** G2
Adda, *river*, Italy, **778** B2
Adda, *river*, Sudan, **806** B3
Addis Ababa *see* Ādīs Ābeba, Ethiopia, **807** E3
Addlestone, England, U.K., **789** G3
Addu Atoll, Maldives, **752** C7
Adel, U.S.A., **835** L4
Adelaide, Australia, **721** H5
Adelaide River, Australia, **720** G1
Adelfia, Italy, **779** F5
Aden, Gulf of, Somalia/Yemen, **756** E6
Aden *see* 'Adan, Yemen, **756** E6
Aderbissinat, Niger, **805** F1
Adh Dhahībāt, Tunisia, **802** B2
Adi, Pulau, *island*, Indonesia, **735** F4
Ādī Ārk'ay, Ethiopia, **807** E2
Ādī Keyih, Eritrea, **807** E2
Ādī Kwala, Eritrea, **807** E2
Ādī Ugrī, Eritrea, **807** E2
Adige, *river*, Italy, **778** C3
Adige, *state*, Italy, **778** C2
Ādīgrat, Ethiopia, **807** E2
Adıguzel Barajı, *dam*, Turkey, **781** G6
Ādilābād, India, **752** D2
Adilang, Uganda, **809** F2
Adin, U.S.A., **828** D6
Adirī, Libya, **802** B3
Adirondack Mountains, *mountain range*, U.S.A., **836** C2
Ādīs Ābeba (Addis Ababa), Ethiopia, **807** E3
Ādīs 'Alem, Ethiopia, **807** E3
Ādīs Zemen, Ethiopia, **807** E2
Adıyaman, Turkey, **760** E5
Adjud, Romania, **780** F2
Admiralty Gulf, Australia, **720** E1
Admiralty Inlet, U.S.A., **828** C2
Admiralty Island, U.S.A., **822** B3
Admiralty Islands, Lord Howe Island, Australia, **721** U14
Admiralty Islands, Papua New Guinea, **726** B3
Ado-Ekiti, Nigeria, **805** F3
Adok, Sudan, **806** D3
Adonara, Pulau, *island*, Indonesia, **734** C5
Ādoni, India, **752** D3
Adoumandjali, Central African Republic, **808** C2
Adour, *river*, France, **774** D5
Adra, Spain, **777** F4
Adranga, Democratic Republic of the Congo, **809** F2
Adrano, Sicilia, Italy, **779** E7
Adrar, *administrative region*, Mauritania, **800** D4
Adrar, Algeria, **801** F3
Adrar, *mountain range*, Mauritania, **800** D4
Adré, Chad, **806** B2
Adria, Italy, **778** D3
Adrian, Michigan, U.S.A., **831** L5
Adrian, Texas, U.S.A., **833** M4
Adriatic Sea, Croatia/Italy, **778** D3
Adun Qulu, China, **746** G2
Adusa, Democratic Republic of the Congo, **809** E2
Adutiškis, Lithuania, **771** N5
Ādwa, Ethiopia, **807** E2
Adwāna, India, **754** B5
Adygeya, Respublika, *republic*, Russian Federation, **782** F4
Adzopé, Côte d'Ivoire, **804** D3
Aegean Sea, Greece/Turkey, **781** E6
Aegviidu, Estonia, **771** M3
Aeron, *river*, Wales, U.K., **788** C2
Afantou, Greece, **781** G7
Afféri, Côte d'Ivoire, **804** D3
Afghanistan, *country*, Asia, **730** H6
Afgooye, Somalia, **807** G4
'Afif, Saudi Arabia, **803** H4
Afikpo, Nigeria, **808** A1
Åfjord, Norway, **768** E5
Aflao, Ghana, **804** E3
Aflou, Algeria, **801** G2
Afmadow, Somalia, **809** H2
Afobaka, Suriname, **850** B2
Afognak Island, U.S.A., **820** D4
Afrânio, Brazil, **851** F5
Āfrēra Terara, *mountain peak*, Eritrea, **807** F2
Afrikanda, Russian Federation, **769** R3
'Afrīn, *river*, Syria/Turkey, **761** D1
'Afrīn, Syria, **761** D1
Afuá, Brazil, **850** C3
'Afula, Israel, **761** C3
Afyon, *province*, Turkey, **781** G6
Afyon, Turkey, **760** D5
Agadez, *department*, Niger, **805** F1
Agadez, Niger, **805** F1
Agadir, Morocco, **800** E2
Agalega Islands, Mauritius, **812** D3
Agana, Guam, **724** C3
Agapovka, Russian Federation, **758** F2
Agar, India, **754** C5
Āgaro, Ethiopia, **807** E3
Agartala, India, **755** G5
Agassiz Fracture Zone, *tectonic feature*, Pacific Ocean, **869** J7
Agate, U.S.A., **833** M2
Agathonisi, *island*, Dodekanisos, Greece, **781** F7
Agats, Indonesia, **735** G4
Agatti Island, India, **752** C4
Agawa, Canada, **831** L2
Agboville, Côte d'Ivoire, **804** D3
Agbulu, Philippines, **740** C2
Ağdam, Azerbaijan, **758** D5
Agde, Cap d', *cape*, France, **775** F5
Agde, France, **775** F5
Agen, France, **774** E4
Āgere Maryam, Ethiopia, **809** G1
Agger, Denmark, **770** D4
Aghla Mountain, *mountain peak*, Ireland, **793** D3
Aghor, Afganistan, **754** A4
Agia Marina, Dodekanisos, Greece, **781** F7
Agiabampo, Estero de, *inlet*, Mexico, **840** C3
Agighiol, Romania, **780** G3
Aginskiy Buryatskiy Avtonomnyy Okrug, *autonomous area*, Russian Federation, **746** F2
Aginskoye, Russian Federation, **746** F2
Agioi Theodoroi, Greece, **781** D7
Agiokampos, Greece, **781** D6
Agios Efstratios, *island*, Greece, **781** E6
Agios Georgios, *island*, Greece, **781** D7
Agios Ioannis, Akra, *point*, Kriti, Greece, **781** E8
Agios Nikolaos, Kriti, Greece, **781** E8
Agios Paraskevi, Greece, **781** F6
Agiou Orous, Kolpos, *bay*, Greece, **781** D5
Agira, Sicilia, Italy, **779** E7
Aglona, Latvia, **771** N4
Agnantero, Greece, **781** C6
Agness, U.S.A., **828** B5
Agnibilékrou, Côte d'Ivoire, **804** D3
Agnita, Romania, **780** E3
Agno, Philippines, **740** B2
Agnone, Italy, **779** E5
Agogo, Ghana, **804** D3
Agostinho, Brazil, **853** E2
Āgra, India, **754** D4
Agri, *river*, Italy, **779** F5
Ağrı Dağı, *mountain peak*, Turkey, **760** F4
Agrigento, Sicilia, Italy, **779** D7
Agrihan, *island*, Northern Mariana Islands, **724** C3
Agrinio, Greece, **781** C6
Ağsu, Azerbaijan, **758** D4
Agua de Dios, Colombia, **848** C3
Agua Prieta, Mexico, **840** C2
Aguada Cecilio, Argentina, **858** E1
Aguadas, Colombia, **848** C3
Aguadilla, Puerto Rico, **837** C2
Aguadulce, Panama, **839** E5
Aguadulce, Providencia, Colombia, **859** C1
Aguamansa, Providencia, Colombia, **859** C1
Aguanaval, *river*, Mexico, **840** E3
Aguanus, *river*, Canada, **827** K4
Aguapeí, *river*, Brazil, **854** C5
Aguapey, *river*, Argentina, **857** F3
Aguaray-guazú, *river*, Paraguay, **857** E2
Águas Formosas, Brazil, **855** F4
Aguascalientes, Mexico, **840** E4
Aguascalientes, *state*, Mexico, **840** E4
Aguda, Punta, *point*, Islas Canarias, Spain, **813** B4
Agudos, Brazil, **857** H2
Águeda, Portugal, **776** C2
Águeda, *river*, Spain, **776** D2
Aguelhok, Mali, **801** G5
Agüenit, Western Sahara, **800** D4
Aguié, Niger, **805** F2
Aguila, U.S.A., **832** G5
Aguilar, Spain, **776** E4
Aguilar de Campóo, Spain, **776** E1
Aguilares, Argentina, **856** D3
Águilas, Spain, **777** G4
Agul, *river*, Russian Federation, **759** P1
Āgula'i, Ethiopia, **807** E2
Agulhas, Cape, South Africa, **810** D5
Agulhas Basin, *underwater feature*, Indian Ocean, **866** A8
Agulhas Negras, *mountain peak*, Brazil, **855** E6
Agulhas Plateau, *underwater feature*, Indian Ocean, **866** A7
Agung, Gunung, *mountain peak*, Indonesia, **737** F5
Agusan, *river*, Philippines, **740** D5
Ahar, Iran, **758** D5
Ahaura, New Zealand, **719** C6
Ahaus, Germany, **772** C2
Ahe, *island*, French Polynesia, **723** G2
Ahipara, New Zealand, **718** D2
Ahipara Bay, New Zealand, **718** D2
Ahititi, New Zealand, **718** E4
Ahlainen, Finland, **771** K2
Ahlat, Turkey, **803** H1
Ahmad Wāl, Pakistan, **754** A3
Ahmadābād, India, **754** C5
Ahmadnagar, India, **752** C2
Ahmadpur, India, **752** D2
Ahmadpur East, Pakistan, **754** B3
Ahmar Mountains, *mountain range*, Ethiopia, **807** F3
Aḥmed al Bāqir, Jabal, *mountain peak*, Jordan, **761** C5
Ahmetli, Turkey, **781** F6
Ahmovaara, Finland, **769** P5
Ahor, India, **754** C4
Ähtäri, Finland, **771** M1
Ahuachapán, El Salvador, **838** C4
Ahualulco, Mexico, **841** E4
Ahun, France, **774** F3
Ahuriri Point, New Zealand, **718** F4
Ahvāz, Iran, **756** E2
Ahvenanmaa (Åland), *island*, Finland, **771** J2
Ahvenanmaan Lääni (Åland), *province*, Finland, **771** J2
Ahvenselkä, Finland, **769** P3
Ai Yin Young, Vietnam, **739** E3
Aiambak, Papua New Guinea, **726** A4
Aiddejavrre, Norway, **769** L2
Aiduna, Indonesia, **735** F4
Aigina, Greece, **781** D7
Aigina, *island*, Greece, **781** D7
Aiginio, Greece, **781** D5
Aigio, Greece, **781** D6
Aigrettes, Pointe des, *point*, Réunion, **813** A1
Aiguá, Uruguay, **857** F5
Aiguillon, France, **774** E4
Ailao Shan, *mountain range*, China, **751** G5
Aileu, Indonesia, **734** D5
Ailigandí, Panama, **839** F5
Ailinglapalap, *island*, Marshall Islands, **725** E4
Ailly-le-Haut-Clocher, France, **789** J4
Ailly-sur-Noye, France, **789** K5
Ailsa Craig, *island*, Scotland, U.K., **792** D5
Aimogasta, Argentina, **856** C3
Ain, *river*, France, **775** G3
Aïn Beïda, Algeria, **801** H1
Aïn Ben Tili, Mauritania, **800** E3
Aïn Beni Mathar, Morocco, **801** F2
'Aïn Defla, Algeria, **801** G1
'Aïn Deheb, Algeria, **801** G2
'Aïn el Hadjel, Algeria, **801** G1
Aïn-M'Lila, Algeria, **801** H1
Aïn Oussera, Algeria, **777** J5
'Aïn Sefra, Algeria, **801** F2
'Aïn Temouchent, Algeria, **801** F1
Ainaži, Latvia, **771** M4
Ainsa, Spain, **777** H1
Ainsworth, U.S.A., **830** D4
Aipe, Colombia, **848** C3
Aiquile, Bolivia, **853** F5
Aïr, Massif de l', *mountain range*, Niger, **805** F1
Airaines, France, **774** E2
Airbangis, Indonesia, **736** B2
Airdrie, Canada, **823** M6
Airdrie, Scotland, U.K., **792** F5
Aire, *river*, France, **775** G2
Aire-sur-l'Adour, France, **774** D5
Airpanas, Indonesia, **734** D4
Airvault, France, **774** D3
Aisch, *river*, Germany, **772** E4
Aisén, *administrative region*, Chile, **858** C3
Aishalton, Guyana, **849** G3
Aisne, *river*, France, **775** F2
Aïssa, Djebel, *mountain peak*, Algeria, **801** F2
Aitana, *mountain peak*, Spain, **777** G3
Aitape, Papua New Guinea, **726** A3
Aitkin, U.S.A., **830** G2
Aitutaki, *island*, Cook Islands, **723** E2
Aiud, Romania, **780** D2
Aiviekste, *river*, Latvia, **771** N4
Aix-en-Provence, France, **775** G5
Aix-les-Bains, France, **775** G4
Āīzawl, India, **755** H5
Aizenay, France, **774** D3
Aizpute, Latvia, **771** K4
Aizu-Wakamatsu, Japan, **745** G3
Aj Bogd Uul, *mountain peak*, Mongolia, **749** G3
Ajā, Egypt, **761** A4
Ajaccio, Corse, France, **779** B5
Ajaccio, Golfe d', *gulf*, Corse, France, **779** B5
Ajaigarh, India, **754** E4

Ajalpán, Mexico, **841** F5
Ajanta, India, **754** C5
Ajanta Range, *mountain range*, India, **754** C5
Ajaria, *autonomous republic*, Georgia, **758** C4
Ajaureforsen, Sweden, **768** G4
Ajax, Mount, *mountain peak*, New Zealand, **719** D6
Ajdābiyā, Libya, **802** D2
Ajdovščina, Slovenia, **778** D3
Ajmah, Jabal al, *plateau*, Egypt, **761** B5
Ajmer, India, **754** C4
Ajnala, India, **754** C3
Ajo, U.S.A., **832** G5
Ak Dağ, *mountain peak*, Turkey, **781** F6
Ak Dağlar, *mountain range*, Turkey, **781** G7
Ak-Dovurak, Russian Federation, **759** N2
Ak-Shyyrak, Kyrgyzstan, **759** K4
Akabira, Japan, **745** H2
Akabli, Algeria, **801** G3
Āk'ak'ī Besek'a, Ethiopia, **807** E3
Akalkot, India, **752** D2
Akanthou, Cyprus, **761** B2
Akaroa, New Zealand, **719** D6
Akaroa Harbour, New Zealand, **719** D6
Akatora, Chaine de l', *mountain range*, Benin, **804** E2
Akbou, Algeria, **801** G1
Akbulak, Kazakhstan, **759** J3
Akçakale, Turkey, **760** E5
Akçay, Turkey, **781** G7
Akdağ, *mountain peak*, Turkey, **781** G6
Akelamo, Indonesia, **735** E2
Akeld, England, U.K., **790** F2
Aken, Germany, **772** F3
Åkersberga, Sweden, **771** J3
Akershus, *county*, Norway, **770** E3
Aketi, Democratic Republic of the Congo, **808** D2
Akhalts'ikhe, Georgia, **758** C4
Akhisar, Turkey, **760** C5
Akhmīm, Egypt, **803** F3
Akhnūr, India, **754** C2
Akhtubinsk, Russian Federation, **758** D3
Aki, Japan, **744** F4
Akiaki, *island*, French Polynesia, **723** H2
Akiéni, Gabon, **808** B3
Akima, *river*, Russian Federation, **746** G1
Akima, Russian Federation, **746** F1
Akimiski Island, Canada, **825** P5
Akita, Japan, **745** H3
Akjoujt, Mauritania, **800** D5
Akka, Morocco, **800** E3
Akkajaure, *lake*, Sweden, **768** H3
Akkavare, *mountain peak*, Sweden, **768** H3
'Akko (Acre), Israel, **761** C3
Aklampa, Benin, **805** E3
Aklavik, Canada, **820** F3
Aknīste, Latvia, **771** M4
Akodia, India, **754** D5
Akoke, Sudan, **806** D3
Akola, India, **754** D5
Akom II, Cameroon, **808** B2
Akonolinga, Cameroon, **808** B2
Akordat, Eritrea, **807** E1
Akören, Turkey, **803** F1
Akot, India, **754** D5
Akot, Sudan, **806** D3
Akoupé, Côte d'Ivoire, **804** D3
Akpatok Island, Canada, **821** N3
Akqi, China, **748** C4
Akra Lithino, Greece, **802** D2
Akranes, Iceland, **768** X7
Akrathos, Akra, *point*, Greece, **781** E5
Åkrehamn, Norway, **770** B3
Akrérèb, Niger, **805** F1
Åkrestrømmen, Norway, **770** E2
Akron, Colorado, U.S.A., **833** M1
Akron, Ohio, U.S.A., **831** N5
Akrotiri, Cyprus, **761** B2
Aksai Chin, *disputed region*, China/India, **754** D2
Aksakal, Turkey, **781** G5
Aksakovo, Bulgaria, **780** F4
Aksaray, Turkey, **760** D5
Aksay, Kazakhstan, **758** E2
Akşehir, Turkey, **760** D5
Akşehir Gölü, *lake*, Turkey, **803** F1
Akseki, Turkey, **803** F1
Aksha, Russian Federation, **746** F2
Aksu, China, **748** D4
Aksu, Kazakhstan, **758** E4
Āksum, Ethiopia, **807** E2
Aktash, Russian Federation, **759** M2
Aktau *see* Aqtaū, W. Kazakhstan, **758** E4
Aktaz, China, **748** E5
Akto, China, **748** B5
Aktyubinsk *see* Aqtöbe, Kazakhstan, **758** F2
Akūbū, Sudan, **806** D3
Akulivik, Canada, **825** Q1
Akure, Nigeria, **805** F3
Akureyri, Iceland, **768** Y7
Akutikha, Russian Federation, **759** L2
Akwa Ibon, *state*, Nigeria, **805** F4
Akwanga, Nigeria, **805** F3
Akxokesay, China, **749** F5
Akyab *see* Sittwe, Myanmar, **741** B3
Al Abyār, Libya, **802** D2
Al Ajfar, Saudi Arabia, **803** H3
Al Akhḍar, Saudi Arabia, **761** D5
Al 'Alamayn, Egypt, **802** E2
Al 'Amārah, Iraq, **803** J2
Al 'Aqabah, Jordan, **761** C5
Al 'Aqīq, Saudi Arabia, **803** H4
Al 'Arīsh, Egypt, **761** B4
Al Artāwīyah, Saudi Arabia, **803** J3
Al 'Azīzīyah, Libya, **802** B2
Al Bāb, Syria, **761** D1
Al Bad', Saudi Arabia, **761** C5
Al Badī', Saudi Arabia, **803** J4
Al Baḥr Al Aḥmar, *state*, Sudan, **803** F5
Al Balyanā, Egypt, **803** F3
Al Bardī, Libya, **802** E2
Al Barun, Sudan, **806** D2
Al Başrah (Basra), Iraq, **803** J2
Al Batrūn, Lebanon, **761** C2
Al Bauga, Sudan, **803** F5
Al Bawīṭī, Egypt, **802** E3
Al Bayḍā', Libya, **802** D2
Al Bayḍā', Yemen, **756** E6
Al Bi'ār, Saudi Arabia, **803** G4
Al Bi'r, Saudi Arabia, **761** D5
Al Birk, Saudi Arabia, **803** H5
Al Biyāḍ, *desert*, Saudi Arabia, **756** E4
Al Buḥayrat, *state*, Sudan, **806** C3
Al Bukayrīyah, Saudi Arabia, **803** H3
Al Burayj, Syria, **761** D2
Al Burmah, Tunisia, **802** A2
Al Buşayyah, Iraq, **803** J2
Al Fāshir, Sudan, **806** C2
Al Fashn, Egypt, **803** F3
Al Fayyūm, Egypt, **803** F3
Al Fāzah, Yemen, **756** D6
Al Firdān, Egypt, **761** B4
Al Fujayrah, United Arab Emirates, **757** G3
Al Fūlah, Sudan, **806** C2
Al Fuqahā', Libya, **802** C3
Al Ghayḍah, Yemen, **756** F5
Al Ghurdaqah, Egypt, **803** F3
Al Ḥadīthah, Iraq, **803** H2
Al Ḥadīthah, Saudi Arabia, **761** D4
Al Ḥamdānīyah, Syria, **761** D2
Al Ḥamīdīyah, Syria, **761** C2
Al Ḥāmmah, Tunisia, **802** A2
Al Ḥammām, Egypt, **802** E2
Al Ḥammāmāt, Tunisia, **779** C7
Al Ḥamrāt, Syria, **761** D2
Al Ḥāmūl, Egypt, **761** A4
Al Ḥanākīyah, Saudi Arabia, **803** H4
Al Ḥasā, Jordan, **761** C4
Al Ḥasakah, Syria, **803** H1
Al Ḥawātah, Sudan, **806** D2
Al Ḥawjā', Saudi Arabia, **803** G3
Al Ḥawṭah, Yemen, **756** E5
Al Ḥayz, Egypt, **802** E3
Al Ḥazm, Saudi Arabia, **761** D5
Al Ḥibāk, *desert*, Saudi Arabia, **756** F5
Al Hijaz, *desert*, Saudi Arabia, **803** G3
Al Ḥillah, Iraq, **803** H2
Al Ḥillah, Sudan, **806** C2
Al Hirmil, Lebanon, **761** D2
Al Ḥişn, Jordan, **761** C3
Al Hoceima, Morocco, **801** F1
Al Ḥudaydah, Yemen, **756** D6
Al Hufūf, Saudi Arabia, **756** E3
Al Ḥumayḍah, Saudi Arabia, **761** C5
Al Ḥumayshah, Yemen, **756** E6
Al Īsāwīyah, Saudi Arabia, **761** D4
Al Iskandarīya (Alexandria), Egypt, **803** E2
Al Ismā'īlīyah (Ismailia), Egypt, **761** B4
Al Jafr, Jordan, **761** D4
Al Jaghbūb, Libya, **802** D3
Al Jahrā', Kuwait, **803** J3
Al Jamm, Tunisia, **802** B1
Al Jawf, Libya, **802** D4
Al Jawf, Saudi Arabia, **803** G3
Al Jazīrah, *state*, Sudan, **806** D2
Al Jithāmīyah, Saudi Arabia, **803** H3
Al Jīzah, Egypt, **761** A5
Al Jubayl, Saudi Arabia, **756** E3
Al Jumūm, Saudi Arabia, **803** G4
Al Junaynah, Sudan, **806** B2
Al Kahfah, Saudi Arabia, **803** H3
Al Kāmil, Oman, **757** G4
Al Kāmilīn, Sudan, **806** D1
Al Karīb, Tunisia, **779** B7
Al Karak, Jordan, **761** C4
Al Karnak, Egypt, **803** F3
Al Kāẓimīyah, Iraq, **803** H2
Al Khābūrah, Oman, **757** G4
Al Khalīl (Hebron), West Bank, **761** C4
Al Khandaq, Sudan, **803** F5
Al Khānkah, Egypt, **761** A4
Al Khārijah, Egypt, **803** F3
Al Kharfah, Saudi Arabia, **803** J4
Al Kharj, Saudi Arabia, **756** E4
Al Khartūm, *state*, Sudan, **806** D1
Al Kharṭūm (Khartoum), Sudan, **806** D1
Al Kharṭūm Baḥr (Khartoum North), Sudan, **806** D1
Al Khaşab, Oman, **757** G3
Al Khawsh, Saudi Arabia, **803** H5
Al Khufrah, Libya, **802** D4
Al Khums, Libya, **802** B2
Al Kidan, *desert*, Saudi Arabia, **757** F4
Al Kiswah, Syria, **761** D3
Al Kūfah, Iraq, **803** H2
Al Kuntillah, Egypt, **761** C5
Al Kūt, Iraq, **803** J2
Al Kuwayt (Kuwait), Kuwait, **803** J3
Al Lādhiqīyah, *district*, Syria, **761** C2
Al Lādhiqīyah (Latakia), Syria, **761** C2
Al Lagowa, Sudan, **806** C2
Al Līth, Saudi Arabia, **803** H4
Al Madāfi', *plateau*, Saudi Arabia, **761** D5
Al Madīnah (Medina), Saudi Arabia, **803** G4
Al Mafraq, Jordan, **761** D3
Al Maḥalla al Kubrá, Egypt, **761** A4
Al Mahrah, *mountain range*, Yemen, **756** F5
Al Majma'ah, Saudi Arabia, **803** J3
Al Manāmah, Bahrain, **756** F3
Al Manāqil, Sudan, **806** D2
Al Manşūrah, Egypt, **761** A4
Al Manzil, Jordan, **761** D4
Al Manzilah, Egypt, **761** A4
Al Ma'qil, Iraq, **803** J2
Al Marāwi'ah, Yemen, **756** D6
Al Māriyah, Oman, **756** F4
Al Marj, Libya, **802** D2
Al Mawşil (Mosul), Iraq, **803** H1
Al Mayādīn, Syria, **803** H2
Al Mazār, Jordan, **761** C4
Al Mazra'ah, Jordan, **761** C4
Al Metlaoui, Tunisia, **802** A2
Al Minyā, Egypt, **803** F3
Al Mismīyah, Syria, **761** D3
Al Mubarraz, Saudi Arabia, **756** E3
Al Mudawwarah, Jordan, **761** C5
Al Muglad, Sudan, **806** C2
Al Mukallā, Yemen, **756** E6
Al Mukhā, Yemen, **756** D6
Al Munastīr, Tunisia, **802** B1
Al Muqdādīyah, Iraq, **803** H2
Al Musayjīd, Saudi Arabia, **803** G4
Al Muwayh, Saudi Arabia, **803** H4
Al Qa'āmīyāt, *physical feature*, Saudi Arabia, **807** G1
Al Qa'āmīyāt, *region*, Saudi Arabia, **756** E5
Al Qaḍārif, *state*, Sudan, **806** E2
Al Qaḍārif, Sudan, **806** E2
Al Qaḍīmah, Saudi Arabia, **803** G4
Al Qadmūs, Syria, **761** D2
Al Qāhirah (Cairo), Egypt, **761** A4
Al Qaḥmah, Saudi Arabia, **803** H5
Al Qā'īyah, Saudi Arabia, **803** H4
Al Qalībah, Saudi Arabia, **761** D5
Al Qāmishlī, Syria, **803** H1
Al Qanṭarah, Egypt, **761** B4
Al Qaryatayn, Syria, **761** D2
Al Qaşabāt, Libya, **802** B2
Al Qaşr, Egypt, **802** E3
Al Qaşrayn, Tunisia, **802** A1
Al Qaṭrānah, Jordan, **761** D4
Al Qaṭrūn, Libya, **802** B4
Al Quşaymah, Egypt, **761** C4
Al Quşayr, Egypt, **803** F3
Al Quṭaynah, Sudan, **806** D2
Al Quṭayfah, Syria, **761** D3
Al Qunayṭirah, *district*, Syria, **761** C3
Al Qunayṭirah, Syria, **761** C3
Al Qunfudhah, Saudi Arabia, **803** H5
Al Qurayyāt, Saudi Arabia, **761** D4
Al Quwayrah, Jordan, **761** C5
Al Ṭawṭah, Yemen, **756** E6
Al Ubayyiḍ (El Obeid), Sudan, **806** D2
Al 'Ulā, Saudi Arabia, **803** G3
Al 'Ulayyah, Saudi Arabia, **803** H5
Al 'Umarī, Jordan, **761** D4
Al 'Uqaylah, Libya, **802** C2
Al Uqşur (Luxor), Egypt, **803** F3
Al 'Urayq, *desert*, Saudi Arabia, **803** G3
Al Uthaylī, Saudi Arabia, **761** D5
Al 'Uthmānīyah, Saudi Arabia, **756** E3
Al 'Uwaynāt, E. Libya, **802** D4
Al 'Uwaynāt, W. Libya, **802** B3
Al 'Uwayqīlah, Saudi Arabia, **803** H2
Al 'Uyūn, N. Saudi Arabia, **803** H3
Al 'Uyūn, W. Saudi Arabia, **803** G4
Al Wīgh, Libya, **802** B4
Al Waḥdah, *state*, Sudan, **806** C3
Al Wajh, Saudi Arabia, **803** G3
Al Wāsiṭah, Egypt, **761** A5
Al Waslātīyah, Tunisia, **779** B8
Al Wazz, Sudan, **806** D2
Al Yamāmah, Saudi Arabia, **756** E4
Ala-Vuokki, Finland, **769** P4
Alabama, *river*, U.S.A., **835** J4
Alabama, *state*, U.S.A., **835** J3
Alabaster, U.S.A., **835** J3
Alaçam Dağları, *mountain range*, Turkey, **781** G6
Alachua, U.S.A., **835** L5
Aladdin, U.S.A., **829** M4
Alaejos, Spain, **776** E2
Alagoas, *state*, Brazil, **855** G2
Alagoinhas, Brazil, **855** F3
Alahärmä, Finland, **769** L5
Alajärvi, Finland, **769** L5
Alajuela, Costa Rica, **838** D5
Alaköl', *lake*, Kazakhstan, **748** D3
Alakurtti, Russian Federation, **769** Q3
Alalau, *river*, Brazil, **849** G4
Alamagan, *island*, Northern Mariana Islands, **724** C3
Ālamat'ā, Ethiopia, **807** E2
Alamdo, China, **750** E3
Alamo, U.S.A., **832** F3
Alamo Lake, U.S.A., **832** G4
Alamogordo, U.S.A., **833** L5
Alamos, Mexico, **840** C3
Alamosa, U.S.A., **833** L3
Åland *see* Ahvenanmaa, *island*, Finland, **771** J2
Åland *see* Ahvenanmaan Lääni, *province*, Finland, **771** J2
Alantika, Monts, *mountain range*, Cameroon, **805** G3
Alanya (Coracesium), Turkey, **761** A1
Alapaha, U.S.A., **835** L4
Alapayevsk, Russian Federation, **758** G1
Alarcón, Embalse de, *reservoir*, Spain, **777** F3
Alarcón, Spain, **777** F3
Alaşehir, Turkey, **781** G6
Alaska, Gulf of, U.S.A., **820** E4
Alaska, *state*, U.S.A., **820** D3
Alaska Peninsula, U.S.A., **820** C4
Alaska Range, *mountain range*, U.S.A., **820** D3
Alassio, Italy, **778** B4
Älät, Azerbaijan, **758** D5
Alatri, Italy, **779** D5
Alatyr', Russian Federation, **758** D2
Alausí, Ecuador, **848** B5
Alavieska, Finland, **769** M4
Alavus, Finland, **771** L1
'Alawīyīn, Jibāl al, *mountain range*, Syria, **761** D2
Alay kyrka, *mountain range*, Kyrgyzstan/Tajikistan, **748** B5
'Ālayh, Lebanon, **761** C3
Alazeya, *river*, Russian Federation, **785** S2
Alba, Italy, **778** A3
Alba, Mount, *mountain peak*, New Zealand, **719** B7
Alba Iulia, Romania, **780** D3
Albacete, Spain, **777** G3
Ålbæk, Denmark, **770** E4
Alban, Canada, **831** N2
Albanel, Lac, *lake*, Canada, **826** E4
Albania, *country*, Europe, **764** F7
Albany, Australia, **720** D5
Albany, Kentucky, U.S.A., **835** K4
Albany, New York, U.S.A., **836** D3

Alton, Missouri, U.S.A., **830** H7
Alton, Utah, U.S.A., **832** G3
Altona, Canada, **824** F7
Altoona, U.S.A., **831** P5
Altos, Brazil, **851** E4
Altötting, Germany, **772** F4
Altraga, Mongolia, **749** H2
Altrincham, England, U.K., **790** F4
Altun Shan, *mountain range*, China, **748** E5
Alturas, U.S.A., **828** D6
Altus, U.S.A., **834** C2
Alu *see* Shortland, *island*, Solomon Islands, **727** A1
Alūksne, Latvia, **771** N4
Alūr, India, **752** D3
Alva, U.S.A., **830** D7
Älvängen, Sweden, **770** F4
Alvarães, Brazil, **849** F5
Alvdal, Norway, **770** E1
Älvdalen, Sweden, **770** G2
Alveley, England, U.K., **788** E2
Alvesta, Sweden, **770** G4
Ålvik, Norway, **770** C2
Alvin, U.S.A., **834** E5
Älvkarleby, Sweden, **771** H2
Älvsborg, *county*, Sweden, **770** F4
Älvsbyn, Sweden, **768** K4
Alwar, India, **754** D4
Alxa Zuoqi, China, **746** D5
Alyth, Scotland, U.K., **792** F4
Alytus, Lithuania, **771** M5
Alzamay, Russian Federation, **759** P1
Alzira, Spain, **777** G3
Am-Dam, Chad, **806** B2
Am Timan, Chad, **806** B2
Am-Zoer, Chad, **806** B2
Amada Gaza, Central African Republic, **808** C2
Amadeus, Lake, Australia, **720** G3
Amadjuak Lake, Canada, **821** M3
Amado, U.S.A., **833** H6
Amadora, Portugal, **776** C3
Amagasaki, Japan, **745** F4
Amager, *island*, Denmark, **770** F5
Amahai, Indonesia, **735** E3
Amakusa-shotō, *islands*, Japan, **744** E4
Åmål, Sweden, **770** F3
Amalfi, Colombia, **848** C2
Amalfi, Italy, **779** E5
Amaliada, Greece, **781** C7
Amamapare, Indonesia, **735** G4
Amambaí, Brazil, **857** F2
Amambaí, *river*, Brazil, **857** F2
Amambaí, Serra de, *mountain range*, Brazil/Paraguay, **857** F2
Amami-shotō, *islands*, Japan, **745** P8
Amamula, Democratic Republic of the Congo, **809** E3
Amanab, Papua New Guinea, **726** A3
Amangeldi, Kazakhstan, **758** H2
Amanqaraghay, Kazakhstan, **758** G2
Amantea, Italy, **779** F6
Amantogay, Kazakhstan, **758** H2
Amanu, *island*, French Polynesia, **723** G2
Amanzimtoti, South Africa, **811** F5
Amapá, Brazil, **850** C2
Amapá, *state*, Brazil, **850** C3
Amapari, *river*, Brazil, **850** C3
Amarante, Brazil, **851** E5
Amarante do Maranhão, Brazil, **850** D4
Amaranth, Canada, **824** E6
Amarapura, Myanmar, **741** C3
Amargosa Valley, U.S.A., **832** E3
Amarillo, U.S.A., **834** B2
Amarkantak, India, **755** E5
Amarnāth, India, **752** C2
Amaro, Monte, *mountain peak*, Italy, **779** E4
Amasya, Turkey, **760** E4
Amatán, Mexico, **841** G5
Amatlán de Cañas, Mexico, **840** D4
Amatrice, Italy, **778** D4
Amaturá, Brazil, **849** E5
Amazon Basin, South America, **846** F4
Amazon Fan, *underwater feature*, Atlantic Ocean, **867** D5
Amazonas, *river*, Brazil/Peru, **847** G4
Amazonas, *state*, Brazil, **849** F5
Āmba Ālagē, *mountain peak*, Ethiopia, **807** E2
Amba Farit, *mountain peak*, Ethiopia, **807** E2
Ambāla, India, **754** D3
Ambāla Sadar, India, **754** D3
Ambalakida, Madagascar, **812** B4
Ambalavao, Madagascar, **812** B5
Ambam, Cameroon, **808** B2
Ambanja, Madagascar, **812** B3
Ambarnyy, Russian Federation, **769** R4
Ambato, Ecuador, **848** B4
Ambato Boeny, Madagascar, **812** B4
Ambatofinandrahana, Madagascar, **812** B5
Ambatolampy, Madagascar, **812** B4
Ambatomainty, Madagascar, **812** B4
Ambatondrazaka, Madagascar, **812** B4
Ambazac, France, **774** E4
Amberg, Germany, **772** E4
Amberg, U.S.A., **831** K3
Ambérieu-en-Bugey, France, **775** G3
Amberley, New Zealand, **719** D6
Ambert, France, **775** F4
Ambidédi, Mali, **804** B2
Ambikāpur, India, **755** E5
Ambilobe, Madagascar, **812** B3
Amble, England, U.K., **791** G2
Ambleside, England, U.K., **790** F3
Ambo, Peru, **852** C3
Amboasary, Madagascar, **812** B6
Ambohidratrimo, Madagascar, **812** B4
Ambohimahasoa, Madagascar, **812** B5
Ambohipaky, Madagascar, **812** A4
Ambohitra, *mountain peak*, Madagascar, **812** B3
Amboise, France, **774** E3
Ambon, Indonesia, **735** E3
Amborompotsy, Madagascar, **812** B5
Ambositra, Madagascar, **812** B5
Ambovombe, Madagascar, **812** B6
Amboy, U.S.A., **832** F4
Ambre, Cap d' *see* Bobaomby, Tanjona, Madagascar, **812** B3
Ambre, Île d', *island*, Mauritius, **813** C1
Ambriz, Angola, **808** B4
Ambrym, *island*, Vanuatu, **727** A2
Ambuaki, Indonesia, **735** F3
Amchitka Island, Aleutian Islands, U.S.A., **816** E3
Amdo, China, **750** D2
Ameca, Mexico, **840** D4
Ameland, *island*, Netherlands, **772** B2
American Falls, U.S.A., **828** H5
American Falls Reservoir, U.S.A., **828** H5
American Fork, U.S.A., **833** H1
American Samoa, *U.S. territory*, Pacific Ocean, **715** H3
Americana, Brazil, **857** H2
Americus, U.S.A., **835** K3
Amersfoort, Netherlands, **772** B2
Amersham, England, U.K., **789** G3
Amery Ice Shelf, Antarctica, **862** F5
Ames, U.S.A., **830** G4
Amesbury, England, U.K., **789** F3
Amfilochia, Greece, **781** C6
Amfissa, Greece, **781** D6
Amga, *river*, Russian Federation, **785** Q4
Amgalang Bulag, China, **747** G2
Amgu, Russian Federation, **745** G1
Amguid, Algeria, **801** H3
Amgun', *river*, Russian Federation, **747** L2
Amherst, Canada, **827** J7
Amiata, Monte, *mountain peak*, Italy, **778** C4
Amidon, U.S.A., **830** B2
Amiens, France, **774** F2
Amindivi Islands, India, **752** C4
Amino, Ethiopia, **809** H2
Aminuis, Namibia, **810** C3
Amirante Isles, Seychelles, **812** C2
Amisk Lake, Canada, **824** C4
Amite, U.S.A., **834** G4
Amla, India, **754** D5
Amlamé, Togo, **804** E3
Åmli, Norway, **770** D3
Amlia Island, Aleutian Islands, U.S.A., **816** F3
Amlwch, Wales, U.K., **790** D4
'Ammān, Jordan, **761** D4
Ammanford, Wales, U.K., **788** C3
Ammarnäs, Sweden, **768** H4
Ammassalik, Greenland, **821** R3
Ammersee, *lake*, Germany, **772** E4
Ammochostos (Famagusta), Cyprus, **761** B2
Ammochostos Bay, Cyprus, **761** C2
Amnat Charoen, Thailand, **739** E3
Amok, Vanuatu, **727** A2
Amolar, Brazil, **854** B5
Amontada, Brazil, **851** F4
Amorgos, *island*, Kyklades, Greece, **781** E7
Amory, U.S.A., **835** H2
Amos, Canada, **826** B5
Åmot, Norway, **770** D3
Åmot, Sweden, **770** H2
Åmotfors, Sweden, **770** F3
Amourj, Mauritania, **804** C1
Ampahana, Madagascar, **812** C3
Ampanavoana, Madagascar, **812** C4
Ampanefena, Madagascar, **812** B3
Ampanihy, Madagascar, **812** A5
Amparafaravola, Madagascar, **812** B4
Amparai, Sri Lanka, **753** E5
Amparo, Brazil, **857** H2
Ampasimanjeva, Madagascar, **812** B5
Ampasimanolotra, Madagascar, **812** B4
Ampato, Nevado, *mountain peak*, Peru, **852** D4
Ampelonas, Greece, **781** D6
Amper, *river*, Germany, **772** E4
Ampisikinana, Madagascar, **812** B3
Amposta, Spain, **777** H2
Ampthill, England, U.K., **789** G2
Amqui, Canada, **826** H5
'Amrān, Yemen, **756** D5
Amrāvati, India, **754** D5
Amreli, India, **754** B5
Amritsar, India, **754** C3
Åmsele, Sweden, **768** J4
Amstein, Germany, **772** D4
Amsterdam, Île, *island*, French Southern and Antarctic Islands, **708** E12
Amsterdam, Netherlands, **772** B2
Amstetten, Austria, **773** G4
Amu Darya, *river*, Turkmenistan/Uzbekistan, **758** G5
Amund Ringnes Island, Canada, **821** K2
Amundsen, Mount, *mountain peak*, Antarctica, **862** G5
Amundsen Gulf, Canada, **820** G2
Amundsen-Scott, *U.S. research station*, Antarctica, **862** D5
Amundsen Sea, Antarctica, **862** A6
Amuntai, Indonesia, **737** F3
Amur, *river*, Russian Federation, **733** Q5
Amurang, Teluk, *bay*, Indonesia, **734** C2
Amurrio, Spain, **777** F1
Amursk, Russian Federation, **747** M2
Amurskaya Oblast', *province*, Russian Federation, **747** K1
Amurzet, Russian Federation, **747** K3
Amvrakikos Kolpos, *bay*, Greece, **781** C6
Amyntaio, Greece, **781** C5
Amyot, Canada, **831** L1
Amyūn, Lebanon, **761** C2
An Hai, Vietnam, **739** F3
An Nabatīyah at Taḩtā, Lebanon, **761** C3
An Nabk, Syria, **761** D3
An Nafūd, *desert*, Saudi Arabia, **803** H3
An Nahūd, Sudan, **806** C2
An Najaf, Iraq, **803** H2
An Nakhl, Egypt, **761** B5
An Nāqūrah, Lebanon, **761** C3
An Nāşirīyah, Iraq, **803** J2
An Nawfalīyah, Libya, **802** C2
An Nīl Al Abyaḑ, *state*, Sudan, **806** D2
An Nimāş, Saudi Arabia, **803** H5
An Nu'ayrīyah, Saudi Arabia, **756** E3
An Teallach, *mountain peak*, Scotland, U.K., **792** D3
Anaco, Venezuela, **849** F2
Anaconda, U.S.A., **828** H3
Anacortes, U.S.A., **828** C2
Anadarko, U.S.A., **834** C2
Anadyr', Russian Federation, **785** U3
Anadyrskiy Zaliv, *bay*, Russian Federation, **820** A3
Anadyrskoye Ploskogor'ye, *plateau*, Russian Federation, **785** T3
Anafi, *island*, Kyklades, Greece, **781** E7
Anagé, Brazil, **855** F4
'Ānah, Iraq, **803** H2
Anaheim, U.S.A., **832** D5
Anahola, Hawaiian Islands, U.S.A., **832** R9
Anajás, Brazil, **850** D3
Anajás, Ilha, *island*, Brazil, **850** C3
Anakāpalle, India, **753** E2
Analalava, Madagascar, **812** B3
Anamã, Brazil, **849** G5
Anambas, Kepulauan, *islands*, Indonesia, **736** D2
Anambra, *state*, Nigeria, **805** F3
Anamu, *river*, Brazil, **850** B3
Anamur, Turkey, **761** B1
Anamur Burnu, *cape*, Turkey, **803** F1
Anan, Japan, **744** F4
Ānand, India, **754** C5
Ānandpur, India, **755** F5
Ananea, Peru, **853** E4
Anantapur, India, **752** D3
Anantnāg, India, **754** C2
Anan'yiv, Ukraine, **780** H2
Anapa, Russian Federation, **782** E4
Anápolis, Brazil, **854** D4
Anār, Iran, **757** G2
Anār Darreh, Afghanistan, **757** H2
Anārak, Iran, **756** F2
Anare Station, Macquarie Island, **720** R11
Anarjokka, *river*, Norway, **769** M2
Ånäset, Sweden, **768** K4
Anatahan, *island*, Northern Mariana Islands, **724** C3
Anatolia, *region*, Turkey, **732** E6
Anatoliki Makedonia Kai Thraki, *administrative region*, Greece, **781** E5
Anatom, *island*, Vanuatu, **727** A3
Anatone, U.S.A., **828** F3
Añatuya, Argentina, **856** D3
Anauá, *river*, Brazil, **849** G4
Anbianbu, China, **746** E5
Anbo, China, **747** H5
Ancasti, Sierra de, *mountain range*, Argentina, **856** D3
Anchau, Nigeria, **805** F2
Anchopaya, Bolivia, **853** E4
Anchorage, U.S.A., **820** E3
Anchorstock Point, Tristan da Cunha, **813** C2
Ancón, Peru, **852** C3
Ancón de Sardinas, Bahía de, *bay*, Ecuador, **848** B4
Ancona, Italy, **778** D4
Ancroft, England, U.K., **790** G2
Ancuabe, Mozambique, **809** G5
Ancud, Chile, **858** C1
Ancud, Golfo de, *gulf*, Chile, **858** C2
Anda, China, **747** J3
Andacollo, Chile, **856** B4
Andahuaylas, Peru, **852** D3
Andalgalá, Argentina, **856** C3
Andalucia, *autonomous community*, Spain, **777** F4
Andalusia, U.S.A., **835** J4
Andaman and Nicobar Islands, India, Indian Ocean, **753** G3
Andaman and Nicobar Islands, *union territory*, India, Indian Ocean, **753** H4
Andaman Basin, *underwater feature*, Indian Ocean, **866** F4
Andaman Islands, Andaman and Nicobar Islands, India, **753** H4
Andaman Sea, Indian Ocean, **738** B3
Andamarca, Bolivia, **853** E5
Andance, France, **775** G4
Andapa, Madagascar, **812** B3
Andarai, Brazil, **855** F3
Andenes, Norway, **768** H2
Andéramboukane, Mali, **805** E1
Andermatt, Switzerland, **775** J3
Andernach, Germany, **772** C3
Anderson, Indiana, U.S.A., **831** L5
Anderson, *river*, Canada, **820** G3
Anderson, South Carolina, U.S.A., **835** L2
Andes, Colombia, **848** C3
Andes, *mountain range*, South America, **847** E4
Andfjorden, *bay*, Norway, **768** H2
Andhra Pradesh, *state*, India, **752** D2
Andijon, Uzbekistan, **748** B4
Andilamena, Madagascar, **812** B4
Andilanatoby, Madagascar, **812** B4
Andīmeshk, Iran, **756** E2

Applecross, Scotland, U.K., **792** D3
Appledore, Devon, England, U.K., **788** C3
Appledore, Kent, England, U.K., **789** H3
Appleton, U.S.A., **831** J3
Approuague, *river*, French Guiana, **850** C2
Apraksin Bor, Russian Federation, **783** C3
Apricena, Italy, **779** E5
Aprilia, Italy, **779** D5
Apsley, Canada, **826** B7
Apt, France, **775** G5
Apucarana, Brazil, **857** G2
Apucarana, Serra da, *mountain range*, Brazil, **857** G2
Apurímac, *river*, Peru, **852** D4
Aqaba, Gulf of, Red Sea, **761** C5
Aqadyr, Kazakhstan, **759** J3
Aqal, China, **748** C4
Aqbalyq, Kazakhstan, **748** C3
Āqchah, Afghanistan, **754** A1
'Aqdā, Iran, **756** F2
Aqitag, *mountain peak*, China, **749** F4
Aqköl, Kazakhstan, **759** J4
Aqmola, *province*, Kazakhstan, **748** A2
Aqmola *see* Astana, Kazakhstan, **759** J2
Aqqikkol Hu, *lake*, China, **748** F5
Aqshataū, Kazakhstan, **748** B3
Aqsorang Biigi, *mountain peak*, Kazakhstan, **748** B2
Aqsū, Aqmola, Kazakhstan, **759** J2
Aqsu, Kazakhstan, **748** C1
Aqsū, Pavlodar, Kazakhstan, **759** K2
Aqsū-Ayuly, Kazakhstan, **748** B2
Aqsūat, Central Shyghys Qazaqstan, Kazakhstan, **748** D3
Aqsūat, E. Shyghys Qazaqstan, Kazakhstan, **748** D2
Aqtasty, Kazakhstan, **759** K2
Aqtaū, E. Kazakhstan, **759** J2
Aqtaū (Aktau), W. Kazakhstan, **758** E4
Aqtöbe (Aktyubinsk), Kazakhstan, **758** F2
Aqtoghay, Pavlodar, Kazakhstan, **759** K2
Aqtoghay, Qaraghandy, Kazakhstan, **748** B2
Aqtoghay, Shyghys Qazaqstan, Kazakhstan, **748** C3
Aquidabán, *river*, Paraguay, **857** F2
Aquidauana, Brazil, **854** B5
Aquidauana, *river*, Brazil, **854** B5
Aquila, Mexico, **840** E5
Aquiles Serdán, Mexico, **840** D2
Aquiraz, Brazil, **851** F4
Aquitaine, *administrative region*, France, **774** D4
Aqyrap, Kazakhstan, **758** F2
Aqzhar, Kazakhstan, **759** L3
Ar-Asgat, Mongolia, **746** D2
Ar Horqin Qi, China, **747** H4
Ar Radīsīya Baḥrī, Egypt, **803** F4
Ar Rahad, Sudan, **806** D2
Ar Rāk, Suquṭrá (Socotra), Yemen, **813** B2
Ar Ramādī, Iraq, **803** H2
Ar Ramlah, Jordan, **761** D5
Ar Ramthā, Jordan, **761** D3
Ar Rank, Sudan, **806** D2
Ar Raqqa, *district*, Syria, **761** E2
Ar Raqqah, Syria, **803** G1
Ar Rass, Saudi Arabia, **803** H3
Ar Rastan, Syria, **761** D2
Ar Rawḍatayn, Kuwait, **803** J3
Ar Riyāḍ (Riyadh), Saudi Arabia, **756** E4
Ar Ru'āt, Sudan, **806** D2
Ar Rub' al Khālī, *desert*, Saudi Arabia, **756** E5
Ar Rubay'īyah, Saudi Arabia, **803** H3
Ar Ruṣayfah, Jordan, **761** D4
Ar Ruṣayriṣ, Sudan, **806** D2
Ar Ruṭbah, Iraq, **803** H2
Ar Ruwayḍah, Saudi Arabia, **756** E4
Ar Ruways, Oman, **756** F4
'Arab, Baḥr al, *river*, Sudan, **806** C2
Arab, U.S.A., **835** J2
'Arab al Mulk, Syria, **761** C2
Arabelo, Venezuela, **849** F3
Arabian Basin, *underwater feature*, Indian Ocean, **866** D3
Arabian Peninsula, Asia, **732** F7
Arabian Sea, Indian Ocean, **732** H8
Arabopó, Venezuela, **849** G3
Araçá, *river*, Brazil, **849** F4
Aracaju, Brazil, **855** G3
Aracati, Brazil, **851** G4
Aracatu, Brazil, **855** F4
Araçatuba, Brazil, **854** C5
Aracena, Spain, **776** D4
Aracena, Sierra de, *mountain peak*, Spain, **776** D4
Aracena, Sierra de, *mountain range*, Spain, **776** D4
Aracruz, Brazil, **855** F5
'Arad, Israel, **761** C4
Arad, Romania, **780** C2
Arada, Chad, **806** B2
'Arādah, Oman, **756** F4
Aradan, Russian Federation, **749** G1
Arafura Sea, Australia/Indonesia, **724** B5
Aragarças, Brazil, **854** C4
Aragats Lerr, *mountain peak*, Armenia, **758** C4
Aragón, *autonomous community*, Spain, **777** G2
Aragón, *river*, Spain, **777** G1
Aragua de Barcelona, Venezuela, **849** F2
Araguacema, Brazil, **854** D2
Araguaçu, Brazil, **854** D3
Araguaia, *river*, Brazil, **854** D2
Araguaína, Brazil, **850** D5
Araguao, Boca, *bay*, Venezuela, **849** G2
Araguari, Brazil, **854** D5
Araguari, *river*, Amapá, Brazil, **850** C3
Araguari, *river*, Minas Gerais, Brazil, **854** D5
Araguatins, Brazil, **850** D4
Araioses, Brazil, **851** E4
Arak, Algeria, **801** G3
Arāk, Iran, **756** E2
Arak, Syria, **761** E2
Arakan, *state*, Myanmar, **741** B4
Arakan Yoma, *mountain range*, Myanmar, **741** B3
Aral, China, **748** D4
Aral Sea, Kazakhstan/Uzbekistan, **758** F3
Aralköl, Kazakhstan, **758** G2
Aralqi, China, **748** E5
Aral'sk, Kazakhstan, **758** G3
Aralsor Köli, *lake*, Kazakhstan, **758** D3
Aramberri, Mexico, **841** F3
Aramia, *river*, Papua New Guinea, **726** A4
Ārān, Iran, **756** F2
Aran Fawddwy, *mountain peak*, Wales, U.K., **788** D2
Aran Island, Ireland, **793** D2
Aran Islands, Ireland, **793** C4
Aranda de Duero, Spain, **777** F2
Aranđelovac, Yugoslavia, **780** C3
Aranjuez, Spain, **777** F2
Aranos, Namibia, **810** C3
Aranyaprathet, Thailand, **738** D3
Arao, Japan, **744** E4
Araouane, Mali, **801** F5
Arapahoe, U.S.A., **830** D5
Arapey Grande, *river*, Uruguay, **857** F4
Arapiraca, Brazil, **855** G2
Arapis, Akra, *point*, Greece, **781** E5
Arapkir, Turkey, **760** E5
Arapongas, Brazil, **857** G2
Araputanga, Brazil, **853** G4
'Ar'ar, Saudi Arabia, **803** H2
Araracuara, Colombia, **848** D4
Araranguá, Brazil, **857** H3
Araraquara, Brazil, **854** D5
Araras, Brazil, **850** B5
Araras, Serra das, *mountain range*, Brazil, **857** G2
Ararat, Australia, **721** J6
Ararat, Mount *see* Ağri Daği, *mountain peak*, Turkey, **760** F4
Arari, Brazil, **851** E4
Araria, India, **755** F4
Araripe, Chapada do, *mountain range*, Brazil, **851** F5
Araripina, Brazil, **851** F5
Aras, *river*, Armenia/Azerbaijan/Iran, **803** J1
Arataca, Brazil, **855** F4
Arataua, *mountain peak*, New Zealand, **718** E4
Aratika, *island*, French Polynesia, **723** G2
Aratika, New Zealand, **719** C6
Arauca, Colombia, **849** D2
Arauca, *river*, Venezuela, **849** E2
Araucanía, *administrative region*, Chile, **856** B6
Arauco, Chile, **856** B5
Arauco, Golfo de, *gulf*, Chile, **856** B5
Arauquita, Colombia, **848** D2
Arāvalli Range, *mountain range*, India, **754** C4
Arawa, Papua New Guinea, **726** E2
Araxá, Brazil, **854** D5
Araxos, Akra, *cape*, Greece, **781** C6
Ārba Minch', Ethiopia, **807** E3
Arbīl, Iraq, **803** H1
Arboga, Sweden, **770** G3
Arborfield, Canada, **824** C5
Arborg, Canada, **824** F6
Arbrå, Sweden, **770** H2
Arbroath, Scotland, U.K., **792** G4
Arcachon, Bassin d', *inlet*, France, **774** D4
Arcachon, France, **774** D4
Arcadia, Florida, U.S.A., **835** M6
Arcadia, Louisiana, U.S.A., **834** F3
Arcata, U.S.A., **828** B6
Arcelia, Mexico, **841** E5
Arch Cape, U.S.A., **828** C4
Archer City, U.S.A., **834** C3
Arcidosso, Italy, **778** C4
Arco, U.S.A., **828** H5
Arcos, Brazil, **854** E5
Arcos de la Frontera, Spain, **776** E4
Arcoverde, Brazil, **851** G5
Arctic Bay, Canada, **821** L2
Arctic Ocean, **863** C4
Arḍ aş Şawwān, *plain*, Jordan, **761** D4
Ardabīl, Iran, **758** D5
Ardakān, Iran, **757** F2
Ardal, Iran, **803** K2
Årdalstangen, Norway, **770** C2
Ardara, Ireland, **793** D3
Ardatov, Russian Federation, **782** F1
Ardbeg, Canada, **831** N3
Ardee, Ireland, **793** F4
Ardennes, *region*, Belgium/France, **766** E6
Ardentes, France, **774** E3
Ardgay, Scotland, U.K., **792** E3
Ardglass, Northern Ireland, U.K., **793** G3
Ardino, Bulgaria, **781** E5
Ardlussa, Scotland, U.K., **792** D4
Ardminish, Scotland, U.K., **792** D5
Ardmore, Ireland, **793** E6
Ardmore, U.S.A., **834** D2
Ardnamurchan, Point of, Scotland, U.K., **792** C4
Ardres, France, **789** J4
Ardrishaig, Orkney, Scotland, U.K., **792** D4
Ardrossan, Scotland, U.K., **792** E5
Ards, *district*, Northern Ireland, U.K., **793** G3
Ards Peninsula, Northern Ireland, U.K., **793** G3
Ardud, Romania, **780** D2
Ardvasar, Scotland, U.K., **792** D3
Åre, Sweden, **768** F5
Areavaara, Sweden, **769** L3
Arebi, Democratic Republic of the Congo, **809** E2
Arecibo, Puerto Rico, **837** C2
Areia Branca, Brazil, **851** G4
Arena, Point, U.S.A., **832** A2
Arena, Punta, *point*, Mexico, **840** C4
Arenales, Cerro, *mountain peak*, Chile, **858** C3
Arenas, Punta de, *point*, Argentina, **858** D4
Arenas de San Pedro, Spain, **776** E2
Arendal, Norway, **770** D3
Arendsee, Germany, **772** E2
Areopoli, Greece, **781** D7
Arequipa, Peru, **852** D4
Arere, Brazil, **850** C3
Arès, France, **774** D4
Arévalo, Spain, **776** E2
Arezzo, Italy, **778** C4
Arga, *river*, Spain, **777** G1
Argalasti, Greece, **781** D6
Argan, China, **748** F4
Argan, China, **759** M4
Argatay, Mongolia, **746** D3
Argens, *river*, France, **775** H5
Argenta, Italy, **778** C3
Argentan, France, **774** D2
Argentina, Argentina, **856** D3
Argentina, *country*, South America, **844** F7
Argentine Plain, *underwater feature*, Atlantic Ocean, **867** D8
Argentino, Lago, *lake*, Argentina, **858** C4
Argentino, *river*, Argentina, **858** C4
Argenton-sur-Creuse, France, **774** E3
Argeş, *river*, Romania, **780** E3
Arghandāb, *river*, Afghanistan, **754** A2
Arghastān, *river*, Afghanistan, **754** A3
Argolikos Kolpos, *bay*, Greece, **781** D7
Argopuro, Gunung, *mountain peak*, Indonesia, **737** F4
Argos, Greece, **781** D7
Argos Orestiko, Greece, **781** C5
Argostoli, Ionioi Nisoi, Greece, **781** C6
Argueil, France, **789** J5
Arguello, Point, U.S.A., **832** C4
Argun', *river*, Russian Federation, **747** H1
Argungu, Nigeria, **805** E2
Argus, Dome, *ice dome*, Antarctica, **862** E5
Arguut, Mongolia, **749** J3
Argyle, Canada, **826** J8
Argyle, Lake, Australia, **720** F2
Argyll, *region*, Scotland, U.K., **792** D4
Argyll and Bute, *local authority*, Scotland, U.K., **792** D4
Arhangay, *province*, Mongolia, **749** J3
Århus, Denmark, **770** E4
Arhust, Mongolia, **746** D3
Ari Atoll, Maldives, **752** C5
Aria, *river*, Papua New Guinea, **726** C4
Ariamsvlei, Namibia, **810** C4
Ariano Irpino, Italy, **779** E5
Arias, Argentina, **856** D4
Ariaú, Brazil, **850** B4
Aribinda, Burkina Faso, **804** D2
Arica, Chile, **853** D5
Arica, Colombia, **848** D5
Arica, Peru, **848** C4
Arichat, Canada, **827** L7
Arid, Cape, Australia, **720** E5
Aride, *island*, Seychelles, **813** A2
Ariguaní, *river*, Colombia, **848** C1
Arīḩā (Jericho), West Bank, **761** C4
Ariki, New Zealand, **719** D5
Arilje, Yugoslavia, **780** C4
Arima, Trinidad, Trinidad and Tobago, **859** C4
Arimo, U.S.A., **829** H5
Arinos, Brazil, **854** D4
Arinos, *river*, Brazil, **854** B3
Ario de Rosales, Mexico, **840** E5
Aripuanã, Brazil, **853** G2
Aripuanã, *river*, Brazil, **853** G2
Ariquemes, Brazil, **853** F2
Arisaig, Scotland, U.K., **792** D4
Arisaig, Sound of, Scotland, U.K., **792** D4
Aristazabel Island, Canada, **822** D5
Aritzo, Sardegna, Italy, **779** B6
Ariza, Spain, **777** F2
Arizaro, Salar de, *salt-pan*, Argentina, **856** C2
Arizona, *state*, U.S.A., **833** H4
Årjäng, Sweden, **770** F3
Arjeplog, Sweden, **768** H3
Arjona, Colombia, **848** C1
Arkadelphia, U.S.A., **834** F2
Arkanū, Jabal, *mountain peak*, Libya, **802** D4
Arkansas, *river*, U.S.A., **819** M5
Arkansas, *state*, U.S.A., **834** F2
Arkansas City, U.S.A., **830** E7
Arkatag Shan, *mountain range*, China, **748** F5
Arkhangel'sk, Russian Federation, **784** F3
Arkhangel'skaya Oblast', *province*, Russian Federation, **783** G2
Arkhangel'skoye, Russian Federation, **758** F2
Arkhara, Russian Federation, **747** K2
Arkhipovka, Russian Federation, **783** C5
Arklow, Ireland, **793** F5
Arkona, Kap, *cape*, Germany, **772** F1
Arkonam, India, **752** D3
Arkösund, Sweden, **771** H3
Arlan, *mountain peak*, Turkmenistan, **758** E5
Arlee, U.S.A., **828** G3
Arles, France, **775** G5
Arli, Burkina Faso, **804** E2
Arlington, Colorado, U.S.A., **833** M2
Arlington, Georgia, U.S.A., **835** K4
Arlington, Texas, U.S.A., **834** D3
Arlington, Virginia, U.S.A., **836** B5
Arlit, Niger, **801** H5
Arlon, Belgium, **772** B4
Armagh, *district*, Northern Ireland, U.K., **793** F3
Armagh, Northern Ireland, U.K., **793** F3
Armagnac, *region*, France, **774** E5
Armant, Egypt, **803** F3

B

Ba, Fiji, **727** A4
Ba, *river*, Vietnam, **739** F3
Bá Thước, Vietnam, **751** H5
Baamonde, Spain, **776** D1
Baardheere, Somalia, **809** H2
Baba Burnu, *point*, Turkey, **781** E6
Bababé, Mauritania, **804** B1
Babaçulândia, Brazil, **850** D5
Babadag, Romania, **780** G3
Babadağ, Turkey, **781** G7
Babadurmaz, Turkmenistan, **758** F5
Babaeski, Turkey, **781** F5
Babahoyo, Ecuador, **848** B4
Babanka, Ukraine, **780** H1
Babanki, Cameroon, **805** G3
Babar, Kepulauan, *islands*, Indonesia, **735** E5
Babati, Tanzania, **809** G3
Babayevo, Russian Federation, **783** E3
Babb, U.S.A., **828** H2
Babbacombe Bay, England, U.K., **788** D4
Babel, Mont de, *mountain peak*, Canada, **826** G4
Babelthuap, *island*, Palau, **724** B4
Babian, *river*, China, **751** G4
Babinavichy, Belarus, **783** C5
Babine Lake, Canada, **822** G4
Babo, Indonesia, **735** F3
Babonde, Democratic Republic of the Congo, **809** E2
Babongo, Cameroon, **805** G3
Baboquivari Peak, *mountain peak*, U.S.A., **833** H6
Baboua, Central African Republic, **808** B1
Babruysk, Belarus, **783** B6
Babushkin, Russian Federation, **746** D2
Babušnica, Yugoslavia, **780** D4
Babuyan Channel, Philippines, **740** C2
Babuyan Islands, Philippines, **740** C2
Bač, Yugoslavia, **780** B3
Bắc Cạn, Vietnam, **739** E1
Bạc Liêu, Vietnam, **739** E4
Bắc Ninh, Vietnam, **739** E1
Bắc Quang, Vietnam, **739** E1
Bacaadweyn, Somalia, **807** G3
Bacabal, Brazil, **851** E4
Bacajá, *river*, Brazil, **850** C4
Bacalar, Mexico, **841** H5
Bacan, Pulau, *island*, Indonesia, **734** D3
Bacao, Philippines, **740** B4
Bacarra, Philippines, **740** C2
Bacău, Romania, **780** F2
Baccarat, France, **775** H2
Bachu, China, **748** C5
Back, *river*, Canada, **820** J3
Bačka Palanka, Yugoslavia, **780** B3
Bačka Topola, Yugoslavia, **780** B3
Backe, Sweden, **768** H5
Bäckefors, Sweden, **770** F3
Bački Petrovac, Yugoslavia, **780** B3
Baco, Mount, *mountain peak*, Philippines, **740** C3
Bacolod, Philippines, **740** C4
Bacqueville-en-Caux, France, **789** H5
Bacungan, Philippines, **740** B4
Bad Axe, U.S.A., **831** M4
Bad Bevensen, Germany, **772** E2
Bad Freienwalde, Germany, **773** G2
Bad Hersfeld, Germany, **772** D3
Bad Ischl, Austria, **772** F5
Bad Kissingen, Germany, **772** E3
Bad Kreuznach, Germany, **772** C4
Bad Mergentheim, Germany, **772** D4
Bad Neustadt an der Saale, Germany, **772** E3
Bad Oldesloe, Germany, **772** E2
Bad Orb, Germany, **772** D3
Bad Reichenhall, Germany, **772** F5
Bad Segeberg, Germany, **772** E2
Bad Waldsee, Germany, **772** D5
Badagara, India, **752** C4
Badahe, China, **751** H4
Badain Jaran Shamo, *desert*, China, **749** J5
Badajós, Amazonas, Brazil, **849** F5
Badajós, Pará, Brazil, **850** D4
Badajoz, Spain, **776** D3
Badalona, Spain, **777** J2
Badanah, Saudi Arabia, **803** H2
Badanloch, Loch, *lake*, Scotland, U.K., **792** E2
Baddo, *river*, Pakistan, **757** H3
Badéguichéri, Niger, **805** F2
Baden, Austria, **773** H5
Baden-Baden, Germany, **772** D4
Baden-Württemberg, *state*, Germany, **772** D4
Badger, Canada, **827** N5
Badin, Pakistan, **754** B4
Badiraguato, Mexico, **840** D3
Badoc, Philippines, **740** C2
Badong, China, **742** B2
Badou, Togo, **804** E3
Badovinci, Yugoslavia, **780** B3
Badr Ḥunayn, Saudi Arabia, **803** G4
Badu Island, Australia, **721** J1
Badulla, Sri Lanka, **753** E5
Baena, Spain, **776** E4
Baeza, Ecuador, **848** C4
Bafang, Cameroon, **808** B1
Bafatá, Guinea-Bissau, **804** B2
Baffa, Pakistan, **754** C2
Baffin, Cape, Canada, **821** M2
Baffin Bay, Canada/Greenland, **821** M2
Baffin Island, Canada, **821** M2
Bafia, Cameroon, **808** B2
Bafilo, Togo, **804** E3
Bafoulabé, Mali, **804** B2
Bafoussam, Cameroon, **808** B1
Bāfq, Iran, **757** G2
Bafra, Turkey, **760** E4
Bafra Burnu, *cape*, Turkey, **760** E4
Bafwasende, Democratic Republic of the Congo, **809** E2
Bagabag, Philippines, **740** C2
Bagac, Philippines, **740** C3
Bagaha, India, **755** F4
Bāgalkot, India, **752** C2
Bagamoyo, Tanzania, **809** G4
Baganga, Philippines, **740** D5
Bagani, Namibia, **810** D2
Bagansiapiapi, Indonesia, **736** C2
Bağarası, Turkey, **781** F7
Bagaroua, Niger, **805** E2
Bagata, Democratic Republic of the Congo, **808** C3
Bagatelle, Réunion, **813** A1
Bagdad, U.S.A., **832** G4
Bagé, Brazil, **857** F4
Bagenkop, Denmark, **770** E5
Bages et de Sigean, Étang de, *lake*, France, **775** F5
Bāgeshwar, India, **754** D3
Baggs, U.S.A., **833** K1
Baggy Point, England, U.K., **788** C3
Bāgh, India, **754** C5
Baghdād, Iraq, **803** H2
Bāghīn, Iran, **757** G2
Baghlān, Afghanistan, **754** B1
Bāghrān, Afghanistan, **754** A2
Bagn, Norway, **770** D2
Bagnères-de-Luchon, France, **774** E5
Bagno di Romagna, Italy, **778** C4
Bago, Philippines, **740** C4
Bagrationovsk, Russian Federation, **771** K5
Bagre, Brazil, **850** C3
Bagua Grande, Peru, **852** B1
Bagudo, Nigeria, **805** E2
Baguio, Philippines, **740** C2
Bagzane, Monts, *mountain peak*, Niger, **805** F1
Bahamas, *country*, Caribbean Sea, **817** R6
Baharampur, India, **755** G4
Bahāwalpur, Pakistan, **754** B3
Bahía, Islas de la, *islands*, Honduras, **838** D3
Bahia, *state*, Brazil, **855** F3
Bahía Asunción, Mexico, **840** B3
Bahía Blanca, Argentina, **856** D6
Bahía Bustamante, Argentina, **858** D2
Bahía de Caráquez, Ecuador, **848** B4
Bahía de los Ángeles, Mexico, **840** B2
Bahia de los Ángeles, U.S.A., **832** G7
Bahía Kino, Mexico, **840** C2
Bahía Laura, Argentina, **858** D3
Bahía Negra, Paraguay, **853** G5
Bahía Thetis, Argentina, **858** E5
Bahía Tortugas, Mexico, **840** B3
Bahir Dar, Ethiopia, **807** E2
Bahn, *river*, Germany, **772** E4
Baḥr al Jabal, *state*, Sudan, **809** F1
Baḥr an Nīl, *state*, Sudan, **803** F5
Bahraich, India, **755** E4
Bahrain, *country*, Asia, **730** F7
Bāhū Kalāt, Iran, **757** H3
Bahushewsk, Belarus, **783** C5
Bai, *river*, China, **742** C1
Bai Shan, *mountain peak*, China, **749** G4
Baia, Romania, **780** G3
Baia de Aramă, Romania, **780** D3
Baia de Arieș, Romania, **780** D2
Baía de Traição, Brazil, **851** G5
Baía dos Tigres, Angola, **810** B2
Baía Farta, Angola, **808** B5
Baia Mare, Romania, **780** D2
Baia Sprie, Romania, **780** D2
Baião, Brazil, **850** D4
Baïbokoum, Chad, **805** H3
Baibu, China, **743** D1
Baicheng, Jilin, China, **747** H3
Baicheng, Xinjiang Uygur Zizhiqu, China, **748** D4
Băicoi, Romania, **780** E3
Baie-Comeau, Canada, **826** G5
Baie-du-Poste, Canada, **826** E4
Baie du Tombeau, Mauritius, **813** C1
Baie-Johan-Beetz, Canada, **827** K4
Baie-St-Paul, Canada, **826** F6
Baie Verte, Canada, **827** N5
Baihao, China, **743** B3
Baihe, Hubei, China, **742** B1
Baihe, Jilin, China, **747** K4
Baijiao, China, **743** A4
Baikal, Lake *see* Baykal, Ozero, *lake*, Russian Federation, **746** D1
Bailang, China, **747** H3
Băile Govora, Romania, **780** E3
Băile Herculane, Romania, **780** D3
Băile Tușnad, Romania, **780** E2
Bailén, Spain, **777** F3
Băilești, Romania, **780** D3
Bailieborough, Ireland, **793** F4
Bailique, Brazil, **850** C3
Bailleul, France, **789** K4
Bailundo, Angola, **808** C5
Baima, Guangdong, China, **743** B3
Baima, Qinghai, China, **751** G2
Baimuru, Papua New Guinea, **726** B4
Bainang, China, **750** D3
Bainbridge, U.S.A., **835** K4
Bainet, Haiti, **839** G3
Baing, Indonesia, **734** C5
Bainville, U.S.A., **829** M2
Baiona, Spain, **776** C1
Baiquan, China, **747** J3
Bā'ir, Jordan, **761** D4
Bairab Co, *lake*, China, **755** E2
Bairagnia, India, **755** F4
Bairiki, Kiribati, **725** F4
Bairin Qiao, China, **747** G4
Bairin Youqi, China, **747** G4
Bairin Zuoqi, China, **747** G4
Bairnsdale, Australia, **721** K6
Bais, France, **774** D2
Baisha, China, **751** H3
Baishan, China, **747** J4
Baishui, *river*, China, **751** H2
Baisogala, Lithuania, **771** L5
Baitang, Guangdong, China, **743** C2
Baitang, Qinghai, China, **751** F2
Baitarani, *river*, India, **755** F5
Baixiang, China, **746** F5
Baixo, Ilhéu de, *island*, Madeira, Portugal, **813** C3
Baixo Longa, Angola, **808** C6
Baiyanghe, China, **748** F4
Baiyin, China, **746** D5
Baiyü, China, **751** F3
Baj Baj, India, **755** G5
Baja, Bahía, *bay*, San Andrés, Colombia, **859** B1
Baja, Hungary, **773** J5
Baja, Punta, *point*, Isla de Pascua (Easter Island), Chile, **859** B2
Baja, Punta, *point*, Mexico, **840** A2
Baja California, *peninsula*, Mexico, **840** B2
Baja California, *state*, Mexico, **840** A2
Baja California Sur, *state*, Mexico, **840** B3
Bājah, Tunisia, **779** B7
Bajamar, Islas Canarias, Spain, **813** A4
Bajestān, Iran, **757** G2
Bājil, Yemen, **756** D6
Bajina Bašta, Yugoslavia, **780** B4
Bajo Baudó, Colombia, **848** C3
Bajo Caracoles, Argentina, **858** C3
Bajoga, Nigeria, **805** G2
Bajovo Polje, Yugoslavia, **780** B4
Bajram Curri, Albania, **780** B4
Bakala, Central African Republic, **806** B3
Bakaoré, Chad, **806** B1
Bakauheni, Indonesia, **736** D4
Bakayan, Gunung, *mountain peak*, Indonesia, **737** G2
Bakchar, Russian Federation, **759** L1
Bakel, Senegal, **804** B2
Baker, California, U.S.A., **832** E4
Baker, *island*, Baker and Howland Islands, **725** G4
Baker, Montana, U.S.A., **829** M3
Baker, Mount, *mountain peak*, U.S.A., **828** D2
Baker and Howland Islands, *U.S. territory*, Pacific Ocean, **715** H1
Baker City, U.S.A., **828** F4
Baker Lake, Canada, **821** K3
Baker Lake, *lake*, Canada, **821** K3
Bakersfield, California, U.S.A., **832** D4
Bakersfield, Texas, U.S.A., **833** M6
Bakhtiyārpur, India, **755** F4
Bakhty, Kazakhstan, **748** D3
Bakı (Baku), Azerbaijan, **758** D4
Bakır, *river*, Turkey, **781** F6
Bakkafjörður, Iceland, **768** Z6
Bakkaflói, *bay*, Iceland, **768** Z6
Bakko, Norway, **770** D3
Bakloh, India, **754** C2
Bako, Côte d'Ivoire, **804** C3
Bako, Ethiopia, **807** E3
Bakony, *mountain range*, Hungary, **773** H5
Bakool, *administrative region*, Somalia, **807** F4
Bakop, Papua New Guinea, **726** D4
Bakouma, Central African Republic, **808** D1
Bakoumba, Gabon, **808** B3
Baku *see* Bakı, Azerbaijan, **758** D4
Bakutis Coast, *region*, Antarctica, **862** B6
Bala, Cerros de, *mountain range*, Bolivia, **853** E3
Bala, Wales, U.K., **788** D2
Balabac, Philippines, **740** B4
Balabac Island, Philippines, **740** B5
Ba'labakk, Lebanon, **761** D2
Balabanovo, Russian Federation, **783** F5
Bālāghāt, India, **754** E5
Bālāghāt Range, *mountain range*, India, **752** C2
Balaguer, Spain, **777** H2
Balaka, Malawi, **809** F5
Balakhta, Russian Federation, **759** N1
Balakovo, Russian Federation, **758** D2
Balambangan, Pulau, *island*, Malaysia, **737** F1
Bălan, Romania, **780** E2
Balanga, Philippines, **740** C3
Balāngīr, India, **755** E5
Balashikha, Russian Federation, **783** F5
Balashov, Russian Federation, **782** F2
Balassagyarmat, Hungary, **773** J4
Balaton, *lake*, Hungary, **773** H5
Balatonszentgyörgy, Hungary, **773** H5
Balazote, Spain, **777** F3
Balbi, Mount, *mountain peak*, Papua New Guinea, **726** E2
Balbina, Brazil, **849** G4
Balbina, Represa de, *reservoir*, Brazil, **849** G4
Balbriggan, Ireland, **793** F4
Balcarce, Argentina, **857** E5
Balchik, Bulgaria, **780** G4
Balclutha, New Zealand, **719** B8
Balcones Escarpment, U.S.A., **834** C5
Bald Knob, U.S.A., **834** G2
Bald Mountain, *mountain peak*, U.S.A., **832** C1
Balderton, England, U.K., **789** G1
Baldock, England, U.K., **789** G3
Baldone, Latvia, **771** M4
Baldwin, Florida, U.S.A., **835** M4
Baldwin, Michigan, U.S.A., **831** L4
Baldwin, Wisconsin, U.S.A., **830** G3
Baldy Peak, *mountain peak*, U.S.A., **833** J5
Baleares, Islas (Balearic Islands), *islands*, Spain, **777** J3
Balearic Islands *see* Baleares, Islas, *islands*, Spain, **777** J3
Baleh, *river*, Malaysia, **737** F2
Baleia, Ponta da, *point*, Brazil, **855** F4
Băleni, Romania, **780** E3
Baler, Philippines, **740** C3
Baler Bay, Philippines, **740** C3
Bāleshwar, India, **755** F5
Baley, Russian Federation, **746** G2
Baléya, Mali, **804** B2
Baléyara, Niger, **805** E2
Balfour, Canada, **823** L7
Balfour, Orkney, Scotland, U.K., **792** G1

Betrandraka, Madagascar, **812** B4
Betroka, Madagascar, **812** B5
Betsiboka, *river*, Madagascar, **812** B4
Bettiah, India, **755** F4
Bettna, Sweden, **771** H3
Bettyhill, Scotland, U.K., **792** E2
Betül Bāzār, India, **754** D5
Betws-y-coed, Wales, U.K., **788** D1
Beulah, U.S.A., **830** B2
Beverley, England, U.K., **791** H4
Beverly, U.S.A., **828** E3
Beverly Hills, U.S.A., **832** D4
Beverstedt, Germany, **772** D2
Bewdley, England, U.K., **788** E2
Bexhill, England, U.K., **789** H4
Bey Dağı, *mountain peak*, Turkey, **760** E5
Beyağaç, Turkey, **781** G7
Beykoz, Turkey, **781** G5
Beyla, Guinea, **804** C3
Bēylul, Eritrea, **807** F2
Beyneu, Kazakhstan, **758** F3
Beyra, Somalia, **807** G3
Beyşehir Gölü, *lake*, Turkey, **760** D5
Bezaha, Madagascar, **812** A5
Bezhanitsy, Russian Federation, **783** B4
Bezhetsk, Russian Federation, **783** F4
Béziers, France, **775** F5
Bhabua, India, **755** E4
Bhadarwāh, India, **754** C2
Bhadra Reservoir, India, **752** C3
Bhadrak, India, **755** F5
Bhadrapur, Nepal, **755** G4
Bhadrāvati, India, **752** C3
Bhāgalpur, India, **755** F4
Bhairab Bāzār, Bangladesh, **750** D4
Bhairahawa, Nepal, **755** E4
Bhakkar, Pakistan, **754** B3
Bhaktapur, Nepal, **755** F4
Bhamo, Myanmar, **741** C2
Bhandāra, India, **754** D5
Bhānvad, India, **754** B5
Bharatpur, India, **754** D4
Bharūch, India, **754** C5
Bhatinda, India, **754** C3
Bhatkal, India, **752** C3
Bhatpara, India, **755** G5
Bhāvnagar, India, **754** C5
Bhawānipatna, India, **755** E6
Bheigeir, Beinn, *mountain peak*, Scotland, U.K., **792** C5
Bheri, *river*, Nepal, **755** E3
Bhilai, India, **755** E5
Bhīlwāra, India, **754** C4
Bhima, *river*, India, **752** C2
Bhīmavaram, India, **753** E2
Bhind, India, **754** D4
Bhīnmāl, India, **754** C4
Bhiwandi, India, **752** C2
Bhiwāni, India, **754** D3
Bhokardan, India, **754** C5
Bhopāl, India, **754** D5
Bhopālpatnam, India, **752** E2
Bhor, India, **752** C2
Bhuban, India, **755** F5
Bhubaneshwar, India, **755** F5
Bhuj, India, **754** B5
Bhumiphon Reservoir, Thailand, **738** C2
Bhusāwal, India, **754** C5
Bhutan, *country*, Asia, **730** L7
Bia, Phou, *mountain peak*, Laos, **739** D2
Biała, *river*, Poland, **773** K4
Biała Piska, Poland, **773** L2
Biała Podlaska, Poland, **773** L2
Białogard, Poland, **773** H2
Białystok, Poland, **773** L2
Biak, Indonesia, **735** G3
Biak, Pulau, *island*, Indonesia, **735** G3
Bianga, Central African Republic, **808** D2
Biankouma, Côte d'Ivoire, **804** C3
Bianzhuang, China, **742** D1
Biaora, India, **754** D5
Biārjomand, Iran, **758** F5
Biaro, Pulau, *island*, Indonesia, **734** D2
Biarritz, France, **774** D5
Biasca, Switzerland, **775** J3
Biaza, Russian Federation, **759** K1
Bibā, Egypt, **803** F3
Bibai, Japan, **745** H2
Bibala, Angola, **808** B5
Bibas, Gabon, **808** B2
Bibbiena, Italy, **778** C4
Bibémi, Cameroon, **805** G3
Biberach an der Riß, Germany, **772** D4
Bibiani, Ghana, **804** D3
Bibirevo, Russian Federation, **783** D4
Biblos *see* Jubayl, Lebanon, **761** C2
Bibury, England, U.K., **789** F3
Bicaz, Romania, **780** F2
Bicester, England, U.K., **789** F3
Biche, Trinidad, Trinidad and Tobago, **859** C4
Bichena, Ethiopia, **807** E2
Bichura, Russian Federation, **746** D2
Bickleigh, Central Devon, England, U.K., **788** D4
Bickleigh, W. Devon, England, U.K., **788** C4
Bida, Nigeria, **805** F3
Bidar, India, **752** D2
Biddeford, U.S.A., **836** E3
Biddle, U.S.A., **829** M4
Biddulph, England, U.K., **788** E1
Bidean nam Bian, *mountain peak*, Scotland, U.K., **792** D4
Bideford, England, U.K., **788** C3
Bidjovagge, Norway, **769** L2
Bidor, Malaysia, **736** C1
Bié, *province*, Angola, **808** C5
Bieber, U.S.A., **828** D6
Biecz, Poland, **773** K4
Biel, Switzerland, **775** H3
Bielefeld, Germany, **772** D3
Bieler See, *lake*, Switzerland, **775** H3
Biella, Italy, **778** B3
Bielsk Podlaski, Poland, **773** L2
Bielsko-Biała, Poland, **773** J4
Biên Hòa, Vietnam, **739** E4
Bienvenue, French Guiana, **850** C2
Bienville, Lac, *lake*, Canada, **826** E2
Biescas, Spain, **777** G1
Bieszczady, *mountain range*, Poland, **773** L4
Biferno, *river*, Italy, **779** E5
Bifoun, Gabon, **808** B3
Big Bar, U.S.A., **832** B1
Big Bay, New Zealand, **719** A7
Big Beaver, Canada, **823** S7
Big Bend, Swaziland, **811** F4
Big Blue, *river*, U.S.A., **830** E5
Big Creek, Canada, **822** H6
Big Creek, U.S.A., **828** G4
Big Falls, U.S.A., **830** G1
Big Lake, U.S.A., **834** B4
Big Piney, U.S.A., **829** J5
Big Quill Lake, Canada, **824** B5
Big Rapids, U.S.A., **831** L4
Big Sand Lake, Canada, **824** E3
Big Sandy, U.S.A., **829** J2
Big Snow Mountain, *mountain peak*, U.S.A., **829** K3
Big South Cape Island (Taukihepa), New Zealand, **719** A8
Big Spring, U.S.A., **834** B3
Big Sur, U.S.A., **832** C3
Big Timber, U.S.A., **829** K4
Big Trout Lake, Canada, **824** K5
Big Trout Lake, *lake*, Canada, **824** J5
Big Trout, *river*, Canada, **825** K4
Big Water, U.S.A., **833** H3
Biga, Turkey, **781** F5
Bigadiç, Turkey, **781** G6
Bigbury Bay, England, U.K., **788** C4
Bigfork, U.S.A., **828** G2
Biggar, Canada, **823** R5
Biggar, Scotland, U.K., **792** F5
Bigge Island, Australia, **720** E1
Biggleswade, England, U.K., **789** G2
Bighorn, *river*, U.S.A., **829** K4
Bighorn Lake, U.S.A., **829** K4
Bighorn Mountains, *mountain range*, U.S.A., **829** L4
Bignona, Senegal, **804** A2
Bigstone, *river*, Canada, **824** G4
Bihać, Bosnia and Herzegovina, **778** E3
Bihār, *state*, India, **755** F4
Bihār Sharif, India, **755** F4
Biharamulo, Tanzania, **809** F3
Bijagós, Arquipélago dos, *islands*, Guinea-Bissau, **804** A2
Bijāpur, India, **752** C2
Bijāwar, India, **754** D4
Bijeljina, Bosnia and Herzegovina, **780** B3
Bijelo Polje, Yugoslavia, **780** B4
Bijie, China, **751** H4
Bijni, India, **755** G4
Bijnor, India, **754** D3
Bikāner, India, **754** C3
Bikar, *island*, Marshall Islands, **725** F3
Bikin, *river*, Russian Federation, **747** L3
Bikin, Russian Federation, **747** L3
Bikini, *island*, Marshall Islands, **724** E3
Bikita, Zimbabwe, **811** F3
Bikoro, Democratic Republic of the Congo, **808** C3
Bikubiti, *mountain range*, Libya, **802** C4
Bílá, Czech Republic, **773** J4
Bila, *river*, Indonesia, **736** B2
Bila Tserkva, Ukraine, **782** D3
Bilaspur, Himāchal Pradesh, India, **754** D3
Bilāspur, Madhya Pradesh, India, **755** E5
Bilauktaung Range, *mountain range*, Myanmar/Thailand, **738** C3
Bilbao, Spain, **777** F1
Bilbays, Egypt, **761** A4
Bilbor, Romania, **780** E2
Bíldudalur, Iceland, **768** X7
Bílé Karpaty, *mountain range*, Slovakia, **773** H4
Bileča, Bosnia and Herzegovina, **778** G4
Bilecik, *province*, Turkey, **781** G5
Bilecik, Turkey, **781** G5
Biled, Romania, **780** C3
Biłgoraj, Poland, **773** L3
Bilhorod-Dnistrovs'kyy, Ukraine, **780** H2
Bili, Democratic Republic of the Congo, **808** E2
Bilibino, Russian Federation, **785** T3
Bilimora, India, **754** C5
Biliran Island, Philippines, **740** D4
Bilisht, Albania, **781** C5
Bill, U.S.A., **829** M5
Bill of Portland, *point*, England, U.K., **788** E4
Bill Williams, *river*, U.S.A., **832** G4
Billericay, England, U.K., **789** H3
Billingham, England, U.K., **791** G3
Billinghay, England, U.K., **789** G1
Billings, U.S.A., **829** K4
Billingshurst, England, U.K., **789** G3
Billond, Denmark, **770** D5
Billsta, Sweden, **768** J5
Bilma, Niger, **802** B5
Bilo gora, *mountain range*, Croatia, **778** F3
Biloela, Australia, **721** L3
Biloku, Guyana, **849** G4
Biloxi, U.S.A., **835** H4
Bilpa Morea Claypan, *lake*, Australia, **721** J3
Bilqas Qism Awwal, Egypt, **761** A4
Bilston, Scotland, U.K., **792** F5
Biltine, Chad, **806** B2
Biltine, *prefecture*, Chad, **806** B2
Bilto, Norway, **768** K2
Bilton, England, U.K., **791** H4
Bilugyun Island, Myanmar, **741** C4
Bilungala, Indonesia, **734** C2
Bilüü, Mongolia, **748** F2
Bilwascarma, Nicaragua, **838** E4
Bilyayivka, Ukraine, **780** H2
Bima, Indonesia, **737** G5
Bimbila, Ghana, **804** E3
Bimbo, Central African Republic, **808** C2
Bimini Islands, Bahamas, **835** N7
Bin Qirdān, Tunisia, **802** B2
Bin Xian, Heilongjiang, China, **747** J3
Bin Xian, Shaanxi, China, **751** J2
Binbrook, England, U.K., **791** H4
Binder, Chad, **805** G3
Bindu, Democratic Republic of the Congo, **808** C4
Bindura, Zimbabwe, **809** F6
Binéfar, Spain, **777** H2
Binga, Monte, *mountain peak*, Mozambique, **811** F2
Binga, Zimbabwe, **811** E2
Bingerville, Côte d'Ivoire, **804** D3
Bingham, England, U.K., **789** G2
Bingham, U.S.A., **833** K5
Binghamton, U.S.A., **836** C3
Bingley, England, U.K., **791** G4
Bingöl, Turkey, **760** F5
Binhai, China, **742** D1
Binjai, Indonesia, **736** B2
Binna, Raas, *point*, Somalia, **807** H2
Binscarth, Canada, **824** D6
Binser, Mount, *mountain peak*, New Zealand, **719** C6
Bint Jubayl, Lebanon, **761** C3
Bintan, Pulau, *island*, Indonesia, **736** D2
Bintang, Gunung, *mountain peak*, Malaysia, **736** C1
Bintuhan, Indonesia, **736** C4
Bintulu, Malaysia, **737** F2
Bintun, Indonesia, **724** B5
Bintuni, Teluk, *bay*, Indonesia, **735** F3
Binyang, China, **742** B4
Binzhou, China, **747** G5
Bío Bío, *administrative region*, Chile, **856** B5
Bio Bio, *river*, Chile, **856** B5
Bioco, Isla de, *island*, Equatorial Guinea, **808** A2
Biograd na Moru, Croatia, **778** E4
Biokovo, *mountain peak*, Croatia, **778** E4
Bīr, India, **752** C2
Bir, Ras, *point*, Djibouti, **807** F2
Bir Di, Sudan, **806** C3
Bir Enzarán, Western Sahara, **800** D4
Bir Ghbalou, Algeria, **777** J4
Bi'r Ḩasanah, Egypt, **761** B4
Bi'r Jifjāfah, Egypt, **761** B4
Bîr Mogreïn, Mauritania, **800** D3
Bira, Indonesia, **734** C4
Bira, Russian Federation, **747** L2
Birāk, Libya, **802** B3
Birao, Central African Republic, **806** B2
Birātnagar, Nepal, **755** F4
Birch, *river*, Canada, **823** N2
Birch Lake, Canada, **824** H6
Birch Mountains, *mountain range*, Canada, **823** M3
Birch River, Canada, **824** D5
Bircot, Ethiopia, **807** F3
Bircza, Poland, **773** L4
Bird Island, South Georgia, **859** A3
Birdsville, Australia, **721** H4
Birecik, Turkey, **803** G1
Bireuen, Indonesia, **736** B1
Birigüi, Brazil, **854** C5
Bīrjand, Iran, **757** G2
Birkeland, Norway, **770** D3
Birkenhead, England, U.K., **790** E4
Birlik, north of Töle Bī, Kazakhstan, **748** B3
Birlik, south of Töle Bī, Kazakhstan, **748** B4
Birmingham, England, U.K., **789** F2
Birmingham, U.S.A., **835** J3
Birnie, *island*, Kiribati, **725** G5
Birnin-Gaouré, Niger, **805** E2
Birnin Gwari, Nigeria, **805** F2
Birnin Kebbi, Nigeria, **805** E2
Birnin Konni, Niger, **805** F2
Birnin Kudu, Nigeria, **805** F2
Birnin-Yauri, Nigeria, **805** E2
Birobidzhan, Russian Federation, **747** L2
Birr, Ireland, **793** E4
Birshoghyr, Kazakhstan, **758** F3
Birsk, Russian Federation, **758** F1
Birstall, England, U.K., **789** F2
Biru, China, **750** E3
Biržai, Lithuania, **771** M4
Birži, Latvia, **771** M4
Bisbee, Arizona, U.S.A., **833** J6
Bisbee, North Dakota, U.S.A., **830** D1
Biscarrosse, France, **774** D4
Biscarrosse et de Parentis, Étang de, *lake*, France, **774** D4
Biscay, Bay of, France, **774** B3
Biscay Plain, *underwater feature*, Atlantic Ocean, **867** G2
Biscotasing, Canada, **831** M2
Bisert', Russian Federation, **758** F1
Bisertsi, Bulgaria, **780** F4
Biševo, *island*, Croatia, **778** F4
Bishan, Singapore, **736** K6
Bishkek, Kyrgyzstan, **748** B4
Bishnupur, India, **755** F5
Bisho, South Africa, **811** E5
Bishop, California, U.S.A., **832** D3
Bishop, Texas, U.S.A., **834** D6
Bishop Auckland, England, U.K., **791** G3
Bishop's Cleeve, England, U.K., **788** E3
Bishop's Lydeard, England, U.K., **788** D3
Bishops Stortford, England, U.K., **789** H3
Bishui, China, **747** H1
Biskra, Algeria, **801** H2
Biskupiec, Poland, **773** K2
Bislig, Philippines, **740** D4
Bismarck, Missouri, U.S.A., **830** H7
Bismarck, North Dakota, U.S.A., **830** C2
Bismarck Archipelago, Papua New Guinea, **726** B3
Bismarck Sea, Papua New Guinea, **724** C6
Bismark, Germany, **772** E2
Bismark Range, *mountain range*, Papua New Guinea, **726** B4
Bismil, Turkey, **803** H1
Bison, U.S.A., **830** B3
Bissau, Guinea-Bissau, **804** A2
Bissaula, Nigeria, **805** G3
Bissikrima, Guinea, **804** B2

Bolena, Democratic Republic of the Congo, **808** C2
Bolesławiec, Poland, **773** G3
Bolgatanga, Ghana, **804** D2
Bolhrad, Ukraine, **780** G3
Boli, China, **747** K3
Boli, Sudan, **806** C3
Bolia, Democratic Republic of the Congo, **808** C3
Boliden, Sweden, **768** K4
Bolinao, Philippines, **740** B2
Bolívar, Bolivia, **853** E3
Bolívar, Colombia, **848** C3
Bolivar, Missouri, U.S.A., **830** G7
Bolívar, Peru, **852** C2
Bolívar, Pico, *mountain peak*, Venezuela, **849** D2
Bolivar, Tennessee, U.S.A., **835** H2
Bolivia, *country*, South America, **845** F5
Boljevac, Yugoslavia, **780** C4
Bolkhov, Russian Federation, **783** F6
Bollnäs, Sweden, **770** H2
Bollons Island, Antipodes Islands, New Zealand, **719** P15
Bollstabruk, Sweden, **771** H1
Bollullos par del Condado, Spain, **776** D4
Bolobo, Democratic Republic of the Congo, **808** C3
Bologna, Italy, **778** C3
Bolognesi, Central Peru, **852** C2
Bolognesi, N. Peru, **852** D2
Bologovo, Russian Federation, **783** C4
Bologoye, Russian Federation, **783** E4
Bolomba, Democratic Republic of the Congo, **808** C2
Bolon', Ozero, *lake*, Russian Federation, **747** M2
Bolon', Russian Federation, **747** M2
Bolondo, Democratic Republic of the Congo, **808** C3
Bolong, Philippines, **740** C5
Bolotnoye, Russian Federation, **759** L1
Bolsena, Italy, **778** D4
Bolsena, Lago di, *lake*, Italy, **778** C4
Bol'shakovo, Russian Federation, **771** K5
Bol'shaya Belaya, *river*, Russian Federation, **746** C1
Bol'shaya Glushitsa, Russian Federation, **758** E2
Bol'shaya Kinel', *river*, Russian Federation, **758** E2
Bol'sherech'ye, Russian Federation, **759** J1
Bol'shevik, Ostrov, *island*, Russian Federation, **785** M2
Bol'shoy Begichev, Ostrov, *island*, Russian Federation, **785** N2
Bol'shoy Kavkaz (Caucasus), *mountain range*, Asia/Europe, **758** D4
Bol'shoy Lyakhovskiy, Ostrov, *island*, Russian Federation, **785** R2
Bol'shoy Uvat, Ozero, *lake*, Russian Federation, **759** H1
Bol'shoy Yenisey, *river*, Russian Federation, **759** P2
Bol'shoye Pole, Russian Federation, **783** B2
Bol'shoye Sorokino, Russian Federation, **759** H1
Bol'shoye Zaborov'ye, Russian Federation, **783** D3
Bolsover, England, U.K., **789** F1
Bolt Head, *point*, England, U.K., **788** D4
Bolton, England, U.K., **790** F4
Bolubolu, Papua New Guinea, **726** C5
Boluntay, China, **749** G5
Boluo, China, **739** G1
Bolva, *river*, Russian Federation, **783** E5
Bolvadin, Turkey, **803** F1
Bolyston, Canada, **827** L7
Bolzano, Italy, **778** C2
Bom Comércio, Brazil, **853** E2
Bom Jardim, Amazonas, Brazil, **853** E2
Bom Jardim, Pará, Brazil, **850** C4
Bom Jesus, Brazil, **857** G3
Bom Jesus da Lapa, Brazil, **855** E3
Bom Retiro, Brazil, **857** H3
Boma, Democratic Republic of the Congo, **808** B4
Bomassa, Congo, **808** C2
Bombala, Australia, **721** K6
Bombay *see* Mumbai, India, **752** C2
Bombay Beach, U.S.A., **832** F5
Bomboma, Democratic Republic of the Congo, **808** C2
Bomi, China, **751** E3
Bomili, Democratic Republic of the Congo, **809** E2
Bømlo, *island*, Norway, **770** B3
Bomongo, Democratic Republic of the Congo, **808** C2
Bon, Cap, *cape*, Tunisia, **779** C7
Bon Air, U.S.A., **836** B6
Bonaire, *island*, Netherlands Antilles, **859** A4
Bonanza, Nicaragua, **838** D4
Bonao, Dominican Republic, **839** H3
Bonaparte, *river*, Canada, **822** J6
Bonaparte Archipelago, *islands*, Australia, **720** E1
Bonaparte Lake, Canada, **822** J6
Bonar Bridge, Scotland, U.K., **792** E3
Bonasse, Trinidad, Trinidad and Tobago, **859** C4
Bonaventure, Canada, **826** J5
Bonavista, Canada, **827** Q5
Bonavista Bay, Canada, **827** Q5
Bondo, Angola, **808** C6
Bondo, Democratic Republic of the Congo, **808** D2
Bondoukou, Côte d'Ivoire, **804** D3
Bondoukui, Burkina Faso, **804** D2
Bondowoso, Indonesia, **737** F4
Bondurant, U.S.A., **829** J5
Bone, Teluk, *bay*, Indonesia, **734** C3
Bonerate, Pulau, *island*, Indonesia, **734** C4
Bo'ness, Scotland, U.K., **792** F4
Bonete, Cerro, *mountain peak*, Argentina, **856** C3
Bonete, Cerro, *mountain peak*, Bolivia, **853** E5
Bonete, Spain, **777** G3
Bonfinópolis, Brazil, **854** D4
Bông Lông, Cambodia, **739** E3
Bonga, Ethiopia, **807** E3
Bongabong, Philippines, **740** C3
Bongandanga, Democratic Republic of the Congo, **808** D2
Bongo, Democratic Republic of the Congo, **808** D2
Bongor, Chad, **805** H2
Bongos, Massif des, *mountain range*, Central African Republic, **806** B3
Bongouanou, Côte d'Ivoire, **804** D3
Bonham, U.S.A., **834** D3
Bonifacio, Corse, France, **779** B5
Bonifacio, Strait of, Mediterranean, **766** E7
Bonifay, U.S.A., **835** K4
Bonin Trench, *underwater feature*, Pacific Ocean, **868** D3
Bonito, Brazil, **854** B5
Bonito, Pico, *mountain peak*, Honduras, **838** D4
Bonn, Germany, **772** C3
Bonners Ferry, U.S.A., **828** F2
Bonneville, France, **775** H3
Bonny, Bight of, *gulf*, Nigeria, **808** A2
Bonny, Nigeria, **808** A2
Bonnyrigg, Scotland, U.K., **792** F5
Bonnyville, Canada, **823** P4
Bono, U.S.A., **834** G2
Bonorva, Sardegna, Italy, **779** B5
Bonoua, Côte d'Ivoire, **804** D3
Bontang, Indonesia, **737** G2
Bontoc, Philippines, **740** C2
Bonyhád, Hungary, **773** J5
Boola, Guinea, **804** C3
Booneville, U.S.A., **835** H2
Bööntsagaan Nuur, *lake*, Mongolia, **749** H3
Boonville, U.S.A., **836** C3
Boorama, Somalia, **807** F3
Boosaaso, Somalia, **807** G2
Boothia, Gulf of, Canada, **821** K2
Boothia Peninsula, Canada, **821** K2
Bootle, England, U.K., **790** E4
Booué, Gabon, **808** B3
Boqueirão, Brazil, **857** G4
Boquete, Panama, **839** E5
Boquillas del Carmen, Mexico, **840** E2
Boquirão, Serra do, *mountain range*, Brazil, **857** F3
Bor, Czech Republic, **772** F4
Bor, Russian Federation, **783** E3
Bor, Sudan, **806** D3
Bor, Turkey, **760** D5
Bor, Yugoslavia, **780** D3
Bor-Üdzüür, Mongolia, **749** G3
Bora Bora, *island*, French Polynesia, **723** F2
Borah Peak, *mountain peak*, U.S.A., **828** H4
Boran, Kazakhstan, **748** E2
Borang, Tanjong, *point*, Indonesia, **735** F4
Borås, Sweden, **770** F4
Borāzjān, Iran, **756** F3
Borba, Brazil, **849** G5
Borborema, Planalto da, *plateau*, Brazil, **847** J4
Borchgrevink Coast, *region*, Antarctica, **862** D8
Bordeaux, France, **774** D4
Borden, Canada, **823** R5
Borden Island, Canada, **820** H2
Bordertown, Australia, **721** J6
Bordj Bou Arreridj, Algeria, **801** G1
Bordj Messouda, Algeria, **801** H2
Bordj Mokhtar, Algeria, **801** G4
Bordj Omar Driss, Algeria, **801** H3
Boré, Mali, **804** D1
Boreray, *island*, Scotland, U.K., **792** B3
Borgarfjörður, Iceland, **768** Z7
Borgarnes, Iceland, **768** X7
Borgefjellet, *mountain range*, Norway, **768** F4
Borger, U.S.A., **834** B2
Borgholm, Sweden, **771** H4
Borgo San Dalmazzo, France, **775** H4
Borgo San Lorenzo, Italy, **778** C4
Borgo Valsugara, Italy, **778** C2
Borgomanero, Italy, **778** B3
Borgund, Norway, **770** C2
Borhoyn Tal, Mongolia, **746** E4
Bori, India, **754** D5
Borisoglebsk, Russian Federation, **782** F2
Borisovo-Sudskoye, Russian Federation, **783** F3
Boriziny, Madagascar, **812** B4
Borja, Peru, **848** C5
Borja, Spain, **777** G2
Borken, Germany, **772** C3
Borkou, *physical feature*, Chad, **802** C5
Borkou-Ennedi-Tibesti, *prefecture*, Chad, **802** C5
Borkum, *island*, Germany, **772** C2
Borlänge, Sweden, **770** G2
Bormio, Italy, **778** C2
Borna, Germany, **772** F3
Borneo, *island*, Brunei/Indonesia/Malaysia, **737** F2
Bornholm, *island*, Denmark, **770** G5
Borno, *state*, Nigeria, **805** G2
Bornova, Turkey, **802** E1
Borodino, Russian Federation, **759** P1
Borodino, Ukraine, **780** G2
Borodinskoye, Russian Federation, **783** B2
Borohoro Shan, *mountain range*, China, **748** D3
Borok, Russian Federation, **783** C3
Boroko, Indonesia, **734** C2
Boromata, Central African Republic, **806** B2
Boromo, Burkina Faso, **804** D2
Borongan, Philippines, **740** D4
Boronów, Poland, **773** J3
Borotou, Côte d'Ivoire, **804** C3
Boroughbridge, England, U.K., **791** G3
Borovichi, Pskovskaya Oblast', Russian Federation, **783** B4
Borovichi, Novgorodskaya Oblast', Russian Federation, **783** D3
Borovoy, Russian Federation, **769** R4
Borovskoy, Kazakhstan, **758** G2
Borre, Denmark, **770** F5
Borrisokane, Ireland, **793** D5
Borrisoleigh, Ireland, **793** E5
Borroloola, Australia, **721** H2
Börrum, Sweden, **771** H3
Borșa, Romania, **780** E2
Borsec, Romania, **780** E2
Børselv, Norway, **769** M1
Borshchiv, Ukraine, **780** F1
Borshchovochnyy Khrebet, *mountain range*, Russian Federation, **747** G1
Borth, Wales, U.K., **788** C2
Börtnan, Sweden, **768** F5
Borūjerd, Iran, **756** E2
Borups Corners, Canada, **824** H7
Borve, Scotland, U.K., **792** C3
Boryslav, Ukraine, **773** L4
Borzya, Russian Federation, **746** G2
Bosa, Sardegna, Italy, **779** B5
Bosagha, Kazakhstan, **748** B3
Bosanska Dubica, Bosnia and Herzegovina, **778** F3
Bosanski Novi, Bosnia and Herzegovina, **778** F3
Bosanski Petrovac, Bosnia and Herzegovina, **778** F3
Bosavi, Mount, *mountain peak*, Papua New Guinea, **726** A4
Boscastle, England, U.K., **788** C4
Boscobel, U.S.A., **830** H4
Bose, China, **751** H5
Boshan, China, **747** G5
Bosherston, Wales, U.K., **788** C3
Bosilegrad, Yugoslavia, **780** D4
Boskamp, Suriname, **850** B2
Boslanti, Suriname, **850** B2
Bosler, U.S.A., **829** M6
Bosna, *river*, Bosnia and Herzegovina, **778** G3
Bosnia and Herzegovina, *country*, Europe, **764** F7
Bosobolo, Democratic Republic of the Congo, **808** C2
Bosporus *see* Istanbul Boğazı, *strait*, Turkey, **781** G5
Bossembélé, Central African Republic, **808** C1
Bossentélé, Central African Republic, **808** C1
Bossier City, U.S.A., **834** F3
Bostan, China, **748** E5
Bostān, Pakistan, **754** A3
Bosten Hu, *lake*, China, **748** E4
Boston, England, U.K., **789** G2
Boston, U.S.A., **836** E3
Boston Bar, Canada, **822** J7
Boston Mountains, *mountain range*, U.S.A., **834** F2
Boston Spa, England, U.K., **791** G4
Bot Makak, Cameroon, **808** B2
Botād, India, **754** B5
Botany Bay, Australia, **721** L5
Boteå, Sweden, **771** H1
Boteka, Democratic Republic of the Congo, **808** C3
Botemola, Democratic Republic of the Congo, **808** C3
Botevgrad, Bulgaria, **780** D4
Bothel, England, U.K., **790** E3
Bothnia, Gulf of, Finland/Sweden, **771** J2
Boticas, Portugal, **776** D2
Botna, *river*, Moldova, **780** G2
Botngård, Norway, **768** D5
Boto-Pasi, Suriname, **850** B2
Botolan, Philippines, **740** C3
Botoșani, Romania, **780** F2
Botou, China, **746** G5
Botsmark, Sweden, **768** K4
Botswana, *country*, Africa, **797** H9
Botte Donato, Monte, *mountain peak*, Italy, **779** F6
Bottenviken Perämeri, *gulf*, Finland/Sweden, **769** L4
Bottineau, U.S.A., **830** C1
Bottrop, Germany, **772** C3
Botucatu, Brazil, **857** H2
Botuporã, Brazil, **855** E3
Bou Ismaïl, Algeria, **777** J4
Bou Izakarn, Morocco, **800** E3
Bou Kadir, Algeria, **777** H4
Bou Naceur, Jbel, *mountain peak*, Morocco, **801** F2
Bou Saâda, Algeria, **777** K5
Bou Salem, Tunisia, **779** B7
Bouaflé, Côte d'Ivoire, **804** C3
Bouaké, Côte d'Ivoire, **804** C3
Bouandougou, Côte d'Ivoire, **804** C3
Bouar, Central African Republic, **808** C1
Bouârfa, Morocco, **801** F2
Bouble, *river*, France, **775** F3
Bouca, Central African Republic, **806** A3
Bouchegouf, Algeria, **779** A7
Boudenib, Morocco, **801** F2
Boudoua, Central African Republic, **808** C2
Bouenza, *administrative region*, Congo, **808** B3
Bougainville Island, Papua New Guinea, **726** E8
Boughessa, Mali, **801** G5
Bougouni, Mali, **804** C2
Bougtob, Algeria, **801** G2
Bougzoul, Algeria, **777** J5
Bouillon, Belgium, **772** B4
Bouira, Algeria, **777** J4
Boulder, Colorado, U.S.A., **833** L1
Boulder, Montana, U.S.A., **829** H3
Boulder, Utah, U.S.A., **833** H3
Boulder, Wyoming, U.S.A., **829** K5
Boulder City, U.S.A, **832** F4
Boulemane, Morocco, **801** F2
Boulia, Australia, **721** H3
Boulmer, England, U.K., **791** G2
Boulogne-Billancourt, France, **774** F2
Boulogne-sur-Mer, France, **774** E1
Boulouba, Central African Republic, **806** B3

Bouloupari, New Caledonia, **727** A3
Boumango, Gabon, **808** B3
Boumba, *river*, Cameroon, **808** B2
Bouna, Côte d'Ivoire, **804** D3
Boundary Peak, *mountain peak*, U.S.A., **832** D3
Boundiali, Côte d'Ivoire, **804** C3
Boundji, Congo, **808** C3
Bounty Islands, New Zealand, **719** N14
Bounty Trough, *underwater feature*, Pacific Ocean, **868** F7
Bourail, New Caledonia, **727** A3
Bourbourg, France, **789** K4
Bourem, Mali, **804** D1
Bourg-en-Bresse, France, **775** G3
Bourg-Saint-Maurice, France, **775** H4
Bourganeuf, France, **774** E4
Bourges, France, **774** F3
Bourget, Lac du, *lake*, France, **775** G4
Bourgogne, *administrative region*, France, **775** F3
Bourke, Australia, **721** K5
Bourne, England, U.K., **789** G2
Bournemouth, England, U.K., **789** F4
Bournemouth, *unitary authority*, England, U.K., **789** F4
Bourtoutou, Chad, **806** B2
Bouse, U.S.A., **832** F5
Boussac, France, **774** F3
Bousso, Chad, **805** H2
Boutilimit, Mauritania, **804** B1
Bouvet Island, *Norwegian dependency*, Atlantic Ocean, **862** D1
Bouza, Niger, **805** F2
Bova Marina, Sicilia, Italy, **779** E7
Bovalino Marina, Italy, **779** F6
Bovallstrand, Sweden, **770** E3
Bøverdal, Norway, **770** D2
Boves, France, **789** K5
Bovina, U.S.A., **833** M4
Bovril, Argentina, **857** E4
Bow Island, Canada, **823** P7
Bowdle, U.S.A., **830** D3
Bowen, Australia, **721** K3
Bowes, England, U.K., **790** F3
Bowie, Arizona, U.S.A., **833** J5
Bowie, Texas, U.S.A., **834** D3
Bowland, Forest of, England, U.K., **790** F4
Bowling Green, Kentucky, U.S.A., **831** K7
Bowling Green, Missouri, U.S.A., **830** H6
Bowling Green, Ohio, U.S.A., **831** M5
Bowman, U.S.A., **830** B2
Bowmanville, Canada, **826** B8
Bowmore, Scotland, U.K., **792** C5
Bowral, Australia, **721** L5
Bowron, *river*, Canada, **822** J5
Boxing, China, **747** G5
Boyang, China, **742** D2
Boyd, Montana, U.S.A., **829** K4
Boyd, Texas, U.S.A., **834** D3
Boyd Lagoon, *lake*, Australia, **720** F4
Boyero, U.S.A., **833** M2
Boyle, Canada, **823** N4
Boyle, Ireland, **793** D4
Boyne, *river*, Ireland, **793** F4
Boyuibe, Bolivia, **853** F5
Boz Dağ, *mountain peak*, Turkey, **781** G7
Bozburun, Turkey, **781** G7
Bozcaada, *island*, Turkey, **781** E6
Bozdoğan, Turkey, **781** G7
Bozeman, U.S.A., **829** J4
Bozhou, China, **742** C1
Bozoum, Central African Republic, **805** H3
Bozova, Turkey, **803** G1
Bozovici, Romania, **780** D3
Bozüyük, Turkey, **781** H6
Bozyazı, Turkey, **761** B1
Brabant Lake, Canada, **824** C3
Brabant-Wallon, *province*, Belgium, **772** B3
Brač, *island*, Croatia, **778** F4
Bracadale, Loch, *inlet*, Scotland, U.K., **792** C3
Bracadale, Scotland, U.K., **792** C3
Bracciano, Italy, **779** D4
Bracciano, Lago di, *lake*, Italy, **779** D4
Bracebridge, Canada, **831** P3
Bräcke, Sweden, **770** G1
Brackendale, Canada, **822** H7
Brackettville, U.S.A., **834** B5
Brackley, England, U.K., **789** F2
Bracknell, England, U.K., **789** G3
Bracknell Forest, *unitary authority*, England, U.K., **789** G3
Braço Menor do Araguaia, *river*, Brazil, **854** C3
Brad, Romania, **780** D2
Bradenton, U.S.A., **835** L6
Bradford, England, U.K., **791** G4
Bradford, U.S.A., **836** D3
Bradford on Avon, England, U.K., **788** E3
Bradwell-on-Sea, England, U.K., **789** H3
Brady, Montana, U.S.A., **829** J2
Brady, Nebraska, U.S.A., **830** C5
Brady, Texas, U.S.A., **834** C4
Brae, Shetland, Scotland, U.K., **792** K7
Brædstrup, Denmark, **770** D5
Braemar, Scotland, U.K., **792** F3
Braga, *district*, Portugal, **776** C2
Braga, Portugal, **776** C2
Bragado, Argentina, **856** E5
Bragança, Brazil, **850** D3
Bragança, *district*, Portugal, **776** D2
Bragança, Portugal, **776** D2
Bragança Paulista, Brazil, **857** H2
Brāhmanbāria, Bangladesh, **750** D4
Brāhmani, *river*, India, **755** F5
Brahmapur, India, **753** F2
Brahmaputra, *river*, Asia, **750** E4; *see also* Yarlung Zangbo, *river*, China, **741** B1
Brăila, Romania, **780** F3
Brailsford, England, U.K., **789** F2
Brainerd, U.S.A., **830** F2
Braintree, England, U.K., **789** H3
Brake (Unterweser), Germany, **772** D2
Brâkna, *administrative region*, Mauritania, **804** B1
Brålanda, Sweden, **770** F3
Brampton, England, U.K., **789** J2
Bramsche, Germany, **772** C2
Bramwell, Australia, **726** A6
Brancaster, England, U.K., **789** H2
Branch, Canada, **827** P6
Branco, *river*, Mato Grosso do Sul, Brazil, **854** B5
Branco, *river*, Roraima, Brazil, **849** G4
Brandberg, *mountain peak*, Namibia, **810** B3
Brandbu, Norway, **770** E2
Brande, Denmark, **770** D5
Brandenburg, *state*, Germany, **772** F2
Brandenburg an der Havel, Germany, **772** F2
Brandesburton, England, U.K., **791** H4
Brandon, Canada, **824** E7
Brandon, England, U.K., **789** H2
Brandon, U.S.A., **836** D3
Brandon Head, *point*, Ireland, **793** B5
Brandon Hill, Ireland, **793** F5
Brandon Mountain, Ireland, **793** B5
Brandvlei, South Africa, **810** D5
Brandywine, U.S.A., **836** B5
Branford, U.S.A., **835** L5
Brani, Pulau, *island*, Singapore, **736** K7
Braniewo, Poland, **773** J1
Brańsk, Poland, **773** L2
Branson, U.S.A., **833** M3
Brantley, U.S.A., **835** J4
Brantôme, France, **774** E4
Brânzeni, Moldova, **780** F1
Bras d'Or Lake, Canada, **827** L7
Bras-Panon, Réunion, **813** A1
Brasil, Brazil, **848** D5
Brasil, Planalto do, *plateau*, Brazil, **855** E4
Brasiléia, Brazil, **853** E3
Brasília, Brazil, **854** D4
Brasília de Minas, Brazil, **855** E4
Brasília Legal, Brazil, **850** B4
Braslaw, Belarus, **771** N5
Braşov, Romania, **780** E3
Brasstown Bald, *mountain peak*, U.S.A., **835** L2
Bratca, Romania, **780** D2
Bratislava, Slovakia, **773** H4
Bratislavský, *administrative region*, Slovakia, **773** H4
Bratsk, Russian Federation, **785** M4
Bratskoye Vodokhranilishche, *reservoir*, Russian Federation, **785** M4
Brattleboro, U.S.A., **836** D3
Brattvåg, Norway, **770** C1
Braunau am Inn, Austria, **772** F4
Braunlage, Germany, **772** E3
Braunschweig, Germany, **772** E2
Braunton, England, U.K., **788** C3
Brava, *island*, Cape Verde, **800** P9
Bravo del Norte, Río, *river*, Mexico, **840** E2
Brawley, U.S.A., **832** F5
Bray, Ireland, **793** F4
Bray, *river*, England, U.K., **788** D3
Bray, U.S.A., **828** D6
Bray-sur-Somme, France, **789** K5
Brazeau, Mount, *mountain peak*, Canada, **823** L5
Brazil, *country*, South America, **844** G5
Brazil, U.S.A., **831** K6
Brazil Basin, *underwater feature*, Atlantic Ocean, **867** E6
Brazilian Highlands, *mountain range*, Brazil, **846** G5
Brazos, *river*, U.S.A., **834** D3
Brazzaville, Congo, **808** C3
Brčko, Bosnia and Herzegovina, **778** G3
Brda, *river*, Poland, **773** H2
Brdów, Poland, **773** J2
Breaksea Island, New Zealand, **719** A7
Bream Bay, New Zealand, **718** E2
Breaza, Romania, **780** E3
Brechfa, Wales, U.K., **788** C3
Brechin, Scotland, U.K., **792** G4
Breckenridge, Minnesota, U.S.A., **830** E2
Breckenridge, Texas, U.S.A., **834** C3
Brecknock, Península, Chile, **858** C5
Břeclav, Czech Republic, **773** H4
Brecon, Wales, U.K., **788** D3
Brecon Beacons, *mountain range*, Wales, U.K., **788** D3
Breda, Netherlands, **772** B3
Bredaryd, Sweden, **770** F4
Bredasdorp, South Africa, **810** D5
Bredbyn, Sweden, **768** J5
Brede, *river*, England, U.K., **789** H4
Bredsel, Sweden, **768** K4
Bredstedt, Germany, **772** D1
Bredy, Russian Federation, **758** G2
Bree, Belgium, **772** B3
Bregalnica, *river*, Macedonia, **780** D5
Bregenz, Austria, **772** D5
Bregovo, Bulgaria, **780** D3
Breiðafjörður, *bay*, Iceland, **768** W7
Breiðdalsvík, Iceland, **768** Z7
Breien, U.S.A., **830** C2
Breivikbotn, Norway, **769** L1
Brejinho de Nazaré, Brazil, **854** D3
Brejo, Brazil, **851** E4
Brekstad, Norway, **768** D5
Brem River, Canada, **822** G6
Bremangerlandet, *island*, Norway, **770** A2
Bremen, Germany, **772** D2
Bremen, *state*, Germany, **772** D2
Bremen, U.S.A., **831** K5
Bremerhaven, Germany, **772** D2
Bremerton, U.S.A., **828** C3
Bremervörde, Germany, **772** D2
Brenham, U.S.A., **834** D4
Brentwood, England, U.K., **789** H3
Brescia, Italy, **778** C3
Bressanone, Italy, **778** C2
Bressay, *island*, Shetland, Scotland, U.K., **792** K7
Bressuire, France, **774** D3
Brest, Belarus, **782** B2
Brest, France, **774** B2
Brestskaya Voblasts', *province*, Belarus, **773** M2
Bretagne, *administrative region*, France, **774** C2
Breteuil, France, **789** K5
Breton, Canada, **823** M5
Breton, Pertuis, *strait*, France, **774** D3
Brett, Cape, New Zealand, **718** E2
Bretton, Wales, U.K., **788** E1
Breueh, Pulau, *island*, Indonesia, **736** A1
Breves, Brazil, **850** C3
Brewster, U.S.A., **830** D5
Brewton, U.S.A., **835** J4
Breynat, Canada, **823** N4
Breytovo, Russian Federation, **783** F3
Brežice, Slovenia, **778** E3
Breznik, Bulgaria, **780** D4
Brezno, Slovakia, **773** J4
Brezoi, Romania, **780** E3
Brezolles, France, **774** E2
Bria, Central African Republic, **806** B3
Briançon, France, **775** H4
Briare, France, **774** F3
Bribri, Costa Rica, **839** E5
Briceni, Moldova, **780** F1
Bricquebec, France, **774** D2
Bride, Isle of Man, **790** D3
Bride, *river*, Ireland, **793** D5
Bridge of Orchy, Scotland, U.K., **792** E4
Bridgeland, U.S.A., **833** H1
Bridgend, Islay, Scotland, U.K., **792** C5
Bridgend, Scotland, U.K., **792** F3
Bridgend, *unitary authority*, Wales, U.K., **788** D3
Bridgend, Wales, U.K., **788** D3
Bridgeport, California, U.S.A., **832** D2
Bridgeport, Connecticut, U.S.A., **836** D4
Bridgeport, Nebraska, U.S.A., **830** B5
Bridgeport, Texas, U.S.A., **834** D3
Bridgeton, U.S.A., **836** C5
Bridgetown, Australia, **720** D5
Bridgetown, Barbados, **837** E3
Bridgetown, Canada, **826** J7
Bridgeville, U.S.A., **832** B1
Bridgewater, Australia, **721** K7
Bridgewater, Canada, **827** J7
Bridgewater, U.S.A., **836** C3
Bridgman, Kap, *cape*, Greenland, **821** S1
Bridgnorth, England, U.K., **788** E2
Bridgton, U.S.A., **836** E2
Bridgwater, England, U.K., **788** D3
Bridgwater Bay, England, U.K., **788** D3
Bridlington, England, U.K., **791** H3
Bridlington Bay, England, U.K., **791** H3
Bridport, England, U.K., **788** E4
Brienz, Switzerland, **775** J3
Brienza, Italy, **779** E5
Brig, Switzerland, **775** H3
Brig Bay, Canada, **827** N4
Brigg, England, U.K., **791** H4
Briggsdale, U.S.A., **833** L1
Brigham City, U.S.A., **829** H6
Brighstone, England, U.K., **789** F4
Brightlingsea, England, U.K., **789** J3
Brighton, England, U.K., **789** G4
Brighton, New Zealand, **719** C7
Brighton, U.S.A., **835** M6
Brighton and Hove, *unitary authority*, England, U.K., **789** G4
Brignoles, France, **775** G5
Brikama, Gambia, **804** A2
Brilhante, *river*, Brazil, **854** B5
Brilon, Germany, **772** D3
Brindisi, Italy, **779** F5
Brinkley, U.S.A., **834** G2
Brionne, France, **774** E2
Briouze, France, **774** D2
Brisbane, Australia, **721** L4
Brisco, Canada, **823** L6
Bristol, Alabama, U.S.A., **835** K4
Bristol, Connecticut, U.S.A., **836** D4
Bristol, England, U.K., **788** E3
Bristol, South Dakota, U.S.A., **830** E3
Bristol, Tennessee/Virginia, U.S.A., **831** M7
Bristol Bay, U.S.A., **820** C4
Bristol Channel, England, U.K., **788** C3
Bristol City, *unitary authority*, England, U.K., **788** E3
Bristow Point, Auckland Islands, New Zealand, **718** J10
Britannia Beach, Canada, **822** H7
British Columbia, *province*, Canada, **822** F4
British Indian Ocean Territory, *U.K. dependency*, Indian Ocean, **708** E9
Britstown, South Africa, **810** D5
Brittas Bay, Ireland, **788** A2
Brive-la-Gaillarde, France, **774** E4
Brixham, England, U.K., **788** D4
Brno, Czech Republic, **773** H4
Broad Bay, Scotland, U.K., **792** C2
Broad Haven, *bay*, Ireland, **793** C3
Broad Haven, Wales, U.K., **788** B3
Broad Law, *mountain peak*, Scotland, U.K., **792** F5
Broadford, Ireland, **793** D5
Broadford, Scotland, U.K., **792** D3
Broadmeadows, New Zealand, **719** E5

C

Caiapônia, Brazil, **854** C4
Caibarién, Cuba, **839** F2
Caicara de Orinoco, Venezuela, **849** E2
Caicó, Brazil, **851** G5
Caicos Islands, Turks and Caicos Islands, **839** G2
Caijiapo, China, **751** H2
Cailan, *river*, China, **748** E4
Cailloma, Peru, **852** D4
Caima, Brazil, **850** C4
Caineville, U.S.A., **833** H2
Cainnyi, China, **751** G2
Caird Coast, *region*, Antarctica, **862** C4
Cairndow, Scotland, U.K., **792** E4
Cairngorm Mountains, Scotland, U.K., **792** F3
Cairnryan, Scotland, U.K., **792** D6
Cairns, Australia, **721** K2
Cairo, U.S.A., **835** K4
Cairo *see* Al Qāhirah, Egypt, **761** A4
Cairo Montenotte, Italy, **778** B3
Caister-on-Sea, England, U.K., **789** J2
Caistor, England, U.K., **791** H4
Caitou, Angola, **808** B5
Caiundo, Angola, **808** C6
Cajacay, Peru, **852** C3
Cajamarca, Peru, **852** B2
Cajarc, France, **774** E4
Cajatambo, Peru, **852** C3
Cajàzeiras, Brazil, **851** F5
Čajetina, Yugoslavia, **780** B4
Čajniče, Bosnia and Herzegovina, **780** B4
Caka, China, **749** H5
Caka Yanhu, *lake*, China, **749** H5
Čakovec, Croatia, **778** F2
Çal, Turkey, **781** G6
Cal Madow, Buuraha, *mountain range*, Somalia, **807** G2
Calabar, Nigeria, **808** A2
Calabogie, Canada, **826** C7
Calabozo, Venezuela, **849** E2
Calabria, *autonomous region*, Italy, **779** F6
Calacoto, Bolivia, **853** E4
Calafat, Romania, **780** D4
Calagua Islands, Philippines, **740** C3
Calahorra, Spain, **777** G1
Calai, Angola, **810** C2
Calais, France, **774** E1
Calalaste, Sierra de, *mountain range*, Argentina, **856** C3
Calama, Brazil, **853** F2
Calama, Chile, **856** C2
Calamar, N. Colombia, **848** C1
Calamar, S. Colombia, **848** D4
Calamba, Philippines, **740** C3
Calamocha, Spain, **777** G2
Calamus, *river*, U.S.A., **830** D4
Călan, Romania, **780** D3
Calanda, Spain, **777** G2
Calandula, Angola, **808** C4
Calang, Indonesia, **736** A1
Calapan, Philippines, **740** C3
Călăraşi, Moldova, **780** G2
Călăraşi, Romania, **780** F3
Calasparra, Spain, **777** G3
Calatagan, Philippines, **740** C3
Calatayud, Spain, **777** G2
Calau, Germany, **773** F3
Calauag, Philippines, **740** C3
Calavite, *cape*, Philippines, **740** B3
Calbayog, Philippines, **740** D3
Calbuco, Chile, **858** C1
Calca, Peru, **852** D3
Calcanhar, Ponta do, *point*, Brazil, **851** G4
Calçoene, Brazil, **850** C2
Calçoene, *river*, Brazil, **850** C2
Calcutta, India, **755** G5
Caldas da Rainha, Portugal, **776** C3
Caldas Novas, Brazil, **854** D4
Caldera, Chile, **856** B3
Caldew, *river*, England, U.K., **790** E3
Caldey Island, Wales, U.K., **788** C3
Caldicot, Wales, U.K., **788** E3
Caldwell, Idaho, U.S.A., **828** F5
Caldwell, Kansas, U.S.A., **830** E7
Caldwell, Texas, U.S.A., **834** D4
Caledon, *river*, South Africa, **811** E5
Caledonia, Canada, **826** J7
Caledonia, U.S.A., **830** H4
Caledonia Hills, Canada, **826** J7
Calella, Spain, **777** J2
Caleta Buena, Chile, **853** D5
Caleta Olivia, Argentina, **858** D3
Calexico, U.S.A., **832** F5
Calf, The, *mountain peak*, England, U.K., **790** F3
Calf of Man, *island*, Isle of Man, **790** D3
Calgary, Canada, **823** M6
Calhan, U.S.A., **833** L2
Calheta, Madeira, Portugal, **813** C3
Calhoun, U.S.A., **835** K2
Cali, Colombia, **848** C3
Calicut *see* Kozhikode, India, **752** C4
Caliente, California, U.S.A., **832** D4
Caliente, Nevada, U.S.A., **832** F3
California, Golfo de, *gulf*, Mexico, **840** B2
California, *state*, U.S.A., **832** D4
California, Trinidad, Trinidad and Tobago, **859** C4
Călimăneşti, Romania, **780** E3
Călimani, Munţii, *mountain range*, Romania, **780** E2
Calintaan, Philippines, **740** C3
Calipatria, U.S.A., **832** F5
Caliper Lake, Canada, **824** H7
Calitzdorp, South Africa, **810** D5
Calkini, Mexico, **841** H4
Callac, France, **774** C2
Callahan, U.S.A., **828** C6
Callan, Ireland, **793** E5
Callander, Scotland, U.K., **792** E4
Callao, Peru, **852** C3
Callaway, U.S.A., **830** F2
Calling Lake, Canada, **823** N4
Callington, England, U.K., **788** C4
Calmar, U.S.A., **830** H4
Calne, England, U.K., **788** E3
Calotmul, Mexico, **841** H4
Caloundra, Australia, **721** L4
Caltagirone, Sicilia, Italy, **779** E7
Caltama, Cerro, *mountain peak*, Bolivia, **853** E5
Caltanissetta, Sicilia, Italy, **779** D7
Calucinga, Angola, **808** C5
Călugăreni, Romania, **780** F3
Calulo, Angola, **808** B5
Calunda, Angola, **808** D5
Calunga, Angola, **808** C6
Caluquembe, Angola, **808** B5
Caluula, Raas, *point*, Somalia, **807** H2
Caluula, Somalia, **807** H2
Calvados Chain, The, *islands*, Papua New Guinea, **721** L1
Calvert, *river*, Australia, **721** H2
Calvert Island, Canada, **822** E6
Calvi, Corse, France, **778** B4
Calvillo, Mexico, **840** E4
Calvinia, South Africa, **810** C5
Calw, Germany, **772** D4
Calzada de Calatrava, Spain, **777** F3
Cam, *river*, England, U.K., **789** H2
Cam Lâm (Cam Ranh), Vietnam, **739** F4
Cẩm Phả, Vietnam, **739** E1
Cam Ranh *see* Cam Lâm, Vietnam, **739** F4
Camabatela, Angola, **808** C4
Camaçari, Brazil, **855** F3
Camacho, Mexico, **840** E3
Camacupa, Angola, **808** C5
Camaguán, Venezuela, **849** E2
Camagüey, Cuba, **839** F2
Camah, Gunung, *mountain peak*, Malaysia, **736** C1
Camamu, Brazil, **855** F3
Camaná, Peru, **852** D4
Camanongue, Angola, **808** D5
Camapuã, Brazil, **854** C5
Camaquã, Brazil, **857** G4
Camaquã, *river*, Brazil, **857** G4
Câmara de Lobos, Madeira, Portugal, **813** C3
Camarat, Cap, *cape*, France, **775** H5
Camarès, France, **774** F5
Camaret-sur-Mer, France, **774** B2
Camarones, Argentina, **858** E2
Camarones, Bahía, *bay*, Argentina, **858** E2
Camarones, *river*, Chile, **853** D5
Camas Valley, U.S.A., **828** C5
Cambará, Brazil, **854** B4
Cambellton, Canada, **826** H6
Camberley, England, U.K., **789** G3
Cambo-les-Bains, France, **774** D5
Cambodia, *country*, Asia, **731** M8
Camborne, England, U.K., **788** B4
Cambrai, France, **775** F1
Cambria, U.S.A., **832** C4
Cambrian Mountains, *mountain range*, Wales, U.K., **788** C3
Cambridge, England, U.K., **789** H2
Cambridge, Idaho, U.S.A., **828** F4
Cambridge, Maryland, U.S.A., **836** B5
Cambridge, Massachusetts, U.S.A., **836** E3
Cambridge, Nebraska, U.S.A., **830** C5
Cambridge, New Zealand, **718** E3
Cambridge, Ohio, U.S.A., **831** N5
Cambridge Bay, Canada, **820** J3
Cambridgeshire, *unitary authority*, England, U.K., **789** G2
Cambulo, Angola, **808** D4
Cambundi-Catembo, Angola, **808** C5
Camden, Alabama, U.S.A., **835** J3
Camden, Arkansas, U.S.A., **834** F3
Camden, Australia, **721** L5
Camden, New Jersey, U.S.A., **836** C5
Camden, South Carolina, U.S.A., **835** M2
Camdenton, U.S.A., **830** G6
Cameia, Angola, **808** D5
Camelford, England, U.K., **788** C4
Çameli, Turkey, **781** G7
Camenca, Moldova, **780** G1
Camerino, Italy, **778** D4
Cameron, Arizona, U.S.A., **833** H4
Camerón, Chile, **858** D4
Cameron, Louisiana, U.S.A., **834** F5
Cameron, Missouri, U.S.A., **830** F6
Cameron, Texas, U.S.A., **834** D4
Cameron Hills, Canada, **823** K1
Cameron Mountains, *mountain range*, New Zealand, **719** A8
Cameroon, *country*, Africa, **796** F6
Cameroon Mountains, Cameroon, **808** A2
Cametá, Brazil, **850** D4
Camiguin Island, Philippines, **740** D4
Camilla, U.S.A., **835** K4
Camiña, Chile, **853** E5
Camiranga, Brazil, **850** D3
Camiri, Bolivia, **853** F5
Camissombo, Angola, **808** D4
Cammarata, Monte, *mountain peak*, Italy, **779** D7
Camocim, Brazil, **851** F4
Camooweal, Australia, **721** H2
Camopi, French Guiana, **850** C2
Camopi, *river*, French Guiana, **850** C2
Camorta Island, Andaman and Nicobar Islands, India, **753** H4
Camotes Islands, Philippines, **740** C4
Camp Verde, U.S.A., **833** H4
Campagne-lès-Hesdin, France, **789** J4
Campana, Argentina, **857** E5
Campana, Isla, *island*, Chile, **858** B3
Campanario, *mountain peak*, Argentina/Chile, **856** B5
Campania, *autonomous region*, Italy, **779** E5
Campbell, Cape, New Zealand, **719** E5
Campbell Island, New Zealand, **718** K11
Campbell Plateau, *underwater feature*, Pacific Ocean, **868** F8
Campbell River, Canada, **822** G6
Campbellsville, U.S.A., **831** L7
Campbeltown, Scotland, U.K., **792** D5
Campeche, Bahía de, *bay*, Mexico, **841** G5
Campeche, Mexico, **841** H5
Campeche, *state*, Mexico, **841** H5
Câmpeni, Romania, **780** D2
Câmpia Turzii, Romania, **780** D2
Campidano, *valley*, Sardegna, Italy, **779** B6
Campillo de Llerena, Spain, **776** D3
Campillos, Spain, **776** E4
Câmpina, Romania, **780** E3
Campina Grande, Brazil, **851** G5
Campina Verde, Brazil, **854** D5
Campinas, Brazil, **857** H2
Campo, Cameroon, **808** A2
Campo Belo, Brazil, **855** E5
Campo Belo do Sul, Brazil, **857** G3
Campo de Diauarem, Brazil, **854** C3
Campo Esperanza, Paraguay, **857** E2
Campo Florido, Brazil, **854** D5
Campo Formoso, Brazil, **855** F3
Campo Gallo, Argentina, **856** D3
Campo Grande, Amazonas, Brazil, **853** G2
Campo Grande, Mato Grosso do Sul, Brazil, **854** B5
Campo Maior, Brazil, **851** E4
Campo Mara, Venezuela, **848** D1
Campo Mourão, Brazil, **857** G2
Campo Novo, Brazil, **857** G3
Campoalegre, Colombia, **848** C3
Campobasso, Italy, **779** E5
Campobello di Licata, Sicilia, Italy, **779** D7
Campos, Brazil, **855** F5
Campos Altos, Brazil, **854** D5
Campos Belos, Brazil, **854** D3
Campos Novos, Brazil, **857** G3
Campos Sales, Brazil, **851** F5
Camprodon, Spain, **777** J1
Câmpulung, Romania, **780** E3
Câmpulung Moldovenesc, Romania, **780** E2
Camrose, Canada, **823** N5
Camrose, Wales, U.K., **788** C3
Camucuio, Angola, **808** B5
Çan, Turkey, **781** F5
Cần Thơ, Vietnam, **739** E4
Canaan, Tobago, Trinidad and Tobago, **859** B4
Canada, *country*, North America, **816** N3
Canadian, *river*, U.S.A., **833** L4
Canadian, U.S.A., **834** B2
Canadian Shield, *physical feature*, Canada, **818** M2
Çanakkale, *province*, Turkey, **781** F6
Çanakkale, Turkey, **781** F5
Canakkale Bogazi, *strait*, Turkey, **781** F5
Canal Flats, Canada, **823** M6
Canala, New Caledonia, **727** A3
Canalejas, Argentina, **856** C5
Canamari, Brazil, **853** E3
Cananea, Mexico, **840** C2
Cananéia, Brazil, **857** H2
Canapiare, Cerro, *mountain peak*, Colombia, **849** E3
Cañar, Ecuador, **848** B5
Canarias, Islas (Canary Islands), *islands*, Spain, Atlantic Ocean, **813** A4
Canarreos, Archipélago de los, *islands*, Cuba, **839** E2
Canary Islands, *see* Canarias Islas, *islands*, Spain, Atlantic Ocean, **813** A4
Canastra, Serra da, *mountain range*, Brazil, **854** D5
Canatlán, Mexico, **840** D3
Canaveral, Cape, U.S.A., **835** M5
Cañaveras, Spain, **777** F2
Canavieiras, Brazil, **855** F4
Canberra, Australia, **721** K6
Canby, California, U.S.A., **828** D6
Canby, Minnesota, U.S.A., **830** E3
Canche, *river*, France, **789** K4
Canchyuaya, Cerros de, *mountain range*, Peru, **852** C2
Cancún, Mexico, **841** J4
Candarave, Peru, **852** D4
Candé, France, **774** D3
Candelaria, Argentina, **857** F3
Candelaria, Mexico, **841** H5
Candelaro, *river*, Italy, **779** E5
Cândido Mendes, Brazil, **850** E3
Candle Lake, Canada, **823** S5
Candon, Philippines, **740** C2
Canelones, Uruguay, **857** F5
Cañete, Chile, **856** B5
Cangallo, Peru, **852** C3
Cangamba, Angola, **808** C5
Cangandala, Angola, **808** C4
Cangombe, Angola, **808** D5
Cangshan, China, **747** H2
Canguaretama, Brazil, **851** G5
Canguçu, Brazil, **857** G4
Canguçu, Serra do, *mountain range*, Brazil, **857** G4
Cangumbe, Angola, **808** C5
Cangwu, China, **742** B4
Cangxi, China, **751** H3
Cangyuan, China, **751** F5
Cangzhou, China, **746** G5
Caniapiscau, Lac, *lake*, Canada, **826** G2
Caniapiscau, *river*, Canada, **821** N4
Canicatti, Sicilia, Italy, **779** D7
Canigou, Pic du, *mountain peak*, France, **774** F5
Canindé, Ceará, Brazil, **851** F4
Canindé, Pará, Brazil, **850** D4
Canindé, *river*, Brazil, **851** E5
Canisp, *mountain peak*, Scotland, U.K., **792** D2
Cañitas de Felipe Pescador, Mexico, **840** E4
Cañizal, Spain, **776** E2
Canmore, Canada, **823** M6
Canna, *island*, Scotland, U.K., **792** C3
Cannanore, India, **752** C4
Cannanore Islands, India, **752** C4

Chelyabinskaya Oblast', *province*, Russian Federation, **758** F2
Chelyuskin, Mys, *cape*, Russian Federation, **785** M2
Chemaïa, Morocco, **800** E2
Chemal, Russian Federation, **759** M2
Chemchâm, Sebkhet, *salt-pan*, Mauritania, **800** D4
Chemin Grenier, Mauritius, **813** C1
Chemnitz, Germany, **772** F3
Chen Barag Qi, China, **747** G2
Chenāb, *river*, Pakistan, **754** B3
Chenachane, Algeria, **801** F3
Ch'ench'a, Ethiopia, **807** E3
Cheney, U.S.A., **828** F3
Ch'eng-kung, Taiwan, **742** E4
Cheng'an, China, **746** F5
Chengde, China, **747** G4
Chengdu, China, **751** H3
Chengele, India, **755** J3
Chenghai, China, **742** D4
Chengjiang, China, **743** C2
Chengkou, China, **742** B2
Chengmai, China, **739** F2
Chennai (Madras), India, **752** E3
Chenxi, China, **742** B3
Chenzhou, China, **742** C3
Chepelare, Bulgaria, **781** E5
Chepén, Peru, **852** B2
Chépénéhé, New Caledonia, **727** A3
Chepes, Argentina, **856** C4
Chepo, Panama, **848** B2
Chepstow, Wales, U.K., **788** E3
Cher, *river*, France, **774** E3
Cheraw, U.S.A., **835** N2
Cherbourg, France, **774** D2
Cherchell, Algeria, **777** J4
Cherekha, *river*, Russian Federation, **783** B4
Cherepanovo, Russian Federation, **759** L2
Cherepovets, Russian Federation, **783** F3
Chéria, Algeria, **801** H1
Cherkessk, Russian Federation, **758** C4
Chern', Russian Federation, **783** F6
Chernevo, Russian Federation, **783** B3
Chernihiv, Ukraine, **782** D2
Chernivets'ka Oblast', *province*, Ukraine, **780** E1
Chernivtsi, Chernivets'ka Oblast', Ukraine, **780** E1
Chernivtsi, Vinnyts'ka Oblast', Ukraine, **780** G1
Chernyakhovsk, Russian Federation, **771** K5
Chernyshevsk, Russian Federation, **746** G1
Chernyy Yar, Russian Federation, **758** D3
Cherokee, Iowa, U.S.A., **830** F4
Cherokee, Oklahoma, U.S.A., **830** D7
Cherokee Sound, Bahamas, **838** F1
Cherrapunji, India, **755** G4
Cherry Creek, U.S.A., **830** C3
Cherryville, Canada, **823** K6
Cherskiy, Russian Federation, **785** T3
Cherskogo, Khrebet, *mountain range*, Russian Federation, **785** Q3
Cherven Bryag, Bulgaria, **780** E4
Chervonohrad, Ukraine, **773** M3
Chervonoznam'yanka, Ukraine, **780** H2
Chervyen', Belarus, **783** B6
Cherykaw, Belarus, **783** C6
Chesapeake, U.S.A., **836** B6
Chesapeake Bay, U.S.A., **836** B5
Chesham, England, U.K., **789** G3
Cheshire, *unitary authority*, England, U.K., **788** E1
Cheshskaya Guba, *bay*, Russian Federation, **784** F3
Cheshunt, England, U.K., **789** G3
Cheste, Spain, **777** G3
Chester, California, U.S.A., **832** C1
Chester, Canada, **827** J7
Chester, England, U.K., **788** E1
Chester, Illinois, U.S.A., **830** J7
Chester, Montana, U.S.A., **829** J2
Chester, South Carolina, U.S.A., **835** M2
Chester-le-Street, England, U.K., **791** G3
Chesterfield, England, U.K., **789** F1
Chesterfield, Îles, *islands*, New Caledonia, **722** A2
Chesterfield Inlet, Canada, **821** K3
Chestnut, U.S.A., **834** F3
Chesuncook Lake, U.S.A., **836** E1
Chet', *river*, Russian Federation, **759** M1
Chetaibi, Algeria, **779** A7
Cheticamp, Canada, **827** L6
Chetlat Island, India, **752** C4
Chetumal, Mexico, **841** H5
Chetwode Island, New Zealand, **719** E5
Chetwynd, Canada, **822** J4
Cheugda, Russian Federation, **747** K2
Cheung Chau, *island*, China, **743** C4
Chevejécure, Bolivia, **853** E4
Chevilly, France, **774** E2
Cheviot, New Zealand, **719** D6
Cheviot, The, *mountain peak*, England, U.K., **790** F2
Cheviot Hills, England, U.K., **790** F2
Che'w Bahir, *lake*, Ethiopia, **809** G2
Chew Magna, England, U.K., **788** E3
Chew Valley Lake, England, U.K., **788** E3
Chewelah, U.S.A., **828** F2
Cheyenne, Oklahoma, U.S.A., **834** C2
Cheyenne, *river*, U.S.A., **829** P4
Cheyenne, Wyoming, U.S.A., **829** M6
Cheyenne Wells, U.S.A., **833** M2
Chhatarpur, India, **754** D4
Chhattīsgarh, *plain*, India, **755** E5
Chhindawāra, India, **754** D5
Chhnăng, *river*, Cambodia, **739** E3
Chhota Udepur, India, **754** C5
Chi-lung, Taiwan, **742** E3
Ch'i-shan, Taiwan, **742** E4
Chia-i, Taiwan, **742** E4
Chiang Dao, Doi, *mountain peak*, Thailand, **738** C2
Chiang Kham, Thailand, **738** D2
Chiang Khan, Thailand, **738** D2
Chiang Mai, Thailand, **738** C2
Chiang Rai, Thailand, **738** C2
Chiange, Angola, **808** B6
Chiapas, *state*, Mexico, **841** G5
Chiari, Italy, **778** B3
Chiautla de Tapia, Mexico, **841** F5
Chiavenna, Italy, **778** B2
Chiba, Japan, **745** H4
Chibemba, Angola, **808** B6
Chibia, Angola, **808** B6
Chibougamau, Canada, **826** D5
Chic-Chocs, Monts, *mountain range*, Canada, **826** H5
Chicago, U.S.A., **831** K5
Chicama, Peru, **852** B2
Chicama, *river*, Peru, **852** B2
Chichagof Island, U.S.A., **822** A3
Chichas, Cordillera de, *mountain range*, Bolivia, **853** E5
Chichāwatni, Pakistan, **754** C3
Chicheng, China, **746** F4
Chichester, England, U.K., **789** G4
Chichi-jima, *island*, Japan, **724** C2
Chichola, India, **754** E5
Chichón, Volcán, *mountain peak*, Mexico, **841** G5
Chickasawhay, *river*, U.S.A., **835** H4
Chickasha, U.S.A., **834** D2
Chickerell, England, U.K., **788** E4
Chiclana de la Frontera, Spain, **776** D4
Chiclayo, Peru, **852** B2
Chico, *river*, Chubut, Argentina, **858** D2
Chico, *river*, Río Negro, Argentina, **858** C2
Chico, *river*, Santa Cruz, Argentina, **858** C3
Chico, *river*, S. Santa Cruz, Argentina, **858** D4
Chico, U.S.A., **832** C2
Chicoa, Mozambique, **809** F6
Chicomba, Angola, **808** B5
Chicotte, Canada, **827** K5
Chicoutimi, Canada, **826** F5
Chicualacuala, Mozambique, **811** F3
Chidambaram, India, **752** D4
Chidenguele, Mozambique, **811** F3
Chidley, Cape, Canada, **821** N3
Chiefland, U.S.A., **835** L5
Chiemsee, *lake*, Germany, **772** F5
Chiengi, Zambia, **809** E4
Chieo Lan Reservoir, Thailand, **738** C4
Chiese, *river*, Italy, **778** C3
Chieti, Italy, **779** E4
Chietla, Mexico, **841** F5
Chifeng, China, **747** G4
Chigorodó, Colombia, **848** C2
Chiguana, Bolivia, **853** E5
Chigubo, Mozambique, **811** F3
Chihuahua, Mexico, **840** D2
Chihuahua, *state*, Mexico, **840** D2
Chihuido Medio, *mountain peak*, Argentina, **856** C6
Chikhachevo, Russian Federation, **783** B4
Chikmagalūr, India, **752** C3
Chikodi, India, **752** C2
Chikoy, *river*, Russian Federation, **746** E2
Chikwa, Zambia, **809** F5
Chikwawa, Malawi, **809** F6
Chila, Angola, **808** B5
Chilakalūrupet, India, **752** E2
Chilapa de Alvarez, Mexico, **841** F5
Chilaw, Sri Lanka, **752** D5
Chilca, Cordillera de, *mountain range*, Peru, **852** D4
Chilcotin, *river*, Canada, **822** G5
Chilcott Island, Coral Sea Islands, **721** K2
Childers, Australia, **721** L4
Childress, U.S.A., **834** B2
Chile, *country*, South America, **845** E7
Chile Basin, *underwater feature*, Pacific Ocean, **869** N6
Chile Chico, Argentina, **858** C3
Chile Rise, *underwater feature*, Pacific Ocean, **869** M7
Chilecito, Argentina, **856** C3
Chilham, England, U.K., **789** H3
Chilia Veche, Romania, **780** G3
Chililabombwe, Zambia, **809** E5
Chilka Lake, India, **755** F6
Chillán, Chile, **856** B5
Chillar, Argentina, **857** E5
Chillicothe, Illinois, U.S.A., **831** J5
Chillicothe, Missouri, U.S.A., **830** G6
Chillicothe, Ohio, U.S.A., **831** M6
Chilliculco, Peru, **853** E4
Chillinji, Pakistan, **754** C1
Chilliwack, Canada, **822** J7
Chilpancingo de los Bravos, Mexico, **841** F5
Chiltal'd, Gora, *mountain peak*, Russian Federation, **769** Q2
Chilubi, Zambia, **809** E5
Chilumba, Malawi, **809** F5
Chimala, Tanzania, **809** F4
Chimán, Panama, **839** F5
Chimanimani, Zimbabwe, **811** F2
Chimayo, U.S.A., **833** L3
Chimborazo, *mountain peak*, Ecuador, **848** B4
Chimbote, Peru, **852** B2
Chiméal, Cambodia, **739** D4
Chimoio, Mozambique, **811** F2
Chin, *state*, Myanmar, **741** B3
China, *country*, Asia, **730** L6
China, Mexico, **841** F3
Chinácota, Colombia, **848** D2
Chinajá, Guatemala, **838** C3
Chinandega, Nicaragua, **838** D4
Chinati Peak, *mountain peak*, U.S.A., **833** L7
Chincha Alta, Peru, **852** C3
Chinchaga, *river*, Canada, **823** K3
Chinchilla, Australia, **721** L4
Chinchilla de Monte Aragón, Spain, **777** G3
Chincholi, India, **752** D2
Chinde, Mozambique, **811** G2
Chindo, *island*, South Korea, **744** D4
Chindu, China, **751** F2
Chindwin, *river*, Myanmar, **741** B2
Chingola, Zambia, **809** E5
Chinguar, Angola, **808** C5
Chinguetti, Mauritania, **800** D4
Chinguil, Chad, **806** A2
Chinhae, South Korea, **744** E4
Chinhoyi, Zimbabwe, **811** F2
Chiniot, Pakistan, **754** C3
Chinipas, Mexico, **840** C3
Chinjan, Pakistan, **754** A3
Chinju, South Korea, **744** E4
Chinle, U.S.A., **833** J3
Chinnūr, India, **752** D2
Chinon, France, **774** E3
Chinook Trough, *underwater feature*, Pacific Ocean, **868** G2
Chinsali, Zambia, **809** F5
Chinsong-ri, North Korea, **744** D2
Chintāmani, India, **752** D3
Chinturu, India, **753** E2
Chioggia, Italy, **778** D3
Chios, Greece, **781** F6
Chios, *island*, Greece, **781** E6
Chipata, Zambia, **809** F5
Chipili, Zambia, **809** E5
Chipinge, Zimbabwe, **811** F3
Chipman, Canada, **823** N5
Chipoia, Angola, **808** C5
Chippenham, England, U.K., **788** E3
Chippewa, *river*, U.S.A., **830** H3
Chippewa Falls, U.S.A., **830** H3
Chipping Campden, England, U.K., **789** F2
Chipping Norton, England, U.K., **789** F3
Chipping Ongar, England, U.K., **789** H3
Chipping Sodbury, England, U.K., **788** E3
Chiprovtsi, Bulgaria, **780** D4
Chiquimula, Guatemala, **838** C4
Chiquinata, Bahía, *bay*, Chile, **852** D5
Chiquinquirá, Colombia, **848** D3
Chirāla, Cape, India, **753** E3
Chirāla, India, **752** E3
Chirāwa, India, **754** C3
Chiradzulu, Malawi, **811** G2
Chiralto, *river*, Mexico, **841** E5
Chiramba, Mozambique, **809** F6
Chirbury, England, U.K., **788** D2
Chirchiq, Uzbekistan, **759** H4
Chiredzi, Zimbabwe, **811** F3
Chirfa, Niger, **802** B4
Chiricahua Peak, *mountain peak*, U.S.A., **833** J6
Chiriguaná, Colombia, **848** D2
Chiriquí, Golfo de, *gulf*, Panama, **839** E6
Chirk, Wales, U.K., **788** D2
Chirmiri, India, **755** E5
Chirnside, Scotland, U.K., **792** G5
Chiromo, Malawi, **809** G6
Chirpan, Bulgaria, **780** E4
Chirripó, Cerro, *mountain peak*, Costa Rica, **838** E5
Chirundu, Zambia, **809** E6
Chisamba, Zambia, **809** E5
Chisasibi, Canada, **825** Q5
Chishmy, Russian Federation, **758** F2
Chisholm, Canada, **823** M4
Chisholm, U.S.A., **830** G2
Chishui, *river*, China, **751** H4
Chişinău (Kishinev), Moldova, **780** G2
Chişineu-Criş, Romania, **780** C2
Chistiān Mandi, Pakistan, **754** C3
Chistopol', Russian Federation, **758** E1
Chistopol'e, Kazakhstan, **758** H2
Chita, Bolivia, **853** E5
Chita, Russian Federation, **785** N4
Chitado, Angola, **808** B6
Chitambo, Zambia, **809** F5
Chitato, Angola, **808** D4
Chitembo, Angola, **808** C5
Chitinskaya Oblast', *province*, Russian Federation, **746** F1
Chitipa, Malawi, **809** F4
Chitobe, Mozambique, **811** F3
Chitose, Japan, **745** H2
Chitrāl, Pakistan, **754** B2
Chitré, Panama, **839** E6
Chittagong, Bangladesh, **750** D5
Chittagong, *division*, Bangladesh, **750** D5
Chittaurgarh, India, **754** C4
Chittoor, India, **752** D3
Chitungwiza, Zimbabwe, **811** F2
Chiume, Angola, **808** D6
Chiure Novo, Mozambique, **809** G5
Chivasso, Italy, **778** A3
Chive, Bolivia, **853** E3
Chivhu, Zimbabwe, **811** F2
Chivington, U.S.A., **833** M2
Chlef, Algeria, **801** G1
Chlef, *river*, Algeria, **777** H4
Chloride, U.S.A., **832** F4
Chmelevoye, Ukraine, **780** H1
Chmielnik, Poland, **773** K3
Choa Chu Kang, Singapore, **736** J6
Chŏâm Ksant, Cambodia, **739** E3
Choapa, *river*, Chile, **856** B4
Chobe, *district*, Botswana, **810** D2
Chocolate Mountains, *mountain range*, U.S.A., **832** F5
Chocontá, Colombia, **848** D3
Chodavaram, India, **753** E2
Chodzież, Poland, **773** H2
Choele Choel, Argentina, **858** E1
Chofombo, Mozambique, **809** F5
Chograyskoye Vodokhranilishche, *reservoir*, Russian Federation, **758** C3
Choiceland, Canada, **824** B5
Choiseul, *island*, Solomon Islands, **727** A1

Cline, U.S.A., **834** B5
Clinton, British Columbia, Canada, **822** J6
Clinton, Iowa, U.S.A., **830** H5
Clinton, Massachusetts, U.S.A., **836** E3
Clinton, Mississippi, U.S.A., **834** G3
Clinton, Missouri, U.S.A., **830** G6
Clinton, Montana, U.S.A., **828** H3
Clinton, North Carolina, U.S.A., **835** N2
Clinton, Oklahoma, U.S.A., **834** C2
Clinton, Ontario, Canada, **831** N4
Clinton, South Carolina, U.S.A., **835** M2
Clipperton Fracture Zone, *tectonic feature*, Pacific Ocean, **869** J4
Clitheroe, England, U.K., **790** F4
Cliza, Bolivia, **853** F4
Clo-oose, Canada, **822** G7
Clogh, Northern Ireland, U.K., **793** F3
Clogheen, Ireland, **793** D5
Clogher Head, *point*, Ireland, **793** F4
Clonakilty, Ireland, **793** D6
Clonakilty Bay, Ireland, **793** D6
Clonbern, Ireland, **793** D4
Cloncurry, Australia, **721** J3
Clones, Ireland, **793** E3
Clonmel, Ireland, **793** E5
Clonroche, Ireland, **793** F5
Cloonbannin, Ireland, **793** C5
Cloppenburg, Germany, **772** D2
Cloquet, U.S.A., **830** G2
Cloridorme, Canada, **826** J5
Clorinda, Argentina, **857** F2
Cloud Peak, *mountain peak*, U.S.A., **829** L4
Clova, Scotland, U.K., **792** F4
Cloverdale, U.S.A., **832** B2
Clovis, U.S.A., **833** M4
Cluanie, Loch, *lake*, Scotland, U.K., **792** D3
Cluff Lake, Canada, **823** Q2
Cluj-Napoca, Romania, **780** D2
Clun, England, U.K., **788** D2
Cluny, France, **775** G3
Clutha, *river*, New Zealand, **719** B7
Clydach, Wales, U.K., **788** D3
Clyde, *river*, Scotland, U.K., **792** F5
Clyde Park, U.S.A., **829** J4
Clyde River, Canada, **821** N2
Clydebank, Scotland, U.K., **792** E5
Clydevale, New Zealand, **719** B8
Clyro, Wales, U.K., **788** D2
Cnoc Moy, Scotland, U.K., **792** D5
Coahuila, *state*, Mexico, **840** E3
Coal, *river*, Canada, **822** E1
Coal River, Canada, **822** F2
Coaldale, U.S.A., **832** E2
Coalgate, U.S.A., **834** D2
Coalinga, U.S.A., **832** C3
Coalville, England, U.K., **789** F2
Coari, Brazil, **849** F5
Coari, Lago de, *lake*, Brazil, **849** F5
Coari, *river*, Brazil, **849** F5
Coast, *province*, Kenya, **809** G3
Coast Mountains, *mountain range*, Canada, **822** C2
Coast Range, *mountain range*, U.S.A., **818** L5
Coatbridge, Scotland, U.K., **792** E5
Coats Island, Canada, **821** L3
Coats Land, *region*, Antarctica, **862** C4
Coatzacoalcos, Mexico, **841** G5
Cobadin, Romania, **780** G3
Cobán, Guatemala, **838** C4
Cobar, Australia, **721** K5
Cobequid Mountains, *mountain range*, Canada, **827** J7
Cobh, Ireland, **793** D6
Cobham, *river*, Canada, **824** G5
Cobija, Bolivia, **853** E3
Cobleskill, U.S.A., **836** C3
Cobourg Peninsula, Australia, **720** G1
Cobram, Australia, **721** K6
Cóbuè, Mozambique, **809** F5
Coburg, Germany, **772** E3
Coburg Island, Canada, **821** M2
Coca, Pizzo di, *mountain peak*, Italy, **778** B2
Cocachacra, Peru, **852** D4
Cocalinho, Brazil, **854** C4
Cochabamba, Bolivia, **853** E4
Cochabamba, *department*, Bolivia, **853** E4
Cochamó, Chile, **858** C1
Cochem, Germany, **772** C3
Cochin, Canada, **823** Q5
Cochin *see* Kochi, India, **752** D4
Cochise, U.S.A., **833** J5
Cochrane, Alberta, Canada, **823** M6
Cochrane, Chile, **858** C3
Cochrane, Ontario, Canada, **825** P7
Cockburn, Canal, *channel*, Chile, **858** C5
Cockburn, Cape, Australia, **735** F5
Cockburn Harbour, Turks and Caicos Islands, **839** H2
Cockburn Town, Bahamas, **838** G1
Cockburnspath, Scotland, U.K., **792** G5
Cockerham, England, U.K., **790** F4
Cockermouth, England, U.K., **790** E3
Coclé del Norte, Panama, **839** E5
Coco, Punta, *point*, Colombia, **848** B3
Coco, *river*, Honduras/Nicaraqua, **838** D4
Coco Channel, Andaman and Nicobar Islands, India, **753** H3
Cocorná, Colombia, **848** C2
Côcos, Brazil, **855** E4
Cocos Bay, Trinidad, Trinidad and Tobago, **859** C4
Cocos (Keeling) Islands, *Australian territory*, Indian Ocean, **720** Q10
Cocos Ridge, *underwater feature*, Pacific Ocean, **869** N4
Cocula, Mexico, **840** E4
Cod, Cape, U.S.A., **836** E3
Cod Island, Canada, **821** N4
Codajás, Brazil, **849** F5
Coddington, England, U.K., **789** G1
Codera, Cabo, *cape*, Venezuela, **849** E1
Codfish Island, New Zealand, **719** A8
Codigoro, Italy, **778** D3
Codlea, Romania, **780** E3
Codó, Brazil, **851** E4
Codrington, Antigua and Barbuda, **837** D2
Codrington, Mount, *mountain peak*, Antarctica, **862** F4
Codsall, England, U.K., **788** E2
Cody, U.S.A., **829** K4
Coe, Glen, *valley*, Scotland, U.K., **792** D4
Coen, Australia, **721** J1
Coeroeni, *river*, Suriname, **850** B2
Coesfeld, Germany, **772** C3
Coetivy Island, Seychelles, **812** D2
Coeur d'Alene, U.S.A., **828** F3
Coeur d'Alene Lake, U.S.A., **828** F3
Coffee Bay, South Africa, **811** E5
Coffeeville, U.S.A., **835** H4
Coffeyville, U.S.A., **830** F7
Coffs Harbour, Australia, **721** L5
Cofrentes, Spain, **777** G3
Cogealac, Romania, **780** G3
Coggeshall, England, U.K., **789** H3
Cognac, France, **774** D4
Cogo, Equatorial Guinea, **808** A2
Cohagen, U.S.A., **829** L3
Coiba, Isla de, *island*, Panama, **839** E6
Coig, *river*, Argentina, **858** C4
Coigeach, Rubha, *point*, Scotland, U.K., **792** D2
Coihaique, Chile, **858** C2
Coimbatore, India, **752** D4
Coimbra, *district*, Portugal, **776** C2
Coimbra, Portugal, **776** C2
Coin, Spain, **776** E4
Coipasa, Lago de, *lake*, Bolivia, **853** E5
Coipasa, Salar de, *salt-pan*, Bolivia, **853** E5
Cojudo Blanco, Cerro, *mountain peak*, Argentina, **858** D3
Cojutepeque, El Salvador, **838** C4
Colac, Australia, **721** J6
Colac Bay, New Zealand, **719** A8
Colares, Brazil, **850** D3
Colatina, Brazil, **855** F5
Colby, U.S.A., **830** C6
Colchester, England, U.K., **789** J3
Cold Lake, Canada, **823** P4
Cold Lake, *lake*, Canada, **823** Q4
Cold Springs, U.S.A., **832** E2
Coldstream, Canada, **823** K6
Coldwater, Kansas, U.S.A., **830** D7
Coldwater, Michigan, U.S.A., **831** L5
Coldwater, Missouri, U.S.A., **830** H7
Colebrook, U.S.A., **836** E2
Coleford, England, U.K., **788** E3
Coleman, U.S.A., **834** C4
Çölemerik, Turkey, **760** F5
Colemon, U.S.A., **831** L4
Coleraine, *district*, Northern Ireland, U.K., **793** F2
Coleraine, Northern Ireland, U.K., **793** F2
Coleridge, Lake, New Zealand, **719** C6
Coles, Punta, *point*, Peru, **852** D4
Colesberg, South Africa, **810** E5
Colfax, California, U.S.A., **832** C2
Colfax, Louisiana, U.S.A., **834** F4
Colfax, Washington, U.S.A., **828** F3
Colhué Huapi, Lago, *lake*, Argentina, **858** D2
Colico, Italy, **778** B2
Colima, Mexico, **840** E5
Colima, *state*, Mexico, **840** D5
Colinas, Brazil, **851** E5
Coll, *island*, Scotland, U.K., **792** C4
Collaguasi, Chile, **853** E5
College Station, U.S.A., **834** D4
Collie, Australia, **720** D5
Collier Bay, Australia, **720** E2
Collingwood, Canada, **831** N3
Collingwood, New Zealand, **719** D5
Collins, Iowa, U.S.A., **830** G5
Collins, Mississippi, U.S.A., **835** H4
Collipulli, Chile, **856** B5
Collooney, Ireland, **793** D3
Colmar, France, **775** H2
Colmonell, Scotland, U.K., **792** E5
Coln, *river*, England, U.K., **789** F3
Colne, England, U.K., **790** F4
Colne, *river*, England, U.K., **789** H3
Cologne *see* Köln, Germany, **772** C3
Colômbia, Brazil, **854** D5
Colombia, Colombia, **848** C3
Colombia, *country*, South America, **845** E3
Colombo, Sri Lanka, **752** D5
Colome, U.S.A., **830** D4
Colomiers, France, **774** E5
Colón, Buenos Aires, Argentina, **856** E4
Colón, Cuba, **839** E2
Colón, Entre Rios, Argentina, **857** E4
Colón, Panama, **839** F5
Colonel Hill, Bahamas, **839** G2
Colonia del Sacramento, Uruguay, **857** F5
Colonia Dora, Argentina, **856** D3
Colonia Josefa, Argentina, **858** E1
Colonia Lavalleja, Uruguay, **857** F4
Colonia Vicente Guerrero, Mexico, **840** A2
Colonsay, *island*, Scotland, U.K., **792** C4
Colorado, *river*, Argentina, **858** E1
Colorado, *river*, Brazil, **853** F3
Colorado, *river*, Mexico/U.S.A., **819** M5
Colorado, *state*, U.S.A., **833** K2
Colorado City, Colorado, U.S.A., **832** G3
Colorado City, Texas, U.S.A., **834** B3
Colorado Desert, U.S.A., **832** E5
Colorado do Oeste, Brazil, **853** G3
Colorado Plateau, U.S.A., **833** H3
Colorado Springs, U.S.A., **833** L2
Colotlán, Mexico, **840** E4
Colquechaca, Bolivia, **853** E5
Colquiri, Bolivia, **853** E4
Colquitt, U.S.A., **835** K4
Colsterworth, England, U.K., **789** G2
Colstrip, U.S.A., **829** L4
Coltishall, England, U.K., **789** J2
Colton, U.S.A., **833** H2
Columbia, District of, *district*, U.S.A., **831** Q6
Columbia, Kentucky, U.S.A., **831** L7
Columbia, Louisiana, U.S.A., **834** F3
Columbia, Mississippi, U.S.A., **834** H4
Columbia, Missouri, U.S.A., **830** G6
Columbia, Mount, *mountain peak*, Canada, **823** L5
Columbia, North Carolina, U.S.A., **836** B7
Columbia, *river*, Canada/U.S.A., **818** L4
Columbia, South Carolina, U.S.A., **835** M3
Columbia, Tennessee, U.S.A., **835** J2
Columbia Basin, U.S.A., **818** M4
Columbia City, U.S.A., **831** L5
Columbia Falls, U.S.A., **828** G2
Columbia Mountains, *mountain range*, Canada, **822** J5
Columbia Plateau, U.S.A., **828** E4
Columbiana, U.S.A., **835** J3
Columbine, Cape, South Africa, **810** C5
Columbus, Georgia, U.S.A., **835** K3
Columbus, Indiana, U.S.A., **831** L6
Columbus, Iowa, U.S.A., **831** J4
Columbus, Mississippi, U.S.A., **835** H3
Columbus, Nebraska, U.S.A., **830** E5
Columbus, New Mexico, U.S.A., **833** K6
Columbus, Ohio, U.S.A., **831** M6
Columbus, Texas, U.S.A., **834** D5
Columbus Point, Tobago, Trinidad and Tobago, **859** B4
Colville, Cape, New Zealand, **718** E3
Colville, *river*, U.S.A., **820** D3
Colville, U.S.A., **828** F2
Colville Lake, Canada, **820** G3
Colwyn Bay, Wales, U.K., **790** E4
Colyford, England, U.K., **788** D4
Comacchio, Italy, **778** D3
Comallo, *river*, Argentina, **858** C1
Coman, Mount, *mountain peak*, Antarctica, **862** B5
Comanche, Oklahoma, U.S.A., **834** D2
Comanche, Texas, U.S.A., **834** C4
Comandante Salas, Argentina, **856** C4
Comănești, Romania, **780** F2
Comarapa, Bolivia, **853** F4
Comarnic, Romania, **780** E3
Comas, Peru, **852** C3
Comayagua, Honduras, **838** D4
Combarbalá, Chile, **856** B4
Combe Martin, England, U.K., **788** C3
Comber, Northern Ireland, U.K., **793** G3
Combermere Bay, Myanmar, **741** B4
Comendador, Dominican Republic, **839** H3
Comeragh Mountains, *mountain range*, Ireland, **793** E5
Comfort, U.S.A., **834** C5
Comfort Bight, Canada, **827** P3
Comino, Capo, *cape*, Sardegna, Italy, **779** B5
Comitán de Domínguez, Mexico, **841** G5
Commanda, Canada, **831** P3
Commandante Luis Piedrabuena, Argentina, **858** D3
Commanders Bay, Aruba, Netherlands, **859** B3
Commerce, U.S.A., **834** E3
Committee Bay, Canada, **821** L3
Como, Italy, **778** B3
Como, Lago di, *lake*, Italy, **778** B3
Comodoro Rivadavia, Argentina, **858** D2
Comoé, *river*, Côte d'Ivoire, **804** D3
Comondú, Mexico, **840** C3
Comoros, *country*, Indian Ocean, **797** K8
Comox, Canada, **822** G7
Compiègne, France, **775** F2
Comprida, Ilha, *island*, Brazil, **857** H2
Comrat, Moldova, **780** G2
Comrie, Scotland, U.K., **792** F4
Côn Sơn, Vietnam, **739** E4
Cona, China, **750** D4
Cona Niyeu, Argentina, **858** D1
Conakry, Guinea, **804** B3
Concarneau, France, **774** C3
Conceição, Brazil, **851** F5
Conceição da Barra, Brazil, **855** F5
Conceição do Araguaia, Brazil, **854** D2
Conceição do Coité, Brazil, **855** F3
Concepción, Argentina, **856** D3
Concepción, Beni, Bolivia, **853** E3
Concepción, Canal, *channel*, Chile, **858** B4

Courtown, Ireland, **793** F5
Coutances, France, **774** D2
Couto Magalhães, Brazil, **854** D2
Coutras, France, **774** D4
Coutts, Canada, **823** N7
Covadonga, Spain, **776** E1
Covasna, Romania, **780** F3
Cove Fort, U.S.A., **832** G2
Coventry, England, U.K., **789** F2
Covilhã, Portugal, **776** D2
Covington, Georgia, U.S.A., **835** L3
Covington, Kentucky, U.S.A., **831** L6
Covington, Michigan, U.S.A., **831** J2
Covington, Tennessee, U.S.A., **835** H2
Cowan, Canada, **824** D5
Cowan, Lake, Australia, **720** E5
Cowargarzê, China, **751** F2
Cowbridge, Wales, U.K., **788** D3
Cowdenbeath, Scotland, U.K., **792** F4
Cowdrey, U.S.A., **833** K1
Cowell, Australia, **721** H5
Cowfold, England, U.K., **789** G4
Cowra, Australia, **721** K5
Cox Lake, U.S.A., **834** D4
Coxim, Brazil, **854** B5
Cox's Bāzār, Bangladesh, **755** G5
Coxwold, England, U.K., **791** G3
Coyah, Guinea, **804** B3
Coyote, U.S.A., **833** K3
Coyotitán, Mexico, **840** D4
Cozad, U.S.A., **830** D5
Cozes, France, **774** D4
Cozhê, China, **750** C2
Cozie, Alpi, *mountain range*, Italy, **778** A3
Cozumel, Isla, *island*, Mexico, **841** J4
Cozumel, Mexico, **841** J4
Crab Island, Rodrigues, **813** B1
Cradock, South Africa, **810** E5
Craig, Alaska, U.S.A., **822** C4
Craig, Colorado, U.S.A., **833** K1
Craigavon, *district*, Northern Ireland, U.K., **793** F3
Craigavon, Northern Ireland, U.K., **793** F3
Craignure, Scotland, U.K., **792** D4
Crail, Scotland, U.K., **792** G4
Crailsheim, Germany, **772** E4
Craiova, Romania, **780** D3
Cramlington, England, U.K., **791** G2
Cranberry Portage, Canada, **824** D4
Cranbrook, Canada, **823** M7
Crandon, U.S.A., **831** J3
Crane, Oregon, U.S.A., **828** E5
Crane, Texas, U.S.A., **833** M6
Cranleigh, England, U.K., **789** G3
Cranston, U.S.A., **836** E4
Craon, France, **774** D3
Crary Mountains, *mountain range*, Antarctica, **862** B6
Crasnoe, Moldova, **780** G2
Crater Lake, U.S.A., **828** C5
Crater Point, Papua New Guinea, **726** D4
Crateús, Brazil, **851** F4
Crathorne, England, U.K., **791** G3
Crati, *river*, Italy, **779** F6
Crato, Brazil, **851** F5
Crauford, Cape, Canada, **821** L2
Craven Arms, England, U.K., **788** E2
Cravo Norte, Colombia, **849** D2
Crawford, U.S.A., **830** B4
Crawfordville, U.S.A., **835** K4
Crawfordsville, U.S.A., **831** K5
Crawley, England, U.K., **789** G3
Crécy-en-Ponthieu, France, **789** J4
Credenhill, England, U.K., **788** E2
Crediton, England, U.K., **788** D4
Cree, *river*, Canada, **823** S2
Cree Lake, Canada, **823** R3
Cree Lake, *lake*, Canada, **823** S3
Creede, U.S.A., **833** K3
Creel, Mexico, **840** D3
Creeslough, Ireland, **793** E2
Creil, France, **774** F2
Crema, Italy, **778** B3
Crémieu, France, **775** G4
Cremona, Italy, **778** B3
Crenshaw, U.S.A., **834** G2
Cres, *island*, Croatia, **778** E3
Crescent, U.S.A., **828** D5
Crescent City, U.S.A., **828** B6
Crescent Junction, U.S.A., **833** J2
Crescent Lake, U.S.A., **835** M5
Crescent Spur, Canada, **822** J5
Crespo, Argentina, **857** E4
Crest, France, **775** G4
Creston, Canada, **823** L7
Creston, Iowa, U.S.A., **830** F5
Creston, Montana, U.S.A., **828** G2
Crestview, U.S.A., **835** J4
Creswell, England, U.K., **789** F1
Crete *see* Kriti, *island*, Greece, **781** E8
Cretin, Cape, Papua New Guinea, **726** B4
Creus, Cabo de, *cape*, Spain, **777** J1
Creuse, *river*, France, **774** E3
Crèvecoeur-le-Grand, France, **789** K5
Crewe, England, U.K., **788** E1
Crewe, U.S.A., **836** A6
Crewkerne, England, U.K., **788** E4
Crianlarich, Scotland, U.K., **792** E4
Criccieth, Wales, U.K., **788** C2
Criciúma, Brazil, **857** H3
Crickhowell, Wales, U.K., **788** D3
Crieff, Scotland, U.K., **792** F4
Criel-sur-Mer, France, **789** J4
Crikvenica, Croatia, **778** E3
Crimean Peninsula *see* Kryms'kyy Pivostriv, *peninsula*, Ukraine, **782** D3
Criquetot-l'Esneval, France, **789** H5
Cristalândia, Brazil, **854** D3
Cristalina, Brazil, **854** D4
Cristalino, *river*, Mato Grosso, Brazil, **854** C3
Cristalino, *river*, Pará, Brazil, **854** B2
Cristino Castro, Brazil, **855** E2
Cristóbal, Punta, *point*, Islas Galápagos (Galapagos Islands), Ecuador, **859** A2
Cristóbal Colón, Pico, *mountain peak*, Colombia, **848** D1
Cristuru Secuiesc, Romania, **780** E2
Criuleni, Moldova, **780** G2
Crixás, Brazil, **854** D4
Crixás Açu, *river*, Brazil, **854** D3
Crna Gora, *mountain range*, Macedonia/Yugoslavia, **780** C4
Crna Gora (Montenegro), *republic*, Yugoslavia, **780** B4
Crni Vrh, *mountain peak*, Romania, **780** D3
Črnomelj, Slovenia, **778** E3
Croatia, *country*, Europe, **764** F6
Crockett, U.S.A., **834** E4
Crofton, U.S.A., **830** E4
Croisette, Cap, *cape*, France, **775** G5
Croix, Lac la, *lake*, Canada/U.S.A., **830** H1
Croker Island, Australia, **720** G1
Cromarty, Scotland, U.K., **792** E3
Crombach, Belgium, **772** B3
Cromer, England, U.K., **789** J2
Cromwell, New Zealand, **719** B7
Crook, England, U.K., **791** G3
Crook, U.S.A., **833** M1
Crooked Island, Bahamas, **839** G2
Crooked Island, China, **743** C4
Crooked River, Canada, **824** C5
Crookham, England, U.K., **790** F2
Crookhaven, Ireland, **793** C6
Crookston, U.S.A., **830** E2
Croom, Ireland, **793** D5
Crosby, U.S.A., **830** G2
Cross City, U.S.A., **835** L5
Cross Fell, *mountain peak*, England, U.K., **790** F3
Cross Inn, Wales, U.K., **788** C2
Cross Lake, Canada, **824** F4
Cross River, *state*, Nigeria, **805** F3
Crossett, U.S.A., **834** G3
Crossgar, Northern Ireland, U.K., **793** G3
Crossgates, Wales, U.K., **788** D2
Crosshaven, Ireland, **793** D6
Crossmaglen, Northern Ireland, U.K., **793** F3
Crossville, U.S.A., **835** K2
Croswell, U.S.A., **831** M4
Crotone, Italy, **779** F6
Crouch, *river*, England, U.K., **789** H3
Crow Agency, U.S.A., **829** L4
Crow Head, *point*, Ireland, **793** B6
Crowborough, England, U.K., **789** H3
Crowell, U.S.A., **834** C3
Crowheart, U.S.A., **829** K5
Crowland, England, U.K., **789** G2
Crowle, England, U.K., **791** H4
Crowley, U.S.A., **834** F4
Crowleys Ridge, *mountain range*, U.S.A., **834** G2
Crown Point, U.S.A., **831** K5
Crowsnest Pass, Canada, **823** M7
Croyde, England, U.K., **788** C3
Croydon, Australia, **721** J2
Croydon, England, U.K., **789** G3
Crozet, Îles, *islands*, French Southern and Antarctic Islands, **708** D13
Crozet Basin, *underwater feature*, Indian Ocean, **866** C7
Crozet Plateau, *underwater feature*, Indian Ocean, **866** C8
Cruachan, Ben, *mountain peak*, Scotland, U.K., **792** D4
Crucero, Peru, **853** D4
Cruillas, Mexico, **841** F3
Crumlin, Northern Ireland, U.K., **793** F3
Crummock Water, *lake*, England, U.K., **790** E3
Crusheen, Ireland, **793** D5
Cruz, Cabo, *cape*, Cuba, **839** F3
Cruz Alta, Brazil, **857** G3
Cruz del Eje, Argentina, **856** D4
Cruzeiro, Brazil, **855** E6
Cruzeiro do Sul, Brazil, **852** D2
Crvenka, Yugoslavia, **780** B3
Crymmych Arms, Wales, U.K., **788** C3
Crystal, U.S.A., **830** E1
Crystal City, U.S.A., **834** C5
Crystal Falls, U.S.A., **831** J2
Csenger, Hungary, **773** L5
Csongrád, Hungary, **773** K5
Csorna, Hungary, **773** H5
Csurgó, Hungary, **773** H5
Cuadrada, Sierra, *mountain range*, Argentina, **858** D2
Cuamba, Mozambique, **809** G5
Cuando, *river*, Angola, **808** D6
Cuando Cubango, *province*, Angola, **808** C6
Cuangar, Angola, **810** C2
Cuango, Angola, **808** C4
Cuanza, *river*, Angola, **808** C4
Cuanza Norte, *province*, Angola, **808** B4
Cuanza Sul, *province*, Angola, **808** B5
Cuarto, *river*, Argentina, **856** D4
Cuatir, *river*, Angola, **808** C6
Cuatro Ciéngas, Mexico, **840** E3
Cuatro Ojos, Bolivia, **853** F4
Cuauhtémoc, Mexico, **840** D2
Cuautla Morelos, Mexico, **841** F5
Cuba, *country*, Caribbean Sea, **817** Q6
Cuba, U.S.A., **833** K3
Cubal, Angola, **808** B5
Cubango, *river*, Angola, **808** C6
Cubará, Colombia, **848** D2
Cuchi, Angola, **808** C5
Cuchillo-Có, Argentina, **856** D6
Cuckfield, England, U.K., **789** G3
Cucuí, Brazil, **849** E4
Cucumbi, Angola, **808** C5
Cúcuta, Colombia, **848** D2
Cuddalore, India, **752** D4
Cuddapah, India, **752** D3
Cudworth, Canada, **823** S5
Cuebe, *river*, Angola, **808** C6
Cuelei, *river*, Angola, **808** C5
Cuéllar, Spain, **776** E2
Cuemba, Angola, **808** C5
Cuenca, Ecuador, **848** B5
Cuenca, Serranía de, *mountain range*, Spain, **777** G2
Cuenca, Spain, **777** F2
Cuencamé, Mexico, **840** E3
Cuernavaca, Mexico, **841** F5
Cuero, U.S.A., **834** D5
Cuervo, U.S.A., **833** L4
Cueto, Cuba, **839** G2
Cugir, Romania, **780** D3
Cuglieri, Sardegna, Italy, **779** B5
Cuiaba, Brazil, **850** A5
Cuiabá, Brazil, **854** B4
Cuiabá de Larga, Brazil, **854** B4
Cuidado, Punta, *point*, Isla de Pascua (Easter Island), Chile, **859** B2
Cuihengcun, China, **743** A4
Cuilcagh, *mountain peak*, Ireland, **793** E3
Cuillin Hills, Scotland, U.K., **792** C3
Cuillin Sound, Scotland, U.K., **792** C3
Cuilo, Angola, **808** C4
Cuiluan, China, **747** K3
Cuimba, Angola, **808** B4
Cuio, Angola, **808** B5
Cuité, Brazil, **851** G5
Cuito, *river*, Angola, **808** C5
Cuito Cuanavale, Angola, **808** C6
Cuiuni, *river*, Brazil, **849** F4
Cujmir, Romania, **780** D3
Cukai, Malaysia, **736** C1
Cul Mor, *mountain peak*, Scotland, U.K., **792** D2
Culasi, Philippines, **740** C4
Culbertson, Montana, U.S.A., **829** M2
Culbertson, Nebraska, U.S.A., **830** C5
Culebra, Sierra de la, *mountain range*, Spain, **776** D2
Culebras, Peru, **852** B2
Culgoa, *river*, Australia, **721** K4
Culiacán, Mexico, **840** D3
Culiacancito, Mexico, **840** D3
Culion Island, Philippines, **740** B4
Cúllar Baza, Spain, **777** F4
Cullen, Scotland, U.K., **792** G3
Cullera, Spain, **777** G3
Cullivoe, Shetland, Scotland, U.K., **792** K7
Cullman, U.S.A., **835** J2
Cullompton, England, U.K., **788** D4
Çullu, Turkey, **803** H1
Cullybackey, Northern Ireland, U.K., **793** F3
Culmstock, England, U.K., **788** D4
Culpeper, U.S.A., **836** B5
Culpepper *see* Darwin, Isla, *island*, Islas Galápagos (Galapagos Islands), Ecuador, **859** A1
Culuene, *river*, Brazil, **854** C3
Cumaná, Venezuela, **849** F1
Cumare, Cerro, *mountain peak*, Colombia, **848** D4
Cumbal, Nevado de, *mountain peak*, Colombia, **848** C4
Cumberland, Bahía, *bay*, Róbinson Crusoe Island, Archipiélago Juan Fernández, Chile, **859** C2
Cumberland, *river*, U.S.A., **834** K1
Cumberland, U.S.A., **836** A6
Cumberland Bay, South Georgia, **859** A3
Cumberland House, Canada, **824** C5
Cumberland Island, U.S.A., **835** M4
Cumberland Lake, Canada, **824** C4
Cumberland Peninsula, Canada, **821** N3
Cumberland Plateau, U.S.A., **835** J3
Cumberland Sound, Canada, **821** N3
Cumbrian Mountains, *mountain range*, England, U.K., **790** E3
Cuminapanema, *river*, Brazil, **850** B3
Cummings, U.S.A., **832** B2
Cumpas, Mexico, **840** C2
Çumra, Turkey, **803** F1
Cumuripa, Mexico, **840** C2
Cunén, Guatemala, **838** C4
Cunene, *province*, Angola, **808** C6
Cunene, *river*, Angola, **808** B6
Cuneo, Italy, **778** A3
Cunnamulla, Australia, **721** K4
Cupar, Scotland, U.K., **792** F4
Cupcina, Moldova, **780** F1
Cupica, Colombia, **848** C2
Cupica, Golfo de, *gulf*, Colombia, **848** B2
Ćuprija, Yugoslavia, **780** C4
Curaçá, Brazil, **855** F2
Curaçao, *island*, Netherlands Antilles, **859** C3
Curacautín, Chile, **856** B6
Curacó, *river*, Argentina, **856** D6
Curaray, *river*, Ecuador/Peru, **848** C4
Curaumilla, Punta, *point*, Chile, **856** B4
Curepipe, Mauritius, **813** C1
Curicó, Chile, **856** B5
Curicuriari, *river*, Brazil, **849** E4
Curieuse, *island*, Seychelles, **813** A2
Curimatá, Brazil, **855** E3
Curimataú, *river*, Brazil, **851** G5
Curitiba, Brazil, **857** H2
Curitibanos, Brazil, **857** G3
Curlew, U.S.A., **828** E2
Curoca, *river*, Angola, **808** B6
Currais Novos, Brazil, **851** G5
Curral Velho, Cape Verde, **800** Q8
Curralinho, Brazil, **850** D3
Currant, U.S.A., **832** F2
Currie, Australia, **721** J6
Currie, U.S.A., **832** F1
Currituck, U.S.A., **836** C6
Curtea de Argeş, Romania, **780** E3
Curtici, Romania, **780** C2
Curtis Island, Australia, **721** L3
Curtis Island, Kermadec Islands, New Zealand, **718** L12

D

Darwin, Isla (Culpepper), *island*, Islas Galápagos (Galapagos Islands), Ecuador, **859** A1
Darwin, Monte, *mountain peak*, Chile, **858** D5
Darwin, Volcán, *mountain peak*, Islas Galápagos (Galapagos Islands), Ecuador, **859** A1
Darya Khān, Pakistan, **754** B3
Dārzin, Iran, **757** G3
Dasāda, India, **754** B5
Dashbalbar, Mongolia, **746** F2
Dashhowuz, Turkmenistan, **758** F4
Dashi, China, **743** A2
Dashitou, Jilin, China, **747** K4
Dashitou, Xinjiang Uygur Zizhiqu, China, **749** F4
Dashizhai, China, **747** H3
Dasht, *river*, Pakistan, **757** H3
Dashuijing, China, **751** G4
Dashuikeng, China, **743** D3
Dasu, Pakistan, **754** C2
Datang, China, **742** B3
Datça, Turkey, **781** F7
Date, Japan, **745** H2
Dateland, U.S.A., **832** G5
Datia, India, **754** D4
Datian, China, **742** D3
Datil, U.S.A., **833** K4
Datong, Qinghai, China, **749** J5
Datong, *river*, China, **749** J5
Datong, Shanxi, China, **746** F4
Datu, Tanjong, *point*, Malaysia, **737** E2
Datu, Teluk, *bay*, Malaysia, **737** E2
Datuk, Tanjong, *point*, Indonesia, **736** C2
Dauban, Mont, *mountain peak*, Seychelles, **813** A2
Daudnagar, India, **755** F4
Daugai, Lithuania, **771** M5
Daugava, *river*, Latvia, **771** M4
Daugavpils, Latvia, **771** N5
Daule, Indonesia, **734** C4
Daun, Gunung, *mountain peak*, Indonesia, **736** C3
Daund, India, **752** C2
Dauphin, Canada, **824** D6
Dauphin Island, U.S.A., **835** H4
Dauphin Lake, Canada, **824** E6
Daura, Nigeria, **805** F2
Dausa, India, **754** D4
Dava, Scotland, U.K., **792** F3
Dāvangere, India, **752** C3
Davao, Philippines, **740** D5
Davao Gulf, Philippines, **740** D5
Dāvarzan, Iran, **758** F5
Davenport, Iowa, U.S.A., **830** H5
Davenport, Washington, U.S.A., **828** F3
Daventry, England, U.K., **789** F2
David, Panama, **839** E5
Davidson, Canada, **823** R6
Davis, *Australian research station*, Antarctica, **862** G5
Davis, Mount, *mountain peak*, U.S.A., **831** P6
Davis, U.S.A., **832** C2
Davis Creek, U.S.A., **828** D6
Davis Inlet, Canada, **827** L2
Davis Mountains, *mountain range*, U.S.A., **833** M6
Davis Sea, Antarctica, **862** G5
Davis Strait, Canada/Greenland, **821** P3
Davlekanovo, Russian Federation, **758** F2
Davos, Switzerland, **775** J3
Davy Lake, Canada, **823** Q2
Dawa, *river*, Ethiopia, **809** G2
Dawanshan Dao, *island*, China, **743** B5
Dawei *see* Tavoy, Myanmar, **738** C3
Dawhinava, Belarus, **771** N5
Dawkah, Oman, **757** F5
Dawlish, England, U.K., **788** D4
Dawn, U.S.A., **834** A2
Dawros Head, *point*, Ireland, **793** D3
Dawson, Canada, **820** F3
Dawson, Georgia, U.S.A., **835** K4
Dawson, Minnesota, U.S.A., **830** E3
Dawson, North Dakota, U.S.A., **830** D2
Dawson Creek, Canada, **822** J4
Dawson Falls, New Zealand, **718** E4
Dawson Inlet, Canada, **824** H1
Dawu, China, **741** D1
Dawu, Hubei, China, **742** C2
Dawu, Sichuan, China, **751** G3
Dawusi, China, **749** F5
Dawwah, Oman, **757** G4
Dax, France, **774** D5
Daxatar, China, **746** E4
Daxin, China, **751** H5
Daxing, China, **746** G5
Daxinggou, China, **747** K4
Daxue Shan, *mountain range*, China, **751** G3
Daya Wan, *bay*, China, **743** D3
Dayangshu, China, **747** J2
Dayao, China, **751** G4
Dayi, China, **751** G3
Daym Zubayr, Sudan, **806** C3
Daymán, Cuchilla del, *mountain range*, Uruguay, **857** F4
Dayong, China, **743** A4
Dayr 'Aṭīyah, Syria, **761** D2
Dayr az Zawr, Syria, **803** H1
Dayr Ḥāfir, Syria, **761** D1
Dayrūṭ, Egypt, **803** F3
Daysland, Canada, **823** N5
Dayton, Ohio, U.S.A., **831** L6
Dayton, Tennessee, U.S.A., **835** K2
Dayton, Washington, U.S.A., **828** F3
Dayton, Wyoming, U.S.A., **829** L4
Daytona Beach, U.S.A., **835** M5
Dayu, China, **742** C3
Dayville, U.S.A., **828** E4
Dazhou, China, **751** H3
De Aar, South Africa, **810** D5
De Funiak Springs, U.S.A., **835** J4
De Goeje Gebergte, *mountain peak*, Suriname, **850** B2
De Jongs, Tanjong, *point*, Indonesia, **735** G4
De Kalb, Illinois, U.S.A., **831** J5
De Kalb, Texas, U.S.A., **834** E3
De Panne, Belgium, **789** K3
De Pere, U.S.A., **831** J3
De Queen, U.S.A., **834** E2
De Tour Village, U.S.A., **831** M3
De Winton, Canada, **823** M6
De Witt, U.S.A., **830** H5
Dead Indian Peak, *mountain peak*, U.S.A., **829** K4
Dead Sea, *lake*, Israel/Jordan, **761** C4
Deadhorse, U.S.A., **820** E2
Deadman Bay, U.S.A., **835** L5
Deadman Butte, *mountain peak*, U.S.A., **829** L5
Deal, England, U.K., **789** J3
Dealul Bălănești, *mountain peak*, Moldova, **780** G2
Deán Funes, Argentina, **856** D4
Dearborn, U.S.A., **831** M4
Dearg, Beinn, *mountain peak*, Highland, Scotland, U.K., **792** E3
Dearg, Beinn, *mountain peak*, Perth and Kinross, Scotland, U.K., **792** F4
Deary, U.S.A., **828** F3
Dease, *river*, Canada, **822** E2
Dease Lake, Canada, **822** E2
Death Valley, U.S.A., **832** E3
Deba, Spain, **777** F1
Debak, Malaysia, **737** E2
Debar, Macedonia, **781** C5
Debark', Ethiopia, **807** E2
Debden, Canada, **823** R5
Deben, *river*, England, U.K., **789** J2
Debenham, England, U.K., **789** J2
Debesy, Russian Federation, **758** E1
Dębica, Poland, **773** K3
Dęblin, Poland, **773** K3
Dębno, Poland, **773** G2
Debrc, Yugoslavia, **780** B3
Debre Birhan, Ethiopia, **807** E3
Debre Mark'os, Ethiopia, **807** E2
Debre Sīna, Ethiopia, **807** E3
Debre Tabor, Ethiopia, **807** E2
Debre Werk', Ethiopia, **807** E2
Debre Zeyit, Ethiopia, **807** E3
Debrecen, Hungary, **773** K5
Debrzno, Poland, **773** H2
Dečani, Yugoslavia, **780** C4
Decatur, Alabama, U.S.A., **835** J2
Decatur, Illinois, U.S.A., **831** J6
Decatur, Indiana, U.S.A., **831** L5
Decatur, Texas, U.S.A., **834** D3
Decazeville, France, **774** F4
Deccan, *plateau*, India, **732** J8
Dechu, India, **754** C4
Decize, France, **775** F3
Decorah, U.S.A., **830** H4
Deddington, England, U.K., **789** F3
Deder, Ethiopia, **807** F3
Dediāpāda, India, **754** C5
Dedo de Deus, *mountain peak*, Brazil, **857** H2
Dédougou, Burkina Faso, **804** D2
Dedovichi, Russian Federation, **783** B4
Dedza, Malawi, **809** F5
Dee, *river*, England, U.K., **790** E4
Dee, *river*, Scotland, U.K., **792** F3
Deel, *river*, Ireland, **793** D5
Deep River, Canada, **826** C6
Deep Valley Bay, St Helena, **813** B3
Deer, *island*, New Caledonia, **722** C3
Deer Lake, Ontario, Canada, **824** G5
Deer Lake, Newfoundland, Canada, **827** N5
Deer Lodge, U.S.A., **828** H3
Deer Park, U.S.A., **828** F3
Deer Peak, *mountain peak*, U.S.A., **828** F4
Defiance, U.S.A., **831** L5
Dêgê, China, **751** F3
Degeberga, Sweden, **770** G5
Degeh Bur, Ethiopia, **807** F3
Degelis, Canada, **826** G6
Degema, Nigeria, **805** F4
Degerfors, Sweden, **770** G3
Deh Bīd, Iran, **756** F2
Deh Shū, Afghanistan, **757** H2
Dehiwala-Mount Lavinia, Sri Lanka, **752** D5
Dehlorān, Iran, **803** J2
Dehra Dūn, India, **754** D3
Dehri, India, **755** F4
Dehua, China, **742** D3
Dehui, China, **747** J3
Dej, Romania, **780** D2
Deje, Sweden, **770** F3
Dejen, Ethiopia, **807** E2
Dejiang, China, **742** B2
Dek'emhāre, Eritrea, **807** E1
Dekese, Democratic Republic of the Congo, **808** D3
Dekina, Nigeria, **805** F3
Dékoa, Central African Republic, **806** A3
Del Norte, U.S.A., **833** K3
Del Rio, U.S.A., **834** B5
Delano, U.S.A., **832** D4
Delano Peak, *mountain peak*, U.S.A., **832** G2
Delārām, Afghanistan, **757** H2
Delareyville, South Africa, **810** E4
Delavan, U.S.A., **831** J4
Delaware, *river*, U.S.A., **836** C4
Delaware, *state*, U.S.A., **836** C5
Delaware, U.S.A., **831** M5
Delaware Bay, U.S.A., **836** C5
Delčevo, Macedonia, **780** D5
Deleau, Canada, **824** D7
Delémont, Switzerland, **775** H3
Délép, Chad, **806** A2
Delft, Netherlands, **772** B2
Delfzijl, Netherlands, **772** C2
Delgado, Cabo, *cape*, Mozambique, **809** H5
Delger Mörön, *river*, Mongolia, **749** H2
Delgermörön, Mongolia, **749** H3
Delhi, India, **754** D3
Delhi, *union territory*, India, **754** D3
Delhi, U.S.A., **833** M3
Délices, French Guiana, **850** C2
Deliceto, Italy, **779** E5
Delījān, Iran, **756** F2
Déline, Canada, **820** G3
Delingha, China, **749** H5
Delisle, Canada, **823** R6
Delitzsch, Germany, **772** F3
Dellys, Algeria, **801** G1
Delmenhorst, Germany, **772** D2
Delnice, Croatia, **778** E3
Deloraine, Canada, **824** D7
Delray Beach, U.S.A., **835** M6
Delsbo, Sweden, **770** H2
Delta, Colorado, U.S.A., **833** J2
Delta, Iowa, U.S.A., **830** G5
Delta, *state*, Nigeria, **805** F3
Delta, Utah, U.S.A., **832** G2
Delta Beach, Canada, **824** E6
Delta Junction, U.S.A., **820** E3
Deltona, U.S.A., **835** M5
Delvāda, India, **754** B5
Delvin, Ireland, **793** E4
Delvinë, Albania, **781** C6
Delyatyn, Ukraine, **780** E1
Demba, Democratic Republic of the Congo, **808** D4
Dembech'a, Ethiopia, **807** E2
Dembī Dolo, Ethiopia, **806** D3
Dembia, Central African Republic, **808** D1
Demerara Plain, *underwater feature*, Atlantic Ocean, **867** D5
Demidov, Russian Federation, **783** C5
Deming, U.S.A., **833** K5
Demini, *river*, Brazil, **849** F4
Demirci, Turkey, **781** G6
Demirköprü Barajı, *dam*, Turkey, **781** G6
Demirköy, Turkey, **780** F5
Demmin, Germany, **772** F2
Democratic Republic of the Congo, *country*, Africa, **797** G7
Demopolis, U.S.A., **835** J3
Dempo, Gunung, *mountain peak*, Indonesia, **736** C3
Demta, Indonesia, **735** H3
Demyansk, Russian Federation, **783** D4
Den Chai, Thailand, **738** D2
Den Helder, Netherlands, **772** B2
Denan, Ethiopia, **807** F3
Denbigh, Canada, **826** C7
Denbigh, Wales, U.K., **788** D1
Denbighshire, *unitary authority*, Wales, U.K., **788** D1
Dendang, Indonesia, **737** D3
Dendâra, Mauritania, **804** C1
Dengfeng, China, **742** C1
Dengi, Nigeria, **805** F3
Dengkou, China, **746** D4
Dêngqên, China, **751** E3
Dengyoufang, China, **746** F4
Dengzhou, China, **742** C1
Denham, Australia, **720** C4
Denia, Spain, **777** H3
Denio Junction, U.S.A., **828** E6
Denison, Iowa, U.S.A., **830** F4
Denison, Texas, U.S.A., **834** D3
Denizli, *province*, Turkey, **781** G7
Denizli, Turkey, **781** G7
Denmark, Australia, **720** D5
Denmark, *country*, Europe, **764** E4
Denmark, U.S.A., **835** M3
Denmark Strait, Greenland/Iceland, **821** S3
Dennehotso, U.S.A., **833** J3
Denny, Scotland, U.K., **792** F4
Denow, Uzbekistan, **758** H5
Denpasar, Indonesia, **737** F5
Dent Island, Auckland Islands, New Zealand, **718** K11
Denton, U.S.A., **834** D3
d'Entrecasteaux, Point, Australia, **716** A5
D'Entrecasteaux Islands, Papua New Guinea, **726** C5
Denver, U.S.A., **833** L2
Denver City, U.S.A., **833** M5
Deoghar, India, **755** F4
Deolāli, India, **754** C6
Deoli, India, **754** D5
Deorī Khās, India, **754** D5
Deoria, India, **755** E4
Deosil, India, **755** E5
Dep, *river*, Russian Federation, **747** K1
Depapre, Indonesia, **735** H3
Depot Peak, *mountain peak*, Antarctica, **862** F4
Deputatskiy, Russian Federation, **785** Q3
Dêqên, China, **751** F3
Deqing, Guangdong, China, **742** B4
Deqing, Zhejiang, China, **742** E2
DeQuincy, U.S.A., **834** F4
Der-Chantecoq, Lac du, *lake*, France, **775** G2
Dera Bugti, Pakistan, **754** B3
Dera Ghāzi Khān, Pakistan, **754** B3
Dera Ismāīl Khān, Pakistan, **754** B3
Derbent, Russian Federation, **758** D4
Derbent, Turkey, **781** G6
Derbent, Uzbekistan, **758** H5
Derbissaka, Central African Republic, **808** D1
Derbur, China, **747** H2
Derby, Australia, **720** E2
Derby, England, U.K., **789** F2
Derby City, *unitary authority*, England, U.K., **789** F2
Derbyshire, *unitary authority*, England, U.K., **789** F1
Déréssa, Chad, **806** B2
Derg, Lough, *lake*, Clare/Galway, Ireland, **793** D5
Derg, Lough, *lake*, Donegal, Ireland, **793** D3
Derg, *river*, Northern Ireland, U.K., **793** E3
Dergachi, Russian Federation, **758** D2
DeRidder, U.S.A., **834** F4
Dermott, U.S.A., **834** B3
Dernberg, Cape, Namibia, **810** B4
Dêrong, China, **751** F3
Déroute, Passage de la, *strait*, Channel Islands/France, **774** C2
Derre, Mozambique, **809** G6
Derri, Somalia, **807** G4
Derry, U.S.A., **836** E3
Derryveagh Mountains, Ireland, **793** D3
Dersingham, England, U.K., **789** H2
Derst, China, **746** F4
Derudeb, Sudan, **803** G5
Derval, France, **774** D3
Derventa, Bosnia and Herzegovina, **778** F3
Derwent, Canada, **823** P5
Derwent, *river*, England, U.K., **791** H4
Derwent Reservoir, England, U.K., **790** F3

Dodson, U.S.A., **829** K2
Doetinchem, Netherlands, **772** C3
Dog Creek, Canada, **822** H6
Dog Island, U.S.A., **835** K5
Dog Lake, Canada, **825** K7
Dogai Coring, *lake*, China, **750** D2
Doğanbey, Aydin, Turkey, **781** F7
Doğanbey, İzmir, Turkey, **781** F6
Dōgo, *island*, Japan, **744** F3
Dogondoutchi, Niger, **805** E2
Dogoumbo, Chad, **805** H2
Doğu Menteşe Dağları, *mountain range*, Turkey, **781** G7
Doğubayazıt, Turkey, **760** F5
Do'gyaling, China, **750** D3
Doha *see* Ad Dawḩah, Qatar, **756** F3
Dohazar, Bangladesh, **755** H5
Doilungdêqên, China, **750** D3
Dokka, Norway, **770** E2
Dokshytsy, Belarus, **771** N5
Dolak, Pulau, *island*, Indonesia, **735** G4
Dolavón, Argentina, **858** E2
Dolbeau, Canada, **826** E5
Dolbenmaen, Wales, U.K., **788** C2
Dolce, Cape, U.S.A., **836** C5
Doldrums Fracture Zone, *tectonic feature*, Atlantic Ocean, **867** D5
Dole, France, **775** G3
Dolgellau, Wales, U.K., **788** D2
Dolianova, Sardegna, Italy, **779** B6
Dolit, Indonesia, **734** D3
Doljevac, Yugoslavia, **780** C4
Dolný Kubín, Slovakia, **773** J4
Dolo Odo, Ethiopia, **809** H2
Dolomiti, *mountain range*, Italy, **778** C2
Doloon, Mongolia, **746** D3
Dolores, Argentina, **857** F5
Dolores, Guatemala, **838** C3
Dolores, Uruguay, **857** E4
Dolphin, Cape, Falkland Islands, **858** F4
Dolphin and Union Strait, Canada, **820** G2
Dolphin Head, *point*, Namibia, **810** B4
Dolyna, Ukraine, **773** L4
Dom, Gunung, *mountain peak*, Indonesia, **735** G3
Dom Pedrito, Brazil, **857** F4
Dom Pedro, Brazil, **851** E4
Domanivka, Ukraine, **780** H2
Domar, China, **750** B2
Domaradz, Poland, **773** L4
Domažlice, Czech Republic, **772** F4
Domba, China, **751** E2
Dombarovskiy, Russian Federation, **758** F2
Dombås, Norway, **770** D1
Dombe, Mozambique, **811** F2
Dombóvár, Hungary, **773** H5
Dome Creek, Canada, **822** J5
Domett, Mount, *mountain peak*, New Zealand, **719** D5
Domeyko, Antofagasta, Chile, **856** C2
Domeyko, Atacama, Chile, **856** B3
Domeyko, Cordillera, *mountain range*, Chile, **856** C2
Domfront, France, **774** D2
Dominica, *country*, Caribbean Sea, **837** D3
Dominica Passage, Caribbean Sea, **837** D3
Dominical, Costa Rica, **838** E5
Dominican Republic, *country*, Caribbean Sea, **817** R7
Dominion, Cape, Canada, **821** M3
Dömitz, Germany, **772** E2
Domnesti, Romania, **780** E3
Domo, Ethiopia, **807** G3
Domodedovo, Russian Federation, **783** F5
Domodossola, Italy, **778** B2
Domokos, Greece, **781** D6
Domoni, Comoros, **812** A3
Dompu, Indonesia, **737** G5
Domuyo, Volcán, *mountain peak*, Argentina, **856** B5
Domžale, Slovenia, **778** E2
Don, Mexico, **840** C3
Don, *river*, France, **774** D3
Don, *river*, Russian Federation, **782** F3
Don, *river*, Scotland, U.K., **792** F3
Donaghmore, Northern Ireland, U.K., **790** B3
Donaldson, U.S.A., **830** E1
Donaldsonville, U.S.A., **834** G4
Donard, Slieve, *mountain peak*, Northern Ireland, U.K., **793** G3
Donau (Danube), *river*, Austria, **773** F4
Donau (Danube), *river*, Germany, **772** E4
Donaueschingen, Germany, **772** D5
Donauwörth, Germany, **772** E4
Doncaster, England, U.K., **791** G4
Dondo, Angola, **808** B4
Dondo, Mozambique, **811** F2
Dondra Head, Sri Lanka, **753** E5
Donduşeni, Moldova, **780** F1
Donegal, *county*, Ireland, **793** D3
Donegal, Ireland, **793** D3
Donegal Bay, Ireland, **793** D3
Donegal Point, Ireland, **793** C5
Donets'k, Ukraine, **782** E3
Dong, *river*, N. China, **749** J4
Dong, *river*, S. China, **743** C2
Đông Hà, Vietnam, **739** E2
Đồng Hới, Vietnam, **739** E2
Đông Nai, *river*, Vietnam, **739** E4
Dong Ujimqin Qi, China, **746** G3
Donga, Nigeria, **805** G3
Dong'an, Heilongjiang, China, **747** L3
Dong'an, Hunan, China, **742** B3
Dongarra, Australia, **720** C4
Dongchuan, China, **751** G4
Dongco, China, **750** C2
Dongfang, China, **739** F2
Dongfanghong, China, **747** L3
Dongfeng, Guangdong, China, **743** A3
Dongfeng, Jilin, China, **747** J4
Donggala, Indonesia, **734** B3
Donggou, China, **744** D3
Dongguan, China, **743** B2
Donghai Dao, *island*, China, **739** F1
Dongjiangkou, China, **742** B1
Dongkou, China, **742** B3
Donglan, China, **751** H4
Dongning, China, **747** K3
Dongnyi, China, **751** G3
Dongo, Angola, **808** C5
Dongo, Democratic Republic of the Congo, **808** C2
Dongou, Congo, **808** C2
Dongping, China, **739** G1
Dongping, Guangdong, China, **742** C4
Dongping, Shandong, China, **742** D1
Dongsanjia, China, **747** J3
Dongshan, China, **742** B4
Dongshan Dao, *island*, China, **742** D4
Dongsheng, China, **746** E5
Dongtai, China, **742** E1
Dongting Hu, *lake*, China, **742** C2
Dongyang, China, **742** E2
Dongying, China, **747** G5
Dongzhi, China, **742** D2
Donji Milanovac, Yugoslavia, **780** D3
Donji Mu, Croatia, **778** F4
Donji Srb, Croatia, **778** E3
Dønna, *island*, Norway, **768** E4
Donna, U.S.A., **834** C6
Donnelly, Canada, **823** L4
Donon, *mountain peak*, France, **775** H2
Donostia-San Sebastián, Spain, **777** F1
Donoughmore, Ireland, **793** D6
Donskoy, Russian Federation, **783** G6
Donsol, Philippines, **740** C3
Donxing, China, **744** E1
Dooagh, Ireland, **793** B4
Doon, Loch, *lake*, Scotland, U.K., **792** E5
Doon, *river*, Scotland, U.K., **792** E5
Doonbeg, Ireland, **793** C5
Doonbeg, *river*, Ireland, **793** C5
Dora, Lake, Australia, **720** E3
Dorchester, England, U.K., **788** E4
Dordabis, Namibia, **810** C3
Dordogne, *river*, France, **774** D4
Dordrecht, Netherlands, **772** B3
Dore, Monts, *mountain range*, France, **774** F4
Doré Lake, Canada, **823** R4
Dores, Scotland, U.K., **792** E3
Dori, Burkina Faso, **804** D2
Dorking, England, U.K., **789** G3
Dormaa Ahenkro, Ghana, **804** D3
Dormans, France, **775** F2
Dornie, Scotland, U.K., **792** D3
Dornoch Firth, *river mouth*, Scotland, U.K., **792** E3
Dornod, *province*, Mongolia, **746** F3
Dornogovĭ, *province*, Mongolia, **746** E3
Doro, Mali, **804** D1
Dorobanţu, Romania, **780** F3
Dorobino, Russian Federation, **783** F6
Dorogobuzh, Russian Federation, **783** D5
Dorohoi, Romania, **780** F2
Dorokhovo, Russian Federation, **783** F5
Dorolemo, Indonesia, **735** E2
Dorotea, Sweden, **768** H4
Dorre Island, Australia, **720** C4
Dorsale, *mountain range*, Tunisia, **802** A1
Dorset, *unitary authority*, England, U.K., **788** E4
Dortmund, Germany, **772** C3
Dorum, Germany, **772** D2
Doruma, Democratic Republic of the Congo, **809** E2
Dos Bahías, Cabo, *cape*, Argentina, **858** E2
dos Bois, *river*, Brazil, **854** D4
Dos de Mayo, Peru, **852** C2
Dos Pozos, Argentina, **858** E2
Dosi, Indonesia, **735** F4
Dospat, Bulgaria, **781** E5
Dosquet, Canada, **826** F6
Dosso, *department*, Niger, **805** E2
Dosso, Niger, **805** E2
Dossor, Kazakhstan, **758** E3
Dostyq, Kazakhstan, **748** D3
Dothan, U.S.A., **835** K4
Douai, France, **775** F1
Douala, Cameroon, **808** A2
Douarnenez, France, **774** B2
Double Cone, *mountain peak*, New Zealand, **719** B7
Double Mer, *river*, Canada, **827** M2
Doubs, *river*, France, **775** G3
Doubtful Sound, New Zealand, **719** A7
Doubtless Bay, New Zealand, **718** D2
Doudeville, France, **789** H5
Douentza, Mali, **804** D2
Douéoulou, New Caledonia, **727** A3
Doughboy Bay, New Zealand, **719** A8
Douglas, Alaska, U.S.A., **822** B2
Douglas, Arizona, U.S.A., **833** J6
Douglas, Georgia, U.S.A., **835** L4
Douglas, Isle of Man, **790** D3
Douglas, North Dakota, U.S.A., **830** C2
Douglas, Scotland, U.K., **792** F5
Douglas, South Africa, **810** D4
Douglas, Wyoming, U.S.A., **829** M5
Douglas City, U.S.A., **832** B1
Douglas Lake, Canada, **822** J6
Douglass, U.S.A., **830** E7
Doullens, France, **774** F1
Doumen, China, **743** A4
Dounreay, Scotland, U.K., **792** F2
Dourados, Brazil, **854** B6
Dourados, *river*, Brazil, **854** B6
Dourados, Serra dos, *mountain range*, Brazil, **857** G2
Dourbali, Chad, **805** H2
Douro, *river*, Portugal, **776** D2
Douze, *river*, France, **774** E5
Dove, *river*, England, U.K., **789** F1
Dover, Delaware, U.S.A., **836** C5
Dover, England, U.K., **789** J3
Dover, New Hampshire, U.S.A., **836** E3
Dover, New Jersey, U.S.A., **836** C4
Dover, Strait of, France/U.K., **789** J4
Dovey, *river*, Wales, U.K., **788** D2
Dovre, Norway, **770** D2
Dowi, Tanjong, *point*, Indonesia, **736** B2
Dowlat Yār, Afghanistan, **754** A2
Dowlatābād, Afghanistan, **754** A1
Down, *district*, Northern Ireland, U.K., **793** G3
Downey, U.S.A., **829** H5
Downham Market, England, U.K., **789** H2
Downpatrick, Northern Ireland, U.K., **793** G3
Downpatrick Head, *point*, Ireland, **793** C3
Downs, U.S.A., **830** D6
Downton, England, U.K., **789** F4
Dowshī, Afghanistan, **754** B2
Dowsk, Belarus, **783** C6
Doyleville, U.S.A., **833** K2
Dōzen, *island*, Japan, **744** F3
Drâa, Hamada du, *plateau*, Algeria, **800** E3
Drac, *river*, France, **775** G4
Dracena, Brazil, **854** C5
Dragalina, Romania, **780** F3
Drăgăşani, Romania, **780** E3
Drăgăneşti-Olt, Romania, **780** E3
Drăgăneşti-Vlaşca, Romania, **780** E3
Dragón, Bocas del, *bay*, Trinidad and Tobago, **849** G1
Dragón, Bocas del, *strait*, Trinidad and Tobago/Venezuela, **837** D4
Dragonada, *island*, Greece, **781** F8
Draguignan, France, **775** H5
Drăguşeni, Romania, **780** F2
Drahichyn, Belarus, **773** M2
Drake, U.S.A., **830** C2
Drake Passage, *strait*, Antarctica, **867** C9
Drakensberg, *mountain range*, South Africa, **799** H10
Drama, Greece, **781** E5
Drammen, Norway, **770** E3
Drangedal, Norway, **770** D3
Draper, U.S.A., **830** C4
Draperstown, Northern Ireland, U.K., **790** B3
Drava, *river*, Croatia/Hungary/Slovenia, **778** F2
Dravograd, Slovenia, **778** E2
Drawa, *river*, Poland, **773** G2
Drawsko, Jezioro, *lake*, Poland, **773** G2
Drayton, U.S.A., **830** E1
Drayton Valley, Canada, **823** M5
Dreikikir, Papua New Guinea, **726** A3
Dremsel, Mount, *mountain peak*, Papua New Guinea, **726** B3
Drenthe, *province*, Netherlands, **772** C2
Drepano, Akra, *point*, Greece, **781** D6
Dresden, Germany, **772** F3
Dretun', Belarus, **783** B5
Dreux, France, **774** E2
Drevsjø, Norway, **770** F2
Drewsey, U.S.A., **828** E5
Dreyers Rock, New Zealand, **719** E5
Driffield, England, U.K., **791** H3
Driftwood, Canada, **825** P7
Driggs, U.S.A., **829** J5
Drimoleague, Ireland, **793** C6
Drin, *river*, Albania, **780** B4
Drina, *river*, Bosnia and Herzegovina/Yugoslavia, **780** B3
Drinit, Gjiri i, *bay*, Albania, **780** B5
Drinizi, *river*, Albania, **780** C5
Drinkwater, Canada, **823** S6
Driva, *river*, Norway, **770** D1
Drniš, Croatia, **778** F4
Drøbak, Norway, **770** E3
Drobeta-Turnu Severin, Romania, **780** D3
Drobin, Poland, **773** K2
Drocea, *mountain peak*, Romania, **780** D2
Drochia, Moldova, **780** F1
Drogheda, Ireland, **793** F4
Drogobych, Ukraine, **773** L4
Droitwich, England, U.K., **788** E2
Drôme, *river*, France, **775** G4
Dromod, Ireland, **793** E4
Dromore, Northern Ireland, U.K., **793** E3
Dromore West, Ireland, **793** D3
Dronfield, England, U.K., **791** G4
Dronne, *river*, France, **774** E4
Dronning Maud Land, *region*, Antarctica, **862** D4
Dropt, *river*, France, **774** E4
Drosendorf, Austria, **773** G4
Drosh, Pakistan, **754** B2
Druif, Aruba, **859** B3
Druimdrishaig, Scotland, U.K., **792** D5
Drumheller, Canada, **823** N6
Drumkeeran, Ireland, **793** D3
Drummond, U.S.A., **828** H3
Drummond Island, U.S.A., **831** L2
Drummondville, Canada, **826** E7
Drummore, Scotland, U.K., **792** E6
Drumnadrochit, Scotland, U.K., **792** E3
Druskininkai, Lithuania, **773** L1
Drut', *river*, Belarus, **783** B6
Druya, Belarus, **771** N5
Druzhba, Ukraine, **782** D2
Drvar, Bosnia and Herzegovina, **778** F3
Drvenik, Croatia, **778** F4
Dry Gut Bay, St Helena, **813** B3
Dry Ridge, U.S.A., **831** L6
Dryanovo, Bulgaria, **780** E4
Drybrough, Canada, **824** D3
Dryden, Canada, **824** H7
Dryden, U.S.A., **833** M6
Drygalski Fjord, *fiord*, South Georgia, **859** A3
Drygarn Fawr, *mountain peak*, Wales, U.K., **788** D2

E

East Angus, Canada, **826** F7
East Antarctica, *region*, Antarctica, **862** E5
East Aurora, U.S.A., **836** A3
East Ayrshire, *local authority*, Scotland, U.K., **792** E5
East Bay, Papua New Guinea, **726** B4
East Bay, U.S.A., **835** H5
East Braintree, Canada, **824** G7
East Cape, New Zealand, **718** G3
East Caroline Basin, *underwater feature*, Pacific Ocean, **868** D4
East Dereham, England, U.K., **789** H2
East Dunbartonshire, *local authority*, Scotland, U.K., **792** E5
East Falkland, *island*, Falkland Islands, **858** G4
East Glacier Park, U.S.A., **828** H2
East Grand Forks, U.S.A., **830** E2
East Grinstead, England, U.K., **789** G3
East Hampton, U.S.A., **836** D4
East Harling, England, U.K., **789** H2
East Indian Ridge, *underwater feature*, Indian Ocean, **866** F6
East Islet, *island*, Ashmore and Cartier Islands, **720** P9
East Jordan, U.S.A., **831** L3
East Kilbride, Scotland, U.K., **792** E5
East Linton, Scotland, U.K., **792** G5
East Liverpool, U.S.A., **831** N5
East Loch Tarbert, *inlet*, Scotland, U.K., **792** C3
East London, South Africa, **811** E5
East Lothian, *local authority*, Scotland, U.K., **792** G4
East Malling, England, U.K., **789** H3
East Mariana Basin, *underwater feature*, Pacific Ocean, **868** E4
East New Britain, *province*, Papua New Guinea, **726** D4
East Pacific Rise, *underwater feature*, Pacific Ocean, **869** L7
East Point, Canada, **827** L6
East Point, Lord Howe Island, Australia, **721** U14
East Point, Tristan da Cunha, **813** C2
East Point, U.S.A., **835** K3
East Poplar, Canada, **823** S7
East Renfrewshire, *local authority*, Scotland, U.K., **792** E5
East Riding of Yorkshire, *unitary authority*, England, U.K., **791** H4
East St Louis, U.S.A., **830** H6
East Sepik, *province*, Papua New Guinea, **726** A3
East Sussex, *unitary authority*, England, U.K., **789** H4
East Tasman Plateau, *underwater feature*, Pacific Ocean, **868** E7
East Timor, *country*, Asia, 734 D5
East Wittering, England, U.K., **789** G4
Eastbourne, England, U.K., **789** H4
Eastend, Canada, **823** Q7
Easter Fracture Zone, *tectonic feature*, Pacific Ocean, **869** K6
Easter Island see Pascua, Isla, *island*, Chile, Pacific Ocean, **859** B2
Eastern, *administrative region*, Ghana, **804** D3
Eastern, *province*, Kenya, **809** G2
Eastern, *province*, Sierra Leone, **804** B3
Eastern, *province*, Zambia, **809** F5
Eastern Cape, *province*, South Africa, **811** E5
Eastern Desert *see* Sharqīyah, Aş-Şahrā' ash, *desert*, Egypt, **761** A5
Eastern Ghats, *mountain range*, India, **752** D3
Eastern Group, *islands*, Bounty Islands, New Zealand, **719** N14
Eastern Group *see* Lau Group, *islands*, Fiji, **727** A4
Eastern Highlands, *province*, Papua New Guinea, **726** B4
Eastland, U.S.A., **834** C3
Eastleigh, England, U.K., **789** F4
Eastmain, Canada, **825** Q5
Eastmain, *river*, Canada, **826** C3
Eastman, U.S.A., **835** L3
Easton, England, U.K., **788** E4
Eastry, England, U.K., **789** J3
Eastwood, England, U.K., **789** F1
Eaton Socon, England, U.K., **789** G2
Eatonton, U.S.A., **835** L3
Eau Claire, Lac à l', *lake*, Canada, **825** S3
Eau Claire, U.S.A., **830** H3
Eauripik, *island*, Micronesia, **724** C4
Eban, Nigeria, **805** E3
Ebano, Mexico, **841** F4
Ebbw Vale, Wales, U.K., **788** D3
Ebebiyin, Equatorial Guinea, **808** B2
Ebeltoft, Denmark, **770** E4
Eberbach, Germany, **772** D4
Eberswalde-Finow, Germany, **773** F2
Ebetsu, Japan, **745** H2
Ebian, China, **751** G3
Ebino, Japan, **744** E4
Ebinur Hu, *lake*, China, **748** D3
Ebolowa, Cameroon, **808** B2
Ebon, *island*, Marshall Islands, **725** E4
Ebony, Namibia, **810** C3
Ebro, *river*, Spain, **766** D7
Ebruchorr, Gora, *mountain peak*, Russian Federation, **769** R3
Ecclefechan, Scotland, U.K., **792** F5
Eccleshall, England, U.K., **788** E2
Eceabat, Turkey, **781** F5
Echinos, Greece, **781** E5
Echt, Netherlands, **772** B3
Echuca, Australia, **721** J6
Écija, Spain, **776** E4
Eckenförde, Germany, **772** D1
Eckington, England, U.K., **788** E2
Écommoy, France, **774** E3
Ecuador, *country*, South America, **845** E4
Écueillé, France, **774** E3
Ēd, Eritrea, **807** F2
Ed, Sweden, **770** E3
Edam, Canada, **823** Q5
Edam, Netherlands, **772** B2
Eday, *island*, Orkney, Scotland, U.K., **792** G1
Eddystone Point, Australia, **721** K7
Ede, Nigeria, **805** E3
Ede Point, Canada, **821** J2
Edéa, Cameroon, **808** A2
Edehon Lake, Canada, **824** F1
Edéia, Brazil, **854** D4
Eden, Australia, **721** K6
Eden, Canada, **824** E6
Eden, *river*, England, U.K., **790** F3
Eden, Texas, U.S.A., **834** C4
Eden, Wyoming, U.S.A., **829** K5
Edenbridge, England, U.K., **789** H3
Edendale, New Zealand, **719** B8
Edenderry, Ireland, **793** E4
Edenton, U.S.A., **836** B6
Eder, *river*, Germany, **772** D3
Edessa, Greece, **781** D5
Edgartown, U.S.A., **836** E4
Edgeley, U.S.A., **830** D2
Edgemont, U.S.A., **830** B4
Edgeøya, *island*, Svalbard, **784** D2
Edgerton, Canada, **823** P5
Edgeworthstown, Ireland, **793** E4
Edina, U.S.A., **830** G5
Edinboro, U.S.A., **831** N5
Edinburgh, Scotland, U.K., **792** F5
Edinburgh, Tristan da Cunha, **813** C2
Edinburgh City, *local authority*, Scotland, U.K., **792** F5
Edineţ, Moldova, **780** F1
Edirne, *province*, Turkey, **781** F5
Edirne, Turkey, **760** C4
Edjeleh, Algeria, **801** H3
Edlingham, England, U.K., **791** G2
Edmond, Kansas, U.S.A., **830** D6
Edmond, Oklahoma, U.S.A., **834** D2
Edmonton, Canada, **823** N5
Edmund Lake, Canada, **824** H4
Edmundston, Canada, **826** G6
Edna, U.S.A., **834** D5
Edo, *state*, Nigeria, **805** F3
Edolo, Italy, **778** C2
Edremit, Turkey, **781** F6
Edremit Körfezi, *bay*, Turkey, **781** F6
Edsbro, Sweden, **771** J3
Edsbyn, Sweden, **770** G2
Edson, Canada, **823** L5
Eduardo Castex, Argentina, **856** D5
Edward VII Land, *region*, Antarctica, **862** C7
Edwards Plateau, U.S.A., **834** B4
Edzo, Canada, **820** H3
Edzouga, Congo, **808** B3
Efate (Vaté), *island*, Vanuatu, **727** A2
Effie, U.S.A., **830** G2
Effingham, U.S.A., **831** J6
Effon-Alaiye, Nigeria, **805** E3
Eforie, Romania, **780** G3
Eg, Mongolia, **746** E2
Egadi, Isole, *islands*, Sicilia, Italy, **779** D7
Egan Range, *mountain range*, U.S.A., **832** F2
Eganville, Canada, **826** C7
Eger, Hungary, **773** K5
Egeria Point, Christmas Island, **720** N8
Egersund, Norway, **770** C3
Egg Island, St Helena, **813** B3
Eggedal, Norway, **770** D2
Eggenfelden, Germany, **772** F4
Egilsstaðir, Iceland, **768** Z7
Egindibulaq, Kazakhstan, **748** C2
Egiyn, *river*, Mongolia, **749** J2
Égletons, France, **774** F4
Eglinton, Northern Ireland, U.K., **793** E2
Eglwys Fach, Wales, U.K., **788** D2
Egmont, Mount (Mount Taranaki), *mountain peak*, New Zealand, **718** E4
Egremont, Canada, **823** N4
Egremont, England, U.K., **790** E3
Eğrigöz Dağı, *mountain range*, Turkey, **781** G6
Egton, England, U.K., **791** H3
Egtved, Denmark, **770** D5
Egypt, *country*, Africa, **796** I14
Eiao, *island*, French Polynesia, **723** G1
Eide, Norway, **768** C5
Eidfjord, Norway, **770** C2
Eidsdal, Norway, **770** C1
Eidsvåg, Norway, **770** D1
Eifel, *mountain range*, Germany, **772** C3
Eigg, *island*, Scotland, U.K., **792** C4
Eight Degree Channel, India/ Maldives, **752** C5
Eights Coast, *region*, Antarctica, **862** B6
Eighty Mile Beach, Australia, **720** E2
Eikefjord, Norway, **770** B2
Eiken, Norway, **770** C3
Eilenburg, Germany, **772** F3
Eiler Rasmussen, Kap, *cape*, Greenland, **821** S1
Eilerts de Haan Gebergte, *mountain range*, Suriname, **850** B2
Eilsleben, Germany, **772** E2
Eina, Norway, **770** E2
Einasleigh, Australia, **721** J2
Einasleigh, *river*, Australia, **721** J2
Einbeck, Germany, **772** D3
Eindhoven, Netherlands, **772** B3
Eirunepé, Brazil, **853** E2
Eisenach, Germany, **772** E3
Eisenstadt, Austria, **773** H5
Eisfeld, Germany, **772** E3
Eišiškės, Lithuania, **771** M5
Eitel, Mount, *mountain peak*, Macquarie Island, **720** R11
Eivinvik, Norway, **770** B2
Eivissa (Ibiza), *island*, Islas Baleares, Spain, **777** H3
Eivissa (Ibiza), Islas Baleares, Spain, **777** H3
Ejea de los Caballeros, Spain, **777** G1
Ejeda, Madagascar, **812** A5
Ejido Insurgentes, Mexico, **840** C3
Ejin Horo Qi, China, **746** E5
Ejin Qi, China, **749** J4
Ejura, Ghana, **804** D3
Ejutla, Mexico, **841** F5
Ekalaka, U.S.A., **829** M4
Ekenäs, Sweden, **770** F3
Ekerem, Turkmenistan, **758** E5
Eket, Nigeria, **808** A2
Eketahuna, New Zealand, **718** E5
Ekibastuz, Kazakhstan, **759** K2
Ekombe, Democratic Republic of the Congo, **808** D2
Ekouamou, Congo, **808** C2
Ekshärad, Sweden, **770** F2
Eksjö, Sweden, **770** G4
Ekuku, Democratic Republic of the Congo, **808** D3
Ekwan, *river*, Canada, **825** M5
El Aaiún (Laâyoune), Western Sahara, **800** D3
El Aargub, Western Sahara, **800** C4
El Abiodh Sidi Cheikh, Algeria, **801** G2
El Adeb Larache, Algeria, **801** H3
El Affroun, Algeria, **777** J4
El Alia, Algeria, **801** H2
El Aouinet, Algeria, **779** A8
El Arco, Mexico, **840** B2
El Banco, Colombia, **848** D2
El Barco de Ávila, Spain, **776** E2
El Baúl, Venezuela, **849** E2
El Bayadh, Algeria, **801** G2
El Bolsón, Argentina, **858** C1
El Burgo de Osma, Spain, **777** F2
El Cabaco, Spain, **776** D2
El Caín, Argentina, **858** D1
El Cajon, U.S.A., **832** E5
El Calafate, Argentina, **858** C4
El Callao, Venezuela, **849** G2
El Campo, U.S.A., **834** D5
El Carmen, Bolivia, **853** F3
El Carmen de Bolívar, Colombia, **848** C2
El Centro, U.S.A., **832** F5
El Cerro, Bolivia, **853** G4
El Cerro del Aripo, *mountain peak*, Trinidad, Trinidad and Tobago, **859** C4
El Cerron, Cerro, *mountain peak*, Venezuela, **849** D1
El Chaparro, Venezuela, **849** F2
El Cocuy, Colombia, **848** D2
El Cove, San Andrés, Colombia, **859** B1
El Cuervo, Mexico, **840** D2
El Cuyo, Mexico, **841** J4
El Desemboque, Mexico, **840** B2
El Difícil, Colombia, **848** C2
El Diviso, Colombia, **848** B4
El Djenoun, Garet, *mountain peak*, Algeria, **801** H4
El Dorado, Arkansas, U.S.A., **834** F3
El Dorado, Kansas, U.S.A., **830** E7
El Dorado, Mexico, **840** D3
El Dorado, Venezuela, **849** G2
El Dorado Springs, U.S.A., **830** G7
El Eglab, *mountain range*, Algeria, **801** E3
El Encanto, Colombia, **848** D4
El Escorial, Spain, **776** E2
El Estor, Guatemala, **838** C4
El Eulma, Algeria, **801** H1
El Fahs, Tunisia, **779** B7
El Fud, Ethiopia, **807** F3
El Fuerte, Mexico, **840** C3
El Goléa, Algeria, **801** G2
El Golfo de Santa Clara, Mexico, **840** B2
El Grado, Spain, **777** H1
El Hadjar, Algeria, **801** H1
El Hank, *mountain range*, Mauritania, **800** E4
El Haouaria, Tunisia, **779** C7
El Harrach, Algeria, **777** J4
El Homr, Algeria, **801** G3
El Jadida, Morocco, **800** E2
El Jaralito, Mexico, **840** D3
El Jicaral, Nicaragua, **838** D4
El Kala, Algeria, **779** B7
El Kef, Tunisia, **779** B7
El Kelaa des Srarhna, Morocco, **800** E2
Ēl Kerē, Ethiopia, **807** F3
Ēl Lēh, Ethiopia, **809** G2
El Limón, Mexico, **841** F4
El Meghaïer, Algeria, **801** H2
El Miamo, Venezuela, **849** G2
El Mojar, Bolivia, **853** F3
El Molinillo, Spain, **776** E3
El Nido, Philippines, **740** B4
El Oasis, Islas Canarias, Spain, **813** B4
El Obeid *see* Al Ubayyiḍ, Sudan, **806** D2
El Oro, Mexico, **840** E3
El Oued, Algeria, **801** H2
El Palmar, Venezuela, **849** G2
El Palmito, Mexico, **840** D3
El Pao, E. Venezuela, **849** F2
El Pao, N. Venezuela, **849** E2
El Paso, U.S.A., **833** K6
El Pensamiento, Bolivia, **853** G4
El Perú, Bolivia, **853** E3
El Portugués, Peru, **852** B2
El Porvenir, Mexico, **840** D2
El Porvenir, Panama, **839** F5
El Potosí, Mexico, **841** E3
El Progreso, Guatemala, **838** C4
El Progreso, Honduras, **838** D4
El Puente, Bolivia, **853** F4
El Puerto de Santa Maria, Spain, **776** D4
El Real, Panama, **839** F5
El Reno, U.S.A., **834** D2
El Rocío, Spain, **776** D4
El Ronquillo, Spain, **776** D4
El Rosario de Arriba, Mexico, **840** B2
El Salado, Argentina, **858** D3
El Salado, Mexico, **841** E3
El Salto, Mexico, **840** D4
El Salvador, Chile, **856** C3
El Salvador, *country*, Central America, **817** P7

Erenhot, China, **746** E4
Eretria, Greece, **781** D6
Ereymentaū, Kazakhstan, **759** J2
Erezée, Belgium, **772** B3
Erfjord, Norway, **770** C3
Erfoud, Morocco, **801** F2
Erfurt, Germany, **772** E3
Ergani, Turkey, **803** G1
Ergel, Mongolia, **746** E4
Ergene, *river*, Turkey, **781** F5
Ērgļi, Latvia, **771** M4
Ergun, *river*, China, **747** H1
Erick, U.S.A., **834** C2
Erickson, Canada, **824** E6
Ericson, U.S.A., **830** D5
Erie, Lake, Canada/U.S.A., **831** N5
Erie, U.S.A., **831** N4
Erîgât, *desert*, Mali, **801** E4
Eriksdale, Canada, **824** E6
Erillas, *mountain peak*, Spain, **776** E3
Erimo, Japan, **745** H2
Erimo-misaki, *point*, Japan, **745** H2
Erin Point, Trinidad, Trinidad and Tobago, **859** C4
Eringsboda, Sweden, **770** G4
Eriskay, *island*, Scotland, U.K., **792** B3
Eritrea, *country*, Africa, **796** J5
Erkowit, Sudan, **803** G5
Erlangen, Germany, **772** E4
Erldunda, Australia, **720** G4
Erlongshan, China, **747** L3
Ermelo, South Africa, **811** F4
Ermenek, Turkey, **803** F1
Ermioni, Greece, **781** D7
Ermoupoli, Kyklades, Greece, **781** E7
Erndtebrück, Germany, **772** D3
Ernée, France, **774** D2
Ernei, Romania, **780** E2
Ernstbrunn, Austria, **773** H4
Erode, India, **752** D4
Eromanga, Australia, **721** J4
Erongo, *administrative region*, Namibia, **810** B3
Erongo, *mountain peak*, Namibia, **810** C3
Errego, Mozambique, **809** G6
Errigal Mountain, *mountain peak*, Ireland, **793** D2
Erris Head, *point*, Ireland, **793** B3
Errol, U.S.A., **836** E2
Erromango, *island*, Vanuatu, **727** A3
Ersekë, Albania, **781** C5
Ershiwuzhan, China, **747** H1
Ershizhan, China, **747** J1
Erskine, U.S.A., **830** E2
Ertai, China, **748** F3
Ertis, Kazakhstan, **759** K2
Ertis, *river*, Kazakhstan, **759** K2
Ertvågøy, *island*, Norway, **768** D5
Eruki, Mount, *mountain peak*, Papua New Guinea, **726** B4
Erval, Brazil, **857** G4
Erwood, Canada, **824** C5
Erythres, Greece, **781** D6
Eryuan, China, **751** F4
Erzgebirge, *mountain range*, Germany, **772** F3
Erzhan, China, **747** J2
Erzin, Russian Federation, **749** G2
Erzincan, Turkey, **760** E5
Erzurum, Turkey, **760** F5
Eržvilkas, Lithuania, **771** L5
Esa'ala, Papua New Guinea, **726** C5
Esashi, N. Hokkaidō, Japan, **745** H1
Esashi, S. Hokkaidō, Japan, **745** H2
Esbjerg, Denmark, **770** D5
Escada, Brazil, **851** G5
Escalada, Spain, **777** F1
Escalante, U.S.A., **833** H3
Escalaplano, Sardegna, Italy, **779** B6
Escalón, Mexico, **840** D3
Escanaba, U.S.A., **831** K3
Eschede, Germany, **772** E2
Escocesa, Bahía, *bay*, Dominican Republic, **839** H3
Escoma, Bolivia, **853** E4
Escondida, Chile, **856** C2
Escondido, U.S.A., **832** E5
Escuinapa, Mexico, **840** D4
Escuintla, Guatemala, **838** C4
Eséka, Cameroon, **808** B2
Eşen, Turkey, **781** G7
Esens, Germany, **772** C2
Eşfahān, Iran, **756** F2
Esfandak, Iran, **757** H3
Esfarāyen, Iran, **758** F5
Esha Ness, *point*, Shetland, Scotland, U.K., **792** K7
Esigodini, Zimbabwe, **811** E3
Esik, Kazakhstan, **748** C4
Esil, Kazakhstan, **758** H2
Esil, *river*, Kazakhstan, **759** H2
Eskdale, *valley*, Scotland, U.K., **792** G5
Eskdalemuir, Scotland, U.K., **792** F5
Eske, Lough, *lake*, Ireland, **793** D3
Esker, Canada, **826** H3
Eskilstuna, Sweden, **770** H3
Eskişehir, Turkey, **760** D5
Esla, *river*, Spain, **776** E1
Eslöv, Sweden, **770** F5
Eşme, Turkey, **781** G6
Esmeralda, Cuba, **839** F2
Esmeralda, Isla, *island*, Chile, **858** B3
Esmeraldas, Ecuador, **848** B4
Espakeh, Iran, **757** H3
Espalion, France, **774** F4
Espanola, Canada, **831** N2
Española, Isla, *island*, Islas Galápagos (Galapagos Islands), Ecuador, **859** A2
Espanola, U.S.A., **833** K3
Esperance, Australia, **720** E5
Esperantinópolis, Brazil, **851** E4
Esperanza, *Argentinian research station*, Antarctica, **862** A4
Esperanza, Mexico, **840** C3
Esperanza, Peru, **852** D2
Esperanza, Santa Cruz, Argentina, **858** C4
Esperanza, Santa Fé, Argentina, **856** E4
Espichel, Cabo, *cape*, Portugal, **776** C3
Espiel, Spain, **776** E3
Espigão, Serra do, *mountain range*, Brazil, **857** G3
Espigão Mestre, *mountain range*, Brazil, **854** E3
Espinhaço, Serra do, *mountain range*, Brazil, **847** H6
Espinilho, Serra do, *mountain range*, Brazil, **857** F3
Espinillo, Argentina, **857** E2
Espinosa, Brazil, **855** E4
Espírito Santo, *state*, Brazil, **855** F5
Espíritu Santo, *island*, Vanuatu, **727** A2
Esplanada, Brazil, **855** G3
Espoo, Finland, **771** M2
Espungabera, Mozambique, **811** F3
Esquel, Argentina, **858** C2
Esquina, Argentina, **857** E4
Esrange, Sweden, **768** K3
Essaouira, Morocco, **800** E2
Essen, Germany, **772** C3
Essequibo, *river*, Guyana, **849** G3
Essex, California, U.S.A., **832** F4
Essex, Montana, U.S.A., **828** H2
Essex, Punta, *point*, Islas Galápagos (Galapagos Islands), Ecuador, **859** A2
Essex, *unitary authority*, England, U.K., **789** H3
Est, Pointe de l', *point*, Canada, **827** L5
Est, *province*, Cameroon, **808** B2
Estaca de Bares, Punta da, *point*, Spain, **776** D1
Estacado, Llano, *plain*, U.S.A., **833** M4
Estados, Isla, de los, *island*, Argentina, **858** E5
Estagel, France, **774** F5
Estaires, France, **789** K4
Estância, Brazil, **855** G3
Estats, Pic d', France/Spain, **777** H1
Estcourt, South Africa, **811** E4
Esteban Rams, Argentina, **856** E3
Estelí, Nicaragua, **838** D4
Estella, Spain, **777** F1
Estepa, Spain, **776** E4
Estépar, Spain, **777** F1
Estepona, Spain, **776** E4
Esterhazy, Canada, **824** C6
Estevan, Canada, **824** C7
Estevan Point, Canada, **822** F7
Estherville, U.S.A., **830** F4
Estill, U.S.A., **835** M3
Estissac, France, **775** F2
Estiva, *river*, Brazil, **851** E5
Eston, Canada, **823** Q6
Estonia, *country*, Europe, **764** G4
Estrées-St-Denis, France, **789** K5
Estrela, Serra da, *mountain range*, Portugal, **776** C2
Estremoz, Portugal, **776** D3
Estrondo, Serra do, *mountain range*, Brazil, **850** D5
Estuaire, *province*, Gabon, **808** A2
Esztergom, Hungary, **773** J5
Etah, India, **754** D4
Etampes, France, **774** F2
Étaples, France, **774** E1
Etāwah, India, **754** D4
Etelä-Suomen Lääni, *province*, Finland, **771** M2
Ethelbert, Canada, **824** D6
Ethiopa, *country*, Africa, **796** J6
Ethiopian Highlands, *mountain range*, Ethiopa, **798** J5
Ethridge, U.S.A., **829** H2
Etive, Loch, *inlet*, Scotland, U.K., **792** D4
Etna, Monte, *mountain peak*, Sicilia, Italy, **779** E7
Etne, Norway, **770** B3
Eton, Canada, **831** L2
Etoumbi, Congo, **808** B2
Étretat, France, **789** H5
Etropole, Bulgaria, **780** E4
Ettelbruck, Luxembourg, **775** H2
Ettington, England, U.K., **789** F2
Etwall, England, U.K., **789** F2
Etzatlan, Mexico, **840** D4
Eu, France, **789** J4
'Eua, *island*, Tonga, **727** B4
'Eua Iki, *island*, Tonga, **727** B4
Euakafa, *island*, Vava'u Group, Tonga, **727** B3
Euboea *see* Evvoia, *island*, Greece, **781** E6
Eucla, Australia, **720** F5
Euclides da Cunha, Brazil, **855** F3
Eufaula, U.S.A., **835** K4
Eufaula Lake, U.S.A., **834** E2
Eugene, U.S.A., **828** C4
Eugenia, Punta, *point*, Mexico, **840** A3
Eunice, Louisiana, U.S.A., **834** F4
Eunice, New Mexico, U.S.A., **833** M5
Eupen, Belgium, **772** B3
Euphrates, *river*, Asia, **732** F6; *see also* Euphrates, *river*, Iraq, **803** H2; Firat, *river*, Turkey, **760** E5; Firat Nehri, *river*, Syria, **803** G1
Eupora, U.S.A., **835** H3
Eura, Finland, **771** L2
Eurajoki, Finland, **771** K2
Eureka, California, U.S.A., **832** A1
Eureka, Canada, **821** L1
Eureka, Montana, U.S.A., **828** G2
Eureka, Nevada, U.S.A, **832** F2
Eureka, Utah, U.S.A., **833** G2
Eureka, Washington, U.S.A., **828** E3
Europa, Île, *island*, Réunion, **811** H3
Europa, Picos de, *mountain peak*, Spain, **776** E1
Eustis, U.S.A., **835** M5
Eutaw, U.S.A., **835** J3
Eutin, Germany, **772** E1
Eutsuk Lake, Canada, **822** F5
Evanger, Norway, **770** C2
Evans, Lac, *lake*, Canada, **826** C4
Evans, Mount, *mountain peak*, U.S.A., **828** H3
Evans Peninsula, Antarctica, **862** A6
Evans Strait, Canada, **821** L3
Evanston, Illinois, U.S.A., **831** K4
Evanston, Wyoming, U.S.A., **829** J6
Evansville, Canada, **831** M3
Evansville, Illinois, U.S.A., **830** J6
Evansville, Indiana, U.S.A., **831** K7
Evaro, U.S.A., **828** G3
Evaton, South Africa, **811** E4
Evaz, Iran, **756** F3
Everest, Mount, *mountain peak*, China, **750** C3
Everett, U.S.A., **828** C3
Evergreen, U.S.A., **835** J4
Evesham, England, U.K., **789** F2
Evijärvi, Finland, **769** L5
Evijärvi, *lake*, Finland, **769** L5
Evinayong, Equatorial Guinea, **808** B2
Evje, Norway, **770** C3
Évora, *district*, Portugal, **776** D3
Évora, Portugal, **776** D3
Evoron, Ozero, *lake*, Russian Federation, **747** M2
Évreux, France, **774** E2
Évry, France, **774** F2
Evvoia (Euboea), *island*, Greece, **781** E6
Ewan, U.S.A., **828** F3
Ewango, Nigeria, **805** F3
Ewaso Ngiro, *river*, Kenya, **809** G2
Ewe, Loch, *inlet*, Scotland, U.K., **792** D3
Ewo, Congo, **808** B3
Exaltación, Bolivia, **853** F3
Exe, *river*, England, U.K., **788** D4
Executive Committee Range, *mountain range*, Antarctica, **862** C7
Exeter, Canada, **831** N4
Exeter, England, U.K., **788** D4
Exminster, England, U.K., **788** D4
Exmoor, *moorland*, England, U.K., **788** D3
Exmore, U.S.A., **836** C6
Exmouth, Australia, **720** C3
Exmouth, England, U.K., **788** D4
Exmouth Gulf, Australia, **720** C3
Exmouth Plateau, *underwater feature*, Indian Ocean, **866** G6
Extremadura, *district*, Spain, **776** D3
Extrême-Nord, *province*, Cameroon, **805** G2
Exu, Brazil, **851** F5
Eyasi, Lake, Tanzania, **809** F3
Eye, Cambridgeshire, England, U.K., **789** G2
Eye, Suffolk, England, U.K., **789** J2
Eye Peninsula, Scotland, U.K., **792** C2
Eyemouth, Scotland, U.K., **792** G5
Eyl, Somalia, **807** G3
Eymet, France, **774** E4
Eynsham, England, U.K., **789** F3
Eyre North, Lake, Australia, **721** H4
Eyre Peninsula, Australia, **721** H5
Eyre South, Lake, Australia, **721** H4
Eyreton, New Zealand, **719** D6
Eysturoy, *island*, Faeroe Islands, **786** D1
Eyumojok, Cameroon, **808** A1
Ezequiel Ramos Mexia, Embalse, *reservoir*, Argentina, **858** D1
Ezere, Latvia, **771** L4
Ezernieki, Latvia, **771** N4
Ezhou, China, **742** C2
Ezine, Turkey, **781** F6

F

Faadhippolhu Atoll, Maldives, **752** C5
Faafxadhuun, Somalia, **809** H2
Faaite, *island*, French Polynesia, **723** G2
Fabens, U.S.A., **833** K6
Fåberg, Norway, **770** E2
Fabiuola, *river*, Spain, **776** D3
Fåborg, Denmark, **770** E5
Fabriano, Italy, **778** D4
Facatativá, Colombia, **848** C3
Fachi, Niger, **805** G1
Facundo, Argentina, **858** C2
Fada, Chad, **802** D5
Fada N'Gourma, Burkina Faso, **804** E2
Faddeyevskiy, Ostrov, *island*, Russian Federation, **785** R2
Faenza, Italy, **778** C3
Faeroe-Iceland Ridge, *underwater feature*, Atlantic Ocean, **867** G1
Faeroe Islands, *Danish territory*, Atlantic Ocean, **786** C2
Fagamalo, Samoa, **727** B1
Făgăraş, Romania, **780** E3
Fagatogo, American Samoa, **727** B2
Fågelberget, Sweden, **768** G4
Fagernes, Oppland, Norway, **770** D2
Fagernes, Troms, Norway, **768** J2
Fagersta, Sweden, **770** G3
Făget, Romania, **780** D3
Faggo, Nigeria, **805** G2
Fagnano, Lago, *lake*, Argentina, **858** D5
Faguibine, Lac, *lake*, Mali, **804** D1
Fagurhólsmýri, Iceland, **768** Y8
Faial, *island*, Azores, Portugal, **800** M7
Faial, Madeira, Portugal, **813** C3
Fā'id, Egypt, **761** B4
Fair Head, *point*, Northern Ireland, U.K., **793** F2
Fairbank, U.S.A., **833** H6
Fairbanks, U.S.A., **820** E3
Fairfax, U.S.A., **830** D4
Fairfield, California, U.S.A., **832** C2
Fairfield, Idaho, U.S.A., **828** G5
Fairfield, Illinois, U.S.A., **831** J6
Fairfield, Iowa, U.S.A., **830** H5
Fairfield, Montana, U.S.A., **829** J3
Fairfield, North Dakota, U.S.A., **830** B2
Fairfield, Texas, U.S.A., **834** D4

G

Gainsborough, England, U.K., **791** H4
Gairdner, Lake, Australia, **721** H5
Gairloch, Scotland, U.K., **792** D3
Gaizhou, China, **747** H4
Gaiziņkalns, *mountain peak*, Latvia, **771** M4
Gakarosa, *mountain peak*, South Africa, **810** D4
Gakem, Nigeria, **805** F3
Gakuch, Pakistan, **754** C1
Gakugsa, Russian Federation, **783** F2
Gal, *river*, Sri Lanka, **753** E5
Gala, China, **755** G3
Galán, Cerro, *mountain peak*, Argentina, **856** C3
Galana, *river*, Kenya, **809** G3
Galand, Iran, **758** F5
Galang, Pulau, *island*, Indonesia, **736** D2
Galápagos, Islas, (Galapagos Islands), *islands*, Ecuador, Pacific Ocean, **859** A1
Galapagos Fracture Zone, *tectonic feature*, Pacific Ocean, **869** J5
Galapagos Islands see Galápagos, Islas, *islands*, Ecuador, Pacific Ocean, **859** A1
Galapagos Rise, *underwater feature*, Pacific Ocean, **869** M5
Galashiels, Scotland, U.K., **792** G5
Galata, Bulgaria, **780** F4
Galata, U.S.A., **829** J2
Galaţi, Romania, **780** G3
Galatista, Greece, **781** D5
Galatone, Italy, **779** G5
Galbally, Ireland, **793** D5
Gáldar, Islas Canarias, Spain, **813** B4
Galdhøpiggen, *mountain peak*, Norway, **770** D2
Galeana, Mexico, **840** D2
Galena, U.S.A., **830** H4
Galeota Point, Trinidad, Trinidad and Tobago, **859** C4
Galera, Punta, *point*, Chile, **858** B1
Galera, Punta, *point*, Ecuador, **848** B4
Galera, Spain, **777** F4
Galera Point, Trinidad, Trinidad and Tobago, **859** C4
Galéria, Corse, France, **779** B4
Galesburg, U.S.A., **830** H5
Galesville, U.S.A., **830** H3
Galeton, U.S.A., **836** B4
Galets, Pointe des, *point*, Réunion, **813** A1
Galguduud, *administrative region*, Somalia, **807** G3
Galicea Mare, Romania, **780** D3
Galicia, *autonomous community*, Spain, **776** D1
Galilee, Sea of *see* Kinneret, Yam, *lake*, Israel, **761** C3
Gallatin, U.S.A., **835** J1
Gallatin Peak, *mountain peak*, U.S.A., **829** J4
Galle, Sri Lanka, **752** E5
Gállego, *river*, Spain, **777** G1
Gallegos, *river*, Argentina, **858** C4
Gallegos, U.S.A., **833** M4
Galley Head, *point*, Ireland, **793** D6
Gallinas, Punta, *point*, Colombia, **848** D1
Gallipoli, Italy, **779** F5
Gallipoli *see* Gelibolu, Turkey, **781** F5
Gallipolis, U.S.A., **831** M6
Gällivare, Sweden, **768** K3
Gällö, Sweden, **768** G5
Galloway, Mount, *mountain peak*, New Zealand, **719** P15
Galloway, Mull of, *point*, Scotland, U.K., **792** E6
Gallup, U.S.A., **833** J4
Galmisdale, Scotland, U.K., **792** C4
Galston, Scotland, U.K., **792** E5
Galtström, Sweden, **771** H1
Galtymore, *mountain peak*, Ireland, **793** D5
Galva, U.S.A., **830** H5
Galveston, U.S.A., **834** E5
Galveston Bay, U.S.A., **834** E5
Gálvez, Argentina, **856** E4
Galway, *county*, Ireland, **793** C4
Galway, Ireland, **793** C4
Galway Bay, Ireland, **793** C4
Gâm, *river*, Vietnam, **739** E1
Gamaches, France, **774** E2
Gamba, China, **755** G3
Gamba, Gabon, **808** A3
Gambang, Malaysia, **736** C2
Gambēla, Ethiopia, **806** D3
Gambia, *country*, Africa, **796** D5
Gambia Plain, *underwater feature*, Atlantic Ocean, **867** F5
Gambier, Îles, *islands*, French Polynesia, **723** H3
Gambo, Canada, **827** P5
Gambo, Central African Republic, **808** D2
Gamboma, Congo, **808** C3
Gamboula, Central African Republic, **808** C2
Gamgadhi, Nepal, **755** E3
Gamleby, Sweden, **770** H4
Gammelstaden, Sweden, **769** L4
Gamph, Slieve, *mountain range*, Ireland, **793** C3
Gamtog, China, **751** F3
Gamud, *mountain peak*, Ethiopia, **809** G2
Gamvik, Norway, **769** P1
Gan, France, **774** D5
Gan, *river*, N. China, **747** J2
Gan, *river*, S. China, **742** C3
Gan Gan, Argentina, **858** D2
Gana, China, **751** G2
Ganado, U.S.A., **833** J4
Gäncä, Azerbaijan, **758** D4
Gancheng, China, **739** F2
Ganda, Angola, **808** B5
Gandadiwata, Gunung, *mountain peak*, Indonesia, **734** B3
Gandajika, Democratic Republic of the Congo, **808** D4
Gandak, *river*, India, **755** F4
Gandāva, Pakistan, **754** A3
Gander, Canada, **827** P5
Gander Bay, Canada, **827** P5
Gandesa, Spain, **777** H2
Gāndhī Sāgar, *lake*, India, **754** C4
Gāndhīdhām, India, **754** B5
Gāndhīnagar, India, **754** C5
Gandía, Spain, **777** G3
Gandu, Brazil, **855** F3
Gangānagar, India, **754** C3
Gangāpur, India, **754** D4
Ganga, *river*, India, **755** E4
Gangala-na-Bodio, Democratic Republic of the Congo, **809** E2
Gangara, Niger, **805** F2
Gangaw, Myanmar, **741** B3
Gangaw Taung, *mountain range*, Myanmar, **741** C2
Gangca, China, **749** J5
Gangdisê Shan, *mountain range*, China, **755** E3
Ganges, France, **775** F5
Ganges, Mouths of the, Bangladesh/India, **732** K7
Ganges, *river*, Bangladesh/India, **741** A3
Ganges Fan, *underwater feature*, Indian Ocean, **866** E4
Gangkou, E. Guangdong, China, **743** D3
Gangkou, W. Guangdong, China, **743** A3
Gangoumen, China, **744** B2
Gangtok, India, **755** G4
Gangu, China, **751** H2
Ganluo, China, **751** G3
Gannan, China, **747** H3
Gannat, France, **775** F3
Gannvalley, U.S.A., **830** D3
Ganq, China, **749** G5
Ganquan, China, **746** E5
Gänserndorf, Austria, **773** H4
Gansu, *province*, China, **749** J5
Gantang, Anhui, China, **742** D2
Gantang, Ningxia Huizu Zizhiqu, China, **746** D5
Ganye, Nigeria, **805** G3
Ganyu, China, **742** D1
Ganyushkino, Kazakhstan, **758** D3
Ganzhou, China, **742** C3
Gao, *administrative region*, Mali, **805** E1
Gao, Mali, **804** D1
Gao Xian, China, **751** H3
Gao'an, China, **742** C2
Gaocheng, China, **746** F5
Gaolan, China, **749** J5
Gaolan Dao, *island*, China, **743** A5
Gaoping, China, **742** C1
Gaoqiao, China, **743** A1
Gaotai, China, **749** H5
Gaotang, China, **746** G5
Gaotouyao, China, **746** E4
Gaoua, Burkina Faso, **804** D2
Gaoyang, China, **746** F5
Gaoyou, China, **742** D1
Gaozhou, China, **742** B4
Gap, France, **775** H4
Gapan, Philippines, **740** C3
Gar, China, **754** E2
Gara, Lough, *lake*, Ireland, **793** D4
Gara Nasa, *mountain peak*, Ethiopia, **806** E3
Garabogazköl Aylagy, *bay*, Turkmenistan, **758** E4
Garacad, Somalia, **807** G3
Garachiné, Panama, **839** F5
Garadag, Somalia, **807** G3
Garafia, Islas Canarias, Spain, **813** A4
Garagum, *desert*, Turkmenistan, **758** F5
Garaina, Papua New Guinea, **726** B5
Garalo, Mali, **804** C2
Garang, China, **749** J5
Garanhuns, Brazil, **855** G2
Garba, Central African Republic, **806** B3
Garba Tula, Kenya, **809** G2
Garbahaarrey, Somalia, **809** H2
Garberville, U.S.A., **832** B1
Garbsen, Germany, **772** D2
Garça, Brazil, **857** H2
Garco, China, **750** D2
Garda, Lago di, *lake*, Italy, **778** C3
Garde, Cap de, *cape* , Algeria, **779** A7
Gardelegen, Germany, **772** E2
Garden City, U.S.A., **830** C7
Garden Corners, U.S.A., **831** K3
Gardey, Argentina, **857** E5
Gardēz, Afghanistan, **754** B2
Gardiner, U.S.A., **829** J4
Gärdnäs, Sweden, **768** G4
Gardner, Colorado, U.S.A., **833** L3
Gardner, Florida, U.S.A., **835** M6
Gardner Pinnacles, *islands*, Hawaiian Islands, U.S.A., **725** H2
Gardone Val Trompia, Italy, **778** C3
Gare Tigre, French Guiana, **850** C2
Garelochhead, Scotland, U.K., **792** E4
Garforth, England, U.K., **791** G4
Gargždai, Lithuania, **771** K5
Garhchiroli, India, **754** E5
Garibaldi, Brazil, **857** G3
Garibaldi, Mount, *mountain peak*, Canada, **822** H7
Garies, South Africa, **810** C5
Garissa, Kenya, **809** G3
Garland, Canada, **824** D6
Garland, North Carolina, U.S.A., **835** N2
Garland, Texas, U.S.A., **834** D3
Garland, Wyoming, U.S.A., **829** K4
Garliava, Lithuania, **771** L5
Garlin, France, **774** D5
Garmisch-Partenkirchen, Germany, **772** E5
Garmo, Norway, **770** D2
Garmsār, Iran, **756** F1
Garner, U.S.A., **830** G4
Garnett, U.S.A., **830** F6
Garnish, Canada, **827** P6
Garnpung Lake, Australia, **721** J5
Garonne, *river*, France, **774** D4
Garoowe, Somalia, **807** G3
Garoua, Cameroon, **805** G3
Garoua Boulaï, Cameroon, **808** B1
Garove Island, Papua New Guinea, **726** C4
Garqu Yan, China, **750** E2
Garrison, Montana, U.S.A., **828** H3
Garrison, North Dakota, U.S.A., **830** C2
Garsen, Kenya, **809** H3
Garsila, Sudan, **806** B2
Garson Lake, Canada, **823** Q3
Garstang, England, U.K., **790** F4
Gartempe, *river*, France, **774** E3
Garth, Wales, U.K., **788** D2
Garut, Indonesia, **737** D4
Garut, Tanjong, *point*, Indonesia, **737** D4
Garvagh, Northern Ireland, U.K., **793** F3
Garve, Scotland, U.K., **792** E3
Garwa, India, **755** E4
Garwolin, Poland, **773** K3
Gary, U.S.A., **831** K5
Garyarsa, China, **754** E3
Garzê, China, **751** G3
Garzón, Colombia, **848** C3
Gascogne, *region*, France, **774** D5
Gascoyne, Golfe de, *gulf*, France, **774** C4
Gascoyne, *river*, Australia, **720** D4
Gashua, Nigeria, **805** G2
Gasim, Indonesia, **735** E3
Gasmata, Papua New Guinea, **726** C4
Gaspé, Canada, **827** J5
Gaspé, Cap de, *cape*, Canada, **827** J5
Gaspé, Péninsule de, Canada, **826** H5
Gasquet, U.S.A., **828** C6
Gassol, Nigeria, **805** G3
Gastonia, U.S.A., **835** M2
Gastouni, Greece, **781** C7
Gastre, Argentina, **858** D2
Gata, Cabo de, *cape*, Spain, **777** F4
Gătaia, Romania, **780** C3
Gataivai, Samoa, **727** B1
Gatchina, Russian Federation, **783** C3
Gate, U.S.A., **830** C7
Gatehouse of Fleet, Scotland, U.K., **792** E6
Gateshead, England, U.K., **791** G3
Gatesville, U.S.A., **834** D4
Gatineau, Canada, **826** D7
Gatún, Lago, *reservoir*, Panama, **839** F5
Gau, *island*, Fiji, **727** A4
Gaua *see* Santa Maria, *island*, Vanuatu, **727** A2
Gauja, *river*, Latvia, **771** N4
Gauley Bridge, U.S.A., **831** N6
Gauribidanūr, India, **752** D3
Gausta, *mountain peak*, Norway, **770** D3
Gāv, *river*, Iran, **756** E1
Gāvbandī, Iran, **756** F3
Gavdopoula, *island*, Greece, **781** D8
Gavdos, *island*, Greece, **781** E8
Gave de Pau, *river*, France, **774** D5
Gaviãozinho, Brazil, **853** E2
Gävle, Sweden, **771** H2
Gävleborg, *county*, Sweden, **770** G2
Gavrilov-Yam, Russian Federation, **783** G4
Gavsele, Sweden, **768** H4
Gāwilgarh Hills, India, **754** D5
Gawler, Australia, **721** H5
Gaxun Nur, *lake*, China, **749** J4
Gaya, India, **755** F4
Gaya, Nigeria, **805** F2
Gaylord, U.S.A., **831** L3
Gaza, Gaza Strip, **761** C4
Gaza, *province*, Mozambique, **811** F3
Gaza Strip, *disputed region*, Asia, **761** B4
Gazanjyk, Turkmenistan, **758** F5
Gazi, Kenya, **809** G3
Gaziantep, Turkey, **760** E5
Gazimur, *river*, Russian Federation, **747** G1
Gazipaşa, Turkey, **761** B1
Gazli, Uzbekistan, **758** G4
Gbadolite, Democratic Republic of the Congo, **808** D2
Gbarnga, Liberia, **804** C3
Gbatala, Liberia, **804** C3
Gboko, Nigeria, **805** F3
Gdańsk, Poland, **773** J1
Gdańska, Zatoka, *gulf*, Poland, **771** J5
Gdov, Russian Federation, **783** A3
Gdynia, Poland, **773** J1
Geary, Canada, **826** H7
Gebo, U.S.A., **829** K5
Gebre Guracha, Ethiopia, **807** E3
Gech'a, Ethiopia, **806** E3
Geddington, England, U.K., **789** G2
Gediz, *river*, Turkey, **781** F6
Gediz, Turkey, **781** G6
Gedlegubē, Ethiopia, **807** G3
Gedney Drove End, England, U.K., **789** H2
Gedo, *administrative region*, Somalia, **809** H2
Gedser, Denmark, **770** E5
Gedser Odde, *cape*, Denmark, **770** E5
Geelong, Australia, **721** J6
Geesaley, Somalia, **807** H2
Geeveston, Australia, **721** K7
Gê'gyai, China, **754** E2
Geidam, Nigeria, **805** G2
Geigar, Sudan, **806** D2
Geikie, *river*, Canada, **824** B3
Geilo, Norway, **770** D2
Geiranger, Norway, **770** C1
Geisenfeld, Germany, **772** E4
Geita, Tanzania, **809** F3
Gejiu, China, **751** G5
Gela, Golfo di, *gulf*, Italy, **779** D7
Gela, Sicilia, Italy, **779** E7
Geladī, Ethiopia, **807** G3
Gelam, Pulau, *island*, Indonesia, **737** E3
Gelang, Tanjong, *point*, Malaysia, **736** C2
Gelderland, *province*, Netherlands, **772** B2
Gelibolu (Gallipoli), Turkey, **781** F5
Gelligaer, Wales, U.K., **788** D3
Gelnica, Slovakia, **773** K4
Gelsenkirchen, Germany, **772** C3
Gem, U.S.A., **830** C6

Gembu, Nigeria, **805** G3
Geme, Indonesia, **734** D1
Gemena, Democratic Republic of the Congo, **808** C2
Gemlik, Turkey, **781** G5
Gen, *river*, China, **747** H2
Gençay, France, **774** E3
General Acha, Argentina, **856** D5
General Alvear, Argentina, **856** C5
General Artigas, Paraguay, **857** F3
General Belgrano, Argentina, **857** E5
General Belgrano II, *Argentinian research station*, Antarctica, **862** C4
General Bernardo O'Higgins, *Chilean research station*, Antarctica, **862** A4
General Carrera, Lago, *lake*, Chile, **858** C3
General Cepeda, Mexico, **840** E3
General Conesa, Buenos Aires, Argentina, **857** F5
General Conesa, Río Negro, Argentina, **858** E1
General Eugenio A. Garay, Paraguay, **853** F5
General Guido, Argentina, **857** F5
General José de San Martín, Argentina, **857** E3
General Juan Madariaga, Argentina, **857** F5
General La Madrid, Argentina, **856** E5
General Lagos, Chile, **853** E4
General Lavalle, Argentina, **857** F5
General Levalle, Argentina, **856** D5
General Martín Miguel de Güemes, Argentina, **856** D2
General Pico, Argentina, **856** D5
General Pinedo, Argentina, **856** E3
General Pinto, Argentina, **856** E5
General Roca, Argentina, **858** D1
General San Martín, *Argentinian research station*, Antarctica, **862** B4
General Santos (Dadiangas), Philippines, **740** D5
General-Toshevo, Bulgaria, **780** G4
General Villegas, Argentina, **856** D5
Geneseo, U.S.A., **830** H5
Genet, Ethiopia, **807** E3
Geneva, Nebraska, U.S.A., **830** E5
Geneva, New York, U.S.A., **836** B3
Geneva, Ohio, U.S.A., **831** N5
Geneva *see* Genève, Switzerland, **775** H3
Genève (Geneva), Switzerland, **775** H3
Gengma, China, **751** F5
Gengwa, Democratic Republic of the Congo, **808** D3
Genhe, China, **747** H2
Genil, *river*, Spain, **776** E4
Gennargentu, Monti del, *mountain peak*, Italy, **779** B5
Genoa, *river*, Argentina, **858** C2
Genoa *see* Genova, Italy, **778** B3
Genova (Genoa), Italy, **778** B3
Genova, Golfo di, *gulf*, Italy, **778** B4
Genovesa, Isla, *island*, Islas Galápagos (Galapagos Islands), Ecuador, **859** A1
Gent, Belgium, **772** A3
Genteng, Indonesia, **736** D4
Genthin, Germany, **772** F2
Genzano di Lucania, Italy, **779** F5
Geographe Bay, Australia, **720** C5
Georga, Zemlya, *island*, Russian Federation, **784** F1
George, Cape, Canada, **827** K6
George, Cape, South Africa, **810** D5
George, Lake, U.S.A., **835** M5
George, *river*, Canada, **821** N4
George, South Africa, **810** D5
George, U.S.A., **828** E3
George V Land, *region*, Antarctica, **862** E7
George Sound, New Zealand, **719** A7
George Town, Australia, **721** K7
George Town, Bahamas, **838** G2
George Town, Cayman Islands, **839** E3
George Town, Malaysia, **736** C1
George von Neumayer, *German research station*, Antarctica, **862** D3
George West, U.S.A., **834** C5
Georgetown, Ascension, **813** A3
Georgetown, Australia, **721** J2
Georgetown, Delaware, U.S.A., **836** C5
Georgetown, Gambia, **804** B2
Georgetown, Guyana, **849** G2
Georgetown, Kentucky, U.S.A., **831** L6
Georgetown, Ohio, U.S.A., **831** M6
Georgetown, St Vincent and the Grenadines, **837** D3
Georgetown, South Carolina, U.S.A., **835** N3
Georgetown, Texas, U.S.A., **834** D4
Georgi Traykov, Bulgaria, **780** F4
Georgia, *country*, Asia, **730** F5
Georgia, *state*, U.S.A., **835** L3
Georgia, Strait of, Canada, **822** G7
Georgian Bay, Canada, **831** N3
Georgiana, U.S.A., **835** J4
Georgievka, Shyghys Qazaqstan, Kazakhstan, **748** D2
Georgievka, Zhambyl, Kazakhstan, **748** B4
Georgina, *river*, Australia, **721** H3
Gera, Germany, **772** F3
Gerace, Italy, **779** F6
Geraki, Greece, **781** D7
Geral, Serra, *mountain range*, Brazil, **847** G6
Geral de Goiás, Serra, *mountain range*, Brazil, **847** H5
Geral do Paraná, Serra, *mountain range*, Brazil, **854** D4
Geraldine, U.S.A., **829** J3
Geraldton, Australia, **720** C4
Geraldton, Canada, **825** L7
Gerede, Turkey, **760** D4
Gereshk, Afghanistan, **754** A3
Gérgal, Spain, **777** F4
Gering, U.S.A., **829** N6
Gerlach, U.S.A., **832** D1
Gerlachovský Štít, *mountain peak*, Slovakia, **773** K4
Germakolo, Indonesia, **735** F3
Germany, *country*, Europe, **764** E5
Germencik, Turkey, **781** F7
Germiston, South America, **811** E4
Gero, Japan, **745** G4
Gers, *river*, France, **774** E5
Gêrzê, China, **755** F2
Gestro, Wabē, *river*, Ethiopia, **807** F3
Geta, Finland, **771** J2
Getafe, Spain, **777** F2
Gethsémani, Canada, **827** L4
Gettysburg, Pennsylvania, U.S.A., **836** B5
Gettysburg, South Dakota, U.S.A., **830** D3
Getz Ice Shelf, Antarctica, **862** B7
Geureudong, Gunung, *mountain peak*, Indonesia, **736** B1
Gevgelija, Macedonia, **781** D5
Gevrai, India, **752** C2
Geyikli, Turkey, **781** F6
Geylang, Singapore, **736** K7
Geyser, U.S.A., **829** J3
Geyve, Turkey, **781** H5
Gföhl, Austria, **773** G4
Ghabāghib, Syria, **761** D3
Ghadāmis, Libya, **802** A2
Ghaddūwah, Libya, **802** B3
Ghāghara, *river*, India, **755** E4
Ghāghra, India, **755** F5
Ghaibi Dero, Pakistan, **754** A4
Ghana, *country*, Africa, **796** E6
Ghanzi, Botswana, **810** D3
Ghanzi, *district*, Botswana, **810** D3
Gharandal, Jordan, **761** C4
Gharb al Istiwā'īyah, *state*, Sudan, **809** E1
Gharb Baḩr al Ghazal, *state*, Sudan, **806** C3
Gharb Dārfūr, *state*, Sudan, **806** B2
Gharb Kurdufān, *state*, Sudan, **806** C2
Ghardaïa, Algeria, **801** G2
Ghardimaou, Tunisia, **779** B7
Ghārib, Jabal, *mountain peak*, Egypt, **761** B5
Gharo, Pakistan, **754** A4
Gharyān, Libya, **802** B2
Ghāt, Libya, **802** B3
Ghazāl, Baḩr al, *river*, Sudan, **806** C3
Ghazaouet, Algeria, **801** F1
Ghāziābād, India, **754** D3
Ghāzīpur, India, **755** E4
Ghazlānī, Jabal, *mountain peak*, Egypt, **761** C5
Ghazlūna, Pakistan, **754** A3
Ghaznī, Afghanistan, **754** B2
Ghazzālah, Saudi Arabia, **803** H3
Gheorgheni, Romania, **780** E2
Gherla, Romania, **780** D2
Ghijduwon, Uzbekistan, **758** G4
Ghilarza, Sardegna, Italy, **779** B5
Ghlo, Beinn a', *mountain peak*, Scotland, U.K., **792** F4
Ghotāru, India, **754** B4
Ghubaysh, Sudan, **806** C2
Ghunthur, Syria, **761** D2
Ghūriān, Afghanistan, **757** H2
Ghuzor, Uzbekistan, **758** H5
Gia Rai, Vietnam, **739** E4
Giang, *river*, Vietnam, **739** E2
Giannitsa, Greece, **781** D5
Giant's Causeway, *physical feature*, Northern Ireland, U.K., **793** F2
Gibara, Cuba, **839** F2
Gibbons, Canada, **823** N5
Gibeon, Namibia, **810** C4
Gibostad, Norway, **768** J2
Gibraleón, Spain, **776** D4
Gibraltar, Gibraltar, **776** E4
Gibraltar, Strait of, Morocco/Spain, **776** E5
Gibraltar, *U.K. dependency*, Europe, **776** E4
Gibson Desert, Australia, **716** B4
Gīdar, Pakistan, **754** A3
Giddalūr, India, **752** D3
Gideälven, *river*, Sweden, **768** J5
Gidolē, Ethiopia, **809** G1
Gien, France, **774** F3
Gießen, Germany, **772** D3
Gifford, Scotland, U.K., **792** G5
Gifford, U.S.A., **828** E2
Gifhorn, Germany, **772** E2
Gifu, Japan, **745** G4
Giganta, Cerro, *mountain peak*, Mexico, **840** C3
Gigante, Colombia, **848** C3
Gigha Island, Scotland, U.K., **792** D5
Giglio, Isola del, *island*, Italy, **779** C4
Gignac, France, **775** F5
Gijón, Spain, **776** E1
Gila, *river*, U.S.A., **833** H5
Gila, Tanjong, *point*, Indonesia, **735** E2
Gila, U.S.A., **833** J5
Gila Bend, U.S.A., **832** G5
Gila Mountains, *mountain range*, U.S.A., **833** H5
Gilău, Romania, **780** D2
Gilbert, *river*, Australia, **721** J2
Gilbert Islands, Kiribati, **725** F5
Gilbués, Brazil, **854** E2
Gildford, U.S.A., **829** J2
Gilé, Mozambique, **809** G6
Gilgandra, Australia, **721** K5
Gilgil, Kenya, **809** G3
Gilgit, Pakistan, **754** C2
Gilgit, *river*, Pakistan, **754** C1
Gill, Lough, *lake*, Ireland, **793** D3
Gill Point, St Helena, **813** B3
Gillam, Canada, **824** G3
Gilleleje, Denmark, **770** F4
Gillette, U.S.A., **829** M4
Gilling West, England, U.K., **791** G3
Gillingham, Dorset, England, U.K., **788** E3
Gillingham, Kent, England, U.K., **789** H3
Gilmer, U.S.A., **834** E3
Gilroy, U.S.A., **832** C3
Gilsland, England, U.K., **790** F3
Giltjaur, Sweden, **768** H4
Giluwe, Mount, *mountain peak*, Papua New Guinea, **726** A4
Gilwern, Wales, U.K., **788** D3
Gīmbī, Ethiopia, **806** E3
Gimli, Canada, **824** F6
Gimo, Sweden, **771** J2
Gimoly, Russian Federation, **769** R5
Gimont, France, **774** E5
Gingoog, Philippines, **740** D4
Ginir, Ethiopia, **807** F3
Gioia del Colle, Italy, **779** F5
Gioia Tauro, Italy, **779** E6
Gīr Hills, India, **754** B5
Girard, U.S.A., **830** J6
Girardville, Canada, **826** E5
Girgir, Cape, Papua New Guinea, **726** B3
Girīdīh, India, **755** F4
Girifalco, Italy, **779** F6
Girón, Ecuador, **848** B5
Girona, Spain, **777** J2
Gironde, *river mouth*, France, **774** D4
Girvan, Scotland, U.K., **792** E5
Girvas, Murmanskaya Oblast', Russian Federation, **769** Q3
Girvas, Respublika Kareliya, Russian Federation, **769** R5
Girvin, U.S.A., **833** M6
Gisborne, New Zealand, **718** G4
Giscome, Canada, **822** H4
Gisenyi, Rwanda, **809** E3
Gislaved, Sweden, **770** F4
Gisors, France, **774** E2
Gitega, Burundi, **809** E3
Giulianova, Italy, **778** D4
Giurgiu, Romania, **780** E4
Givors, France, **775** G4
Giyani, South Africa, **811** F3
Giyon, Ethiopia, **807** E3
Gīzāb, Afganistan, **754** A2
Gizo, Solomon Islands, **727** A1
Giżycko, Poland, **773** K1
Gjirokastër, Albania, **781** C5
Gjoa Haven, Canada, **821** K3
Gjøra, Norway, **770** D1
Gjøvik, Norway, **770** E2
Gjuhëzës, Kepi i, *cape*, Albania, **781** B5
Glace Bay, Canada, **827** M6
Glacier, Canada, **823** L6
Glacier, U.S.A., **828** D2
Glad', Russian Federation, **783** D3
Glad Valley, U.S.A., **830** C3
Gladstad, Norway, **768** E4
Gladstone, Canada, **824** E6
Gladstone, Michigan, U.S.A., **831** K3
Gladstone, New Mexico, U.S.A., **833** M3
Gladstone, Queensland, Australia, **721** L3
Gladstone, South Australia, Australia, **721** H5
Gláma, *mountain peak*, Iceland, **768** X7
Glåma, *river*, Norway, **770** E2
Glamis, Scotland, U.K., **792** F4
Glåmos, Norway, **770** E1
Glan, Philippines, **740** D5
Glanaruddery Mountains, Ireland, **793** C5
Glanton, England, U.K., **791** G2
Glarner Alpen, *mountain range*, Switzerland, **775** J3
Glarus, Switzerland, **775** J3
Glasbury, Wales, U.K., **788** D2
Glasgow, Kentucky, U.S.A., **831** L7
Glasgow, Montana, U.S.A., **829** L2
Glasgow, Scotland, U.K., **792** E5
Glasgow, Virginia, U.S.A., **831** P7
Glasgow City, *local authority*, Scotland, U.K., **792** E5
Glaslyn, Canada, **823** Q5
Glass Butte, *mountain peak*, U.S.A., **828** D5
Glassboro, U.S.A., **836** C5
Glastonbury, England, U.K., **788** E3
Glazov, Russian Federation, **784** G4
Gleisdorf, Austria, **773** G5
Glen Canyon, *gorge*, U.S.A., **833** H3
Glen Cove, U.S.A., **836** D4
Glen Falls, U.S.A., **836** D3
Glen Innes, Australia, **721** L4
Glen Ullin, U.S.A., **829** P3
Glenavy, New Zealand, **719** C7
Glenbarr, Scotland, U.K., **792** D5
Glencross, U.S.A., **830** C3
Glendale, Arizona, U.S.A., **833** G5
Glendale, California, U.S.A., **832** D4
Glendambo, Australia, **721** H5
Glendive, U.S.A., **829** M3
Glendo, U.S.A., **829** M5
Glendon, Canada, **823** P4
Gleneagles, Scotland, U.K., **792** F4
Glenelg, *river*, Australia, **721** J6
Glenfield, U.S.A., **830** D2
Glenfinnan, Scotland, U.K., **792** D4
Glengad Head, *point*, Ireland, **793** E2
Glengarriff, Ireland, **793** C6
Glenluce, Scotland, U.K., **792** E6
Glennallen, U.S.A., **820** E3
Glennamaddy, Ireland, **793** D4
Glennville, U.S.A., **835** M4
Glenorchy, New Zealand, **719** B7
Glenrock, U.S.A., **829** M5
Glenrothes, Scotland, U.K., **792** F4
Glenties, Ireland, **793** D3
Glentworth, Canada, **823** R7
Glenville, U.S.A., **835** K3
Glenwood, Arkansas, U.S.A., **834** F2
Glenwood, Iowa, U.S.A., **830** F5
Glenwood, Minnesota, U.S.A., **830** F3
Glenwood, New Mexico, U.S.A., **833** J5

Grim, Cape, Australia, 716 D6
Grimari, Central African Republic, 805 J3
Grimma, Germany, 772 F3
Grimmen, Germany, 772 F1
Grimsby, England, U.K., 791 H4
Grimshaw, Canada, 823 L3
Grimsstaðir, Iceland, 768 Y7
Grimstad, Norway, 770 D3
Grindavík, Iceland, 768 X8
Grindsted, Denmark, 770 D5
Grinnell, U.S.A., 830 G5
Grintavec, mountain peak, Slovenia, 778 E2
Griquatown, South Africa, 810 D4
Gris Nez, Cap, cape, France, 789 J4
Grise Fiord, Canada, 821 L2
Grisslehamn, Sweden, 771 J2
Groais Island, Canada, 827 P4
Grobiņa, Latvia, 771 K4
Grødes, Norway, 770 C2
Grodków, Poland, 773 H3
Groesbeek, Netherlands, 772 B3
Groix, Île de, island , France, 774 C3
Grójec, Poland, 773 K3
Grong, Norway, 768 F4
Groningen, Netherlands, 772 C2
Groningen, province, Netherlands, 772 C2
Groningen, Suriname, 850 B2
Groote Eylandt, island, Australia, 721 H1
Grootfontein, Namibia, 810 C2
Gropniţa, Romania, 780 F2
Grose Morne, mountain peak, Canada, 827 N5
Gross Ums, Namibia, 810 C3
Grossa, Punta, point, Islas Baleares, Spain, 777 H3
Grosser Arber, mountain peak, Germany, 772 F4
Grosseto, Italy, 778 C4
Großglockner, mountain peak, Austria, 772 F5
Groswater Bay, Canada, 827 N2
Groton, U.S.A., 830 D3
Grov, Norway, 768 H2
Grove City, U.S.A., 831 N5
Grove Hill, U.S.A., 835 J4
Grover City, U.S.A., 832 C4
Groznyy, Russian Federation, 758 D4
Grua, Norway, 770 E2
Grudovo, Bulgaria, 780 F4
Grudziądz, Poland, 773 J2
Gruinard Bay, Scotland, U.K., 792 D3
Grums, Sweden, 770 F3
Grünau, Namibia, 810 C4
Gruvberget, Sweden, 770 H2
Gruža, Yugoslavia, 780 C4
Gruzdžiai, Lithuania, 771 L4
Gryfice, Poland, 773 G2
Gryllefjord, Norway, 768 H2
Gryt, Sweden, 771 H3
Grytøya, island, Norway, 768 H2
Grytviken, South Georgia, 859 A3
Grytviken, U.K. research station, Antarctica, 862 A2
Guacanayabo, Golfo de, gulf, Cuba, 839 F2
Guachipas, Argentina, 856 D2
Guaçu, river, Brazil, 857 F2
Guadajoz, river, Spain, 776 E4
Guadalajara, Mexico, 840 E4
Guadalajara, Spain, 777 F2
Guadalcanal, island, Solomon Islands, 727 A1
Guadalimar, river, Spain, 777 F3
Guadalmena, Embalse de, reservoir, Murcia, 777 G3
Guadalmena, river, Spain, 777 F3
Guadālmez, river, Spain, 776 E3
Guadalope, river, Spain, 777 G2
Guadalquivir, river, Spain, 776 E4
Guadalupe, Baja California, Mexico, 840 A1
Guadalupe, Isla, island, Mexico, 817 M6
Guadalupe, Nuevo Léon, Mexico, 840 E4
Guadalupe, Spain, 776 E3
Guadalupe Aguilera, Mexico, 840 D3
Guadalupe Victoria, Mexico, 840 D3
Guadarrama, Sierra de, mountain range, Spain, 777 F2
Guadeloupe, French department, Caribbean Sea, 817 S7
Guadeloupe Passage, Caribbean Sea, 837 D2
Guadiana, river, Portugal/Spain, 766 D4
Guadix, Spain, 777 F4
Guafo, Boca del, river mouth, Chile, 858 B2
Guafo, Isla, island, Chile, 858 B2
Guaíba, Brazil, 857 G4
Guaimaca, Honduras, 838 D4
Guáimaro, Cuba, 839 F2
Guaiquinima, Cerro, mountain peak, Venezuela, 849 F3
Guaira, Brazil, 857 F2
Guaitecas, Islas, islands, Chile, 858 B2
Guajará-Mirim, Brazil, 853 F3
Guajarraã, Brazil, 853 E2
Guajira, Península de, Colombia, 848 D1
Gualaceo, Ecuador, 848 B5
Gualdo Tadino, Italy, 778 D4
Gualeguay, Argentina, 857 E4
Gualeguay, river, Argentina, 857 E4
Gualeguaychú, Argentina, 857 E4
Gualicho, Salina, salt-pan, Argentina, 858 E1
Gualjaina, Argentina, 858 C2
Guallatiri, Volcán, mountain peak, Chile, 853 E5
Guam, U.S. territory, Pacific Ocean, 724 C3
Guamini, Argentina, 856 D5
Guamúchil, Mexico, 840 C3
Guan Xian, China, 751 G3
Guanabacoa, Cuba, 839 E2
Guanaja, Honduras, 838 D3
Guanajuato, Mexico, 841 E4
Guanajuato, state, Mexico, 841 E4
Guanambi, Brazil, 855 E4
Guanare, Venezuela, 849 E2
Guanarito, Venezuela, 849 E2
Guanay, Sierra, mountain range, Venezuela, 849 E3
Guandacol, Argentina, 856 C3
Guane, Cuba, 838 D2
Guang'an, China, 751 H3
Guangchang, China, 742 D3
Guangde, China, 742 D2
Guangdegong, China, 747 G4
Guangdong, province, China, 742 C4
Guangfeng, China, 742 D2
Guanghai, China, 742 C4
Guangning, China, 742 C4
Guangrao, China, 747 G5
Guangshui, China, 742 C2
Guangxi Zhuangzu Zizhiqu, autonomous region, China, 742 B3
Guangyuan, China, 751 H2
Guangze, China, 742 D3
Guangzhou (Canton), China, 743 A2
Guanhães, Brazil, 855 E5
Guanhu, China, 742 D1
Guanipa, river, Venezuela, 849 F2
Guanlan, China, 743 C3
Guantánamo, Cuba, 839 G2
Guanting, China, 751 G2
Guanyinge, China, 743 D2
Guanyun, China, 742 D1
Guapay, river see Grande, river, Bolivia, 853 F5
Guapi, Colombia, 848 C3
Guápiles, Costa Rica, 838 E5
Guapo Bay, Trinidad, Trinidad and Tobago, 859 C4
Guaporé, river, Bolivia/Brazil, 853 F3
Guara, Sierra de, mountain peak, Spain, 777 G1
Guarabira, Brazil, 851 G5
Guaranda, Ecuador, 848 B4
Guarapari, Brazil, 855 F5
Guarapuava, Brazil, 857 G2
Guaraqueçaba, Brazil, 857 H2
Guaratinguetá, Brazil, 855 E6
Guaratuba, Brazil, 857 H2
Guarayos, Bolivia, 853 E3
Guarda, district, Portugal, 776 D2
Guarda, Portugal, 776 D2
Guarda Mor, Brazil, 854 D4
Guárico, river, Venezuela, 849 E2
Guarita, river, Brazil, 857 G3
Guarujá, Brazil, 857 H2
Guasacavi, Cerro, mountain peak, Colombia, 849 E3
Guasave, Mexico, 840 C3
Guasdualito, Venezuela, 849 D2
Guasipati, Venezuela, 849 G2
Guatemala, country, Central America, 817 P7
Guatemala, Guatemala, 838 C4
Guatemala Basin, underwater feature, Pacific Ocean, 869 M4
Guateng, province, South Africa, 811 E4
Guatrache, Argentina, 856 D5
Guatuaro Point, Trinidad, Trinidad and Tobago, 859 C4
Guaviare, river, Colombia, 849 D3
Guaxupé, Brazil, 854 D5
Guayabero, river, Colombia, 848 D3
Guayaguayare, Trinidad, Trinidad and Tobago, 859 C4
Guayama, Puerto Rico, 837 C2
Guayaquil, Ecuador, 848 B5
Guayaquil, Golfo de, gulf, Ecuador, 848 B5
Guayaramerin, Bolivia, 853 F3
Guaycurú, river, Argentina, 857 E3
Guaymas, Mexico, 840 C3
Guayquiraró, river, Argentina, 857 E4
Guba, Ethiopia, 806 E2
Guban, physical feature, Somalia, 807 F2
Gubbio, Italy, 778 D4
Guben, Germany, 773 G3
Gubi, Nigeria, 805 F2
Gubin, Poland, 773 G3
Gubio, Nigeria, 805 G2
Gucheng, China, 742 B1
Gudivāda, India, 753 E2
Gudiyattam, India, 752 D3
Güdür, India, 752 D3
Gudvangen, Norway, 770 C2
Guékédou, Guinea, 804 B3
Guélengdeng, Chad, 805 H2
Guelma, Algeria, 801 H1
Guelmim, Morocco, 800 D3
Guelta Zemmur, Western Sahara, 800 D3
Guemar, Algeria, 801 H2
Güémez, Mexico, 841 F4
Guéné, Benin, 805 E2
Guer, France, 774 C3
Guéra, prefecture, Chad, 806 A2
Guerara, Algeria, 801 G2
Guercif, Morocco, 801 F2
Guéret, France, 774 E3
Guernsey, island, Channel Islands, 774 C2
Guernsey, U.S.A., 829 M5
Guérou, Mauritania, 804 B1
Guerrero, state, Mexico, 841 E5
Guerrero Negro, Mexico, 840 B3
Gueugnon, France, 775 G3
Guéyo, Côte d'Ivoire, 804 C3
Gugê, mountain peak, Ethiopia, 807 E3
Guguan, island, Northern Mariana Islands, 724 C3
Guguang, Gunung, mountain peak, Indonesia, 737 G2
Guhāgar, India, 752 C2
Guhakolak, Tanjong, point, Indonesia, 736 D4
Gui, river, China, 742 B3
Guía de Isora, Islas Canarias, Spain, 813 A4
Guiana Highlands, South America, 847 F3
Guichi, China, 742 D2
Guichón, Uruguay, 857 F4
Guidari, Chad, 805 H3
Guide, China, 751 G2
Guider, Cameroon, 805 G3
Guidimaka, administrative region, Mauritania, 804 B1
Guiding, China, 751 H4
Guigang, China, 742 B4
Guiglo, Côte d'Ivoire, 804 C3
Guijuelo, Spain, 776 E2
Guildford, England, U.K., 789 G3
Guiler, China, 747 H3
Guilford, U.S.A., 836 F2
Guilin, China, 742 B3
Guillaume-Delisle, Lac, lake, Canada, 825 S3
Guillestre, France, 775 H4
Guimarães, Brazil, 851 E4
Guimarães, Portugal, 776 C2
Guimbiri, Mont, mountain peak, Cameroon, 805 G4
Guinan, China, 751 G2
Guindulman, Philippines, 740 D4
Guinea, country, Africa, 796 D5
Guinea Basin, underwater feature, Atlantic Ocean, 867 G5
Guinea-Bissau, country, Africa, 796 D5
Guinée-Forestière, administrative area, Guinea, 804 C3
Guinée-Maritime, administrative region, Guinea, 804 B2
Güines, Cuba, 839 E2
Guingamp, France, 774 C2
Guinguinéo, Senegal, 804 A2
Guiping, China, 742 B4
Guir, Oued, river, Algeria/Morocco, 801 F2
Guiratinga, Brazil, 854 C4
Güiria, Venezuela, 849 F1
Guisanbourg, French Guiana, 850 C2
Guisborough, England, U.K., 791 G3
Guise, France, 775 F2
Guishan Dao, island, China, 743 B4
Guist, England, U.K., 789 H2
Guitinguitin, Mount, mountain peak, Philippines, 740 C3
Guitiriz, Spain, 776 D1
Guiuan, Philippines, 740 D4
Guixi, China, 742 D2
Guiyang, Guizhou, China, 751 H4
Guiyang, Hunan, China, 742 C3
Guizhou, China, 743 A3
Guizhou, province, China, 751 H4
Gujarāt, state, India, 754 B5
Gujrānwāla, Pakistan, 754 C2
Gujrāt, Pakistan, 754 C2
Gulang, China, 749 J5
Gulbarga, India, 752 D2
Gulbene, Latvia, 771 N4
Gul'cha, Kyrgyzstan, 759 J4
Gulf, province, Papua New Guinea, 726 B5
Gulf Shores, U.S.A., 835 J4
Gulfport, U.S.A., 835 H4
Gulin, China, 751 H4
Guling, China, 742 C2
Guliston, Uzbekistan, 759 H4
Gull Bay, Canada, 825 K7
Gullspång, Sweden, 770 G3
Güllük Körfezi, bay, Turkey, 781 F7
Gülnar, Turkey, 761 B1
Gülpınar, Turkey, 781 F6
Gülshat, Kazakhstan, 759 J3
Gulu, Uganda, 809 F2
Gülübovo, Bulgaria, 780 E4
Gulyantsi, Bulgaria, 780 E4
Gumal, river, Pakistan, 754 B2
Gumare, Botswana, 810 D2
Gumarino, Russian Federation, 769 R5
Gumbiri, mountain peak, Sudan, 809 F2
Gumdag, Turkmenistan, 758 E5
Gumel, Nigeria, 805 F2
Gumia, India, 755 F5
Gumla, India, 755 F5
Gummi, Nigeria, 805 F2
Gümüşhane, Turkey, 760 E4
Guna, India, 754 D4
Guna Terara, mountain peak, Ethiopia, 807 E2
Güncang, China, 750 E3
Gunda, Russian Federation, 746 E1
Güney, Turkey, 781 G6
Güneydoğu Toroslar, mountain range, Turkey, 760 E5
Gungu, Democratic Republic of the Congo, 808 C4
Gunja, Croatia, 778 G3
Gunnarn, Sweden, 768 H4
Gunnbjørn Fjeld, mountain peak, Greenland, 821 R3
Gunnedah, Australia, 721 L5
Gunners Quoin, island, Mauritius, 813 C1
Gunnilbo, Sweden, 770 G3
Gunnison, Colorado, U.S.A., 833 K2
Gunnison, Utah, U.S.A., 833 H2
Guntakal, India, 752 D3
Guntersville Lake, U.S.A., 835 J2
Guntur, India, 752 E2
Gunung, Tanjong, point, Indonesia, 737 E2
Gunungsitoli, Indonesia, 736 B2
Gunungsugih, Indonesia, 736 D4
Gunupur, India, 753 E2
Guojiadian, China, 744 D2
Guoyang, China, 742 D1
Gura Galbenei, Moldova, 780 G2
Gura Humorului, Romania, 780 E2
Gurais, India, 754 C2
Gurban Obo, China, 746 F4
Gurbantünggüt Shamo, desert, China, 748 E3
Güre, Turkey, 781 G6
Gurgaon, India, 754 D3
Gurgei, Jabal, mountain peak, Sudan, 806 B2
Gurguéia, river, Brazil, 851 E5
Gurha, India, 754 B4
Guri, Embalse de, reservoir, Venezuela, 849 F2
Gurinhatã, Brazil, 854 D5
Gurk, Austria, 773 G5
Guro, Mozambique, 811 F2
Gurskoye, Russian Federation, 747 M2
Gürsu, Turkey, 781 G5
Guru Sikhar, mountain peak, India, 754 C4
Gurué, Mozambique, 809 G6
Gürün, Turkey, 760 E5
Gurupá, Brazil, 850 C3
Gurupi, Brazil, 854 D3
Gurupi, river, Brazil, 850 D4
Gurupi, Serra do, mountain range, Brazil, 850 D4
Guruve, Zimbabwe, 811 F2
Gurvan Sayhan Uul, mountain range, Mongolia, 749 J4

Gus'-Khrustal'nyy, Russian Federation, **782** F1
Gusau, Nigeria, **805** F2
Gusev, Russian Federation, **771** L5
Gushan, China, **747** H5
Gushi, China, **742** C1
Gushiago, Ghana, **804** D3
Gusinoozersk, Russian Federation, **746** D2
Guspini, Sardegna, Italy, **779** B6
Gustav Holm, Kap, *cape*, Greenland, **821** R3
Gustavsberg, Sweden, **771** J3
Güstrow, Germany, **772** F2
Gutay, Russian Federation, **746** E2
Guthrie, Oklahoma, U.S.A., **834** D2
Guthrie, Texas, U.S.A., **834** B3
Gutian, China, **742** D3
Gutu, Zimbabwe, **811** F2
Guwāhāti, India, **755** G4
Guyana, *country*, South America, **845** G3
Guyang, China, **746** E4
Guymon, U.S.A., **830** C7
Guyot, Mount, *mountain peak*, U.S.A., **835** L2
Guyuan, China, **746** D5
Güzelbağ, Turkey, **761** A1
Guzhu, China, **743** D1
Guzmán, Mexico, **840** D2
Gvarv, Norway, **770** D3
Gwa, Myanmar, **741** B4
Gwadabawa, Nigeria, **805** F2
Gwādar, Pakistan, **757** H3
Gwalior, India, **754** D4
Gwanda, Zimbabwe, **811** E3
Gwane, Democratic Republic of the Congo, **809** E2
Gwatar Bay, Iran/Pakistan, **757** H4
Gwawele, Democratic Republic of the Congo, **809** E2
Gwda, *river*, Poland, **773** H2
Gweebarra Bay, Ireland, **793** D3
Gweedore, Ireland, **793** D2
Gweru, Zimbabwe, **811** E2
Gweta, Botswana, **810** E3
Gwinn, U.S.A., **831** K2
Gwinner, U.S.A., **830** E2
Gwoza, Nigeria, **805** G2
Gwynedd, *unitary authority*, Wales, U.K., **788** D2
Gyaca, China, **750** E3
Gyagartang, China, **751** G2
Gyangzê, China, **750** D3
Gyaring, China, **751** F2
Gyaring Co, *lake*, China, **750** D3
Gyaring Hu, *lake*, China, **751** F2
Gyawa, China, **751** G3
Gyda, Russian Federation, **784** J2
Gydanskiy Poluostrov, *peninsula*, Russian Federation, **784** J2
Gyirong, China, **750** C3
Gyitang, China, **751** F3
Gyldenløves Fjord, Greenland, **821** Q3
Gyljen, Sweden, **769** L3
Gympie, Australia, **721** L4
Gyomaendrőd, Hungary, **773** K5
Gyöngyös, Hungary, **773** J5
Gypsumville, Canada, **824** E6
Győr, Hungary, **773** H5
Gytheio, Greece, **781** D7
Gyula, Hungary, **773** K5
Gyumri, Armenia, **758** C4
Gyzylarbat, Turkmenistan, **758** F5

H

Hà Đông, Vietnam, **739** E1
Hà Giang, Vietnam, **739** E1
Hà Nam, Vietnam, **739** E1
Hà Nôi (Hanoi), Vietnam, **739** E1
Hà Tiên, Vietnam, **739** E4
Hş Tĩnh, Vietnam, **739** E2
Häädemeeste, Estonia, **771** M3
Haag in Oberbayern, Germany, **772** F4
Haakon VII Sea, Antarctica, **862** D3
Ha'alaufuli, Vava'u Group, Tonga, **727** B3
Ha'apai Group, *islands*, Tonga, **722** D3
Haapajärvi, Finland, **769** M5
Haapavesi, Finland, **769** M4
Haapsalu, Estonia, **771** L3
Haarlem, Netherlands, **772** B2
Haast, New Zealand, **719** B6
Ha'atua, Tongatapu Group, Tonga, **727** B4
Hab, *river*, Pakistan, **754** A4
Habaswein, Kenya, **809** G2
Ḥabbān, Yemen, **756** E6
Ḥabbānīyah, Iraq, **803** H2
Habirag, China, **746** F4
Hacha, Colombia, **848** C4
Hachijō-jima, *island*, Japan, **745** G3
Hachinohe, Japan, **745** H2
Hackås, Sweden, **768** G5
Hackness, England, U.K., **791** H3
Hacufera, Mozambique, **811** F3
Hadagang, China, **747** K3
Hadarba, Ras, *point*, Sudan, **803** G4
Hadat, China, **747** G2
Ḥadbaram, Oman, **757** G5
Ḥadd, Ra's al, *cape*, Oman, **757** G4
Ḥaddā', Saudi Arabia, **803** G4
Haddiscoe, England, U.K., **789** J2
Haddunmahti Atoll, Maldives, **752** C6
Hadejia, Nigeria, **805** G2
Ḥadera, Israel, **761** C3
Haderslev, Denmark, **770** D5
Hadgaon, India, **752** D2
Hadīboh, Suquṭrá (Socotra), Yemen, **813** B2
Hadilik, China, **748** E5
Hadleigh, England, U.K., **789** H2
Hadley Bay, Canada, **820** J2
Ḥaḍramawt, *region*, Yemen, **756** E5
Hadseløya, *island*, Norway, **768** F2
Hadsund, Denmark, **770** E4
Hadyach, Ukraine, **782** D2
Haedo, Cuchilla de, *mountain range*, Brazil/Uruguay, **857** F4
Haeju, North Korea, **744** D3
Haenam, South Korea, **744** D4
Ḥafar al Bāṭin, Saudi Arabia, **803** J3
Hafik, Turkey, **803** G1
Ḥafīrat al 'Aydā, Saudi Arabia, **803** G3
Hāfizābād, Pakistan, **754** C2
Hāflong, India, **750** E4
Hafnarfjörður, Iceland, **768** X7
Hafnir, Iceland, **768** X8
Hagen, Germany, **772** C3
Hagenow, Germany, **772** E2
Hāgere Hiywet, Ethiopia, **807** E3
Hagerman, Idaho, U.S.A., **828** G5
Hagerman, New Mexico, U.S.A., **833** L5
Hagerstown, U.S.A., **836** B5
Hagetmau, France, **774** D5
Hagfors, Sweden, **770** F3
Hagi, Japan, **744** E4
Hagi-zaki, *point*, Japan, **744** E4
Hagley, England, U.K., **788** E2
Hags Head, *point*, Ireland, **793** C5
Hague, Canada, **823** R5
Hague, Cap de la, *cape*, France, **774** D2
Hague, U.S.A., **830** D2
Haguenau, France, **775** H2
Hagunia, Western Sahara, **800** D3
Haha-jima, *island*, Japan, **724** C2
Hahót, Hungary, **773** H5
Hải Phòng, Vietnam, **739** E1
Hai'an, China, **742** E1
Hai'an Shan, *mountain range*, China, **743** C3
Haicheng, China, **747** H4
Haifa *see* Ḥefa, Israel, **761** C3
Haifeng, China, **742** C4
Haikang, China, **742** B4
Haikou, China, **739** F1
Ḥā'il, Saudi Arabia, **803** H3
Hailar, China, **747** G2
Hailar, *river*, China, **747** H2
Hailin, China, **747** K3
Hails, China, **746** D4
Hailsham, England, U.K., **789** H4
Hailun, China, **747** J3
Hailuoto, Finland, **769** M4
Hailuoto, *island*, Finland, **769** M4
Haimen, China, **742** E2
Hainan, *province*, China, **739** F2
Hainan Dao, *island*, China, **739** F2
Hainaut, *province*, Belgium, **772** A3
Haindi, Liberia, **804** B3
Haines City, U.S.A., **835** M5
Haines Junction, Canada, **820** F3
Haining, China, **742** E2
Haīpur, Pakistan, **754** C2
Haitan Dao, *island*, China, **742** D3
Haiti, *country*, Caribbean Sea, **817** R7
Haitou, China, **739** F2
Haiyan, China, **742** E2
Haiyang, China, **747** H5
Haiyuan, China, **746** D5
Ḥajar, Al, *mountain range*, Oman, **757** G4
Hajdúböszörmeny, Hungary, **773** K5
Hajdúszoboszló, Hungary, **773** K5
Hajhir, *mountain range*, Suquṭrá (Socotra), Yemen, **813** B2
Ḥājī Ebrāhīm, Kūhe, *mountain peak*, Iran/Iraq, **803** H1
Hājīpur, India, **750** C4
Ḥajj 'Abd Allāh, Sudan, **806** D2
Ḥajjah, Yemen, **756** D5
Hajnówka, Poland, **773** L2
Haju, China, **749** H4
Hajuu-Ulaan, Mongolia, **746** E3
Hajuu-Us, Mongolia, **746** D3
Haka, Myanmar, **741** B3
Hakkas, Sweden, **768** K3
Hakkstabben, Norway, **769** L1
Hakodate, Japan, **745** H2
Hakupu, Niue, **718** M13
Hāla, Pakistan, **754** B4
Ḥalab (Aleppo), Syria, **761** D1
Ḥalab, *district*, Syria, **761** D1
Ḥalabān, Saudi Arabia, **803** H4
Ḥalabjah, Iraq, **803** J1
Halagigie Point, Niue, **718** M13
Ḥalā'ib, Sudan, **803** G4
Ḥālat 'Ammār, Saudi Arabia, **761** D5
Ḥalbā, Lebanon, **761** D2
Halban, Mongolia, **749** H2
Halberstadt, Germany, **772** E3
Halbrite, Canada, **824** C7
Halcon, Mount, *mountain peak*, Philippines, **740** C3
Haldde, *mountain peak*, Norway, **769** L2
Halden, Norway, **770** E3
Haldwāni, India, **754** D3
Hale, England, U.K., **790** F4
Halesowen, England, U.K., **788** E2
Halesworth, England, U.K., **789** J2
Ḥalfa'al Jadīdah, Sudan, **806** E1
Halfmoon Bay, New Zealand, **719** B8
Haliburton, Canada, **826** B7
Haliburton Highlands, *mountain range*, Canada, **826** B7
Halifax, Canada, **827** K7
Halifax, England, U.K., **791** G4
Halitpaşa, Turkey, **781** F6
Halkirk, Scotland, U.K., **792** F2
Hall Beach, Canada, **821** L3
Hall Islands, Micronesia, **724** D4
Hall Peninsula, Canada, **821** N3
Halla-san, *mountain peak*, South Korea, **744** D4
Halland, *county*, Sweden, **770** F4
Halle, Germany, **772** E3
Halle (Westfalen) Germany, **772** D2
Hällefors, Sweden, **770** G3
Hallen, Sweden, **768** G5
Hallencourt, France, **789** J5
Hällestad, Sweden, **770** G3
Hallettsville, U.S.A., **834** D5
Halley, *U.K. research station*, Antarctica, **862** C4
Halliday, U.S.A., **830** B2
Hallingskarvet, *mountain peak*, Norway, **770** C2
Hällnäs, Sweden, **768** J4
Hallock, U.S.A., **830** E1
Halls Creek, Australia, **720** F2
Hallsberg, Sweden, **770** G3
Hallstavik, Sweden, **771** J2
Hallworthy, England, U.K., **788** C4
Halma, U.S.A., **830** E1
Halmahera, Pulau, *island*, Indonesia, **734** D2
Halmahera Sea, Indonesia, **724** A5
Halmeu, Romania, **780** D2
Halmstad, Sweden, **770** F4
Hals, Denmark, **770** E4
Hal'shany, Belarus, **771** N5
Halstad, U.S.A., **830** E2
Halstead, England, U.K., **789** H3
Halsua, Finland, **769** M5
Halswell, New Zealand, **719** D6
Haltang, *river*, China, **749** G5
Halti, *mountain peak*, Finland, **768** K2
Halton, *unitary authority*, England, U.K., **790** F4
Haltwhistle, England, U.K., **790** F3
Halwell, England, U.K., **788** D4
Hàm Yên, Vietnam, **739** E1
Hamada, Japan, **744** F4
Hamadān, Iran, **756** E2
Hamaguir, Algeria, **801** F2
Ḥamāh, *district*, Syria, **761** D2
Ḥamāh, Syria, **761** D2
Hamam, Turkey, **761** D1
Hamamatsu, Japan, **745** G4
Hamar, Norway, **770** E2
Ḥamāṭah, Jabal, *mountain peak*, Egypt, **803** F4
Hamatombetsu, Japan, **745** H1
Hambantota, Sri Lanka, **753** E5
Hamburg, Arkansas, U.S.A., **834** G3
Hamburg, California, U.S.A., **828** C6
Hamburg, Germany, **772** E2
Hamburg, *state*, Germany, **772** D2
Ḥamḍah, Saudi Arabia, **803** H5
Ḥamdānah, Saudi Arabia, **803** H5
Hamdibey, Turkey, **781** F6
Hämeenkyrö, Finland, **771** L2
Hämeenlinna, Finland, **771** M2
Hameln, Germany, **772** D2
Hamersley Range, *mountain range*, Australia, **716** A4
Hamhŭng, North Korea, **744** D3
Hami, China, **749** G4
Hamilton, Alabama, U.S.A., **835** J2
Hamilton, Australia, **721** J6
Hamilton, Canada, **831** P4
Hamilton, Montana, U.S.A., **828** G3
Hamilton, Mount, *mountain peak*, Macquarie Island, **720** R11
Hamilton, New Zealand, **718** E3
Hamilton, Ohio, U.S.A., **831** L6
Hamilton, Scotland, U.K., **792** E5
Hamilton, Washington, U.S.A., **828** C2
Hamilton City, U.S.A., **832** C2
Hamilton Inlet, Canada, **827** M3
Hamina, Finland, **771** N2
Hamīrpur, India, **754** D3
Hamlet, North Carolina, U.S.A., **835** N2
Hamlet, North Dakota, U.S.A., **830** B1
Hamm, Germany, **772** C3
Ḥammām, Syria, **761** E2
Hammamet, Golfe de, *gulf*, Tunisia, **802** B1
Ḥammār, Hawr al, *lake*, Iraq, **803** J2
Hammarstrand, Sweden, **768** H5
Hammerdal, Sweden, **768** G5
Hammerfest, Norway, **769** L1
Hammond, Indiana, U.S.A., **831** K5
Hammond, Louisiana, U.S.A., **834** G4
Hammond, Montana, U.S.A., **829** M4
Hammonton, U.S.A., **836** C5
Hampden, Canada, **827** N5
Hampden, New Zealand, **719** C7
Hampden, U.S.A., **830** D1
Hampshire, *unitary authority*, England, U.K., **789** F3
Hampton, Canada, **826** J7
Hampton, Iowa, U.S.A., **830** G4
Hampton, New Hampshire, U.S.A., **836** E3
Hampton, Oregon, U.S.A., **828** D5
Hampton, South Carolina, U.S.A., **835** M3
Hampton, Virginia, U.S.A., **836** B6
Hampton Butte, *mountain peak*, U.S.A., **828** D5
Ḥamrā', Al Ḥamādah al, *plateau*, Libya, **802** B3
Hamrångefjärden, Sweden, **771** H2
Ḥamrat ash Shaykh, Sudan, **806** C2
Hamstreet, England, U.K., **789** H3
Han, *river*, China, **742** B1
Han, *river*, South Korea, **744** D3
Han Pijesak, Bosnia and Herzegovina, **778** G3
Han Sum, China, **747** G3
Hana, Hawaiian Islands, U.S.A., **832** R9
Hanahan, Papua New Guinea, **726** E2
Ḥanak, Saudi Arabia, **803** G3
Hanalei, Hawaiian Islands, U.S.A., **832** R9
Hanamaki, Japan, **745** H3
Hâncești, Moldova, **780** G2
Hanceville, Canada, **822** H6
Hancheng, China, **742** B1
Handa Island, Scotland, U.K., **792** D2
Handan, China, **746** F5
Handeni, Tanzania, **809** G4
Handlová, Slovakia, **773** J4
HaNegev, *desert*, Israel, **761** C4
Hanestad, Norway, **770** E2
Hanford, U.S.A., **832** D3
Hanga-Roa, Isla de Pascua (Easter Island), Chile, **859** B2
Hangay, *province*, Mongolia, **749** J3
Hangayn Nuruu, *mountain range*, Mongolia, **749** H3
Hanggin Houqi, China, **746** D4
Hanggin Qi, China, **746** E5
Hangu, China, **746** G5
Hangu, Pakistan, **754** B2
Hangzhou, China, **742** E2

I

J

Jēkabpils, Latvia, **771** M4
Jektvik, Norway, **768** F3
Jeldesa, Ethiopia, **807** F3
Jelenia Góra, Poland, **773** G3
Jelgava, Latvia, **771** L4
Jeli, Malaysia, **736** C1
Jellicoe, Canada, **825** L7
Jemaluang, Malaysia, **736** C2
Jember, Indonesia, **737** F5
Jeminay, China, **748** E3
Jempang, Danau, *lake*, Indonesia, **737** F3
Jena, Germany, **772** E3
Jendouba, Tunisia, **779** B7
Jenner, Canada, **823** P6
Jennings, U.S.A., **834** F4
Jenpeg, Canada, **824** E4
Jensen, U.S.A., **833** J1
Jepara, Indonesia, **737** E4
Jepua, Finland, **769** L5
Jequié, Brazil, **855** F3
Jequitaí, Brazil, **855** E4
Jequitinhonha, Brazil, **855** F4
Jequitinhonha, *river*, Brazil, **855** F4
Jerada, Morocco, **801** F2
Jerbar, Sudan, **809** F1
Jérémie, Haiti, **839** G3
Jeremoabo, Brazil, **855** F3
Jerez de García Salinas, Mexico, **840** E4
Jeréz de la Frontera, Spain, **776** D4
Jergucat, Albania, **781** C6
Jericho *see* Arīḥā, West Bank, **761** C4
Jerilderie, Australia, **721** K6
Jerome, U.S.A., **828** G5
Jerramungup, Australia, **720** D5
Jersey, *island*, Channel Islands, **774** C2
Jersey City, U.S.A., **836** C4
Jersey Shore, U.S.A., **836** B4
Jerseyville, U.S.A., **830** H6
Jerumenha, Brazil, **851** E5
Jerusalem *see* Yerushalayim, Israel, **761** C4
Jesi, Italy, **778** D4
Jessen, Germany, **772** F3
Jessheim, Norway, **770** E2
Jessore, Bangladesh, **750** D5
Jesup, U.S.A., **835** M4
Jesús María, Argentina, **856** D4
Jesús María, Boca de, *river mouth*, Mexico, **841** F3
Jetait, Canada, **824** D3
Jetmore, U.S.A., **830** D6
Jetpur, India, **754** B5
Jever, Germany, **772** C2
Jeziorak, Jeziora, *lake*, Poland, **773** J2
Jha Jha, India, **755** F4
Jhābua, India, **754** C5
Jhal, Pakistan, **754** A3
Jhang Sadr, Pakistan, **754** C3
Jhānsi, India, **754** D4
Jhārsuguda, India, **755** F5
Jhatpat, Pakistan, **754** B3
Jhelum, Pakistan, **754** C2
Jhelum, *river*, Pakistan, **754** C2
Jhenida, Bangladesh, **750** D5
Jhumri Tilaiyā, India, **755** F4
Ji Xian, Shanxi, China, **746** E5
Ji Xian, Tianjin Shi, China, **746** G4
Jia Xian, China, **746** E5
Jiaganj-Azimganj, India, **755** G4
Jiahe, Guangdong, China, **743** A2
Jiahe, Hunan, China, **742** C3
Jialing, *river*, China, **751** H3
Jiamusi, China, **747** K3
Ji'an, Jiangxi, China, **742** C3
Ji'an, Jilin, China, **747** J4
Jianchuan, China, **751** F4
Jiande, China, **742** D2
Jiang'an, China, **751** H3
Jiange, China, **751** H2
Jianggao, China, **743** A2
Jianghua, China, **742** B3
Jiangjin, China, **751** H3
Jiangjunmiao, China, **748** F3
Jiangle, China, **742** D3
Jiangling, China, **742** C2
Jiangluo, China, **751** H2
Jiangmen, China, **742** C4
Jiangsu, *province*, China, **742** D1
Jiangxi, *province*, China, **742** C3
Jiangxigou, China, **749** J5
Jiangyin, China, **742** E2
Jiangyou, China, **751** H3
Jianhu, China, **742** D1
Jianli, China, **742** C2
Jianning, China, **742** D3
Jian'ou, China, **742** D3
Jianquanzi, China, **749** H4
Jianshi, China, **742** B2
Jianshui, China, **751** G5
Jianyang, Fujian, China, **742** D3
Jianyang, Sichuan, China, **751** H3
Jiaocheng, China, **746** F5
Jiaohe, Hebei, China, **746** G5
Jiaohe, Jilin, China, **747** J4
Jiaojiang, China, **742** E2
Jiaokou, China, **746** E5
Jiaoling, China, **742** D3
Jiaonan, China, **747** G6
Jiaozhou, China, **747** H5
Jiaozuo, China, **742** C1
Jiasa, China, **751** G4
Jiashan, Anhui, China, **742** D1
Jiashan, Zhejiang, China, **742** E2
Jiashi, China, **748** C5
Jiawang, China, **742** D1
Jiaxing, China, **742** E2
Jiayin, China, **747** K2
Jiayuguan, China, **749** H5
Jiazi, China, **742** D4
Jibou, Romania, **780** D2
Jiddah (Jedda), Saudi Arabia, **803** G4
Jiddat al Ḥarāsīs, *desert*, Oman, **757** G5
Jiddī, Jabal al, *mountain peak*, Egypt, **761** B4
Jiekkevarre, *mountain peak*, Norway, **768** J2
Jieshi Wan, *bay*, China, **742** C4
Jieshou, China, **742** C1
Iešjavrre, *lake*, Norway, **769** M2
Jiexiu, China, **746** E5
Jieyang, China, **742** D4
Jieznas, Lithuania, **771** M5
Jigawa, *state*, Nigeria, **805** F2
Jigzhi, China, **751** G2
Jihlava, Czech Republic, **773** G4
Jihlava, *river*, Czech Republic, **773** G4
Jihočeský, *administrative region*, Czech Republic, **773** F4
Jihomoravský, *administrative region*, Czech Republic, **773** G4
Jijel, Algeria, **801** H1
Jijiga, Ethiopia, **807** F3
Jilf al Kabīr, Haḍabat al, *plain*, Egypt, **802** E4
Jili Hu, *lake*, China, **748** E3
Jilib, Somalia, **809** H2
Jilin, China, **747** J4
Jilin, *province*, China, **747** J4
Jiloca, *river*, Spain, **777** G2
Jilong, China, **743** D3
Jīma, Ethiopia, **807** E3
Jimaní, Haiti, **839** H3
Jimbolia, Romania, **780** C3
Jimena de la Frontera, Spain, **776** E4
Jiménez, Mexico, **840** D3
Jimenez, Philippines, **740** C4
Jimo, China, **747** H5
Jimsar, China, **748** F3
Jimulco, *mountain peak*, Mexico, **840** E3
Jinan, China, **746** G5
Jinchai, China, **742** B3
Jinchang, China, **749** J5
Jincheng, China, **742** C1
Jinchuan, China, **751** G3
Jīnd, India, **754** D3
Jindřichuv Hradec, Czech Republic, **773** G4
Jing Xian, Anhui, China, **742** D2
Jing Xian, Hunan, China, **742** B3
Jingbian, China, **746** E5
Jingchuan, China, **751** H2
Jingde, China, **742** D2
Jingdezhen, China, **742** D2
Jinggu, China, **751** G5
Jinghai, Guangdong, China, **742** D4
Jinghai, Tianjin Shi, China, **746** G5
Jinghe, China, **748** D3
Jinghong, China, **751** G5
Jingmen, China, **742** C2
Jingning, China, **751** H2
Jingshan, China, **742** C2
Jingtai, China, **746** D5
Jingxi, China, **751** H5
Jingyu, China, **747** J4
Jingyuan, China, **746** D5
Jingzhi, China, **747** G5
Jinhua, China, **742** D2
Jining, Nei Mongol Zizhiqu, China, **746** F4
Jining, Shandong, China, **742** D1
Jinja, Uganda, **809** F2
Jinjiang, Fujian, China, **742** D3
Jinjiang, Yunnan, China, **751** G4
Jinjuling, China, **743** B3
Jinka, Ethiopia, **809** G1
Jinkouhe, China, **751** G3
Jinkuang, China, **751** G3
Jinmen Dao, *island*, Taiwan, **742** D3
Jinotega, Nicaragua, **838** D4
Jinotepe, Nicaragua, **838** D5
Jinsha, China, **751** H4
Jinsha (Yangtze), *river*, China, **751** F3
Jinshantun, China, **747** K3
Jinshi, China, **742** B2
Jinta, China, **749** H5
Jintan, China, **742** D2
Jintang, China, **751** H3
Jinxi, Jiangshi, China, **742** D3
Jinxi, Liaoning, China, **747** H4
Jinxiang, China, **742** D1
Jinzhou, S. Liaoning, China, **747** H5
Jinzhou, W. Liaoning, China, **747** H4
Jipijapa, Ecuador, **848** B4
Jirin Gol, China, **746** G3
Jirjā, Egypt, **803** F3
Jirriiban, Somalia, **807** G3
Jishan, China, **742** B1
Jishou, China, **742** B2
Jisr ash Shughūr, Syria, **761** D2
Jitra, Malaysia, **736** C1
Jiu, *river*, Romania, **780** D3
Jiu'ao Dao, *island*, China, **743** B4
Jiucai Ling, *mountain peak*, China, **742** B3
Jiudengkou, China, **746** D5
Jiufo, China, **743** B2
Jiuhe, China, **743** D2
Jiujiang, China, **742** C2
Jiuling Shan, *mountain range*, China, **742** C2
Jiulong, China, **751** G3
Jiulong (Kowloon), China, **743** C4
Jiuquan, China, **749** H5
Jiutai, China, **747** J3
Jiuyuhang, China, **742** D2
Jiuzhan, Heilongjiang, China, **747** J2
Jiuzhan, Jilin, China, **747** J4
Jiuzhou, China, **751** H4
Jiwani, Pakistan, **757** H3
Jiwen, China, **747** H2
Jixi, Anhui, China, **742** D2
Jixi, Heilongjiang, China, **747** K3
Jixian, China, **747** K3
Jīzān, Saudi Arabia, **803** H5
Jizzakh, Uzbekistan, **758** H4
Joaçaba, Brazil, **857** G3
Joal-Fadiout, Senegal, **804** A2
João Pessoa, Brazil, **851** G5
João Pinheiro, Brazil, **854** D4
Joaquín V. González, Argentina, **856** D2
Jobat, India, **754** C5
Jock, Sweden, **769** L3
Jódar, Spain, **777** F4
Jodhpur, India, **754** C4
Joensuu, Finland, **771** P1
Jōetsu, Japan, **745** G3
Jofane, Mozambique, **811** F3
Jogbani, India, **755** F4
Jogbura, Nepal, **754** E3
Jõgeva, Estonia, **771** N3
Jogues, Canada, **825** N7
Johannesburg, South Africa, **811** E4
Johannesburg, U.S.A., **832** E4
John Day, *river*, U.S.A., **828** D4
John o'Groats, Scotland, U.K., **792** F2
Johnson, Pico de, *mountain peak*, Mexico, **840** B2
Johnson City, Kansas, U.S.A., **833** N3
Johnson City, Tennessee, U.S.A., **831** M7
Johnsons Crossing, Canada, **822** C1
Johnston, Wales, U.K., **788** B3
Johnston Atoll, *U.S. territory*, Pacific Ocean, **725** H3
Johnstone, Scotland, U.K., **792** E5
Johnstown, Ireland, **793** E5
Johor, Selat, *strait*, Malaysia/Singapore, **736** J6
Johor, *state*, Malaysia, **736** C2
Johor Baharu, Malaysia, **736** C2
Jõhvi, Estonia, **771** N3
Joigny, France, **775** F3
Joinville, Brazil, **857** H3
Joinville, France, **775** G2
Jokkmokk, Sweden, **768** J3
Jökulsá á Brú, *river*, Iceland, **768** Z7
Jolfā, Iran, **758** D5
Joliet, U.S.A., **831** J5
Joliette, Canada, **826** E6
Jolo, Philippines, **740** C5
Jolo Island, Philippines, **740** C5
Jombo, *river*, Angola, **808** C5
Jomppala, Finland, **769** N2
Jonava, Lithuania, **771** M5
Jondal, Norway, **770** C2
Jonê, China, **751** G2
Jones, Cape, Canada, **821** K3
Jones Sound, Canada, **821** L2
Jonesboro, Arkansas, U.S.A., **834** G2
Jonesboro, Louisiana, U.S.A., **834** F3
Jonesville, U.S.A., **835** M2
Joniškis, Lithuania, **771** L4
Jönköping, *county*, Sweden, **770** F4
Jönköping, Sweden, **770** G4
Jonquière, Canada, **826** F5
Joplin, Missouri, U.S.A., **830** F7
Joplin, Montana, U.S.A., **829** J2
Jora, India, **754** D4
Jordan, *country*, Asia, **730** E7
Jordan, *river*, Israel/Jordan, **761** C4
Jordan, U.S.A., **829** L3
Jordan Valley, U.S.A., **828** F5
Jordão, *river*, Brazil, **857** G2
Jordet, Norway, **770** F2
Jorhāt, India, **755** H4
Jormlien, Sweden, **768** G4
Jörn, Sweden, **768** K4
Joroinen, Finland, **771** N1
Jos, Nigeria, **805** F3
José Agustín Palacios, Bolivia, **853** E3
José Bonifácio, Brazil, **853** G3
José de San Martín, Argentina, **858** C2
José Pedro Varela, Uruguay, **857** F4
Joselândia, Brazil, **854** B4
Joseni, Romania, **780** E2
Joseph, Lake, Canada, **826** J3
Joseph, U.S.A., **828** F4
Joseph Bonaparte Gulf, Australia, **720** F1
Josephstaal, Papua New Guinea, **726** B4
Josipdol, Croatia, **778** E3
Jössefors, Sweden, **770** F3
Jostedalsbreen, *glacier*, Norway, **770** C2
Jotunheimen, *mountain range*, Norway, **770** D2
Jouberton, South Africa, **811** E4
Joukokylä, Finland, **769** P4
Joussard, Canada, **823** M4
Joutsa, Finland, **771** N2
Joutseno, Finland, **771** P2
Joutsijärvi, Finland, **769** P3
Jowai, India, **755** H4
Joyce, U.S.A., **828** C2
Joyeuse, France, **775** G4
Jreïda, Mauritania, **800** C5
Ju Xian, China, **742** D1
Juan de Fuca, Strait of, Canada/U.S.A., **828** B2
Juan de Nova, Île, *island*, Réunion, **812** A4
Juan Fernández, Archipiélago, *islands*, Chile, **845** D7
Juanjuí, Peru, **852** C2
Juankoski, Finland, **769** P5
Juárez, Sierra de, *mountain range*, Mexico, **840** A1
Juazeiro, Brazil, **855** F2
Juazeiro do Norte, Brazil, **851** F5
Juazohn, Liberia, **804** C3
Juba, Sudan, **809** F2
Jubayl, Egypt, **761** B5
Jubayl (Biblos), Lebanon, **761** C2
Jubb al Jarrāḥ, Syria, **761** D2
Jubba, *river*, Somalia, **809** H2
Jubbada Dhexe, *administrative region*, Somalia, **809** H2
Jubbada Hoose, *administrative region*, Somalia, **809** H2
Jubbah, Saudi Arabia, **803** H3
Jubilee Lake, Australia, **720** F4
Júcar, *river*, Spain, **777** G3
Juçara, Brazil, **855** F3
Juchitán de Zaragoza, Mexico, **841** G5
Juchitlán, Mexico, **840** D4
Jucurucu, *river*, Brazil, **855** F4
Judenburg, Austria, **773** G5
Judian, China, **751** F4
Juh, China, **746** E5
Juigalpa, Nicaragua, **838** D4
Juillac, France, **774** E4
Juiná, *river*, Brazil, **853** G3
Juist, *island*, Germany, **772** C2
Juiz de Fora, Brazil, **855** E5
Jujuy, *province*, Argentina, **856** C2
Julaca, Bolivia, **853** E5
Julau, Malaysia, **737** E2
Jule, Norway, **768** F4
Juli, Peru, **853** E4
Julia Creek, Australia, **721** J3
Juliaca, Peru, **853** D4
Julianadorp, Curaçao, Netherlands Antilles, **859** C3
Julianadorp, Netherlands, **772** B2
Julianatop, *mountain peak*, Suriname, **850** B2
Jülich, Germany, **772** C3
Julijske Alpe, *mountain range*, Slovenia, **778** D2
Jullouville, France, **774** D2
Jullundur, India, **754** C3
Julwānia, India, **754** C5
Jumbilla, Peru, **852** C1
Jumilla, Spain, **777** G3
Juminen, Finland, **769** N5
Jun Bulen, China, **747** G3
Jūnāgadh, India, **754** B5
Junāgarh, India, **755** E6
Junan, China, **742** D1
Junaynah, Ra's al, *mountain peak*, Egypt, **761** B5
Juncal, Cerro, *mountain peak*, Chile, **856** B4
Junction, Texas, U.S.A., **834** C4
Junction, Utah, U.S.A., **833** G2
Junction City, U.S.A., **828** C4
Jundiaí, Brazil, **857** H2

K

Konos, Papua New Guinea, 726 C3
Konosha, Russian Federation, 783 H2
Konotop, Ukraine, 782 D2
Konqi, *river*, China, 748 F4
Końskie, Poland, 773 K3
Konso, Ethiopia, 809 G1
Konstanz, Germany, 772 D5
Konta, India, 753 E2
Kontagora, Nigeria, 805 F2
Kontiolahti, Finland, 769 P5
Kontiomäki, Finland, 769 P4
Konttajärvi, Finland, 769 M3
KonTum, Vietnam, 739 F3
Konya, Turkey, 760 D5
Koocanusa, Lake, U.S.A., 828 G2
Koor, Indonesia, 735 F3
Kooskia, U.S.A., 828 G3
Kootenay Lake, Canada, 823 L7
Kopaki, New Zealand, 718 E4
Kopaonik, *mountain range*, Yugoslavia, 780 C4
Kopargo, Benin, 804 E3
Kópasker, Iceland, 768 Y6
Kopayhorod, Ukraine, 780 F1
Köpbirlik, Kazakhstan, 759 K3
Köpenick, Germany, 772 F2
Koper, Slovenia, 778 D3
Kopiago, Papua New Guinea, 726 A4
Köping, Sweden, 770 H3
Koplik, Albania, 780 B4
Kopor'ye, Russian Federation, 783 B3
Koppa, India, 752 C3
Koppang, Norway, 770 E2
Kopparberg, Sweden, 770 G3
Kopparnäs, Sweden, 768 K4
Kopperå, Norway, 768 E5
Koprivnica, Croatia, 778 F2
Köprübaşı, Turkey, 781 G6
Kop'yevo, Russian Federation, 759 M2
Korab (Maja e Korbit), *mountain peak*, Albania/ Macedonia, 780 C5
K'orahē, Ethiopia, 807 F3
Koramlik, China, 748 E5
Korangal, India, 752 D2
Korba, India, 755 E5
Korba, Tunisia, 779 C7
Korbach, Germany, 772 D3
Korbenichi, Russian Federation, 783 E2
Korbol, Chad, 806 A3
Korçë, Albania, 781 C5
Korčula, *island*, Croatia, 778 F4
Korčulanski Kanal, *channel*, Croatia, 778 F4
Korea Bay, China/North Korea, 744 C3
Korea Strait, Japan/South Korea, 744 E4
Korem, Ethiopia, 807 E2
Koremoa, New Zealand, 718 D3
Korenica, Croatia, 778 E3
Korgas, China, 748 D3
Korgen, Norway, 768 F3
Korhogo, Côte d'Ivoire, 804 C3
Korido, Indonesia, 735 F3
Korim, Indonesia, 735 G3
Korinthiakos Kolpos, *gulf*, Greece, 781 D6
Korinthos (Corinth), Greece, 781 D7
Kőris-hegy, *mountain peak*, Hungary, 773 H5
Kōriyama, Japan, 745 H3
Korkuteli, Turkey, 760 D5
Korla, China, 748 E4
Kormakitis, Cape, Cyprus, 761 B2
Körmend, Hungary, 773 H5
Kornat, *island*, Croatia, 778 E4
Kórnik, Poland, 773 H2
Kornsjø, Norway, 770 E3
Koro, *island*, Fiji, 727 A4
Koro, Mali, 804 D2
Koro Toro, Chad, 806 A1
Köroğlu Dağları, *mountain range*, Turkey, 760 D4
Korogwe, Tanzania, 809 G4
Koronadal, Philippines, 740 D5
Koroni, Greece, 781 C7
Koronia, Limni, *lake*, Greece, 781 D5
Koror, Palau, 724 B4
Körös, *river*, Hungary, 773 K5
Korosten', Ukraine, 782 C2
Korostyn', Russian Federation, 783 C3
Korovou, Fiji, 727 A4
Korpikå, Sweden, 769 L4
Korpilahti, Finland, 771 M1
Korpilombolo, Sweden, 769 L3
Korsberga, Sweden, 770 G4
Korskrogen, Sweden, 770 G2
Korsnäs, Finland, 771 K1
Korsør, Denmark, 770 E5
Kortesjärvi, Finland, 769 L5
Korti Linchang, China, 748 E2
Kortrijk, Belgium, 772 A3
Koryakskoye Nagor'ye, *mountain range*, Russian Federation, 785 T3
Korycin, Poland, 773 L2
Korzybie, Poland, 773 H1
Kos, Dodekanisos, Greece, 781 F7
Kos, *island*, Dodekanisos, Greece, 781 F7
Kosan, North Korea, 747 J5
Kosaya Gora, Russian Federation, 783 F5
Kościan, Poland, 773 H2
Kościerzyna, Poland, 773 J1
Kosciusko, U.S.A., 835 H3
Kosciuszko, Mount, *mountain peak*, Australia, 716 D5
Kose, Estonia, 771 M3
Kosh-Agach, Russian Federation, 759 M2
Koshikijima-rettō, *islands*, Japan, 744 E5
Košice, Slovakia, 773 K4
Košický, *administrative region*, Slovakia, 773 K4
Kosiv, Ukraine, 780 E1
Kosjerići, Yugoslavia, 780 B4
Koskenkylä, Finland, 771 M2
Koskenpää, Finland, 771 M1
Koski, Finland, 771 L2
Kosŏng, North Korea, 744 E3
Kosŏng, South Korea, 744 E4
Kosovo, *province*, Yugoslavia, 780 C4
Kosovska Mitrovica, Yugoslavia, 780 C4
Kosrae, *island*, Micronesia, 724 E4
Kossou, Lac de, *lake*, Côte d'Ivoire, 804 C3
Kostajnica, Croatia, 778 F3
Kostenets, Bulgaria, 780 D4
Kostinbrod, Bulgaria, 780 D4
Kostolac, Yugoslavia, 780 C3
Kostomuksha, Russian Federation, 769 Q4
Kostonjärvi, *lake*, Finland, 769 P4
Kostroma, Russian Federation, 784 F4
Kostryzń, Poland, 773 G2
Kostyantynivka, Ukraine, 780 H2
Koszalin, Poland, 773 H1
Koszyce, Poland, 773 K3
Kot Diji, Pakistan, 754 B4
Kot Kapūra, India, 754 C3
Kot Pūtli, India, 754 D4
Kota, India, 754 C4
Kota Baharu, Malaysia, 736 C1
Kota Kinabalu, Malaysia, 737 G1
Kota Tinggi, Malaysia, 736 C2
Kotaagung, Indonesia, 736 D4
Kotabaru, Indonesia, 737 G3
Kotabumi, Indonesia, 736 D4
Kotamobagu, Indonesia, 734 D2
Kotanopan, Indonesia, 736 B2
Kotapinang, Indonesia, 736 C2
Kotare, New Zealand, 718 E4
Kotel, Bulgaria, 780 F4
Kotel'nich, Russian Federation, 784 F4
Kotel'nyy, Ostrov, *island*, Russian Federation, 785 Q2
Kothāpet, India, 752 D2
Köthen, Germany, 772 F3
Kotido, Uganda, 809 F2
Kotila, Finland, 769 P4
Kotka, Finland, 771 N2
Kotlas, Russian Federation, 784 F3
Kotli, India, 754 C2
Kotlik, U.S.A., 820 C3
Kotly, Russian Federation, 783 B3
Koton-Karifi, Nigeria, 805 F3
Kotor, Yugoslavia, 780 B4
Kotor Varoš, Bosnia and Herzegovina, 778 F3
Kotouba, Côte d'Ivoire, 804 D3
Kotovs'k, Ukraine, 782 C3
Kotri, Pakistan, 754 B4
Kotri, *river*, India, 750 B5
Kottagūdem, India, 752 E2
Kottapatnam, India, 752 E3
Kottayam, India, 752 D4
Kotto, *river*, Central African Republic, 806 B3
Kotuy, *river*, Russian Federation, 785 M3
Kotzebue, U.S.A., 820 C3
Kotzebue Sound, U.S.A., 820 C3
Kou Senjaq, Iraq, 803 H1
Kouandé, Benin, 805 E2
Kouango, Central African Republic, 808 D1
Koubia, Guinea, 804 B2
Koudougou, Burkina Faso, 804 D2
Koufalia, Greece, 781 D5
Kouilou, *administrative region*, Congo, 808 B3
Kouilou, *river*, Congo, 808 B3
Kouka, Burkina Faso, 804 D2
Koulamoutou, Gabon, 808 B3
Koulikoro, *administrative region*, Mali, 804 C2
Koulikoro, Mali, 804 C2
Koum, Cameroon, 805 G3
Koumac, New Caledonia, 727 A3
Koumbia, Guinea, 804 B2
Koumogo, Chad, 806 A3
Koumra, Chad, 805 H3
Koundâra, Guinea, 804 B2
Koundougou, Burkina Faso, 804 D2
Koungheul, Senegal, 804 B2
Kountze, U.S.A., 834 E4
Koupéla, Burkina Faso, 804 D2
Kourou, French Guiana, 850 C2
Kouroussa, Guinea, 804 C2
Koussanar, Senegal, 804 B2
Kousséri, Cameroon, 805 G2
Koussi, Emi, *mountain peak*, Chad, 802 C5
Koutiala, Mali, 804 C2
Koutsochero, Greece, 781 D6
Kouvola, Finland, 771 N2
Kovačica, Yugoslavia, 780 C3
Kovarzino, Russian Federation, 783 G2
Kovaskiy, Mys, *cape*, Russian Federation, 785 S2
Kovda, Russian Federation, 769 R3
Kovdor, Russian Federation, 769 Q3
Kovdozero, Ozero, *lake*, Russian Federation, 769 Q3
Kovel', Ukraine, 782 B2
Kovel', Ukraine, 773 M3
Kovera, Russian Federation, 783 D2
Kovero, Finland, 771 Q1
Kovzhskoye, Ozero, *lake*, Russian Federation, 783 F2
Kowal, Poland, 773 J2
Kowary, Poland, 773 G3
Kowloon *see* Jiulong, China, 743 C4
Kowon, North Korea, 744 D3
Kowt-e 'Ashrow, Afghanistan, 754 B2
Koxlax, China, 748 D5
Köyceğiz, Turkey, 781 G7
Köyceğiz Gölü, *lake*, Turkey, 781 G7
Koyna Reservoir, India, 752 C2
Koynare, Bulgaria, 780 E4
Koyukuk, *river*, U.S.A., 820 D3
Kozani, Greece, 781 C5
Kozara, *mountain range*, Bosnia and Herzegovina, 778 F3
Kozel'sk, Russian Federation, 783 E5
Kozhikode (Calicut), India, 752 C4
Kozienice, Poland, 773 K3
Kozloduy, Bulgaria, 780 D4
Kozlovo, Russian Federation, 783 G2
Koz'modem'yansk, Russian Federation, 758 D1
Kpalimé, Togo, 804 E3
Kpandae, Ghana, 804 D3
Kpandu, Ghana, 804 E3
Kra, Isthmus of, Malaysia/ Thailand, 738 C4
Kra Buri, Thailand, 738 C4
Krabi, Thailand, 738 C4
Krâchéh, Cambodia, 739 E3
Kräckelbäcken, Sweden, 770 G2
Kragerø, Norway, 770 D3
Kragujevac, Yugoslavia, 780 C3
Krakatau, *mountain peak*, Indonesia, 736 D4
Kraków, Poland, 773 J3
Kralendijk, Bonaire, Netherlands Antilles, 859 A4
Kralendijk, Netherlands Antilles, 837 B3
Kralendijk Punt, *point*, Bonaire, Netherlands Antilles, 859 A4
Kraljevica, Croatia, 778 E3
Kraljevo, Yugoslavia, 780 C4
Kralovice, Czech Republic, 772 F4
Kranidi, Greece, 781 D7
Kranj, Slovenia, 778 E2
Kranji Reservoir, Singapore, 736 J6
Krapina, Croatia, 778 E2
Krapkowice, Poland, 773 H3
Krāslava, Latvia, 771 N5
Krasni Okny, Ukraine, 780 G2
Kraśnik, Poland, 773 L3
Krasnoarmeysk, Kazakhstan, 759 H2
Krasnoarmeysk, Russian Federation, 783 G4
Krasnodar, Russian Federation, 758 B3
Krasnodarskiy Kray, *territory*, Russian Federation, 782 E3
Krasnodarskoye Vodokhranilishche, *reservoir*, Russian Federation, 782 E3
Krasnodarskoye Vodokhranilishche, Russian Federation, 758 B3
Krasnokamensk, Russian Federation, 747 G2
Krasnomayskiy, Russian Federation, 783 E4
Krasnopollye, Belarus, 783 C6
Krasnoshchel'ye, Russian Federation, 769 T3
Krasnoslobodsk, Russian Federation, 758 C2
Krasnoyarsk, Russian Federation, 759 N1
Krasnoyarskiy Kray, *territory*, Russian Federation, 759 N2
Krasnoyarskoye Vodokhranilishche, *lake*, Russian Federation, 759 N2
Krasnoye Selo, Russian Federation, 783 C3
Krasnystaw, Poland, 773 L3
Krasnyy Kholm, Russian Federation, 783 F3
Krasnyy Yar, Russian Federation, 759 J1
Krasukha, Russian Federation, 783 E3
Kratovo, Macedonia, 780 D4
Krau, Indonesia, 735 H3
Kravanh, Chuŏr Phnum, *mountain range*, Cambodia, 739 D3
Kraynovka, Russian Federation, 758 D4
Krechetovo, Russian Federation, 783 G2
Krefeld, Germany, 772 C3
Kremenchuk, Ukraine, 782 D3
Kremintsi, Ukraine, 780 E1
Kreml', Russian Federation, 769 S4
Kremlin, U.S.A., 829 J2
Kremmling, U.S.A., 833 K1
Krems an der Donau, Austria, 773 G4
Kresna, Bulgaria, 781 D5
Kresstsy, Russian Federation, 783 D3
Krestena, Greece, 781 C7
Kresty, Russian Federation, 783 F5
Kretinga, Lithuania, 771 K5
Kribi, Cameroon, 808 A2
Krieglach, Austria, 773 G5
Krikellos, Greece, 781 C6
Kril'on, Mys, *cape*, Russian Federation, 745 H1
Krimml, Austria, 772 E5
Krishna, *river*, India, 752 D2
Krishnadevipeta, India, 753 E2
Krishnagiri, India, 752 D3
Krishnanagar, India, 755 G5
Krishnarāja Sagara, *lake*, India, 752 C3
Kristiansand, Norway, 770 C3
Kristianstad, *county*, Sweden, 770 F4
Kristianstad, Sweden, 770 G5
Kristiansund, Norway, 768 C5
Kristiinankaupunki, Finland, 771 K1
Kristineberg, Sweden, 768 J4
Kristinehamn, Sweden, 770 G3
Kriti, *administrative region*, Greece, 781 E8
Kriti (Crete), *island*, Greece, 781 E8
Kriva Palanka, Macedonia, 780 D4
Krivoles, Russian Federation, 783 D6
Krivosheino, Russian Federation, 759 L1
Krk, Croatia, 778 E3
Krk, *island*, Croatia, 778 E3
Krka, *river*, Croatia, 778 F4
Kroken, Norway, 768 G4
Krokom, Sweden, 768 G5
Krokowa, Poland, 773 J1
Kroksjö, Sweden, 768 H4
Kronach, Germany, 772 E3
Krŏng Kaôh Kŏng, Cambodia, 739 D4
Kronoberg, *county*, Sweden, 770 F4
Kronoby, Finland, 769 L5
Kronotskiy Zaliv, *bay*, Russian Federation, 785 T4
Kronprins Olav Kyst, *region*, Antarctica, 862 F4
Kronprinsesse Martha Kyst, *region*, Antarctica, 862 C4
Kroonstad, South Africa, 811 E4
Kropotkin, Russian Federation, 782 F3
Krosno, Poland, 773 K4
Krosno Odrzańskie, Poland, 773 G2
Krotoszyn, Poland, 773 H3
Krško, Slovenia, 778 E2
Krugersdorp, South Africa, 811 E4
Kruhlaye, Belarus, 783 B5
Krui, Indonesia, 736 C4
Krujë, Albania, 781 B5
Krumbach (Schwaben), Germany, 772 E4
Krumë, Albania, 780 C4
Krumovgrad, Bulgaria, 781 E5
Krung Thep (Bangkok), Thailand, 738 D3

Kyela, Tanzania, **809** F4
Kyenjojo, Uganda, **809** F2
Kyindwe, Myanmar, **741** B3
Kyklades (Cyclades), *islands*, Greece, **781** E7
Kyle of Lochalsh, Scotland, U.K., **792** D3
Kyleakin, Scotland, U.K., **792** D3
Kyll, *river*, Germany, **772** C3
Kyllini Oros, *mountain peak*, Greece, **781** D7
Kylmälä, Finland, **769** N4
Kymi, Greece, **781** E6
Kyŏnggi-man, *bay*, South Korea, **744** D3
Kyŏngju, South Korea, **744** E4
Kyŏngsŏng, North Korea, **744** E2
Kyōto, Japan, **745** F4
Kyparissia, Greece, **781** C7
Kyparissiakos Kolpos, *bay*, Greece, **781** C7
Kyra, Russian Federation, **746** E2
Kyra Panagia, *island*, Greece, **781** E6
Kyren, Russian Federation, **749** J2
Kyrenia Range, *mountain range*, Cyprus, **761** B2
Kyrgyz Ala Too, *mountain range*, Kazakhstan/Kyrgyzstan, **748** B4
Kyrgyzstan, *country*, Asia, **730** J5
Kyritz, Germany, **772** F2
Kyrksæterøra, Norway, **768** D5
Kyrnasivka, Ukraine, **780** G1
Kyrnychky, Ukraine, **780** G3
Kyrönjoki, *river*, Finland, **769** L5
Kyshtovka, Russian Federation, **759** K1
Kythira, Greece, **781** D7
Kythira, *island*, Greece, **781** D7
Kythnos, *island*, Kyklades, Greece, **781** E7
Kythrea, Cyprus, **761** B2
Kyuquot Sound, Canada, **822** F7
Kyushe, Kazakhstan, **758** F3
Kyūshū, *island*, Japan, **744** F4
Kyushu-Palau Ridge, *underwater feature*, Pacific Ocean, **868** D3
Kyustendil, Bulgaria, **780** D4
Kyyiv (Kiev), Ukraine, **782** D2
Kyyivs'ke, Vodoskhovyshche, *reservoir*, Ukraine, **782** C2
Kyyjärvi, Finland, **769** M5
Kyzyl, Russian Federation, **759** N2
Kyzyl-Kiya, Kyrgyzstan, **759** J4
Kzyl-Orda *see* Qyzylorda, Kazakhstan, **758** H4
Kyzyldangi, Gora, *mountain peak*, Tajikistan, **759** J5
Kyzylkum, Peski, *desert*, Kazakhstan/Uzbekistan, **758** G4

L

La Almunia de Doña Godina, Spain, **777** G2
La Asunción, Venezuela, **849** F1
La Banda, Argentina, **856** D3
La Bañeza, Spain, **776** E1
La Barge, U.S.A., **829** J5
La Belle, U.S.A., **835** M6
La Blanquilla, *island*, Venezuela, **849** F1
La Boquilla del Conchos, Mexico, **840** D3
La Brea, Trinidad, Trinidad and Tobago, **859** C4
La Brède, France, **774** D4
La Calera, Chile, **856** B4
La Capelle, France, **775** F2
La Carlota, Argentina, **856** D4
La Carolina, Spain, **777** F3
La Ceiba, Honduras, **838** D4
La Charité-sur-Loire, France, **775** F3
La Châtre, France, **774** E3
La Chorrera, Colombia, **848** D4
La Chorrera, Panama, **839** F5
La Ciudad, Mexico, **840** D4
La Cocha, Argentina, **856** D3
La Concepción, Panama, **839** E5
La Corey, Canada, **823** P4
La Crescent, U.S.A., **830** H4
La Croisière, France, **774** E3
La Crosse, Kansas, U.S.A., **830** D6
La Crosse, Wisconsin, U.S.A., **830** H4
La Cruz, Argentina, **857** F3
La Cruz, Colombia, **848** C4
La Cruz, Mexico, **840** D4
La Cumbre, Volcán, *mountain peak*, Islas Galápagos (Galapagos Islands), Ecuador, **859** A2
La Dorada, Colombia, **848** C3
La Escala, Spain, **777** J1
La Esmeralda, Paraguay, **856** D2
La Esmeralda, Venezuela, **849** F3
La Esperanza, Argentina, **858** D1
La Esperanza, Bolivia, **853** F4
La Esperanza, Honduras, **838** C4
La Estrella, Argentina, **856** D2
La Estrella, Bolivia, **853** F4
La Falda, Argentina, **856** D4
La Fayette, U.S.A., **835** K2
La Fé, Isla de la Juventud, Cuba, **839** E2
La Fé, W. Cuba, **838** D2
La Flèche, France, **774** D3
La Foa, New Caledonia, **727** A3
La Forestière, French Guiana, **850** B2
La Fría, Venezuela, **848** D2
La Galite, *island*, Tunisia, **779** B7
La Giandola, France, **775** H5
La Gloria, Colombia, **848** D2
La Goulette, Tunisia, **779** C7
La Grande, U.S.A., **828** E4
La Grande Deux, Réservoir de, Canada, **826** C3
La Grande Rivière, *river*, Canada, **825** Q5
La Grande Trois, Réservoir de, Canada, **826** D3
La Grange, Georgia, U.S.A., **835** K3
La Grange, Texas, U.S.A., **834** D5
La Grange, Wyoming, U.S.A., **829** M6
La Grave, France, **775** H4
La Guardia, Chile, **856** C3
La Guerche-de-Bretagne, France, **774** D3
La Habana (Havana), Cuba, **839** E2
La Horqueta, Venezuela, **849** G2
La Huaca, Peru, **852** B1
La Jagua de Ibirico, Colombia, **848** D2
La Jara, U.S.A., **833** L3
La Joya, Mexico, **840** D3
La Joya, Peru, **852** D4
La Junta, U.S.A., **833** M3
La Laguna, Argentina, **856** D4
La Laguna, Islas Canarias, Spain, **813** A4
La Laja, Chile, **856** B5
La Libertad, Guatemala, **838** C3
La Ligua, Chile, **856** B4
La Linea de la Concepción, Spain, **776** E4
La Loberia, Argentina, **858** E1
La Loche, Canada, **823** Q3
La Loma, San Andrés, Colombia, **859** B1
La Maddalena, Sardegna, Italy, **779** B5
La Malbaie, Canada, **826** F6
La Martre, Canada, **821** N5
La Mejorada, Peru, **852** C3
La Merced, Peru, **852** C3
La Moure, U.S.A., **830** D2
La Mula, Mexico, **840** D2
La Mure, France, **775** G4
La Nava de Ricomalillo, Spain, **776** E3
La Negra, Chile, **856** B2
La Noria, Mexico, **840** D4
La Oliva, Islas Canarias, Spain, **813** B4
La Orchila, *island*, Venezuela, **849** E1
La Oroya, Peru, **852** C3
La Paca, Spain, **777** G4
La Palma, *island*, Islas Canarias, Spain, **813** A4
La Palma, Panama, **839** F5
La Paloma, Uruguay, **857** F5
La Pampa, *province*, Argentina, **856** D5
La Paragua, Venezuela, **849** F2
La Paz, Bahía de, *bay*, Mexico, **840** C3
La Paz, Bolivia, **853** E4
La Paz, *department*, Bolivia, **853** E4
La Paz, Entre Rios, Argentina, **857** E4
La Paz, Mendoza, Argentina, **856** C4
La Paz, Mexico, **840** C3
La Paz, Providencia, Colombia, **859** C1
La Pedrera, Colombia, **849** E4
La Perla, Mexico, **840** D2
La Perouse Strait, Japan/Russian Federation, **745** H1
La Pesca, Mexico, **841** F4
La Piedad Cavadas, Mexico, **840** E4
La Pine, U.S.A., **828** D5
La Plaine, Dominica, **837** D3
La Plaine des Cafres, Réunion, **813** A1
La Plata, Argentina, **857** F5
La Plata, Colombia, **848** C3
La Pobla de Segur, Spain, **777** H1
La Possession, Réunion, **813** A1
La Potherie, Lac, *lake*, Canada, **825** T2
La Pryor, U.S.A., **834** C5
La Push, U.S.A., **828** B3
La Quiaca, Argentina, **856** D2
La Rioja, Argentina, **856** C3
La Rioja, *autonomous community*, Spain, **777** F1
La Rioja, *province*, Argentina, **856** C3
La Rivière, Canada, **824** E7
La Roca de la Sierra, Spain, **776** D3
La Roche, New Caledonia, **727** A3
La Roche-Chalais, France, **774** D4
La Roche-sur-Yon, France, **774** D3
La Rochelle, France, **774** D3
La Roda, Spain, **777** F3
La Romana, Dominican Republic, **839** H3
La Ronge, Canada, **823** S4
La Rosita, Mexico, **840** E2
La Sábana, Argentina, **857** E3
La Salle, Canada, **824** F7
La Salle, U.S.A., **831** J5
La Sarre, Canada, **826** B5
La Scie, Canada, **827** P5
La Serena, Chile, **856** B3
La Seu d'Urgell, Spain, **777** H1
La Solana, Spain, **777** F3
La Spezia, Italy, **778** B3
La Tagua, Colombia, **848** C4
La Teste, France, **774** D4
La Toma, Argentina, **856** D4
La Tortuga, *island*, Venezuela, **849** F1
La Troya, *river*, Argentina, **856** C3
La Tuque, Canada, **826** E6
La Unión, Bolivia, **853** G4
La Unión, Chile, **858** C1
La Unión, Colombia, **848** C4
La Unión, Mexico, **840** E5
La Unión, Peru, **852** C2
La Urbana, Venezuela, **849** E2
La Vega, Haiti, **839** H3
La Ventana, Mexico, **841** E4
La Vibora, Mexico, **840** E3
La Victoria, Venezuela, **849** E1
La Yarada, Peru, **852** D5
Laage, Germany, **772** F2
Laascaanood, Somalia, **807** G3
Laâyoune *see* El Aaiún, Western Sahara, **800** D3
Labasa, Fiji, **727** A4
Labé, Guinea, **804** B2
Labe (Elbe), *river*, Czech Republic, **773** G3
Labelle, Canada, **826** D6
Labin, Croatia, **778** E3
Labinsk, Russian Federation, **758** C4
Labis, Malaysia, **736** C2
Labo, Mount, *mountain peak*, Philippines, **740** C3
Labo, Philippines, **740** C3
Laboulaye, Argentina, **856** D5
Labrador, *region*, Canada, **821** N4
Labrador City, Canada, **826** H3
Labrador Sea, Canada/Greenland, **821** P4
Lábrea, Brazil, **853** F2
Labrit, France, **774** D4
Labu, Indonesia, **736** D3
Labuan, *federal territory*, Malaysia, **737** F1
Labudalin, China, **747** H2
Labuha, Indonesia, **734** D3
Labuhanbajo, Indonesia, **734** B5
Labuhanbilik, Indonesia, **736** C2
Labuhanhaji, Indonesia, **736** B2
Labuhanmeringgai, Indonesia, **736** D4
Labuk, Teluk, *bay*, Malaysia, **737** G1
Labyrinth Lake, Canada, **824** A1
Labytnangi, Russian Federation, **784** H3
Laç, Albania, **781** B5
Lac, *prefecture*, Chad, **805** G2
Lac du Bonnet, Canada, **824** F6
Lac-Édouard, Canada, **826** E6
Lac-Gatineau, Canada, **826** D6
Lac La Biche, Canada, **823** P4
Lac la Hache, Canada, **822** J6
Lac-Saguay, Canada, **826** D6
Lacanau, Étang de, *lake*, France, **774** D4
Lacanau, France, **774** D4
Lacaune, France, **774** F5
Laccadive Islands *see* Lakshadweep Islands, India, Indian Ocean, **752** B4
Lacha, Ozero, *lake*, Russian Federation, **783** G2
Lachlan, *river*, Australia, **721** K5
Lachung, India, **755** G4
Läckö, Sweden, **770** F3
Laclede, U.S.A., **828** F2
Lacombe, Canada, **823** N5
Laconi, Sardegna, Italy, **779** B6
Laconia, U.S.A., **836** E3
Lacre Punt, *point*, Bonaire, Netherlands Antilles, **859** A4
Lada, *river*, Russian Federation, **783** D3
Ladākh Range, *mountain range*, India, **754** D2
Ladismith, South Africa, **810** D5
Ladispoli, Italy, **779** D5
Lādnūn, India, **754** C4
Ladozhskoye Ozero, *lake*, Russian Federation, **783** C2
Ladrillero, Golfo, *gulf*, Chile, **858** B3
Ladron Peak, *mountain peak*, U.S.A., **833** K4
Ladushkin, Russian Federation, **771** K5
Ladva, Russian Federation, **783** E2
Ladvozero, Russian Federation, **769** P4
Lady Barron, Australia, **721** K7
Ladybank, Scotland, U.K., **792** F4
Ladysmith, Canada, **822** H7
Ladysmith, South Africa, **811** E4
Ladysmith, U.S.A., **830** H3
Ladyzhyn, Ukraine, **780** G1
Ladyzhynka, Ukraine, **780** H1
Lae, Papua New Guinea, **726** B4
Lærdalsøyri, Norway, **770** C2
Læsø, *island*, Denmark, **770** E4
Lævvajok, Norway, **769** N2
Lafayette, Indiana, U.S.A., **831** K5
Lafayette, Louisiana, U.S.A., **834** G4
Lafia, Nigeria, **805** F3
Lafiagi, Nigeria, **805** F3
Lagamar, Brazil, **854** D5
Lagan', Russian Federation, **758** D3
Lagan, Sweden, **770** F4
Lagarto, Brazil, **855** G3
Lagbar, Senegal, **804** B1
Lågen, *river*, Norway, **770** D2
Lagg, Scotland, U.K., **792** D5
Laggan, Loch, *lake*, Scotland, U.K., **792** E4
Laggan, Scotland, U.K., **792** E3
Laghouat, Algeria, **801** G2
Lagkadas, Greece, **781** D5
Lago Agrio, Ecuador, **848** C4
Lago Ranco, Chile, **858** C1
Lagoa Santa, Brazil, **855** E5
Lagoa Vermelha, Brazil, **857** G3
Lagonegro, Italy, **779** E5
Lagong, Pulau, *island*, Indonesia, **737** E2
Lagonoy, Philippines, **740** C3
Lagonoy Gulf, Philippines, **740** C3
Lagos, Nigeria, **805** E3
Lagos, Portugal, **776** C4
Lagos, *state*, Nigeria, **805** E3
Lagos de Moreno, Mexico, **840** E4
Lagosa, Tanzania, **809** E4
Lagrange, Australia, **720** E2
Lagrasse, France, **774** F5
Lagrave, Mont, *mountain peak*, Mauritius, **813** C1
Lagrave, Pointe, *point*, Mauritius, **813** C1
Laguiole, France, **774** F4
Laguna, Brazil, **857** H3
Laguna, Ilha da, *island*, Brazil, **850** C3
Laguna, U.S.A., **833** K4
Laguna de Perlas, Nicaragua, **838** E4
Laguna Grande, Argentina, **858** C3
Laguna Madre, *bay*, U.S.A., **834** D6
Lagunas, Chile, **853** E5
Lagunas, Peru, **848** C5
Lagunillas, Bolivia, **853** F5
Lagunillas, Venezuela, **848** D1
Laha, China, **747** J2
Lahad Datu, Malaysia, **737** G1
Lahaina, Hawaiian Islands, U.S.A., **832** R9
Lahat, Indonesia, **736** C3
Lahe, Myanmar, **741** B2
Lahewa, Indonesia, **736** B2
Laḥij, Yemen, **756** D6
Lahn, *river*, Germany, **772** D3
Laholm, Sweden, **770** F4
Laholmsbukten, *bay*, Sweden, **770** F4
Lahore, Pakistan, **754** C3
Lahr, Germany, **772** C4
Lahri, Pakistan, **754** B3
Lāhrūd, Iran, **758** D5
Lahti, Finland, **771** M2
Laï, Chad, **805** H3
Lai Châu, Vietnam, **739** D1
Lai-hka, Myanmar, **741** C3
Laiagam, Papua New Guinea, **726** A4
Lai'an, China, **742** D1
Laifeng, China, **742** B2
L'Aigle, France, **774** E2

Lincolnshire, *unitary authority*, England, U.K., **791** H4
Lincolnshire Wolds, *region*, England, U.K., **791** H4
Lind, U.S.A., **828** E3
Linden, Guyana, **849** G2
Linden, U.S.A., **835** J3
Lindesberg, Sweden, **770** G3
Lindi, *administrative region*, Tanzania, **809** G4
Lindi, Tanzania, **809** G4
Lindian, China, **747** J3
Lindisfarne, England, U.K., **791** G2
Lindos, Dodekanisos, Greece, **781** G7
Lindozero, Russian Federation, **769** R5
Lindsay, Canada, **826** B7
Lindsay, Montana, U.S.A., **829** M3
Lindsay, Oklahoma, U.S.A., **834** D2
Lindsborg, U.S.A., **830** E6
Line Islands, Kiribati, **725** J4
Linfen, China, **746** E5
Linganamakki Reservoir, India, **752** C3
Lingayen, Philippines, **740** C3
Lingayen Gulf, Philippines, **740** C2
Lingbao, China, **742** B1
Lingbi, China, **742** D1
Lingen, Germany, **772** C2
Lingfield, England, U.K., **789** G3
Lingga, Kepulauan, *islands*, Indonesia, **736** D3
Lingga, Pulau, *island*, Indonesia, **736** D3
Lingkabau, Malaysia, **737** G1
Lingle, U.S.A., **829** M5
Lingomo, Democratic Republic of the Congo, **808** D2
Lingqiu, China, **746** F5
Lingshan, China, **742** B4
Lingshi, China, **746** E5
Lingshui, China, **739** F2
Lingtai, China, **751** H2
Linguère, Senegal, **804** A1
Lingwu, China, **746** D5
Lingyuan, China, **747** G4
Linhai, Heilongjiang, China, **747** J2
Linhai, Zhejiang, China, **742** E2
Linhares, Brazil, **855** F5
Linhe, China, **746** D4
Linjiang, Gonsu, China, **751** H2
Linjiang, Jilin, China, **747** J4
Linköping, Sweden, **770** G3
Linkou, China, **747** K3
Linkuva, Lithuania, **771** L4
Linnhe, Loch, *inlet*, Scotland, U.K., **792** D4
Linosa, Isola di, *island*, Isole Pelagie, Italy, **779** D8
Linova, Belarus, **773** M2
Linping, China, **742** E2
Linqing, China, **746** F5
Linqu, China, **744** B3
Linquan, China, **742** C1
Lins, Brazil, **854** D5
Linsell, Sweden, **770** F1
Linshu, China, **742** D1
Linshui, China, **751** H3
Linta, *river*, Madagascar, **812** A5
Lintan, China, **751** G2
Lintao, China, **751** G2
Linton, Indiana, U.S.A., **831** K6
Linton, North Dakota, U.S.A., **830** C2
Lintong, China, **742** B1
Linxi, Hebei, China, **747** G5
Linxi, Nei Mongol Zizhiqu, China, **747** G4
Linxia, China, **751** G2
Linyanti, *river*, Botswana/Namibia, **810** D2
Linyi, Shanxi, China, **742** B1
Linyi, S. Shandong, China, **742** D1
Linyi, N. Shandong, China, **746** G5
Linyou, China, **751** H2
Linz, Austria, **773** G4
Linze, China, **749** J5
Lioboml', Ukraine, **773** M3
Lion, Golfe du, *gulf*, France, **775** F5
Lioua, Chad, **805** G2
Liouesso, Congo, **808** C2
Lipa, Philippines, **740** C3
Lipany, Slovakia, **773** K4
Lipari, Isola, *island*, Italy, **779** E6
Lipari, Italy, **779** E6
Lipcani, Moldova, **780** F1
Liperi, Finland, **769** P5
Lipetsk, Russian Federation, **782** E2
Lipetskaya Oblast', *province*, Russian Federation, **783** G6
Liphook, England, U.K., **789** G3
Lipiany, Poland, **773** G2
Lipin Bor, Russian Federation, **783** F2
Liping, China, **742** B3
Lipki, Russian Federation, **783** F6
Lipljan, Yugoslavia, **780** C4
Lipnica, Poland, **773** J2
Lipno, Poland, **773** J2
Lipobane, Ponta, *point*, Mozambique, **809** G6
Lipova, Romania, **780** C2
Lippe, *river*, Germany, **772** C3
Lipsk, Poland, **773** L2
Liptougou, Burkina Faso, **804** E2
Liptovský Mikuláš, Slovakia, **773** J4
Lipu, China, **742** B3
Lira, Uganda, **809** F2
Liranga, Congo, **808** C3
Lircay, Peru, **852** C3
Liria, Sudan, **809** F2
Lisala, Democratic Republic of the Congo, **808** D2
Lisbellaw, Northern Ireland, U.K., **793** E3
Lisboa, *district*, Portugal, **776** C3
Lisboa (Lisbon), Portugal, **776** C3
Lisbon *see* Lisboa, Portugal, **776** C3
Lisbon, U.S.A., **831** N5
Lisburn, *district*, Northern Ireland, U.K., **793** G3
Lisburn, Northern Ireland, U.K., **793** F3
Lisburne, Cape, U.S.A., **820** C3
Liscannor Bay, Ireland, **793** C5
Lisco, U.S.A., **830** B5
Lisdoonvarna, Ireland, **793** C4
Lishi, China, **746** E5
Lishu, China, **747** J4
Lishui, China, **742** D2
Lisianski, *island*, Hawaiian Islands, U.S.A., **725** G2
Lisieux, France, **774** E2
Liskeard, England, U.K., **788** C4
Liski, Russian Federation, **782** E2
Lismore, Australia, **721** L4
Lismore, Ireland, **793** E5
Lisnaskea, Northern Ireland, U.K., **793** E3
Liss, England, U.K., **789** G3
Lister, Mount, *mountain peak*, Antarctica, **862** D7
Listowel, Ireland, **793** C5
Lit, Sweden, **768** G5
Litang, Guangxi Zhuangzu Zizhiqu, China, **742** B4
Litang, Sichuan, China, **751** G3
Līṭānī, *river*, Lebanon, **761** C3
Litani, *river*, Suriname, **850** B2
Litchfield, Illinois, U.S.A., **831** J6
Litchfield, Nebraska, U.S.A., **830** D5
Lithakia, Ionioi Nisoi, Greece, **781** C7
Lithgow, Australia, **721** L5
Lithino, Akra, *point*, Kriti, Greece, **781** E8
Lithuania, *country*, Europe, **764** G4
Litovko, Russian Federation, **747** L2
Little Aden, Yemen, **756** D6
Little Andaman, *island*, Andaman and Nicobar Islands, India, **753** H4
Little Cayman, *island*, Cayman Islands, **839** E3
Little Coco Island, Myanmar, **753** H3
Little Colorado, *river*, U.S.A., **833** H4
Little Current, Canada, **831** N3
Little Falls, Minnesota, U.S.A., **830** F3
Little Falls, New York, U.S.A., **836** C3
Little Fort, Canada, **822** J6
Little Grand Rapids, Canada, **824** G5
Little Inagua Island, Bahamas, **839** G2
Little Kanawha, *river*, U.S.A., **831** N6
Little Lake, U.S.A., **832** E4
Little Mecatina, *river*, Canada, **827** L3
Little Minch, The, *strait*, Scotland, U.K., **792** B3
Little Missouri, *river*, U.S.A., **830** B2
Little Nicobar, *island*, Andaman and Nicobar Islands, India, **753** H5
Little Oakley, England, U.K., **789** J3
Little Ouse, *river*, England, U.K., **789** H2
Little Quill Lake, Canada, **824** B6
Little Rock, U.S.A., **834** F2
Little Sachigo Lake, Canada, **824** H4
Little Sioux, *river*, U.S.A., **830** E4
Little Smoky, Canada, **823** L4
Little Smoky, *river*, Canada, **823** K4
Little Tobago, *island*, Tobago, Trinidad and Tobago, **859** B4
Little Wabash, *river*, U.S.A., **831** J6
Littleborough, England, U.K., **790** F4
Littlefield, Arizona, U.S.A., **832** G3
Littlefield, Texas, U.S.A., **833** M5
Littlehampton, England, U.K., **789** G4
Littlemore, England, U.K., **789** F3
Littleport, England, U.K., **789** H2
Littoral, *province*, Cameroon, **808** A2
Litunde, Mozambique, **809** G5
Liu, *river*, China, **750** E3
Liuba, Gansu, China, **749** J5
Liuba, Shaanxi, China, **751** H2
Liucheng, China, **742** B3
Liuhe, China, **747** J4
Liuhu, China, **747** H3
Liujiang, China, **742** B3
Liulin, China, **746** E5
Liupanshui, China, **751** H4
Liushuquan, China, **749** G4
Liuxi, *river*, China, **743** A2
Liuxihe Reservoir, China, **743** B1
Liuyang, China, **742** C2
Liuyuan, China, **749** G4
Liuzhou, China, **742** B3
Livada, Romania, **780** D2
Livadiya, Russian Federation, **747** L4
Livāni, Latvia, **771** N4
Livanovka, Kazakhstan, **758** G2
Live Oak, U.S.A., **835** L4
Lively Island, Falkland Islands, **858** F4
Livermore, Mount, *mountain peak*, U.S.A., **833** L6
Liverpool, Canada, **827** J7
Liverpool, England, U.K., **790** F4
Liverpool Bay, England, U.K., **790** E4
Livingston, Guatemala, **838** C4
Livingston, Lake, U.S.A., **834** E4
Livingston, Montana, U.S.A., **829** J4
Livingston, Texas, U.S.A., **834** E4
Livingstone, Zambia, **811** E2
Livingstonia, Malawi, **809** F5
Livno, Bosnia and Herzegovina, **778** F4
Livo, Finland, **769** N4
Livonia, U.S.A., **831** M4
Livorno, Italy, **778** C4
Livramento do Brumado, Brazil, **855** F3
Liwale, Tanzania, **809** G4
Lixi, China, **751** G4
Lixouri, Ionioi Nisoi, Greece, **781** C6
Liyang, China, **742** D2
Lizard, England, U.K., **788** B5
Lizard Point, England, U.K., **788** B5
Lizotte, Canada, **826** E5
Iizuka, Japan, **744** E4
Ljig, Yugoslavia, **780** C3
Ljubljana, Slovenia, **778** E2
Ljubovija, Yugoslavia, **780** B3
Ljugarn, Sweden, **771** J4
Ljungan, *river*, Sweden, **771** H1
Ljungby, Sweden, **770** F4
Ljungdalen, Sweden, **768** F5
Ljusdal, Sweden, **770** H2
Ljusnan, *river*, Sweden, **770** G2
Ljustorp, Sweden, **771** H1
Llagostera, Spain, **777** J2
Llaima, Volcán, *mountain peak*, Chile, **856** B6
Llanaelhaearn, Wales, U.K., **788** C2
Llanarth, Wales, U.K., **788** C2
Llanarthney, Wales, U.K., **788** C3
Llanbadarn-fawr, Wales, U.K., **788** C2
Llanbedrog, Wales, U.K., **788** C2
Llanberis, Wales, U.K., **788** C1
Llanbister, Wales, U.K., **788** D2
Llandeilo, Wales, U.K., **788** D3
Llandissilio, Wales, U.K., **788** C3
Llandovery, Wales, U.K., **788** D3
Llandrillo, Wales, U.K., **788** D2
Llandrindod Wells, Wales, U.K., **788** D2
Llandudno, Wales, U.K., **790** E4
Llandwrog, Wales, U.K., **788** C1
Llandysul, Wales, U.K., **788** C2
Llanelli, Wales, U.K., **788** C3
Llanelltyd, Wales, U.K., **788** D2
Llanerchymedd, Wales, U.K., **790** D4
Llanfair Caereinion, Wales, U.K., **788** D2
Llanfair Talhaiarn, Wales, U.K., **788** D1
Llanfair-yn-Neubwll, Wales, U.K., **790** D4
Llanfairfechan, Wales, U.K., **788** D1
Llanfairpwllgwyngyll, Wales, U.K., **788** C1
Llanfihangel-ar-Arth, Wales, U.K., **788** C2
Llanfyllin, Wales, U.K., **788** D2
Llangadfan, Wales, U.K., **788** D2
Llangadog, Wales, U.K., **788** D3
Llangeler, Wales, U.K., **788** C2
Llangelynin, Wales, U.K., **788** C2
Llangfre Head, *point*, Wales, U.K., **790** D4
Llangoed, Wales, U.K., **790** D4
Llangollen, Wales, U.K., **788** D2
Llangurig, Wales, U.K., **788** D2
Llanidloes, Wales, U.K., **788** D2
Llanleigh Head, *point*, Wales, U.K., **788** C2
Llanllyfni, Wales, U.K., **788** C1
Llannor, Wales, U.K., **788** C2
Llano, U.S.A., **834** C4
Llanos, *region*, Colombia/Venezuela, **846** E3
Llanquihué, Lago, *lake*, Chile, **858** C1
Llanrhystyd, Wales, U.K., **788** C2
Llanrwst, Wales, U.K., **788** D1
Llansannan, Wales, U.K., **788** D1
Llansawel, Wales, U.K., **788** C2
Llantrisant, Wales, U.K., **788** D3
Llantwit Major, Wales, U.K., **788** D3
Llanuwchllyn, Wales, U.K., **788** D2
Llanwenog, Wales, U.K., **788** C2
Llanwnda, Wales, U.K., **788** C1
Llanwnog, Wales, U.K., **788** D2
Llanwrtyd Wells, Wales, U.K., **788** D2
Llata, Peru, **852** C2
Lleida, Spain, **777** H2
Llera de Canales, Mexico, **841** F4
Llerena, Spain, **776** D3
Lleyn Peninsula, Wales, U.K., **788** C2
Llica, Bolivia, **853** E5
Llíria, Spain, **777** G3
Llorente, Philippines, **740** D4
Lloydminster, Canada, **823** Q5
Llullaillaco, Volcán, *mountain peak*, Argentina/Chile, **856** C2
Llyn Alaw, *lake*, Wales, U.K., **790** D4
Lo Wu, China, **743** C3
Loa, *river*, Chile, **856** C2
Loa, U.S.A., **833** H2
Loa Mauna, *mountain peak*, Hawaiian Islands, U.S.A., **832** R10
Loano, Italy, **778** B3
Lobatse, Botswana, **811** E4
Löbau, Germany, **773** G3
Lobaye, *prefecture*, Central African Republic, **808** C2
Loberia, Argentina, **857** E6
Łobez, Poland, **773** G2
Lobito, Angola, **808** B5
Lobitos, Peru, **852** B1
Lobo, Philippines, **740** C3
Lobo, U.S.A., **833** L6
Lobos, Argentina, **857** E5
Lobos, *island*, Islas Canarias, Spain, **813** B4
Lobos, Punta de, *point*, Chile, **856** B5
Lobskoye, Russian Federation, **769** S5
Locarno, Switzerland, **775** J3
Locate, U.S.A., **829** M3
Lochaline, Scotland, U.K., **792** D4
Lochboisdale, Scotland, U.K., **792** B3
Lochcarron, Scotland, U.K., **792** D3
Lochearnhead, Scotland, U.K., **792** E4
Loches, France, **774** E3
Lochgelly, Scotland, U.K., **792** F4
Lochgilphead, Scotland, U.K., **792** D4
Lochgoilhead, Scotland, U.K., **792** E4
Lochinver, Scotland, U.K., **792** D2
Lochmaben, Scotland, U.K., **792** F5
Lochmaddy, Scotland, U.K., **792** B3
Lochnagar, *mountain peak*, Scotland, U.K., **792** F4
Łochów, Poland, **773** K2
Lochranza, Scotland, U.K., **792** D5
Lochy, Loch, *lake*, Scotland, U.K., **792** E3
Lock Haven, U.S.A., **836** B4
Lockeford, U.S.A., **832** C2
Lockeport, Canada, **826** J8
Lockerbie, Scotland, U.K., **792** F5

Lovelock, U.S.A., **832** D1
Lovere, Italy, **778** C3
Loviisa, Finland, **771** N2
Lovington, U.S.A., **833** M5
Lövnäs, Kopperberg, Sweden, **770** F2
Lövnäs, Norbotten, Sweden, **768** H3
Lovozero, Ozero, *lake*, Russian Federation, **769** S3
Lovozero, Russian Federation, **769** S2
Lovrin, Romania, **780** C3
Lövstabruk, Sweden, **771** H2
Lóvua, Lunda Norte, Angola, **808** D4
Lóvua, Moxico, Angola, **808** D5
Low, Canada, **826** D7
Low, Cape, Canada, **821** L3
Lowa, Democratic Republic of the Congo, **809** E3
Lowa, *river*, Democratic Republic of the Congo, **809** E3
Lowell, U.S.A., **828** G3
Löwenberg, Germany, **772** F2
Lower Arrow Lake, Canada, **823** K7
Lower Hutt, New Zealand, **719** E5
Lower Lake, U.S.A., **832** B2
Lower Lough Erne, *lake*, Northern Ireland, U.K., **793** E3
Lower Peirce Reservoir, Singapore, **736** K6
Lower Red Lake, U.S.A., **830** F2
Lowestoft, England, U.K., **789** J2
Łowicz, Poland, **773** J2
Lowman, U.S.A., **828** G4
Lowrah, *river*, Afghanistan, **754** A3
Lowther, Canada, **825** N7
Lowville, U.S.A., **836** C3
Loxton, South Africa, **810** D5
Loxur, China, **751** G2
Loyal, Ben, *mountain peak*, Scotland, U.K., **792** E2
Loyal Valley, U.S.A., **834** C4
Loyalty Islands *see* Loyauté, Îles, *islands*, New Caledonia, **727** A3
Loyauté, Îles (Loyalty Islands), New Caledonia, **727** A3
Loymola, Russian Federation, **783** C2
Loyne, Loch, Scotland, U.K., **792** D3
Lozère, Mont, *mountain peak*, France, **775** F4
Loznica, Yugoslavia, **780** B3
Loznitsa, Bulgaria, **780** F4
Lozoyuela, Spain, **777** F2
Lučenec, Slovakia, **773** J4
Lua Nova, Brazil, **850** B4
Luacano, Angola, **808** D5
Lualuba, *river*, Democratic Republic of the Congo, **809** E2
Luama, *river*, Democratic Republic of the Congo, **809** E3
Luampa, *river*, Zambia, **808** D5
Luan Xian, China, **747** G5
Lu'an, China, **742** D2
Luan, China, **746** G4
Luanchuan, China, **742** B1
Luanda, Angola, **808** B4
Luanda, *province*, Angola, **808** B4
Luando, Angola, **808** C5
Luando, *river*, Angola, **808** C5
Luanguinga, *river*, Angola, **808** D5
Luangwa, *river*, Zambia, **809** F5
Luangwa, Zambia, **811** F2
Luanjing, China, **746** D5
Luanshya, Zambia, **809** E5
Luanza, Democratic Republic of the Congo, **809** E4
Luapula, *province*, Zambia, **809** E5
Luar, Danau, *lake*, Indonesia, **737** F2
Luar *see* Horsburgh Island, Cocos (Keeling) Islands, **720** Q10
Luarca, Spain, **776** D1
Luashi, Democratic Republic of the Congo, **808** D5
Luau, Angola, **808** D5
Lubāna, Latvia, **771** N4
Lubāns, *lake*, Latvia, **771** N4
Luba, Equatorial Guinea, **808** A2
Lubaczów, Poland, **773** L3
Lubalo, Angola, **808** C4
Lubango, Angola, **808** B5
Lubang Islands, Philippines, **740** B3
Lubao, Democratic Republic of the Congo, **809** E4
Lubartów, Poland, **773** L3
Lubawa, Poland, **773** J2
Lübben, Germany, **773** F3
Lubbock, U.S.A., **834** B3
Lübeck, Germany, **772** E2
Lübecker Bucht, *bay*, Germany, **772** E1
Lubefu, Democratic Republic of the Congo, **808** D3
Lubefu, *river*, Democratic Republic of the Congo, **808** D3
Lubero, Democratic Republic of the Congo, **809** E3
Lubin, Poland, **773** H3
Lublin, Poland, **773** L3
Lubliniec, Poland, **773** J3
Lubnān, Jabal, *mountain range*, Lebanon, **761** C3
Lubny, Ukraine, **782** D3
Lubsko, Poland, **773** G3
Lubuagan, Philippines, **740** C2
Lubudi, Democratic Republic of the Congo, **809** E4
Lubumbashi, Democratic Republic of the Congo, **809** E5
Lubungu, Zambia, **809** E5
Lubutu, Democratic Republic of the Congo, **809** E3
Łuby, Poland, **773** J2
Lucala, Angola, **808** C4
Lucan, Ireland, **793** F4
Lücaoshan, China, **749** G5
Lucapa, Angola, **808** D4
Lucca, Italy, **778** C4
Lucélia, Brazil, **854** C5
Lucena, Philippines, **740** C3
Lucena, Spain, **776** E4
Lucera, Italy, **779** E5
Lucerna, Peru, **853** E3
Luchang, China, **751** G4
Lüchow, Germany, **772** E2
Luchuan, China, **742** B4
Lucie, *river*, Suriname, **850** B2
Lucile, U.S.A., **828** F4
Lucira, Angola, **808** B5
Luckau, Germany, **772** F3
Luckeesarai, India, **755** F4
Luckenwalde, Germany, **772** F2
Lucknow, India, **754** E4
Luçon, France, **774** D3
Lucrecia, Cabo, *cape*, Cuba, **839** G2
Lucusse, Angola, **808** D5
Luda Kamchiya, *river*, Bulgaria, **780** F4
Ludden, U.S.A., **830** D2
Lüderitz, Namibia, **810** C4
Lüderitz Bay, Namibia, **810** B4
Ludhiāna, India, **754** C3
Ludian, China, **751** G4
Ludington, U.S.A., **831** K4
Ludlow, California, U.S.A., **832** E4
Ludlow, Colorado, U.S.A., **833** L3
Ludlow, England, U.K., **788** E2
Ludlow, Vermont, U.S.A., **836** D3
Ludowici, U.S.A., **835** M4
Luduș, Romania, **780** E2
Ludvika, Sweden, **770** G2
Ludwigsburg, Germany, **772** D4
Ludwigshafen am Rhein, Germany, **772** D4
Ludwigslust, Germany, **772** E2
Ludza, Latvia, **771** N4
Luebo, Democratic Republic of the Congo, **808** D4
Lueki, Democratic Republic of the Congo, **809** E3
Luena, Angola, **808** C5
Luepa, Venezuela, **849** G3
Lüeyang, China, **751** H2
Lufeng, China, **742** C4
Lufkin, U.S.A., **834** E4
Luga, *river*, Russian Federation, **783** B3
Luga, Russian Federation, **783** B3
Lugait, Philippines, **740** D4
Lugano, Switzerland, **775** J3
Luganville, Vanuatu, **727** A2
Lugela, Mozambique, **809** G6
Lughaye, Somalia, **807** F2
Lugnaquillia, *mountain peak*, Ireland, **793** F5
Lugo, Italy, **778** C3
Lugo, Spain, **776** D1
Lugoj, Romania, **780** C3
Lügovoy, Kazakhstan, **759** J4
Lugu, China, **750** C2
Luhačovice, Czech Republic, **773** H4
Luhans'k, Ukraine, **782** E3
Luhombero, Tanzania, **809** G4
Luhuo, China, **751** G3
Lui, Ben, *mountain peak*, Scotland, U.K., **792** E4
Luia, *river*, Mozambique, **809** F6
Luiana, Angola, **810** D2
Luikonlahti, Finland, **769** P5
Luing, *island*, Scotland, U.K., **792** D4
Luís Correia, Brazil, **851** F4
Luitpold Coast, *region*, Antarctica, **862** C4
Luiza, Democratic Republic of the Congo, **808** D4
Luján, Argentina, **856** C4
Lujiang, China, **742** D2
Lukachek, Russian Federation, **747** L1
Lukala, Democratic Republic of the Congo, **808** B4
Lukavac, Bosnia and Herzegovina, **778** G3
Lukengo, Democratic Republic of the Congo, **809** E4
Lukeville, U.S.A., **832** G6
Lukhovitsy, Russian Federation, **783** G5
Lŭki, Bulgaria, **780** E5
Lukolela, Democratic Republic of the Congo, **808** C3
Lukovit, Bulgaria, **780** E4
Lukovnikovo, Russian Federation, **783** E4
Łuków, Poland, **773** L3
Lukula, Democratic Republic of the Congo, **808** B4
Lukulu, Zambia, **808** D5
Lukumburu, Tanzania, **809** G4
Lukunor, *island*, Micronesia, **724** D4
Lukwasa, India, **754** D4
Luleå, Sweden, **769** L4
Luleälven, *river*, Sweden, **768** K4
Lüleburgaz, Turkey, **781** F5
Luliang, China, **751** G4
Lüliang Shan, *mountain range*, China, **746** E5
Lulimba, Democratic Republic of the Congo, **809** E3
Luling, U.S.A., **834** D5
Lulonga, Democratic Republic of the Congo, **808** C2
Lulua, *river*, Democratic Republic of the Congo, **808** D4
Lülung, China, **750** C3
Luma, American Samoa, **727** B2
Lumbala Kaquengue, Angola, **808** D5
Lumbala N'guimbo, Angola, **808** D5
Lumberton, Mississippi, U.S.A., **835** H4
Lumberton, North Carolina, U.S.A., **835** N2
Lumbrales, Spain, **776** D2
Lumbrera, Argentina, **856** D2
Lumbres, France, **789** K4
Lumding, India, **755** H4
Lumecha, Tanzania, **809** G5
Lumimba, Zambia, **809** F5
Lumo, *island*, Micronesia, **724** C4
Lumphăt, Cambodia, **739** E3
Lumsden, Canada, **823** S6
Lumsden, New Zealand, **719** B7
Lumut, Gunung, *mountain peak*, Indonesia, **737** F3
Lumut, Tanjong, *point*, Indonesia, **736** D3
Lün, Mongolia, **746** D3
Lunan Bay, Scotland, U.K., **792** G4
Lund, Sweden, **770** F5
Lunda Norte, *province*, Angola, **808** C4
Lunda Sul, *province*, Angola, **808** D5
Lundazi, Zambia, **809** F5
Lunde, Sweden, **771** H1
Lundy, *island*, England, U.K., **788** C3
Lune, *river*, England, U.K., **790** F3
Lüneburg, Germany, **772** E2
Lunenburg, Canada, **827** J7
Lunéville, France, **775** H2
Lung Kwu Tan, China, **743** B4
Lungdo, China, **750** B2
Lunggar, China, **750** B3
Lungi, Sierra Leone, **804** B3
Lunglei, India, **755** H5
Lungsang, China, **750** D3
Luning, China, **751** G3
Luning, U.S.A., **832** D2
Lūnkaransar, India, **754** C3
Lunsar, Sierra Leone, **804** B3
Luntai, China, **748** E4
Lunz am See, Austria, **773** G5
Luo, *river*, China, **746** E5
Luobei, China, **747** K3
Luobuzhuang, China, **748** F5
Luochuan, China, **742** B1
Luodian, China, **751** H4
Luoding, China, **742** B4
Luofu Shan, *mountain peak*, China, **743** B2
Luofu Shan, *mountain range*, China, **743** C2
Luogang, China, **743** B2
Luogosanto, Sardegna, Italy, **779** B5
Luohe, China, **742** C1
Luonan, China, **742** B1
Luoning, China, **742** B1
Luoping, China, **751** H4
Luoshan, China, **742** C1
Luotian, China, **742** C2
Luoxiao Shan, *mountain range*, China, **742** C3
Luoyang, China, **742** C1
Luoyuan, China, **742** D3
Luozi, Democratic Republic of the Congo, **808** B3
Lupane, Zimbabwe, **811** E2
Lupeni, Romania, **780** D3
Lupilichi, Mozambique, **809** G5
Luqu, China, **751** G2
Luray, U.S.A., **830** D6
Lure, France, **775** H3
Lure, Montagne de, *mountain peak*, France, **775** G4
Luremo, Angola, **808** C4
Lurgan, Northern Ireland, U.K., **793** F3
Luribay, Bolivia, **853** E4
Lurín, Peru, **852** C3
Lúrio, Mozambique, **809** H5
Lurton, U.S.A., **834** F2
Lusahunga, Tanzania, **809** F3
Lusaka, *province*, Zambia, **809** E6
Lusaka, Zambia, **809** E6
Lusambo, Democratic Republic of the Congo, **808** D3
Lusangi, Democratic Republic of the Congo, **809** E3
Luseland, Canada, **823** Q5
Lusengo, Democratic Republic of the Congo, **808** C2
Lushi, China, **742** B1
Lushnjë, Albania, **781** B5
Lushoto, Tanzania, **809** G3
Lushui, China, **751** F4
Lüshun, China, **747** H5
Lusk, U.S.A., **829** M5
Lūt, Dasht-e, *desert*, Iran, **757** G2
Lūţak, Iran, **757** H2
Lutembo, Angola, **808** D5
Lutherstadt Eisleben, Germany, **772** E3
Lutherstadt Wittenberg, Germany, **772** F3
Lütian, China, **743** B1
Lutiba, Democratic Republic of the Congo, **809** E3
Lütjenburg, Germany, **772** E1
Lutnes, Norway, **770** F2
Luton, England, U.K., **789** G3
Luton, *unitary authority*, England, U.K., **789** G3
Lutong, Malaysia, **737** F1
Lutselk'e, Canada, **820** H3
Lutshima, Democratic Republic of the Congo, **808** C4
Luts'k, Ukraine, **782** C2
Lutterworth, England, U.K., **789** F2
Lutto, *river*, Finland, **769** P2
Lututów, Poland, **773** J3
Lützow Holmbukta, *bay*, Antarctica, **862** F3
Luumaki, Finland, **771** N2
Luuq, Somalia, **809** H2
Luverne, Alabama, U.S.A., **835** J4
Luverne, Minnesota, U.S.A., **830** E4
Luvozero, Russian Federation, **769** Q4
Luvua, *river*, Democratic Republic of the Congo, **809** E4
Luvuei, Angola, **808** D5
Luwero, Uganda, **809** F2
Luwuk, Indonesia, **734** C3
Luxembourg, *country*, Europe, **764** E6
Luxembourg, Luxembourg, **775** H2
Luxembourg, *province*, Belgium, **772** B4
Luxeuil-les-Bains, France, **775** H3
Luxi, E. Yunnan, China, **751** G4
Luxi, Hunan, China, **742** B2
Luxi, W. Yunnan, China, **751** F4
Luxor *see* Al Uqşur, Egypt, **803** F3
Luyamba, Democratic Republic of the Congo, **809** E3
Luz-Saint-Sauveur, France, **774** D5
Luza, Russian Federation, **784** F3
Luzern, Switzerland, **775** J3
Luzhitsa, Russian Federation, **783** B3
Luzhou, China, **751** H3
Luziânia, Brazil, **854** D4
Luzilândia, Brazil, **851** E4
Luzon, *island*, Philippines, **740** C2
Luzon Strait, Philippines/Taiwan, **733** N7
Luzy, France, **775** F3
L'viv, Ukraine, **782** B3
L'vivsk'a Oblast', *province*, Ukraine, **773** L4
Lyady, Russian Federation, **783** B3
Lyakhovskiye Ostrova, *islands*, Russian Federation, **785** Q2
Lyall, Mount, *mountain peak*, Campbell Island, New Zealand, **718** K11
Lyall, Mount, *mountain peak*, New Zealand, **719** A7
Lyamtsa, Russian Federation, **769** T4
Lyaskelya, Russian Federation, **783** C2
Lyaskovets, Bulgaria, **780** E4

M

Magat, *river*, Philippines, **740** C2
Magbakele, Democratic Republic of the Congo, **808** D2
Magburaka, Sierra Leone, **804** B3
Magdagachi, Russian Federation, **747** J1
Magdalena, Argentina, **857** F5
Magdalena, Bolivia, **853** F3
Magdalena, Isla, *island*, Chile, **858** C2
Magdalena, Mexico, **840** C2
Magdalena, *river*, Colombia, **848** D2
Magdalena, *river*, Mexico, **840** C2
Magdalena, U.S.A., **833** K4
Magdalena Tequisistlán, Mexico, **841** G5
Magdeburg, Germany, **772** E2
Magdelaine Cays, *islands*, Coral Sea Islands, **721** L2
Magee Island, Northern Ireland, U.K., **793** G3
Magelang, Indonesia, **737** E4
Magerøya, *island*, Norway, **769** M1
Maggiorasca, Monte, *mountain peak*, Italy, **778** B3
Maggiore, Lago, *lake*, Italy, **778** B3
Maggiore, Monte, *mountain peak*, Italy, **779** E5
Maghāghah, Egypt, **803** F3
Maghama, Mauritania, **804** B1
Maghārah, Jabal, *mountain peak*, Egypt, **761** B4
Magherafelt, *district*, Northern Ireland, U.K., **793** F3
Magherafelt, Northern Ireland, U.K., **793** F3
Maghull, England, U.K., **790** F4
Magilligan Point, Northern Ireland, U.K., **793** F2
Mágina, *mountain peak*, Spain, **777** F4
Maglić, *mountain peak*, Bosnia and Herzegovina, **778** G4
Maglie, Italy, **779** G5
Magma Point, Papua New Guinea, **726** C4
Magna, U.S.A., **833** G1
Magnetic Island, Australia, **721** K2
Magnetity, Russian Federation, **769** R2
Magnitogorsk, Russian Federation, **758** F2
Magnolia, U.S.A., **834** F3
Mago, *island*, Fiji, **727** A4
Màgoé, Mozambique, **809** F6
Magog, Canada, **826** E7
Magpie, Canada, **827** J4
Magpie, Lac, *lake*, Canada, **827** J4
Magrath, Canada, **823** N7
Magta' Lahjar, Mauritania, **804** B1
Maguarinho, Cabo, *cape*, Brazil, **850** D3
Magude, Mozambique, **811** F4
Magumeri, Nigeria, **805** G2
Maguse Lake, Canada, **824** G1
Magwe, *division*, Myanmar, **741** B3
Magwe, Myanmar, **741** B3
Magyichaung, Myanmar, **741** B3
Maha Sarakham, Thailand, **739** D2
Mahābād, Iran, **758** D5
Mahabe, Madagascar, **812** B4
Mahābhārat Lekh, *mountain range*, Nepal, **755** E3
Mahabo, Madagascar, **812** A5
Mahaboboka, Madagascar, **812** A5
Mahadday Weyne, Somalia, **807** G4
Mahagi Port, Democratic Republic of the Congo, **809** F2
Mahaicony, Guyana, **850** B1
Mahājan, India, **754** C3
Mahajanga, Madagascar, **812** B4
Mahajanga, *province*, Madagascar, **812** B4
Mahakam, *river*, Indonesia, **737** F2
Mahalapye, Botswana, **811** E3
Mahalevona, Madagascar, **812** B4
Mahallāt, Iran, **756** F2
Mahānadi, *river*, India, **755** F5
Mahanoro, Madagascar, **812** B4
Mahārājganj, Bihār, India, **755** F4
Mahārājganj, Uttar Pradesh, India, **755** E4
Mahārāshtra, *state*, India, **752** C2
Maharès, Tunisia, **801** J2
Mahavelona, Madagascar, **812** B4
Maḥbūb, Sudan, **806** C2
Mahbūbnagar, India, **752** D2
Mahdia, Guyana, **849** G3
Mahdia, Tunisia, **802** B1
Mahe, India, **752** C4
Mahé, *island*, Seychelles, **813** A2
Mahébourg, Mauritius, **813** C1
Mahenge, Tanzania, **809** G4
Maheno, New Zealand, **719** C7
Mahesāna, India, **754** C5
Mahi, *river*, India, **754** C5
Mahia, New Zealand, **718** F4
Mahia Peninsula, New Zealand, **718** F4
Mahilyow, Belarus, **783** C6
Mahilyowskaya Voblasts', *province*, Belarus, **783** C6
Mahina, Mali, **804** B2
Maḥmūd-e Rāqī, Afghanistan, **754** B2
Mahmūdābād, India, **754** E4
Mahmudia, Romania, **780** G3
Mahnomen, U.S.A., **830** F2
Mahoba, India, **754** D4
Mahoenui, New Zealand, **718** E4
Mahón, Islas Baleares, Spain, **777** K3
Mahora, Spain, **777** G3
Mahou, Mali, **804** D2
Mahrāt, Jabal, *mountain range*, Yemen, **756** F5
Mahroni, India, **754** D4
Mahuanggou, China, **749** G5
Mahuva, India, **754** B5
Mahwa, India, **754** D4
Mai-Ndombe, Lac, *lake*, Democratic Republic of the Congo, **808** C3
Maiao, *island*, French Polynesia, **723** F2
Maicao, Colombia, **848** D1
Maîche, France, **775** H3
Maicuru, *river*, Brazil, **850** B3
Maidenhead, England, U.K., **789** G3
Maidi, Indonesia, **734** D2
Maidstone, Canada, **823** Q5
Maidstone, England, U.K., **789** H3
Maiduguri, Nigeria, **805** G2
Maignelay-Montigny, France, **789** K5
Maigualida, Sierra, *mountain range*, Venezuela, **849** F3
Maihar, India, **754** E4
Maihiá, Venezuela, **849** F3
Maikala Range, *mountain range*, India, **754** E5
Mailsi, Pakistan, **754** C3
Main, *river*, Germany, **772** D4
Main-a-Dieu, Canada, **827** M6
Main Brook, Canada, **827** N4
Maine, Gulf of, U.S.A., **836** G3
Maine, *state*, U.S.A., **836** F2
Maine Hanari, Cerro, *mountain peak*, Colombia, **848** D4
Maïné-Soroa, Niger, **805** G2
Mainit, Lake, Philippines, **740** D4
Mainland, *island*, Orkney, Scotland, U.K., **792** F1
Mainland, *island*, Shetland, Scotland, U.K., **792** K7
Mainpuri, India, **754** D4
Maintirano, Madagascar, **812** A4
Mainz, Germany, **772** D4
Maio, *island*, Cape Verde, **800** Q8
Maipú, Argentina, **857** F5
Maipú, Volcán, *mountain peak*, Argentina/Chile, **856** C5
Maipuri Landing, Guyana, **849** G3
Maisí, Cuba, **839** G2
Maitencillo, Chile, **856** B4
Maitengwe, Botswana, **811** E3
Maitland, New South Wales, Australia, **721** L5
Maitland, South Australia, Australia, **721** H5
Maizuru, Japan, **745** F4
Maja e Korbit *see* Korab, *mountain peak*, Albania/ Macedonia, **780** C5
Majardah, Monts de la, *mountain range*, Algeria, **779** A7
Majardah, *river*, Tunisia, **802** A1
Majāz al Bāb, Tunisia, **779** B7
Majdanpek, Yugoslavia, **780** C3
Majene, Indonesia, **734** B3
Majevica, *mountain range*, Bosnia and Herzegovina, **778** G3
Majī, Ethiopia, **806** E3
Majia, *river*, China, **746** G5
Majiagang, China, **747** L3
Majiang, China, **742** B4
Majie, China, **751** H5
Majitang, China, **742** B2
Major, Canada, **823** Q6
Major, Puig, *mountain peak*, Islas Baleares, Spain, **777** J3
Major Buratovich, Argentina, **858** E1
Major Lake, Macquarie Island, **720** R11
Majuro, *island*, Marshall Islands, **725** F4
Makīnsk, Kazakhstan, **759** J2
Maka, Senegal, **804** B2
Maka, Solomon Islands, **727** A1
Makabana, Congo, **808** B3
Makaha, Hawaiian Islands, U.S.A., **832** R9
Makak, Cameroon, **808** B2
Makale, Indonesia, **734** B3
Makamba, Burundi, **809** E3
Makanza, Democratic Republic of the Congo, **808** C2
Makapu Point, Niue, **718** M13
Makaraka, New Zealand, **718** F4
Makarakomburu, Mount, *mountain peak*, Solomon Islands, **727** A1
Makarska, Croatia, **778** F4
Makar'yevskaya, Russian Federation, **783** E2
Makasar Selat, *strait*, Indonesia, **734** B3
Makassar *see* Ujungpandang, Indonesia, **734** B4
Makatea, *island*, French Polynesia, **723** G2
Makaw, Myanmar, **741** C2
Makefu, Niue, **718** M13
Makeni, Sierra Leone, **804** B3
Makhachkala, Russian Federation, **758** D4
Makikihi, New Zealand, **719** C7
Makindu, Kenya, **809** G3
Makira, *island*, Solomon Islands, **727** A1
Makiyivka, Ukraine, **782** E3
Makkah (Mecca), Saudi Arabia, **803** G4
Makkola, Finland, **771** P2
Makkovik, Cape, Canada, **827** M2
Makó, Hungary, **773** K5
Makokou, Gabon, **808** B2
Makongolosi, Tanzania, **809** F4
Makoro, Democratic Republic of the Congo, **809** E2
Makotipoko, Congo, **808** C3
Makoua, Congo, **808** C3
Maków Mazowiecki, Poland, **773** K2
Makra, *island*, Kyklades, Greece, **781** E7
Makrakomi, Greece, **781** D6
Makrany, Belarus, **773** M3
Makronisi, *island*, Kyklades, Greece, **781** E7
Maksatikha, Russian Federation, **783** E4
Maksi, India, **754** D5
Maksimikha, Russian Federation, **746** E1
Maksimovka, Russian Federation, **745** G1
Maksudangarh, India, **754** D4
Makthar, Tunisia, **779** B8
Mākū, Iran, **758** C5
Makumbako, Tanzania, **809** F4
Makumbi, Democratic Republic of the Congo, **808** D4
Makungo, Somalia, **809** H2
Makunguwiro, Tanzania, **809** G5
Makurazaki, Japan, **744** E5
Makurdi, Nigeria, **805** F3
Makushino, Russian Federation, **758** H1
Mala, Peru, **852** C3
Mala, Punta, *point*, Panama, **839** F6
Mala, *river*, Peru, **852** C3
Malå, Sweden, **768** J4
Mala Kapela, *mountain range*, Croatia, **778** E3
Mala Vyska, Ukraine, **780** H1
Malabang, Philippines, **740** D5
Malabar, Mount, *mountain peak*, Lord Howe Island, Australia, **721** U14
Malabo, Equatorial Guinea, **808** A2
Malacca, Strait of, Indonesia/ Malaysia, **736** B1
Malacky, Slovakia, **773** H4
Malad City, U.S.A., **829** H5
Maladzyechna, Belarus, **771** N5
Málaga, Spain, **776** E4
Malaga, U.S.A., **833** L5
Malagarasi, Tanzania, **809** F4
Malahide, Ireland, **793** F4
Malaimbandy, Madagascar, **812** B5
Malaita, *island*, Solomon Islands, **727** A1
Malakāl, Sudan, **806** D3
Malākhera, India, **754** D4
Malakula, *island*, Vanuatu, **727** A2
Malalamai, Papua New Guinea, **726** B4
Malali, Guyana, **849** G3
Malam, Papua New Guinea, **726** A5
Malån, *river*, Sweden, **768** J4
Malang, Indonesia, **737** F4
Malanje, Angola, **808** C4
Malanje, *province*, Angola, **808** C4
Malanville, Benin, **805** E2
Malanzán, Argentina, **856** C4
Mälaren, *lake*, Sweden, **771** H3
Malargüe, Argentina, **856** C5
Malartic, Canada, **826** B5
Malaryta, Belarus, **773** M3
Malaso, *river*, Indonesia, **734** B3
Malatayur, Tanjong, *point*, Indonesia, **737** F3
Malatya, Turkey, **760** E5
Malaut, India, **754** C3
Malavalli, India, **752** D3
Malawali, Pulau, *island*, Malaysia, **737** G1
Malawi, *country*, Africa, **797** J8
Malawi, Lake, Malawi, **809** F5
Malawiya, Sudan, **806** E1
Malay Peninsula, Malaysia/ Thailand, **733** M9
Malaya Vishera, Russian Federation, **783** D3
Malaybalay, Philippines, **740** D4
Malāyer, Iran, **756** E2
Malayiwan, China, **751** F2
Malaysia, *country*, Asia, **731** N9
Malazgirt, Turkey, **803** H1
Malbork, Poland, **773** J1
Malden Island, Kiribati, **725** J5
Maldives, *country*, Asia, **730** J9
Maldon, England, U.K., **789** H3
Maldonado, Uruguay, **857** F5
Malè, Italy, **778** C2
Male, Maldives, **752** C5
Male Atoll, Maldives, **752** C5
Malé Karpaty, *mountain range*, Slovakia, **773** H4
Malea, Gunung, *mountain peak*, Indonesia, **736** B2
Maleas, Akra, *point*, Greece, **781** D7
Mālegaon, India, **754** C5
Malek Dīn, Afghanistan, **754** B2
Malela, Democratic Republic of the Congo, **809** E3
Malema, Mozambique, **809** G5
Malemba Nkulu, Democratic Republic of the Congo, **809** E4
Malen'ga, Russian Federation, **769** T5
Målerås, Sweden, **770** G4
Maleta, Russian Federation, **746** E2
Malgomaj, *lake*, Sweden, **768** G4
Malha, Sudan, **806** C1
Malheur Lake, U.S.A., **828** E5
Malheureux, Cap, *cape*, Mauritius, **813** C1
Mali, *country*, Africa, **796** E5
Mali, Democratic Republic of the Congo, **809** E3
Mali, Guinea, **804** B2
Mali Kanal, *canal*, Yugoslavia, **780** B3
Mali Kyun (Tavoy Island), *island*, Myanmar, **738** C3
Maliangping, China, **742** B2
Maliaohe, China, **743** D3
Målilla, Sweden, **770** G4
Malimba, Monts, *mountain range*, Democratic Republic of the Congo, **809** E4
Malin Head, *point*, Ireland, **793** E2
Malin More, Ireland, **793** D3
Malindang, Mount, *mountain peak*, Philippines, **740** C4
Malindi, Kenya, **809** H3
Malinga, Gabon, **808** B3
Malingsbo, Sweden, **770** G3
Malinoa, *island*, Tonga, **727** B4
Malinovka, Russian Federation, **759** M2
Malipo, China, **751** H5
Maliq, Albania, **781** C5
Malita, Philippines, **740** D5
Maljamar, U.S.A., **833** M5
Mālkāngiri, India, **753** E2
Malkāpur, India, **754** D5
Malkara, Turkey, **781** F5
Malkhanskiy Khrebet, *mountain range*, Russian Federation, **746** D2
Mallaig, Scotland, U.K., **792** D3
Mallard, U.S.A., **830** F4
Mallawī, Egypt, **803** F3
Mallorca, *island*, Islas Baleares, Spain, **777** J3
Mallow, Ireland, **793** D5
Mallwyd, Wales, U.K., **788** D2
Malm, Norway, **768** E4
Malmal, Papua New Guinea, **726** C4
Malmanoury, French Guiana, **850** C2
Malmberget, Sweden, **768** K3
Malmédy, Belgium, **772** C3

Manuelzinho, Brazil, **850** B5
Manui, Pulau, *island*, Indonesia, **734** C3
Manūjān, Iran, **757** G3
Manukau, New Zealand, **718** E3
Manukau Harbour, New Zealand, **718** D3
Manundi, Tanjong, *point*, Indonesia, **735** F3
Manunui, New Zealand, **718** E4
Manuoha, *mountain peak*, New Zealand, **718** F4
Manus, *province*, Papua New Guinea, **726** B3
Manus Island, Papua New Guinea, **726** B3
Manvel, U.S.A., **830** E1
Manville, U.S.A., **829** M5
Manyara, Lake, Tanzania, **809** G3
Manyas, Turkey, **781** F5
Manych-Gudilo, Ozero, *lake*, Russian Federation, **782** F3
Manyoni, Tanzania, **809** F4
Mânzai, Pakistan, **754** B3
Manzanares, Spain, **777** F3
Manzanilla Point, Trinidad, Trinidad and Tobago, **859** C4
Manzanillo, Cuba, **839** F2
Manzanillo, Mexico, **840** D5
Manzariyeh, Iran, **756** F2
Manzhouli, China, **746** G2
Manzil Bū Ruqaybah, Tunisia, **802** A1
Manzini, Swaziland, **811** F4
Mao, Chad, **805** H2
Maobosheng, China, **749** J5
Maoke, Pegunungan, *mountain range*, Indonesia, **735** G4
Maomao Shan, *mountain peak*, China, **749** J5
Maoming, China, **742** B4
Maotou Shan, *mountain peak*, China, **751** G4
Mapai, Mozambique, **811** F3
Mapi, Indonesia, **735** G4
Mapi, *river*, Indonesia, **735** G4
Mapinhane, Mozambique, **811** G3
Mapire, Venezuela, **849** F2
Mapiri, Bolivia, **853** E4
Maple Creek, Canada, **823** Q7
Maple Inlet, Canada, **824** G1
Maplesville, U.S.A., **835** J3
Mapmaker Seamounts, *underwater feature*, Pacific Ocean, **868** F3
Maprik, Papua New Guinea, **726** A3
Mapua, New Zealand, **719** D5
Mapuera, *river*, Brazil, **850** B3
Mapulanguene, Mozambique, **811** F3
Maputo, Mozambique, **811** F4
Maputo, *province*, Mozambique, **811** F4
Maqanshy, Kazakhstan, **748** D3
Maqat, Kazakhstan, **758** E3
Maqên, China, **751** G2
Maqen Gangri, *mountain peak*, China, **751** F2
Maqnā, Saudi Arabia, **761** C5
Maqu, China, **751** G2
Maqueda, Spain, **776** E2
Maquela do Zombo, Angola, **808** C4
Maquinchao, Argentina, **858** D1
Mar Chiquita, Laguna, *lake*, Argentina, **856** D4
Mar del Plata, Argentina, **857** F5
Mar Menor, *lake*, Spain, **777** G4
Mara, *administrative region*, Tanzania, **809** F3
Mara, Guyana, **849** H2
Mara, South Africa, **811** E3
Maraã, Brazil, **849** F4
Marabá, Brazil, **850** D4
Maracá, Ilha de, *island*, Brazil, **850** C2
Maraçacumé, *river*, Brazil, **850** D4
Maracaibo, Lago de, *lake*, Venezuela, **848** D2
Maracaibo, Venezuela, **848** D1
Maracaju, Brazil, **854** B5
Maracajú, Serra de, *mountain range*, Brazil, **854** B5
Maracanã, Brazil, **850** D3
Maracanaquará, Planalto, *plateau*, Brazil, **850** C3
Maracás, Chapada de, *mountain range*, Brazil, **855** F3
Maracay, Venezuela, **849** E1
Marādah, Libya, **802** C3
Maradi, *department*, Niger, **805** F2
Maradi, Niger, **805** F2
Marāgheh, Iran, **758** D5
Maragogipe, Brazil, **855** F3
Marahuaca, Cerro, *mountain peak*, Venezuela, **849** F3
Marais des Cygnes, *river*, U.S.A., **830** F6
Marajó, Baía de, *bay*, Brazil, **850** D3
Marajó, Ilha de, *island*, Brazil, **850** C3
Maralal, Kenya, **809** G2
Marali, Central African Republic, **806** A3
Maramasike, *island*, Solomon Islands, **727** A1
Maran, Malaysia, **736** C2
Marana, U.S.A., **833** H5
Marand, Iran, **758** D5
Maranguape, Brazil, **851** F4
Maranhão, Barragem de, *reservoir*, Portugal, **776** D3
Maranhão, *river*, Brazil, **854** D4
Maranhão, *state*, Brazil, **851** E4
Maranoa, *river*, Australia, **721** K4
Marañón, *river*, Peru, **848** C5
Marão, *mountain peak*, Portugal, **776** D2
Marapanim, Brazil, **850** D3
Marapi, Gunung, *mountain peak*, Indonesia, **736** C3
Mărășești, Romania, **780** F3
Marathon, Canada, **825** L7
Marathon, Florida, U.S.A., **835** M7
Marathon, Texas, U.S.A., **833** M6
Marathonas, Greece, **781** E6
Maratua, Pulau, *island*, Indonesia, **737** G2
Maraú, Brazil, **855** F4
Marau Point, New Zealand, **718** G4
Maravari, Solomon Islands, **727** A1
Marawi, Philippines, **740** D4
Marawi, Sudan, **803** F5
Mar'ayt, Yemen, **756** F5
Marbella, Spain, **776** E4
Marble Bar, Australia, **720** D3
Marble Canyon, *gorge*, U.S.A., **833** G3
Marble Falls, U.S.A., **834** C4
Marble Hall, South Africa, **811** E3
Marburg, Germany, **772** D3
Marburg, South Africa, **811** F5
Marcali, Hungary, **773** H5
Marcelândia, Brazil, **854** B3
March, England, U.K., **789** H2
Marche, *autonomous state*, Italy, **778** D4
Marche-en-Famenne, Belgium, **772** B3
Marchena, Isla, *island*, Islas Galápagos (Galapagos Islands), Ecuador, **859** A1
Marcigny, France, **775** G3
Marcinkonys, Lithuania, **773** M1
Marcona, Peru, **852** C4
Marcos Juárez, Argentina, **856** D4
Mărculești, Moldova, **780** G2
Mardan, Pakistan, **754** B2
Mardin, Turkey, **760** F5
Maré, *island*, New Caledonia, **727** A3
Maree, Loch, *lake*, Scotland, U.K., **792** D3
Mareeba, Australia, **721** K2
Maremma, *mountain range*, Italy, **778** C4
Maresfield, England, U.K., **789** H3
Mareyes, Argentina, **856** C4
Marfa, U.S.A., **833** L6
Margaree Forks, Canada, **827** L6
Margaret River, Australia, **720** D5
Margarita, Isla de, *island*, Venezuela, **849** F1
Margate, England, U.K., **789** J3
Margeride, Monts de la, *mountain range*, France, **775** F4
Marghita, Romania, **780** D2
Margie, U.S.A., **830** G1
Margosatubig, Philippines, **740** C5
Mārgow, Dasht-e, *desert*, Afghanistan, **757** H2
Marguerite, Canada, **822** H5
Marhoum, Algeria, **801** F2
Mari, Papua New Guinea, **726** A5
Maria, Îles, *islands*, French Polynesia, **723** F3
Maria, *island*, French Polynesia, **723** H3
Maria Byrd Land, *region*, Antarctica, **862** C6
María Elena, Chile, **856** C2
Maria Grande, Argentina, **857** E4
Maria Island, Australia, **721** H1
Maria van Diemen, Cape, New Zealand, **718** C2
Mariana Trough, *underwater feature*, Pacific Ocean, **868** D4
Marianao, Cuba, **839** E2
Marianna, Arkansas, U.S.A., **834** G2
Marianna, Florida, U.S.A., **835** K4
Mariannelund, Sweden, **770** G4
Mariano Loza, Argentina, **857** E3
Mariánské Lázně, Czech Republic, **772** F4
Mariato, Punta, *point*, Panama, **839** E6
Mariazell, Austria, **773** G5
Ma'rib, Yemen, **756** E5
Maribor, Slovenia, **778** E2
Maricopa, U.S.A., **832** D4
Marie Anne, *island*, Seychelles, **813** A2
Maridi, Sudan, **809** E2
Marie Valdemar, Kap, *cape*, Greenland, **821** T2
Mariefred, Sweden, **771** H3
Marielund, Sweden, **768** H4
Mariental, Namibia, **810** C3
Mariestad, Sweden, **770** F3
Marietta, Georgia, U.S.A., **835** K2
Marietta, West Virginia, U.S.A., **831** N6
Marigot, St Martin, Guadeloupe, **837** D2
Mariinsk, Russian Federation, **759** M1
Marijampolė, Lithuania, **771** L5
Marília, Brazil, **857** H2
Marimba, Angola, **808** C4
Marín, Spain, **776** C1
Marina, U.S.A., **832** C3
Marina di Leuca, Italy, **779** G6
Marina di Ragusa, Italy, **779** E7
Marina di Ravenna, Italy, **778** D3
Mar''ina Horka, Belarus, **783** B6
Marinduque Island, Philippines, **740** C3
Marineo, Sicilia, Italy, **779** D7
Marinette, U.S.A., **831** K3
Maringá, Brazil, **857** G2
Maringuè, Mozambique, **811** F2
Marinovka, Kazakhstan, **759** H2
Marion, Indiana, U.S.A., **831** L5
Marion, Lake, U.S.A., **835** M3
Marion, Ohio, U.S.A., **831** M5
Marion, South Carolina, U.S.A., **835** N2
Marion, Virginia, U.S.A., **831** N7
Maripa, Venezuela, **849** F2
Maripasoula, French Guiana, **850** B2
Mariposa, U.S.A., **832** C3
Marisa, Indonesia, **734** C2
Mariscal Estigarribia, Paraguay, **856** E2
Maritsa, *river*, Bulgaria, **780** E4
Maritsa, *river*, Greece, **781** F5
Mariupol', Ukraine, **782** E3
Marīvān, Iran, **758** D5
Mariveles, Philippines, **740** C3
Mariy El, Respublika, *republic*, Russian Federation, **758** D1
Märjamaa, Estonia, **771** M3
Mark Twain Lake, U.S.A., **830** G6
Marka, Somalia, **807** F4
Markala, Mali, **804** C2
Markam, China, **751** F3
Mārkāpur, India, **752** D3
Markaryd, Sweden, **770** F4
Marked Tree, U.S.A., **834** G2
Market Deeping, England, U.K., **789** G2
Market Drayton, England, U.K., **788** E2
Market Harborough, England, U.K., **789** G2
Market Rasen, England, U.K., **791** H4
Market Weighton, England, U.K., **791** H4
Markethill, Northern Ireland, U.K., **793** F3
Markit, China, **748** C5
Markopoulo, Greece, **781** D7
Markounda, Central African Republic, **805** H3
Markoy, Burkina Faso, **804** D2
Marksville, U.S.A., **834** F4
Marktredwitz, Germany, **772** F4
Marla, Australia, **720** G4
Marlborough, England, U.K., **789** F3
Marlborough, Guyana, **849** G2
Marlborough Downs, *region*, England, U.K., **789** F3
Marle, France, **775** F2
Marlin, U.S.A., **834** D4
Marlinton, U.S.A., **831** P6
Marlow, England, U.K., **789** G3
Marma, Sweden, **771** H2
Marmagoa, India, **752** C3
Marmande, France, **774** E4
Marmara, Sea of *see* Marmara Denizi, *sea*, Turkey, **781** F5
Marmara, Turkey, **781** F5
Marmara Adası, *island*, Turkey, **781** F5
Marmara Denizi (Sea of Marmara), *sea*, Turkey, **781** F5
Marmaraereğlisi, Turkey, **781** F5
Marmaris, Turkey, **781** G7
Marmarth, U.S.A., **830** B2
Marmion, Lake, Australia, **720** E4
Marmolada, *mountain peak*, Italy, **778** C2
Marnay, France, **775** G3
Marne, *river*, France, **775** G2
Marne-la-Vallée, France, **774** F2
Maro, Chad, **806** A3
Maroantsetra, Madagascar, **812** B4
Maroanui, *mountain peak*, New Zealand, **718** F4
Marofa, *mountain peak*, Portugal, **776** D2
Marokau, *island*, French Polynesia, **723** G2
Marolambo, Madagascar, **812** B5
Maromokotro, *mountain peak*, Madagascar, **812** B3
Maromony, Lohatanjona, *cape*, Madagascar, **812** B3
Marondera, Zimbabwe, **811** F2
Maroni, *river*, French Guiana, **850** B2
Maroochydore, Australia, **721** L4
Maropiu, New Zealand, **718** D2
Maros, Indonesia, **734** B4
Maroseranana, Madagascar, **812** B4
Marotiri, *island*, French Polynesia, **723** G3
Maroua, Cameroon, **805** G2
Marovato, Madagascar, **812** B3
Marovoay, Madagascar, **812** B4
Marowijne, *river*, Suriname, **850** B2
Marple, England, U.K., **790** F4
Marquesas Fracture Zone, *tectonic feature*, Pacific Ocean, **869** J5
Marquette, U.S.A., **831** K2
Marquise, France, **774** E1
Marquises, Îles, *islands*, French Polynesia, **723** H1
Marracuene, Mozambique, **811** F4
Marradi, Italy, **778** C3
Marrah, Jabal, *mountain range*, Sudan, **806** B2
Marrakech (Marrakesh), Morocco, **800** E2
Marrakesh *see* Marrakech, Morocco, **800** E2
Marree, Australia, **721** H4
Marrehan, *mountain range*, Somalia, **809** H2
Marroqui o de Tarifa, Punta, *point*, Spain, **776** D5
Marrupa, Mozambique, **809** G5
Mars Bay, Ascension, **813** A3
Marsá al 'Alam, Egypt, **803** F3
Marsá al Burayqah, Libya, **802** C2
Marsá Maṭrūḥ, Egypt, **802** E2
Marsabit, Kenya, **809** G2
Marsala, Sicilia, Italy, **779** D7
Marsberg, Germany, **772** D3
Marsden, Canada, **823** Q5
Marseille, France, **775** G5
Marseille-en-Beauvaisis, France, **789** J5
Marsh Harbour, Bahamas, **838** F1
Marsh Island, U.S.A., **834** F5
Marshall, Arkansas, U.S.A., **834** F2
Marshall, Canada, **823** Q5
Marshall, Minnesota, U.S.A., **830** F3
Marshall, Missouri, U.S.A., **830** G6
Marshall, Texas, U.S.A., **834** E3
Marshall Islands, *country*, Pacific Ocean, **715** \ g1
Marshalltown, U.S.A., **830** G4
Marshavitsy, Russian Federation, **783** B4
Marshfield, Missouri, U.S.A., **830** G7
Marshfield, Wisconsin, U.S.A., **830** H3
Marsimang, Tanjong, *point*, Indonesia, **735** E3
Marsland, U.S.A., **830** B4
Marsoui, Canada, **826** H5
Märsta, Sweden, **771** H3
Marstein, Norway, **770** C1
Martaban, Gulf of, Myanmar, **738** C2
Martano, Italy, **779** G5
Martapura, Kalimantan Selatan, Indonesia, **737** F3
Martapura, Sumatera Selatan, Indonesia, **736** D4
Marten Falls, Canada, **825** M6
Marten River, Canada, **831** P2
Martha's Vineyard, *island*, U.S.A., **836** E4
Martigny, Switzerland, **775** H3
Martigues, France, **775** G5
Martin, Lake, U.S.A., **835** K3

Martin, Slovakia, **773** J4
Martin, South Dakota, U.S.A., **830** C4
Martin, Tennessee, U.S.A., **835** H1
Martin Peninsula, Antarctica, **862** B6
Martina, Greece, **781** D6
Martinborough, New Zealand, **719** E5
Martinez de la Torre, Mexico, **841** F4
Martinique, *French department*, Caribbean Sea, **837** D3
Martinique Passage, Caribbean Sea, **837** D3
Martinsburg, Pennsylvania, U.S.A., **831** P5
Martinsburg, West Virginia, U.S.A., **836** B5
Martinsicuro, Italy, **778** D4
Martinsville, Indiana, U.S.A., **831** K6
Martinsville, Virginia, U.S.A., **831** P7
Martley, England, U.K., **788** E2
Martock, England, U.K., **788** E4
Martos, Spain, **777** F4
Martre, Lac la, *lake*, Canada, **820** G3
Martti, Finland, **769** P3
Marttila, Finland, **771** L2
Mart'yanovo, Russian Federation, **783** C4
Martynovo, Russian Federation, **759** M2
Maruim, Brazil, **855** G3
Marutea, *island*, French Polynesia, **723** H3
Marv Dasht, Iran, **756** F3
Marvine, Mount, *mountain peak*, U.S.A., **833** H2
Mary, Turkmenistan, **758** G5
Maryborough, Australia, **721** L4
Marydale, South Africa, **810** D4
Mar'yevka, Russian Federation, **758** D2
Maryhill, U.S.A., **828** D4
Maryland, *state*, U.S.A., **836** B5
Marypark, Scotland, U.K., **792** F3
Maryport, England, U.K., **790** E3
Marystown, Canada, **827** P6
Marysvale, U.S.A., **833** G2
Marysville, California, U.S.A., **832** C2
Marysville, Kansas, U.S.A., **830** E6
Marysville, Ohio, U.S.A., **831** M5
Marysville, Washington, U.S.A., **828** C2
Maryville, Missouri, U.S.A., **830** F5
Maryville, Tennessee, U.S.A., **835** K2
Masachapa, Nicaragua, **838** D5
Masaka, Uganda, **809** F3
Masākin, Tunisia, **802** B1
Masalembu, Kepulauan, *islands*, Indonesia, **737** F4
Masallı, Azerbaijan, **758** D5
Masan, South Korea, **744** E4
Masasi, Tanzania, **809** G5
Masavi, Bolivia, **853** F5
Masaya, Nicaragua, **838** D5
Masbate, Philippines, **740** C3
Masbate Island, Philippines, **740** C3
Mascara, Algeria, **801** G1
Mascarene Islands, Mauritius, **812** D5
Mascarene Plain, *underwater feature*, Indian Ocean, **866** C6
Mascarene Plateau, *underwater feature*, Indian Ocean, **866** C5
Mascasín, Argentina, **856** C4
Masel'gskaya, Russian Federation, **769** S5
Maseno, Kenya, **809** F2
Maseru, Lesotho, **811** E4
Masham, England, U.K., **791** G3
Mashan, China, **747** K3
Mashava, Zimbabwe, **811** F3
Mashhad, Iran, **758** F5
Mashiz, Iran, **757** G3
Mashonaland Central, *province*, Zimbabwe, **809** F6
Mashonaland East, *province*, Zimbabwe, **811** F2
Mashonaland West, *province*, Zimbabwe, **809** E6
Mashra'ar Raqq, Sudan, **806** C3
Masi, China, **743** C2
Masi, Norway, **769** L2
Masi-Manimba, Democratic Republic of the Congo, **808** C3
Masiaca, Mexico, **840** C3
Masindi, Uganda, **809** F2
Maşīrah, Jazīrat, *island*, Oman, **757** G4
Maşīrah, Khalīj, *bay*, Oman, **757** G5
Masisea, Peru, **852** C2
Masisi, Democratic Republic of the Congo, **809** E3
Masjed Soleymān, Iran, **756** E2
Mask, Lough, *lake*, Ireland, **793** C4
Maskanah, Syria, **761** E2
Maslenica, Croatia, **778** E3
Masoala, Tanjona, *cape*, Madagascar, **812** C4
Masoarivo, Madagascar, **812** A4
Mason, U.S.A., **834** C4
Mason City, U.S.A., **830** G4
Mason Hall, Tobago, Trinidad and Tobago, **859** B4
Maspalomas, Islas Canarias, Spain, **813** A4
Masqaţ (Muscat), Oman, **757** G4
Massa, Italy, **778** C4
Massachusetts, *state*, U.S.A., **836** D3
Massachusetts Bay, U.S.A., **836** E3
Massadona, U.S.A., **833** J1
Massafra, Italy, **779** F5
Massaguet, Chad, **805** H2
Massakory, Chad, **805** H2
Massangena, Mozambique, **811** F3
Massango, Angola, **808** C4
Massangulo, Mozambique, **809** G5
Massapê, Brazil, **851** F4
Massassa-Lewémé, Congo, **808** B3
Massawa, Eritrea, **807** E1
Massawa Channel, Eritrea, **807** E1
Massenya, Chad, **805** H2
Masset, Canada, **822** C4
Massif Central, *mountain range*, France, **775** F4
Massif de la Hotte, Haiti, **839** G3
Massigui, Mali, **804** C2
Massina, Mali, **804** C2
Massinga, Mozambique, **811** G3
Massingir, Mozambique, **811** F3
Mastābah, Saudi Arabia, **803** G4
Masters, U.S.A., **833** L1
Masterton, New Zealand, **719** E5
Mastic Point, Bahamas, **838** F1
Mastrevik, Norway, **770** B2
Mastūj, Pakistan, **754** C1
Mastūj, *river*, Pakistan, **754** B1
Mastung, Pakistan, **754** A3
Mastūrah, Saudi Arabia, **803** G4
Masty, Belarus, **773** M2
Masuda, Japan, **744** E4
Masugnsbyn, Sweden, **769** L3
Masurai, Gunung, *mountain peak*, Indonesia, **736** C3
Masvingo, *province*, Zimbabwe, **811** F3
Masvingo, Zimbabwe, **811** F3
Maşyāf, Syria, **761** D2
Mata Utu, Wallis and Futuna, **725** G6
Matabeleland North, *province*, Zimbabwe, **811** E2
Matabeleland South, *province*, Zimbabwe, **811** E3
Matachewan, Canada, **831** N2
Matadi, Democratic Republic of the Congo, **808** B4
Matagalpa, Nicaragua, **838** D4
Matagami, Canada, **826** C5
Matagami, Lac, *lake*, Canada, **826** B5
Matagorda Island, U.S.A., **834** D5
Matagorda, U.S.A., **834** E5
Mataiva, *island*, French Polynesia, **723** G2
Matakana Island, New Zealand, **718** F3
Matakaoa Point, New Zealand, **718** G3
Matala, Angola, **808** B5
Matam, Senegal, **804** B1
Matamata, New Zealand, **718** E3
Matamec, Canada, **826** J4
Matamey, Niger, **805** F2
Matamoros, Coahuila, Mexico, **840** E3
Matamoros, Tamaulipas, Mexico, **841** F3
Matana, Danau, *lake*, Indonesia, **734** C3
Matane, Canada, **826** H5
Matanzas, Cuba, **839** E2
Mataquito, *river*, Chile, **856** B5
Matara, Sri Lanka, **752** E5
Mataragka, Greece, **781** C6
Mataram, Indonesia, **737** G5
Mataranka, Australia, **720** G1
Matarape, Teluk, *bay*, Indonesia, **734** C3
Mataró, Spain, **777** J2
Matas Blancas, Islas Canarias, Spain, **813** B4
Matata, New Zealand, **718** F3
Mataura, New Zealand, **719** B8
Mataura, *river*, New Zealand, **719** B7
Mataveri, Isla de Pascua (Easter Island), Chile, **859** B2
Matawai, New Zealand, **718** F4
Matay, Kazakhstan, **748** C3
Mategua, Bolivia, **853** F3
Matehuala, Mexico, **841** E4
Matelot, Trinidad, Trinidad and Tobago, **859** C4
Matema, Tanzania, **809** F4
Matemanga, Tanzania, **809** G5
Matemateaonga, *mountain peak*, New Zealand, **718** E4
Matera, Italy, **779** F5
Matese, Monti del, *mountain peak*, Italy, **779** E5
Mátészalka, Hungary, **773** L5
Mateur, Tunisia, **779** B7
Matfors, Sweden, **771** H1
Matha, France, **774** D4
Matheson, Canada, **825** P7
Mathews, U.S.A., **836** B6
Mathis, U.S.A., **834** D5
Mathura, India, **754** D4
Mati, Philippines, **740** D5
Matías Romero, Mexico, **841** G5
Matinha, Brazil, **850** E4
Matīši, Latvia, **771** M4
Matkuli, India, **754** D5
Mātli, Pakistan, **754** B4
Matlock, England, U.K., **789** F1
Matnog, Philippines, **740** D3
Mato Grosso, Brazil, **853** G4
Mato Grosso, Planalto do, *plateau*, Brazil, **847** G5
Mato Grosso, *state*, Brazil, **854** B3
Mato Grosso do Sul, *state*, Brazil, **854** B5
Matola, Mozambique, **811** F4
Matomb, Cameroon, **808** B2
Matru, Sierra Leone, **804** B3
Matsiatra, *river*, Madagascar, **812** B5
Matsue, Japan, **744** F4
Matsumae, Japan, **745** H2
Matsumoto, Japan, **745** G3
Matsusaka, Japan, **745** G4
Matsuyama, Japan, **744** F4
Mattagami, *river*, Canada, **825** P7
Mattawa, Canada, **826** B6
Matterhorn, *mountain peak*, Italy/Switzerland, **766** E6
Matterhorn, *mountain peak*, U.S.A., **828** G6
Matthew Town, Bahamas, **839** G2
Matthews Ridge, Guyana, **849** G2
Mattice, Canada, **825** N7
Mattmar, Sweden, **768** F5
Mattoon, U.S.A., **831** J6
Mattsmyra, Sweden, **770** G2
Matucana, Peru, **852** C3
Matuka, *island*, Fiji, **727** A4
Matumbo, Angola, **808** C5
Maturín, Venezuela, **849** F2
Matutum, Mount, *mountain peak*, Philippines, **740** D5
Mau, India, **755** E4
Mau Rānipur, India, **754** D4
Maúa, Mozambique, **811** G1
Maubourguet, France, **774** E5
Maud, *river*, Canada, **820** J3
Maudaha, India, **754** E4
Maués, Brazil, **850** B4
Maug, *island*, Northern Mariana Islands, **724** C2
Mauga Silisili, *mountain peak*, Samoa, **727** B1
Mauganj, India, **755** E4
Maughold Head, *point*, Isle of Man, **790** D3
Maui, *island*, Hawaiian Islands, U.S.A., **832** R9
Mauke, *island*, Cook Islands, **723** F3
Maule, *administrative region*, Chile, **856** B5
Maule, *river*, Chile, **856** B5
Maullín, Chile, **858** C1
Maulyneill, Ireland, **793** C6
Maumakeogh, *mountain peak*, Ireland, **793** C3
Maumee, U.S.A., **831** M5
Maumere, Indonesia, **734** C5
Maumturk Mountains, Ireland, **793** C4
Maun, Botswana, **810** D2
Maungatua, *mountain peak*, New Zealand, **719** C7
Maunu, Sweden, **769** L2
Maupihaa, *island*, French Polynesia, **723** F2
Maupin, U.S.A., **828** D4
Maupiti, *island*, French Polynesia, **723** F2
Maures, Massif des, *mountain peak*, France, **775** H5
Mauri, *river*, Bolivia, **853** E4
Mauriac, France, **774** F4
Maurice, Lake, Australia, **720** G4
Maurine, U.S.A., **830** B3
Mauritania, *country*, Africa, **796** D5
Mauritius, *country*, Indian Ocean, **797** L8
Mauritius Trench, *underwater feature*, Indian Ocean, **866** C6
Mauron, France, **774** C2
Maury Seachannel, *underwater feature*, Atlantic Ocean, **867** F2
Mauston, U.S.A., **830** H4
Mauterndorf, Austria, **772** F5
Mauzé-sur-le-Mignon, France, **774** D3
Mavago, Mozambique, **809** G5
Mavasjaure, *lake*, Sweden, **768** H3
Mavengue, Angola, **808** C6
Mavinga, Angola, **808** D6
Mawa, Democratic Republic of the Congo, **809** E2
Mawanga, Democratic Republic of the Congo, **808** C4
Mawasangka, Indonesia, **734** C4
Mawei, China, **751** H4
Māwiyah, Yemen, **756** D6
Mawshij, Yemen, **756** D6
Mawson, *Australian research station*, Antarctica, **862** F4
Mawson Coast, *region*, Antarctica, **862** F4
Mawson Peak, *mountain peak*, Heard and McDonald Islands, **720** S12
Mawson Peninsula, Antarctica, **862** E8
Max, U.S.A., **830** C2
Maxaas, Somalia, **807** G4
Maxbass, U.S.A., **824** D7
Maxcanú, Mexico, **841** H4
Maxmo, Finland, **769** L5
Maxwell, California, U.S.A., **832** B2
Maxwell, New Mexico, U.S.A., **833** L3
Mayāmey, Iran, **758** F5
Maya, China, **751** G2
Maya, Pulau, *island*, Indonesia, **737** E3
Maya, *river*, Russian Federation, **785** Q4
Maya Mountains, *mountain range*, Belize/Guatemala, **838** C3
Mayaguana Island, Bahamas, **839** G2
Mayagüez, Puerto Rico, **837** C2
Mayahi, Niger, **805** F2
Mayama, Congo, **808** B3
Mayaro Bay, Trinidad, Trinidad and Tobago, **859** C4
Maybell, U.S.A., **833** J1
Maybole, Scotland, U.K., **792** E5
Maych'ew, Ethiopia, **807** E2
Maydh, Somalia, **807** G2
Mayenne, France, **774** D2
Mayenne, *river*, France, **774** D2
Mayer, U.S.A., **833** G4
Mayevo, Russian Federation, **783** B4
Mayfield, New Zealand, **719** C6
Mayfield, U.S.A., **831** J7
Mayhan, Mongolia, **749** J3
Mayhill, U.S.A., **833** L5
Maying, China, **751** H2
Maykop, Russian Federation, **758** C4
Mayluu-Suu, Kyrgyzstan, **748** B4
Maymyo, Myanmar, **741** C3
Maynooth, Canada, **826** C7
Mayo, Canada, **820** F3
Mayo, *county*, Ireland, **793** C4
Mayo, *river*, Argentina, **858** C2
Mayo, *river*, Mexico, **840** C3
Mayo, U.S.A., **835** L4
Mayo Alim, Cameroon, **805** G3
Mayo Belwa, Nigeria, **805** G3
Mayo Darlé, Cameroon, **805** G3
Mayo-Kébbi, *prefecture*, Chad, **805** G3
Mayo Mayo, Bolivia, **853** F3
Mayoko, Congo, **808** B3
Mayong, China, **743** B2
Mayor Island (Tuhua), New Zealand, **718** F3
Mayor Pablo Lagerenza, Paraguay, **853** G5
Mayotte, *French territory*, Indian Ocean, **812** B3
Mayoworth, U.S.A., **829** L5
Mayqayyng, Kazakhstan, **748** B2
Mayraira Point, Philippines, **740** C2
Maysville, Kentucky, U.S.A., **831** M6
Maytiguid Island, Philippines, **740** B4
Mayumba, Gabon, **808** B3
Mayville, North Dakota, U.S.A., **830** E2
Maywood, U.S.A., **830** C5
Maza, Argentina, **856** D5
Mazabuka, Zambia, **809** E6

Mazagão, Brazil, **850** C3
Mazagón, Spain, **776** D4
Mazama, U.S.A., **828** D2
Mazán, Peru, **848** D5
Mazar, China, **748** C5
Mazār-e Sharīf, Afghanistan, **754** A1
Mazara del Vallo, Sicilia, Italy, **779** D7
Mazarredo, Argentina, **858** D3
Mazarrón, Golfo de, *gulf*, Spain, **777** G4
Mazarrón, Spain, **777** G4
Mazaruni, *river*, Guyana, **849** G3
Mazatán, Mexico, **840** C2
Mazatenango, Guatemala, **838** C4
Mazatlán, Mexico, **840** D4
Mazatzal Peak, *mountain peak*, U.S.A., **833** H4
Mažeikiai, Lithuania, **771** L4
Mazha, China, **743** C2
Mazı, Turkey, **781** F7
Mazirbe, Latvia, **771** L4
Mazo Cruz, Peru, **853** E4
Mazocahui, Mexico, **840** C2
Mazomora, Tanzania, **809** G4
Mazong Shan, *mountain peak*, China, **749** H4
Mazunga, Zimbabwe, **811** E3
Mazyr, Belarus, **782** C2
Mbabane, Swaziland, **811** F4
Mbahiakro, Côte d'Ivoire, **804** D3
Mbaïki, Central African Republic, **808** C2
Mbakaou, Lac de, *lake*, Cameroon, **805** G3
Mbaké, Senegal, **804** A2
Mbala, Zambia, **809** F4
Mbalabala, Zimbabwe, **811** E3
Mbalam, Cameroon, **808** B2
Mbale, Uganda, **809** F2
Mbalmayo, Cameroon, **808** B2
Mbalo, Solomon Islands, **727** A1
Mbamba Bay, Tanzania, **809** F5
Mbandaka, Democratic Republic of the Congo, **808** C2
Mbang, Cameroon, **808** B2
Mbanga, Cameroon, **808** A2
M'banza Congo, Angola, **808** B4
Mbarara, Uganda, **809** F3
Mbari, *river*, Central African Republic, **806** B3
Mbata, Central African Republic, **808** C2
Mbati, Zambia, **809** F5
Mbatto, Côte d'Ivoire, **804** D3
Mbatuna, Solomon Islands, **727** A1
Mbé, Cameroon, **805** G3
Mbemburu, *river*, Tanzania, **809** G5
Mbengué, Côte d'Ivoire, **804** C2
Mbeya, *administrative region*, Tanzania, **809** F4
Mbeya, Tanzania, **809** F4
Mbi, *river*, Central African Republic, **806** A4
Mbigou, Gabon, **808** B3
Mbinda, Congo, **808** B3
Mbinga, Tanzania, **809** G5
Mbizi, Zimbabwe, **811** F3
Mboki, Central African Republic, **809** E1
Mbomo, Congo, **808** B2
Mbomou, *prefecture*, Central African Republic, **808** D1
Mbouda, Cameroon, **808** B1
Mbour, Senegal, **804** A2
Mbout, Mauritania, **804** B1
Mbozi, Tanzania, **809** F4
Mbridge, *river*, Angola, **808** B4
Mbuji-Mayi, Democratic Republic of the Congo, **808** D4
Mbulu, Tanzania, **809** G3
Mburuku, Solomon Islands, **727** A1
Mbuyuni, Tanzania, **809** G4
Mbwamaji, Tanzania, **809** G4
Mchinga, Tanzania, **809** G4
Mchinji, Malawi, **809** F5
Mdandu, Tanzania, **809** F4
Mdantsane, South Africa, **811** E5
M'Daourouch, Algeria, **801** H1
Meacham, Canada, **823** S5
Mead, Lake, U.S.A., **832** F3
Meade, U.S.A., **830** C7
Meadow Creek, Canada, **823** L6
Meadow Lake, Canada, **823** Q4
Meadville, U.S.A., **831** N5
Meagaidh, Creag, *mountain peak*, Scotland, U.K., **792** E4
Mealy Mountains, *mountain range*, Canada, **827** M3
Mearim, *river*, Brazil, **850** D5
Measham, England, U.K., **789** F2
Meath, *county*, Ireland, **793** F4
Meaux, France, **775** F2
Mebo, Gunung, *mountain peak*, Indonesia, **735** F3
Mecca *see* Makkah, Saudi Arabia, **803** G4
Mechanicsburg, Ohio, U.S.A., **831** M5
Mechanicsville, Iowa, U.S.A., **830** H5
Mechelen, Belgium, **772** B3
Mecheria, Algeria, **801** F2
Méchiméré, Chad, **805** H2
Mecklenburg-Vorpommern, *state*, Germany, **772** E2
Mecklenburger Bucht, *bay*, Germany, **772** E1
Meconta, Mozambique, **809** G5
Mecuburi, Mozambique, **809** G5
Mecula, Mozambique, **809** G5
Medak, Croatia, **778** E3
Medan, Indonesia, **736** B2
Médanos, Argentina, **858** E1
Medanosa, Punta, *point*, Argentina, **858** E3
Medawachchiya, Sri Lanka, **752** E4
Médéa, Algeria, **801** G1
Medellín, Colombia, **848** C2
Medenine, Tunisia, **802** B2
Mederdra, Mauritania, **804** A1
Medford, Oregon, U.S.A., **828** C5
Medford, Wisconsin, U.S.A., **830** H3
Medgidia, Romania, **780** G3
Media Luna, Argentina, **856** C5
Medias, Romania, **780** E2
Medicine Bow, U.S.A., **829** L6
Medicine Bow Mountains, *mountain range*, U.S.A., **829** L6
Medicine Bow Peak, *mountain peak*, U.S.A., **829** L6
Medicine Hat, Canada, **823** P6
Medicine Lodge, U.S.A., **830** D7
Medina *see* Al Madīnah, Saudi Arabia, **803** G4
Medina, U.S.A., **836** A3
Medina de Rioseco, Spain, **776** E2
Medina del Campo, Spain, **776** E2
Médina Gounas, Senegal, **804** B2
Medina Sidonia, Spain, **776** E4
Medinaceli, Spain, **777** F2
Medininkai, Lithuania, **771** M5
Medinipur, India, **755** F5
Mediterranean Ridge, *underwater feature*, Mediterranean Sea, **867** J3
Mediterranean Sea, Africa/Asia/Europe, **766** E8
Medley, Canada, **823** P4
Mednyy, Ostrov, *island*, Russian Federation, **785** T4
Medora, U.S.A., **830** B2
Médouneu, Gabon, **808** B2
Medveđa, Yugoslavia, **780** C4
Medveditsa, *river*, Russian Federation, **782** F2
Medvezh'i, Ostrova, *islands*, Russian Federation, **785** S2
Medvezh'yegorsk, Russian Federation, **769** S5
Medway, *unitary authority*, England, U.K., **789** H3
Medwin Point, Christmas Island, **720** N8
Medyn', Russian Federation, **783** E5
Medzilaborce, Slovakia, **773** K4
Meekatharra, Australia, **720** D4
Meeker, U.S.A., **833** K1
Meelpaeg Lake, Canada, **827** N5
Meerut, India, **754** D3
Meeteetse, U.S.A., **829** K4
Mega, Ethiopia, **809** G2
Mega, Indonesia, **735** E3
Megali Panagia, Greece, **781** D5
Megalo, Ethiopia, **807** F3
Megalopoli, Greece, **781** D7
Meganisi, *island*, Ionioi Nisoi, Greece, **781** C6
Megara, Greece, **781** D6
Meghalaya, *state*, India, **755** G4
Megisti (Kastellotizon), *island*, Greece, **781** G7
Mehadia, Romania, **780** D3
Mehamn, Norway, **769** N1
Mehar, Pakistan, **754** A4
Meharry, Mount, *mountain peak*, Australia, **720** D3
Mehdia, Algeria, **801** G1
Mehetia, *island*, French Polynesia, **723** G2
Mehr Jān, Iran, **757** G2
Mehrān, Iran, **756** E2
Mehtarlām, Afghanistan, **754** B2
Mei-nung, Taiwan, **742** E4
Meia Ponte, *river*, Brazil, **854** D5
Meicheng, China, **742** D2
Meiganga, Cameroon, **805** G3
Meighen Island, Canada, **821** J1
Meigu, China, **751** G3
Meihekou, China, **747** J4
Meiktila, Myanmar, **741** B3
Meiningen, Germany, **772** E3
Meira, Spain, **776** D1
Meishan, China, **751** G3
Meißen, Germany, **772** F3
Meizhou, China, **742** D3
Meizhou Wan, *bay*, China, **742** D3
Mejicana, *mountain peak*, Argentina, **856** C3
Mejillones, Chile, **856** B2
Mejillones del Sur, Bahía de, *bay*, Chile, **856** B2
Mejit, *island*, Marshall Islands, **725** F3
Mékambo, Gabon, **808** B2
Mek'elē, Ethiopia, **807** E2
Mekerrhane, Sebkha, *salt-pan*, Algeria, **801** G3
Mékhé, Senegal, **804** A1
Mekhtar, Pakistan, **754** B3
Meknès, Morocco, **801** E2
Mekong, *river*, Asia, **733** M8; *see also* Lancang, *river*, China, **751** F3; Mènam Khong, *river*, Laos, **739** E3
Mekongga, Gunung, *mountain peak*, Indonesia, **734** C3
Mekongga, Pegunungan, *mountain range*, Indonesia, **734** C3
Melaka, Malaysia, **736** C2
Melaka, *state*, Malaysia, **736** C2
Melanesia, *islands*, Pacific Ocean, **716** E1
Melanesian Basin, *underwater feature*, Pacific Ocean, **868** E4
Melapalawam, India, **752** D4
Melba, U.S.A., **828** F5
Melbourn, England, U.K., **789** H2
Melbourne, Australia, **721** J6
Melbourne, U.S.A., **835** M5
Melbu, Norway, **768** G2
Melchhām, Nepal, **755** E3
Melchor, Isla, *island*, Chile, **858** B2
Melchor Múzquiz, Mexico, **841** E3
Melchor Ocampo, Mexico, **840** E3
Meldal, Norway, **768** D5
Meldorf, Germany, **772** D1
Meldrum Bay, Canada, **831** M3
Mele, Vanuatu, **727** A2
Meleuz, Russian Federation, **758** F2
Mélèzes, Rivière aux, *river*, Canada, **821** M4
Mélfi, Chad, **806** A2
Melfi, Italy, **779** E5
Melfjorden, Norway, **768** F3
Melfort, Canada, **824** B5
Melgaço, Brazil, **850** C3
Melgar de Fernamental, Spain, **776** E1
Melham, *river*, England, U.K., **789** H2
Melide, Spain, **776** C1
Meligalas, Greece, **781** C7
Melilla, *enclave*, Spain, N. W. Africa, **801** F1
Melimoyu, Monte, *mountain peak*, Chile, **858** C2
Melintang, Danau, *lake*, Indonesia, **737** F3
Melipilla, Chile, **856** B4
Melita, Canada, **824** D7
Melitopol', Ukraine, **782** E3
Melivoia, Greece, **781** E5
Melk, Austria, **773** G4
Melka Guba, Ethiopia, **809** G2
Melksham, England, U.K., **788** E3
Mellakoski, Finland, **769** M3
Mellerud, Sweden, **770** F3
Mellette, U.S.A., **830** D3
Mellilä, Finland, **771** L2
Mellizo Sur, Cerro, *mountain peak*, Chile, **858** C3
Mělník, Czech Republic, **773** G3
Melo, Uruguay, **857** F4
Meloco, Mozambique, **809** G5
Melong, Cameroon, **808** A1
Melrhir, Chott, *lake*, Algeria, **801** H2
Melrose, Scotland, U.K., **792** G5
Melsisi, Vanuatu, **727** A2
Melstone, U.S.A., **829** L3
Meltaus, Finland, **769** M3
Meltham, England, U.K., **791** G4
Melton, Australia, **721** J6
Melton Mowbray, England, U.K., **789** G2
Meltosjärvi, Finland, **769** M3
Meluco, Mozambique, **809** G5
Melun, France, **774** F2
Melūr, India, **752** D4
Melville, Canada, **824** C6
Melville, Cape, Australia, **721** J1
Melville, Lake, Canada, **827** M3
Melville, U.S.A., **830** D2
Melville Bay, Australia, **721** H1
Melville Island, Australia, **720** G1
Melville Island, Canada, **820** H2
Melville Peninsula, Canada, **821** L3
Melvin, Lough, *lake*, Ireland/Northern Ireland, **793** D3
Memala, Indonesia, **737** F3
Memaliaj, Albania, **781** C5
Memba, Baía de, *bay*, Mozambique, **809** H5
Memba, Mozambique, **809** H5
Membalong, Indonesia, **737** D3
Memingen, Germany, **772** E5
Memori, Tanjong, *point*, Indonesia, **735** F3
Mempawah, Indonesia, **737** E2
Memphis, Missouri, U.S.A., **830** G5
Memphis, Tennessee, U.S.A., **834** H2
Memphis, Texas, U.S.A., **834** B2
Mena, U.S.A., **834** E2
Menahga, U.S.A., **830** F2
Menai Bridge, Wales, U.K., **788** C1
Ménaka, Mali, **805** E1
Mènam Khong (Mekong), *river*, Asia, **739** E3
Menanga, Indonesia, **734** D3
Menard, U.S.A., **834** C4
Menard Fracture Zone, *tectonic feature*, Pacific Ocean, **869** K8
Menawashei, Sudan, **806** B2
Mendī, Ethiopia, **806** E3
Mendam, Papua New Guinea, **726** B3
Mendawai, *river*, Indonesia, **737** F3
Mende, France, **775** F4
Mendebo, *mountain range*, Ethiopia, **807** E3
Mendenhall, U.S.A., **834** H4
Méndez, Mexico, **841** F3
Mendi, Papua New Guinea, **726** A4
Mendip Hills, England, U.K., **788** E3
Mendocino, Cape, U.S.A., **832** A1
Mendocino, U.S.A., **832** B2
Mendocino Fracture Zone, *tectonic feature*, Pacific Ocean, **869** H2
Mendol, Pulau, *island*, Indonesia, **736** C2
Mendota, U.S.A., **831** J5
Mendoza, Argentina, **856** C4
Mendoza, *province*, Argentina, **856** C5
Mene de Mauroa, Venezuela, **849** D1
Mene Grande, Venezuela, **848** D2
Menemen, Turkey, **781** F6
Menesjärvi, Finland, **769** N2
Menfi, Sicilia, Italy, **779** D7
Mengcheng, China, **742** D1
Menggala, Indonesia, **736** D4
Menghai, China, **751** G5
Mengla, China, **751** G5
Mengshan, China, **742** B3
Mengyin, China, **742** D1
Mengzhe, China, **751** G5
Mengzi, China, **751** G5
Menheniot, England, U.K., **788** C4
Menindee, Australia, **721** J5
Menindee Lake, Australia, **721** J5
Mennecy, France, **774** F2
Menno, U.S.A., **830** E4
Menominee, *river*, U.S.A., **831** J3
Menomonee Falls, U.S.A., **831** J4
Menongue, Angola, **808** C5
Menorca, *island*, Islas Baleares, Spain, **777** K2
Mentawai, Selat, *strait*, Indonesia, **736** B3
Mentone, U.S.A., **833** M6
Mentor, U.S.A., **831** N5
Menyapa, Gunung, *mountain peak*, Indonesia, **737** G2
Menyapa, *river*, Indonesia, **737** G2
Menyuan, China, **749** J5
Menza, *river*, Russian Federation, **746** E2
Menza, Russian Federation, **746** E2
Menzel Temime, Tunisia, **779** C7
Menzies, Australia, **720** E4
Menzies, Mount, *mountain peak*, Antarctica, **862** F5
Meoqui, Mexico, **840** D2
Meponda, Mozambique, **809** F5
Meppel, Netherlands, **772** C2
Meppen, Germany, **772** C2
Mequinenza, Embalse de, *reservoir*, Spain, **777** G2
Merak, Indonesia, **736** D4
Merano, Italy, **778** C2
Meratus, Pegunungan, *mountain range*, Indonesia, **737** F3

Mordoviya, Respublika, *republic*, Russian Federation, **758** C2
More, Ben, *mountain peak*, Scotland, U.K., **792** C4
More Assynt, Ben, Scotland, U.K., **792** E2
Møre og Romsdal, *county*, Norway, **770** C1
Moreau, *river*, U.S.A., **830** B3
Morebattle, Scotland, U.K., **792** G5
Morecambe, England, U.K., **790** F3
Morecambe Bay, England, U.K., **790** E3
Moree, Australia, **721** K4
Morehead, Papua New Guinea, **726** A5
Morehead, U.S.A., **831** M6
Morehead City, U.S.A., **836** B7
Morelia, Mexico, **841** E5
Morella, Spain, **777** G2
Morelos, *state*, Mexico, **841** F5
Morena, India, **754** D4
Morena, Sierra, *mountain range*, Spain, **776** D3
Moreni, Romania, **780** E3
Morerú, *river*, Brazil, **853** G3
Moresby Island, Canada, **822** C5
Moreton-in-Marsh, England, U.K., **789** F3
Moreton Island, Australia, **721** L4
Moretonhampstead, England, U.K., **788** D4
Moretta, Italy, **778** A3
Moreuil, France, **789** K5
Morgan City, U.S.A., **834** G5
Morgan Hill, U.S.A., **832** C3
Morgan Island, Heard and McDonald Islands, **720** S12
Morganton, U.S.A., **835** L2
Morges, Switzerland, **775** H3
Morghāb, *river*, Afghanistan, **754** A2
Mori, Japan, **745** H2
Moriah, Tobago, Trinidad and Tobago, **859** B4
Moriani-Plage, Corse, France, **779** B4
Moribaya, Guinea, **804** C3
Moricetown, Canada, **822** F4
Morichal, Colombia, **849** D3
Moriki, Nigeria, **805** F2
Morioka, Japan, **745** H3
Morjärv, Sweden, **769** L3
Morlaix, France, **774** C2
Morley, Canada, **823** M6
Morley, England, U.K., **791** G4
Morningside, Canada, **823** N5
Mornington, Isla, *island*, Chile, **858** B3
Mornington Island, Australia, **721** H2
Moro, Pakistan, **754** A4
Moro, U.S.A., **828** D4
Moro Gulf, Philippines, **740** C5
Morobe, Papua New Guinea, **726** B4
Morobe, *province*, Papua New Guinea, **726** B4
Morocco, *country*, Africa, **796** E4
Morocco, U.S.A., **831** K5
Morococha, Peru, **852** C3
Morogoro, *administrative region*, Tanzania, **809** G4
Morogoro, Tanzania, **809** G4
Morokweng, South Africa, **810** D4
Moroleón, Mexico, **841** E4
Morombe, Madagascar, **812** A5
Morón, Cuba, **839** F2
Mörön, Hentiy, Mongolia, **746** E3
Mörön, Hövsgöl, Mongolia, **749** J2
Morón de la Frontera, Spain, **776** E4
Morona, Ecuador, **848** C5
Morondava, Madagascar, **812** A5
Morondo, Côte d'Ivoire, **804** C3
Moroni, Comoros, **812** A3
Morotai, Pulau, *island*, Indonesia, **735** E2
Moroto, *mountain peak*, Uganda, **809** F2
Moroto, Uganda, **809** F2
Morozovsk, Russian Federation, **782** F3
Morpará, Brazil, **855** E3
Morpeth, England, U.K., **791** G2
Morphou, Cyprus, **761** B2
Morphou Bay, Cyprus, **761** B2
Morrilton, U.S.A., **834** F2
Morrin, Canada, **823** N6
Morrinhos, Brazil, **854** D4
Morrinsville, New Zealand, **718** E3
Morris, Illinois, U.S.A., **831** J5
Morris, Minnesota, U.S.A., **830** F3
Morris, Pennsylvania, U.S.A., **836** B4
Morristown, New Jersey, U.S.A., **836** C4
Morristown, Tennessee, U.S.A., **835** L1
Morro, Sierra del, *mountain peak*, Argentina, **856** D4
Morro Bay, U.S.A., **832** C4
Morro d'Anta, Brazil, **855** F5
Morro do Chapéu, Brazil, **855** F3
Morro Jable, Islas Canarias, Spain, **813** B4
Morrón, *mountain peak*, Spain, **777** F4
Morrosquillo, Golfo de, *gulf*, Colombia, **848** C2
Morrumbala, Mozambique, **811** G2
Morrumbene, Mozambique, **811** G3
Morshansk, Russian Federation, **782** F2
Morshyn, Ukraine, **773** L4
Morson, Canada, **824** G7
Mørsvik, Norway, **768** G3
Mortagne-sur-sèvre, France, **774** D3
Mortara, Italy, **778** B3
Morte Bay, England, U.K., **788** C3
Morteau, France, **775** H3
Mortehoe, England, U.K., **788** C3
Morteros, Argentina, **856** D4
Mortes, Rio das, *river*, Brazil, **854** C3
Mortimers, Bahamas, **839** G2
Mortlock Islands, Micronesia, **724** D4
Morton, England, U.K., **789** G2
Morton, Minnesota, U.S.A., **830** F3
Morton, Texas, U.S.A., **833** M5
Morton, Washington, U.S.A., **828** C3
Mortyq, Kazakhstan, **758** F2
Moruga, Trinidad, Trinidad and Tobago, **859** C4
Morungole, *mountain peak*, Uganda, **809** F2
Morvan, *region*, France, **775** F3
Morvern, *region*, Scotland, U.K., **792** D4
Morville, England, U.K., **788** E2
Morwell, Australia, **721** K6
Mor'ye, Russian Federation, **783** C2
Mosal'sk, Russian Federation, **783** E5
Mosbach, Germany, **772** D4
Mosborough, England, U.K., **791** G4
Mosby, U.S.A., **829** L3
Moscow *see* Moskva, Russian Federation, **783** F4
Moscow, U.S.A., **828** F3
Moscow University Ice Shelf, Antarctica, **862** F7
Mosel, *river*, Germany, **772** C4
Moselle, *river*, France, **775** H2
Moses Lake, *lake*, U.S.A., **828** E3
Moses Lake, U.S.A., **828** E3
Mosetse, Botswana, **811** E3
Moshchnyy, Ostrov, *island*, Russian Federation, **771** N2
Moshi, Tanzania, **809** G3
Mosina, Poland, **773** H2
Mosjøen, Norway, **768** F4
Moskenesøya, *island*, Norway, **768** E3
Moskosel, Sweden, **768** J4
Moskovskaya Oblast', *province*, Russian Federation, **783** F5
Moskva, *river*, Russian Federation, **783** F5
Moskva (Moscow), Russian Federation, **783** F4
Mosonmagyaróvár, Hungary, **773** H5
Mosqueiro, Brazil, **850** D3
Mosquera, Colombia, **848** B3
Mosquero, U.S.A., **833** M4
Mosquito Bay, Canada, **825** Q1
Mosquitos, Golfo de los, *gulf*, Panama, **839** E5
Moss, Norway, **770** E3
Mossat, Scotland, U.K., **792** G3
Mossburn, New Zealand, **719** B7
Mossel Bay, South Africa, **810** D5
Mossendjo, Congo, **808** B3
Mossman, Australia, **721** K2
Mossoró, Brazil, **851** G4
Mossuril, Mozambique, **809** H5
Mostaganem, Algeria, **801** G1
Mostar, Bosnia and Herzegovina, **778** F4
Mostardas, Brazil, **857** G4
Mostove, Ukraine, **780** H2
Mostys'ka, Ukraine, **773** L4
Mosul *see* Al Mawşil, Iraq, **803** H1
Mosŭlp'o, South Korea, **744** D4
Møsvatn, *lake*, Norway, **770** C3
Mot'a, Ethiopia, **807** E2
Mota del Cuervo, Spain, **777** F3
Motala, Sweden, **770** G3
Moth, India, **754** D4
Motherwell, Scotland, U.K., **792** F5
Motilla del Palancar, Spain, **777** G3
Motiti Island, New Zealand, **718** F3
Motokwe, Botswana, **810** D3
Motovskiy Zaliv, *bay*, Russian Federation, **769** R2
Motril, Spain, **777** F4
Motru, Romania, **780** D3
Mott, U.S.A., **830** B2
Mottola, Italy, **779** F5
Motu, *river*, New Zealand, **718** F4
Motu Iti, *island*, Isla de Pascua (Easter Island), Chile, **859** B2
Motu Nui, *island*, Isla de Pascua (Easter Island), Chile, **859** B2
Motu One, *island*, French Polynesia, **723** F2
Motu Tautara, *island*, Isla de Pascua (Easter Island), Chile, **859** B2
Motueka, New Zealand, **719** D5
Motunau Beach, New Zealand, **719** D6
Motunui, New Zealand, **718** E4
Motupena Point, Papua New Guinea, **726** E2
Mou, New Caledonia, **727** A3
Mouali Gbangba, Congo, **808** C2
Mouanko, Cameroon, **808** A2
Mouchalagane, *river*, Canada, **826** G3
Moudjéria, Mauritania, **800** D5
Mouhijärvi, Finland, **771** L2
Mouila, Gabon, **808** B3
Moulins, France, **775** F3
Moulmein, Myanmar, **738** C2
Moultrie, Lake, U.S.A., **835** M3
Moultrie, U.S.A., **835** L4
Mound City, Illinois, U.S.A., **831** J7
Mound City, South Dakota, U.S.A., **830** C3
Moundou, Chad, **805** H3
Moundsville, U.S.A., **831** N6
Moŭng Roessei, Cambodia, **739** D3
Mount Airy, U.S.A., **831** N7
Mount Ayr, U.S.A., **830** F5
Mount Barker, Australia, **720** D5
Mount Bellew, Ireland, **793** D4
Mount Caramel Junction, U.S.A., **832** G3
Mount Carroll, U.S.A., **830** J4
Mount Cook, New Zealand, **719** C6
Mount Currie, Canada, **822** H6
Mount Darwin, Zimbabwe, **811** F2
Mount Dora, U.S.A., **833** M3
Mount Forest, Canada, **831** N4
Mount Gambier, Australia, **721** J6
Mount Hagen, Papua New Guinea, **726** B4
Mount Horeb, U.S.A., **830** J4
Mount Hutt, New Zealand, **719** C6
Mount Ida, U.S.A., **834** F2
Mount Isa, Australia, **720** H3
Mount Magnet, Australia, **720** D4
Mount Pearl, Canada, **827** Q6
Mount Pleasant, Iowa, U.S.A., **830** H5
Mount Pleasant, Pennsylvania, U.S.A., **831** P5
Mount Pleasant, South Carolina, U.S.A., **835** N3
Mount Pleasant, Texas, U.S.A., **834** E3
Mount Pleasant, Utah, U.S.A., **833** H2
Mount St George, Tobago, Trinidad and Tobago, **859** B4
Mount Shasta, U.S.A., **828** C6
Mount Sterling, U.S.A., **831** M6
Mount Union, U.S.A., **831** Q5
Mount Vernon, Alabama, U.S.A., **835** H4
Mount Vernon, Illinois, U.S.A., **831** J6
Mount Vernon, Ohio, U.S.A., **831** M5
Mount Vernon, Oregon, U.S.A., **828** E4
Mountain City, U.S.A., **828** G6
Mountain Home, Arkansas, U.S.A., **834** F1
Mountain Home, Idaho, U.S.A., **828** G5
Mountain Lake, U.S.A., **830** F4
Mountain View, Hawaiian Islands, U.S.A., **832** R10
Mountain View, U.S.A., **833** H1
Mountmellick, Ireland, **793** E4
Mountrath, Ireland, **793** E4
Mount's Bay, England, U.K., **788** B4
Mountshannon, Ireland, **793** D5
Mountsorrel, England, U.K., **789** F2
Moura, Australia, **721** K3
Moura, Brazil, **849** G4
Moura, Chad, **806** B2
Moura, Portugal, **776** D3
Mourão, Portugal, **776** D3
Mouray, Chad, **806** B2
Mourdi, Dépression du, *depression*, Chad, **802** D5
Mourdiah, Mali, **804** C2
Mourea, New Zealand, **718** F4
Mourne Mountains, *mountain range*, Northern Ireland, U.K., **793** F3
Mousehole, England, U.K., **788** B4
Mousgougou, Chad, **805** H2
Moussoro, Chad, **805** H2
Moutamba, Congo, **805** G5
Moûtiers, France, **775** H4
Moutsamoudou, Comoros, **812** A3
Mouy, France, **789** K5
Mouydir, Monts du, *mountain range*, Algeria, **801** G4
Mouzaki, Greece, **781** C6
Mouzarak, Chad, **805** H2
Moville, Ireland, **793** E2
Moxico, *province*, Angola, **808** D5
Moxotó, *river*, Brazil, **855** F2
Moyalē, Ethiopia, **809** G2
Moyamba, Sierra Leone, **804** B3
Moyen Atlas, *mountain range*, Morocco, **801** E2
Moyen Chari, Chad, **806** A3
Moyen-Ogooué, *province*, Gabon, **808** B3
Moyenne-Guinée, *administrative region*, Guinea, **804** B2
Moyie, Canada, **823** M7
Moyie Springs, U.S.A., **828** F2
Moyle, *district*, Northern Ireland, U.K., **793** F2
Moylough, Ireland, **793** D4
Moyo, Uganda, **809** F2
Moyobamba, Peru, **852** C2
Møysalen, *mountain peak*, Norway, **768** G2
Moyto, Chad, **805** H2
Moyu, China, **748** C5
Moyvally, Ireland, **793** F4
Moyynqum, *desert*, Kazakhstan, **759** H4
Moyynty, Kazakhstan, **748** B3
Mozăceni, Romania, **780** E3
Mozambique, *country*, Africa, **797** J9
Mozambique Channel, East Africa, **811** G3
Mozambique Fracture Zone, *tectonic feature*, Indian Ocean, **866** B7
Mozambique Plateau, *underwater feature*, Indian Ocean, **866** B7
Mozhaysk, Russian Federation, **783** F5
Mozhga, Russian Federation, **758** E1
Mpala, Democratic Republic of the Congo, **809** E4
Mpanda, Tanzania, **809** F4
Mpandamatenga, Zimbabwe, **811** E2
Mpé, Congo, **808** B3
Mpen, India, **755** J4
Mpen, Myanmar, **741** C2
Mpessoba, Mali, **804** C2
Mpigi, Uganda, **809** F2
Mpika, Zambia, **809** F5
Mporokoso, Zambia, **809** F4
Mpouya, Congo, **808** C3
Mpulungu, Zambia, **809** F4
Mpumalanga, *province*, South Africa, **811** E4
Mpwapwa, Tanzania, **809** G4
Mrągowo, Poland, **773** K2
Mrakovo, Russian Federation, **758** F2
Mrežičko, Macedonia, **781** C5
Mrkonjić Grad, Bosnia and Herzegovina, **778** F3
Msata, Tanzania, **809** G4
Mshinskaya, Russian Federation, **783** B3
M'Sila, Algeria, **801** G1
Msta, *river*, Russian Federation, **783** D3
Mstsislaw, Belarus, **783** C5
Msuna, Zimbabwe, **811** E2
Mtama, Tanzania, **809** G5
Mtsensk, Russian Federation, **783** F6
Mtwara, *administrative region*, Tanzania, **809** G5
Mtwara, Tanzania, **809** H5
Mú, *mountain peak*, Portugal, **776** C4
Mu, *river*, Myanmar, **741** B3
Mu'a, Tongatapu Group, Tonga, **727** B4

N

Naples, Idaho, U.S.A., **828** F2
Naples *see* Napoli, Italy, **779** E5
Napo, China, **751** H5
Napo, *river*, Ecuador/Peru, **848** C4
Napoleon, North Dakota, U.S.A., **830** D2
Napoleon, Ohio, U.S.A., **831** L5
Napoli, Golfo di, *gulf*, Italy, **779** E5
Napoli (Naples), Italy, **779** E5
Napuka, *island*, French Polynesia, **723** G2
Nara, Japan, **745** F4
Nara, Mali, **804** C1
Narach, Belarus, **771** N5
Narach, Vozyera, *lake*, Belarus, **771** N5
Naracoorte, Australia, **721** J6
Nārāinpur, India, **755** E6
Naran Bulag, China, **746** F3
Naranjal, Ecuador, **848** B5
Naranjo, Mexico, **840** C3
Naranjos, Mexico, **841** F4
Narasannapeta, India, **753** F2
Narasapur, India, **753** E2
Narasun, Russian Federation, **746** F2
Narathiwat, Thailand, **738** D5
Narberth, Wales, U.K., **788** C3
Narbonne, France, **775** F5
Narborough, England, U.K., **789** H2
Narbuvollen, Norway, **770** E1
Narcea, *river*, Spain, **776** D1
Naré, Argentina, **856** E4
Nares Land, *island*, Greenland, **821** P1
Nares Plain, *underwater feature*, Atlantic Ocean, **867** C4
Nares Strait, Canada/Greenland, **821** M2
Narew, *river*, Poland, **773** L2
Nargund, India, **752** C3
Narhamcha, Sebkha, *salt-pan*, Mauritania, **800** C5
Nāri, *river*, Pakistan, **754** B3
Narib, Namibia, **810** C3
Narimanov, Russian Federation, **758** D3
Narin, *river*, China, **749** G5
Nariz, Pico, *mountain peak*, Chile, **858** C4
Nārkanda, India, **754** D3
Narkatiāganj, India, **755** F4
Narmada, *river*, India, **754** C5
Narni, Italy, **779** D4
Naro-Fominsk, Russian Federation, **783** F5
Narok, Kenya, **809** G3
Narooma, Australia, **721** L6
Närpes, Finland, **771** K1
Narrabri, Australia, **721** K5
Narrandera, Australia, **721** K5
Narrogin, Australia, **720** D5
Narromine, Australia, **721** K5
Narrows, U.S.A., **831** N7
Narsarsuaq, Greenland, **821** Q3
Narsimhapur, India, **754** D5
Narsinghdi, Bangladesh, **750** D5
Narsinghgarh, India, **754** D5
Nart, China, **746** F4
Nart, Mongolia, **746** D2
Narva, Estonia, **771** P3
Narva, Russian Federation, **759** N1
Narva Laht, *bay*, Estonia/Russian Federation, **771** N3
Narvacan, Philippines, **740** C2
Narvik, Norway, **768** H2
Nar'yan Mar, Russian Federation, **784** G3
Naryn, Kyrgyzstan, **759** K4
Naryn, *river*, Kyrgyzstan, **748** B4
Naryn, Russian Federation, **749** G2
Naryn Qum, *desert*, Kazakhstan, **758** D3
Narynqol, Kazakhstan, **759** L4
Näsåker, Sweden, **768** H5
Nasau, Fiji, **727** A4
Năsăud, Romania, **780** E2
Nasawa, Vanuatu, **727** A2
Naschitti, U.S.A., **833** J3
Nashoba, U.S.A., **834** E2
Nashua, U.S.A., **836** E3
Nashville, Illinois, U.S.A., **831** J6
Nashville, Tennessee, U.S.A., **835** J1
Nashwauk, U.S.A., **830** G2
Našice, Croatia, **778** G3
Nāsik, India, **754** C5
Nāşir, Sudan, **806** D3
Naskaupi, *river*, Canada, **827** K2
Nasondoye, Democratic Republic of the Congo, **808** E5
Nasorolevu, *mountain peak*, Fiji, **727** A4
Nāsriganj, India, **755** F4
Nass, *river*, Canada, **822** E4
Nassarawa, Nigeria, **805** F3
Nassau, Bahamas, **838** F1
Nassau, Bahía, *bay*, Chile, **858** D5
Nassau, *island*, Cook Islands, **725** H6
Nasser, Lake, Egypt, **803** F4
Nässjö, Sweden, **770** G4
Nastapoca, *river*, Canada, **825** S3
Nastapoka Islands, Canada, **825** R3
Nasugbu, Philippines, **740** C3
Nasva, Russian Federation, **783** C4
Nata, Botswana, **811** E3
Nata, Tanzania, **809** F3
Natagaima, Colombia, **848** C3
Natal, Brazil, **851** G4
Natal, Indonesia, **736** B2
Natal Basin, *underwater feature*, Indian Ocean, **866** B6
Natalia, U.S.A., **834** C5
Naţanz, Iran, **756** F2
Natashquan, Canada, **827** K4
Natashquan, *river*, Canada, **827** L4
Natchez, U.S.A., **834** G4
Natchitoches, U.S.A., **834** F4
Natewa Bay, Fiji, **727** A4
National Capital District, *province*, Papua New Guinea, **726** B5
Natitingou, Benin, **804** E2
Natividade, Brazil, **854** D3
Natoma, U.S.A., **830** D6
Nátora, Mexico, **840** C2
Natron, Lake, Tanzania, **809** G3
Nattam, India, **752** D4
Nattaung, *mountain peak*, Myanmar, **741** C4
Nattavaara, Sweden, **768** K3
Natuna Besar, Pulau, *island*, Indonesia, **737** D1
Naucelle, France, **774** F4
Nauchas, Namibia, **810** C3
Nauen, Germany, **772** F2
Naujan, Lake, Philippines, **740** C3
Naulila, Angola, **808** B6
Naumburg, Germany, **772** E3
Nā'ūr, Jordan, **761** C4
Naurskaya, Russian Federation, **758** D4
Nauru, *country*, Pacific Ocean, **715** F2
Nauru, *island*, Pacific Ocean, **724** E5
Nāushahra, India, **754** C2
Naushahro Firoz, Pakistan, **754** B4
Naustdal, Norway, **770** B2
Nauta, Peru, **848** D5
Nautla, Mexico, **841** F4
Nautsi, Russian Federation, **769** P2
Navahermosa, Spain, **776** E3
Navahrudak, Belarus, **773** M2
Navajo, U.S.A., **833** J4
Navajo Reservoir, U.S.A., **833** K3
Naval, Philippines, **740** D4
Navalmoral de la Mata, Spain, **776** E3
Navalvillar de Pela, Spain, **776** E3
Navan, Ireland, **793** F4
Navapolatsk, Belarus, **783** B5
Navarin, Mys, *cape*, Russian Federation, **820** A3
Navarino, Isla, *island*, Chile, **858** D5
Navarra, *autonomous community*, Spain, **777** G1
Navasota, *river*, U.S.A., **834** D4
Navassa Island, *U.S. territory*, Caribbean Sea, **839** G3
Naver, Loch, *lake*, Scotland, U.K., **792** E2
Naver, *river*, Scotland, U.K., **792** E2
Navesti, *river*, Estonia, **771** M3
Navia, *river*, Spain, **776** D1
Navia, Spain, **776** D1
Navidad, Chile, **856** B4
Naviti, *island*, Fiji, **727** A4
Năvodari, Romania, **780** G3
Navojoa, Mexico, **840** C3
Navsāri, India, **754** C5
Navua, Fiji, **727** A4
Nawá, Syria, **761** D3
Nawabganj, Bangladesh, **750** D4
Nawābshāh, Pakistan, **754** B4
Nawāda, India, **755** F4
Nāwah, Afghanistan, **754** A2
Nawalgarh, India, **754** C4
Nawāpāra, India, **755** E5
Nawoiy, Uzbekistan, **758** H4
Naws, Ra's, *cape*, Oman, **757** G5
Naxçivan, *autonomous state*, Azerbaijan, **758** D5
Naxçıvan, Azerbaijan, **758** D5
Naxos, *island*, Kyklades, Greece, **781** E7
Naxos, Kyklades, Greece, **781** E7
Nāy Band, E. Iran, **757** G2
Nāy Band, Kūh-e, *mountain peak*, Iran, **757** G2
Nāy Band, S. Iran, **756** F3
Naya, Colombia, **848** C3
Naya Chor, Pakistan, **754** B4
Nayar, Mexico, **840** D4
Nayarit, *state*, Mexico, **840** D4
Nayau, *island*, Fiji, **727** A4
Nayoro, Japan, **745** H1
Nāyudupeta, India, **752** D3
Nazaré, Bahia, Brazil, **855** F3
Nazaré, Pará, Brazil, **850** C5
Nazaré, Portugal, **776** C3
Nazareth *see* Naẕerat, Israel, **761** C3
Nazarovo, Russian Federation, **759** N1
Nazca, Peru, **852** C4
Nazca Ridge, *underwater feature*, Pacific Ocean, **869** N6
Naze, The, *point*, England, U.K., **789** J3
Naẕerat (Nazareth), Israel, **761** C3
Nazilli, Turkey, **781** G7
Naziya, Russian Federation, **783** C3
Nazko, Canada, **822** H5
Nazko, *river*, Canada, **822** H5
Nazran', Russian Federation, **758** D4
Nazrēt, Ethiopia, **807** E3
Nazyvayevsk, Russian Federation, **759** J1
Nchelenge, Zambia, **809** E4
Ncojane, Botswana, **810** D3
Ncue, Equatorial Guinea, **808** B2
N'dalatando, Angola, **808** B4
Ndali, Benin, **805** E3
Ndélé, Central African Republic, **806** B3
Ndélélé, Cameroon, **808** B2
Ndendé, Gabon, **808** B3
Ndjamena, Chad, **805** H2
Ndji, *river*, Central African Republic, **806** B3
Ndjolé, Gabon, **808** B3
Ndjounou, Gabon, **808** B3
Ndola, Zambia, **809** E5
Nduye, Democratic Republic of the Congo, **809** E2
Nea Alikarnassos, Kriti, Greece, **781** E8
Nea Anchialos, Greece, **781** D6
Nea Artaki, Greece, **781** D6
Nea Makri, Greece, **781** D6
Nea Moudania, Greece, **781** D5
Nea Zichni, Greece, **781** D5
Neagh, Lough, *lake*, Northern Ireland, U.K., **793** F3
Neah Bay, U.S.A., **828** B2
Neale, Lake, Australia, **720** G3
Neapoli, Kriti, Greece, **781** E8
Neapoli, Peloponnisos, Greece, **781** D7
Near Islands, U.S.A., **785** U4
Neath, *river*, Wales, U.K., **788** D3
Neath, Wales, U.K., **788** D3
Neath Port Talbot, *unitary authority*, Wales, U.K., **788** D3
Nebbi, Uganda, **809** F2
Nebbou, Burkina Faso, **804** D2
Nebe, Indonesia, **734** C5
Nebitdag, Turkmenistan, **758** E5
Neblina, Pico da, *mountain peak*, Brazil, **849** E4
Nebolchi, Russian Federation, **783** D3
Nebraska, *state*, U.S.A., **830** D5
Nebraska City, U.S.A., **830** F5
Nebrodi, Monti, *mountain range*, Sicilia, Italy, **779** E7
Nechi, *river*, Colombia, **848** C2
Necker, *island*, Hawaiian Islands, U.S.A., **725** H2
Necochea, Argentina, **857** E6
Necton, England, U.K., **789** H2
Nedas, *river*, Greece, **781** C7
Nédéley, Chad, **806** A1
Nêdong, China, **750** D3
Nedstrand, Norway, **770** B3
Nedumangād, India, **752** D4
Needham Market, England, U.K., **789** J2
Needles, Canada, **823** K7
Needles, The, *point*, England, U.K., **789** F4
Needles, U.S.A., **832** F4
Neegro, Qooriga, *bay*, Somalia, **807** G3
Neepawa, Canada, **824** E6
Neftçala, Azerbaijan, **758** D5
Neftekamsk, Russian Federation, **758** E1
Nefyn, Wales, U.K., **788** C2
Negēlē, Ethiopia, **807** E3
Negage, Angola, **808** C4
Négala, Mali, **804** C2
Negara, Indonesia, **737** F5
Negeri Sembilan, *state*, Malaysia, **736** C2
Negomane, Mozambique, **809** G5
Negombo, Sri Lanka, **752** D5
Negotin, Yugoslavia, **780** D3
Negra, Cordillera, *mountain range*, Peru, **852** B2
Negra, Punta, *point*, Peru, **852** B1
Negreşti, Romania, **780** F2
Negreşti-Oaş, Romania, **780** D2
Negreni, Romania, **780** E3
Negritos, Peru, **852** B1
Negro, *river*, Amazonas, Brazil, **849** G5
Negro, *river*, Bolivia, **853** F4
Negro, *river*, Choco, Argentina, **857** E3
Negro, *river*, Mato Grosso do Sul, Brazil, **854** B5
Negro, *river*, Paraguay, **857** E2
Negro, *river*, Rio Negro, Argentina, **858** D1
Negro, *river*, Uruguay, **857** F4
Negros, *island*, Philippines, **740** C4
Negru Vodă, Romania, **780** G4
Neguac, Canada, **826** J6
Nehbandān, Iran, **757** H2
Nehe, China, **747** J2
Nehoiu, Romania, **780** F3
Nehone, Angola, **808** C6
Nei Mongol Gaoyuan, *plateau*, China, **749** J4
Nei Mongol Zizhiqu (Inner Mongolia), *autonomous region*, China, **746** F4
Neiafu, Vava'u Group, Tonga, **727** B3
Neiba, Dominican Republic, **839** H3
Neiden, Norway, **769** P2
Neidersachsen, *state*, Germany, **772** D2
Neiges, Piton des, *mountain peak*, Réunion, **813** A1
Neihart, U.S.A., **829** J3
Neijiang, China, **751** H3
Neilingding Dao, *island*, China, **743** B4
Neiße, *river*, Germany, **773** G3
Neiva, Colombia, **848** C3
Neixiang, China, **742** B1
Nejanilini Lake, Canada, **824** F2
Nek'emtē, Ethiopia, **807** E3
Nekoma, U.S.A., **830** D1
Neksø, Denmark, **770** G5
Nelidovo, Russian Federation, **783** D4
Neligh, U.S.A., **830** D4
Nellore, India, **752** E3
Nelson, Canada, **823** L7
Nelson, Cape, Papua New Guinea, **726** C5
Nelson, England, U.K., **790** F4
Nelson, Estrecho, *strait*, Chile, **858** B4
Nelson, New Zealand, **719** D5
Nelson, *river*, Canada, **824** G3
Nelson House, Canada, **824** E4
Nelspruit, South Africa, **811** F4
Nelyan Point, Philippines, **740** B4
Néma, Mauritania, **804** C1
Neman, Russian Federation, **771** L5
Nembe, Nigeria, **805** F4
Nembrala, Indonesia, **734** C5
Nemea, Greece, **781** D7
Nemegos, Canada, **831** M2
Nemenčinė, Lithuania, **771** M5
Nemor, *river*, China, **747** J2
Nemunas, *river*, Lithuania, **771** L5
Nemuro, Japan, **745** J2
Nemyriv, Ukraine, **773** L3
Nen, *river*, China, **747** J2
Nenagh, Ireland, **793** D5
Nendo, *island*, Solomon Islands, **724** E6
Nene, *river*, England, U.K., **789** G2
Nenjiang, China, **747** J2
Nenthead, England, U.K., **790** F3
Neo Karlovasi, Dodekanisos, Greece, **781** F7
Neola, U.S.A., **833** H1
Neos Marmaras, Greece, **781** D5
Neosho, *river*, U.S.A., **830** F7
Neosho, U.S.A., **830** F7
Nepālganj, Nepal, **755** E3
Nepal, *country*, Asia, **730** K7
Nepean Island, Norfolk Island, **721** T13
Nepeña, Peru, **852** B2
Nephi, U.S.A., **833** H2
Nephin, *mountain peak*, Ireland, **793** C3
Nephin Beg Range, *mountain range*, Ireland, **793** C3
Nepisiguit, *river*, Canada, **826** H6
Nepomuk, Czech Republic, **772** F4
Nérac, France, **774** E4
Nerang, Australia, **721** L4

Nerchinsk, Russian Federation, **746** G1
Nereta, Latvia, **771** M4
Nereto, Italy, **778** D4
Neriquinha, Angola, **808** D6
Neris, *river*, Lithuania, **771** M5
Nerja, Spain, **777** F4
Nerl', *river*, Russian Federation, **783** F4
Nerópolis, Brazil, **854** D4
Neryungri, Russian Federation, **785** P4
Nesbyen, Norway, **770** D2
Nesebŭr, Bulgaria, **780** F4
Nesflaten, Norway, **770** C3
Nesjøen, *lake*, Norway, **768** E5
Nesna, Norway, **768** F3
Ness, Loch, *lake*, Scotland, U.K., **792** E3
Ness City, U.S.A., **830** D6
Nesseby, Norway, **769** P1
Nesterov, Russian Federation, **771** L5
Netanya, Israel, **761** C3
Netherlands, *country*, Europe, **764** E5
Netherlands Antilles, *Netherlands autonomous region*, Caribbean Sea, **844** F2
Neto, *river*, Italy, **779** F6
Nettilling Lake, Canada, **821** M3
Neubrandenburg, Germany, **772** F2
Neubukow, Germany, **772** E1
Neuchâtel, Lac de, *lake*, Switzerland, **775** H3
Neuchâtel, Switzerland, **775** H3
Neuenhagen bei Berlin, Germany, **773** F2
Neufchâteau, France, **775** G2
Neufchâtel-en-Bray, France, **774** E2
Neumünster, Germany, **772** D1
Neung-sur-Beuvron, France, **774** E3
Neunkirchen, Germany, **772** C4
Neuquén, Argentina, **858** D1
Neuquén, *province*, Argentina, **858** C1
Neuquén, *river*, Argentina, **856** C5
Neuruppin, Germany, **772** F2
Neusiedler See, *lake*, Austria, **773** H5
Neuss, Germany, **772** C3
Neustadt am Rübenberge, Germany, **772** D2
Neustadt in Holstein, Germany, **772** E1
Neustrelitz, Germany, **772** F2
Neuville-lès-Dieppe, France, **789** J5
Neuwied, Germany, **772** C3
Nevşehir, Turkey, **803** F1
Neva, *river*, Russian Federation, **783** C3
Nevada, Cerro, *mountain peak*, Argentina, **856** C5
Nevada, Sierra, *mountain peak*, Argentina, **856** C3
Nevada, Sierra, *mountain range*, Spain, **777** F4
Nevada, Sierra, *mountain range*, U.S.A., **832** C2
Nevada, *state*, U.S.A., **832** E2
Nevada, U.S.A., **830** F7
Nevada del Cocuy, Sierra, *mountain peak*, Colombia, **848** D2
Nevado, Cerro, *mountain peak*, Colombia, **848** C3
Nevado, Sierra del, *mountain range*, Argentina, **856** C5
Neve, Serra da, *mountain range*, Angola, **808** B5
Nevel', Russian Federation, **783** B4
Nevers, France, **775** F3
Nevesinje, Bosnia and Herzegovina, **778** G4
Nevinnomyssk, Russian Federation, **758** C4
Nevis, Ben, *mountain peak*, Scotland, U.K., **792** E4
Nev'yansk, Russian Federation, **758** G1
New Albany, Indiana, U.S.A., **831** L6
New Albany, Mississippi, U.S.A., **835** H2
New Albany, Pennsylvania, U.S.A., **836** B4
New Alresford, England, U.K., **789** F3
New Amsterdam, Guyana, **849** H2
New Bedford, U.S.A., **836** E4
New Berlin, U.S.A., **836** C3
New Bern, U.S.A., **836** B7
New Boston, U.S.A., **834** E3
New Braunfels, U.S.A., **834** C5
New Britain, *island*, Papua New Guinea, **726** C4
New Britain, U.S.A., **836** D4
New Brunswick, *province*, Canada, **826** H6
New Bussa, Nigeria, **805** E3
New Caledonia, *French territory*, Pacific Ocean, **714** E3
New Caledonia Basin, *underwater feature*, Pacific Ocean, **868** E6
New Castle, Kentucky, U.S.A., **831** L6
New Castle, Pennsylvania, U.S.A., **831** N5
New Cumnock, Scotland, U.K., **792** E5
New Dayton, Canada, **823** N7
New Deer, Scotland, U.K., **792** G3
New Delhi, India, **754** D3
New Ellenton, U.S.A., **835** M3
New England, U.S.A., **830** B2
New Galloway, Scotland, U.K., **792** E5
New Georgia, *island*, Solomon Islands, **727** A1
New Georgia Group, *islands*, Solomon Islands, **727** A1
New Georgia Sound (The Slot), *channel*, Solomon Islands, **727** A1
New Germany, Canada, **827** J7
New Glasgow, Canada, **827** K7
New Grant, Trinidad, Trinidad and Tobago, **859** C4
New Guinea, *island*, Indonesia/Papua New Guinea, **726** A4
New Hampshire, *state*, U.S.A., **836** E3
New Hampton, U.S.A., **830** G4
New Hanover, *island*, Papua New Guinea, **726** C3
New Haven, U.S.A., **836** D4
New Hazelton, Canada, **822** F4
New Iberia, U.S.A., **834** G5
New Ireland, *island*, Papua New Guinea, **726** C3
New Ireland, *province*, Papua New Guinea, **726** D3
New Jersey, *state*, U.S.A., **836** C5
New Lexington, U.S.A., **831** M6
New Liskeard, Canada, **831** P2
New London, Connecticut, U.S.A., **836** D4
New London, Iowa, U.S.A., **830** H5
New London, Wisconsin, U.S.A., **831** J3
New Meadows, U.S.A., **828** F4
New Mexico, *state*, U.S.A., **833** K4
New Milford, U.S.A., **836** C4
New Milton, England, U.K., **789** F4
New Mirpur, India, **754** C2
New Orleans, U.S.A., **834** G5
New Paltz, U.S.A., **836** C4
New Pitsligo, Scotland, U.K., **792** G3
New Plymouth, New Zealand, **718** E4
New Providence, *island*, Bahamas, **838** F1
New Quay, Wales, U.K., **788** C2
New Richmond, Canada, **826** J5
New Richmond, U.S.A., **830** G3
New Rockford, U.S.A., **830** D2
New Romney, England, U.K., **789** H4
New Ross, Ireland, **793** F5
New Salem, U.S.A., **830** C2
New Sarepta, Canada, **823** N5
New Scone, Scotland, U.K., **792** F4
New Smyrna Beach, U.S.A., **835** M5
New South Wales, *state*, Australia, **721** J5
New Underwood, U.S.A., **830** B3
New Waterford, Canada, **827** L6
New York, *state*, U.S.A., **836** B3
New York, U.S.A., **836** D4
New Zealand, *country*, Pacific Ocean, **715** F6
Newala, Tanzania, **809** G5
Newark, Delaware, U.S.A., **836** C5
Newark, New Jersey, U.S.A., **836** C4
Newark, New York, U.S.A., **836** B3
Newark-on-Trent, England, U.K., **789** G1
Newberg, U.S.A., **828** C4
Newberry, U.S.A., **835** M2
Newbiggin-by-the-sea, England, U.K., **791** G2
Newbridge, Ireland, **793** F4
Newburgh, Scotland, U.K., **792** F4
Newburgh, U.S.A., **836** C4
Newbury, England, U.K., **789** F3
Newby Bridge, England, U.K., **790** F3
Newcastle, Australia, **721** L5
Newcastle, Canada, **826** J6
Newcastle, Northern Ireland, U.K., **793** G3
Newcastle, South Africa, **811** E4
Newcastle, U.S.A., **829** M5
Newcastle Emlyn, Wales, U.K., **788** C2
Newcastle-under-Lyme, England, U.K., **788** E1
Newcastle upon Tyne, England, U.K., **791** G3
Newcastle West, Ireland, **793** C5
Newcastleton, Scotland, U.K., **792** G5
Newcomb, U.S.A., **833** J3
Newell, U.S.A., **830** B3
Newenham, Cape, U.S.A., **820** C4
Newent, England, U.K., **788** E3
Newfolden, U.S.A., **830** E1
Newfoundland, *island*, Canada, **827** N5
Newfoundland, *province*, Canada, **821** N4
Newham, England, U.K., **791** G2
Newhaven, England, U.K., **789** H4
Newington, South Africa, **811** F3
Newinn, Ireland, **793** E5
Newman, Australia, **720** D3
Newman, U.S.A., **831** K6
Newmarket, Canada, **831** P3
Newmarket, England, U.K., **789** H2
Newmarket, Ireland, **793** C5
Newmarket on Fergus, Ireland, **793** D5
Newnan, U.S.A., **835** K3
Newnham, England, U.K., **788** E3
Newport, Arkansas, U.S.A., **834** G2
Newport, Essex, England, U.K., **789** H3
Newport, Isle of Wight, England, U.K., **789** F4
Newport, Kentucky, U.S.A., **831** L6
Newport, Mayo, Ireland, **793** C4
Newport, New Hampshire, U.S.A., **836** D3
Newport, Newport, Wales, U.K., **788** E3
Newport, Oregon, U.S.A., **828** B4
Newport, Pembrokeshire, Wales, U.K., **788** C2
Newport, Rhode Island, U.S.A., **836** E4
Newport, Shropshire, England, U.K., **788** E2
Newport, Tennessee, U.S.A., **835** L2
Newport, Tipperary, Ireland, **793** D5
Newport, *unitary authority*, Wales, U.K., **788** D3
Newport, Vermont, U.S.A., **836** D2
Newport, Washington, U.S.A., **828** F2
Newport Bay, Wales, U.K., **788** B2
Newport News, U.S.A., **836** B6
Newport Pagnell, England, U.K., **789** G2
Newquay, England, U.K., **788** B4
Newry, Northern Ireland, U.K., **793** F3
Newry and Mourne, *district*, Northern Ireland, U.K., **793** F3
Newry Canal, Northern Ireland, U.K., **790** B3
Newton, England, U.K., **790** F4
Newton, Illinois, U.S.A., **831** J6
Newton, Iowa, U.S.A., **830** G5
Newton, Kansas, U.S.A., **830** E6
Newton, Mississippi, U.S.A., **835** H3
Newton Abbot, England, U.K., **788** D4
Newton Aycliffe, England, U.K., **791** G3
Newton Stewart, Scotland, U.K., **792** E6
Newtonmore, Scotland, U.K., **792** E3
Newtown, England, U.K., **788** E2
Newtown, Wales, U.K., **788** D2
Newtown Mount Kennedy, Ireland, **793** F4
Newtown St Boswells, Scotland, U.K., **792** G5
Newtownabbey, *district*, Northern Ireland, U.K., **793** F3
Newtownabbey, Northern Ireland, U.K., **793** G3
Newtownards, Northern Ireland, U.K., **793** G3
Newtownbutler, Northern Ireland, U.K., **793** E3
Newtownstewart, Northern Ireland, U.K., **793** E3
Neyland, Wales, U.K., **788** C3
Neyrīz, Iran, **757** F3
Neyshābūr, Iran, **758** F5
Neyva, *river*, Russian Federation, **758** G1
Neyveli, India, **752** D4
Neyyāttinkara, India, **752** D4
Nezperce, U.S.A., **828** F3
Nezvys'ko, Ukraine, **780** E1
Ngabang, Indonesia, **737** E2
Ngabé, Congo, **808** C3
Ngabordamlu, Tanjong, *point*, Indonesia, **735** F4
Ngagahtawng, Myanmar, **741** C2
Ngakawau, New Zealand, **719** C5
Ngala, Nigeria, **805** G2
Ngalipaeng, Indonesia, **734** D2
Ngam, Chad, **805** H2
Ngama, Chad, **805** H2
Ngamiland, *district*, Botswana, **810** D2
Ngamo, Zimbabwe, **811** E2
Ngamring, China, **750** C3
Ngangala, Sudan, **809** F2
Nganglong Kangri, *mountain range*, China, **754** E2
Ngangzê Co, *lake*, China, **750** C3
Ngao, Thailand, **738** D2
Ngaoundal, Cameroon, **805** G3
Ngaoundéré, Cameroon, **805** G3
Ngara, Tanzania, **809** F3
Ngatik, *island*, Micronesia, **724** D4
Ngauruhoe, Mount, *mountain peak*, New Zealand, **718** E4
Ngbala, Congo, **808** B2
Nggatokae, *island*, Solomon Islands, **727** A1
Nghĩa Ðàn, Vietnam, **739** E2
Ngo, Congo, **808** C3
Ngoc Linh, *mountain peak*, Vietnam, **739** E3
Ngomedzap, Cameroon, **808** B2
Ngong, Cameroon, **805** G3
Ngoni, Tanjong, *point*, Indonesia, **735** F4
Ngoqumaima, China, **750** C2
Ngoring, China, **751** F2
Ngorkou, Mali, **804** D1
Ngoso, Democratic Republic of the Congo, **808** C3
Ngoto, Central African Republic, **808** C2
Ngouma, Mali, **804** D1
Ngounié, *province*, Gabon, **808** B3
Ngoura, Chad, **805** H2
Ngouri, Chad, **805** H2
Ngourti, Niger, **805** G1
Ngouyo, Central African Republic, **809** E1
Ngudu, Tanzania, **809** F3
Nguia Bouar, Central African Republic, **808** B1
Nguigmi, Niger, **805** G2
Ngulu, *island*, Micronesia, **724** B4
Ngum, *river*, Laos, **739** D2
Ngundu, Zimbabwe, **811** F3
Nguru, Nigeria, **805** G2
Ngwedaung, Myanmar, **741** C4
Ngwezi, *river*, Zambia, **811** E2
Nha Trang, Vietnam, **739** F3
Nhabe, *river*, Botswana, **810** D3
Nhachengue, Mozambique, **811** G3
Nhamalábue, Mozambique, **811** G2
Nhamatanda, Mozambique, **811** F2
Nhamundá, Brazil, **850** B4
Nhamundá, *river*, Brazil, **850** B3
N'harea, Angola, **808** C5
Nhecolândia, Brazil, **854** B5
Nhill, Australia, **721** J6
Nhulunbuy, Australia, **721** H1
Nia-Nia, Democratic Republic of the Congo, **809** E2
Niafounké, Mali, **804** D1
Niagara Escarpment, Canada, **831** N3
Niagara Falls, Canada/U.S.A., **831** P4
Niagassola, Guinea, **804** C2
Niakaramandougou, Côte d'Ivoire, **804** C3
Niamey, Niger, **805** E2
Niandankoro, Guinea, **804** C2
Niangara, Democratic Republic of the Congo, **809** E2
Niangniangba, China, **751** H2
Niangoloko, Burkina Faso, **804** D2
Nianzishan, China, **747** H3
Niari, *administrative region*, Congo, **808** B3
Nias, Pulau, *island*, Indonesia, **736** B2

O

Ohau, New Zealand, **718** E5
Ohaupo, New Zealand, **718** E3
O'Higgins, Cabo, *cape*, Isla de Pascua (Easter Island), Chile, **859** B2
O'Higgins, Lago, *lake*, Chile, **858** B3
O'Higgins, Punta, *point*, Róbinson Crusoe Island, Archipiélago Juan Fernández, Chile, **859** C2
Ohio, *river*, U.S.A., **819** Q5
Ohio, *state*, U.S.A., **831** M5
'Ohonua, Tongatapu Group, Tonga, **727** B4
Ohře, *river*, Czech Republic, **773** F3
Ohrid, Lake *see* Ohridsko Jezero, *lake*, Macedonia, **781** C5
Ohrid, Macedonia, **781** C5
Ohridsko Jezero (Lake Ohrid), *lake*, Macedonia, **781** C5
Ohura, New Zealand, **718** E4
Oiapoque, Brazil, **850** C2
Oijärvi, Finland, **769** N4
Oil City, U.S.A., **831** P5
Oir, Beinn an, *mountain peak*, Scotland, U.K., **792** C5
Oise, *river*, France, **775** F2
Oisemont, France, **789** J5
Ōita, Japan, **744** E4
Oiti Oros, *mountain peak*, Greece, **781** D6
Öje, Sweden, **770** F2
Ojibwa, U.S.A., **830** H3
Ojinaga, Mexico, **840** D2
Ojo de Laguna, Mexico, **840** D2
Ojos del Salado, *mountain peak*, Argentina/Chile, **856** C3
Öjung, Sweden, **770** G2
Ok Tedi, Papua New Guinea, **726** A4
Oka, *river*, Russian Federation, **783** F5
Okaba, Indonesia, **735** G5
Okahandja, Namibia, **810** C3
Okaihau, New Zealand, **718** D2
Okak Islands, Canada, **821** N4
Okakarara, Namibia, **810** C3
Okanagan Lake, Canada, **828** E2
Okaputa, Namibia, **810** C3
Okāra, Pakistan, **754** C3
Okarito Lagoon, *bay*, New Zealand, **719** B6
Okaukuejo, Namibia, **810** C2
Okavango, *administrative region*, Namibia, **810** C2
Okavango, *river*, Southern Africa, **799** G8
Okavango Delta, Botswana, **810** D2
Okawa Point, Chatham Islands, New Zealand, **719** Q16
Okaya, Japan, **745** G3
Okayama, Japan, **744** F4
Okazize, Namibia, **810** C3
Okeechobee, Lake, U.S.A., **835** M6
Okeechobee, U.S.A., **835** M6
Okehampton, England, U.K., **788** C4
Okemah, U.S.A., **834** D2
Okha, Russian Federation, **785** R4
Okhaldhungā, Nepal, **755** F4
Okhotsk, Russian Federation, **785** R4
Okhotsk, Sea of *see* Okhotskoye More, *sea*, Russian Federation, **785** R4
Okhotskoye More (Sea of Okhotsk), *sea*, Russian Federation, **785** R4
Okhtan-Yarvi, Ozero, *lake*, Russian Federation, **769** Q4
Oki-shotō, *islands*, Japan, **744** F3
Okinawa, Japan, **745** N8
Okinawa-jima, *island*, Japan, **745** P8
Okinawa-shotō, *islands*, Japan, **745** N8
Okino-Tori-shima, *island*, Japan, **724** B2
Okinoerabu-jima, *island*, Japan, **745** P8
Okiore, New Zealand, **718** F4
Oklahoma, *state*, U.S.A., **834** C2
Oklahoma City, U.S.A., **834** D2
Okmulgee, U.S.A., **834** E2
Okondja, Gabon, **808** B3
Okotoks, Canada, **823** M6
Okoyo, Congo, **808** C3
Okpo, Myanmar, **741** B4
Okreek, U.S.A., **830** C4
Oksbøl, Denmark, **770** D5
Øksfjord, Norway, **769** L1
Oktyabr'sk, Kazakhstan, **758** F3
Oktyabr'skiy, Russian Federation, **758** E2
Oktyabr'skoy Revolyutsii, Ostrov, *island*, Russian Federation, **784** L2
Okučani, Croatia, **778** F3
Okulovka, Russian Federation, **783** D3
Okurcalar, Turkey, **761** A1
Okushiri-tō, *island*, Japan, **745** G2
Okuta, Nigeria, **805** E3
Ola, U.S.A., **828** F4
ûlafsfjörður, Iceland, **768** Y6
Olaine, Latvia, **771** L4
Olal, Vanuatu, **727** A2
Olanchito, Honduras, **838** D4
Öland, *island*, Sweden, **771** H4
Olanga, *river*, Finland/Russian Federation, **769** Q3
Olathe, U.S.A., **830** F6
Olavarría, Argentina, **857** E5
Olbia, Sardegna, Italy, **779** B5
Old Crow, Canada, **820** F3
Old Faithful, U.S.A., **829** J4
Old Forge, U.S.A., **836** C3
Old Head of Kinsale, *point*, Ireland, **793** D6
Old Leake, England, U.K., **789** H1
Old Orchard Beach, U.S.A., **836** E3
Old Town, U.S.A., **836** F2
Old Wives Lake, Canada, **823** R6
Oldcastle, Ireland, **793** E4
Oldenburg in Holstein, Germany, **772** E1
Olderfjord, Norway, **769** M1
Oldervik, Norway, **768** J2
Oldham, England, U.K., **790** F4
Oldmeldrum, Scotland, U.K., **792** G3
Olds, Canada, **823** M6
Öldziyt, Arhangay, Mongolia, **749** J2
Öldziyt, Dorngovĭ, Mongolia, **746** E3
Olean, U.S.A., **836** A3
Olecko, Poland, **773** L1
Olekminsk, Russian Federation, **785** P3
Oleksandriya, Ukraine, **782** D3
Olenegorsk, Russian Federation, **769** R2
Olenek, *river*, Russian Federation, **785** N3
Olenino, Russian Federation, **783** D4
Olenitsa, Russian Federation, **769** S3
Oleniy, Ostrov, *island*, Russian Federation, **769** S4
Olen'ya Rechka, Russian Federation, **749** G1
Oléron, Île d', *island*, France, **774** D4
Oles'ko, Ukraine, **773** M4
Oleśnica, Poland, **773** H3
Olesno, Poland, **773** J3
Ølfjellet, *mountain peak*, Norway, **768** G3
Olga, Mount *see* Katatjuta, *mountain peak*, Australia, **720** G4
Ol'ga, Russian Federation, **747** L4
Ol'ginsk, Russian Federation, **747** L1
Ölgiy, Mongolia, **748** F2
Ølgod, Denmark, **770** D5
Olhava, Finland, **769** M4
Olib, *island*, Croatia, **778** E3
Olímpia, Brazil, **854** D5
Olinalá, Mexico, **841** F5
Olinda, Brazil, **851** G5
Olinga, Mozambique, **809** G6
Olingskog, Sweden, **770** G2
Oliva, Argentina, **856** D4
Oliva, Cordillera de, *mountain range*, Argentina/Chile, **856** C3
Oliva, Spain, **777** G3
Olivares, Cerro de, *mountain peak*, Argentina/Chile, **856** C4
Olivares de Júcar, Spain, **777** F3
Olive, U.S.A., **829** M4
Olive Hill, U.S.A., **831** M6
Oliveira, Brazil, **855** E5
Oliveira dos Brejinhos, Brazil, **855** E3
Olivenza, Spain, **776** D3
Oliver, Canada, **823** K7
Oliver Lake, Canada, **824** C3
Ölkeyek, *river*, Kazakhstan, **758** G3
Ol'khon, Ostrov, *island*, Russian Federation, **746** D1
Olkusz, Poland, **773** J3
Ollagüe, Chile, **853** E5
Ollagüe, Volcán, *mountain peak*, Bolivia/Chile, **853** E5
Ollita, Cordillera de, *mountain range*, Argentina/Chile, **856** B4
Ollombo, Congo, **808** C3
Olmedo, Spain, **776** E2
Olmillos de Sasamon, Spain, **777** F1
Olmos, Peru, **852** B1
Olney, England, U.K., **789** G2
Olney, U.S.A., **831** J6
Olofström, Sweden, **770** G4
Olomane, *river*, Canada, **827** L4
Olomouc, Czech Republic, **773** H4
Olonets, Russian Federation, **783** D2
Olongapo, Philippines, **740** C3
Olonzac, France, **774** F5
Oloron-Sainte-Marie, France, **774** D5
Olosega, *island*, American Samoa, **727** B2
Olot, Spain, **777** J1
Olovo, Bosnia and Herzegovina, **778** G3
Olovyannaya, Russian Federation, **746** F2
Olpe, Germany, **772** C3
Ol'sha, Russian Federation, **783** C5
Olsztyn, Poland, **773** K2
Olsztynek, Poland, **773** K2
Olt, *river*, Romania, **780** E3
Olten, Switzerland, **775** H3
Oltenița, Romania, **780** F3
Oltina, Romania, **780** F3
Olton, U.S.A., **834** A2
Olutlanga Island, Philippines, **740** C5
Olympia, U.S.A., **828** C3
Olympic Mountains, *mountain range*, U.S.A., **828** C3
Olympos, *mountain peak*, Cyprus, **761** B2
Olympos, Oros (Mount Olympus), *mountain peak*, Greece, **766** G7
Olympus, Mount, *mountain peak*, U.S.A., **828** C3
Olympus, Mount *see* Olympos Oros, *mountain peak*, Greece, **766** G7
Olyutorskiy, Mys, *cape*, Russian Federation, **785** U4
Om', *river*, Russian Federation, **759** L1
Om Häjer, Eritrea, **807** E2
Oma, China, **755** E2
Ōma, Japan, **745** H2
Oma, Russian Federation, **784** F3
Ōmagari, Japan, **745** H3
Omagh, *district*, Northern Ireland, U.K., **793** E3
Omagh, Northern Ireland, U.K., **793** E3
Omaguas, Peru, **848** D5
Omaha, U.S.A., **830** F5
Omaheke, *administrative region*, Namibia, **810** C3
Omak, U.S.A., **828** E2
Omakau, New Zealand, **719** B7
Omakere, New Zealand, **718** F5
Oman, *country*, Asia, **730** G8
Oman, Gulf of, Arabian Peninsula/Iran, **757** G4
Omarama, New Zealand, **719** B7
Omaruru, Namibia, **810** C3
Omate, Peru, **852** D4
Ombalantu, Namibia, **810** B2
Ombella-Mpoko, *prefecture*, Central African Republic, **808** C1
Ombersley, England, U.K., **788** E2
Ombo, *island*, Norway, **770** B3
Omboué, Gabon, **808** A3
Ombu, China, **750** C3
Omdurman *see* Umm Durmān, Sudan, **806** D1
Ometepec, Mexico, **841** F5
Omineca, *river*, Canada, **822** G4
Omineca Mountains, *mountain range*, Canada, **822** F3
Omiš, Croatia, **778** F4
Ömnögovĭ, *province*, Mongolia, **749** J4
Omo, *river*, Ethiopia, **807** E3
Omoku, Nigeria, **805** F3
Omolon, *river*, Russian Federation, **785** S3
Ömossa, Finland, **771** K1
Omsk, Russian Federation, **759** J2
Omskaya Oblast', *province*, Russian Federation, **759** J1
Omsukchan, Russian Federation, **785** S3
Ōmura, Japan, **744** E4
Omurtag, Bulgaria, **780** F4
Omusati, *administrative region*, Namibia, **810** B2
Ōmuta, Japan, **744** E4
Omutinskiy, Russian Federation, **758** H1
Ona, *river*, Russian Federation, **748** F2
Onalaska, U.S.A., **830** H4
Onaping Lake, U.S.A., **831** N2
Onavas, Mexico, **840** C2
Onaway, U.S.A., **831** L3
Oncativo, Argentina, **856** D4
Onchan, Isle of Man, **790** D3
Oncócua, Angola, **808** B6
Ondangwa, Namibia, **810** C2
Ondava, *river*, Slovakia, **773** K4
Onder, India, **754** D4
Ondjiva, Angola, **808** C6
Ondo, Nigeria, **805** E3
Ondo, *state*, Nigeria, **805** E3
Öndörhaan, Mongolia, **746** E3
Öndörhushuu, Mongolia, **746** F3
Ondozero, Ozero, *lake*, Russian Federation, **769** R5
One and Half Degree Channel, Maldives, **752** C6
100 Mile House, Canada, **822** J6
Onega, *river*, Russian Federation, **767** H3
Oneida, U.S.A., **836** C3
Oneida Lake, U.S.A., **836** B3
O'Neill, U.S.A., **830** D4
Onekotan, Ostrov, *island*, Russian Federation, **785** S5
Oneonta, Alabama, U.S.A., **835** J3
Oneonta, New York, U.S.A., **836** C3
Onești, Romania, **780** F2
Onetar, Vanuatu, **727** A2
Onevai, *island*, Tonga, **727** B4
Onezhskaya Guba, *bay*, Russian Federation, **769** S4
Onezhskiy Poluostrov, *peninsula*, Russian Federation, **769** T4
Onezhskoye Ozero, *lake*, Russian Federation, **783** E2
Onga, Gabon, **808** B3
Ongandjera, Namibia, **810** B2
Onggunoi, Indonesia, **734** D2
Ongi, Mongolia, **749** J3
Ongiyn, *river*, Mongolia, **749** J3
Ongjin, North Korea, **744** D3
Ongniud Qi, China, **747** G4
Ongole, India, **752** E3
Ongon, Mongolia, **749** J3
Onguday, Russian Federation, **748** E2
Onida, U.S.A., **830** C3
Onitsha, Nigeria, **805** F3
Ono, *island*, Fiji, **727** A4
Ōnojō, Japan, **744** E4
Onokhoy, Russian Federation, **746** E2
Onon, *river*, Mongolia, **746** E2
Onor, China, **747** H2
Onotoa, *island*, Kiribati, **725** F5
Ons, Illa de, *island*, Spain, **776** C1
Onseepkans, South Africa, **810** C4
Onslow, Australia, **720** D3
Onslow Bay, U.S.A., **835** P2
Ontario, Lake, Canada/U.S.A., **826** B8
Ontario, *province*, Canada, **825** K6
Ontario, U.S.A., **828** F4
Ontonagon, U.S.A., **831** J2
Ontong Java, *island*, Solomon Islands, **724** E5
Ontur, Spain, **777** G3
Onverwacht, Suriname, **850** B2
Onycha, U.S.A., **835** J4
Oodnadatta, Australia, **721** H4
Oodweyne, Somalia, **807** G3
Oologah Lake, U.S.A., **830** F7
Oost-Vaanderen, *province*, Belgium, **772** A3
Oostende, Belgium, **772** A3
Oostpunt, *point*, Curaçao, Netherlands Antilles, **859** C3
Ootsa Lake, Canada, **822** F5
Opal, U.S.A., **829** J6
Opala, Democratic Republic of the Congo, **808** D3
Opari, Sudan, **809** F2
Opasatika, Canada, **825** N7
Opatija, Croatia, **778** E3
Opatów, Poland, **773** K3
Opava, Czech Republic, **773** H4
Opelika, U.S.A., **835** K3
Opelousas, U.S.A., **834** F4
Opheim, U.S.A., **829** L2
Ophir, Gunung, *mountain peak*, Indonesia, **736** C2
Opienge, Democratic Republic of the Congo, **809** E2
Opinaca, Réservoir, Canada, **826** C3
Opobo, Nigeria, **808** A2
Opochka, Russian Federation, **783** B4
Opoczno, Poland, **773** K3
Opole, Poland, **773** H3
Opole Lubelskie, Poland, **773** K3
Opotiki, New Zealand, **718** F4
Opp, U.S.A., **835** J4
Oppdal, Norway, **770** D1
Oppland, *county*, Norway, **770** D2
Opsa, Belarus, **771** N5
Opua, New Zealand, **718** E2
Opunake, New Zealand, **718** D4
Opuwo, Namibia, **810** B2
Oq-Suu, *river*, Tajikistan, **759** J5
Oracle, U.S.A., **833** H5
Oradea, Romania, **780** C2
Orahov Do, Bosnia and Herzegovina, **778** F4
Orahovac, Yugoslavia, **780** C4

Orahovica, Croatia, **778** F3
Orai, India, **754** D4
Oral, Kazakhstan, **758** E2
Oran, Algeria, **801** F1
Orange, Australia, **721** K5
Orange, Cabo, *cape*, Brazil, **850** C2
Orange, France, **775** G4
Orange, Louisiana, U.S.A., **834** F4
Orange, *river*, Namibia/South Africa, **810** C4
Orange, Virginia, U.S.A., **836** A5
Orange Walk, Belize, **838** C3
Orangeburg, U.S.A., **835** M3
Orangerie Bay, Papua New Guinea, **726** C5
Orango, *island*, Guinea-Bissau, **804** A2
Oranienburg, Germany, **772** F2
Oranje Gebergte, *mountain range*, Suriname, **850** B2
Oranjemund, Namibia, **810** C4
Oranjestad, Aruba, **859** B3
Oranmore, Ireland, **793** D4
Oransbari, Indonesia, **735** F3
Orap, Vanuatu, **727** A2
Orapa, Botswana, **811** E3
Orăştie, Romania, **780** D3
Orava, *river*, Slovakia, **773** J4
Oraviţa, Romania, **780** C3
Orawia, New Zealand, **719** A8
Orbec, France, **774** E2
Orbetello, Italy, **779** C4
Órbigo, *river*, Spain, **776** E1
Orbost, Australia, **721** K6
Orcadas, *Argentinian research station*, Antarctica, **862** B3
Orchard, Idaho, U.S.A., **828** G5
Orchard, Nebraska, U.S.A., **830** D4
Orcotuna, Peru, **852** C3
Ord, *river*, Australia, **720** F2
Orderville, U.S.A., **832** G3
Ordes, Spain, **776** C1
Ordu, Turkey, **760** E4
Ordway, U.S.A., **833** M2
Orealla, Guyana, **849** H3
Orebić, Croatia, **778** F4
Örebro, *county*, Sweden, **770** G3
Örebro, Sweden, **770** G3
Oredezh, *river*, Russian Federation, **783** C3
Oredezh, Russian Federation, **783** C3
Oregon, *state*, U.S.A., **828** D4
Oregon, U.S.A., **831** J4
Oregon City, U.S.A., **828** C4
Oregon Inlet, U.S.A., **836** C7
Orekhovo-Zuyevo, Russian Federation, **783** G5
Orel, Russian Federation, **782** E2
Orellana, N. Peru, **852** B1
Orellana, on Ucayali, *river*, Peru, **852** C2
Ören, Turkey, **781** F7
Orenburg, Russian Federation, **758** F2
Orenburgskaya Oblast', *province*, Russian Federation, **758** E2
Orense, Argentina, **857** E6
Orepuki, New Zealand, **719** A8
Orere, New Zealand, **718** E3
Orestiada, Greece, **781** F5
Oreti, *river*, New Zealand, **719** B7
Orford, England, U.K., **789** J2
Orford Ness, *spit*, England, U.K., **789** J2
Organ, U.S.A., **833** K5
Organabo, French Guiana, **850** C2
Orgaz, Spain, **777** F3
Orgil, Mongolia, **749** H2
Órgiva, Spain, **777** F4
Örgön, Mongolia, **749** J3
Orhaneli, Turkey, **781** G6
Orhei, Moldova, **780** G2
Orhon, *river*, Mongolia, **746** D2
Orhontuul, Mongolia, **746** D2
Orhy, Pic d', *mountain peak*, France/Spain, **777** G1
Orick, U.S.A., **828** B6
Oriental, Cordillera, *mountain range*, Bolivia, **847** F5
Oriental, Cordillera, *mountain range*, Colombia, **847** E3
Oriente, Argentina, **856** E6
Orihuela, Spain, **777** G3
Orillia, Canada, **831** P3
Orimattila, Finland, **771** M2
Orin, U.S.A., **829** M5
Orinduik, Guyana, **849** G3
Orinoco, *river*, Venezuela, **847** F3
Oriomo, Papua New Guinea, **726** A5
Orissa, *state*, India, **753** E2
Orissaare, Estonia, **771** L3
Oristano, Golfo di, *gulf*, Italy, **779** A6
Oristano, Sardegna, Italy, **779** B6
Orivesi, *lake*, Finland, **771** P1
Oriximina, Brazil, **850** B3
Orizaba, Mexico, **841** F5
Orizaba, Pico de *see* Citlaltepetl, Volcán, *mountain peak*, Mexico, **841** F5
Orkanger, Norway, **768** D5
Örkelljunga, Sweden, **770** F4
Orkla, *river*, Norway, **768** D5
Orkney, *local authority*, Scotland, U.K., **792** F1
Orkney Islands, Scotland, U.K., **792** F1
Orla, U.S.A., **833** M6
Orlândia, Brazil, **854** D5
Orlando, U.S.A., **835** M5
Orléans, France, **774** E3
Orleans, U.S.A., **836** F4
Orlické hory, *mountain range*, Czech Republic, **773** H3
Orlik, Russian Federation, **749** H1
Orlovka, Russian Federation, **759** K1
Orlovskaya Oblast', *province*, Russian Federation, **783** E6
Ormāra, Pakistan, **757** H3
Ormea, Italy, **778** A3
Ormoc, Philippines, **740** D4
Ormond Beach, U.S.A., **835** M5
Ormskirk, England, U.K., **790** F4
Ormylia, Greece, **781** D5
Ørnes, Norway, **768** F3
Orneta, Poland, **773** K1
Ornö, *island*, Sweden, **771** J3
Örnsköldsvik, Sweden, **768** J5
Oro *see* Northern, *province*, Papua New Guinea, **726** C5
Orobie, Alpi, *mountain range*, Italy, **778** B3
Orocué, Colombia, **848** D2
Orodara, Burkina Faso, **804** D2
Orofino, U.S.A., **828** F3
Orog Nuur, *lake*, Mongolia, **749** H3
Orogrande, U.S.A., **833** K5
Oromocto, Canada, **826** H7
Oron, Israel, **761** C4
Oron, Nigeria, **808** A2
Oron, *river*, Jordan, **761** C4
Orona, *island*, Kiribati, **725** G5
Oroquieta, Philippines, **740** C4
Orós, Açude, *reservoir*, Brazil, **851** F5
Orosei, Golfo di, *gulf*, Sardegna, Italy, **779** B5
Orosei, Sardegna, Italy, **779** B5
Orosháza, Hungary, **773** K5
Orovada, U.S.A., **828** F6
Oroville, Lake, U.S.A., **832** C2
Oroville, U.S.A., **832** C2
Orpesa, Spain, **777** H2
Orphir, Orkney, Scotland, U.K., **792** F2
Orqen Zizhiqi, China, **747** H2
Orqohan, China, **747** H2
Orr, Mount, *mountain peak*, New Zealand, **719** C7
Orrin, *river*, Scotland, U.K., **792** E3
Orsa, Sweden, **770** G2
Orsha, Belarus, **783** C5
Örsjö, Sweden, **770** G4
Orsk, Russian Federation, **758** F2
Orşova, Romania, **780** D3
Ørsta, Norway, **770** C1
Ørsted, Denmark, **770** E4
Örsundsbro, Sweden, **771** H3
Orta, Lago d', *lake*, Italy, **778** B3
Orta Nova, Italy, **779** E5
Ortaca, Turkey, **781** G7
Orte, Italy, **779** D4
Ortegal, Cabo, *cape*, Spain, **776** C1
Orthez, France, **774** D5
Ortigueira, Spain, **776** D1
Orting, U.S.A., **828** C3
Ortiz, Mexico, **840** C2
Ortiz, Venezuela, **849** E2
Ortoire, *river*, Trinidad, Trinidad and Tobago, **859** C4
Orton, England, U.K., **790** F3
Ortón, *river*, Bolivia, **853** E3
Ortona, Italy, **779** E4
Ortonville, U.S.A., **830** E3
Örträsk, Sweden, **768** J4
Orulgan, Khrebet, *mountain range*, Russian Federation, **785** P3
Orūmīyeh, Daryācheh-ye, *lake*, Iran, **803** J1
Orūmīyeh (Urmia), Iran, **803** H1
Oruro, Bolivia, **853** E4
Oruro, *department*, Bolivia, **853** E5
Orust, *island*, Sweden, **770** E3
Orvieto, Italy, **778** C4
Orville Coast, *region*, Antarctica, **862** B5
Orwell, U.S.A., **831** N5
Oryakhovo, Bulgaria, **780** D4
Orynyn, Ukraine, **780** F1
Orzysz, Poland, **773** K2
Os, Norway, **770** E1
Osa, Península de, Costa Rica, **838** E5
Osa, Russian Federation, **758** F1
Osage, U.S.A., **830** G4
Ōsaka, Japan, **745** F4
Osakarovka, Kazakhstan, **748** B2
Osawatomie, U.S.A., **830** F6
Osby, Sweden, **770** G4
Oscar, French Guiana, **850** C2
Osceola, U.S.A., **830** E5
Oschiri, Sardegna, Italy, **779** B5
Oscoda, U.S.A., **831** M3
Osečina, Yugoslavia, **780** B3
Osen, Norway, **768** E4
Osera, Spain, **777** G2
Osh, Kyrgyzstan, **759** J4
Oshakati, Namibia, **810** C2
Oshamambe, Japan, **745** H2
Oshana, *administrative region*, Namibia, **810** C2
Oshawa, Canada, **831** P4
Oshikango, Namibia, **810** C2
Oshikoto, *administrative region*, Namibia, **810** C2
Oshkosh, Nebraska, U.S.A., **830** B5
Oshkosh, Wisconsin, U.S.A., **831** J3
Oshogbo, Nigeria, **805** E3
Oshwe, Democratic Republic of the Congo, **808** C3
Osiān, India, **754** C4
Osie, Poland, **773** J2
Osijek, Croatia, **778** G3
Oskaloosa, U.S.A., **830** G5
Oskarshamn, Sweden, **770** H4
Oskarström, Sweden, **770** F4
Oskélanéo, Canada, **826** D5
Öskemen, Kazakhstan, **748** D2
Oslo, *county*, Norway, **770** E3
Oslo, Norway, **770** E3
Oslofjorden, *fiord*, Norway, **770** E3
Osmānābād, India, **752** D2
Osmaniye, Turkey, **760** E5
Os'mino, Russian Federation, **783** B3
Osnabrück, Germany, **772** D2
Oso, U.S.A., **828** D2
Osogovske Planine, Bulgaria/Macedonia, **780** D4
Osório, Brazil, **857** G3
Osorno, Chile, **858** C1
Osorno, Volcán, *mountain peak*, Chile, **858** C1
Osoyoos, Canada, **823** K7
Ossa, Mount, *mountain peak*, Australia, **721** K7
Ossa, *mountain peak*, Portugal, **776** D3
Ossa de Montiel, Spain, **777** F3
Ossabaw Island, U.S.A., **835** M4
Osse, *river*, France, **774** E5
Ossima, Papua New Guinea, **726** A3
Ossjøen, *lake*, Norway, **770** E2
Östansjö, Sweden, **768** J4
Ostashkov, Russian Federation, **783** D4
Östavall, Sweden, **770** G1
Østby, Norway, **768** E5
Oster, *river*, Russian Federation, **783** D6
Øster Vrå, Denmark, **770** E4
Osterburg, Germany, **772** E2
Österbybruk, Sweden, **771** H2
Österbymo, Sweden, **770** G4
Österdalälven, *river*, Sweden, **770** F2
Østerdalen, *valley*, Norway, **770** E2
Österfärnebo, Sweden, **771** H2
Östergötland, *county*, Sweden, **770** G3
Östersund, Sweden, **768** G5
Østfold, *county*, Norway, **770** E3
Ostfriesische Inseln, *islands*, Germany, **772** C2
Östhammar, Sweden, **771** J2
Ostiglia, Italy, **778** C3
Ostrava, Czech Republic, **773** J4
Ostrogozhsk, Russian Federation, **782** E2
Ostróda, Poland, **773** K2
Ostrołęka, Poland, **773** K2
Ostrov, Pskovskaya Oblast', Russian Federation, **783** B4
Ostrov, Vologodskaya Oblast', Russian Federation, **783** F3
Ostrów Mazowiecka, Poland, **773** K2
Ostrów Wielkopolski, Poland, **773** H3
Ostrowiec Świętokrzyski, Poland, **773** K3
Ostrzeszów, Poland, **773** J3
Osttirol, *region*, Austria, **772** F5
Ostuni, Italy, **779** F5
Osŭm, *river*, Bulgaria, **780** E4
Ōsumi-shotō, *islands*, Japan, **744** E5
Osun, *state*, Nigeria, **805** E3
Osuna, Spain, **776** E4
Oswego, U.S.A., **836** B3
Oswestry, England, U.K., **788** D2
Oświęcim, Poland, **773** J3
Otago Peninsula, New Zealand, **719** C7
Otaika, New Zealand, **718** E2
Otaki, New Zealand, **719** E5
Otakiri, New Zealand, **718** F3
Otar, Kazakhstan, **748** B4
Otaru, Japan, **745** H2
Otavalo, Ecuador, **848** B4
Otavi, Namibia, **810** C2
Otelnuk, Lac, *lake*, Canada, **826** G1
Oţelu Roşu, Romania, **780** D3
Otematata, New Zealand, **719** C7
Otepää, Estonia, **771** N3
Othello, U.S.A., **828** E3
Othonoi, *island*, Ionioi Nisoi, Greece, **781** B6
Oti, *river*, Togo, **804** E2
Otish, Monts, *mountain range*, Canada, **826** F3
Otjiwarongo, Namibia, **810** C3
Otjozondjupa, *administrative region*, Namibia, **810** C2
Otley, England, U.K., **791** G4
Otnes, Norway, **770** E2
Otog Qi, China, **746** E5
Otog Qianqi, China, **746** D5
Otorohanga, New Zealand, **718** E4
Otorokua Point, New Zealand, **719** B6
Otra, *river*, Norway, **770** C3
Otrabanda, Curaçao, Netherlands Antilles, **859** C3
Otranto, Italy, **779** G5
Otranto, Strait of, Albania/Italy, **766** F7
Otsego, U.S.A., **831** L4
Otta, Norway, **770** D2
Otta, *river*, Norway, **770** C1
Ottawa, Canada, **826** D7
Ottawa, *river*, Canada, **826** C6
Ottawa, U.S.A., **830** F6
Ottawa Islands, Canada, **825** P2
Ottenby, Sweden, **770** H4
Otterburn, England, U.K., **790** F2
Otterndorf, Germany, **772** D2
Otterøy, Norway, **768** E4
Otterup, Denmark, **770** E5
Ottery, *river*, England, U.K., **788** C4
Otukpa, Nigeria, **805** F3
Otumpa, Argentina, **856** D3
Oturkpo, Nigeria, **805** F3
Otuzco, Peru, **852** B2
Otway, Bahía, *bay*, Chile, **858** B4
Otway, Cape, Australia, **721** J6
Otyniya, Ukraine, **780** E1
Ötztaler Alpen, *mountain range*, Austria, **772** E5
Ou, *river*, China, **742** E2
Ōu-sanmyaku, *mountain range*, Japan, **745** H2
Ouachita, Lake, U.S.A., **834** F2
Ouachita, *river*, U.S.A., **834** F3
Ouachita Mountains, *mountain range*, U.S.A., **834** E2
Ouadane, Mauritania, **800** D4
Ouadda, Central African Republic, **806** B3
Ouaddaï, *prefecture*, Chad, **806** B2
Ouagadougou, Burkina Faso, **804** D2
Ouahigouya, Burkina Faso, **804** D2
Ouaka, *prefecture*, Central African Republic, **808** D1
Oualâta, Mauritania, **804** C1
Ouallam, Niger, **805** E2
Ouanary, French Guiana, **850** C2
Ouanda Djallé, Central African Republic, **806** B3
Ouandago, Central African Republic, **806** A3
Ouando, Central African Republic, **809** E1
Ouango, Central African Republic, **808** D2
Ouangolodougou, Côte d'Ivoire, **804** C3
Ouaqui, French Guiana, **850** C2
Ouargaye, Burkina Faso, **804** E2
Ouargla, Algeria, **801** H2
Ouarkziz, Jebel, *mountain range*, Algeria/Morocco, **800** E3
Ouarzazate, Morocco, **800** E2
Oudtshoorn, South Africa, **810** D5
Oued Rhiou, Algeria, **777** H5
Ouégoa, New Caledonia, **727** A3
Ouélésébougou, Mali, **804** C2
Ouessa, Burkina Faso, **804** D2
Ouessant, Île d', *island*, France, **774** B2
Ouésso, Congo, **808** C2

Ouest, *province*, Cameroon, **808** B1
Oughter, Lough, *lake*, Ireland, **793** E3
Oughterard, Ireland, **793** C4
Ouham, *prefecture*, Central African Republic, **805** H3
Ouham-Pendé, *prefecture*, Central African Republic, **805** H3
Ouidah, Benin, **805** E3
Oujda, Morocco, **801** F2
Oujeft, Mauritania, **800** D5
Oulad Teima, Morocco, **800** E2
Oulainen, Finland, **769** M4
Ould Yenjé, Mauritania, **804** B1
Ouled Djellal, Algeria, **801** H2
Oulton Broad, England, U.K., **789** J2
Oulu, Finland, **769** M4
Oulujärvi, *lake*, Finland, **769** N4
Oulujoki, *river*, Finland, **769** M4
Oulun Lääni, *province*, Finland, **769** N4
Oulx, Italy, **778** A3
Oum-Chalouba, Chad, **806** B1
Oum el Bouaghi, Algeria, **801** H1
Oum-Hadjer, Chad, **806** A2
Oumm ed Droûs Guebli, Sebkhet, *salt-pan*, Mauritania, **800** D4
Oumm ed Droûs Telli, Sebkhet, *salt-pan*, Mauritania, **800** D4
Ounane, Djebel, *mountain peak*, Algeria, **801** H3
Ounara, Morocco, **800** E2
Ounasjoki, *river*, Finland, **769** M3
Oundle, England, U.K., **789** G2
Oungre, Canada, **824** C7
Ounianga Kébir, Chad, **802** D5
Ounianga Sérir, Chad, **802** D5
Oupu, China, **747** J1
Ouray, U.S.A., **833** K2
Ourém, Brazil, **850** D3
Ourense, Spain, **776** D1
Ouricurí, Brazil, **851** F5
Ouro Prêto, Brazil, **855** E5
Ourville-en-Caux, France, **789** H5
Ouse, *river*, E. Sussex, England, U.K., **789** H4
Ouse, *river*, Yorkshire, England, U.K., **791** H4
Outakoski, Finland, **769** N2
Outaouais, Rivière des, *river*, Canada, **826** B6
Outardes Quatre, Réservoir, Canada, **826** G4
Outer Hebrides, *islands*, Scotland, U.K., **792** B3
Outjo, Namibia, **810** C3
Outokumpu, Finland, **769** P5
Outram, New Zealand, **719** C7
Ouvéa, *island*, New Caledonia, **727** A3
Ouyen, Australia, **721** J6
Ovacık, Turkey, **803** G1
Ovada, Italy, **778** B3
Ovaka, *island*, Vava'u Group, Tonga, **727** B3
Ovalau, *island*, Fiji, **727** A4
Ovalle, Chile, **856** B4
Ovan, Gabon, **808** B2
Ovando, U.S.A., **828** H3
Ovar, Portugal, **776** C2
Oveng, Cameroon, **808** B2
Overbister, Orkney, Scotland, U.K., **792** G1
Øverbygd, Norway, **768** J2
Overijssel, *province*, Netherlands, **772** C2
Överkalix, Sweden, **769** L3
Overland Park, U.S.A., **830** F6
Overlander Roadhouse, Australia, **720** C4
Overton, U.S.A., **832** F3
Overton, Wales, U.K., **788** E2
Övertorneå, Sweden, **769** L3
Överturingen, Sweden, **770** G1
Överum, Sweden, **770** H4
Övgödiy, Mongolia, **749** H2
Ovidiopol', Ukraine, **780** H2
Ovidiu, Romania, **780** G3
Oviedo, Spain, **776** E1
Ovino, Russian Federation, **783** D3
Ovišі, Latvia, **771** K4
Ovoot, Mongolia, **746** F3
Övör-Ereen, Mongolia, **746** F2
Övre Soppero, Sweden, **768** K2
Övt, Mongolia, **749** J3
Owaka, New Zealand, **719** B8
Owando, Congo, **808** C3
Owase, Japan, **745** G4
Owase-zaki, *point*, Japan, **745** G4
Owego, U.S.A., **836** B3
Owel, Lough, *lake*, Ireland, **793** E4
Owen, Mount, *mountain peak*, New Zealand, **719** D5
Owen Fracture Zone, *tectonic feature*, Indian Ocean, **866** C4
Owen Head, *point*, New Zealand, **719** B8
Owen Sound, Canada, **831** N3
Owen Stanley Range, *mountain range*, Papua New Guinea, **716** D2
Owenga, Chatham Islands, New Zealand, **719** Q16
Owens, U.S.A., **836** B5
Owens Lake, U.S.A., **832** E3
Owensboro, U.S.A., **831** K7
Owerri, Nigeria, **808** A1
Owl, *river*, Alberta, Canada, **823** P4
Owl, *river*, Manitoba, Canada, **824** H3
Owo, Nigeria, **805** F3
Owosso, U.S.A., **831** L4
Owyhee, Lake, U.S.A., **828** F5
Owyhee, *river*, U.S.A., **828** F5
Owyhee, U.S.A., **828** F6
Oxapampa, Peru, **852** C3
Oxbow, Canada, **824** C7
Oxelösund, Sweden, **771** H3
Oxford, Canada, **827** K7
Oxford, England, U.K., **789** F3
Oxford, Mississippi, U.S.A., **835** H2
Oxford, Nebraska, U.S.A., **830** D5
Oxford, New Zealand, **719** D6
Oxford, North Carolina, U.S.A., **831** P7
Oxford Lake, Canada, **824** G4
Oxfordshire, *unitary authority*, England, U.K., **789** F3
Oxnard, U.S.A., **832** D4
Oxted, England, U.K., **789** H3
Oxylithos, Greece, **781** E6
Oyama, Japan, **745** G3
Oyapok, Baie d', *bay*, French Guiana, **850** C2
Oyapok, *river*, French Guiana, **850** C2
Oyat', *river*, Russian Federation, **783** E2
Øye, Norway, **770** D2
Oyem, Gabon, **808** B2
Oyen, Canada, **823** P6
Øyeren, *lake*, Norway, **770** E3
Oykel, *river*, Scotland, U.K., **792** E3
Oykel Bridge, Scotland, U.K., **792** E3
Oyo, Congo, **808** C3
Oyo, Nigeria, **805** E3
Oyo, *state*, Nigeria, **805** E3
Oyón, Peru, **852** C3
Oyster Island, Myanmar, **741** B4
Oysterville, U.S.A., **828** B3
Oytal, Kazakhstan, **759** J4
Oytal, Kyrgyzstan, **759** J4
Oytograk, China, **748** D5
Oyyl, Kazakhstan, **758** E3
Oyyl, *river*, Kazakhstan, **758** E3
Ozamiz, Philippines, **740** C4
Ozark Plateau, U.S.A., **834** E1
Ozarks, Lake of the, U.S.A., **830** G6
Ozbaşı, Turkey, **781** F7
üzd, Hungary, **773** K4
Özen, Kazakhstan, **758** E4
Ozernoy, Mys, *cape*, Russian Federation, **785** T4
Ozersk, Russian Federation, **771** L5
Ozery, Russian Federation, **783** G5
Özgön, Kyrgyzstan, **759** J4
Ozhukarai, India, **752** D3
Ozieri, Sardegna, Italy, **779** B5
Ozimek, Poland, **773** J3
Ozinki, Russian Federation, **758** D2
Ozizweni, South Africa, **811** F4
Ozona, U.S.A., **834** B4
Ozuluama, Mexico, **841** F4

P

Pa, *river*, China, **743** A1
Pa-an, Myanmar, **741** C4
Paamiut, Greenland, **821** Q3
Paarl, South Africa, **810** C5
Paavola, Finland, **769** M4
Pabbay, *island*, Central Western Isles, Scotland, U.K., **792** B3
Pabbay, *island*, S. Western Isles, Scotland, U.K., **792** B4
Pabianice, Poland, **773** J3
Pābna, Bangladesh, **750** D5
Pabradė, Lithuania, **771** M5
Pacaás Novos, Serra dos, *mountain range*, Brazil, **853** F3
Pacaraima, Serra, *mountain range*, Brazil/Venezuela, **847** F3
Pacasmayo, Peru, **852** B2
Pacheco, Isla, *island*, Chile, **858** B4
Pachino, Sicilia, Italy, **779** E7
Pachitea, *river*, Peru, **852** C2
Pachmarhi, India, **754** D5
Pachuca, Mexico, **841** F4
Pacific Antarctic Ridge, *underwater feature*, Pacific Ocean, **868** G8
Pacific Ocean, **868** F4
Pacific Ranges, *mountain range*, Canada, **822** F6
Pacitan, Indonesia, **737** E5
Packwood, U.S.A., **828** D3
Pacov, Czech Republic, **773** G4
Pacoval, Brazil, **850** B4
Pacoval, *river*, Brazil, **850** B4
Padam, India, **754** D2
Padamarang, Pulau, *island*, Indonesia, **734** C4
Padang, Indonesia, **736** C3
Padang, Pulau, *island*, Indonesia, **736** C2
Padangsidempuan, Indonesia, **736** B2
Padangtikar, Pulau, *island*, Indonesia, **737** E3
Padany, Russian Federation, **769** R5
Padasjoki, Finland, **771** M2
Padauari, Pico, *mountain peak*, Brazil, **849** F4
Padauari, *river*, Brazil, **849** F4
Padcaya, Bolivia, **853** F5
Paddle Prairie, Canada, **823** L3
Paderborn, Germany, **772** D3
Padilla, Bolivia, **853** F5
Padina, Romania, **780** F3
Padova, Italy, **778** C3
Padrão, Ponta do, *point*, Angola, **808** B4
Padre Island, U.S.A., **834** D6
Padrón, Spain, **776** C1
Padstow, England, U.K., **788** C4
Padsvillye, Belarus, **771** N5
Paducah, Kentucky, U.S.A., **831** J7
Paducah, Texas, U.S.A., **834** B2
Paektu-san, *mountain peak*, North Korea, **744** F1
Paeroa, *mountain peak*, New Zealand, **718** F4
Paeroa, New Zealand, **718** E3
Pafos, Cyprus, **761** B2
Pafuri, Mozambique, **811** F3
Pag, Croatia, **778** E3
Pag, *island*, Croatia, **778** E3
Paga, Indonesia, **734** C5
Paga Conta, Brazil, **850** B4
Pagadian, Philippines, **740** C5
Pagai Selatan, Pulau, *island*, Indonesia, **736** B3
Pagai Utara, Pulau, *island*, Indonesia, **736** B3
Pagan, *island*, Northern Mariana Islands, **724** C3
Pagan, Myanmar, **741** B3
Pagaralam, Indonesia, **736** C4
Pagasitikos Kolpos, *bay*, Greece, **781** D6
Pagatan, Indonesia, **737** F3
Page, U.S.A., **833** H3
Pagėgiai, Lithuania, **771** K5
Paget, Mount, *mountain peak*, South Georgia, **859** A3
Pago Pago, American Samoa, **727** B2
Pagoda Peak, *mountain peak*, U.S.A., **833** K1
Pagon, Gunung, *mountain peak*, Brunei, **737** F1
Pagri, China, **750** D4
Pahala, Hawaiian Islands, U.S.A., **832** R10
Pahang, *river*, Malaysia, **736** C2
Pahang, *state*, Malaysia, **736** C2
Pahlāgaon, Andaman and Nicobar Islands, India, **753** H3
Pahoa, Hawaiian Islands, U.S.A., **832** R10
Pahute Peak, *mountain peak*, U.S.A., **828** E6
Paiaguás, Brazil, **854** B5
Paide, Estonia, **771** M3
Paige, U.S.A., **834** D4
Paignton, England, U.K., **788** D4
Paihia, New Zealand, **718** E2
Päijänne, *lake*, Finland, **771** M2
Pail, Pakistan, **754** C2
Pailin, Cambodia, **739** D3
Paillaco, Chile, **858** C1
Pailolo Channel, Hawaiian Islands, U.S.A., **832** R9
Paimio, Finland, **771** L2
Paimpol, France, **774** C2
Painan, Indonesia, **736** C3
Paine, Chile, **856** B4
Painswick, England, U.K., **788** E3
Painted Desert, U.S.A., **833** H3
Paintsville, U.S.A., **831** M7
País Vasco, *autonomous community*, Spain, **777** F1
Paisley, Scotland, U.K., **792** E5
Paisley, U.S.A., **828** D5
Paita, Peru, **852** B1
Paitan, China, **743** B2
Paitan, Teluk, *bay*, Malaysia, **737** G1
Paittasjärvi, Sweden, **769** L2
Pajala, Sweden, **769** L3
Paján, Ecuador, **848** B4
Pájara, Islas Canarias, Spain, **813** B4
Pajares, Spain, **776** E1
Pajeú, *river*, Brazil, **851** G5
Pak Khat, Thailand, **739** D2
Pak Tam Chung, China, **743** C4
Pak Thong Chai, Thailand, **738** D3
Pakaraima Mountains, *mountain range*, Guyana, **849** G3
Pakaur, India, **755** F4
Pakch'ŏn, North Korea, **744** D3
Paki, Nigeria, **805** F2
Pakistan, *country*, Asia, **730** H7
Pakokku, Myanmar, **741** B3
Pakotai, New Zealand, **718** D2
Pakrac, Croatia, **778** F3
Paks, Hungary, **773** J5
Pakuli, Indonesia, **734** B3
Pakuratahi, New Zealand, **719** E5
Pakxé, Laos, **739** E3
Pala, Chad, **805** G3
Pala, U.S.A., **832** E5
Palacios, U.S.A., **834** D5
Palafrugell, Spain, **777** J2
Palaiochora, Kriti, Greece, **781** D8
Palairos, Greece, **781** C6
Palaiseau, France, **774** F2
Pālakollu, India, **753** E2
Palamas, Greece, **781** D6
Palame, Brazil, **855** G3
Palamós, Spain, **777** J2
Palampur, India, **754** D2
Palanan Point, Philippines, **740** C2
Palanga, Lithuania, **771** K5
Palangkaraya, Indonesia, **737** F3
Pālanpur, India, **754** C4
Palapye, Botswana, **811** E3
Palatka, U.S.A., **835** M5
Palau, *country*, Pacific Ocean, **714** C1
Palau, Sardegna, Italy, **779** B5
Palau Islands, Palau, **724** B4
Palaui Island, Philippines, **740** C2
Palaw, Myanmar, **738** C3
Palawan, *island*, Philippines, **740** B4
Palawan Passage, Philippines, **740** B4
Palawan Trough, *underwater feature*, South China Sea, **868** B4
Palayankottai, India, **752** D4
Paldiski, Estonia, **771** M3
Pale, Bosnia and Herzegovina, **778** G4
Paleleh, Pegunungan, *mountain range*, Indonesia, **734** C2
Palembang, *river*, Indonesia, **736** D3
Palen Lake, U.S.A., **832** F5
Palena, Chile, **858** C2
Palena, Lago, *lake*, Chile, **858** C2
Palencia, Spain, **776** E1
Palenque, Panama, **839** F5
Palermo, Sicilia, Italy, **779** D6
Palestine, Lake, U.S.A., **834** E3
Palestine, U.S.A., **834** E4
Paletwa, Myanmar, **741** B3
Pālghāt, India, **752** D4
Palgrave Point, Namibia, **810** B3
Pāli, India, **754** C4
Paliki, Russian Federation, **783** E6
Palikir, Micronesia, **724** D4
Palinuro, Italy, **779** E5
Paliouri, Akra, *point*, Greece, **781** D6
Palisade, U.S.A., **830** C5
Pālitāna, India, **754** B5
Pāliyād, India, **754** B5
Palk Strait, India/Sri Lanka, **752** D4
Palkino, Russian Federation, **783** B4
Palkonda, India, **753** E2
Pālkonda Range, *mountain range*, India, **752** D3
Pallas Grean, Ireland, **793** D5
Pallastunturi, *mountain peak*, Finland, **769** M2
Pallës, Bishti i, *point*, Albania, **781** B5
Pallisa, Uganda, **809** F2
Palliser, Cape, New Zealand, **719** E5
Palliser Bay, New Zealand, **719** E5
Pallu, India, **754** C3
Palm Bay, U.S.A., **835** M6
Palm Beach, U.S.A., **835** M6
Palm-Mar, Islas Canarias, Spain, **813** A4
Palm Springs, U.S.A., **832** E5
Palma, Mozambique, **809** H5
Palma, *river*, Brazil, **854** D3
Palma de Mallorca, Spain, **777** J3

Parsons, U.S.A., **830** F7
Partanna, Sicilia, Italy, **779** D7
Pårtefjällen, *mountain peak*, Sweden, **768** H3
Parthenay, France, **774** D3
Partizansk, Russian Federation, **747** L4
Partizánske, Slovakia, **773** J4
Partney, England, U.K., **789** H1
Partry, Ireland, **793** C4
Partry Mountains, *mountain range*, Ireland, **793** C4
Paru, *river*, Brazil, **850** C3
Paru de Este, *river*, Brazil, **850** B3
Paru de Oeste, *river*, Brazil, **850** B3
Parvatsar, India, **754** C4
Paryang, China, **755** E3
Pas-en-Artois, France, **789** K4
Pasadena, California, U.S.A., **832** D4
Pasadena, Texas, U.S.A., **834** E5
Paşalimanı Adası, *island*, Turkey, **781** F5
Pasapuat, Indonesia, **736** C3
Paşayiğit, Turkey, **781** F5
Pascagoula, U.S.A., **835** H4
Paşcani, Romania, **780** F2
Pasco, U.S.A., **828** E3
Pascoal, Monte, *mountain peak*, Brazil, **855** F4
Pascua, Isla de (Easter Island), *island*, Chile, Pacific Ocean, **859** B2
Pasewalk, Germany, **773** G2
Pasfield Lake, Canada, **824** B2
Pasha, *river*, Russian Federation, **783** D2
Pasha, Russian Federation, **783** D2
Pāsighāt, India, **755** H3
Pasir Panjang, Singapore, **736** J7
Pasir Puteh, Malaysia, **736** C1
Pasir Ris, Singapore, **736** K6
Pasirpengarayan, Indonesia, **736** C2
Påskallavik, Sweden, **770** H4
Pasłęk, Poland, **773** J1
Pasley, Cape, Australia, **716** B5
Pasni, Pakistan, **757** H3
Paso Caballos, Guatemala, **838** C3
Paso de Indios, Argentina, **858** D2
Paso de los Libres, Argentina, **857** F3
Paso de los Toros, Uruguay, **857** F4
Paso de Patria, Paraguay, **857** E3
Paso Socompa, Chile, **856** C2
Pasrūr, Pakistan, **754** C2
Passage Point, Canada, **820** H2
Passau, Germany, **772** F4
Passero, Capo, *cape*, Sicilia, Italy, **779** E7
Passi, Philippines, **740** C4
Passo Fundo, Brazil, **857** G3
Passos, Brazil, **854** D5
Pastavy, Belarus, **771** N5
Pastaza, *river*, Peru, **848** C5
Pasto, Colombia, **848** C4
Pastos Bons, Brazil, **851** E5
Pasu, India, **748** B5
Pasu, Pakistan, **754** C1
Pasuruan, Indonesia, **737** F4
Pasvalys, Lithuania, **771** M4
Pasvikelva, *river*, Norway, **769** P2
Pásztó, Hungary, **773** J5
Pata, Central African Republic, **806** B3
Pata, Senegal, **804** B2
Patagonia, U.S.A., **833** H6
Patah, Gunung, *mountain peak*, Indonesia, **736** C4
Patamea, Samoa, **727** B1
Pātan, Gujarat, India, **754** C5
Pātan, Madhya Pradesh, India, **754** D5
Pātan, Nepal, **755** F4
Patani, Indonesia, **735** E2
Patay, Argentina, **856** D3
Patay, France, **774** E2
Patchway, England, U.K., **788** E3
Patea, New Zealand, **718** E4
Patea, *river*, New Zealand, **718** E4
Pategi, Nigeria, **805** F3
Pateley Bridge, England, U.K., **791** G3
Paterno, Sicilia, Italy, **779** E7
Paterson, U.S.A., **836** C4
Pathfinder Reservoir, U.S.A., **829** L5
Pathiu, Thailand, **738** C4
Patía, *river*, Colombia, **848** B4
Patiāla, India, **754** D3
Patience, French Guiana, **850** C2
Patikul, Philippines, **740** C5
Patmos, *island*, Dodekanisos, Greece, **781** F7
Patna, India, **755** F4
Patnos, Turkey, **803** H1
Patoka Lake, U.S.A., **831** K6
Patos, Albania, **781** B5
Patos, Brazil, **851** G5
Patos, Lagoa dos, *lagoon*, Brazil, **857** G4
Patos de Minas, Brazil, **854** D5
Patquía, Argentina, **856** C4
Patra, Greece, **781** C6
Patricio Lynch, Isla, *island*, Chile, **858** B3
Patrington, England, U.K., **791** H4
Patrocínio, Brazil, **854** D5
Pattani, Thailand, **738** D5
Pattaya, Thailand, **738** D3
Patten, U.S.A., **836** F1
Patterdale, England, U.K., **790** F3
Patti, Sicilia, Italy, **779** E6
Pattisson, Cape, Chatham Islands, New Zealand, **719** Q16
Pattoki, Pakistan, **754** C3
Patton Escarpment, *underwater feature*, Pacific Ocean, **869** K2
Patuākhāli, Bangladesh, **750** D5
Patuca, Punta, *point*, Honduras, **838** D4
Patuca, *river*, Honduras, **838** D4
Patūr, India, **754** D5
Patzcuaro, Mexico, **840** E5
Pau, France, **774** D5
Paucarbamba, Peru, **852** C3
Paucartambo, Peru, **852** D3
Pauillac, France, **774** D4
Pauini, Brazil, **853** E2
Pauini, *river*, Brazil, **853** E2
Pauk, Myanmar, **741** B3
Pauksa Taung, *mountain peak*, Myanmar, **741** B4
Paulatuk, Canada, **820** G3
Paulden, U.S.A., **832** G4
Paulista, Brazil, **851** G5
Paulistana, Brazil, **855** F2
Paulo Afonso, Brazil, **855** F2
Paulo, *river*, Bolivia, **853** G4
Pauls Valley, U.S.A., **834** D2
Păuneşti, Romania, **780** F2
Paungbyin, Myanmar, **741** B2
Paungde, Myanmar, **741** B4
Paup, Papua New Guinea, **726** A3
Paurī, India, **754** D4
Pauri, India, **754** D3
Pauto, *river*, Colombia, **848** D3
Pauträsk, Sweden, **768** H4
Pāvagada, India, **752** D3
Pavão, Brazil, **855** F4
Pavia, Italy, **778** B3
Pavilion, Canada, **822** J6
Pavilly, France, **789** H5
Pāvilosta, Latvia, **771** K4
Pavlikeni, Bulgaria, **780** E4
Pavlodar, Kazakhstan, **759** K2
Pavlodar, *province*, Kazakhstan, **748** C2
Pavlogradka, Russian Federation, **759** J2
Pavlohrad, Ukraine, **782** E3
Pavlovac, Croatia, **778** F3
Pavlovo, Russian Federation, **782** F1
Pavlovsk, Russian Federation, **759** L2
Pavlovskaya, Russian Federation, **782** E3
Pavón, Colombia, **848** D3
Pavullo nel Frignano, Italy, **778** C3
Pawan, *river*, Indonesia, **737** E3
Pawhuska, U.S.A., **830** E7
Pawnee, *river*, U.S.A., **830** C6
Paximadia, *island*, Greece, **781** E8
Paxoi, *island*, Ionioi Nisoi, Greece, **781** B6
Pay, Russian Federation, **783** E2
Paya Lebar, Singapore, **736** K6
Payagyi, Myanmar, **741** C4
Payakumbuh, Indonesia, **736** C3
Payne, Lac, *lake*, Canada, **825** S2
Paynes Creek, U.S.A., **832** C1
Paynton, Canada, **823** Q5
Payong, Tanjong, *point*, Malaysia, **737** F2
Pays de la Loire, *administrative region*, France, **774** D3
Paysandú, Uruguay, **857** E4
Payson, U.S.A., **833** H4
Payún, Cerro, *mountain peak*, Argentina, **856** C5
Payung, Indonesia, **736** D3
Paz de Ariporo, Colombia, **848** D3
Paz de Río, Colombia, **848** D2
Pazardzhik, Bulgaria, **780** E4
Pazarlar, Turkey, **781** G6
Pazaryeri, Turkey, **781** G6
Pazin, Croatia, **778** D3
Pea, Tongatapu Group, Tonga, **727** B4
Peace, *river*, Canada, **823** L3
Peace Point, Canada, **823** N2
Peace River, Canada, **823** L3
Peacehaven, England, U.K., **789** G4
Peach Springs, U.S.A., **832** G4
Peak, The, *mountain peak*, Ascension, **813** A3
Peal de Becerro, Spain, **777** F4
Peale, Mount, *mountain peak*, U.S.A., **833** J2
Pearce, U.S.A., **833** J6
Pearl, *river*, U.S.A., **834** G4
Pearl *see* Zhu, *river*, China, **743** B2
Pearl City, Hawaiian Islands, U.S.A., **832** R9
Pearl Harbor, Hawaiian Islands, U.S.A., **832** R9
Pearsall, U.S.A., **834** C5
Pearson, U.S.A., **835** L4
Peary Channel, Canada, **821** J2
Peary Land, *region*, Greenland, **821** R1
Peawanuck, Canada, **825** M4
Pebane, Mozambique, **809** G6
Pebas, Peru, **848** D5
Pebble Island, Falkland Islands, **858** F4
Peć, Yugoslavia, **780** C4
Peçanha, Brazil, **855** E5
Peças, Ilha das, *island*, Brazil, **857** H2
Pechenga, *river*, Russian Federation, **769** Q2
Pechenga, Russian Federation, **769** Q2
Pechenicheno, Russian Federation, **783** D5
Pechenizhyn, Ukraine, **780** E1
Pechora, *river*, Russian Federation, **784** G3
Pechora, Russian Federation, **784** G3
Pechory, Russian Federation, **783** A4
Peck, U.S.A., **831** M4
Pecka, Yugoslavia, **780** B3
Pecos, *river*, U.S.A., **833** L4
Pecos, U.S.A., **833** M6
Pécs, Hungary, **773** J5
Pedasí, Panama, **839** E6
Pedder, Lake, Australia, **721** J7
Pededze, *river*, Estonia/Latvia, **771** N4
Pedernales, Dominican Republic, **839** H3
Pedernales, Mexico, **840** D2
Pedhoulas, Cyprus, **761** B2
Pediva, Angola, **808** B6
Pedra Azul, Brazil, **855** F4
Pedra Lume, Cape Verde, **800** Q8
Pedras Negras, Brazil, **853** F3
Pedraza La Vieja, Venezuela, **848** D2
Pedregal, Venezuela, **849** D1
Pedregulho, Brazil, **854** D5
Pedreiras, Brazil, **851** E4
Pedrero, Meseta el, *plateau*, Argentina, **858** D3
Pedriceña, Mexico, **840** E3
Pedro Afonso, Brazil, **854** D2
Pedro Chico, Colombia, **848** D4
Pedro de Valdivia, Chile, **856** C2
Pedro Gomes, Brazil, **854** B4
Pedro Juan Caballero, Paraguay, **857** F2
Pedro Osorio, Brazil, **857** G4
Pedro II, Brazil, **851** F4
Peebles, Canada, **824** C6
Peebles, Scotland, U.K., **792** F5
Peekskill, U.S.A., **836** D4
Peel, Isle of Man, **790** D3
Peel, *river*, Canada, **820** F3
Peel Sound, Canada, **821** K2
Peene, *river*, Germany, **772** F2
Peenemünde, Germany, **773** G1
Peerless, U.S.A., **823** S7
Peetz, U.S.A., **833** M1
Pegasus Bay, New Zealand, **719** D6
Pegnitz, Germany, **772** E4
Pego, Spain, **777** G3
Pegu, *division*, Myanmar, **741** C4
Pegu, Myanmar, **741** C4
Pegu Yoma, *mountain range*, Myanmar, **741** B4
Pegwell Bay, England, U.K., **789** J3
Pehlivanköy, Turkey, **781** F5
Pehuajó, Argentina, **856** E5
Peipohja, Finland, **771** L2
Peipsi Järv, *lake*, Estonia, **771** N3
Peiraias (Piraeus), Greece, **781** D7
Peitz, Germany, **773** G3
Peixe, Brazil, **854** D3
Peixe, do, *river*, Brazil, **854** C4
Peixe, *river*, Brazil, **854** C6
Pejirá, Sierra de, *mountain range*, Venezuela, **848** D2
Pekalongan, Indonesia, **737** E4
Pekan, Malaysia, **736** C2
Pekanbaru, Indonesia, **736** C2
Peking *see* Beijing, China, **746** G5
Peklino, Russian Federation, **783** D6
Peksha, *river*, Russian Federation, **783** G4
Pelabuhanratu, Indonesia, **736** D4
Pelabuhanratu, Teluk, *bay*, Indonesia, **736** D4
Pelagie, Isole, *islands*, Sicilia, Italy, **779** D8
Pelawanbesar, Indonesia, **737** G2
Pelée, Montagne, *mountain peak*, Martinique, **837** D3
Pelee Island, Canada, **831** M5
Peleng, Pulau, *island*, Indonesia, **734** C3
Peleng, Selat, *strait*, Indonesia, **734** C3
Pelhřimov, Czech Republic, **773** G4
Pelican Mountains, *mountain range*, Canada, **823** M4
Pelican Rapids, Canada, **824** D5
Peligro, Punta del, *point*, Islas Canarias, Spain, **813** A4
Pelkosenniemi, Finland, **769** N3
Pell City, U.S.A., **835** J3
Pellegrini, Lago, *lake*, Argentina, **858** D1
Pello, Finland, **769** M3
Pellworm, *island*, Germany, **772** D1
Pelly, *river*, Canada, **820** F3
Pelly Bay, Canada, **821** L3
Pelly Crossing, Canada, **820** F3
Pelona Mountain, *mountain peak*, U.S.A., **833** J5
Peloponnisos, *administrative region*, Greece, **781** C7
Peloritani, Monti, *mountain range*, Sicilia, Italy, **779** E7
Pelotas, Brazil, **857** G4
Peltovuoma, Finland, **769** M2
Pemali, Tanjong, *point*, Indonesia, **734** C4
Pemangkat, Indonesia, **737** E2
Pematangsiantar, Indonesia, **736** B2
Pemba, Baía de, *bay*, Mozambique, **809** H5
Pemba, Mozambique, **809** H5
Pemba Island, Tanzania, **809** G4
Pemberton, Canada, **822** H6
Pembine, U.S.A., **831** K3
Pembre, Indonesia, **735** G4
Pembrey, Wales, U.K., **788** C3
Pembroke, Canada, **826** C7
Pembroke, Wales, U.K., **788** C3
Pembroke Dock, Wales, U.K., **788** C3
Pembrokeshire, *unitary authority*, Wales, U.K., **788** B3
Pen-y-ghent, *mountain peak*, England, U.K., **790** F3
Peña de Francia, *mountain peak*, Spain, **776** D2
Peña Nevada, Cerro, *mountain peak*, Mexico, **841** F4
Penafiel, Portugal, **776** C2
Peñafiel, Spain, **776** E2
Penal, Trinidad, Trinidad and Tobago, **859** C4
Penalva, Brazil, **850** E4
Penamacor, Portugal, **776** D2
Penang *see* Pinang, Pulau, *island*, Malaysia, **736** B1
Penanjung, Teluk, *bay*, Indonesia, **737** E4
Penápolis, Brazil, **854** C5
Peñaranda de Bracamonte, Spain, **776** E2
Peñarroya, *mountain peak*, Spain, **777** G2
Penarth, Wales, U.K., **788** D3
Peñas, Cabo, *cape*, Argentina, **858** D4
Peñas, Cabo de, *cape*, Spain, **776** E1
Penas, Golfo de, *gulf*, Chile, **858** B3
Peñas, Punta, *point*, Venezuela, **859** C4
Pend Oreille Lake, U.S.A., **828** F2
Pendang, Indonesia, **737** F3
Pendleton, U.S.A., **828** E4
Pendroy, U.S.A., **828** H2
Peneda, *mountain peak*, Portugal, **776** C2
Penetanguishene, Canada, **831** P3
P'eng-hu Lieh-tao (Pescadores), *island*, Taiwan, **742** D4
P'eng-hu Tao, *island*, Taiwan, **742** D4
Peng Xian, China, **751** G3
Penganga, *river*, India, **754** D5
Penge, Democratic Republic of the Congo, **808** D4
Penglai, China, **747** H5
Pengshui, China, **742** B2
Pengxi, China, **751** H3
Peniche, Portugal, **776** C3
Penicuik, Scotland, U.K., **792** F5

Picton, Canada, **826** C8
Picton, Isla, *island*, Chile, **858** D5
Picton, New Zealand, **719** D5
Picton, U.S.A., **836** B2
Picún Leufú, Argentina, **858** D1
Picún Leufú, *river*, Argentina, **858** C1
Pidārak, Pakistan, **757** H3
Pidi, Democratic Republic of the Congo, **809** E4
Pidurutalagata, *mountain peak*, Sri Lanka, **753** E5
Pie Town, U.S.A., **833** J4
Piedmont, Alabama, U.S.A., **835** K3
Piedmont, South Dakota, U.S.A., **830** B3
Piedrabuena, Spain, **776** E3
Piedrahita, Spain, **776** E2
Piedras, de las, *river*, Peru, **852** D3
Piedras Negras, Coahuila, Mexico, **841** E2
Piedras Negras, Veracruz, Mexico, **841** F5
Pieksämäki, Finland, **771** N1
Pielavesi, Finland, **769** N5
Pielinen, *lake*, Finland, **769** P5
Piemonte, *autonomous region*, Italy, **778** A3
Pieniężno, Poland, **773** K1
Pierce, U.S.A., **828** G3
Pierceland, Canada, **820** J4
Pierowall, Orkney, Scotland, U.K., **792** F1
Pierre, U.S.A., **830** C3
Pierrelatte, France, **775** G4
Pierreville, Canada, **826** E6
Pierrot Island, Rodrigues, **813** B1
Pierson, Canada, **824** D7
Piet Retief, South Africa, **811** F4
Pietarsaari, Finland, **769** L5
Pietermaritzburg, South Africa, **811** F4
Pietersburg, South Africa, **811** E3
Pieve di Cadore, Italy, **778** D2
Pigeon, *river*, Canada, **824** F5
Pigeon Point, Tobago, Trinidad and Tobago, **859** B4
Pigüé, Argentina, **856** D5
Pihāni, India, **754** E4
Pihlajavesi, Finland, **771** M1
Pihtipudas, Finland, **769** M5
Piippola, Finland, **769** N4
Pijijiapan, Mexico, **841** G6
Pikalevo, Russian Federation, **783** E3
Pikangikum, Canada, **824** H6
Piketberg, South Africa, **810** C5
Pikeville, U.S.A., **831** M7
Pikine, Senegal, **804** A2
Pikit, Philippines, **740** D5
Pikou, China, **747** H5
Pikounda, Congo, **808** C2
Pikwitonei, Canada, **824** F4
Pila, Argentina, **857** E5
Piła, Poland, **773** H2
Pilagá, *river*, Argentina, **857** E2
Pilão Arcado, Brazil, **855** E2
Pilar, Argentina, **857** E5
Pilar, Cabo, *cape*, Chile, **858** B4
Pilar, Paraguay, **857** E3
Pilaya, *river*, Bolivia, **853** F5
Pilbara, *region*, Australia, **720** D3
Pilcaniyeu, Argentina, **858** C1
Pilcomayo, *river*, Argentina/Bolivia/Paraguay, **853** F5
Pīleru, India, **752** D3
Pili, Philippines, **740** C3
Pīlībhīt, India, **754** D3
Pilica, *river*, Poland, **773** K3
Pillar Bay, Ascension, **813** A3
Pillcopata, Peru, **852** D3
Pilões, Serra dos, *mountain range*, Brazil, **854** D4
Pilón, Cuba, **839** F3
Pilot Mound, Canada, **824** E7
Pilot Rock, U.S.A., **828** E4
Pilsen *see* Plzeň, Czech Republic, **772** F4
Pilzno, Poland, **773** K4
Pima, U.S.A., **833** J5
Pimenta Bueno, Brazil, **853** G3
Pimperne, England, U.K., **788** E4
Pimpri-Chinchwad, India, **752** C2
Pináculo, Cerro, *mountain peak*, Argentina, **858** C4
Pinamalayan, Philippines, **740** C3
Pinang (Penang), Pulau, *island*, Malaysia, **736** B1
Pinang, *state*, Malaysia, **736** B1
Pinangah, Malaysia, **737** G1
Pinar del Río, Cuba, **838** E2
Pınarhisar, Turkey, **781** F5
Piñas, Ecuador, **848** B5
Pinatubo, Mount, *mountain peak*, Philippines, **740** C3
Pinchbeck, England, U.K., **789** G2
Pincher Creek, Canada, **823** N7
Pindaré, *river*, Brazil, **850** D4
Pindaré-Mirim, Brazil, **850** E4
Pindi Gheb, Pakistan, **754** C2
Pindobal, Brazil, **850** D4
Pindos Oros (Pindus Mountains), *mountain range*, Albania, **781** C5
Pindushi, Russian Federation, **769** S5
Pindwāra, India, **754** C4
Pine, Cape, Canada, **827** Q6
Pine, U.S.A., **833** H4
Pine Bluff, U.S.A., **834** F2
Pine Creek, Australia, **720** G1
Pine Dock, Canada, **824** F6
Pine Hills, U.S.A., **835** M5
Pine Point, Canada, **823** M1
Pine Ridge, U.S.A., **830** B4
Pine River, Canada, **824** D6
Pine Springs, U.S.A., **833** L6
Pinedale, Arizona, U.S.A., **833** H4
Pinedale, Wyoming, U.S.A., **829** K5
Pinehouse Lake, Canada, **823** R4
Pinehouse Lake, *lake*, Canada, **823** R4
Pineimuta, *river*, Canada, **825** K5
Pineios, *river*, Greece, **781** D6
Pinerolo, Italy, **778** A3
Pines, Isle of *see* Pins, Île des, *island*, New Caledonia, **727** A3
Pinetop-Lakeside, U.S.A., **833** J4
Pineville, U.S.A., **834** F4
Pinewood, Canada, **824** G7
Piney, France, **775** G2
Ping, Mae Nam, *river*, Thailand, **738** C2
P'ing-tung, Taiwan, **742** E4
Ping'an, China, **743** C2
Pingchang, China, **751** H3
Pingdi, China, **743** C3
Pingdingshan, China, **742** C1
Pingdu, China, **747** G5
Pingelap, *island*, Micronesia, **724** E4
Pingguo, China, **751** H5
Pinghai, China, **743** D3
Pinghe, China, **742** D3
Pinghu, Guangdong, China, **743** C3
Pinghu, Zhejiang, China, **742** E2
Pingjiang, China, **742** C2
Pingle, China, **742** B3
Pingli, China, **742** B1
Pingliang, China, **751** H2
Pingling, China, **743** C1
Pingluo, China, **746** D5
Pingquan, China, **747** G4
Pingree, U.S.A., **830** D2
Pingsha, China, **742** C4
Pingshan, China, **743** C3
Pingtan, Fujian, China, **742** D3
Pingtan, Guangdong, China, **743** D2
Pingwu, China, **751** H2
Pingxiang, Guangxi Zhuangzu Zizhiqu, China, **751** H5
Pingxiang, Jiangxi, China, **742** C3
Pingxiang, Vietnam, **739** E1
Pingyang, China, **742** E3
Pingyao, China, **746** F5
Pingyi, China, **742** D1
Pingyin, China, **746** G5
Pingyuanjie, China, **751** G5
Pingzhuang, China, **747** G4
Pinheiro, Brazil, **850** E4
Pinheiro Machado, Brazil, **857** G4
Pinhel, Portugal, **776** D2
Pinhoe, England, U.K., **788** D4
Pini, Pulau, *island*, Indonesia, **736** B2
Pinjarra, Australia, **720** D5
Pink, *river*, Canada, **824** B3
Pink Mountain, Canada, **822** H3
Pinlebu, Myanmar, **741** B2
Pinnacle, *mountain peak*, New Zealand, **719** D5
Pinnes, Akra, *point*, Greece, **781** E5
Pinoso, Spain, **777** G3
Pins, Île des (Isle of Pines), *island*, New Caledonia, **727** A3
Pinsk, Belarus, **782** C2
Pinta, Isla, *island*, Islas Galápagos (Galapagos Islands), Ecuador, **859** A1
Pintados, Chile, **853** E5
Pintamo, Finland, **769** N4
Pintatu, Indonesia, **734** D2
Pinto, Argentina, **856** D3
Pintuyan, Philippines, **740** D4
Pinzón, Isla, *island*, Islas Galápagos (Galapagos Islands), Ecuador, **859** A2
Piombino, Italy, **778** C4
Pioneer Fracture Zone, *tectonic feature*, Pacific Ocean, **869** H2
Pioner, Ostrov, *island*, Russian Federation, **784** K2
Pionerskiy, Russian Federation, **771** K5
Piopio, New Zealand, **718** E4
Piotrków Trybunalski, Poland, **773** J3
Piperi, *island*, Greece, **781** E6
Pipestone, Canada, **824** D7
Pipestone, *river*, Canada, **823** R3
Pipestone, U.S.A., **830** E3
Pipili, India, **755** F5
Pipiriki, New Zealand, **718** E4
Pipmuacan, Réservoir, Canada, **826** F5
Pipri, India, **755** E4
Piquiri, *river*, Brazil, **857** G2
Pīr Panjāl Range, *mountain range*, India, **754** C2
Piracanjuba, Brazil, **854** D4
Piracicaba, Brazil, **857** H2
Piracicaba, *river*, Brazil, **857** H2
Piraçununga, Brazil, **854** D5
Piracuruca, Brazil, **851** F4
Piraeus *see* Peiraias, Greece, **781** D7
Piraí do Sul, Brazil, **857** H2
Pirajuí, Brazil, **854** D5
Pirané, Argentina, **857** E2
Piranhas, Brazil, **854** C4
Piranhas, *river*, Brazil, **851** G5
Pirapó, *river*, Brazil, **857** G2
Pirapora, Brazil, **855** E4
Piratini, Brazil, **857** G4
Piratini, *river*, Brazil, **857** G4
Piray, *river*, Bolivia, **853** F4
Piray Guazu, *river*, Argentina, **857** F3
Pires do Rio, Brazil, **854** D4
Piripiri, Brazil, **851** F4
Piripiri, New Zealand, **718** F5
Píritu, Venezuela, **849** E1
Pirizal, Brazil, **854** B4
Pirmasens, Germany, **772** C4
Pirna, Germany, **773** F3
Pirnmill, Scotland, U.K., **792** D5
Pirón, *river*, Spain, **776** E2
Pirongia Mountain, *mountain peak*, New Zealand, **718** E3
Pirot, Yugoslavia, **780** D4
Pirovac, Croatia, **778** E4
Pirttikoski, Finland, **769** N3
Pirttikylä, Finland, **771** K1
Piru, Indonesia, **735** E3
Pisa, Italy, **778** C4
Pisa, Mount, *mountain peak*, New Zealand, **719** B7
Pisagua, Chile, **853** D5
Pisco, Peru, **852** C3
Pisco, *river*, Peru, **852** C3
Písek, Czech Republic, **773** G4
Pisgah, Mount, *mountain peak*, New Zealand, **719** C7
Pishchanka, Ukraine, **780** G1
Pising, Indonesia, **734** C4
Piso Firme, Bolivia, **853** G3
Pissos, France, **774** D4
Pistayarvi, Ozero, *lake*, Russian Federation, **769** Q4
Piste, Mexico, **841** H4
Pisticci, Italy, **779** F5
Pistoia, Italy, **778** C4
Pistol River, U.S.A., **828** B5
Pisuerga, *river*, Spain, **776** E1
Pisz, Poland, **773** K2
Pita, Guinea, **804** B2
Pitaga, Canada, **826** J3
Pital, Cerro El, *mountain peak*, El Salvador, **838** C4
Pital, Mexico, **841** H5
Pitalito, Colombia, **848** C4
Pitanga, Brazil, **857** G2
Pitangui, Brazil, **855** E5
Pitcairn Island, Pitcairn Islands, **723** J3
Pitcairn Islands, *U.K. dependency*, Pacific Ocean, **723** J3
Piteå, Sweden, **768** K4
Piteälven, *river*, Sweden, **768** J4
Pitești, Romania, **780** E3
Pithiviers, France, **774** F2
Pitkyaranta, Russian Federation, **783** C2
Pitlochry, Scotland, U.K., **792** F4
Pitoa, Cameroon, **805** G3
Pitomača, Croatia, **778** F3
Pitrufquén, Chile, **858** C1
Pitscottie, Scotland, U.K., **792** G4
Pitt Island, Canada, **822** D5
Pitt Island, Chatham Islands, New Zealand, **719** Q16
Pitt Strait, Chatham Islands, New Zealand, **719** Q16
Pittentrail, Scotland, U.K., **792** E3
Pittsburgh, U.S.A., **831** N5
Pittsfield, U.S.A., **836** D3
Pium, Brazil, **854** D3
Piura, Peru, **852** B1
Pivijay, Colombia, **848** C1
Pivka, Slovenia, **778** E3
Pixa, China, **748** C5
Pixoyal, Mexico, **841** H5
Pizacoma, Peru, **853** E4
Pizhi, Nigeria, **805** F3
Pizzo, Italy, **779** F6
Placentia, Canada, **827** Q6
Placentia Bay, Canada, **827** P6
Placer, Philippines, **740** C4
Placerville, California, U.S.A., **832** C2
Placerville, Colorado, U.S.A., **833** J2
Plácido de Castro, Brazil, **853** E3
Plačkovica, *mountain peak*, Macedonia, **781** D5
Plains, Kansas, U.S.A., **830** C7
Plains, Texas, U.S.A., **833** M5
Plainview, U.S.A., **834** B2
Plakoti, Cape, Cyprus, **761** B2
Plampang, Indonesia, **737** G5
Plana, Bosnia and Herzegovina, **778** G4
Planaltina, Brazil, **854** D4
Planeta Rica, Colombia, **848** C2
Plano, U.S.A., **834** D3
Plantation, U.S.A., **835** M6
Plaquemine, U.S.A., **834** G4
Plasencia, Spain, **776** D2
Plastun, Russian Federation, **745** G1
Plata, Río de la, *estuary*, Argentina/Uruguay, **847** G7
Platanos, Greece, **781** C7
Plateau, *state*, Nigeria, **805** F3
Plateaux, *administrative region*, Congo, **808** B3
Platičevo, Yugoslavia, **780** B3
Platina, U.S.A., **832** B1
Plato, Colombia, **848** C2
Platte, *river*, U.S.A., **830** D5
Platte Island, Seychelles, **812** D2
Platteville, U.S.A., **830** H4
Plattsburgh, U.S.A., **836** D2
Plau, Germany, **772** F2
Plauen, Germany, **772** F3
Plauer See, *lake*, Germany, **772** F2
Plav, Yugoslavia, **780** B4
Plava, *river*, Russian Federation, **783** F6
Pļaviņas, Latvia, **771** M4
Plavsk, Russian Federation, **783** F6
Plây Cu (Pleiku), Vietnam, **739** F3
Playa Blanca, Islas Canarias, Spain, **813** B4
Playas, Ecuador, **848** B5
Playas Lake, U.S.A., **833** J6
Plaza Huincul, Argentina, **858** D1
Pld'ma, Russian Federation, **783** E2
Pleasant Plains, U.S.A., **834** G2
Pleasant Valley, U.S.A., **828** F4
Pleasanton, U.S.A., **834** C5
Plechý, *mountain peak*, Czech Republic, **773** F4
Plei Câ'n, Vietnam, **739** E3
Pleiku *see* Plây Cu, Vietnam, **739** F3
Plenty, Bay of, New Zealand, **718** F3
Plentywood, U.S.A., **829** M2
Plessisville, Canada, **826** F6
Pleszew, Poland, **773** H3
Plétipi, Lac, *lake*, Canada, **826** F4
Pleven, Bulgaria, **780** E4
Plevna, U.S.A., **829** M3
Plitvice, Croatia, **778** E3
Pljevlja, Yugoslavia, **780** B4
Ploaghe, Sardegna, Italy, **779** B5
Płock, Poland, **773** J2
Ploërmel, France, **774** C3
Ploiești, Romania, **780** F3
Plomari, Greece, **781** F6
Plomb du Cantal, *mountain peak*, France, **774** F4
Plön, Germany, **772** E1
Płońsk, Poland, **773** K2
Plopeni, Romania, **780** E3
Ploskosh', Russian Federation, **783** C4
Ploskoye, Russian Federation, **783** E5
Plotava, Russian Federation, **759** L2
Plotnikovo, Russian Federation, **759** L1
Płoty, Poland, **773** G2
Plouaret, France, **774** C2
Ploudalmézeau, France, **774** B2
Plovdiv, *administrative region*, Bulgaria, **780** E4
Plovdiv, Bulgaria, **780** E4
Plummer, U.S.A., **828** F3
Plumpton, England, U.K., **790** F3
Plumtree, Zimbabwe, **811** E3
Plungė, Lithuania, **771** K5
Plyeshchanitsy, Belarus, **771** N5
Plymouth, England, U.K., **788** C4
Plymouth, Indiana, U.S.A., **831** K5
Plymouth, Massachusetts, U.S.A., **836** E4
Plymouth, Montserrat, **837** D2
Plymouth, Tobago, Trinidad and Tobago, **859** B4
Plymouth, *unitary authority*, England, U.K., **788** C4
Plympton, England, U.K., **788** C4

Purari, *river*, Papua New Guinea, **726** B4
Purcell, U.S.A., **834** D2
Purcell Mountains, *mountain range*, Canada, **823** L6
Purekkari neem, *point*, Estonia, **771** M3
Purén, Chile, **856** B6
Purgatoire, *river*, U.S.A., **833** M3
Puri, India, **755** F6
Purificación, Mexico, **840** D5
Purna, India, **754** D6
Purnach, *river*, Russian Federation, **769** U3
Pūrnia, India, **755** F4
Purranque, Chile, **858** C1
Puruarán, Mexico, **841** E5
Purukcahu, Indonesia, **737** F3
Puruliya, India, **755** F5
Purus, *river*, Brazil, **849** F5
Puruvesi, *lake*, Finland, **771** P1
Pŭrvomay, Bulgaria, **780** E4
Purwakarta, Indonesia, **737** D4
Purwokerto, Indonesia, **737** E4
Pusad, India, **754** D6
Pusan, South Korea, **744** E4
Pushkin, Russian Federation, **783** C3
Pushlakhta, Russian Federation, **769** T4
Pushnoy, Russian Federation, **769** S4
Püspökladány, Hungary, **773** K5
Pustaya Guba, Russian Federation, **769** R3
Pustoshka, Russian Federation, **783** B4
Pu'tai, Taiwan, **742** E4
Putao, Myanmar, **741** C2
Putaruru, New Zealand, **718** E4
Putia, Indonesia, **734** D3
Putian, China, **742** D3
Putina, Peru, **853** E4
Puting, Tanjong, *point*, Indonesia, **737** E3
Putla, Mexico, **841** F5
Putlitz, Germany, **772** F2
Putnam, U.S.A., **834** C2
Putorana, Plato, *mountain range*, Russian Federation, **784** L3
Putorino, New Zealand, **718** F4
Putre, Chile, **853** E5
Puttalam, Sri Lanka, **752** D4
Puttalam Lagoon, Sri Lanka, **752** D4
Puttgarden, Germany, **772** E1
Puttūr, India, **752** C3
Putumayo, *river*, Colombia/Peru, **848** C4
Putus, Tanjong, *point*, Indonesia, **737** E3
Putussibau, Indonesia, **737** F2
Putyla, Ukraine, **780** E2
Puukkokumpu, Finland, **769** M4
Puula, *lake*, Finland, **771** N2
Puumala, Finland, **771** P2
Puuwai, Hawaiian Islands, U.S.A., **832** Q9
Puvirnituq, Canada, **825** R1
Puyang, China, **742** C1
Puyehue, Chile, **858** C1
Puyo, Ecuador, **848** C4
Puysegur Point, New Zealand, **719** A8
Pwani, *administrative region*, Tanzania, **809** G4
Pweto, Democratic Republic of the Congo, **809** E4
Pwllheli, Wales, U.K., **788** C2
Pyal'ma, Russian Federation, **769** S5
Pyamalaw, *river*, Myanmar, **741** B4
Pyaozero, Ozero, *lake*, Russian Federation, **769** Q3
Pyapon, Myanmar, **741** B4
Pyasinskiy Zaliv, *bay*, Russian Federation, **784** J2
Pyatigorsk, Russian Federation, **758** C4
Pyawbwe, Myanmar, **741** C3
Pyazhelka, Russian Federation, **783** E2
Pyè (Prome), Myanmar, **741** B4
Pyhäjärvi, Finland, **769** N5
Pyhäjoki, Finland, **769** M4
Pyhäjoki, *river*, Finland, **769** M4
Pyhältö, Finland, **771** N2
Pyhäntä, Finland, **769** N4
Pyhäranta, Finland, **771** K2
Pyhäselkä, Finland, **771** Q1
Pyhäselkä, *lake*, Finland, **771** P1
Pyhätunturi, *mountain peak*, Finland, **769** N3
Pyinmana, Myanmar, **741** C4
Pyle, Wales, U.K., **788** D3
Pylkönmäki, Finland, **769** M5
Pylos, Greece, **781** C7
Pymatuning Reservoir, U.S.A., **831** N5
Pyramid Island, Chatham Islands, New Zealand, **719** Q16
Pyramid Lake, U.S.A., **832** D1
Pyramid Point, Ascension, **813** A3
P'yŏnggang, North Korea, **744** D3
P'yŏngsŏng, North Korea, **744** D3
P'yŏngt'aek, South Korea, **744** D3
P'yŏngyang, North Korea, **744** D3
Pyrenees, *mountain range*, Andorra/France/Spain, **766** D7
Pyrgetos, Greece, **781** D6
Pyrgi, Greece, **781** E6
Pyrgos, Greece, **781** C7
Pyrzyce, Poland, **773** G2
Pyshna, Belarus, **783** B5
Pyttegga, *mountain peak*, Norway, **770** C1
Pyu, Myanmar, **741** C4
Pyuntaza, Myanmar, **741** C4
Pyzdry, Poland, **773** H2

Q

Qaanaag (Thule), Greenland, **821** N2
Qabanbay, Kazakhstan, **748** D3
Qabātiyah, West Bank, **761** C3
Qābis, Tunisia, **802** B2
Qāḑub, Suquţrá (Socotra), Yemen, **813** B2
Qā'en, Iran, **757** G2
Qagan, China, **747** G2
Qagan Nur, China, **746** F4
Qagan Nur, *lake*, China, **746** F4
Qagan Teg, China, **746** F4
Qagca, China, **751** F2
Qaidam Pendi, *basin*, China, **749** G5
Qakar, China, **748** D5
Qala'an Naḩl, Sudan, **806** D2
Qalāt, Afghanistan, **754** A2
Qal'at al Ḩiṣn, Syria, **761** D2
Qal'at Bīshah, Saudi Arabia, **803** H5
Qal'at Şāliḩ, Iraq, **803** J2
Qalba Zhotasy, *mountain range*, Kazakhstan, **748** D2
Qal'eh Shahr, Afghanistan, **754** A2
Qal'eh-ye Now, Afghanistan, **757** H2
Qal'eh-ye Sarkārī, Afghanistan, **754** A2
Qallābāt, Sudan, **806** E2
Qalyūb, Egypt, **761** A4
Qamalung, China, **751** F2
Qamar, Ghubbat al, *bay*, Oman/Yemen, **756** F5
Qambar, Pakistan, **754** A4
Qamdo, China, **751** F3
Qamīnis, Libya, **802** C2
Qandahār, Afghanistan, **754** A3
Qandala, Somalia, **807** G2
Qanshenggel, Kazakhstan, **748** B3
Qapqal, China, **748** D4
Qapshaghay, Kazakhstan, **748** C4
Qapshaghay Bögeni, *reservoir*, Kazakhstan, **748** C3
Qaqortoq, Greenland, **821** Q3
Qarabas, Kazakhstan, **748** B2
Qaraböget, Kazakhstan, **748** A3
Qarabulaq, Almaty, Kazakhstan, **748** C3
Qarabulaq, Shyghys Qazaqstan, Kazakhstan, **748** E3
Qarabulaq, Yuzhnyy Qazaqstan, Kazakhstan, **759** H4
Qarabutaq, Kazakhstan, **758** G3
Qaraghandy, *province*, Kazakhstan, **748** B2
Qaraghandy (Karaganda), Kazakhstan, **748** B2
Qaraghayly, Kazakhstan, **748** B2
Qārah, Egypt, **802** E3
Qarak, China, **748** C5
Qarakŭl, *lake*, Tajikistan, **748** B5
Qaraqamys, Kazakhstan, **758** E3
Qarasor Köli, Kazakhstan, **748** B2
Qaratal, *river*, Kazakhstan, **748** C3
Qaratöbe, Kazakhstan, **758** E3
Qaraūyl, Kazakhstan, **748** C2
Qarazhal, Kazakhstan, **748** A2
Qardho, Somalia, **807** G3
Qarqan, *river*, China, **748** E5
Qarqaraly, Kazakhstan, **748** B2
Qarqi, Central Xinjiang Uygur Zizhiqu, China, **748** E4
Qarqi, W. Xinjiang Uygur Zizhiqu, China, **748** D4
Qarsan, China, **747** H3
Qarshi, Uzbekistan, **758** H5
Qarţabā, Lebanon, **761** C2
Qaryat al Qaddāḩiyah, Libya, **802** C2
Qasigiannguit (Christianshåb), Greenland, **821** P3
Qaskeleng, Kazakhstan, **748** C4
Qaşr Ḩamām, Saudi Arabia, **803** J4
Qaşr al Farāfirah, Egypt, **802** E3
Qaţanā, Syria, **761** D3
Qaţānan, Ra's, *point*, Suquţrá (Socotra), Yemen, **813** B2
Qatar, *country*, Asia, **730** F7
Qaţmah, Syria, **761** D1
Qaţrūyeh, Iran, **757** F3
Qattara Depression, Egypt, **802** E2
Qawz Rajab, Sudan, **806** E1
Qaynar, Kazakhstan, **748** C2
Qaysar, Kuh-e, *mountain peak*, Afghanistan, **754** A2
Qayū, China, **750** E3
Qazimämmäd, Azerbaijan, **758** D5
Qazvīn, Iran, **758** D5
Qeh, China, **749** J4
Qeqertarsuaq (Disko), *island*, Greenland, **821** P2
Qeqertarsuaq, Greenland, **821** P3
Qeqertarsuatsiaat, Greenland, **821** P3
Qeqertarsuup Tunua, *bay*, Greenland, **821** P3
Qeshm, Jazīreh-ye, *island*, Iran, **757** G3
Qêyi, China, **751** G3
Qeyşār, Afghanistan, **754** A2
Qeẓi'ot, Israel, **761** C4
Qi Xian, Henan, China, **742** C1
Qi Xian, Shaanxi, China, **746** F5
Qian Shan, *mountain range*, China, **747** H4
Qian Xian, China, **742** B1
Qian'an, China, **747** J3
Qianjiang, Sichuan, China, **742** B2
Qianjiang, Hubei, China, **742** C2
Qianning, China, **751** G3
Qianshan, China, **743** B4
Qiansuo, China, **751** G4
Qianwei, China, **751** G3
Qianxi, China, **751** H4
Qianyang, China, **751** H2
Qi'ao, China, **743** B4
Qi'ao Dao, *island*, China, **743** B4
Qiaotou, China, **743** C2
Qiaowan, China, **749** H4
Qiaozhen, China, **746** E5
Qibilī, Tunisia, **802** A2
Qichun, China, **742** C2
Qidaogou, China, **747** J4
Qidong, Hunan, China, **742** C3
Qidong, Jiangsu, China, **742** E2
Qidukou, China, **751** E2
Qiemo, China, **748** E5
Qigan, China, **743** A1
Qihregt, China, **746** F4
Qijiang, China, **751** H3
Qijiaojing, China, **749** F4
Qijing, China, **743** B1
Qila Abdullāh, Pakistan, **754** A3
Qila Saifullāh, Pakistan, **754** B3
Qilian, China, **749** J5
Qilian Shan, *mountain range*, China, **749** H5
Qiman, China, **748** D4
Qimen, China, **742** D2
Qin, *river*, China, **742** C1
Qin Ling, *mountain range*, China, **733** M6
Qin Xian, China, **746** F5
Qinā, Egypt, **803** F3
Qin'an, China, **751** H2
Qing'an, China, **747** J3
Qingchengzi, China, **747** H4
Qingdao, China, **747** H5
Qinggang, China, **747** J3
Qinghai, *province*, China, **751** E2
Qinghai Hu, *lake*, China, **749** H5
Qinghe, China, **748** F3
Qinghemen, China, **747** H4
Qingjian, China, **746** E5
Qingshui, China, **749** H5
Qingshuihe, Nei Mongol Zizhiqu, China, **746** E5
Qingshuihe, Qinghai, China, **751** F2
Qingtian, China, **742** E2
Qingtongxia, China, **746** D5
Qingxi, China, **743** C3
Qingxu, China, **746** F5
Qingyang, China, **746** D5
Qingyuan, Guangdong, China, **742** C4
Qingyuan, Liaoning, China, **747** J4
Qingyuan, Zhejiang, China, **742** D3
Qingzang Gaoyuan (Plateau of Tibet), *plateau*, China, **750** C2
Qingzhou, China, **744** B3
Qinhuangdao, China, **747** G5
Qinyang, China, **742** C1
Qinyuan, China, **746** F5
Qinzhou, China, **742** B4
Qinzhou Wan, *bay*, China, **739** F1
Qionghai, China, **739** F2
Qionglai, China, **751** G3
Qiongzhou Haixia, *strait*, China, **739** F1
Qiqian, China, **747** H1
Qiqihar, China, **747** H3
Qīr, Iran, **756** F3
Qiryat Gat, Israel, **761** C4
Qishi, China, **743** C2
Qitai, China, **748** F3
Qitaihe, China, **747** K3
Qiubei, China, **751** H4
Qixia, China, **747** H5
Qiyahe, China, **747** H1
Qiyang, China, **742** B3
Qizhan, China, **747** J2
Qom, Iran, **756** F2
Qomo, China, **750** E3
Qomsheh, Iran, **756** F2
Qongj, China, **746** E4
Qoraqalpoghiston, Respublika, *autonomous republic*, Uzbekistan, **758** F4
Qorveh, Iran, **803** J1
Qosköl, Kazakhstan, **758** H3
Qostanay (Kustanay), Kazakhstan, **758** G2
Qotanqaraghay, Kazakhstan, **748** E2
Qu Xian, China, **751** H3
Quabbin Reservoir, U.S.A., **836** D3
Quảng Ngãi, Vietnam, **739** F3
Quanzhou, Fujian, China, **742** D3
Quanzhou, Guangxi Zhuangzu Zizhiqu, China, **742** B3
Qu'Appelle, *river*, Canada, **824** C6
Quaqtaq, Canada, **821** N3
Quaraí, Brazil, **857** F4
Quaraí, *river*, Brazil/Uruguay, **857** F4
Quarles, Pegunungan, *mountain range*, Indonesia, **734** B3
Quarry Hills, New Zealand, **719** B8
Quartier Militaire, Mauritius, **813** C1
Quartu Sant'Elena, Sardegna, Italy, **779** B6
Quartzsite, U.S.A., **832** F5
Quartzite Mountain, *mountain peak*, U.S.A., **832** E3
Quatre Bornes, Mauritus, **813** C1
Quatsino, Canada, **822** F6
Quba, Azerbaijan, **758** D4
Qūchān, Iran, **758** F5
Queanbeyan, Australia, **721** K6
Québec, Canada, **826** F6
Québec, *province*, Canada, **826** F4
Quebracho Coto, Argentina, **856** D3
Quebradas, Guatemala, **838** C4
Qued Zem, Morocco, **800** E2
Quedal, Cabo, *cape*, Chile, **858** B1
Quedlinburg, Germany, **772** E3
Queen Bess, Mount, *mountain peak*, Canada, **822** G6
Queen Charlotte, Canada, **822** D5
Queen Charlotte Bay, Falkland Islands, **858** E4
Queen Charlotte Islands, Canada, **822** C5
Queen Charlotte Mountains, *mountain range*, Canada, **822** C5
Queen Charlotte Sound, Canada, **822** E6
Queen Elizabeth Islands, Canada, **821** J2
Queen Mary Land, *region*, Antarctica, **862** F6
Queen Mary's Peak, *mountain peak*, Tristan da Cunha, **813** C2
Queen Maud Bay, South Georgia, **859** A3
Queen Maud Gulf, Canada, **821** J3
Queen Maud Mountains, *mountain range*, Antarctica, **862** D6
Queenborough, England, U.K., **789** H3
Queensbury, New Zealand, **719** B7
Queensland, *state*, Australia, **721** J3
Queenstown, Australia, **721** K7
Queenstown, New Zealand, **719** B7
Queenstown, South Africa, **811** E5
Queguay Grande, *river*, Uruguay, **857** F4
Quehué, Argentina, **856** D5
Queilén, Chile, **858** C2
Queimadas, Brazil, **855** F3
Quela, Angola, **808** C4
Quelimane, Mozambique, **811** G2

R

Raroia, *island*, French Polynesia, **723** G2
Rarotonga, *island*, Cook Islands, **723** F3
Ra's Ajdīr, Tunisia, **802** B2
Ra's an Naqb, Jordan, **761** C5
Ra's at Tīn, Libya, **760** B6
Ras Dashen Terara, *mountain peak*, Ethiopia, **807** E2
Râs el Mâ, Mali, **804** D1
Ra's Ghārib, Egypt, **803** F3
Ra's Maṭārimah, Egypt, **761** B5
Ra's Sudr, Egypt, **761** B5
Ra's Tannūrah, Saudi Arabia, **756** E3
Raša, Croatia, **778** E3
Rasa, Punta, *point*, Argentina, **858** E1
Rasa Island, Philippines, **740** B4
Râşcani, Moldova, **780** F2
Raseiniai, Lithuania, **771** L5
Rashād, Sudan, **806** D2
Rashaant, Bayan-Ölgiy, Mongolia, **749** F3
Rashaant, Dundgovĭ, Mongolia, **746** D3
Rashm, Iran, **757** F1
Rasht, Iran, **758** D5
Rasi Salai, Thailand, **739** E3
Rāsk, Iran, **757** H3
Raška, Yugoslavia, **780** C4
Råsken, *river*, Norway, **770** C2
Râşnov, Romania, **780** E3
Raso, Cabo, *cape*, Argentina, **858** E2
Rastede, Germany, **772** D2
Rastegai'sa, *mountain peak*, Norway, **769** N2
Råstojaure, *lake*, Sweden, **768** K2
Rasu, Monte, *mountain peak*, Sardegna, Italy, **779** B5
Rasūl, Pakistan, **754** C2
Rat Islands, United States of America, **785** U4
Rata, New Zealand, **718** E5
Rata, Tanjong, *point*, Indonesia, **736** D4
Rätan, Sweden, **770** G1
Ratanpur, India, **755** E5
Ratchaburi, Thailand, **738** C3
Rāth, India, **754** D4
Rath Luirc, Ireland, **793** D5
Rathangan, Ireland, **793** E4
Rathbun Lake, U.S.A., **830** G5
Rathdowney, Ireland, **793** E5
Rathdrum, Ireland, **793** F5
Rathenow, Germany, **772** F2
Rathfriland, Northern Ireland, U.K., **793** F3
Rathkeale, Ireland, **793** D5
Rathlin Island, Northern Ireland, U.K., **793** F2
Rathvilly, Ireland, **793** F5
Rathwell, Canada, **824** E7
Rätische Alpen, *mountain range*, Switzerland, **775** J3
Ratlām, India, **754** C5
Ratnāgiri, India, **752** C2
Ratne, Ukraine, **773** M3
Ratodero, Pakistan, **754** B4
Raton, U.S.A., **833** L3
Rättvik, Sweden, **770** G2
Ratz, Mount, *mountain peak*, Canada, **822** C3
Raub, Malaysia, **736** C2
Raub, U.S.A., **830** B2
Rauch, Argentina, **857** E5
Raufarhöfn, Iceland, **768** Z6
Raukumara Range, *mountain range*, New Zealand, **718** F4
Rauland, Norway, **770** D3
Rauma, Finland, **771** K2
Rauma, *river*, Norway, **770** D1
Raunds, England, U.K., **789** G2
Raung, Gunung, *mountain peak*, Indonesia, **737** F5
Raurkela, India, **755** F5
Răut, *river*, Moldova, **780** G2
Rautavaara, Finland, **769** P5
Rautjärvi, Finland, **771** P2
Rava-Rus'ka, Ukraine, **773** L3
Ravalli, U.S.A., **828** G3
Rāvar, Iran, **757** G2
Ravelo, Bolivia, **853** F5
Ravendale, U.S.A., **832** C1
Ravenglass, England, U.K., **790** E3
Ravenna, Italy, **778** D3
Ravensburg, Germany, **772** D5
Ravenshoe, Australia, **721** K2
Ravensthorpe, Australia, **720** E5
Ravenswood, U.S.A., **831** N6
Rāvi, *river*, India/Pakistan, **754** C3
Rawa Mazowiecka, Poland, **773** K3
Rawaki (Phoenix), *island*, Kiribati, **725** G5
Rāwalpindi, Pakistan, **754** C2
Rawāndūz, Iraq, **803** H1
Rawarra, *river*, Indonesia, **735** F3
Rawas, Indonesia, **735** F3
Rāwatsār, India, **754** C3
Rawḩah, Saudi Arabia, **803** H5
Rawicz, Poland, **773** H3
Rawlins, U.S.A., **829** L6
Rawson, Argentina, **858** E2
Rawtenstall, England, U.K., **790** F4
Rawu, China, **751** F3
Ray, Cape, Canada, **827** M6
Ray, U.S.A., **830** B1
Raya, Gunung, *mountain peak*, Indonesia, **737** F3
Raya, Tanjong, *point*, Aceh, Indonesia, **736** B2
Raya, Tanjong, *point*, Sumatera Selatan, Indonesia, **736** D3
Raychikhinsk, Russian Federation, **747** K2
Raydah, Yemen, **756** D5
Rayleigh, England, U.K., **789** H3
Raymond, Canada, **823** N7
Raymond, U.S.A., **828** C3
Raymondville, U.S.A., **834** D6
Raymore, Canada, **824** B6
Raynesford, U.S.A., **829** J3
Rayong, Thailand, **738** D3
Raystown Lake, U.S.A., **836** A4
Raz, Pointe du, *point*, France, **774** B3
Ražanj, Yugoslavia, **780** C4
Razelm, Lacul, *lake*, Romania, **780** G3
Razgrad, Bulgaria, **780** F4
Razim, Lacul, *lagoon*, Romania, **782** C4
Razlog, Bulgaria, **780** D5
Razmak, Pakistan, **754** B2
Ré, Île de, *island*, France, **774** D3
Reading, England, U.K., **789** G3
Reading, U.S.A., **836** C4
Reading, *unitary authority*, England, U.K., **789** G3
Readstown, U.S.A., **830** H4
Real, Cordillera, *mountain range*, Bolivia, **853** E4
Realicó, Argentina, **856** D5
Reao, *island*, French Polynesia, **723** H2
Rebbenesøy, *island*, Norway, **768** H1
Rebecca, Lake, Australia, **720** E5
Reboly, Russian Federation, **769** Q5
Rebordelo, Portugal, **776** D2
Rebun-tō, *island*, Japan, **745** H1
Recess, Ireland, **793** C4
Rechane, Russian Federation, **783** C4
Recherche, Archipelago of, *islands*, Australia, **720** E5
Recife, Brazil, **851** G5
Recife, Cape, South Africa, **811** E5
Récifs, Île aux, *island*, Seychelles, **813** A2
Recinto, Chile, **856** B5
Recklinghausen, Germany, **772** C3
Reconquista, Argentina, **857** E3
Recreio, Brazil, **853** G2
Recreo, Argentina, **856** D3
Red, *river*, Minnesota, U.S.A., **830** E2
Red, *river*, Oklahoma, U.S.A., **834** C2
Red Bank, New Jersey, U.S.A., **836** C4
Red Bank, Tennessee, U.S.A., **835** K2
Red Bay, Canada, **827** N4
Red Bluff, U.S.A., **832** B1
Red Cloud, U.S.A., **830** D5
Red Deer, Canada, **823** N5
Red Deer, *river*, Alberta, Canada, **823** N6
Red Deer, *river*, Saskatchewan, Canada, **824** C5
Red Deer Lake, Canada, **824** D5
Red Elm, U.S.A., **830** C3
Red Indian Lake, Canada, **827** N5
Red Lake, Canada, **824** H6
Red Lake Road, Canada, **824** H7
Red Lodge, U.S.A., **829** K4
Red Rock, British Columbia, Canada, **822** H5
Red Rock, Ontario, Canada, **831** J1
Red Sea, Africa/Asia, **756** C4
Red Sucker Lake, Canada, **824** G4
Red Wing, U.S.A., **830** G3
Redang, Pulau, *island*, Malaysia, **736** C1
Redbird, U.S.A., **829** M5
Redcar, England, U.K., **791** G3
Redcar and Cleveland, *unitary authority*, England, U.K., **791** G3
Redcliff, Canada, **823** P6
Redcliff, Zimbabwe, **811** E2
Redding, California, U.S.A., **832** B1
Redding, Iowa, U.S.A., **830** F5
Redditch, England, U.K., **789** F2
Redditt, Canada, **824** G7
Rede, *river*, England, U.K., **790** F2
Redenção, Brazil, **850** C5
Redenção de Gurguéia, Brazil, **855** E2
Redeyef, Tunisia, **801** H2
Redfield, New York, U.S.A., **836** C3
Redfield, South Dakota, U.S.A., **830** D3
Redhead, Trinidad, Trinidad and Tobago, **859** C4
Redhill, England, U.K., **789** G3
Rédics, Hungary, **773** H5
Redkino, Russian Federation, **783** F4
Redland, Orkney, Scotland, U.K., **792** F1
Redlynch, England, U.K., **789** F4
Redmond, U.S.A., **828** D4
Redon, France, **774** C3
Redonda, *island*, Antigua and Barbuda, **837** D2
Redonda, Punta, *point*, Isla de Pascua (Easter Island), Chile, **859** B2
Redondo, Portugal, **776** D3
Redruth, England, U.K., **788** B4
Redstone, Canada, **822** H5
Redwood City, U.S.A., **832** B3
Redwood Valley, U.S.A., **832** B2
Red'ya, *river*, Russian Federation, **783** C4
Ree, Lough, *lake*, Ireland, **793** E4
Reed City, U.S.A., **831** L4
Reedpoint, U.S.A., **829** K4
Reedsburg, U.S.A., **830** H4
Reedsport, U.S.A., **828** B5
Reedville, U.S.A., **836** B6
Reefton, New Zealand, **719** C6
Reform, U.S.A., **835** J3
Regeb, Sudan, **806** B2
Regen, Germany, **772** F4
Regen, *river*, Germany, **772** F4
Regensburg, Germany, **772** F4
Regent, U.S.A., **830** B2
Reggane, Algeria, **801** G3
Reggane, Sebkha, *lake*, Algeria, **801** F3
Reggio di Calabria, Italy, **779** E6
Reggio nell' Emilia, Italy, **778** C3
Reghin, Romania, **780** E2
Regina, Brazil, **850** C2
Regina, Canada, **824** B6
Régina, French Guiana, **850** C2
Regina, U.S.A., **833** K3
Regna, Sweden, **770** G3
Reharaka, Madagascar, **812** A4
Rehli, India, **754** D5
Rehoboth, Namibia, **810** C3
Reḥovot, Israel, **761** C4
Reichenau, Switzerland, **775** J3
Reichenbach, Germany, **772** F3
Reidsville, U.S.A., **831** P7
Reigate, England, U.K., **789** G3
Reigh, Rubha, *point*, Scotland, U.K., **792** C3
Reilly Hill, U.S.A., **830** B5
Reims, France, **775** G2
Reina Adelaida, Archipiélago de la, *islands*, Chile, **858** B4
Reinbek, Germany, **772** E2
Reindeer, *river*, Canada, **824** C4
Reindeer Lake, Canada, **824** C3
Reinga, Cape, New Zealand, **718** D2
Reinosa, Spain, **776** E1
Reinøy, *island*, Norway, **768** J2
Reinsfjell, *mountain peak*, Norway, **768** E5
Reisaelva, *river*, Norway, **768** K2
Reisjärvi, Finland, **769** M5
Reisseck, *mountain peak*, Austria, **778** D2
Reisterstown, U.S.A., **836** B5
Reitoru, *island*, French Polynesia, **723** G2
Rejunya, Venezuela, **849** F3
Rekovac, Yugoslavia, **780** C4
Relizane, Algeria, **801** G1
Rémalard, France, **774** E2
Remanso, Brazil, **855** E2
Rembang, Indonesia, **737** E4
Remennikovo, Russian Federation, **783** B4
Rémire, French Guiana, **850** C2
Remiremont, France, **775** H2
Remo, *mountain peak*, Italy, **779** D4
Rempang, Pulau, *island*, Indonesia, **736** C2
Remscheid, Germany, **772** C3
Rena, Norway, **770** E2
Renam, Myanmar, **741** C2
Rencēni, Latvia, **771** M4
Rend Lake, U.S.A., **831** J6
Renda, Latvia, **771** L4
Rendova, *island*, Solomon Islands, **727** A1
Rendsburg, Germany, **772** D1
Renfrew, Canada, **826** C7
Renfrewshire, *local authority*, Scotland, U.K., **792** E5
Rengat, Indonesia, **736** C3
Rengo, Chile, **856** B5
Renhua, China, **742** C3
Reni, Ukraine, **780** G3
Renmark, Australia, **721** J5
Rennebu, Norway, **770** D1
Rennell, *island*, Solomon Islands, **727** A1
Rennes, France, **774** D2
Rennie, Canada, **824** G7
Reno, U.S.A., **832** D2
Renovo, U.S.A., **836** B4
Renqiu, China, **746** G5
Renshan, China, **743** D3
Renshou, China, **751** H3
Rensjön, Sweden, **768** J2
Renwer, Canada, **824** D5
Réo, Burkina Faso, **804** D2
Reo, Indonesia, **734** C5
Répcelak, Hungary, **773** H5
Repetek, Turkmenistan, **758** G5
Republic, U.S.A., **828** E2
Repulse Bay, Canada, **821** L3
Repvåg, Norway, **769** M1
Requena, Peru, **852** D1
Requena, Spain, **777** G3
Réquista, France, **774** F4
Rere, Solomon Islands, **727** A1
Resang, Tanjong, *point*, Malaysia, **736** C2
Resen, Macedonia, **781** C5
Reserva, Brazil, **857** G2
Reserve, Canada, **824** C5
Reserve, U.S.A., **829** M2
Resistencia, Argentina, **857** E3
Reşiţa, Romania, **780** C3
Resko, Poland, **773** G2
Resolute, Canada, **821** K2
Resolution Island, Canada, **821** N4
Resolution Island, New Zealand, **719** A7
Resseta, *river*, Russian Federation, **783** E6
Restigouche, *river*, Canada, **826** H6
Restinga, Punta, *point*, Islas Canarias, Spain, **813** A4
Retalhuleu, Guatemala, **838** C4
Reteag, Romania, **780** E2
Retén Llico, Chile, **856** B5
Retford, England, U.K., **791** H4
Rethel, France, **775** G2
Rethymno, Kriti, Greece, **781** E8
Retz, Austria, **773** G4
Réunion, *French department*, Indian Ocean, **813** A1
Reus, Spain, **777** H2
Reutlingen, Germany, **772** D4
Revda, Russian Federation, **769** S3
Revelstoke, Canada, **823** K6
Reventazón, Peru, **852** B2
Revermont, *region*, France, **775** G3
Revillagigedo, Islas, *islands*, Mexico, **817** M7
Revivim, Israel, **761** C4
Revúboè, *river*, Mozambique, **809** F6
Revúca, Slovakia, **773** K4
Rewa, India, **755** E4
Rewāri, India, **754** D3
Rexburg, U.S.A., **829** J5
Rexford, U.S.A., **828** G2
Rey, Isla del, *island*, Panama, **839** F5
Rey Bouba, Cameroon, **805** G3
Reyes, Bolivia, **853** E4
Reyes, Point, U.S.A., **832** B3
Reyes, Punta dos, *point*, Chile, **856** B2
Reyhanlı, Turkey, **761** D1
Reykhólar, Iceland, **768** X7
Reykjanes Ridge, *underwater feature*, Atlantic Ocean, **867** E2
Reykjavík, Iceland, **768** X7
Reynosa, Mexico, **841** F3
Rēzekne, Latvia, **771** N4
Rezina, Moldova, **780** G2
Rgotina, Yugoslavia, **780** D3
Rhayader, Wales, U.K., **788** D2
Rhein, *river*, Austria, **775** J3
Rhein, *river*, Germany, **772** C3
Rhein, *river*, Switzerland, **775** J3
Rheine, Germany, **772** C2
Rheinland-Pfalz, *state*, Germany, **772** C3
Rheinwaldhorn, *mountain peak*, Switzerland, **775** J3
Rhiconich, Scotland, U.K., **792** E2
Rhin, *river*, France, **775** H3
Rhine, *river*, Europe, **766** E5; *see also* Rhein, *river*, Austria, **775** J3; Rhein, *river*, Germany, **772** C3; Rhein, *river*, Switzerland, **775** J3; Rhin, *river*, France, **775** H3
Rhinelander, U.S.A., **831** J3
Rhino Camp, Uganda, **809** F2
Rhinow, Germany, **772** F2
Rhir, Cap, *cape*, Morocco, **800** D2

Rognan, Norway, **768** G3
Rogne, Norway, **770** D2
Rohat, India, **754** C4
Rohatyn, Ukraine, **773** M4
Rohri, Pakistan, **754** B4
Rohtak, India, **754** D3
Rohuküla, Estonia, **771** L3
Roi Et, Thailand, **739** D2
Roing, India, **755** H3
Roja, Latvia, **771** L4
Rojas, Argentina, **856** E5
Rojhān, Pakistan, **754** B3
Rojo, Cabo, *cape*, Mexico, **841** F4
Rokan, *river*, Indonesia, **736** C2
Rokhmoyva, Gora, *mountain peak*, Russian Federation, **769** P3
Rokiškis, Lithuania, **771** M5
Rokkasho, Japan, **745** H2
Rola Co, *lake*, China, **750** D2
Rolândia, Brazil, **857** G2
Rôlas, Ilhéu das, *island*, São Tomé and Príncipe, **813** C4
Røldal, Norway, **770** C3
Roll, U.S.A., **834** C2
Rolla, Missouri, U.S.A., **830** H7
Rolla, North Dakota, U.S.A., **830** D1
Rollag, Norway, **770** D2
Rolleston, Mount, *mountain peak*, New Zealand, **719** C6
Rollet, Canada, **826** B6
Rolvsøya, *island*, Norway, **769** L1
Roma, Australia, **721** K4
Roma, Lesotho, **811** E4
Roma (Rome), Italy, **779** D5
Roma, Sweden, **771** J4
Roma, U.S.A., **834** C6
Romaine, *river*, Canada, **827** K4
Roman, Romania, **780** F2
Roman-Kosh, Hora, *mountain peak*, Ukraine, **782** D4
Romanche Fracture Zone, *tectonic feature*, Atlantic Ocean, **867** E5
Romania, *country*, Europe, **764** G6
Romano, Cape, U.S.A., **835** L7
Romano, Cayo, *island*, Cuba, **839** F2
Romanovka, Russian Federation, **746** F1
Rombebai, Danau, *lake*, Indonesia, **735** G3
Romblon, Philippines, **740** C3
Rome, Alabama, U.S.A., **835** J4
Rome, New York, U.S.A., **836** C3
Rome, Oregon, U.S.A., **828** F5
Rome *see* Roma, Italy, **779** D5
Romney, U.S.A., **831** P6
Romny, Russian Federation, **747** K2
Romny, Ukraine, **782** D2
Rømø, *island*, Denmark, **770** D5
Rompin, *river*, Malaysia, **736** C2
Romsey, England, U.K., **789** F3
Romuli, Romania, **780** E2
Ron Phibun, Thailand, **738** C4
Ronan, U.S.A., **828** G3
Ronas Hill, Shetland, Scotland, U.K., **792** K7
Roncador, Serra do, *mountain range*, Brazil, **854** C4
Ronda, Serrania de, *mountain range*, Spain, **776** E4
Ronda, Spain, **776** E4
Rønde, Denmark, **770** E4
Rondon do Pará, Brazil, **850** D4
Rondônia, *state*, Brazil, **853** F3
Rondonópolis, Brazil, **854** B4
Rondslottet, *mountain peak*, Norway, **770** D2
Rông, Kaôh, *island*, Cambodia, **738** D4
Rong, *river*, China, **742** B3
Rong Xian, China, **742** B4
Rong'an, China, **742** B3
Rongbaca, China, **751** F3
Rongcheng, China, **747** H5
Ronge, Lac la, *lake*, Canada, **823** S4
Rongelap, *island*, Marshall Islands, **724** E3
Rongjiang, China, **742** B3
Rongklang, *mountain range*, Myanmar, **741** B3
Rongqi, China, **743** A3
Rongxar, China, **750** C3
Rønne, Denmark, **770** G5
Ronne Entrance, *strait*, Antarctica, **862** B5
Ronne Ice Shelf, Antarctica, **862** C5
Ronneby, Sweden, **770** G4
Rønnede, Denmark, **770** F5
Rönnöfors, Sweden, **768** F5
Ronuro, *river*, Brazil, **854** B3
Rookery Point, Tristan da Cunha, **813** C2
Roorkee, India, **754** D3
Roosendaal, Netherlands, **772** B3
Roosevelt, Arizona, U.S.A., **833** H5
Roosevelt, Mount, *mountain peak*, Canada, **822** G2
Roosevelt, Utah, U.S.A., **833** J1
Roosevelt Island, Antarctica, **862** D7
Ropeid, Norway, **770** C3
Roper, *river*, Australia, **720** G1
Roper Bar, Australia, **721** G1
Ropi, *mountain peak*, Finland, **768** K2
Roquefort, France, **774** D4
Roraima, Monte, *mountain peak*, Guyana, **849** G3
Roraima, *state*, Brazil, **849** G4
Røros, Norway, **770** E1
Rørvik, Norway, **768** E4
Ros', Belarus, **773** M2
Rosa, Cabo, *cape*, Islas Galápagos (Galapagos Islands), Ecuador, **859** A2
Rosa, Monte, *mountain peak*, Italy, **778** A3
Rosa, Punta, *point*, Mexico, **840** C3
Rosa de los James, Islas Canarias, Spain, **813** B4
Rosa Zárate, Ecuador, **848** B4
Rosal de la Frontera, Spain, **776** D4
Rosalia, Punta, *point*, Isla de Pascua (Easter Island), Chile, **859** B2
Rosalia, U.S.A., **828** F3
Rosana, Brazil, **857** G2
Rosantos, Punta, *point*, Mexico, **840** C3
Rosario, Argentina, **856** E4
Rosário, Brazil, **851** E4
Rosario, Cayo del, *island*, Cuba, **839** E2
Rosario, Paraguay, **857** F2
Rosario, Sinaloa, Mexico, **840** D4
Rosario, Sonora, Mexico, **840** C3
Rosario, Venezuela, **848** D1
Rosario de la Frontera, Argentina, **856** D2
Rosario de Lerma, Argentina, **856** D2
Rosario del Tala, Argentina, **857** E4
Rosário do Sul, Brazil, **857** F4
Rosário Oeste, Brazil, **854** B4
Rosarito, Baja California, Mexico, **840** B2
Rosarito, Baja California Sur, Mexico, **840** C3
Roscoe, New York, U.S.A., **836** C4
Roscoe, South Dakota, U.S.A., **830** D3
Roscoff, France, **774** C2
Roscommon, *county*, Ireland, **793** D4
Roscommon, Ireland, **793** D4
Roscrea, Ireland, **793** E5
Rose, *island*, American Samoa, **725** H6
Rose, U.S.A., **834** E1
Rose Belle, Mauritius, **813** C1
Rose Blanche, Canada, **827** M6
Rose Peak, *mountain peak*, U.S.A., **833** J5
Rose Prairie, Canada, **822** J3
Rose Valley, Canada, **824** C5
Roseau, Dominica, **837** D3
Roseau, U.S.A., **830** F1
Rosebud, Canada, **823** N6
Roseburg, U.S.A., **828** C5
Rosedale Abbey, England, U.K., **791** H3
Rosehearty, Scotland, U.K., **792** G3
Rosemarkie, Scotland, U.K., **792** E3
Rosemary, Canada, **823** N6
Rosenberg, U.S.A., **834** E5
Rosendal, Norway, **770** C3
Rosenheim, Germany, **772** F5
Roses, Golfo de, *gulf*, Spain, **777** J1
Roseto degli Abruzzi, Italy, **778** D4
Rosetown, Canada, **823** Q6
Roseville, U.S.A., **830** H5
Rosh Pinah, Namibia, **810** C4
Rosières-en-Santerre, France, **789** K5
Rosignol, Guyana, **849** H2
Roșiorii de Vede, Romania, **780** E3
Rositsa, Bulgaria, **780** F4
Roskilde, Denmark, **770** F5
Roslavl', Russian Federation, **783** D6
Ross, Mount, *mountain peak*, New Zealand, **719** E5
Ross, New Zealand, **719** C6
Ross, Point, Norfolk Island, **721** T13
Ross, U.S.A., **830** B1
Ross Bay Junction, Canada, **826** H3
Ross Carbery, Ireland, **793** C6
Ross Hill, *mountain peak*, Christmas Island, **720** N8
Ross Ice Shelf, Antarctica, **862** D6
Ross Island, Antarctica, **862** D7
Ross-on-Wye, England, U.K., **788** E3
Ross River, Canada, **820** F3
Ross Sea, Antarctica, **862** C7
Rossan Point, Ireland, **793** C3
Rossano, Italy, **779** F6
Rossel Island, Papua New Guinea, **726** D5
Rossignol, Lake, Canada, **826** J7
Rossington, England, U.K., **791** G4
Rosslare, Ireland, **793** F5
Rosslare Harbour, Ireland, **793** F5
Rosso, Mauritania, **804** A1
Rossosh', Russian Federation, **782** E2
Rosston, U.S.A., **830** D7
Røssvatnet, *lake*, Norway, **768** F4
Rostāq, Afganistan, **754** B1
Rosthern, Canada, **823** R5
Rostock, Germany, **772** F1
Rostov, Russian Federation, **783** G4
Rostov-na-Donu, Russian Federation, **758** B3
Rostovskaya Oblast', *province*, Russian Federation, **758** B3
Røsvik, Norway, **768** G3
Roswell, Georgia, U.S.A., **835** K2
Roswell, New Mexico, U.S.A., **833** L5
Rota, *island*, Northern Mariana Islands, **724** C3
Rotenburg (Wümme), Germany, **772** D2
Rothbury, England, U.K., **791** G2
Rothbury Forest, England, U.K., **791** G2
Rothenburg ob der Tauber, Germany, **772** E4
Rothera, *U.K. research station*, Antarctica, **862** A4
Rotherham, England, U.K., **791** G4
Rothes, Scotland, U.K., **792** F3
Rothesay, Scotland, U.K., **792** D5
Rothwell, England, U.K., **789** G2
Roti, *island*, Indonesia, **734** C5
Roti, Selat, *strait*, Indonesia, **734** C5
Rotokohu, New Zealand, **719** C5
Rotomanu, New Zealand, **719** C6
Rotondella, Italy, **779** F5
Rotondo, Monte, *mountain peak*, Corse, France, **779** B4
Rotorua, Lake, New Zealand, **718** F3
Rotorua, New Zealand, **718** F4
Rott, *river*, Germany, **772** F4
Rotterdam, Netherlands, **772** B3
Rottweil, Germany, **772** D4
Rotuma, *island*, Fiji, **725** F6
Roubaix, France, **775** F1
Rouen, France, **774** E2
Rouge, Le Piton, *mountain peak*, Réunion, **813** A1
Rouge, Pointe, *point*, Réunion, **813** A1
Rough River Lake, U.S.A., **831** K7
Rouleau, Canada, **823** S6
Round Island, Mauritius, **813** C1
Round Mountain, *mountain peak*, Australia, **721** L5
Round Mountain, U.S.A., **832** C1
Round Rock, Arizona, U.S.A., **833** J3
Round Rock, Texas, U.S.A., **834** D4
Roundup, U.S.A., **829** K3
Roura, French Guiana, **850** C2
Rous, Península, Chile, **858** D5
Rousay, *island*, Orkney, Scotland, U.K., **792** F1
Rouyn-Noranda, Canada, **826** B5
Rovaniemi, Finland, **769** M3
Rovereto, Italy, **778** C3
Roverud, Norway, **770** F2
Rovigo, Italy, **778** C3
Rovinari, Romania, **780** D3
Rovinj, Croatia, **778** D3
Rovkuly, Russian Federation, **769** Q4
Rovuma, *river*, Mozambique/Tanzania, **809** G5
Roxas, Palawan Island, Philippines, **740** B4
Roxas, Panay Island, Philippines, **740** C4
Roxborough, Tobago, Trinidad and Tobago, **859** B4
Roxby Downs, Australia, **721** H5
Roy, Montana, U.S.A., **829** K3
Roy, New Mexico, U.S.A., **833** L4
Royal Leamington Spa, England, U.K., **789** F2
Royal Tunbridge Wells, England, U.K., **789** H3
Royale, Isle, *island*, U.S.A., **831** J2
Royalton, U.S.A., **836** D3
Royalty, U.S.A., **833** M6
Royan, France, **774** D4
Roybridge, Scotland, U.K., **792** E4
Roye, France, **775** F2
Royston, England, U.K., **789** G2
Royston, U.S.A., **835** L2
Rožaj, Yugoslavia, **780** C4
Różan, Poland, **773** K2
Rozdil'na, Ukraine, **780** H2
Rozhniv, Ukraine, **780** E1
Rožňava, Slovakia, **773** K4
Roznov, Romania, **780** F2
Rrëshen, Albania, **780** B5
Rtishchevo, Russian Federation, **758** C2
Ružomberok, Slovakia, **773** J4
Ruabon, Wales, U.K., **788** D2
Ruacana, Namibia, **810** B2
Ruahine, New Zealand, **718** E4
Ruahine Range, *mountain range*, New Zealand, **718** F5
Ruakaka, New Zealand, **718** E2
Ruapehu, Mount, *mountain peak*, New Zealand, **717** G5
Ruapuke Island, New Zealand, **719** B8
Ruatahuna, New Zealand, **718** F4
Ruawai, New Zealand, **718** E3
Ruba, Belarus, **783** C5
Rubi, Democratic Republic of the Congo, **809** E2
Rubio, *mountain peak*, Spain, **777** F2
Rubtsovsk, Russian Federation, **759** L2
Ruby, U.S.A., **820** D3
Ruby Mountains, *mountain range*, U.S.A., **832** F1
Rucăr, Romania, **780** E3
Rucava, Latvia, **771** K4
Rucheng, China, **742** C3
Rūdbār, Afghanistan, **757** H2
Rudewa, Tanzania, **809** F5
Rudkøbing, Denmark, **770** E5
Rudky, Ukraine, **773** L4
Rudna Glava, Yugoslavia, **780** D3
Rudnaya Pristan', Russian Federation, **745** F1
Rudnya, Russian Federation, **783** C5
Rudnytsya, Ukraine, **780** G1
Rūdnyy, Kazakhstan, **758** G2
Rudo, Bosnia and Herzegovina, **780** B4
Rudong, China, **742** E1
Rue, France, **789** J4
Rufā'ah, Sudan, **806** D2
Ruffec, France, **774** E3
Rufiji, *river*, Tanzania, **809** G4
Rufino, Argentina, **856** D5
Rufisque, Senegal, **804** A2
Rufrufua, Indonesia, **735** F3
Rufunsa, Zambia, **809** E6
Rugāji, Latvia, **771** N4
Rugao, China, **742** E1
Rugby, England, U.K., **789** F2
Rugby, U.S.A., **830** D1
Rugeley, England, U.K., **789** F2
Rugozero, Russian Federation, **769** R4
Ruguy, Russian Federation, **783** D3
Ruhengeri, Rwanda, **809** E3
Ruhnu, *island*, Estonia, **771** L4
Ruhu, China, **743** C2
Rui'an, China, **742** E3
Ruichang, China, **742** C2
Ruidosa, U.S.A., **833** L7
Ruidoso, U.S.A., **833** L5
Ruijin, China, **742** D3
Ruili, China, **751** F4
Ruivo de Santana, Pico, *mountain peak*, Madeira, Portugal, **813** C3
Ruiz, Mexico, **840** D4
Ruiz, Nevado del, *mountain peak*, Colombia, **848** C3
Rūjiena, Latvia, **771** M4
Ruka, Finland, **769** P3
Ruki, *river*, Democratic Republic of the Congo, **808** C3
Rukungiri, Uganda, **809** E3
Rukwa, *administrative region*, Tanzania, **809** F4
Rukwa, Lake, Tanzania, **809** F4
Rum Cay, *island*, Bahamas, **838** G2
Ruma, Yugoslavia, **780** B3
Rumah Kulit, Malaysia, **737** F2
Rumbek, Sudan, **806** C3

S

St-Georges, French Guiana, **850** C2
St George's, Grenada, **837** D3
St George's Bay, Canada, **827** M5
St George's Channel, Ireland/Wales, **788** A3
St Germans, England, U.K., **788** C4
Saint-Gilles-les Bains, Réunion, **813** A1
Saint-Girons, France, **774** E5
St Govan's Head, *point*, Wales, U.K., **788** C3
St Gregory, Mount, *mountain peak*, Canada, **827** M5
St Helena, *island*, Atlantic Ocean, **813** B3
St Helena, *U.K. dependency*, Atlantic Ocean, **797** E8
Saint Helena Bay, South Africa, **810** C5
St Helens, Australia, **721** K7
St Helens, England, U.K., **790** F4
St Helens, Mount, *mountain peak*, U.S.A., **828** C3
St Helens, U.S.A., **828** C4
St Helier, Jersey, Channel Islands, **774** C2
St Hilary, England, U.K., **788** B4
St-Hyacinthe, Canada, **826** E7
St Ignace, U.S.A., **831** L3
St Ignace Island, Canada, **825** K7
St Ishmael, Wales, U.K., **788** C3
St Ive, England, U.K., **788** C4
St Ives, Cambridgeshire, England, U.K., **789** G2
St Ives, Cornwall, England, U.K., **788** B4
St Ives Bay, England, U.K., **788** B4
Saint-Jean, Lac, *lake*, Canada, **826** F5
St Jean Baptiste, Canada, **824** F7
Saint-Jean-d'Angély, France, **774** D4
Saint-Jean-de-Maurienne, France, **775** H4
Saint-Jean-de-Monts, France, **774** C3
Saint-Jean-Pied-de-Port, France, **774** D5
St-Jean-Port-Joli, Canada, **826** F6
St-Jean-sur-Richelieu, Canada, **826** E7
St-Jérôme, Canada, **826** D7
St Joe, U.S.A., **828** F3
Saint John, Canada, **826** H7
St John, Cape, Canada, **827** P4
St John, *river*, U.S.A., **836** F1
St John, U.S.A., **828** F3
St John Island, Canada, **827** N4
St John's, Antigua and Barbuda, **837** D2
St John's, Canada, **827** Q6
Saint Johns, U.S.A., **833** J4
St John's Chapel, England, U.K., **790** F3
St John's Point, Ireland, **793** D3
St Johnsbury, U.S.A., **836** D2
St Joseph, Lake, Canada, **824** J6
Saint-Joseph, New Caledonia, **727** A3
Saint-Joseph, Réunion, **813** A1
Saint Joseph, Trinidad, Trinidad and Tobago, **859** C4
St Joseph, U.S.A., **830** F6
St Joseph Point, U.S.A., **835** K5
Saint-Junien, France, **774** E4
St Just, England, U.K., **788** B4
Saint-Just-en-Chaussée, France, **789** K5
St Keverne, England, U.K., **788** B4
St Kitts and Nevis, *country*, Caribbean Sea, **817** S7
St Laurent, Canada, **824** F6
St-Laurent du Maroni, French Guiana, **850** C2
St Lawrence, Canada, **827** P6
St Lawrence, Gulf of, Canada, **827** K5
St Lawrence, *river*, Canada/U.S.A., **836** C2
St Lawrence Island, U.S.A., **820** B3
St Lawrence Seaway, *river*, Canada/U.S.A., **826** D7
St Léonard, Canada, **826** H6
Saint-Leu, Réunion, **813** A1
St Lewis, *river*, Canada, **827** N3
Saint-Lô, France, **774** D2
St Louis, Canada, **823** S5
Saint-Louis, Réunion, **813** A1
Saint-Louis, Senegal, **804** A1
St Louis, U.S.A., **830** H6
St Lucia, *country*, Caribbean Sea, **817** S7
St Lucia, Lake, South Africa, **811** F4
St Lucia Channel, Caribbean Sea, **837** D3
St Maarten, *island*, Netherlands Antilles, **837** D2
St Magnus Bay, Shetland, Scotland, U.K., **792** K7
Saint-Malo, France, **774** D1
Saint-Malo, Golfe de, *gulf*, France, **774** C2
Saint-Marc, Haiti, **839** G3
Saint-Marcel, Mont, *mountain peak*, French Guiana, **850** C2
Saint-Marcellin, France, **775** G4
St Margaret's Hope, Orkney, Scotland, U.K., **792** G2
St Maries, U.S.A., **828** F3
Saint Marks, U.S.A., **835** K4
St Martin, Channel Islands, **788** E5
St Martin, *island*, Guadeloupe, **837** D2
St Martin, Lake, Canada, **824** E6
Saint-Martory, France, **774** E5
St Mary, Mount, *mountain peak*, New Zealand, **719** B7
St Mary, U.S.A., **828** H2
St Mary Peak, *mountain peak*, Australia, **721** H5
St Mary's, Cape, Canada, **827** P6
St Marys, Ohio, U.S.A., **831** L5
St Mary's, Orkney, Scotland, U.K., **792** G2
St Marys, Pennsylvania, U.S.A., **831** P5
St Marys, *river*, Canada, **827** K7
St Marys, Trinidad, Trinidad and Tobago, **859** C4
St Mary's Bay, Canada, **827** Q6
Saint-Mathieu, Pointe de, *point*, France, **774** B2
St Matthew Island, U.S.A., **820** B3
St Matthias Group, *islands*, Papua New Guinea, **726** C3
St Mawes, England, U.K., **788** B4
St-Michel-des-Saints, Canada, **826** E6
Saint-Mihiel, France, **775** G2
Saint Moritz, Switzerland, **775** J3
Saint-Nazaire, France, **774** C3
Saint-Nectaire, France, **775** F4
St Neots, England, U.K., **789** G2
Saint-Nicolas d'Aliermont, France, **789** J5
Saint-Niklaas, Belgium, **772** B3
Saint-Omer, France, **774** F1
St Osyth, England, U.K., **789** J3
Saint-Palais, France, **774** D5
St-Pascal, Canada, **826** G6
St Paul, Arkansas, U.S.A., **834** F2
St Paul, Canada, **823** P5
Saint Paul, Cape, Ghana, **804** E3
St Paul, Minnesota, U.S.A., **830** G3
St Paul, Nebraska, U.S.A., **830** D5
Saint-Paul, Réunion, **813** A1
St-Paul, *river*, Canada, **827** M3
Saint-Péray, France, **775** G4
St Peter, U.S.A., **830** G3
St Peter in the Wood, Channel Islands, **788** E5
St Peter Port, Guernsey, Channel Islands, **774** C2
St Peters, Canada, **827** K6
St Petersburg *see* Sankt-Peterburg, Russian Federation, **783** C3
St Petersburg, U.S.A., **835** L6
Saint-Philippe, Réunion, **813** A1
St Philips, Canada, **824** D6
Saint-Pierre, Réunion, **813** A1
St Pierre, St Pierre and Miquelon, **827** N6
St Pierre and Miquelon, *French territorial collectivity*, Atlantic Ocean, **817** T4
Saint-Pierre-Église, France, **789** F5
Saint-Pierre-en-Port, France, **789** H5
St Pierre Island, Seychelles, **812** C2
Saint-Pol-sur-Mer, France, **789** K3
Saint-Pol-sur-Ternoise, France, **789** K4
St Pölten, Austria, **773** G4
Saint-Pons-de-Thomières, France, **774** F5
Saint-Pourçain-sur-Sioule, France, **775** F3
St Quentin, Canada, **826** H6
Saint-Quentin, France, **775** F2
Saint-Riquier, France, **789** J4
Saint-Saëns, France, **789** J5
St Sampson, Channel Islands, **788** E5
Saint-Sauveur-sur-Tinée, France, **775** H4
St-Siméon, Canada, **826** G6
St Simons Island, U.S.A., **835** M4
St Stephen, Canada, **826** H7
St Stephen, U.S.A., **835** N3
St Theresa Point, Canada, **824** G5
St Thomas, Canada, **831** N4
St Thomas, U.S.A., **830** E1
Saint-Tropez, France, **775** H5
Saint-Vaast-la-Hougue, France, **774** D2
Saint-Valéry-en-Caux, France, **774** E2
Saint-Valéry-sur-Somme, France, **774** E1
Saint-Vallier, France, **775** G3
St Vincent, Gulf, Australia, **721** H5
St Vincent and the Grenadines, *country*, Caribbean Sea, **817** S7
St Vincent Passage, Caribbean Sea, **837** D3
Saint-Vivien-de-Médoc, France, **774** D4
St Walburg, Canada, **823** Q5
St Xavier, U.S.A., **829** L4
Saint-Yrieix-la-Perche, France, **774** E4
Sainte-Adresse, France, **789** H5
Sainte-Anne, Lac, *lake*, Canada, **826** H4
Ste-Agathe-des-Monts, Canada, **826** D6
Sainte-Énimie, France, **775** F4
Sainte-Marie, Martinique, **837** D3
Sainte-Marie, Réunion, **813** A1
Sainte-Mère-Église, France, **789** F5
Sainte-Rose, Guadeloupe, **837** D2
Sainte-Rose, Réunion, **813** A1
Ste-Rose-du-Lac, Canada, **824** E6
Sainte-Suzanne, Réunion, **813** A1
Saintes, France, **774** D4
Saintes-Maries-de-la-Mer, France, **775** G5
Saintfield, Northern Ireland, U.K., **793** G3
Sāipal, *mountain peak*, Nepal, **755** E3
Saipan, *island*, Northern Mariana Islands, **724** C3
Saipan, Northern Mariana Islands, **724** C3
Sajam, Indonesia, **735** F3
Sajama, Bolivia, **853** E5
Sajama, Nevado, *mountain peak*, Bolivia, **853** E5
Sājir, Ra's, *cape*, Oman, **756** F5
Sājūr, *river*, Syria/Turkey, **761** D1
Saka, Ethiopia, **807** E3
Sakākah, Saudi Arabia, **803** H3
Sakakawea, Lake, U.S.A., **830** C2
Sakami, Lac, *lake*, Canada, **826** C3
Sakami, *river*, Canada, **826** D3
Sakaraha, Madagascar, **812** A5
Sakassou, Côte d'Ivoire, **804** C3
Sakata, Japan, **745** G3
Saketa, Indonesia, **734** D3
Sakété, Benin, **805** E3
Sakha, Respublika, *republic*, Russian Federation, **785** P3
Sakhalin, Ostrov, *island*, Russian Federation, **785** R4
Sakht-Sar, Iran, **758** E5
Şäki, Azerbaijan, **758** D4
Saki, Nigeria, **805** E3
Šakiai, Lithuania, **771** L5
Sakishima-shotō, *islands*, Japan, **745** M8
Sakleshpur, India, **752** C3
Sakmara, *river*, Russian Federation, **758** F2
Sakon Nakhon, Thailand, **739** E2
Sakra, Pulau, *island*, Singapore, **736** J7
Sakrivier, South Africa, **810** D5
Sakura, Japan, **745** H4
Säkylä, Finland, **771** L2
Sal, *island*, Cape Verde, **800** Q8
Sal Rei, Cape Verde, **800** Q8
Šal'a, Slovakia, **773** H4
Sala, Sweden, **770** H3
Sala y Gómez, *Chilean dependency*, Pacific Ocean, **709** P11
Salacgrīva, Latvia, **771** M4
Salada, Bahía, *bay*, Chile, **856** B3
Saladas, Argentina, **857** E3
Saladillo, Argentina, **857** E5
Saladillo, *river*, Córdoba, Argentina, **856** D4
Saladillo, *river*, Santa Fé, Argentina, **857** E4
Saladillo, *river*, Santiago del Estero, Argentina, **856** D3
Salado, *river*, Buenos Aires, Argentina, **857** E5
Salado, *river*, Formosa, Argentina, **857** E2
Salado, *river*, Mexico, **841** E3
Salado, *river*, Rio Nego, Argentina, **858** E1
Salado, *river*, Santiago del Estero, Argentina, **856** D3
Saladougou, Guinea, **804** C2
Salaga, Ghana, **804** D3
Sala'ilua, Samoa, **727** B1
Salal, Chad, **805** H2
Şalālah, Oman, **757** F5
Salālah, Sudan, **803** G4
Salamá, Guatemala, **838** C4
Salamanca, Chile, **856** B4
Salamanca, Mexico, **841** E4
Salamanca, Spain, **776** E2
Salamat, *prefecture*, Chad, **806** B2
Salamaua, Papua New Guinea, **726** B4
Salamina, Colombia, **848** C3
Salamiyah, Syria, **761** D2
Salamo, Papua New Guinea, **726** C5
Salani, Samoa, **727** B1
Salantai, Lithuania, **771** K4
Salas, Spain, **776** D1
Salas de los Infantes, Spain, **777** F1
Salatiga, Indonesia, **737** E4
Sălătrucu, Romania, **780** E3
Salau, France, **774** E5
Salavat, Russian Federation, **758** F2
Salawati, Pulau, *island*, Indonesia, **735** E3
Salāya, India, **754** B5
Salazar, Argentina, **856** D5
Salazie, Réunion, **813** A1
Salbris, France, **774** F3
Salcea, Romania, **780** F2
Šalčininkai, Lithuania, **771** M5
Salcombe, England, U.K., **788** D4
Sălcuța, Romania, **780** D3
Salda Gölü, *lake*, Turkey, **781** G7
Saldaña, Colombia, **848** C3
Saldanha, South Africa, **810** C5
Saldungaray, Argentina, **856** E6
Saldus, Latvia, **771** L4
Sale, Australia, **721** K6
Sale, England, U.K., **790** F4
Salehurst, England, U.K., **789** H4
Salekhard, Russian Federation, **784** H3
Salelologa, Samoa, **727** B1
Salem, Illinois, U.S.A., **831** J6
Salem, India, **752** D4
Salem, Missouri, U.S.A., **830** H7
Salem, Ohio, U.S.A., **831** N5
Salem, Oregon, U.S.A., **828** C4
Salem, South Dakota, U.S.A., **830** E4
Salemi, Sicilia, Italy, **779** D7
Salen, Scotland, U.K., **792** D4
Sälen, Sweden, **770** F2
Salernes, France, **775** H5
Salerno, Golfo di, *gulf*, Italy, **779** E5
Salerno, Italy, **779** E5
Salford, England, U.K., **790** F4
Salgado, *river*, Brazil, **851** F5
Salgótarján, Hungary, **773** J4
Salgueiro, Brazil, **851** F5
Salibea, Trinidad, Trinidad and Tobago, **859** C4
Salida, U.S.A., **833** L2
Salihli, Turkey, **781** G6
Salihorsk, Belarus, **782** C2
Salima, Malawi, **809** F5
Salina, Arizona, U.S.A., **833** J3
Salina, Isola, *island*, Italy, **779** E6
Salina, Kansas, U.S.A., **830** E6
Salina, Utah, U.S.A., **833** H2
Salina Cruz, Mexico, **841** G5
Salinas, Brazil, **855** E4
Salinas, Cabo de, *cape*, Islas Baleares, Spain, **777** J3
Salinas, Ecuador, **848** B5
Salinas, Pampa de la, *plain*, Argentina, **856** C4
Salinas, Punta, *point*, Dominican Republic, **839** H3
Salinas, Punta, *point*, Róbinson Crusoe Island, Archipiélago Juan Fernández, Chile, **859** C2
Salinas, U.S.A., **832** C3
Salinas de Garci Mendoza, Bolivia, **853** E5
Salinas de Hidalgo, Mexico, **840** E4
Salinas ó Lachay, Punta, *point*, Peru, **852** B3
Salinas Peak, *mountain peak*, U.S.A., **833** K5
Saline Bay, Trinidad, Trinidad and Tobago, **859** C4
Saline Lake, U.S.A., **834** F4
Salinitas, Chile, **856** B2
Salinópolis, Brazil, **850** D3
Salisbury, England, U.K., **789** F3
Salisbury, Maryland, U.S.A., **836** C5
Salisbury, North Carolina, U.S.A., **835** M2

Salisbury Island, Canada, **821** M3
Salisbury Plain, England, U.K., **789** E3
Săliște, Romania, **780** D3
Salitre, *river*, Brazil, **855** F3
Şalkhad, Syria, **761** D3
Salla, Finland, **769** P3
Salliqueló, Argentina, **856** D5
Sallisaw, U.S.A., **834** E2
Salluit, Canada, **821** M3
Sallūm, Sudan, **803** G5
Sally's Cove, Canada, **827** N5
Salmās, Iran, **760** F5
Salmi, Russian Federation, **783** C2
Salmi, Sweden, **768** K2
Salmon, *river*, U.S.A., **828** F4
Salmon, U.S.A., **828** H4
Salmon Arm, Canada, **823** K6
Salmon Peak, *mountain peak*, U.S.A., **834** B5
Salmon River Mountains, *mountain range*, U.S.A., **828** F4
Salo, Finland, **771** L2
Saloinen, Finland, **769** M4
Salonica *see* Thessaloniki, Greece, **781** D5
Salonta, Romania, **780** C2
Salor, *river*, Spain, **776** D3
Salsacate, Argentina, **856** D4
Sal'sk, Russian Federation, **782** F3
Salso, *river*, Sicilia, Italy, **779** D7
Salsomaggiore Terme, Italy, **778** B3
Salt, *river*, U.S.A., **833** H5
Salt Basin, U.S.A., **833** L6
Salt Flat, U.S.A., **833** L6
Salt Lake City, U.S.A., **833** H1
Salta, Argentina, **856** D2
Salta, *province*, Argentina, **856** D2
Saltash, England, U.K., **788** C4
Saltburn-by-the-Sea, England, U.K., **791** H3
Saltcoats, Scotland, U.K., **792** E5
Saltee Islands, Ireland, **793** F5
Saltillo, Mexico, **841** E3
Salto, Argentina, **857** E5
Salto, *river*, Italy, **779** D4
Salto, Uruguay, **857** F4
Salto da Divisa, Brazil, **855** F4
Salto del Guairá, Paraguay, **857** F2
Salto Santiago, Represa de, *reservoir*, Brazil, **857** G2
Salton Sea, *lake*, U.S.A., **832** E5
Saltpond, Ghana, **804** D3
Saltvik, Finland, **771** K2
Saluafata, Samoa, **727** B1
Saluda, U.S.A., **835** M3
Salūm, Khalīj as, *gulf*, Egypt/Libya, **802** E2
Sālūmbar, India, **754** C4
Saluzzo, Italy, **778** A3
Salvacion, Philippines, **740** D4
Salvador, Brazil, **855** F3
Salvaterra, Brazil, **850** D3
Salvatierra, Mexico, **841** E4
Salviac, France, **774** E4
Salween, *river*, Asia, **733** L7; *see also* Nu, *river*, China, **751** F3; Thanlwin, *river*, Myanmar, **741** C4
Salyan, Azerbaijan, **758** D5
Salzburg, Austria, **772** F5
Salzburg, *state*, Austria, **772** F5
Salzgitter, Germany, **772** E2
Salzkammergut, *region*, Austria, **773** F5
Salzwedel, Germany, **772** E2
Sām, India, **754** B4
Sam A Tsuen, China, **743** C3
Sam Rayburn Reservoir, U.S.A., **834** E4
Sầm Sơn, Vietnam, **739** E2
Samagaltay, Russian Federation, **759** N2
Samaipata, Bolivia, **853** F5
Samal Island, Philippines, **740** D5
Samalaeulu, Samoa, **727** B1
Samālūț, Egypt, **803** F3
Samaná, Bahía de, *bay*, Dominican Republic, **839** H3
Samandağı, Turkey, **761** C1
Samangān, Afghanistan, **754** B2
Samar, *island*, Philippines, **740** D4
Samara, Russian Federation, **758** E2
Samarai, Papua New Guinea, **726** C5
Samariapo, Venezuela, **849** E3
Samarinda, Indonesia, **737** G3
Samarqand, Uzbekistan, **758** H5
Sāmarrā', Iraq, **803** H2
Samarskaya Oblast', *province*, Russian Federation, **758** D2
Samasodu, Solomon Islands, **727** A1
Samastipur, India, **755** F4
Samataitai, Samoa, **727** B1
Samatau, Samoa, **727** B1
Samba, Democratic Republic of the Congo, **809** E3
Samba Cajú, Angola, **808** C4
Sambaliung, Pegunungan, *mountain range*, Indonesia, **737** G2
Sambalpur, India, **755** F5
Sambar, Tanjong, *point*, Indonesia, **737** E3
Sambas, Indonesia, **737** E2
Sambau, Indonesia, **736** D3
Sambava, Madagascar, **812** C3
Sāmbhar, India, **754** C4
Sambir, Ukraine, **773** L4
Sambito, *river*, Brazil, **851** F5
Sambo, Angola, **808** C5
Samborombón, Bahía, *bay*, Argentina, **857** F5
Sambre, *river*, France, **775** F1
Sambro, Canada, **827** K7
Samch'ŏk, South Korea, **744** E3
Samdari, India, **754** C4
Same, Tanzania, **809** G3
Samer, France, **789** J4
Samfya, Zambia, **809** E5
Samḥah, *island*, Suquṭrá (Socotra), Yemen, **813** B2
Sami, India, **754** B5
Samia, Tanjong, *point*, Indonesia, **734** C2
Samijiyŏn, North Korea, **747** K4
Samka, Myanmar, **741** C3
Samnū, Libya, **802** B3
Samoa, *country*, Pacific Ocean, **715** H3
Samobor, Croatia, **778** E3
Samokov, Bulgaria, **780** D4
Šamorín, Slovakia, **773** H4
Samos, Dodekanisos, Greece, **781** F7
Samos, *island*, Dodekanisos, Greece, **781** F7
Samosir, Pulau, *island*, Indonesia, **736** B2
Samothraki, *island*, Greece, **781** E5
Sampit, Indonesia, **737** F3
Sampit, *river*, Indonesia, **737** F3
Sampit, Teluk, *bay*, Indonesia, **737** F3
Sampun, Papua New Guinea, **726** D4
Sampwe, Democratic Republic of the Congo, **809** E4
Samsang, China, **750** B3
Samsø Bælt, *strait*, Denmark, **770** E5
Samsu, North Korea, **744** E2
Samsun, Turkey, **760** E4
Samucumbi, Angola, **808** C5
Samui, Ko, *island*, Thailand, **738** D4
Samut Prakan, Thailand, **738** D3
Samut Sakhon, Thailand, **738** D3
Samut Songkhram, Thailand, **738** D3
San, Mali, **804** D2
San, *river*, Cambodia, **739** E3
San Agustín, Argentina, **857** E5
San Agustín de Valle Fértil, Argentina, **856** C4
San Ambrosio, Isla, *island*, Chile, **845** E6
San Andreas, U.S.A., **832** C2
San Andrés, Bahía de, *bay*, San Andrés, Colombia, **859** B1
San Andrés, Bolivia, **853** F4
San Andrés, *island*, Colombia, Caribbean Sea, **859** B1
San Andres, Philippines, **740** C3
San Andrés, San Andrés, Colombia, **859** B1
San Andrés Tuxtla, Mexico, **841** G5
San Angelo, U.S.A., **834** B4
San Antonio, Belize, **838** C3
San Antonio, Bolivia, **853** F4
San Antonio, Cabo, *cape*, Cuba, **838** D2
San Antonio, Catamarca, Argentina, **856** D3
San Antonio, Chile, **856** B4
San Antonio, Mount, *mountain peak*, U.S.A., **832** E4
San Antonio, San Luis, Argentina, **856** C4
San Antonio, U.S.A., **834** C5
San Antonio, Venezuela, **849** E3
San Antonio Abad, Islas Baleares, Spain, **777** H3
San Antonio Bay, Philippines, **740** B4
San Antonio de Caparo, Venezuela, **848** D2
San Antonio de los Cobres, Argentina, **856** C2
San Antonio de Tamanaco, Venezuela, **849** E2
San Antonio Oeste, Argentina, **858** E1
San Ardo, U.S.A., **832** C3
San Augustin, Cape, Philippines, **740** D5
San Bartolo, Mexico, **841** E4
San Bartolomeo in Galdo, Italy, **779** E5
San Benedetto del Tronto, Italy, **778** D4
San Bernando, Argentina, **856** E3
San Bernardino, U.S.A., **832** E4
San Bernardino Mountains, *mountain range*, U.S.A., **832** E4
San Bernardo, Chile, **856** B4
San Bernardo, Mexico, **840** D3
San Blás, Archipiélago, *islands*, Panama, **839** F5
San Blas, Nayarit, Mexico, **840** D4
San Blas, Sinaloa, Mexico, **840** C3
San Borja, Bolivia, **853** E4
San Buenaventura, Mexico, **840** E3
San Camilo, Argentina, **856** E2
San Carlos, Argentina, **856** C4
San Carlos, Bolivia, **853** F4
San Carlos, Chile, **856** B5
San Carlos, Luzon Island, Philippines, **740** C3
San Carlos, Mexico, **841** F3
San Carlos, N. Venezuela, **849** E2
San Carlos, Negros Island, Philippines, **740** C4
San Carlos, Nicaragua, **838** D5
San Carlos, *river*, Paraguay, **857** E2
San Carlos, S. Venezuela, **849** E4
San Carlos, Uruguay, **857** F5
San Carlos, U.S.A., **833** H5
San Carlos Centro, Argentina, **856** E4
San Carlos de Bariloche, Argentina, **858** C1
San Carlos de Bolívar, Argentina, **856** E5
San Carlos del Zulia, Venezuela, **848** D2
San Ciro de Acosta, Mexico, **841** F4
San Clemente, Chile, **856** B5
San Clemente, *island*, U.S.A., **832** D5
San Clemente, Spain, **777** F3
San Clemente, U.S.A., **832** E5
San Cristóbal, Argentina, **856** E4
San Cristóbal, Bolivia, **853** E5
San Cristóbal, Dominican Republic, **839** H3
San Cristóbal, Isla, *island*, Islas Galápagos (Galapagos Islands), Ecuador, **859** A2
San Cristóbal, Venezuela, **848** D2
San Cristóbal de las Casas, Mexico, **841** G5
San Diego, California, U.S.A., **832** E5
San Diego, Texas, U.S.A., **834** C6
San Dimas, Mexico, **840** D3
San Donà di Piave, Italy, **778** D3
San Estanislao, Paraguay, **857** F2
San Esteban de Gormaz, Spain, **777** F2
San Felipe, Baja California, Mexico, **840** B2
San Felipe, Chile, **856** B4
San Felipe, Guanajuato, Mexico, **841** E4
San Felipe, Providencia, Colombia, **859** C1
San Felipe, Venezuela, **849** E1
San Felipe de Jesús, Mexico, **840** D3
San Feliu de Guíxols, Spain, **777** J2
San Félix, Isla, *island*, Chile, **845** D6
San Fernando, Argentina, **857** E5
San Fernando, Central Luzon Island, Philippines, **740** C3
San Fernando, Chile, **856** B5
San Fernando, Mexico, **841** F3
San Fernando, N. Luzon Island, Philippines, **740** C2
San Fernando, Spain, **776** D4
San Fernando, Trinidad, Trinidad and Tobago, **859** C4
San Fernando de Apure, Venezuela, **849** E2
San Fernando de Atabapo, Venezuela, **849** E3
San Fernando del Valle de Catamarca, Argentina, **856** D3
San Fidel, U.S.A., **833** K4
San Francique, Trinidad, Trinidad and Tobago, **859** C4
San Francisco, Argentina, **856** D4
San Francisco, Cabo de, *cape*, Ecuador, **848** B4
San Francisco, Mexico, **840** B2
San Francisco, Panama, **839** E5
San Francisco, Philippines, **740** C3
San Francisco, U.S.A., **832** B3
San Francisco de Macorís, Dominican Republic, **839** H3
San Francisco de Paula, Cabo, *cape*, Argentina, **858** D3
San Francisco del Chañar, Argentina, **856** D3
San Francisco del Oro, Mexico, **840** D3
San Gabriel, Ecuador, **848** C4
San Germán, Puerto Rico, **837** C2
San Gil, Colombia, **848** D2
San Hipólito, Punta, *point*, Mexico, **840** B3
San Ignacio, Belize, **838** C3
San Ignacio, Beni, Bolivia, **853** F4
San Ignacio, Paraguay, **857** F3
San Ignacio, Peru, **852** B1
San Ignacio, Santa Cruz, Bolivia, **853** G4
San Ildefonso, Cape, Philippines, **740** C2
San Javier, Bolivia, **853** F4
San Javier, Chile, **856** B5
San Javier, Misiones, Argentina, **857** F3
San Javier, Santa Fé, Argentina, **857** E4
San Javier, Spain, **777** G4
San Jerónimo, Serranía de, *mountain range*, Colombia, **848** C2
San Joaquin, *river*, U.S.A., **832** C3
San Joaquin Valley, U.S.A., **832** C3
San Jorge, Argentina, **856** E4
San Jorge, Golfo de, *gulf*, Argentina, **858** D3
San Jorge, Golfo de, *gulf*, Spain, **777** H2
San Jorge, *river*, Colombia, **848** C2
San José, Costa Rica, **838** D5
San José, Golfo, *gulf*, Argentina, **858** E2
San José, Isla, *island*, Mexico, **840** C3
San José, Isla, *island*, Panama, **839** F5
San Jose, Luzon Island, Philippines, **740** C3
San Jose, Mindoro Island, Philippines, **740** C3
San Jose, Panay Island, Philippines, **740** C4
San José, Spain, **777** F4
San Jose, U.S.A., **832** C3
San José, Volcán, *mountain peak*, Chile, **856** B4
San José de Amacuro, Venezuela, **849** G2
San José de Chiquitos, Bolivia, **853** G4
San José de Dimas, Mexico, **840** C2
San José de Feliciano, Argentina, **857** E4
San José de Gracia, Baja California Sur, Mexico, **840** B3
San José de Gracia, Sinaloa, Mexico, **840** D3
San José de Guanipa, Venezuela, **849** F2
San José de Jáchal, Argentina, **856** C4
San José de la Dormida, Argentina, **856** D4
San José de la Mariquina, Chile, **858** C1
San José de Mayo, Uruguay, **857** F5
San José de Ocuné, Colombia, **849** D3
San José de Quero, Peru, **852** C3
San José de Raíces, Mexico, **841** E3
San Jose del Boqueron, Argentina, **856** D3
San José del Cabo, Mexico, **840** C4
San José del Guaviare, Colombia, **848** D3
San José del Progreso, Mexico, **841** F5
San Jose Island, U.S.A., **834** D6
San Juan, Argentina, **856** C4
San Juan, Cabo, *cape*, Argentina, **858** E5
San Juan, Cabo, *cape*, Equatorial Guinea, **808** A2
San Juan, Dominican Republic, **839** H3
San Juan, Peru, **852** C4
San Juan, Pico, *mountain peak*, Cuba, **839** E2
San Juan, *province*, Argentina, **856** C4
San Juan, Puerto Rico, **837** C2
San Juan, Punta, *point*, Isla de Pascua (Easter Island), Chile, **859** B2
San Juan, *river*, Costa Rica/Nicaragua, **838** D5
San Juan, U.S.A., **833** H3
San Juan, Venezuela, **849** F3

San Juan Bautista, Islas Baleares, Spain, **777** H3
San Juan Bautista, Paraguay, **857** F3
San Juan Bautista, Róbinson Crusoe Island, Archipiélago Juan Fernández, Chile, **859** C2
San Juan Bautista Tuxtepec, Mexico, **841** F5
San Juan de Guadalupe, Mexico, **840** E3
San Juan de los Cayos, Venezuela, **849** E1
San Juan de los Morros, Venezuela, **849** E2
San Juan de Salvamento, Argentina, **858** E5
San Juan del Norte, Nicaragua, **838** E5
San Juan del Río, Durango, Mexico, **840** D3
San Juan del Río, Queretaro, Mexico, **841** F4
San Juan del Sur, Nicaragua, **838** D5
San Juan Mountains, *mountain range*, U.S.A., **833** K3
San Juancito, Honduras, **838** D4
San Juanico, Punta, *point*, Mexico, **840** B3
San Justo, Argentina, **856** E4
San Lázaro, Cabo, *cape*, Mexico, **840** B3
San Lorenzo, Argentina, **856** E4
San Lorenzo, Beni, Bolivia, **853** F4
San Lorenzo, Ecuador, **848** B4
San Lorenzo, Monte, *mountain peak*, Chile, **858** C3
San Lorenzo, *mountain peak*, Spain, **777** F1
San Lorenzo, Paraguay, **857** F2
San Lorenzo, Peru, **853** E3
San Lorenzo, Tarija, Bolivia, **853** F5
San Lucas, Baja California Sur, Mexico, **840** B3
San Lucas, Bolivia, **853** F5
San Lucas, Cabo, *cape*, Mexico, **840** C4
San Lucas, S. Baja California Sur, Mexico, **840** C4
San Lucas Ojitlán, Mexico, **841** F5
San Luis, Argentina, **856** C4
San Luis, Guatemala, **838** C3
San Luis, Lago de, *lake*, Bolivia, **853** F3
San Luis, Mexico, **840** D3
San Luis, *province*, Argentina, **856** C4
San Luís, San Andrés, Colombia, **859** B1
San Luis, Sierra de, *mountain range*, Argentina, **856** D4
San Luis de la Paz, Mexico, **841** E4
San Luis del Palmar, Argentina, **857** E3
San Luis Obispo, U.S.A., **832** C4
San Luis Potosí, Mexico, **841** E4
San Luis Potosí, *state*, Mexico, **841** E4
San Luis Río Colorado, Mexico, **840** B1
San Luisito, Mexico, **840** B2
San Marco, Capo, *cape*, Italy, **779** D7
San Marcos, Guatemala, **838** C4
San Marcos, Mexico, **841** F5
San Marcos, U.S.A., **834** D5
San Marino, *country*, Europe, **764** F7
San Marino, San Marino, **778** D4
San Martín, Argentina, **856** D3
San Martin, Cape, U.S.A., **832** B4
San Martín, Colombia, **848** D3
San Martin, Lago, *lake*, Argentina, **858** C3
San Martín, *river*, Bolivia, **853** F4
San Martín De Los Andes, Argentina, **858** C1
San Martín de Valdeiglesias, Spain, **776** E2
San Mateo, U.S.A., **832** B3
San Matías, Bolivia, **853** G4
San Matías, Golfo, *gulf*, Argentina, **858** E1
San Mauricio, Venezuela, **849** E2
San Miguel, Bolivia, **853** G4
San Miguel, El Salvador, **838** C4
San Miguel, *island*, U.S.A., **832** C4
San Miguel, Panama, **839** F5
San Miguel, Peru, **852** D3
San Miguel, *river*, Bolivia, **853** F4
San Miguel, *river*, Colombia/Ecuador, **848** C4
San Miguel, *river*, Mexico, **840** C2
San Miguel Bay, Philippines, **740** C3
San Miguel de Huachi, Bolivia, **853** E4
San Miguel de Tucumán, Argentina, **856** D3
San Miguel del Monte, Argentina, **857** E5
San Miguelito, Bolivia, **853** E3
San Miguelito, Panama, **839** F5
San Millán, *mountain peak*, Spain, **777** F1
San Nicolás, Bahía, *bay*, Peru, **852** C4
San Nicolas, *island*, U.S.A., **832** C5
San Nicolás de los Arroyos, Argentina, **857** E4
San Nicolás de Tolentino, Islas Canarias, Spain, **813** B4
San Pablo, Beni, Bolivia, **853** F4
San Pablo, Philippines, **740** C3
San Pablo, Potosí, Bolivia, **853** E5
San Patricio, U.S.A., **833** L5
San Pedro, Belize, **838** D3
San Pedro, Bolivia, **853** F4
San Pedro, Buenos Aires, Argentina, **857** E4
San-Pédro, Côte d'Ivoire, **804** C4
San Pedro, Jujuy, Argentina, **856** D2
San Pedro, Mexico, **840** C4
San Pedro, Misiones, Argentina, **857** F3
San Pedro, Paraguay, **857** F2
San Pedro, *river*, Cuba, **839** F2
San Pedro *see* Bulalacao, Philippines, **740** C3
San Pedro, Sierra de, *mountain range*, Spain, **776** D3
San Pedro, Volcán, *mountain peak*, Chile, **856** C1
San Pedro de Arimena, Colombia, **848** D3
San Pedro de Atacama, Chile, **856** C2
San Pedro de Las Bocas, Venezuela, **849** F2
San Pedro de las Colonias, Mexico, **840** E3
San Pedro de Macorís, Dominican Republic, **839** H3
San Pedro Sula, Honduras, **838** D4
San Pedro Tapanatepec, Mexico, **841** G5
San Pedro Totalapan, Mexico, **841** F5
San Pietro, Isola di, *island*, Italy, **779** A6
San Quintín, Mexico, **840** B2
San Rafael, Argentina, **856** C5
San Rafael, Bolivia, **853** G4
San Rafael, Cerro, *mountain peak*, Paraguay, **857** F3
San Rafael, Venezuela, **848** D1
San Rafael Knob, *mountain peak*, U.S.A., **833** H2
San Ramón, Beni, Bolivia, **853** F3
San Ramón, Santa Cruz, Bolivia, **853** F4
San Ramón de la Nueva Orán, Argentina, **856** D2
San Remigio, Philippines, **740** C4
San Remo, Italy, **778** A4
San Román, Cabo, *cape*, Venezuela, **849** D1
San Roque, Argentina, **857** E3
San Saba, U.S.A., **834** C4
San Salvador, Argentina, **857** E4
San Salvador, El Salvador, **838** C4
San Salvador, Isla, *island*, Islas Galápagos (Galapagos Islands), Ecuador, **859** A1
San Salvador, *island*, Bahamas, **838** G2
San Salvador de Jujuy, Argentina, **856** D2
San Sebastián, Argentina, **858** D4
San Sebastián, Bahía, *gulf*, Argentina, **858** D4
San Sebastián de la Gomera, Islas Canarias, Spain, **813** A4
San Severo, Italy, **779** E5
San Telmo, Mexico, **840** A2
San Telmo, Punta, *point*, Mexico, **840** D5
San Tin, China, **743** C4
San Valentín, Monte, *mountain peak*, Chile, **858** C3
San Vicente, El Salvador, **838** C4
San Vicente, Mexico, **840** A2
San Vicente de Cañete, Peru, **852** C3
San Vicente de Toranzo, Spain, **777** F1
San Vicente del Caguán, Colombia, **848** C3
San Vincenzo, Italy, **778** C4
San Vito, Capo, *cape*, Sicilia, Italy, **779** D6
San Ysidro, U.S.A., **833** K4
Şan'ā', Yemen, **756** D5
Sanaag, *administrative region*, Somalia, **807** G2
SANAE IV, *South African research station*, Antarctica, **862** D3
Sanaga, *river*, Cameroon, **808** B2
Sanaigmore, Scotland, U.K., **792** C5
Sanana, Pulau, *island*, Indonesia, **734** D3
Sanandaj, Iran, **758** D5
Sanandita, Bolivia, **853** F5
Sanāw, Yemen, **756** F5
Sanchahe, China, **747** J3
Sanchakou, China, **748** C5
Sanchidrián, Spain, **776** E2
Sānchor, India, **754** B4
Sanchursk, Russian Federation, **758** D1
Sanco Point, Philippines, **740** D4
Sancti Spíritus, Cuba, **839** F2
Sand, Hedmark, Norway, **770** E2
Sand, Rogaland, Norway, **770** C3
Sand Hill, *river*, Canada, **827** N3
Sand Hills, U.S.A., **830** B4
Sand Springs, Montana, U.S.A., **829** L3
Sand Springs, Oklahoma, U.S.A., **834** D1
Sandai, Indonesia, **737** E3
Sandakan, Malaysia, **737** G1
Sândăn, Cambodia, **739** E3
Sandane, Norway, **770** C2
Sandanski, Bulgaria, **781** D5
Sandaré, Mali, **804** B2
Sandarne, Sweden, **771** H2
Sanday, *island*, Orkney, Scotland, U.K., **792** G1
Sanday Sound, Orkney, Scotland, U.K., **792** G1
Sandbach, England, U.K., **788** E1
Sandbukta, Norway, **768** K2
Sanddøla, *river*, Norway, **768** F4
Sande, Sogn og Fjordane, Norway, **770** B2
Sande, Vestfold, Norway, **770** E3
Sandefjord, Norway, **770** E3
Sandell Bay, Macquarie Island, **720** R11
Sanders, U.S.A., **833** J4
Sanderson, U.S.A., **833** M6
Sandfire Roadhouse, Australia, **720** E2
Sandgerði, Iceland, **768** X7
Sandhead, Scotland, U.K., **792** E6
Sandhurst, England, U.K., **789** G3
Sandia, Peru, **853** E4
Sandıklı, Turkey, **781** H6
Sandīla, India, **754** E4
Sanding, Pulau, *island*, Indonesia, **736** C3
Sandlake, U.S.A., **828** C4
Sandnäset, Sweden, **768** H5
Sandnes, Norway, **770** B3
Sandness, Shetland, Scotland, U.K., **792** K7
Sandnessjøen, Norway, **768** F4
Sandoa, Democratic Republic of the Congo, **808** D4
Sandomierz, Poland, **773** K3
Sândominic, Romania, **780** E2
Sandön, *island*, Sweden, **769** L4
Sandoná, Colombia, **848** C4
Sandovo, Russian Federation, **783** F3
Sandow, Mount, *mountain peak*, Antarctica, **862** G5
Sandown, England, U.K., **789** F4
Sandoy, *island*, Faeroe Islands, **786** D2
Sandplace, England, U.K., **788** C4
Sandpoint, U.S.A., **828** F2
Sandray, *island*, Scotland, U.K., **792** B4
Sandsend, England, U.K., **791** H3
Sandspit, Canada, **822** D5
Sandstone, U.S.A., **830** G2
Sandu, China, **742** C3
Sandusky, Michigan, U.S.A., **831** M4
Sandusky, Ohio, U.S.A., **831** M5
Sandusky, *river*, U.S.A., **831** M5
Sandverhaar, Namibia, **810** C4
Sandvik, Sweden, **771** H4
Sandvika, Norway, **768** F5
Sandviken, Sweden, **771** H2
Sandwich, England, U.K., **789** J3
Sandwich Bay, Canada, **827** N3
Sandwich Bay, Namibia, **810** B3
Sandwick, Scotland, U.K., **792** K7
Sandy, England, U.K., **789** G2
Sandy, U.S.A., **828** C4
Sandy Bay, Macquarie Island, **720** R11
Sandy Bay, St Helena, **813** B3
Sandy Cape, Australia, **721** L3
Sandy Lake, Australia, **720** E2
Sandy Lake, *lake*, Canada, **824** H5
Sandy Lake, Newfoundland, Canada, **827** N5
Sandy Lake, Ontario, Canada, **824** H5
Sandy Point, Tristan da Cunha, **813** C2
Sandykgachy, Turkmenistan, **758** G5
Sanford, Florida, U.S.A., **835** M5
Sanford, Maine, U.S.A., **836** E3
Sanford, North Carolina, U.S.A., **835** N2
Sang, Loi, *mountain peak*, Myanmar, **741** C3
Sangān, Kūh-e, *mountain peak*, Afghanistan, **757** H2
Sangar, Russian Federation, **785** P3
Sangay, Volcán, *mountain peak*, Ecuador, **848** B4
Sângeorgiu de Pădure, Romania, **780** E2
Sângeorz-Băi, Romania, **780** E2
Sanger, U.S.A., **832** D3
Sângerei, Moldova, **780** G2
Sangerhausen, Germany, **772** E3
Sanggarpar, China, **751** G2
Sanggau, Indonesia, **737** E2
Sangha, *administrative region*, Congo, **808** C2
Sangha, Burkina Faso, **804** E2
Sangha-Mbaéré, *prefecture*, Central African Republic, **808** C2
Sānghar, Pakistan, **754** B4
Sangihe, Pulau, *island*, Indonesia, **734** D2
Sanginkylä, Finland, **769** N4
Sangis, Sweden, **769** L4
Sangiyn Dalay, Mongolia, **749** H3
Sangkha, Thailand, **739** D3
Sāngli, India, **752** C2
Sangmélima, Cameroon, **808** B2
Sango, Zimbabwe, **811** F3
Sāngola, India, **752** C2
Sangonera, *river*, Spain, **777** G4
Sangre de Cristo Mountains, *mountain range*, U.S.A., **833** L2
Sangre Grande, Trinidad, Trinidad and Tobago, **859** C4
Sangri, China, **750** D3
Sangruma, China, **751** F2
Sangrūr, India, **754** C3
Sangsang, China, **750** C3
Sangue, *river*, Brazil, **853** H3
Sangwali, Namibia, **810** D2
Sangzhi, China, **742** B2
Sanibel Island, U.S.A., **835** L6
Sanikiluaq, Canada, **825** Q3
Sanje, Tanzania, **809** G4
Sanjiachang, China, **751** G4
Sanjiao, China, **743** A3
Sanjō, Japan, **745** G3
Sankarankovil, India, **752** D4
Sankt Gallen, Switzerland, **775** J3
Sankt Peter-Ording, Germany, **772** D1
Sankt-Peterburg (St Petersburg), Russian Federation, **783** C3
Sanlúcar de Barrameda, Spain, **776** D4
Sanluri, Sardegna, Italy, **779** B6
Sanmen Dao, *island*, China, **743** D4
Sanmen Wan, *bay*, China, **742** E2
Sanmenxia, China, **742** B1
Sanming, China, **742** D3
Sänna, Sweden, **770** G3
Sannār, Sudan, **806** D2
Sânnicolau Mare, Romania, **780** C2
Sanniki, Poland, **773** J2
Sanniquellie, Liberia, **804** C3
Sanok, Poland, **773** L4
Sanquhar, Scotland, U.K., **792** F5
Sansepolcro, Italy, **778** D4
Sansha Wan, *bay*, China, **742** D3
Sanski Most, Bosnia and Herzegovina, **778** F3
Sansui, China, **742** B3
Sansuri, *mountain peak*, North Korea, **747** H4
Sant' Antioco, Isola di, *island*, Sardegna, Italy, **779** B6
Sant' Antioco, Sardegna, Italy, **779** B6
Sant' Arcangelo, Italy, **779** F5
Sant Carles de la Ràpita, Spain, **777** H2

São Miguel dos Campos, Brazil, **855** G2
São Nicolau, *island*, Cape Verde, **800** P8
São Paulo, Brazil, **857** H2
São Paulo, *state*, Brazil, **857** H2
São Paulo de Olivença, Brazil, **849** E5
São Pedro, Brazil, **849** G5
São Pedro, *river*, Brazil, **851** F5
São Pedro do Sul, Portugal, **776** C2
São Raimundo das Mangabeiras, Brazil, **850** E5
São Raimundo Nonato, Brazil, **855** E2
São Romão, Amazonas, Brazil, **853** E1
São Romão, Minas Gerais, Brazil, **855** E4
São Roque, Cabo de, *cape*, Brazil, **851** G4
São Sebastião, Ilha de, *island*, Brazil, **857** J2
São Sebastião, Pará, Brazil, **850** C4
São Sebastião, Rondônia, Brazil, **853** G2
São Sebastiao da Boa Vista, Brazil, **850** D3
São Sebastião do Paraíso, Brazil, **854** D5
São Sepé, Brazil, **857** G4
São Simão, Brazil, **854** C5
São Tiago, *island*, Cape Verde, **800** Q8
São Tomé, Cabo de, *cape*, Brazil, **855** F5
São Tomé, *island*, São Tomé and Príncipe, **813** C4
São Tomé, Pico de, *mountain peak*, São Tomé and Príncipe, **813** C4
São Tomé, São Tomé and Príncipe, **813** C4
São Tomé and Príncipe, *country*, Atlantic Ocean, **797** F6
São Vicente, Brazil, **857** H2
São Vicente, Cabo de, *cape*, Portugal, **776** C4
São Vicente, *island*, Cape Verde, **800** P8
São Vicente, Madeira, Portugal, **813** C3
Saona, Isla, *island*, Dominican Republic, **839** H3
Saône, *river*, France, **775** G3
Sapanca, Turkey, **781** H5
Sapanda, Papua New Guinea, **726** B4
Sapele, Nigeria, **805** F3
Sapello, U.S.A., **833** L4
Sapelo Island, U.S.A., **835** M4
Sapernoye, Russian Federation, **783** C2
Sapes, Greece, **781** E5
Saposoa, Peru, **852** C2
Sapphire Mountains, *mountain range*, U.S.A., **828** G3
Sappho, U.S.A., **828** B2
Sapporo, Japan, **745** H2
Sapri, Italy, **779** E5
Sapucaia, Brazil, **850** B4
Sapulpa, U.S.A., **834** D1
Sapulut, Malaysia, **737** G1
Saqqez, Iran, **758** D5
Sar Bīsheh, Iran, **757** G2
Šar Planina, *mountain range*, Macedonia/Yugoslavia, **780** C4
Sara, Philippines, **740** C4
Sarāb, Iran, **803** J1
Saraburi, Thailand, **738** D3
Saraby, Norway, **769** L1
Saragosa, U.S.A., **833** M6
Saraguro, Ecuador, **848** B5
Saraipāli, India, **755** E5
Säräisniemi, Finland, **769** N4
Sarajärvi, Finland, **769** N4
Sarajevo, Bosnia and Herzegovina, **778** G4
Saraktash, Russian Federation, **758** F2
Saramati, *mountain peak*, Myanmar, **741** B2
Saran, Gunung, *mountain peak*, Indonesia, **737** E3
Saranac Lake, U.S.A., **836** C2
Sarandë, Albania, **781** C6
Sarandi, Brazil, **857** G3
Sarandí del Yi, Uruguay, **857** F4
Sarandí Grande, Uruguay, **857** F4
Sarangani Islands, Philippines, **740** D5
Sārangarh, India, **755** E5
Sārangpur, India, **754** D5
Saransk, Russian Federation, **782** G2
Sarapul, Russian Federation, **758** E1
Sarasota, U.S.A., **835** L6
Sarata, Ukraine, **780** G2
Saratoga, U.S.A., **829** L6
Saratok, Malaysia, **737** E2
Saratov, Russian Federation, **758** D2
Saratovskaya Oblast', *province*, Russian Federation, **758** D2
Sarāvān, Iran, **757** H3
Saravan, Laos, **739** E3
Sarawak, *state*, Malaysia, **737** F2
Saray, Turkey, **781** F5
Saraya, Senegal, **804** B2
Sarāyā, Syria, **761** C2
Sarayakpınar, Turkey, **780** F5
Sarayköy, Turkey, **781** G7
Sarayönü, Turkey, **760** D5
Sarbāz, Iran, **757** H3
Sárbogárd, Hungary, **773** J5
Sarco, Chile, **856** B3
Sardārpur, India, **754** C5
Sardārshahr, India, **754** C3
Sardegna, *autonomous region*, Italy, **779** B5
Sardegna (Sardinia), *island*, Italy, **779** C5
Sardinata, Colombia, **848** D2
Sardinata, Ensenada de, *bay*, San Andrés, Colombia, **859** B1
Sardinia *see* Sardegna, *island*, Italy, **779** C5
Sardis Lake, U.S.A., **835** H2
Sar-e Pol, Afghanistan, **754** A1
Sargent, U.S.A., **830** D5
Sargodha, Pakistan, **754** C2
Sarh, Chad, **806** A3
Sarhro, Jebel, *mountain range*, Morocco, **800** E2
Sārī, Iran, **758** E5
Saria, *island*, Dodekanisos, Greece, **781** F8
Sarichioi, Romania, **780** G3
Sarigan, *island*, Northern Mariana Islands, **724** C3
Sarıgöl, Turkey, **781** G6
Sarıkaya, Turkey, **803** G1
Sarikei, Malaysia, **737** E2
Sarıkemer, Turkey, **781** F7
Sarıköy, Turkey, **781** F5
Sarimbun Reservoir, Singapore, **736** J6
Sarina, Australia, **721** K3
Sariñena, Spain, **777** G2
Sariwon, North Korea, **744** D3
Sarıyer, Turkey, **781** G5
Sark, *Guernsey dependency*, English Channel, **774** C2
Sarkāri Tala, India, **754** B4
Särkijärvi, Finland, **769** L3
Särkisalmi, Finland, **771** P2
Şarkışla, Turkey, **803** G1
Şarköy, Turkey, **781** F5
Sărmaşu, Romania, **780** E2
Sarmi, Indonesia, **735** G3
Sarmiento, Argentina, **858** D2
Särna, Sweden, **770** F2
Sarnen, Switzerland, **775** J3
Sarnia, Canada, **831** M4
Sarny, Ukraine, **782** C2
Särö, Sweden, **770** E4
Saros Körfezi, *bay*, Turkey, **781** F5
Sárospatak, Hungary, **773** K4
Sarowbī, Afghanistan, **754** B2
Sarpsborg, Norway, **770** E3
Sarqan, Kazakhstan, **748** C3
Sarre, England, U.K., **789** J3
Sarrebourg, France, **775** H2
Sarriá, Spain, **776** D1
Sarroch, Sardegna, Italy, **779** B6
Sartène, Corse, France, **779** B5
Sarthe, *river*, France, **774** D3
Saru, *river*, Japan, **745** H2
Saruhanlı, Turkey, **781** F6
Sárvár, Hungary, **773** H5
Sarvestān, Iran, **756** F3
Sárvíz, *river*, Hungary, **778** G2
Särvsjö, Sweden, **770** F1
Sary-Tash, Kyrgyzstan, **748** B5
Saryesik-Atyraū Qumy, *desert*, Kazakhstan, **748** B3
Saryg-Sep, Russian Federation, **749** G2
Saryözek, Kazakhstan, **748** C3
Saryqopa Köli, *lake*, Kazakhstan, **758** G2
Saryshagan, Kazakhstan, **748** B3
Sarysu, *river*, Kazakhstan, **748** A2
Sarzhal, Kazakhstan, **748** C2
Sasak, Indonesia, **736** B3
Sasamungga, Solomon Islands, **727** A1
Sasar, Tanjong, *point*, Indonesia, **734** C5
Sasarām, India, **755** E4
Sasebo, Japan, **744** E4
Saser Kangri, *mountain peak*, India, **754** D2
Saskatchewan, *province*, Canada, **823** R4
Saskatchewan, *river*, Canada, **823** S5
Saskatoon, Canada, **823** R5
Saslaya, Cerro, *mountain peak*, Nicaragua, **838** D4
Sasolburg, South Africa, **811** E4
Sasovo, Russian Federation, **782** F2
Sassandra, Côte d'Ivoire, **804** C4
Sassari, Sardegna, Italy, **779** B5
Sassnitz, Germany, **772** F1
Sasstown, Liberia, **804** C4
Sasyk, Ozero, *lake*, Ukraine, **780** G3
Sasyqköl, *lake*, Kazakhstan, **748** D3
Sata-misaki, *point*, Japan, **744** E5
Satāna, India, **754** C5
Satanta, U.S.A., **830** C7
Satapuala, Samoa, **727** B1
Sātāra, India, **752** C2
Sataua, Samoa, **727** B1
Satawal, *island*, Micronesia, **724** C4
Sätbaev, Kazakhstan, **758** H3
Säter, Sweden, **770** G2
Satipo, Peru, **852** C3
Sātmala Hills, India, **754** C5
Satna, India, **754** E4
Sátoraljaújhely, Hungary, **773** K4
Sātpura Range, *mountain range*, India, **754** C5
Satrokala, Madagascar, **812** B5
Satti, India, **754** D2
Sattūr, India, **752** D4
Satu Mare, Romania, **780** D2
Satun, Thailand, **738** D5
Satupa'itea, Samoa, **727** B1
Sauce, Argentina, **857** E4
Saucillo, Mexico, **840** D2
Sauda, Norway, **770** C3
Saūdakent, Kazakhstan, **759** H4
Saudi Arabia, *country*, Asia, **730** F7
Sauêruiná, (Papagaio), *river*, Brazil, **853** G3
Saugstad, Mount, *mountain peak*, Canada, **822** F5
Saül, French Guiana, **850** C2
Sauldre, *river*, France, **774** E3
Saulgau, Germany, **772** D4
Saulieu, France, **775** G3
Saulkrasti, Latvia, **771** M4
Sault Ste Marie, Canada, **831** L2
Sault Ste Marie, U.S.A., **831** L2
Saumlaki, Indonesia, **735** E4
Saumur, France, **774** D3
Saunders, Cape, Australia, **717** G6
Saundersfoot, Wales, U.K., **788** C3
Saurimo, Angola, **808** D4
Sauvo, Finland, **771** L2
Sauzé-Vaussais, France, **774** E3
Savá, Honduras, **838** D4
Sava, *river*, Europe, **766** F6
Savage, U.S.A., **829** M3
Savageton, U.S.A., **829** M5
Savai'i, *island*, Samoa, **727** B1
Savalou, Benin, **805** E3
Savaneta, Aruba, **859** B3
Savanna-la-Mar, Jamaica, **839** F3
Savannah, Georgia, U.S.A., **835** M3
Savannah, Missouri, U.S.A., **830** F6
Savannah, *river*, U.S.A., **835** M3
Savannah, Tennessee, U.S.A., **835** H2
Savannakhét, Laos, **739** E2
Savant Lake, Canada, **824** J6
Sāvantvādi, India, **752** C3
Såvar, Sweden, **768** K5
Savaştepe, Turkey, **781** F6
Savè, Benin, **805** E3
Save, *river*, Mozambique, **811** F3
Sāveh, Iran, **756** F2
Savelugu, Ghana, **804** D3
Savenay, France, **774** D3
Săveni, Romania, **780** F2
Saverdun, France, **774** E5
Savikylä, Finland, **769** P5
Savissivik, Denmark, **821** N2
Savitaipale, Finland, **771** N2
Šavnik, Yugoslavia, **780** B4
Savona, Canada, **822** J6
Savona, Italy, **778** B3
Savonlinna, Finland, **771** P2
Savonranta, Finland, **771** P1
Savran', Ukraine, **780** H1
Sävsjö, Sweden, **770** G4
Savu Sea, Indonesia, **734** C5
Savukoski, Finland, **769** P3
Savusavu, Fiji, **727** A4
Savuti, Botswana, **810** D2
Saw, Myanmar, **741** B3
Sawākin, Sudan, **803** G5
Sawan, Myanmar, **741** C2
Sawankhalok, Thailand, **738** C2
Sawatch Range, *mountain range*, U.S.A., **833** K2
Sawbill, Canada, **826** H3
Sawdā', Jabal, *mountain peak*, Saudi Arabia, **803** H5
Sawdā', Qurnat as, *mountain peak*, Lebanon, **761** D2
Sawdirī, Sudan, **806** C2
Sawel Mountain, *mountain peak*, Northern Ireland, U.K., **790** A3
Sawi, Ao, *bay*, Thailand, **738** C4
Şawqirah, Ghubbat, *bay*, Oman, **757** G5
Sawston, England, U.K., **789** H2
Sawtell, Australia, **721** L5
Sawu, *island*, Indonesia, **720** E1
Sawu, Pulau, *island*, Indonesia, **734** C5
Saxilby, England, U.K., **789** G1
Saxmundham, England, U.K., **789** J2
Saxnäs, Sweden, **768** G4
Say, Niger, **805** E2
Sayán, Peru, **852** C3
Sayaq, Kazakhstan, **748** C3
Sayaxché, Guatemala, **838** C3
Şaydā (Sidon), Lebanon, **761** C3
Sayghān, Afghanistan, **754** A2
Sayḥūt, Yemen, **756** F5
Sāylac, Somalia, **807** F2
Säyneinen, Finland, **769** P5
Saynshand, Dornogovī, Mongolia, **746** E3
Saynshand, Ömnögovī, Mongolia, **749** J4
Sayn-Ust, Mongolia, **749** G3
Sayötesh, Kazakhstan, **758** E4
Sayqal, Baḩr, *lake*, Syria, **761** D3
Sayram Hu, *lake*, China, **748** D3
Sayre, U.S.A., **834** C2
Sayula, Mexico, **840** E5
Sayula de Alemán, Mexico, **841** G5
Sayward, Canada, **822** G6
Saywūn, Yemen, **756** E5
Sazan, *island*, Albania, **781** B5
Sazonovo, Russian Federation, **783** E3
Sbaa, Algeria, **801** F3
Sbega, Russian Federation, **747** G1
Sbeïtla, Tunisia, **802** A1
Scafell Pike, *mountain peak*, England, U.K., **790** E3
Scalasaig, Scotland, U.K., **792** C4
Scalby, England, U.K., **791** H3
Scalloway, Shetland, Scotland, U.K., **792** K7
Scalp, *mountain peak*, Ireland, **793** D5
Scalpay, *island*, Scotland, U.K., **792** C3
Scammon Bay, U.S.A., **820** C3
Scandia, Canada, **823** N6
Scandinavia, *region*, Europe, **766** F3
Scansano, Italy, **778** C4
Scanzano, Italy, **779** F5
Scapa Flow, *bay*, Orkney, Scotland, U.K., **792** F2
Scarba, *island*, Scotland, U.K., **792** D4
Scarborough, England, U.K., **791** H3
Scarborough, Tobago, Trinidad and Tobago, **859** B4
Scargill, New Zealand, **719** D6
Scarp, *island*, Scotland, U.K., **792** B2
Scarth, Canada, **824** D7
Schaffhausen, Switzerland, **775** J3
Schärding, Austria, **778** D1
Schefferville, Canada, **826** H2
Scheibbs, Austria, **773** G5
Schelde, *river*, Belgium, **772** A3
Schell Creek Range, *mountain range*, U.S.A., **832** F2
Schenectady, U.S.A., **836** C3
Scheveningen, Netherlands, **772** B2
Schiermonnikoog, Netherlands, **772** C2
Schitu Duca, Romania, **780** F2
Schleiden, Germany, **772** C3
Schleswig, Germany, **772** D1
Schleswig-Holstein, *state*, Germany, **772** D1
Schongau, Germany, **772** E5
Schooner, Caleta, *bay*, San Andrés, Colombia, **859** B1
Schouten Islands, Papua New Guinea, **726** B3
Schrader, Mount, *mountain peak*, Papua New Guinea, **726** B4
Schroffenstein, *mountain peak*, Namibia, **810** C4
Schulenburg, U.S.A., **834** D5
Schuler, Canada, **823** P6
Schurz, U.S.A., **832** D2
Schuyler, U.S.A., **830** E5
Schwabach, Germany, **772** E4
Schwäbisch Hall, Germany, **772** D4
Schwäbische Alb, *mountain range*, Germany, **772** D4
Schwaner, Pegunungan, *mountain range*, Indonesia, **737** E3
Schwarzwald, *mountain range*, Germany, **766** E6
Schwaz, Austria, **772** E5
Schwedt, Germany, **773** G2

Šėta, Lithuania, **771** M5
Sète, France, **775** F5
Sete Lagoas, Brazil, **855** E5
Setermoen, Norway, **768** J2
Setesdal, *valley*, Norway, **770** C3
Sétif, Algeria, **801** H1
Settat, Morocco, **800** E2
Setté Cama, Gabon, **808** A3
Settle, England, U.K., **790** F3
Setúbal, Baía de, *bay*, Portugal, **776** C3
Setúbal, *district*, Portugal, **776** C3
Setúbal, Portugal, **776** C3
Seui, Sardegna, Italy, **779** B6
Seul, Lac, *lake*, Canada, **824** H6
Sevana Lich, *lake*, Armenia, **758** D4
Sevastopol', Ukraine, **782** D4
Seven Persons, Canada, **823** P7
Seven Sisters Peaks, *mountain peak*, Canada, **822** E4
Sevenoaks, England, U.K., **789** H3
Severn, *river*, Canada, **825** K4
Severn, *river*, Wales, U.K., **788** D2
Severn Lake, Canada, **824** J4
Severnaya Osetiya-Alaniya, Respublika, *republic*, Russian Federation, **758** C4
Severnaya Zemlya, *islands*, Russian Federation, **785** M1
Severnoye, Novosibirskaya Oblast', Russian Federation, **759** K1
Severnoye, Orenburgskaya Oblast', Russian Federation, **758** E2
Severnyye Uvaly, *mountain range*, Russian Federation, **784** F4
Severobaykal'sk, Russian Federation, **785** M4
Severočeský, *administrative region*, Czech Republic, **773** F3
Severodvinsk, Russian Federation, **784** F3
Severomoravský, *administrative region*, Czech Republic, **773** H4
Severomorsk, Russian Federation, **769** R2
Severo-Sibirskaya Nizmennost', Russian Federation, **784** K2
Severo-Yeniseyskiy, Russian Federation, **784** L3
Severo-Zadonsk, Russian Federation, **783** G5
Severy, U.S.A., **830** E7
Sevettijärvi, Finland, **769** P2
Sevi, Russian Federation, **749** G1
Sevier, *river*, U.S.A., **832** G2
Sevier Desert, U.S.A., **832** G2
Sevier Lake, U.S.A., **832** G2
Sevilla, Colombia, **848** C3
Sevilla, Spain, **776** E4
Sevlievo, Bulgaria, **780** E4
Sevnica, Slovenia, **778** E2
Sèvre Niortaise, *river*, France, **774** D3
Sevryukovo, Russian Federation, **783** F5
Seward, U.S.A., **820** E3
Seward Peninsula, Canada, **820** C3
Sexsmith, Canada, **823** K4
Seybaplaya, Mexico, **841** H5
Seychelles, *country*, Indian Ocean, **797** L7
Seychellois, Morne, *mountain peak*, Seychelles, **813** A2
Seydişehir, Turkey, **803** F1
Seyðisfjörður, Iceland, **768** Z7
Seymor, U.S.A., **831** L6
Seymour, Australia, **721** K6
Seymour, U.S.A., **834** C3
Seyssel, France, **775** G4
Sežana, Slovenia, **778** D3
Sézanne, France, **775** F2
Sezze, Italy, **779** D5
Sfakia, Kriti, Greece, **781** E8
Sfântu Gheorghe, Central Romania, **780** E3
Sfântu Gheorghe, E. Romania, **780** G3
Sfax, Tunisia, **802** B2
Sgurr Mor, *mountain peak*, Scotland, U.K., **792** D3
Sha, *river*, China, **742** D3
Sha Tau Kok *see* Shatoujiao, China, **743** C3
Sha Tin, China, **743** C4
Sha Xian, China, **742** D3
Shaanxi, *province*, China, **746** E5
Shaba, *administrative region*, Democratic Republic of the Congo, **809** E4
Shabaqua Corners, Canada, **824** K7
Shabeellaha Dhexe, *administrative region*, Somalia, **807** G4
Shabeellaha Hoose, *administrative region*, Somalia, **807** F4
Shabeelle, *river*, Somalia, **807** F4
Shabelē, Wabē, *river*, Ethiopia, **807** F3
Shabla, Bulgaria, **780** G4
Shabla, Nos, *point*, Bulgaria, **780** G4
Shabogamo Lake, Canada, **826** H3
Shabunda, Democratic Republic of the Congo, **809** E3
Shache, China, **748** C5
Shackleton Coast, *region*, Antarctica, **862** D6
Shackleton Ice Shelf, Antarctica, **862** G6
Shackleton Range, *mountain range*, Antarctica, **862** C4
Shadehill, U.S.A., **830** B3
Shadrinsk, Russian Federation, **758** G1
Shadwān, Jazīrat, *island*, Egypt, **803** F3
Shaftesbury, England, U.K., **788** E3
Shag Point, New Zealand, **719** C7
Shagamu, *river*, Canada, **825** L4
Shagari, Nigeria, **805** F2
Shaghan, Kazakhstan, **748** C2
Shaghan, *river*, Kazakhstan, **748** C2
Shāh, *river*, Iran, **758** D5
Shah Alam, Malaysia, **736** C2
Shāhāda, India, **754** C5
Shahany, Ozero, *lake*, Ukraine, **780** H3
Shahbā', Syria, **761** D3
Shāhbandar, Pakistan, **754** A4
Shahdol, India, **755** E5
Shahe, Guangdong, China, **743** A2
Shahe, Hebei, China, **746** F5
Shāhganj, India, **755** E4
Shaḥḥāt, Libya, **802** D2
Shāhjahānpur, India, **754** D4
Shāhpur, India, **752** D2
Shāhpur Chākar, Pakistan, **754** B4
Shāhpura, Madhya Pradesh, India, **754** E5
Shāhpura, N. Rājasthān, India, **754** C4
Shāhpura, S. Rājasthān, India, **754** C4
Shahrak, Afghanistan, **754** A2
Shahr-e Kord, Iran, **756** F2
Shajing, northeast of Yonghan, Guangdong, China, **743** C1
Shajing, southeast of Taiping, Guangdong, China, **743** B3
Shaka, Ras, *point*, Kenya, **809** H3
Shakhovskaya, Russian Federation, **783** E4
Shakhtinsk, Kazakhstan, **748** B2
Shakhty, Russian Federation, **782** F3
Shakhun'ya, Russian Federation, **784** F4
Shakopee, U.S.A., **830** G3
Shalday, Kazakhstan, **748** C2
Shallotte, U.S.A., **835** N3
Shalqar, Kazakhstan, **758** F3
Shal'skiy, Russian Federation, **783** E2
Shaluli Shan, *mountain range*, China, **751** F3
Shalya, Russian Federation, **758** F1
Shām, Bādiyat ash (Syrian Desert), *desert*, Asia, **761** D3
Shām, Jabal ash, *mountain peak*, Oman, **757** G4
Sham Tseng, China, **743** C4
Shamāl Baḩr al Ghazal, *state*, Sudan, **806** C3
Shamāl Dārfūr, *state*, Sudan, **802** E5
Shamāl Kurdufān, *state*, Sudan, **806** C1
Shamattawa, Canada, **824** H4
Shamattawa, *river*, Canada, **825** M4
Shambu, Ethiopia, **807** E3
Shāmkūh, Iran, **758** F5
Shāmli, India, **754** D3
Shammar, Jabal, *mountain range*, Saudi Arabia, **803** G3
Shāmpur, India, **754** D4
Shamrock, U.S.A., **834** B2
Shamsābād, India, **754** D5
Shamva, Zimbabwe, **809** F6
Shan, *state*, Myanmar, **751** F5
Shan State, *state*, Myanmar, **741** C3
Shan Xian, China, **742** C1
Sha'nabī, Jabal ash, *mountain peak*, Tunisia, **802** A1
Shandī, Sudan, **803** F5
Shandan, China, **749** J5
Shandon, U.S.A., **832** C4
Shandong, *province*, China, **747** G5
Shangcai, China, **742** C1
Shangcheng, China, **742** C2
Shangchuan Dao, *island*, China, **742** C4
Shangdu, China, **746** F4
Shanggao, China, **742** C2
Shanghai, China, **742** E2
Shanghang, China, **742** D3
Shanghe, China, **746** G5
Shangkuli, China, **747** H2
Shangnan, China, **742** B1
Shangombo, Zambia, **808** D6
Shangqiu, China, **742** C1
Shangrao, China, **742** D2
Shangyu, China, **742** E2
Shangyun, China, **751** F5
Shangzhi, China, **747** J3
Shangzhou, China, **742** B1
Shanhaiguan, China, **747** H4
Shanhetun, China, **747** J3
Shani, Nigeria, **805** G2
Shanklin, England, U.K., **789** F4
Shankou, China, **749** G4
Shanlaragh, Ireland, **793** C6
Shannon, Mouth of the, *river mouth*, Ireland, **793** B5
Shannon, North Island, New Zealand, **718** E5
Shannon, *river*, Ireland, **793** D4
Shannon, South Island, New Zealand, **719** C7
Shannon Ø, *island*, Greenland, **821** T2
Shanshan, China, **748** F4
Shantarskiye Ostrova, *islands*, Russian Federation, **785** Q4
Shantou, China, **742** D4
Shanwei, China, **742** C4
Shanxi, *province*, China, **751** J2
Shanya, *river*, Russian Federation, **783** E5
Shanyang, China, **742** B1
Shanyin, China, **746** F5
Shaodong, China, **742** B3
Shaoguan, China, **742** C3
Shaowu, China, **742** D3
Shaoxing, China, **742** E2
Shaoyang, China, **742** B3
Shap, England, U.K., **790** F3
Shapa, China, **742** B4
Shapinsay, *island*, Orkney, Scotland, U.K., **792** G1
Shapki, Russian Federation, **783** C3
Shaqrā', Saudi Arabia, **803** J3
Shaqrā', Yemen, **756** E6
Shaquanzi, China, **748** D3
Shar, Kazakhstan, **748** D2
Shar, *river*, Kazakhstan, **748** D2
Sharafah, Sudan, **806** C2
Sharashova, Belarus, **773** M2
Sharbaqty, Kazakhstan, **759** K2
Sharbulag, Mongolia, **749** G2
Share, Nigeria, **805** E3
Sharga, Bulgan, Mongolia, **749** J2
Sharga, Govĭ-Altay, Mongolia, **749** G3
Sharga, Hövsgöl, Mongolia, **749** H2
Sharhorod, Ukraine, **780** G1
Sharhulsan, Mongolia, **746** D3
Shari, Japan, **745** J2
Shark Bay, Australia, **720** C4
Sharkawshchyna, Belarus, **771** N5
Sharlyk, Russian Federation, **758** E2
Sharm ash Shaykh, Egypt, **761** C6
Sharon Springs, U.S.A., **830** C6
Sharpe Lake, Canada, **824** H4
Sharq al Istiwā'īyah, *state*, Sudan, **809** E1
Sharqī, Jabal ash, *mountain range*, Lebanon/Syria, **761** D3
Sharqīyah, Aş-Şahrā' ash, *desert*, Egypt, **761** A5
Shar'ya, Russian Federation, **784** F4
Sharyn, *river*, Kazakhstan, **748** C4
Sharypovo, Russian Federation, **759** M1
Shashamenē, Ethiopia, **807** E3
Shashe, *river*, Botswana/Zimbabwe, **811** E3
Shashi, China, **742** C2
Shasta, Mount, *mountain peak*, U.S.A., **828** C6
Shasta Lake, U.S.A., **832** B1
Shatou, China, **743** A3
Shatoujiao (Sha Tau Kok), China, **743** C3
Shatsk, Russian Federation, **782** F2
Shats'k, Ukraine, **773** L3
Shatura, Russian Federation, **783** G5
Shaunavon, Canada, **823** Q7
Shawan, Guangdong, China, **743** A3
Shawan, Sichuan, China, **751** G3
Shawano, U.S.A., **831** J3
Shawmarīyah, Jabal ash, *mountain range*, Syria, **761** D2
Shawmut, U.S.A., **829** K3
Shawnee, U.S.A., **834** D2
Shaxi, China, **743** A3
Shayang, China, **742** C2
Shaybārā, *island*, Saudi Arabia, **803** G3
Shaykh, Jabal ash, *mountain peak*, Syria, **761** C3
Shaykh Miskin, Syria, **761** D3
Shchelkovo, Russian Federation, **783** G5
Shchūchinsk, Kazakhstan, **759** J2
Shchuch'ye, Russian Federation, **758** G1
Shchuchyn, Belarus, **773** M2
She Xian, China, **742** D2
Shebalino, Russian Federation, **759** M2
Sheberghān, Afghanistan, **754** A1
Sheboygan, U.S.A., **831** K4
Shebunino, Russian Federation, **745** H1
Shediac, Canada, **827** J6
Sheelin, Lough, *lake*, Ireland, **793** E4
Sheenjek, *river*, U.S.A., **820** E3
Sheep Haven, *bay*, Ireland, **793** D2
Sheerness, England, U.K., **789** H3
Sheet Harbour, Canada, **827** K7
Shefar'am, Israel, **761** C3
Sheffield, Alabama, U.S.A., **835** J2
Sheffield, England, U.K., **791** G4
Sheffield, Iowa, U.S.A., **830** G4
Sheffield, Pennsylvania, U.S.A., **831** P5
Sheffield, Texas, U.S.A., **833** N6
Sheho, Canada, **824** C6
Shehong, China, **751** H3
Shek Kong, China, **743** C4
Shek Pik, China, **743** B4
Shek Uk Shan, *mountain peak*, China, **743** C4
Shekhūpura, Pakistan, **754** C3
Shekou, China, **743** B4
Sheksna, Russian Federation, **783** G3
Shelagskiy, Mys, *cape*, Russian Federation, **785** U2
Shelburne, Canada, **826** J8
Shelburne Bay, Australia, **721** J1
Shelby, U.S.A., **829** J2
Shelbyville, Illinois, U.S.A., **831** J6
Shelbyville, Indiana, U.S.A., **831** L6
Shelbyville, Lake, U.S.A., **831** J6
Shelbyville, Tennessee, U.S.A., **835** J2
Sheldon, U.S.A., **830** F4
Sheldrake, Canada, **826** J4
Shelek, Kazakhstan, **748** C4
Shelek, *river*, Kazakhstan, **748** C4
Shelekhov, Russian Federation, **746** D1
Shelikhova, Zaliv, *gulf*, Russian Federation, **785** S3
Shelikof Strait, U.S.A., **820** D4
Shell, U.S.A., **829** L4
Shellbrook, Canada, **823** R5
Shelley, U.S.A., **829** H5
Shelokhovskaya, Russian Federation, **783** G2
Shelton, U.S.A., **828** C3
Shemonaïkha, Kazakhstan, **748** D2
Shenandoah, U.S.A., **830** F5
Shenandoah Mountains, *mountain range*, U.S.A., **831** P6
Shendam, Nigeria, **805** F3
Sheng Xian, China, **742** E2
Shengang, China, **743** B2
Shengena, *mountain peak*, Tanzania, **809** G3
Shëngjin, Albania, **780** B5
Shengze, China, **742** E2
Shenjingzi, China, **747** J3
Shenkursk, Russian Federation, **784** F3
Shenmu, China, **746** E5
Shenshu, China, **747** K3
Shenwan, China, **743** A4
Shenyang, China, **747** H4
Shenzhen, China, **743** C3
Sheopur, India, **754** D4
Shepetivka, Ukraine, **782** C2
Shepparton, Australia, **721** K6
Sheppey, Isle of, England, U.K., **789** H3
Shepton Mallet, England, U.K., **788** E3
Sherard, Cape, Canada, **821** M2
Sherborne, England, U.K., **788** E4
Sherbro Island, Sierra Leone, **804** B3

Songnim, North Korea, **744** D3
Songo, Angola, **808** B4
Songo, Mozambique, **809** F6
Songpan, China, **751** G2
Songsak, India, **755** G4
Songxi, China, **742** D3
Songzi, China, **742** B2
Sonid Youqi, China, **746** F4
Sonid Zuoqi, China, **746** F4
Sonipat, India, **754** D3
Sonkajärvi, Finland, **769** N5
Sonkovo, Russian Federation, **783** F4
Sonmiāni Bay, Pakistan, **754** A4
Sonmiāni, Pakistan, **754** A4
Sono, do, *river*, Brazil, **854** D3
Sonoita, U.S.A., **833** H6
Sonoma, U.S.A., **832** B2
Sonora, Bahía, *bay*, San Andrés, Colombia, **859** B1
Sonora, California, U.S.A., **832** C3
Sonora, *river*, Mexico, **840** C2
Sonora, *state*, Mexico, **840** B2
Sonora, Texas, U.S.A., **834** B4
Sonoran Desert, U.S.A., **832** F5
Sonostrov, Russian Federation, **769** S3
Sonoyta, Mexico, **840** B2
Sonskiy, Russian Federation, **759** N2
Sonsón, Colombia, **848** C3
Sonsonate, El Salvador, **838** C4
Sonsorol, *island*, Palau, **724** B4
Sooke, Canada, **822** H7
Sop Huai, Thailand, **738** C2
Sopachuy, Bolivia, **853** F5
Sopki, Russian Federation, **783** C4
Sopokha, Russian Federation, **769** S5
Sopot, Bulgaria, **780** E4
Sopot, Poland, **773** J1
Sopot, Yugoslavia, **780** C3
Sopron, Hungary, **773** H5
Sor, *river*, Portugal, **776** C3
Sör-dellen, *lake*, Sweden, **771** H2
Sør-Flatanger, Norway, **768** E4
Sør-Rondane, *mountain range*, Antarctica, **862** E3
Sør-Trøndelag, *county*, Norway, **768** E5
Sora, Italy, **779** D5
Sorāh, Pakistan, **754** B4
Söråker, Sweden, **771** H1
Sorang, Kazakhstan, **748** B2
Sorata, Bolivia, **853** E4
Sorbe, *river*, Spain, **777** F2
Sørbovag, Norway, **770** B2
Sörbygden, Sweden, **770** H1
Sorel, Canada, **826** E6
Sorell, Australia, **721** K7
Sorgono, Sardegna, Italy, **779** B5
Soria, Spain, **777** F2
Sørli, Norway, **768** F4
Soro, India, **755** F5
Soro, Pakistan, **754** A3
Soroca, Moldova, **780** G1
Sorocaba, Brazil, **857** H2
Sorochinsk, Russian Federation, **758** E2
Sorok, Russian Federation, **749** J1
Sorokino, Russian Federation, **783** B4
Sorol, *island*, Micronesia, **724** C4
Sorong, Indonesia, **735** E3
Sorot', *river*, Russian Federation, **783** B4
Soroti, Uganda, **809** F2
Sørøya, *island*, Norway, **769** L1
Sørøysundet, *channel*, Norway, **769** L1
Sørreisa, Norway, **768** J2
Sorrento, Italy, **779** E5
Sorsatunturi, *mountain peak*, Finland, **769** P3
Sorsele, Sweden, **768** H4
Sorsogon, Philippines, **740** D3
Sortavala, Russian Federation, **783** C2
Sortland, Norway, **768** G2
Sørvågen, Norway, **768** F3
Sørvika, Norway, **770** E1
Sosanpal, India, **753** E2
Sösdala, Sweden, **770** F4
Sösjöfjällen, *mountain peak*, Sweden, **768** F5
Sosneado, Cerro, *mountain peak*, Argentina, **856** C5
Sosnovets, Russian Federation, **769** S4
Sosnovyy, Russian Federation, **769** R3
Sosnovyy Bor, Russian Federation, **783** B3
Sosnowiec, Poland, **773** J3
Sospel, France, **775** H5
Sotkamo, Finland, **769** P4
Soto, Curaçao, Netherlands Antilles, **859** C3
Soto La Marina, Mexico, **841** F4
Sotomayor, Colombia, **848** C4
Sotra, *island*, Norway, **770** B2
Sotteville-lès-Rouen, France, **789** J5
Sotuf, Adrar, *mountain range*, Western Sahara, **800** C4
Sotuta, Mexico, **841** H4
Souanké, Congo, **808** B2
Soubré, Côte d'Ivoire, **804** C3
Souda, Kriti, Greece, **781** E8
Soufli, Greece, **781** F5
Soufrière, *mountain peak*, St Vincent and the Grenadines, **837** D3
Sougéta, Guinea, **804** B2
Sougueur, Algeria, **801** G1
Souillac, France, **774** E4
Souillac, Mauritius, **813** C1
Souk Ahras, Algeria, **801** H1
Souk-el-Arba-du-Rharb, Morocco, **801** E2
Sŏul (Seoul), South Korea, **744** D3
Sour el Ghozlane, Algeria, **777** J4
Soure, Brazil, **850** D3
Souris, Canada, **824** D7
Sousa, Brazil, **851** F5
Sousse, Tunisia, **802** B1
South Africa, *country*, **797** H9
South Andaman, *island*, Andaman and Nicobar Islands, India, **753** H4
South Australia, *state*, Australia, **720** G4
South Australian Basin, *underwater feature*, Indian Ocean, **866** H7
South Ayrshire, *local authority*, Scotland, U.K., **792** E5
South Baldy, *mountain peak*, U.S.A., **833** K5
South Bay, Canada, **824** H6
South Bend, Indiana, U.S.A., **831** K5
South Bend, Washington, U.S.A., **828** C3
South Boston, U.S.A., **831** P7
South Bruny Island, Australia, **721** K7
South Cape, New Zealand, **719** A8
South Carolina, *state*, U.S.A., **834** M2
South Cave, England, U.K., **791** H4
South China Basin, *underwater feature*, South China Sea, **868** B3
South China Sea, China/ Philippines/Vietnam, **733** N8
South Dakota, *state*, U.S.A., **830** C3
South Downs, *region*, England, U.K., **789** G4
South East, *district*, Botswana, **811** E3
South East Bay, Ascension, **813** A3
South East Cape, Australia, **721** K7
South East Harbour, Campbell Island, New Zealand, **718** K11
South East Head, *point*, Ascension, **813** A3
South Elmsall, England, U.K., **791** G4
South Fork, U.S.A., **833** K3
South Georgia, *island*, South Georgia and South Sandwich Islands, **845** J9
South Georgia and South Sandwich Islands, *U.K. dependency*, Atlantic Ocean, **845** J9
South Georgia Ridge, *underwater feature*, Atlantic Ocean, **867** D9
South Gloucestershire, *unitary authority*, England, U.K., **788** E3
South Harris, *island*, Scotland, U.K., **792** B3
South Harting, England, U.K., **789** G4
South Haven, U.S.A., **831** K4
South Henik Lake, Canada, **824** F1
South Hill, U.S.A., **836** A6
South Horr, Kenya, **809** G2
South Indian Lake, Canada, **824** E3
South Island (Atas), Cocos (Keeling) Islands, **720** Q10
South Island, New Zealand, **719** D6
South Junction, Canada, **824** G7
South Keeling Islands, Cocos (Keeling) Islands, **720** Q10
South Knife, *river*, Canada, **824** F2
South Korea, *country*, Asia, **731** P6
South Lake Tahoe, U.S.A., **832** C2
South Lanarkshire, *local authority*, Scotland, U.K., **792** E5
South Miami, U.S.A., **835** M7
South Molton, England, U.K., **788** D3
South Nahanni, *river*, Canada, **820** G3
South Negril Point, Jamaica, **839** F3
South Orkney Islands, Antarctica, **862** A3
South Ossetia, *former autonomous republic*, Georgia, **758** C4
South Pacific Ocean, **717** J5
South Pass City, U.S.A., **829** K5
South Petherton, England, U.K., **788** E4
South Platte, *river*, U.S.A., **830** C5
South Platte, U.S.A., **829** M7
South Point, Ascension, **813** A3
South Point, Christmas Island, **720** N8
South Promontory, *point*, Snares Islands, New Zealand, **718** H9
South Ronaldsay, *island*, Orkney, Scotland, U.K., **792** G2
South Sandwich Islands, South Georgia and South Sandwich Islands, **845** K9
South Sandwich Trench, *underwater feature*, Atlantic Ocean, **867** E9
South Saskatchewan, *river*, Canada, **823** Q6
South Seal, *river*, Canada, **824** E2
South Shetland Islands, Antarctica, **862** A4
South Shields, England, U.K., **791** G3
South Taranaki Bight, *gulf*, New Zealand, **718** D4
South Twin Island, Canada, **825** Q5
South Tyne, *river*, England, U.K., **790** F3
South Uist, *island*, Scotland, U.K., **792** B3
South Wabasca Lake, Canada, **823** N4
South West Bay, Ascension, **813** A3
South West Cape, Auckland Islands, New Zealand, **718** J10
South West Point, Macquarie Island, **720** R11
South West Point, St Helena, **813** B3
South Wootton, England, U.K., **789** H2
South Yorkshire, *unitary authority*, England, U.K., **791** G4
Southam, England, U.K., **789** F2
Southampton, Canada, **831** N3
Southampton, England, U.K., **789** F4
Southampton, U.S.A., **836** D4
Southampton City, *unitary authority*, England, U.K., **789** F4
Southampton Island, Canada, **821** L3
Southard, Mount, *mountain peak*, Antarctica, **862** E8
Southaven, U.S.A., **834** H2
Southbridge, U.S.A., **836** E3
Southeast Indian Ridge, *underwater feature*, Indian Ocean, **866** E7
Southeast Pacific Basin, *underwater feature*, Pacific Ocean, **869** M7
Southend, Canada, **824** C3
Southend, Scotland, U.K., **792** D5
Southend-on-Sea, England, U.K., **789** H3
Southend-on-Sea, *unitary authority*, England, U.K., **789** H3
Southern, *administrative region*, Malawi, **809** F6
Southern, *district*, Botswana, **810** D3
Southern, *province*, Sierra Leone, **804** B3
Southern, *province*, Zambia, **809** E6
Southern Alps, *mountain range*, New Zealand, **717** F6
Southern Cook Islands, Cook Islands, **723** F2
Southern Cross, Australia, **716** A6
Southern Highlands, *province*, Papua New Guinea, **726** A4
Southern Indian Lake, Canada, **824** E3
Southern Ocean, **708** D14
Southern Uplands, *mountain range*, Scotland, U.K., **792** E5
Southery, England, U.K., **789** H2
Southey, Canada, **824** B6
Southminster, England, U.K., **789** H3
Southport, Australia, **721** K7
Southport, England, U.K., **790** E4
Southport, U.S.A., **835** N3
Southwell, England, U.K., **789** G1
Southwest Indian Ridge, *underwater feature*, Indian Ocean, **866** B7
Southwest Pacific Basin, *underwater feature*, Pacific Ocean, **869** H7
Southwest Point, Papua New Guinea, **726** B3
Southwold, England, U.K., **789** J2
Sovata, Romania, **780** E2
Sovdozero, Russian Federation, **769** R5
Sovetsk, Russian Federation, **771** K5
Sovetskiy, Russian Federation, **783** B2
Sowa Pan, *lake*, Botswana, **811** E3
Soweto, South Africa, **811** E4
Soyaló, Mexico, **841** G5
Soyda, *river*, Russian Federation, **783** F2
Soyo, Angola, **808** B4
Sozaq, Kazakhstan, **759** H4
Sozh, *river*, Belarus, **783** C6
Sozopol, Bulgaria, **780** F4
Spain, *country*, Europe, **764** D8
Spalding, Canada, **824** B5
Spalding, England, U.K., **789** G2
Spanish, Canada, **831** M2
Spanish Fork, U.S.A., **833** H1
Spanish Peak, *mountain peak*, U.S.A., **828** E4
Spanish Town, Jamaica, **839** F3
Sparks, U.S.A., **832** D2
Sparta, U.S.A., **835** K2
Sparta *see* Sparti, Greece, **781** D7
Spartanburg, U.S.A., **835** M2
Spartel, Cap, *cape*, Morocco, **776** D5
Sparti (Sparta), Greece, **781** D7
Spartivento, Capo, *cape*, Italy, **779** F7
Sparwood, Canada, **823** M7
Spas-Demensk, Russian Federation, **783** D5
Spassk, Russian Federation, **759** M2
Spasskaya Guba, Russian Federation, **769** R5
Spassk-Dal'niy, Russian Federation, **747** L3
Spatha, Akra, *point*, Kriti, Greece, **781** D8
Spean Bridge, Scotland, U.K., **792** E4
Spearfish, U.S.A., **830** B3
Spearman, U.S.A., **830** C7
Speculator, U.S.A., **836** C3
Speery Island, St Helena, **813** B3
Speightstown, Barbados, **837** E3
Spencer, Idaho, U.S.A., **829** H4
Spencer, Iowa, U.S.A., **830** F4
Spencer, West Virginia, U.S.A., **831** N6
Spencer Gulf, Australia, **721** H6
Spencerville, New Zealand, **719** D6
Spences Bridge, Canada, **822** J6
Spennymoor, England, U.K., **791** G3
Sperrin Mountains, *mountain range*, Northern Ireland, U.K., **793** E3
Spetses, Greece, **781** D7
Spetses, *island*, Greece, **781** D7
Speyer, Germany, **772** D4
Speyside, Tobago, Trinidad and Tobago, **859** B4
Spiekeroog, *island*, Germany, **772** C2
Spili, Kriti, Greece, **781** E8
Spilsby, England, U.K., **789** H1
Spin Būldak, Afghanistan, **754** A3
Spinazzola, Italy, **779** F5
Spirit River, Canada, **823** K4
Spirits Bay, New Zealand, **718** D2
Spiritwood, Canada, **823** R5
Spit Point, Heard and McDonald Islands, **720** S12
Spitsbergen, *island*, Svalbard, **784** C2
Spittal an der Drau, Austria, **772** F5
Spittal of Glenshee, Scotland, U.K., **792** F4
Split, Croatia, **778** F4
Split Lake, Canada, **824** F3
Spofford, U.S.A., **834** B5
Spofforth, England, U.K., **791** G4
Špoği, Latvia, **771** N4
Spokane, U.S.A., **828** F3

T

Tahlequah, U.S.A., **834** E2
Tahoe, Lake, U.S.A., **832** C2
Tahoe City, U.S.A., **832** C2
Tahoka, U.S.A., **834** B3
Taholah, U.S.A., **828** B3
Tahora, New Zealand, **718** E4
Tahoua, *department*, Niger, **805** E1
Tahoua, Niger, **805** F2
Ţahţā, Egypt, **803** F3
Tahuamanu, *river*, Bolivia/Peru, **853** E3
Tahuatu, *island*, French Polynesia, **723** G2
Tahulandang, Pulau, *island*, Indonesia, **734** D2
Tahuna, Indonesia, **734** D2
Tahuna, New Zealand, **718** E3
Taï, Côte d'Ivoire, **804** C3
T'ai-chung, Taiwan, **742** E3
Tai Hu, *lake*, China, **742** E2
Tai Long, China, **743** C4
Tai Long Wan, *bay*, China, **743** C4
Tai Mo Shan, *mountain peak*, China, **743** C4
T'ai-nan, Taiwan, **742** E4
Tai O, China, **743** B4
Tai Pang Wan, *bay*, China, **743** C3
T'ai-pei, Taiwan, **742** E3
Tai Po, China, **743** C4
Tai Po Tsai, China, **743** C4
T'ai-tung, Taiwan, **742** E4
Tai'an, China, **746** G5
Taibai, China, **746** E5
Taibai Shan, *mountain peak*, China, **751** H2
Taibus Qi, China, **746** F4
Taieri, *river*, New Zealand, **719** C7
Taigu, China, **746** F5
Taihang Shan, *mountain range*, China, **746** F5
Taihape, New Zealand, **718** E4
Taihe, Anhui, China, **742** C1
Taihe, Guangdong, China, **743** A2
Taihe, Jiangxi, China, **742** C3
Taihu, China, **742** D2
Taikang, China, **742** C1
Taikkyi, Myanmar, **741** B4
Tailai, China, **747** H3
Tailem Bend, Australia, **721** H6
Taimei, China, **743** C2
Tain, Scotland, U.K., **792** E3
Tainaro, Akra, *point*, Greece, **781** D7
Taining, China, **742** D3
Taiping, Guangdong, China, **743** B3
Taiping, Guangxi Zhuangzu Zizhiqu, China, **751** H5
Taiping, Malaysia, **736** C1
Taipingchang, China, **743** A2
Tairua, New Zealand, **718** E3
Tais, Indonesia, **736** C4
Taishan, China, **742** C4
Taissy, France, **775** G2
Taitao, Península de, Chile, **858** B3
Taivalkoski, Finland, **769** P4
Taivassalo, Finland, **771** K2
Taiwan, *country*, Asia, **731** P7
Taiwan Strait, China/Taiwan, **742** D4
Taiyanggou, China, **747** J2
Taiyuan, China, **746** F5
Taizhou, China, **742** D1
Ta'izz, Yemen, **756** D6
Tajarhi, Libya, **802** B4
Tajikistan, *country*, Asia, **730** J6
Tajitos, Mexico, **840** B2
Tajo, *river*, Spain, **766** D8
Tajumulco, Volcán, *mountain peak*, Guatemala, **838** C4
Tajuña, *river*, Spain, **777** F2
Tak, Thailand, **738** C2
Takāb, Iran, **758** D5
Takabba, Kenya, **809** H2
Takaka, New Zealand, **719** D5
Takamaka, Réunion, **813** A1
Takamaka, Seychelles, **813** A2
Takamatsu, Japan, **744** F4
Takanabe, Japan, **744** E4
Takaoka, Japan, **745** G3
Takapuna, New Zealand, **718** E3
Takaroa, *island*, French Polynesia, **723** G2
Takasaki, Japan, **745** G3
Takatokwane, Botswana, **810** D3
Takayama, Japan, **745** G3
Takefu, Japan, **745** G4
Takengon, Indonesia, **736** B1
Tākestān, Iran, **758** D5
Takêv, Cambodia, **739** E4
Takhteh Pol, Afghanistan, **754** A3
Takikawa, Japan, **745** H2
Takis, Papua New Guinea, **726** C4
Takla Lake, Canada, **822** G4
Taklimakan Shamo, *desert*, China, **748** D5
Takoradi, Ghana, **804** D4
Taksimo, Russian Federation, **785** N4
Takua Pa, Thailand, **738** C4
Takum, Nigeria, **805** F3
Takutea, *island*, Cook Islands, **723** F2
Tala, Uruguay, **857** F5
Talacasto, Argentina, **856** C4
Talachyn, Belarus, **783** B5
Talagang, Pakistan, **754** C2
Tālah, Tunisia, **802** A1
Talaimannar, Sri Lanka, **752** D4
Talakan, Russian Federation, **747** L2
Talangbatu, Indonesia, **736** D4
Talara, Peru, **852** B1
Talarrubias, Spain, **776** E3
Talas, Kyrgyzstan, **748** B4
Talasea, Papua New Guinea, **726** C4
Talaud, Kepulauan, *islands*, Indonesia, **734** D1
Talavera de la Reina, Spain, **776** E3
Talawdī, Sudan, **806** D2
Talaya, Russian Federation, **759** P1
Talca, Chile, **856** B5
Talcahuano, Chile, **856** B5
Tālcher, India, **755** F5
Taldom, Russian Federation, **783** F4
Taldykorgan *see* Taldyqorghan, Kazakhstan, **748** C3
Taldyqorghan (Taldykorgan), Kazakhstan, **748** C3
Tālesh, Iran, **758** D5
Talgarth, Wales, U.K., **788** D3
Talghar, Kazakhstan, **748** C4
Talhār, Pakistan, **754** B4
Tali Post, Sudan, **809** F1
Taliabu, Pulau, *island*, Indonesia, **734** D3
Tālīkota, India, **752** D2
Talitsa, Russian Federation, **758** G1
Taljāpur, India, **752** D2
Tall 'Afar, Iraq, **803** H1
Talladega, U.S.A., **835** J3
Tallahassee, U.S.A., **835** K4
Tallinn, Estonia, **771** M3
Tallow, Ireland, **793** E5
Tallsjö, Sweden, **768** J4
Tallulah, U.S.A., **834** G3
Talluskylä, Finland, **769** N5
Tălmaciu, Romania, **780** E3
Tal'menka, Russian Federation, **759** L2
Talo, *mountain peak*, Ethiopia, **807** E2
Taloda, India, **754** C5
Tāloqān, Afganistan, **754** B1
Talparo, Trinidad, Trinidad and Tobago, **859** C4
Talshand, Mongolia, **749** H3
Talsi, Latvia, **771** L4
Taltal, Chile, **856** B2
Taluk, Indonesia, **736** C3
Talvikyulya, Russian Federation, **769** P2
Tam Kỳ, Vietnam, **739** F3
Tamacuari, Pico, *mountain peak*, Brazil/Venezuela, **849** F4
Tamakautoga, Niue, **718** M13
Tamalameque, Colombia, **848** D2
Tamale, Ghana, **804** D3
Tamana, *island*, Kiribati, **725** F5
Tamanhint, Libya, **802** B3
Tamanrasset, Algeria, **801** H4
Tamanthi, Myanmar, **741** B2
Tamar, *river*, England, U.K., **788** C4
Tamarin, Mauritius, **813** C1
Tamási, Hungary, **773** J5
Tamaulipas, Sierra de, *mountain range*, Mexico, **841** F4
Tamaulipas, *state*, Mexico, **841** F3
Tamazula, Mexico, **840** D3
Tambach, Kenya, **809** G2
Tambacounda, Senegal, **804** B2
Tambey, Russian Federation, **784** J2
Tambo, *river*, Peru, **852** D4
Tambo Grande, Peru, **852** B1
Tambohorano, Madagascar, **812** A4
Tambora, Gunung, *mountain peak*, Indonesia, **737** G5
Tamboril, Brazil, **851** F4
Tamboura, Central African Republic, **809** E1
Tambov, Russian Federation, **782** F2
Tambovskaya Oblast', *province*, Russian Federation, **758** C2
Tambre, *river*, Spain, **776** C1
Tambura, Sudan, **809** E1
Tâmchekket, Mauritania, **804** B1
Tame, Colombia, **848** D2
Tamgak, Adrar, *mountain peak*, Niger, **801** H5
Tamgué, Massif du, *mountain range*, Guinea, **804** B2
Tamgué, Mont du, *mountain peak*, Guinea, **804** B2
Tamiang, Ujung, *point*, Indonesia, **736** B1
Tamil Nādu, *state*, India, **752** D3
Tamiš, *river*, Yugoslavia, **780** C3
Tamitatoala (Batovi), *river*, Brazil, **854** B3
Tamitsa, Russian Federation, **769** U4
Ţāmiyah, Egypt, **761** A5
Tamlelt, Plaine de, *plain*, Morocco, **801** F2
Tammisaari, Finland, **771** L3
Tampa, U.S.A., **835** L5
Tampa Bay, U.S.A., **835** L6
Tampere, Finland, **771** L2
Tampico, Mexico, **841** F4
Tampico, U.S.A., **829** L2
Tampines, Singapore, **736** K6
Tampo, Indonesia, **734** C4
Tampoc, *river*, French Guiana, **850** C2
Tamsalu, Estonia, **771** N3
Tamshiyacu, Peru, **848** D5
Tamuín, Mexico, **841** F4
Tamulol, Indonesia, **735** E3
Tamworth, Australia, **721** L5
Tamworth, England, U.K., **789** F2
Tân An, on Song Vam Co Tay, Vietnam, **739** E4
Tân An, Vietnam, **739** E4
Tan-shui, Taiwan, **742** E3
Tan-Tan, Morocco, **800** D3
Tana, Lake *see* T'ana Hāyk', *lake*, Ethiopia, **807** E2
Tana, Norway, **769** P1
Tana, *river*, Kenya, **809** G3
T'ana Hāyk' (Lake Tana), *lake*, Ethiopia, **807** E2
Tanabe, Japan, **745** F4
Tanahbala, Pulau, *island*, Indonesia, **736** B3
Tanahgrogot, Indonesia, **737** G3
Tanahjampea, Pulau, *island*, Indonesia, **734** B4
Tanahmasa, Pulau, *island*, Indonesia, **736** B3
Tanahmerah, Indonesia, **735** H4
Tanami Desert, Australia, **716** C3
Tanana, *river*, U.S.A., **820** E3
Tanana, U.S.A., **820** D3
Tanat, *river*, Wales, U.K., **788** D2
Tanbei, China, **743** A3
Tanch'ŏn, North Korea, **744** E2
Tanda, Côte d'Ivoire, **804** D3
Tanda, India, **755** E4
Tandag, Philippines, **740** D4
Tandaltī, Sudan, **806** D2
Tăndărei, Romania, **780** F3
Tandil, Argentina, **857** E5
Tandil, Sierra del, *mountain range*, Argentina, **857** E5
Tandjilé, *prefecture*, Chad, **805** H3
Tandjungpinang, Indonesia, **736** D2
Tando Ādam, Pakistan, **754** B4
Tando Allāhyār, Pakistan, **754** B4
Tando Bāgo, Pakistan, **754** B4
Tanen Taunggyi, *mountain range*, Thailand, **738** C2
Tanezrouft, *mountain range*, Algeria, **801** F4
Tanezrouft Tan-Ahenet, *mountain range*, Algeria, **801** F4
Tang, *river*, China, **742** C1
Tanga, *administrative region*, Tanzania, **809** G4
Tanga, Tanzania, **809** G4
Tanga Islands, Papua New Guinea, **726** D3
Tangail, Bangladesh, **750** D4
Tanganyika, Lake, E. Africa, **799** J7
Tangaroa, Volcán, *mountain peak*, Isla de Pascua (Easter Island), Chile, **859** B2
Tangen, Norway, **770** E2
Tanger (Tangier), Morocco, **801** E1
Tangermünde, Germany, **772** E2
Tanggo, China, **750** E3
Tanggor, China, **751** G2
Tanggula Shan, *mountain range*, China, **750** D2
Tanggulashan, China, **750** E2
Tanghe, China, **742** C1
Tangier *see* Tanger, Morocco, **801** E1
Tangjia, China, **743** B4
Tangjiang, China, **742** C3
Tangmai, China, **751** E3
Tangnag, China, **751** G2
Tangoio, New Zealand, **718** F4
Tangra Yumco, *lake*, China, **750** C3
Tangse, Indonesia, **736** A1
Tangshan, China, **747** G5
Tangtang, China, **743** B1
Tangtouxia, China, **743** C3
Tangu, Papua New Guinea, **726** B4
Tangung, Indonesia, **737** G2
Tangxia, China, **743** B2
Tangyin, China, **742** C1
Tangyuan, China, **747** K3
Tanhua, Finland, **769** N3
Tanimbar, Kepulauan, *islands*, Indonesia, **735** E4
Tanisapata, Indonesia, **735** F3
Tanjungbalai, Indonesia, **736** B2
Tanjungpandan, Indonesia, **737** D3
Tanjungredeb, Indonesia, **737** G2
Tanjungselor, Indonesia, **737** G2
Tānk, Pakistan, **754** B2
Tankhoy, Russian Federation, **746** D2
Tankse, India, **754** D2
Tanna, *island*, Vanuatu, **727** A3
Tannadice, Scotland, U.K., **792** G4
Tännäs, Sweden, **770** F1
Tannila, Finland, **769** M4
Tannūrah, Ra's, *cape*, Saudi Arabia, **756** F3
Tanout, Niger, **805** F2
Tanque al Revés, Mexico, **840** E3
Ţanţā, Egypt, **761** A4
Tantoyuca, Mexico, **841** F4
Tanuanella, Sardegna, Italy, **779** B5
Tanumshede, Sweden, **770** E3
Tanunak, U.S.A., **820** C3
Tanzania, *country*, Africa, **797** J7
Tanzhou, north of Zhongshan, Guangdong, China, **743** A3
Tanzhou, south of Zhongshan, Guangdong, China, **743** A4
Tao, Ko, *island*, Thailand, **738** D4
Tao, *river*, Central China, **751** G2
Tao, *river*, N. China, **742** C3
Tao'er, *river*, China, **747** H3
Taojiang, China, **742** C2
Taonan, China, **747** H3
Taongi, *island*, Marshall Islands, **725** E3
Taormina, Sicilia, Italy, **779** E7
Taos, U.S.A., **833** L3
Taoudenni, Mali, **801** F4
Taounate, Morocco, **801** F2
Taourirt, Morocco, **801** F2
Taouz, Morocco, **801** F2
T'ao-yüan, Taiwan, **742** E3
Taoyuan, China, **742** B2
Tap Mun Chau, *island*, China, **743** C4
Tapa, Estonia, **771** M3
Tapajós, *river*, Brazil, **850** B4
Tapaktuan, Indonesia, **736** B2
Tapalqué, Argentina, **857** E5
Tapan, Indonesia, **736** C3
Tapanahoni, *river*, Suriname, **850** B2
Tapanui, New Zealand, **719** B7
Tapanuli, Teluk, *bay*, Indonesia, **736** B2
Tapará, Serra do, *mountain range*, Brazil, **850** C4
Tapauá, Brazil, **853** F1
Tapauá, *river*, Brazil, **853** E2
Tapaulama, Tanjong, *point*, Indonesia, **734** C3
Tapera, Brazil, **857** G3
Tapes, Brazil, **857** G4
Tapeta, Liberia, **804** C3
Tapi, *river*, India, **754** C5
Tapis, Gunung, *mountain peak*, Malaysia, **736** C2
Tapolca, Hungary, **773** H5
Tappahannock, U.S.A., **836** B6
Tapuae-o-Uenuku, *mountain peak*, New Zealand, **719** D5
Tapul Group, *islands*, Philippines, **740** B5
Tapul Island, Philippines, **740** C5
Tapurucuara, Brazil, **849** F4
Taqab, Sudan, **803** F5
Taquari, Brazil, **854** C4
Taquari, *river*, Mato Grosso do Sul, Brazil, **854** B5
Taquari, *river*, Rio Grande do Sul, Brazil, **857** G3
Taquaritinga, Brazil, **854** D5
Tara, *river*, Russian Federation, **759** K1
Tara, Russian Federation, **759** J1
Taraba, *state*, Nigeria, **805** G3
Tarabuco, Bolivia, **853** F5
Ţarābulus (Tripoli), Lebanon, **761** C2
Ţarābulus (Tripoli), Libya, **802** B2
Taraclia, Moldova, **780** G3
Taradale, New Zealand, **718** F4
Tarāghin, Libya, **802** B3

Télagh, Algeria, **801** F2
Télataï, Mali, **805** E1
Telč, Czech Republic, **773** G4
Telchac Puerto, Mexico, **841** H4
Telciu, Romania, **780** E2
Telde, Islas Canarias, Spain, **813** B4
Tele, *river*, Democratic Republic of the Congo, **808** D2
Telefomin, Papua New Guinea, **726** A4
Telegraph Creek, Canada, **822** D3
Telêmaco Borba, Brazil, **857** G2
Telemark, *county*, Norway, **770** C3
Telemba, Russian Federation, **746** F1
Télemsès, Niger, **805** E1
Telén, Argentina, **856** D5
Telenești, Moldova, **780** G2
Teleorman, *river*, Romania, **780** E3
Telerhteba, Djebel, *mountain peak*, Algeria, **801** H4
Teles Pires (São Manuel), *river*, Brazil, **850** B5
Telescope Peak, *mountain peak*, U.S.A., **832** E3
Telford, England, U.K., **788** E2
Telford and Wrekin, *unitary authority*, England, U.K., **788** E2
Telica, Nicaragua, **838** D4
Teljo, Jabal, *mountain peak*, Sudan, **806** C2
Telkwa, Canada, **822** F4
Telmen Nuur, *lake*, Mongolia, **749** H2
Telok Blangah, Singapore, **736** J7
Teloloapan, Mexico, **841** F5
Telsen, Argentina, **858** D2
Telšiai, Lithuania, **771** L5
Telukbatang, Indonesia, **737** E3
Telukdalam, Indonesia, **736** B2
Telupid, Malaysia, **737** G1
Tema, Ghana, **804** E3
Temagami, Canada, **831** P2
Temagami, Lake, Canada, **831** N2
Tematangi, *island*, French Polynesia, **723** G3
Temax, Mexico, **841** H4
Tembagapura, Indonesia, **735** G4
Tembesi, *river*, Indonesia, **736** C3
Tembhurni, India, **752** C2
Tembilahan, Indonesia, **736** C3
Tembisa, South Africa, **811** E4
Tembito, Indonesia, **734** C2
Tembleque, Spain, **777** F3
Tembo, Democratic Republic of the Congo, **808** C4
Tembo Aluma, Angola, **808** C4
Temecula, U.S.A., **832** E5
Téméra, Mali, **804** D1
Temerin, Yugoslavia, **780** B3
Temerloh, Malaysia, **736** C2
Temirtaū, Kazakhstan, **748** B2
Témiscaming, Canada, **826** B6
Temoe, *island*, French Polynesia, **723** H3
Temora, Australia, **721** K5
Temósachic, Mexico, **840** D2
Tempe, Danau, *lake*, Indonesia, **734** B4
Tempe, U.S.A., **833** H5
Tempio Pausania, Sardegna, Italy, **779** B5
Temple, U.S.A., **834** D4
Temple Bar, Wales, U.K., **788** C2
Temple Ewell, England, U.K., **789** J3
Temple Sowerby, England, U.K., **790** F3
Templemore, Ireland, **793** E5
Templeton, Wales, U.K., **788** C3
Templetouhy, Ireland, **793** E5
Templin, Germany, **772** F2
Tempoal, Mexico, **841** F4
Tempué, Angola, **808** C5
Temska, Yugoslavia, **780** D4
Temuco, Chile, **858** C1
Temuka, New Zealand, **719** C7
Ten Degree Channel, Andaman and Nicobar Islands, India, **753** G4
Ten Sleep, U.S.A., **829** L4
Ten Thousand Islands, U.S.A., **835** M7
Tena, Ecuador, **848** C4
Tenāli, India, **752** E2
Tenamatua, Gunung, *mountain peak*, Indonesia, **734** C3
Tenasserim, *division*, Myanmar, **738** C3
Tenbury Wells, England, U.K., **788** E2
Tenby, Wales, U.K., **788** C3
Tendaho, Ethiopia, **807** F2
Tende, France, **775** H4
Tendō, Japan, **745** H3
Tendoy, U.S.A., **828** H4
Tendrara, Morocco, **801** F2
Ténenkou, Mali, **804** C2
Tenerife, *island*, Islas Canarias, Spain, **813** A4
Ténès, Algeria, **801** G1
Teng Xian, China, **742** B4
Tengchong, China, **751** F4
Tengeh Reservoir, Singapore, **736** J6
Tengiz Köli, *lake*, Kazakhstan, **759** H2
Tengréla, Côte d'Ivoire, **804** C2
Tenhola, Finland, **771** L2
Tenja, Croatia, **778** G3
Tenke, Democratic Republic of the Congo, **809** E5
Tenkiller Ferry Lake, U.S.A., **834** E2
Tenkodogo, Burkina Faso, **804** D2
Tenmarou, Vanuatu, **727** A2
Tenna, *river*, Italy, **778** D4
Tennant Creek, Australia, **720** G2
Tennessee, *river*, U.S.A., **835** H2
Tennessee, *state*, U.S.A., **835** J2
Tennevoll, Norway, **768** H2
Tenniöjoki, *river*, Finland/Russian Federation, **769** P3
Tenojoki, *river*, Finland, **769** N2
Tenosique de Pino Suárez, Mexico, **841** H5
Tenryū, *river*, Japan, **745** G4
Tensed, U.S.A., **828** F3
Tenstrike, U.S.A., **830** F2
Tenterden, England, U.K., **789** H3
Tenterfield, Australia, **721** L4
Tentolomatinan, Gunung, *mountain peak*, Indonesia, **734** C2
Tentudia, *mountain peak*, Spain, **776** D3
Teodoro Sampaio, Brazil, **857** G2
Teófilo Otoni, Brazil, **855** F4
Teopisca, Mexico, **841** G5
Tepa, Indonesia, **735** E4
Tepa Point, Niue, **718** M13
Tepasto, Finland, **769** M3
Tepatitlán, Mexico, **840** E4
Tepehuanes, Mexico, **840** D3
Tepelenë, Albania, **781** B5
Tepequém, Brazil, **849** G3
Tepequém, Serra, *mountain range*, Brazil, **849** G3
Tepic, Mexico, **840** D4
Teploye, Russian Federation, **783** F6
Tepoto, *island*, French Polynesia, **723** G2
Tepsa, Finland, **769** M3
Téra, Niger, **804** E2
Tera, *river*, Spain, **776** D1
Tera Nova Bay, *Italian research station*, Antarctica, **862** D7
Teraina, *island*, Kiribati, **725** H4
Teramo, Italy, **778** D4
Teratyn, Poland, **773** L3
Terceira, *island*, Azores, Portugal, **800** M7
Teregova, Romania, **780** D3
Terengganu, *state*, Malaysia, **736** C1
Terenos, Brazil, **854** B5
Teresina, Brazil, **851** E4
Teresópolis, Brazil, **855** E6
Terespol, Poland, **773** L2
Terevaka, *mountain peak*, Isla de Pascua (Easter Island), Chile, **859** B2
Terevinto, Bolivia, **853** F4
Tergun Daba Shan, *mountain range*, China, **749** G5
Teriberka, *river*, Russian Federation, **769** S2
Teriberka, Russian Federation, **769** S2
Teriberskiy, Mys, *cape*, Russian Federation, **769** S2
Terlingua, U.S.A., **833** M7
Termas de Río Hondo, Argentina, **856** D3
Terminillo, Monte, *mountain peak*, Italy, **779** D4
Términos, Laguna de, *lagoon*, Mexico, **841** H5
Termit-Kaoboul, Niger, **805** G1
Termiz, Uzbekistan, **754** A1
Termoli, Italy, **779** E5
Tern, *island*, Hawaiian Islands, U.S.A., **725** H2
Ternate, Indonesia, **734** D2
Terneuzen, Netherlands, **772** A3
Terney, Russian Federation, **745** G1
Terni, Italy, **779** D4
Ternivka, Ukraine, **780** G1
Ternopil', Ukraine, **782** C3
Terpeniya, Mys, *cape*, Russian Federation, **785** R5
Terra Firma, South Africa, **810** D4
Terrace, Canada, **822** E4
Terrace Bay, Canada, **825** L7
Terracina, Italy, **779** D5
Terråk, Norway, **768** F4
Terralba, Sardegna, Italy, **779** B6
Terrassa, Spain, **777** H2
Terre Adélie, *region*, Antarctica, **862** E7
Terre Haute, U.S.A., **831** K6
Terrebonne Bay, U.S.A., **834** G5
Terreton, U.S.A., **828** H5
Terrington St Clement, England, U.K., **789** H2
Terry, Mississippi, U.S.A., **834** G3
Terry, Montana, U.S.A., **829** M3
Terschelling, *island*, Netherlands, **772** B2
Tertenia, Sardegna, Italy, **779** B6
Teruel, Spain, **777** G2
Tervel, Bulgaria, **780** F4
Tērvete, Latvia, **771** L4
Tervo, Finland, **769** N5
Tervola, Finland, **769** M3
Tešanj, Bosnia and Herzegovina, **778** F3
Teseney, Eritrea, **807** E1
Teshig, Mongolia, **749** J2
Teshikaga, Japan, **745** J2
Teshio, *river*, Japan, **745** H1
Teskey Ala-Too, *mountain range*, Kyrgyzstan, **748** C4
Teslin, Canada, **822** C1
Teslin Lake, Canada, **822** C1
Tesouro, Brazil, **854** C4
Tesovo Netyl'skiy, Russian Federation, **783** C3
Tessalit, Mali, **801** G4
Tessaoua, Niger, **805** F2
Tessin, Germany, **772** F1
Test, *river*, England, U.K., **789** F3
Tét, Hungary, **773** H5
Tetas, Punta, *point*, Chile, **856** B2
Tetbury, England, U.K., **788** E3
Tete, Mozambique, **809** F6
Tete, *province*, Mozambique, **809** F6
Tête Jaune Cache, Canada, **823** K5
Tetepare, *island*, Solomon Islands, **727** A1
Tetere, Solomon Islands, **727** A1
Teteven, Bulgaria, **780** E4
Tetiaroa, *island*, French Polynesia, **723** G2
Tetney, England, U.K., **791** H4
Teton, U.S.A., **829** J5
Tetonia, U.S.A., **829** J5
Tetouan (Tetuán), Morocco, **801** E1
Tetovo, Macedonia, **780** C4
Tetrino, Russian Federation, **769** U3
Tetuán *see* Tetouan, Morocco, **801** E1
Teuco, *river*, Argentina, **856** E2
Teulada, Capo, *cape*, Italy, **779** B6
Teulada, Sardegna, Italy, **779** B6
Teulon, Canada, **824** F6
Teutoburger Wald, *mountain range*, Germany, **772** C2
Teuva, Finland, **771** K1
Teverya, Israel, **761** C3
Teviotdale, *valley*, Scotland, U.K., **792** G5
Tevriz, Russian Federation, **759** J1
Tewkesbury, England, U.K., **788** E3
Têwo, China, **751** G2
Texarkana, U.S.A., **834** E3
Texas, Australia, **721** L4
Texas, *state*, U.S.A., **833** M5
Texas City, U.S.A., **834** E5
Texas Creek, U.S.A., **833** L2
Texel, *island*, Netherlands, **772** B2
Texhoma, U.S.A., **830** C7
Texoma, Lake, U.S.A., **834** D2
Teyateyaneng, Lesotho, **811** E4
Teziutlan, Mexico, **841** F5
Tezpur, India, **755** H4
Tha-anne, *river*, Canada, **824** E1
Tha Song Yang, Thailand, **738** C2
Tha Tum, Thailand, **739** D3
Thabana-Ntlenyana, *mountain peak*, Lesotho, **811** E4
Thabazimbi, South Africa, **811** E3
Thabong, South Africa, **811** E4
Thabt, Jabal ath, *mountain peak*, Egypt, **761** C5
Thagaya, Myanmar, **741** C4
Thái Nguyên, Vietnam, **739** E1
Thailand, *country*, Asia, **731** L8
Thailand, Gulf of, South East Asia, **738** D4
Thal, Pakistan, **754** B2
Thale, Germany, **772** E3
Thamarit, Oman, **807** H1
Thame, England, U.K., **789** G3
Thames, Firth of, *bay*, New Zealand, **718** E3
Thames, New Zealand, **718** E3
Thames, *river*, Canada, **831** N4
Thames, *river*, England, U.K., **789** H3
Than Kyun, *island*, Myanmar, **738** C4
Thāna Ghāzi, India, **754** D4
Thāne, India, **752** C2
Thānesar, India, **754** D3
Thanh Hóa, Vietnam, **739** E2
Thánh Lang Xã, Vietnam, **739** E2
Thanh Phố Hồ Chí Minh (Saigon), Vietnam, **739** E4
Thanjāvur, India, **752** D4
Thanlwin (Salween), *river*, Myanmar, **741** C1
Thāno Būla Khān, Pakistan, **754** A4
Thap Sakae, Thailand, **738** C4
Thar Desert, India/Pakistan, **754** B4
Thargomindah, Australia, **721** J4
Tharthār, Buḩayrat ath, *lake*, Iraq, **803** H2
Tharwānīyah, Oman, **757** F4
Thasos, Greece, **781** E5
Thasos, *island*, Greece, **781** E5
Thatcham, England, U.K., **789** F3
Thaton, Myanmar, **741** C4
Thatta, Pakistan, **754** A4
Thau, Bassin de, *lake*, France, **775** F5
Thaxted, England, U.K., **789** H3
The Dalles, U.S.A., **828** D4
The Forks, New Zealand, **719** C6
The Hague *see* 's-Gravenhage, Netherlands, **772** B2
The Pas, Canada, **824** D5
The Valley, Anguilla, **837** D2
Thedford, U.S.A., **830** C5
Theinkun, Myanmar, **738** C4
Thekulthili Lake, Canada, **823** P1
Thelon, *river*, Canada, **820** J3
Theniet el Had, Algeria, **801** G1
Thenon, France, **774** E4
Theodore, Canada, **824** C6
Theodore Roosevelt, *river*, Brazil, **853** G2
Theodore Roosevelt Lake, U.S.A., **833** H5
Thermaïkos Kolpos, *bay*, Greece, **781** D5
Thermo, Greece, **781** C6
Thermopolis, U.S.A., **829** K5
Thesiger Bay, Canada, **820** G2
Thessalia, *administrative region*, Greece, **781** D6
Thessalon, Canada, **831** M2
Thessaloniki (Salonica), Greece, **781** D5
Thet, *river*, England, U.K., **789** H2
Thetford, England, U.K., **789** H2
Thetford Mines, Canada, **826** F6
Thibodaux, U.S.A., **834** G5
Thief River Falls, U.S.A., **830** E1
Thiene, Italy, **778** C3
Thiers, France, **775** F4
Thiès, Senegal, **804** A2
Thika, Kenya, **809** G3
Thimphu, Bhutan, **741** A2
Thio, New Caledonia, **727** A3
Thionville, France, **775** H2
Thira (Santorini), *island*, Kyklades, Greece, **781** E7
Thirsk, England, U.K., **791** G3
Thiruvananthapuram (Trivandrum), India, **752** D4
Thiruvattiyur, India, **752** E3
Thisted, Denmark, **770** D4
Thisvi, Greece, **781** D6
Thiva, Greece, **781** D6
Thiviers, France, **774** E4
Þjórsá, *river*, Iceland, **768** Y7
Thlewiaza, *river*, Canada, **824** F1
Thohoyandou, South Africa, **811** F3
Thới Bình, Vietnam, **739** E4
Thomas, U.S.A., **831** P6
Thomaston, Alabama, U.S.A., **835** J3
Thomaston, Georgia, U.S.A., **835** K3
Thomastown, Ireland, **793** E5
Thomasville, Alabama, U.S.A., **835** J4
Thomasville, Georgia, U.S.A., **835** K4
Thompson, Canada, **824** F4
Thompson Falls, U.S.A., **828** G3
Thompson Peak, *mountain peak*, U.S.A., **828** C6
Thompson Point, Canada, **824** H2
Thomson, *river*, Australia, **721** J3
Thomson, U.S.A., **835** L3
Thoreau, U.S.A., **833** J4
Þorlákshöfn, Iceland, **768** X8
Thornaby on Tees, England, U.K., **791** G3

04 B3
02 D2
…e Australes, Îles, French Polynesia,
…3

Tottori, Japan, **744** F4
Touba, Côte d'Ivoire, **804** C3
Touba, Senegal, **804** A2
Toubkal, Jebel, *mountain peak*, Morocco, **800** E2
Touboro, Cameroon, **805** H3
Toucy, France, **775** F3
Tougan, Burkina Faso, **804** D2
Touggourt, Algeria, **801** H2
Tougué, Guinea, **804** B2
Touho, New Caledonia, **727** A3
Touil, Mauritania, **804** B1
Toukoto, Mali, **804** C2
Toul, Cairn, *mountain peak*, Scotland, U.K., **792** F3
Toul, France, **775** G2
Toulépleu, Côte d'Ivoire, **804** C3
Toulon, France, **775** G5
Toulouse, France, **774** E5
Toumodi, Côte d'Ivoire, **804** C3
Toungo, Nigeria, **805** G3
Toungoo, Myanmar, **741** C4
Tourba, Chad, **805** H2
Touriñán, Cabo, *cape*, Spain, **776** C1
Tourlaville, France, **774** D2
Tournai, Belgium, **772** A3
Tournavista, Peru, **852** C2
Touros, Brazil, **851** G4
Tourouvre, France, **774** E2
Tours, France, **774** E3
Toury, France, **774** E2
Tous, Embalse de, *reservoir*, Spain, **777** G3
Toussiana, Burkina Faso, **804** D2
Toussidé, Pic, *mountain peak*, Chad, **802** C4
Toussoro, Mont, *mountain peak*, Central African Republic, **806** B3
Touws River, South Africa, **810** D5
Töv, *province*, Mongolia, **746** D3
Tovar, Venezuela, **848** D2
Tovarkovskiy, Russian Federation, **783** G6
Towada, Japan, **745** H2
Towanda, U.S.A., **836** B4
Towcester, England, U.K., **789** G2
Townsville, Australia, **721** K2
Towot, Sudan, **806** D3
Towrzi, Afghanistan, **754** A3
Towson, U.S.A., **836** B5
Towuti, Danau, *lake*, Indonesia, **734** C3
Toxkan, *river*, China, **748** C4
Toyah, U.S.A., **833** M6
Toyama, Japan, **745** G3
Toyama-wan, *bay*, Japan, **745** G3
Toyohashi, Japan, **745** G4
Toyo'oka, Japan, **744** F4
Toyota, Japan, **745** G4
Töysä, Finland, **771** L1
Trà Vinh, Vietnam, **739** E4
Trabanca, Spain, **776** D2
Trabzon, Turkey, **760** E4
Tracadie, Canada, **826** J6
Tracy, U.S.A., **830** F3
Traer, U.S.A., **830** G4
Traiguén, Chile, **856** B6
Trail, Canada, **823** L7
Trail, U.S.A., **828** C5
Trail City, U.S.A., **830** C3
Traill Ø, *island*, Greenland, **821** S2
Traisen, Austria, **773** G4
Tralee, Ireland, **793** C5
Tramore, Ireland, **793** E5
Tranås, Sweden, **770** G3
Trancas, Argentina, **856** D3
Trang, Thailand, **738** C5
Tranomaro, Madagascar, **812** B5
Tranoroa, Madagascar, **812** B5
Tranøy, Norway, **768** G2
Tranqueras, Uruguay, **857** F4
Transantarctic Mountains, *mountain range*, Antarctica, **862** D5
Transtrand, Sweden, **770** F2
Trapani, Sicilia, Italy, **779** D6
Trarza, *administrative region*, Mauritania, **800** C5
Trasimeno, Lago, *lake*, Italy, **778** C4
Trat, Thailand, **739** D3
Traunsee, *lake*, Austria, **773** F5
Travemünde, Germany, **772** E2
Travers City, U.S.A., **831** L3
Travnik, Bosnia and Herzegovina, **778** F3
Trawsfynydd, Llyn, *reservoir*, Wales, U.K., **788** C2
Trawsfynydd, Wales, U.K., **788** D2
Treasury Islands, Solomon Islands, **727** A1
Třebíč, Czech Republic, **773** G4
Trebinje, Bosnia and Herzegovina, **778** G4
Trebisacce, Italy, **779** F6
Trebišov, Slovakia, **773** K4
Treble Mountain, *mountain peak*, New Zealand, **719** A7
Trebnje, Slovenia, **778** E3
Trechado, U.S.A., **833** J4
Tredegar, Wales, U.K., **788** D3
Tregaron, Wales, U.K., **788** D2
Tregony, England, U.K., **788** C4
Treig, Loch, *lake*, Scotland, U.K., **792** E4
Treinta-y-Tres, Uruguay, **857** F4
Trelew, Argentina, **858** E2
Trelleborg, Sweden, **770** F5
Trelleck, Wales, U.K., **788** E3
Tremadoc Bay, Wales, U.K., **788** C2
Tremiti, Isole, *islands*, Italy, **779** E4
Tremp, Spain, **777** H1
Trenary, U.S.A., **831** K2
Trenčianský, *administrative region*, Slovakia, **773** H4
Trenčín, Slovakia, **773** J4
Trenque Lauquen, Argentina, **856** D5
Trent, *river*, England, U.K., **791** H4
Trentino-Alto Adige, *autonomous region*, Italy, **778** C2
Trento, Italy, **778** C2
Trenton, Canada, **826** C7
Trenton, Michigan, U.S.A., **831** M4
Trenton, Missouri, U.S.A., **830** G5
Trenton, New Jersey, U.S.A., **836** C4
Trepassey, Canada, **827** Q6
Tres Arroyos, Argentina, **857** E6
Tres Cerros, Argentina, **858** D3
Três Corações, Brazil, **855** E5
Tres Esquinas, Colombia, **848** C4
Tres Isletas, Argentina, **856** E3
Três Lagoas, Brazil, **854** C5
Tres Lagos, Argentina, **858** C3
Tres Lomas, Argentina, **856** D5
Tres Mapajos, Bolivia, **853** F3
Tres Marías, Islas, *islands*, Mexico, **840** D4
Três Marias, Represa, *reservoir*, Brazil, **855** E5
Tres Montes, Península, Chile, **858** B3
Tres Picos, Cerro, *mountain peak*, Argentina, **856** E6
Tres Picos, Mexico, **841** G6
Tres Piedras, U.S.A., **833** L3
Três Pontas, Brazil, **854** E5
Tres Puntas, Cabo, *cape*, Argentina, **850** E3
Três Rios, Brazil, **855** E6
Tres Valles, Mexico, **841** F5
Tresfjord, Norway, **770** C1
Tretten, Norway, **770** E2
Treviglio, Italy, **778** B3
Treviso, Italy, **778** D3
Trevose Head, *point*, England, U.K., **788** B4
Trévoux, France, **775** G4
Trgovište, Yugoslavia, **780** D4
Tria Nisia, *island*, Kyklades, Greece, **781** F7
Tribal Areas, *province*, Pakistan, **754** B2
Tribune, U.S.A., **830** C6
Tricase, Italy, **779** G6
Trichonida, Limni, *lake*, Greece, **781** C6
Trichūr, India, **752** D4
Trier, Germany, **772** C4
Trieste, Golfo di, *gulf*, Italy, **778** D3
Trieste, Italy, **778** D3
Triglav, *mountain peak*, Slovenia, **778** D2
Trigno, *river*, Italy, **779** E5
Trikala, Greece, **781** C6
Trikomo, Cyprus, **761** B2
Trikora, Puncak, *mountain peak*, Indonesia, **735** G4
Trilj, Croatia, **778** F4
Trim, Ireland, **793** F4
Trimdon, England, U.K., **791** G3
Trincomalee, Sri Lanka, **753** E4
Trindade, Brazil, **854** D4
Trindade, *island*, Brazil, Atlantic Ocean, **709** T10
Tring, England, U.K., **789** G3
Trinidad, Bolivia, **853** F4
Trinidad, California, U.S.A., **828** B6
Trinidad, Colombia, **848** D3
Trinidad, Colorado, U.S.A., **833** L3
Trinidad, Cuba, **839** F2
Trinidad, Golfo, *gulf*, Chile, **858** B3
Trinidad, *island*, Trinidad and Tobago, **859** C4
Trinidad, Uruguay, **857** F4
Trinidad and Tobago, *country*, Caribbean Sea, **817** S7
Trinity, *river*, U.S.A., **834** E4
Trinity Bay, Canada, **827** Q6
Trinity Hills, *mountain peak*, Trinidad, Trinidad and Tobago, **859** C4
Trino, Italy, **778** B3
Triolet, Mauritius, **813** C1
Tripa, *river*, Indonesia, **736** B1
Tripoli, Greece, **781** D7
Tripoli *see* Ţarābulus, Lebanon, **761** C2
Tripoli *see* Ţarābulus, Libya, **802** B2
Tripura, *state*, India, **755** G5
Tristan da Cunha, *island*, St Helena, **813** C2
Tristan da Cunha, *St Helena dependency*, Atlantic Ocean, **797** D10
Triunfo, *river*, Brazil, **850** C5
Trivandrum *see* Thiruvananthapuram, India, **752** D4
Trivento, Italy, **779** E5
Trnava, Slovakia, **773** H4
Trnavský, *administrative region*, Slovakia, **773** H4
Trobriand Islands, Papua New Guinea, **726** C5
Troebratskiy, Kazakhstan, **758** H2
Trofors, Norway, **768** F4
Trogir, Croatia, **778** F4
Troglav, *mountain peak*, Bosnia and Herzegovina, **778** F4
Troia, Italy, **779** E5
Trois Bassins, Réunion, **813** A1
Trois Fourches, Cap des, *cape*, Morocco, **777** F5
Trois-Pistoles, Canada, **826** G5
Trois-Rivières, Canada, **826** E6
Troisdorf, Germany, **772** C3
Troitsk, Russian Federation, **758** G2
Troitskoye, Russian Federation, **747** M2
Trollhättan, Sweden, **770** F3
Trombetas, *river*, Brazil, **850** B3
Tromelin Île, *island*, Réunion, **812** C4
Tromen, Volcán, *mountain peak*, Argentina, **856** B5
Troms, *county*, Norway, **768** J2
Tromsø, Norway, **768** J2
Tromvik, Norway, **768** J2
Tron, *mountain peak*, Norway, **770** E1
Tronador, Cerro, *mountain peak*, Chile, **858** C1
Trondheim, Norway, **768** E5
Trönninge, Sweden, **770** F4
Troodos, Cyprus, **761** B2
Troodos Mountains, *mountain range*, Cyprus, **761** B2
Troon, Scotland, U.K., **792** E5
Tropaia, Greece, **781** C7
Tropeiros, Serra dos, *mountain range*, Brazil, **855** E4
Trostan, *mountain peak*, Northern Ireland, U.K., **793** F2
Trou d'Eau Dolce, Mauritius, **813** C1
Trout Creek, Canada, **826** B7
Trout Creek, U.S.A., **828** G3
Trout Lake, Canada, **823** L6
Trout Lake, *lake*, Northwest Territories, Canada, **822** J1
Trout Lake, *lake*, Ontario, Canada, **824** H6
Trout Lake, U.S.A., **828** D4
Trouville-sur-Mer, France, **774** E2
Trowbridge, England, U.K., **788** E3
Troy, Alabama, U.S.A., **835** K4
Troy, Montana, U.S.A., **828** G2
Troy, New York, U.S.A., **836** D3
Troy Peak, *mountain peak*, U.S.A., **832** F2
Troyan, Bulgaria, **780** E4
Troyanka, Ukraine, **780** H1
Troyes, France, **775** G2
Troyits'ke, Ukraine, **780** H2
Trstenik, Yugoslavia, **780** C4
Trsteno, Croatia, **778** F4
Truckee, U.S.A., **832** C2
Trujillo, Honduras, **838** D4
Trujillo, Peru, **852** B2
Trujillo, Spain, **776** E3
Trujillo, Venezuela, **849** D2
Trumann, U.S.A., **834** G2
Trumbull, Mount, *mountain peak*, U.S.A., **832** G3
Trŭn, Bulgaria, **780** D4
Truro, Canada, **827** K7
Truro, England, U.K., **788** B4
Trus Madi, Gunung, *mountain peak*, Malaysia, **737** G1
Truşeşti, Romania, **780** F2
Truskmore, *mountain peak*, Ireland, **793** D3
Trutch, Canada, **822** H3
Truth or Consequences, U.S.A., **833** K5
Trutnov, Czech Republic, **773** G3
Truyère, *river*, France, **774** F4
Trwyn Cilan, *point*, Wales, U.K., **788** C2
Tryavna, Bulgaria, **780** E4
Tryon, U.S.A., **830** C5
Trysilelva, *river*, Norway, **770** E2
Tryškiai, Lithuania, **771** L4
Tržac, Bosnia and Herzegovina, **778** E3
Trzcianka, Poland, **773** H2
Trzciel, Poland, **773** G2
Trzebnica, Poland, **773** H3
Tsagaan-Olom, Mongolia, **749** H3
Tsagaan Ovoo, Mongolia, **749** J3
Tsagaanchuluut, Mongolia, **749** H3
Tsagaandörvölj, Mongolia, **746** E3
Tsagaannuur, Bayan-Ölgiy, Mongolia, **748** F2
Tsagaannuur, Dornod, Mongolia, **747** G3
Tsagan Aman, Russian Federation, **758** D3
Tsakir, Russian Federation, **749** J2
Tsåktso, *mountain peak*, Sweden, **768** K2
Tsaratanana, Madagascar, **812** B4
Tsaris Mountains, Namibia, **810** C3
Tsebrykove, Ukraine, **780** H2
Tseel, Mongolia, **749** G3
Tsengel, Mongolia, **749** J2
Tsentral'nyy, Russian Federation, **759** M1
Tses, Namibia, **810** C4
Tsetseng, Botswana, **810** D3
Tsetserleg, Mongolia, **749** J3
Tsévié, Togo, **804** E3
Tshabong, Botswana, **810** D4
Tshane, Botswana, **810** D3
Tshela, Democratic Republic of the Congo, **808** B3
Tshibala, Democratic Republic of the Congo, **808** D4
Tshibwika, Democratic Republic of the Congo, **808** D4
Tshikapa, Democratic Republic of the Congo, **808** D4
Tshilenge, Democratic Republic of the Congo, **808** D4
Tshimbalanga, Democratic Republic of the Congo, **808** D4
Tshimbo, Democratic Republic of the Congo, **809** E4
Tshimbulu, Democratic Republic of the Congo, **808** D4
Tshinsenda, Democratic Republic of the Congo, **809** E5
Tshokwane, South Africa, **811** F3
Tshootsha, Botswana, **810** D3
Tsiigehtchic, Canada, **820** F3
Tsimlyanskoye Vodokhranilishche, *reservoir*, Russian Federation, **758** C3
Tsineng, South Africa, **810** D4
Tsiombe, Madagascar, **812** B6
Tsiribihina, *river*, Madagascar, **812** A4
Tsiribihina, Tanjona, *cape*, Madagascar, **812** A4
Tsiroanomandidy, Madagascar, **812** B4
Tsivil'sk, Russian Federation, **758** D1
Tsolo, South Africa, **811** E5
Tsoohor, Mongolia, **746** D4
Tsuchiura, Japan, **745** H3
Tsuen Wan, China, **743** C4
Tsumeb, Namibia, **810** C2
Tsumis Park, Namibia, **810** C3
Tsumkwe, Namibia, **810** D2
Tsuruga, Japan, **745** G4
Tsuruoka, Japan, **745** G3
Tsushima, *island*, Japan, **744** E4
Tsuyama, Japan, **744** F4
Tu, *river*, Myanmar, **741** C3
Tuai, New Zealand, **718** F4
Tuakau, New Zealand, **718** E3
Tuam, Ireland, **793** D4
Tuamarina, New Zealand, **719** D5
Tuamotu, Archipel des, *islands*, French Polynesia, **723** G2
Tuan, Tanjong, *point*, Malaysia, **736** C2
Tuâ'n Giáo, Vietnam, **739** D1
Tuangku, Pulau, *island*, Indonesia, **736** B2
Tu'anuku, Vava'u Group, Tonga, **727** B3
Tuao, Philippines, **740** C2
Tuaran, Malaysia, **737** G1
Tuas, Singapore, **736** J7
Tuba City, U.S.A., **833** H3
Tuban, Indonesia, **737** F4
Tubarão, Brazil, **857** H3
Ţubarjal, Saudi Arabia, **761** E4
Ţūbās, West Bank, **761** C3
Tübingen, Germany, **772** D4
Tubmanburg, Liberia, **80**[illegible]
Tubou, Fiji, **727** A4
Tubruq, Libya, **80**[illegible]
Tubuai, Îles *s*[illegible] *islands*, [illegible] **723** [illegible]

U

V

Victoria, Chile, **856** B6
Victoria, Isla, *island*, Chile, **858** B2
Victoria, Lake, Tanzania/Uganda, **809** F3
Victoria, Malaysia, **737** F1
Victoria, Mount, *mountain peak*, Myanmar, **741** B3
Victoria, Mount, *mountain peak*, New Zealand, **719** D6
Victoria, Mount, *mountain peak*, Papua New Guinea, **726** B5
Victoria, *river*, Australia, **720** G2
Victoria, Romania, **780** E3
Victoria, Seychelles, **813** A2
Victoria, Sierra de la, *mountain range*, Argentina, **857** F2
Victoria, *state*, Australia, **721** J6
Victoria, U.S.A., **834** D5
Victoria Falls, Zimbabwe, **811** E2
Victoria Island, Canada, **820** H2
Victoria Lake, Canada, **827** N5
Victoria Land, *region*, Antarctica, **862** E7
Victoria Peak, *mountain peak*, Belize, **838** C3
Victoria Peak, *mountain peak*, Philippines, **740** B4
Victoria Peak, *mountain peak*, U.S.A., **833** L6
Victoria Point, Macquarie Island, **720** R11
Victoria River Wayside Inn, Australia, **720** G2
Victoria West, South Africa, **810** D5
Victoriaville, Canada, **826** F6
Victorica, Argentina, **856** D5
Victorville, U.S.A., **832** E4
Victory, Mount, *mountain peak*, Papua New Guinea, **726** C5
Vicuña Mackenna, Argentina, **856** D4
Vida, U.S.A., **828** C4
Vidal, U.S.A., **832** F4
Vidalia, U.S.A., **835** L3
Vidamlya, Belarus, **773** L2
Videbæk, Denmark, **770** D4
Videle, Romania, **780** E3
Vidigueira, Portugal, **776** D3
Vidin, Bulgaria, **780** D4
Vidio, Cabo, *cape*, Spain, **776** D1
Vidlin, Shetland, Scotland, U.K., **792** K7
Vidlitsa, Russian Federation, **783** D2
Vidsel, Sweden, **768** K4
Vidukle, Lithuania, **771** L5
Viduša, *mountain range*, Bosnia and Herzegovina, **778** G4
Vidzy, Belarus, **771** N5
Viedma, Argentina, **858** E1
Viedma, Lago, *lake*, Argentina, **858** C3
Vieja, Sierra, *mountain range*, U.S.A., **833** L6
Viekšniai, Lithuania, **771** L4
Vienna *see* Wien, Austria, **773** H4
Vienne, France, **775** G4
Vienne, *river*, France, **774** E3
Vientiane *see* Viangchan, Laos, **739** D2
Viento, Cordillera del, *mountain range*, Argentina, **856** B5
Vieremä, Finland, **769** N5
Vierwaldstätter See, *lake*, Switzerland, **775** J3
Vierzon, France, **774** F3
Viesīte, Latvia, **771** M4
Vieste, Italy, **779** F5
Việt Tri, Vietnam, **739** E1
Vietas, Sweden, **768** J3
Vietnam, *country*, Asia, **731** M8
Vieux Fort, St Lucia, **837** D3
Vif, France, **775** G4
Viga, Philippines, **740** D3
Vigan, Philippines, **740** C2
Vigia, Brazil, **850** D3
Vigía Chico, Mexico, **841** J5
Vignacourt, France, **789** K4
Vignemale, *mountain peak*, France/Spain, **777** G1
Vignola, Italy, **778** C3
Vigo, Spain, **776** C1
Vihanti, Finland, **769** M4
Vihāri, Pakistan, **754** C3
Vihiers, France, **774** D3
Vihtari, Finland, **771** P1
Vihti, Finland, **771** M2
Viiala, Finland, **771** L2
Viipustunturit, *mountain peak*, Finland, **769** M2
Viitasaari, Finland, **769** M5
Viitna, Estonia, **771** N3
Vijāpur, India, **754** C5
Vijayawāda, India, **752** E2
Vík, Iceland, **768** Y8
Vik, Norway, **768** F4
Vika, Sweden, **770** G2
Vikajärvi, Finland, **769** N3
Vikanes, Norway, **770** B2
Vikārābād, India, **752** D2
Vikeke, Indonesia, **734** D5
Vikersund, Norway, **770** E3
Vikhren, *mountain peak*, Macedonia, **781** D5
Viking, Canada, **823** P5
Vikna, *island*, Norway, **768** E4
Vikran, Norway, **768** J2
Viksjö, Sweden, **771** H1
Viksøyri, Norway, **770** C2
Vila Bittencourt, Brazil, **849** E4
Vila da Ribeira Brava, Cape Verde, **800** Q8
Vila de Sena, Mozambique, **811** G2
Vila do Bispo, Portugal, **776** C4
Vila Franca de Xira, Portugal, **776** C3
Vila Nova, Brazil, **850** B4
Vila Real, *district*, Portugal, **776** D2
Vila Real, Portugal, **776** D2
Vila Velha, Amapá, Brazil, **850** C2
Vila Velha, Espíritu Santo, Brazil, **855** F5
Vilacaya, Bolivia, **853** F5
Vilaine, *river*, France, **774** D2
Viļaka, Latvia, **771** N4
Vilakalaka, Vanuatu, **727** A2
Vilaller, Spain, **777** H1
Vilanandro, Tanjona, *cape*, Madagascar, **812** A4
Vilanculos, Mozambique, **811** G3
Viļāni, Latvia, **771** N4
Vilanova i la Geltrú, Spain, **777** H2
Vilar Formoso, Portugal, **776** D2
Vilātikkulam, India, **752** D4
Vilcabamba, Cordillera, *mountain range*, Peru, **852** D3
Vilhelmina, Sweden, **768** H4
Vilhena, Brazil, **853** G3
Viliya, *river*, Belarus, **782** C2
Viljandi, Estonia, **771** M3
Vilkaviškis, Lithuania, **771** L5
Vilkija, Lithuania, **771** L5
Villa Abecia, Bolivia, **853** F5
Villa Ahumada, Mexico, **840** D2
Villa Ángela, Argentina, **856** E3
Villa Berthet, Argentina, **856** E3
Villa Constitución, Argentina, **856** E4
Villa de Alvarez, Mexico, **840** E5
Villa de Cos, Mexico, **840** E4
Villa de Tamazulapan, Mexico, **841** F5
Villa del Rosario, Argentina, **856** D4
Villa Dolores, Argentina, **856** D4
Villa Flores, Mexico, **841** G5
Villa Florida, Paraguay, **857** F3
Villa Gesell, Argentina, **857** F5
Villa Hayes, Paraguay, **857** F2
Villa Huidobro, Argentina, **856** D5
Villa Iris, Argentina, **856** D6
Villa Juárez, Mexico, **841** E3
Villa María, Argentina, **856** D4
Villa Martín, Bolivia, **853** E5
Villa Mazán, Argentina, **856** C3
Villa Nueva, Argentina, **856** C4
Villa Ocampo, Argentina, **857** E3
Villa Ocampo, Mexico, **840** D3
Villa Ojo de Agua, Argentina, **856** D3
Villa Oropeza, Bolivia, **853** F5
Villa Regina, Argentina, **858** D1
Villa San José, Argentina, **857** E4
Villa Tehuelche, Chile, **858** C4
Villa Unión, Argentina, **856** C3
Villa Unión, Durango, Mexico, **840** D4
Villa Unión, Sinaloa, Mexico, **840** D4
Villa Valeria, Argentina, **856** D5
Villa Viscarra, Bolivia, **853** F4
Villablino, Spain, **776** D1
Villacarrillo, Spain, **777** F3
Villacastín, Spain, **776** E2
Villach, Austria, **773** F5
Villada, Spain, **776** E1
Villagarcía de Arousa, Spain, **776** C1
Villagra, Bahía, *bay*, Róbinson Crusoe Island, Archipiélago Juan Fernández, Chile, **859** C2
Villagrán, Mexico, **841** F3
Villaguay, Argentina, **857** E4
Villahermosa, Mexico, **841** G5
Villahermosa, Spain, **777** F3
Villahoz, Spain, **777** F1
Villajoyosa, Spain, **777** G3
Villalba, Spain, **776** D1
Villaldama, Mexico, **841** E3
Villalonga, Argentina, **858** E1
Villalpando, Spain, **776** E2
Villamalea, Spain, **777** G3
Villamartín, Spain, **776** E4
Villamontes, Bolivia, **853** F5
Villandraut, France, **774** D4
Villano, Ecuador, **848** C4
Villanueva, Colombia, **848** D1
Villanueva, Mexico, **840** E4
Villanueva de Córdoba, Spain, **776** E3
Villanueva de la Serena, Spain, **776** E3
Villanueva del Fresno, Spain, **776** D3
Villány, Hungary, **773** J6
Villapalacios, Spain, **777** F3
Villar, Bolivia, **853** F5
Villarrica, Chile, **858** C1
Villarrica, Lago, *lake*, Chile, **858** C1
Villarrica, Paraguay, **857** F2
Villarrica, Volcán, *mountain peak*, Chile, **858** C1
Villarrobledo, Spain, **777** F3
Villasis, Philippines, **740** C3
Villavicencio, Colombia, **848** D3
Villazón, Bolivia, **853** F6
Ville-Marie, Canada, **826** B6
Villedieu-les-Poêles, France, **774** D2
Villefranche-de-Rouergue, France, **774** F4
Villefranche-sur-Saône, France, **775** G3
Villemontel, Canada, **826** B5
Villena, Spain, **777** G3
Villeneuve-sur-Lot, France, **774** E4
Villers-Bocage, France, **774** D2
Villers-Bretonneux, France, **789** K5
Villeurbanne, France, **775** G4
Villingen-Schwenningen, Germany, **772** D4
Villisca, U.S.A., **830** F5
Vilnius, Lithuania, **771** M5
Vilppula, Finland, **771** M2
Vils, *river*, Germany, **772** E4
Vilsbiburg, Germany, **772** F4
Vilshofen, Germany, **772** F4
Vilusi, Yugoslavia, **778** G4
Vilyeyka, Belarus, **771** N5
Vilyuy, Russian Federation, **785** P3
Vimianzo, Spain, **776** C1
Vimieiro, Portugal, **776** D3
Vimmerby, Sweden, **770** G4
Vimoutiers, France, **774** E2
Viña del Mar, Chile, **856** B4
Vinanivao, Madagascar, **812** C4
Vinaròs, Spain, **777** H2
Vincennes, U.S.A., **831** K6
Vincennes Bay, Antarctica, **862** G6
Vindelälven, *river*, Sweden, **768** H3
Vindeln, Sweden, **768** J4
Vindhya Range, *mountain range*, India, **732** J7
Vineland, U.S.A., **836** C5
Vinga, Romania, **780** C2
Vingåker, Sweden, **770** G3
Vinh, Vietnam, **739** E2
Vĩnh Long, Vietnam, **739** E4
Vinica, Macedonia, **780** D5
Vinita, U.S.A., **830** F7
Vinje, Norway, **770** C2
Vinkovci, Croatia, **778** G3
Vinnitsy, Russian Federation, **783** E2
Vinnyts'ka Oblast', *province*, Ukraine, **780** G1
Vinnytsya, Ukraine, **782** C3
Vinson Massif, *mountain peak*, Antarctica, **862** C5
Vinstra, Norway, **770** D2
Vinsulla, Canada, **822** J6
Vinza, Congo, **808** B3
Vinzili, Russian Federation, **758** H1
Vipiteno, Italy, **778** C2
Virac, Philippines, **740** D3
Viramgām, India, **754** C5
Virandozero, Russian Federation, **769** S4
Viranşehir, Turkey, **760** E5
Virden, Canada, **824** D7
Vire, France, **774** D2
Virei, Angola, **808** B6
Vireši, Latvia, **771** N4
Virgem da Lapa, Brazil, **855** E4
Virgin Islands, *U.K. dependency*, Caribbean Sea, **817** S7
Virgin Islands, *U.S. territory*, Caribbean Sea, **817** S7
Virginia, Ireland, **793** E4
Virginia, South Africa, **811** E4
Virginia, *state*, U.S.A., **831** P7
Virginia, U.S.A., **830** G2
Virginia Beach, U.S.A., **836** B6
Virginia City, U.S.A., **832** D2
Virihaure, *lake*, Sweden, **768** H3
Virma, Russian Federation, **769** S4
Virolanti, Finland, **771** N2
Viroqua, U.S.A., **830** H4
Virovitica, Croatia, **778** F3
Virserum, Sweden, **770** G4
Virtaniemi, Finland, **769** P2
Virtsu, Estonia, **771** L3
Virttaa, Finland, **771** L2
Virú, Peru, **852** B2
Vis, *island*, Croatia, **778** F4
Visaginas, Lithuania, **771** N5
Visale, Solomon Islands, **727** A1
Visalia, U.S.A., **832** D3
Visayan Sea, Philippines, **740** C4
Visby, Sweden, **771** J4
Viscount, Canada, **823** S6
Viscount Melville Sound, Canada, **820** H2
Višegrad, Bosnia and Herzegovina, **780** B4
Viseu, Brazil, **850** D3
Viseu, *district*, Portugal, **776** D2
Viseu, Portugal, **776** D2
Vişeu de Sus, Romania, **780** E2
Vishākhapatnam, India, **753** E2
Vishnevaya, Russian Federation, **783** F5
Vīshnevka, Kazakhstan, **759** J2
Vislanda, Sweden, **770** G4
Visoko, Bosnia and Herzegovina, **778** G4
Vissefjärda, Sweden, **770** G4
Visso, Italy, **778** D4
Vit, *river*, Bulgaria, **780** E4
Viterbo, Italy, **779** D4
Viti Levu, *island*, Fiji, **727** A4
Vitichi, Bolivia, **853** F5
Vitigudino, Spain, **776** D2
Vitina, Bosnia and Herzegovina, **778** F4
Vitis, Austria, **773** G4
Vítor, Peru, **852** D4
Vitória, Espírito Santo, Brazil, **855** F5
Vitória, Pará, Brazil, **850** C4
Vitória da Conquista, Brazil, **855** F4
Vitória do Mearim, Brazil, **851** E4
Vitoria-Gasteiz, Spain, **777** F1
Vitorog, *mountain peak*, Bosnia and Herzegovina, **778** F3
Vitré, France, **774** D2
Vitry-le-François, France, **775** G2
Vitsyebsk, Belarus, **783** C5
Vitsyebskaya Voblasts', *province*, Belarus, **771** N5
Vittangi, Sweden, **768** K3
Vitteaux, France, **775** G3
Vittoria, Sicilia, Italy, **779** E7
Vityaz Trench, *underwater feature*, Pacific Ocean, **868** F5
Vivarais, Monts du, *mountain range*, France, **775** G4
Viveiro, Spain, **776** D1
Vivian, Canada, **824** F7
Vivian, U.S.A., **830** C4
Viviers, France, **775** G4
Vivigani, Papua New Guinea, **726** C5
Vivo, South Africa, **811** E3
Vivonne, France, **774** E3
Vizcaíno, Sierra, *mountain range*, Mexico, **840** B3
Vize, Turkey, **781** F5
Vizianagaram, India, **753** E2
Vižinada, Croatia, **778** D3
Viziru, Romania, **780** F3
Vizzini, Sicilia, Italy, **779** E7
Vjosë, *river*, Albania, **781** B5
Vlaams Brabant, *province*, Belgium, **772** B3
Vlădeasa, *mountain peak*, Romania, **780** D2
Vladičin Han, Yugoslavia, **780** C4
Vladikavkaz, Russian Federation, **758** C4
Vladimir, Russian Federation, **782** F1
Vladimirci, Yugoslavia, **780** B3
Vladimirovo, Bulgaria, **780** D4
Vladimirskaya Oblast', *province*, Russian Federation, **783** G4
Vladivostok, Russian Federation, **747** K4
Vladychnoye, Russian Federation, **783** G3
Vlasenica, Bosnia and Herzegovina, **778** G3
Vlašić, *mountain peak*, Bosnia and Herzegovina, **778** F3
Vlasotince, Yugoslavia, **780** D4
Vlieland, *island*, Netherlands, **772** B2
Vlissingen, Netherlands, **772** A3
Vlorë, Albania, **781** B5
Vltava, *river*, Czech Republic, **773** G4
Voćin, Croatia, **778** F3
Vöcklabruck, Austria, **772** F4
Vodla, *river*, Russian Federation, **783** F2
Vodlozero, Ozero, *lake*, Russian Federation, **769** T5
Vogel, Cape, Papua New Guinea, **726** C5
Vogelsberg, *mountain peak*, Germany, **772** D3
Voghera, Italy, **778** B3
Voh, New Caledonia, **727** A3
Vohilava, Madagascar, **812** B5

W

X

Y